Environmental Ethics

DIVERGENCE
AND
CONVERGENCE

Environmental Ethics

DIVERGENCE AND CONVERGENCE

Susan J. Armstrong
Humboldt State University
Richard G. Botzler
Humboldt State University

McGraw-Hill, Inc.

New York St. Louis San Francisco Auckland Bogotá
Caracas Lisbon London Madrid Mexico City Milan
Montreal New Delhi San Juan Singapore
Sydney Tokyo Toronto

Environmental Ethics
Divergence and Convergence

Acknowledgments appear on pages 567–570, and
on this page by reference.

2 3 4 5 6 7 8 9 0 DOH DOH 9 0 9 8 7 6 5 4 3

ISBN 0-07-002608-4

This book was set in Times Roman by Ruttle, Shaw,
& Wetherill, Inc.
The editors were Cynthia Ward and John M. Morriss;
the production supervisor was Friederich W. Schulte.
The cover was designed by Carla Bauer.
Project supervision was done by Ruttle, Shaw, & Wetherill, Inc.
R. R. Donnelley & Sons Company was printer and
binder.

Cover photo credit: Laren McIntyre, Woodfin,
Camp, & Associates, Inc.

Library of Congress Cataloging-in-Publication Data

Environmental ethics: divergence and convergence/[compiled by]
   Susan J. Armstrong, Richard G. Botzler.
       p.   cm.
       Includes bibliographical references.
       ISBN 0-07-002608-4
       1. Human ecology—Moral and ethical aspects.   2. Human ecology—
History.   I. Armstrong, Susan J. (Susan Jean)   II. Botzler,
Richard George, (date).
GF80.E585   1993
179'.1—dc20   92-35126

SUSAN J. ARMSTRONG is Professor of Philosophy and Women's Studies at Humboldt State University. She received her Ph.D. degree in Philosophy from Bryn Mawr College in 1976. During graduate school she was manager of *The Review of Metaphysics*. She has published articles in *Environmental Ethics, The Journal of Wildlife Diseases, The Trumpeter,* and *Process Studies* and contributed book reviews to several other publications. She was nominated for Outstanding Professor in 1989. She has developed several environmental studies programs at Humboldt State University and is active in local environmental organizations. This is her first book.

RICHARD G. BOTZLER is Professor of Wildlife at Humboldt State University and the editor for the *Journal of Wildlife Diseases.* He served as a Fulbright Fellow to the Federal Republic of Germany in 1981-1982 and has authored publications in wildlife diseases, tissue immunity, and environmental ethics. He was selected as Outstanding Professor for the 20-campus California State University for 1992.

CONTENTS

Environmental Ethics: Divergence and Convergence is intended as a comprehensive, balanced introduction to the field of environmental ethics for upper-division undergraduate students. It also may be useful for lower-division courses and for introductory courses at the graduate level. This text is appropriate for use in courses dealing with environmental ethics from a theoretical perspective. It also can serve as a foundation for courses that address specific environmental problems.

Both of us have been professionally involved in environmental ethics since the 1970s. Susan's dissertation *The Rights of Nonhuman Beings: A Whiteheadian Study* was copyrighted in 1976 and may be the first dissertation in environmental ethics, though it emphasizes animals and plants. Rick has taught an environmental ethics course since 1977. This book is based on our experience of team-teaching environmental ethics since 1983. All except the most recent articles have been tested in the classroom for effective use.

Environmental Ethics: Divergence and Convergence offers the instructor a number of features not available in other texts:

- A structure and standardized terminology for this developing field;
- Contemporary essays (for 1993);
- Instructional aids for each chapter: chapter introductions and individual headnote introductions to each essay, discussion questions for each essay, a class exercise for each chapter, and annotated recommended readings;
- A multidisciplinary approach to environmental ethics incorporating natural science, social science, aesthetic, ethical, and religious perspectives;
- Non-Western as well as Western religious and cultural perspectives;

- Ecofeminist perspectives;
- Editorship by both a philosopher and a scientist, and;
- Focus on the students' development of their own environmental ethic. This goal is furthered by the solicitation of student perspectives, reactions, and experiences in the discussion questions, as well as by the selection of readings that are well-written and accessible to upper-division students.

Since the development of such a comprehensive text is beyond the abilities of one or even two editors, we gratefully acknowledge the help of many others. We acknowledge the encouragement and contributions of those who have helped us formulate the design of this text: Tom Birch, J. Baird Callicott, Jim Cheney, Patsy Hallen, Eugene Hargrove, Edward Johnson, Max Oelschlaeger, Holmes Rolston III, Mark Sagoff, Ariel Kay Salleh, Karen J. Warren, and Anthony Weston. We also thank those who have helped us in choosing individual readings: Allen Carlson, Bill Devall, Michael Goodman, Ramachandra Guha, William Herbrechtsmeier, Freya Matthews, Ernest Partridge, and George Sessions. Special thanks are due to Nelson Black at McGraw-Hill.

Susan also wishes to thank those she is most closely associated with for their endurance of her many hours in her office and at times for even offering encouragement: her children Tom, Liz, Alex, and Emily (some of whom are grown and some even recycling). Rick is particularly grateful to his wife, Sally, whose unflagging support, salient insights, and editorial skills helped make his contributions to this project a reality.

We have benefitted greatly from the criticisms and suggestions of professional colleagues and students in the construction of this book. However, any errors herein are entirely our own.

In one sense, a book of this nature is never completed, but must continually evolve to serve its users in this rapidly changing field. We invite you, both professional colleagues and students, to help enhance its value. Tell us what aspects you found helpful and what you believe could be improved. The topic of environmental ethics is of such importance, it de-serves the best that each of us can bring to its development.

Susan J. Armstrong
Richard G. Botzler

Since the first Earth Day in 1970, the world has lost nearly 200 million hectares of tree cover (roughly the size of the United States east of the Mississippi River). Deserts have expanded by over 120 million hectares. Thousands of plant and animal species no longer exist; at least 140 plant and animal species become extinct each day. Over 1.6 billion people have been added to the world's population, more than inhabited the planet in 1900, and one in three children is malnourished. Freshwater fish are declining in many areas; a worldwide decline in amphibians has been observed in recent years. Approximately 480 billion tons of topsoil have been lost.[1] Such facts have led to the perception of many that the planet is experiencing a serious environmental crisis.

The 1990s are a crucial decade. The East-West ideological conflict, which dominated world concerns for over a generation, has ended. No one can know what new political alignments will emerge in the future. But there is one certainty: unprecedented worldwide environmental damage has continued despite the efforts of legislators, agencies, environmental organizations, and individuals. The most important struggle now and for the foreseeable future is to prevent further environmental degradation, and even to reverse this trend. Such changes require international cooperation, including changes in the world economy and in political priorities. Environmental sustainability is emerging as a key principle on which this change must be based.[2] Out of this concern for the enormous environmental destruction brought about by humans has emerged a new field of philosophical inquiry: environmental ethics.

---

1. Lester R. Brown et al., *State of the World 1992,* W.W. Norton, New York, 1992, pp. 3–26.

2. *Ibid.,* chapter 3, 9–10.

WHAT IS ENVIRONMENTAL ETHICS?

Environmental ethics is the field of inquiry that addresses the ethical responsibilities of human beings for the natural environment. It is concerned with values: Does nature have value that extends beyond its obvious role of meeting human needs? Do some parts of nature have more value than others? What is the responsibility of humans towards nature and natural entities? While the field took its name from the 1979 creation of the journal *Environmental Ethics,* we recognize that this field is not limited to ethical inquiry only, but also is embedded in a larger matrix of aesthetic, religious, scientific, economic, and political considerations.

ENVIRONMENTAL ETHICS IS A DEVELOPING FIELD

Environmental ethics encompasses a surprising richness and diversity of responses to the concerns raised by the environmental crisis. As a distinctive discipline, it probably did not develop much before 1970. Environmental ethics deals with a global subject matter in a world that is just beginning to develop the ability to engage in global cooperation. No one set of ideas has been persuasive in convincing the majority of environmentally aware scholars that it holds the key to the right relationship to the environment. As such, the field is still in a stage of active growth and development and offers a variety of exciting ideas.

ENVIRONMENTAL ETHICS IS INTERDISCIPLINARY

Because environmental ethics concerns the human relationship to the environment, it includes all of the major perspectives on this relationship: scientific, ethical, aesthetic, political, economic, and religious. One-sided or narrow perspectives simply do not adequately address the subject matter.

Environmental ethics draws on a variety of insights. Some perspectives draw heavily on scientific insights with an emphasis on methods founded on reason, logic, objectivity, and repeatability. Other perspectives draw more heavily on intuition, emotion, imagination, artistic and religious insights, and everyday experience. Scholars in the area of environmental ethics come from a variety of disciplines—philosophy, science, art, economics, history, religion, to name a few—and the methods associated with these fields often differ. Thus, a great deal of interdisciplinary work is being done in environmental ethics.

ENVIRONMENTAL ETHICS IS MULTICULTURAL

The environmental crisis is international. It no longer is possible for any one society to live without having a significant impact on others. The political, economic, religious, moral, and aesthetic traditions, as well as institutional structures in both Western and non-Western societies, must be sympathetically addressed and understood to successfully develop a respectful and workable international environmental ethic. A multicultural perspective provides richer resources from which both Western and non-Western societies can draw to reframe and resolve environmental problems. Issues of justice in the distribution of resources, both between existing countries and between existing generations and those of the future, require attention and action.

ENVIRONMENTAL ETHICS IS TRANSFORMATIVE

Because environmental ethics has emerged in response to global environmental crisis, many proposals address the need for a transformation of human experience. Traditional economic arrangements that ignore environmental consequences, traditional political arrangements that impose artificial territorial limits on continuous physical processes and systems,

and traditional philosophic and religious theories that consider human beings in isolation from their natural surroundings are all being examined and modified. The incorporation of environmental concerns into these traditional theories is not just a minor shift of emphasis, but a substantial change in approach.

ENVIRONMENTAL ETHICS: DIVERGENCE AND CONVERGENCE

We have subtitled this book ''Divergence and Convergence'' because of its double aim. First, we want to offer readings that represent the major philosophical approaches to environmental ethics, including anthropocentrism, individualism, ecocentrism, ecofeminism, and several based on both Western and non-Western religious traditions. We believe that each of these approaches can be held by intellectually sincere people. We have sought to include the writings of those scholars that best help the reader evaluate the relative strengths and weaknesses of each position.

Second, we believe that some of these approaches have begun to converge in important ways. As you consider each chapter, we suggest that you keep this convergence in mind. Note that while theoretical approaches differ, the policy recommendations or conduct based on these approaches sometimes are relatively similar. This convergence is important because it indicates that similar constructive changes in the human treatment of the environment can result from more than one philosophical approach to environmental ethics.

FEATURES OF THIS BOOK

We have edited this book as an aid to developing your own environmental ethic. To do so, we include essays encompassing the major approaches to environmental ethics. The chapter introductions not only introduce specific readings, but also provide brief orientations to the entire field addressed by the readings.

The suggestions for further reading at the end of each chapter include only a small portion of what is available, but they will provide a good foundation in each area. Many also contain valuable bibliographies for further reference. The discussion questions at the end of each reading will help you assess the strengths and weaknesses of the various philosophical approaches, as well as encourage you to evaluate the ideas presented. The class exercise suggested for each chapter will help you confront some of the issues raised in the chapter while exchanging ideas with your classmates.

YOUR CONTRIBUTION TO ENVIRONMENTAL ETHICS

Deep, fundamental changes such as those described above originate in the minds and lives of individuals. As you examine your own beliefs and conduct, you will influence your friends and family. Your choice of courses and career will influence educational institutions. Your conduct as a consumer will influence manufacturers and advertising firms. Your vote will influence the composition of planning commissions, city councils, county boards of supervisors, representatives, governors, and presidents. Your choices are crucial to formulating the direction your society takes in addressing the many significant problems that face it. Your choices are crucial to the lives of your children and their children, to wildlife, and to the health of forests and oceans. Your responsibility is indeed a heavy one, but its very weight and urgency, if accepted in a thoughtful spirit, can help enrich your life and the lives of many others with greater meaning and value.

Environmental Ethics

DIVERGENCE
AND
CONVERGENCE

CHAPTER ONE

The Role of Science

Science offers a perspective that strongly influences environmental decisions. In this chapter we define science and summarize the scientific method, clarifying their relationship to resource management and environmental decision making. Some ethical issues concerning science and use of the scientific method to solve environmental problems are explored.

SCIENCE AND THE SCIENTIFIC METHOD

Most environmental decisions depend on having accurate knowledge about the physical world, the choices available, and the consequences of taking these various choices. The knowledge about the physical world falls in the realm of science. Thus, to make sound environmental judgments, one must have a basic understanding of science, and the methods on which it is based.

The concept of science is described in such diverse ways that it is difficult to provide a simple definition. Etymologically, the word *science* is derived from the Latin *scientia,* meaning "knowledge," and from *scire,* meaning "to know." The term *science* originally referred to the state or fact of knowing, and was contrasted with the notions of intuition or belief (Webster's New Twentieth Century Dictionary, 2nd ed.).

The realm of science deals with the objects and events of the physical world. Conversely, science traditionally has avoided topics not open to concrete analysis, such as moral or aesthetic values, notions of divinity, and metaphysics in general. The goals of science are to discover knowledge about the world, to fit this knowledge into conceptual schemes, and to discover the relationships among these schemes so that we may accurately describe, explain, and make predictions about the physical world.

Science can be divided into a variety of disciplines. One major division distinguishes empirical from nonempirical sciences. Nonempirical sciences begin with basic theorems or assumed truths, and apply logic to develop new truths and insights. Examples include formal logic and some types of theoretical mathematics. In contrast, empirical sciences use observations and experiments, along with logic, to develop new insights.

Empirical sciences can be divided further into the natural and social sciences. Natural sciences include the physical, earth, and life sciences. Social sciences include economics, political science, sociology, and history, among others. Some disciplines, such as psychology, may be represented in both categories.

Numerous fields of study incorporate more than

one branch of science, e.g., biophysics and geochemistry. Ecology, which can be defined as the study of how living things interact with each other and their environments, also is an example. It has strong roots in the life sciences, but also draws on other natural sciences (e.g., geochemistry), and more recently has developed ties to the social sciences.

For many, the term *science* refers primarily to the organized body of knowledge describing the physical world. However, others maintain that a proper definition of science must include the methods through which this knowledge is gained. The scientific method provides a process for testing hypotheses about the physical world; the role of the scientific method has more to do with correcting false ideas than establishing probable truth. Much of the work in science is directed to ruling out untenable ideas until a core of theories remains which are difficult or impossible to disprove. These persisting ideas form the foundation of our scientific perspectives—unless or until they too are disproved, and replaced by theories which provide better descriptions, explanations, and predictions about the world. Some scholars disagree about whether there are consistent differences between the natural and social sciences in the types of knowledge, or in the techniques used to gather knowledge. One suggestion is that empathy is a quality emphasized more in the social sciences than in the natural sciences.

There is no standard description of the scientific method. In the first essay, Lyman McDonald provides one current model of the scientific method in operation. McDonald offers valuable insights on the application, strengths, and limitations of the process, and includes some natural resource issues to illustrate the methodology.

For some, science is seen as approaching certain absolute truths. However, other scholars disagree with this perspective. Some argue that science progresses through series of elaborate systems of theory and methodology based on predominantly subjective interpretations scientists make of new, paradigmatic experiments and insights. The process of changing systems entails subjective and political elements. In this view, newer systems may solve some problems better than previous ones did, but they are not necessarily more accurate in describing reality. The selection by Leslie Stevenson in this chapter explores some of these notions. See also the works by Kuhn, Lakatos and Musgrave, and Popper in the section, For Further Reading, at the end of this chapter.

Scientists traditionally have focused on the cognitive aspects of their work. Recently, many have become more involved with the social and ethical implications of their research.

IS SCIENCE VALUE NEUTRAL?

Much of the confidence in the scientific method as a process for solving environmental problems is based on the assumption that researchers can address important issues without being biased by their own personal values. Is this a safe assumption?

Ideally, the scientist is said to be motivated by a love of truth for its own sake, unbiased by any personal preferences or cultural beliefs. Stevenson challenges this image in his essay, arguing that scientific research cannot be value-neutral because, as a human activity, it constantly involves choices of how to spend time, energy, money, and other resources. Since all of these resources are limited, the scientist's personal values contribute significantly to the choices made.

Holmes Rolston III asserts that scientists constantly are challenged to make value-laden decisions. Using Yellowstone National Park as an example, Rolston argues that the professional interests of scientists involved in a study must be compatible with the mission of the supervising agencies, the goals of any outside funding agencies, the constraints of good field biology, and the integrity of the ecosystems studied. Thus, value judgments need to be made at several levels.

Donald A. Brown identifies several sources of pressure that serve to separate empirical information from values considerations and to emphasize technical considerations in the processes of environmental regulation and decision making. Brown argues that this is wrong, and that skills are needed for dealing more openly with both the value dimensions and scientific dimensions of environmental concerns.

SHOULD HUMAN VALUES DETERMINE THE COURSE OF NATURE?

There often is a conflict among scholars on the extent to which humans should use available scientific knowledge to intervene in natural processes, especially in wilderness regions. Rolston points out that scientific management of natural systems is a means to an end, but does not replace the need to make value judgments of what the ends should be, and whether the ends should include or exclude human intervention. Rolston advocates that humans should not attempt to manage nature, as in the case of Yellowstone, but instead should learn to trust and to appreciate nature as it unfolds.

ECOLOGY AS A MODEL FOR LIVING

Many writers of current environmental literature build on the images of order, harmony, and integration often described in natural communities as models of how humans ought to relate to the natural world. Can the science of ecology provide a conceptual framework useful in helping humans live in harmony with nature?

Some scholars use a holistic perspective of the biosphere commonly presented in ecology as a sci-

entific basis for criticizing environmental decision making and practices. Ecology has been called ''the subversive science'' because its findings frequently are used to challenge political, economic, and ethical perspectives in contemporary society. Ecological principles often are cited in challenging the value-neutral positions commonly associated with science, and a number of philosophers have argued that these principles provide bases for new moral attitudes and political expectations.

These perspectives run counter to the traditional view that science cannot serve as a source of values: science may aid in predicting the outcomes of various decisions, but it first is necessary to select the moral values used, to determine which outcomes are acceptable. Rolston stresses this point in his essay.

According to Worster, even if one were willing to draw on science as a source of values, ecology cannot provide the philosophical model necessary to help humans live harmoniously with nature, because the current theoretical framework of ecology is undergoing some sweeping changes. Earlier views of holistic natural communities working in stable associations are being replaced by images of nature as fundamentally erratic, discontinuous, chaotic, and unpredictable. These images do not support the vision of a peaceful union between humans and nature. If Worster is correct, this shift could have a powerful impact on the direction of the environmental movement.

The Role of Statistics and the Scientific Method in the Art of Problem Solving

Lyman McDonald

Lyman McDonald (b. 1941) is President of Western EcoSystems Technology, Inc., and Professor of Statistics and Zoology at the University of Wyoming, Cheyenne. In this paper, McDonald presents a formal model for using prior knowledge, logical reasoning, and the scientific method for discovering new information and solving environmental problems.

McDonald uses three key terms in his model: "conjecture" (a broad idea or solution to a problem), "hypothesis" (a specific question used to rule out or test a conjecture), and "theory" (a formal and logical interpretation of prior facts and knowledge). McDonald's model offers a process for problem solving with several critical phases: clearly identifying a scientific or management objective, assimilating prior knowledge by logical reasoning, providing a variety of conjectured solutions to the objective through brainstorming and other strategies for tapping subconscious ideas, and supporting or rejecting the conjecture through logical reasoning or application of the scientific method. McDonald recommends that when there is not an adequate opportunity to rigorously test a conjecture by logic or the scientific method before a management decision is required, managers often should implement what they consider to be the best conjectured solution, and use the eventual results of that choice as a basis for formulating future conjectures.

POSTULATES:

1. There is no single, simple "scientific method" for gaining new knowledge.
2. "Theory" is not on the frontier of new knowledge.
3. College graduates (at least new B.S. graduates) are poorly trained in the art of gaining new knowledge.

Hopefully, this list of postulates will catch your attention and stimulate discussion—if so, one of my objectives for participating in the symposium is satisfied. I believe the postulates to be true and will attempt to clarify my position on each as well as explain my understanding of the overall role of statistics and the scientific method in problem solving. The discussion is applicable in all areas of science and management but is particularly important when considering the art of gaining new knowledge for the management of impacted wildlife populations.

Three main scientific methods have been recognized (Romesburg 1981). I have attempted to simultaneously integrate all three into the model presented in this paper.

I define "theory" to be the formalization and logical presentation of prior knowledge, or as the first definition in Webster's New Collegiate Dictionary states "the analysis of a set of facts in their relation to one another". In this sense, postulate 2 is clearly true. Theory is not on the frontier of new knowledge. However, a clear understanding of prior knowledge and, hence, theory is essential for progress in the discovery of new information.

In defense of postulate 3, university and college classes usually present facts, laws, and theories. Little is presented on how those facts, laws, and theories were conjectured and proven (if indeed they were proven). It follows that little is taught about the process of discovery of new facts, laws, and theories.

A MODEL FOR THE ART OF GAINING NEW KNOWLEDGE

Three individuals having considerable influence on my thinking are Deming (1965), Romesburg (1981), and Borgman (1982). Romesburg's paper gives a review of the literature for the interested reader.

Consider a problem that you have solved by discovery of new information and analyze the steps involved in first obtaining the solution and then in justifying it to others. Similarly, consider a management decision for which you had responsibility. I would appreciate communicating with you if it is found that the model presented is inappropriate. A flow diagram of the model (Figure 1) helps to explain my ideas on the art of using prior knowledge, logical reasoning,

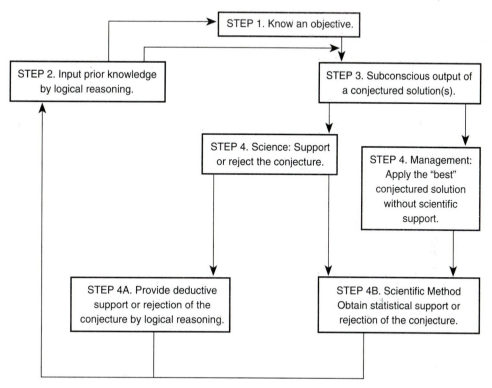

FIGURE 1

Flow diagram of a model for the art of solving problems.

and the scientific method for solving problems. Five examples will be presented to help clarify the model. But first, briefly consider each of the steps.

Step 1 is to know an objective. For example, the objective may be to solve a management problem, make one more step in a mathematical model, or devise a testable hypothesis that is true if a certain conjecture is correct.

Step 2 is logical input of prior knowledge. The individual must have some background knowledge obtained by study, review of related studies, talking with peers, review of projections made by mathematical models (computer simulations), analysis of pilot data, etc. With concentration and plain hard work it may be possible to make it past Step 2.

Step 3, subconscious output of conjectured solutions, may not occur! The mind must be given time

to create. I agree with Borgman (1982) that this nonverbal, almost mystical component of the process is real and absolutely necessary. It cannot be forced to occur although it will not occur unless one holds the ideas in mind and concentrates on obtaining a solution. Often a conjectured solution will occur when one is not actively trying to solve the problem. It is a phenomenon that must be experienced to be understood. I tell my students to work hard, concentrate, and have faith that solutions will come.

The word "conjecture" has been selected for the output of Step 3. Other words that could be used here but might lead to confusion in the model are: theory or hypothesis (assumed for sake of argument), unproven assumption, and speculation. In this sense, theory is on the frontier of new knowledge, but I reserve the word for formal presentation of a concise systematic view of the subject (Step 2). The word hypothesis has similarly been reserved for use in Step 4B, the "scientific method."

In "science" the next step is to support or reject the conjectured solution by logical reasoning (Step 4A) or to support or reject the conjecture by a statistical inference (Step 4B, the scientific method). For the result to be accepted (published), this step must be made. Problems are broken down into small discrete steps that can be attacked in this manner.

Individuals should expect to find themselves at Step 3 with no deductive or statistical argument to support their position. It is a natural and essential part of the discovery process. One just knows he is correct and all that is left is to work out the deductive argument or to wait on the data for a statistical inference. Of course, this is never mentioned in a technical report. We always report the objective (Step 1), literature review (Step 2), methods and materials (Step 4B), results (i.e., statistical inferences, Step 4B) and conclusions. Seldom if ever is there a discussion of circumstances behind discovery of the solution (Step 3) or how the idea for a testable hypothesis arose. I realize these points belong to the nonverbal part of our intellect but they may be the most important part of the art of gaining new knowledge.

In "management" many problems are so large that entire ecosystems are influenced by the conjectured "best" alternative. The mind (at least my mind) cannot comprehend how a deductive or statistical argument could possibly "prove" that the conjectured solution is the best management decision. Usually several variables are simultaneously under study, some of which are difficult or impossible to quantify, and no single objective function exists to maximize or minimize. Also, as Romesburg (1981) points out, decisions are based on perceived relative "values" of alternatives, not data. In addition, the value of an alternative may change over time.

I have drawn the flow diagram to indicate that the conjectured solution is applied to the management problem without benefit of scientific support. However, with careful planning and some desire, testable hypotheses or long term trend studies can usually be devised for study of consequences of the decision.

For example, if the decision is made to erect artificial nest structures for eagles, one might compare long term fledging rates of eagles using such structures and of eagles using natural structures. Similarly, long term trend data on density of small mammals in reclaimed areas might be compared to similar data from undisturbed areas. At a later date, new information will be available for improvement of future management decisions.

Finally, the cycle is completed when conclusions are drawn and the results are added to the theory covering prior knowledge.

A flow diagram for the scientific method (Step 4B, Figure 1) is given in Figure 2. Steps I and II of the scientific method actually require a cycle(s) through the model outlined in Figure 1 because we have unsolved problems! To make progress we must devise testable hypotheses that are true if the conjectured solution is correct and design feasible experiments that will yield unbiased data for statistical inferences. Either indirect support for the conjecture is obtained or the conjecture is rejected by the statistical inferences of Step IV.

Step IV (Figure 2) is the only part of the whole process that is typically addressed in statistics courses. However, in all fairness, I am unaware of any college course that addresses the whole learning and problem solving process.

Two examples from my experiences on an advisory team for the Wyoming Game and Fish Department and 3 examples from consulting and research projects conducted at the University of Wyoming are given to illustrate steps in the model (Figure 1).

Example 1—New knowledge for management of a rare species. Assume the objective is to prove the existence or non-existence of black-footed ferrets (*Mustela nigripes*) on a white-tailed prairie dog (*Cynomys leucurus*) town in Wyoming.

With this objective (Step 1), one faces a critical shortage of information that is based on the scientific method. Additional statistical inferences were impossible prior to November, 1981, because no ferrets existed for study (Schroeder and Martin 1982). Cycles through the learning process were

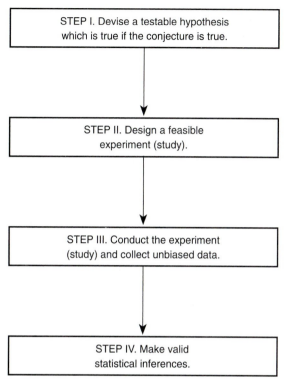

```
┌─────────────────────────────────────┐
│  STEP I. Devise a testable hypothesis │
│  which is true if the conjecture is true. │
└─────────────────────────────────────┘
                    │
                    ▼
┌─────────────────────────────────────┐
│      STEP II. Design a feasible       │
│         experiment (study).           │
└─────────────────────────────────────┘
                    │
                    ▼
┌─────────────────────────────────────┐
│     STEP III. Conduct the experiment  │
│     (study) and collect unbiased data. │
└─────────────────────────────────────┘
                    │
                    ▼
┌─────────────────────────────────────┐
│        STEP IV. Make valid            │
│        statistical inferences.        │
└─────────────────────────────────────┘
```

FIGURE 2

Flow diagram of a model for the scientific method.

made but with conclusions based on studies of black-tailed prairie dogs (*Cynomys ludovicianus*) (Hillman 1968), other mustelids, or from general knowledge of biological systems. Undoubtedly conjectures were made (Step 3) that were simply stymied for lack of adequate input for deductive inferences (Step 4A), or because of a lack of experimental results necessary for statistical inferences (Step 4B). Also, conjectured solutions were applied to meet management objectives without benefit of adequate scientific support. I am unaware of when Clark and Campbell (1982) arrived at the conjecture that the best time to search for ferret sign (tracks, digging, etc.) was immediately after a fresh snowfall. Probably they were not the first to make the conjecture but without the opportunity for making statistical inferences, the idea

would likely lie dormant. Also, the conjecture may have been simply an opportunistic hunch since the Meeteetse ferret population was discovered in early winter. At any rate, deductive logic combined with inductive reasoning from field data now leads one to the conclusion that if ferrets are present, winter searches have a higher probability of yielding proof of existence than do searches in other seasons. As we cycle through the learning process, (e.g., determine the likelihood that a ferret will be above ground on a given night) additional knowledge will be gained to better meet the objective.

Example 2—Management decision concerning a rare species. A problem faced by the Wyoming Game and Fish Department in the spring of 1982 concerned whether or not to allow researchers to trap and radio-collar black-footed ferrets in the Meeteetse population (Step 1). Members of the advisory and research teams possessed at least some of the necessary prior knowledge (Step 2) for conjecturing alternative decisions (Step 3). Providing the list of alternative decisions is the most important step in the problem solving process. If good alternatives are not conjectured it is impossible to make a good decision! Among the alternatives considered were: (1) allow no trapping; (2) trap and radio-collar a small number of adult males, after the reproductive season; (3) trap and radio-collar a small number of young animals of both sexes; and (4) both 2 and 3. Other alternatives were discussed and with additional homework, perhaps better ones would have been proposed. At any rate, picking the ''best'' alternative from the list became the objective.

Solution of the management problem now deviates from solution of a scientific problem in that the management decision is based on perceived relative ''values'' of the alternatives. Some disadvantages of trapping were: non-zero probability of accidental deaths of animals; increased chances of spread of disease; and unknown effects of increased human disturbances. Advantages included better data on: migration and survival of young ferrets, movements, prey needs (as far as can be determined from observed hunting behavior), and evaluation of current practices for ferret searches on other sites. Based on the perceived values, the committee advised the Wyoming Game and Fish Department to follow alternative 3. Scientific proof that this was the "best" alternative seems to be impossible. Clearly, in this case, data will be collected enabling tests of certain hypotheses that will either indirectly support the conclusion that a good decision was made or directly support lthe conclusion that it was a poor decision.

Example 3—An unsolved problem. One of the graduate students at the University of Wyoming is considering the objective of development of a mathematical population dynamics model that will better model the effects of genetics in small populations such as ferret populations and transplanted populations. At the present time the student is stuck at Step 2. It is impossible to reach Step 3 with his present background, but with desire, proper coursework, literature review, and evaluation of present models, he will make Steps 3 and 4. Of course, he is not as convinced of this as I am. The phenomenon has to be experienced to be fully understood. Meanwhile, faith and hard work are in order.

Example 4—Development of baseline data. Specifically, the objective (Step 1) was to determine the distribution and relative densities of mountain lions (*Felis concolor*) in Wyoming by an inexpensive, quick method. The objective was stated by Dale Strickland of the Wyoming Game and Fish Department in 1980 after management of the species became the responsibility of the department. I consulted with Dale on the project and eventually Richard Berg, a student at the University of Wyoming, was involved. Between the three of us we should have had the necessary prior knowledge (Step 2) to suggest some solutions, but conjectures (Step 3) do not necessarily come to mind. The mind must be given time to create and the conjectures will likely come to the conscience when one is not actively trying to solve the problem. Eventually,

the suggestion was made that we use a mail survey of (1) professional biologists and foresters, (2) trappers and lion hunters, (3) outfitters and (4) farmers and ranchers with questions on where and when lions had been sighted during the last ten years. Certainly the conjectured solution is imperfect, providing only indirect evidence on distribution and relative abundance of lions. Another characteristic of Step 3 is that once a solution has been conjectured, it is often so simple that you hesitate to tell others how long it took to arrive at it. Estimable parameters for testing hypotheses concerning distribution and density were established (part I of Figure 2) and a deductive argument was made that the survey provided unbiased data. Statistical inferences in part IV were relatively straight forward given unbiased data and proper sampling techniques.

Finally, the circle was completed with the input of the new knowledge into Steps 1 and 2 for meeting a new objective. Lions have been sighted in all appropriate habitat of Wyoming during the last ten years. The number of sightings per year increased during this period, and areas with the highest numbers of lion sightings were identified (Berg 1981). This new input was assembled with other knowledge to begin another round where the objective was to select a study site and design a more intensive capture-recapture study.

Example 5—New knowledge in a mathematical modeling problem. The objective was to determine a way to combine band return data from Canada Geese (*Branta canadensis*) banded in Wyoming with capture-recapture data on the same populations to better estimate mortality rates.

This objective (Step 1) was first stated in 1977 in a contract between the Wyoming Game and Fish Department and the University of Wyoming. At the time the contract was awarded, it was impossible to make progress toward the objective. Neither the graduate student, Stephanie Zowada Mardekian, nor I had the necessary prior knowledge. By studying the literature, taking courses, looking at data, talking to other people who had worked

on the models, thinking about the problem and educating me, Stephanie paid her dues (Step 2). Finally, late in the winter of 1979 part of a key to one solution of the problem (perhaps not the optimum solution) occurred to us while we were casually discussing the project after attending a rather dry seminar on another topic (Step 3). It was necessary to slightly modify the initial conjectured solution but we know it was basically correct. In fact, Stephanie and I required several days to tie up all loose ends in a neat, deductive mathematical proof (Step 4A). And even then, one weak link in the argument was discovered and corrected by a referee before the results were published (Mardekian and McDonald 1981).

CONCLUDING REMARKS

Many researchers seem to be afraid to admit that they must depend on logical reasoning for problem solving. The comment I hear is, ''we want a non-subjective procedure for making the decision''. Such a position is both impossible and undesirable. Even the choice and use of a statistical inference procedure is a subjective decision. As long as the biologist is willing to personally shoulder the responsibility for a subjective conclusion and can explain the steps in the reasoning, he should have no argument with the statistician.

One reason it is difficult for the steps in Figures 1 and 2 to be recognized is that we often cycle through the steps several times in one data analysis session. If a large set of reliable data exists, and if the proper background information is available (i.e., if Step 2 is automatic), the objectives, conjectured solutions, and testable hypotheses can arise very quickly and be evaluated statistically using the available data. Students may find themselves in this position because they often enter research projects at the data collection stage and without the required knowledge to contribute to the learning process. After some additional years of study, and with a good data set, everything may suddenly fall into place and they are able to cycle through the discovery process.

LITERATURE CITED

Berg, R.L. 1981. A mail survey for information on the distribution of mountain lions in Wyoming. M.S. Thesis, University of Wyoming, Laramie, WY. 94pp.

Borgman, L. 1982. Zen and statistical research. Presented at the Spring Meeting of the Colorado-Wyoming Chapter of the American Statistical Association, April 30, 1982, Boulder, CO.

Clark, T.W. and T.M. Campbell. 1982. The Meeteetse black-footed ferret conservation studies. Progress report July 22, 1982. Wyoming Game and Fish Department, Cheyenne, Wyoming.

Deming, W.E. 1965. Principles of professional statistical practice. *Annuals of Math. Statist.* 36:1883-1990.

Hillman, C.N. 1968. Field observations of black-footed ferret in South Dakota. *Trans. N. Amer. Wildl. and Nat. Res. Conf.* 33:433-443.

Mardekian, S.Z. and L.L. McDonald. 1981. Simultaneous analysis of band-recovery and life-recapture data. *J. Wildl. Manage.* 45:484-488.

Romesburg, H.C. 1981. Wildlife Science: gaining reliable knowledge. *J. Wildl. Manage.* 45:293-313

Schroeder, M.H. and S. Martin. 1982. Search for the black-footed ferret succeeds. *Wyo. Wildl.* 46(7):8-9.

DISCUSSION TOPICS

1. Give examples of ways in which a person's personal preferences or cultural stereotypes might affect the solutions reached after using McDonald's model of the scientific method. How might the possibility of biased solutions be reduced?

READING 2

Is Scientific Research Value-Neutral?

Leslie Stevenson

Leslie F. Stevenson is a member of the Department of Logic and Metaphysics at The University, St. Andrews, Fife, Scotland. In this reading, Stevenson challenges three assumptions commonly made about the value-free nature of science.

The first assumption Stevenson challenges is that while science discovers facts, there can be no scientific investigation of values influencing how those facts should be used. In contrast, Stevenson asserts both that science may not be as objective as many adherents claim, and that values may have an objective component that can be empirically analyzed.

The second assumption Stevenson challenges is that the only value recognized by the scientist, as a scientist, is to pursue the truth for its own sake. Stevenson argues that scientists are susceptible to pressures to compete for professional advancement and reputation, both of which are determined primarily by outside forces. Likewise, scientists depend upon research funding, which often is granted for projects promising some beneficial application of the results. Such funding rarely is value-free.

The third assumption the author challenges is that the application of scientific knowledge can and should be democratically decided by society as a whole. Stevenson points out that there is no such thing as ''society'' deciding. Rather, it generally is government agencies, universities, or other public and private institutions which decide these matters; the general public exercises little control over the direction of contemporary research or its applications.

A conventional view of scientific research, or at least of the 'pure' kind traditionally done in universities, is that it is a completely value-free activity. The white coat of the scientist has been taken as a sign of the purity of his motives, in the sense that he is devoted only to the pursuit of knowledge for its own sake. Beneficial (or sinister) applications of his work may come, but that is said to be not his concern: he is supposed to seek only for truth, for objective knowledge of the world. But when we realize how many of the world's scientists are presently working in the so-called 'defence' industries, the supposed purity of scientific activity can begin to look very mythical indeed.[1] Even if we look at research which is supposedly directed to more peaceful and benign purposes, such as in medicine, we may feel qualms about the

ways in which drug companies pursue profit, and about how the latest high technology treatments may contribute more to the fame of their creators than to the happiness of their patients.

The story of Frankenstein is an early expression of trepidation not just about misapplications of science, but about the process of scientific research itself. The image of the scientist there presented by Mary Shelley is of someone determined to gain knowledge of, and power over, some hidden and potentially dangerous aspect of nature: someone so obsessed with his project that he is prepared to risk the safety of himself, his collaborators, and perhaps his very society, in testing to the utmost his mental power to understand and his physical power to intervene.

> So much has been done . . . more, far more, will I achieve; treading in the steps already marked, I will pioneer a new way, explore unknown powers, and unfold to the world the deepest mysteries of creation.

So says Frankenstein at the outset of his research. But when he has 'discovered the causes of generation and life' and made himself 'capable of bestowing animation unpon lifeless matter,' he immediately proceeds to try out his powers, and the mis-shapen monster he creates gets quite out of his control and ends up destroying all that is most dear to him, so that afterwards he says:

> Learn from me . . . how dangerous is the acquirement of knowledge, and how much happier that man is who believes his native town to be the world, than he who aspires to become greater than his nature will allow.[2]

Thus by 1816 we find the early seventeenth-century optimism of Francis Bacon about the 'effecting of all things possible,'[3] the social benefits of the application of scientific knowledge, already very much clouding over.

Nowadays, when we think of the tremendous scientific technique that has been devoted to perfecting nuclear bombs and their delivery systems, of the research now being conducted into the militarization of space and into chemical and biological weapons, and into the possibilities for genetic engineering to produce new variants of living species, then the Franken-stein image of scientific research may seem more appropriate than that of white-coated purity.[4] Recalling the Biblical story of the garden of Eden, some may even begin to wonder whether there is some knowledge which it is better that we should not have.

However, the conventional response to such pessimism dismisses it as quite unnecessarily apocalyptic.[5] A distinction is commonly made between pure science on the one hand and applied science or technology on the other. It is said, first, that science offers us objective knowledge of how the world works, and hence of what would be the consequences of various possible interventions in it. But it is implied, by contrast, that there can be no such 'objective knowledge' of whether we *should* make any particular interventions: a sharp distinction between facts and values is thought to rule out any knowledge of the latter, so that the adoption of values is a matter of merely 'subjective' individual opinion.

It is said, second, that the only value recognized by the scientist as such is the value of knowledge for its own sake: he may welcome the possibility of applications of his research, but as a scientist he is a scholar devoted purely to the extension of human knowledge as an end in itself, like the philologist, the medieval historian, and the pure mathematician.

> Whoever, in the pursuit of science, seeks after immediate practical utility, may generally rest assured that he will seek in vain. All that science can achieve is a perfect knowledge and a perfect understanding of the action of natural and moral forces. Each individual student must be content to find his reward in rejoicing over new discoveries, as over new victories of mind over reluctant matter, or in enjoying the aesthetic beauty of a well-ordered field of knowledge, where the connection and filiation of every detail is clear to the mind, he must rest satisfied with the consciousness that he too has contributed something to the increasing fund of knowledge on which the dominion of man over all the forces hostile to intelligence reposes.[6]

The third element of the conventional wisdom is that the applications of scientific knowledge are for 'society' to decide: the technologist is the servant of other people, applying his expertise towards ends that are chosen in whatever way it is that individuals and institutions decide what to aim at. Some may think there is knowledge of the right way for human beings to live—whether derived from a sacred book, a church, a theocracy of mullahs, the ideology of a ruling party, or an inspired leader—and all these can apply scientific knowledge towards their various ends. Those more sceptical of the possibility of knowledge of values typically appeal to the ideal of democracy at this point, and suggest that the ends to which scientific knowledge is to be applied should be decided by some democratic process by which decisions emerge from the mass of individual, 'subjective,' opinions.

But all three elements of this conventional picture are very much open to question. Let us take them in reverse order. There is, of course, no such thing as 'society' deciding: there are only the decisions of various institutions—governments, companies, universities, etc. And there are good reasons for wondering how far contemporary scientific research and its technological application is—or could be—under the democratic control of the citizens who contribute to its costs and are likely to be affected by its results. Much vital research is now conducted under conditions of military or industrial secrecy, and by the time its results become publicly known it is too late for anyone to argue that the effort and resources might have been better directed elsewhere. Such can be the situation facing a newly-elected politician being briefed about the technological programmes which have been going on behind the scenes. He will be advised by authoritative experts that 'this is a project on which much has already been spent, which is soon to come to fruition, and which it would be madness to abandon at this late stage, just when we are about to gain an advantage over our rivals.' The very nature of modern technology—the long lead-time needed for development, the large numbers of people with specialist expertise who have to be committed to it, and the very high costs of the process—means that it acquires a momentum of its own which makes it extremely difficult for any outside force, even a clear majority of public opinion, to stop. Another factor favouring those responsible for directing research is that because of its very technical nature and of the secrecy which usually surrounds it, they can usually retain the initiative in how the matter is presented to the public. With the aid of those skilled in the mass media, public opinion can be 'moulded.'[7]

Let us consider now the second point of the conventional picture: the claim that the only thing valued by the scientist is knowledge for its own sake. It would have to be a very 'pure' scientist indeed who was content to hide his light under a bushel, who did not care about his scientific reputation, his professional advancement, and the power and rewards which this can bring. But the areas in which appointments, promotion, fame, and reward are to be found are determined by social forces outside the individual scientist. Perhaps in the past the relevant audience was simply the professional judgment of fellow-scientists, and the resources necessary for research could be provided by the average university laboratory. But for many parts of science the picture has now changed enormously—the era of 'big science' has come. The leading edges of research and development have got to the point where to push them further forward requires large teams of specialists, and supplies of extremely expensive equipment. This means that hard choices have now to be faced about the direction and funding of research. Because of the huge costs involved, the concentration of research into larger units and its control by large institutions seem inevitable. Since the state itself is increasingly involved, there comes to be a political element in decision-making even about pure scientific research.

So even though the scientist may wish to say that his only professional commitment is to the increase of human knowledge, he will now have to recognize that the funds for his research will probably be given with a fairly close eye to possible applications, be they military, industrial, medical, or whatever. Such research cannot be said to be value-free. By accepting funds from certain sources, and agreeing to make his results available to them, the scientist is participating in social processes by which knowledge, and hence power, is given to certain social groups rather than others.[8] The scientist may have to make a difficult choice between doing his research under these conditions, or not doing it at all. By his participation in the process as actually institutionalized, he displays tacit acceptance of the values of those institutions.

The Frankenstein image never was very plausible for the average *individual* scientist—and the occasional fanatic is fairly easily controlled. What we surely need to worry about much more is the power of the institutions which increasingly direct scientific research—the research councils, the commercial companies and corporations, the rich private foundations, the weapons laboratories, the armed services, the defence departments, the state itself. Such bodies may be made up of reasonably well-meaning individuals, each of them earning their living and doing their duty as they conceive of it, yet the institutions can act like corporate Frankensteins, pursuing power or profit regardless of social consequences.

Let us return now to the first element in the conventional picture of the value-neutrality of science. A sharp distinction between facts and values has been commonplace in twentieth-century thought—not just in the philosophies of positivism and existentialism which have dramatized it most, but as a background assumption which conditions much everyday thinking. But there is of course a major philosophical issue here—the common assumption of the subjectivity of all values should certainly not be allowed to pass without question. For this represents a major claim in the theory of meaning, knowledge, and metaphysics—a philosophical thesis that there is some crucially important difference between the standards governing science and ethics. The philosophical debate about the objectivity of values which has been going on since Socrates at least shows no sign of flagging.

This is not the place to try to extend that debate. But it is worth noting here that there are two ways in which the allegedly unique objectivity of science might be rejected. It may be suggested that science does not really have the kind of objectivity commonly attributed to it, or it might be claimed that discussion of values can in principle attain an objectivity not significantly lower-grade than that of science. Examples of the latter kind of argument can be found in the work of Hilary Putnam[9] and of Jürgen Habermas.[10] Both writers question what Habermas calls 'scientism'—the typical positivist assumption that our very standard of what is to count as knowledge should be defined in terms of the natural sciences: they thus attack the first element in our conventional picture above. Habermas recommends 'reflection' on the ends of our actions, and in particular on the applications which we may consider making of scientific knowledge; his hope seems to be that if only the conditions of communication of knowledge, opinion, and argument were ideal, then the discussion of values could approach in rationality to the standard commonly recognized in the sciences. But adequate discussion of Habermas or Putnam would take us beyond the scope of this paper.

The objectivity of science itself has been questioned by some, and it is appropriate to review their arguments briefly here. Paul Feyerabend adopts a radically relativist position, according to which science is just one tradition amongst others, such as ancient or primitive world-views, or religious or political belief-systems within Western culture.[11] His crucial claim is that these various 'traditions' cannot be rationally compared for truth, since all such judgments about truth or rationality can only be made from within one tradition. Along with this Protagorean relativism, Feyerabend recommends 'political relativism', namely a 'free society' in which all traditions are given equal rights, equal access to education and other positions of power. This would involve a separation between science and state, like that presently acknowledged between religion and state in most Western democracies.

This splendidly provocative challenge to the conventional wisdom about the rationally of scientific method deserves a careful answer, and has received more than one.[12] But the following point is worth making here. If Feyerabend is to be entitled to make a distinction between comparing rival theories within a tradition, and the alleged impossibility of any rational comparison between traditions themselves, he had better have a clearly-articulated criterion of identity for 'traditions.' He has to be able to tell us when a change in concepts or beliefs is merely a change

within a tradition, and when it constitutes a change *of* tradition. Which description, for example, would he apply to the Copernican revolution in astronomy, to the advent of Darwinian theory or of relativity physics, or to the difference between organic and psychodynamic accounts of mental illness? Unless Feyerabend can give us a principled way of answering such questions, his claims about the limitation of rationality to within traditions are mere formal schemas, empty of real content.

Some years earlier, Herbert Marcuse conducted a verbal onslaught on scientific and technical rationality and its social consequences which is perhaps even more radical than that of Feyerabend.[13] In his chapter on 'technological rationality and the logic of domination' he claims that the way in which 'scientific-technical rationality and manipulation are welded together into new forms of social control' is not just the result of a specific social application of science, but was already 'inherent in pure science.' He asserts: 'the science of nature develops under the technological a priori which projects nature as potential instrumentality, stuff of control and organization' and 'science, by virtue of its own method and concepts, has projected and promoted a universe in which the domination of nature has remained linked to the domination of man'. Yet, he says, things could be radically different, for the structure of the scientific project could change: 'its hypotheses, without losing their rational character, would develop in an essentially different experimental context (that of a pacified world); consequently, science would arrive at essentially different concepts of nature and establish essentially different facts'.

Marcuse's vision of an alternative form of science, which would establish different concepts and facts from those presently acknowledged, also seems very schematic and philosophically undefended. He owes us an account of what he sees as definitive of science in whatever forms it may take, and of which features of present-day science he thinks could alter, and how. I do not see that he does more than gesture at this. Of course, research might be pursued in some areas rather than others—for reasons of finance, social need, military pressure, ethical restrictions, or scientific fashionability. But Marcuse's thesis appears to be (if we take seriously the last sentence quoted from him above) that even on a given topic, an alternative way of doing science would yield different theories about the nature of the world. And presumably he does not mean just that there can be complementary theories of the same phenomenon (such as wave- or particle theories of light)—I take it that such differences would for him be *within* the 'domineering' way of doing science, to which he wants to suggest a radical alternative. But unless he can characterize this with more than abstract words like 'being', 'logos,' and 'eros,' we can be forgiven for wondering whether he really has an alternative to offer.

More recently, Jeremy Rifkin has published a manifesto in which he declares himself a 'heretic' about the worthwhileness of our whole present scientific enterprise.[14] He argues that we must rethink our basic assumptions about the pursuit of knowledge (not just our use of technology, and our economic systems), and he suggests that it is possible 'for the mind to think in a radically different way.' Ever since Bacon's time, we have been seeking scientific knowledge for its instrumental value, but 'instead of pursuing knowledge to gain power and control, we could just as well pursue knowledge to experience empathy and participation.' But Rifkin does not in this short popular book make it clear whether he has in mind a different epistemology of science, or just a different kind of *motivation* for pursuing and applying scientific knowledge as standardly understood.

Nicholas Maxwell has made a similar-sounding plea (at much greater length, and with pretensions to philosophical depth) for a total transformation of our attitude to scientific knowledge.[15] He argues that instead of the 'philosophy of knowledge' (which would seem to be his version of the conventional image of science which I have been attacking above) we should espouse the 'philosophy of wisdom,' by which Maxwell means, in brief summary, that we should 'give absolute intellectual priority to our life and its problems'—the idea seems to be that all inquiry should be aimed *directly* at goals of human value. But later it emerges that Maxwell is committed to more than a change in the motivation of scientific research, for he disputes the standard epistemology of science, which

he labels 'minimal standard empiricism.' He claims to show that 'empirical considerations alone cannot decide what theories are to be accepted and rejected in science: metaphysical considerations concerning the comprehensibility of the universe must be taken into account in addition.' Maxwell thus takes us back into Feyerabendian territory, into issues in the basic epistemology of science which have already received extended philosophical consideration and which deserve more.

I mention these various writers here not just because they sense that there are problems about the way in which science is currently being applied, but because they make interesting and controversial claims about how the roots of those problems lie in philosophical assumptions about the nature of science, and of knowledge generally. These radical thinkers raise questions about science and its applications which are hardly mentioned by academically more prestigious philosophers of science.[16] But it is one thing to ask good questions, and another thing to give good answers to them. The comments above give us reason to wonder whether either Feyerabend or Marcuse has a coherent philosophical position to defend. The programmatic remarks of Rifkin, and the more verbose 'philosophy of wisdom' of Maxwell, leave it unclear whether they want to question not just the wisdom of our present applications of science, but the validity of scientific method as the way to find out the truth about the material world.

It is one thing to question the usefulness or point of any particular programme of scientific research, but quite another to question the epistemology of scientific method itself. Let us try to distinguish the different basic questions here. We can ask (about any given topic):

1. *What is true?*

and, if we want to know the answer, we will be led to ask:

2. *How can we know what is true?* (What is the way to find out?)

That scientific method (in the general sense) is the answer to the second question is not doubted except by Feyerabend and his ilk—but still, this is a perfectly serious philosophical question which merits a more considered response than I can attempt to give here.

But even if we take it that there is a truth about a certain matter, and that scientific method is the way to discover what it is, it does not follow that it is worth anyone's while to find it out. The average weight of the pebbles on a beach can be estimated, but unless this fact is thought to be relevant to testing some wider theory, why should anyone bother to make the measurements? So we can also ask (about a given topic):

3. *Why should anyone want to know?*—and more concretely: *Who* wants to know, and why?

Yet any sort of scientific inquiry takes someone's time and effort (and usually costs some money). Even the nineteenth-century rural dean, botanizing on weekdays, can reasonably be asked why he should spend his time on this rather than something else (like ministering to the needs of his parishioners, perhaps). So even if we allow that there is *some* intrinsic value (perhaps fairly minimal—such as satisfying someone's curiosity, or extending the sum total of human knowledge) in knowing the truth about anything, we can still ask:

4. *Is it worth the costs of finding out?*

There are various different kinds of cost that may be involved, not all of them monetary. As noted above, there now tend to be very high financial costs in pursuing research; but there are many other factors which have to be weighed in the balance when answering questions of type 4. Sometimes there are safety risks in experimentation itself (e.g., when dealing with radiation, poisons, viruses or microbes); and these often cannot be realistically estimated in advance of the results of the research (consider the famous controversy of the 1970s about the unknown risks of the new techniques of genetic engineering).[17] Sometimes there are ethical values which people may recognize, and yet hotly disagree whether the interest and possible benefits of scientific research should be allowed to override them in particular cases (e.g., animal suffering, fairness to human patients, honesty to subjects of experiments in social psychology, privacy of individual lives).

Even when a given individual or institution can answer question 4 to their own satisfaction, it does not follow that their answer will be equally acceptable to others. In military or commercial competition, one group wants to know something, but does *not* want its rivals to know it. Question 3 thus becomes vital. As noted above, the institutions funding research typically have interests in utilizing the knowledge gained, so it may in practice be possible to get results only on the condition that they are made available exclusively to a certain defence department or industrial company. A scientist may want to know something, both for its own intrinsic interest, and for the possibility of beneficial applications, and yet the institutional or social situation may be such that he must have serious doubts about whether the knowledge may not be misused. One may have excellent reason to suspect that the military or the corporation will use one's discoveries and inventions for their own purposes, with which one may well disagree. Or one may have good reason to predict that a new technique will be used in a certain society in ways one might not approve of—e.g., the availability of procedures to determine the sex of the foetus may lead, in countries where male children are perferred, to widespread abortion of female foetuses. And even if one does not have *specific* misuses in mind, there may be social choices, which on the whole we might prefer *not* to have to face, which could be forced on us simply by the further advance of scientific understanding. For example, however scientifically interesting the mechanisms of human genetics may be, do we really want to be given the opportunity of, and hence the responsibility for, deciding the genetic characteristics of our offspring?

Scientific research cannot, then, be value-neutral. The general reason for this is that it is a human activity, and therefore involves choices how to spend time, energy, and resources. The special reasons are those adverted to in this paper, more peculiar to the institutional character of scientific research in the late twentieth century and beyond. Besides continuing epistemological and metaphysical inquiry into scientific method, there is pressing need for philosophical discussion of under what conditions further scientific knowledge is likely to be worth the various costs of getting it.[18]

NOTES

1. It is obviously hard to quantify exactly, but Barry Barnes, for one, suggests that at least one third of worldwide expenditure on research and development should be reckoned as military in nature (and that in Britain the proportion is more than half). See his *About Science* (Oxford: Blackwell, 1985), p. 29.

2. Mary Shelley, *Frankenstein* (1816, Oxford University Press ed.), pp. 48, 52, 57.

3. Francis Bacon, *New Atlantis* (1627).

4. Some writers identify here a compulsive masculine urge to penetrate the innermost secrets of passive feminine nature. See Brian Easlea, *Fathering the Unthinkable* (London: Pluto Press, 1983), an account of the invention of the atomic and hydrogen bombs in terms of such aggressively masculine motives. At the beginning of the modern scientific era, Bacon in *The Masculine Birth of Time* made a more peaceful and domestic application of the metaphor of scientific masculinity: 'what I purpose is to unite you with things themselves in a chaste, holy, and legal wedlock; and from this association you will secure an increase beyond all the hopes and prayers of ordinary marriages, to wit, a blessed race of Heroes or Supermen who will overcome the immeasurable helplessness and poverty of the human race'—translated in Benjamin Farrington, *The Philosophy of Francis Bacon* (Chicago: Phoenix Books, 1966), p. 72.

5. Peter Medawar wrote eloquently: 'To deride the hope of progress is the ultimate fatuity, the last word in poverty of spirit and meanness of mind' (in 'On ''The Effecting of All Things Possible,'' ' reprinted in *Pluto's Republic* (Oxford: Clarendon Press, 1982) and in *The Hope of Progress.*

6. H. von Helmholtz in *Popular Lectures on Scientific Subjects,* 1st series (London/New York, 1893); quoted in J. R. Ravetz, *Scientific Knowledge and its Social Problems* (Oxford: Oxford University Press, 1971), p. 39.

7. For example, consider how America's present strategic defence initiative has come to be popularly labelled the 'star wars' programme—thus associating it in the public mind with popular science-fiction films, conveying the impression of something futuristic, exciting, even entertaining, and in which good can be guaranteed to defeat evil in the end. Consider, too, how the vast investment in the SDI programme will limit the options open to Reagan's successor in 1989.

8. Consider, e.g., the £20-million deal between Oxford University and the Squibb Corporation (the world's seventh largest drug company) reported in *New Scientist 116,* No. 1583 (22/10/87). The company will provide a new building for the Department of Pharmacology, and will support research into treatment for brain diseases, in return for intellectual property rights on relevant results—researchers must keep them secret for long enough for the company to take out patents.

9. H. Putnam, *Reason, Truth and History* (Cambridge: Cambridge University Press, 1981), esp. ch. 6.

10. J. Habermas, *Knowledge and Human Interests* (Boston: Beacon Press, 1971).

11. P. Feyerabend, *Against Method* (London: NLB, 1975), esp. ch. 18; and *Science in a Free Society* (London: NLB, 1978), esp. pt. 2.

12. W. Newton-Smith, *The Rationality of Science* (London: Routledge & Kegan Paul, 1981), ch. VI.

13. H. Marcuse, *One-Dimensional Man* (London: Routledge & Kegan Paul, 1964), esp. ch. 6.

14. J. Rifkin, *Declaration of a Heretic* (London: Routledge & Kegan Paul, 1985).

15. N. Maxwell, *From Knowledge to Wisdom* (Oxford: Blackwell, 1984).

16. An exception to this generalization is I. Hacking, 'Weapons Research and the Form of Scientific Knowledge,' *Canadian Journal of Philosophy,* suppl. vol. 12 (1986); pp. 237-60.

17. See S. Krinsky, *Genetic Alchemy: The Social History of the DNA Controversy* (Boston: MIT Press, 1982).

18. An early version of this paper was presented to an Anglo-French colloquium on social aspects of science in the University of Lille in May 1985, and an abbreviated version of the first few pages appeared in *New Scientist,* 1 September 1988.

DISCUSSION TOPICS

1. What factors should be considered and who should be given responsibility for decisions about engaging in controversial areas of environmental research such as certain applications of genetic engineering? Explain your reasoning.

2. Do you agree with Stevenson that the general public exercises little control over the direction of contemporary research and its applications? Should the general public have more control? Why or why not? If greater public involvement were to become a priority, what guidelines would you recommend?

3. If Stevenson is correct in asserting that science is not value-free, how might the results of scientific research on environmental topics be presented to provide value-neutral information? Explain your reasoning.

Ethics, Science, and Environmental Regulation

Donald A. Brown

Donald A. Brown is Chief of Central Region Litigation in the Pennsylvania Department of Environmental Resources, and has been an environmental lawyer with the states of New Jersey and Pennsylvania.

Brown identifies some problems in this reading that result from relegating complex environmental problems to scientific experts. In particular, he argues that the ethical issues embedded in many complex environmental problems often become hidden or distorted by the methods and communication styles of both science and administration. For example, factual information related to environmental decisions often is difficult or impossible to separate from value considerations. In many cases value issues are translated into economic frames of reference and then are used by technical experts in a scheme to maximize market efficiency by satisfying the greatest number of individual preferences—a classic utilitarian perspective; Brown points out a number of weaknesses with this approach. He also decries the recent trend at both the state and federal levels to perform mandatory cost-benefit analyses on environmental decisions despite the many weaknesses of this approach.

Brown notes that the increasing pressures brought by regulated industries to restrict the regulatory activities of the government make it almost impossible for environmental administrators to adopt new regulations without first establishing strong political support for those regulations. He argues that current pressures for this type of "regulatory reform" may lead to increased environmental abuses.

Brown delineates the ways in which technical analyses often are written in technological terms only, omitting important social and ethical considerations. He also cautions that risk assessments of environmental issues may be distorted and outlines six concerns he believes should be addressed when making them.

Brown argues that value issues become distorted or ignored when laws place the burden of proof to show possible risk or injury on regulating government agencies. The complexities involved impede government agencies in making a case that risk or injury may occur.

Brown concludes that value distortions sometimes result from the narrow scientific training of most scientists. He advocates that citizens develop the technical skills required for addressing the important ethical and value dimensions of environmental issues, and he offers five recommendations for facilitating this process.

INTRODUCTION

Are important ethical and values questions distorted through the relegation of environmental problems to the language systems of technical "experts"? Does our growing faith in science often lead to confusion about important environmental issues? Many authors have written extensively about the impoverishment of human communication through the use of technology-laden language and the development of value-neutral sciences to analyze human value problems. Jurgen Habermas, for instance, has asserted that science and technology are sources of systematically distorted communication that prevents the attainment of consensus on political issues.[1] Communication about environmental problems and issues is particularly susceptible to the distortion that follows from the uncritical use of the language of science because of the technical complexity of most environmental problems and the accompanying need to relegate all complex environmental problems to "technical experts." In this article I explore some of the more frequent ways in which the translation of environmental problems into the language and methods of science all too often distorts the value questions inherent in environmental problems. By exposing the many ways in which questions of value are lost or distorted in technical discourse about environmental problems, I hope to help restore value questions to their appropriate central status in environmental policy making.

THE REGULATORY SETTING

We all know that the new age of science, computers, space missions, biotechnology, star wars weapons

---

1. Jurgen Habermas, *Toward a Rational Society: Student Protest, Science, and Politics* (Boston: Beacon Press, 1970).

and other goodies of post-industrial society creates potential for new man-made environmental and social disasters. The dangers posed by hazardous chemicals, endangered and vanishing species of flora and fauna, the potential depletion of the ozone layer, the ever increasing contamination of domestic water supplies, problems relating to nuclear power, and the most recent concern over the gradual heating of the global weather patterns caused by the ''green-house effect'' are examples of pressing ecological problems thrust upon society for the first time during the second half of the twentieth century. These problems are characterized by levels of complexity and uncertainty never before experienced by any society. Because faith in science is at an all time high, we tend not to blame the engineer or scientist for these problems. Instead, we believe that science will tell us which problems should be of concern and what steps should be taken to protect us.

In the United States the usual response to these complex problems has been to create complex laws that empower administrative agencies staffed largely by engineers, scientists, lawyers, and, with greater frequency, economists, to ''regulate'' these problems. Although many of the goals of public policy are set out in the authorizing legislation, very often much of the public policy is determined by administrative rule making.[2] For example, some environmental laws require the government to promulgate rules to balance health benefits against costs, such as the Toxic Substances Control Act,[3] while others appear to allow for considerations of health only, e.g., section 109(b)(1) of the Clean Air Act.[4] Even though environmental administrators are in this way constrained by the authorizing legislation in promulgating environmental rules, all the major environmental statutes give government agencies much discretion in formulating the final rules, for example, by allowing agencies to decide which pollutants shall be regulated or by allowing administrators to identify what levels of pollution are acceptable. For instance, under the Clean Air Act national ambient air standards are set at a level which ''in the judgment of the administrator . . . allow an adequate margin of safety'' and a hazardous air pollutant is designated by ''the judgment of the administrator.''[5]

According to the model for an administrative agency accepted by most lawyers, administrators, and political scientists, the administrative expert breaks down all environmental problems into an ''objective'' technical problem and a ''subjective'' policy component. In developing policy the administrator looks at the guidance contained in the legislation and then applies the ''objective'' technical facts to the decision rule found in the policy-defining legislation. In this way, agency technicians apply science derived ''facts'' to politically derived rules. The model envisioned in this conventional view of administrative decision making assumes that the technical problems under consideration can be dealt with in technical, analytical terms and that the values of the administrator and the value problems embedded in the environmental controversy can be eliminated from the administrative process. Does the relegation of these ''fact-value'' questions to ''technical'' experts systematically distort the important values and ethical questions that are necessarily embedded in the environmental questions under consideration? I believe that the answer is clear.

DEFINITION OF TERMS—ETHICS AND SCIENCE DISTINGUISHED

For purposes of definition, by ethics I mean the domain of inquiry that attempts to answer the question ''What is good?'' Ethical statements are propositions of the form that such and such is good or bad, right or wrong, obligatory or nonobligatory. Ethics should be

---

2. During the late 1970s and early 1980s many parties called for regulatory reform to curb the alleged abuse of discretion by administrative agencies in rule making. If all policy choices are made by authorizing legislation, then there is no need for regulatory reform to control administrative discretion. It is therefore assumed to be axiomatic that agencies have great discretion in writing environmental regulations and designing environmental regulatory programs.

3. 15 U.S.C. §2605(a).

4. 42 U.S.C. §7409.

5. U.S.C. §7409(b)(I); *Lead Industries v. EPA,* 645 F.2d 1130 (1980), *cert. den'd;* 449 U.S. 102 (1980); 42 U.S.C. §7412(A)(I).

distinguished from the social sciences, such as sociology and psychology, which attempt to determine why individuals or groups make statements about what is good, right, or obligatory. Furthermore, ethics is concerned with ''prescriptive'' statements, which attempt to transcend relative cultural and individual positions. Science, as used in this essay, is the discipline that attempts to make ''descriptive'' statements about the nature of reality through analysis of facts and experience. Science and its derivative technologies attempt to describe objectively, through an empirical methodology, facts and relationships between facts, and the laws of nature that govern the universe.

It is generally accepted that science cannot deduce prescriptive statements from facts.[6] That is, one cannot deduce ''ought'' from ''is'' without supplying a new minor premise. One cannot introduce an evaluative term, such as ''optimal solution,'' into the conclusion of an argument if the prior premises of that argument are entirely nonevaluative (e.g., dose-response statistics). Although a description of certain facts may suggest an ethical position, one cannot through a description of the facts alone deduce an ethical conclusion. An ethical system such as utilitarianism may provide the minor premise needed for ethical reasoning. For instance, if one concludes that option ''A'' will create the greatest happiness, by applying the utilitarian maxim that one should choose the option that creates the greatest happiness, one can conclude that option ''A'' is the optimal solution. From a proposition that such and such a problem creates a particular risk, one cannot, however, deduce whether that risk is acceptable without first deciding

on certain criteria for acceptability. Therefore, on this largely traditional view of the logic of ethics, science cannot answer ethical questions all by itself.

This is not to say, however, that science is irrelevant to ethics. Ethics is concerned with the ends that should be chosen by people. Science is extremely important in most environmental ethical discussions because, once a particular goal is chosen, science can evaluate various means that are available to achieve the goal. Science can also analyze which ends are feasible. If a society determines that it is good to build a nuclear power plant, for instance, science can analyze what structures or what types of institutions most effectively and safely achieve the type of power plant described by the community. Science can also help determine what environmental impacts the community should expect from the power plant. On this view, however, science cannot fully determine whether the power plant should be built, precisely because no amount of descriptive analysis can logically certify a prescriptive course of action. Science is thus obviously fundamental to the description of the environmental problems discussed in this essay and is particularly useful in identifying, for example, the health risks that certain projects pose. Those who are interested in a full discussion of values positions in environmental policy making, therefore, are not anti-scientific. In fact, sound scientific analysis is essential in any attempt to fully define most of environmental ethical questions considered here.

If we agree that the question of whether society should use nuclear power is essentially an ethical question, while admitting that science is extremely important in analyzing the facts, and thereby giving content to the ethical question, it must be admitted that there is no generally accepted consensus in the philosophical community about which ethical system to apply to any given problem. Several major philosophical systems attempt to define good, including utilitarianism, Kantian ethics, natural rights, and Rawlsian contract theory, just to name a few. Some philosophers assert that ethical assertions should be treated as nothing more than the emotive preferences of the person making the assertion on the grounds that they are entirely subjective and relative to the person

---

6. The relationship between facts and ethical positions is of considerable controversy within the philosophical community. See, for example, J. Baird Callicott, ''Hume's *Is/Ought* Dichotomy and the Relation of Ecology to Leopold's Land Ethic,'' *Environmental Ethics* 4 (1982): 163-174. Although certain linguistic philosophers have held that moral reasoning made by individuals does not rely on deductive models, in which ethical conclusions follow from ethical principles. I believe that it is particularly important in developing public policy that those who make ethical assertions be required to expose ethical premises that support ethical conclusions. Also see Don E. Marrietta, Jr., ''Knowledge And Obligation in Environmental Ethics: A Phenomenological Approach,'' *Environmental Ethics* 4 (1982): 153-162.

making the value judgment. Additionally, it is some-times difficult to determine which facts should be considered and what weight should be given to these facts in any ethical calculus. Because most of the dominant Western philosophical systems make human interests the measure of value, human interests, some critics argue, are the only interests considered in Western ethical systems, with the result that such concerns as the rights of animals are not appropriately included in traditional ethical debate. In the last ten years, as concerns about environmental problems has increased, environmental philosophers have attempted to create new ethical approaches to these complex environmental problems. Because there are so many approaches, showing that there are ethical questions that have not been adequately considered in public policy formulation is far easier than finding ethical solutions to these questions.

THE SEPARATION OF FACTS AND VALUES IN THE ADMINISTRATIVE PROCESS

One of the most common ways in which value issues are hidden in environmental public policy making develops out of the expectation that the technical analysts can isolate the "facts" under dispute and employ these "facts" in accordance with the "value" formula given in the enabling legislation. The separation of "fact" and "value" issues, however, is often difficult, if not impossible. Philosophers who have been concerned about how people understand facts, a topic studied within a branch of philosophy called hermeneutics, have come to realize that what one sees is usually a product of cultural tradition; there are no acts of pure perception that are not dependent on prior value choices. In this context, the decision about which "facts" to focus on in the analytical state of research cannot avoid value questions. For example, should the environmental impact analysis of a dam consider protection of the habitats of deer and elk or should it consider potential destruction of the habitats of skunk or coyote? The decision of what to study is frequently a question of value, not of fact.

Second, the decision about what resources will be used in performing the analyses of the facts is ultimately a value decision for which there is usually no objective standard. In a recent book entitled *Making Bureaucracies Think,* Serge Taylor reports that the determination of what methods and resources the Army Corps of Engineers will employ to predict the environmental impacts of a project often results from a negotiated settlement between the environmental analyst and the project manager, and frequently depends upon such nonscientific criteria as the amount of budget money that is available to perform the analysis.[7]

Many of the "facts" that the analyst attempts to collect for use in policy calculations are not susceptible to purely objective analysis. For instance, it is impossible to determine the visual impact of a water diversion project upstream from a dam, for there are simply no "objective" criteria for beauty or ugliness. Separating "facts" from values is also often impossible because the gathering of the facts must rest on hard-to-test or even presently untestable assumptions about the way the world works. The facts at issue in environmental disputes are very often nothing more than guesses based on high-level speculation. Likewise, how facts are arrayed by technical expert are often not policy neutral. A report by the Center for Philosophy and Public Policy entitled *Faith in Science* concludes that

> simply knowing some action will result in the deaths of some people who would not have otherwise died does not tell us whether the act is murder, killing, allowing some people to die, or even saving lives. . . . No matter how "neutral" the scientific work is, there may be no neutral description of it that can be incorporated into policy discussions. The psychological literature on decision making shows that people's preferences are often determined by the way a choice is described to them and can change under different descriptions that appear to be equivalent.[8]

Analysis of environmental "facts" usually requires prior value decisions about level of detail, burden-of-proof, and quality of data. Thus, a value choice

---

7. Serge Taylor, *Making Bureaucracies Think* (Stanford: Stanford University Press, 1984).
8. Claudia Mills, "Faith in Science," *Report From the Center for Philosophy and Public Policy* 5 (1985): 1.

is implicit in almost every choice the technical analyst makes. But for reasons discussed later, these value choices are rarely identified in the technical analysis or in the public policy debate.

THE TRANSLATION OF ALL VALUE QUESTIONS INTO ECONOMIC LANGUAGE

Another way in which values questions are distorted in the technical process into which they are relegated is through the translation of value questions to economic language. When technical experts recognize that particular value questions have to be considered in environmental decision making, the values are usually discussed in terms of economic considerations, in terms of costs and benefits and efficient markets. Although economics, as social science, is a valid attempt to describe and predict what will happen within a society if it chooses certain economic behaviors, many economists do not hesitate to make prescriptive statements about economic behavior. Many economists, for example, assert that the option that makes the most efficient use of resources ought to be the preferred option. Once an economist makes an ''ought'' statement, however, he or she is tacitly assuming some ethical position. When such recommendations are made, economists are choosing one ethical approach over others, and that approach is most often some form of utilitarianism. The underlying assumption of utilitarianism is that an option should be chosen that creates the greatest happiness for the greatest number of people. Since an efficient market maximizes happiness by satisfying the greatest number of individual preferences, the economist usually asserts that the option which maximizes the efficiency of the market place is the ''optimal'' solution. This is a utilitarian formulation of the good.[9] It is a different formulation than other ethical formulations, and to the extent that the value assumption is not identified

and remains hidden, the ethical basis for the final decision is never exposed, and other viable approaches are completely ignored.

The utilitarian approach raises additional ethical problems that cannot easily be answered from within a utilitarian system.[10] A utilitarian, for instance, must decide which alternatives will be entertained in the utilitarian calculus, which consequences of a given action will be considered, whose assessments of harms and benefits will be allowed, and what time scale will be used in assessing those consequences. The utilitarian framework, therefore, often rests upon imprecise judgments independent of, and prior to, the utility calculus itself.

Utilitarian methodology, moreover, cannot easily accommodate the rights individuals may have either to be protected from certain pollutants or to be spared from death-threatening situations. Most contemporary philosophers hold that utilitarian approaches must be supplemented by other ethical approaches, such as a Kantian approach, which stress such concepts as rights, justice, and due process as fundamental. The Kantian would resist many developmental strategies that may be justifiable on utilitarian grounds. More importantly, the utilitarian approach often assumes that various questions can be reduced to a quantifiable amount. Quantification of environmental or health benefits, however, is often difficult and sometimes impossible. For instance, what is the value of human life? Even if the problem of quantification can be solved, utilitarianism is still incapable of answering how benefits or costs should be distributed among potential losers and winners.[11] As a result, most commentators agree that a utilitarian analysis must be supplemented by concepts of distributive justice. Nevertheless, almost all value discussions one

9. For a discussion of economic theory and utilitarian ethics see Mark Sagoff, ''At The Shrine of Our Lady of Fatima or Why Political Questions Are Not All Economic,'' *Arizona Law Review* 23 (1981): 1283-1298, and ''Economic Theory and Environmental Law,'' *Michigan Law Review* 79 (1981): 1393-1419.

10. See Alasdair MacIntyre, ''Utilitarianism and Cost/Benefit Analysis: An Essay on the Relevance of Moral Philosophy to Bureaucratic Theory,'' in K.M. Sayre et al., *Values in the Electric Power Industry* (Notre Dame: University of Notre Dame Press, 1977).

11. See David Harrison, Jr. and Paul R. Partner, ''Who Loses From Reform of Environmental Regulation,'' in Wesley A. Magat, ed., *Reform of Environmental Regulation* (Cambridge, Mass.: Ballinger Publishing, 1982).

encounters in the environmental public policy debate are limited to some variant of the utilitarian approach. Although more sophisticated utilitarian approaches are capable of dealing with some of the problems mentioned above, all too frequently the value analyses one actually finds in the environmental public policy debates are over-simplified utilitarian calculations that more sophisticated utilitarians would likely reject.

THE PRESSURE TO MAKE DECISIONS THROUGH ANALYSIS OF COSTS AND BENEFITS

One manifestation of the propensity to discuss all value questions in economic terms is the recent ascendency of cost-benefit analysis as the paradigmatic decision-making tool. Although most academic observers agree that cost-benefit analysis as a descriptive tool may initially be helpful to decision makers, provided that the ethical limitations of this approach are understood, most philosophers agree that mandatory cost-benefit analysis should not be used as a prescriptive decision-making tool. It is ironic that despite the fact that much has been written in the philosophical community of late about the weakness of cost-benefit analysis as a prescriptive decision-making tool, because of inherent difficulties in dealing with certain values questions and in quantifying benefits, governments with increasing frequency are being required to perform mandatory cost-benefit analysis. For instance, the federal government is required to perform mandatory cost-benefit analysis as a decision tool by Executive Order 12291, issued by Ronald Reagan in 1981,[12] and many states now require mandatory cost-benefit analysis by law or executive order.

The value approach encountered in mandatory cost-benefit analysis often involves the assumption that values are nothing more than subjective preferences that can be determined in market situations. This position, however, ignores the view of many

philosophers, namely, that values are not only subjective preferences, but also have an objective content— that is, that value claims are not just felt; that they are capable of being judged to be sound or unsound. Seen in this way, value claims are more than individual preferences. Pricing mechanisms measuring preferences measure only the intensity of wants; they cannot evaluate which beliefs are morally superior. For instance, the right of an individual to be protected from PCBs in his or her water supply may be greater than the utility of such protection recognized by the market place. Such cases show that ethical questions are not reducible to questions of economics understood as efficient markets. Nevertheless, all one usually hears during the public policy debate on environmental issues is oversimplified versions of the utilitarian economic approach.

THE PRESSURE FOR REGULATORY REFORM

Another cause of value distortion is pressure for reform to limit governmental regulatory activity. Most state governments and the federal government have been acutely aware of the pressure for strong regulatory reform that has existed since the middle of the 1970s. It has been so strong in the last five years that no administrator can long survive without giving considerable attention to reform issues. As a result, the rule-making activities of almost all government agencies now include elaborate public participation procedures, ''sunset'' provisions which require that all programs be reviewed on a periodic basis, various legislative oversight provisions, and mandatory cost-benefit analysis procedures.

The net effect of all of these reforms has been the creation of a climate in which it is almost impossible for an environmental administrator to adopt a regulation without first establishing a strong political consensus that the regulation is ''necessary.'' Lobbyists for regulated industries, nevertheless, continue to call for regulatory reform as an important political priority on the grounds that environmental agencies axiomatically always adopt regulations that are unnecessary and that go far beyond the intent of the authorizing legislation. As a result, there has been significant and

---

12. Comptrollers Report to the Congress, *Cost-Benefit Analysis Can Be Useful in Assessing Environmental Regulations Despite Limitations,* U.S. General Accounting Office, GAO/RCED-84-62.

continuing effort on the part of government to ''reform'' environmental rule making. Although some of this reform is valid, much of it is not. According to Webster's dictionary, *reform* means ''to amend or improve by change or removal of faults or abuses.'' The most recent pressure to reform environmental regulation, nonetheless, has been directed at establishing a considerably restricted meaning for the word. Those who have been pushing most vigorously for environmental regulatory reform usually assert that rational decision making should rely on such procedures as mandatory cost-benefit analysis and that rule making should be prohibited unless government agencies can clearly demonstrate that a particular activity creates a serious environmental problem with a high degree of scientific certainty. ''Regulatory reform,'' therefore, is often a euphemism for mandatory cost-benefit analysis and strict quantitative risk assessment approaches.

Regulary reform so constituted is a force aimed at preventing government agencies from making decisions when those decisions cannot be quantitatively justified in accordance with a very specific methodology. Whenever such regulatory reform is adopted, the government expert is then under considerable pressure to quantify and balance all issues on a single scale. As a result of this pressure, administrators are forced to reduce all aspects of each problem to some common measure in terms of which ''objective'' comparisons can be made. According to some common versions of this approach, all of the ''fuzzy'' values, such as rights, are either reduced to ''hard data'' or ignored, and the objectified values are measured in terms of prices as determined in market situations. When values cannot be ignored or quantified as prices, they are then translated into matters of human personal preference. The transformation of these values into personal preference, in turn, serves to discredit policy choices based on general principles believed to hold universally, such as theories of distributive justice.

In most cases, regulatory reform as it has most recently been formulated obscures rather than clarifies the kinds of ethical concerns and issues discussed in this essay. Although regulatory reform in its broadest sense, as the ''improving'' and ''removing of abuses,'' should be a goal of all concerned citizens, current pressure for regulatory reform may actually create significant abuses by forcing administrative officials to balance things which should not be compared on the same scale, to quantify values arbitrarily which are inherently unquantifiable, and to use a decision methodology which distorts interests and values concerns.

THE TENDENCY OF TECHNICAL ANALYSIS TO BE INCOMPLETE

Value distortions also appear in environmental public policy making when incomplete technical analyses are performed. One of the primary causes of incomplete technical analyses is the tendency of analysts to examine environmental problems exclusively in terms of their own disciplines. To illustrate this common phenomenon, let us consider the following twist in the ancient story of the blindmen and the elephant. Four specially trained blindmen are asked to examine an elephant and describe what it is after touching it. The first blindman, who is specially trained to examine legs, determines that the elephant is cylindrical in shape and has a body of considerable mass. The second blindman who is specially trained to examine surface texture, asserts that elephants are large masses of wrinkled soft material. The third blindman who is specially trained to find tails, examines the tail of the elephant and asserts that the major characteristic of an elephant is a long flexible structure having the thickness of a two-inch rope. The fourth blindman who is specially trained to be sensitive to smell, asserts that the distinguishing characteristic of an elephant is its unique mixture of organic, peanut, and haylike fragrances.

The regulation of the nuclear power industry in this country provides a dramatic example of the tendency of the technical community to concentrate on those aspects of a problem that are best understood by the persons responsible for the analysis. Almost all of the debate on nuclear energy has been centered on the risk of accidents that can cause a release of radiation. However, accident-induced radiation releases are not the only reason why many are concerned about the wisdom of nuclear power. Some are very concerned about the relationship between nuclear power plant development and the resultant loss of ability to control the spread of nuclear weapons. Some commentators have ranked the policy importance of nuclear power risks in the following (decreasing) order: proliferation, theft, sabotage, accidents, routine emissions.[13] Nuclear engineering data is only very useful at the lower end of the policy importance continuum. However, since the nuclear power debate is usually conducted by a technical community trained to think about how to build a nuclear power plant, and thereby to minimize the risk of accidents, the debate concerning nuclear power has largely ignored the nuclear proliferation issue. This sort of tunnel vision may yet prove to be the most serious folly of all.

The technical community often focuses on those aspects of a problem it knows something about while ignoring others. It is true, of course, that no one person can fully be an expert on all of the many issues and factual questions that are of concern. What the public usually sees, however, is a debate about a narrow range of the technical issues with the participants in the debate acting as though they understand and are dealing with all that should be of concern to the public. In this way, the public policy debate is often a language game in which the jargon of the specialty of the analysts sets the allowable limits of where to start and stop the investigation. Value conflicts which should be resolved politically are then hidden in what look like rational and objective calculations.

K. S. Shrader-Frechette has discussed still another variant of incomplete analysis, what she calls the fallacy of unfinished business.[14] This fallacy arises out of the assumption that technical and environmental problems have only technical, but not social, ethical, or political solutions. The fallacy of unfinished business is the practice of formulating questions about environmental issues in such a way that the answers

necessarily include technical solutions for the problems identified. An example given by the author focuses on whether "to store radioactive waste in salt mines, or in deep drilled wells, in solidified ceramic form or as a liquid double-walled steel tanks."[15] Although the question posed in this way requires a technical solution,

> the really intractable problem is not the technical one of what storage technique to adopt, but the ethical and social one, such as what risk we can impose on future generations and how we ought to determine the acceptability of a given risk. We have not answered questions such as these in part because we have been asking, not wrong questions but incomplete ones, questions that are epistemologically loaded, questions that presuppose a definition of a given problem for which only an answer in terms of the technological status quo counts as a solution.[16]

As another example, Shrader-Frechette asks whether we ought "to develop coal or nuclear fission in the United States Ohio River basin area, in order to meet the electric power demand between now and the year 2000?"[17] She points out that precisely because the formulation of this technological question allows only for a technical answer in terms either of coal or nuclear fission, the EPA assessment of this question ignores alternative ethical, social, and political solutions to problems such as the conservation of energy.

The propensity to ask the incomplete question is built into the way that we develop new technology and solve technological problems. When a technology goes wrong, someone schooled in that technology is brought in to fix or analyze that technology. Likewise, when a technology is under consideration for future use, someone knowledgeable about that technology is often asked to assess that technology. The result is public policy that does not consider other potentially appropriate options. Once again the ethical questions posed by the public policy issue are confused by the process of relegating the problem to a narrow technical eite.

13. Dorothy Nelkin, "Thoughts on the Proposed Science Court," *Technology and Human Values* 18 (1977): 22.

14. K.S. Shrader-Frechette, "Environmental Impact Assessment and the Fallacy of Unfinished Business," *Environmental Ethics* 4 (1982): 37–47.

15. Ibid., p. 37.
16. Ibid., p. 38.
17. Ibid., p. 38.

Finally, there is the problem of time pressure. The technical expert within a government agency is usually under pressure to make a technical assessment of alternatives in a timely fashion and to ignore any arbitrariness in so doing. This pressure tends to force the technical expert to analyse only what is genuinely predictable and calculable. Since a known technology is usually taken to be more predictable than alternatives that depend upon social or moral considerations, the technical expert usually focuses his or her attention on those alternatives that are most easily calculable and predictable, namely alternative technologies.

DISTORTIONS CAUSED BY NARROW FOCUS ON RISK ASSESSMENT

Value questions can also be distorted in risk assessment studies. It is often asserted in environmental public policy debates that a comparison of the risks associated with the technology in question with the risks posed by other activities is of central importance to responsible environmental decision making. Quantitative risk assessment is a statistical process that uses data from laboratory tests, epidemiological studies, or material failure rates to predict the probability of health costs that result from the use of various chemicals or technologies. Many technical experts act as if a weighing of risks is all that is necessary to give direction to public policy questions. It is often stated, for example, that nuclear power is an acceptable energy option because the risks involved with it compare favorably to risks created by the mining and burning of coal. The basic argument presumably is that because more people will die from mining and burning coal than will die from exposure to an operational nuclear power plant, nuclear power is the acceptable energy option. Although on the surface such straightforward reliance on quantitative risk assessment seems reasonable, the approach, nevertheless, frequently ignores many ethical problems that need to be taken into consideration in the policy debate.[18]

These problems include the following:

(1) *Problems of scientific uncertainty.* Risk assessment involves so much scientific uncertainty that comparison of risks may often be no better than intuitive speculation. In some cases, for instance, risk assessment depends on the evaluation of epidemiological data about rates of exposure in laboratory animal experiments. There are many reasons why uncertainties arise: (a) epidemiological data relating to dose rates to human disease does not exist for most problems; (b) there are significant problems in extrapolating from animals to humans; (c) effects of exposure may take years or generations to materialize; (d) human experimentation is excluded on ethical grounds; and finally (e) experiments must often assume an average dose rate, thereby providing little or no information about very high dose rates. Because of these kinds of uncertainties, quantitative risk assessment cannot be relied upon to support the fine distinctions required for accurate public policy decision making.

(2) *Questions concerning the distribution of harm.* If a particular hazard is not equally distributed among subgroups in a population, certain ethical questions arise. For instance, migrant farm workers may be exposed to pesticides when picking oranges in concentrations thousands of times higher than those of city dwellers whose rate is determined solely by eating an occasional breakfast orange. Considerations of due process of other rights theories may require that the migrant worker be protected from a pesticide in addition to the average consumer of oranges.

(3) *The need to distinguish accepted risks from those that are not accepted.* When a hazard is not well understood by the public that will bear the risks, questions arise about due process and the protection of individual rights. A risk that is voluntarily accepted is different in kind from a risk that is involuntarily forced upon someone.[19] For instance, someone may accept the risk associated with his or her decision to smoke cigarettes alone, but resent the additional risks

---

18. See James P. Leape ''Quantitative Risk Assessment in Regulation of Carcinogens,'' *Harvard Environmental Law Review* 4 (1980): 86-116.

19. Mark Sagoff, ''On Markets for Risk,'' *Maryland Law Review* 41 (1982): 755–773.

imposed by others who smoke in the same room. Free and informed consent to risks from toxic substances in the environment is not a realistic goal, since most exposure is indirect, involuntary, and difficult to observe.

(4) *The need to consider the type of harm that will be created by the risk.* Risks that are grave and dangerous are different in kind from risks that involve less dire consequences. If certain activities create a risk of death, even though that risk may be small, that risk may be more objectionable than a risk of sickness, even though the risk associated with the sickness has a higher probability. The risk of a nuclear power plant accident, for example, although perhaps small, may be more objectionable than the risk to the public of an explosion at a fossil fuel plant.

(5) *The need to distinguish background facts from ethical questions.* Questions of risk often confuse the normal with the moral. We often hear comparisons of a new risk with background conditions. Although we have no choice but to accept the background conditions, the new risks may, nevertheless, be objectionable. If one person in 100,000 dies because of background radiation from the atmosphere, it does not necessarily follow that it is ethically appropriate to choose deliberately to expose people to low levels of radiation that are likely to produce a rate of death from increased exposure equal to or less than one death in 100,000.

(6) *The need to describe criteria for acceptability of risks.* The term *acceptable risks* includes a normative dimension that is not usually defended in public policy debate. For example, risks to a small proportion of a human population are often asserted to be "acceptable." When large numbers of humans are involved, however, there can be a considerable number of statistical casualties. If the government accepts that one in 100,000 people will get cancer from a particular activity, it is willing to permit 2,500 cancer deaths in the United States. Despite the low risk statistically, few people would consider so many deaths to be a clearly "acceptable" risk. Nevertheless, small numerical risks may encourage policy makers to believe that they can responsibly proceed with an activity in some cases when it is not actually warranted. For instance, the Rasmussen Report, the report relied upon by the Nuclear Regulatory Commission before the accident at Three Mile Island, predicted that the probability of a meltdown was one in 17,000. Although this seemed to suggest a reasonable risk associated with nuclear power plant failure, when one added this risk to the risks of all other power plants that were expected to be in existence by the time the report was published, the risk increased to one meltdown every five years.[20]

DISTORTIONS CAUSED BY IMPROPER PLACEMENT OF BURDEN OF PROOF

Another way in which value questions get distorted in public debate is through the improper placement of burden of proof. Because of the complexity of many public health and environmental issues and because of the economic consequences to those who are regulated when government action is taken, many of the laws that authorize government regulation put the burden of proof of showing risk or injury on the government agencies responsible for the rule making. Since the incredible complexities involved make it almost impossible for the party with the burden of proof to sustain that burden, government has been scandalously slow in regulating such substances as pesticides.[21] In such cases, there are so many technical difficulties with mathematical models, dose-response assumptions, and the statistical analysis that problems can nearly always be quickly identified by those who want to assert that the burden of proof has not been met. Precisely because of the inherent complexities of these issues, guesswork at almost all stages of problem analysis is necessary, with potential for mistakes in either direction.

If the benefit of the doubt does not go to the public, then those interested in restraining government can, with little effort, regularly suceed in preventing government regulation. Scientists inside and outside the

---

20. K.S. Shrader-Frechette, *Nuclear Power and Public Policy* (Dordreut and Boston: D. Riechel Publishing Company, 1980). See also Ernest Partridge's review of the book in *Environmental Ethics* 4 (1982): 261–271.

21. See James H. Ware, "Health Risk Assessment: The Role of Statistical Analysis," in Magat, *Reform of Environmental Regulation.*

agency are very skilled in exposing technical weaknesses in an adversary's position, particularly when that adversary is viewed to have the burden of proof. Moreover, greater weight and authority is given to those insiders and outsiders that are viewed to have the greater technical resources, frequently a decisive advantage to those who can muster more resources than the government. As a result, government is often troubled about what to do when its knowledge is viewed to be inadequate but it is under pressure to take action. In such situations, however, the value questions that are created by inadequate information are very rarely identified as such. Instead, the public debate focuses on the "technical" aspects of the issue under consideration.

At various times the burden of proof shifts back and forth between government and regulated industry. For instance, although a permit applicant may be viewed to have the burden of showing that a new plant will not create a water pollution problem from a point source discharge, the permit reviewer may assume a presumption of innocence about the "nonpoint" pollution discharges to the stream. As Serge Taylor points out in *Making Bureaucracies Think,* burden of proof questions are often level of detail questions. In many permit review situations, when government is faced with the question of whether it has enough information at the proper level of detail to make an informed decision, it decides not to require additional information on the grounds that it is too costly.

The very posing of environmental questions in terms of empirical science often has the effect of enhancing the expectation that the agency technical analysts will be able to determine the environmental impacts of various projects with available methodologies. When public expectation is created in this way, the government may assume a burden of proof that it cannot meet, especially if the theoretical basis for predicting outcomes is not available. For instance, when a government agency accepts the responsibility for deciding whether a low-level waste dump will have adverse environmental impacts, the government may be assuming a burden of proof for which existing technology cannot provide answers with an acceptable level of scientific certainty. Because most environmental impact analysis is discussed in "science-like" terminology, notwithstanding the fact that the scientific predictive basis is sometimes so weak that prediction is not much better than untutored intuitive speculation, there is, nevertheless, nearly always a strong, but unfounded, belief in the credibility of the analysis that shifts burden of proof to the analyst. Since scientists in environmental agencies are usually not in a position to suspend judgment until all of the proof is in, nor to wait out the long latency periods that may be necessary to determine whether the project will create the expected outcomes, the "science-like" jargon of the analysis is misleading. Environmental impact analysis should be distinguished from other areas of science in which the scientist can selectively focus on problems that can be settled by verifiable scientific procedures.

Because of the scientific uncertainty in environmental problems, technical experts within government have often refused to act out of fear that they will enrage a legislator who will then have them fired if it is discovered that they have imposed unsupportable costs upon a constituent. This reluctance is also consistent with most scientific training. The scientist is trained to be very conservative in asserting cause and effect relationships. No traditionally trained scientist will act quickly if there is reason to suspect uncertainty about the cause of an environmental problem. If a position, once taken, is later discredited by subsequent scientific research, the technical person who suggested the cause and effect relationship may suffer significant peer sanctions for being associated with a faulty scientific hypothesis.

VALUE DISTORTIONS CAUSED BY THE TECHNICAL TRAINING OF THE ANALYST

Another cause of value distortion in environmental analysis is the narrow scientific training of most scientists. Scientists are taught to value scientific truths above other truths because, ideally, scientific truths are usually never accepted until they have been publicly tested. In contrast, since the "truth" of ethical positions cannot be empirically verified in the same way, and is therefore less "objective" than scientific truth, many scientifically trained people express open hostility to ethical discourse and value judgments. Ethical questions are often called "soft" or "fuzzy" in contrast with scientific questions and solutions that are supposed to be "hard." As a result, quantitative criteria tend to crowd out qualitative criteria. Because quantitative disputes can be resolved on technical grounds and value disputes cannot, disagreements tend to get settled on analytical technical grounds.

Some technically trained administrators go so far as to equate rationality with science and irrationality or raw emotion with ethics on the grounds that value questions cannot be decided scientifically. Those who do not go quite this far, nevertheless, often act as if ethical questions are less significant or less relevant than the "hard" scientific facts. Engineers often express open hostility and frustration with having to analyze the value questions that are raised in environmental impact analysis. On one occasion, for example, an environmental engineer who was given the task of analyzing the aesthetic impact of a substantial reduction in water flow on the Great Falls of the Passaic River in New Jersey in a proposed water diversion project asserted that aesthetic values were "Mickey Mouse" and that environmental groups that were raising aesthetic issues were being "irrational."

Because of the primacy given to scientific truths by technically trained persons, issues that can be dealt with on quantitative terms are more sympathetically considered than issues that involve more difficult qualitative or ethical concerns. Most environmental administrators, for instance, will deal more quickly, seriously, and sympathetically with an issue requiring the setting of standards for bacteria to prevent *living* people from getting a water-borne disease than they will with issues involving our duty to future generations to preserve wilderness areas or save species form extinction.

Scientists are trained to report impersonal data from which all subjective elements have been removed, to reduce all issues to a scale that can be quantitatively manipulated, to think of nature as lifeless substance with measurable analytic parameters, and to transform social questions into technical questions. When a problem has been reduced to quantitative terms, to the language of science and mathematics, technically trained people almost invariably critique the mathematical model exclusively on a scientific-mathematical basis, omitting any critique of the transformation of the qualitative values into quantitative terms. For example, although there was much discussion within the New Jersey Department of Environmental Protection during the 1970s about the science of modeling a river in order to predict pollution loads and set water-quality based effluent limitations, there was almost no discussion during that time about the ethical assumptions of the model, even though the model included provisions for distributing available stream capacity among various industrial and domestic users and for reserving the river's pollution-absorbing capacity for future use. In distributing loads among users and reserving stream capacity for future use the engineers had to make value judgments and to translate those value judgments into quantitative factors that could be incorporated into the model. Although these factors had far-reaching consequences, never to my knowledge did any of the technical staff challenge the value assumptions that were used in determining them. This situation was startling, I believe, given the fact that at one point the model permitted all domestic sewage treatment plants in New Jersey to use as much of a stream's assimilative capacity as they needed provided that they employed a minimum secondary treatment, while industrial users, on the other hand, were required to accept whatever effluent limitations were necessary to meet stream standards after ten percent of New Jersey's stream capacity was reserved for *all* future uses. In the end, the public policy considerations that had the most important long-term consequences were based upon the value premises of a few engineers that were never disclosed, discussed, or critiqued by any of the technical experts inside or outside the agency.

RECOMMENDATIONS

Although it is admittedly important that we continue our attempts to enhance our analytical power to make mathematical estimates of risks, costs, and outcomes, it is even more important that we at long last develop the technical skill to deal with the ethical and value dimensions of our environmental problems. To this end, I recommend the following measures, which, if they are to be successful, require not only improvements in public policy procedures within government, but also the active support and involvement of concerned citizens.

First, environmental decision makers must come to understand value questions. At a minimum, concerned citizens must demand that environmental decision makers are capable of distinguishing issues of fact from ethical issues. In addition, it is vitally important to make sure that ethical questions and various ethical positions are adequately considered in environmental decision-making processes. To this end, persons concerned about environmental ethical issues should vigorously include themselves in debates about public policy and refuse to accept a narrow utilitarian calculus as the sole basis for a rational choice.

Second, ethical positions must be disclosed. As government inevitably increases its ability to calculate costs and benefits, reform of environmental rule making must insure that value assumptions are disclosed as part of the decision-making process. For example, if a given chemical is not going to be regulated because a human life has been assigned a value of $75,000, then surely that fact must be disclosed. Similarly, in risk assessments the value assumptions included in any risk comparison should be disclosed as well as the timetables used to calculate the consequences of any activity and any alternatives to that activity. Better access to information is a precondition of public decisions on regulatory standards.

Third, solutions to environmental problems must consider social alternatives. Everyone should strive to see that public policy questions are as open as possible to social as well as technical solutions. Environmental administrators should not adopt a technical solution unti they have fully examined, identified, and rejected all possible social solutions.

Fourth, economic analyses must expose their value assumptions. Interested parties should critique all cost-benefit analyses in order to identify the basic ethical assumptions and presumptions. Citizens should resist any law that requires that all environmental decisions be made strictly in accordance with a cost-benefit calculation.

Finally, environmental decisions must be viewed primarily as ethical choices. It is important in an age of increasing scientific complexity that interested parties attempt to understand the value positions and ethical issues that lie underneath scientifically derived policy choices. Experts and concerned citizens must realize that crucial policy choices concerning environmental pollution, nuclear power, and toxic chemicals are value judgments, matters of morality, social and political judgments. In a democracy these judgments should not be made by ''experts,'' but rather by the people and their elected representatives. As long as the value component of environmental decision making is relegated to technical experts, who are not experts in ethics and value studies, and indeed are reluctant by training and disposition to deal with value issues at all, environmental policy that is critically flawed by value distortions will continue to be the rule, not the exception.

DISCUSSION TOPICS

1. Using a traditional view on the logic of ethics, Brown argues that science alone cannot address ethical questions adequately. Do you agree? What exceptions might there be to this position? Support your answers.
2. In the process of evaluating environmental decisions, what weight should be accorded values concerns compared with technical concerns? Explain the reasons for your position. What guidelines would you devise to help environmental administrators give greater weight to values concerns?

READING 4

Biology and Philosophy in Yellowstone

Holmes Rolston III

Holmes Rolston III (b. 1932) is Professor of Philosophy at Colorado State University, Fort Collins, Colorado. He has written extensively about environmental values and ethics.

Rolston describes how diverse perspectives from biology, philosophy, history, and social forces have combined to create a complex controversy surrounding the National Park Service's policy of "Let Nature Take Its Course" in Yellowstone National Park. In his analysis of this controversy, Rolston identifies and clarifies several significant issues involving both science and values.

Rolston distinguishes three connotations of the term "natural," each with different implications for evaluating human action in relation to the rest of nature. He acknowledges how difficult it is for humans to fully understand the effects of great time spans, large biotic regions, and complex ecological relationships; and he suggests that "bigscale biology" requires different levels of conceptualization than do organismic and molecular biology. Rolston describes how value considerations, political issues, and social forces influence decisions on the research conducted by ecologists.

Rolston explores the intriguing question of whether certain negative human qualities which sometimes are infused with the conduct of scientific work, such as political infighting, arrogance, and use of raw power, may not ultimately have an overall positive effect on scientific advancement. He concludes that such was not the case in the controversy at Yellowstone.

When comparing the relative merits of management versus preservation in Yellowstone Park, Rolston concludes that it is best to preserve and appreciate nature rather than to manage it for other human goals.

Yellowstone National Park is a place to go on vacation. Yet a philosopher or biologist will find work to do here—challenges so fundamental that we hardly have intellectual resources adequate to the task. In the field, forest, and range, our theories will look different. For the trip you are about to take, be forewarned. An excursion into biology and philosophy in Yellowstone, at times a pleasant diversion, is also a risky adventure into poorly mapped terrain. In Yellowstone you can get lost—philosophically and biologically, as well as geographically.

That has already happened in fact, and the trip to be taken here will be one of rescue as well as exploration. For several years Alston Chase, with a doctorate in philosophy from Princeton, also degrees from Harvard and Oxford, former professor of philosophy (Macalester College), and sometime wilderness guide, has been trying to rescue biologists in Yellowstone, who, he fears, have gone astray. They did not get lost all by themselves, however; Chase thinks environmental philosophers helped misguide them (Chase 1987; 1988). Unfortunately, as happens sometimes with would-be rescuers, Chase has gotten confused himself in the Yellowstone terrain. Then too, there are degrees of being lost, and the park naturalists, if sometimes disoriented, may not in recent times have been entirely lost. Nor were the environmentalists.

Yellowstone is significant for what it is—vast and spectacular, the largest, nearest intact ecosystem in the temperature zone of Earth, visited by millions—and for what it represents: the oldest national park in the world and a model for the world of enlightened care for fauna, flora, and ecosystems. So Chase's search, and ours, is globally and nationally important—the more so because in this region, in the wild, we can find our way only with an environmental ethic that joins biology and philosophy in ways as yet not well mapped.

VALUING NATURE

In Yellowstone we find that science is necessary but not sufficient for valuing nature. There is public debate about whether the massive fires last summer were a good thing—for humans, for the fauna, the flora, for the ecosystem. John Varley, Chief of Research at Yellowstone Park claims, "The ecological story . . . has been a very positive thing" (in Stuebner, 1988). Governor Cecil Andrus of Idaho, Interior Secretary under President Carter, replies, "To let fires burn in July and August is ridiculous" (in Egan, 1988). Chase (1988) finds the present policy neither biologically nor philosophically sound. Once we judged fires to be bad and suppressed them; now it is clear that fires are sometimes good and fire suppression bad. The Department of Interior has appointed a review panel to mix biology and philosophy and decide how much fire is a good thing.

We permitted an epidemic of pinkeye to destroy half the bighorn herd, intending to strengthen the species, thinking it good to let nature take its course. We rescued a grizzly sow and her three cubs stranded after the spring ice breakup on Frank Island in Yellowstone Lake, hoping to save the species, not letting nature take its course. A park official forbade four compassionate snowmobilers from either rescuing or mercy-killing a bison that had fallen through the ice into a river; this seeming callousness was castigated in national newscasts. Once we judged predators to be a bad thing, and eliminated them; now it is clear that the human policy, not the predators, was bad. After fire suppression, the absence of wolves is the greatest department from a natural ecosystem in Yellowstone. But do we want to reintroduce the wolf?

Carved in stone on the gateway Yellowstone Arch, we assert that Yellowstone is preserved ''for the benefit and enjoyment of the people'' by Act of Congress. But to think that this place ought to be only a ''pleasuring-ground'' (U.S. Congress 1872, par. 1) has come to seem shallow, humanistic arrogance; we value it also as a deeper token and symbol, an archetype of the primeval. ''The primary purpose of Yellowstone National Park is to preserve natural ecosystems and opportunities for visitors to see and appreciate scenery and native plant and animal life as it occurred in primitive America'' (Cole, 1969). It ought to be a biotic whole, a ''natural community'' (Leopold *et al.,* 1963; p. 13), untrammeled by humans, where nature takes its course and humans learn to take pleasure in it. ''The primary purpose of the National Park Service in administering natural areas is to maintain an area's ecosystem in as nearly pristine a condition as possible'' (Houston, 1971).

What we ought to have in Yellowstone, Chase never tires of saying, is sound scientific management. What we have instead, he thinks, is an inflexible ideology—let nature take its course. The policy is ''that the biotic associations within each park be maintained, or where necessary recreated, as nearly as possible in the condition that prevailed when the area was first visited by the white man'' (Leopold *et al.,* 1963; p. 3). That, Chase laments, is philosophy dressed up like biology, holding that whatever is natural ought to be. It is a natural religion, faith in nature, ''a metaphysical ideal'' (Chase, 1987; p. 177) that results in less and less scientific management and culminates,

disastrously, in no management at all. With managers immobilized by a gospel of noninterference with nature, the park is being destroyed. Chase concludes by carving an epitaph for the park: ''Victim of an Environmental Ideal'' (1987; p. 375). Ideally, for Chase, management ought to be ''scientific'' and ignore the word ''natural'' altogether (1987; pp. 175-77).

What eludes Chase is that urging scientific management is an instrumental, not an intrinsic, value judgment. To instruct managers to be scientific is to set only strategic not ultimate goals for them. Science can be used to determine what the spontaneous course of nature was, is, or will be, in order to determine how far human alterations have and will upset it and how far we can restore the original course. But do we value that nature course at Yellowstone? That is a philosophical question. Science can report how far the dynamic biological integrity is gone and whether there is any use trying to recover it. If not, we might scientifically manage what remains, to maximize the show of pseudo-wildlife and to maximize the human pleasures produced. But do we value here a scientifically managed zero—a pleasuring grounds for tourists? That also is a philosophical question.

The Yellowstone philosophy is: let nature take its course—at least in this largest, nearest intact temperate ecosystem remaining on Earth. Such trusting of nature values biology. This might be philosophically wise (were it possible), but biologically foolish, if nature here can no longer take its course and we have assumed an unrealistic goal of primitiveness. Whether the Yellowstone ecosystem, though invaded by human interruptions, has enough recuperative power to heal itself without remedial help is a biological question. Biologists in Yellowstone have believed so at some points, not others, but they have never disclaimed appropriate remedial help, although they have regularly said that the less remedial help the better. That nature, invaded by human interruptions, is impossible to restore to at least relatively natural conditions is a claim in biology, pure and applied, which biologists in Yellowstone are reluctant to hold. They want to maximize restoration, rather than settle for a compromised nature. At the same time they want the minimal restoration it takes to get the maximum recovery of nature. Where they cannot now regain processes like those operating before the human alterations, they may prefer to give the remaining natural processes free rein, rather than to manipulate them.

Chase alleges that Yellowstone biologists/managers value natural regulation, no matter what happens to wildlife or to the pleasures of tourists. Park policy lets nature take its course and allows most wildlife to vanish, except for the over-populating elk. That policy lets bison drown, bighorns die of pinkeye, grizzlies go extinct. Chase urges scientific management for the benefit of wildlife and the people. He cannot envision the possibility that so far as we can restore or mimic natural regulation, this is for the long-term benefit of wildlife and best for the deepest needs of park visitors. Perhaps it is our human duty here as well. He fails to see that a simultaneously wild and scientifically managed fauna is a contradiction in terms, a logical and managerial impossibility.

Do we prefer a natural grizzly bear population, if we can have one, reduced but viable, at risk of losing grizzlies? Do we augment the population to insure survival? Is a bear, with human interruptions compensated for by feeding, too much a compromised bear? Have we a duty to save the species, even if this requires feeding centers in the wilderness ecosystem, an ecosystem that we also have a duty to preserve as pristine as possible? The soundest scientific management cannot answer these questions. Philosophical analysis is required.

THE CONCEPT OF THE NATURAL

All organisms produce waste naturally, humans too; so garbage is as natural as scat. Hence, bears at a Yellowstone dump feeding on oranges from Florida and bananas from Honduras are feeding naturally. ''Believing garbage to be artificial was, therefore, not a scientific hypothesis but a cultural bias'' (Chase, 1987; p. 177).

On the other hand, since Yellowstone has obviously been affected by humans, nothing here is truly natural, and Chase disparages trying to maintain any primeval landscape as ''romantic myth'' (Chase, 1987; p. 46), in contrast to sound scientific manage-

ment. The goal of the Wilderness Act of 1964 is to preserve wilderness areas ''untrammeled by man,'' which environmentalists interpret as appropriate respect for the biological integrity of place. But this, Chase claims, is an ''illusion'' driven by an ideology, not science at all. The Leopold report too speaks of creating ''a reasonable illusion of primitive America'' (Leopold *et al.,* 1963, p. 4). *Newsweek* calls pristine parks ''the grand illusion'' (Adler, 1986).

Events may be said to be natural in different senses; unless we discriminate among these everyone will get lost (Rolston, 1986; 1988; pp. 32-44). (1) In a law-of-nature sense, all human (and nonhuman) activities are natural; neither humans producing nor bears eating garbage breaks any laws of nature. Nor does hands-on scientific management. It is impossible to be unnatural. (2) Another sense is at issue in Yellowstone. Spontaneous events in wild nature are natural; in contrast, deliberate human activities and their intended or unintended results are artificial, that is, artifacts. Plastic bags with leftover Froot Loops dumped in the middle of the Yellowstone forest are unnatural. Since all actions of human agents interrupt spontaneous nature, it is impossible for managers to be completely natural. The Yellowstone ecosystem has often been interrupted; therefore that nature can simply take its course there is an illusion, a romantic myth. Even protection intervenes: Yellowstone runs by Act of Congress. Certainly scientific management is unnatural. (3) But there is also a relative sense of ''natural,'' one consistent with human management. Some human interventions are more, others less natural, depending on the degree to which they fit in with, mimic, or restore spontaneous nature. Any paint on a campground water tank is unnatural, but green is more natural than chartreuse. Restoration of wolves as predators would be more natural than culling elk by sharp-shooters.

Given these distinctions, it does not help to label all restored nature faked, myth, or ideology. Compared with pristine nature, there is diminished naturalness, but the naturalness that remains is not illusory. Some processes were never tampered with; even restored processes, though minus their original historical genesis, are relatively more natural. A broken arm, reset and healed, is relatively more natural than an artificial limb, though both have been medically manipulated. The arm, decades later, is not a ''reasonable illusion'' of a pristine arm. Except for hairline bone scars it may be indistinguishable from the arm nature gave. Likewise with a restored forest or range, the historical genesis has been partially interrupted. But henceforth, deliberately put back in place, spontaneous nature takes over as before. Trees blow over in storms, coyotes hunt ground squirrels, lightning causes burns, natural selection resumes.

SCOPE, SIZE, AND SCALE

In Yellowstone, we get lost in bigscale biology. . . . We are not going to find our way in Yellowstone until philosophers and scientists face the difficulties of regional field biology—beyond laboratory, experimental, specialized, or theoretical biology—and find that on the real Earth bigscale biology is as fundamental as anything organismic or molecular. Contrasted with much academic biology, in Yellowstone the emphases are different; there is no talk of selfish genes, sociobiology, kin selection, DNA. Life in the park goes on of course at the molecular level, but here we see landscapes, ecosystems—regionally enough to wonder whether the gene's eye view is itself myopic.

We need to know how three tropic levels interact: vegetation, herbivores, carnivores—how far the carnivores are a determinant of herbivore population size, and herbivores, in turn, a determinant of vegetative condition. Subtract carnivores. What will be the vegetation-herbivore interactions? Subtract the herbivores (an exclosure experiment) and watch the vegetation, but this experiment of course misleads us, since the grasses and forbs have co-evolved with grazing ungulates. Subtract an unknown depth of soil and nutrient capacities that have eroded away as a result of overgrazing. Add (or subtract) errors due to the reliability/unreliability of historical population estimates over the last century. Add disease organisms and parasites; some native, some exotic, with their effects on ungulates stress-aggravated.

Factor in another determinant: fire. Fire resets aspen succession, and the browsing elk depend on twigs

to supply critical winter nitrogen for gut bacteria that digest dry cellulose. Subtract the fires the white man has suppressed, clearly unnatural; but should we add in the fires the Indians once started? The Indians started fires elsewhere, but how many fires did they start here? How did that affect this particular ecosystem? Factor out fire suppression for a century, add fires back for a decade—but only lightning burns, with no prescribed burns that might repair a century of fire suppression.

Grizzlies have been feeding for a century at the remote garbage dumps. Add the extra food, subtract for any adverse nutritional effect. Also subtract food no longer obtained on now lost habitat. Is there a concentration effect, beneficial or harmful? After closing the dumps, the grizzlies decline in weight and in fertility, but were these higher than normal before, due to the artificial feeding? How many bears are not at the dumps? In decline, are there mechanisms that will compensate with higher birthrates? To what extent have the increased elk, trout, and bison populations replaced the garbage lost since 1970? Add or subtract fire suppression again, depending on what this has done to the always somewhat marginal bear habitat—the lack of fires perhaps permitting a whitebark pine infestation with bark beetle, with the pine nut a principal fall food. Perhaps what the grizzlies lost from fire suppression is compensated for by more elk carcasses to scavenge. Will they switch from a vegetarian diet? Or do the elk eat vegetation that the grizzlies might otherwise eat? The bear feed in part on introduced trout. Are these an added source of nutrition or do they merely replace native trout that were there before?

Can the really big mammals, any more than the migrating birds, really be said to inhabit an ecosystem? Grizzly bears and wolves range over a landscape; they need a biome, perhaps half a continent, in which to evolve. Is the aspen decline due to overgrazing by elk or to fire suppression of serial species that are maintained by fire?

These questions of biology do not model well on computers nor at the genetic or specific level. They reveal how little we know about community structure, succession, evolution at the ecosystem level—a humbling reminder in these days of spectacular molecular biology, and bold, quantitative evolutionary theory, sociobiology, kin selection theory. It is difficult to establish causal connections in an equilibrating ecosystem, a network of forces pushing and pulling at interweaving levels of structure and process, often with multiple homeostatic peaks. One is dealing with historical ecology, with systems of great complexity, with elements of randomness and openness. Yellowstone may not be a closed, determinate system. It has historically contingent, narrative elements. These park managers face some of the most difficult and unresolved questions anywhere in biology. Philosophers ought to sympathize if biologists in Yellowstone sometimes get lost.

NATURAL AND CULTURAL HISTORY

To biology on regional scales we must add biology on historical scales, about which, again, we are often ignorant. On this idiographic landscape in Northwest Wyoming, we know less than we wish about what was happening in spontaneous nature, which is one reason why we cannot predict the outcomes of our management interventions. Yellowstone was tundra 10,000 years ago. The carnivore-herbivore-vegetation-climate interactions have been dynamically altering on the scale of centuries. The American West is a relatively recent landscape, drying out since pluvial Pleistocene times, resulting, for example, in fish speciation more rapid than any known elsewhere among other vertebrates.

Since the Pleistocene, natural history here has been entwined with human history. The Indians long hunted on foot and were partially responsible for some extinctions. There is archaeological evidence of periodic hunting by Indians throughout the park, although apparently not for elk, which may have been sparse here (Wright, 1984). Indian hunting patterns depended on their tribal confederations, their disputes and agreements. They sometimes set fires to increase browse and game. For a century before white men really knew the area, Indians hunted on introduced Spanish horses, about the same period of time that smallpox and other European-introduced diseases began to decimate Indian populations here.

Discovery of Indian impacts, more or less, does not require giving up an illusion of the primitive for sound scientific management. Yellowstone with Indians was relatively natural; Yellowstone minus Indians may nevertheless be a viable ecosystem. It is a mistake to think that the goal at Yellowstone "should be to preserve, or where necessary to recreate, the ecologic scene as viewed by the European visitors" (Leopold *et al.,* 1963; p. 13), as though Yellowstone natural history had only a past and no future. That is not historical enough, nor do we wish to preserve Indian impacts.

What our philosophy ought to value here is dynamic *natural* history. In Yellowstone, biology and philosophy meet in a proper-named place. Real biology is never abstract; it is on the ground in locale, on landscape. Bison frequent Hayden Valley; elk, Lamar Valley. Biology is a historical science in a way that physics is not. What we are preserving is this place, with its uniqueness. Let nature take its course *here.*

YELLOWSTONE BIOLOGY AND SOCIAL FORCES

Our journey across this wild landscape brings into view, surprisingly, the confluence of biology, philosophy, and society. Recently, we have discovered how biological science is driven by social forces—by the needs of medical technology, of agriculture and industry, by funds available for molecular genetics, but not for biogeography or taxonomy. Biology has become less pure and more pragmatic. Starker Leopold, at a meeting of research scientists and management biologists of the National Park Service, insisted that biological research, according to park policy, must be "mission-oriented," rather than "science for science's sake" (Leopold, 1968). That seems plausible; one does not want irrelevant research. But once we see the sociology of science, we must look further to see whether biological theories are proposed in part because they are politically and bureaucratically convenient. What happens to research that questions management policy? That threatens careers? Chase alleges that the bureaucracy suppressed dissent. They used their permitting and funding authority to shut out independent research that might challenge their theories.

John and Frank Craighead, especially Frank, claimed their research indicated a need for supplemental feeding, at least during a period of weaning from the dumps, but this was contrary to park service policy (except in last resort). How does the demand for "mission-oriented" research fit with the further recommendation of the Robbins' report that "the Park Service should make every effort to support and accommodate independent research effort" and "honor the basic freedom of the independent investigator to pursue his objectives, within the limits of these responsibilities (not to harm the parks), without interference" (NAS, 1963; p. xiii, p. 68, p. 62)? Somehow, the career interests of scientists must line up with the bureaucratic mission, both line up with funding sources, and all three line up with field biology, as well as with the integrity of the fauna, flora, ecosystems under study, before biology in Yellowstone can make any progress. At least forty research projects are current on Yellowstone's northern range, and a summary of them does seem to strike a balance between inside and outside researchers and funding, without compromising the need for mission orientation (NPS, 1987).

It is difficult enough to establish causal hypotheses in an equilibrating ecosystem, with networks of forces pushing and pulling at multiple levels of structure and process. The difficulty in biology is compounded as we discover how biologists must work in networks of personal and political forces pushing and pulling at multiple societal levels. Should they orient (taxpayer funded) research guided by what the public wants, what their supervisors want, or what they think best, based on their scientific judgments? Should bear and wolf policy be determined primarily on biological grounds? What weight, if any, should be given to protecting humans, to protecting the Park from torts and litigation? Should biologists risk testing whether more bison can overwinter within the park, since if bison leave the park, they may spread brucellosis to domestic cattle, causing them to miscarry? If a few cows are found infected, Montana law can require a rancher to destroy his entire herd. Ethics constrains the testing of biological hypotheses.

These biologists are all philosophical realists in their view of their science. They think to describe how nature takes its course. But the course they themselves follow is so mission oriented, pragmatically guided, bureaucracy thwarted, buffeted by political fortunes, funding dependent, and ethically constrained that it is a wonder that scientists here find their way through field biology at all. The bewildering is not just the wilderness but the culture that drives the science and philosophy here.

EVOLUTIONARY PHILOSOPHY OF SCIENCE

In relation to the Yellowstone controversies, we can explore theories in philosophy of science that biological science develops through competition, interest groups, and partisan advocacy, as much as through reason and empirical evidence. Such philosophy of science is "naturalistic," "not rationalistic." David L. Hull's *Science as a Process,* the most recent example, is "an account of science that is structurally similar to biological evolution" (1988; p. 3, p. 520), using an evolutionary model of competitive selection processes to understand biologists and the history of biology, as well as natural history and field biology. In Hull's model, what goes on in scientific society at Yellowstone, including the bewildering bureaucratic, political, personal elements just noted, is an analogue of what goes on in the Yellowstone wilderness itself—the survival of the fittest.

By Hull's account, although we might view such behavior with some dismay, "the political infighting, the name-calling, the parody and ridicule, the arrogance, elitism, and use of raw power" belong in science. This is not simply because scientists are human too and fail to live up to their ideals.

> I argue an even stronger thesis: some of the behavior that appears to be the most improper actually facilitates the manifest goals of science. . . . Objective knowledge results in science not despite bias and commitment but because of them. . . . The existence and ultimate rationality of science can be explained in terms of bias, jealousy, and irrationality. . . . Those who make the greatest contributions . . . frequently behave the most deplorably (1988; pp. 31-32).

We can use Chase's adventures to evaluate this Darwinized philosophy of biological science, and vice versa. Does Chase's method teach us something descriptively and prescriptively about how biological science and philosophical analysis are and ought to be done? Chase hopes to rescue lost biologists and environmental philosophers, to improve the state of the science and the art. He seems to be testing the views of others. He uses logic when logic serves, data when data serve, but as readily rhetoric, innuendo, selective weighting of evidence, humor, emotional appeal—almost anything that needles his opponents, whom he judges to be blind and hellbent in their non-management philosophy, their know-nothing and know-too-much biology. He attacks persons sooner than arguments. Does this method produce any reliable analysis of causes and effects in Yellowstone biology, or of the social forces and their connections, or of the values and arguments employed in environmental philosophy?

Chase is relentlessly one-sided and mean spirited. Everybody comes off badly—except the few who aid Chase in the pursuit of his thesis. Almost every chapter title is pejorative.

His strategy is more satire than argument. Satire is what it takes when arguments are falling on deaf ears. Did not Jesus ridicule the Pharisees for straining at gnats and swallowing camels, looking for dust specks in the eyes of others while they had logs jammed into their own? There is something comic about chicken liberation and rights for rocks. But satire is no substitute for argument. Satire attacks persons; what one really wants is to assess the logic and interactions of biology and philosophy here.

Scientific knowledge, Hull claims, does not grow because scientists are interested in truth for truth's sake. It grows when scientists are pushy about their own views, their careers at stake with their theories, fighting for their own interests as much as for the truth. "One of the strengths of science is that it does not require that scientists be unbiased, only that different scientists have different biases" (1988; p. 22). Better science will get selected in the melee. Science grows not "*in spite of*" these seeming flaws but "*because of*" them. If so, the situation Chase alleges and deplores in Yellowstone is the norm, with Chase's "infighting and personal vendettas" (Hull, 1988; p. 26) more of the same—and biology and philosophy here the better for it.

By Chase's account, bias, personal commitment, and self interest have been inseparably entwined with objective science here, but lamentably not laudably, for neither Chase nor the biologists he criticizes would think of these as norms. Hull might be right so far as one can make a case that the pulling and hauling of these forces driving biology in Yellowstone has been constructive. Certainly much has been learned about Yellowstone in this century, during which those in a position to know well the fights in wildlife management have called them "range wars" (Despain *et al.*, 1986; p. 112). But biology can advance here only when in this fighting the better argued claim, based on better evaluation of evidence, is being selected. It is hard to see how Chase's animosity helps the process of discovery. Hull's "because of" may be necessary, but it cannot be sufficient for the positive growth of biology. There is nothing about being obnoxious as such that produces sounder argument.

Even if, as a result of his attack, Chase proves to be among the causes of better biology and philosophy in Yellowstone, he himself cannot be relied on rationally to assess biological causal networks or the history and internal logic of biology and philosophy here. A park service rebuttal of Chase's factual errors and distortions as he relates the grizzly episodes is much longer than Chase's original account (NPS, 1986). Others who are more constrained by balanced weighing of evidence and cogency of argument will have to find these things out. Rational assessment of truth is further required, supported by and superposed on partisan advocacy. Chase seldom finds his way this far. For most of their routes, biologists and philosophers in Yellowstone will have to make progress *in spite of*, not because of him.

PLAYING GOD

When we analyze Chase's deliberately abrasive central metaphor, we discover that "playing God" is empty of descriptive or normative, scientific or ethical content. Therefore it does nothing to help orient us. Discoveries in biology and philosophy in Yellowstone must be made in spite of the metaphor, not because of it. It does not illuminate any issues, either in theory or practice; it does not even mark wrong directions of travel. Playing God is intervening to improve the ecosystem for humans; playing God is restoring the ecosystem; playing God is letting nature take its course. In ''giving a blank check to nature,'' ''in taking a passive role they would not have stopped playing God'' (1987; p. 41). Having faith in nature, pantheism, or leaving it to the Creator—these are still playing God. Playing God is hands-on management; playing God is hands-off management. The Europeans who came to improve hunting were playing God. ''The Indians, too, knew how to play God'' (1987; p. 97).

So what is not playing God? What would Chase do? Of all the options that Chase considers, the one he seems to recommend would most deify resource managers; strong, scientific management. We never have a careful definition of the accusative metaphor that alleges bad biology and bad philosophy. The phrase operates to condemn, not to analyze; to attack people, not to reform policies. It operates psychologically, not logically, and for that reason it cannot advance the search for better biology or philosophy in Yellowstone.

LOVING YELLOWSTONE

Truth for truth's sake is not all biologists and philosophers want in Yellowstone; they want truth for Yellowstone's sake—whether or not they push their careers. If philosophers of biology cannot find this objective concern elsewhere in biology, they ought to visit Yellowstone. At the start this is surely Chase's quest too; he leaves academic philosophy for life in the wilderness. He leaves the wilderness to fight for its perservation. He claims that he gives his career to Yellowstone. But, alas, he gets lost. He loses appropriate respect for the naturalists who also have loved Yellowstone. At the end, it is not really clear whether Chase has an environmental ethic; he disdains most of the biology and philosophy, the biologists and phi-

losophers he surveys. He disdains letting nature take its course in favor of sound scientific management—as if that were an ethic that valued wildness. He does not trust the naturalists, but, worse, he does not trust nature.

In Yellowstone, if not also elsewhere, managerial control is not love; biology and philosophy here ought to seek to appreciate, rather than to manipulate. Restorative love is sometimes in order; after that, letting nature take its course is the appropriate form of caring for the great bear, the wapiti, the aspin, *Ursus arctos, Cervus canadensis, Populus tremuloides,* for the ecosystem, for the land, for this wild place.

REFERENCES

Adler, J., M. Hager, and J. Copeland: 1986, 'The Grand Illusion,' *Newsweek,* 28 July, pages 48-51 (vol. 108, no. 4).

Chase, A.: 1987, *Playing God in Yellowstone: The Destruction of America's First National Park,* Harcourt Brace Jovanovich, New York.

Chase, A.: 1988, 'Neither Fire Suppression Nor Natural Burn Is a Sound Scientific Option,' *New York Times,* 18 September, p. 24.

Cole, G. F.: 1969, 'Elk and the Yellowstone Ecosystem,' Yellowstone Library, Yellowstone National Park, February.

Despain, D., D. Houston, M. Meagher, and P. Schullery: 1986, *Wildlife in Transition: Man and Nature on Yellowstone's Northern Range,* Roberts Rinehart, Boulder, CO.

Egan, T.: 1988, 'Ethic of Protecting Land Fueled Yellowstone Fires,' *New York Times,* 22 September, p. 1, p. 12.

Houston, D.B.: 1971, 'Ecosystems of National Parks,' *Science* 172, pp. 648-651.

Hull, D.L.: 1988, *Science as a Process: An Evolutionary Account of the Social and Conceptual Development of Science.* University of Chicago Press, Chicago.

Leopold, A.S.: 1968, 'The View from Berkeley and Madison,' in *Proceedings of the Meeting of Research Scientists and Management Biologists of the National Park Service.* Horace M. Albright Training Center, Grand Canyon National Park, April 6, 7, 8.

Leopold, A.S., S.A. Cain, C.M. Cottam, I.N. Gabrielson, and T.L. Kimball: 1963, *Wildlife Management in the National Parks,* Report of the Advisory Board on Wildlife Management to Secretary of Interior Udall, March 4, U.S. Government Printing Office, Washington.

National Academy of Sciences (NAS): 1963, *A Report by the Advisory Committee to the National Park Service on Research of the National Academy of Sciences-National Research Council* (Robbins Report). National Academy of Sciences-National Research Council, Washington, D.C.

National Park Service (NPS): 1986, *A Detailed Response from the National Park Service to 'The Grizzly and the Juggernaut.'* Yellowstone National Park, WY.

National Park Service (NPS): 1987, *Elk and Vegetation Research Relevant to Yellowstone's Northern Range: Project Summaries.* Yellowstone National Park, WY.

Rolston, H.: 1986, 'Can and Ought We to Follow Nature?' In *Philosophy Gone Wild,* Prometheus Books, Buffalo, NY.

Rolston, H.: 1988, *Environmental Ethics: Duties to and Values in the Natural World.* Temple University Press, Philadelphia.

Stuebner, S.: 1988, 'Diverse Species Thrive after Fire Burns Forest,' *The Coloradoan,* Gannett News Service, 18 September.

U.S. Congress: 1872, Yellowstone Park Act. U.S. Statutes at Large, vol. 17 (1873), ch. 24, pp. 32-33.

Wright, G.A.: 1984, *People of the High Country: Jackson Hole Before the Settlers.* Peter Lang, New York.

DISCUSSION TOPICS

1. Evaluate Rolston's assertion that, ''in Yellowstone, . . . managerial control is not love.'' Under what conditions do you believe it is, and is not, appropriate for humans to manipulate and manage nature? Explain your position.

2. What is your opinion about Rolston's proposal that negative human behaviors such as political infighting, ridicule, arrogance, or the raw use of power may ultimately promote and enhance scientific advancement in environmental and other research? Support your perspective.

READING 5

The Ecology of Order and Chaos

Donald Worster

Donald Worster (b. 1941) is Professor of History at the University of Kansas, Laurence, and has written a number of books and articles on environmental history. Worster believes that the persistent enthusiasm shown for the field of ecology lies in a hope that science can offer moral enlightenment allowing humans to work and live in equilibrium and harmony with the rest of nature. Tracing the history of ideas in ecology, Worster notes that from its beginnings ecological thought has emphasized the equilibrium, harmony, and order of nature.

Recent ecologists, such as Eugene P. Odum, strengthened this perception by arguing that nature's strategy leads to mutualism and cooperation among the organisms inhabiting an area, and that a point of "homeostasis" ultimately is reached in which interrelatedness and cooperation allow the living organisms in an ecosystem to manage it for maximum efficiency and mutual benefit. Odum cites high species diversity and minimal loss of nutrients to the outside as key indicators of ecological order.

Since the early 1970s, this view of ecology has been challenged. Worster documents the emergence of "patch theory" in which nature is depicted as composed of mosaics of environmental conditions continually changing through time and space. Here the parts, including various species, function independently of one another. Ecologists increasingly have portrayed the natural world as existing in a state of flux dominated by chaos and disharmony. Thus, Worster concludes that ecology no longer offers a sound philosophical basis for the hope that a harmonious equilibrium between humans and nature can be restored—if it ever existed.

The science of ecology has had a popular impact unlike that of any other academic field of research. Consider the extraordinary ubiquity of the word itself: it has appeared in the most everyday places and the most astonishing, on day-glo T-shirts, in corporate advertising, and on bridge abutments. It has changed the language of politics and philosophy—springing up in a number of countries are political groups that are self-identified as "Ecology Parties." Yet who ever proposed forming a political party named after comparative linguistics or advanced paleontology? On several continents we have a philosophical movement termed "Deep Ecology," but nowhere has anyone announced a movement for "Deep Entomology" or "Deep Polish Literature." Why has this funny little word, ecology, coined by an obscure 19th-century German scientist, acquired so powerful a cultural resonance, so widespread a following?

Behind the persistent enthusiasm for ecology, I believe, lies the hope that this science can offer a great deal more than a pile of data. It is supposed to offer a pathway to a kind of moral enlightenment that we can call, for the purposes of simplicity, "conservation." The expectation did not originate with the public but first appeared among eminent scientists within the field. For instance, in his 1935 book *Deserts on the March*, the noted University of Oklahoma, and later Yale, botanist Paul Sears urged Americans to take ecology seriously, promoting it in their universities and making it part of their governing process. "In Great Britain," he pointed out,

> the ecologists are being consulted at every step in planning the proper utilization of those parts of the Empire not yet settled, thus . . . ending the era of haphazard exploitation. There are hopeful, but all too few signs that our own national government realizes the part which ecology must play in a permanent program.[1]

Sears recommended that the United States hire a few thousand ecologists at the county level to advise citizens on questions of land use and thereby bring an end to environmental degradation; such a brigade, he thought, would put the whole nation on a biologically and economically sustainable basis.

In a 1947 addendum to his text, Sears added that ecologists, acting in the public interest, would instill in the American mind that "body of knowledge," that "point of view, which peculiarly implies all that is meant by conservation."[2] In other words, by the time of the 1930s and 40s, ecology was being hailed as a much needed guide to a future motivated by an ethic of conservation. And conservation for Sears meant restoring the biological order, maintaining the health of the land and thereby the well-being of the nation, pursuing by both moral and technical means a lasting equilibrium with nature.

While we have not taken to heart all Sears's suggestions—have not yet put any ecologists on county payrolls, with an office next door to the tax collector and sheriff—we have taken a surprisingly long step in his direction. Every day in some part of the nation, an ecologist is at work writing an environmental impact report or monitoring a human disturbance of the landscape or testifying at a hearing.

Twelve years ago I published a history, going back to the 18th century, of this scientific discipline and its ideas about nature.[3] The conclusions in that book still strike me as being, on the whole, sensible and valid: that this science has come to be a major influence on our perception of nature in modern times; that its ideas, on the other hand, have been reflections of ourselves as much as objective apprehensions of nature; that scientific analysis cannot take the place of moral reasoning; that science, including the science of ecology, promotes, at least in some of its manifestations, a few of our darker ambitions toward nature and therefore itself needs to be morally examined and critiqued from time to time. Ecology, I argued, should never be taken as an all-wise, always trustworthy guide. We must be willing to challenge this authority, and indeed challenge the authority of science in general; not be quick to scorn or vilify or behead, but simply, now and then, to question.

During the period since my book was published, there has accumulated a considerable body of new thinking and new research in ecology. In this essay I mean to survey some of that recent thinking, contrasting it with its predecessors, and to raise a few of the same questions I did before. Part of my argument will be that Paul Sears would be astonished, and perhaps dismayed, to hear the kind of advice that ecological experts have to give these days. Less and less do they offer, or even promise to offer, what he would consider to be a program of moral enlightenment—of "conservation" in the sense of a restored equilibrium between humans and nature.

There is a clear reason for that outcome, I will argue, and it has to do with drastic changes in the ideas that ecologists hold about the structure and function of the natural world. In Sears's day ecology was basically a study of equilibrium, harmony, and order; it had been so from its beginnings. Today, however, in many circles of scientific research, it has become a study of disturbance, disharmony, and chaos, and coincidentally or not, conservation is often not even a remote concern.

At the time *Deserts on the March* appeared in print, and through the time of its second and even third edition, the dominant name in the field of American ecology was that of Frederic L. Clements, who more than any other individual introduced scientific ecology into our national academic life. He called his approach "dynamic ecology," meaning it was concerned with change and evolution in the landscape. At its heart Clements's ecology dealt with the process of vegetational succession—the sequence of plant communities that appear on a piece of soil, newly made or disturbed, beginning with the first pioneer communities that invade and get a foothold.[4] Here is how I have defined the essence of the Clementsian paradigm:

> Change upon change became the inescapable principle of Clements's science. Yet he also insisted stubbornly and vigorously on the notion that the natural landscape must eventually reach a vaguely final climax stage. Nature's course, he contended, is not an aimless wandering to and fro but a steady flow toward stability that can be exactly plotted by the scientist.[5]

Most interestingly, Clements referred to that final climax stage as a "superorganism," implying that the assemblage of plants had achieved the close integration of parts, the self-organizing capability, of a single animal or plant. In some unique sense, it had become a live, coherent thing, not a mere collection of atomistic individuals, and exercised some control over the nonliving world around it, as organisms do.

Until well after World War II Clements's climax theory dominated ecological thought in this country.[6] Pick up almost any textbook in the field written forty, or even thirty, years ago, and you will likely find mention of the climax. It was this theory that Paul Sears had studied and took to be the core lesson of ecology that his county ecologists should teach their fellow citizens: that nature tends toward a climax state and that, as far as practicable, they should learn to respect and preserve it. Sears wrote that the chief work of the scientist ought to be to show "the unbalance which man has produced on this continent" and to lead people back to some approximation of nature's original health and stability.[7]

But then, beginning in the 1940s, while Clements and his ideas were still in the ascendent, a few scientists began trying to speak a new vocabulary. Words like "energy flow," "trophic levels," and "ecosystem" appeared in the leading journals, and they indicated a view of nature shaped more by physics than botany. Within another decade or two nature came to be widely seen as a flow of energy and nutrients through a physical or thermodynamic system. The early figures prominent in shaping this new view included C. Juday, Raymond Lindeman, and G. Evelyn Hutchinson. But perhaps its most influential exponent was Eugene P. Odum, hailing from North Carolina and Georgia, discovering in his southern saltwater marshes, tidal estuaries, and abandoned cotton fields the animating, pulsating force of the sun, the global flux of energy. In 1953 Odum published the first edition of his famous textbook, *The Fundamentals of Ecology.*[8] In 1966 he became president of Ecological Society of America.

By now anyone in the United States who regularly reads a newspaper or magazine has come to know at least a few of Odum's ideas, for they furnish the main themes in our popular understanding of ecology, beginning with the sovereign idea of the ecosystem. Odum defined the ecosystem as "any unit that includes all of the organisms (i.e., the 'community') in a given area interacting with the physical environment so that a flow of energy leads to clearly defined trophic structure, biotic diversity, and material cycles (i.e., exchange of materials between living and nonliving parts) within the system."[9] The whole earth, he argued, is organized into an interlocking series of such "ecosystems," ranging in size from a small pond to so vast an expanse as the Brazilian rainforest.

What all those ecosystems have in common is a "strategy of development," a kind of game plan that gives nature an overall direction. That strategy is, in Odum's words, "directed toward achieving as large and diverse an organic structure as is possible within the limits set by the available energy input and the prevailing physical conditions of existence."[10] Every single ecosystem, he believed, is either moving toward or has already achieved that goal. It is a clear, coherent, and easily observable strategy; and it ends in the happy state of order.

Nature's strategy, Odum added, leads finally to a world of mutualism and cooperation among the organisms inhabiting an area. From an early stage of competing against one another, they evolve toward a more symbiotic relationship. They learn, as it were, to work together to control their surrounding environment, making it more and more suitable as a habitat, until at last they have the power to protect themselves from its stressful cycles of drought and flood, winter and summer, cold and heat. Odum called that point "homeostasis." To achieve it, the living components of an ecosystem must evolve a structure of interrelatedness and cooperation that can, to some extent, manage the physical world—manage it for maximum efficiency and mutual benefit.

I have described this set of ideas as a break from the past, but that is misleading. Odum may have used different terms than Clements, may even have had a radically different vision of nature at times; but he did not repudiate Clements's notion that nature moves toward order and harmony. In the place of the theory of the "climax" stage he put the theory of the "mature ecosystem." His nature may have appeared more as an automated factory than as a Clementsian superorganism, but like its predecessor it tends toward order.

The theory of the ecosystem presented a very clear set of standards as to what constituted order and disorder, which Odum set forth in the form of a "tabular model of ecological succession." When the ecosystem reaches its end point of homeostasis, his table shows, it expends less energy on increasing production and more on furnishing protection from external vicissitudes: that is, the biomass in an area reaches a steady level, neither increasing nor decreasing, and the emphasis in the system is on keeping it that way—on maintaining a kind of no-growth economy. Then the little, aggressive, weedy organisms common at an early stage in development (the r-selected species) give way to larger, steadier creatures (K-selected species), who may have less potential for fast growth and explosive reproduction but also better talents at surviving in dense settlements and keeping the place on an even keel.[11] At that point there is supposed to be more diversity in the community—i.e., a greater array of species. And there is less loss of nutrients to the outside; nitrogen, phosphorous, and calcium all stay in circulation within the ecosystem rather than leaking out. Those are some of the key indicators of ecological order, all of them susceptible to precise measurement. The suggestion was implicit but clear that if one interfered too much with nature's strategy of development, the effects might be costly: a serious loss of nutrients, a decline in species diversity, an end to biomass stability. In short, the ecosystem would be damaged.

The most likely source of that damage was no mystery to Odum: it was human beings trying to force up the production of useful commodities and stupidly risking the destruction of their life support system.

> Man has generally been preoccupied with obtaining as much "production" from the landscape as possible, by developing and maintaining early successional types of ecosystems, usually monocultures. But, of course, man does not live by food and fiber alone; he also needs a balanced CO_2-O_2 atmosphere, the climatic buffer provided by oceans and masses of vegetation, and clean (that is, unproductive) water for cultural and industrial uses. Many essential life-cycle resources, not to mention recreational and esthetic needs, are best provided man by the less "productive" landscapes. In other words, the landscape is not just a supply depot but is also the *oikos*—the home—in which we must live.[12]

Odum's view of nature as a series of balanced ecosystems, achieved or in the making, led him to take a strong stand in favor of preserving the landscape in as nearly natural a condition as possible. He suggested the need for substantial restraint on human activity—for environmental planning "on a rational and scientific basis." For him as for Paul Sears, ecology must be taught to the public and made the foundation of education, economics, and politics; America and other countries must be "ecologized."

Of course not every one who adopted the ecosystem approach to ecology ended up where Odum did. Quite the contrary, many found the ecosystem idea a wonderful instrument for promoting global technocracy. Experts familiar with the ecosystem and skilled in its manipulation, it was hoped in some quarters, could manage the entire planet for improved efficiency. "Governing" all of nature with the aid of rational science was the dream of these ecosystem technocrats.[13] But technocratic management was not the chief lesson, I believe, the public learned in Professor Odum's classroom; most came away devoted, as he was, to preserving large parts of nature in an unmanaged state and sure that they had been given a strong scientific rationale, as well as knowledge base, to do it. We must defend the world's endangered ecosystems, they insisted. We must safeguard the integrity of the Greater Yellowstone ecosystem, the Chesapeake Bay ecosystem, the Serengeti ecosystem. We must protect species diversity, biomass stability and calcium recycling. We must make the world safe for K-species.[14]

That was the rallying cry of environmentalists and ecologists alike in the 1960s and early 1970s, when it seemed that the great coming struggle would be between what was left of pristine nature, delicately balanced in Odum's beautifully rational ecosystems, and a human race bent on mindless, greedy destruction. A decade or two later the situation has changed considerably. There are still environmental threats around, to be sure, and they are more dangerous than ever. The newspapers inform of us of continuing disasters like the massive 1989 oil spill in Alaska's Prince William Sound, and reporters persist in using words like "ecosystem" and "balance" and "fragility" to describe such disasters. So do many scientists, who continue to acknowledge their theoretical indebtedness to Odum. For instance, in a recent British poll, 447 ecologists out of 645 questioned ranked the "ecosystem" as one of the most important concepts their discipline has contributed to our understanding of the natural world; indeed, ''ecosystem'' ranked first on their list, drawing more votes than nineteen other leading concepts.[15] But all the same, and despite the persistence of environmental problems, Odum's ecosystem is no longer the main theme in research or teaching in the science. A survey of recent ecology textbooks shows that the concept is not even mentioned in one leading work and has a much diminished place in the others.[16]

Ecology is not the same as it was. A rather drastic change has been going on in this science of late—a radical shifting away from the thinking of Eugene Odum's generation, away from its assumptions of order and predictability, a shifting toward what we might call a new *ecology of chaos.*

In July 1973, the *Journal of the Arnold Arboretum* published an article by two scientists associated with the Massachusetts Audubon Society, William Drury and Ian Nisbet, and it challenged Odum's ecology fundamentally. The title of the article was simply ''Succession,'' indicating that old subject of observed sequences in plant and animal associations. With both Frederic Clements and Eugene Odum, succession has been taken to be the straight and narrow road to equilibrium. Drury and Nisbet disagreed completely with that assumption. Their observations, drawn particularly from northeastern temperate forests, strongly suggested that the process of ecological succession does not lead anywhere. Change is without any determinable direction and goes on forever, never reaching a point of stability. They found no evidence of any progressive development in nature: no progressive increase over time in biomass stabilization, no progressive diversification of species, no progressive movement toward a greater cohesiveness in plant and animal communities, nor toward a greater success in regulating the environment. Indeed, they found none of the criteria Odum had posited for mature ecosystems. The forest, they insisted, no matter what its age, is nothing but an erratic, shifting mosaic of trees and other plants. In their words, ''most of the phenomena of succession should be understood as resulting from the differential growth, differential survival, and perhaps differential dispersal of species adapted to grow at different points on stress gradients.''[17] In other

words, they could see lots of individual species, each doing its thing, but they could locate no emergent collectivity, nor any strategy to achieve one.

Prominent among their authorities supporting this view was the nearly forgotten name of Henry A. Gleason, a taxonomist who, in 1926, had challenged Frederic Clements and his organismic theory of the climax in an article entitled, ''The Individualistic Concept of the Plant Association.'' Gleason had argued that we live in a world of constant flux and impermanence, not one tending toward Clements's climaxes. There is no such thing, he argued, as balance or equilibrium or steady-state. Each and every plant association is nothing but a temporary gathering of strangers a clustering of species unrelated to one another, here for a brief while today, on their way somewhere else tomorrow. ''Each . . . species of plant is a law unto itself,'' he wrote.[18] We look for cooperation in nature and we find only competition. We look for organized wholes, and we can discover only loose atoms and fragments. We hope for order and discern only a mishmash of conjoining species, all seeking their own advantage in utter disregard of others.

Thanks in part to Drury and Nisbet, this ''individualistic'' view was reborn in the mid-1970s and, during the past decade, it became the core idea of what some scientists hailed as a new, revolutionary paradigm in ecology. To promote it, they attacked the traditional notion of succession; for to reject that notion was to reject the larger idea that organic nature tends toward order. In 1977 two more biologists, Joseph Connell and Ralph Slatyer, continued the attack, denying the old claim that an invading community of pioneering species, the first stage in Clements's sequence, works to prepare the ground for its successors, like a group of Daniel Boones blazing the trail for civilization. The first comers, Connell and Slatyer maintained, manage in most cases to stake out their claims and successfully defend them; they do not give way to a later, superior group of colonists. Only when the pioneers die or are damaged by natural disturbances, thus releasing the resources they have monopolized, can latecomers find a foothold and get established.[19]

As this assault on the old thinking gathered momentum, the word "disturbance" began to appear more frequently in the scientific literature and be taken far more seriously. "Disturbance" was not a common subject in Odum's heyday, and it almost never appeared in combination with the adjective "natural." Now, however, it was as though scientists were out looking strenuously for signs of disturbance in nature—especially signs of disturbance that were not caused by humans—and they were finding it everywhere. During the past decade those new ecologists succeeded in leaving little tranquility in primitive nature. Fire is one of the most common disturbances they noted. So is wind, especially in the form of violent hurricanes and tornadoes. So are invading populations of microorganisms and pests and predators. And volcanic eruptions. And invading ice sheets of the Quaternary Period. And devastating droughts like that of the 1930s in the American West. Above all, it is these last sorts of disturbances, caused by the restlessness of climate, that the new generation of ecologists have emphasized. As one of the most influential of them, Professor Margaret Davis of the University of Minnesota, has written: "For the last 50 years or 500 or 1,000—as long as anyone would claim for 'ecological time'—there has never been an interval when temperature was in a steady state with symmetrical fluctuations about a mean. . . . Only on the longest time scale, 100,000 years, is there a tendency toward cyclical variation, and the cycles are asymmetrical, with a mean much different from today."[20]

One of the most provocative and impressive expressions of the new post-Odum ecology is a book of essays edited by S.T.A. Pickett and P.S. White, *The Ecology of Natural Disturbance and Patch Dynamics* (published in 1985). I submit it as symptomatic of much of the thinking going on today in the field. Though the final section of the book does deal with ecosystems, the word has lost much of its former meaning and implications. Two of the authors in fact open their contribution with a complaint that many scientists assume that "homogeneous ecosystems are a reality," when in truth "virtually all naturally occurring and man-disturbed ecosystems are mosaics of environmental conditions." "Historically," they write, "ecologists have been slow to recognize the importance of disturbances and the heterogeneity they generate." The reason for this slowness? "The majority of both theoretical and empirical work has been dominated by an equilibrium perspective."[21] Repudiating that perspective, these authors take us to the tropical forests of South and Central America and to the Everglades of Florida, showing us instability on every hand: a wet, green world of continual disturbance—or as they prefer to say, " of perturbations." Even the grasslands of North America, which inspired Frederic Clements's theory of the climax, appear in this collection as regularly disturbed environments. One paper describes them as a "dynamic, fine-textured mosaic" that is constantly kept in upheaval by the workings of badgers, pocket gophers, and mound-building ants, along with fire, drought, and eroding wind and water.[22] The message in all these papers is consistent: The climax notion is dead, the ecosystem has receded in usefulness, and in their place we have the idea of the lowly "patch." Nature should be regarded as a landscape of patches, big and little, patches of all textures and colors, a patchwork quilt of living things, changing continually through time and space, responding to an unceasing barrage of perturbations. The stitches in that quilt never hold for long.

Now, of course, scientists have known about gophers and winds, the Ice Age and droughts for a considerable time. Yet heretofore they have not let those disruptions spoil their theories of balanced plant and animal associations, and we must ask why that was so. Why did Clements and Odum tend to dismiss such forces as climatic change, at least of the less catastrophic sort, as threats to the order of nature? Why have their successors, on the other hand, tended to put so much emphasis on those same changes, to the point that they often see nothing but instability in the landscape?

One clue comes from the fact that many of these disturbance boosters are not and have never been ecosystem scientists; they received their training in the subfield of population biology and reflect the growing confidence, methodological maturity, and influence of the subfield.[23] When they look at a forest, the population ecologists see only the trees. See them and count them—so many white pines, so many hemlocks, so many maples and birches. They insist that if we know all there is to know about the individual species that constitute a forest, and can measure their lives in precise, quantitative terms, we will know all there is to know about that forest. It has no "emergent" or organismic properties. It is not some whole greater than the sum of its parts, requiring "holistic" understanding. Outfitted with computers that can track the life histories of individual species, chart the rise and fall of populations, they have brought a degree of mathematical precision to ecology that is awesome to contemplate. And what they see when they look at population histories for any patch of land is wildly swinging oscillations. Populations rise and populations fall, like stock market prices, auto sales, and hemlines. We live, they insist, in a non-equilibrium world.[24]

There is another reason for the paradigmatic shift I have been describing, though I suggest it quite tentatively and can offer only sketchy evidence for it. For some scientists, a nature characterized by highly individualistic associations, constant disturbance, and incessant change may be more ideologically satisfying than Odum's ecosystem, with its stress on cooperation, social organization, and environmentalism. A case in point is the very successful popularizer of contemporary ecology, Paul Colinvaux, author of *Why Big Fierce Animals Are Rare* (1978). His chapter on succession begins with these lines: "If the planners really get hold of us so that they can stamp out all individual liberty and do what they like with our land, they might decide what whole counties full of inferior farms should be put back into forest." Clearly, he is not enthusiastic about land-use planning or forest restoration. And he ends that same chapter with these remarkably revealing and self-assured words:

> We can now ... explain all the intriguing, predictable events of plant successions in simple, matter of fact, Darwinian ways. Everything that happens in successions comes about because of the different species go about earning their livings as best they may, each in its own individual manner. What look like community properties are in fact the summed results of all these bits of private enterprise.[25]

Apparently, if this example is any indication, the social Darwinists are back on the scene, and at least some of them are ecologists, and at least some of their opposition to Odum's science may have to do with a revulsion toward its political implications, including its attractiveness for environmentalists. Colinvaux is very clear about the need to get some distance between himself and groups like the Sierra Club.

I am not alone in wondering whether there might be a deeper, half-articulated ideological motive generating the new direction in ecology. The Swedish historian of science, Thomas Söderqvist, in his recent study of ecology's development in his country, concludes that the present generation of evolutionary ecologists

> seem to do ecology for fun only, indifferent to practical problems, including the salvation of the nation. They are mathematically and theoretically sophisticated, sitting indoors calculating on computers, rather than traveling out in the wilds. They are individualists, abhorring the idea of large-scale ecosystem projects. Indeed, the transition from ecosystem ecology to evolutionary ecology seems to reflect the generational transition from the politically consciousness generation of the 1960s to the 'yuppie' generation of the 1980s.[26]

That may be an exaggerated characterization, and I would not want to apply it to every scientist who has published on patch dynamics or disturbance regimes. But it does draw our attention to an unmistakable attempt by many ecologists to disassociate themselves from reform environmentalism and its criticisms of human impact on nature.

I wish, however, that the emergence of the new post-Odum ecology could be explained so simply in those two ways: as a triumph of reductive population dynamics over holistic consciousness, or as a triumph of social Darwinist or entrepreneurial ideology over a commitment to environmental preservation. There is, it seems, more going on than that, and it is going on all through the natural sciences—biology, astronomy, physics—perhaps going on through all modern technological societies. It is nothing less than the discovery of chaos. Nature, many have begun to believe is *fundamentally* erratic, discontinuous, and unpredictable. It is full of seemingly random events that elude our models of how things are supposed to work. As a result, the unexpected keeps hitting us in the face. Clouds collect and disperse, rain falls or doesn't fall, disregarding our careful weather predictions, and we cannot explain why. Cars suddenly bunch up on the freeway, and the traffic controllers fly into a frenzy. A man's heart beats regularly year after year, then abruptly begins to skip a beat now and then. A ping pong ball bounces off the table in an unexpected direction. Each little snowflake falling out of the sky turns out to be completely unlike any other. Those are ways in which nature seems, in contrast to all our previous theories and methods, to be chaotic. If the ultimate test of any body of scientific knowledge is its ability to predict events, then all the sciences and pseudo-sciences—physics, chemistry, climatology, economics, ecology—fail the test regularly. They all have been announcing laws, designing models, predicting what an individual atom or person is supposed to do; and now, increasingly, they are beginning to confess that the world never quite behaves the way it is supposed to do.

Making sense of this situation is the task of an altogether new kind of inquiry calling itself the science of chaos. Some say it portends a revolution in thinking equivalent to quantum mechanics or relativity. Like those other 20th-century revolutions, the science of chaos rejects tenets going back as far as the days of Sir Isaac Newton. In fact, what is occurring may be not two or three separate revolutions but a single revolution against all the principles, laws, models, and applications of classical science, the science ushered in by the great Scientific Revolution of the 17th century.[27] For centuries we have assumed that nature, despite a few appearances to the contrary, is a perfectly predictable system of linear, rational order. Give us an adequate number of facts, scientists have said, and we can describe that order in complete detail—can plot the lines along which everything moves and the speed of that movement and the collisions that will occur. Even Darwin's theory of evolution, which in the last century challenged much of the Newtonian worldview, left intact many people's confidence that order would prevail at last in the evolution of life; that out of the tangled history of competitive struggle

would come progress, harmony, and stability. Now that traditional assumption may have broken down irretrievably. For whatever reason, whether because empirical data suggests it or because extrascientific cultural trends do—the experience of so much rapid social change in our daily lives—scientists are beginning to focus on what they had long managed to avoid seeing. The world is more complex than we ever imagined, they say, and indeed, some would add, ever can imagine.[28]

Despite the obvious complexity of their subject matter, ecologists have been among the slowest to join the cross-disciplinary science of chaos. I suspect that the influence of Clements and Odum, lingering well into the 1970s, worked against the new perspective, encouraging faith in linear regularities and equilibrium in the interaction of species. Nonetheless, eventually there arrived a day of conversion. In 1974 the Princeton mathematical ecologist Robert May published a paper with the title, ''Biological Populations with Nonoverlapping Generations: Stable Points, Stable Cycles, and Chaos.''[29] In it he admitted that the mathematical models he and others had constructed were inadequate approximations of the ragged life histories of organisms. They did not fully explain, for example, the aperiodic outbreaks of gypsy moths in eastern hardwood forests or the Canadian lynx cycles in the subartic. Wildlife populations do not follow some simple Malthusian pattern of increase, saturation, and crash.

More and more ecologists have followed May and begun to try to bring their subject into line with chaotic theory. William Schaefer is one of them; though a student of Robert MacArthur, a leader of the old equilibrium school, he has been lately struck by the same anomaly of unpredictable fluctuations in populations as May and others. Though taught to believe in ''the so-called 'Balance of Nature','' he writes, ''. . . the idea that populations are at or close to equilibrium,'' things now are beginning to look very different.[30] He describes himself has having to reach far across the disciplines, to make connections with concepts of chaos in the other natural sciences, in order to free himself from his field's restrictive past.

The entire study of chaos began in 1961, with

efforts to simulate weather and climate patterns on a computer at MIT. There, meteorologist Edward Lorenz came up with his now famous ''Butterfly Effect,'' the notion that a butterfly stirring the air today in a Beijing park can transform storm systems next month in New York City. Scientists call this phenomenon ''sensitive dependence on initial conditions.'' What it means is that tiny differences in input can quickly become substantial differences in output. A corollary is that we cannot know, even with all our artificial intelligence apparatus, every one of the tiny differences that have occurred or are occurring at any place or point in time; nor can we know which tiny differences will produce which substantial differences in output. Beyond a short range, say, of two or three days from now, our predictions are not worth the paper they are written on.

The implications of this ''Butterfly Effect'' for ecology are profound. If a single flap of an insect's wings in China can lead to a torrential downpour in New York, then what might it do to the Greater Yellowstone Ecosystem? What can ecologists possibly know about all the forces impinging on, or about to impinge on, any piece of land? What can they safely ignore and what must they pay attention to? What distant, invisible, minuscule events may even now be happening that will change the organization of plant and animal life in our back yards? This is the predicament, and the challenge, presented by the science of chaos, and it is altering the imagination of ecologists dramatically.

John Muir once declared, ''When we try to pick out anything by itself, we find it hitched to everything else in the universe.''[31] For him, that was a manifestation of an infinitely wise plan in which everything functioned with perfect harmony. The new ecology of chaos, though impressed like Muir with interdependency, does not share his view of ''an infinitely wise plan'' that controls and shapes everything into order. There is no plan, today's scientists say, no harmony apparent in the events of nature. If there is order in the universe—and there will no longer be any science if all faith in order vanishes—it is going to be much more difficult to locate and describe than we thought.

For Muir, the clear lesson of cosmic complexity was that humans ought to love and preserve nature just as it is. The lessons of the new ecology, in contrast, are not at all clear. Does it promote, in Ilya Prigogine and Isabelle Stenger's words, ''a renewal of nature,'' a less hierarchical view of life, and a set of ''new relations between man and nature and between man and man''?[32] Or does it increase our alienation from the world, our withdrawal into postmodernist doubt and self-consciousness? What is there to love or preserve in a universe of chaos? How are people supposed to behave in such a universe? If such is the kind of place we inhabit, why not go ahead with all our private ambitions, free of any fear that we may be doing special damage? What, after all, does the phrase ''environmental damage'' mean in a world of so much natural chaos? Does the tradition of environmentalism to which Muir belonged, along with so many other nature writers and ecologists of the past—people like Paul Sears, Eugene Odum, Aldo Leopold, and Rachel Carson—make sense any longer? I have no space here to attempt to answer those questions or to make predictions but only issue a warning that they are too important to be left for scientists alone to answer. Ecology today, no more than in the past, can be assumed to be all-knowing or all-wise or eternally true.

Whether they are true or false, permanent or passingly fashionable, it does seem entirely possible that these changes in scientific thinking toward an emphasis on chaos will not produce any easing of the environmentalist's concern. Though words like ecosystem or climax may fade away and some new vocabulary take their place, the fear of risk and danger will likely become greater than ever. Most of us are intuitively aware, whether we can put our fears into mathematical formulae or not, that the technological power we have accumulated is *destructively* chaotic; not irrationally, we fear it and fear what it can to do us as well as the rest of nature.[33] It may be that we moderns, after absorbing the lessons of today's science, find we cannot love nature quite so easily as Muir did; but it may also be that we have discovered more reason than ever to respect it—to respect its baffling complexity, its inherent unpredictability, its daily turbulence. And to flap our own wings in it a little more gently.

NOTES

1. Paul Sears. *Deserts on the March,* 3rd ed. (Norman: University of Oklahoma Press, 1959), p. 162.
2. Ibid., p. 177.
3. Donald Worster, *Nature's Economy: A History of Ecological Ideas* (New York: Cambridge University Press, 1977)
4. This is the theme in particular of Clement's book *Plant Succession* (Washington: Carnegie Institution, 1916).
5. Worster, p. 210.
6. Clements's major rival for influence in the United States was Henry Chandler Cowles of the University of Chicago, whose first paper on ecological succession appeared in 1899. The best study of Cowles's ideas is J. Ronald Engel, *Sacred Sands: The Struggle for Community in the Indiana Dunes* (Middletown, CT: Wesleyan University Press, 1983), pp. 137-59. Engel describes him as having a less deterministic, more pluralistic notion of succession, one that "opened the way to a more creative role for human beings in nature's evolutionary adventure." (p. 150). See also Ronald C. Tobey, *Saving the Prairies: The Life Cycle of the Founding School of American Plant Ecology, 1895-1955* (Berkeley: University of California, 1981).
7. Sears, p. 142.
8. This book was co-authored with his brother Howard T. Odum, and it went through two more editions, the last appearing in 1971.
9. Eugene P. Odum, *Fundamentals of Ecology* (Philadelphia: W.B. Saunders, 1971), p. 8.
10. Odum. "The Strategy of Ecosystem Development," *Science,* 164 (18 April 1969): 266.
11. The terms "K-selection" and "r-selection" came from Robert MacArthur and Edward O. Wilson, *Theory of Island Biogeography* (Princeton: Princeton University Press, 1967). Along with Odum, MacArthur was the leading spokesman during the 1950s and 60s for the view of nature as a series of thermodynamically balanced ecosystems.
12. Odum, "Strategy of Ecosystem Development," p. 266. See also Odum, "Trends Expected in Stressed Ecosystems." *BioScience,* 35 (July/August 1985): 419-422.
13. A book of that title was published by Earl P. Murphy, *Governing Nature* (Chicago: Quadrangle Books, 1967). From time to time, Eugene Odum himself seems to have caught that ambition or leant his support to it,

and it was certainly central to the work of his brother, Howard T. Odum. On this theme see Peter J. Taylor, "Technocratic Optimism, H. T. Odum, and the Partial Transformation of Ecological Metaphor after World War II," *Journal of the History of Biology,* 21 (Summer 1988): 213-244.
14. A very influential popularization of Odum's view of nature (though he is never actually referred to in it) is Barry Commoner's *The Closing Circle: Nature, Man, and Technology* (New York: Alfred A. Knopf, 1971). See in particular the discussion of the four "Laws" of ecology, pp. 33-46.
15. Communication from Malcolm Cherrett, *Ecology,* 70 (March 1989): 41-42.
16. See Michael Begon, John L. Harper, and Colin R. Townsend, *Ecology: Individuals, Populations, and Communities* (Sunderland, Mass.: Sinauer, 1986). In another textbook, Odum's views are presented critically as the traditional approach: R. J. Putnam and S. D. Wratien, *Principles of Ecology* (Berkeley: University of California Press, 1984). More loyal to the ecosystem model are Paul Ehrlich and Jonathan Roughgarden. *The Science of Ecology* (New York: Macmillan, 1987); and Robert Leo Smith, *Elements of Ecology,* 2nd ed. (New York: Harper & Row, 1986), though the latter admits that he has shifted from an "ecosystem approach" to more of an "evolutionary approach" (p. xiii).
17. William H. Drury and Ian C. T. Nisbet, "Succession," *Journal of the Arnold Arboretum,* 54 (July 1973); 360.
18. H. A. Gleason, "The Individualistic Concept of the Plant Association," *Bulletin of the Torrey Botanical Club,* 53 (1926): 25. A later version of the same article appeared in *American Midland Naturalist,* 21 (1939): 92-110.
19. Joseph H. Connell and Ralph O. Slatyer, "Mechanisms of Succession in Natural Communities and Their Role in Community Stability and Organization." *The American Naturalist,* 111 (November-December 1977): 1119-1144.
20. Margaret Bryan Davis, "Climatic instability, Time Lags, and Community Disequilibrium," in *Community Ecology,* ed. Jared Diamond and Ted J. Case (New York: Harper & Row, 1986), p. 269.
21. James R. Karr and Kathryn E. Freemark. "Disturbance and Vertebrates: An Integrative Perspective." *The Ecology of Natural Disturbance and Patch Dynamics,* eds., S. T. A. Pickett and P. S. White (Orlando, Fla.: Academic Press, 1985), pp. 154-55. The Odum school of thought is, however, by no means silent. Another

recent compilation has been put together in his honor, and many of its authors express a continuing support for his ideas: L. R. Porneroy and J. J. Alberts, eds., *Concepts of Ecosystem Ecology: A Comparative View* (New York: Springer-Verlag, 1988).

22. Orie L. Loucks, Mary L. Plumb-Menties, and Deborah Rogers, ''Gap Processes and Large-Scale Disturbances in Sand Prairies,'' *ibid.,* pp. 72-85.

23. For the rise of population ecology see Sharon E. Kingsland, *Modeling Nature: Episodes in the History of Populaton Ecology* (Chicago: University of Chicago Press, 1985).

24. An influential exception to this tendency is F. H. Bormann and G. E. Likens, *Pattern and Process in a Forested Ecosystem* (New York: Springer-Verlag, 1979), which proposes in Chap. 6 the model of a ''shifting mosaic steady-state.'' See also P. Yodzis, ''The Stability of Real Ecosystems,'' *Nature,* 289 (19 February 1981): 674-76.

25. Paul Colinvaux, *Why Big Fierce Animals Are Rare: An Ecologist's Perspective* (Princeton: Princeton University Press, 1978), pp. 117, 135.

26. Thomas Söderqvist, *The Ecologists: From Merry Naturalists to Saviours of the Nation. A Sociologically informed narrative survey of the ecologization of Sweden, 1895-1975.* (Stockholm: Almqvist & Wiksell International, 1986), p. 281.

27. This argument is made with great intellectual force by Stengers, (Boulder: Shambala/ New Science Library, 1984). Prigogine won the Nobel Prize in 1977 for his work on the thermodynamics of nonequilibrium systems.

28. An excellent account of the change in thinking is James Gleick, *Chaos: The Making of a New Science* (New York: Viking, 1987). I have drawn on his explanation extensively here. What Gleick does not explore are the striking intellectual parallels between chaotic theory in science and post-modern discourse in literature and philosophy. Post-Modernism is a sensibility that has abandoned the historic search for unity and order in nature, taking an ironic view of existence and debunking all established faiths. According to Todd Gitkin. ''Post-Modernism reflects the fact that a new moral structure has not yet been built and our culture has not yet found a language for articulating the new understandings we are trying, haltingly, to live with. It objects to all principles, all commitments, all crusades— in the name of an unconscientious evasion.'' On the other hand, and more positively, the new sensibility leads to emphasis on democratic coexistence: ''a new

'moral ecology'—that in the preservation of the other is a condition for the preservation of the self.'' Gitkin, ''Post-Modernism: The Stenography of Surfaces,'' *New Perspectives Quarterly,* 6 (Spring 1989): 57, 59.

29. The paper was published in Science, 186 (1974): 645-647. See also Robert M. May, ''Simple Mathematical Models with Very Complicated Dynamics,'' *Nature,* 261 (1976): 459-67. Gleick discusses May's work in *Chaos,* pp. 69-80.

30. W. M. Schaeffer, ''Chaos in Ecology and Epidemiology,'' in *Chaos in Biological Systems,* ed., H. Degan, A. V. Holden, and L. F. Olsen (New York: Plenum Press, 1987), p. 233. See also Schaeffer, ''Order and Chaos in Ecological Systems,'' *Ecology,* 66 (February 1985): 93-106.

31. John Muir, *My First Summer in the Sierra* (1911; Boston: Houghton Mifflin, 1944), p. 157.

32. Prigogine and Stengers, pp. 312-13.

33. Much of the alarm that Sears and Odum, among others, expressed has shifted to a global perspective, and the oder equilibrium thinking has been taken up by scientists concerned about the geo- and biochemical condition of the planet as a whole and about human threats, particularly from the burning of fossil fuels, to its stability. One of the most influential texts in this new development is James Lovelock's *GAIA: A New Look at Life on Earth* (Oxford: Oxford University Press, 1979). See also Edward Goldsmith, ''Gaia: Some implications for Theoretical Ecology,'' *The Ecologist,* 18, nos. 2/3 (1988): 64-74.

DISCUSSION TOPICS

1. Assume that Worster is correct, and that the natural world increasingly will be portrayed in ecological theory as dominated by chaos and disharmony. How might this perspective affect the environmental movement in Western society? How might it affect your personal values? Support your positions.

CLASS DISCUSSION

1. Some scholars consider the field of ecology to be a rich source of principles about how humans ought to relate to the natural world. It also has been argued that humans need to learn to trust nature more fully. Other scholars, however, believe that human moral values should be derived independently of nature; Worster maintains that ecology does not offer a coherent set of moral precepts. To what degree is it appropriate to use principles from the field of ecology as guidelines for human moral values? Support your opinions.

2. There is a proposal to dam a river for the purpose of generating electricity in your region. The dam will generate about 20 megawatts of electricity annually, with little pollution produced. The resulting 12,000-ha (approximately 30,000-acre) reservoir of water is estimated to bring in about 600,000 visitor-days and $2 million to the region annually from increased recreational use of the region.

   What other social, ethical and aesthetic values might need to be considered with this proposal? How would you rank these latter values in relation to each other? How would you rank them in relation to the identified economic and technical values of the project? How might your opinion be influenced if you had the opportunity to acquire ownership of a motel in that region? Support your reasoning.

CLASS EXERCISES

1. Use McDonald's model to design a process for investigating one of the following two problems.
   (a) Conjecture: grazing inhibits the growth of grasses.
      Hypothesis: Shafts of grass subject to grazing (or clipping) will show less total growth in a week's time than shafts left ungrazed (or unclipped).
   (b) Conjecture: the early bird gets the worm.
      Hypothesis: There is no difference in the success of robins in catching worms before 9 A.M., compared to after 9 A.M.
   (Note that one can test the hypothesis that there *is* a difference in results between two test groups, or one can test the null hypothesis that there is *no* difference. In each case one determines whether the hypothesis can be falsified.)
2. Develop a conjecture and test a hypothesis of your own.

FOR FURTHER READING

Crawford-Brown, Douglas J., and Neil E. Pearce. ''Sufficient Proof in the Scientific Justification of Environmental Actions.'' *Environmental Ethics* 11: 153-167, 1989. The authors explore the points at which evidence is used to support inferences about environmental affects in environmental risk analysis, with the purpose of providing a framework for evaluating how evidence may provide a sufficient basis for ethical decisions for environmental actions.

Dobzhansky, Theodosius. *The Biology of Ultimate Concern* (Perspectives in Humanism). New York: The New American Library, 1967. An evolutionary biologist seeks to examine some of the philosophical implications of biology and anthropology. He integrates the thoughts of Teilhard de Chardin.

Feyerabend, Paul. *Farewell to Reason.* New York: Verso, 1987. A series of essays addressing cultural diversity and cultural exchange. The author criticizes two ideas: the idea of objectivity and the idea of reason. The idea of objectivity is that a claim can be made that something is valid independent of human expectations, attitudes, and wishes. The idea of rationality is that there is one correct procedure.

Goodlad, J.S.R.: *Science for Non-scientists.* London: Oxford University Press, 1973. The author presents an overview of the objectives and limitations of science for nonspecialists.

Haught, John F. ''The Emergent Environment and the Problem of Cosmic Purpose.'' *Environmental Ethics* 8: 139-150, 1986. The author challenges whether scientific materialism can consistently sustain an environmental concern. The author calls for a new vision that is more supportive of an environmental concern. He builds on Whitehead's integration of modern science, philosophy, and religion for a workable ethic.

Hempel, Carl G. *Aspects of Scientific Explanation.* New York: The Free Press, 1965. A series of essays on the philosophy of science. The author provides an excellent overview of how science works. Sections include confirmation, induction, and rational belief; structure and function of scientific concepts and theories; and scientific explanations.

Kuhn, Thomas S. *Structure of Scientific Revolutions,* 2nd ed. Chicago: University of Chicago Press, 1970. The book that caused a major rethinking of the image of science, and how it works.

Laudan, Larry. *Progress and Its Problems: Toward a Scientific Theory of Growth.* Berkeley Calif.: University of

California Press, 1977. The author incorporates and evaluates the contributions of many science philosophers, including Hempel, Kuhn, Buchdahl, Feyerabend, Popper, Lakatos, and Grünbaum, in developing a model for scientific progress and discussion of its applications.

Laudan, Larry. *Science and Values.* Berkeley, Calif.: University of California Press, 1984. Despite the implications of the title, the author does not address ethical values and science. Rather, he addresses cognitive values in the shaping of scientific rationality. Laudan believes that the perspectives of Kuhn are deeply flawed.

Leiss, William. *The Domination of Nature.* New York: George Braziller, 1972. Identifies some historical foundations of human domination of nature and argues that dominating nature cannot lead to fulfilling common expectations such as satisfaction of material needs and establishment of social tranquility.

Lemons, John. ''Atmospheric Carbon Dioxide: Environmental Ethics and Environmental Facts.'' *Environmental Ethics* 5: 21-32, 1983. In the context of atmospheric carbon dioxide, addresses the issue about making decisions in the absence of sufficient factual information, and offers suggestions on how this might be done.

McLaughlin, Andrew. ''Images and Ethics of Nature.'' *Environmental Ethics* 7: 293-320, 1985. Challenges a common view in science that nature is devoid of meaning or value, and that, consequently, moral limits on the human manipulation of nature are irrational. Provides three alternative images of nature.

Rescher, Nicholas. *Scientific Progress.* Pittsburgh: University of Pittsburgh Press, 1978. The author addresses the future of scientific progress. He builds on the work of Gottfried Leibniz to evaluate the productive aspects of scientific inquiry, input and output; he also addresses the economics of scientific research, building on the work of Charles Peirce.

Richards, Stewart. *Philosophy and Sociology of Science,* 2nd ed. New York: Basil Blackwell, 1987. Richards challenges the notion of the neutrality of science. A major contention of the author is that the quality and breadth of the education of scientists will have a marked effect on the quality of judgments they can later make.

Rolston, Holmes, III. ''Science-based Versus Traditional Values,'' in *Ethics of Environment and Development: Global Challenge and International Response,* J. Ronald Engel and Joan Gibb Engel, eds. London: Belhaven Press, Pinter Publishers, 1990. Rolston addresses whether science-based values occupy a privileged position as criteria against which our traditional cultural values are to be tested, and concludes there is no simple answer because of the pluralistic nature of both science-based and traditional values.

Rorty, Richard. *Philosophy and the Mirror of Nature.* Princeton, N.J.: Princeton University 1979. The author offers thoughtful and thought-provoking assessments of the assumptions behind modern philosophy, and the language–fact distinction, in a criticism of traditional expressicism.

Ruse, Michael. *Taking Darwin Seriously: A Naturalistic Approach to Philosophy.* Oxford: Basil Blackwell, 1986. The author seeks to develop a consistent and satisfying philosophy founded on evolutionary biology. He questions whether ethics can be placed on an evolutionary foundation, and argues that knowledge, including ethics, is shaped by the human evolutionary past. He develops an evolutionary-based ethic patterned after Hume.

Sagoff, Mark. ''Fact and Value in Ecological Science.'' *Environmental Ethics* 7: 99-116, 1985. Sagoff develops the roles that ecology can play in the human relationship with nature.

Suppe, Frederick, ed. *The Structure of Scientific Theories.* Urbana, Ill.: University of Illinois Press, 1977. The author summarizes a summary of the conference on the structure of scientific theories held at the University of Illinois in 1969. Includes 15 contributors addressing both traditional and alternative perspectives.

Thomas, Lewis. *The Lives of a Cell: Notes of a Biology Watcher.* New York: The Viking Press, 1974. The author presents a delightful series of 29 essays on biology, mixed with personal perceptions of values and interpretations of life. An excellent introduction to biological thought by a master storyteller.

Toulmin, Stephen. *The Philosophy of Science.* London: Hutchinson & Co., 1967. The types of arguments and methods scientists employ in actual practice are presented. Using examples, the author lays out the basic logic of the physical sciences. He identifies what questions must be asked to most readily understand a scientific theory. Includes chapters on discovery, laws of nature, theories and maps, and uniformity and determinism.

Van Fraassen, Bas C. *The Scientific Image.* Oxford: Oxford University Press, 1980. In developing an alternative to scientific realism, the author presents three theories: a theory of empirical import, a theory of scientific explanations, and a theory of the explication of probability as it occurs within physical theory.

CHAPTER TWO

The Role of Moral Philosophy

In this chapter we discuss some central concepts in moral philosophy as it concerns the environment, including what a good moral judgment is, whether we should expect to find one over-arching moral theory applicable to all of our moral concerns, and several concepts of natural value.

Moral philosophy can be defined as the search for knowledge of the good life and of right conduct. Its subject matter is human conduct as it relates to the attainment of moral value, and its methodology is the systematic questioning and critical examination of our beliefs and values, including their consistency with each other and their implications for action.

Moral philosophy differs from the empirical sciences in both its subject matter and specific methodology. It is often characterized as ''prescriptive'' rather than ''descriptive''; rather than describing human behavior as done in the social sciences, moral philosophers evaluate such behavior in the light of moral principles and norms. Moral philosophers are concerned with how human beings ought to act, rather than how human beings do act.

Moral philosophy encompasses two main levels: ''meta-ethics'' and ''normative ethics.'' Meta-ethics is concerned with the justification of moral judgments, in other words, the correct method for answering moral questions, as well as a conceptual analysis of such morally crucial terms as ''value'' and ''rights-holder.'' Asking whether moral questions are ultimately to be answered by personal opinion or cultural bias is a meta-ethical inquiry. Normative ethics, on the other hand, concerns practical questions such as ''What should I do?'' or ''Is it right for anyone to steal in such a situation''? An appropriate meta-ethical question would be, ''What is meant by 'right' ''?

The essays in this chapter are all meta-ethical and pose questions on the nature of morality and moral theory. The selection by Tom Regan, ''Ethical Thinking and Theory,'' discusses the definition of a good moral judgment, regardless of the particular theory or principle in question. Christopher Stone's essay, ''Moral Pluralism and the Course of Environmental Ethics,'' makes the meta-ethical argument that we should adopt a stance of moral pluralism and use different theories for different areas of our lives rather than limit ourselves to one moral theory. Jim Cheney's essay, ''Postmodern Environmental Ethics: Ethics as Bioregional Narrative,'' makes the meta-ethical argument that ethics should be pursued in terms of ''local truth,'' in which concepts resonate with the local geography and culture. Anthony Weston's essay, drawn from "Before Environmental Ethics," stresses the role of ethical thinking in developing moral values. In their essays, Holmes Rolston III and J. Baird Callicott each address the concept of natural value in a way applicable to a number of different theories.

KINDS OF VALUE

The term *value* is derived from the Latin *valere,* to be worth, to be strong. Value refers to the strength of a thing, what it can carry for us, what it can mean to us, what it is worth. Defining the nature of value is a task of metaphysics, the philosophical study of reality. Understanding the nature of value has important consequences not only for ethics, but for any area of evaluation and decision making.

Three key terms commonly used in discussing value are "intrinsic," "inherent," and "instrumental." There often is disagreement among philosophers on the meaning of these terms. For example, some writers use "inherent value" and "intrinsic value" interchangeably, whereas others distinguish between them. However, there is a consensus emerging in the field of environmental ethics, and so we define these terms as follows:

1. *Intrinsic value:* the value of an object which is independent of the presence of a valuer. For example, a planet consisting only of plants or even of rocks without sentient beings might be said by some to have intrinsic value. Holmes Rolston argues for this position in his essay "Values Gone Wild."
2. *Inherent value:* value which requires the presence of a valuer who can appreciate the object or experience. In this sense, a wilderness area can have inherent value only if there is a being who can recognize its value. It is not necessary for the being to be present at that area to value it, however. J Baird Callicott presents this view in "The Intrinsic Value of Nonhuman Species."
3. *Instrumental value:* the value of an object or experience in serving as a means to accomplish a

goal which has intrinsic or inherent value. For example, a human being might use a stand of timber as a source of money to increase the comfort and material quality of her life. The instrumental value of the timber allows the individual to attain an experience of well-being, and the experience of well-being for many is of inherent value. Thus, the stand of timber is said to serve an instrumental value.

An additional concept basic to the study of natural value is that of "naturalistic fallacy," sometimes identified with the "is-ought dichotomy" discerned by David Hume, a prominent eighteenth century Scottish philosopher (1711-1776).[1] The naturalistic fallacy consists of arguing from what is biologically or culturally "natural," from what "is," to what we "ought" to do.[2] In other words, a movement is made from what is descriptively true of the world to a prescriptive claim. Whether or not a thinker considers such an argument to be valid depends on the thinker's view of the relationship between morality and the world. Philosophers such as Plato and Kant see reason as having a transcendental or autonomous nature, standing over against what is and upholding ideals of what we ought to do, regardless of what has been done in the past or is currently being done. They note that we are blamed or praised for our actions, whereas natural processes are not subject to moral praise and blame. Similarly, according to the great British philosopher Alfred North Whitehead (1851–1947), moral judgments are a contrast of what is, with the apprehension of what ideally ought to be. In such theories, human beings are portrayed as not simply part of nature but as partaking of an ideal rational order, in terms of which what is "natural" might well be morally wrong. For example, it may be natural

---

1. Callicott and others argue that the naturalistic fallacy is a different issue and is most accurately associated with the ethics of G.E. Moore. See Callicott, "Hume's Is/Ought Dichotomy," *Environmental Ethics* 4 (1982): 163–174, especially pp. 166–167.

2. In this sense Hume commits the naturalistic fallacy, since he derives moral imperatives from the cultural traditions of his society, hence from how people do in fact act.

to have as many children as possible, but it may in fact be immoral to do so in today's overcrowded world.

However, there is an ancient and robust moral tradition of ''natural law'' and ''natural order,'' in which it is argued that the only way to know what we should do is to understand what the world truly is. According to this approach our deepest moral guidance comes from understanding nature and our ''natural'' place in it. The land ethic of Leopold and the deep ecology movement (Chapter 8) as well as the aesthetic recommendations of thinkers such as Carlson (Chapter 3) rely on a concept of intuition of what is ''natural.''[3]

ARE MORAL JUDGMENTS UNIVERSAL?

Another important meta-ethical question is whether value judgments and particularly moral judgments are ''universal'' or ''relative,'' ''objective'' or ''subjective.'' These terms are used in many different ways by different thinkers. Currently there seem to be four main approaches:

1. *Traditional relativism,* according to which the truth or falsity of moral judgments are relative to either the individual making the judgment or the culture of which he or she is a part.[4]
2. *Contextualism,* according to which the truth or falsity of moral judgments is tied to the place (geographical and historical) in which the moral judgments occur.

   ''Narrative contextualism'' is a form of contextualism which emphasizes that moral terms are not abstractions such as ''good'' but are conveyed by means of stories.

3. *Pluralism,* according to which the truth or falsity of a moral judgment is decided by reference to a universal standard with limited applicability: different planes or moral frameworks. These different moral frameworks exist side by side, each governing its own set of relationships, such as those with future generations, those with sentient creatures, and those with inanimate beings.[5]
4. *Universalism,* according to which the truth or falsity of moral judgments is decided by reference to a universal moral standard, applicable to all individuals and cultures.

The various theories sketched above differ partly because they involve different views of what ''reason'' is. What is the relationship of reason to the rest of human life? How important are the cultural milieu, the geographical place, the gender, the ethnicity, the personality of the reasoner? Is reason capable of presenting us with ''abstract'' truth, independent of context? In this chapter, Tom Regan presents a traditional view of reason as requiring impartiality and consistency. Christopher Stone and Jim Cheney argue for contextualism and pluralism—approaches which reject the goal of one universal moral theory. Anthony Weston emphasizes the dependence of concepts of reason and value on human practices and institutions.

In his essay, Jim Cheney attacks the idea of objective, universal principles and offers instead a contextual approach. Environmental ethics is understood as ''bioregional narrative'' or ''ethical vernacular,'' inextricably linked to the place from which it was developed, although Cheney believes that bioregional narratives possess enough generality to allow for cross-cultural understanding. Christopher Stone's essay raises the issue of pluralism in a different way. Stone agrees with Cheney that we should give up the

---

3. For further discussion see the exchange between J. Baird Callicott and Kristin Shrader-Frechette in *Between the Species* 6, No. 4 (Fall 1990); 185–196.

4. For a clear discussion of why traditional relativism in both its forms is unsatisfactory, see James Rachels, *The Elements of Moral Philosophy* New York: McGraw-Hill, 1986), Chapters 2 and 3.

5. Christopher Stone states that, strictly speaking, moral pluralism is consistent with either relativism or moral realism (universalism). For the sake of displaying possible moral theories, pluralism is treated here as a form of moral realism. See Christopher Stone, *Earth and Other Ethics: The Case for Moral Pluralism* (New York: Harper & Row, 1987), pp. 246–247.

search for one universal moral theory, not because of the interrelationship of self and place, but because of the existence of different domains of experience, different kinds of things. Some moral theories are applicable to our dealings with the environment, for example, whereas others are appropriate to dealings with our immediate family. While Cheney's "local truth" might be thought of as cultural relativism because it is context-dependent, Stone's view is not necessarily relativist. There may be really right an-

swers, but the answers are limited in their applicability to certain kinds of things.[6]

---

6. For a forceful critique of both Cheney and Stone, see J. Baird Callicott, "The Case Against Moral Pluralism," *Environmental Ethics* 12, No. 2 (1990): 99–124; James C. Anderson, "Moral Planes and Intrinsic Values," *Environmental Ethics* 13 No. 1: 49–58 also finds Stone's pluralism unsatisfactory. For a critique of Callicott's critique, see Anthony Weston, "On Callicott's Case against Moral Pluralism," *Environmental Ethics* 13, No. 3 (1991): 283–287.

Values Gone Wild

Holmes Rolston III

Holmes Rolston III (b. 1932), Professor of Philosophy at Colorado State University, develops an account of nature as having intrinsic value. In his article ''Values Gone Wild,'' Rolston explicitly rejects Hume's split between fact and value and argues that this split is a cultural artifact which should be ignored. Rolston shows how environmental ethics challenges the narrow boundaries of anthropocentric and anthropogenic thinking, that is, of natural value as either restricted to human interests, or as based on human valuers.

    Rolston views the phenomenon of human consciousness as an outgrowth, a ''storied achievement,'' of natural selection. He sees in natural selection a process wherein value decisions are continually made by all organisms. Components of ecosystems have instrumental, survival value to other components and to the systems as such. Value as ''what makes a favorable difference'' no longer requires a beholder but simply a holder.

For the trip you are about to take I offer myself as a wilderness guide. Nowadays it is easier to get lost conceptually in wildlands than physically. A century ago the challenge was to know where you were geographically in a blank spot on the map, but today we are bewildered philosophically in what has long been mapped as a moral blank space. Despite our scientific and cultural taming of wildness we still wander, confused over how to value it. Values run off our maps. In journeys there, ''value'' changes its meaning, as does the word ''wild.'' Travelers need pathfinding through strange places.

VALUING OUR SOURCES AND RESOURCES

Before I can lead you into the deep wilderness of values, we will have to make our way past a misguided route. It may seem to keep us oriented to value wildlands as *resources*. With soil, timber, or game the meaning of ''resource'' is clear enough. Humans tap into spontaneous nature, dam water, smelt ores, domesticate, manage, and harvest, redirecting natural courses to become resources. No longer wild, they come under our control. But when we try to speak of wilderness as a ''resource'' the term soon goes kerflooey. Notice the oddity of this resource relationship, which will prove a key for unlocking anthropocentric presumptions about value.

A park ranger may interpret the Tetons as a scientific, recreational, or aesthetic resource, but by the time she calls it a philosophical or religious resource, the term is eating up everything, as if humans have no other operating modes *vis-à-vis* wilderness. Have her notice that resources come in two kinds: the ordinary kind that are rearranged into artifacts, and the extraordinary, wild type that we impact as little as possible. The botanist in Cascade Canyon or the mountaineer atop the Grand Teton find both places important precisely as not consumed. Contrary to typical resource use, we visit wildness on its own terms and do not reform it to ours. The conceptually wild turn is when humans, ordinarily valuing resources of the kind they can make over, here value what they will not disturb lest they devalue it. Under the standard doctrine, we wanted potatoes but the fields grew worthless brush. We wanted logs dovetailed around us as a home, but the world gave only standing trees. We labored to make value. Under the revised claim, pure wildness can be a good thing. These places change us, not we them.

Well, some reply, nature offers some resources that take no redoing or consuming, only looking and enjoying. Most are commodities to be drawn upon, but others are amenities left as is. Perhaps this revision in the logic of ''resource'' will solve our problem. Wilderness is important only as a resource in our society.

> Wilderness is for people. This is a principle that bears restating. The preservation goals established for such areas are designed to provide values and benefits to society.... Wilderness is not set aside for the sake of its flora or fauna, but for people.[1]

We must recognize various kinds of instrumental value. The commonest kind modifies natural courses, but an infrequent sort needs only to take natural things as they are. We capture wilderness instrumentally for human experience, though we never lay a hand on it and tread lightly afoot. So why is it not a resource?

Still, two deeper worries begin to loom. One is that the resource orientation is only a half truth and afterward *logically* misguided. The other is that, taken for the whole truth, it is *ethically* misguided. Unfortunately, these troubles intertwine, because everything is defined in relation to us.

We can continue by noticing how the claim, ''Everything is a resource, really,'' parallels a more familiar claim, ''Everyone is selfish, really.'' Here philosophers have better mapped how logical difficulties are ingrown with ethical ones. The egoist begins by citing how persons regularly pursue self-interest and then turns to apparent altruism. Mother Teresa has labored among the poor in Calcutta and Charles Lindbergh in later years turned to the defense of wildlife. But both received self-fulfillment from their efforts. The Marines who died on Iwo Jima had their families at stake, which it was in their enlightened self-interest to protect. The claim expands to digest all counter-evidence, redefining ''selfish'' to embrace all conduct, reinterpreting motives or imagining hidden ones until it becomes a presumption brought to experience. Afterward, there is no point in examining further cases. Willy-nilly, everything is twisted to fit the selfishness gestalt.

''Everything is a resource, really.'' The argument cites how humans redirect nature to their benefit, and then turns to apparent nonresources. Nevada authorities labor to save the Devil's Hole pupfish, which requires reduced water drawdown for ranching. Southwestern developers agree not to build the Marble Canyon Dam, and members of the Wilderness Society contribute money to save wilderness, some nearby which they expect to visit, and some Alaskan which they do not. But some humans are fascinated by the pupfish, run rafts down the Grand Canyon, visit the Indian Peaks, enjoy knowing the Alaskan wilds are there, and hope their children may visit them. SUPPORT WATCHABLE WILDLIFE! That slogan from the Oregon Department of Fish and Wildlife is a commendable step away from fish you catch and game you shoot, both to consume. But *watchable* wildlife is a resource for looking. In every case humans enter into some self-fulfilling relationship. What we want is high quality wilderness experience that improves human life.

Use of the word ''resource'' gradually changes until nothing can be comprehended outside such a relationship, no matter if the paramount emotion becomes the appreciating of these realms for what they are in themselves. One ponders the pupfish, the Supai and Redwall strata in Marble Gorge, spends a lonesome weekend amidst glacier-cut scenery in the Indian Peaks, wondering if a grandchild might ever share such feelings on Alaskan slopes, steadily stretched out of local concerns to the age-long flows of life over time. But these are resource relationships! Logically, the claim has become trivial, redefining as resource whatever one ''takes in,'' whether food or scenery. Ethically, valuing has ''gone wild'' in the haywire sense because it has become so nonnegotiably anthropocentric that we cannot let values go wild in any naturalistic sense.

What if a daughter should say to her mother, ''You know you are a resource, really,'' or a communicant, approaching the altar, were to think how the priest, in transforming bread and wine, was making better resources out of them? Before parents and the sacred, one is not so much looking to *resources* as to *sources,* seeking relationships in an elemental stream of being with transcending integrities. Our place in the natural world necessitates resource relationships, but there comes a point when we want to know how we belong in this world, not how it belongs to us. We want to get ourselves defined in relation to nature, not just to define nature in relation to us.

We Americans preserve our historical parks at Lexington or Appomattox to remember our origins, but we would be shortsighted not to set aside wilderness as the profoundest museum of all, a relic of how the world was in 99.99 percent of past time, the crucible in which we were forged. A historical park is a place to recall our sources, our national story; but we need ''genesis parks'' to recall our natural history.

Wilderness is the first legacy, the grand parent, and offers dramatic contacts with ultimacies not found in town.

Why should it seem so logical to call even our wild natural sources a resource? To answer we must look for a still deeper presumption brought to experience: the conviction that value emerges with the satisfaction of human interest. Only positive human mental states have noninstrumental value. Take away our selection and feeling, and intrinsic value vanishes. If so, nature as the source of valued experiences must be only instrumental, and therefore a resource even if of an anomalous kind. But what if this too is logically misguided? In that case, to force everything into the all-purpose resource formula is only for those who have no better logical model for appreciating wild places. It sounds humane, yet it keeps alive a humanist illusion. But to overthrow the nature-as-mere-resource paradigm we will need a more comprehensive, non-anthropocentric theory of value.

The key idea we are following is of nature as a *source of values,* including our own. Nature is a generative process to which we want to relate ourselves and by this to find relationships to other creatures. Value includes far more than a simplistic human-interest satisfaction. Value is a multifaceted idea with structures that root in natural sources. Wilderness is valuationally complex, as it is scientifically complex. Tracking these components will require triangulation from three points, the notions of *roots, neighbors,* and *aliens.* After that, we will see whether there is any unifying systemic structure. Notice how value is indeed beginning to go wild. Extending beyond the reach of human domestication and experience, it begins to have a life of its own in spontaneous nature.

VALUING ROOTS, NEIGHBORS, AND ALIENS

We can represent the logical paths ahead, both those of discovery and justification, as in Figure 1. We began with values all in the human orbit, and all outside valueless except as resources brought in instru-

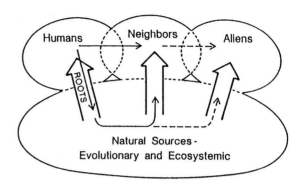

FIGURE 1

mentally. But now values leave the human circle; they go wild. Our paths of discovery (the line arrows) follow value back into its roots, but these same evolutionary sources have generated neighbors and aliens in the planetary ecosystem we coinhabit. Paths stretch around toward these regions, zones we can also visit by crossing diffuse boundaries into territories shared with these neighbors and occupied by aliens. The theory and its implications are suggested by an originating source area with three broad lines of production (the wide arrows).

On these paths leading progressively toward wilder territories, need we take any precautions about crossing illegitimately a forbidden boundary? For (some will warn) one cannot move from bare facts in nature to what is of value there, nor to what conduct persons ought to undertake, without committing the naturalistic fallacy. At this point I am going to say only that the signs posted that forbid trespassing this boundary are themselves cultural artifacts (deriving as they do from certain theories about ethics, about the moral neutrality of nature, value as human-interest satisfaction, etc.), and this guide recommends that we ignore (as wilderness travelers often do) the cultural prohibitions about where one can and cannot legitimately go. Let us undergo the wilderness experience first hand, and only then think back whether we have made any logical mistakes or gone into territory we ought not to have visited in quest of value. I have proposed to lead you into wild experiences, and only in retrospect, not in prospect, can we intelligently argue about what has happened in passing from *is* to *ought*.

Wildness Is a Place of *Roots* in Historical and Ongoing Senses

We stay oriented by thinking of a visit to the birthplace. Here historical value blends with that order of value we owe to parents. Value leaves culture to return to natal mysteries, to primitive archetypes. Wilderness is the incubating matrix that served as the production site of the human race. Stopping at a spring, I meet a salamander and am struck by its tiny finger-like feet. As I dip water, I notice in my hand the same digital pattern, in modified but unmistakably kindred form. I catch my reflection to compare facial patterns. How far back in geologic time must go that bilateral symmetry of eyes, nose, mouth! Even now beneath my cerebrum lies a remnant reptilian brain, essential to my cognitive and emotional humanity.[2] So much of what we most radically value arose anciently in the spontaneous wild, but is presumed in the routine of culture.

Wildness does not merely lie behind, it remains the generating matrix. Laden with my pack, moving briskly along, I turn my thoughts to respiration. Present in every cell containing a respiratory chain—from microbes to humans—is an electron carrier called the cytochrome-c molecule that evolved over 1.5 billion years ago.[3] Given that I plainly value respiration for myself, and that evolution has conserved this molecule since before plants and animals diverged, it seems some sort of wild type in value. If I become winded, my body is facing another problem. The citric acid cycle, which follows glycolysis in the processing of food molecules and is a more recently evolved skill, is not generating enough ATP for the demands of my skeletal muscle, and so my metabolism switches to make lactate rather than sending pyruvate into the citric acid cycle. The lactate leaks out of the muscle cells and is carried to the liver, which can process it.[4] Short of oxygen and pushed for energy, my body

reverts to a use of glycolysis first learned before there was atmospheric oxygen and since kept and modified for emergency situations.

Turning to the extrasomatic ecosystem, all flesh is grass, including my own, using "grass" to refer to the photosynthetic base of the biomass. All flesh is wind, remembering its nitrogen and oxygen components; there would be no protein without the nitrogen fixers, no respiration without the oxygen releasers. Resting at an overlook, I may take in the greenness, autotrophs feeding the heterotrophs, which rot to nourish the autotrophs, and realize that when higher forms evolved, the lower were not all left behind. Many remain as essentials in an ecological web. They can do without my cultures, but I cannot do without their kind of world, which forms my pyramidal community. In wildness, one learns to value the compound units of integrated biological achievement. . . .

Wildness is a living museum of our roots. The experiences humans have there are to be valued because we learn where we came from and who we are. But it is crude to say this only makes a resource out of wilderness, misguided by the belief that value can appear only in human experience. We are here realizing that nature is an originating *source* of value first, and only later and secondarily a *resource*. We are *experiencing roots,* and this experiencing is to be valued, but what the experiencing is *of*—these *wild generative roots* at work before humans arrived—has delivered to us much of value, processes the benefits of which are at work within us whether we are aware of them or not.

This sort of experience moves value outside ourselves. It forces a redistribution and redefinition of value. Value is not just a human product. We realize this by learning how we humans, including much that we value in ourselves, are natural products, and are thereby alerted to look for other natural productions of value. Such nonhuman values, as we track them here, are first discovered in these roots, but the path does not end there. It leads secondly to wild neighbors and on beyond to paths more foreign and difficultly explored.

Wildness Is a Place of *Neighbors* in a Sense Gone Wild

This requires a sympathetic turning to value what does not stand directly in our lineage or underpinning, but is enough like ourselves that we are drawn by spill-over to shared phenomena manifest in others. The principle of universalizability demands that I recognize corresponding values in fellow persons. But need this apply only with reciprocating moral agents? Growth in ethical sensitivity has often required enlarging the circle of neighbors, and are there no neighbors in the wild? They are not moral agents; that is part of what their wildness means. But have they no values to consider? This great natural source (Figure 1) that has generated us all continues to flow in others, not into humans alone. There is a great similarity between humans and other organisms, whether at experiential, psychological, or biological levels. If I value these qualities in myself, by parity of reasoning I should likewise value them when manifested in other organisms.

Animals take an interest in affairs that affect them. They hunt and flee, grow tired, thirsty, and hot. They seek shelter, play, wag tails, scratch, suffer injury, and lick their wounds. The salamander reacts first by freezing, then fleeing. In judging such actions, we must guard against the pathetic fallacy. A moose does not suffer winter cold as we do; perhaps the warbler is not glad when it sings. But we must not commit the humanistic fallacy of supposing no naturalistic analogues of what humans plainly value. We have every logical and psychological reason to posit degrees of kinship.

Endorphins—natural analogues of morphine—are produced by human brains upon injury and stress. These compounds buffer pain, are important for emotional stability, and are implicated in certain "good feelings," like those involved in the euphoria of the wilderness experience under stress. They are found widely in the nervous systems of vertebrates—mammals, reptiles, amphibians, birds, fish—and in some invertebrates, for example, earthworms. The endorphin level in a frightened mouse rises.[5] Additionally, mice have the neural receptors for Librium and Valium. The trip into wildness, we were saying, reawak-ens bodily experience. There is the climb, the heat, the cold; we need water, food, shelter. We think more about endurance and fatigue, sureness and fear, comfort and pain. Such experiences bring appreciation of our own natural endowments, but if they serve that end alone, we are too humanistic. Enjoying the tonic of wildness, feeling more alive without quite knowing why, endorphin levels rising, we ought to make value judgments in kinship with all embodied being, just because we are stripped to gutsy, animal elements.

This sense of kinship need not be restricted to shared subjectivity, for it can be somatic. Consider the development of muscle and fat, both outside the central nervous system. The university-educated mind tends to value brainpower and to devalue muscle and fat, but this opinion will be challenged in the wild. Brainpower follows and coevolves with muscle. The mind is useless unless it can act, while the power to move can be of value even when governed by mere instinct. Seen at the molecular level, the coordinated muscle cells with their interdigitating fibers, A-bands and I-bands, the myosin that splits ATP to drive push-pull contractions, are hardly less an evolutionary achievement than is the nervous system. Contact with animal strength and grace, flight and fury, makes it difficult to maintain that the relevant senses of kinship here are only subjective.

Muscle cannot move without energy, and energy can be in short supply in winter. The fat cell evolves to store energy in compact form, and thus to power muscle months after energy intake. As night falls I begin to shiver, using muscle to generate heat. But some animals do not shiver. The brown fat cell, modified from the ordinary fat cell, is present in hibernators, seals, ground squirrels, bats, in the young of rabbits, cats, sheep, and newborn humans who cannot yet shiver. Brown adipose tissue appears late in evolution and forms a heating jacket that provides the capacity to survive the cold when in thermogenic response fats burn without forming ATP, thereby generating heat more efficiently.[6] If I judge that muscle and fat have no value as unfelt spontaneous processes, I begin to wonder whether I am myopically biased toward sentience. Perhaps value judgments need to be made not merely on the basis of *sympathy* for sentient kin, but on the basis of what biologists call *sympatry,* shared organic origins.

Some will find it incoherent and nonsensical, wild in a logically wayward sense, to speak of objective value in embodied being, for (say they) there is no value without awareness. Nonneural animals may have sensory receptors, but these are mere stimulus response mechanisms. But why cannot values be located outside the nervous system? In fact, at the metabolic level we gain the fullest sense of shared biological powers. The marsh hawk and the ground squirrel are enemies because they are somatically kindred; it is the protein muscle and the fat in the squirrel that the hawk can use. One could label all this so much resource use, and then stipulate that values necessitate sentient awareness. Objective organic processes form roots, precursors of value, but valueless in themselves, becoming of value only when experience is superadded. But the more one studies organic bodies, the less evidently this is the most plausible route for mapping value. It starts with a psychological or hedonic result of the biological processes, values this experiential effect, and devalues the productive causes except in terms of a late conclusion, in which, subjectively, we happen to stand. It takes a derived thing as the only thing that really counts.

In one sense, the choice between broader, objective and more restricted, subjective accounts of value does not matter. Even if value is defined as interest satisfaction, it has here become nonhuman. Intrinsic value lies in worthwhile experiences, which wild animals sometimes have, although somatically we can speak only instrumentally of the power to produce such experiences. But specify, if you wish, that muscle and fat, food and hemoglobin have only instrumental value, they are still out there in the wildlands apart from human awareness, instrumental to experienced intrinsic values that take place irrespective of human visitors, although humans do not enjoy realization of this except as they visit. But in another sense, somatic achievements such as autotrophic, muscular, or energetic self-reliance introduce us to a more comprehensive notion of value. Value arises with organic problem-solving, perceived or not, a notion we must yet refine. An achievement of this sort has value of

itself, being worthwhile as a significant adventure of life, although it will inevitably also be contributory to some further achievement. But we will be better prepared for this account after making our way through some yet wilder places.

Wildness Is a Place Where We Encounter *Aliens*

The previous triangulation points (roots and neighbors) unite us with wildness, but now we turn to loving differences, even to respecting otherness we cannot love. On the first and second nights backpacking, there is a restored sense of belonging, but by the third night the country becomes foreign. Man is not the measure of things. J. B. S. Haldane was asked by some theologians what he had learned about God from biology. He replied that God has "an inordinate fondness for beetles."[7] Perhaps three-fourths of the known animals are insects, by some criteria the most successful form of life, and a disproportionate number are *Coleoptera.* God went wild making beetles. Evolution went wild in speciation. Some will stall here, but wild creatures can stretch us out of ourselves into the depth and breadth of being. We seek values that cannot be shared, altruistic encounters of the strangest kind. . . .

Our duty before wildness is ambiguous. In the beginning we respect the coyote, the spider, even the bacterium by grading how much they are kin, possessing smaller amounts what we have a lot more of—biochemistry, mobility, complexity, information, skill, sentience, freedom, language, consciousness. But afterward we find this demeaning, leading to pity because they took a form inferior to our own. We insult them by calling them static lines or dead ends in the evolutionary process. What we must rather learn is to respect their own integrity, nonhuman manifestations of what Aristotle would call *arete,* excellences in kind. Wild creatures are not nature at a suboptimal level. They are humble creatures, but they can also humble humans whose values have grown too proudly provincial.

Humans are nature's richest achievement but not nature's only achievement, and in unresolved tension with our lofty rank we have to judge that diversity in being is richer than would be a world with only humans. Even if by some wizardry one could, one ought not to kiss toads into men. Nature has done that over evolutionary time, but has also taken other twists in value. These creatures improve the world just by being there, and thus alien nature is a form of wealth. We can be exalted by those of low degree; we can exalt those of low degree.

Whatever is wary, as sentient or instinctive wildness is, has a value set of its own. So the salamander first froze and then fled at the spring. The wildness by which it escapes is objective evidence of value alien to my own. But owning a value set is not merely a feature of the rapidly mobile. Every genetic set proclaims a life way, and thus makes an assertive claim over its surroundings. Every genetic set is a proportional set, a *normative* (nonmoral) set, proposing what *ought* to be, beyond what *is,* on the basis of its encoded information. So it grows, reproduces, repairs its wounds, and resists death. Wildness, activity outside the scope of human concern, is not a sign of something valueless, but of foreign freedom, of spontaneous autonomy and self-maintenance.

These things are not merely to be valued *for me and my kind* (as resources), not even as goods *of my kind* (sharing sentience or fat cells), but as goods *of their kind, as good kinds* without consideration of their kinship. At our departure value was restricted to human affairs, and later shared with neighboring organisms. With still deeper penetration into wildness, value becomes alien. Yet the human genius is such that we can nonetheless manage to cross these thresholds (through science, imagination, wilderness adventure, ethical sensitivity) and glimpse these wildest values. Value attaches to experience but also to shared somatic skills. Value attaches even to the cleverness of alien forms. Value is sometimes anthropomorphic, but can be morphic in any formed integrity. *Value is storied achievement.* With this definition we can reach a fundamental motif, which could be widely woven through culture and might be deployed even into inorganic realms, though we are tracing it here only organically. Even the inanimate planetary system is sometimes impelled, energized toward *created form,*

storied developments, works of genius, and, in due course, toward the evolution of the genera and of sentient genius. Interest satisfaction is only a lately formed subset of this richer principle. Continuing our search we must set individuals in their ecosystems and evaluate their evolutionary sources. Once again, the terrain we push through is wild and alien to the cultured mind.

SURVIVAL VALUE REVISITED—ORGANIC AND SYSTEMIC ACHIEVEMENTS

A formidable emotion before nature is a kind of horror at the anarchy and relentless struggle in a world that opposes either by its indifference or by its hostility. Once, as a college youth, I killed an opossum that seemed sluggish and then did an autopsy. He was infested with a hundred worms! Grisly and pitiful, he seemed a sign of the whole wilderness, hardly a place of roots, hardly neighborly, but too alien to value. Each is ringed about with competitors and limits, forced to do or die. Physical nature, from which are wrested the materials of life, is brute fact and brutally there, caring naught and always threatening. Organic nature is savage; life preys on life. Perhaps we can reconcile ourselves to alien value in individuals. The opossum in its marsupial being is a good kind; even the worms defend their genetic sets and manifest biochemical skills. But the systemic source that they of necessity inhabit seems ugly, evil, wild. They do not live in a good place.

The wilderness contains only the thousandth part of creatures that sought to be, but rather became seeds eaten, young fallen to prey or disease. The Darwinian revolution has revealed that the governing principle is survival in a world thrown forward in chaotic contest, with much randomness and waste besides. The wilderness teems with its kinds but is a vast graveyard with a hundred species laid waste for one or two that survive. T. H. Huxley reacted that the values society most cherishes depend ''not on imitating the cosmic process, still less in running away from it, but in combating it.''[8] If so, can there be value in the wild holocaust, any reason for society to preserve or admire it? . . .

The diagram we need now (Figure 2) modifies our earlier sketch. Small circles (○) show intrinsic values, small arrows (→) instrumental values, both as individual achievements. The three wide arrows represent what we call systemic achievement.

The cutthroat portrait does not mean there are no valuers in the wild; it portrays too many claimants contesting scarce worth. Life is never self-contained but incessantly moves through its environment, ingesting and eliminating it. Rocks attach no value to the environment, but coyotes must eat. Where anything is being made a resource of, just this claiming of the environment as nutrient source and sink reveals valuational systems in interaction. Perhaps we can return to the resource notion, which at the start we had to get past, now finding it a key to the larger dynamics of the system. . . .

What seems waste in the rabbit life stream is nutrient within the coyote stream, and even the rabbit population benefits by the ongoing selection over mutants. The surplus of offspring is cut back by premature death, but this cutback is executed unawares by the coyotes so as, on statistical average, to leave the smarter, faster, more fertile, efficient, and wary. The rabbits suffer for the coyotes, but not entirely; they collectively gain from their pains. The surplus of young permits both mutational advance and the synthesis of biotic materials with higher forms at the top of the pyramid. This produces further demands on coyotes, and the coevolutionary race goes on.

Nature treats any particular individual with a momentary life, but life is a propagating wave over time. Located in individuals, value is also consigned to a stream. Even species regularly come and go, typically over five to fifty million years. Some become extinct without issue, but over longstanding trends nature transforms others to increase the numbers of species present in each later epoch, as well as their richness. Even the few crashes and mass extinctions, though setbacks, have reset life's directions, as happened at the ends of the Permian and Cretaceous periods. Retrenchments in the quantity of life were followed by explosive inventiveness in its quality. The mammals came into their own, triggered by wiping out the dinosaurs, even while reptiles and amphibians, and their

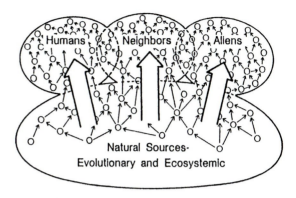

FIGURE 2

descendants, the birds, remain important in our ecosystems. So I have at once to respect salamanders and to be glad nature sacrificed cold-blooded forms for hot-blooded developments beyond.

Wildness is an unquenchable, pro-life force in this respect, however groping, blind, and unmerciful it may otherwise seem. Survival value has its upstrokes, and we reach the paradox that out of seeming disorder order comes the more. There flows this great river of life, strangely wild flowing because it flows as it were uphill, negentropically from nonbeing to being, from nonlife to objective life and on to subjective life. Nature is full of crooked, winding paths. Some are wayward lines; some prove routes to interesting places, and some are ascents to summits. Wildness is a place of new arrivals, as much as of survivals.

An individual's life is a defense of its value set, a concrete attempt at problem-solving, instantiating an intrinsic value. But an individual's death, by which such value collapses, is a contribution to values being defended by others who recycle its materials, energy, and information. Overall, the myriad individual passages through life and death upgrade the system. Value has to be something more, something opposed to what any individual actor likes or selects, since even struggle and death, which are never approved, are ingredients used instrumentally to produce still higher intrinsic values. Things good in themselves and of their kinds are not permitted to have such integrity alone, but are required to be good in their niche, good corporately. This can seem in morally wild disregard for their individuality, treating each as a means to an end. But the whole system in turn generates more and higher individuality. Problem-solving is a function of the system too as it recycles, recovers from setbacks, speciates, increases sentience and complexity, pulls conflicts into harmony, and redeems life from an ever-pressing death. The systemic source interblends intrinsic and instrumental values.

As we earlier met it, value is what makes a favorable difference to an organism's life, whether microbes using compasses or humans enjoying their wilderness roots, no matter whether instrumentally or intrinsically conceived. But as we now enlarge it, value is what makes a favorable difference to an ecosystem, enriching it, making it more beautiful, diverse, harmonious, intricate. Here a disvalue to an individual may be a value in the system and will result in values carried to other individuals. Intrinsic value exists only as embedded in instrumental value. No organism is a mere instrument, for each has its integral intrinsic value. But it can also be sacrificed in behalf of another life course, when its intrinsic value collapses, becomes extrinsic, and is in part instrumentally transported to another organism. When we interpret this transfer between individuals systemically, the life stream flows up an ecological pyramid over evolutionary time. The incessant making use of resources unifies the intrinsic and instrumental distinctions (the small circles and arrows of Figure 2) and the result is the broad arrows of storied achievement by the great wild Source. Value as storied achievement is a property alike of organisms and the evolutionary ecosystem. Against the standard view that value requires a *beholder,* we see how value requires only a *holder,* which can be an individual, but can be also the historic system that carries value to and through individuals.

There is nothing secondary about instrumental value. When resource use is found omnipresent in the system, it loses its sting. Although there is something wrong with making everything else a resource for humans, there is nothing wrong with something being an instrumental resource for others. We think that a person is narrow and selfish who cultivates intrinsic worth and withdraws from seeking any instrumental value in the community. A person's intrinsic worth—for example, creative ability—is not separable from the power to confer a benefit on others. Excellence does not consist in what a thing is merely for itself, but in what it is for others. This is true of persons, animals, and plants. Excellence is not a matter of encapsulated being, but of fittedness into a pervasive whole.

Like instrumental and intrinsic values, the *is* and the *is good* have evolved together, and are even now experienced together. The recommendation that one ought to value these events follows from a discovery of their goodness in place, which is not so much by argument as by adventure that experiences their origins, structures, and environmental locations. We find value holders defending their values and fitted into the large narratives of life. Natural *facts* of this kind are *storied doings* (Latin: *factum,* a deed) with their *value* (Latin: *valere,* to be worth) integral to their having managed to happen. In such a story every achievement is to be viewed intrinsically and instrumentally.

A wilderness guide can only exhibit examples from nature and then ask what reasons remain for asserting that storied achievement is not of value. The reason traditionally so called is that value lies in (human-) interest satisfaction. But that now seems only a stipulation born of prejudice or shortsightedness. Interest satisfaction is one among other values, and this better theory retains all we want from the narrower predecessor. Approbation and pleasure are only later parts of the story, and storied achievement can take place using, in the absence of, in indifference to, and even in opposition to interest satisfaction. Wildness first seems a chaos where nothing is given but everything is fought for. But afterward we learn how in the struggle everything vital has been given. In one sense wildness is the most *valuable* realm of all, the struggling womb *able* to generate all these adventures in *value,* whether involving roots, neighbors, or aliens. Thus the experienced wilderness traveler finds that the trespassing signs posted between the *is* and the *ought* are nothing but cultural artifacts. . . .

A singular feature of human psychology and morality is how we can value wild things not for ourselves, but for what they are in themselves, estimating our own place in nature when so doing. Animal species, though out there in the wild, cannot appreciate wildness beyond their own territories. But humans can value wild roots, neighbors, and aliens independently of whether a particular phenomenon affects our survival, well-being, or convenience. Resource relationships are set aside, and we look at the world with moral judgment. Nor is this merely at the individual level, valuing kinds in themselves, but it is also at the global level, for we alone are able to see past the atomistic struggles into the production of value in the evolutionary ecosystem. We do not have survival value revisited, but survival value transcended. We have a novel arrival indeed. We reach an almost supernatural altruism, unprecedented on the planet.

Humans are disjoined from nature not merely because we form cultures and dramatically rebuild our environment. We are still more unnatural creatures when we post boundaries for our cultures and designate wilderness that we resolve not to rebuild. At this point, I do want to grade the human excellence over the other creatures. On the one hand, this human evaluation of the world expresses itself as a late-coming consequence of, rather than claiming itself as an exemption to, a value-generating creativity inherent in nature. On the other hand, this human excellence is exceptional. Nature takes a wild turn, an idiographic and historic one in ethical achievement. The story comes to a head in humans, although the story is vastly more than its heading in humans. Persons count, but not so much that nothing else counts; and persons count for more when they can count something else. . . .

NOTES

For critical discussion see Anthony Weston, "Beyond Intrinsic Value: Pragmatism in Environmental Ethics," *Environmental Ethics* 7 (1985): 321-339.

1. John C. Hendee, George H. Stankey, and Robert C. Lucas, *Wilderness Management* (Washington, D.C.: USDA Forest Service Miscellaneous Publication No. 1365, 1978), pp. 140-141.

2. Paul D. MacLean, "The Triune Brain, Emotion, and Scientific Bias," in Francis O. Schmitt, ed., *The Neurosciences Second Study Program* (New York: Rockefeller University Press, 1970), pp. 336-349.

3. Lubert Stryer, *Biochemistry* (San Francisco: W.H. Freeman & Co., 1975), pp. 351-352.

4. Ibid., pp. 373-374.

5. J. Alumets, R. Hakanson, F. Sundler, and J. Thorell, "Neuronal Localization of Immunoreactive Enkephalin and β-endorphin in the Earthworm," *Nature* 279 (28 June 1979): 805-806; K.A. Miczek, M.L. Thompson, and L. Schuster, "Opioid-Like Analgesia in Defeated Mice," *Science* 215 (1982): 1520-1522.

6. Olov Lindberg, ed., *Brown Adipose Tissue* (New York: American Elsevier Publishing Co., 1970); Julie Ann Miller, "Getting Warm," *Science News* 111, No. 3 (15 January 1977): 42-43.

7. Quoted in G.E. Hutchinson, "Homage to Santa Rosalia, or Why Are There So Many Kinds of Animals?" *American Naturalist* 93 (1959): 145-159, on p. 146.

8. T.H. Huxley, *Evolution and Ethics* (New York: D. Appleton & Co., 1894), p. 83.

DISCUSSION TOPICS

1. Rolston disagrees with the view that everything is a resource, and says that this view parallels the position that everything we do is selfish. What connections do you see between the two views?

2. Rolston urges that we extend our idea of value to include "organic problem-solving" whether involving awareness or not. Do you agree? Why or why not?

3. While acknowledging the intrinsic value of individuals, Rolston also asserts that ecosystems have intrinsic value. Is it inconsistent to maintain both positions? Explain.

4. Rolston rejects the naturalistic fallacy as a "cultural artifact." Does his argument convince you? Explain your position.

5. Rolston says: "Persons count, but not so much that nothing else counts; and persons count for more when they can count something else." Restate this idea in your own words, and consider whether you agree.

On the Intrinsic Value of Nonhuman Species

J. Baird Callicott

J. Baird Callicott (b. 1941) is Professor of Philosophy and Natural Resources at the University of Wisconsin, Stevens Point. He has edited and written a number of important books and articles concerning environmental ethics.

In the excerpt from his essay "On the Intrinsic Value of Nonhuman Species," Callicott argues for an "anthropogenic" theory of value, in which human consciousness is the source of all value. Callicott argues that while all value is anthropogenic, value can be either inherent or instrumental. While he refers to this theory as that of "truncated intrinsic value," we will use "inherent value" (as defined in the introduction to Chapter 2) to characterize his position.

Callicott builds his position on that of David Hume, Charles Darwin, and Aldo Leopold and argues that it is consistent with ecological and evolutionary theories of human development. The human capacity for "disinterested sympathy" for other human beings has developed over the ages and can be extended into "bio-empathy," the recognition of the inherent value of nonhumans, both at the species and individual level. Callicott argues that his theory avoids relativism because of the "consensus of feeling" issuing from the "human psychological profile" or human nature, which transcends cultural differences. He points out that all cultures abhor murder, theft, dishonesty, and so forth. Normal human psychological characteristics have been fixed by natural selection.

. . . Something is intrinsically valuable if it is valuable *in* and *for* itself—if its value is not derived from its utility, but is independent of any use or function it may have in relation to something or someone else. In classical philosophical terminology, an intrinsically valuable entity is said to be an "end-in-itself," not just a "means" to another's ends.

Most systems of modern ethics, both formal philosophical systems (e.g., Kant's deontology), and less

formal popular systems (e.g., the Christian ethic), take it for granted that human beings are intrinsically valuable, that, in other words, each human being is valuable in and for himself/herself independently of any contribution s/he may make to the welfare of another person or to society collectively. We may not discard or destroy worn-out, broken, or imperfectly made human beings as we might tools in similar condition because human beings are, it is almost universally supposed, intrinsically—not, like tools or "resources," merely instrumentally—valuable. . . .

A fundamental doctrine of modern science remains a formidable obstacle . . . to all the heroic attempts of philosophers to establish the existence, and adequately explain the nature, of intrinsic value, the value of something in and for itself. The objective physical world is sharply distinguished from subjective consciousness in the metaphysical posture of modern science as originally formulated by Descartes. Thought, feeling, sensation, and value have ever since been, from the point of view of Scientific Naturalism, regarded as confined to the subjective realm of consciousness. The objective, physical world is therefore value-free from a scientific point of view.

Quantum theory, relativity, and the other revolutionary developments of post-modern science are said to have invalidated the Cartesian distinction between the subjective and the objective domains, and hence to promise profound consequences not only for epistemology and ontology, but for value theory as well.[1] The axiological consequences of postmodern science, however, remain at this point programmatic; they have not been worked out in any detail, and seem, in any case, remote and metaphorical. Further, in the structure of science itself, quantum theory has little direct relationship to or influence on biology. Hence, at the level of organization with which we are concerned, the macroscopic world of terrestrial life and the value of its component species, the classical attitude that nature is value-neutral remains a virtually unchallenged dogma of the scientific world view. From this perspective, the attribution of intrinsic value to species, as to anything else under the sun, is doomed at the outset to failure. . . .

I concede that, from the point of view of Scientific Naturalism, the *source* of all value is human consciousness, but it by no means follows that the *locus* of all value is consciousness itself or a mode of consciousness like reason, pleasure, or knowledge. In other words, something may be valuable only because someone values it, but it may also be valued for itself, not for the sake of any subjective experience (pleasure, knowledge, aesthetic satisfaction, etc.) it may afford the valuer. Value may be subjective and affective, but it is intentional, not self-referential. For example, a newborn infant is valuable to its parents for its own sake as well as for the joy or any other experience it may afford them. In and of itself an infant child is as value-neutral as a stone or a hydrogen atom, considered in strict accordance with the subject-object/fact-value dichotomy of modern science. Yet we still may wish to say that a newborn infant is "intrinsically valuable" (even though its value depends, in the last analysis, on human consciousness) in order to distinguish the *noninstrumental* value it has for its parents, relatives, and the human community generally from its actual or potential instrumental value—the pleasure it gives its parents, the pride it affords its relatives, the contribution it may make to society, etc. In so doing, however, "intrinsic value" retains only half its traditional meaning. An intrinsically valuable thing on this reading is valuable *for* its own sake, *for* itself, but it is not valuable *in* itself, i.e., completely independently of any consciousness, since no value can in principle, from the point of view of classical normal science, be altogether independent of a valuing consciousness. Nonhuman species, I argue, may possess intrinsic value in this truncated sense, which is consistent with the world view of Scientific Naturalism. Indeed, my suggestion is that the world view of modern science not only *allows* for the intrinsic value of nonhuman species in this limited sense, but its cosmological, evolutionary, and ecological perspectives actually *foster* such value. . . .

There remains [after consideration of alternative views—eds.] a modern moral metaphysic which has been largely ignored or dismissed by the philosophical community, but which has survived largely in biological discussions of moral or moral-like phenomena. Hume's grounding of morality in feeling or emotion has been the basis for several recent attempts to explain the intrinsic value of other species. Ac-

cording to Hume, one may have a strong emotional attachment to one's own interests, but such an attachment is entirely contingent. It is possible, indeed, that one may also have strong feelings for the interests of other beings.[2] Sometimes these overcome the self-regarding passions and issue in behavior which we praise as "heroic," "noble," or "saintly" (or condemn as "foolhardy" or "daft").

Hume's famous sharp distinction between fact and value, his is/ought dichotomy, has made his moral metaphysic more appealing and useful to scientists interested in moral phenomena than any other philosophical analysis of ethics, since in science nature is conceived to be an objective and, more to the point so far as our interests are concerned, value-free system. From the scientific point of view, nature throughout, from atoms to galaxies, is an orderly, objective, axiologically neutral domain. Value is, as it were, projected onto natural objects or events by the subjective feelings of observers. If all consciousness were annihilated at a stroke, there would be no good and evil, no beauty and ugliness, no right and wrong; only impassive phenomena would remain. Accordingly, it has been characteristic of evolutionary biological thought about moral phenomena to follow Hume (whether deliberately or not) and treat moral valuation and behavior as both subjective and affective.

One of the more conspicuous problems for an evolutionary biological account of animal behavior is this: How is it possible to account for the existence of something like morality or ethics among human beings and their prehuman ancestors in a manner consistent with evolutionary theory? One would suppose, given the struggle for existence, that hostile, aggressive traits would be of great advantage to individuals in competition with one another for limited resources and that therefore such traits would be represented in ever increasing magnitude in future generations. As time goes on we should see less inclination toward "moral" behavior, rather than, as the history of civilization seems to indicate (though cynics might well contest this point), more. At this late date, in any case, all human beings, indeed all animals, should be thoroughly rapacious and utterly merciless. Kindness, pity, generosity, benevolence, justice, and similar dispositions should have been nipped in the bud as soon as they appeared, winnowed by the remorseless and impersonal principle of natural selection.

Charles Darwin himself tackled this problem in *The Descent of Man.*[3] He begins with the observation that for many species, and especially mammals, prolonged parental care is necessary to ensure reproductive success. Such care is motivated by a certain strong emotion which adult mammals (in some species perhaps only the females) experience toward their offspring—parental love. Selection for this capacity would affect a species' psychological profile since it would strongly contribute to inclusive fitness (not necessarily prolonged individual survival, so much as reproductive success).

Once established, Darwin argued, the "parental and filial affections" permitted the formation of small social units originally consisting, presumably, of parent(s) and offspring. The survival advantages to the individual of membership in a protective social unit, like a family group, are obvious and would tend to conserve slight variations of the parent-child emotional bond, such as affection for other kin—siblings, uncles, aunts, cousins, and so on. Those individuals in whom these affections were strongest would form the most closely knit family and clan bonds. Now, these and similar "social sentiments" or "social instincts," such as "the all-important emotion of sympathy," Darwin reasoned, "will have been increased through natural selection; for those communities which included the greatest number of the most sympathetic members would flourish best, and rear the greatest number of offspring."[4]

As family group competes with family group, ironically, the same principles which at first would seem to lead to greater intolerance and rapacity lead instead to increased affection, kindness, and sympathy, for now the struggle for limited resources is understood to be pursued collectively, and groups with "the greatest number of the most sympathetic members" may be supposed to out-compete those whose members are quarrelsome and disagreeable. "No tribe," Darwin tells us, "could hold together if murder, robbery, treachery, etc., were common; consequently, such crimes within the limits of the same tribe 'are branded with everlasting infamy'; but excite no such

sentiment beyond these limits."[5] Indeed, beyond these limits, it remains biologically important for the passions of aggression, rage, and bloodlust to come into play.

Not only was there selective pressure for *more intense* sympathy and affection within group boundaries, there was selective pressure for more widely cast social sentiments, since in competition among the most internally peaceable and cooperative groups the larger will win out. "As man advances in civilization, and small tribes are united into larger communities, the simplest reason would tell each individual that he ought to extend his social instincts and sympathies to all the members of the same nation though personally unknown to him [and unrelated to him genetically]."[6]

Unlike both the (Benthamic) utilitarian and (Kantian) deontological schools of modern moral philosophy, the Humean-Darwinian natural history of morals does not regard egoism as the only geniune and self-explanatory value. Selfishness and altruism are equally primitive and both are explained by natural selection. Self-assertion and aggressiveness are necessary for survival to reproductive age and to reproductive success, but so are caring, cooperativeness, and love.

Darwin's account of the origin and evolution of morals obviously involves the current biological anathema of "group selection," i.e., natural selection operating with respect to groups rather than to individual phenotypes who are the immediate carriers of these genes.[7] A more rigorous theoretical account of social-moral phenomena has recently been provided by social evolutionary theorists.[8] Darwin's classical account, however, is an indispensable ingredient in the theoretical structure of Aldo Leopold's "land ethic" (which contains a plea for the "biotic right" of other species to exist) and it is the basis for Paul and Anne Ehrlich's argument for the "rights" of species to exist, as well. . . .

Thus I think we have found . . . an axiology which faithfully articulates and adequately grounds the moral intuition that nonhuman species have "intrinsic value." They may not be valuable *in* themselves, but they may certainly be valued *for* themselves. According to this expanded Humean account, value is, to be sure, humanly conferred, but not necessarily homocentric. We certainly experience strong self-oriented feelings and appraise other things in reference to our human interests. But we experience certain distinct disinterested affections as well. We can foster, for example, the welfare of our own kin at considerable cost or even sacrifice to ourselves. We are capable of a disinterested sympathy and selfless charity to persons unrelated and unknown to us. According to Hume, the ''intrinsic value'' we attribute to all human beings is a projection or objectification of this ''sentiment of humanity.''

The philosophical and popular disagreement about which beings are intrinsically valuable, though all value is itself affective, is, according to this theory, a matter of *cognitive* rather than affective differences. The human capacity for the moral sentiments upon which intrinsic value depends is fairly uniform (because it is a genetically fixed psychological characteristic like sexual appetite) and roughly equally distributed throughout the human population. To whom or to what these affections are directed, however, is an open matter, a matter of cognitive representation— of ''nurture,'' not ''nature.'' A person whose social and intellectual horizons are more or less narrow regards only a more or less limited set of persons and a more or less social whole to be intrinsically valuable. To perceive nonhuman species as intrinsically valuable involves, thus, not only the moral sentiments, but an expansive cognitive representation of nature.

The Humean/Darwinian bio-empathetic moral metaphysic, based upon naturally selected ''moral sentiments,'' provides a theory according to which species qua species may have ''intrinsic value.'' That is, they may be valued for themselves. Because the theory is humanly grounded, though not humanly centered, it does not impel us toward some detached and impersonal axiological reference point and thus submerge the value of the present ecosystem in a temporally and spatially infinite cosmos, as Holistic Rationalism does. Our social affections are extended to our fellow members and to the social whole of which we are part. The tribesmen who stand helplessly by and witness the ''extinction'' of their cul-

ture, as so many nineteenth-century Native Americans unfortunately had to do, take little comfort in knowing that another cultural order will replace their own. Similarly, this is the biotic community of which we are a part, these are our companions in the odyssey of evolution, and it is to them, not to any future complement, that our loyalties properly extend.

Hume's grounding of morality in feeling or emotion has usually been regarded by the philosophical community as leading inevitably to an irresponsible ethical relativism.[9] If good and evil, right and wrong, are, like beauty and ugliness, in the eye of the beholder, then there can be no moral truths. We could no more reject as mistaken the opinion that matricide, say, is good, than the opinion that Picasso's Cubist paintings are ugly.

While Hume's theory of morality is certainly an emotive theory, it does not necessarily collapse into emotive relativism. Hume provides for a functional equivalent of objective moral truths by what may be called a ''consensus of feeling.'' The human psychological profile in certain crucial respects is standardized, fixed. Unlike aesthetic judgments, which notoriously vary widely from culture to culture and within the same culture from person to person, moral judgments (allowing for certain peripheral divergencies) are both culturally and individually invariant. Christian cultures may regard polygamy with horror while Muslim cultures may approve it. Still, all cultures abominate murder, theft, treachery, dishonesty, and the other cardinal vices. Certainly individuals differ in the degree to which they are endowed with the moral sentiments. Still, just as we can speak of certain normal physical proportions and conditions among human beings, while allowing for all sorts of variations, so we can speak of a certain normal human affective profile, while allowing for all sorts of variations. Some people are tall, others are short, and both the tall and the short are normal. Then there are giants and midgets. Similarly, some people are overflowing with moral sentiments while others experience them far less intensely and are more possessed by self-love. Depraved criminals, for example, exceed the limits of normality. They are the psychological equivalent of the physically freakish. Their emotional responses are not untrue, but, by the human consensus of feeling, they are "wrong," morally, if not epistemically.

For Hume the "universality" of human moral dispositions was an ad hoc fact. Darwin completed Hume's theory by explaining how such a standardization came about. Like the complex of normal human physical characteristics, normal human psychological characteristics, including the moral sentiments, were fixed by natural (and perhaps by sexual) selection.

Still it may seem defeating to say that the nonutilitarian value of other forms of life is ultimately emotional, that it rests upon feeling, that species are valuable and we ought to save them simply because we have an affection for them. This would be defeating if there were some viable alternative and if emotivism implied moral relativism. But according to the Humean-Darwinian axiology, the only tenable axiology from the general perspective of traditional normal science, all value is affective. The intrinsic value we attribute to individual human beings and to humanity expresses only our feelings for co-members of our global village and for our human community. I remain convinced therefore that the Humean-Darwinian moral metaphysic is, intellectually, the most coherent and defensible axiology and, practically, the most convincing basis for an environmental ethic which includes intrinsic value for nonhuman species. . . .

NOTES

1. See, for example, Holmes Rolston III, "Are Values in Nature Subjective or Objective," *Environmental Ethics* 4 (1982): 125-151; and Don E. Marietta, Jr., "Knowledge and Obligation in Environmental Ethics: A Phenomenological Approach," *Environmental Ethics* 4 (1982): 153-162.
2. Cf. David Hume, *A Treatise of Human Nature* (Oxford: The Clarendon Press, 1960), Bk. III, Pt. I.
3. Charles Darwin, *The Descent of Man and Selection in Relation to Sex,* second edition (New York: J.A. Hill, 1904), p. 97.
4. Ibid., p. 107.
5. Ibid., p. 118.
6. Ibid., p. 124.

7. Darwin seems both aware and forthright about his dependency on the concept of group selection in his account of the origin and evolution of morals: "We have now seen that actions are regarded by savages, and were probably so regarded by primeval man, as good or bad, solely as they obviously affect the welfare of the tribe,— nor that of the species, nor that of the individual member of the species. This conclusion agrees well with the belief that the so-called moral sense is aboriginally derived from the social instincts, for both relate at first exclusively to the community" (ibid., p. 120). V.C. Wynne-Edwards, *Animal Dispersion in Relation to Social Behavior* (Edinburgh: Oliver and Boyd, 1962), provides the most celebrated recent support for group selection. Wynne-Edwards was refuted to the satisfaction at least of most biologists by G.C. Williams in *Adaptation and Natural Selection: A Critique of Some Current Evolutionary Thought* (Princeton: Princeton University Press, 1966) and ever since, the concept of group selection has been avoided by most evolutionary theorists and certainly by sociobiologists. For a recent summary discussion see Michael Ruse, *Sociobiology: Sense or Nonsense?* (Boston: D. Reidel, 1979).
8. Most notably by W.D. Hamilton, "The Genetical Theory of Social Behavior," *Journal of Theoretical Biology* 7 (1964): 1-32; R.L. Trivers, "The Evolution of Reciprocal Altruism," *Quarterly Review of Biology* 46 (1971): 35-57; Edward O. Wilson, *Sociobiology: The New Synthesis* (Cambridge: Harvard University Press, 1975). Ruse, *Sociobiology: Sense or Nonsense?* Provides a thorough bibliography.
9. See the discussion of Hume in W.D. Hudson, *Modern Moral Philosophy* (Garden City: Anchor Books, 1970), for a good summary of professional opinion.

DISCUSSION TOPICS

1. Give your own example of something with Callicott's "truncated intrinsic" or inherent value.
2. Describe Darwin's account of the evolutionary development of morality. Do you agree that it produces a "consensus of feeling"?
3. According to Callicott, why is Hume's fact-value distinction so attractive to modern science?
4. What weaknesses do you find in Callicott's theory of bioempathy?

Ethical Thinking and Theory

Tom Regan

Tom Regan (b. 1938) is Professor of Philosophy at North Carolina State University at Raleigh. He is a prominent and eloquent advocate of animal rights. In "The Bird in the Cage: A Glimpse of My Life" in Between the Species *2, Nos. 1-2: 42-49; 90-99 (1986) he shares his moral journey leading to his commitment to animal rights.*

In the following excerpt from The Case for Animal Rights, *he discusses six characteristics of a good moral judgment: conceptual clarity, information, rationality, impartiality, coolness, and use of valid moral principles. Regan maintains that in order to evaluate moral principles, we should apply tests of consistency, adequacy of scope, precision, and conformity with our moral intuitions.*

THE IDEAL MORAL JUDGMENT

I shall begin by attempting to answer the question, What requirements would someone have to meet to make an ideal moral judgment? Considered ideally, that is, what are the conditions that anyone would have to satisfy to reach a moral judgment as free from fault and error as possible? Now, by its very nature, an *ideal* moral judgment is just that—an ideal. Perhaps no one ever has met or ever will completely meet all the requirements set forth in the ideal. But that does not make it irrational to strive to come as close as possible to fulfilling it. If we can never quite get to the finish, we can still move some distance from the starting line.

There are at least six different ideas that must find a place in a description of the ideal moral judgment. A brief discussion of each follows.

Conceptual Clarity

The importance of conceptual clarity is obvious. If someone tells us that euthanasia is always wrong, we cannot determine whether that statement is true before

we understand what euthanasia is. Similar remarks apply to other controversies. In the case of abortion, for example, many think the question turns on whether the fetus is a person; and that will depend on what a person is—that is, on how the concept "person" should be analyzed. Clarity by itself may not be enough, but thought cannot get far without it.

Information

We cannot answer moral questions in our closets. Moral questions arise in the real world, and a knowledge of the real-world setting in which they arise is essential if we are seriously to seek rational answers to them. For example, in the debate over the morality of capital punishment, some people argue that convicted murderers ought to be executed because, if they are not, they may be (and often are) paroled; and if they are paroled, they are more likely to kill again than are other released felons. Is this true? Is this a fact? We have to come out of our closets to answer this (or to find the answer others have reached on the basis of their research); and answer it we must if we are to reach an informed judgment about the morality of capital punishment. The importance of getting the facts, of being informed, is not restricted just to the case of capital punishment by any means. It applies all across the broad sweep of moral inquiry.

Rationality

Rationality is a difficult concept to analyze. Fundamentally, however, it involves the ability to recognize the connection between different ideas, to understand that if some statements are true, then some other statements must be true while others must be false. Now, it is in logic that rules are set forth that tell us when statements do follow from others, and it is because of this that a person who is rational often is said to be logical. When we speak of the need to be rational, then, we are saying that we need to observe the rules of logic. To reach an ideal moral judgment, therefore, we must not only strive to make our judgment against a background of information and conceptual clarity;

we must also take care to explore how our beliefs are logically related to other things that we do or do not believe. For example, imagine that Lee thinks all abortions are morally wrong; and suppose that his wife, Mary, recently has had an abortion. Then Lee is not being rational or logical if he also believes that there was nothing immoral about Mary's abortion. Rationally he cannot believe this while believing the other things we assume he believes. Logically, it is impossible for both of the following statements to be true: (1) All abortions are morally wrong, and (2) Mary's abortion was not morally wrong. Whenever someone is committed to a group of beliefs that cannot possibly all be true at the same time, that person is said to be committed to a *contradiction*. Lee, then, is committed to a contradiction. To fall short of the ideal moral judgment by committing oneself to a contradiction is to fall as short as one possibly can.

Impartiality

Partiality involves favoring someone or something above others. For example, if a father is partial to one of his children, then he will be inclined to give the favored child more than he gives his other children. In some cases, perhaps, partiality is a fine thing; but a partiality that excludes even thinking about or taking notice of others is far from what is needed in an ideal moral judgment. That someone has been harmed, for example, always seems to be a relevant consideration, whether this someone is favored by us or not. In striving to reach the correct answer to moral questions, therefore, we must strive to guard against extreme, unquestioned partiality; otherwise we shall run the risk of having our judgment clouded by bigotry and prejudice.

The idea of impartiality is at the heart of what sometimes is referred to as the *formal principle of justice*, the principle that justice is the similar, and injustice the dissimilar, treatment of similar individuals. This principle is said to express the formal principle of justice because by itself it does not specify what factors are relevant for determining what makes individuals similar or dissimilar. To decide this, one would have to supplement the formal principle of justice with a substantive or normative interpretation of justice. . . . Even at this juncture, however, we can recognize the rich potential the formal principle of justice can have in arguments about moral right and wrong. For example, if someone were to say that causing suffering is wrong when humans are made to suffer but not wrong in the case of animals, it would be apposite to ask why the two cases are dissimilar. For they must be dissimilar if, as we are assuming, dissimilar treatment is allowed. If, in reply to our question, we were told that the difference is that human beings suffer in the one case but animals suffer in the other, then it would again be apposite to ask why a biological difference, a difference that relates to the species to which humans and animals happen to belong, can make any moral difference to the morality of the treatment in the two cases. If to cause suffering is wrong, then it is wrong no matter who is made to suffer, and the attempt to limit its wrongness only to human beings is a symptom of one's showing unquestioned partiality for the members of one's own species. While the formal principle of justice does not by itself tell us what are the relevant factors for determining when treatment is similar or dissimilar, that principle must be observed if we are to make the ideal moral judgment. Not to observe it is a symptom of prejudice or bias, rational defects that must be identified and overcome if we are to make the best moral judgment we can. I will have occasion to refer to the formal principle of justice in a number of places in what follows.

Coolness

All of us know what it is like to do something in the heat of anger that we later regret. No doubt we have also had the experience of getting so excited that we do something that later on we wish we had not done. Emotions are powerful forces, and though life would be a dull wasteland without them, we need to appreciate that the more volatile among them can mislead us; strong emotion is not a reliable guide to doing (or judging) what is best. This brings us to the need to be ''cool.'' *Being cool* here means ''not being in an emotionally excited state, being in an emotionally calm state of mind.'' The idea is that the hotter (the more emotionally charged) we are, the more likely we are to reach a mistaken moral conclusion, while the cooler (the calmer) we are, the greater the chances that we will avoid making mistakes.

The position is borne out by common experience. People who are in a terribly excited state may not be able to retain their rationality. Because of their deep emotional involvement, they may not be able to attain impartiality; and because they are in an excited emotional state, they may not even care about learning what happened or why. Like the proverb about shooting first and asking questions later, a lack of coolness can easily lead people to judge first and ask about the facts afterwards. The need to be cool, then, seems to merit a place on our list.

Valid Moral Principles

The concept of a moral principle has been analyzed in different ways. At least this much seems clear, however: for a principle to qualify as a *moral* principle (as distinct from, say, a scientific or a legal principle), it must prescribe that all moral agents are required to act in certain ways, thereby providing, so we are to assume, rational guidance in the conduct of life. More will be said about moral principles and moral agents in the sequel. For the present it will suffice to say that moral agents are those who can bring impartial reasons (i.e., reasons that respect the requirement of impartiality) to bear on deciding how they ought to act. Individuals who lack the ability to understand or act on the basis of impartial reasons (e.g., young children) fail to qualify as moral agents: they cannot meaningfully be said to have obligations or to do, or fail to do, what is morally right or wrong. Only moral agents have this status, and moral principles apply only to the determination of how moral agents may behave.

How does the idea of a valid moral principle relate to the concept of an ideal moral judgment? In an ideal moral judgment, it is not enough that the judgment be based on complete information, complete impartiality, complete conceptual clarity, and so forth. It is also essential that the judgment be based on a *valid* or *correct* moral principle(s). Ideally, one wants not only

to make the correct judgment but to make it for the correct reasons. But which among the many possible moral principles we might accept are the correct or most reasonable ones? This is a question we cannot answer merely by saying which principles we *happen* to prefer, or which ones all or most people *happen* to accept, or which principles some alleged moral authority issues. These ways of answering moral questions have previously been eliminated from serious consideration. What is needed are criteria for rationally evaluating and choosing between competing ethical principles. In the section that follows various criteria are characterized and their appropriateness defended. No claim to completeness is made, nor are the several criteria ranked systematically in terms of their respective weight or importance, though some suggestions will be made in this regard. It will be enough for our present and future purposes to make the case for the reasonableness of the criteria about to be discussed.

CRITERIA FOR EVALUATING MORAL PRINCIPLES

Consistency

A minimum requirement for any ethical principle is that it be consistent. Consistency concerns the *possible conjoint* truth of two or more statements. Any combination of two or more statements (let us refer to this as *any set of statements*) is consistent if and only if it is possible that all the statements constituting the set can be true at the same time. Here is an example of a consistent set. (It is assumed that ''Jack'' refers to one, and ''Jill'' refers to another, individual, at the same time, in the same circumstances).

Set A (1): Jack is taller than Jill.
(2): Jill is shorter than Jack.

Here is an example of an inconsistent set.

Set B (3): Jack is taller than Jill.
(4): Jill is taller than Jack.

Set A is consistent because it is possible for both (1) and (2) to be true at the same time: there is nothing involved in (1)'s being true that automatically or necessarily makes (2) false, and vice versa—the conjunction of (1) and (2) is *not* a contradiction—though neither (1) nor (2) must be true (for it might be that Jack and Jill are the same height). Set B is inconsistent, however, because if (3) were true, then (4) would have to be false, and if (4) were true, then (3) would have to be false; necessarily, that is, (3) and (4) cannot both be true; the conjunction of (3) and (4) *is* a contradiction.

Now, a valid moral principle must be consistent. This is true because such a principle aims at providing us with a basis by reference to which we may rationally decide which actions are right and which are wrong. If, however, a proposed principle turns out to be inconsistent, then its failure in this regard would undermine the very point of having an ethical principle in the first place—namely, to provide rational guidance in the determination of what is right and wrong.

One way of arguing that a proposed principle is inconsistent is to show that it implies that the very same act can be both right and wrong. One (but by no means not the only) interpretation of the view called *ethical relativism* has this implication. On this interpretation, an act is right or wrong whenever the majority in any given society approves or disapproves of it, respectively. It is important to be clear about what, on this interpretation, ethical relativism comes to. The claim is not that a given act is *thought* to be right in a given society if the majority approves of it; nor is it that the act of which a given society's majority approves is right *in that society*; rather, an act *is unqualifiedly right,* according to the interpretation presently under review, whenever the majority of the members of any given society happen to approve of it.

This way of viewing right and wrong does imply that the very same act can be both right and wrong. To make this clearer, suppose that the majority in one society happens to approve of killing and eating foreigners, while the majority in another society happens to disapprove of it. Then it follows, given the interpretation of ethical relativism we are discussing, both

that (a) killing and eating foreigners is right, and that (b) it is not the case that killing and eating foreigners is right. The principle implies, that is, that *both* (a) *and* (b) are true. However, since (a) and (b) are *inconsistent,* they *cannot* both be true. Neither, then, can ethical relativism, as understood here, be a valid ethical principle.

Adequacy of Scope

A further legitimate requirement is that an ethical principle have adequate scope. The reason for this should be clear when we recall that ethical principles are supposed to provide us with practical guidance in the determination of what is right and wrong. Since we find ourselves in a great variety of circumstances in which we have to make such determinations, a given principle will succeed in providing guidance to the extent that it can be applied in these circumstances, and this will depend on the principle's scope. The wider a principle's scope, the greater its potential use; the narrower its scope, the narrower its range of applications. Though it is not possible to legislate exactly how wide a principle's scope must be if it is to qualify as adequate, the case for viewing adequacy of scope as a relevant criterion is reasonable, something we will see more clearly as we proceed.

Precision

What we want from an ethical principle is not vague direction concerning a broad range of cases: we expect specific or determinate direction. Without this precision, a principle's usefulness will be seriously diminished. It is of little help, for example, to be told to ''Love your neighbor'' or ''Do no harm'' if we are not told, in a clear and helpful way, what ''love'' and ''harm''—and ''neighbor,'' for that matter!—are supposed to mean. If a principle is vague in what it requires, in a significant range of cases, we will be uncertain of what it requires; and to the extent we are uncertain, we will also be unsure about what we must do to follow the principle's direction in the present or whether we have complied with the principle by acting as we have in the past. A reasonable degree of precision, then, is a legitimate requirement for any ethical principle. At the same time, too much precision, or precision of the wrong sort, are illegitimate requirements. Ethics is not geometry. We should not expect or require definitions of moral concepts (e.g., of ''love'' or ''harm'') to be as exact as definitions of geometrical concepts (e.g., of ''square'' or ''circle''); nor should we require that moral principles be as precise, or that they be demonstrable in the same way, as the Pythagorean Theorem. Always we must keep Aristotle's sage advice in mind: ''It is the mark of an educated man to look for precision in each class of things just so far as the nature of the subject admits.'' We shall have occasion to remind ourselves of this elemental wisdom on more than one occasion in the sequel.

Conformity with Our Intuitions

One final basis for evaluating competing ethical principles concerns whether they conform with our moral intuitions. This is by far the most controversial criterion we will discuss and use. Some philosophers flatly reject it as a reasonable test. Others insist on its validity. Whichever position one does or should take, it is essential to clarify what it means in the present context. This is more than idle semantic curiosity. The notion of intuition has been understood in different ways in moral philosophy, some of which are logically distinct from, and thus ought not be confused with, the sense in which this notion is used when ''appeals to intuition'' are recognized as a legitimate way to test ethical principles. The highly influential twentieth-century English philosopher G. E. Moore, for example, uses the word *intuition* to refer to those ethical propositions that, on his view, are ''incapable of proof,'' while a contemporary of Moore's, W. D. Ross, characterizes moral intuitions as ''self evident'' moral truths. Whatever else one might wish to say about either Moore's view of intuition, or Ross's, or both, it is abundantly clear, as will be seen more fully in what follows, that neither Moore's sense nor Ross's is what is meant when one asks whether a given ethical principle conforms with our moral intuitions or holds

that conformity with them is a legitimate test of an ethical principle's rational credentials.

A third sense in which 'intuition' is sometimes used in moral philosophy is to mean ''our unexamined moral convictions,'' including our initial response or immediate reactions to hard moral cases. It is in this sense that the word is used when people are asked, What are your intuitions?, after an unusual case or situation has been described (e.g., a case where a man has to kill and eat his own grandson in order to survive, and the question is whether he ought to). This sense of 'intuition', certainly is distinct from either Moore's or Ross's, since in responding to the question by giving our initial response we are far from committing ourselves to the view that what we say is self-evidently true or that it is unprovable. Even more important, our intuitions in this sense are our *prereflective judgments* about what is right or wrong. When we are asked about our intuitions in this sense, in other words, we are not being asked to say what we think *after* we have given the question a good deal of thought—*after* we have tried, to the best of our ability, to make an ideal moral judgment about the case. On the contrary, what we are being asked is what we think *before* we have thought about the case in any considerable detail and thus before we have made a concerted effort to make an ideal moral judgment about it. For convenience, let us refer to intuitions in this sense as *prereflective intuitions.* Like Moore's and Ross's understanding of intuition, this prereflective sense also is not the sense involved, when we require that ethical principles conform to our moral intuitions.

The sense that is involved is what we shall term *the reflective sense.* In this sense, our intuitions are those moral beliefs we hold *after* we have made a conscientious effort to satisfy five of the previously listed criteria of making an ideal moral judgment. It is to be assumed, that is, that we have conscientiously endeavored to think about our beliefs coolly, rationally, impartially, with conceptual clarity, and with as much relevant information as we can reasonably acquire. The judgments we make *after* we have made this effort are not our ''gut responses,'' nor are they merely expressions of what we *happen* to believe; they are our *considered* beliefs, beliefs we hold when, and only when, we have done our best to be impartial, rational, cool, and so forth. To test alternative moral principles by how well they conform with our reflective intuitions is thus to test them against our considered beliefs, and, other things being equal between two competing moral principles (i.e., assuming that the two are equal to scope, precision, and consistency), the principle that matches our reflective intuitions best is rationally to be preferred.

Theoretically, however, it is possible that a given principle might pass all the tests for evaluating an ethical principle and yet fail to match one or a few of those beliefs we initially regard as considered beliefs. Moreover, it may also be true that we know of no other moral principle demonstrably better than this principle when it comes to meeting the appropriate criteria for evaluating moral principles, that can account for these intuitions. In that case we should be highly skeptical of those beliefs initially construed as considered beliefs. If no otherwise satisfactory moral principle can be shown to match them, then wisdom would dictate that we agree that, try as we have, we have erred in our intitial assessment of these beliefs. Those beliefs we initially identify as considered beliefs, in other words, can themselves be shown to stand in need of revision or abandonment. What we must strive to achieve, to use a helpful expression of the Harvard philosopher John Rawls, is ''reflective equilibrium'' between our considered beliefs, on the one hand, and our moral principles, on the other. Some of these beliefs may have to be discounted because they cannot be made to fit any principle that is satisfactory in other respects, and some of these principles will have to be dismissed because they fail to match intuitions that can be accommodated by principles that are otherwise satisfactory. No principle is shown to be invalid, therefore, *merely* on the grounds that it fails to match each and every reflective intuition. But a principle *is* shown to be invalid if it fails to match our intuitions *in a broad range of cases*, assuming that these intuitions *are* matched by an alternative principle that is validated by appeals to other

relevant criteria. When ''the appeal to our intuitions'' is understood as an appeal to our considered beliefs, beliefs that stand up under the heat of our best reflective consideration, in the sense and in the manner explained, we should not surrender requiring conformity with these beliefs as a legitimate test of the validity of moral principles unless we are given a good argument against doing so.

DISCUSSION TOPICS

1. State Regan's six criteria for a good moral judgment. Should any be eliminated? Has he missed anything?
2. State your current environment ethic in the form of one or more moral principles. Evaluate your ethic according to Regan's criteria of consistency, adequacy of scope, precision, and conformity with your intuitions. Does your ethic require revision of any of your previously unexamined beliefs or those of your friends?
3. Can Stone's moral pluralism and Cheney's contextualism meet Regan's criterion of consistency?

READING 9

Moral Pluralism and the Course of Environmental Ethics

Christopher D. Stone

Christopher D. Stone (b. 1937) is Professor of Law at the University of Southern California School of Law. He is one of the originators of environmental ethics and is known for his essay ''Should Trees Have Standing?— Toward Legal Rights for Natural Objects,'' Southern California Law Review 45 (1972): 450-501. *In the following essay he attacks the idea of environmental ethics as involving ''invariant moral principles'' which are capable of guiding us through all moral dilemmas to the one right answer. Such a view is ''moral monism,'' which assumes that an entity is morally significant only if it possesses a particular moral property such as sentience or consciousness.*

He criticizes the attempt to include nonhumans in human-based moral theories as being forced and inadequate. Stone points out the varied activities and kinds of things with which ethics is concerned and argues that a better approach is to conceive of morality as consisting of several distinct "frameworks" or "domains," each with its own appropriate principles. Frameworks vary according to "grains of description," "mood," and "logical texture." He recognizes the probability of conflict between domains, but does not believe that such conflict makes pluralism untenable.

THE METAETHICAL ASSUMPTIONS

... What are environmental ethicists trying to achieve, and what are the standards for success? In other words, what, more exactly, is an ethics supposed to look like and do? To illustrate, for years environmental ethicists have been stimulated by Aldo Leopold's conviction that we should develop a "land ethic." But how much thought has been given to what such a project implies? Are the proponents of a land ethic committed to coming up with a capacious replacement for all existing ethics, one capable of mediating all moral questions touching man, beast and mountain, but by reference to a grander, more all-encompassing set of principles? Or can the land ethic be an ethic that governs man's relations with land alone, leaving intact other principles to govern actions touching humankind (and yet others for actions touching, say, lower animals, and so on)?

If we are implying that there are different ethics, then there are a host of questions to face. What is an ethical system, and what are its minimum requirements? Need its "proofs" be as irresistible as a geometry's? Is it required to provide for each moral dilemma that it recognizes as a dilemma one right, tightly defined answer? Or is it enough to identify several courses of action equally acceptable, perhaps identifying for elimination those that are wrong or unwelcome? How—by reference to what elements—can one ethic differ from another? What possibilities

of conflicting judgments are introduced by multiple frameworks, and how are they to be resolved?

These are among the questions that, sooner or later, environmental ethicists will have to confront. Upon their answer hinges nothing less than the legitimacy of environmental ethics as a distinct enterprise.

MORAL MONISM

The environmental ethics movement has always known that if it is to succeed, it has to challenge the prevailing orthodoxy. But the orthodoxy it has targeted is only the more obvious one, the orthodoxy of morals: that man is the measure (and not merely the measurer) of all value. Certainly calling that gross presumption to question is a valid part of the program. But the orthodoxy we have to question first is that of metaethics—of how moral philosophy ought to be conducted, of the ground rules.

Note that I am not claiming that we lack controversy at the level of *morals.* There is no shortage of lively contention in the philosophy literature. But underneath it all there is a striking, if ordinarily only implicit agreement on the metaethical sense of mission. It is widely presumed, by implication when it is not made explicit, that the ethicist's task is to put forward and defend a single overarching principle (or coherent body of principles), such as utilitarianism's "greatest good for the greatest number" or Kant's categorical imperative, and to demonstrate how it (the one correct viewpoint) guides us through all moral dilemmas to the one right solution.

This attitude, which I call moral monism, implies that in defending, say, the preservation of a forest or the protection of a laboratory animal, we are expected to bring our argument under the same principles that dictate our obligations to kin or the just deserts of terrorists. It suggests that moral considerateness is a matter of either-or; that is, the single viewpoint is presumably built upon a single salient moral property, such as, typically, sentience, intelligence, being the subject of a conscious life, etc. Various entities (depending on whether they are blessed with the one salient property) are *either* morally relevant (each in the same way, according to the same rules) *or* utterly inconsiderate, out in the moral cold.[1]

Environmentalists, more than most philosophers, have at least an intuitive reason for supposing that this attitude is mistaken, for it is they whom the attitude is the first to bridle. Environmentalists wonder about the possible value in a river (or in preserving a river), but cannot rationalize those feelings in the familiar anthropocentric terms of pains and life-projects that they would apply to their own situations. By contrast, mainstream ethicists, concentrating on interpersonal relations, constrict their attention to a relatively narrow and uncontroversial band or morally salient qualities. Persons can speak for themselves, exercise moral choice, and—because they share a community—assert and waive many sorts of claims that are useful in governing their reciprocal relationships. Orthodox ethics has understandably tended to identify all ethics with this one set of morally salient properties: the paradigmatic moral problems have historically been interpersonal problems; the paradigmatic rules, person-regarding.

Thus, while vying camps have arisen within the orthodox tradition, none is ordinarily forced to account for the significance of properties that lie outside the common pool of human attributes. It is only when one starts to wonder about exotic clients, such as future generations, the dead, embryos, animals, the

spatially remote, tribes, trees, robots, mountains, and art works, that the assumptions which unify ordinary morals are called into question. Need the rules that apply be in some sense, and at some level of generality, "the same" in all cases? The term *environmental ethics* suggests the possibility of a distinct moral regime for managing our way through environment-affecting conduct. But in what respects that regime is distinct from other regimes and how conflicts among the regimes are to be mediated are crucial matters that have not been generally and directly addressed.

In default of well-worked out answers, the prevailing strategy of those who represent nonhumans is one of extension: to force one of the familiar person-oriented frameworks outward and apply one of the familiar arguments to some nonhuman entity. But such arguments too often appear just that—forced. Utilitarianism's efforts to draw future generations under its mantle (a relatively easy extension, one would suppose) ties it in some awkward, if not paradoxical knots. Do we include, for example, those who might be born—obliging us to bring as many as possible of them into existence in order to aggregate more pleasures? Nor is it clear that utilitarianism, unqualified by a complex and ill-fitting rights appendage, can satisfy the concerns that drive the animal liberation movement.

The shortcomings of (let us call it) moral extensionism[2] are not peculiar to utilitarianism. Extensions of utilitarianism's principal contenders all require, in various ways and with various justifications, putting oneself in the place of another to test whether we can really wish the conduct under evaluation if we assume the other's position, role, and/or natural endowment. While such hypothetical trading of places and comparable techniques of thought experiment are always problematical, they are most satisfactory when we are trading places with (or universalizing about) persons who share our culture, and whose interests, values, and tastes we can therefore presume with some confidence. But even that slender

---

1. Consider the argument that a proponent of using animals in medical research throws up to the animal rights advocate: "If all forms of animal life . . . must be treated equally, and if therefore . . . the pains of a rodent count equally with the pains of a human, we are forced to conclude (1) that neither humans nor rodents possess rights, or (2) that rodents possess all the rights that humans possess." Carl Cohen, "The Case for the Use of Animals in Biomedical Research," *New England Journal of Medicine* 315 (1986): 865, 867. An alternative "pluralist" position would examine the possibility that a laboratory bred animal has rights, but not the same as humans. The rodent might have no "right" to life, but have a "right" to be free from suffering. This distinction could be operationalized by saying that the proponent of an experiment that took a laboratory animal's life painlessly would only have to show a clear likelihood of an advance of human welfare; animal suffering, however, would (alternatively) never be allowed, or allowed only when it could be shown that there was a very high probability that the experiment would result in the saving of human lives or the reduction of human suffering—never because it would alleviate mere inconveniences in human life, such as baggy eyelids.

---

2. The term was suggested to me by Holmes Rolston.

assurance is destined to erode the further we venture beyond the domain of the most familiar natural persons. With what conviction can we trade places with members of spatially and temporally remote cultures, or with our own descendants in some future century? And, of course, if we wish to explore our obligations in regard to the dead, trees, rocks, fetuses, artificial intelligence, species, or corporate bodies, trading places is essentially a blind alley. It is one thing to put oneself in the shoes of a stranger, perhaps even in the hooves of a horse—but quite another to put oneself in the banks of a river.

Certainly, the fact that orthodox moral philosophies, each with its own ordinary-person orientation, have difficulty accommodating various nonhumans is not, in itself, proof that the conventional moral schools are wrong, or have to be amended beyond recognition. One alternative, the position of an ardent adherent to one of the predominant schools, is that any unconventional moral client that it cannot account for, except perhaps in a certain limited way, cannot (save in that limited way) have any independent moral significance or standing.

But there is another response to the dilemma, one that is more challenging to the assumptions that dominate conventional moral thought. In accordance with this approach we need to ask several new questions. How imperialistic need a moral framework be? Need we accept as inevitable that there be one set of axioms or principles or paradigm cases for all morals—operable across all moral activities and all diverse entities? Are we constrained to come forward with a single coherent set of principles that will govern throughout, so that any ethic we champion has to absorb its contenders with a more general, abstract and plenary intellectual framework? My own view is that monism's ambitions, to unify all ethics within a single framework capable of yielding the one right answer to all our quandaries, are simply quixotic.

First, the monist's mission sits uneasily with the fact that morality involves not one, but several distinguishable *activities*—choosing among courses of conduct, praising and blaming actors, evaluating institutions, and so on. Is it self-evident that someone who is, say, utilitarian in his or her act evaluation is

committed to utilitarianism in the grading of character?

Second, we have to account for the *variety of things* whose considerateness commands some intuitive appeal: normal persons in a common moral community, persons remote in time and space, embryos and fetuses, nations and nightingales, beautiful things and sacred things. Some of these things we wish to account for because of their high degree of intelligence (higher animals); with others, sentience seems the key (lower life); the moral standing of membership groups, such as nation-states, cultures, and species has to stand on some additional footing, since the group itself (the species, as distinct from the individual whale) manifests no intelligence and experiences no pain. Other entities are genetically human, either capable of experiencing pain (advanced fetuses) or nonsentient (early embryos), but lack, at the time of our dealings with them, full human capacities. Trying to force all these diverse entities into a single mold—the one big, sparsely principled comprehensive theory—forces us to disregard some of our moral intuitions, and to dilate our overworked person-wrought precepts into unhelpfully bland generalities. The commitment is not only chimerical; it imposes strictures on thought that stifle the emergence of more valid approaches to moral reasoning.

MORAL PLURALISM

The alternative conception toward which I have been inviting discussion, what I call *moral pluralism*,[3] takes exception to monism point by point. It refuses to presume that all ethical activities (evaluating acts,

---

3. Moral pluralism ought not to be confused with moral relativism, the view, roughly, that all morals are context-dependent. A pluralist can be agnostic with respect to the moral realist position that there are absolutely true answers to moral quandaries, as invariable across time, space, and communities as the value of pi. There may be ''really right'' and not just relatively right answers, but the way to find them is by reference not to one single principle, constellation of concepts, etc., but by reference to several distinct frameworks, each appropriate to its own domain of entities and/or moral activities (evaluating character, ranking options for conduct, etc.).

actors, social institutions, rules, states of affairs, etc.) are in all contexts (in normal interpersonal relations, across large spaces and many generations, between species) determined by the same features (intelligence, sentience, capacity for emotions, life) or even that they are subject, in each case, to the same over-arching principles (utilitarianism, Kantianism, non-maleficence, etc.). Pluralism invites us to conceive the intellectual activities of which morals consist as being partitioned into several distinct frameworks, each governed by its own appropriate principles.

Certainly, one would expect pain-regarding principles to emerge as pivotal in establishing obligations toward all those things that experience pain. Not pain alone, but preferences of some sort, e.g., the projection of a life plan, have to be accounted for in our relations with a second level of creature. Still richer threads (such as a sense of justice, and rights of a sort that can be consensually created, extinguished, traded, and waived) form the fabric of the moral tapestry that connects humans who share a common moral community. Other principles, perhaps invoking respect for life, for a natural unfolding, seem fit as a basis for forming our relations with plants.[4] Indeed, should we pursue this path, we would multiply subdivisions even within the interpersonal realm. The Kantians, emphasizing the place of nonwelfarist duties, make rightful ado about our not saving our child from drowning because it is "best on the whole." But this does not mean that classic utilitarianism is wrong. Maybe it is of only limited force in parsing out obligations among associates and kin. Utilitarianism strikes me as having considerable validity for legislation (an activity) affecting large numbers of largely unrelated persons (an entity set) who are therefore relatively unacquainted with each other's cardinal preferences.

That monism should have become so firmly established in morals is understandable (it echoes one God, one grand unified theory), but is hardly inevitable. Geometers have long relinquished the belief that Euclid's is the only geometry.

> This discovery led to the pluralization of mathematics (itself already a strangely plural noun); where we once had geometry, we now have geometries and, ultimately, algebras rather than algebra, and number systems rather than a number system.[5]

A comparable partitioning has taken place in the empirical and social sciences. The body politic is commonly viewed as being comprised of groups: groups of humans, each of which is made up of more groups, groups of cells, molecules, atoms, and subatomic particles, and/or waves. What happens at one level of description is undoubtedly a product, in some complex way, of what is occurring at another. Many, perhaps most scientists feel that "in principle" there is a single unifying body of law—the laws of nature—that at some level of simple generality hold throughout. If so, one may harbor the hope not only of abolishing all lingering pockets of ignorance and chaos, but of connecting phenomena on every plane with phenomena on another, of someday unifying, say, the laws that govern the movement of subatomic particles with those that govern social conduct. But we are far from it. What we actually work with, for all intents and purposes, and to almost everyone's satisfaction, are separate bodies of law and knowledge.

The issue I am raising is this. If, as I maintain, ethics comprises several activities and if it has to deal with subject matters as diverse as persons, dolphins, cultural groups, and trees, why has ethics not pursued the same path as the sciences—or, rather, paths? That is, why not explore the possibility that ethics can also be partitioned?

---

4. See Paul W. Taylor, *Respect for Nature* (Princeton: Princeton University Press, 1986); J.L. Arbor presents a coherent and persuasive plea for plants—coldly logical, however heartfelt—in "Animal Chauvinism, Plant-Regarding Ethics, and the Torture of Trees," *Australasian Journal of Philosophy* 64 (1986): 335.

5. Steen, "Mathematics Today," pp. 4–5. To pursue the mathematical model for a further moment, Godel and others have laid to rest the hope of ever producing a complete and consistent formal system powerful enough to prove or to refute every statement it can formulate. Although what happens in math is hardly a conclusive model of what should go on in morals, it does make one wonder how much of moral philosophy implicitly proceeds on the assumption that a morality not only has axioms (or even solider starting points), but that they are axioms more powerful than math's! And if that is not the assumption, what takes its place?

Perhaps the analogy is simply too weak. However free science may be to partition, one might argue, ethics appears to be under peculiarly strong constraints to remain monistic. The argument might go like this. Alternative descriptions of how the world is (or might be) can peacefully coexist over a broad latitude without logical conflict—e.g., in most contexts, one can indulge either in a particle or a wave version of light without chafing. And even where apparently irreconcilable conflict does erupt at one level (say, at the subatomic) the participants at other levels (those doing cellular biology) can ordinarily remain agnostic. By contrast, ethics (one is tempted to say) is not merely descriptive. It has as its ultimate aim choosing the right *action*. Unlike describing, in which subtly overlapping nuances of adjective and predicate are tolerable, acting seems to lend itself to, if not to demand, binary yes/no, right/wrong alternatives.

If this is the argument why morals require monism, it appears to me unpersuasive. There is, to begin with, the question of agenda: one wants from moral reasoning not merely the verdict, whether or not to do act *a*, but also what the choice set is: *a, b, c, . . .*? Moral thought is a service when it is populating and clarifying the range of morally creditable alternatives. Hence, attention to plural approaches would find justification if, by stimulating us to define and come at problems from different angles, it were to advance our grasp of alternatives.[6]

Perhaps most importantly, let us remind ourselves that actions are in the physical world; the evaluation of them is intellectual. Many persons (are these the ''moralists''?) would probably be pleased if our moral reasoning had the power to map a unique, precise

moral evaluation for each alternative action. It would give us much the same pleasure (tinged with a not entirely ingenuous surprise) that mathematicians derive from confirmation that the world ''out there,'' while theoretically at liberty to go its own haphazard way, is conforming in general to the elegant inventions of our intellects.[7] Why, when we set out to apply our best moral theories to the unruly world of human conduct should we confidently expect more—a more meticulous isomorphism, more freedom from inconsistency, more power of resolution?

Specifically, it may be a (not terribly interesting) truth that an act can be defined in such a way that we are left with no alternative but to do it or not—a feature of the world that makes monism superficially attractive. But even if so, it is a fact about the world that our best moral reasoning may just not be able to rise to or to map. The rightness and wrongness of some acts may lie beyond our power to deduce or otherwise discover. Key moral properties may not lend themselves to produce a transitive ordering across the choice set.

THE VARIABLES

If we are to explore bringing our relations with different sorts of things under different moral governances, then we face the question: by reference to what intellectual elements might governances vary domain to domain?

(a) *Grain of description.* Morals is concerned with comparing actions, characters, and states of affairs. To compare alternatives, as a logical first step, we have to settle upon the appropriate vocabulary of description. For example, in evaluating our impact on humans, we consistently adopt a grain of description that individuates organisms: each person counts equally. In evaluating other actions, there is often intuitive support for some other unit, e.g., the hive or the herd or the habitat. I am not claiming that these

---

6. Note that this rationale for pluralism could be endorsed on heuristic grounds by a monist, even by a moral realist who presumed (as I do not) that all the candidates for truth *disclosed* by this many-angled attack on the problem will in the end be submitted to a single adjudicatory principle to decide which of them is *uniquely and truly right.* Compare the position Paul Feyerabend adopts with respect to the natural sciences, viz., that the history of sciences reveals an incompleteness and even inconsistency of each framework which should be regarded as routine and inevitable, and that a pluralism of theories and metaphysical viewpoints should be nourished as a means of advancing on the truth. Feyerabend, *Against Method* (London: Verso, 1978): 35-53.

7. See E.P. Wigner, ''The Unreasonable Effectiveness of Mathematics in the Natural Sciences,'' in Wigner, *Symmetries and Reflections* (Cambridge: M.I.T. Press, 1970).

intutitions are self-validating, only that they, and their implications, merit sustained and systematic attention. Each vying grain of description is integral to a separate editorial viewpoint. Suppose that a bison naturally (of its own action) faces drowning in a river in a national park. Should we rescue it, or let "nature take its course"? One viewpoint emphasizes the individual animal; another (favored, apparently, by the park service)[8] consigns the individual animal to the background and emphasizes the larger unit, the park ecosystem. Another viewpoint emphasizes species. Each focus brings along its allied constellation of concepts. In invoking the finer grain, focusing upon the individual animal, we scan for such properties as the animal's capacity to feel pain, its intelligence, its understanding of the situation, and its suffering. None of these terms apply to the park. Instead, the ecosystem version brings out stability, resilience, uniqueness, and energy flow.

(b) *Mood.* What I mean by mood may best be illustrated by a contrast between morals and law. Law, like morals, often speaks in negative injunctions, i.e., "Thou shalt not kill . . ." and "Thou shalt not park in the red zone. . . ." But the law always proceeds to specify, in each case, a sanction which expresses the relative severity of the offense, viz., ". . . or face the death penalty," ". . . or face a $12 fine." The result is a legal discussion endowed with fine-tuned nuances. By contrast, much of moral philosophy, inspirited with monism, is conducted at a level of abstraction at which every act is assumed to be either-or, either good or bad; there is either a duty to do *x* or a duty not to do *x*; a right to *y* or no right to *y*. Monist moral discourse, then, lacks the refinements of expression that enrich legal discourse. As long as monism reigns, significant distinctions between cases, distinctions marked by nuances of feeling and belief that moral reflection might investigate and amplify, lack a semantic foothold.

By contrast, pluralism welcomes diversified material out of which moral judgments can be fashioned, particularly as we cross from one domain to another.

Moral regard for lakes may seem silly—or even unintelligible—if we are required to flesh it out by reference to the same rules, and express our judgments in the same mood, as those that apply to a person. But there are prospective middle grounds. Our lake-affecting actions might have to be judged in terms of distinct deontic operators understood to convey a relatively lenient mood, perhaps something like "that which is morally welcome" or that which will bring credit or discredit to our character.

(c) *Logical (formal) texture.* Every system of intellectual rules is girded on a number of properties that endow it with a distinct logical texture. These range from whether it is subject to closure (whether it is capable of yielding one unique solution for each question that can be opened within it) to its attitude on contradictions and inconsistencies. As to closure, the monist implicitly assumes that morals must be modelled on ordinary arithmetic. There is one and only one solution to 4 + 7; so too there should be, for each dilemma of morals, one right answer. And monism rejects, too, any system of ethical postulates from which we could derive conflicting and contradictory prescriptions. After all, what would we think of a system of geometry from whose postulates we could derive both that two triangles were, and that they were not, congruent?

Pluralism is not so dogmatic—or perhaps one should just say not so "optimistic"—about the prospects of assimilating morals to (slightly idealized conceptions of) arithmetic or geometry. We simply may not be able to devise a single system of morals, operative throughout, that is subject to closure, and in which the laws of noncontradiction[9] and excluded middle[10] are in vigilant command.[11]

---

8. See Jim Robbins, "Do not Feed the Bears?" *Natural History,* January 1984, p. 12.

9. The law of contradiction holds that it cannot be the case that both a proposition *p* and its negation −*p* are true.

10. The law of excluded middle maintains that either a proposition *p* or its negation −*p* must be true; there is no middle possibility.

11. See Freidrich Waismann, "Language Strata," in *Logic and Language,* ed: Anthony Flew (New York: Anchor Books, 1965), p. 237. The notion I present of multiple conceptual planes with systematically varying formal requirements owes much to Waismann's musings about "language strata."

RECONCILING THE DIFFERENCES

There are many problems with this pluralistic approach. Many of the stumbling blocks—those that I could identify by myself, or with a little help from my friends—are dealt with in *Earth and Other Ethics.*[12] It can be defended from the obvious charge that it must stumble into moral relativism of the rankest sort.[13] But it faces comparable problems that are not so easy to dismiss. It would appear that a pluralist, analyzing some choice situation in one framework (say, one that accounts for species in an appropriate way) may conclude that act *a* is right. The same person, analyzing the situation in another framework (one built, say, from a person-regarding viewpoints) concludes *b*. Are not such conflicts paralyzing? And do they not therefore render pluralism methodologically unacceptable?

To begin with, the fact that morals might admit of several allowable viewpoints does not mean that each and every dilemma will require several competing analyses. Assuming that remotely probable and minimal consequences can be ignored, some choices may be carried through solely within one framework. For example, whatever morality has to say about whether to uproot an individual plant could be provided, presumably, by the appropriate one-plant framework. No excursion into the agent's obligations to the plant's species, or to mankind, or to kin or whatever would be called for.

We can anticipate myriad other circumstances in which thorough analysis requires defining and processing the situation in each of several frameworks. But in some subset of those situations each of the various analyses will endorse the same action. We all know that vegetarianism, for example, can be supported both within a framework that posits the moral considerateness of animals and one that values humans alone, viz., that by eating animals the planet uses protein inefficiently, therefore reducing aggregate human welfare, even robbing badly undernour-

ished persons of a minimally human existence. (What we do not know—and ought to examine—is why approaching such a question from several angles, a technique well-accepted in other areas,[14] should be indicted as an ignoble and impure way to go about doing philosophy).

There is a third set of cases in which more than one framework will appear appropriate, and the different frameworks, rather than mutually endorsing the same result, reinforce different, even inconsistent actions. The potential for conflicts is there—but no more so than in any moral system that deems the proper choice to be a function of several independent criteria: welfare maximization, duties to kin, respect for life, the values of community and friendship. How do we "combine," where rights analysis says one thing, utility analysis, another?

One possibility is to formulate a lexical ordering rule. For example, our obligations to neighbor-persons, as determined on a framework built on neo-Kantian principles, might claim priority up to the point where our neighbor-persons have reached a certain level of comfort and protection. But when that level has been reached, considerations of, say, species preservation as determined per another framework, or of future generations per another, would be brought into play.

One might claim, with partial justification, that in those circumstances in which we accepted mediation by reference to a master rule, we are reintroducing a sort of monism "after all." But even in these cases, it is an "after all" significant enough to keep pluralism from collapsing into monism. Under monism, a problem is defined appropriately for evaluation by the relevant standard, in such a way that all the "irrelevant" descriptions are left behind from the outset.

---

12. Christopher D. Stone, *Earth and Other Ethics* (New York: Harper & Row, 1987).

13. See note 3 above.

14. I do not mean only lawyers, who do this sort of thing unabashedly all of the time. As for the natural sciences, see Feyerabend, *Against Method.* In mathematics, Gorg Polya, *How to Solve It* (Princeton: Princeton University Press, 1957) is a classic exposition of how mathematicians may stalk a single problem with widely assorted techniques (indirect proofs, reductio ad absurdums, analogy), ultimately to be convinced of the truth of a solution by the dual standards of formal proof and intuition.

The problem, so defined, is worked through to solution without further distraction. Under pluralism, a single situation, variously described, may produce several analyses and various conclusions. If a master rule is to be introduced, it is to be introduced only after the separate reasoning processes have gone their separate ways to yield a conflicting set of conclusions, *a, b, c, d.* The master rule is brought to bear on that set, none of whose members would necessarily have been constructed had the procedure been subjected to the monist stricture that a single standard, such as utilitarianism, had to be applied consistently and exclusively from the start.

Finally, and most troublesomely, there are quandaries for which each of our multiple analyses not only endorse inconsistent actions, but for which no lexical rule is available, and for which further intuitive reflection[15] reveals no further, best-of-all, alternative. We can imagine as a ''worst case scenario'' an outcome not merely of the form *a* is mandatory per one framework and *b* is mandatory per the other (and we cannot do both), but rather of the form *a* is mandatory and −*a* is mandatory (*a* is impermissible). One must, and must not, pull the trigger. What then?

This much is clear: those two edicts, taken together, tell us (logically) nothing. We would say of the total system of beliefs that it had *disappointed us in the particular case.* We would have to agree, too, that if such out-and-out conflicts were in each and every case endemic to pluralist methodology, the whole system we constructed, would have to be abandoned. But suppose that such outcomes, while possible, should prove exceptional. Then we could regard their occasional occurrences as a particularly poignant indication of the total system's indeterminacy.

This prospect illustrates one of the principal monist-pluralist dividing lines referred to earlier: How fatal is it to a system of moral rules if it fails to furnish a single unambiguous answer to each choice we recognize as morally significant? If we cannot devise a whale-regarding moral framework that gives us one confident right answer to every action affecting whales, do we have to withdraw whales from consideration (except as resources in a human-oriented framework) entirely? If our whale-regarding and our person-regarding edicts conflict, does one or the other or both of the systems responsible have to be dismantled?

As I have already indicated, such a standard, if to be applied with an even hand (and fin) throughout, would cramp the range of morals significantly. Better to come right out and consider the alternative: that we may have to abandon the ambition to find perfect consistency and the ''one right answer'' to every moral quandary, either because a single answer does not exist, or because our best analytical methods are not up to finding it.[16]

In some circumstances, if we can identify and eliminate the options that are morally unacceptable, we may have gone as far as moral thought can take us. It may be that the choices that remain are equally good or equally evil or equally perplexing.[17]

This does not mean that as a moral community we are relieved from striving for a higher, if ultimately imperfect consensus on progressively better answers.[18] Nor does it mean that, as regards the indeterminate set, one can be arbitrary—as though, from that point on, flipping a coin is as good as we can do.

---

15. I mean by intuitive reflection a process of analysis that leads to a right-feeling judgment, but one for which, even after the conclusion, we cannot offer any proof, perhaps not even specify the premises.

16. As Hilary Putnam puts it, ''The question whether there is one objectively best morality or a number of objectively best moralities which, hopefully, agree on a good many principles or in a good many cases, is simply the question whether, given the desiderata . . . [of] the enterprise . . . will it turn out that these desiderata select a best morality or a group of moralities which have a significant measure of agreement on a number of significant questions.'' Hilary Putnam, *Meaning and the Moral Sciences* (Boston: Routledge & Kegan Paul, 1978), p. 84.

17. See Leibniz's stumper: ''It is certain that God sets greater store by a man than a lion; nevertheless it can hardly be said with certainty that God prefers a single man in all respects to the whole of lion-kind.'' *Theodicy,* trans. E. M. Hoggard (New Haven: Yale University Press, 1952), Sec. 118.

18. One might even expect this endeavor to take the form of integrating, or at least striving to integrate, originally independent ''plural'' frameworks into something grander and more unified— much as the theoretical physicist will continue to scout about for a grand unified field theory. But in the meantime, the practical and even playful work of significance will take place on humbler levels.

It is by the choices we affirm in this zone of ultimate uncertainty that we have our highest opportunity to exercise our freedoms and define our characters. Particularly as the range of moral considerateness is extended outward from those who are (in various ways) "near" us, people who take morals seriously, who are committed to giving good reasons, will come to irreconcilably conflicting judgments on many issues. But the main question now is this: what model of decision process provides the best prospect for constructing the best answers reason can furnish?

DISCUSSION TOPICS

1. What does Stone mean by "grain of description," "mood," and "logical texture"? Give your own example of each.

2. In your view, is Stone's pluralism really moral relativism? Why or why not?

3. In an article critical of Stone's pluralism (footnote 6 to the chapter introduction), J. Baird Callicott argues that because different moral theories imply different metaphysical systems, moral pluralism would require an impossible shift between different metaphysical views. In considering this objection, give an example of an environmental problem which might be best decided using a zoocentric individualism (Chapter 7) and one which might be best decided using a land ethic approach (Chapter 8). Then explain how the metaphysical view underlying zoocentric individualism differs from that of the land ethic. Is it possible or desirable for one person to switch between these views in order to decide how to deal with the two environmental problems?

Postmodern Environmental Ethics: Ethics as Bioregional Narrative

Jim Cheney

Professor Jim Cheney (b. 1941) teaches at the University of Wisconsin at Waukesha. His interests include feminism and American Indian philosophies in addition to environmental ethics. In the following essay he attacks modernism, *a term which refers to "the world view which has developed out of the seventeenth-century Galilean-Cartesian-Baconian-Newtonian science"[1] and which today is still the dominant world view. According to modern science, nature is mechanistic, devoid of purpose, freedom, and feelings. The self is understood to be an isolated mind. Cheney refers to modernism as "totalizing" because it claims to capture everything in its abstract net, disregarding individual differences. Modernism is "foundationalist" because modernism claims to present fundamental, "essential" knowledge of the ultimate truth—the one true story. Modernism is "colonizing" because it abstracts concepts and theories from the settings in which they have developed and forces them upon the minds of people in other places.*

Postmodernism is the twentieth century countermovement to modernism which has occurred in philosophy, history, architecture, sociology, the psychology of science, and in the sciences themselves. Philosophically, the term refers to two different movements. "Deconstructive postmodernism" deconstructs or eliminates concepts such as God, self, purpose, a real world, and truth as correspondence, on the basis that such concepts are socially constructed. "Constructive postmodernism" revises modern concepts in important ways but maintains that there is a world beyond human language and society which can be apprehended and spoken of and perhaps to.

In his essay Cheney advocates a constructive postmodernism in which concepts are "contextual": inseparable from geography and historical experience.

---

1. David Ray Griffin, ed., *The Reenchantment of Science* (Albany: State University of New York Press, 1988), p. x. See also Griffin's other publications in the Suny Series in Constructive Postmodern Thought.

Instead of imposing a universal system on individuals, language articulates individual experience without distorting or repressing it. Such language takes the form of narrative, "storied residence" (Rolston), and myth. In environmental ethics, this contextualizing discourse is expressed as bioregionalism, in which we ground ourselves in our relation to the land. The human-land community provides moral instruction in fostering individual and community health. The land is not "Mother Earth," carrying the ambivalent projection of the human mother, but the nurturing other in a sense wider than the human. We experience the local, bioregional truth of our intersection with the land.

The landscape and the language are the same,
And we ourselves are language and are land.

Conrad Aiken[1]

I can only answer the question "What am I to do?" if I can answer the prior question "Of what story or stories do I find myself a part?" . . . Mythology, in its original sense, is at the heart of things.

Alasdair MacIntyre[2]

An environmental ethic does not want to abstract out universals, if such there be, from all this drama of life, formulating some set of duties applicable across the whole. . . . The logic of the home, the ecology, is finally narrative. . . . If a holistic ethic is really to incorporate the whole story, it must systematically embed itself in historical eventfulness. Else it will not really be objective. It will not be appropriate, well adapted, for the way humans actually fit into their niches.

Holmes Rolston III[3]

The move from is to ought, which logicians have typically thought it their job to solve before any naturalistic ethics could be judged sound, is transformed into movement along a story line.

Holmes Rolston III[4]

In *A Sand County Almanac* Aldo Leopold offers the following general principle: "A thing is right when it tends to preserve the integrity, stability, and beauty of the biotic community. It is wrong when it tends otherwise."[5] Holmes Rolston III suggests that we understand this principle as "deeply embedded in

[Leopold's] love for the Wisconsin sand counties,''[6] that we understand it as belonging to Leopold's ''storied residence'' in those counties. Rather than view it simply as a universal norm perhaps *suggested* to Leopold by his life and work, we are urged to understand it as inflected by historicity, as *essentially* tied to place and Leopold's narrative embeddedness in, and understanding of, the sand counties of Wisconsin.

Rolston's notion of ''storied residence'' can be understood as urging environmental ethicists to make the postmodern turn. It can also be understood in the spirit of Alasdair MacIntyre's recent insistence upon the central importance of narrative to ethical thought, an insistence which is, likewise, a rejection of modernist ethical thought. In this paper I pick up on Rolston's suggestion in an indirect way by sketching a path for a postmodernism which makes use of certain notions current in contemporary environmentalism. In so doing, my hope is that this transformed postmodernism will, in turn, have a transformative effect on environmental ethics which, protestations to the contrary notwithstanding, has almost always been conceived of in modernist ethical terms. In reconstructing postmodernism I am at the same time setting an agenda for reconceiving environmental ethics in contextual and postmodern terms.

In a recent article, Biddy Martin and Chandra Talpade Mohanty state with admirable clarity both the limitations and potential of postmodernism for feminist discourse in particular (and, by implication, for any discourse aimed at the deconstruction of totalizing and colonizing discourse). In discussing the work of Minnie Bruce Pratt, Martin and Mohanty contrast her insistence upon ''our responsibility for remapping boundaries and renegotiating connections'' with

> the more abstract critiques of ''feminism'' and the charges of totalization that come from the ranks of antihumanist intellectuals. For without denying the importance of their vigilante attacks on humanist beliefs in ''man'' and Absolute Knowledge wherever they appear, it is equally important to point out the political limitations of an insistence on ''indeterminacy'' which implicitly, when not explicitly, denies the critic's own situatedness in the social, and in effect refuses to acknowledge the critic's own institutional home.[7]

The project that emerges from the acknowledgement of situatedness while refusing modernist essentialism and totalization is that of initiating a ''complicated working out of the relationship between home, identity, and community that calls into question the notion of a coherent, historically continuous, stable identity and works to expose the political stakes concealed in such equations.'' This is accomplished by grounding the narrative account not in a ''coherent, historically continuous, stable identity'' but rather

> in the geography, demography, and architecture of the communities that are [Pratt's] ''homes''; these factors function as an organizing mode in the text, providing a specific concreteness and movement for the narrative.

Further,

> Geography, demography, and architecture, as well as the configuration of her relationships to particular people . . . serve to indicate the fundamentally relational nature of identity and the negations on which the assumption of a singular, fixed, and essential self is based.

Relations to people are elaborated ''through spatial relations and historical knowledges,'' the importance of which ''lies in the contextualization of [those relations], and the consequent avoidance of any purely psychological explanation.''

Narrative is the key then, but it is narrative grounded in geography rather than in a linear, essentialized, narrative self. The narrative style required for situating ourselves without making essentializing or totalizing moves is an elaboration of relations which forgoes the coherence, continuity, and consistency insisted on by totalizing discourse. Our position, our *location,* is understood in the elaboration of relations in a nonessentializing narrative achieved through a grounding in the geography of our lives. Self and geography are bound together in a narrative which locates us in the moral space of defining relations. ''*Psychology without ecology is lonely* and vice versa.''[8] *Mind*scapes are as multiple as the *land*scapes which ground them. Totalizing masculine discourse (and essentializing feminist discourse) give way to a contextualized discourse of place.

Why a discourse or narrative of relation to place?

And what is meant by 'place' here? We can work toward an answer to these questions by considering some of the possible alternatives for a contextualizing narrative as the means for locating oneself in a moral space out of which a whole and healthy self, community, and earth can emerge.

The fragility of the inturning process, the internal narrative in isolation from community and world is obvious. A particularly poignant example of this fragility is related by Edith Cobb in her book *The Ecology of Imagination in Childhood*. She relates the story of Alice, a child she describes as ''surrounded by empty psychological space''; her narrative construction of self had to operate entirely within the confines of her own interior space. The result (or actuality) of this is schizophrenia. In extreme cases such as this it is brought home to us that what we take to be the interior space of the self, our individual essence, is really an internalized landscape or, better, one term of a constructed narrative of self-in-place. Cobb's account of Alice's life brings this out clearly. In one situation only is Alice embedded in a geography larger than her own closed-in self. This occurs in yearly visits to the family summer home, when a ''sea change'' comes over her in the context of an immersion in the natural world. Alice's lyrical portrait of these summers poignantly illustrates the necessity of landscape for the coherent construction of a self:

Canoes. Water against the paddle pushing ahead, home late, moon on the water, crickets singing, stumbling up the path carrying blankets. . . . Michigan and Michigan again, always different, each year it changed—it didn't change, I did, a new me in the same place. Each summer I would wonder what would happen . . . each one with something new, unexpected, exciting, for me to have and to remember, never lose it, always have it, in me, never forget it, just think about it, relive it over and over, love it and keep it, part of me . . . for me, *is me*.[9]

As the reality of the natural world of Alice's summer home slips away, leaving Alice ''surrounded by empty psychological space,'' the writing changes:

Twisting, revolving, rotating, squirming, wriggling, slithering, shaky . . . water breaking, sliding past, new water passing by, turning white, turning black, turning green, turning blue, going far away, never come back, off to nowhere . . .

The writing deteriorates further: ''dissipation,'' Cobb says, ''of all solidity into shapeless feeling; helpless longing follows, ending on a note of bewildered exhaustion.''[9] The necessity of landscape for the construction of self is clear—''psychology without ecology is lonely.''

What happens when the landscape includes only the human community and its institutions? Here Martin and Mohanty's analysis of Pratt's autobiographical narrative is illuminating. We have looked at the positive side of narrative contextualized by reference to geography. There is a negative aspect, however, when that geography is one of human making:

The very stability, familiarity, and security of these physical structures are undermined by the discovery that these buildings and streets witnessed and obscured particular race, class, and gender struggles. The realization . . . politicizes and undercuts any physical anchors she might use to construct a coherent notion of home or her identity in relation to it.

This cultural geography serves as well to indicate

the negations on which the assumption of a singular, fixed, and essential self is based. For the narrator, such negativity is represented by a rigid identity such as that of her father, which sustains its appearance of stability by defining itself in terms of what it is not. . . . The ''self'' in this narrative is not an essence or truth concealed by patriarchal layers of deceit and lying in wait of discovery, revelation or birth.

It is this very conception of self that Pratt likens to entrapment. When ''unity is exposed to be a potentially repressive fiction'' in this way, one of the critical functions of narrative is to undercut such identities, such ''homes'':

''The system'' is revealed to be not one but multiple, overlapping, intersecting systems or relations that are historically constructed and recreated through everyday practices and interactions, and that implicate the individual in contradictory ways. . . .

Community, then, is the product of work, of struggle, it is inherently unstable, contextual, it has to be constantly reevaluated in relation to critical political priorities. . . . There is also, however, a strong suggestion that community is related to experience, to history. For if identity and community are not the product of essential connections, neither are they merely the product of political urgency or necessity. For Pratt, they are a constant recontextualizing of the relationship between personal/group history and political priorities.

Within the geography of human landscape the contextual voice can emerge in clarity and health only through a ''constant recontextualizing'' which prevents the oppressive and distorting overlays of cultural institutions (representing a return of the repressed) from gathering false, distorting, and unhealthy identities out of ''the positive desire for unity, for Oneness.''[10]

Is there any setting, any landscape, in which contextualizing discourse is not constantly in danger of falling prey to the distortions of essentializing, totalizing discourse? Perhaps not. A partial way out might be envisioned, however, if we expand the notion of a contextualizing narrative of place so as to include nature—nature as one more player in the construction of community. My suggestion is that a postmodernist emphasis on contextualism and narrative as a means of locating oneself offers us an alternative mode of understanding bioregionalism and, conversely, that bioregionalism is a natural extension of the line of thought being developed by those advocating a view of ethics as contextualist and narrative. What I propose is that we extend these notions of context and narrative outward so as to include not just the human community, but also the land, one's community in a larger sense.[11] Bioregions provide a way of grounding narrative without essentializing the idea of self, a way of mitigating the need for ''constant recontextualization'' to undercut the oppressive and distorting overlays of cultural institutions.

Listen to the following passage concerning the Ainu, the indigenous people of Japan (The Kamui referred to are spirits of natural phenomena—everything is a Kamui for the Ainu.):

> The Ainu believed that the housefire was an eye of the Kamui that watched and welcomed all game that entered through the hunting window. As game entered through the hunting window . . . the fire reported its treatment

back to the appropriate Kamui community. Fire is the appropriate witness for the *resource,* flickering warm light rising from the broken limbs of trees. . . . The mythic images circle and knot together into a reality that is a story, a parable, where facts are legendary incidents, not data.[12]

One significant feature of this passage is that it locates moral imperatives in the watchful eye of the housefire. The reality that is knit together as story and parable carries not the ''intrinsic value'' so much discussed in the literature in environmental ethics, but rather actual moral *instruction.* An important aspect of the construction or evolution of mythic images is their ability to articulate such moral imperatives and to carry them in such a way that they actually *do* instruct; that they *locate* us in a *moral* space which is at the same time the space we live in physically; that they locate us in such a way that these moral imperatives have the lived reality of fact. In the case of the Ainu this is achieved, in part, by including all of nature within the moral community.[13] For a genuinely contextualist ethic to include the land, the land must *speak* to us; we must stand in *relation* to it; it must *define* us, and we it.

A striking feature of contextualized language, particularly in traditional cultures such as those of American Indians, is that it

> bridges subject and object worlds, inner and outer. Language is the path, the game trail, the river, the reverie between them. It shimmers there, revealing and nourishing their interdependence. Each word *bears* and *locates* our meetings with the world. A word is a dipped breath, a bit of spirit (*inspire, expire*) wherein we hear the weather. Our ''tongues'' taste the world we eat. At root [this] language is sacramental.[14]

This observation is commonplace concerning discourse in traditional cultures. The construction of the modernist subject has been a long time in the making. It took much time and cultural effort to generate the intuitive ''obviousness'' of the Cartesian privatized self. The modernist period in philosophy, with its creation of absolute subjectivity and the need for a foundationalist epistemology to regain connection with the world, is only the latest installment in the story of the cultural construction of the subjective self.

As an example of language which "bridges subject and object worlds" Tom Jay refers to the place of the salmon in the lives of Northwest Coast Indians, the way in which what is said and done in relationship to salmon incorporates an understanding, including a *moral* understanding, of health—health in self, community, earth and the relationships between these.

> [S]almon . . . are literal *embodiments* of the wisdom of the *locale,* the resource. The salmon are the wisdom of the northwest biome. They are the old souls, worshipful children of the land. *Psychology without ecology is lonely* and vice versa. The salmon is not merely a projection, a symbol of some inner process, it is rather the embodiment of the soul that nourishes us all. . . . [T]o the original peoples of the Pacific Northwest, salmon were not merely food. To them, salmon were people who lived in houses far away under the sea. Each year they undertook to visit the human people because the Indian peoples always treated them as honored guests. When the salmon people traveled, they donned their salmon disguises and these they left behind perhaps in the way we leave flowers or food when visiting friends. To the Indians the salmon were a resource in the deep sense, great generous beings whose gifts gave life. The salmon were energy: not "raw" energy, but intelligent perceptive energy. The Indians understood that salmon's gift involved them in an ethical system that resounded in every corner of their locale. The aboriginal landscape was a democracy of spirits where everyone listened, careful not to offend the *resource* they were a working part of.[15]

This understanding of the salmon performs a major integrative function in Northwest Coast Indian society. It is this integrative function which is the criterion which guides development of the image.

We in the postmodernist West are only beginning to see such possibilities in language. Postmodernism makes possible for us the conception of language conveying an understanding of self, world, and community which is consciously tuned to, and shaped by, considerations of the health and well-being of individual, community, and land and our ethical responsibilities to each. This postmodernist possibility is an actuality in the world of tribal myth and ritual.[16]

The current emphasis in contemporary feminist thought on contextualism, narrative discourse, standpoint epistemologies, and "cultural and discursive birthplaces"[17] helps give us access to the discourse of tribal peoples, with which it has significant affinities. Likewise, the role of the land in tribal discourse as well as the details of its narrative and mythic style can significantly inform postmodernist thought on discourse. The postmodernist account of ethics as bioregional narrative which I explore in this paper owes much to meditation on the role of land in tribal discourse.

It has often been noticed that mythical cosmologies carry thought, that they are the vehicles of richly textured understandings of human nature and community cohesion. John Wisdom and Paul Ricoeur, for example, have noted the quite sophisticated and complex understandings of human psychology embedded in Christian cosmology.[18] The difficulty with that cosmology in particular is in its relationship to the land. It has been argued by Shepard[19] and others that although the religion of the Desert Fathers *was* a response to the desert landscape, it was often one of denial, one which set culture over and against nature, history over and against cyclical mythologies firmly embedded in place. James Hillman has noted that monotheism functions as a mechanism to deny the voices of polytheism, those voices which speak from all dimensions and aspects of one's experience of, and relation to, the world; voices which, if allowed to speak, would tell not only of distortions, but of the health that is there, or might be there.[20] These voices can also be found in a monotheistic cosmology, but they come through indirection or as background, subliminal, buried, as in dreams. The monotheistic overlay, the narrative of a totalizing history, a salvation history rooted in the beyond of a father god distinct from his creation, is a rejection of precisely those elements which make mythical images bearers of health, images which gather to themselves knowledge of place and its health, community and the dynamics of community health—all woven together in a narrative that *instructs* by locating us in a moral space in which moral imperatives are present to the community with the force and presence of reality, of fact. The mythic images and narratives which gather to themselves knowledge of place and community and the health of each must be free of the influence of such world-denying and self-truncating projects so they can be responsive to world and self. And they must be rich and complex enough to articulate an understanding of both self and world and to weave them together into a unity in which an understanding of self and community *is* an understanding of the place in which life is lived out and in which an understanding of place *is* an understanding of self and community.

Where are *we* to find those "mythic images" which "circle and knot together into a reality" that is life-giving, healthy, liberating? Where we must look is to the *mind*scape/*land*scape which emerges from our narrative and mythical embeddedness in some particular place. This begins with the inscribing of the nervous system *in* the landscape; the body is the instrument of our knowledge of the world.[21]

With language comes a taxonomy of the world, an ordering of our cosmos, and a positioning of ourselves within this matrix. Eventually the cosmos comes to express a moral order—it instructs us in virtue of its very manner of containing us. It is critical that just as the infant passes from the nurturing womb into a nurturing relationship with the first caretaker(s), so the child must pass from this to a sense of embeddedness in a nurturing cosmos. Shepard claims that without this there is fixation at the earlier developmental level, a fixation on ambivalences engendered in relation to one's first nurturer(s) which would have been resolved by passing into what he calls the "earth matrix." This second "grounding" or "bonding" to the earth matrix nourishes the growing child in ways that the earlier bonding cannot achieve by itself. By satsifying emerging urges, the earlier bonding is incorporated in the latter bonding; the ambivalences which begin to emerge do not become objects of fixation. The result is not an *identification* with nature; identification is an essentializing move motivated by attempts to deal with ambivalence. As Shepard notes, the lovers of the earth and the destroyers of the earth often have one thing in common: the attempt to handle ambivalence without resolving it, using the defective tools of identification or dichotomization, respectively.[22] What one should do is *relate* to nature as "satisfying other."

Shepard's account of the ways in which we have lost this bioregional connectedness is instructive, for it points to the difficulties that must be faced in the "constant recontextualization" discussed by Martin and Mohanty as well as to some features of "storied residence" that might temper these difficulties. The central claim is that when social structures emerged in an agrarian society which no longer allowed for the broadening of the child's relationship from the human nurturer to nature as the nurturing other in a wider sense, the image of the mother, with all its ambivalence, was *projected* onto nature. The result was a *representation* of the mother rather than a clear vision of nature as nurturer but *not* mother. The whole complex of Mother Earth imagery is the result of this projection, making Mother Earth the object of highly ambivalent attitudes and behavior. The love-hate relationship to nature and the need to dominate nature seems to begin precisely with the rise into prominence of Mother Earth imagery.[23] To resolve this particular problem it should not be necessary to return to a preagrarian, gatherer-hunter life. It *is* necessary, however, that we do not take existing, humanly constructed models such as machines, words, and human society as our models and metaphors of order, for these already embed our projections and carry with them the return of the repressed. One consequence of this tendency is a literalization of nature at the conscious level and its use as a projection screen by unconscious processes. Bioregionalism could help turn this around if it were understood in light of the kind of contextualist approach I have been advocating.

The cosmos constructed as a result of a sense of embeddedness in the "earth matrix" first nourishes and later instructs. "Through myth and its ritual enactments," Shepard says, "natural things are not only themselves but a speaking." Passage into adolescence *not* marked by ambivalence and fixation at earlier levels precludes perception of the world as an illusion to be transcended. Rather than graduating "*from* the world," Shepard says, the child graduates "into its significance."[24]

That this second grounding is in the natural world is important. As the ground out of which we have evolved, it can be satisfying in a way that no substitute for this matrix could be. What is desired is a complex system of images or myths of the humanland community which *instructs* and does so in a way that is felt to be both obligatory and fostering of individual and community health. These purposes can be accomplished best when the community has before it a coherent model of health to draw on. When this model is the one within which, and in interaction with which, both the individual and the community must live, we get precisely the images we need to mediate our relationships to one another and to the land. But nature must be transformed in image to perform this function. A Western scientific description of the specifics of the ecosystem within which one lives is not adequate. It provides the wrong kind of myth. It can and ought to *inform* our construction of appropriate mythical images, but it cannot function as the centerpiece of a viable environmental ethic, much less a *mythos* for our times. Elizabeth Bird asks whether we would want "the world [that] ecology would construct for us if it were to win political hegemony in the sciences?"[25] The *mythos* into which modern ecology is drawn in the minds of many radical environmentalists is that of organicism, the "dream of natural (unforced) community":

> For many radical and antiliberal thinkers, including many feminists considering sciences and technologies, [organicism] has . . . appeared to be an alternative to both antagonistic opposition and to regulatory functionalism. It is easy to forget that organicism is a form of longing for a spontaneous and always healthy body, a perfect opposite to the technicist and reductionist boogey man. . . . Organicism is the analytical longing . . . for purity outside the disruptions of the "artificial." It is the reversed, mirror image of other forms of longing for transcendence.[26]

The integrity of the Western scientific model must, for the purposes I have been sketching (but not for all purposes), give way to the requirement of the health and well-being of individual, community, and land in the construction of an image of nature (with us in it) which effectively instructs.[27] If value is implicit in our descriptions of the world and our place in it, then the narratives we construct will embody value and orient us.

What we want then is language that grows out of experience and articulates it, language intermediate between self and world, their *intersection,* carrying knowledge of both, knowledge charged with valuation and instruction. This is language in which "the clues to the meaning of life [are] embodied in natural things, where everyday life [is] inextricable from spiritual significance and encounter."[28] The vision received in the American Indian vision quest, for example, is a culturally mediated intersection of self and world. It is a gift and must be located in the world. It is important not to conceive of these images as projections; they are intersections, encounters. This way of putting it acknowledges both our active construction of reality and nature's role in these negotiations. We should say with Aiken that "the landscape and the language are the same,/And we ourselves are language and are land."[29] Such language mediates experience and the world with language alive and responsive to our interaction with the world, language which articulates not the *logos* of the system as we in the West have come to understand this, but our *telos* within it. It is a language of instruction; and in order to instruct it must embed an understanding of self and world and the relation between the two. The task then is to tell the best stories we can. The tales we tell of our, and our communities', "storied residence" in place are tales not of universal truth, but of local truth, bioregional truth.

The notion of a mythic, narrative, and bioregional construction of self and community, and the "storied residence" out of which action proceeds, has a close affinity with, and relevance to, feminist postmodernist attempts to deal with the "fractured identities" of multiple female voices in the wake of the deconstruction of patriarchal totalizing and essentializing discourse. Listen to the following comparison of Australian aboriginal people with the villager/farmer:

> [For the aboriginal peoples the] topographic features and creatures were diffused throughout a vast region. They were not all visible at once and human products were always mixed with the nonhuman. The villager[s by contrast] did not rove through these physical extensions of the self; [they] occupied them. [The aborigine] seemed to inhabit the land like a blood corpuscle, while the farmer [by contrast] was centered in it and could scan it as a whole.[30]

The gatherer-hunter who wanders through "physical extensions of the self" "like a blood corpuscle" is certainly not subject to many of the essentializing pressures brought to bear on "civilized" people since the agrarian revolution. The "centered" point of view of the farmer and the diminished natural landscape available for articulating both self and community (as well as its virtual replacement by a humanly-contrived world) are simply the first of many such pressures. The totalizing, essentializing discourse of patriarchal consciousness is the latest of such pressures. Dismantling patriarchal discourse is not likely by itself to eliminate the forces of essentialization and totalization. If the above description is right, the price that was paid by the human move away from the gatherer-hunter condition was precisely the setting in motion of those forces of essentialization and totalization. In the modern world the constant "recontextualization" that Martin and Mohanty speak of is likely to be an ever necessary feature of attempts to produce health and well-being. The concept of "storied residence" or "bioregional narrative" that I have been articulating seems increasingly important once we see the omnipresent nature of the forces of essentialization and totalization. In fact, "storied residence" seems to be a necessary part of the deconstructive process, the dismantling of the manifestations of these forces.

But beyond the project of deconstruction is the goal of health and well-being, which is the primary reason for introducing the idea of bioregional narrative. Authentic existence is not a matter of discovering a "real" self (it is still a social self, a construct); there is just the project of bringing into being healthy communities, healthy selves—an *achievement,* not a discovery of something that is hidden, covered over. But landscapes can be hard, or diminished and distorted, and the health in them and, consequently, in us comes at a price and only with much labor.

What has emerged is a conception of bioregional truth, local truth, or ethical vernacular.[31] The fractured identities of postmodernism, I suggest, can build health and well-being by means of a bioregional contextualization of self and community. The voices of health will be as various and multiple as the landscapes which give rise to them—landscapes which function as metaphors of self and community and

figure into those mythical narratives which give voice to the emergence of self and community. The notion of socially constructed selves gives way to the idea of bioregionally constructed selves and communities. In this way, bioregionalism can "ground" the construction of self and community without the essentialization and totalization typical of the various "groundings" of patriarchal culture.

CONCLUDING REMARKS

My objective in this paper has been to suggest a direction for postmodernism which at the same time sets an agenda for any environmental ethic that opts for the postmodern turn. The central notion of such an ethic, I have suggested, is that of bioregional narrative. In setting this agenda I have for the most part bypassed the difficulties attendant upon the satisfactory articulation of this notion and its embeddedness in an environmental ethic. Bioregional narratives are normative; and they are the subject of social negotiation. What I *have* been at pains to do is to avoid the foundationalist suggestion that these narratives are *givens* from which ethical injunctions *follow,* to resist, that is, a form of naturalism which would preclude the social negotiation of the stories we tell and the concepts of health and well-being embedded in them.[32]

Inevitably, the charge of parochialism will be leveled against the conception of ethics as bioregional narrative presented in this paper. The charge, however, is no more valid than related charges raised against Thomas Kuhn's view that objectivity and rationality in the sciences are based on social consensus. As Sabina Lovibond puts it, "[t]he idea of rationality as resting upon consensus . . . does not imply that the *fact* of consensus need carry any weight with us in any particular piece of thinking."[33]

Lovibond's distinction between "transcendental parochialism" and "empirical parochialism" is relevant here. Our beliefs and concerns, she says, "will necessarily be the beliefs, etc. of creatures with a certain physical constitution and a certain ecological location." Acceptance of this view, in turn,

> amounts to an acquiescence in what we might describe as a "transcendental parochialism": a renunciation of

the (ascetically-motivated) impulse to escape from the conceptual scheme to which, as creatures with a certain kind of body and environment, we are transcendentally related.

However,

as long as we can form the concrete conception of a less arbitrary description of the world—as long as we can find other rational persons or communities, by reference to whose world-view new symptoms of (empirical) parochialism in our own world-view can be identified—there will still be ground to cover in order to emancipate ourselves from such parochialism. Only when we have exhausted the supply of dialectical material may we follow the Quinean course of 'acquiescing in our mother tongue and taking its words at face value.'[34]

In a similar vein, Nancy Fraser and Linda J. Nicholson ask: "How can we combine a postmodernist incredulity toward metanarratives with social-critical power?"

A first step is to recognize . . . that postmodern critique need forswear neither large historical narratives nor analyses of societal macrostructures. . . . However, . . . not just any kind of theory will do. Rather, theory here would be explicitly historical, attuned to the cultural specificity of different societies and periods and to that of different groups within societies and periods. . . . Moreover, postmodern . . . theory would be nonuniversalist. When its focus became cross-cultural or transepochal, its mode of attention would be comparativist rather than universalizing, attuned to changes and contrasts instead of to covering laws.[35]

NOTES

1. Conrad Aiken, quoted in Edith Cobb, *The Ecology of Imagination in Childhood* (New York: Columbia University Press 1977), p. 67.

2. Alasdair MacIntyre, *After Virtue* (Notre Dame, Indiana: University of Notre Dame Press, 1984), p. 216.

3. Holmes Rolston III, "The Human Standing in Nature: Storied Fitness in the Moral Observer," in Wayne Summer, Donald Callen, and Thomas Attig, eds., *Values and Moral Standing* (Bowling Green, Ohio: The Applied Philosophy Program, Bowling Green State University, 1986), pp. 97–98.

4. Holmes Rolston III, *Environmental Ethics: Duties to and Values in the Natural World* (Philadelphia: Temple University Press, 1988), p. 342.

5. Aldo Leopold, *A Sand County Almanac* (New York: Ballantine Books, 1970), p. 262.

6. Rolston, "Human Standing in Nature," p. 100.

7. Biddy Martin and Chandra Talpade Mohanty, "Feminist Politics: What's Home Got to Do with It?" in Teresa de Lauretis, ed., *Feminist Studies/Critical Studies* (Bloomington: Indiana University Press, 1986), pp. 193–94. Quotations in the next paragraph are from pp. 195–200. See also Alcoff, "Cultural Feminism."

8. Tom Jay, "The Salmon of the Heart," in Finn Wilcox aned Jeremiah Gorsline, eds. *Working the Woods, Working the Sea* (Port Townsend, Washington: Empty Bowl, 1986), p. 112.

9. Edith Cobb, *The Ecology of Imagination in Childhood* (New York: Columbia University Press, 1977), pp. 76–77 (emphasis added).

10. Martin and Mohanty, "Home," pp. 196–197, 204, 208, 209–210.

11. This theme is beautifully developed by Barry Lopez, "Landscape and Narrative," in Barry Lopez, *Crossing Open Ground* (New York: Random House, 1989), pp. 61–71.

12. Jay, "Salmon," p. 117.

13. See Gary Snyder, *The Practice of the Wild* (Berkeley: North Point Press, 1990), pp. 86–87.

14. Jay, "Salmon," pp. 101–102.

15. Ibid., p. 112.

16. This is not to say, however, that such potential is in fact realized by all tribal cultures. There are, even in tribal cultures, various pressures at work which all-too-often result in, for example, male dominance, erosion of female power, and dramatic increases in the level of inter- and intratribal violence. The anthropologist Peggy Reeves Sanday, in her wide-ranging, cross-cultural study of tribal cultures (*Female Power and Male Dominance: On the origins of sexual inequality* [Cambridge: Cambridge University Press, 1981]), provides a perceptive account of the conditions under which such deterioration either takes place or is held at bay. Such factors include recentness of migration to a new home, environmental stress, reproductive difference, and the type of story of origin told by the culture. The interaction between these and other factors in producing or precluding domination and violence is complex. Even under the best of conditions some form of culturally constructed vigilance seems necessary. In many Native American tribes this takes the form of the

trickster or clown. For excellent literary examples, see Gerald Vizenor, *The Trickster of Liberty: Tribal Heirs to a Wild Baronage* (Minneapolis: University of Minnesota Press, 1988) and *The Heirs of Columbus* (Hanover, NH: University Press of New England, 1991), Anne Cameron, *Daughters of Copper Woman* (Vancouver: Press Gang Publishers, 1981), pp. 107–114; and Hyemeyohsts Storm, *Song of Heyoehkah* (New York: Ballantine Books, 1981). See also, Paul Radin, *The Trickster: A Study in American Indian Mythology* (London: Routledge & Kegan Paul Ltd., 1956) and Barbara Babcock-Abrahams, " 'A Tolerated Margin of Mess': The Trickster and His Tales Reconsidered," *Journal of the Folklore Institute* 11 (1975): 147–186.

17. See Sandra Harding, *The Science Question in Feminism* (Ithaca: Cornell University Press, 1986); Carol Gilligan, *In a Different Voice: Psychological Theory and Women's Development* (Cambridge: Harvard University Press, 1982); Terry Winant, "The Feminist Standpoint: A Matter of Language," *Hypatia* 2 (1987): 123–148.

18. John Wisdom, "Gods," *Proceedings of the Aristotelian Society* 45 (1944–45): 185–206; Paul Ricoeur, *The Symbolism of Evil* (Boston: Beacon Press, 1967).

19. Paul Shepard, *Nature and Madness* (San Francisco: Sierra Club Books, 1982), chapter 3.

20. James Hillman, *Re-Visioning Psychology* (New York: Harper and Row, 1975).

21. I use the paradoxical-sounding phrase "inscribing of the nervous system *in* the landscape" to avoid the modernist empiricism which would be suggested were I to interchange "nervous system" and "landscape." See David Abram, "The Perceptual Implications of Gaia," *The Ecologist* 15 (1985): 96–103, for an overview of some of the literature concerning the views (1) that perception must be studied as an attribute of an organism and its environment taken together, (2) that psyche is a property of the ecosystem as a whole, and (3) that the intellect is an elaboration of creativity at the level of bodily experience.

22. Shepard, *Nature and Madness*, p. 123.

23. As an aside to this account see Sam Gill, *Mother Earth: An American Story* (Chicago: University of Chicago Press, 1987), p. 6 and *passim*, who argues that "Mother Earth, as she has existed in North America, cannot be adequately and understood and appreciated apart from the complex history of the encounter between Native Americans and Americans of European ancestry, nor apart from comprehending that the scholarly enterprise

that has sought to describe her has had a hand in bringing her into existence, a hand even in introducing her to Native American peoples."

24. Shepard, *Nature and Madness*, p. 9.

25. Elizabeth Ann R. Bird, "The Social Construction of Nature: Theoretical Approaches to the History of Environmental Problems," *Environmental Review* 11 (1987): 262.

26. Donna Haraway, "Primatology Is Politics by Other Means," in Ruth Bleier, ed., *Feminist Approaches to Science* (New York: Pergamon Press, 1984), pp. 86, 96.

27. For an account of the way in which ecosystem ecology, for example, *can* (and ought to) inform the construction of an environmental ethic, see Jim Cheney, "Callicott's 'Metaphysics of Morals'," *Environmental Ethics* 13 (1991): 318–325.

28. Shepard, *Nature and Madness*, p. 6.

29. See note 1.

30. Shepard, *Nature and Madness*, pp. 23–24.

31. My thanks to Carolyn Merchant for suggesting the wonderful term "ethical vernacular."

32. See Cheney, "Callicott's 'Metaphysics of Morals'," pp. 318–325.

33. Sabina Lovibond, *Realism and Imagination in Ethics* (Minneapolis: University of Minnesota Press, 1983), p. 148.

34. Ibid., pp. 210 and 217. The phrase from W.V.O. Quine is from *Ontological Relativity* (New York: Columbia University Press, 1969), p. 49. Lovibond's book provides a thorough-going defense of the metaethical framework within which my notion of ethics as bioregional narrative has been developed.

35. Nancy Fraser and Linda J. Nicholson, "Social Criticism without Philosophy: An Encounter between Feminism and Postmodernism," in Linda J. Nicholson, ed., *Feminism/Postmodernism* (New York: Routledge, 1990), p. 34.

DISCUSSION TOPICS

1. Write a short paragraph in which you attempt to define your "self." Is your definition modernist or postmodernist?

2. Write a bioregional narrative on the subject of the right human relationship to the place in which you live.

3. How does Cheney's postmodern environmental

ethics avoid the is/ought dichotomy or the naturalistic fallacy?

4. Explain the defects of modernism as noted by Cheney. Do you agree or disagree with his view? Is there anything positive to be said for modernism?

5. Can you think of any dangers in the idea of "bioregional narrative" or "local truth"?

█████████ **READING 11** █████████

Before Environmental Ethics

Anthony Weston

Anthony Weston is Associate Professor of Philosophy at SUNY-Stony Brook, New York. His courses include environmental ethics, philosophy of education, and philosophy of medicine and other courses at the intersection of philosophy and the social sciences. He has recently published Toward Better Problems *(Philadelphia: Temple University Press, 1992). Reading II is a shortened version of an article to appear in* Environmental Ethics *14 (1992). A book partly based on these themes is in the works.*

Weston maintains that environmental ethics involves the development of a new set of values in a world which is deeply anthropocentric. He points to the experimentation and uncertainty which accompanied the development of the rights of persons in order to illustrate that values are dependent on human practices and institutions. Ethics, including environmental ethics, should not limit itself to the systematic application of established values, but should express and experiment with new values. Ethical arguments should be read as creative, open-ended challenges and proposals. Weston suggests that Aldo Leopold's land ethic, for example, should not be considered an entirely new theory but rather as opening new approaches to thinking about the land.

Since according to Weston environmental ethics is in its infancy, we should view environmental ethics as an "umbrella" field which includes a variety of approaches, and we should resist premature attempts to systematize it. The development of enabling environmental practices is one important and creative approach. New practices such as the creation of quiet zones or mixed communities of humans and nonhumans may lead to the discovery of new or stronger environmental values.

Environmental ethics has seldom viewed the development of values themselves as an evolutionary process. Actually, though, even our patron saint viewed them this way. "Nothing as important as an ethic is ever 'written'," insisted Aldo Leopold, and again: ethics "evolves in the minds of a thinking community".[1] This evolution, he adds, "never stops."

These lines come from the very same essay that ends with that all-too-familiar proposal, "A thing is right when it tends to preserve the integrity, stability, and beauty of the biotic community." Today that proposal is perpetually quoted as if it were a formula for a final and complete environmental ethic. Other philosophers have their own favorite formulae. Yet suppose instead that we took the more evolutionary Leopold—the tentative, provisional, nonformulaic Leopold—more seriously. Suppose that we view new sets of values as only gradually taking shape, as deeply interwoven with constantly-evolving institutions, experiences, and practices. How would environmental ethics look then?

It might seem that little would change. After all, a similar sociological view of the development of values is already widespread in contemporary mainstream ethics[2] which has nonetheless managed in practice to keep on plowing more or less the familiar old theoretical furrows. But there is a radical difference between mainstream ethics and environmental ethics. Mainstream ethics generally deals with sets of values that have long since consolidated. The familiar ethics of persons, for example, took shape several centuries ago with the rise of Protestantism and capitalism. Environmental ethics, by contrast, is only now entering what we could call an "originary" stage. Therefore, while mainstream ethics can perhaps ignore the evolutionary side of values, taking them for the most part as "given," environmental ethics—so I will argue—cannot. The consequences of paying attention to these evolutionary processes turn out to be quite radical.

THE PRACTICE OF ETHICS AT ORIGINARY STAGES

Let us turn our attention to the appropriate *comportment* for ethics at the "originary states" of the development of values: stages at which new values are only beginning to be constituted and consolidated. Let us take as a working example the ethics of person just mentioned. We must try, then, to place ourselves back at the time when respect for persons, and indeed persons themselves, were far less secure: not at all so fixed, secure, or "natural" as they now seem, but strange, forced, truncated, the way they must have seemed to, say, Calvin's contemporaries. Our question then is: how should—how *could*—a proto-ethics of persons proceed in such a situation?

For one thing, the early stages in the development of such a new set of values require a great deal of exploration and metaphor in ethical notions. Only later can they be allowed to harden into analytic categories. For example, although the concept of "rights" of persons now may be invoked with a fair degree of rigor, through most of its history it played a much more open-ended role, allowing the possibility of treating whole new classes of people as rights-holders—slaves, foreigners, non-property-owners, women—in ways previously unheard of, and ways that, speaking literally, were misuses of the concept. (" 'Barbarian rights'? But the very concept of 'barbarian' precludes being one of 'us,' i.e. Greeks, i.e. rights-holders . . .") This malleable rhetoric of rights also *created* "rights-holders," and thus literally helped create persons themselves. To persuade someone that she has a right to something, for example, or to persuade a whole class or group that their rights have been violated, may dramatically change their behavior, and ultimately reconstructs their belief-systems and experiences of themselves as well. Even now the creative and rhetorical possibilities of the concept of rights are not exhausted. We might read the sweeping and inclusive notion of rights in *The United Nations Declaration of Human Rights* in this light, for instance, rather than dismissing it, as do more legalistic thinkers, as conceptually confused.[3]

Moreover, the process of co-evolving values and practices at originary stages is seldom a smooth process of progressively filling in a kind of outline that is obvious from the start. Instead we see a variety of fairly incompatible outlines coupled with a wide range of protopractices, even social experiments of various sorts, all contributing to a kind of cultural working-through of a new set of possibilities. Those that ultimately prevail will, among other things, re-write the history of the others, so that the less successful practices and experiments are eventually smoothed over, obscured—much as successful scientific paradigms, according to Kuhn, rewrite their own pasts so that in retrospect their evolution seems much smoother, more necessary, and more univocal than it actually was. Great moments in the canonical history of rights, for example, include the Declaration of Independence and the Declaration of the Rights of Man, capitalism's institutionalization of rights to property and wealth, and now the occasional defense of a non-positivistic notion of rights for international export. *Not* included are the utopian socialists' many experimental communities, which often explicitly embraced (what *became*) non-standard, in fact anti-capitalistic notions of rights, or such sustained and massive struggles as the labor movement's organization around working-persons' rights or the various modern attempts by most social democracies to institutionalize rights to health care.

A long period of experimentation and uncertainty, then, ought to be expected and even welcomed in the originary stages of any new ethics. Remember that even the most currently familiar aspects of personhood co-evolved with a particular, complex, and even wildly improbable set of ideas and practices. Protestantism contributed not just a theology, and not just Calvin's peculiar and (if Max Weber is right) peculiarly world-historical "inner-world asceticism," but also such seemingly simple projects as an accessible Bible in the vernacular. Imagine the extraordinary impact of reading the holy text oneself, of being offered or pushed into an individual relation to God after centuries of only the most mediated access. Imagine the extraordinary self-preoccupation created by having to choose for the first time between rival versions of the same revelation, with not only one's eternal soul in the balance but often one's earthly life as well. Only against such a background of practice did it become possible to begin to experience oneself as an individual, separate from others, autonomous, beholden to inner voices and something we now call ''one's own values,'' and bearing the responsibility for one's choices. Only then, in short, did there appear on the scene not only the now-familiar ethics of persons but also persons themselves.

RETHINKING ENVIRONMENTAL ETHICS

Again, we now look at the evolution of such values mostly from the far side. It is therefore easy to miss the fundamental contingency of those values and their dependence upon practices, institutions, and experiences that were for their time genuinely uncertain and exploratory. Reading a little sociology might restore some of that sense of contingency. In a way, though, that very turn to another discipline is also precisely the problem. We are too used to an easy division of labor that leaves philosophical ethics only the systematic tasks, articulating a set of values that is already solidified and middle-aged, and abandons originary questions to the social sciences.

Looking at such periods of uncertainty from the far side, as it were, tends to incapacitate us on the near side. Ethics itself no longer knows how to deal with values that are *now* entering an originary stage. Even when systematic ethics is out of its depth, we continue to imagine that it is the only kind of ethics there is. We continue to regard the contingency, open-endedness, and uncertainty of ''new'' values as an objection to them, ruling them out of ethical court entirely, or else as a kind of embarassment to be quickly papered over with an ethical theory. We forget that every value that we now so confidently theorize about, as well as our theories themselves, had first a long period of gestation as well as a callow youth. Moreover, should we remember this much, we may simply want to tactfully withdraw from the scene: to wait a few centuries, with respect to the currently ''new'' values, before we think we can ''do ethics'' at all. But we do not always have that luxury.

The rest of the argument then is simple. *Environmental* values are in fact at an originary stage. This I

take to be the premise of most contemporary work in the field. But we can hardly confine ourselves to merely systematizing values that for the most part do not even exist. We also do not have the luxury of a few centuries' wait before we can break out the old familiar tools. We had better look for new tools instead. Whether any kind of latter-day theorizing is appropriate in environmental ethics is therefore very much an open question. Indeed, that we know how to proceed at *all* is very much an open question.

We might draw three conclusions paralleling those just drawn about ethics at previous originary stages. First and fundamentally, if environmental ethics is indeed at an originary stage, we can have only the barest sense of what ethics for a culture truly beyond anthropocentrism would actually look like. Calvinism and capitalism did not simply actualize some preexisting or easily anticipated notion of persons, but rather played a part in the larger *co-evolution* of respect for persons and persons themselves. What would emerge could only be imagined in advance in the dimmest of ways, or not imagined at all. Similarly, we are only now embarking on an attempt to move beyond anthropocentrism, and we simply cannot predict in advance where even another century, say, will take us.

When anthropocentrism is finally cut down to size, for example, there is no reason to think that what we will have or need in its place is something called ''*non*-anthropocentrism'' at all—as if that characterization would even begin to be useful in a culture for which anthropocentrism were indeed transcended. It may not be any kind of ''centrism'' whatsoever: i.e., some form of hierarchically structured ethics. It is already clear that hierarchy is not the only option.[4]

Second and correlatively, exploration and metaphor become crucial in environmental ethics. Only later can we harden originary notions into precise analytic categories. Any attempt to appropriate the moral force of rights-language for (much of) the transhuman world, for example, ought to be expected from the start to be *im*precise, literally ''confused.'' ('' 'Animal rights'? But the very concept of 'animal' precludes being one of 'us', i.e., persons, i.e., rights-holders . . .'') It need not be meant as a description of prevailing practice, but should be read instead as an attempt to *change* the prevailing practice. Christopher Stone's book *Should Trees Have Standing?—Toward Legal Rights for Natural Objects,* for example, is making a revisionist proposal about legal arrangements, not offering an analysis of the existing concept of rights.[5]

Something similar should be understood when we are invited to conceive not only animals or trees as rights-holders, but the land as a community and the planet as a person. Again, the force of all such arguments should be understood to be rhetorical, in a non-pejorative, pragmatic sense: the arguments are to be read as suggestive and open-ended sorts of challenges, even proposals for Deweyan kinds of social reconstruction, rather than attempts to demonstrate particular conclusions on the basis of premises supposed to be already accepted.[6] The force of these arguments lies in the way they open up the possibility of new connections, not in the way they settle or ''close'' any questions. Their work is more creative than summative; more prospective than retrospective. Their chief function is to provoke, to loosen up the language and correspondingly our thinking, to fire the imagination: to *open* questions, not to settle them.

The founders of environmental ethics were explorers along these lines. I want to return for a moment to Aldo Leopold: I think it is vital to reclaim him from the theorists. Bryan Norton reminds us, for example, that Leopold's appeal to the ''integrity, stability, and beauty of the biotic community'' occurs in the midst of a discussion of purely economic constructions of the land. It is best read, says Norton, as a kind of counterbalance and challenge to the excesses of pure commercialism, rather than as a grand criterion for moral action all by itself. John Rodman agrees, arguing that Leopold's work should be read as an environmental ethic *in process,* complicating the anthropocentric picture more or less from within, rather than as a kind of proto-system, simplifying and unifying an entirely new picture, that can be progressively refined in the way that utilitarian and deontological theories have been refined over the last century.[7] And I have already cited Leopold's own insistence that ''the land ethic [is] a product of social evolution.''

He continues: ''Only the most superficial student of history supposes that Moses ''wrote'' the Decalogue; it evolved in the minds of the thinking community, and Moses wrote a tentative summary of it. . . .''[8] Surely he thinks of himself as (merely) doing the same. It would be better to regard Leopold not as purveying a general ethical theory at all, but rather as simply opening some questions, unsettling some assumptions, prying the door loose just far enough to lead, in time, to much wilder and certainly more diverse suggestions or ethical standards.

A third general conclusion is this. As I put it above, the process of evolving values and practices at originary stages is seldom a smooth process of progressively filling in a fairly obvious earlier outline. At originary stages, again, we should instead expect a variety of fairly incompatible outlines coupled with a wide range of proto-practices, even social experiments of various sorts, all contributing to a kind of cultural working-through of a new set of possibilities. In environmental ethics, then, we arrive at exactly the opposite view from J. Baird Callicott, for example, who insists that we attempt to formulate, right now, a complete, unified, ''closed'' (his term) theory of environmental ethics. Callicott even argues that contemporary environmental ethics should not tolerate more than one basic type of value, insisting on a ''univocal'' environmental ethic.[9] In fact, however, as I argued above, originary stages are the worst possible times to demand that we all speak with one voice. Once a set of values is culturally consolidated it may well be possible, perhaps even necessary, to reduce them to some kind of consistency. But environmental values are unlikely to be in such a position for a very long time. The necessary period of ferment, cultural experimentation, and *multi*-vocality is only *beginning.* So Callicott is right, perhaps, about the demands of systematic ethical theory at late cultural stages. But he is wrong—indeed wildly wrong—about what stage environmental values have actually reached.

ENABLING ENVIRONMENTAL PRACTICE

Space for some analogues to the familiar theories does remain in the alternative environmental ethics envisioned here. I have argued that they are unreliable guides to the ethical future, but they might well be viewed as another kind of ethical experiment or proposal: rather like, for example, the work of the utopian socialists. However unrealistic, they may nonetheless play a historical and transitional role: highlighting new possibilities, inspiring reconstructive experiments, even perhaps eventually provoking environmental ethics' equivalent of a Marx.

It should be clear, though, that the kind of constructive activity suggested by the argument offered here goes far beyond the familiar theories as well. Rather than systematizing environmental values, again, the overall project at this stage must be to begin to *coevolve* those values with practices and institutions that make them even *un*systematically possible. It is this point that I now want to develop. I offer one specific example of such a coevolutionary practice. I have to insist that is by no means the only example. Indeed the best thing that could be hoped, in my view, is the emergence of many others. But it is *one* example, and it may be a good example to help clarify how such approaches might look, and thus to clear the way for more.

A central part of the challenge is to create the social, psychological, and phenomenological preconditions—the conceptual, experiential, or even quite literal ''Space''—for new or stronger environmental values to evolve. This is what I will call ''enabling'' such values; we may call the practical project *enabling environmental practice*. The specific example I propose is this. Consider the attempt to create actual, physical spaces for the emergence of trans-human experience: *places* within which some return to the experience of and immersion in natural settings is possible. Suppose in particular that certain places are set aside as quiet zones: places where automobile engines and lawnmowers and low-flying airplanes are not allowed, and yet places where people will live.

On one level the aim is modest: simply to make it possible to hear the birds and the winds and the silence once again. If bright outside lights were also banned, one could see the stars at night and feel the slow pulsations of the light over the seasons. A little creative zoning, in short, could make space for increasingly divergent styles of living on the land: experi-

ments in recycling and energy self-sufficiency, for example; mixed communities of humans and other species; serious ''re-inhabitation,'' though perhaps with more emphasis on place and community than upon the individual re-inhabitors; the ''ecosteries'' that have been proposed on the model of monasteries; or other possibilities not yet even imagined.[10]

This is not a utopian proposal. Unplug a few outdoor lights, reroute some roads, and in some places of the country we could already have a first approximation. In gardening, meanwhile, we already experience some semblance of mixed communities. Practices like beekeeping already model a symbiotic relation with the ''biotic community.'' It is not hard to work out policies to protect and extend such practices.

Enabling environmental practice is of course a *practice.* That does not mean that it is not also philosophical. ''Theory'''' and ''practice'' interpenetrate here. In the abstract, for example, the concept of ''natural settings'' just invoked has been acrimoniously debated, and the best-known positions are unfortunately more or less the extremes. ''Social Ecologists'' insist that no environment is ever purely natural, that human beings have already remade the entire world, and that the challenge is really to get the process under socially progressive and politically inclusive control. Some ''Deep Ecologists,'' by contrast, argue that only wilderness is the ''real world.''[11] Both ''deep'' and ''social'' views have something to offer. But it may be that only from the point of view of practice, even so simple a practice as the attempt to create ''quiet places,'' might we finally achieve the necessary distance to take what we can from the purely philosophical debate, and also to go beyond it toward a better set of questions and answers.

Both views, for example, unjustly discount ''encounter.'' On the one hand, non-anthropocentrism should not become anti-anthropocentrism: the aim is not to push humans out of the picture entirely, but rather to open up the possibility of reciprocity *between* humans and the rest of nature. But reciprocity does require a space not wholly permeated by humans either. What we need to explore are possible realms of *interaction*. Probably we should say that both the wilderness and the city are ''real worlds,'' if we must talk in such terms at all; but we must insist that there are still others also, and at present the most necessary of these are places where humans and other creatures, honored in their wildness and potential reciprocity, can come together, perhaps warily but at least openly.

As paradigmatic for philosophical engagement in this key we could take the work of Wendell Berry. Berry writes, for example, of what he calls "the phenomenon of edge or margin, that we know to be one of the powerful attractions of a diversified landscape, both to wildlife and to humans." "Margins" are places where domesticity and wildness meet. Mowing his small hayfield with a team of horses, Berry encounters a hawk who lands close to him, watching carefully but without fear. The hawk comes, he says,

> because of the conjunction of the small pasture and its wooded borders, of open hunting ground and the security of trees. . . . The human eye itself seems drawn to such margins, hungering for the difference made in the countryside by a hedgy fencerow, a stream, or a grove of trees. These margins are biologically rich, the meeting of two kinds of habitat.[12]

The hawk would not have come, he says, if the field had been larger, or if there had been no trees, or if he had been plowing with a tractor. Interaction is a fragile thing, and we need to pay careful attention to its preconditions. As Berry shows, this is a deeply philosophical and phenomenological project as well as a "practical" one—but nonetheless it always revolves around and refers back to practice. Without actually maintaining a farm, he would know very little of what he knows. The hawk would not—*could* not—have come to him.

Once again, this is only one example. Margins can't be the whole story. Many creatures avoid them; that is why the spotted owl's survival depends on large tracts of old-growth forest. Again, though it is *part* of the story, and a part given particularly short shrift, it seems, by all sides in the current debate.

There is no space here to develop the kind of philosophy of "practice" that would be necessary to fully work out these points. But we must at least note two opposite pitfalls in speaking of practice. First, again, it is not as if we come to this practice already knowing what values we will find or exemplify there.

Too often the notion of "practice" in contemporary philosophy has degenerated into "application," i.e., of prior principles or theories. At best it might include a space for feedback from practice to principle or theory. Something more radical is meant here. Practice is the opening of the "space" for interaction, for the re-emergence of a larger world. It is a kind of exploration. We do not know in advance what we will find. Berry had to *learn*, for example, about "margins." Gary Snyder and others propose Buddhist terms to describe the necessary attitude: a kind of mindfulness, attentiveness: what Tom Birch is calling the "primary sense" of the notion of "consideration."[13]

On the other hand, this sort of open-ended practice does not mean reducing our own activity to zero, as in some form of quietism. I do not mean that we must simply "open, and it will come," or that there is likely to be any single and simple set of values that somehow emerges once we merely get out of the way. Berry's view is that a more open-ended and respectful relation to nature requires constant and creative *activity*: in his case, constant presence in nature, constant interaction with his own animals, maintenance of a place that maximizes "margins." Others will (should, must) choose other ways. The crucial thing, again, is that humans must neither monopolize the picture entirely nor absent ourselves from it completely, but rather to try to live in interaction, to create a space for genuine encounter as part of our on-going reconstruction of our own lives and practices. What will come of such encounters, what will emerge from such sustained interactions, again, we cannot yet say.

No doubt it will be argued that Berry is necessarily an exception, that small unmechanized farms are utterly anachronistic and that any real maintenance of "margins" or space for "encounter" is unrealistic in mass society. Perhaps. But these are claims that are also open to argumentation and experiment, and one might even partially define an enabling environmental practice precisely by its having something practical to offer on the other side of these two automatically accepted commonplaces. Christopher Alexander and his colleagues, in *A Pattern Language* and elsewhere, for example, remind us how profoundly even the simplest features of houses, streets, and cities structure our experience of nature—and can be consciously redesigned to change those experiences. Windows on two sides of a room make it possible for natural light to suffice for daytime illumination. Buildings should be built on those parts of the land that are in the worst condition, not the best, leaving the most healthy and beautiful parts alone while improving the worse-off ones. On a variety of grounds they argue for the presence of still and moving water throughout the city, for extensive common land, "accessible green," sacred sites and burial grounds within the city as well, and so on. If we built mindfully, Alexander and his colleagues argue, maintaining and even expanding "margins," even with high human population densities, is not only possible but easy.[14] But we do have to put our theories to the side and begin to pay attention.

NOTES

1. Aldo Leopold, *Sand County Almanac* (Oxford University Press, 1949), p. 225.
2. This point is argued at length in Part III of the full version of this paper, appearing in *Environmental Ethics* 14 (1992).
3. While Hugo Bedau (in "International Human Rights," in Tom Regan and Donald Vandeveer, eds., *And Justice Toward All: New Essays in Philosophy and Public Policy* (Totowa, NJ: Rowman and Littlefield, 1982)) calls the *Declaration* "the triumphant product of several centuries of political, legal, and moral inquiry into . . . 'the dignity and worth of the human person' " (p. 298), he goes on to assert that "It is . . . doubtful whether the General Assembly that proclaimed the UN Declaration understood what a human right is," since in the document rights are often stated loosely and in many different modalities, such as "ideals, purposes, or aspirations" rather than just "as rights," and at the same time the Declaration allows considerations of general welfare to limit rights, which seems to undercut their function as protectors of individuals against such rationales (p. 302n). *Contra* Bedau, however, I am suggesting that the General Assembly understood "what rights are" very well. Rights-language is a broad-based moral language with multiple purposes and constituencies: in some contexts a counterweight to the typically self-serving utilitarian rhetoric of the powers that be; in others a provocation to think serious about even such much-mocked ideas as a right to a paid vacation; etc.

4. See for example Bernard Williams, *Ethics and the Limits of Philosophy* (Harvard University Press, 1985); Walzer's *Spheres of Justice* again; and Karen Warren, "The Power and Promise of Ecofeminism," *Environmental Ethics* 12 No. 2 (Summer 1990): 125–146.
5. Christopher Stone, *Should Trees Have Standing?—Toward Legal Rights for Natural Objects* (Los Altos: Wm Kaufmann, 1974). G.E. Varner, in "Do Species Have Standing?," *Environmental Ethics* 9, No. 1 (Spring 1987): 57–72, points out that the creation of new legal rights—as for example in the Endangered Species Act—helps expand what W.D. Lamont calls our "stock of ethical ideas—the mental capital, so to speak, with which [one] begins the business of living." There is no reason that the law must merely reflect "growth" that has already occurred, as opposed to motivating some growth itself.
6. See Chaim Perelman, *The Realm of Rhetoric* (Notre Dame: University of Notre Dame Press, 1982) and C. Perelman and L. Olbrechts-Tyteca, *The New Rhetoric* (Notre Dame: University of Notre Dame Press, 1969) for an account of rhetoric that resists the usual Platonic disparagement.
7. Norton, "Conservation and Preservation: A Conceptual Rehabilitation," *Environmental Ethics* 8, No. 3 (Fall 1986): 195–220; Rodman "Four Forms of Ecological Consciousness Reconsidered," in Donald Scherer and Thomas Attig, *Ethics and the Environment* (Englewood Cliffs, N.J.: Prentice-Hall, 1983): pp. 89–92.
8. Leopold, *Sand County Almanac,* p. 225.
9. J. Baird Callicott, "The Case Against Moral Pluralism," *Environmental Ethics* 12, No. 2 (Summer 1990): 99–124.
10. On "ecosteries," see Alan Drengson, "The Ecostery Foundation of North America: Statement of Philosophy," *The Trumpeter* 7, No. 1 (Winter 1990): 12–16. On "reinhabitation" a good starting-point is Peter Berg, "What is Bioregionalism?", *The Trumpeter* 8, No. 1 (Winter 1991): 6–12.
11. See, for instance, Dave Foreman, "Reinhabitation, Biocentrism, and Self-Defense," *Earth First!* (1 August 1987); Murray Bookchin, "Which Way for the US Greens?" *New Politics* 11, No. 2 (Winter 1989); and Bill Devall, "Deep Ecology and its Critics," *Earth First!* (22 December 1987).
12. Wendell Berry, "Getting Along with Nature," in *Home Economics* (San Francisco: North Point Press, 1987), p. 13.
13. Gary Snyder, "Good, Wild, Sacred," in *The Practice*

of the Wild (San Francisco: North Point Press, 1990); Tom Birch, "Universal Consideration," paper presented for the International Society for environmental Ethics, American Philosophical Association, 27 December 1990; Jim Cheney, "Ecofeminism and Deep Ecology," *Environmental Ethics* 9, No. 2 (1987): 115–145. Snyder also speaks of "grace" as the primary "practice of the wild"; Doug Peacock (in *Grizzly Years*) insists upon "interspecific tact"; Berry writes of an "etiquette" of nature, Birch of "generosity of spirit" and "considerateness." All of these terms have their home in a discourse of manners and personal bearing, rather than moral discourse as usually conceived by ethical philosophers. We are not speaking of some universal categorical obligation, but of something much closer to us, bound up with who we are and how we immediately bear ourselves in the world—though not necessarily any more "optional" for all that.

14. Christopher Alexander, et al., *A Pattern Language* (New York: Oxford University Press, 1977). On windows, see sections 239, 159, and 107; on "site repair", section 104; on water in the city, sections 25, 64, and 71; on "accessible green," sections 51 and 60; on "holy ground," sections 24, 66, and 70.

DISCUSSION TOPICS

1. Do you agree with Weston that values such as the right to life do not exist independently of human history and institutions? Explain your reasoning.
2. Can you think of any aspects of your culture which are not anthropocentric?
3. What kinds of environmental practices have you engaged in? Are there some you would like to try out?

CHAPTER EXERCISE

1. Consider a grove of alder trees in a remote watershed, which has never (and never will be) observed by human beings. Do the trees have value? What kind? Give reasons for your answer.
2. Consider the moral judgment "It is wrong to cause the extinction of a species." What are some reasons for and against such a judgment? Classify your reasons according to whether they assume traditional relativism, universalism, contextualism, or pluralism.

FOR FURTHER READING

Armstrong-Buck, Susan. "What Process Philosophy Can Contribute to the Land Ethic and Deep Ecology." *The Trumpeter* 8, No. 1 (Winter 1991): 29–34. Discusses some weaknesses of Callicott's and Rolston's positons on value and presents a brief introduction to the advantages of process metaphysics in clarifying the concept of self in deep ecology.

Birch, Tom. "Universal Consideration: All the Way Down with Considerability." *Environmental Ethics* (in press). An important article, arguing for the view that the search for a criterion of moral considerability or of intrinsic value should be abandoned because it is based on the Western project of domination: who can join the elite club? Birch urges that human beings adopt the practice of meaningful attending (universal consideration).

Cheney, Jim. "Callicott's Metaphysic of Morals." *Environmental Ethics* 13, No. 4 (1991): 311–325. Cheney argues that Callicott's appeal to the biosocial moral theory, according to which obligations are determined by the community of which we are a part, fails to resolve potential conflicts between types of communities. Cheney also argues that while human obligations to ecosystems cannot be directly derived from descriptions of ecosystems, there are important interactions.

Disch, Robert, ed. *The Ecological Conscience: Values for Survival.* Englewood Cliffs, N.J.: Prentice-Hall, 1970. Contains some accessible, classic essays on ecological values.

The Monist 75 (1992). Special issue, edited by J. Baird Callicott, on natural value theory.

Norton, Bryan G. *Why Preserve Natural Variety?* Princeton, New Jersey: Princeton University Press, 1987. A valuable discussion of types of values, including demand values, amenity values, and transformative values. Norton argues that preservation of habitats is the best way to preserve biodiversity.

Partridge, Ernest. "Values in Nature: Is Anybody There?" *Philosophical Inquiry* 8, Nos. 1–2 (1986): 96–110. A strong argument for inherent value in nature.

Rolston, Holmes, III. *Environmental Ethics.* Philadelphia: Temple University Press, 1988. The most complete account so far of the notion of intrinsic natural value. A subtle and complex study with ample use of biological examples.

Stone, Christopher D. *Earth and Other Ethics: The Case for Moral Pluralism.* New York; Harper and Row, 1987. An important attack on moral monism; Stone explains the advantages of a more flexible approach.

CHAPTER THREE

The Aesthetic Value of Nature

. . . [T]he ultimate historical foundations of nature preservation are aesthetic. . . .

Eugene Hargrove
Foundations of Environmental Ethics, p. 168

In this chapter seven characteristics of aesthetic experience are presented. We also describe how the aesthetic experience of nature differs from the aesthetic experience of art objects. Finally we consider the experiences of nature as sacred and as wilderness.

CHARACTERISTICS OF AESTHETIC EXPERIENCE

Aesthetic[1] experience, like all experience, has both an objective aspect, determined by the characteristics of the object, and a subjective aspect, referring to the characteristics, states of mind, and interests of the subject or observer. Aesthetic experience, however, differs from other experience in important ways.[2] First, aesthetic experience requires an attitude of ''disinterest''—an interest that is nonpractical and nonu-

tilitarian. Aesthetically, an object or event is valued for its own sake, rather than for its potential use. Thus aesthetic experience is either intrinsically or inherently valuable, as discussed in Chapter 2.

Second, aesthetic experience is a sympathetic, contemplative, receptive experience, in which the observer lets the object or event be itself. The observer seeks to understand or relate to the object on its own terms.

Third, aesthetic experience is centered in the present moment, rather than in the past or future. The observer is concerned primarily with what an object or event is in itself, rather than with what caused it or what consequences the object or event might have.

Fourth, aesthetic experience concerns particular object or event, or a particular kind of object or event. Aesthetically, the observer does not engage the object (or kind of object) as merely an instance or example of a general principle, as would be the case in scientific inquiry. Rather, the focus is on the uniqueness of the object.

Fifth, aesthetic experience entails delight in harmony and complex unity. In aesthetic feeling a goal is to avoid both discord (the lack of a unifying pattern) and monotony (a boring or repetitive pattern). The observer recognizes an organizing structure or pattern that unifies many parts.

---

1. A.G. Baumgarten coined the term in 1750; it is based on the Greek *aistheikos,* meaning sense perception.

2. The following discussion draws from Jerome Stolnitz, ''The Aesthetic Attitude,'' in *Aesthetics and the Philosophy of Art Criticism* (New York: Houghton Mifflin, 1960).

Sixth, aesthetic experience can involve primarily the spontaneous feelings of the observer, but it can also include a distinctly conceptual aspect.[3] The conceptual aspect may involve reflection upon the fruitfulness of that experience in leading to additional experiences of value. Recognition of both emotive and conceptual aspects of aesthetic experience allows the postulation that nonhuman sentient organisms may have aesthetic experiences. Examples might include the paintings of captive chimpanzees and elephants, as well as the bowers, decorations, dances, and paintings of bower birds.[4]

Seventh, aesthetic experience can be of any object or event, as long as we encounter the object with disinterested, sympathetic attention. There are no specific properties which an object or event must possess in order to be considered aesthetic. The object can be sensuous, perceivable with the five senses, or an intellectual one, apprehended only with the mind. Because most cultures have considered the mind to be superior to the body, intellectual beauty such as that found in mathematical systems generally has been thought to be a higher form of beauty than is sensuous beauty. For example, Edna St. Vincent Millay wrote, "Euclid alone has looked upon beauty bare."[5]

THE BEAUTY OF NATURE

Although the aesthetic appreciation of art has been evident for millenia, the appreciation of natural beauty in the West has developed very slowly.[6] In medieval and Renaissance art, nature was only the background to human activity, and a symbolic one at that. Nature was either a source of the "mirror of God," or simply hard work and danger for human beings; nature was not something of interest in its own right. As Callicott points out in his essay "The Land Aesthetic," the enjoyment of natural beauty for its own sake developed from a tradition of landscape painting in the seventeenth century; its origin lies in the "picturesque" as formed by the history of painting.[7] So strong is that art historical influence that it has been claimed that only those areas deemed picturesque owing to having been painted by a notable artist have been given protected status as parks or wilderness areas![8] In the eighteenth century, garden activities and games became popular, and cities began to include trees in their urban planning. In the mid-eighteenth to the mid-nineteenth centuries many people traveled to beautiful places, and enjoyed the emerging activities of landscape gardening and landscape architecture. In the nineteenth century the development of natural science contributed to the recognition of the scientifically "interesting" as an aesthetic category in addition to the traditional categories of the beautiful, the sublime, and the picturesque.[9]

How does an aesthetic experience of nature differ from one of human-made art? One essential difference is that of *participation.* Nature surrounds, involves all of our senses, and sustains us in a way no painting, poem, or sculpture can. In experiencing natural beauty the observer may experience himself or herself as a living creature dependent upon the soil, plants, water, air, and light. Some contemporary thinkers have suggested a "habitat theory" of landscape beauty, according to which we admire environments where we feel safe.[10] We like landscapes in which we have both vision ("prospect") and protec-

3. Charles Hartshorne, *Born to Sing: An Interpretation and World Survey of Bird Song* (Bloomington, Ind., Indiana University Press, 1973).

4. A.J. Marshall, *Bower-Birds: Their Displays and Breeding Cycles* (Oxford, Clarendon Press, 1954). Jared Diamond, "Art of the Wild," *Discover* (February 1991): 79-85 discusses chimp and elephant art. Elephant art is also extensively and perceptively discussed by David Gucwa and James Ehmann in *To Whom It May Concern: An Investigation of the Art of Elephants* (New York: W.W. Norton, 1985).

5. Edna St. Vincent Millay, "Euclid Alone Has Looked on Beauty Bare," in Louis Untermeyer, ed., *Modern American Poetry* (New York: Harcourt, Brace and Co., 1942).

6. In Japan and China the admiration of wild mountain landscapes has existed since ancient times.

7. Marcia M. Eaton, *Aesthetics and the Good Life* (London: Fairleigh Dickinson University Press, 1989).

8. Eugene Hargrove, *Foundations of Environmental Ethics* (Englewood Cliffs, N.J.: Prentice-Hall, 1989), p. 106, fn. 47.

9. Hargrove, *Foundations of Environmental Ethics,* pp. 88–92.

10. Jay Appleton, *The Experience of Landscape* (London: John Wiley & Sons, 1975).

tion. This participatory quality of our experience of nature might explain what Carlson in his essay, "Appreciation and the Natural Environment," terms "positive aesthetics," in which our task is to learn to understand why nature (untouched by human beings) is always beautiful. Perhaps we experience untouched nature as beautiful because healthy natural cycles promote human well-being.

Second, nature is *frameless*.[11] The experience of nature provides surprises, whereas art objects often have spatial and temporal boundaries. The aesthetic experience of nature requires an alertness to new experiences, arising from the dynamism of natural processes and from the fact that the observer can choose any point of observation. In his essay on Leopold's natural aesthetic, Callicott notes the aesthetic excitement of the "noumena" of the land—the hidden, unpredictable presence of wolves and bears, loons and cutthroat trout.

These characteristics of participation and framelessness are evident in recent "earth art," in which natural objects are inseparable from the work of art and in which the art is often bound to its site.[12]

Third, the *independent existence* of natural objects is crucial to the aesthetic experience of nature. We value the self-creating, continuous history of natural objects. We value the non-human origin, the "naturalness" of nature. Our delight at a stand of trees is changed into something else if we are informed that the trees are plastic. Eugene Hargrove builds on this centrality of existence in his essay, "The Ontological Argument for the Preservation of Nature."

11. R.W. Hepburn, "Aesthetic Appreciation of Nature," in *Contemporary Aesthetics*, ed. Matthew Lipman (Boston: Allyn & Bacon, Inc., 1973), pp. 340–354.

12. Yrjo Sepanmaa, *The Beauty of Environment* (Helsinki: Suomalainen Tiedeakatemia, 1986), pp. 39-40, discusses the works of Christo and the Finnish artists Lanu and Lukkela. James Turrell's work at Roden Crater in Arizona, an extinct cinder cone, is described in Craig Adcock, *James Turrell: The Art of Light and Space* (Berkeley: University of California Press, 1990). Turrell has purchased the site and is building underground chambers to be aligned with the sun. See also John Beardsley, *Earthworks and Beyond: Contemporary Art in the Landscape* (New York: Abbeville Press, 1984); Alan Sonfist, ed., *Art in the Land: A Critical Anthology of Environmental Art* (New York: E.P. Dutton, 1983).

Fourth, the *connectedness and complexity* of natural systems are fundamental parts of our aesthetic experience of nature. In his essay Allen Carlson points out that we diminish natural objects if we abstract or remove them from the system that produced and sustains them. Natural objects are always part of a larger whole, and the understanding of that whole is necessary for an adequate appreciation of the objects. Since natural systems are the subject matter of the natural sciences, these sciences play a significant role in both developing appropriate aesthetic categories for natural beauty and in training individuals to appreciate how natural objects exemplify these categories. While aesthetic traditions in art history cannot be disregarded in appreciating natural beauty, the natural sciences provide additional categories of appreciation and also function analogous to courses in art history in training the observer to perceive and interpret natural beauty.

Fifth, because of the connectedness within natural systems, an aesthetic experience of nature has a *normative* character based on the health of continuous, self-sufficient natural cycles. Qualities such as integrity, stability, and appropriateness of part to whole characterize natural systems.

Sixth, nature provides *transcendence* of ordinary experience. Nature has been interpreted not only as picturesque or beautiful, but as "sublime," as inspiring feelings of awe and grandeur. Great storms at sea, waterfalls, and ranges of towering mountains often were considered sublime, particularly in the eighteenth and nineteenth centuries. Although the term is no longer much used, feelings of awe and grandeur appear in the contemporary appreciation of wilderness and the associated sense of nature as sacred. In wild places human experience is transcended. We can experience humility in the face of the nonhuman and a liberation from human planning and conventional human thinking. We apprehend something approaching a cosmic order and ultimate meaning.

The essays by the nineteenth century American writers John Muir and Henry David Thoreau—"Walking" by Thoreau and Muir's "A Near View of the High Sierra"—exemplify a deep appreciation for wilderness and its revelations of what makes for a truly satisfying human life. Annie Dillard in her essay, ''Seeing'' eloquently represents those in the twentieth century who continue to seek ultimate, divine meaning in nature.

In ''Seeing Nature Whole'' John Fowles points out the connection between the inner ''green man or woman,'' our wild feelings and creativity, and the outer green of the forest. Fowles maintains that only art is capable of apprehending nature in its ''individual presentness'' of ongoing creativity.

Walking

Henry David Thoreau

Henry David Thoreau (1817-1862) is generally considered the greatest American nature writer. His best-known work, Walden, *has influenced several generations through its call to a life of natural simplicity, harmony, and spiritual liberty. For Thoreau, nature teaches us how to wake up from our slothful, conventional everyday consciousness and to live out our own, original lives.*

Thoreau's essay "Walking" is one of the best expressions of his love for wilderness. The walking he speaks of occurs in two dimensions: that of country paths and that of spiritual paths. Thoreau tells the reader that a walk requires the readiness to leave familiar, ordinary life and to venture into the "springs of life."

For Thoreau the wildest is the most alive, the wildest being found in natural vitality and creativity. The natural for Thoreau is not other than the human: "a good book is as natural as a wild-flower." He seeks the poet who can transplant words to his page "with earth adhering to the roots"; he speaks of the "awful ferity [wildness] with which good men and lovers meet." The wildness of instinct spurs his neighbor's cow to swim a swollen river; it also lives in the perfect flowers of the tallest, unseen branches of a white pine. Thoreau invites us to walk, so that we might hear "the gospel according to the moment."

I wish to speak a word for Nature, for absolute freedom and wildness, as contrasted with a freedom and culture merely civil—to regard man as an inhabitant, or a part and parcel of Nature, rather than a member of society. I wish to make an extreme statement, if so I may make an emphatic one, for there are enough champions of civilization: the minister and the school committee and every one of you will take care of that.

I have met with but one or two persons in the course of my life who understood the art of Walking, that is, of taking walks—who had a genius, so to speak, for *sauntering,* which word is beautifully derived "from idle people who roved about the country, in the Middle Ages, and asked charity, under pretense of going *à la Sainte Terre,"* to the Holy Land, till the children exclaimed, "There goes a *Sainte-Terrer,"* a Saunterer, a Holy-Lander. They who never go to the Holy Land in their walks, as they pretend, are indeed mere idlers and vagabonds; but they who do go there are saunterers in the good sense, such as I mean. Some, however, would derive the word from *sans terre,* without land or a home, which, therefore, in the good sense, will mean, having no particular home, but equally at home everywhere. For this is the secret of successful sauntering. He who sits still in a house all the time may be the greatest vagrant of all; but the saunterer, in the good sense, is no more vagrant than the meandering river, which is all the while sedulously seeking the shortest course to the sea. But I prefer the first, which, indeed, is the most probable derivation. For every walk is a sort of crusade, preached by some Peter the Hermit in us, to go forth and reconquer this Holy Land from the hands of the Infidels.

It is true, we are but faint-hearted crusaders, even the walkers, nowadays, who undertake no persevering, never-ending enterprises. Our expeditions are but tours, and come round again at evening to the old hearth-side from which we set out. Half the walk is but retracing our steps. We should go forth on the shortest walk, perchance, in the spirit of undying adventure, never to return—prepared to send back our embalmed hearts only as relics to our desolate kingdoms. If you are ready to leave father and mother, and brother and sister, and wife and child and friends, and never see them again—if you have paid your debts, and made your will, and settled all your affairs, and are a free man, then you are ready for a walk. . . .

But the walking of which I speak has nothing in it akin to taking exercise, as it is called, as the sick take medicine at stated hours—as the swinging of dumbbells or chairs; but is itself the enterprise and adventure of the day. If you would get exercise, go in search of the springs of life. Think of a man's swinging dumb-bells for his health, when those springs are bubbling up in far-off pastures unsought by him!

Moreover, you must walk like a camel, which is

said to be the only beast which ruminates when walking. When a traveler asked Wordsworth's servant to show him her master's study, she answered, ''Here is his library, but his study is out of doors.''

Living much out of doors, in the sun and wind, will no doubt produce a certain roughness of character—will cause a thicker cuticle to grow over some of the finer qualities of our nature, as on the face and hands, or as severe manual labor robs the hands of some of their delicacy of touch. So staying in the house, on the other hand, may produce a softness and smoothness, not to say thinness of skin, accompanied by an increased sensibility to certain impressions. Perhaps we should be more susceptible to some influences important to our intellectual and moral growth, if the sun had shone and the wind blown on us a little less: and no doubt it is a nice matter to proportion rightly the thick and thin skin. But methinks that is a scurf that will fall off fast enough—that the natural remedy is to be found in the proportion which the night bears to the day, the winter to the summer, thought to experience. There will be so much the more air and sunshine in our thoughts. The callous palms of the laborer are conversant with finer tissues of self-respect and heroism, whose touch thrills the heart, than the languid fingers of idleness. That is mere sentimentality that lies abed by day and thinks itself white, far from the tan and callus of experience.

When we walk, we naturally go to the fields and woods: what would become of us, if we walked only in a garden or a mall? Even some sects of philosophers have felt the necessity of importing the woods to themselves, since they did not go to the woods. ''They planted groves and walks of Platanes,'' where they took *subdiales ambulationes* in porticos open to the air. Of course it is of no use to direct our steps to the woods, if they do not carry us thither. I am alarmed when it happens that I have walked a mile into the woods bodily, without getting there in spirit. In my afternoon walk I would fain forget all my morning occupations and my obligations to society. But it sometimes happens that I cannot easily shake off the village. The thought of some work will run in my head and I am not where my body is—I am out of my senses. In my walks I would fain return to my senses.

What business have I in the woods, if I am thinking of something out of the woods? I suspect myself, and cannot help a shudder, when I find myself so implicated even in what are called good works—for this may sometimes happen.

My vicinity affords many good walks; and though for so many years I have walked almost every day, and sometimes for several days together, I have not yet exhausted them. An absolutely new prospect is a great happiness, and I can still get this any afternoon. Two or three hours' walking will carry me to as strange a country as I expect ever to see. A single farmhouse which I had not seen before is sometimes as good as the dominions of the King of Dahomey. There is in fact a sort of harmony discoverable between the capabilities of the landscape within a circle of ten miles' radius, or the limits of an afternoon walk, and the threescore years and ten of human life. It will never become quite familiar to you.

Nowadays almost all man's improvements, so called, as the building of houses and the cutting down of the forest and of all large trees, simply deform the landscape, and make it more and more tame and cheap. A people who would begin by burning the fences and let the forest stand! I saw the fences half consumed, their ends lost in the middle of the prairie, and some worldly miser with a surveyor looking after his bounds, while heaven had taken place around him, and he did not see the angels going to and fro, but was looking for an old post-hole in the midst of paradise. I looked again, and saw him standing in the middle of a boggy Stygian fen, surrounded by devils, and he had found his bounds without a doubt, three little stones, where a stake had been driven, and looking nearer, I saw that the Prince of Darkness was his surveyor.

I can easily walk ten, fifteen, twenty, any number of miles, commencing at my own door, without going by any house, without crossing a road except where the fox and the mink do: first along by the river, and then the brook, and then the meadow and the woodside. There are square miles in my vicinity which have no inhabitant. From many a hill I can see civilization and the abodes of man afar. The farmers and their works are scarcely more obvious than woodchucks and their burrows. Man and his affairs, church and state and school, trade and commerce, and manufactures and agriculture, even politics, the most alarming of them all—I am pleased to see how little space they occupy in the landscape. Politics is but a narrow field, and that still narrower highway yonder leads to it. I sometimes direct the traveler thither. If you would go to the political world, follow the great road—follow that market-man, keep his dust in your eyes, and it will lead you straight to it; for it, too, has its place merely, and does not occupy all space. I pass from it as from a bean-field into the forest, and it is forgotten. In one half-hour I can walk off to some portion of the earth's surface where a man does not stand from one year's end to another, and there, consequently, politics are not, for they are but as the cigar-smoke of a man. . . .

At present, in this vicinity, the best part of the land is not private property; the landscape is not owned, and the walker enjoys comparative freedom. But possibly the day will come when it will be partitioned off into so-called pleasure-grounds, in which a few will take a narrow and exclusive pleasure only—when fences shall be multiplied, and man-traps and other engines invented to confine men to the *public* road, and walking over the surface of God's earth shall be construed to mean trespassing on some gentleman's grounds. To enjoy a thing exclusively is commonly to exclude yourself from the true enjoyment of it. Let us improve our opportunities, then, before the evil days come.

What is it that makes it so hard sometimes to determine whither we will walk? I believe that there is a subtle magnetism in Nature, which, if we unconsciously yield to it, will direct us aright. It is not indifferent to us which way we walk. There is a right way; but we are very liable from heedlessness and stupidity to take the wrong one. We would fain take that walk, never yet taken by us through this actual world, which is perfectly symbolical of the path which we love to travel in the interior and ideal world; and sometimes, no doubt, we find it difficult to choose our direction, because it does not yet exist distinctly in our idea.

When I go out of the house for a walk, uncertain as yet whither I will bend my steps, and submit myself to my instinct to decide for me, I find, strange and whimsical as it may seem, that I finally and inevitably settle southwest, toward some particular wood or meadow or deserted pasture or hill in that direction. My needle is slow to settle—varies a few degrees, and does not always point due southwest, it is true, and it has good authority for this variation, but it always settles between west and south-southwest. The future lies that way to me, and the earth seems more unexhausted and richer on that side. The outline which would bound my walks would be, not a circle, but a parabola, or rather like one of those cometary orbits which have been thought to be non-returning curves, in this case opening westward, in which my house occupies the place of the sun. I turn round and round irresolute sometimes for a quarter of an hour, until I decide, for a thousandth time, that I will walk into the southwest or west. Eastward I go only by force; but westward I go free. Thither no business leads me. It is hard for me to believe that I shall find fair landscapes or sufficient wildness and freedom behind the eastern horizon. I am not excited by the prospect of a walk thither; but I believe that the forest which I see in the western horizon stretches uninterruptedly toward the setting sun, and there are no towns nor cities in it of enough consequence to disturb me. Let me live where I will, on this side is the city, on that the wilderness, and ever I am leaving the city more and more, and withdrawing into the wilderness. I should not lay so much stress on this fact, if I did not believe that something like this is the prevailing tendency of my countrymen. I must walk toward Oregon, and not toward Europe. And that way the nation is moving, and I may say that mankind progress from east to west. Within a few years we have witnessed the phenomenon of a southeastward migration, in the settlement of Australia; but this affects us as a retrograde movement, and, judging from the moral and physical character of the first generation of Australians, has not yet proved a successful experiment. The eastern Tartars think that there is nothing west beyond Thibet. ''The world ends there,'' say they; ''beyond there is nothing but a shoreless sea.'' It is unmitigated East where they live.

We go eastward to realize history and study the

works of art and literature, retracing the steps of the race; we go westward as into the future, with a spirit of enterprise and adventure. The Atlantic is a Lethean stream, in our passage over which we have had an opportunity to forget the Old World and its institutions. If we do not succeed this time, there is perhaps one more chance for the race left before it arrives on the banks of the Styx; and that is in the Lethe of the Pacific, which is three times as wide. . . .

The West of which I speak is but another name for the Wild; and what I have been preparing to say is, that in Wildness is the preservation of the World. Every tree sends its fibres forth in search of the Wild. The cities import it at any price. Men plow and sail for it. From the forest and wilderness come the tonics and barks which brace mankind. Our ancestors were savages. The story of Romulus and Remus being suckled by a wolf is not a meaningless fable. The founders of every state which has risen to eminence have drawn their nourishment and vigor from a similar wild source. It was because the children of the Empire were not suckled by the wolf that they were conquered and displaced by the children of the northern forests who were.

I believe in the forest, and in the meadow, and in the night in which the corn grows. We require an infusion of hemlock spruce or arbor-vitæ in our tea. There is a difference between eating and drinking for strength and from mere gluttony. The Hottentots eagerly devour the marrow of the koodoo and other antelopes raw, as a matter of course. Some of our northern Indians eat raw the marrow of the Arctic reindeer, as well as various other parts, including the summits of the antlers, as long as they are soft. And herein, perchance, they have stolen a march on the cooks of Paris. They get what usually goes to feed the fire. This is probably better than stall-fed beef and slaughter-house pork to make a man of. Give me a wildness whose glance no civilization can endure— as if we lived on the marrow of koodoos devoured raw.

There are some intervals which border the strain of the wood thrush, to which I would migrate—wild lands where no settler has squatted; to which, methinks, I am already acclimated.

The African hunter Cumming tells us that the skin of the eland, as well as that of most other antelopes just killed, emits the most delicious perfume of trees and grass. I would have every man so much like a wild antelope, so much a part and parcel of nature, that his very person should thus sweetly advertise our senses of his presence, and remind us of those parts of nature which he most haunts. I feel no disposition to be satirical, when the trapper's coat emits the odor of musquash even; it is a sweeter scent to me than that which commonly exhales from the merchant's or the scholar's garments. When I go into their wardrobes and handle their vestments, I am reminded of no grassy plains and flowery meads which they have frequented, but of dusty merchants' exchanges and libraries rather.

A tanned skin is something more than respectable, and perhaps olive is a fitter color than white for a man—a denizen of the woods. ''The pale white man!'' I do not wonder that the African pitied him. Darwin the naturalist says, ''A white man bathing by the side of a Tahitian was like a plant bleached by the gardener's art, compared with a fine, dark green one, growing vigorously in the open fields.''

Ben Jonson exclaims,—

''How near to good is what is fair!''

So I would say,—

How near to good is what is *wild!*

Life consists with wildness. The most alive is the wildest. Not yet subdued to man, its presence refreshes him. One who pressed forward incessantly and never rested from his labors, who grew fast and made infinite demands on life, would always find himself in new country or wilderness, and surrounded by the raw material of life. He would be climbing over the prostrate stems of primitive forest-trees.

Hope and the future for me are not in lawns and cultivated fields, not in towns and cities, but in the impervious and quaking swamps. When, formerly, I have analyzed my partiality for some farm which I had contemplated purchasing, I have frequently found that I was attracted solely by a few square rods of impermeable and unfathomable bog—a natural sink in one corner of it. That was the jewel which dazzled me. I derive more of my subsistence from the swamps which surround my native town than from the cultivated gardens in the village. There are no richer parterres to my eyes than the dense beds of dwarf andromeda (*Cassandra calyculata*) which cover these tender places on the earth's surface. Botany cannot go farther than tell me the names of the shrubs which grow there—the high blueberry, panicled andromeda, lambkill, azalea, and rhodora—all standing in the quaking sphagnum. I often think that I should like to have my house front on this mass of dull red bushes, omitting other flower plots and borders, transplanted spruce and trim box, even graveled walks—to have this fertile spot under my windows, not a few imported barrowfuls of soil only to cover the sand which was thrown out in digging the cellar. Why not put my house, my parlor, behind this plot, instead of behind that meagre assemblage of curiosities, that poor apology for a Nature and Art, which I call my front yard? It is an effort to clear up and make a decent appearance when the carpenter and mason have departed, though done as much for the passer-by as the dweller within. The most tasteful front-yard fence was never an agreeable object of study to me; the most elaborate ornaments, acorn tops, or what not, soon wearied and disgusted me. Bring your sills up to the very edge of the swamp, then (though it may not be the best place for a dry cellar), so that there be no access on that side to citizens. Front yards are not made to walk in, but, at most, through, and you could go in the back way.

Yes, though you may think me perverse, if it were proposed to me to dwell in the neighborhood of the most beautiful garden that ever human art contrived, or else of a Dismal Swamp, I should certainly decide for the swamp. How vain, then, have been all your labors, citizens, for me!

My spirits infallibly rise in proportion to the outward dreariness. Give me the ocean, the desert, or the wilderness! In the desert, pure air and solitude compensate for want of moisture and fertility. The traveler Burton says of it: ''Your *morale* improves; you become frank and cordial, hospitable and single-minded. . . . In the desert, spirituous liquors excite only disgust. There is a keen enjoyment in a mere animal existence.'' They who have been traveling long on the steppes of Tartary say, ''On reëntering cultivated lands, the agitation, perplexity, and turmoil of civilization oppressed and suffocated us; the air seemed to fail us, and we felt every moment as if about to die of asphyxia.'' When I would recreate myself, I seek the darkest wood, the thickest and most interminable and, to the citizen, most dismal, swamp. I enter a swamp as a sacred place, a *sanctum sanctorum*. There is the strength, the marrow, of Nature. The wildwood covers the virgin mould, and the same soil is good for men and for trees. A man's health requires as many acres of meadow to his prospect as his farm does loads of muck. There are the strong meats on which he feeds. A town is saved, not more by the righteous men in it than by the woods and swamps that surround it. A township where one primitive forest waves above while another primitive forest rots below—such a town is fitted to raise not only corn and potatoes, but poets and philosophers for the coming ages. In such a soil grew Homer and Confucius and the rest, and out of such a wilderness comes the Reformer eating locusts and wild honey.

To preserve wild animals implies generally the creation of a forest for them to dwell in or resort to. So it is with man. A hundred years ago they sold bark in our streets peeled from our own woods. In the very aspect of those primitive and rugged trees there was, methinks, a tanning principle which hardened and consolidated the fibres of men's thoughts. Ah! already I shudder for these comparatively degenerate days of my native village, when you cannot collect a load of bark of good thickness, and we no longer produce tar and turpentine.

The civilized nations—Greece, Rome, England—have been sustained by the primitive forests which anciently rotted where they stand. They survive as long as the soil is not exhausted. Alas for human culture! little is to be expected of a nation, when the vegetable mould is exhausted, and it is compelled to make manure of the bones of its fathers. There the poet sustains himself merely by his own superfluous fat, and the philosopher comes down on his marrow-bones. . . .

In literature it is only the wild that attracts us. Dullness is but another name for tameness. It is the uncivilized free and wild thinking in Hamlet and the

Iliad, in all the scriptures and mythologies, not learned in the schools, that delights us. As the wild duck is more swift and beautiful than the tame, so is the wild—the mallard—thought, which 'mid falling dews wings its way above the fens. A truly good book is something as natural, and as unexpectedly and unaccountably fair and perfect, as a wild-flower discovered on the prairies of the West or in the jungles of the East. Genius is a light which makes the darkness visible, like the lightning's flash, which perchance shatters the temple of knowledge itself—and not a taper lighted at the hearth-stone of the race, which pales before the light of common day.

English literature, from the days of the minstrels to the Lake Poets—Chaucer and Spenser and Milton, and even Shakespeare, included—breathes no quite fresh and, in this sense, wild strain. It is an essentially tame and civilized literature, reflecting Greece and Rome. Her wilderness is a greenwood, her wild man a Robin Hood. There is plenty of genial love of Nature, but not so much of Nature herself. Her chronicles inform us when her wild animals, but not when the wild man in her, became extinct.

The science of Humboldt is one thing, poetry is another thing. The poet to-day, notwithstanding all the discoveries of science, and the accumulated learning of mankind, enjoys no advantage over Homer.

Where is the literature which gives expression to Nature? He would be a poet who could impress the winds and streams into his service, to speak for him; who nailed words to their primitive senses, as farmers drive down stakes in the spring, which the frost has heaved; who derived his words as often as he used them—transplanted them to his page with earth adhering to their roots; whose words were so true and fresh and natural that they would appear to expand like the buds at the approach of spring, though they lay half smothered between two musty leaves in a library—aye, to bloom and bear fruit there, after their kind, annually, for the faithful reader, in sympathy with surrounding Nature.

I do not know of any poetry to quote which adequately expresses this yearning for the Wild. Approached from this side, the best poetry is tame. I do not know where to find in any literature, ancient or modern, any account which contents me of that Nature with which even I am acquainted. You will perceive that I demand something which no Augustan nor Elizabethan age, which no *culture,* in short, can give. Mythology comes nearer to it than anything. How much more fertile a Nature, at least, has Grecian mythology its root in than English literature! Mythology is the crop which the Old World bore before its soil was exhausted, before the fancy and imagination were affected with blight; and which it still bears, wherever its pristine vigor is unabated. All other literatures endure only as the elms which overshadow our houses; but this is like the great dragon-tree of the Western Isles, as old as mankind, and, whether that does or not, will endure as long; for the decay of other literatures makes the soil in which it thrives.

The West is preparing to add its fables to those of the East. The valleys of the Ganges, the Nile, and the Rhine having yielded their crop, it remains to be seen what the valleys of the Amazon, the Plate, the Orinoco, the St. Lawrence, and the Mississippi will produce. Perchance, when, in the course of ages, American liberty has become a fiction of the past—as it is to some extent a fiction of the present—the poets of the world will be inspired by American mythology.

The wildest dreams of wild men, even, are not the less true, though they may not recommend themselves to the sense which is most common among Englishmen and Americans to-day. It is not every truth that recommends itself to the common sense. Nature has a place for the wild clematis as well as for the cabbage. Some expressions of truth are reminiscent—others merely *sensible,* as the phrase is—others prophetic. Some forms of disease, even, may prophesy forms of health. The geologist has discovered that the figures of serpents, griffins, flying dragons, and other fanciful embellishments of heraldry, have their prototypes in the forms of fossil species which were extinct before man was created, and hence "indicate a faint and shadowy knowledge of a previous state of organic existence." The Hindoos dreamed that the earth rested on an elephant, and the elephant on a tortoise, and the tortoise on a serpent; and though it may be an unimportant coincidence, it will not be out of place here to state, that a fossil tortoise has lately been discovered in Asia large enough to support an elephant. I confess that I am partial to these wild fancies, which transcend the order of time and development. They are the sublimest recreation of the intellect. The partridge loves peas, but not those that go with her into the pot.

In short, all good things are wild and free. There is something in a strain of music, whether produced by an instrument or by the human voice—take the sound of a bugle in a summer night, for instance—which by its wildness, to speak without satire, reminds me of the cries emitted by wild beasts in their native forests. It is so much of their wildness as I can understand. Give me for my friends and neighbors wild men, not tame ones. The wildness of the savage is but a faint symbol of the awful ferity with which good men and lovers meet.

I love even to see the domestic animals reassert their native rights—any evidence that they have not wholly lost their original wild habits and vigor; as when my neighbor's cow breaks out of her pasture early in the spring and boldly swims the river, a cold, gray tide, twenty-five or thirty rods wide, swollen by the melted snow. It is the buffalo crossing the Mississippi. This exploit confers some dignity on the herd in my eyes—already dignified. The seeds of instinct are preserved under the thick hides of cattle and horses, like seeds in the bowels of the earth, an indefinite period.

Any sportiveness in cattle is unexpected. I saw one day a herd of a dozen bullocks and cows running about and frisking in unwieldy sport, like huge rats, even like kittens. They shook their heads, raised their tails, and rushed up and down a hill, and I perceived by their horns, as well as by their activity, their relation to the deer tribe. But, alas! a sudden loud *Whoa!* would have damped their ardor at once, reduced them from venison to beef, and stiffened their sides and sinews like the locomotive. Who but the Evil One has cried ''Whoa!'' to mankind? Indeed, the life of cattle, like that of many men, is but a sort of locomotiveness; they move a side at a time, and man, by his machinery, is meeting the horse and the ox half-way. Whatever

part the whip has touched is thenceforth palsied. Who would ever think of a *side* of any of the supple cat tribe, as we speak of a *side* of beef?

I rejoice that horses and steers have to be broken before they can be made the slaves of men, and that men themselves have some wild oats still left to sow before they become submissive members of society. Undoubtedly, all men are not equally fit subjects for civilization; and because the majority, like dogs and sheep, are tame by inherited disposition, this is no reason why the others should have their natures broken that they may be reduced to the same level. Men are in the main alike, but they were made several in order that they might be various. If a low use is to be served, one man will do nearly or quite as well as another; if a high one, individual excellence is to be regarded. Any man can stop a hole to keep the wind away, but no other man could serve so rare a use as the author of this illustration did. Confucius says, ''The skins of the tiger and the leopard, when they are tanned, are as the skins of the dog and the sheep tanned.'' But it is not the part of a true culture to tame tigers, any more than it is to make sheep ferocious; and tanning their skins for shoes is not the best use to which they can be put. . . .

Here is this vast, savage, howling mother of ours, Nature, lying all around, with such beauty, and such affection for her children, as the leopard; and yet we are so early weaned from her breast to society, to that culture which is exclusively an interaction of man on man—a sort of breeding in and in, which produces at most a merely English nobility, a civilization destined to have a speedy limit.

In society, in the best institutions of men, it is easy to detect a certain precocity. When we should still be growing children, we are already little men. Give me a culture which imports much muck from the meadows, and deepens the soil—not that which trusts to heating manures, and improved implements and modes of culture only! . . .

I would not have every man nor every part of a man cultivated, any more than I would have every acre of earth cultivated: part will be tillage, but the greater part will be meadow and forest, not only serving an immediate use, but preparing a mould against a distant future, by the annual decay of the vegetation which it supports.

There are other letters for the child to learn than those which Cadmus invented. The Spaniards have a good term to express this wild and dusky knowledge, *Gramática parda,* tawny grammar, a kind of mother-wit derived from that same leopard to which I have referred.

We have heard of a Society for the Diffusion of Useful Knowledge. It is said that knowledge is power, and the like. Methinks there is equal need of a Society for the Diffusion of Useful Ignorance, what we will call Beautiful Knowledge, a knowledge useful in a higher sense: for what is most of our boasted so-called knowledge but a conceit that we know something, which robs us of the advantage of our actual ignorance? What we call knowledge is often our positive ignorance; ignorance our negative knowledge. By long years of patient industry and reading of the newspapers—for what are the libraries of science but files of newspapers?—a man accumulates a myriad facts, lays them up in his memory, and then when in some spring of his life he saunters abroad into the Great Fields of thought, he, as it were, goes to grass like a horse and leaves all his harness behind in the stable. I would say to the Society for the Diffusion of Useful Knowledge, sometimes,—Go to grass. You have eaten hay long enough. The spring has come with its green crop. The very cows are driven to their country pastures before the end of May; though I have heard of one unnatural farmer who kept his cow in the barn and fed her on hay all the year round. So, frequently, the Society for the Diffusion of Useful Knowledge treats its cattle.

A man's ignorance sometimes is not only useful, but beautiful—while his knowledge, so called, is oftentimes worse than useless, besides being ugly. Which is the best man to deal with—he who knows nothing about a subject, and, what is extremely rare, knows that he knows nothing, or he who really knows something about it, but thinks that he knows all?

My desire for knowledge is intermittent, but my desire to bathe my head in atmospheres unknown to my feet is perennial and constant. The highest that we can attain to is not Knowledge, but Sympathy with Intelligence. I do not know that his higher knowledge amounts to anything more definite than a novel and grand surprise on a sudden revelation of the insufficiency of all that we called Knowledge before—a discovery that there are more things in heaven and earth than are dreamed of in our philosophy. It is the lighting up of the mist by the sun. . . .

It is remarkable how few events or crises there are in our histories, how little exercised we have been in our minds, how few experiences we have had. I would fain be assured that I am growing apace and rankly, though my very growth disturb this dull equanimity—though it be with struggle through long, dark, muggy nights or seasons of gloom. It would be well if all our lives were a divine tragedy even, instead of this trivial comedy or farce. Dante, Bunyan, and others appear to have been exercised in their minds more than we: they were subjected to a kind of culture such as our district schools and colleges do not contemplate. Even Mahomet, though many may scream at his name, had a good deal more to live for, aye, and to die for, than they have commonly.

When, at rare intervals, some thought visits one, as perchance he is walking on a railroad, then, indeed, the cars go by without his hearing them. But soon, by some inexorable law, our life goes by and the cars return.

> Gentle breeze, that wanderest unseen,
> And bendest the thistles round Loira of storms,
> Traveler of the windy glens,
> Why hast thou left my ear so soon?

While almost all men feel an attraction drawing them to society, few are attracted strongly to Nature. In their reaction to Nature men appear to me for the most part, notwithstanding their arts, lower than the animals. It is not often a beautiful relation, as in the case of the animals. How little appreciation of the beauty of the landscape there is among us! We have to be told that the Greeks called the world Κόσμος, Beauty, or Order, but we do not see clearly why they did so, and we esteem it at best only a curious philological fact.

For my part, I feel that with regard to Nature I live a sort of border life, on the confines of a world into which I make occasional and transient forays only, and my patriotism and allegiance to the state into whose territories I seem to retreat are those of a moss-trooper. Unto a life which I call natural I would gladly follow even a will-o'-the-wisp through bogs and sloughs unimaginable, but no moon nor firefly has shown me the causeway to it. Nature is a personality so vast and universal that we have never seen one of her features. The walker in the familiar fields which stretch around my native town sometimes finds himself in another land than is described in their owners' deeds, as it were in some faraway field on the confines of the actual Concord, where her jurisdiction ceases, and the idea which the word Concord suggests ceases to be suggested. These farms which I have myself surveyed, these bounds which I have set up, appear dimly still as through a mist: but they have no chemistry to fix them; they fade from the surface of the glass, and the picture which the painter painted stands out dimly from beneath. The world with which we are commonly acquainted leaves no trace, and it will have no anniversary.

I took a walk on Spaulding's Farm the other afternoon. I saw the setting sun lighting up the opposite side of a stately pine wood. Its golden rays straggled into the aisles of the wood as into some noble hall. I was impressed as if some ancient and altogether admirable and shining family had settled there in that part of the land called Concord, unknown to me,—to whom the sun was servant,—who had not gone into society in the village,—who had not been called on. I saw their park, their pleasure-ground, beyond through the wood, in Spaulding's cranberry-meadow. The pines furnished them with gables as they grew. Their house was not obvious to vison; the trees grew through it. I do not know whether I heard the sounds of a suppressed hilarity or not. They seemed to recline on the sunbeams. They have sons and daughters. They are quite well. The farmer's cart-path, which leads directly through their hall, does not in the least put them out, as the muddy bottom of a pool is sometimes seen through the reflected skies. They never heard of Spaulding, and do not know that he is their neigh-

bor—notwithstanding I heard him whistle as he drove his team through the house. Nothing can equal the serenity of their lives. Their coat-of-arms is simply a lichen. I saw it painted on the pines and oaks. Their attics were in the tops of the trees. They are of no politics. There was no noise of labor. I did not perceive that they were weaving or spinning. Yet I did detect, when the wind lulled and hearing was done away, the finest imaginable sweet musical hum—as of a distant hive in May—which perchance was the sound of their thinking. They had no idle thoughts, and no one without could see their work, for their industry was not as in knots and excrescences embayed.

But I find it difficult to remember them. They fade irrevocably out of my mind even now while I speak, and endeavor to recall them and recollect myself. It is only after a long and serious effort to recollect my best thoughts that I become again aware of their co-habitancy. If it were not for such families as this, I think I should move out of Concord.

We are accustomed to say in New England that few and fewer pigeons visit us every year. Our forests furnish no mast for them. So, it would seem, few and fewer thoughts visit each growing man from year to year, for the grove in our minds is laid waste—sold to feed unnecessary fires of ambition, or sent to mill—and there is scarcely a twig left for them to perch on. They no longer build nor breed with us. In some more genial season, perchance, a faint shadow flits across the landscape of the mind, cast by the *wings* of some thought in its vernal or autumnal migration, but, looking up, we are unable to detect the substance of the thought itself. Our winged thoughts are turned to poultry. . . .

We hug the earth—how rarely we mount! Methinks we might elevate ourselves a little more. We might climb a tree, at least. I found my account in climbing a tree once. It was a tall white pine, on the top of a hill; and though I got well pitched, I was well paid for it, for I discovered new mountains in the horizon which I had never seen before—so much more of the earth and the heavens. I might have walked about the foot of the tree for threescore years and ten, and yet I certainly should never have seen them. But, above all, I discovered around me—it was near the end of June—on the ends of the topmost branches only, a few minute and delicate red cone-like blossoms, the fertile flower of the white pine looking heavenward. I carried straightway to the village the topmost spire, and showed it to stranger jurymen who walked the streets—for it was court week—and to farmers and lumber-dealers and wood-choppers and hunters, and not one had ever seen the like before, but they wondered as at a star dropped down. Tell of ancient architects finishing their works on the tops of columns as perfectly as on the lower and more visible parts! Nature has from the first expanded the minute blossoms of the forest only toward the heavens, above men's heads and unobserved by them. We see only the flowers that are under our feet in the meadows. The pines have developed their delicate blossoms on the highest twigs of the wood every summer for ages, as well over the heads of Nature's red children as of her white ones; yet scarcely a farmer or hunter in the land has ever seen them.

Above all, we cannot afford not to live in the present. He is blessed over all mortals who loses no moment of the passing life in remembering the past. Unless our philosophy hears the cock crow in every barn-yard within our horizon, it is belated. That sound commonly reminds us that we are growing rusty and antique in our employments and habits of thought. His philosophy comes down to a more recent time than ours. There is something suggested by it that is a newer testament—the gospel according to this moment. He has not fallen astern; he has got up early and kept up early, and to be where he is is to be in season, in the foremost rank of time. It is an expression of the health and soundness of Nature, a brag for all the world—healthiness as of a spring burst forth, a new fountain of the Muses, to celebrate this last instant of time. Where he lives no fugitive slave laws are passed. Who has not betrayed his master many times since last he heard that note?

The merit of this bird's strain is in its freedom from all plaintiveness. The singer can easily move us to tears or to laughter, but where is he who can excite in us a pure morning joy? When, in doleful dumps, breaking the awful stillness of our wooden sidewalk on a Sunday, or, perchance, a watcher in the house of mourning, I hear a cockerel crow far or near, I think to myself, "There is one of us well, at any rate,"—and with a sudden gush return to my senses.

We had a remarkable sunset one day last November. I was walking in a meadow, the source of a small brook, when the sun at last, just before setting, after a cold, gray day, reached a clear stratum in the horizon, and the softest, brightest morning sunlight fell on the dry grass and on the stems of the trees in the opposite horizon and on the leaves of the shrub oaks on the hillside, while our shadows stretched long over the meadow eastward, as if we were the only motes in its beams. It was such a light as we could not have imagined a moment before, and the air also was so warm and serene that nothing was wanting to make a paradise of that meadow. When we reflected that this was not a solitary phenomenon, never to happen again, but that it would happen forever and ever, an infinite number of evenings, and cheer and reassure the latest child that walked there, it was more glorious still.

The sun sets on some retired meadow, where no house is visible, with all the glory and splendor that it lavishes on cities, and perchance as it has never set before—where there is but a solitary marsh hawk to have his wings gilded by it, or only a musquash looks out from his cabin, and there is some little black-veined brook in the midst of the marsh, just beginning to meander, winding slowly round a decaying stump. We walked in so pure and bright a light, gilding the withered grass and leaves, so softly and serenely bright, I thought I had never bathed in such a golden flood, without a ripple or a murmur to it. The west side of every wood and rising ground gleamed like the boundary of Elysium, and the sun on our backs seemed like a gentle herdsman driving us home at evening.

So we saunter toward the Holy Land, till one day the sun shall shine more brightly than ever he has done, shall perchance shine into our minds and hearts, and light up our whole lives with a great awakening light, as warm and serene and golden as on a bankside in autumn.

DISCUSSION TOPICS

1. What might Thoreau mean by saying "In my walks I would fair return to my senses"?
2. What might Thoreau mean by saying that "to enjoy a thing exclusively is commonly to exclude yourself from the true enjoyment of it"? Do you agree with him?
3. Thoreau states that "in Wildness is the preservation of the world." What reasoning does he present in support of this assertion?
4. Thoreau urges us to walk toward the Holy Land. What does he mean by "Holy Land"? Have you ever taken such a walk?
5. Who lives at Spaulding's Farm?

READING 13

A Near View of the High Sierra

John Muir

Born in Scotland, John Muir (1838-1914) labored on a pioneer Wisconsin farm and wandered alone in the wilds of Canada, walked a thousand miles from Wisconsin to the Gulf of Mexico, and delighted in the glories of the Sierra Nevada mountains of California. For Muir the natural world was both a laboratory for scientific research and a temple for worship. Almost every step in the mountains brought him a fresh revelation. His writings for periodicals in the late nineteenth century had wide influence. He was a prime mover in the national park system, and played a central role in preserving what is now Yosemite National Park. He was president of the Sierra Club from its founding in 1892 until his death. Muir's writings continue to inspire his readers to a deeper appreciation of what wilderness offers the solitary adventurer.

In "A New View of the High Sierra" Muir describes

his descent into Yosemite Valley after one of his expeditions into the high country in the early 1870s. He describes his meeting with two artists and his agreement to guide them to a "landscape suitable for a large painting." Leaving them at their work, Muir proceeds on a perilous climb up the glacier-clad Mt. Ritter. He provides a vivid description of the sensory and emotional richness of his mountaineering experience. Muir finds that his strenuous journey into wild beauty both leads him far out of himself and feeds his sense of who he really is.

Early one bright morning in the middle of Indian summer, while the glacier meadows were still crisp with frost crystals, I set out from the foot of Mount Lyell, on my way down to Yosemite Valley, to replenish my exhausted store of bread and tea. I had spent the past summer, as many preceding ones, exploring the glaciers that lie on the head waters of the San Joaquin, Tuolumne, Merced, and Owen's rivers; measuring and studying their movements, trends, crevasses, moraines, etc., and the part they had played during the period of their greater extension in the creation and development of the landscapes of this alpine wonderland. . . .

To artists, few portions of the High Sierra are, strictly speaking, picturesque. The whole massive uplift of the range is one great picture, not clearly divisible into smaller ones; differing much in this respect from the older, and what may be called, riper mountains of the Coast Range. All the landscapes of the Sierra, as we have seen, were born again, remodeled from base to summit by the developing ice-floods of the last glacial winter. But all these new landscapes were not brought forth simultaneously; some of the highest, where the ice lingered longest, are tens of centuries younger than those of the warmer regions below them. In general, the younger the mountain-landscapes—younger, I mean, with reference to the time of their emergence from the ice of the glacial period—the less separable are they into artistic bits capable of being made into warm, sympathetic, lovable pictures with appreciable humanity in them.

Here, however, on the head waters of the Tuolumne, is a group of wild peaks on which the geologist may say that the sun has but just begun to shine, which is yet in a high degree picturesque, and in its main features so regular and evenly balanced as almost to appear conventional—one somber cluster of snow-laden peaks with gray pine-fringed granite bosses braided around its base, the whole surging free into the sky from the head of a magnificent valley, whose lofty walls are beveled away on both sides so as to embrace it all without admitting anything not strictly belonging to it. The foreground was now aflame with autumn colors, brown and purple and gold, ripe in the mellow sunshine; contrasting brightly with the deep, cobalt blue of the sky, and the black and gray, and pure, spiritual white of the rocks and glaciers. Down through the midst, the young Tuolumne was seen pouring from its crystal fountains, now resting in glassy pools as if changing back again into ice, now leaping in white cascades as if turning to snow; glid-ing right and left between granite bosses, then sweep-ing on through the smooth, meadowy levels of the valley, swaying pensively from side to side with calm, stately gestures past dipping willows and sedges, and around groves of arrowy pine; and throughout its whole eventful course, whether flowing fast or slow, singing loud or low, ever filling the landscape with spiritual animation, and manifesting the grandeur of its sources in every movement and tone.

Pursuing my lonely way down the valley, I turned again and again to gaze on the glorious picture, throw-ing up my arms to inclose it as in a frame. After long ages of growth in the darkness beneath the glaciers, through sunshine and storms, it seemed now to be ready and waiting for the elected artist, like yellow wheat for the reaper; and I could not help wishing that I might carry colors and brushes with me on my trav-els, and learn to paint. In the mean time I had to be content with photographs on my mind and sketches in my note-books. At length, after I had rounded a precipitous headland that puts out from the west wall of the valley, every peak vanished from sight, and I pushed rapidly along the frozen meadows, over the divide between the waters of the Merced and Tuol-umne, and down through the forests that clothe the slopes of Cloud's Rest, arriving in Yosemite in due time—which, with me, is *any* time. And, strange to say, among the first people I met here were two artists

who, with letters of introduction, were awaiting my return. They inquired whether in the course of my explorations in the adjacent mountains I had ever come upon a landscape suitable for a large painting; whereupon I began a description of the one that had so lately excited my admiration. Then, as I went on further and further into details, their faces began to glow, and I offered to guide them to it, while they declared that they would gladly follow, far or near, whithersoever I could spare the time to lead them.

Since storms might come breaking down through the fine weather at any time, burying the colors in snow, and cutting off the artists' retreat, I advised getting ready at once.

I led them out of the valley by the Vernal and Nevada Falls, thence over the main dividing ridge to the Big Tuolumne Meadows, by the old Mono trail, and thence along the upper Tuolumne River to its head. This was my companions' first excursion into the High Sierra, and as I was almost always alone in my mountaineering, the way that the fresh beauty was reflected in their faces made for me a novel and inter-esting study. They naturally were affected most of all by the colors—the intense azure of the sky, the pur-plish grays of the granite, the red and browns of dry meadows, and the translucent purple and crimson of huckleberry bogs; the flaming yellow of aspen groves, the silvery flashing of the streams, and the bright green and blue of the glacier lakes. But the general expres-sion of the scenery—rocky and savage—seemed sadly disappointing; and as they threaded the forest from ridge to ridge, eagerly scanning the landscapes as they were unfolded, they said: ''All this is huge and sublime, but we see nothing as yet at all available for effective pictures. Art is long, and art is limited, you know; and here are foregrounds, middle-grounds, backgrounds, all alike; bare rock-waves, woods, groves, diminutive flecks of meadow, and strips of glittering water.'' ''Never mind,'' I replied, ''only bide a wee, and I will show you something you will like.''

At length, toward the end of the second day, the Sierra Crown began to come into view, and when we had fairly rounded the projecting headland before mentioned, the whole picture stood revealed in the flush of the alpenglow. Their enthusiasm was excited beyond bounds, and the more impulsive of the two, a young Scotchman, dashed ahead, shouting and gesticulating and tossing his arms in the air like a madman. Here, at last, was a typical alpine landscape.

After feasting awhile on the view, I proceeded to make camp in a sheltered grove a little way back from the meadow, where pine-boughs could be obtained for beds, and where there was plenty of dry wood for fires, while the artists ran here and there, along the river-bends and up the sides of the cañon, choosing foregrounds for sketches. After dark, when our tea was made and a rousing fire had been built, we began to make our plans. They decided to remain several days, at the least, while I concluded to make an excursion in the meantime to the untouched summit of Ritter.

It was now about the middle of October, the springtime of snow-flowers. The first winter-clouds had already bloomed, and the peaks were strewn with fresh crystals, without, however, affecting the climbing to any dangerous extent. And as the weather was still profoundly calm, and the distance to the foot of the mountain only a little more than a day, I felt that I was running no great risk of being storm-bound.

Mount Ritter is king of the mountains of the middle portion of the High Sierra, as Shasta of the north and Whitney of the south sections. Moreover, as far as I know, it had never been climbed. I had explored the adjacent wilderness summer after summer; but my studies thus far had never drawn me to the top of it. Its height above sea-level is about 13,300 feet, and it is fenced round by steeply inclined glaciers, and cañons of tremendous depth and ruggedness, which render it almost inaccessible. But difficulties of this kind only exhilarate the mountaineer.

Next morning, the artists went heartily to their work and I to mine. Former experiences had given good reason to know that passionate storms, invisible as yet, might be brooding in the calm sun-gold; therefore, before bidding farewell, I warned the artists not to be alarmed should I fail to appear before a week or ten days, and advised them, in case a snow-storm should set in, to keep up big fires and shelter themselves as best they could, and on no account to become

frightened and attempt to seek their way back to Yosemite alone through the drifts.

My general plan was simply this: to scale the cañon wall, cross over to the eastern flank of the range, and then make my way southward to the northern spurs of Mount Ritter in compliance with the intervening topography; for to push on directly southward from camp through the innumerable peaks and pinnacles that adorn this portion of the axis of the range, however interesting, would take too much time, besides being extremely difficult and dangerous at this time of year.

All my first day was pure pleasure; simply mountaineering indulgence, crossing the dry pathways of the ancient glaciers, tracing happy streams, and learning the habits of the birds and marmots in the groves and rocks. Before I had gone a mile from camp, I came to the foot of a white cascade that beats its way down a rugged gorge in the cañon wall, from a height of about nine hundred feet, and pours its throbbing waters into the Tuolumne. I was acquainted with its fountains, which, fortunately, lay in my course. What a fine traveling companion it proved to be, what songs it sang, and how passionately it told the mountain's own joy! Gladly I climbed along its dashing border, absorbing its divine music, and bathing from time to time in waftings of irised spray. Climbing higher, higher, new beauty came streaming on the sight: painted meadows, late-blooming gardens, peaks of rare architecture, lakes here and there, shining like silver, and glimpses of the forested middle region and the yellow lowlands far in the west. Beyond the range I saw the so-called Mono Desert, lying dreamily silent in thick purple light—a desert of heavy sun-glare beheld from a desert of ice-burnished granite. Here the waters divide, shouting in glorious enthusiasm, and falling eastward to vanish in the volcanic sands and dry sky of the Great Basin, or westward to the Great Valley of California, and thence through the Bay of San Francisco and the Golden Gate to the sea.

Passing a little way down over the summit until I had reached an elevation of about 10,000 feet, I pushed on southward toward a group of savage peaks that stand guard about Ritter on the north and west, groping my way; and dealing instinctively with every obstacle as it presented itself. Here a huge gorge would be found cutting across my path, along the dizzy edge of which I scrambled until some less precipitous point was discovered where I might safely venture to the bottom and then, selecting some feasible portion of the opposite wall, reascend with the same slow caution. Massive, flat-topped spurs alternate with the gorges, plunging abruptly from the shoulders of the snowy peaks, and planting their feet in the warm desert. These were everywhere marked and adorned with characteristic sculptures of the ancient glaciers that swept over this entire region like one vast ice-wind, and the polished surfaces produced by the ponderous flood are still so perfectly preserved that in many places the sunlight reflected from them is about as trying to the eyes as sheets of snow.

God's glacial-mills grind slowly, but they have been kept in motion long enough in California to grind sufficient soil for a glorious abundance of life, though most of the grist has been carried to the lowlands, leaving these high regions comparatively lean and bare; while the post-glacial agents of erosion have not yet furnished sufficient available food over the general surface for more than a few tufts of the hardiest plants, chiefly carices and eriogonæ. . . . In so wild and so beautiful a region was spent my first day, every sight and sound inspiring, leading one far out of himself, yet feeding and building up his individuality.

Now came the solemn, silent evening. Long, blue, spiky shadows crept out across the snow-fields, while a rosy glow, at first scarce discernible, gradually deepened and suffused every mountain-top, flushing the glaciers and the harsh crags above them. This was the alpenglow, to me one of the most impressive of all the terrestrial manifestations of God. At the touch of this divine light, the mountains seemed to kindle to a rapt, religious consciousness, and stood hushed and waiting like devout worshipers. Just before the alpenglow began to fade, two crimson clouds came streaming across the summit like wings of flame, rendering the sublime scene yet more impressive; then came darkness and the stars. . . .

I made my bed in a nook of the pine-thicket, where the branches were pressed and crinkled overhead like a roof, and bent down around the sides. These are the best bedchambers the high mountains afford—snug as squirrel-nests, well ventilated, full of spicy odors, and with plenty of wind-played needles to sing one asleep. I little expected company, but, creeping in through a low side-door, I found five or six birds nestling among the tassels. The night-wind began to blow soon after dark; at first only a gentle breathing, but increasing toward midnight to a rough gale that fell upon my leafy roof in ragged surges like a cascade, bearing wild sounds from the crags overhead. The waterfall sang in chorus, filling the old ice-fountain with its solemn roar, and seeming to increase in power as the night advanced—fit voice for such a landscape. I had to creep out many times to the fire during the night, for it was biting cold and I had no blankets. Gladly I welcomed the morning star.

The dawn in the dry, wavering air of the desert was glorious. Everything encouraged my undertaking and betokened success. There was no cloud in the sky, no storm-tone in the wind. Breakfast of bread and tea was soon made. I fastened a hard, durable crust to my belt by way of provision, in case I should be compelled to pass a night on the mountain-top; then, securing the remainder of my little stock against wolves and wood-rats, I set forth free and hopeful.

How glorious a greeting the sun gives the mountains! To behold this alone is worth the pains of any excursion a thousand times over. The highest peaks burned like islands in a sea of liquid shade. Then the lower peaks and spires caught the glow, and long lances of light, streaming through many a notch and pass, fell thick on the frozen meadows. The majestic form of Ritter was full in sight, and I pushed rapidly on over rounded rock-bosses and pavements, my iron-shod shoes making a clanking sound, suddenly hushed now and then in rugs of bryanthus, and sedgy lake-margins soft as moss. . . .

On the southern shore of a frozen lake, I encountered an extensive field of hard, granular snow, up which I scampered in fine tone, intending to follow it to its head, and cross the rocky spur against which it leans, hoping thus to come direct upon the base of the main Ritter peak. The surface was pitted with oval hollows, made by stones and drifted pine-needles that had melted themselves into the mass by the radiation of absorbed sun-heat. These afforded good footholds, but the surface curved more and more steeply at the head, and the pits became shallower and less abundant, until I found myself in danger of being shed off like avalanching snow. I persisted, however, creeping on all fours, and shuffling up the smoothest places on my back, as I had often done on burnished granite, until, after slipping several times, I was compelled to retrace my course to the bottom, and make my way around the west end of the lake, and thence up to the summit of the divide between the head waters of Rush Creek and the northernmost tributaries of the San Joaquin.

Arriving on the summit of this dividing crest, one of the most exciting pieces of pure wilderness was disclosed that I ever discovered in all my mountaineering. There, immediately in front, loomed the majestic mass of Mount Ritter, with a glacier swooping down its face nearly to my feet, then curving westward and pouring its frozen flood into a dark blue lake, whose shores were bound with precipices of crystalline snow; while a deep chasm drawn between the divide and the glacier separated the massive picture from everything else. I could see only the one sublime mountain, the one glacier, the one lake; the whole veiled with one blue shadow—rock, ice, and water close together without a single leaf or sign of life. After gazing spellbound, I began instinctively to scrutinize every notch and gorge and weathered buttress of the mountain, with reference to making the ascent. The entire front above the glacier appeared as one tremendous precipice, slightly receding at the top, and bristling with spires and pinnacles set above one another in formidable array. Massive lichen-stained battlements stood forward here and there, hacked at the top with angular notches, and separated by frosty gullies and recesses that have been veiled in shadow ever since their creation; while to right and left, as far as I could see, were huge, crumbling buttresses, offering no hope to the climber. . . .

I could not distinctly hope to reach the summit from this side, yet I moved on across the glacier as if driven by fate. Contending with myself, the season is too far spent, I said, and even should I be successful, I might be storm-bound on the mountain; and in the cloud-darkness, with the cliffs and crevasses covered with snow, how could I escape! No; I must wait till next summer. I would only approach the mountain now, and inspect it, creep about its flanks, learn what I could of its history, holding myself ready to flee on the approach of the first storm-cloud. But we little know until tried how much of the uncontrollable there is in us, urging across glaciers and torrents, and up dangerous heights, let the judgment forbid as it may.

I succeeded in gaining the foot of the cliff on the eastern extremity of the glacier, and there discovered the mouth of a narrow avalanche gully, through which I began to climb, intending to follow it as far as possible, and at least obtain some fine wild views for my pains. . . .

I thus made my way into a wilderness of crumbling spires and battlements, built together in bewildering combinations, and glazed in many places with a thin coating of ice, which I had to hammer off with stones. The situation was becoming gradually more perilous; but, having passed several dangerous spots, I dared not think of descending; for, so steep was the entire ascent, one would inevitably fall to the glacier in case a single misstep were made. . . .

At length, after attaining an elevation of about 12,800 feet, I found myself at the foot of a sheer drop in the bed of the avalanche channel I was tracing, which seemed absolutely to bar further progress. It was only about forty-five or fifty feet high, and somewhat roughened by fissures and projections; but these seemed so slight and insecure, as footholds, that I tried hard to avoid the precipice altogether, by scaling the wall of the channel on either side. But, though less steep, the walls were smoother than the obstructing rock, and repeated efforts only showed that I must either go right ahead or turn back. The tried dangers beneath seemed even greater than that of the cliff in front; therefore, after scanning its face again and again, I began to scale it, picking my holds with intense caution. After gaining a point about half-way to the top, I was suddenly brought to a dead stop, with arms outspread, clinging close to the face of the rock, unable to move hand or foot either up or down. My doom appeared fixed. I *must* fall. There would be a moment of bewilderment, and then a lifeless rumble down the one general precipice to the glacier below.

When this final danger flashed upon me, I became

nerve-shaken for the first time since setting foot on the mountains, and my mind seemed to fill with a stifling smoke. But this terrible eclipse lasted only a moment, when life blazed forth again with preternatural clearness. I seemed suddenly to become possessed of a new sense. The other self, bygone experiences, Instinct, or Guardian Angel—call it what you will—came forward and assumed control. Then my trembling muscles became firm again, every rift and flaw in the rock was seen as through a microscope, and my limbs moved with a positiveness and precision with which I seemed to have nothing at all to do. Had I been borne aloft upon wings, my deliverance could not have been more complete.

Above this memorable spot, the face of the mountain is still more savagely hacked and torn. It is a maze of yawning chasms and gullies, in the angles of which rise beetling crags and piles of detached boulders that seem to have been gotten ready to be launched below. But the strange influx of strength I had received seemed inexhaustible. I found a way without effort, and soon stood upon the topmost crag in the blessed light.

How truly glorious the landscape circled around this noble summit!—giant mountains, valleys innumerable, glaciers and meadows, rivers and lakes, with the wide blue sky bent tenderly over them all. But in my first hour of freedom from that terrible shadow, the sunlight in which I was laving seemed all in all.

Looking southward along the axis of the range, the eye is first caught by a row of exceedingly sharp and slender spires, which rise openly to a height of about a thousand feet, above a series of short, residual glaciers that lean back against their bases; their fantastic sculpture and the unrelieved sharpness with which they spring out of the ice rendering them peculiarly wild and striking. These are ''The Minarets.'' Beyond them you behold a sublime wilderness of mountains, their snowy summits towering together in crowded abundance, peak beyond peak, swelling higher, higher as they sweep on southward, until the culminating point of the range is reached on Mount Whitney, near the head of the Kern River, at an elevation of nearly 14,700 feet above the level of the sea. . . .

Lakes are seen gleaming in all sorts of places— round, or oval, or square, like very mirrors; others

narrow and sinuous, drawn close around the peaks like silver zones, the highest reflecting only rocks, snow, and the sky. But neither these nor the glaciers, nor the bits of brown meadow and moorland that occur here and there, are large enough to make any marked impression upon the mighty wilderness of mountains. The eye, rejoicing in its freedom, roves about the vast expanse, yet returns again and again to the fountain peaks. Perhaps some one of the multitude excites special attention, some gigantic castle with turret and battlement, or some Gothic cathedral more abundantly spired than Milan's. But, generally, when looking for the first time from an all-embracing standpoint like this, the inexperienced observer is oppressed by the incomprehensible grandeur, variety, and abundance of the mountains rising shoulder to shoulder beyond the reach of vision; and it is only after they have been studied one by one, long and lovingly, that their far-reaching harmonies become manifest. Then, penetrate the wilderness where you may, the main telling features, to which all the surrounding topography is subordinate, are quickly perceived, and the most complicated clusters of peaks stand revealed harmoniously correlated and fashioned like works of art—eloquent monuments of the ancient ice-rivers that brought them into relief from the general mass of the range. The cañons, too, some of them a mile deep, mazing wildly through the mighty host of mountains, however lawless and ungovernable at first sight they appear, are at length recognized as the necessary effects of causes which followed each other in harmonious sequence—Nature's poems carved on tables of stone—the simplest and most emphatic of her glacial compositions.

Could we have been here to observe during the glacial period, we should have overlooked a wrinkled ocean of ice as continuous as that now covering the landscapes of Greenland; filling every valley and cañon with only the tops of the fountain peaks rising darkly above the rock-encumbered ice-waves like islets in a stormy sea—those islets the only hints of the glorious landscapes now smiling in the sun. Standing here in the deep, brooding silence all the wilderness seems motionless, as if the work of creation were done. But in the midst of this outer steadfastness we know there is incessant motion and change. Ever and anon, avalanches are falling from yonder peaks. These cliff-bound glaciers, seemingly wedged and immovable, are flowing like water and grinding the rocks beneath them. The lakes are lapping their granite shores and wearing them away, and every one of these rills and young rivers is fretting the air into music, and carrying the mountains to the plains. Here are the roots of all the life of the valleys, and here more simply than elsewhere is the eternal flux of nature manifested. Ice changing to water, lakes to meadows, and mountains to plains. And while we thus contemplate Nature's methods of landscape creation, and, reading the records she has carved on the rocks, reconstruct, however imperfectly, the landscapes of the past, we also learn that as these we now behold have succeeded those of the preglacial age, so they in turn are withering and vanishing to be succeeded by others yet unborn.

But in the midst of these fine lessons and landscapes, I had to remember that the sun was wheeling far to the west, while a new way down the mountain had to be discovered to some point on the timber line where I could have a fire; for I had not even burdened myself with a coat. I first scanned the western spurs, hoping some way might appear through which I might reach the northern glacier, and cross its snout; or pass around the lake into which it flows, and thus strike my morning track. This route was soon sufficiently unfolded to show that, if practicable at all, it would require so much time that reaching camp that night would be out of the question. I therefore scrambled back eastward, descending the southern slopes obliquely at the same time. Here the crags seemed less formidable, and the head of a glacier that flows northeast came in sight, which I determined to follow as far as possible, hoping thus to make my way to the foot of the peak on the east side, and thence across the intervening cañons and ridges to camp.

The inclination of the glacier is quite moderate at the head, and, as the sun had softened the *névé,* I made safe and rapid progress, running and sliding, and keeping up a sharp outlook for crevasses. . . .

Night drew near before I reached the eastern base of the mountain, and my camp lay many a rugged mile to the north; but ultimate success was assured. It was now only a matter of endurance and ordinary mountain-craft. The sunset was, if possible, yet more beautiful than that of the day before. The Mono landscape seemed to be fairly saturated with warm, purple light. The peaks marshaled along the summit were in shadow, but through every notch and pass streamed vivid sun-fire, soothing and irradiating their rough, black angles, while companies of small luminous clouds hovered above them like very angels of light. . . . I discovered the little pine thicket in which my nest was, and then I had a rest such as only a tired mountaineer may enjoy. After lying loose and lost for awhile, I made a sunrise fire, went down to the lake, dashed water on my head, and dipped a cupful for tea. The revival brought about by bread and tea was as complete as the exhaustion from excessive enjoyment and toil. Then I crept beneath the pine-tassels to bed. The wind was frosty and the fire burned low, but my sleep was none the less sound, and the evening constellations had swept far to the west before I awoke.

After thawing and resting in the morning sunshine, I sauntered home—that is, back to the Tuolumne camp—bearing away toward a cluster of peaks that hold the fountain snows of one of the north tributaries of Rush Creek. Here I discovered a group of beautiful glacier lakes, nestled together in a grand amphitheater. Toward evening, I crossed the divide separating the Mono waters from those of the Tuolumne, and entered the glacier basin that now holds the fountain snows of the stream that forms the upper Tuolumne cascades. This stream I traced down through its many dells and gorges, meadows and bogs, reaching the brink of the main Tuolumne at dusk.

A loud whoop for the artists was answered again and again. Their camp-fire came in sight, and half an hour afterward I was with them. They seemed unreasonably glad to see me. I had been absent only three days; nevertheless, though the weather was fine, they had already been weighing chances as to whether I would ever return, and trying to decide whether they should wait longer or begin to seek their way back to the lowlands. Now their curious troubles were over. They packed their precious sketches, and next morning we set out homeward bound, and in two days entered the Yosemite Valley from the north by way of Indian Cañon.

DISCUSSION TOPICS

1. Muir's writing contains scientific observation, aesthetic delight, religious inspiration, and moral instruction. Find a passage in the reading which illustrates each of the four perspectives.
2. Muir's anthropomorphism is out of fashion today. Find an example in the essay and consider its effect on the reader. In your view, does it add or detract from the vividness of his account?
3. Describe Muir's experience of danger on the cliff face. How did he react to the situation? How would you have reacted?
4. What process of change in perception does Muir describe regarding the ''incomprehensible grandeur'' of the view from the top of Mt. Ritter?
5. Why do you think Muir climbs Mt. Ritter without bringing a coat or blanket?

READING 14

John Muir on Mount Ritter: A New Wilderness Aesthetic

Philip G. Terrie

Philip G. Terrie (b. 1948) is Professor of English and American Studies at Bowling Green State University. In the following essay he maintains that Muir added a new dimension to the aesthetic appreciation of nature because Muir rejected the romantic view of nature as scenery. ''Romantic'' travelers appreciated the pleasing visual aspects of nature, but did not apprehend the geological and biological processes. Muir was aware that most people would overlook or reject natural processes such as complex, ongoing glaciation and the ever-present possibility of death of the individual creature.

While John Muir has been the subject of considerable scholarly scrutiny in recent years, we have yet to arrive at a complete understanding of his response to nature.[1] One reason is that we are often too eager to portray him as a radical, late twentieth-century environmentalist; radical he was, but in his time and place. Another problem—and the one to be addressed here—is the failure to put his narratives into the context of nineteenth-century American wilderness literature, of which there is a substantial cañon. Muir was writing in the framework of an established tradition, and one of the more radical features of his own narratives is the way they depart from the conventions of that tradition. Except for the 1984 study by Michael P. Cohen, I know of no serious effort to understand Muir in the larger context of nineteenth-century wilderness literature.

Beginning in the early decades of the nineteenth century, literate Americans showed an increasing fascination wih their wilderness. Eventually this interest evolved its own distinct literature, which existed on both a popular and an elite cultural level. Examples of these would be Joel T. Headley's *The Adirondack; Or, Life in the Woods,* published in 1849, a book which was reissued, reprinted, expanded, and plagiarized in numerous editions over a period of some thirty-five years, and Thoreau's *The Maine Woods,* published in 1864. I have written elsewhere about the conventions of this literature and cannot describe them in much detail here, but it is important to summarize their aesthetic traditions because this article argues that John Muir was intentionally departing from the accepted, and was thus adding an imaginative and radically new dimension to wilderness literature and aesthetics.[2]

A key element of the romantic response to wilderness was the characteristically turgid reaction to scenery. Invoking the aesthetic vocabulary of Edmund Burke, romantic travelers used Burke's categories of the sublime and the beautiful to reduce the American wilderness to something familiar that they could appreciate.[3] The Burkean aesthetic, in its emphasis on the scenic and pictorial, encouraged a distinction between scenery and wilderness. When romantic travelers encountered landscapes which failed to fit the

Burkean scheme of the sublime and the beautiful or the later distillation of these under the rubric of the picturesque, their disgust at discovering phenomena such as thick woods, dead trees, swamps, or barren mountains emphasizes how the appeal of the cult of scenery was its usefulness in mediating between the romantic consciousness and the reality of nature.

Romantics were searching for *scenes*, for certain arrangements of water, rocks, or trees. When they found what they were looking for, they responded enthusiastically. But when the reality of nature disappointed them, they were often dismayed and disoriented. Romantics were especially dispirited by the omnipresence of death in nature, by the usually unacknowledged implication that nature was constantly changing. Unlike scenes, which were static, nature was in process. Hence even so sensitive a romantic as Thoreau could be horrified by the sense of the inhospitality of nature he perceived on Mount Katahdin. Thoreau's disorientation stemmed from his discovery that nature was indeed in flux and not permanent and scenic.[4] Thoreau, at least, honestly confronted his feelings at finding untrammeled nature to be something considerably more complex, not to say threatening, than the two-dimensional nature of mere scenery, and he showed his loss of psychological equilibrium in the broken syntax of his well-known description of the Katahdin wilderness. But most other romantics either denied the reality of nature by converting it to word pictures or simply rejecting it altogether when they deemed it lacking. . . .

[R]omantic travelers encountering swamps or bogs, where dead trees and an oppressive sense of process characterized the scene, often withdrew in horror and used the same vocabulary: the words "dreary" and "desolate" were applied to both deserts and swamps—anything failing to be conventionally scenic.

It was against this tradition that John Muir was rebelling. Muir's intellectual debt to the romantics, chiefly Emerson, is well known. He never abandoned the Emersonian belief in the transcendence to be found in nature. But what is to be emphasized here is how Muir rejected the romantic inclination to dwell on scenes and suggested instead that the truly tran-

scendent appreciation of nature occurred only when one opened his or her perceiving faculties to all of nature. Muir often pointed out the inadequacy of conventional aesthetics in appreciating the true meaning of the wilderness. In describing the various landscapes of the California wilderness, Muir frequently lamented that a desert or a bog or some other scene would be ignored by most people. Writing about the high glacial lakes, he says, "At first sight, they seem pictures of pure bloodless desolation, miniature arctic seas, bound in perpetual ice and snow." Phrases like "at first sight" appear over and over again in Muir: in each case he avers that the untrained eye, dictated to by conventional aesthetic standards, misses much of nature. Describing the high passes, he declares that the ordinary traveler would find them "cold, dead, gloomy," but that the person who truly sees finds them to be among "the finest and most telling examples of Nature's love." "At first sight," writes Muir of Red Lake, "it seems rather dull and forbidding."[5]

Muir's message was that we should learn to appreciate all of nature and not be shackled by convention. The wilderness aesthetic advanced by Muir is a liberating way of perceiving nature.[6] It permits us to find pleasure in forms of nature hitherto despised. Of course, Muir continued to insist on the kind of transcendent value in nature which had appealed to the romantics of the previous generation. His narratives are full of reveries and transcendental moments inspired by the divinity of nature. But to this Muir added the further perception and appreciation of nature's processes. To Muir the discovery of process was the key to the transcendental experience. Muir explicitly argued that the clearest perception of nature combined the spirituality of the transcendentalist with the discriminating eye of the scientist.

Much of the Sierra consists of spectacular scenery quite within the conventions of traditional aesthetics. But here, too, Muir declared, new eyes, new ways of perceiving the landscape led to deeper understandings. One of the best examples of this is his often-anthologized and much-discussed description of the view from Mount Ritter. In this chapter of *The Mountains of California*, Muir describes the events of a period of a few days in October in the early 1870s. At the outset, he is descending from one of his expeditions in the high country, pondering the wonders of the landscape. He then encounters two artists looking for the picturesque, leads them to a high meadow, and sets out for a solo climb of Mount Ritter. The title of the chapter on Mount Ritter, ''A Near View of the High Sierra,'' announces Muir's intention to emphasize aesthetics and the importance of reexamination of the way we perceive nature, with the words ''Near View'' suggesting the need to look at nature more closely. ''To artists,'' he says, implying the inadequacy of current values in appreciating the true glories of the California mountains, ''few portions of the High Sierra are, strictly speaking, picturesque.'' Artists miss the total meaning of nature by trying to compartmentalize it: ''The whole massive uplift of the range is one great picture, not clearly divisible into smaller ones.''[7]

To underscore yet further his intention to develop a new aesthetic, Muir describes himself early in the chapter responding to a particular view as if he too were a merely pictorial artist: ''Pursuing my lonely way down the valley, I turned again and again to gaze on the glorious picture, throwing up my arms to enclose it as in a frame. After long ages of growth in the darkness beneath the glaciers, through sunshine and storms, it seemed now to be ready for the elected artist, like yellow wheat for the reaper; and I could not help wishing that I might carry colors and brushes with me on my travels, and learn to paint.'' But as he goes on to demonstrate, it is not via paint and brushes that one truly captures the landscape; it is through the deeper acceptance of nature's processes. In the rest of the episode he shows that he is indeed the ''elected artist,'' and he further shows the irrelevance of accepted aesthetic norms by introducing immediately after the scene just quoted a pair of artists seeking scenery ''suitable for a large painting.'' By thus displacing the urge to capture the scene in a painting onto the artist, Muir thus explicitly sets up a contrast between their perceptions and his, and suggests that his response to nature is an evolving one while theirs is static.[8]

Muir agrees to guide the artists back into the high

country and wastes little time in showing the superiority of his perceptions to theirs. He rapturously describes the autumn colors: ''the intense azure of the sky, the purplish grays of the granite, the red and browns of dry meadows, and the translucent purple and crimson of huckleberry bogs.'' None of this satisfies the unnamed artists, however, who find the scenery ''disappointing'' and lament that they see '' 'nothing as yet at all available for effective pictures.' ''[9]

When Muir and his painters finally come upon a truly startling view, their respective responses reveal profoundly different attitudes toward nature: the artists scurry about ''choosing foregrounds for sketches,'' while Muir decides to undertake a perilous mid-October ascent of a previously unclimbed peak. The artists are trapped in a sense of nature as scenery, while Muir embraces an opportunity to enter into nature. The anticipated dangers of such an adventure ''only exhilarate the mountaineer,'' and early the ''[n]ext morning, the artists went heartily to their work and I to mine.''[10]

During the two days it takes Muir to reach Ritter, he describes the scenery in conventional vocabulary. To the south at one point, he spots a group of ''savage peaks.'' The twilight renders a ''sublime scene,'' while that night ''[s]omber peaks, hacked and shattered, circled half-way around the horizon, wearing a savage aspect.'' Invoking a Ruskinian vocabulary, he describes a ''wilderness of crumbling spires and battlements.''[11]

Shortly before reaching the summit, Muir endures a memorable scrape with death. Trying to scale a sheer cliff, he finds himself suddenly unable to locate another hand-hold: ''After gaining a point about half-way to the top, I was suddenly brought to a dead stop, with arms outspread, clinging close to the face of the rock, unable to move hand or foot either up or down. My doom appeared fixed. I must fall.'' Then a burst of new energy rushes through him: ''I seemed suddenly to become possessed of a new sense.'' With renewed vigor he scrambles to the summit. The language of the entire affair suggests that this brief encounter with his own mortality has been a truly spiritual experience. There he is, hugging the cliff as if crucified, fearing his own imminent death, when "The other self, bygone experiences, Instinct, or Guardian Angel—call it what you will—came forward and assumed control. . . . Had I been borne aloft upon wings, my deliverance could not have been more complete."[12]

In addition to other possibilities, this episode seems to encapsulate Muir's argument favoring the need for new perceptions, responses to nature moving beyond the conventions of romantic wilderness literature. The essential ingredient in the new response is an acceptance of nature's processes, of which the death of the individual creature is the most profound and the most difficult to embrace.[13] Muir uses this episode to indicate what he already knows: that death is ubiquitous in nature and that one of the reasons why conventional aesthetics failed to comprehend all of nature was the reluctance of romantics to acknowledge the inevitability of transience and process. The epiphanic nature of the experience explains the radical change in vocabulary and overall response adopted soon after he reaches the top.

Once on the summit, he retreats momentarily to a Ruskinian vocabulary emphasizing architectural detail: one peak is a "gigantic castle with turret and battlement," another a "Gothic cathedral more abundantly spired than Milan's." He quickly drops this stock vocabulary and notes yet again how the scenery hides its deepest meanings from the untrained eye. Neither mysticism nor conventional aesthetics is enough to elicit the truth of the landscape. The eye of empiricism provides the ingredient needed for total perception, and the process of glaciation explains the hitherto unintelligible. In the following long quotation, a reader may note the emphasis on accurate perception and on the glacier as the chief symbol of the natural processes creating the landscape.

> [W]hen looking for the first time from an all-embracing standpoint like this, the inexperienced viewer is oppressed by the incomprehensible grandeur, variety, and abundance of the mountains rising shoulder to shoulder beyond the reach of vision; and it is only after they have been studied one by one, long and lovingly, that their far-reaching harmonies become manifest. Then, penetrate the wilderness where you may, the main telling features, to which all the surrounding topography is subordinate, are quickly perceived, and the most complicated clusters of peaks stand revealed harmoniously correlated and fashioned like works of art—eloquent monuments of the ancient ice-rivers that brought them into relief from the general mass of the range. The cañons, too, some of them a mile deep, mazing wildly through the mighty host of mountains, however lawless and ungovernable at first sight they appear, are at length recognized as the necessary effects of causes which followed each other in harmonious sequence—Nature's poems carved on tables of stone—the simplest and most emphatic of her glacial compositions.[14]

The glacier, then, the crucial symbol in Muir's aesthetic, produces the geological process which unifies and explains the landscape, and contemplating it leads to a moment of supreme transcendence. It is interesting to note that Muir was the first to suspect the existence of living glaciers in the Sierra, and that he deduced their existence on the basis of his personal examination of the landscape.[15] When he did discover actual glaciers, they confirmed the value of his empirical powers. The landscape makes sense only in terms of the glacier; grasping this explanation in turn leads to a discovery of "Nature's poems," the imaginative correlation of Nature's harmonies.

Muir goes on to contemplate further the significance—both geological and mystical—of the glacier. Thinking about the eons required for glacial action to produce the landscape before him, he transcends ordinary time:

> Could we have been here to observe during the glacial period, we should have overlooked a wrinkled ocean of ice as continuous as that now covering the landscapes of Greenland; filling every valley and cañon with only the tops of the mountain peaks rising darkly above the rock-encumbered ice-waves like islets in a stormy sea—those islets the only hints of the glorious landscapes now smiling in the sun. Standing here in the deep brooding silence all the wilderness seems motionless, as if the work of creation were done.

The shift in tense and mood here is critical. The passage begins in a conditional past tense; then the condition of the introductory clause is imaginatively satisfied, and the verbs become present indicative. Muir imagines himself back in the glacial era.

But in the midst of this outer steadfastness we know there is incessant motion and change. Ever and anon, avalanches are falling from yonder peaks. These cliff-bound glaciers, seemingly wedged and immovable, are flowing like water and grinding the rocks beneath them.[16]

Inspired spiritually by contemplation of one of nature's most awesome processes, Muir speeds up time so that a glacier seems to move like water.[17] The imagination, properly aware of process, supplies the understanding of the landscape unavailable to conventional aesthetics. Elevating his imagined account of the shaping of the landscape even further, Muir embraces the transience of the scene before him, finding in that very mutability the essence of all of nature's meaning.

> The lakes are lapping their granite shores and wearing them away, and every one of these rills and young rivers is fretting the air into music, and carrying the mountains to the plains. Here are the roots of all the life of the valleys, and here more simply than elsewhere is the eternal flux of nature manifested. Ice changing to water, lakes to meadows, and mountains to plains. And while we thus contemplate Nature's methods of landscape creation, and, reading the records she has carved on the rocks, reconstruct, however imperfectly, the landscapes of the past, we also learn that as these we now behold have succeeded those of the pre-glacial age, so they in turn are withering and vanishing to be succeeded by others yet unborn.[18]

In Muir's descriptions of the Sierra, the function of the glacier achieved divine status. The existence of glaciers, either in the present or in the remote geological past, explained everything. All rock formations, from the tiniest striations to the grandeur of Yosemite's Half Dome, were "glacier monuments." Whenever Muir employed the Ruskinian vocabulary of Gothic architecture, the sculptor was the glacier. In addition to determining the location of lakes, meadows, and streams, the courses of ancient glaciers also accounted for the distributions of such apparently unrelated phenomena as certain tree species and a particular kind of mountain squirrel. Indeed, insisted Muir, "The key to this beautiful harmony [meaning all the perfection of animate and inanimate nature] is

the ancient glaciers." The glacier was Muir's key to beginnings and ends, to the endless cycles of life and death.

The essential lesson of the glacier is that nature is never static, that all things visible eventually pass away to be succeeded by subsequent forms or generations. Muir, in a way impossible for the antebellum romantic traveler, accepted process and by implication accepted the concept of cyclical time. Whereas the romantic thought in terms of linear time which began at the creation and proceeded toward a divinely appointed end, Muir was able to imagine time in terms of endlessly repeating cycles. Muir's sense of time, in other words, was more natural, based on a keen observation of how natural process dictates a reality wherein life depends on death and decay.

In nearly all his descriptions of the natural phenomena of the Sierra, Muir advanced this notion of cycles. He dwelt on how the cycles of the year are both beautiful and, simultaneously, dependent on death: at a glacial meadow,

> [i]n June small flecks of the dead, decaying sod begin to appear, gradually widening and uniting with one another, covered with creeping rags of water during the day, and ice by night, looking as hopeless and unvital as crushed rocks just emerging from the darkness of the glacial period. . . . The ground seems twice dead. Nevertheless the annual resurrection is drawing near.

The lakes themselves go through a similar cycle of life, decay, and death:

> . . . while its shores are being enriched, the soil-beds creep out with incessant growth, contracting its area, while the lighter mud particles deposited on the bottom cause it to grow constantly shallower, until at length the last remnant of the lake vanishes,—closed forever in ripe and natural old age. And now its feeding-stream goes winding on without halting through the new gardens and groves that have taken its place.[19]

In contrast, the notion of a lake turning boggy was repugnant to the romantic traveler.

With Muir, as with Emerson, vision is the crucial faculty. Like most romantics Emerson believed that children, uncorrupted by worldly concerns, have a purer, more honest perception of nature than adults have. "Few adult persons," insisted Emerson, "can see nature," and he further declared that any disaster was tolerable except the loss of sight.[20] But Muir was thinking of a way of seeing purer than that attributed by Emerson even to children. Muir was able to see both the transcendent essence of nature as well as the objective reality. Indeed, it was his fascination with all the details and processes of nature which led him to his transcendent moments. In a passage reminscent of Emerson's "transparent eyeball" conceit, Muir emphasizes the importance of the faculty of sight, stresses both the mystic and the substantive, and suggests how sight properly exercised leads to a moment of unity with nature: exploring a glacial meadow, "notwithstanding the scene is so impressively spiritual, and you seem dissolved in it, yet everything about you is beating with warm, terrestrial human love and life substantial and familiar. . . . You are all eye, sifted through and through with light and beauty."[21]

Returning from Ritter to his neglected painters, Muir notes one final time how their response to nature falls short of his. Upon their first seeing him, "They seemed unreasonably glad to see me." They have been fretting about Muir's safety, uncomfortable with the possibility of death in the wilderness. Their apprehensions have ruined their tranquility and prevented them from appreciating their opportunity to immerse themselves in the wilderness. Once their guide is safely back with them, Muir notes, with some condescension, "their curious troubles were over." As they prepare to descend from the mountains, he adds, now with overt sarcasm, "They packed their precious sketches."[22]

NOTES

1. Stephen Fox, *John Muir and His Legacy: The American Conservation Movement* (Boston, MA; Little, Brown and Company, 1981); Michael P. Cohen, *The Pathless Way: John Muir and American Wilderness.* (Madison, WI: University of Wisconsin Press, 1984); Frederick Turner, *Rediscovering America: John Muir in His Time and Ours* (New York, NY: Viking, 1985). On the need for more work on Muir, see Frederick Turner, "Toward Future Muir Biographies: Problems and Prospects," *The Pacific Historian* 29 (Summer/Fall, 1985): 157-166.

2. Joel T. Headley, *The Adirondack: Or, Life in the Woods* (New York, NY: Baker and Scribner, 1849). Henry David Thoreau, *The Maine Woods* (Princeton, NJ: Princeton University Press, 1972). Philip G. Terrie, *Forever Wild: Environmental Aesthetics and the Adirondack Forest Preserve* (Philadelphia, PA: Temple University Press, 1985), pp. 44–67. See also, among others, Hans Huth, *Nature and the American: Three Centuries of Changing Attitudes* (Berkeley, CA: University of California Press, 1957), pp. 30–53, 71-104; Roderick Nash, *Wilderness and the American Mind,* 3rd ed. (New Haven, CT: Yale University Press, 1983), pp. 44-46; Elizabeth McKinsey, *Niagra Falls: Icon of the American Sublime* (New York, NY: Cambridge University Press, 1985), pp. 41-125.

3. Edmund Burke, *A Philosophical Enquiry into the Origins of Our Ideas of the Sublime and Beautiful,* ed. James T. Boulton (New York, NY: Columbia University Press, 1958).

4. Thoreau, *The Maine Woods,* pp. 69-71. For a good analysis of Thoreau's experience on Katahdin, see James McIntosh, *Thoreau as Romantic Naturalist* (Ithaca, NY: Cornell University Press, 1974), pp. 179-215.

5. John Muir, *The Mountains of California* (Berkeley, CA: Ten Speed Press, 1977), pp. 258-279, 285.

6. The wilderness aesthetic advanced by Muir bears a striking resemblance to Aldo Leopold's land ethic: see J. Baird Callicott, "The Land Aesthetic," *Environmental Review* 7 (Winter 1983): 345-358.

7. Muir, p. 49.

8. Muir, pp. 50, 51; Cohen, pp. 70-80, 242-243, discusses in detail Muir's account of the ascent of and the view from Mount Ritter. Cohen finds, as I do, that Muir reached the summit with an "awakened consciousness" as he writes on p. 71, and that Muir intentionally contrasted his aesthetic with that of the two artists. But Cohen does not attribute the distinction. as I do, to Muir's awareness of process.

9. Muir, pp. 51, 52.

10. Muir, p. 53.

11. Muir, pp. 55, 57, 63.

12. Muir, pp. 64, 65.

13. Cohen, p. 70.

14. Muir, pp. 68, 69.

15. For a discussion of the spiritual significance of the

glacier in Muir's scheme of nature, see Paul D. Sheats, ''John Muir's Glacial Gospel,'' *The Pacific Historian* 29 (Summer/Fall 1985): 42-53. Sheats also notes the importance of Muir's scientific training in his later response to nature, observes Muir's conviction that too many people ''failed to recognize the true order of a mountain landscape,'' and points to the glacier as they key to seeing nature's ''essential harmony'' (p. 49). Sheats does not discuss the Mount Ritter episode, however. On Muir's hypothesizing on the existence of Sierra glaciers and his subsequent discovery of them, see Fox, pp. 20-25. One of the chief influences on Muir in his thinking abut the role of natural processes in shaping the landscape was probably George Perkins Marsh's *Man and Nature: Or Physical Geography as Modified by Human Action* (New York, NY: Charles Scribner, 1864). Marsh argued that all of nature's parts were interdependent and that new life or growth always depended on death and decay. While Marsh's primary aim in writing *Man and Nature* was to warn mankind against upsetting the capacity of nature to satisfy agricultural needs, his work has important aesthetic implications, which I believe Muir was virtually the first to recognize. See my discussion of Marsh in *Forever Wild*, pp. 81-86.

16. Muir, p. 69.
17. Cohen, p. 74. The chief distinction between Cohen's reading of this episode and mine is that whereas Cohen (with logic I do not question) sees it as part of a spiritual journey, I want to add to that what I believe to have been Muir's calculated effort to replace conventional aesthetics with his own more comprehensive wilderness aesthetic.
18. Muir, pp. 69-70.
19. Muir, pp. 133,104.
20. Ralph Waldo Emerson, *Nature, The Complete Works of Ralph Waldo Emerson*, Centenary Edition, (Boston, MA: Houghton Mifflin, 1903-1904), Vol. I, p. 9.
21. Muir, p. 128.
22. Muir, p. 73.

DISCUSSION TOPICS

1. What are two of the contrasts which Terrie identifies between the aesthetic perceptions of the landscape artists and Muir?
2. Terrie points out that Muir's fascination with the

empirical details of natural processes allowed him to experience transcendent moments. Find two examples in Muir's essay of this connection between empirical observation and transcendence.

READING 15

Seeing

Annie Dillard

Born in Pittsburgh in 1945, Annie Dillard is the author of six books, including Teaching a Stone to Talk *and* Tickets for a Prayer Wheel. *In the following chapter from* Pilgrim at Tinker Creek, *which received the 1975 Pulitzer Prize in general nonfiction, she contrasts several different kinds of ''seeing.''*

Seeing involves the readiness to be surprised by a sudden glimpse of a muskrat kit or a tree momentarily full of red-winged blackbirds. Seeing also is the heightened perception which results from loving something enough to devote one's time to it, whether it is grasses or snakes. Seeing requires attention, since nature conceals much in its constantly moving complexity.

Dillard meditates on the qualities of light—how too much light blinds. She meditates, too, on those who experienced sight only in adulthood, through removal of cataracts. For these newly sighted people, vision is ''pure sensation unencumbered by meaning.'' Their vision is almost unimaginably vivid.

It is by labeling that most people notice what they see. But the newly sighted see directly, without the intermediary of words. Dillard describes her attempts to see this direct way, to see ''the tree with the lights in it.'' She attempts to fully respond to the beauty of the world, an experience in which she not only sees but is seen.

When I was six or seven years old, growing up in Pittsburgh, I used to take a precious penny of my own and hide it for someone else to find. It was a curious compulsion; sadly, I've never been seized by it since.

For some reason I always "hid" the penny along the same stretch of sidewalk up the street. I would cradle it at the roots of a sycamore, say, or in a hole left by a chipped-off piece of sidewalk. Then I would take a piece of chalk, and, starting at either end of the block, draw huge arrows leading up to the penny from both directions. After I learned to write I labeled the arrows: SURPRISE AHEAD or MONEY THIS WAY. I was greatly excited, during all this arrow-drawing, at the thought of the first lucky passer-by who would receive in this way, regardless of merit, a free gift from the universe. But I never lurked about. I would go straight home and not give the matter another thought, until, some months later, I would be gripped again by the impulse to hide another penny.

It is still the first week in January, and I've got great plans. I've been thinking about seeing. There are lots of things to see, unwrapped gifts and free surprises. The world is fairly studded and strewn with pennies cast broadside from a generous hand. But—and this is the point—who gets excited by a mere penny? If you follow one arrow, if you crouch motionless on a bank to watch a tremulous ripple thrill on the water and are rewarded by the sight of a muskrat kit paddling from its den, will you count that sight a chip of copper only, and go your rueful way? It is dire poverty indeed when a man is so malnourished and fatigued that he won't stoop to pick up a penny. But if you cultivate a healthy poverty and simplicity, so that finding a penny will literally make your day, then, since the world is in fact planted in pennies, you have with your poverty bought a lifetime of days. It is that simple. What you see is what you get.

I used to be able to see flying insects in the air. I'd look ahead and see, not the row of hemlocks across the road, but the air in front of it. My eyes would focus along that column of air, picking out flying insects. But I lost interest, I guess, for I dropped the habit. Now I can see birds. Probably some people can look at the grass at their feet and discover all the crawling creatures. I would like to know grasses and sedges—and care. Then my least journey into the world would be a field trip, a series of happy recognitions. Thoreau,

in an expansive mood, exulted, "What a rich book might be made about buds, including, perhaps, sprouts!" It would be nice to think so. I cherish mental images I have of three perfectly happy people. One collects stones. Another—an Englishman, say—watches clouds. The third lives on a coast and collects drops of seawater which he examines microscopically and mounts. But I don't see what the specialist sees, and so I cut myself off, not only from the total picture, but from the various forms of happiness.

Unfortunately, nature is very much a now-you-see-it, now-you-don't affair. A fish flashes, then dissolves in the water before my eyes like so much salt. Deer apparently ascend bodily into heaven; the brightest oriole fades into leaves. These disappearances stun me into stillness and concentration, they say of nature that it conceals with a grand nonchalance, and they say of vision that it is a deliberate gift, the revelation of a dancer who for my eyes only flings away her seven veils. For nature does reveal as well as conceal: now-you-don't-see-it, now-you-do. For a week last September migrating red-winged blackbirds were feeding heavily down by the creek at the back of the house. One day I went out to investigate the racket; I walked up to a tree, an Osage orange, and a hundred birds flew away. They simply materialized out of the tree. I saw a tree, then a whisk of color, then a tree again. I walked closer and another hundred blackbirds took flight. Not a branch, not a twig budged: the birds were apparently weightless as well as invisible. Or, it was as if the leaves of the Osage orange had been freed from a spell in the form of red-winged blackbirds; they flew from the tree, caught my eye in the sky, and vanished. When I looked again at the tree the leaves had reassembled as if nothing had happened. Finally I walked directly to the trunk of the tree and a final hundred, the real diehards, appeared, spread, and vanished. How could so many hide in the tree without my seeing them? The Osage orange, unruffled, looked just as it had looked from the house, when three hundred red-winged blackbirds cried from its crown. I looked downstream where they flew, and they were gone. Searching, I couldn't spot one. I wandered downstream to force them to play their hand, but they'd crossed the creek and scattered. One show to a customer. These appearances catch at my throat; they are the free gifts, the bright coppers at the roots of trees.

It's all a matter of keeping my eyes open. Nature is like one of those line drawings of a tree that are puzzles for children: Can you find hidden in the leaves a duck, a house, a boy, a bucket, a zebra, and a boot? Specialists can find the most incredibly well-hidden things. A book I read when I was young recommended an easy way to find caterpillars to rear: you simply find some fresh caterpillar droppings, look up, and there's your caterpillar. More recently an author advised me to set my mind at ease about those piles of cut stems on the ground in grassy fields. Field mice make them; they cut the grass down by degrees to reach the seeds at the head. It seems that when the grass is tightly packed, as in a field of ripe grain, the blade won't topple at a single cut through the stem, instead, the cut stem simply drops vertically, held in the crush of grain. The mouse severs the bottom again and again, the stem keeps dropping an inch at a time, and finally the head is low enough for the mouse to reach the seeds. Meanwhile, the mouse is positively littering the field with its little piles of cut stems into which, presumably, the author of the book is constantly stumbling. . . .

The lover can see, and the knowledgeable. I visited an aunt and uncle at a quarter-horse ranch in Cody, Wyoming. I couldn't do much of anything useful, but I could, I thought, draw. So, as we all sat around the kitchen table after supper, I produced a sheet of paper and drew a horse. ''That's one lame horse,'' my aunt volunteered. The rest of the family joined in: ''Only place to saddle that one is his neck''; ''Looks like we better shoot the poor thing, on account of those terrible growths.'' Meekly, I slid the pencil and paper down the table. Everyone in that family, including my three young cousins, could draw a horse. Beautifully. When the paper came back it looked as though five shining, real quarter horses had been corraled by mistake with a papier-mâché moose; the real horses seemed to gaze at the monster with a steady, puzzled air. I stay away from horses now, but I can do a creditable goldfish. The point is that I just don't know what the lovers knows; I just can't see the artificial

obvious that those in the know construct. The herpetologist asks the native, ''Are there snakes in that ravine?'' ''Nosir.'' And the herpetologist comes home with, yessir, three bags full. Are there butterflies on that mountain? Are the bluets in bloom, are there arrowheads here, or fossil shells in the shale?

Peeping through my keyhole I see within the range of only about thirty percent of the light that comes from the sun; the rest is infrared and some little ultraviolet, perfectly apparent to many animals, but invisible to me. A nightmare network of ganglia, charged and firing without my knowledge, cuts and splices what I do see, editing it for my brain. Donald E. Carr points out that the sense impressions of one-celled animals are *not* edited for the brain: ''This is philosophically interesting in a rather mournful way, since it means that only the simplest animals perceive the universe as it is.'' . . .

Where Tinker Creek flows under the sycamore log bridge to the tear-shaped island, it is slow and shallow, fringed thinly in cattail marsh. At this spot an astonishing bloom of life supports vast breeding populations of insects, fish, reptiles, birds, and mammals. On windless summer evenings I stalk along the creek bank or straddle the sycamore log in absolute stillness, watching for muskrats. The night I stayed too late I was hunched on the log staring spellbound at spreading, reflected stains of lilac on the water. A cloud in the sky suddenly lighted as if turned on by a switch; its reflection just as suddenly materialized on the water upstream, flat and floating, so that I couldn't see the creek bottom, or life in the water under the cloud. Downstream, away from the cloud on the water, water turtles smooth as beans were gliding down with the current in a series of easy, weightless push-offs, as men bound on the moon. I didn't know whether to trace the progress of one turtle I was sure of, risking sticking my face in one of the bridge's spider webs made invisible by the gathering dark, or take a chance on seeing the carp, or scan the mudbank in hope of seeing a muskrat, or follow the last of the swallows who caught at my heart and trailed it after them like streamers as they appeared from directly below, under the fog, flying upstream with their tails forked, so fast. . . .

At last I stared upstream where only the deepest violet remained of the cloud, a cloud so high its underbelly still glowed feeble color reflected from a hidden sky lighted in turn by a sun halfway to China. And out of that violet, a sudden enormous black body arced over the water. I saw only a cylindrical sleekness. Head and tail, if there was a head and tail, were both submerged in cloud. I saw only one ebony fling, a headlong dive to darkness; then the waters closed, and the lights went out.

I walked home in a shivering daze, up hill and down. Later I lay open-mouthed in bed, my arms flung wide at my sides to steady the whirling darkness. At this latitude I'm spinning 836 miles an hour round the earth's axis; I often fancy I feel my sweeping fall as a breakneck arc like the dive of dolphins, and the hollow rushing of wind raises hair on my neck and the side of my face. In orbit around the sun I'm moving 64,800 miles an hour. The solar system as a whole, like a merry-go-round unhinged, spins, bobs, and blinks at the speed of 43,200 miles an hour along a course set east of Hercules. Someone has piped, and we are dancing a tarantella until the sweat pours. I open my eyes and I see dark, muscled forms curl out of water, with flapping gills and flattened eye. I close my eyes and I see stars, deep stars giving way to deeper stars, deeper stars bowing to deepest stars at the crown of an infinite cone.

"Still," wrote van Gogh in a letter, "a great deal of light falls on everything." If we are blinded by darkness, we are also blinded by light. When too much light falls on everything, a special terror results. Peter Freuchen describes the notorious kayak sickness to which Greenland Eskimos are prone. "The Greenland fjords are peculiar for the spells of completely quiet weather, when there is not enough wind to blow out a match and the water is like a sheet of glass. The kayak hunter must sit in his boat without stirring a finger so as not to scare the shy seals away. . . . The sun, low in the sky, sends a glare into his eyes, and the landscape around moves into the realm of the unreal. The reflex from the mirror-like water hypnotizes him, he seems to be unable to move, and all of a sudden it is as if he were floating in a bottomless void, sinking, sinking, and sinking. . . . Horror-stricken, he tries to stir, to cry out, but he cannot, he is completely paralyzed, he just falls and falls." Some hunters are especially cursed with this panic, and bring ruin and sometimes starvation to their families. . . .

Darkness appalls and light dazzles; the scrap of visible light that doesn't hurt my eyes hurts my brain. What I see sets me swaying. Size and distance and the sudden swelling of meanings confuse me, bowl me over. I straddle the sycamore log bridge over Tinker Creek in the summer. I look at the lighted creek bottom: snail tracks tunnel the mud in quavering curves. A crayfish jerks, but by the time I absorb what has happened, he's gone in a billowing smokescreen of silt. I look at the water: minnows and shiners. If I'm thinking minnows, a carp will fill my brain till I scream. I look at the water's surface: skaters, bubbles, and leaves sliding down. Suddenly, my own face, reflected, startles me witless. Those snails have been tracking my face! Finally, with a shuddering wrench of the will, I see clouds, cirrus clouds. I'm dizzy, I fall in. This looking business is risky. . . .

I reel in confusion; I don't understand what I see. With the naked eye I can see two million light-years to the Andromeda galaxy. Often I slop some creek water in a jar and when I get home I dump it in a white china bowl. After the silt settles I return and see tracings of minute snails on the bottom, a planarian or two winding round the rim of water, roundworms shimmying frantically, and finally, when my eyes have adjusted to these dimensions, amoebae. At first the amoebae look like muscae volitantes, those curled moving spots you seem to see in your eyes when you stare at a distant wall. Then I see the amoebae as drops of water congealed, bluish, translucent, like chips of sky in the bowl. At length I choose one individual and give myself over to its idea of an evening. I see it dribble a grainy foot before it on its wet, unfathomable way. Do its unedited sense impressions include the fierce focus of my eyes? Shall I take it outside and show it Andromeda, and blow its little endoplasm? I stir the water with a finger, in case it's running out of oxygen. Maybe I should get a tropical aquarium with motorized bubblers and lights, and keep this one for a pet. Yes, it would tell its fissioned descendants, the universe is two feet by five, and if your listen closely you can hear the buzzing music of the spheres. . . .

I chanced on a wonderful book by Marius von Senden, called *Space and Sight.* When Western surgeons discovered how to perform safe cataract operations, they ranged across Europe and America operating on dozens of men and women of all ages who had been blinded by cataracts since birth. Von Senden collected accounts of such cases; the histories are fascinating. Many doctors had tested their patients' sense perceptions and ideas of space both before and after the operations. The vast majority of patients, of both sexes and all ages, had, in von Senden's opinion, no idea of space whatsoever. Form, distance, and size were so many meaningless syllables. A patient "had no idea of depth, confusing it with roundness." Before the operation a doctor would give a blind patient a cube and a sphere; the patient would tongue it or feel it with his hands, and name it correctly. After the operation the doctor would show the same objects to the patient without letting him touch them; now he had no clue whatsoever what he was seeing. One patient called lemonade "square" because it pricked on his tongue as a square shape pricked on the touch of his hands. Of another postoperative patient, the doctors writes, "I have found in her no notion of size, for example, not even within the narrow limits which she might have encompassed with the aid of touch. Thus when I asked her to show me how big her mother was, she did not stretch out her hands, but set her two index-fingers a few inches apart." Other doctors reported their patients' own statements to similar effect. "The room he was in . . . he knew to be but part of the house, yet he could not conceive that the whole house could look bigger"; "Those who are blind from birth . . . have no real conception of height or distance. A house that is a mile away is thought of as nearby, but requiring the taking of a lot of steps. . . . The elevator that whizzes him up and down gives no more sense of vertical distance than does the train of horizontal."

For the newly sighted, vision is pure sensation unencumbered by meaning: "The girl went through the experience that we all go through and forget, the moment we are born. She saw, but it did not mean

anything but a lot of different kinds of brightness." Again, "I asked the patient what he could see; he answered that he saw an extensive field of light, in which everything appeared dull, confused, and in motion. He could not distinguish objects." Another patient saw "nothing but a confusion of forms and colours." When a newly sighted girl saw photographs and paintings, she asked, " 'Why do they put those dark marks all over them?' 'Those aren't dark marks,' her mother explained, 'those are shadows. That is one of the ways the eye knows that things have shape. If it were not for shadows many things would look flat.' 'Well, that's how things do look,' Joan answered. 'Everything looks flat with dark patches.' " . . .

In general the newly sighted see the world as a dazzle of color-patches. They are pleased by the sensation of color, and learn quickly to name the colors, but the rest of seeing is tormentingly difficult. Soon after his operation a patient "generally bumps into one of these colour-patches and observes them to be substantial, since they resist him as tactual objects do. In walking about it also strikes him—or can if he pays attention—that he is continually passing in between the colours he sees, that he can go past a visual object, that a part of it then steadily disappears from view; and that in spite of this, however he twists and turns—whether entering the room from the door, for example, or returning back to it—he always has a visual space in front of him. Thus he gradually comes to realize that there is also a space behind him, which he does not see."

The mental effort involved in these reasonings proves overwhelming for many patients. It oppresses them to realize, if they ever do at all, the tremendous size of the world, which they had previously conceived of as something touchingly manageable. It oppresses them to realize that they have been visible to people all along, perhaps unattractively so, without their knowledge or consent. A disheartening number of them refuse to use their new vision, continuing to go over objects with their tongues, and lapsing into apathy and despair. "The child can see, but will not make use of his sight. Only when pressed can he with difficulty be brought to look at objects in his neighbourhood; but more than a foot away it is impossible to bestir him to the necessary effort.'' Of a twenty-one-year-old girl, the doctor relates, ''Her unfortunate father, who had hoped for so much from this operation, wrote that his daughter carefully shuts her eyes whenever she wishes to go about the house, especially when she comes to a staircase, and that she is never happier or more at ease than when, by closing her eyelids, she relapses into her former state of total blindness.'' A fifteen-year-old boy, who was also in love with a girl at the asylum for the blind, finally blurted out, ''No, really, I can't stand it any more; I want to be sent back to the asylum again. If things aren't altered, I'll tear my eyes out.'' . . .

On the other hand, many newly sighted people speak well of the world, and teach us how dull is our own vision. To one patient, a human hand, unrecognized, is ''something bright and then holes.'' Shown a bunch of grapes, a boy calls out, ''It is dark, blue and shiny. . . . It isn't smooth, it has bumps and hollows.'' A little girl visits a garden. ''She is greatly astonished, and can scarcely be persuaded to answer, stands speechless in front of the tree, which she only names on taking hold of it, and then as 'the tree with the lights in it.' '' Some delight in their sight and give themselves over to the visual world. Of a patient just after her bandages were removed, her doctor writes, ''The first things to attract her attention were her own hands; she looked at them very closely, moved them repeatedly to and fro, bent and stretched the fingers, and seemed greatly astonished at the sight.'' One girl was eager to tell her blind friend that ''men do not really look like trees at all,'' and astounded to discover that her every visitor had an utterly different face. Finally, a twenty-two-year-old girl was dazzled by he world's brightness and kept her eyes shut for two weeks. When at the end of that time she opened her eyes again, she did not recognize any objects, but, ''the more she now directed her gaze upon everything about her, the more it could be seen how an expression of gratification and astonishment overspread her features; she repeatedly exclaimed: 'Oh God! How beautiful!' ''

I saw color-patches for weeks after I read this wonderful book. It was summer; the peaches were ripe in the valley orchards. When I woke in the morning, color-patches wrapped round my eyes, intricately, leaving not one unfilled spot. All day long I walked among shifting color-patches that parted before me like the Red Sea and closed again in silence, transfigured, wherever I looked back. Some patches swelled and loomed, while others vanished utterly, and dark marks flitted at random over the whole dazzling sweep. But I couldn't sustain the illusion of flatness. I've been around for too long. Form is condemned to an eternal danse macabre with meaning: I couldn't unpeach the peaches. Nor can I remember ever having seen without understanding; the color-patches of infancy are lost. My brain then must have been smooth as any balloon. I'm told I reached for the moon; many babies do. But the color-patches of infancy swelled as meaning filled them; they arrayed themselves in solemn ranks down distance which unrolled and stretched before me like a plain. The moon rocketed away. I live now in a world of shadows that shape and distance color, a world where space makes a kind of terrible sense. What gnosticism is this, and what physics? The fluttering patch I saw in my nursery window—silver and green and shape-shifting blue—is gone; a row of Lombardy poplars takes its place, mute, across the distant lawn. That humming oblong creature pale as light that stole along the walls of my room at night, stretching exhilaratingly around the corners, is gone, too, gone the night I ate of the bittersweet fruit, put two and two together and puckered forever my brain. Martin Buber tells this tale: ''Rabbi Mendel once boasted to his teacher Rabbi Elimelekh that evenings he saw the angel who rolls away the light before the darkness, and mornings the angel who rolls away the darkness before the light. 'Yes,' said Rabbi Elimelekh, 'in my youth I saw that too. Later on you don't see these things any more.' ''

Why didn't someone hand those newly sighted people paints and brushes from the start, when they still didn't know what anything was? Then maybe we all could see color-patches too, the world unraveled from reason, Eden before Adam gave names. The scales would drop from my eyes; I'd see trees like men walking; I'd run down the road against all orders, hallooing and leaping.

Seeing is of course very much a matter of verbalization. Unless I call my attention to what passes before my eyes, I simply won't see it. It is, as Ruskin says, "not merely unnoticed, but in the full, clear sense of the word, unseen." My eyes alone can't solve analogy tests using figures, the ones which show, with increasing elaborations, a big square, then a small square in a big square, then a big triangle, and expect me to find a small triangle in a big triangle. I have to say the words, describe what I'm seeing. If Tinker Mountain erupted, I'd be likely to notice. But if I want to notice the lesser cataclysms of valley life, I have to maintain in my head a running description of the present. It's not that I'm observant; it's just that I talk too much. Otherwise, especially in a strange place, I'll never know what's happening. Like a blind man at the ball game, I need a radio.

When I see this way I analyze and pry. I hurl over logs and roll away stones; I study the bank a square foot at a time, probing and tilting my head. Some days when a mist covers the mountains, when the muskrats won't show and the microscope's mirror shatters, I want to climb up the blank blue dome as a man would storm the inside of a circus tent, wildly, dangling, and with a steel knife claw a rent in the top, peep, and, if I must, fall.

But there is another kind of seeing that involves a letting go. When I see this way I sway transfixed and emptied. The difference between the two ways of seeing is the difference between walking with and without a camera. When I walk with a camera I walk from shot to shot, reading the light on a calibrated meter. When I walk without a camera, my own shutter opens, and the moment's light prints on my own silver gut. When I see this second way I am above all an unscrupulous observer.

It was sunny one evening last summer at Tinker Creek; the sun was low in the sky, upstream. I was sitting on the sycamore log bridge with the sunset at my back, watching the shiners the size of minnows who were feeding over the muddy sand in skittery schools. Again and again, one fish, then another, turned for a split second across the current and flash! the sun shot out from its silver side. I couldn't watch for it. It was always just happening somewhere else, and it drew my vision just as it disappeared: flash, like a sudden dazzle of the thinnest blade, a sparking over

a dun and olive ground at chance intervals from every direction. Then I noticed white specks, some sort of pale petals, small, floating from under my feet on the creek's surface, very slow and steady. So I blurred my eyes and gazed towards the brim of my hat and saw a new world. I saw the pale white circles roll up, roll up, like the world's turning, mute and perfect, and I saw the linear flashes, gleaming silver, like stars being born at random down a rolling scroll of time. Something broke and something opened. I filled up like a new wineskin. I breathed an air like light; I saw a light like water. I was the lip of a fountain the creek filled forever; I was ether, the leaf in the zephyr; I was flesh-flake, feather, bone.

When I see this way I see truly. As Thoreau says, I return to my senses. I am the man who watches the baseball game in silence in an empty stadium. I see the game purely; I'm abstracted and dazed. When it's all over and the white-suited players lope off the green field to their shadowed dugouts, I leap to my feet; I cheer and cheer.

But I can't go out and try to see this way. I'll fail, I'll go mad. All I can do is try to gag the commentator, to hush the noise of useless interior babble that keeps me from seeing just as surely as a newspaper dangled before my eyes. The effort is really a discipline requiring a lifetime of dedicated struggle; it marks the literature of saints and monks of every order East and West, under every rule and no rule, discalced and shod. The world's spiritual geniuses seem to discover universally that the mind's muddy river, this ceaseless flow of trivia and trash, cannot be dammed, and that trying to dam it is a waste of effort that might lead to madness. Instead you must allow the muddy river to flow unheeded in the dim channels of consciousness; you raise your sights; you look along it, mildly, acknowledging its presence without interest and gazing beyond it into the realm of the real where subjects and objects act and rest purely, without utterance. "Launch into the deep," says Jacques Ellul, "and you shall see."

The secret of seeing is, then, the pearl of great price. If I thought he could teach me to find it and keep it forever I would stagger barefoot across a hundred deserts after any lunatic at all. But although the pearl may be found, it may not be sought. The literature of illumination reveals this above all: although it comes to those who wait for it, it is always, even to the most practiced and adept, a gift and a total surprise. I return from one walk knowing where the killdeer nests in the field by the creek and the hour the laurel blooms. I return from the same walk a day later scarcely knowing my own name. Litanies hum in my ears; my tongue flaps in my mouth Ailinon, alleluia! I cannot cause light; the most I can do is try to put myself in the path of its beam. It is possible, in deep space, to sail on solar wind. Light, be it particle or wave, has force; you rig a giant sail and go. The secret of seeing is to sail on solar wind. Hone and spread your spirit till you yourself are a sail, whetted, translucent, broadside to the merest puff.

When her doctor took her bandages off and led her into the garden, the girl who was no longer blind saw ''the tree with the lights in it.'' It was for this tree I searched through the peach orchards of summer, in the forests of fall and down winter and spring for years. Then one day I was walking along Tinker Creek thinking of nothing at all and I saw the tree with the lights in it. I saw the backyard cedar where the mourning doves roost charged and transfigured, each cell buzzing with flame. I stood on the grass with the lights in it, grass that was wholly fire, utterly focused and utterly dreamed. It was less like seeing than like being for the first time seen, knocked breathless by a powerful glance. The flood of fire abated, but I'm still spending the power. Gradually the lights went out in the cedar, the colors died, the cells unflamed and disappeared. I was still ringing. I had been my whole life a bell, and never knew it until at that moment I was lifted and struck. I have since only very rarely seen the tree with the lights in it. The vision comes and goes, mostly goes, but I live for it, for the moment when the mountains open and a new light roars in spate through the crack, and the mountains slam.

DISCUSSION TOPICS

1. Give an example of how being a specialist in a scientific field might add to one's happiness in experiencing nature. Have you had such an experience arising from your education?
2. Dillard suggests that the lover possesses a keener sight than the rest of us. What characteristics does the sight of a lover have?
3. How does seeing ''the tree with the lights in it'' contrast with seeing based on verbalization?
4. Do you agree with Dillard that the experience of the newly sighted is more ''real'' than that of us who have been sighted since birth? Why or why not?
5. Someone has said that ''Dillard is always seeking and Muir is always finding.'' Seeking and finding what? Do you agree with this evaluation of the two writers?

READING 16

Seeing Nature Whole

John Fowles

John Fowles (b. 1926) is a prominent British novelist, poet, and essayist. He is perhaps best known for his book, The French Lieutenant's Woman *(1969). In the following excerpt from ''Seeing Nature Whole,'' he provides a historical commentary on the intimate relationship between human and nonhuman nature. He argues that the major reason for the contemporary loss of connection with nature in Western society is the devaluing of art in the last 150 years in favor of a one-sided emphasis on scientific technique. Because Fowles views art and nature as ''siblings,'' he argues that Westerners also have cut themselves off from nature, in its ''immediate presentness.'' Artistic creation is the externalization of private self-discovery, requiring the ''green chaos'' of the wilds of the mind. All individuals, whether or not they engage in art, experience the nightly world of dreams, the mysterious processes of the individual mind. Science, on the other hand, bypasses the private in its interest in the general. Science is allied with our addiction to purpose, to finding a reason, function, or quantifiable yield. Thus, for Fowles, science represents a threat to the individual, the subjective, and the wild.*

Fowles believes that the contemporary world is still medieval in its fear of untamed nature as a "green cloak for Satan." Wilderness and forest are needed more than ever in order for human beings to retain their humanity, their green man and woman.

. . . There is something in the nature of nature, in its presentness, its seeming transience, its creative ferment and hidden potential, that corresponds very closely with the wild, or green-man, part of our own psyches; and it is a something that disappears as soon as it is relegated to an automatic pastness, a status of merely classifiable *thing,* image taken *then.* "Thing" and "then" attract each other. If it is thing, it was then; if it was then, it is thing. We lack trust in the present, this moment, this actual seeing, because our culture tells us to trust only the reported back, the publicly framed, the edited, the thing set in the clearly artistic or the clearly scientific angle of perspective. One of the deepest lessons we have to learn is that nature, of its nature, resists this. It waits to be seen otherwise, in its individual presentness and from our individual presentness. . . .

The threat to us in the coming millennium lies not in nature seen as rogue shark but in our growing emotional and intellectual detachment from it—and I do not think the remedy lies solely in the success or failure of the conservation movement. It lies as much in our being able to admit the debit side of scientific revolution, and especially the changes it has effected in our modes of perceiving and of experiencing the world as individuals.

Science is centrally, almost metaphysically, obsessed by general truths, by classifications that stop at the species, by functional laws whose worth is valued by their universality; by statistics, where a Bach or a da Vinci is no more than a quotum, a hole in a computer tape. The scientist has even to generalize himself, to subtract all personal feeling from the conduct of experiment and observation and from the enunciation of its results. He may study individuals, but only to help establish more widely applicable laws

and facts. Science has little time for minor exceptions. But all nature, like all humanity, is made of minor exceptions, of entities that in some way, however scientifically disregardable, do not conform to the general rule. A belief in this kind of exception is as central to art as a belief in the utility of generalization is to science; indeed one might almost call art that branch of science that present science is prevented, by its own constricting tenets and philosophies (that old *hortus conclusus* again), from reaching.

I see little hope of any recognition of this until we accept three things about nature. One is that knowing it fully is an art as well as a science. The second is that the heart of this art lies in our own personal nature and its relationship to other nature—never in nature as a collection of "things" outside us. The last is that this kind of knowledge, or relationship, is not reproducible by any other means—by painting, by photography, by words, by science itself. They may encourage, foster, and help induce the art of the relationship; but they cannot reproduce it, any more than a painting can reproduce a symphony, or the reverse. In the end they can serve only as an inferior substitute, especially if we use them as some people use sexual relationships, merely to flatter and justify ourselves.

There is a deeper wickedness still in Voltaire's unregenerate animal. It won't be owned, or more precisely, it will not be disanimated, unsouled, by the manner in which we try to own it. When it is owned, it disappears. Perhaps nowhere is our human mania for possessing, our delusion that what is owned cannot have a soul of its own, more harmful to us. This disanimation justified all the horrors of the African slave trade. If the black man is so stupid that he can be enslaved, he cannot have the soul of a white man, he must be mere animal. We have yet to cross the threshold of emancipating mere animals; but we should not forget what began the emancipation of the slaves in Britain and America. It was not science or scientific reason, but religious conscience and fellow-feeling.

Unlike white sharks, trees do not even possess the ability to defend themselves when attacked; what arms they sometimes have, like thorns, are static; and their size and immobility means they cannot hide.

They are the most defenseless of creation in regard to man, universally placed by him below the level of animate feeling, and so the most prone to destruction. Their main evolutionary defense, as with many social animals, birds, and fishes, lies in their innumerability, that is, in their capacity to reproduce—in which, for trees, longevity plays a major part. Perhaps it is this passive, patient nature of their system of self-preservation that has allowed man, despite his ancient fears of what they may harbor in terms of other nature (and supernature), to forgive them in one aspect, to see something that is also protective, maternal, even womblike in their silent depths.

All through history trees have provided sanctuary and refuge for both the justly and the unjustly persecuted and hunted. In the wood I know best there is a dell, among beeches, at the foot of a chalk cliff. Not a person a month goes there now, since it is well away from any path. But three centuries ago it was crowded every Sunday, for it is where the Independents came, from miles around along the border of Devon and Dorset, to hold their forbidden services. There are freedoms in woods that our ancestors perhaps realized more fully than we do. I used this wood, and even this one particular dell, in *The French Lieutenant's Woman,* for scenes that it seemed to me, in a story of self-liberation, could have no other setting.

This is the main reason I see trees, the wood, as the best analogue of prose fiction. All novels are also, in some way, exercises in attaining freedom—even when, at an extreme, they deny the possibility of its existence. Some such process of retreat from the normal world—however much the theme and surface is to be of the normal world—is inherent in any act of artistic creation, let alone that specific kind of writing that deals in imaginary situations and characters. And a part of that retreat must always be into a ''wild,'' or ordinarily repressed and socially hidden, self: into a place always a complexity beyond daily (or artistic) reality, never fully comprehensible, mappable, explicable, eternally more potential than realized, yet where no one will ever penetrate as far as we have. It is our passage, our mystery alone, however miserable the account that is brought out for the world to see or hear or read second-hand.

The artist's experience here is only a special—unusually prolonged and self-conscious—case of the universal individual one. The return to the green chaos, the deep forest and refuge of the unconscious, is a nightly phenomenon, and one that psychiatrists—and torturers—tell us is essential to the human mind. Without it, it disintegrates and goes mad. If I cherish trees beyond all personal (and perhaps rather peculiar) need and liking of them, it is because of this, their natural correspondence with the greener, more mysterious processes of mind—and because they also seem to me the best, most revealing messengers to us from all nature, the nearest its heart.

No religion is the only religion, no church the true church; and natural religion, rooted in love of nature, is no exception. But in all the long-cultivated and economically exploited lands of the world our woodlands are the last fragments of comparatively unadulterated nature, and so the most accessible outward correlatives and providers of the relationship, the feeling, the knowledge that we are in danger of losing: the last green churches and chapels outside the walled civilization and culture we have made with our tools. And this is so however far we may have fled, or evolved away from knowledge of, attachment to, interest in the wild—or use of its imagery to describe our more hidden selves and mental quirks.

To see woods and forests merely scientifically, economically, topographically, or aesthetically—not to understand that their greatest utility lies not in the facts derivable from them, or in their timber and fruit, or their landscape charm, or their utility as subject matter for the artist—proves the gathering speed with which we are retreating into outer space from all other life on this planet.

Of course there are scientists who are aware of this profoundest and most dangerous of all our alienation, and warn us of it; or who see hope in a rational remedy, in more education and knowledge, in committee and legislation. I wish them well in all of that, but I am a pessimist; what science and ''reason'' caused, they cannot alone cure. As long as nature is seen as in some way outside us, frontiered and foreign, *separate,* it is lost both to us and in us. The two natures, private and public, human and nonhuman, cannot be divorced; any more than nature, or life itself, can ever be truly understood vicariously, solely through other people's eyes and knowledge. Neither art nor science, however great, however profound, can finally help.

I pray my pessimism is exaggerated, and that we shall recover from this folly resenting the fact that we are, for all practical purposes, caged on our planet, of pretending that our life on it is a temporary inconvenience in a place we have outgrown, a boardinghouse we shall soon be leaving, and for whose other inhabitants and whose contents we need have neither respect nor concern. Scientists speak of biological processes re-created in the laboratory as being done *in vitro*—in glass, not in nature. The evolution of human mentality has put us all *in vitro* now, behind the glass wall of our own ingenuity.

There is a spiritual corollary to the way we are currently deforesting and denaturing our planet. In the end what we must most defoliate and deprive is ourselves. We might as soon start collecting up the world's poetry, every line and every copy, to burn it in a final pyre—and think we should lead richer and happier lives thereafter.

DISCUSSION TOPICS

1. Have you experienced connections between wild nature and your own inner creativity? What do you think is the importance of this connection?
2. Do you agree with Fowles that art is needed to truly appreciate nature? Explain your reasoning.
3. Is Fowles right that the future threat to human beings is in the growing detachment from nature? Do you see such detachment in yourself or the people around you?

Appreciation and the Natural Environment

Allen Carlson

Allen Carlson (b. 1943) teaches philosophy at the University of Alberta, Canada and has been a prominent voice in the field of natural aesthetics. In the following essay he examines and rejects the object paradigm of aesthetic appreciation because it abstracts the object from its surroundings. The landscape paradigm assumes a specific standpoint, involving a static two-dimensional representation of design and color. Carlson recommends instead the environmental model, in which the environment itself comes to the foreground of our attention. Our knowledge of the particular environment, drawn from common sense and science, will provide the appropriate aesthetic categories.

In this section I consider some paradigms of aesthetic appreciation which *prima facie* seem applicable as models for the appreciation of the natural environment. In this I follow tradition to some extent in that these paradigms are ones which have been offered as or assumed to be appropriate models for the appreciation of nature. However, I think we will discover that these models are not as promising as they may initially appear to be.

The first such paradigm I call the object model. In the artworld non-representational sculpture best fits this model of appreciation. When we appreciate such sculpture we appreciate it as the actual physical object which it is. The qualities to be aesthetically appreciated are the sensuous and design qualities of the actual object and perhaps certain abstract expressive qualities. The sculpture need not represent anything external to itself; it need not lead the appreciator beyond itself: it may be a self-contained aesthetic unit. Consider a Brancusi sculpture, for example, the famous *Bird In Space* (1919). It has no representational connections with the rest of reality and no relational con-

nections with its immediate surroundings and yet it has significant aesthetic qualities. It glistens, has balance and grace, and expresses flight itself.

Clearly it is possible to aesthetically appreciate an object of nature in the way indicated by this model. For example, we may appreciate a rock or a piece of driftwood in the same way as we appreciate a Brancusi sculpture: we actually or contemplatively remove the object from its surroundings and dwell on its sensuous and design qualities and its possible expressive qualities. Moreover, there are considerations which support the plausibility of this model for appreciation of the natural environment. First, natural objects are in fact often appreciated in precisely this way: mantel pieces are littered with pieces of rock and driftwood. Second, the model fits well with one feature of natural objects: such objects, like the Brancusi sculpture, do not have representational ties to the rest of reality. Third and most important, the model involves an accepted, traditional aesthetic approach. As Sparshott notes, ''When one talks of the aesthetic this or that, one is usually thinking of it as entering into a subject/object relation.''[1]

In spite of these considerations, however, I think there are aspects of the object model which make it inappropriate for nature. . . . [T]he object model imposes a certain limitation on our appreciation of natural objects. The limitation is the result of the removal of the object from its surroundings which the object model requires in order even to begin to provide answers to questions of what and how to appreciate. But in requiring such a removal the object model becomes problematic. The object model is most appropriate for those art objects which are self-contained aesthetic units. These objects are such that neither the environment of their creation nor the environment of their display are aesthetically relevant: the removal of a self-contained art object from its environment of creation will not vary its aesthetic qualities and the environment of display of such an object should not affect its aesthetic qualities. However, natural objects possess what we might call an organic unity with their environment of creation: such objects are a part of and have developed out of the elements of their environments by means of the forces at work within those environments. Thus the environments of creation are aesthetically relevant to natural objects. And for this reason the environments of display are equally relevant in virtue of the fact that these environments will be either the same as or different from the environments of creation. In either case the aesthetic qualities of natural objects will be affected. Consider again our rock: on the mantel it may seem wonderfully smooth and gracefully curved and expressive of solidity, but in its environment of creation it will have more and different aesthetic qualities—qualities which are the product of the relationship between it and its environment. It is here expressive of the particular forces which shaped and continue to shape it and displays for aesthetic appreciation its place in and its relation to its environment. Moreover, depending upon its place in that environment it may not express many of those qualities, for example, solidity, which it appears to express when on the mantel.

I conclude that the object model, even without changing nature into art, faces a problem as a paradigm for the aesthetic appreciation of nature. The problem is a dilemma: either we remove the object from its environment or we leave it where it is. If the object is removed, the model applies to the object and suggests answers to the questions of what and how to appreciate. But the result is the appreciation of a comparatively limited set of aesthetic qualities. On the other hand if the object is not removed, the model seemingly does not constitute an adequate model for a very large part of the appreciation which is possible. Thus it makes little headway with the what and how questions. In either case the object model does not provide a successful paradigm for the aesthetic appreciation of nature. It appears after all not a very ''curious limitation'' that when our attention is directed specifically toward the objects in the environment it is not called the love of nature.

The second paradigm for the aesthetic appreciation of nature I call the scenery or landscape model. In the artworld this model of appreciation is illustrated by landscape painting; in fact the model probably owes its existence to this art form. In one of its favored senses ''landscape'' means a prospect—usually standpoint and distance; a landscape painting is traditionally a representation of such a prospect.[2] When aesthetically appreciating landscape paintings (or any representative paintings, for that matter) the emphasis is not on the actual object (the painting) nor on the object represented (actual prospect); rather it is on the representation of the object and its represented features. Thus in landscape painting the appreciative emphasis is on those qualities which play an essential role in representing a prospect: visual qualities related to coloration and overall design. These are the qualities which are traditionally significant in landscape painting and which are the focus of the landscape model of appreciation. We thus have a model of appreciation which encourages perceiving and appreciating nature as if it were a landscape painting, as a grandiose prospect seen from a specific standpoint and distance. It is a model which centers attention on those aesthetic qualities of color and design which are seen and seen at a distance.

It is quite evident that the scenery or landscape model has been historically significant in our aesthetic appreciation of nature.[3] For example, this model was evident in the eighteenth and nineteenth centuries in the use of the ''Claude-glass,'' a small, tinted, convex mirror with which tourists viewed the landscape. Thomas West's popular guidebook to the Lake District (first published in 1778) says of the glass:

> ... where the objects are great and near, it removes them to a due distance, and shews them in the soft colours of nature, and most regular perspective the eye can perceive, art teach, or science demonstrate ... to the glass is reserved the finished picture, in highest colouring, and just perspective.[4]

In a somewhat similar fashion, the modern tourist reveals his preference for this model of appreciation by frequenting ''scenic viewpoints'' where the actual space between the tourist and the prescribed ''view'' often constitutes ''a due distance'' which aids the impression of ''soft colours of nature, and the most regular perspective the eye can perceive, art teach, or science demonstrate.'' And the ''regularity'' of the perspective is often enhanced by the positioning of the viewpoint itself. Moreover, the modern tourist also desires ''the finished picture, in highest colouring, and just perspective''; whether this be the ''scene'' framed and balanced in his camera's viewfinder, the result of this in the form of a kodachrome slide, and/or the ''artistically'' composed postcard and calendar reproductions of the ''scene'' which often attract more appreciation than that which they ''reproduce.'' R. Rees has described the situation as follows:

> . . . the taste has been for a view, for scenery, not for landscape in the original Dutch—and present geographical—meaning of term, which denotes our ordinary, everyday surroundings. The average modern sightseer, unlike many of the Romantic poets and painters who were accomplished naturalists, is interested *not* in natural forms and processes, but in a prospect.[5]

It is clear that in addition to being historically important, the landscape model, like the object model, gives us at least initial guidelines as to what and how to appreciate in regard to nature. We appreciate the natural environment as if it were a landscape painting. The model requires dividing the environment into scenes or blocks of scenery, each of which is to be viewed from a particular point by a viewer who is separated by the appropriate spatial (and emotional)? distance. A drive through the country is not unlike a walk through a gallery of landscape paintings. When seen in this light, this model of appreciation causes a certain uneasiness in a number of thinkers. Some, such as ecologist Paul Shepard, seemingly believe this kind of appreciation of the natural environment so misguided that they entertain doubts about the wisdom of *any* aesthetic approach to nature.[6] Others find the model to be ethically suspect. For example, after pointing out that the modern sightseer is interested only in a prospect, Rees concludes:

> In this respect the Romantic Movement was a mixed blessing. In certain phases of its development it stimulated the movement for the protection of nature, but in its picturesque phase it simply confirmed our anthropocentrism by suggesting that nature exists to please as well as to serve us. Our ethics, if the word can be used to describe our attitudes and behaviour toward the environment, have lagged behind our aesthetics. It is an unfortunate lapse which allows us to abuse our local environments and venerate the Alps and the Rockies.[7]

What has not been as generally noted, however, is that this model of appreciation is suspect not only on ethical grounds, but also on aesthetic grounds. The model requires us to view the environment as if it were a static representation which is essentially ''two dimensional.'' It requires the reduction of the environment to a scene or view. But what must be kept in mind is that the environment is not a scene, not a representation, not static, and not two dimensional. The point is that the model requires the appreciation of the environment not as what it is and with the qualities it has, but rather as something which it is not and with qualities it does not have. The model is in fact inappropriate to the actual nature of the object of appreciation. Consequently it not only, as the object model, unduly limits our appreciation—in this case to visual qualities related to coloration and overall design, it also misleads it. Hepburn puts this point in a general way:

> Supposing that a person's aesthetic education . . . instills in him the attitudes, the tactics of approach, the expectations proper to the appreciation of art works only, such a person will either pay very little aesthetic heed to natural objects or else heed them in the wrong way. He will look—and of course look in vain—for what can be found and enjoyed only in art.[8]

I conclude that the landscape model, as the object model, is inadequate as a paradigm for the aesthetic appreciation of nature. However, the reason for its inadequacy is instructive. The landscape model is inadequate because it is inappropriate to the nature of the natural environment. Perhaps to see what and how to appreciate in respect to the natural environment, we must consider the nature of that environment more carefully. In this regard there are two rather obvious points which I wish to emphasize. The first is that the natural environment is an environment; the second is that it is natural.

When we conceptualize the natural environment as ''nature'' I think we are tempted to think of it as an object. When we conceptualize it as ''landscape'' we are certainly led to thinking of it as scenery. Consequently perhaps the concept of the ''natural environment'' is somewhat preferable. At least it makes explicit that it is an environment which is under consideration. The object model and the landscape model each in its own way fail to take account of this. But what is involved in taking this into account? Here I wish initially to follow up some remarks made by Sparshott. He suggests that to consider something environmentally is primarily to consider it in regard to the relation of "self to setting," rather than "subject to object" or "traveler to scene."[9] An environment is the setting in which we exist as a "sentient part"; it is our surroundings. Sparshott points out that as our surroundings, our setting, the environment is that which we take for granted, that which we hardly notice—it is necessarily unobtrusive. If any one part of it becomes obtrusive, it is in danger of being seen as an object or a scene, not as our environment. As Sparshott says, "When a man starts talking about 'environmental values' we usually take him to be talking about aesthetic values of a background sort. . . ."[10]

I suggest then that the beginning of an answer to the question to *how* to aesthetically appreciate an environment is something like the following: We must experience our background setting in all those ways in which we normally experience it, by sight, smell, touch, and whatever. However, we must experience it not as unobtrusive background, but as obtrusive foreground! What is involved in such an "act of aspection" is not completely clear. Dewey gives us an idea in remarks such as:

> To grasp the sources of esthetic experience it is . . . necessary to have recourse to animal life below the human scale. . . . The live animal is fully present, all there, in all of its actions: in its wary glances, its sharp sniffing, its abrupt cocking of ears. All senses are equally on the *qui vive.*[11]

And perhaps the following description by Yi-Fu Tuan gives some further indication:

> An adult must learn to be yielding and careless like a child if he were to enjoy nature polymorphously. He needs to slip into old clothes so that he could feel free to stretch out on the hay beside the brook and bathe in a meld of physical sensations: the smell of the hay and of horse dung; the warmth of the ground, its hard and soft contours; the warmth of the sun tempered by breeze; the tickling of an ant making its way up the calf of his

leg; the play of shifting leaf shadows on his face; the sound of water over the pebbles and boulders, the sound of cicadas and distant traffic. Such an environment might break all the formal rules of euphony and aesthetics, substituting confusion for order, and yet be wholly satisfying.[12]

Tuan's account as to how to appreciate fits well with our earlier answer to the question of what to appreciate, *viz.,* everything. This answer, of course, will not do. We cannot appreciate everything; there must be limits and emphasis in our aesthetic appreciation of nature as there are in our appreciation of art. Without such limits and emphases our experience of the natural environment would be *only* "a meld of physical sensations" without any meaning or significance. It would be a Jamesian "blooming buzzing confusion" which truly substituted "confusion for order" and which, I suspect contra to Tuan, would not be wholly satisfying. Such experience would be too far removed from our aesthetic appreciation of art to merit the label "aesthetic" or even the label "appreciation." Consider again the case of art. In this case, . . . the boundaries and foci of aesthetic significance of works of art are a function of the type of art in question, *e.g.,* paintings end at their frames and their colors are significant. . . . The natural environment is not a work of art. As such it has no boundaries or foci of aesthetic significance which are given as a result of our creation nor of which we have knowledge because of our involvement in such creation.

The fact that nature is natural—not our creation—does not mean, however, that we must be without knowledge of it. Natural objects are such that we can discover things about them which are independent of any involvement by us in their creation. Thus although we have not created nature, we yet know a great deal about it. This knowledge, essentially common sense/scientific knowledge, seems to me the only viable candidate for playing the role in regard to the appreciation of nature which our knowledge of types of art, artistic traditions, and the like plays in regard to the appreciation of art. Consider the aesthetic appreciation of an environment such as that described by Tuan. We experience the environment as obtrusive foreground—the smell of the hay and of the horse dung, the feel of the ant, the sound of the cicadas and of the distant traffic all force themselves upon us. We experience a ''meld of sensations'' but, as noted, if our state is to be aesthetic appreciation rather than just the having of raw experience, the meld cannot be simply a ''blooming buzzing confusion.'' Rather it must be what Dewey called a consummatory experience: one in which knowledge and intelligence transform raw experience by making it determinate, harmonious, and meaningful. For example, in order for there to be aesthetic appreciation we must recognize the smell of the hay and that of the horse dung and perhaps distinguish between them; we must feel the ant at least as an insect rather than as, say, a twitch. Such recognizing and distinguishing results in certain aspects of the obtrusive foreground becoming foci of aesthetic significance. Moreover, they are natural foci appropriate to the particular natural environment we are appreciating. Likewise our knowledge of the environment may yield certain appropriate boundaries or limits to the experience. For example, since we are aesthetically appreciating a certain kind of environment, the sound of cicadas may be appreciated as a proper part of the setting, while the sound of the distant traffic is excluded much as we ignore the coughing in the concert hall.

What I am suggesting is that the question of *what* to aesthetically appreciate in the natural environment is to be answered in a way analogous to the similar question about art. The difference is that in the case of the natural environment the relevant knowledge is the common sense/scientific knowledge which we have discovered about the environment in question. This knowledge gives us the appropriate foci of aesthetic significance and the appropriate boundaries of the setting so that our experience becomes one of aesthetic appreciation. If to aesthetically appreciate art we must have knowledge of artistic traditions and styles within those traditions, to aesthetically appreciate nature we must have knowledge of the different environments of nature and of the systems and elements within those environments. In the way in which the art critic and the art historian are well equipped to aesthetically appreciate art, the naturalist and the ecologist are well equipped to aesthetically appreciate nature.[13]

The point I have now made about what to appreciate in nature also has ramifications for how to appreciate nature. When discussing the nature of an environment, I suggested that Tuan's description seems to indicate a general act of aspection appropriate for any environment. However, since natural environments differ in type it seems that within this general act of aspection there might be differences which should be noted. To aesthetically appreciate an environment we experience our surroundings as obtrusive foreground allowing our knowledge of that environment to select certain foci of aesthetic significance and perhaps exclude others, thereby limiting the experience. But certainly there are also different kinds of appropriate acts of aspection which can likewise be selected by our knowledge of environments. Ziff tells us to look for contours in the Florentine school and for color in a Bonnard, to survey a Tintoretto and to scan a Bosch. Consider different natural environments. It seems that we must survey a prairie environment, looking at the subtle contours of the land, feeling the wind blowing across the open space, and smelling the mix of prairie grasses and flowers. But such an act of aspection has little place in a dense forest environment. Here we must examine and scrutinize, inspecting the detail of the forest floor, listening carefully for the sounds of birds and smelling carefully for the scent of spruce and pine. Likewise, the description of environmental appreciation given by Tuan, in addition to being a model for environmental acts of aspection in general, is also a description of the act of aspection appropriate for a particular kind of environment—one perhaps best described as pastoral. Different natural environments require different acts of aspection; and as in the case of what to appreciate, our knowledge of the environment in question indicates how to appreciate, that is, indicates the appropriate act of aspection.

The model I am thus presenting for the aesthetic appreciation of nature might be termed the environmental model. It involves recognizing that nature is an environment and thus a setting within which we exist and which we normally experience with our complete range of senses as our unobtrusive background. But our experience being aesthetic requires unobtrusive background to be experienced as obtrusive foreground. The result is the experience of a ''blooming, buzzing confusion'' which in order to be appreciated must be tempered by the knowledge which we have discovered about that natural environment so experienced. Our knowledge of the nature of the particular environments yields the appropriate boundaries of appreciation, the particular foci of aesthetic significance, and the relevant act or acts of aspection for that type of environment. We thus have a model which begins to give answers to the questions of what and how to appreciate in respect to the natural environment and which seems to do so with due regard for the nature of that environment. And this is important not only for aesthetic but also for moral and ecological reasons.

In this paper I have attempted to open discussion on the questions of what and how to aesthetically appreciate in regard to nature. In doing so I have argued that two traditional approaches, each of which more or less assimilates the appreciation of nature to the appreciation of certain art forms, leave much to be desired. However, the approach which I have suggested, the environmental model, yet follows closely the general structure of our aesthetic appreciation of art. This approach does not depend on an assimilation of natural objects to art objects or of landscapes to scenery, but rather on an application of the general structure of aesthetic appreciation of art to something which is not art. What is important is to recognize that nature is an environment and is natural, and to make that recognition central to our aesthetic appreciation. Thereby we will aesthetically appreciate nature for what is and for the qualities it has. And we will avoid being the person described by Hepburn who ''will either pay very little aesthetic heed to natural objects or else heed them in the wrong way,'' who ''will look—and of course look in vain—for what can be found and enjoyed only in art.''[14]

NOTES

1. F.E. Sparshott, ''Figuring the Ground: Notes on Some Theoretical Problems of the Aesthetic Environment,'' *Journal of Aesthetic Education* (1972): 13.
2. This favored sense of ''landscape'' is brought out by Yi-Fu Tuan. See *Topophilia: A Study of Environmental Perception, Attitudes, and Values* (Englewood Cliffs, 1974), pp. 132-133, or ''Man and Nature: An Eclectic Reading,'' *Landscape,* Vol. 15 (1966): 30.
3. For a good, brief discussion of this point, see R. Rees, ''The Scenery Cult: Changing Landscape Tastes over Three Centuries,'' *Landscape,* Vol. 19 (1975). Note the following remarks by E. H. Gombrich in ''The Renaissance Theory of Art and the Rise of Landscape,'' *Norm and Form: Studies in the Art of the Renaissance* (London, 1971), pp. 117-118: ''. . . I believe that the idea of natural beauty as an inspiration of art . . . is, to say the least, a very dangerous oversimplification. Perhaps it even reverses the actual process by which man discovers the beauty of nature. We call a scenery 'picturesque' . . . if it reminds us of paintings we have seen. . . . Similarly, so it seems, the discovery of Alpine scenery does not precede but follows the spread of prints and paintings with mountain panoramas.''
4. Thomas West, *Guide to the Lakes* (London, 1778) as quoted in J.T. Ogden, ''From Spatial to Aesthetic Distance in the Eighteenth Century,'' *Journal of the History of Ideas,* Vol. XXXV (1974), 66-67.
5. R. Rees, ''The Taste for Mountain Scenery,'' *History Today,* Vol. XXV (1975): 312.
6. Paul Shepard, *The Tender Carnivore and the Sacred Game* (New York, 1973), pp. 147-148. Shepard made this position more explicit at a lecture at Athabasca University, Edmonton, Alberta, November 16, 1974.
7. Rees, ''Mountain Scenery,'' op. cit., p. 312. Ethical worries are also expressed by Tuan, *Topophilia,* op. cit., Chapter 8, and R.A. Smith and C.M. Smith, ''Aesthetics and Environmental Education,'' *Journal of Aesthetic Education* (1970): 131-132. Smith and Smith put the point as follows: ''Perhaps there is a special form of arrogance in experiencing nature strictly in the categories of art, for the attitude involved here implies an acceptance, though perhaps only momentarily, of the notion that natural elements have been arranged for the sake of the man's aesthetic pleasure. It is possible that this is what Kant had in mind when he said that in the appreciation of natural beauty one ought not assume that nature has fashioned its forms for our delight and that, instead, 'it is we who receive nature with favour, and not nature that does us a favour.' ''
8. R.W. Hepburn, ''Aesthetic Appreciation of Nature,'' *Aesthetics and the Modern World,* ed. H. Osborne (London, 1968), p. 53. Hepburn implicitly argues that our aesthetic appreciation of nature is enhanced by our ''realizing'' that an object is what it is and has the qualities which it has. See pp. 60-65.

9. Sparshott, op. cit, pp. 12-13. Sparshott also considers other possible relations which are not directly relevant here. Moreover, I suspect he considers the "traveler to scene" relation to be more significant than I do.
10. Ibid., pp. 17-18.
11. John Dewey, *Art as Experience* (New York, 1958), especially Chapters I-III, pp. 18–19.
12. Tuan, *Topophilia*, op. cit., p. 96.
13. I have in mind here individuals such as John Muir and Aldo Leopold. See, for example, Leopold's *A Sand County Almanac*.
14. Hepburn, op. cit., p. 53.

DISCUSSION TOPICS

1. Using a natural setting you know as an example, describe how a person might use object, landscape, and environmental paradigms to appreciate it.
2. Does Carlson's position give any guidance regarding the interactions of human beings with nature?

READING 18

The Land Aesthetic

J. Baird Callicott

J. Baird Callicott (b. 1941) is Professor of Philosophy and Natural Resources at the University of Wisconsin at Stevens Point. He is an influential environmental philosopher, whose works include In Defense of the Land Ethic *(1989) and* Ecological Insights *(1992). In the following essay Callicott summarizes the Western aesthetic experience of nature as it emerged in landscape painting of the seventeenth century. Callicott argues that Leopold's ideas constitute the first autonomous natural aesthetic, based on evolutionary and ecological biology. Evolutionary literacy can transform the perception of nature into something deeper than immediate sensory experience.*

Callicott describes his visit to a bog as an example of the appreciation of places which are not sensuously delightful but are nevertheless beautiful—beautiful because ecological science reveals the connectedness of their living components, their "fittingness," analogous to a work of art.

Callicott highlights Leopold's idea of certain species as "noumena" of the land, its hidden, nonquantifiable essences. Callicott renames these noumena "aesthetic indicator species."

Aldo Leopold is best known for the land ethic. He also developed an equally original and revolutionary "land aesthetic." Leopold's land aesthetic, however, has not enjoyed the same attention and celebrity as his land ethic, probably for two reasons. First, because—unlike the land ethic, which is concentrated in a single *Sand County Almanac* essay and labeled as such—the land esthetic is scattered throughout that book and Leopold's other writings, most of which, until recently, have been unavailable to all but the most dedicated scholars; and second, because aesthetics is usually regarded as an even less rigorous and certainly less important subject than ethics. While we earnestly debate matters of right and wrong, most of us have little to say about beauty, natural or artistic, except "ah" or "wow". And besides, what practical differences does aesthetic evaluation make? Such expressions as "to each his (or her) own" and "there's no accounting for taste" are not tolerated in the universe of ethical discourse, but they are virtual truisms in the realm of the aesthetic.

Aesthetics generally is a poor step-sister, a despised and neglected subject of theoretical discussion, in the general field of philosophy. Natural aesthetics is in even worse straits since what little aesthetic theory there is has centered almost entirely on art—painting, sculpture, architecture, drama, literature, dance, music, and more recently, cinema.[1] Indeed, during the twentieth century, "aesthetics" has become practically synonymous with "art criticism."

I suppose artifact aestheticians could make a persuasive case for the importance of artifactual aesthetics in the face of general neglect, but I can certainly say that natural aesthetic evaluation—albeit inarticulate and uncritical—has made a terrific difference to American conservation policy and land management. One of the main reasons that we have set aside certain natural areas as national, state, and county parks is because they are considered beautiful. In the conservation and resource management arena, historically, natural aesthetics has, indeed, been much more important than environmental ethics. Many more of our conservation and management decisions have been motivated by aesthetical rather than ethical values, by beauty instead of duty. What kinds of country we consider to be exceptionally beautiful makes a huge difference when we come to decide which places to save, which to restore or enhance, and which to allocate to other uses. Therefore, a sound natural aesthetics is crucial to sound conservation policy and land management.

Primarily, what I shall do here is assemble and juxtapose the scattered fragments of Leopold's land esthetic in *A Sand County Almanac,* in *Round River*, and in the new collection of his literary and philosophical papers, *The River of the Mother of God and Other Essays by Aldo Leopold,* that Susan Flader and I have edited for the University of Wisconsin Press, and abstract from them a systematic theory of natural beauty and the criteria for its appreciation. One cannot, however, begin to comprehend the originality of Leopold's contribution to the appreciation of natural beauty without some knowledge of how prevailing conventional tastes in natural beauty came to be what they are.

First of all, I think that the appreciation of natural beauty, now as common as Sierra Club calendars, PBS television programs, and L. L. Bean catalogues, is a relatively recent cultural achievement in the West. A negative thesis like this would be hard to verify short of an exhaustive review of classical and Medieval art and literature. So I state it only as a hypothesis and hope some hapless graduate student will devote a dissertation to trying to prove me wrong.

One does not have to search very far, however, in the ancient and Medieval art and literature of China and Japan to find a rich tradition of landscape drawing and painting, nature poetry, and the attendant philosophical analysis of why misty mountains are so enthralling, cherry blossoms so heart-stopping, and rushing brooks so captivating.

But what does Homer have to say about the beauty of Ilium or the island of Circe? A little, but not much. Sappho is without peer in her description of feminine pulchritude, a form of natural beauty to be sure, but she scarcely notices the charms of her native Lesbos. Plato is as flipped out about the beauty of boys as Sappho of girls, but what does he have to say about why the Attic landscape or the Aegean coast are so special? Nothing at all. How about Aristotle? He wrote philosophy's first treatise on aesthetics. But it's all about poetry.

Read the Old Testament. Do you find any celebration or analysis of natural beauty? As in contemporaneous Greek literature, maybe some passing notice of it, here and there in the psalms, but no sustained celebration, and certainly no analysis or criticism. How about the New Testament—the Gospels, or Epistles, or Revelation? Forget it.

In the Church-dominated Middle Ages, sensitivity to natural beauty was, in fact, regarded as vaguely sinful or at best a worldly distraction from the soul's proper preoccupation with its spiritual pilgrimage. In Medieval painting the natural world is pictured as a symbolic backdrop for the artists' central religious motifs. Indeed, it seems that in Western civilization, prior to the seventeenth century, nature was simply not a source of much aesthetic experience. If true, this realization is monumental, even shocking, given the nearly universal susceptibility to natural beauty ambient today in Western culture.

In the West susceptibility to natural beauty was, as Christopher Hussey points out, ancillary to the representation of nature in the exciting new genre of painting for which the name ''landscape'' was coined: ''It was not until Englishmen [as well as other Westerners] became familiar with the landscapes of Claude Lorraine and Salvatore Rosa, Ruysdael and Hobbema, that they were able to receive any [aesthetical] pleasure from their [natural] surroundings.'' Hence, cultivated Europeans began ''viewing and criticizing nature as if it were an infinite series of more or less well composed subjects for painting.''[2]

This, in short, is what seems to have happened in the strange history of natural beauty in the West. People saw landscape paintings in galleries, enjoyed an aesthetic experience, and so turned to the painters' motifs for a similar gratification. Natural beauty thus shown forth in the West, but, like the moon, by a borrowed light.

A device of the period, the Claude glass, named for the seventeenth-century French landscape artist, Claude Lorraine, tells the whole story. The new natural aesthetes carried the rectangular, slightly concave, tinted mirror with them into the countryside. Upon finding a suitably picturesque prospect, they turned their backs to it and rear-viewed its image in the Claude-glass. Thus framed, the natural landscape looked almost (but of course not quite) pretty as a picture.

European landscape painting itself, however, did not originate as a response to a sudden, spontaneous discovery of the beauty of nature, on the part of a few inspired individuals. Rather, the painters were providing, some of them quite consciously, a concrete representation of the abstract picture of nature emerging in the scientific revolution taking place during that period. In the new science, nature was objectified, separated, and distanced from the subjective observer. And it was mathematized. Linear perspective in painting, the principal means by which artists achieved a realistic representation, is, formally speaking, an exercise in projective geometry. Linear perspective in landscape, also creates an implied subject, an observer, who looks on, but is not personally situated or actively involved in the pictorial space.

The "picturesque" aesthetic, as the name suggests, self-consciously canonized as beautiful natural "scenes" or "landscapes" suitable as motifs for pictures. It was formulated in William Gilpin's *Three Essays on Picturesque Beauty* first published in 1792 and Uvedale Prince's *Essay on the Picturesque,* first published in 1794. The aesthetic analysis of nature was thus largely cast in terms of the colors, tones, textures, relative size, and arrangement or "composition" of topographical masses like mountains, valleys, lakes, woods, meadows, fields, streams, and so on.

John Muir provides an amusing and revealing illustration of the aesthetic appraisal of nature through categories developed for the aesthetic appraisal of pictures in *The Mountains of California.* Muir, whose own natural aesthetic tastes were quite catholic, nevertheless, knew well enough that practically everyone else's natural aesthetic tastes were thoroughly driven by landscape art. He discovered, near the headwaters of the Tuolumne, an alpine environment "in a high degree picturesque and in its main features so regular and evenly balanced as almost to appear conventional." Muir did not paint, but considered learning how, since "it seemed now to be ready and waiting for the elected artist." As luck would have it, upon emerging into the Yosemite Valley, he met two artists looking for just such a model as he had found. So they agreed to go have a look at it with Muir as their guide. It was a long hike in and the artists began to be discouraged. According to Muir, "the general expression of the scenery—rocky and savage—seemed sadly disappointing; and as they threaded the forest from ridge to ridge, eagerly scanning the landscapes as they were unfolded, they said: 'All this is huge and sublime, but we see nothing at all yet for effective pictures. Art is long and art is limited, you know; and here are foregrounds, middle grounds, and backgrounds all alike; bare rockwaves, woods, groves, diminutive flecks of meadow, and strips of glittering water.' " But when they finally reached the vista that Muir had in mind, "their enthusiasm was excited beyond bounds . . . [one] dashed ahead, shouting and gesticulating and tossing his arms in the air like a madman. Here at last was a typical alpine landscape."

Hussey argues that from the mid-eighteenth to the mid-nineteenth century all the arts—painting, poetry, the novel, architecture, even music—coalesced around the picturesque aesthetic and that it also spawned two new popular activities: aesthetic travel (or rustic tourism) and the aesthetic management of nature, revealingly called then as now, "landscape gardening" (in England) or "landscape architecture" (in the U.S.).

While painting and the other arts moved on to other fashions—Romanticism, Impression, Cubism, Abstract Expressionism, etc.—and artifactual aesthetic theory in the work of John Ruskin, Clive Bell, Roger Fry, George Santayana, and others kept abreast, popular taste in nature remained more or less tied to the picturesque.[3] And natural aesthetic theory languished.

Hence we continue to admire and preserve primarily "landscapes," "scenery," and "views" according to essentially eighteenth century standards of taste inherited from Gilpin, Price, and their contemporaries. Our tastes in natural beauty may now be broader than the very specific canons demanded by Muir's two artists, but they still remain fixed on visual and formal properties.

The word "landscape," as I just pointed out, was first coined to refer to a genre of painting. But it soon began to be used derivatively to refer to the actual countryside. In English one can hardly begin to speak about the beauty of nature without lapsing into referring to the countryside as "the landscape." That we call the aesthetic management of nature "*landscape* architecture" continues, I suspect, insidiously to tether that discipline to the picturesque aesthetic or at least to a more general concern with the visual characteristics of a piece of land. I don't know, in this case, what's in a name—how much the name "landscape architecture" continues to affect the attitudes and values of the discipline; although, as I just admitted, I do have my suspicions. In classic landscape architecture, certainly, visual qualities were of predominant concern and design considerations could be expressed in such terms as vista, view, and scene—with foreground, middle ground, and background; subtle symmetry of side screening; tension of vertical and horizontal line, relieved by arcs, curves, and diagonals; harmonious patterns of color; variety, movement, and so on. Today, significantly, the avant-garde wing of the discipline seems to be moving in the direction to which Leopold pointed at mid-century.

To sum up my historical review, Western appreciation of natural beauty is recent and derivative from art. The prevailing natural aesthetic, therefore, is not autonomous: it does not flow naturally from nature itself; it is not directly oriented to nature on nature's own terms; nor is it well informed by the ecological and evolutionary revolutions in natural history. It is superficial and narcissistic. In a word, it is trivial.

Naturally occurring scenic or picturesque "landscapes" are regarded, like the art they imitate, to be precious cultural resources and are stored, accordingly, in "museums" (the national parks) or private

"collections" (the "landscaped" estates of the wealthy). They are visited and admired by patrons just like their originals deposited in the actual museums in urban centers. Nonscenic, nonpicturesque nonlandscapes are aesthetic nonresources and thus become available for less exalted uses. While land must be used, it is well within our means to save, restore, and aesthetically manage representative nonscenic, nonpicturesque nonlandscapes—swamps and bogs, dunes, scrub, prairie, bottoms, flats, deserts, and so on as aesthetic amenities—just as we preserve intact representative scenic ones. Aldo Leopold's land aesthetic provides a seminal autonomous natural aesthetic theory which may help to awaken our response to the potential of these aesthetically neglected communities.

Leopold shows us that an autonomous natural aesthetic could involve so much more than the visual appeal of natural environments. One is in the landscape, i.e., in the natural environment, as the mobile center of a three-dimensional, multisensuous experiential continuum. The appreciation of an environment's natural beauty could involve the ears (the sounds of rain, insects, birds, or silence itself), the surface of the skin (the warmth of the sun, the chill of the wind, the texture of grass, rock, sand, etc.), the nose and tongue (the fragrance of flowers, the odor of decay, the taste of saps and waters)—as well as the eyes. Most of all it could involve the mind, the faculty of cognition. For Leopold, as for his contemporaries in structural design, form follows function. The aesthetic appeal of country, in other words, should have less to do with its adventitious colors and shapes or its scenic expanses and picturesque proportions than with the integrity of its evolutionary heritage and ecological processes.

Leopold was, apparently, well aware of the primacy of artifactual aesthetics in Western civilization and thus, as an expository device, he approaches natural aesthetics via analogy with the more familiar branch.

He remarks, "our ability to perceive quality in nature begins, as in art, with the pretty" (exemplified by, for example, "landscaped" English gardens). "It proceeds through successive stages of the beautiful

. . .'' (exemplified by, say, the naturally ''pictur-esque'' Yosemite Valley, high Alpine ''scenery,'' ''sublime'' sequoia groves, etc.), ''to values as yet uncaptured by language.''[4] Leopold then goes on to capture, in his own compact, descriptive prose, the subtler gamut of aesthetic quality in a nonlandscape which the conventional painting-mediated natural aesthetic finds plain, if not odious—a crane marsh.

Among gallery goers there are also those whose taste is limited to the pretty (to naive, realistic, still-life, and portraiture, for example). Then, there are those capable of appreciating successive stages of the beautiful present in ''modern art'' (Cezanne, Picasso, or Pollack), whether pretty or not. As in art, the ca-pacity to actualize the aesthetic potentialities of land which go beyond the pretty and the picturesque re-quires some cultivation of sensibility. One must ac-quire ''a refined taste in natural objects'':[6]

> The taste for country displays the same diversity in es-thetic competence among individuals as the taste for opera, or oils. There are those who are willing to be herded in droves through 'scenic' places; who find mountains grand if they be proper mountains with wa-terfalls, cliffs, and lakes. To such the Kansas plains are tedious.[5]

For Leopold the Kansas plains are aesthetically exciting less for what is directly seen (or, indeed, otherwise sensuously experienced) than for what is known of their history and biology: ''They see the endless corn, but not the heave and the grunt of ox teams breaking the prairie. . . . They look at the low horizon, but they cannot see it, as de Vaca did, under the bellies of the buffalo.''[6]

In ''Marshland Elegy'' Leopold beautifully illus-trates the impact of an evolutionary biological literacy on perception. Wisconsin's first settlers called sand-hill cranes ''red shitepokes'' for the rusty clay stain their ''battleship gray'' feathers acquire in summer.[7] The Wisconsin homesteaders saw red shitepokes as just large birds in the way of farm progress. But ev-olutionary literacy can alter and deepen perception:

> Our appreciation of the crane grows with the slow un-raveling of earthly history. His tribe, we now know, stems out of the remote Eocene. The other members of the fauna in which he originated are long since entombed

within the hills. When we hear his call we hear no mere bird. We hear the trumpet in the orchestra of evolution. He is the symbol of our untamable past, of that incredible sweep of millennia which underlies the daily affairs of birds and men.[8]

Ecology, as Leopold pictures it, is the biological science which runs at right angles to evolution.[9] Ev-olution lends to perception a certain depth, ''that in-credible sweep of millennia,'' while ecology provides it breadth: Wild things do not exist in isolation from one another. They are ''interlocked in one humming community of cooperations and competitions, one biota.''[10] Hence the crane, no mere bird, lends ''a paleontological patent of nobility'' to its marshy hab-itat.[11] We cannot love cranes and hate marshes. The marsh itself is now transformed by the presence of cranes from a ''waste,'' ''God-forsaken'' mosquito swamp, into a thing of precious beauty.[12]

The crane is also a species native to its marshy habitat. Many pretty plants and animals are not. From the point of view of the land aesthetic, the attractive purple flower of centauria or the vivid orange of hawk weed might actually spoil rather than enhance a field of (otherwise) native grasses and forbes. Leopold writes lovingly of draba, pasque-flowers, sylphium, and many other pretty and not-so-pretty native plants, but with undisguised contempt for peonies, downy chess or cheat grass, foxtail, and other European im-ports and stowaways. He takes delight in the sky dance of the native woodcock and the flight plan of a fleeing partridge, but not (hunter though he may have been) in, say, the evasive maneuvers of the imported oriental ring-necked pheasant.

In an (until just now) unpublished 1936 lecture entitled ''Means and Ends in Wild Life Manage-ment,'' Leopold frankly declares that while ''our tools are scientific . . . our output is weighed in esthetic satisfaction rather than economic pounds or dol-lars.''[13] Then he briefly sets out a few criteria for evaluating the aesthetic significance of wildlife spe-cies. One such criterion he denominates ''artistic value,'' by which he seems to mean things like the colorful plumage and musical songs of birds—the sorts of sensory qualities that wildlife and art might have in common. But that is the least important cri-terion for the aesthetic appraisal of wildlife. More important is "personality" or "character" which we perceive of the species, not the individual animal—the resourcefulness of the fox, the grace of the deer, and so on. Leopold identifies, further, "scarcity value"—both natural scarcity, as in the case of the badger, or humanly induced rarity as in the case of the Carolina parakeet—as a criterion of the natural aesthetics of wildlife. Further still, the wilder the animal, the less tolerant of man and his works—such as the grizzly bear as opposed to the black bear and the timber wolf as opposed to the coyote—the more aesthetically valuable. And of course the native species, once again, is to be prized over the exotic.

Ecology, history, paleontology, geology, biogeography—each forms of knowledge or cognition—penetrate the surface provided by direct sensory experience and supply substance to "scenery." Leopold was quite consciously aware of the profound transformation in general sensibility that he was calling for. In another (until now) unpublished piece from the 1930s, "Land Pathology," Leopold lampoons the conventional taste for "scenery" immured in the National Parks as "an epidemic of esthetic rickets."[14] In the almanac, similarly, he disparaged "that underaged brand of esthetics which limits the definition of 'scenery' to lakes and pine trees".[15] "In country," he writes, "a plain exterior often conceals hidden riches."[16] To get at these hidden riches takes more than a gaze at a scenic view through a car window or camera view finder. To promote appreciation of nature is "a job not of building roads into lovely country, but of building receptivity into the still unlovely human mind."[17]

Leopold's land aesthetic, like his land ethic, is self-consciously informed by evolutionary and ecological biology. It involves a subtle interplay between conceptual schemata and sensuous experience. Experience, as the British Empiricists insisted, informs thought. That is true and obvious to everyone. What is not so immediately apparent is that thought equally and reciprocally informs experience. The "world," as we drink it in through our senses, is first filtered, structured, and arranged by the conceptual framework or cognitive set we bring to it, prior, not necessarily to all, but to any articulate experience.

This was Kant's great and lasting contribution to philosophy, his self-styled "Copernican revolution" of philosophy. Kant believed that the cognitive conditions of experience were *a priori*—universal and necessary—but that proved to be a narrowly parochial judgment. The discovery by anthropologists of very different "cultural worlds" or "world views" and subsequent revolutionary changes in Western science affecting even the fundamental experiential parameters of space and time relativized Kant's transcendental "aesthetic" and "logic." His basic revolutionary idea, though, remains very much intact. What one experiences is as much a product of how one thinks as the condition of one's senses and the specific content of one's environment.

Leopold is quite consciously aware of the interplay between the creative or active cognitive component of experience and the receptive or passive sensory component. He imagines what Daniel Boone's experience of nature must have been like as an outdoorsman living before the advent of an evolutionary-ecological biology:

> Daniel Boone's reaction depended not only on the quality of what he saw, but on the quality of the mental eye with which he saw it. Ecological science has wrought a change in the mental eye. It has disclosed origins and functions for what to Boone were only facts. It has disclosed mechanisms for what to Boone were only attributes. We have no yardstick to measure this change, but we may safely say that, as compared with the competent ecologist of the present day, Boone saw only the surface of things. The incredible intricacies of the plant and animal community—the intrinsic beauty of the organism called America, then in the full bloom of her maidenhood—were as invisible and incomprehensible to Daniel Boone as they are today to Babbitt. The only true development in American [aesthetic] resources is the development of the perceptive faculty in Americans. All of the other acts we grace by that name are, at best, attempts to retard or mask the process of dilution.[18]

Thus, while an autonomous natural aesthetic, as I earlier pointed out, must free itself from the prevailing visual bias and involve all sensory modalities, it is not enough to simply open the senses to natural stimuli and enjoy. A complete natural aesthetic, like a complete artifactual aesthetic, shapes and directs sensation, often in surprising ways. It is possible, in certain

theoretical contexts, to enjoy and appreciate disso-
nance in music or the clash of color and distortion of
eidetic form in painting. Similarly, in natural aesthetics, it is possible to appreciate and relish certain environmental experiences which are not literally plea-
surable or sensuously delightful.

For example, I am acquainted with a certain northern bog which is distinguished from the others in its
vicinity by the presence of pitcher plants, an endangered species of floral insectivore. I visit this bog at
least once each season. The plants themselves are not,
by garden standards, beautiful. They are a dark red in
color, less brilliant than maple leaves in autumn, and
humbly hug the low bog floor. They lie on a bed of
sphagnum moss in the deep shade of fifty-foot, ruler-
straight tamaracks. To reach the bog I must wade
across its mucky moat, penetrate a dense thicket of
tag alders and in summer fight off mosquitoes, black
and deer flies. My shoes and trousers get wet; my skin
gets scratched and bitten. The experience is certainly
not spectacular or, for that matter, particularly pleasant; but it is always somehow satisfying aesthetically.
The moss bed on which the pitcher plants grow is
actually floating. It undulates sensually as I walk
through. I smell the sweet decay aroma of the peat
and hear the whining insects (in season). I run my
finger down and then up the vulva-shaped interior of
a pitcher plant's leaf—turned insect trap—to feel the
grain of the fibers which keep the insects from crawling out again. It is silky smooth on the way in, bristled
on the way out. I look through the trees, beyond, to
the adjoining pond. I dig my hand into the moss and
bring up a brown rotting mass. I sometimes see a blue
heron lift itself off the shore into the air with a single
silent stroke of its great wings or see the glint and
splash of a northern pike out on the pond. I feel the
living bark of the tamaracks, precariously anchored
on a floating island. In spring and summer everything
is drably green or brown except the sky, and the
pitcher plants. Fall is the most colorful, the tamaracks
are a "smoky gold." In winter everything shades
from black to white. Yet there is a rare music in this
place. It is orchestrated and deeply moving.

The beauty of this bog is not serial—an aggregate
of interesting objects, like specimens displayed in
cases in a natural history museum, nor is it phenomenological—a variety of sensory stimuli or "sense
data"; rather its beauty is a function of the palpable
organization and closure of the interconnected living
components. The sphagnum moss and the chemical
regime it imposes constitutes the basis of this small,
tight community. The tamaracks are a second major
factor. The flora and fauna of the stories between are
characteristic of, and some like the pitcher plants are
unique to, this sort of community. There is a sensible
fittngness, a unity there, not unlike that of a good
symphony or tragedy. But these connections and relations are not directly sensed in the aesthetic moment,
they are *known* and *projected,* in this case by me. It
is this conceptual act that completes the sensory experience and causes it to be distinctly aesthetic . . .
instead of merely uncomfortable.

Given the Western heritage, it is, perhaps, impossible to express and analyze natural aesthetic experience except by analogy with artifactual aesthetic experience. Leopold's evolutionary-ecological
aesthetic is, yielding to this expository necessity, perhaps more akin to aural aesthetics than to visual aesthetics. Few authors have expressed the sense of the
familiar metaphor "harmony of nature" with more
authority and grace than he:

> The song of a river ordinarily means the tune that waters
> play on rock, root, and rapid . . .
>
> This song of the waters is audible to every ear, but
> there is other music in these hills, by no means audible
> to all. To hear even a few notes of it you must first live
> here for a long time, and you must know the speech of
> hills and rivers. Then on a still night, when the campfire
> is low and the Pleiades have climbed over rimrocks, sit
> quietly and listen for a wolf to howl, and think hard of
> everything you have seen and tried to understand. Then
> you may hear it—a vast pulsing harmony—its score
> inscribed on a thousand hills, its notes the lives and
> deaths of plants and animals, its rhythms spanning the
> seconds and the centuries.[19]

In 1935 Leopold traveled abroad for the first time,
studying forestry and wildlife management in Germany. This experience inspired a piece entitled "Wilderness," which has now also been published for the
first time in the new collection of his essays. As in the
almanac's haunting "Marshland Elegy," Leopold
fuses the evolutionary and ecological dimensions of

informed perception. He expresses his displeasure with the intensively managed German "forest landscape deprived of a certain exuberance which arises from a rich variety of plants fighting with each other for a place in the sun."[20] Maintenance of an excessively high deer herd had resulted in "an illusive burglary of esthetic wealth . . . an unnatural simplicity and monotony in the vegetation of the forest floor, which is still further aggravated by the too-dense shade cast by the artificially crowded trees, and by the soil-sickness . . . arising from conifers."[21] But species diversity, the lack of which is discernible to the ecological eye, is an evolutionary legacy. "It is almost, he suggests, as if the geological clock had been set back to those dim ages when there were only pines and ferns."[22] And, as in the almanac's "Song of the Gavilan," he expresses his (this time negative) aesthetic response with an even more powerful musical metaphor: "I never realized before that the melodies of nature are music only when played against the undertones of evolutionary history. In the German forest one now hears only a dismal fugue out of the timeless reaches of the carboniferous."[23]

In addition to this general Kantian emphasis on the cognitive dimension of natural aesthetic experience, Leopold has formulated a quite specialized and somewhat technical natural aesthetic category, "the noumenon," also ultimately inspired by the philosophy of Kant. To an academic historian of philosophy, Leopold may seem simply to have misappropriated Kant's term. By "noumenon" Kant meant a purely intelligible object, a thing-in-itself (*Ding an sich*) which was beyond human ken. Only phenomena are present to human consciousness, according to Kant. In Leopold's general sense of the term, however, the noumena of land are quite actual or physical (and therefore, strictly speaking, phenomenal). Nonetheless, in a metaphorical way, they constitute the "essence" of the countryside. In this sense Leopold's usage observes the spirit of Kant's definition, if not the letter. Here is how Leopold introduces the term, "noumenon" in *Sand Country:*

> The physics of beauty is one department of natural science still in the Dark Ages. Not even the manipulators of bent space have tried to solve its equations. Everybody knows, for example, that the autumn landscape in

the north woods is the land, plus a red maple, plus a ruffed grouse. In terms of conventional physics, the grouse represents only a millionth of either the mass or the energy of an acre. Yet subtract the grouse and the whole thing is dead. An enormous amount of some kind of motive power has been lost.

> It is easy to say that the loss is all in our mind's eye, but is there any sober ecologist who will agree? He knows full well that there has been an ecological death, the significance of which is inexpressible in terms of contemporary science. A philosopher has called this imponderable essence the *noumenon* of material things. It stands in contradistinction to *phenomenon,* which is ponderable and predictable, even to the tossings and turnings of the remotest star.

> The grouse is the noumenon of the north woods, the blue jay of the hickory groves, the whiskey-jack of the muskegs, the piñonero of the juniper foothills. . . .[24]

And we could go on: the cutthroat trout of high mountain streams, the sand hill crane of northern marshes, the pronghorn antelope of the high plains, the loon of glacial lakes, the alligator of southeastern swamps, etc., etc. We might call these noumena more precisely, though less arrestingly, "aesthetic indicator species." They supply the hallmark, the imprimatur, to their respective ecological communities. If they be missing, then the rosy glow of perfect health, as well as aesthetic excitement, is absent from the countryside. Like the elusive mountain lion and timber wolf, they need not be seen or heard to grace and enliven their respective habitats. It is enough merely to *know* that they are present.

In "Wilderness," Leopold expresses an aesthetic dissatisfaction not only with "what the geometrical mind has done to German rivers," but also with the decidedly picturesque German countryside, because "to the critical eye, there is something lacking that should not be."[25] In addition to much of the native flora, many species of native fauna, especially predators, had been extirpated from the German *Walder* by "cubistic forestry" and by the "misguided zeal of the game-keeper and herdsman." Leopold laments especially the absence of "the great owl or 'Uhu,'" more often heard than seen, "without whose vocal austerity the winter night becomes a mere blackness."[26] The Uhu, we realize, is, for Leopold, the noumenon of the German forests.

To sum up, the land aesthetic, desultorily and intermittently developed in *A Sand County Almanac,* in *Round River,* and now in *The River of the Mother of God* is a new natural aesthetic, the first, to my knowledge, to be informed by ecological and evolutionary natural history and thus the only genuinely autonomous natural aesthetic in Western philosophical literature: It does not treat natural beauty as subordinate to or derivative from artifactual beauty. However, because natural beauty has traditionally and historically been treated as a reflection of artifactual beauty, the land aesthetic is perforce developed by analogy with artifactual aesthetics. Though more analogous to an aesthetic of music, the land aesthetic is no more aurally biased than visually biased. It involves all sensory modalities equally and indiscriminately.

The popularly prevailing natural aesthetic, the scenic or picturesque aesthetic, frames nature, as it were, and deposits it in ''galleries''—the national parks—for most ordinary folk, far from home. We herd in droves to Yellowstone, Yosemite, and the Smokies to gaze at natural beauty and, home again, despise the river bottoms, fallow fields, bogs, and ponds on the back forty. The land aesthetic enables us to mine the hidden riches of the ordinary; it ennobles the commonplace; it brings natural beauty literally home from the hills.

The land aesthetic is sophisticated and cognitive, not naive and hedonic; it delineates a refined taste in natural environments and a cultivated natural sensibility. The basis of such refinement or cultivation is natural history, and more especially, evolutionary and ecological biology. The crane, for example, is no mere bird because of its known, not directly sensed, phylogenetic antiquity and, thus, the experience of cranes is especially aesthetically satisfying only to those who have a paleontological dimension to their outlook. The experience of a marsh or bog is aesthetically satisfying less for what is literally sensed than what is known or schematically imagined of its ecology. Leopold enters a caveat, however, to the cognitive stress of the land aesthetic:

> Let no man jump to the conclusion that Babbitt must take his Ph.D. in ecology before he can 'see' his country. On the contrary, the Ph.D. may become as callous as an

undertaker to the mysteries at which he officiates. Like all real treasures of the mind, perception can be split into infinitely small fractions without losing its quality. The weeds in a city lot convey the same lesson as the redwoods; the farmer may see in his cow-pasture what may not be vouchsafed to the scientist adventuring in the South Seas. Perception, in short, cannot be purchased with either learned degrees or dollars; it grows at home as well as abroad, and he who has a little may use it to as good advantage as he who has much. As a search for perception, the recreational stampede is footless and unnecessary.[27]

Finally and, practically speaking, more importantly, the land aesthetic is not biased in favor of some natural communities or some places and not others. Leopold in his discussion and I in mine have dwelt on wetlands (marshes and bogs) because they are characteristic of Wisconsin (where I also live) and also because, since they are so thoroughly unaesthetic, as measured by conventional canons of landscape beauty, they highlight certain contrasts between the picturesque aesthetic and the land aesthetic. But conventionally beautiful environments—alpine communities, for example—are, for that reason, not the less land aesthetically interesting. All biocoenoses from arctic tundra to tropical rainforest and from deserts to swamps can be aesthetically appealing upon the land aesthetic. Hence, no matter where one may live, one's environment holds the potential for natural aesthetic experience.

NOTES

1. Some recent exceptions include Marjorie Hope Nicholson, *Mountain Gloom, Mountain Glory: The Development of the Aesthetics of the Infinite* (Ithaca, NY: Cornell University Press, 1969); Ian McHarg, *Design with Nature* (Garden City, NY: Doubleday and Co., 1971); Paul Shepard, *Man in the Landscape: A Historic View of the Esthetics of Nature* (New York: Alfred Knopf, 1967); Yi-Fu Tuan, *Topophilia: A Study of Environmental Perception, Attitudes, and Values* (Englewood Cliffs, NJ: Prentice Hall, 1974); Mark Sagoff, ''On Preserving the Natural Environment,'' *The Yale Law Journal* 84 (1974): 245–267; Ronald Rees, ''The Taste for Mountain Scenery,'' *History Today* 25

(1975): 305–312; Eugene C. Hargrove, ''The Historical Foundations of American Environmental Attitudes,'' *Environmental Ethics* 1 (1979): 209–240 and ''Anglo-American Land Use Attitudes,'' *Environmental Ethics* 2 (1980): 121–148; Allen Carlson, ''Appreciation and the Natural Environment,'' *The Journal of Aesthetics and Art Criticism* 37 (1979): 267–275, ''Nature, Aesthetic Judgment, and Objectivity,'' *The Journal of Aesthetics and Art Criticism* 40 (1981): 15–27, ''Nature and Positive Aesthetics,'' *Environmental Ethics* 6 (1984): 5–34; Barbara Novak, *Nature and Culture: American Landscape Painting 1825–1875* (New York: Oxford University Press, 1980); J. Baird Callicott, ''Aldo Leopold's Land Aesthetic and Agrarian Land Use Values,'' *Journal of Soil and Water Conservation* 38 (1983): 329–332; Philip G. Terrie, *Forever Wild: Environmental Aesthetics and the Adirondack Forest Preserve* (Philadelphia, PA: Temple University Press, 1985); Holmes Rolston, III, some essays in *Philosophy Gone Wild* (Buffalo, NY: Prometheus Books, 1986).

2. Christopher Hussey, *The Picturesque: Studies in a Point of View* (London: G. P. Putnam's Sons, 1927) pp. 1–2.

3. R. Rees, ''Mountain Scenery,'' argues that, if anything, taste in natural ''landscapes'' has degenerated to what was known in the picturesque aesthetic literature as ''a prospect,'' i.e., a viewpoint or scene.

4. Aldo Leopold, *A Sand County Almanac: And Sketches Here and There* (New York: Oxford University Press, 1949), p. 96.

5. Aldo Leopold, *The Round River,* pp. 32–33.

6. Ibid., p. 33.

7. Leopold, *Sand County,* p. 99.

8. Ibid., p. 96.

9. Leopold, *Round River,* p. 159.

10. Ibid., p. 148.

11. Leopold, *Sand County,* p. 97.

12. Wetlands to those farmers wearing economic blinders (by no means all farmers) are, in my neck of the woods, regularly referred to as ''waste'' lands, because they are not in ''production,'' i.e., not cultivated.

13. Aldo Leopold, ''Means and Ends in Wildlife Management'' in Susan L. Flader and J. Baird Callicott, eds., *The River of the Mother of God and Other Essays by Aldo Leopold* (Madison: University of Wisconsin Press, 1991), p. 236.

14. Aldo Leopold, ''Land Pathology,'' in *The River of the Mother of God,* p. 216.

15. Leopold, *Sand County,* p. 191.

16. Leopold, *Round River,* p. 33.

17. Leopold, *Sand County,* p. 177.

18. Ibid., p. 174.

19. Ibid., p. 149.

20. Aldo Leopold, ''Wilderness,'' in *The River of the Mother of God,* p. 229.

21. Ibid. p. 228.

22. Ibid. p. 229.

23. Ibid.

24. Leopold, *Sand County,* pp. 138–139.

25. Leopold, ''Wilderness,'' pp. 226–227.

26. Ibid., p. 228.

27. Leopold, *Sand County,* p. 174.

DISCUSSION TOPICS

1. According to Leopold, what contributions to aesthetic experience can be made by ''evolutionary literacy'' in the observer? Give an example.

2. In your view, is the ''picturesque'' sense of natural beauty, which Callicott dates from the seventeenth century, still dominant in the West? What role does the picturesque play in your own experience of natural beauty?

3. Explain Leopold's idea of the ''noumena'' of various ecological communities and give an example from your own geographical area.

4. Compare the overall tone of Leopold's land aesthetic with the essays of Thoreau, Muir, and Dillard. How prominent are the biological, moral, emotional, spiritual, and traditionally aesthetic perspectives in the various writers?

5. Compare the aesthetic appreciation of nature in Leopold's land aesthetic with Carlson's ''environmental model.'' Are they saying the same things?

The Ontological Argument for the Preservation of Nature

Eugene C. Hargrove

Eugene C. Hargrove (b. 1944) teaches philosophy at the University of North Texas in Denton, Texas, and is editor of Environmental Ethics. *In the following chapter from* Foundations of Environmental Ethics, *he presents an argument that human beings are obligated to ensure the continuation of nature in its natural form.*

Hargrove begins from the premise that human beings have a duty to promote and preserve both artistic and natural beauty. He notes that preserving natural beauty is difficult because existence is more fundamental in natural objects than in art objects. Whereas an art object is imagined before it exists, a natural object is more than a human being's concept of it. The human mind cannot comprehend the complexity of natural objects. The beauty of nature arises from its self-creation. The existence of a natural object includes its history. Hargrove uses the example of the alligator to clarify his point. In the three cases of a wild, farmed and plastic alligator, we see three different things. The authentic physical existence of the wild alligator, continuous with its past, is crucial to the full aesthetic appreciation of the alligator.

Traditionally, the *onotological argument* refers to various proofs of the existence of God, according to which it is asserted that the essence of God requires His existence. These proofs are metaphysical arguments without direct ethical implications. The ontological argument for the preservation of nature, in contrast, is primarily aesthetic and ethical, not metaphysical. It is not intended to prove that nature exists, which is taken as a given, but to show that humans have a duty to act so as to ensure the continuation of nature in its appropriate, natural form. . . .

Existence plays a more fundamental role in natural objects than in art objects. As noted earlier, an art object is an entity whose essence precedes its existence. An art object is made in the same way that

Sartre's paper cutter is made. The beauty of the art object exists in imagination before the object itself comes to be. In contrast, a natural object is an entity whose existence precedes its essence. In this case, the beauty has no prior existence in imagination and in fact no prior existence of any kind. It emerges only when the natural object takes physical form. This is a critical difference between natural and artistic beauty. It is better for artistic beauty to exist physically; nevertheless, because it has preexistence in imagination, its beauty is not directly or entirely dependent on the process of physical actualization. This point is especially clear in the case of nonpermanent, or ephemeral, earthworks, for example, Christo's *Valley Curtain*. As Peter Humphrey notes in his interesting examination of earthworks, he, like most people, became aware of this work of art by looking at plans of it in a special exhibit in a museum. In this context he goes on to ask ''how important . . . our *knowledge* that there really was an enormous, orange curtain near Rifle, Colorado,'' is to our aesthetic appreciation of it after the fact, and concludes ''that there's a possibility worth considering that such knowledge doesn't matter.''[1] I am inclined to agree. If one thinks of the plans for the curtain as analogous to an ideal landscape painting, the plans themselves can be appreciated as an art object independent of whether they were or are ever carried out. Similarly, sketches for a work of art that was never finished can often serve as an adequate source for the beauty that would have been in the original. Such is not the case, however, with natural beauty. Since natural beauty does not have preexistence in the imagination or in artist sketches, it must exist physically in order to exist in any sense at all.

This is an important ontological difference. In criticizing the traditional ontological argument, Kant argues that existence is not a true predicate on the grounds that ''the real contains no more than the merely possible.'' Since a hundred coins that physically exist do not possess any properties that are not contained in our concept of them, the physical existence of the coins is irrelevant to their properties and to predicates expressing those properties.[2] Kant's point is certainly correct with regard to objects created by humans, in which the concept precedes their creation, and would also be true of nature, for example, in a universe without evolution in which natural form was fixed and immutable, but it is not true of the objects in the natural world in the universe we actually live in. Our concepts of natural objects rarely, if ever, include all the properties those objects possess. A real, existing tree is more than a human's concept of it. For this reason, if existence is not itself a property, not a predicate of the tree, the tree's existence is nevertheless tied up with the tree's other properties in a way that the properties of the coins are not tied up with their existence.

The problem being addressed here stems directly from the limitations of the human mind, both conceptually and imaginatively. The human mind has great difficulty dealing with complexity, which is, of course, one of nature's chief characteristics. In science, humans have progressed by employing a reductionist method, by breaking nature's complexity down into its simple parts. Although this method has been very productive, it has provided a distorted and simplified picture of nature. In art, likewise, humans have progressed through simplification. The creative impulse in nature is toward the realization of beauty through the generation of complex forms and relations. The creative impulse in humans, resulting from the limitations of their minds, is, in contrast, toward the realization of simplified beauty. This trend is obvious not only in nonrepresentational art but in representational art as well. Nonrepresentational art tends to focus on simple geometric forms. While representational art tries to depict nature accurately, it must do so in a manner that presents forms that are simpler and less detailed than those of the original objects in nature. The result is art that suggests the complexity of nature but does not capture its complete reality. This is true not only of painting but also of landscape gardening, in which the elements of nature itself are used. The assemblage of the simple elements, the various plants and animals, does not produce the real thing. As landscape gardeners learned when they first began trying to imitate wild nature, they could not duplicate the inner processes, the inner reality. The methods used to produce formal gardens

were also required to produce informal ones. Without careful attention, the gardens collapsed into chaos. . . . Complexity is a distinguishing feature of natural beauty that irredeemably sets it apart from the artistic beauty of human beings. . . . Nature knows best (or perhaps does best) in part because whatever it does through creative indifference is beautiful but also, more importantly, because the end result is a creative output that is far too complex for humans to reproduce, to go beyond, or even fully to participate in; as such, it is unique and irreplaceable. We find in the writings of philosophers such as Moore and Passmore and scientists such as Shaler, who are willing to talk about the beauty of the Earth, a willingness to accept the view that humans have a duty to improve on the beauty of nature. Such a duty makes sense insofar as artistically created human beauty is considered to be a special case within the realm of natural beauty. The generation of beauty through simplification is, of course, aesthetically valuable and something that nature can take credit for, not only because complex nature is what humans react against but also because it is the biological source of human beings and all their activity, aesthetic and otherwise. Such a duty, however, does not make sense if it calls for human involvement in the creative process of nonhuman nature, given the vast difference in the approaches of nature and humankind. Since attempts to improve natural beauty will distort, transform, and even destroy that beauty, our duty should not be to improve but rather to promote and preserve through action and inaction that does not restrict, impinge on, redirect, or bring to an end the geological and biological activity on which the indifference of natural creativity depends.

In rejecting the duty to improve nature in favor of one to promote and preserve it, we have to be careful that we do so for the right reasons. The fact that we cannot improve nature in terms of nature's own standards is, of course, an important reason, but it is not the primary one. To attempt to manipulate nature, even for aesthetic reasons, alters nature adversely from an aesthetic standpoint. Historically, manipulation of nature, even to improve it, has been considered subjugation or domination. Such manipulation limits the freedom of nature, which in turn reduces its ability to be creative. The beauty of nature arises out of self-creation, which requires freedom from nonnatural influence. Our appreciation of the beauty of nature is not focused simply on the direct sensory awareness of the moment but is also filtered through an understanding and appreciation of the creative forces that produced that moment in nature's history. Just as we want an art object to be original, the actual result of the artistic process, we want the beauty of nature to be authentic, the result of natural processes only.

The authenticity of nature arises out of the fact that its existence precedes its essence. Nature is not simply a collection of natural objects; it is a process that progressively transforms those objects, retaining some, altering and discarding others, as it selectively unfolds and actualizes its possibilities. Although many natural objects are destroyed in this way, the loss is not complete, for they remain part of the ongoing natural history that constitutes the essence of nature. Nature aesthetically is not simply what exists at this point in time; it is also the entire series of events and undertakings that have brought it to that point. When we admire nature, we also admire that history. When we interfere with nature, regardless of whether our intentions are good or not, we create a break in that natural history. We cannot help nature with its plans, for it does not have any plans. When we make plans to help or improve nature, the plans are not nature's but our own, and the result is the stifling of natural creativity and the transformation of the natural objects influenced into human artifacts. No matter how natural they may look, they are no longer original, no longer authentic: Their ontological status has been altered; they have become objects whose essence has preceded their existence.

One of the best examples of the effect of human interference on existence, or being, of wild nature is an analysis by Bruce Foltz of an exchange between Charles Park, a geologist working for a mining company, and David Brower, an environmentalist. In response to a comment by Park that he could not understand why a mining operation that was not visible in a wilderness area should ruin the quality of that area, Brower responded that "the mood would go." Foltz comments on this exchange as follows:

What Park utterly fails to see, and what Brower merely touches upon, is that the mining operation does not let the mountain *be* a mountain. It is not just the mood of the mountain which is transformed, but its very being. Even the regions which Park would regard as completely unaffected are installed within the mining district, i.e., as the *nonproductive parts* of the installation itself. Glacier Peak would be in this instance precisely a copper mining district, deriving its being from that of the operation.

Understand from this perspective, the notion of "restoration" in such a case also becomes incoherent; beyond our knowledge of the complexities of ecological succession, it must be seen that something which has been subjected to the domination of technology in this manner—which has become a resource whose yield has been challenged forth, extracted, and delivered—cannot be simply released back into its own being through technological planning. As "restored," the mountain preserves its status as a technological reserve. Ontologically, the only difference is that it is now an *exhausted* mining district.

In contrast, Foltz maintains, a firepit made by Native Americans would not have such an effect, for

it has neither provoked the earth, nor forced anything from it. . . . It is not a question here of releasing the site of the fire from the grip of technique, since from the beginning the excavation has allowed the earth to remain earth.[3]

Numerous other examples of the effect of human activity on the reality of natural entities can easily be developed. Consider the differences between the lobo or gray wolf, the coyote, and the domestic dog. The dog is pure and simply a human artifact, bred through artificial selection over hundreds of thousands of years. It is not a part of human history, not natural history. The coyote continues to be a part of natural history, but its status, despite its popularity as an environmentalist symbol, is questionable. There is considerable evidence that extensive efforts in this century to exterminate the coyote, for example, by killing off the less intelligent members of the species, have altered the evolutionary direction of the coyote in a way that is inadvertently similar to artificial selection. Is the coyote a triumph of wild nature over humankind or a mixed creature that is partially humanized and on its way to becoming a human artifact like the dog?

No unequivocal answer is possible. The lobo has retained its natural purity through extinction, but once again, by the hand of man. It remains a part of natural history, but it is a strand unnaturally severed. Its reality now is completely limited to our human concept of it, since its additional properties were lost with its extinction. Unlike species that naturally become extinct, it is not imbedded in the natural history that has followed its demise, except by omission.

What nature has lost in the extinction of the lobo can be made clearer by an examination of an animal that has survived many geological and biological epochs and remains a very visible part of our current era: the alligator. Consider the following cases: (1) an alligator in Okefenokee Swamp in Georgia, (2) an alligator on an alligator farm in Florida, and (3) a plastic alligator that is part of the safari boat ride at Walt Disney World. The alligator in the swamp has both a contemporary and historical reality. It is first of all, a part of wild nature as it exists today; it is a representative of a species and an element in a natural ecosystem. Second, it is a direct and recognizable descendant of a creature that was both a contemporary and perhaps even a predecessor of the dinosaurs. A glimpse of that period of natural history is stored in that alligator. As a reference to that period, it and other such animals provide a depth, temporal unity, and an enlarged sense of reality to nature, aesthetically and ontologically, just as reference to past events in human history provides depth, temporal unity, and a sense of reality in a work of literature. The alligator on the alligator farm is physically identical to the wild alligator and to this extent is still a "real" alligator. It retains some of the natural history of its wild counterpart. Robbed of its natural surroundings and deprived of the opportunity to learn and carry out much of its natural behavior, however, it is a creature in transition, waiting for its transformation into a consumer product, from gatorburgers to purses and shoes, and ultimately into a biologically restructured human artifact, like the domestic cow, that can more efficiently and inexpensively yield up its instrumental value to humankind. With the plastic alligator, the connection with nature and natural history is completely severed, and no trace of the "real" alligator remains, even aesthetically. When one sees the alligator open its mouth as the safari boat turns a corner on the ride, no images of contemporary wild nature or of the dinosaurs of natural history come to mind. These have been replaced by another history, evolutionary, to be sure, but not natural, beginning with the first experimental Mickey Mouse cartoons and highlighted by such Disney animated features as *Snow White and the Seven Dwarfs, Peter Pan,* and *The Jungle Book.* Like the medieval Christian looking at a picture of a fish and thinking about the Bible, the amusement park visitor has dropped the "real" alligator out of his or her aesthetic experience.

What these examples collectively reveal is that authentic physical existence plays a more fundamental role in the creation of beauty in nature and the aesthetic appreciation of that beauty than it does in art. In terms of bare or mere existence, what exists probably does not matter. When humans look at nature, however, contrary to the teachings of early modern philosophy and physics, they do not see it as bare, valueless matter. Rather they see it as natural objects composed of large numbers of properties, historically generated in accordance with natural processes—and very strictly speaking, as Berkeley points out, they see these objects not simply in terms of those properties but also *as* those objects. In this way, existence and essence become inseparable, and concern for the continued existence of the objects is expressed in terms of those properties in the context of aesthetic, moral, and scientific valuational frameworks.

Recognition of the special significance of propertied physical existence in aesthetic experiences and in nature preservation provides the final element in the ontological argument for the preservation of nature, which can now be summarized as follows: (1) Humans have a duty to promote and preserve the existence of good in the world; (2) beauty, both artistic and natural, is part of that good; (3) natural beauty (in a broad sense that includes scientifically interesting properties of natural objects) is, in most cases, as valuable as artistic beauty and therefore as worthy of being promoted and preserved on nonexistential grounds; and (4) because the creation of natural beauty is fundamentally contingent upon physical existence, in a way that art is not—that is, because the existence of nature precedes its essence—(a) the need to preserve natural objects and systems is greater than the need to preserve works of art, and, therefore, (b) the obligation to promote and preserve natural objects, all things (including values) being equal, takes precedence over the obligation to preserve works of art on existential grounds alone.

This argument does not mean that we always have a duty to promote and preserve everything in nature or that the promotion and preservation of works of art does not come first in many cases, but it does mean that if we have a duty to promote and preserve artistic beauty, we ought to recognize a similar duty to promote and preserve natural beauty, in part for much the same reasons that we recognize a duty with regard to art and in addition for distinctive reasons concerning the ontological status of natural existence.

NOTES

1. Peter Humphrey, ''The Ethics of Earthworks,'' *Environmental Ethics* 7 (1985): 20.
2. Kemp Smith (New York: St. Martin's Press, 1965), p. 505.
3. Bruce V. Foltz, ''On Heidegger and the Interpretation of Environmental Crisis,'' *Environmental Ethics* 6 (1984): 330.

DISCUSSION TOPICS

1. According to Hargrove, how does natural beauty differ from artistic beauty with regard to artistic imagination?
2. Do you agree with Hargrove that complexity is a distinguishing feature of natural beauty? Give an example which supports your view.
3. Explain what Hargrove means by ''the beauty of nature arises out of self-creation.''
4. Do you find Hargrove's argument persuasive? Do you think it would persuade others?
5. (*For Small group discussion*): Suppose you are observing a stand of trees, and are then informed that the trees are made of plastic. In what respects would your perceptions of the trees change?

CLASS EXERCISE

Instructional exercise goals:
(1) To highlight several aspects of an aesthetic experience: unity, diversity of parts, and intensity of affect.
(2) To increase student awareness of the pervasiveness of aesthetic experience, something often undernoticed in the contemporary world; and
(3) To highlight similarities and contrasts between experiences of human-made activities and natural processes.

We suggest this activity be used after reading and discussion of the Introduction, but before assignment of individual authors.

PROCEDURE: Divide the class into groups of three to five students. Select at least four different kinds of situations which might give rise to aesthetic perceptions, several human-made and several natural. Suggestions:

a football game
a rock concert
a familiar movie
a dinner of several courses
a solitary canoe trip on a wilderness lake
a thunderstorm in a forest
a spectacular sunset in the desert

Ask each group to answer one or more of the following questions:

1. What is the overall emotional tone, mood, or flavor of the experience? Name some feelings involved in the experience. Describe the sensory qualities: visual, auditory, touch, taste, odor. Are there imaginative qualities in the experience?
2. What is the structure or pattern of the experience? How does it hang together? Are there distinct parts within the structure? If so, name them. Does the experience have a culmination or closure?
3. Consider how biological, historical, or other knowledge would heighten or diminish the aesthetic experience.

FOR FURTHER READING

Abram, David, ''Merleau-Ponty and the Voice of the Earth,'' *Environmental Ethics* 10.2 (1988): 101–120. Abram argues that Merleau-Ponty brings a clarified epistemology and language of perceptual experience to philosophical ecology.

Eaton, Marcia Muelder. *Aesthetics and the Good Life.* London: Fairleigh Dickinson University Press, 1989. A defense of aesthetic experience as delight in the intrinsic features of objects or events as based on the history of values. Chapters 3 and 4 are concerned with environmental aesthetics.

Elliot, Robert. "Faking Nature." *Inquiry* 25: 81-92, 1982. An argument for the value of "naturalness" as based on the history of the thing or system in question.

Hargrove, Eugene C. *Foundations of Environmental Ethics.* Englewood Cliffs, N.J.: Prentice-Hall, 1989. An important account of environmental ethics from the perspective of the history of ideas, emphasizing aesthetics.

Hartshorne, Charles. *Born to Sing: An Interpretation and World Survey of Bird Song.* Bloomington: Indiana University Press, 1973. An account of aesthetic phenomena with focus on bird song by the foremost living process philosopher.

Hepburn, R.W. "Aesthetic Appreciation of Nature," in *Contemporary Aesthetics,* Matthew Lipman, ed. Boston: Allyn & Bacon, Inc., 1973, pp. 340-354. Emphasizes similarities and differences between aesthetic experiences of human-made and natural objects.

Kilham, Lawrence. "Instinct for Beauty and Love of Animals," *Defenders* 63, No. 3: 38-40, 1988. A brief, charming essay illustrating the "innateness" of the sense of beauty.

Norton, Bryan G. "Thoreau's Insect Analogies: Or, Why Environmentalists Hate Mainstream Economists." *Environmertal Ethics* 13, No. 3: 235-251, 1991. An interpretation of Thoreau's mature thought as recommending naturalistic observation as the key to perceptual and psychological transformation. Norton argues that neoclassical economists cannot capture this value of transforming preferences.

Sepanmaa, Yrjo. *The Beauty of Environment: A General Model for Environmental Aesthetics.* Helsinki: Suomalainen Tiedeakatemia, 1986. A groundbreaking, thorough consideration of the environment as an aesthetic object, including brief sections on education and the influencing of taste. Sepanmaa argues that ecology provides the norm for beauty in nature. The book's conceptual structure and sentence transitions are sometimes hard to follow. Includes a comprehensive bibliography covering the years 1840–1985.

Stolnitz, Jerome, "The Aesthetic Attitude," in *Aesthetics and the Philosophy of Art Criticism.* Boston: Houghton Mifflin Co., 1960. A concise introduction to some important characteristics of aesthetic experience.

Thomas, John C. "Values, the Environment and the Creative Act." *Journal of Speculative Philosophy* 4, No. 4: 323-336, 1990. Thomas argues that human beings are essentially aesthetic and that overemphasis on moral value alienates human beings from natural being.

CHAPTER FOUR

Historical Context

The major secular and religious historical ideas which have contributed to current Western attitudes toward the environment are identified in the readings of this chapter. Authors from several of the readings offer suggestions for approaching the current environmental crisis, based on their historical analyses.

HISTORICAL FOUNDATIONS FOR CURRENT WESTERN ENVIRONMENTAL PERPECTIVES

In the first essay, ''The Ancient Roots of Our Ecological Crisis,'' J. Donald Hughes proposes that the foundations for the attitude that nature is something to be conquered, used, and dominated lie deep within the ancient world. In very early times, followers of animism viewed the natural world as having certain human qualities and containing sacred objects which deserved respect or worship. However, this attitude gradually was replaced by other perspectives in many areas. The transcendent monotheism of Israel encouraged the belief that nature was not divine, but merely a lower form of creation. Later, Greek philosophers replaced traditional mythology and religion with an emphasis on reason, and perceived the environment as an object for rational analysis. The notion that all things exist to serve the needs of humans is a perspective articulated by some Greek philosophers which has persisted through the centuries.

The Romans formed attitudes remarkably similar to those held in modern Western societies; they treated nature as one of their conquered provinces, for their profit and economic benefit. In contrast, early Christians lived in a world they viewed as temporary, and often considered the things of this world to be irrelevant or even a barrier to salvation. Hughes concludes that the modern ecological crisis can be traced to several sources, but that it was strongly influenced by the attitudes developed in ancient Greece and Rome.

J. Donald Hughes and Jim Swan analyze in their essay, ''How Much of the Earth Is Sacred Space?'' the differing notions of sacred space in Native American and European cultures. For many traditional Native Americans, all of the earth is sacred, with some locations holding special significance and spiritual power. Among Europeans, there have been changing views. The early Greeks set aside many sacred spaces as specific sanctuaries or tracts of agricultural land consecrated to local deities. Among the early Hebrews, there was one sacred space, the temple of Jerusalem. To later Christians, only church structures and property were sacred. Finally, proponents of capitalism held that land was not sacred, but a commodity like any other economic resource. The tragic conflicts later occurring between Europeans and Native Americans were based to a large degree on their differing perspectives of sacred space.

In his essay, "Transformations of the Earth: Toward an Agroecological Perspective in History" Donald Worster focuses on the relationship between agricultural production and human attitudes toward nature throughout history. He proposes that the shift from subsistence agriculture to a capitalist mode of production was a change of great significance, replacing traditional values with the attitude that land was a commodity to be used for personal gain. Carolyn Merchant in her essay, "Gender and Environmental History" extends Worster's ideas by noting that many current attitudes toward nature can be better understood by tracing the changing roles and relationships between men and women in earlier societies.

Eugene Hargrove proposes in his essay, "Anglo-American Land Use" that current attitudes in the United States which support the powerful position of landowners were influenced by several sources. German and Saxon freemen developed the notion that working a plot of land was the basis for claiming continued use of that land. Freemen also introduced two important policies: primogeniture, in which the oldest child inherited the family land, and taxation, which began as voluntary offerings to local nobles. These policies expedited the shift from a society with many small landholders to one with a few, powerful landowners. County courts (moots) evolved from the freemen's custom of consulting with neighbors to settle disputes. Created originally as a convenience for landholding freemen, county courts in contemporary Western society still tend to favor the interests of landowners over the concerns of other citizens.

Thomas Jefferson was a strong advocate for establishing small freehold farmsteads (allodiums) held with little obligation to any governing authority. He predicted that independent landowners would develop a mature sense of appreciation for the land and would institute wise long-term land use practices.

John Locke advocated that the right to own and use land was determined by a farmer's labor, and that society should have little or no role in managing a landowner's property. These precedents still influence policies today. Hargrove concludes that policies supporting the powerful position of landowners in contemporary Western society are primarily based on such past precedents, rather than on thoughtfully considered positions.

Neil Evernden asserts in his essay, "Nature in Industrial Society" that the term "nature" has many different connotations in industrial society; he analyzes how the concept has changed over time. In contrast to the themes presented by the other scholars in this chapter, Evernden suggests that there has been a recent shift in perspectives in Western society, from viewing nature as intrinsically valuable to viewing it primarily as a means for human survival. Evernden describes how this shift was influenced by the publication of Rachel Carson's *Silent Spring* (Boston: Houghton Mifflin, 1962).

CONTRIBUTIONS OF RELIGIOUS AND SECULAR PHILOSOPHIES TO WESTERN ENVIRONMENTAL ATTITUDES

An issue stimulated by the Lynn White, Jr., debate is the relative contribution of Judeo-Christian religious beliefs to current Western attitudes toward the environment.[1] This issue will be addressed again in Chapter 10.

With the exception of the essays by Hughes, and Hughes and Swan, all of the scholars in this chapter identify only secular ideas as contributing to current Western attitudes. Hughes identifies ideological precursors to contemporary views in Western society in the attitudes and practices of the Judeo-Christian heritage, but he argues that as much or more can be traced to ancient Greek and Roman perspectives. Hughes and Swan compare both religious and secular ideas, and conclude that the emergence of European nation-

---

1. Lynn White, Jr.: "The Historical Roots of Our Ecological Crisis," *Science* 155 (1967): 1203-1207.

alism and secular capitalism finally undermined the notion of land as having sacred qualities.

PERSPECTIVES REACHED FROM HISTORICAL ANALYSES

Based on his study of ancient civilizations, Hughes offers several recommendations to assist Western society in solving its current ecological crisis. First, he proposes that humans today adopt the attitude of respect for the earth and for nature that was more commonly held by societies in the past. For example, contemporary proponents of Judaism and Christianity could enlarge their notions of responsibility to God to include a sense of stewardship toward the whole created natural world. Second, Hughes recommends that a concerted effort should be made to better understand past and present ecological relationships, before more environmental damage occurs. Third, he argues that rejecting modern technology will not prevent environmental degradation nor assure a proper balance of humans with nature. Instead, each human community should find ways to use its technology in a fashion that minimizes its destructive impact on the natural environment, and enhances its relationships with nature in order to benefit both the human community and the environment. Finally, based on the severity of current environmental problems and the available options, Hughes recommends that humans accept limitations on their exploitation of the natural world.

Hughes and Swan suggest that Western society would benefit if it accepted the ancient Native American perspective that all the earth is sacred. They affirm the Native American values that wilderness is sacred, that visits to sacred places can enhance wisdom and health, and that humans are not superior to other species but, rather, fellow members of the natural world.

Worster believes that an ecological perspective must be included for a proper environmental historical study of agroecosystems. He thinks that an ecological perspective could contribute to a historical interpretation of the past few centuries that would be darker and less complacent than humans have known. Merchant points out that the changing roles of both women and men have influenced human relationships and attitudes toward nature, and that a gender perspective is required for a balanced and complete picture of human interactions with nature.

Hargrove concludes that government regulation of individual, private landowners has been ineffective because, from the beginning of American government, representation at state and federal levels usually has been based on landownership; this has assured control of the legislatures by the rural community. Public officials elected by landowners have not effectively regulated private landowners.

Evernden proposes that the view humans hold of nature will affect their idea of what constitutes proper behavior toward nature. In the modern industrial state, humans view nature primarily as composed of impersonal objects. Evernden proposes two alternative perspectives that could enlarge this limited view. One is to extend a separate sense of selfhood to nature (nature-as-self); the other is to learn to appreciate the uncanny and unpredictable elements of nature (nature-as-miracle).

The Ancient Roots of Our Ecological Crisis

J. Donald Hughes

J. Donald Hughes (b. 1932) is Professor of History at the University of Denver, Colorado. He has written extensively on the ecological perceptions and environmental impacts of ancient civilizations.

Hughes believes that a human community's relationship to the natural environment is influenced by a number of factors: the community members' attitudes toward nature, their knowledge and understanding of nature's balance and structure, their uses of technology, and their ability to exert control over the actions of individual members that are directed toward the environment.

Hughes identifies animism, Judeo-Christian beliefs, and Greek and Roman philosophies as the dominant factors influencing Western attitudes toward nature. He notes that early Near Eastern civilizations gathered much information about the natural world through trial and error investigations. The Greeks were the first to apply a consistently rational approach to the study of nature; they sought explanations based on reason for all natural phenomena. Under the Romans, interest in research and discovery declined as thinkers often chose to build on older foundations rather than to seek new knowledge. The human relationship to the natural environment worsened under Christianity, since the world often was viewed as temporary and even as a barrier to salvation. Contemporary Western society has supported an intensified interest in developing accurate knowledge about the world in diverse arenas.

The technologies of older civilizations and their impacts on nature are minor compared with those of contemporary industrial nations. Hughes notes that technological progress often was very slow in ancient societies, because of a common practice of not pursuing inventions. In contrast, the Romans' attitudes, and emphasis on highly developed technology were closest to those of contemporary Western society.

According to Hughes, ancient civilizations were able to exert considerable social control because most ancient peoples perceived themselves primarily as members of their societies, and only secondarily as autonomous individuals. Later, Greek and Roman governments established some policies in agriculture and natural resource use, but allowed citizens many choices. In contrast, modern industrialized nations have surpassed all previous societies in their degree of organization and social control. Yet, they have been slow to implement steps to protect the environment. Among modern democracies, environmental policies can be established only with broad-based public support, which often faces opposition from powerful interest groups. Likewise, the former totalitarian states had not always made environmental protection a high priority.

The damaging changes being suffered today by the natural environment are far more rapid and widespread than anything known in ancient times. Today deforestation proceeds on a worldwide scale, the atmosphere becomes more turbid and opaque every year, the oceans are being polluted on a massive scale, species of animals and plants are being wiped out at a rate unmatched in history, and the earth is being plundered in many other ways. But although the peoples of ancient civilizations were unfamiliar with such recent discoveries as radioactivity, insecticides, and the internal combustion engine, they faced problems sometimes analogous to those the modern world faces, and we may look to the ancients in order to see the beginnings of many of our modern difficulties with an environment which is decaying because of human misuse.

A human community determines its relationship to the natural environment in many ways. Among the most important are its members' attitudes toward nature, the knowledge of nature and the understanding of its balance and structure which they attain, the technology they are able to use, and the social control the community can exert over its members to direct their actions which affect the environment. The ancient world shows us the roots of our present problems in each of these areas.

In a well-known and often reprinted article, ''The Historical Roots of Our Ecologic Crisis,''[1] Lynn White traced modern Western attitudes toward the natural world back to the Middle Ages. But both medieval and modern attitudes have ancient roots. Greece and Rome, as well as Judaism and Christianity, helped to form our habitual ways of thinking about nature. And it is evident that the modern ecological crisis is to a great extent the result of attitudes which see nature as something to be freely conquered, used, and dominated without calculation of the resultant cost to mankind and the earth.

These attitudes stem from similar ideas which were held by the ancient peoples who have most influenced us. Animism, which saw the natural world as sharing human qualities and treated things and events in nature as sacred objects of respect or worship, was the dominant attitude in early antiquity and persisted almost everywhere in the Mediterranean world, but it gradually gave way to other ways of thinking. In Israel, transcendent monotheism replaced animism's "world full of gods." Instead of being divine in itself, nature was seen as a lower order of creation, given as a trust to mankind with accountability to God. But in the later history of that idea, people tended to take the command to have dominion over the earth as blanket permission to do what they wished to the environment, conveniently forgetting the part about accountability to God, or else interpreting most human activities as improvements in nature and therefore pleasing to God.

Perhaps even more important in the history of human attitudes toward nature was the departure from animism made by the Greek philosophers. Rejecting traditional mythological and religious explanations of the natural world, they insisted on the ability of the human mind to discover the truth about nature through the use of reason. Instead of a place filled with spiritual being, or beings, a theater of the gods, the environment was to them an object of thought and rational analysis. Worship of nature became mere ritual, supposedly replaced with philosophical understanding. Since, in the words of Protagoras, "man is the measure of all things,"[2] it followed that all things have usefulness to mankind as their reason for existence. This idea has persisted in Western thought in various forms until the present, for the belief that everything in nature must justify its existence by its purposeful relationship to mankind is firmly, though perhaps implicitly, held by most people.

What was for the Greeks a philosophical opinion became for the Romans a practical reality. Early Roman animism was overcome less by the ingestion of Greek ideas than by the Romans' own demonstrated ability to dominate and to turn most things to their own profit, but both Greek influence and Roman practicality helped the Romans to develop attitudes toward nature which are remarkably similar to those expressed and demonstrated today. The Romans treated the natural environment as if it were one of their conquered provinces. If they needed any justification of this beyond their own pragmatism and cupidity, they could find it in Greek philosophy, which reached them in a late, skeptical form that had removed the sacred from nature and made nature an object of manipulation in thought and, by extension, in action. Our Western attitudes can be traced most directly to the secular, businesslike Romans. Today the process of dominating the earth is seen not as a religious crusade following a biblical commandment but as a profitable venture seeking economic benefit. In this, we are closer to the Romans than to any other ancient people, and in this we demonstrate to a great extent our heritage from them.

Attitudes alone do not determine the way a human community will interact with the natural environment. People whose religion teaches them to treat the world as a sacred place may still manage to make their surroundings a scene of deforestation and erosion, because good intentions toward nature are not enough if they are not informed by accurate knowledge about nature and its workings.

The earlier civilizations of the Near East accumulated a vast amount of information about the world through trial and error, and the information was passed on through tradition. Some of what they thought they knew was correct and useful, and much was colorfully inaccurate, interwoven with myth and folk stories.

A few Greek thinkers were the first to approach the natural world in a consistently rational fashion, demanding that reasonable explanations be found for all natural phenomena. This enabled them to begin the process of gaining knowledge which eventually developed into what might be called the scientific method. Many of the Greek thinkers were also careful observers of nature and attempted to check their ideas against what could be observed, but all of them held rational thought to be superior to what could be seen in the world and assumed that the inner workings of the human mind are congruent with the outer workings of the universe. This assumption, along with the antipathy of Greek thinkers toward work done with the hands, limited the range of their discoveries and led them into some fallacious speculations. Nonetheless, the discoveries of the Greek philosophers and scientists are many and impressive.

Unfortunately, research and discovery in this field gradually diminished under the Romans, who were collectors of older bits of information about the world of nature rather than discoverers of new knowledge. A few Greek scientists continued to work under the Roman Empire, but the Romans themselves produced few creative thinkers in this field. With the advent of Christianity, the situation worsened. Living in a world which they believed to be temporary, early Christians seemed to regard study of the things of this world to be irrelevant, if not a positive barrier on the way to salvation. "The wisdom of this world is foolishness,"[3] said Paul. He spoke in a somewhat different connection, but the Christians of the later Roman Empire, with very few outstanding exceptions, tended to look at all scientific inquiry in the spirit of that statement.

The modern world, having revived the works of the ancient Greeks, has gone beyond them in developing a rigorous methodology for gaining knowledge about the natural environment. The extent and accuracy of the understanding of nature that is available today is truly impressive, but far from complete. Much remains to be discovered about the circulation of the earth's atmosphere, weather, and the effects of pollution of various kinds on climate, for example. The behavior of species of animals and the interaction of all forms of life in an ecosystem are only imperfectly understood. Governments and institutions have not always seen the relevance of such knowledge, and support for research has been a sometime thing. At the same time, human activities are inexorably destroying the last few examples of relatively undisturbed ecosystems that remain on earth, so that soon they will no longer be available for study. Brazilians

are proclaiming that the Amazon rain forest will be gone in thirty years, to give one example, and no one can accurately predict what effects that massive change will have on South America and the world. Careful study is still needed.

The speed, scope, and intensity of interaction with the natural environment are crucially determined by the level of technology available to a human community. Using human and animal motive power and the energy of water, wind, and fire with the relatively simple tools and machines that had been invented, the ancient peoples constructed huge monuments which still impress us, but their level of interaction with the natural environment was relatively low as compared with that of modern industrial society. The changes wrought in the environment by ancient civilizations are massive indeed, but involved centuries or millennia for their accomplishment. Today more significant changes take place in months or years—or even seconds, in the case of atomic explosions. While the real extent and nature of the impact of ancient technology must not be underestimated, what impresses us almost as much is the failure of the ancients to pursue inventions, and the slow rate of technological change that resulted. Of all ancient peoples, the Romans possessed the most highly developed technology, and in this respect they are closest to us. Their machines for war, construction, and industry foreshadowed some that are still in use today. The fact that ancient peoples absorbed and survived changes in the technology of war and peace cannot be of much comfort to us today, because the rapidity, size, and power of such changes today are of an entirely different order from anything experienced in ancient times.

Another factor determining the way a human community will interact with the natural environment is the degree of organization and social control the community possesses. This is true because environmental ends desired for the good of the community may involve sacrifices on the part of its individual members, sacrifices which they would not make without some degree of social encouragement or coercion. The early civilizations of the river valleys, for example, had to be able to call for large expenditures of human energy on the construction of canals which seemed to benefit the entire society. Ancient civilizations were able to exert a considerable degree of social control because the vast majority of ancient people regarded themselves primarily as parts of their societies, and only secondarily, if at all, as individuals. Each person had a place in the social hierarchy which was rigidly defined and rarely changed. This was true of the pharaonic autocracy of Egypt, perhaps the most marked example of social control in the ancient world. But Egypt suffered periodic breakdowns in social control, and no ancient civilization could have channeled the actions of its citizens with regard to the environment to the extent that is at least theoretically possible today.

All ancient societies depended to a large extent on slave labor, a fact which seems to indicate an extreme degree of social control, until it is remembered that the majority of slaves were owned by citizens, not by the state, and that citizens were to a surprising degree able to pursue their private goals, at least in Greece and Rome.

As indicated in the preceding chapters, Greek and Roman governments established policies in the fields of agriculture, forestry, mining, and commerce, but citizens were allowed a wide latitude of choice within certain guidelines. Greek citizens had carefully defined duties to the community, but the city-states are noted for the freedom they allowed. The later Roman Empire tried to interfere in and control the lives of its citizens to an unusual extent; the edicts of Diocletian attempted to stabilize occupations, regulate prices, and control religion, while his secret police kept him informed of activities dangerous to the state. But no ancient autocracy remotely approached the ability of a modern industrial state to keep informed about its citizens and see that they performed their social duties. Greece operated without imprisonment as a punishment, and the Roman Empire supported itself financially without an income tax. The degree of control that can be exercised in the modern world by governments with electronic surveillance, computers, chemical and psychological methods, bureaucracies, police, deportations, and prisons is unmatched by anything seen before in world history. In democracies, environmental policies can be established only when widespread public support for them exists. Over

the last few decades, such policies have in part been established even over the opposition of powerful pressure groups. Some needed measures have been blocked by the same groups or by the tendency of the public to prefer short-term personal gains to long-term benefit for society. Totalitarian states such as the Soviet Union have also taken some steps to preserve the environment, but we have not yet seen a major government take all of the steps which seem called for in the present ecological dilemma. Neither in ancient times nor in modern times have human communities become fully aware of the role which their relationship to the natural environment plays in their long-term welfare and even survival.

One conclusion which seems clear to this author is that the modern ecological crisis grew out of roots which lie deep in the ancient world, particularly in Greece and Rome. The problems of human communities with the natural environment did not begin suddenly with the ecological awakening of the 1960s, nor indeed with the onset of the Industrial Revolution or the Christian Middle Ages. Mankind has been challenged to find a way of living with nature from the earliest times, and many of our habitual answers to that challenge received their first conscious formulation within ancient societies, especially the classical civilizations.

At this point, one might well ask whether this study of ancient civilizations has produced any insights which might be of use in meeting the present crisis. If our ecological crisis has ancient roots, it might also be possible to learn from some of the successes and failures of ancient civilizations as we look to the future.

First of all, it might be possible for people today to recover something like the attitude of respect for the earth and nature that was felt by many in ancient societies. This could come not as a renaissance of animism, or a revival of ancient religions which have lost their ability to infuse human minds, but as a new insight compatible with many religions and philosophies. Judaism and Christianity could expand their concepts of human stewardship to recapture the biblical inclusion of the whole created natural world within the responsibility of people to God. Islam has its own unique insights along similar lines. Others will be impressed by Albert Schweitzer's demonstration that the concept of reverence for life serves as a basis for philosophical ethics. Eastern philosophies, which have long contained attitudes toward nature which emphasize harmony, respect, and refusal to exploit, might find ways to realize their insights. Recent interest in the American Indian feeling for the land and its creatures reveals that the native Americans had ecological wisdom which can be studied and emulated. Better attitudes toward the natural environment will have to develop in a pluralistic human community, as people of varying traditions and points of view come to see the necessity of caring for the earth in order to preserve life itself and improve the quality of life.

Second, a concentrated effort to study the natural environment in all of its facets and interrelationships is needed. This is particularly crucial at the present moment, before much of the evidence about nature is altered, marred, or erased by human activities. These activities themselves and their effects upon the natural environment must also be investigated thoroughly. No wise environmental policy can be based on ignorance of the workings of nature. So that we may learn from what mankind has experienced through millennia of interaction with nature, more research is needed into the ecological relationships of past human societies, to correct and fill out the broad outline which is presented here.

Third, each human community must seek a viable relationship with the natural environment at the level made possible by the technology available to it. A study of ancient civilizations should demonstrate that a rejection of modern technology or an attempt to turn back the clock would not in itself assure a proper balance with nature or prevent environmental degradation. Rather, we should find ways to use our technological abilities in order to minimize the destructive impact of our civilization upon the natural environment and to enhance our relationship with nature in ways which are beneficial both to people and to the environment. This would no doubt mean that some possible avenues of technological development ought to be abandoned, and that human population ought to

be stabilized at some optimum size. No level of technology could support an unlimited increase of human numbers without catastrophic damage to the natural world and resultant crisis for mankind.

Finally, as human beings, we must be willing to accept freely certain limitations on our actions which affect the earth. In democracies, these limitations can be based on public awareness of the magnitude of environmental problems and of the options which exist to meet them. The alternatives to freely chosen environmental policies, consistently administered, are probably few. History does not provide us with an example of an ecologically aware dictatorship, willing to coerce its people to take the courses of action which it deems necessary for survival in balance with nature, but such a government is certainly a future possibility somewhere in the world, unpleasant as it may be to contemplate. History does, however, provide us with many examples of ancient peoples who failed to adapt themselves to live in harmony with the ecosystems within which they found themselves, who depleted their environment, exhausted their resources, and exist today only as ruins within eroded and desiccated landscapes. That fate might also await our own civilization, but this time on a global scale. Ancient history is a warning and a challenge to our attitudes, our ability to understand, our technological competence, and our willingness to make far-reaching decisions. The challenge will not go away, and the response we will make is not yet clear.

NOTES

1. Lynn White, ''The Historical Roots of Our Ecologic Crisis,'' *Science* 155 (1967): 1203-1207.
2. Plato *Theaetetus* 160D (15).
3. 1 Cor. 3:19.

DISCUSSION TOPICS

1. How are our current attitudes toward the environment like those held by the ancient Romans? What are some of the implications of these similarities?
2. Hughes calls attention to the great increase in government control over citizens in modern Western

society. In what ways do you believe that increasing or decreasing governmental control would affect the quality of environmental policies in Western society?

READING 21

How Much of the Earth is Sacred Space?

J. Donald Hughes and Jim Swan

In this essay, Hughes and Swan define sacred space as "a place where humans find a manifestation of divine power, where they experience a sense of connectedness to the universe." The authors trace the notion of sacred space as it has been presented both in Native American and European cultures. For many Native Americans, all of the earth is sacred, with some locations holding special significance and spiritual power.[1]

Among the ancient Greeks, sacred space was land consecrated to the gods or goddesses as sanctuaries, or lands dedicated to them. Early Hebrews centralized worship of God to one sacred space: the temple of Jerusalem. Among early Christians, nature did not specifically contain sacred space; however, churches, monasteries, and cloisters provided sacred places consecrated by ecclesiastical authorities. The development of nationalism in Europe subsequently undermined the notion that even church land was sacred space, and through the tenets of capitalism, land became a commodity similar to other economic resources.

Hughes and Swan believe that the eventual meeting between Europeans and Native Americans was foredoomed to tragedy. Native Americans were incredulous that Mother Earth could be divided along imaginary lines and sold. Europeans were shocked that Native Americans came back to hunt and use the lands they had "sold," and that they did not respect and follow the principle of private landownership. Although the reservation system could have helped maintain Native American sacred spaces, the reservations failed because European Americans placed a higher value on exploiting the resources of Native American lands than on honoring their treaties or on recognizing the value and importance of sacred property boundaries. Instituting national parks and forests protected some sacred lands, but made little provision for the Native Americans who lived on them.

Current laws in the United States generally are directed toward specific parcels of land, and fail to recognize the Native American concept that all the earth is sacred. Hughes and Swan note the growing conviction among some members of the environmental movement that the earth—particularly wilderness—is sacred, and they encourage dialogue on that issue.

---

1. Hughes and Swan cite Chief Seattle as an important source for Native American views. It should be noted that their citation for Chief Seattle's ideas, W.C. Vanderwerth, ed., *Indian Oratory: Famous Speeches by Noted Indian Chieftains* (Norman: University of Oklahoma Press, 1971), probably presents an authentic version of Chief Seattle's thoughts. The famous environmental speech, also known as the "Fifth Gospel," which commonly is attributed to Chief Seattle actually was written over 100 years later by Ted Perry, a screenwriter (Rudolf Kaiser, "A Fifth Gospel, Almost: Chief Seattle's Speech(es): American Origins and European Reception," in Christian F. Feest, ed., *Indians and Europe: An Interdisciplinary Collection of Essays* (Aachen: Rader Verlag, 1987). Also, see J. Baird Callicott, "American Indian Land Wisdom? Sorting Out the Issues," *Journal of Forest History* 33 (1989): 35-42; and Eugene Hargrove, "The Gospel of Chief Seattle is a Hoax," *Environmental Ethics* 11 (1989): 195-196.

One of the happiest events of recent years was the return of Blue Lake to the Taos Pueblo. This locality is a holy place for the Taos people, one of whom said, "We go there and talk to our Great Spirit in our own language, and talk to Nature and what is going to grow."[1] In giving back the lake and the forest surrounding it, Congress acknowledged, as it later did more explicitly in the American Indian Religious Freedom Act,[2] that Native American Indian tribes recognize certain places as sacred space, an attitude which is found in all tribes. The Lakota and others have a spiritual relationship to Mato Tipi (Bear Butte) in the Black Hills, and both the Navajo and Hopi regard the San Francisco Peaks near Flagstaff as sacred, although the courts have been remiss in protecting them from desecration.

Sacred space is a place where human beings find a manifestation of divine power, where they experience a sense of connectedness to the universe. There, in some special way, spirit is present to them. People in many parts of the world and in all times have come to designate some places as sacred: in Japan, Mount Fuji is a *kami* or shrine; an island in Lake Titicaca is for the Aymara an altar to the Sun God, Inti; and the Bimin-Kukusmin of Papua New Guinea, revere the area around a spring of ritual oil.[3] Such examples could be multiplied.

But when one asks a traditional Indian, "How much of the earth is sacred space?" the answer is unhesitating: "All." As Chief Seattle, a Suquamish of the Puget Sound area, told the governor of Washington, "Every part of this soil is sacred in the estimation of my people."[4] When tribal elders speak of Mother Earth, they are not using a metaphor. They perceive that earth is a living being, sacred in all her parts. Black Elk, a Lakota holy man, addressed her in these words: "Every step we take upon You should be done in a sacred manner; each step should be as a prayer."[5] For this reason Smohalla, a Wanapum shaman of the upper Columbia River country, required his followers to use the gentle digging stick instead of the plow, which tears Mother Earth's bosom like a knife. He also forbade them to mine, because that would be to dig under her skin for her bones.[6] Those venerable teachers knew that one could experience a sense of connectedness to the universe virtually anywhere, so there were no boundaries or places that were not sacred.

The last sentence does not contradict what was said before about sacred spaces. In the traditional Indian view, all of nature is sacred, but in certain spots the spirit power manifests itself more clearly, more readily. It is to those places that a person seeking a vision would make a quest. They were localities where the great events of tribal history and the era of creation took place. They were associated with particular beings, whom one ought not even to name unless one were prepared to encounter the energy they wielded, which could either strengthen or destroy. So the Indian view of the universe is that of a sacred continuum that contains foci of power.

Again, this conception of the earth is widespread among traditional peoples around the world and through history. The ancient Chinese practice of *Feng Shui* (geomancy) treats the landscape as a network of potent spots connected by lines of energy.[7] One would be foolish, its practitioners believed, to ignore this sacred geography when locating a house, road, or temple. The Greek philosopher Plato affirmed that the earth is a living organism, alive in every part, and also that there are particular locations where spiritual powers operate positively or negatively. In the *Laws,* he advised founders of cities to take careful account of these influences.[8]

But this is not the only approach that has been taken to sacred space. The Old World produced in ancient times another view that contrasts strongly with the North American Indian version, and which has had a pervasive influence in the history of western thought. That is the idea of sanctuary, an area marked off so as to be separated from the space around it, usually by a wall. The Greek word for such a place, *temenos,* is instructive because it derives from the verb *temnō,* meaning "I cut off." The Latin word *templum,* the root of the word "temple," also means "a part cut off" or "a space marked out." Once dedicated by the proper authorities, such a precinct was protected by all the sanctions of religious custom and local law.

The places chosen were almost always distinguished by some natural feature: an impressive grove of large old trees, a spring, a lake, a fissure in the earth, or a mountain peak. These were often landscapes of great natural beauty. In locating and marking a *temenos,* the seers took account of the lay of the land and the mountain forms visible from it. Within the boundary, all human use other than religious worship was forbidden. There was to be no cutting or removal of wood, no hunting, grazing, or cultivation. The only building permitted was a shelter for the statue of god or goddess. What we call a temple is such a structure, but for the ancients the enclosure itself, and everything within it, served as the temple. There the god lived and became manifest. And there a fugitive could seek sanctuary, a sick person could ask for healing, and anyone seeking wisdom—that is, to know the will of the gods—could sleep overnight in expectation of a meaningful dream. There were hundreds of those places in the ancient world.

Another type of sacred space that deserves mention is a tract of agricultural land dedicated to a god or goddess, the produce of which served as an offering. The Linear B tablets record such land use in ancient Crete. In Athens, the Council of the Areopagus had jurisdiction over groves of sacred olive trees, whose oil was reserved for sacrifices, prize for the winners of the Panathenaic Games, and other purposes sacred to the goddess Athena. The institution of "God's Acre" had a long subsequent history in Europe.

Even within the great ancient cities, sacred spaces retained something of the natural. Babylonian ziggurats were crowned by groves of trees, Egyptian temples were graced with sacred lakes and gardens, and the Acropolis of Athens had its sacred caves, spring, and cypress trees. Those places had to be walled both for protection and to distinguish the sacred space within from the congested streets outside.

But the practice of setting physical boundaries for sacred spaces gives another answer, contrasting with that of the American Indians, to the question, "How much of the world is sacred?" That answer is: "As much as has been consecrated to the gods." Outside the limits, the gods no longer protected the earth, and people were free to use it as they saw fit. Inside the *temenos,* there might be glimpsed a holy light, but outside shone only the ordinary light of day. Thus an enormous step had been taken toward desacralizing nature, but it is also true that the boundaries themselves had been endowed with a numinous quality.

In order to understand how the concept of sacred space entered the medieval and modern mind, one must consider how the Hebrews transformed it. The psalmist proclaimed that all the earth, in a certain sense, is sacred: "The earth is the Lord's and the fullness thereof, the world and those who dwell therein."[9] The early Hebrews had their sacred places: Sinai, where God gave the commandments to Moses, and Bethel, where Jacob had wrestled with the angel. But the dominant view in Judaism held that God the

Creator is not to be identified with His creation, even though it might serve as a marvelous sign of His power and benevolence. Since God is transcendent, He cannot be said to dwell in any spot on earth in an ontological sense. The Hebrews experienced a long struggle with the religions of the surrounding peoples, who worshipped in sacred groves and high places. God had commanded the destruction of those sanctuaries.

The designation of sacred spaces like those of the Canaanites might have suggested that God is present in the natural world in a more intimate way than Judaism was ready to affirm. Since all the world belongs to God, the designation of a particular locale as sacred space could be arbitrary. To avoid the confusion caused by having many sanctuaries, which might have implied to the common people that many gods were being worshipped, the religious authorities under King Josiah centralized the sacrificial worship of the one God in a single space: the Temple of Jerusalem. Even though Mount Zion was undoubtedly a sacred place before it was reconsecrated for the Temple, the Judaic belief was that it was holy because it had been sanctified by God's people at God's command, not because of any special sacredness inherent in the spot. So while the Greeks may be said to have *recognized* sacred space in the landscape, the Hebrews *declared* the Temple space to be sacred.

Christianity took a further step. The early missionaries were anxious that their converts from paganism should not confuse the creation with the creator. Paul the Apostle taught that the natural world had fallen along with mankind and needed to be redeemed through the work of Christ. John urged the Christians not "to love the world or the things in the world."[10] By "world," John doubtlessly meant "non-Christian society," but the Church has insisted on taking the word to mean "the creation." "God who made the world . . . does not live in shrines made by mankind."[11]

It is true that the New Testament does not teach that nature is evil, but that even in its fallen state it exhibits the eternal power and deity of God. Within the first few centuries, however, many Christians were convinced that the natural world was the province of the devil, the adversary of God. Although that idea is not really orthodox, because the sacraments show natural creation as a vehicle of the grace of God, the conception of the world that has fallen into the power of darkness was an image that shaped the imagination of medieval European Christianity. Basil said Satan's "dominion extends over all the earth,"[12] and Synesius of Cyrene prayed to be released from "the demon of the earth, the demon of matter, . . . who stands athwart the ascending path."[13]

The Christians of that time, therefore, were not encouraged to look for sacred space within the world of nature. For them, the churches and monasteries were sacred space, with the enclosed cloisters and churchyards that adjoined them, filled with trees that sheltered the burial places of the sainted dead. They were oases of sanctity in a desert of evil. As outposts of heaven on a fallen earth, they could be established anywhere, though it was considered an act of merit to locate them on the former sites of pagan temples as signs of the victory of Christianity over the demonic gods.

But older attitudes of the pagan converts often surfaced, and some earlier practices continued in the new sacred spaces. From a distance, the appearance of the new sanctuaries was not unlike that of the old, with a sacred building standing within a grove of trees, surrounded by a wall. They still look so today. And within, the right of sanctuary was often given, and those suffering from various maladies were allowed to sleep there in the expectation that God would send them dreams as a means of healing. Once consecrated, they required a different behavior inside the walls, including cloister or churchyard, from that allowed outside. The threshold of the church divided two quite different kinds of space, and boundaries retained a religious sanction.

By the time the Europeans were ready to invade the homeland of the American Indians, the idea of sacred space as a distinct area consecrated by ecclesiastical authority was firmly established. In addition, the concept of a boundary as a sacrosanct limit, whether marked by a wall or an imaginary line, had the force of millennia of tradition. The meeting of the two peoples was foredoomed to tragedy, since the

Indians had no way to grasp the alien concept; and because the program of the Europeans amounted to cultural genocide, they had little interest in Indian ideas of the sacred.

A further development, however, was taking place in Europe in regard to sacred space, and that was the final step in desacralizing nature. Nationalism placed the claims of the State above those of the Church, effectively denying that even Church land was sacred space. And rising capitalism defined land as a commodity, subject to division and sale, no more sacred than any other economic resource. The Church perforce acquiesced in both of those developments. But the old sense of the inviolability of boundaries persisted; now they were boundaries of nations or of private land rather than religious sanctuaries, but the new order believed in them as firmly as the old. Trespass, the violation of boundaries, was still as heinous a sin.

Indians encountered the strange desire of the Europeans to buy land almost as soon as the foreigners appeared on their coasts. It happened again and again, whether in the "sale" of Manhattan Island or in William Penn's "treaty" in Pennsylvania. The Indians seem to have regarded such arrangements as permission for specific uses of the land, not as "conveyance in fee simple." Indians were incredulous at the idea that the earth could be divided by a line drawn on a map. How could Mother Earth be cut up in that way? In the opening years of the nineteenth century, Tecumseh said, "Sell a country? Why not sell the air, the clouds, and the great sea as well as the earth?"[14] He was protesting not against commercialism, but sacrilege.

For their part, Europeans were shocked at the failure of Indians to respect their boundaries. To Europeans, treaty lines embodied the integrity of the nation state and therefore were inviolable, even if they crossed territory that a European had not seen. Similarly, property lines demanded the same respect as the principle of private ownership itself, and the fact that Indians would return to the hunt on their traditional tribal lands after they had become royal, public, or private property was to Europeans an inexcusable trespass of the limits. For the Europeans to violate the boundaries in the other direction was not a similar trespass in their own minds, because they had convinced themselves that the Indians did not really "occupy" or "use" the land. Indian sacred space was not respected because Indian religions were regarded not as "real" religions, but "superstitions," and Indians were expected to accept the new order, either by adopting European-American ways or by withdrawing beyond the frontiers.

The Indian reservation, as an area set aside within recognized boundaries, represents something of an anomaly within the context of the European-American view. Once the limits had been set, and the Indians recognized as the proper occupants of the enclosed land, all the forces of legality and centuries of customary attitudes should have caused Americans to respect the reservations. That they did not, shows that the economic culture of the late nineteenth-century and early twentieth-century America placed a higher value on the acquisition and exploitation of resources located on Indian lands than on the ideals of sacred property boundaries and whatever relict religious feelings might still have attached to them.

An engine for the destruction of reservations, the General Allotment Act of 1887, was a pious fraud imposing American law on Indian tradition. The congressional advocates of the measure claimed that it would acculturate the Indians by giving them property, but after its enactment, the administrators of allotment managed to alienate two-thirds of all Indian land within fifty years. That process showed no concern for the preservation of Indian sacred sites. Indeed, Indian religions were specifically denied the protection of the First Amendment to the United States Constitution during the same period, and an effort was made to stamp them out through proscription of the religions themselves and the reeducation of Indian children.

At the same time, a similar desire to exploit natural resources was altering the American landscape and destroying the character of the Indians' sacred places. "Wilderness" is a western idea, but it is clear that Indian holy places tended to be unspoiled areas, so that the exploitation of wilder country infringed upon many if not most of them. But also during the late nineteenth and early twentieth centuries, what might be regarded as a resurgence of the idea of demarcating sacred spaces appeared in America. That was the movement to preserve natural areas as national parks, forests, and wilderness areas. While it might not seem at first glance that those reservations are sacred in the sense used here, many of the most vocal exponents of the new conservation were motivated in large part by a concern for the sacred. True, that concern was not an expression of ecclesiastical religion, but of what has been called civil religion because it involved secular governmental action for conservation. But "civil religion" as a term does not quite capture the way in which they had recovered the perception of sacred space. Deeply religious, the conservationists were highly orthodox. They found their temples in the wilderness, not in churches. And they did regard wild nature as sacred.

John Muir, whose role in the creation and protection of national parks was enormous, believed that what he was doing was saving sacred spaces. He spoke of mountains and meadows as places of healing, renewal, and worship. What better statement, if the sacred is a feeling of connectedness with the all, than Muir's words, "The clearest way into the Universe is through a forest wilderness."[15] Mircea Eliade connects the sacred with the times and places of creation; Muir found Eden in the wild places, saying, "I have discovered that I also live in 'creation's dawn.'"[16] "In God's wildness," he added, "lies the hope of the world."[17] And when Hetch Hetchy—a miniature valley like the more famous Yosemite, located in the same national park and one of the places he honored most—was threatened with flooding for a reservoir to supply the city of San Francisco, he stated the principle of its sacredness unequivocally:

> These temple destroyers, devotees of ravaging commercialism, seem to have a perfect contempt for Nature, and, instead of lifting their eyes to the God of the mountains, lift them to the Almighty Dollar. Dam Hetch Hetchy! As well dam for water-tanks the people's cathedrals and churches, for no holier temple has ever been consecrated by the heart of man.[18]

Why did the conservation movement in America go so far in its perception of the sacred beyond its precedents in the Old World? George Catlin, Henry Thoreau, Muir, John Wesley Powell, and others among its leaders knew American Indians well and reflected upon Indian ideas in their writings. Catlin, the artist whose work did so much to rescue the culture of Indians in the 1830s from oblivion, was the person who first suggested that a national park be set aside to preserve not just the landscape and wildlife, but also the way of life of the Plains Indians.[19] Thoreau spent months in wild country with the Algonquian Indian guide, Joe Polis. Muir stayed for a while among the Tlingits of Alaska, found their ideas of nature and wild animals very much like his own, and was adopted into the tribe.[20] Powell was fluent in Paiute and published perceptive translations of Indian poetry.[21] Those lovers of nature were putting down spiritual roots in the land, and encountering the fact that Indian tribes had already established a relationship with the earth through thousands of years of tradition.

But when national parks and forests were created, unfortunately little provision was made for the Indian people who lived in them. In actual practice, the Park and Forest Services worked out a method of issuing special use permits for Indians who lived in or used the areas, although there were a few cases of attempted eviction like the repeated endeavors to remove the Havasupai settlement from Grand Canyon Village. Especially important is the fact that the outstanding natural features that caused the parks to be created were usually themselves sacred places in tribal traditions.

Indians generally understood that the parks and forests had been established to protect the land, animals, and plants within them. From the Indian standpoint, it was good to have the areas protected because their integrity as sacred space required that forest and park lands be maintained in the natural state. But the natives were frustrated by the way the laws were administered to interfere with their religions, as well as their traditional hunting and fishing rights. As a member of the Crow tribe stated:

> The Laws that protect birds, animals, plants and our Mother Earth from people who have no respect for these things serve to inhibit the free exercise of religion . . . and free access to religious sites when these American Indians pose no threat to them.[22]

For most of this century, no consistent policy granted Indians access to their sacred spaces, and developments such as roads, spraying and removal of trees, ski areas, other recreational facilities, and river channelization and dams, often committed desecrations in Indian eyes.

In recent years, a more considerate attitude has been reflected in congressional action, although it still remains to be put into practice fully. The American Indian Religious Freedom Act of 1978 (AIRFA) guarantees the right to ''believe, express, and exercise the traditional religions of the American Indian, Eskimo, Aleut, and Native Hawaiian.''[23] The law charges all United States governmental agencies to consult traditional religious leaders in order to preserve Native American religious rights and practices, and to inventory all sacred places on federal lands and come up with proposed policies of management that will preserve the traditional religious values and practices associated with them. The law, it seemed, came none too soon, because the surviving American Indian sacred spaces have never been so threatened with desecration or outright destruction as they now are. The law recognizes that all communities are equally entitled to protection of their freedom of religion, and that in applying this principle to Native Americans, the government must acknowledge the special role of sacred spaces.

But court cases brought under AIRFA to protect sacred sites have failed, with one or two notable exceptions. Among the unsuccessful cases were attempts to protect Navajo rights of worship at Rainbow Bridge, Utah; to save Cherokee sites threatened with flooding by the Tellico Dam in Tennessee; to prevent intrusion of a ski resort into San Francisco Peaks, Arizona, an area sacred to both Hopis and Navajos; and to allow undisturbed ceremonies by Lakota and Cheyenne people at Bear Butte, South Dakota.[24] In these cases, use by the general public in the form of reservoirs or recreational facilities took precedence over Native American religious rights. Even in a case that succeeded, where the Yurok, Karok, and Tolowa tribes of northern California managed to block construction of a road near their traditional mountain prayer sites, their First Amendment rights, not AIRFA, were held to be decisive.[25] One case where

AIRFA appears to have helped was in the denial of a license for Northern Lights, Inc., to build a water project that would have destroyed Kootenai Falls, Idaho, a sacred place for the Kootenai tribe.[26]

The weaknesses of AIRFA are that it is only an advisory resolution of Congress directed at federal agencies, which means it can be ignored with impunity; that it has no enforcement provisions; and that it offers no help in weighing American Indian religious rights against other rights and interests. A federal agency may comply with AIRFA by considering Indian rights; it does not have to decide that they take precedence over skiing, dirt-biking, or electrical power generation. American Indian religious freedom in regard to sacred places can only be guaranteed by a new, stronger, and more carefully drafted law.

But underlying the ineffectiveness of AIRFA is a failure to recognize the difference between the American Indian and European concepts of sacred space. In the successful Yurok-Karok-Tolowa case, usually called the "G-O Road Case," the court defined sacred space in terms of the federal land survey, in a decision quoted here in part:

> It is hereby ordered that the defendants are permanently enjoined from constructing the Chimney Rock Section of the G-O Road and/or any alternative route . . . which would traverse the high country, which constitutes [specified] sections in Six Rivers Forest. . . . It is further hereby ordered that the defendants are permanently enjoined from engaging in commercial timber harvesting.[27]

The decision also requires preparation of Environmental Impact Statements for other future plans in the general area. The provisions resemble those that have been used in demarcating sacred land in the European tradition. The modern officials, without realizing it, are acting like ancient Greeks delimiting a *temenos*. Unlike the Greeks and in accord with modern secular thought, they are doing so without really believing that there is anything inherently sacred inside the lines they are drawing.

Traditional Indians, on the other hand, are faced with difficult alternatives. They can accept the decisions of land managers and/or bring cases to court like the G-O Road Case, thus contenting themselves with saving a few shattered fragments of their heritage and leaving unchallenged the non-Indian idea that sacred space is as much as has been set aside, and no more. This course has the advantage of using federal law to achieve a measure of justice. But another alternative would be to insist on the ancient Indian conception that all the earth is sacred. Taken seriously, this second course could open a dialogue and raise the national consciousness of Indian values. Some tribal elders have already begun to do the latter, as Robert S. Michaelsen indicates in an important recent article:

> Some traditionalists have claimed that in keeping with their religion, *all* land on which the tribe has lived, celebrated, and worshipped in the past is sacred and hence essential to tribal free exercise of religion. Such a claim was made before the Federal agencies Task Force by the combined nineteen Pueblo representatives and in Senate testimony on the [AIRFA] resolution by Yakima representatives. It has also been made in court by the Sioux, the Hopi, and the Navajo.[28]

It has been reported that Hopi spokesmen lay claim, in spirit, to the entire North American continent. In the Ghost Dance, Indians of many tribes prayed for the renewal of the whole land, and the spirit of that prayer did not die at the first Wounded Knee.

The federal law, of course, lacks the same vision. Without realizing it, Congress promised far more than can be delivered. It has recognized that the Indian consensus—that certain lands are sacred—can be respected and protected as long as it does not seriously interfere with the rights and interests of others. But Congress and the courts have not even begun to deal with the basic traditional tribal principle that Mother Earth, as a holistic entity, is sacred.

Another fact has to be considered. There are a large, vocal, and increasingly influential number of people in America today who are recovering the ancient idea of the sacredness of the earth. They hold, not as a fad or pose, but as a deep conviction, that wilderness is sacred ground, and that visits to places of power enhance wisdom and health. They advocate that we shoud learn to know the earth, and the plants and animals that inhabit it, in the places where we live. They feel, as Indians long have felt, that human beings are not the lords of creation but fellow creatures with the bears, the ravens, and the running streams.

Who are these people? They have as yet no name and no church, and perhaps they never will. Gary Snyder is one of them, and Paul Winter is another. It is interesting that the first who come to mind are a poet and a musician. Another, the writer Wendell Berry, speaks characteristically of agricultural land and inhabited space. The idea that holiness inheres in the place where one lives is alien to the European tradition, for in that tradition sacred space is sundered, set aside, a place one goes only to worship. But to live in what one regards as sacred space is the most forceful affirmation of the sacredness of the whole earth. Snyder has made a deep and sympathetic study of Indian traditions, and both Winter and Berry acknowledge the closeness of their ideas to Indian insights.[29]

We are now at the point where those people can talk with traditional Native American elders. The Indian sacred places that remain, the places of power within the sacred continuum, must be preserved. A conversation on how to amend and strengthen the AIRFA offers at least a place to start. A better law would give leverage to people who believe in the sacredness of those places. It is encouraging that, as in the G-O Road case, environmental groups and Indian tribes have joined together. That cooperation has happened because both Indians and environmentalists wish to keep the sacred space in its natural condition. And their motives for wanting to do so, while not identical, are not incompatible either.

The situation should encourage the two groups to engage in a wider dialogue, one in which non-Indians may learn something about the Indian conception of sacred space, while Indians can hear other Americans who feel that many of the same spaces are sacred. Some of the sites, by their nature, must be kept secret and closed to outsiders, a need envisioned by AIRFA and honored in some court cases. In the Kootenai case, for example, tribal elders were allowed to give ''limited distribution'' testimony that presumably located sites and documented their sacred character; the testimony did not become part of the published court record, however, and its secrecy was preserved. But many of the places that need protection are great shrines that should be held open for most of the year as places where all people may seek wisdom and health. Of course, this must be done in a way that would prevent gross intrusions, vandalism, and theft of holy objects by visitors who did not honor sacred space.

The dialogue has begun. All those who participate in it should be willing to learn. Recent developments in science have shown some support for the Indian view of sacred space. By understanding ecology, we learn the intimate way that all parts of the biosphere are interconnected. Life on earth, as ecologists see it, forms a net in which there are important foci of energy. We cannot allow the net to be broken in too many places without destroying the most basic processes that sustain us. The atmospheric chemist James Lovelock and the biologist Lynn Margulis have advanced a theory called the Gaia hypothesis.[30] This postulates that the living systems of the earth—the animals and plants collectively called the biosphere—regulate physical systems such as temperature and the balance of gases and acidity in the atmosphere so as to protect and support life.

If we grant the truth of the Gaia hypothesis for a moment, it seems that we humans are likely to act to keep the planetary system functioning only if we recognize that every part of it is sacred in the sense of being connected to the whole. Whether we are Indians or others, we can agree with the words of John Muir, ''we all dwell in a house of one room—the world with the firmament for its roof—and we are sailing the celestial spaces without leaving any track.''[31] We will know that all decisions affecting any part of the natural environment are decisions about sacred space. Thus the visions of the tribal elders can combine with the most daring new conceptions of ecological scientists to show us how to see wholeness—the holiness—of the earth, and how we must act while we live together here.

NOTES

1. John Collier, *On the Gleaming Way* (Denver, 1962), 124.
2. Public Law 95-341, Senate Joint Resolution 102, 42 U.S.C. par. 1996, August 11, 1978.
3. Fitz John Porter Poole, ''Erosion of a Sacred Land-

scape,'' in Michael Tobias, ed., *Mountain Peoples: Profiles of Twentieth Century Adaptation* (Norman, forthcoming from University of Oklahoma Press).

4. W.C. Vanderwerth, ed., *Indian Oratory: Famous Speeches by Noted Indian Chieftains* (Norman, 1971), 120-121.

5. Black Elk, as quoted in Joseph Epes Brown, *The Sacred Pipe* (Norman, 1953), 12-13.

6. James Mooney, ''The Ghost-dance Religion,'' *Fourteenth Annual Report of the Bureau of Ethnology* (Washington, , DC, 1896), 724.

7. Ernest John Eitel, *Feng-Shui: or, the Rudiments of Natural Science in China* (London, 1873).

8. Plato, *The Laws,* 5.747 D-E.

9. Psalm 24:1.

10. I John 2:15.

11. Acts 17:24.

12. J. P. Migne, ed., *Patrologiae Cursus Completus,* Greek Series, vol. 31 (Rome, 1800), 352A.

13. Synesius of Cyrene, *The Essays and Hymns of Synesius of Cyrene,* trans. A. Fitzgerald, vol. 1 (Oxford, 1930), Hymn IV, pp. 240 ff.

14. Glenn Tucker, *Tecumseh: Vision of Glory* (Indianapolis, 1956), 163.

15. Edwin Way Teale, ed., *The Wilderness World of John Muir* (Boston, 1954), 312.

16. Ibid., 311.

17. Ibid., 315.

18. Ibid., 320.

19. George Catlin, *Letters and Notes on the Manners, Customs, and Condition of the North American Indians,* vol. 1 (1841; reprint, Minneapolis, 1965), 261-262.

20. John Muir, *The Writings of John Muir,* manuscript ed., vol. 3 (Boston, 1916), 208-211.

21. John Wesley Powell, *First Annual Report of the Bureau of American Ethnology* (Washington, DC, 1881), 23.

22. Hearings, Senate Committee on Indian Affairs, Joint Resolution 102, February 24, 1978, quoted in *American Indian Religious Freedom Act Report,* P.L. 95-341, Federal Agencies Task Force, Chairman, Cecil D. Andrus, Secretary of the Interior (Washington, DC, 1979), Appendix A, 1.

23. See note 2.

24. *Badoni v. Higginson,* 638 F.2d 172 (10th Cir. 1980), *cert. denied,* 452 U.S. 954 (1981), regarding Navajo rights at Rainbow Bridge, Utah; *Sequoyah v. Tennessee Valley Authority,* 620 F.2d 1159 (6th Cir. 1980), *cert. denied,* 449 U.S. 953 (1980), regarding Cherokee rights in the Little Tennessee Valley; *Wilson v. Block,* 708 F.2d 735 (D.C. Cir. 1983), regarding Hopi and Navajo rights in the San Francisco Peaks, Arizona; and *Frank Fools Crow v. Gullet,* 706 F.2d 856 (8th Cir. 1983), regarding Lakota Sioux and Cheyenne rights at Bear Butte, South Dakota.

25. *Northwest Indian Cemetery Protective Association v. Peterson,* 565 F.Supp. 586 (N.D. California 1983).

26. Northern Lights, Inc., Project No. 2752-000, 27 Federal Energy Regulatory Commission, par. 63,024, April 23, 1984.

27. See note 25.

28. Robert S. Michaelson, ''The Significance of the American Indian Religious Freedom Act of 1978.'' *Journal of the American Academy of Religion* 52 (no. 1, 1984), 93-115, quotation pp. 108-109.

29. Gary Snyder, ''Good, Wild, Sacred,'' *The CoEvolution Quarterly* (Fall 1983), 8-17; Paul Winter, *Missa Gaia: Earth Mass* (Litchfield, CT: Living Music records, 1982), see notes in 33-rpm disk version; Wendell Berry, *The Gift of Good Land* (San Francisco, 1981), 267-281, and Berry, ''The Body and the Earth,'' in *The Unsettling of America: Culture and Agriculture* (New York, 1978), 97-140.

30. James E. Lovelock, *Gaia: A New Look at Life on Earth* (Oxford, 1979).

31. Teale, *Wilderness World of John Muir,* 310.

DISCUSSION TOPICS

1. Considering the definition provided by Hughes and Swan, to what degree do you believe that the earth contains sacred space?

2. What policies do you believe could enhance the respectful interaction of Native American and European American cultural groups with regard to present and future land use in North America?

Transformations of the Earth: Toward an Agroecological Perspective in History

Donald Worster

Donald Worster (b. 1941) is the Hall Distinguished Professor of American History at the University of Kansas. He has written extensively in the area of environmental history.

Worster describes environmental history as a relatively new field which emerged in the 1970s. The environmental historian's goal is to identify the role and place of nature in human life. Worster notes that the field of environmental history encompasses three realms of inquiry: discovering the structure and distribution of natural environments of the past; understanding how production technology has restructured human-ecological relations; and identifying human patterns of perception, ideology, and value toward the environment. In this reading, Worster focuses on the second realm, analyzing agricultural production as an ecological phenomenon.

Worster defines agroecosystems as domesticated ecosystems managed for the purpose of feeding humans. An agroecosystem always is simpler than the original natural ecosystem, and commonly is a system of export which runs the risk of losing productivity if the nutrients lost to cultivation are not replaced. In the agroecosystems of subsistence cultures, it has been common for most people to raise only what they themselves can consume; thus, the overall natural diversity and complexity of nature usually is preserved.

However, in the eighteenth and nineteenth centuries, a radical transformation occurred, and subsistence agriculture was replaced by a capitalist mode of production. With capitalism, the notion of using the land as a commodity for the purpose of personal gain was introduced. Emotional and ethical values previously associated with the land were set aside when the market economy began to flourish. Specialization resulted in large-scale monocultures, and capitalist agroecosystems resulted in a radical simplification of natural ecosystems. Using wheat farming in the western plains of North America as a case study, Worster outlines the impacts of production technology on the environment, and describes

how these impacts restructured human-ecological relationships in the United States.

Forty years ago a wise, visionary man, the Wisconsin wildlife biologist and conservationist Aldo Leopold, called for ''an ecological interpretation of history,'' by which he meant using the ideas and research of the emerging field of ecology to help explain why the past developed the way it did.[1] At that time ecology was still in its scientific infancy, but its promise was bright and the need for its insights was beginning to be apparent to a growing number of leaders in science, politics, and society. It has taken a while for historians to heed Leopold's advice, but at last the field of environmental history has begun to take shape and its practitioners are trying to build on his initiative. . . .

This new history rejects the common assumption that human experience has been exempt from natural constraints, that people are a separate and uniquely special species, that the ecological consequences of our past deeds can be ignored. The older history could hardly deny that people have been living for a long while on this planet, but its general disregard of that fact suggested that they were not and are not truly part of the planet. Environmental historians, on the other hand, realize that scholarship can no longer afford to be so naïve.

The field of environmental history began to take shape in the 1970s, as conferences on the global predicament were assembling and popular environmentalist movements were gathering momentum. It was a response to questions that people in many nations were beginning to ask: How many humans can the biosphere support without collapsing under the impact of their pollution and consumption? Will man-made changes in the atmosphere lead to more cancer or poorer grain harvests or the melting of the polar ice caps? Is technology making people's lives more dangerous, rather than more secure? Does *Homo sapiens* have any moral obligations to the earth and its circle of life, or does that life exist merely to satisfy

---

1. Aldo Leopold, *A Sand County Almanac, and Sketches Here and There* (1949); reprint, New York, 1987), 205.

the infinitely expanding wants of our own species? History was not alone in being touched by the rising concern; scholars in law, philosophy, economics, sociology, and other areas were likewise responsive. It is surely a permanent response, gaining significance as the questions prompting it increase in urgency, frequency, and scope. Environmental history was born out of a strong moral concern and may still have some political reform commitments behind it, but as it has matured, it has become an intellectual enterprise that has neither any simple, nor any single, moral or political agenda to promote. Its goal is to deepen our understanding of how humans have been affected by their natural environment through time, and conversely and perhaps more importantly in view of the present global predicament, how they have affected that environment and with what results.[2]

Much of the material for environmental history, coming as it does from the accumulated work of geographers, natural scientists, anthropologists, and others, has been around for generations and is merely being absorbed into historical thinking in the light of recent experience. It includes data on tides and winds, ocean currents, the position of continents in relation to each other, and the geological and hydrological forces creating the planet's land and water base. It includes the history of climate and weather, as these have made for good or bad harvests, sent prices up or down, promoted or ended epidemics, or led to population increase or decline. All these have been powerful influences on the course of history, and they continue to be so. In a somewhat different category from these physical factors are the living resources of the earth, or the biota, which the ecologist George Woodwell calls the most important of all to human

well-being: the plants and animals that, in his phrase, "maintain the biosphere as a habitat suitable for life."[3] Those living resources have also been more susceptible to human manipulation than nonbiological factors, and at no point more so than today. We must include the phenomenon of human reproduction as a natural force giving form to history, and by no means a negligible force, as the last few decades of explosive global fertility have amply demonstrated.

Defined in the vernacular then, environmental history deals with the role and place of nature in human life. It studies all the interactions that societies in the past have had with the nonhuman world, the world we have not in any primary sense created. The technological environment, the cluster of things that people have made, which can be so pervasive as to constitute a kind of "second nature" around them, is also part of this study, but in the very specific sense that technology is a product of human culture as conditioned by the nonhuman environment. But with such phenomena as the desert and the water cycle, we encounter autonomous, independent energies that do not derive from the drives and inventions of any culture. It might be argued that as the human will increasingly makes its imprint on forests, gene pools, and even oceans, there is no practical way to distinguish between the natural and the cultural. However, most environmental historians would argue that the distinction is worth keeping, for it reminds us that not all the forces at work in the world emanate from humans. Wherever the two spheres, the natural and the cultural, confront or interact with one another, environmental history finds its essential themes.

There are three levels on which the new history proceeds, each drawing on a range of other disciplines and requiring special methods of analysis. The first involves the discovery of the structure and distribution of natural environments of the past. Before one can write environmental history one must first understand nature itself—specifically, nature as it was or-

2. The best effort to trace the emergence of the field, at least in one influential part of the world, is Richard White, "American Environmental History: The Development of a New Historical Field," *Pacific Historical Review,* 54 (August 1985): 297-335. White argues that the study of frontier and western history has been the formative influence on this field. Another important source of ideas, quite removed from the influence of Frederick Jackson Turner, has been French historians and geographers, particularly Fernand Braudel, Lucien Febvre, and Emmanuel Le Rov Ladurie, all associated with the journal *Annales.*

3. George Woodwell, "On the Limits of Nature," in *The Global Possible: Resources, Development, and the New Century,* ed. Robert Repetto (New Haven, 1985), 47.

ganized and functioning in past times. The task is more difficult than might first appear, for although nature, like society, has a story of change to tell, there are few written records to reveal most of that story. To make such a reconstruction, consequently, the environmental historian must turn for help to a wide array of the natural sciences and must rely on their methodologies, sources, and evidence, though now and then the documentary materials with which historians work can be a valuable aid to the scientists' labors.[4]

The second level of environmental history is more fully the responsibility of the historian and other students of society, for it focuses on productive technology as it interacts with the environment. For help on understanding this complicated level, in which tools, work, and social relations are intermixed, historians in the new field have begun to turn to the extensive literature dealing with the concept of ''modes of production,'' emphasizing (as most of those who use the phrase have not) that those modes have been engaged not merely in organizing human labor and machinery but also in transforming nature.[5] Here the focus is on understanding how technology has restructured human ecological relations, that is, with analyzing the various ways people have tried to make nature over into a system that produces resources for their consumption. In that process of transforming the earth, people have also restructured themselves and their social relations. A community organized to catch fish at sea may have had very different institutions, gender roles, or seasonal rhythms from those of one raising sheep in high mountain pastures. A hunting society may have had a very different configuration from that of a peasant agricultural one. On this level of inquiry, one of the most interesting questions is who has gained and who has lost power as modes of productions have changed.[6] . . .

Finally, forming a third level for the environmental historian is that more intangible, purely mental type of encounter in which perceptions, ideologies, ethics, laws, and myths have become part of an individual's or group's dialogue with nature. People are continually constructing cognitive maps of the world around them, defining what a resource is, determining which sorts of behavior may be environmentally degrading and ought to be prohibited, and generally choosing the ends to which nature is put. Such patterns of human perception, ideology, and value have often been highly consequential, moving with all the power of great sheets of glacial ice, grinding and pushing, reorganizing and recreating the surface of the planet.

The great challenge in the new history does not lie in merely identifying such levels of inquiry, but in deciding how and where to make connections among them. . . .

The gathering strength of the human imagination over nature is so obvious and dramatic that it is in no danger of being neglected by historians. What has been neglected, however, or left conceptually underdeveloped, is the second level of inquiry I mentioned. And it is to that middle level, the analysis of modes of production as ecological phenomena, and particularly as they are articulated in agriculture, that the rest of this essay is devoted. The intention here is not to make a definitive theoretical statement about this subject, but to review, especially with nonspecialists in mind, some of the broader themes and to identify areas where more research is needed.

---

4. A good guide to this field is J. Robert Dodd and Robert J. Stanton, *Paleoecology: Concepts and Applications* (New York, 1981).

5. The phrase ''modes of production'' originated with Karl Marx, who used it in more than one way. In some cases he was referring to ''the material mode,'' defined by G.A. Cohen as ''the way men work with their productive forces, the kinds of material process they set in train, the forms of specialization and division of labour among them.'' In other cases, Marx employed the phrase to denote ''social properties of the production process,'' including the purpose controlling production (whether for use or exchange), the form of the producer's surplus labor, and the means of exploiting producers. Then, again, at times he seems to have meant both material and social aspects at once. See G.A. Cohen, *Karl Marx's Theory of History: A Defense* (Princeton, 1978), 79-84.

6. Useful theoretical background for this study are Julian H. Steward, *The Theory of Culture Change: The Methodology of Multilinear Evolution* (Urbana, 1955), 30-42; and Marvin Harris, *Cultural Materialism: The Struggle for a Science of Culture* (New York, 1979), 46-76.

Humans have extracted an extraordinarily diverse array of resources from the natural world, and the number and magnitude of them is growing all the time. But the most basic and revealing of them in the study of human ecology have been the resources we call food. Every group of people in history has had to identify such resources and create a mode of production to get them from the earth and into their bellies. Moreover, it is through that process that they have been connected in the most vital, constant, and concrete way to the natural world. Few of those modes of producing food, however, have been approached by historians from an ecological perspective. If we are to make further progress in understanding the linkages human beings make to nature, developing that perspective and applying it to food production must be one of the major activities of the new field.

To undertake this project, the historian might begin by adopting the scientist's concept of the *ecosystem* and then asking how it might be applied to the agriculture practiced in any setting or period. There is a tall pile of books and scientific papers on the complicated ways in which ecosystems are structured, work, and evolve; but in simplest terms, one might define an ecosystem as the collective entity of plants and animals interacting with one another and the nonliving (abiotic) environment in a given place. Some ecosystems are fairly small and easily demarcated, like a single pond in New England, while others are sprawling and ill defined, as hugely ambiguous as the Amazonian rain forest or the Serengeti plain. Until rather recently, all those ecosystems have been understood by ecologists to have self-equilibrating powers, like automatic mechanisms that slow themselves when they get too hot or speed up when they begin to sputter and stall. Outside disturbances might affect equilibrium, throwing the system temporarily off its regular rhythm, but always (or almost always) it was supposed to return to some steady state. The number of species constituting an ecosystem was believed to fluctuate around some determinable point, the flow of nutrients and energy through the system staying more or less constant. A dominant concern among ecologists has been to explain how such systems manage to cohere, to maintain order and balance, in the midst of all the perturbations to which they are subject.[7]

But historians wanting to undertake an ecological analysis should be aware that lately the conventional ecosystem model sketched above has been coming under considerable criticism from some scientists, and there is no longer any consensus on how it functions or how resilient it is. Are ecosystems as stable as scientists have assumed, the critics ask, or are they all susceptible to easy upset? Is it accurate to describe them as firmly balanced and orderly until humans arrive on the scene, as some of the older textbooks suggested, or is human disturbance only one of the many sources of instability in nature? Even more disputed are these questions: How and when do people begin to produce changes in ecosystems that might be called damaging, and when does that damage become irreversible? No one really disputes that the death of all its trees, birds, and insects would mean the death of a rain forest, or that the draining of a pond would spell the end of that ecosystem; but most changes, induced by humans or otherwise, are not so catastrophic, and the concept of damage has no clear definition or easy method of measurement. Dependent as it is on ecological theory for assistance in analysis and explanation, the new field of environmental history finds itself in a very awkward position—caught in the middle of a revisionist swing that has left in some disarray the notion of what an ecosystem is and how it works, that has even cast doubt on such old intuitive notions as ''the balance of nature'' and the role of diversity in promoting ecological stability.[8]

---

7. The classic explication of the ecosystem concept is Eugene Odum, *Fundamentals of Ecology* (Philadelphia, 1971), 8-23.

8. The debate is summarized in Paul R. Ehrlich and Jonathan Roughgarden, *The Science of Ecology* (New York, 1987), 541-552. Detailed criticisms of the stable ecosystem idea include Robert May, *Stability and Complexity in Model Ecosystems* (Princeton, 1973); Paul Colinvaux, *Why Big Fierce Animals Are Rare* (Princeton, 1978), 199-211; Margaret B. Davis, ''Climatic Instability, Time Lags, and Community Disequilibrium,'' in *Community Ecology*, ed. Jared Diamond and Ted J. Case (New York, 1986), 269-284; and S.J. McNaughton, ''Diversity and Stability,'' *Nature* (May 19, 1988): 204-205.

Historians have long had to deal with such revisionism in their own field and are only too familiar with the resulting confusion. Learning from that experience, they should not rush to assume that the latest scientific paper on the ecosystem is the true gospel or that yesterday's notions are now completely wrong; on the other hand, if they want to work collaboratively with scientists, they must be careful not to borrow their ideas of nature unthinkingly or innocently from outmoded textbooks or discarded models.

Those theoretical disputes should not obscure the fact that ecological science continues to describe a natural world that is marvelously organized and vital to human existence. Nature, in the eyes of most ecologists, is not an inert or formless or incoherent world that awaits the hand of people. It is a world of living things that are constantly at work, in discernible patterns, producing goods and services that are essential for the survival of one another. Microorganisms, for example, are endlessly busy breaking down organic matter to form the constituents of soil, and other organisms in turn make use of that soil for their own nutrition and growth. The science of ecology still reveals a realm beyond our human economies, and beyond the work we do in them, a realm that has been described as a vast, elaborate, complex ''economy of nature,'' an organized realm that is working energetically and skillfully to satisfy the needs of all living things, creating what might be called the indispensable ''values'' of existence. Without the smooth functioning of that greater economy, without those values that are brought into being by a hardworking nature, no group of people could survive for an hour, and the making of history would come to an abrupt end.

An ecosystem then is a subset of the global economy of nature—a local or regional system of plants and animals working together to create the means of survival. Starting from this understanding, the historian ought to ask how we can best proceed from the ecosystem concept to understand the human past more completely. Taking that next step requires us to adopt still another concept—what some have begun to call an *agroecosystem,* which, as the name suggests, is an ecosystem reorganized for agricultural purposes—a domesticated ecosystem. It is a restruc-

turing of the trophic processes in nature, that is, the processes of food and energy flow in the economy of living organisms. Everywhere such a restructuring involves forcing the productive energies in some ecosystem to serve more exclusively a set of conscious purposes often located outside it—namely, the feeding and prospering of a group of humans. Whatever its place in time, whether its human designers are primitive or advanced, every agroecosystem has at least two general characteristics. It is always a truncated version of some original natural system: There are fewer species interacting within it, and many lines of interaction have been shortened and directed one way. Commonly, it is a system of export, some of the foodstuffs produced being harvested and removed, sometimes only a little distance to a village of folk agriculturists, sometimes a good way off to an international port, in either case leaving the system in danger of becoming depleted and degraded. To survive for very long, the agroecosystem must achieve a balance between its exports and imports, or it loses its productivity and people slide downward into poverty and hunger.[9]

Though something of a human artifact, the agroecosystem remains inescapably dependent on the natural world—on photosynthesis, biochemical cycles, the stability of the atmosphere, and the services of nonhuman organisms. It is a rearrangement, not a repeal, of natural processes. That is as true of a modern factory farm in California or a Douglas fir plantation in Oregon as it is of an ancient rice paddy in China. Whatever the differences among agroecosystems, they are all subject to the laws of ecology, and those same laws govern wild forests, grasslands, savannahs, and heaths, determining just how stable or resilient or sustainable they are as collective entities. . . .

Wheat, corn, and rice, the most widely cultivated

---

9. Eugene P. Odum, ''Properties of Agroecosystems,'' in *Agricultural Ecosystems: Unifying Concepts,* ed. Richard Lowrance, Benjamin R. Stinner, and Garfield J. House (New York, 1986), 5-11. See also George Cox and Michael Atkins, *Agricultural Ecology* (San Francisco, 1979). The scientific pioneers in applying ecology to agriculture were Karl H.W. Klages, *Ecological Crop Geography* (New York, 1942); and Wolfgang Tischler, *Agrookologie* (Jena, 1965).

cereals, have all been carried far from their points of origin and have replaced native vegetation over vast expanses of the earth's surface. As outsiders, they have in many cases thrived exceptionally well in their new settings, freed as they have been from the animal grazers and nibblers and the plant competitors that once kept them in check. In other cases, however, the newcomers have not been so well adapted to their new environment, or at least not so well adapted as the native plants; hence a great deal of effort must be given to securing them against destructive forces, adapting them as well as human ingenuity can, trying to replicate in mere decades or centuries of breeding what it may have taken nature millions of years to evolve, never letting one's vigilance rest. Likewise, the native fauna have been radically diminished, even in many cases exterminated, on every continent by clearance for agriculture, and new fauna—including a plague of insect pests—have appeared over time to thrive in those contrived agroecosystems. Tracing such ecological transformations ought to be the first and most essential step in writing the history of the planet.

Anthropologists and archaeologists are still debating the causes of the Neolithic revolution, which took place some ten thousand years ago in the Middle East (later in other areas), and conclusive support for any theory as to why humans gave up a hunting and gathering life for shifting, or later more settled, farming may always be hard to come by. One of the standard hypotheses starts with a shortage in food supplies brought on by population growth, a situation that may have happened in many places and at different times in prehistory but supposedly always had that same demographic pressure behind it. The hypothesis has plenty of critics, and it is not a matter that historians can pretend to settle, though it may be that historical studies of agricultural change in developing countries in recent centuries can be suggestive. One of the most influential agricultural theorists, the Danish economist Ester Boserup, has followed precisely that strategy and has concluded that population pressure has always been the key force behind land-use intensification, compelling groups to cultivate crops in the

first place and then, as the pressure continues, to work harder and harder at the task, developing new skills as they go along and organizing themselves into larger work units. Sheer necessity, in other words, has been the mother of ecological innovation in preindustrial conditions.[10]

All the while they are rearranging the native flora and fauna to produce more food, people are forced to adapt to local conditions of soil, climate, and water. One might even call such conditions the soft determinants of human existence, for they significantly influence how and where people get their living and what kind of living it is.

No people can do without a little soil. Before people began farming on it, topsoil may have required thousands of years to develop, accumulating at the rate of a mere fraction of an inch per century. One of the greatest challenges posed any community is to maintain that fertility under its contrived food system, and the historian must study the techniques by which the community does so, whether through fallowing, green-manuring, legume planting, or plowing human and animal excrement back into the soil, as well as the consequences that follow when it is not done. The second critical factor, climate, has until recently been well beyond human control; therefore the vulnerability of the agroecosystem to natural forces has been greatest here. Water has been less sovereign. It was one of the earliest forces of nature to come under human management, though here too a scarcity or an

---

10. Mark Nathan Cohen, *The Food Crisis in Prehistory: Overpopulation and the Origins of Agriculture* (New Haven, 1977), 18-70; D.C. Darlington, "The Origins of Agriculture," *Natural History,* 79 (May 1970): 46-57; Stuart Struever, ed., *Prehistoric Agriculture* (Garden City, 1971); Kent V. Flannery, "The Origins of Agriculture," *Annual Review of Anthropology,* 2 (1973): 271-310; Ester Boserup, *The Conditions of Agricultural Growth: The Economics of Agrarian Change under Population Pressure* (Chicago, 1965); Ester Boserup, "The Impact of Scarcity and Plenty on Development," in *Hunger and History: The Impact of Changing Food Productions and Consumption Patterns of Society,* ed., Robert I. Rotberg and Theodore K. Rabb (Cambridge, Eng., 1983), 185-209. Boserup denies that there are any ultimate environmental limits on population growth: scarcity, in her view, always generates greater innovation and abundance.

excess has, at many times and places, put severe constraints on social development.[11]

Unquestionably, all agriculture has brought revolutionary changes to the planet's ecosystems; and, most agroecologists would agree, those changes have often been destructive to the natural order and imperfect in design and execution. Yet as they have gained understanding of how agricultural systems have interacted with nature, scientists have discovered plenty of reasons to respect the long historical achievement of billions of anonymous traditional farmers. As Miguel A. Altieri writes, ''Many farming practices once regarded as primitive or misguided are being recognized as sophisticated and appropriate. Confronted with specific problems of slope, flooding, droughts, pests, diseases and low soil fertility, small farmers throughout the world have developed unique management systems to overcome these constraints.'' One of the most impressive and yet common of such managerial techniques is to diversify the crops under cultivation; traditional Filipino farmers, for example, raise as many as forty separate crops in a single swidden at the same time. The advantages of such diversification include making more efficient use of light, water, and nutrients by cultivating plants of different height, canopy structure, and nutrient requirements, thus harvesting greater total yields per hectare; leaving more nitrogen in the soil from intercropped legumes; and achieving more effective soil cover, pest control, and weed suppression.[12]

The landscapes that resulted from such traditional practices were carefully integrated, functional mosaics that retained much of the wisdom of nature; they were based on close observation and imitation of the natural order. Here a field was selected and cleared for intensive crop production; there a forest was preserved as supply of fuel and mast; over there a patch of marginal land was used for pasturing livestock. What may have appeared scattered and happenstance in the premodern agricultural landscape always had a structure behind it—a structure that was at once the product of nonhuman factors and of human intelligence, working toward a mutual accommodation. In many parts of the world that agroecosystem took thousands of years to achieve, and even then it never reached any perfect resting point.[13] Rises and falls in human numbers, vagaries of weather and disease, external pressures of wars and taxes, tragedies of depletion and collapse, all kept the world's food systems in a constant state of change. Yet, examined over the long duration, they had two remarkably persistent, widely shared characteristics, whether they were in medieval Sweden or ancient Sumer, in the Ohio River valley or the Valley of Mexico, whether the systems were based on maize or wheat or cassava. First, traditional agroecosystems were based on a predominately subsistence strategy in which most people raised what they themselves consumed, though now and then they may have sent some of their surplus off to cities for the sake of trade or tribute. Second, subsistence-oriented agroecosystems, despite making major changes in nature, nonetheless preserved much of its diversity and complexity, and that achievement was a source of social stability, generation following generation.

---

11. One inch of soil may form under natural conditions over three hundred to one thousand years; good farming can speed up this process. See Norman Hudson, *Soil Conservation* (Ithaca, 1971), 38. See also M. Witkamp, ''Soils as Components of Ecosystems,'' *Annual Review of Ecology and Systematics,* 2 (1971): 85-110. On the role of climate in history see, for example, Reid Bryson and Thomas J. Murray, *Climates of Hunger: Mankind and the World's Changing Weather* (Madison, 1977); and Robert I. Rotberg and Theodore K. Rabb, eds., *Climate and History: Studies in Interdisciplinary History* (Princeton, 1981). On the major types of water control in history, see Donald Worster, *Rivers of Empire: Water, Aridity, and the American West* (New York, 1985), 17-60.

12. Miguel A. Altieri, *Agroecology: The Scientific Basis of Alternative Agriculture* (Boulder, 1987), 69-71; Harold C. Conklin, ''An Ethnological Approach to Shifting Agriculture,'' in *Environment and Cultural Behavior,* ed. A.P. Vayda (New York, 1979), 228.

---

13. One of the best descriptions of the mosaic in traditional agriculture can be found in Georges Bertrand, ''Pour une histoire ecologique de la France rurale,'' in *Histoire de la France rurale,* ed. Georges Duby (3 vols., Paris, 1975), I, 96-102. See also E. Estyn Evans, ''The Ecology of Peasant Life in Western Europe,'' in *Man's Role in Changing the Face of the Earth,* ed. Thomas, 217-239. The incredibly long-lived agricultural systems of East Asia, as they existed before the twentieth century forced decisive changes on them, are described in Franklin H. King, *Farmers of Forty Centuries* (Madison, 1911).

So it was, that is, until the modern era and the rise of the capitalist mode of production. Beginning in the fifteenth century and accelerating in the eighteenth and nineteenth centuries, the structure and dynamics of agroecosystems began to change radically. I believe the capitalist reorganization carried out in those years and beyond into our own time brought as sweeping and revolutionary a set of land-use changes as did the Neolithic revolution. Despite its importance, we have not yet fully understood why this second revolution occurred nor asked what its effect has been on the natural environment. I submit that the single most important task for scholars in the history of modern agroecology is to trace what Karl Polanyi has called ''the great transformation,'' both in general planetary terms and in all its permutations from place to place.[14] . . .

An adequate definition of the capitalist transformation of nature is a larger order than I can here undertake to fill, but a few preliminary thoughts may clarify what is meant. In the first place, a distinction must be made between markets and the market system or economy. The new order was not a matter of the existence of isolated markets here and there, but of an entire economy designed according to a simplified, idealized model of human behavior: the meeting of a buyer and a seller for the purpose of freely maximizing personal wealth. The most satisfactory definition of that market economy, one that captures its underlying moral essence, is Polanyi's:

> The transformation implies a change in the motive of action on the part of members of society: for the motive of subsistence that of gain must be substituted. All transactions are turned into money transactions, and these in turn require that a medium of exchange be introduced into articulation of industrial life. All incomes must derive from the sale of something or other, and whatever the actual source of a person's income, it must be regarded as resulting from sale. . . . But the most startling peculiarity of the system lies in the fact that, once it is established, it must be allowed to function without outside interference.

As Polanyi explains, capitalism was distinctive in that it was unabashedly based ''on a motive only rarely acknowledged as valid in the history of human societies, and certainly never before raised to the level of a justification of action and behavior in everyday life, namely, gain.''[15]

Capitalism introduced still another innovation, one that would change profoundly the way people related to nature in general: It created for the first time in history a general market in land. All the complex forces and interactions, beings and processes, that we term ''nature'' (sometimes even elevate to the honorific status of a capitalized ''Nature'') were compressed into the simplified abstraction, ''land.'' Though not truly a commodity in the ordinary sense, that is, something produced by human labor for sale on the market, land became ''commodified''; it came to be regarded as though it were a commodity and by that manner of thinking was made available to be traded without restraint. Whatever emotional meanings that land had held for the self and its identity, whatever moral regard it had engendered, now was suppressed so that the market economy could function freely. The environmental implications in such a mental change are beyond easy reckoning.[16]

What actually happened to the world of nature, once it has been reduced to the abstraction ''land,'' is one of the most interesting historical problems presented by the capitalist transformation and will require a great deal more research by environmental historians. There are many possible lines for that research to take, but among the most promising is an inquiry into the restructuring of agroecosystems that capitalism promoted. First in England and then in every part of the planet, agroecosystems were rationally and systematically reshaped in order to intensify, not merely the production of food and fiber, but the accumulation of personal wealth.

Despite many variations in time and place, the capitalistic agroecosystem shows one clear tendency

14. Karl Polanyi, *The Great Transformation: The Political and Economic Origins of Our Time* (New York, 1944).

15. Polanyi, *Great Transformation,* 30, 41.

16. For an insightful discussion of the new market in land, see William Cronon, *Changes in the Land: Indians, Colonials, and the Ecology of New England* (New York, 1983), 54-81.

over the span of modern history: a movement toward the radical simplification of the natural ecological order in the number of species found in an area and the intricacy of their interconnections. As markets developed and transportation improved, farmers increasingly concentrated their energies on producing a smaller and smaller number of crops to sell for profit. They became, in short, specialists in production, even to the point of producing virtually nothing for their own direct personal consumption. But that is not all: the land itself evolved into a set of specialized instruments of production. What had once been a biological community of plants and animals so complex that scientists can hardly comprehend it, what had been changed by traditional agriculturists into a still highly diversified system for growing local foodstuffs and other materials, now increasingly became a rigidly contrived apparatus competing in widespread markets for economic success. In today's parlance we call this new kind of agroecosystem a *monoculture,* meaning a part of nature that has been reconstituted to the point that it yields a single species, which is growing on the land only because somewhere there is strong market demand for it. Although farmers in isolated rural neighborhoods may have continued to plant a broad, multispecies spectrum of crops, the trend over the past two hundred years or so has been toward the establishment of monocultures on every continent. As Adam Smith realized back in the eighteenth century, specialization is at the very heart of the capitalist mode of production. It should not be surprising then that it would eventually become the rule in agriculture and land use as it is in manufacturing.[17]

In Smith's day, however, the trend in the new agriculture toward a massive loss of ecological com-plexity was not easy to foresee. On the contrary, it was obscured for a long while by the discovery and colonization of the Americas by the European nations, which suddenly made available to farmers a dazzling array of new plant species to try out in their fields: maize, potatoes, tobacco, to name some of the more valuable among them. On both sides of the Atlantic, agroecosystems might now contain more kinds of plants than ever before. That outcome was part of a more general process of global biological exchange, migration, and mixing that occurred with the great discoveries and the subsequent migration of Europeans all over the globe, reversing, as Alfred Crosby has written, the effects of continental drift and geographical isolation that had obtained for millions of years.[18] Thomas Jefferson's enthusiasm for introducing mulberry trees and silkworm cultivation from China into Virginia was only one example of what seemed, in the early days of modern farming, to be the possibility of a new plentitude in production. There was more variety in the modern agricultural market economy, considered as a whole, than in each of the scattered traditional economies of the past—a broader base for consumers than even the Philippine farmer enjoyed with his dozens of varieties growing in the forest clearings. Ironically, however, the individual producer had less biotic complexity to deal with on a given acre than before; his fenced and deeded lands became, in ecological terms, depauperate environments.

Another reason for the long obscurity in capitalistic agriculture's trend toward radical simplification was the near-simultaneous rise of modern science, both practical and theoretical, and its application to the problems of agriculture. The "agricultural revo-

17. On monocultures, see Lech Ryszkowski, ed., *Ecological Effects of Intensive Agriculture* (Warsaw, 1974). This authority observes that Soviet bloc nations have followed the West in adopting monocultural farming, with many of the same environmental ill effects. See also Tim P. Bayliss-Smith, *The Ecology of Agricultural Systems* (Cambridge, 1982), 83-97, which deals with a Russian collective farm. Since Marxists accede to the view that capitalism achieves the final technological domination of nature and argue that communism is simply a rearrangement of the ownership of the technology, it is hardly surprising that they have not repre-sented any real alternative from an ecological standpoint. On specialization in the pinmaker's trade as a model of capitalist development, as perceived in 1776, see Adam Smith, *An Inquiry into the Nature and Causes of the Wealth of Nations* (New York, 1937), 4-5.

18. Alfred Crosby, Jr., "The British Empire as a Product of Continental Drift," In *Environmental History: Critical Issues in Comparative Perspective,* ed. Kendall E. Bailes (Lanham, 1985), 553-576.

lution'' that began in England during the eighteenth century was a double-sided phenomenon: one half of it was capitalistic, the other scientific, and the two halves have never been altogether compatible. In the early years of their relationship, scientifically inclined reformers taught traditional English farmers, faced with declining soil fertility and low output, to rotate their fields between arable and grass to improve livestock husbandry and augment their manure supplies, and to cultivate root crops such as turnips to feed their cattle and legumes such as clover to add nitrogen to the soil.[19] Today those innovations would be viewed as sound ecological practices—real improvements over archaic methods. Unquestionably, they also improved productivity and added to England's economic growth. For a while, they held considerable appeal for profit-seeking entrepreneurs, who preached the gospel of turnips and clover across the English countryside. But in later periods most farmers in England and North America drifted away from those reforms, for example, replacing nitrogen-building root crops with chemical fertilizers. A biology-inspired system of farming, based on careful field rotations and striving for a better balance between plants and animals, failed to establish a secure, lasting, dependable hold on the imagination of capitalist landowners. The reason was that, over the long run, such farming too often interfered with the more compelling system of the market economy. There have been, in other words, two kinds of logic in modern agriculture—that of the scientist and that of the capitalist—and they have not agreed much of the time.[20]

My own research into the restructuring of ecosystems by capitalistic farming has dealt mainly with the raising of wheat on the western plains of North America in the twentieth century. Like any single case, it can afford only a partial understanding of ecological tendencies in the capitalist mode; but wheat provides much of the world's basic nutrition, and patterns of growing and consuming it may be taken as symptomatic of the whole modern mode of food and fiber production. The history of the Great Plains region followed a familiar line of development: It began with a rapid and drastic destruction of ecological complexity and the substitution of a single marketable species (indeed, a single variety of that single species in many instances) over a wide acreage. In their preagricultural state the Plains, though seeming bare and monotonous to many travelers, were in reality a highly diversified environment, containing hundreds of grasses, forbs, and sedges, some of them annuals, some perennials, together with large and small herbivores, and further up the trophic ladder, populations of carnivores and decomposers, which consume the herbivores and return their matter to the soil. From Texas northward into Canada that ecosystem, or more accurately, that series of ecosystems, gave way to wheat and a scattering of other crops. Not everything of the older order disappeared, but a large portion of it did, and some of it may have disappeared forever.[21]

The process of rigorous environmental simplification began among the sodbusters who first appeared on the Plains in the 1870s, looking for a crop they could raise and ship back east on the railroads. The process took a great leap forward during World War I when markets in wheat boomed, and it continued into the late 1920s. Most striking was the fact that livestock—the principal remaining fauna in most

19. Sources for this discussion include J.D. Chambers and G.E. Mingay, *The Agricultural Revolution, 1750–1880* (New York, 1966), 54-76; Eric Kerridge, *The Agricultural Revolution* (London, 1967), 181-348; G.E. Fussell, ''Science and Practice in Eighteenth-Century British Agriculture,'' *Agricultural History,* 43 (January 1969): 7-18; and D.B. Grigg, *The Agricultural Systems of the World: An Evolutionary Approach* (London, 1974), 152-186.

20. I do not deny that science has become, in many places and ways, a handmaiden of modern market agriculture; see, for example, the criticisms of two scientists: Richard Levins and Richard Lewontin, *The Dialectical Biologist* (Cambridge, Mass., 1985).

21. Donald Worster, *Dust Bowl: The Southern Plains in the 1930s* (New York, 1979). The literature on the ecology and human settlement of the Great Plains is voluminous. Good introductions include Walter Prescott Webb, *The Great Plains* (Boston, 1931); James C. Malin, *The Grassland of North America: Prolegomena to Its History* (Lawrence, 1947); and Brian W. Blouet and Frederick C. Luebke, eds., *The Great Plains: Environment and Culture* (Lincoln, 1979). About the adjoining corn belt, which has much in common with the Plains, see Allan N. Auclair, ''Ecological Factors in the Development of Intensive Management Ecosystems in the Midwestern United States,'' *Ecology,* 57 (Late Spring 1976): 431-444.

agroecosystems—were from the outset a minor, and diminishing, part of the Plains farmstead. Cattle, pigs, sheep, and chickens were seldom found in more than token numbers on those farms or soon disappeared if they were. They were a distraction from the main business of raising grain. Of course, they did show up in other places, including livestock ranches in the region, but in spectacularly large numbers, in gatherings of thousands of animals, all one species again. The most important result of that severing of agroecosystems by the sharp knife of economic specialization was to make the maintenance of soil fertility and stability harder. Plains and prairie topsoils are deep—one to two feet on average—and they could grow a lot of crops before productivity began to decline. Eventually, though, the farmer must put back in what he took out; if there were no bison or cattle or prairie dogs to do that for him, he must buy some other sort of fertilizer on the national or world market; in effect, he must buy fossil fuels, for modern synthetic fertilizer is made from natural gas.[22] When the Plains farmer was forced to do that, he came to depend on an often remote, impersonal network of credit suppliers, manufacturers, and trading corporations, and he could only hope that what he could buy from them would be as good for the soil as the bison's great splats of dung had been.

The vulnerabilities inherent in modern monoculture now have a long history to be studied and understood. They include an unprecedented degree of susceptibility to disease, predation, and pest population explosions; a heightened overall instability in the system; a constant tendency of the human manager to take risks for short-term profit, including mining the soil (and in the American West mining a limited underground water resource); an increasing reliance on technological substitutes for natural plant and animal services; a reliance on chemical inputs that have often been highly toxic to humans and other organisms; a

dependence on imports from distant regions to keep the local system functioning; and finally, a demand for capital and expertise that fewer and fewer individual farmers could meet.[23] This last characteristic is one of the earliest to show up and has been widely studied in rural history, though seldom from an ecological point of view. Farming communities reflect the biological systems they rest on. A society cannot radically diminish the diversity of natural ecosystems for the sake of maximum crop production, nor keep the land regimented for profit, nor augment the flow of energy through the system by introducing fossil fuels without changing the rhythms and diversity and structure of power within its various communities. An ecological approach helps explain why capitalistic agriculture has had its peculiar social effects as well as its managerial problems.

I have not yet mentioned what turned out to be the most serious vulnerability of all in Great Plains farming: its susceptibility to wind erosion and dust storms of the kind that wracked the region in the 1930s, storms that followed hard on the extension of wheat farming into high-risk areas in the preceding decades. The dirty thirties were an unmitigated ecological disaster for the Plains; in fact they were one of the worst environmental catastrophes in recorded human experience. In part, of course, the disaster was due to drought, the most severe drought in some two hundred years of the region's climate. But it was also the result of the radically simplified agroecosystem the Plains farmers had tried to create. What they demonstrated in the 1930s was that reducing the land to the single species of wheat did not provide an adequate buffer

---

22. John S. Steinhart and Carol E. Steinhart, "Energy Use in the U.S. Food System," *Science*, April 19, 1974, pp. 307-316; William Lockeretz, ed., *Agriculture and Energy* (New York, 1977); David Pimentel. "Energy Flow in Agroecosystems," in *Agricultural Ecosystems,* ed. Lowrance, Stinner, and House, 121-132.

23. David Pimentel et al., "Land Degradation: Effects on Food and Energy Resources," *Science* (Oct. 8, 1976): 149-155. These authors argue that due to intensive, continuous cultivation, annual sediment loss via surface runoff increased from about 3 billion tons nationally in the 1930s to 4 billion tons in recent years. Other scientific critiques of modern agriculture appear in Miguel A. Altieri, Deborah K. Letourneau, and James R. Davis, "Developing Sustainable Agroecosystems." *Bioscience,* 33 (January 1983); 45-49; and Stephen R. Gliessman, "An Agroecological Approach to Sustainable Agriculture," in *Meeting the Expectations of the Land: Essays in Sustainable Agriculture and Stewardship,* ed. Wes Jackson, Wendell Berry, and Bruce Colman (San Francisco, 1984), 160-171.

between themselves and drought. Wheat was a splended species for making money, but taken alone, planted on immense expanses of plowed acres from which so many other, better-adapted forms of life had been eliminated, it proved to be a poor defense when the rains failed.[24] And therein lies one of the most important lessons we can find in the history of the new mode of production: it had the capability of making the earth yield beans or corn or wheat in quantities never before seen, and of creating more wealth and better nutrition for more people than any traditional agroecosystem could boast. But the other side of that impressive success was (and is) a tendency to bet high against nature, to raise the stakes constantly in a feverish effort to keep from folding—and sometimes to lose the bet and lose big.

Neither ecology nor history, nor the two working together, can reveal unequivocally whether modern capitalistic land use has been a success or a failure; the question is too large for an easy answer and the criteria for judgment too numerous. But they can make the point that scholars ought to begin to address the issue and also that the conventional answers, which have generally been laudatory and narrowly focused on economic or technological efficiency, need to be supplemented by an ecological perspective. From that vantage the historical interpretation of the past few centuries is likely to be a darker, less complacent one than we have known.

This blooming, buzzing, howling world of nature that surrounds us has always been a force in human life. It is so today, despite all our efforts to free ourselves from that dependency, and despite our frequent unwillingness to acknowledge our dependency until it is too late and a crisis is upon us. Environmental history aims to bring back into our awareness that significance of nature and, with the aid of modern science, to discover some fresh truths about ourselves and our past. We need that understanding in a great many places: for instance, in little Haiti, which has been undergoing a long, tragic spiral into poverty,

disease, and land degradation, and in the rain forests of Borneo as they have passed from traditional tribal to modern corporate ownership and management. In both of those cases, the fortunes of people and land have been as inseparably connected as they have been on the Great Plains, and in both the world market economy has created or intensified an ecological problem. Whatever terrain the environmental historian chooses to investigate, he has to address the age-old predicament of how humankind can feed itself without degrading the primal source of life. Today as ever, that problem is the fundamental challenge in human ecology, and meeting it will require knowing the earth well—knowing its history and knowing its limits.

DISCUSSION TOPICS

1. Propose an alternative to the capitalist mode of production that would be a workable foundation for agricultural production in the modern world. How do the strengths and weaknesses of this alternative compare with the strengths and weaknesses of capitalism?

READING 23

Gender and Environment History

Carolyn Merchant

Carolyn Merchant (b. 1936) is Professor of Environmental History, Philosophy and Ethics in the Department of Conservation and Resource Studies, University of California, Berkeley, California. She has written extensively in the area of ecofeminism, and has served on the executive committee of the American Society for Environmental History.

Merchant believes that the three realms of environmental history presented by Worster (ecology, production, and cognition) would benefit from gender analyses. In addition, she proposes that an analysis of

---

reproduction is needed. Merchant asserts that the shifts in power described by Worster occurred not only between indigenous and invading cultures, but between men and women as well.

"As it was the intuitive foresight of [Isabella of Spain] which brought the light of civilization to a great continent, so in great measure, will it fall to woman in her power to educate public sentiment to save from rapacious waste and complete exhaustion the resources upon which depend the welfare of the home, the children, and the children's children." So wrote Lydia Adams-Williams, self-styled feminist conservation writer, in 1908. Her compatriot Mrs. Lovell White of California argued that reversing the destruction of the earth brought about by "men whose souls are gang-saws" was a project that required the best efforts of women. These women of the Progressive conservation crusade of the early twentieth century exemplify an overtly feminist perspective on the environment.[1]

Donald Worster's "Transformations of the Earth," while a rich and provocative approach to the field of environmental history, lacks a gender analysis. His conceptual levels of ecology (natural history), production (technology and its socioeconomic relations), and cognition (the mental realm of ideas, ethics, myths, and so on) are a significant framework for research and writing in this emerging field. His use of the mode-of-production concept in differing ecological and cultural contexts and his account of the changing history of ecological ideas in his major books have propelled environmental history to new levels of sophistication.

A gender perspective can add to his conceptual framework in two important ways. First, each of his three categories can be further illuminated through a gender analysis; second, in my view, environmental history needs a fourth analytical level, that of reproduction, which interacts with the other three levels.[2] What could such a perspective contribute to the framework Worster has outlined?

Women and men have historically had different roles in production relative to the environment. In subsistence modes of production such as those of native peoples, women's impact on nature is immediate and direct. In gathering-hunting-fishing economies, women collect and process plants, small animals, bird eggs, and shellfish and fabricate tools, baskets, mats, slings, and clothing, while men hunt larger animals, fish, construct weirs and hut frames, and burn forests and brush. Because water and fuelwood availability affect cooking and food preservation, decisions over environmental degradation that dictate when to move camp and village sites may lie in the hands of women. In horticultural communities, women are often the primary producers of crops and fabricators of hoes, planters, and digging sticks, but when such economies are transformed by markets, the cash economies and environmental impacts that ensue are often controlled by men. Women's access to resources to fulfill basic needs may come into direct conflict with male roles in the market economy, as in Seneca women's loss of control over horticulture to male agriculture and male access to cash through greater mobility in nineteenth-century America or in India's chipco (tree-hugging) movement of the past decade, wherein women literally hugged trees to protest declining access to fuelwood for cooking as male-dominated lumbering expanded.[3]

---

1. Carolyn Merchant, "Women of the Progressive Conservation Movement, 1900–1916," *Environmental Review,* 8 (Spring 1984): 57-85, esp. 65, 59.

---

2. For a more detailed discussion, see Carolyn Merchant, "The Theoretical Structure of Ecological Revolutions," *ibid.,* 11 (Winter 1987): 251-274. For a discussion of theoretical frameworks for environmental history, see Barbara Leibhardt, "Interpretation and Causal Analysis: Theories in Environmental History," *ibid.,* 12 (Spring 1988): 23-36.

3. Sandra Marburg, "Women and Environment: Subsistence Paradigms, 1850–1950," *ibid.,* 8 (Spring 1984): 7-22; Diane Rothenberg, "Erosion of Power: An Economic Basic for the Selective Conservativism of Seneca Women in the Nineteenth Century," *Western Canadian Journal of Anthropology,* 6 (1976): 106-122; Vandana Shiva, *Staying Alive: Women, Ecology, and Development* (London, 1988); Mona Etienne and Eleanor Leacock, eds., *Women and Colonization: Anthropological Perspectives* (New York, 1980).

In the agrarian economy of colonial and frontier America, women's outdoor production, like men's, had immediate impact on the environment. While men's work in cutting forests, planting and fertilizing fields, and hunting or fishing affected the larger homestead environment, women's dairying activities, free-ranging barnyard fowl, and vegetable, flower, and herbal gardens all affected the quality of the nearby soils and waters and the level of insect pests, altering the effects of the microenvironment on human health. In the nineteenth century, however, as agriculture became more specialized and oriented toward market production, men took over dairying, poultry-raising, and truck farming, resulting in a decline in women's outdoor production. Although the traditional contributions of women to the farm economy continued in many rural areas and some women assisted in farm as well as home management, the general trend toward capitalist agribusiness increasingly turned chickens, cows, and vegetables into efficient components of factories within fields managed for profits by male farmers.[4]

In the industrial era, as middle-class women turned more of their energies to deliberate child rearing and domesticity, they defined a new but still distinctly female relation to the natural world. In their socially constructed roles as moral mothers, they often taught children about nature and science at home and in the elementary schools. By the Progressive era, women's focus on maintaining a home for husbands and children led many women such as those quoted above to spearhead a nationwide conservation movement to save forest and waters and to create national and local parks. Although the gains of the movement have been attributed by historians to men such as President Theodore Roosevelt, forester Gifford Pinchot, and preservationist John Muir, the efforts of thousands of women were directly responsible for many of the country's most significant conservation achievements. Women writers on nature such as Isabella Bird, Mary Austin, and Rachel Carson have been among the most influential commentators on the American response to nature.[5]

Worster's conceptual framework for environmental history can thus be made more complete by including a gender analysis of the differential effects of women and men on ecology and their differential roles in production. At the level of cognition as well, a sensitivity to gender enriches environmental history. Native Americans, for example, construed the natural world as animated and created by spirits and gods. Origin myths included tales of mother earth and father sky, grandmother woodchucks and coyote tricksters, corn mothers and tree spirits. Such deities mediated between nature and humans, inspiring rituals and behaviors that helped to regulate environmental use and exploitation. Similar myths focused planting, harvesting, and first fruit rituals among native Americans and in such Old World cultures as those in ancient Mesopotamia, Egypt, and Greece, which symbolized nature as a mother goddess. In Renaissance Europe the earth was conceptualized as a nurturing mother (God's vice-regent in the mundane world) and the cosmos as an organism having a body, soul, and spirit. An animate earth and an I/thou relationship between humans and the world does not prevent the exploitation of resources for human use, but it entails an ethic of restraint and propitiation by setting up religious rituals to be followed before mining ores, damming brooks, or planting and harvesting crops. The human relationship to the land is intimately connected to daily survival.[6]

---

4. Carolyn Merchant, *Ecological Revolutions: Nature, Gender, and Science in New England* (Chapel Hill, 1989); Corlann Gee Bush, ''The Barn Is His, the House Is Mine,'' in *Energy and Transport,* ed. George Daniels and Mark Rose (Beverly Hills, 1982), 235-259; Carolyn E. Sachs, *The Invisible Farmers: Women in Agricultural Production* (Totowa, 1983).

5. Merchant, ''Women of the Progressive Conservation Movement''; Vera Norwood, ''Heroines of Nature: Four Women Respond to the American Landscape,'' *Environmental Review,* 8 (Spring 1984): 34-56.

6. Paula Gunn Allen, *The Sacred Hoop: Recovering the Feminine in American Indian Traditions* (Boston, 1984); Riane Eisler, *The Chalice and the Blade* (San Franciso, 1988); Pamela Berger, *The Goddess Obscured: Transformation of the Grain Protectress from Goddess to Saint* (Boston, 1985); Janet Bord and Colin Bord, *Earth Rites: Fertility Practices in Pre-Industrial Britain* (London, 1982); Carolyn Merchant, *The Death of Nature: Women, Ecology, and the Scientific Revolution* (San Franciso, 1980).

When mercantile capitalism, industrialization, and urbanization began to distance increasing numbers of male elites from the land in seventeenth-century England and in nineteenth-century America, the mechanistic framework created by the ''fathers'' of modern science legitimated the use of nature for human profit making. The conception that nature was dead, made up of inert atoms moved by external forces, that God was an engineer and mathematician, and that human perception was the result of particles of light bouncing off objects and conveyed to the brain as discrete sensations meant that nature responded to human interventions, not as active participant, but as passive instrument. Thus the way in which world views, myths, and perceptions are constructed by gender at the cognitive level can be made an integral part of environmental history.[7]

While Worster's analytical levels of ecology, production, and cognition may be made more sophisticated by including a gender analysis, ideas drawn from feminist theory suggest the usefulness of a fourth level of analysis—reproduction—that is dialectically related to the other three. First, all species reproduce themselves generationally and their population levels have impacts on the local ecology. But for humans, the numbers that can be sustained are related to the mode of production: More people can occupy a given ecosystem under a horticultural than a gathering-hunting-fishing mode, and still more under an industrial mode. Humans reproduce themselves biologically in accordance with the social and ethical norms of the culture into which they are born. Native peoples adopted an array of benign and malign population control techniques such as long lactation, abstention, coitus interruptus, the use of native plants to induce abortion, infanticide, and senilicide. Carrying capacity, nutritional factors, and tribally accepted customs dictated the numbers of infants that survived to adulthood in order to reproduce the tribal whole. Colonial Americans, by contrast, encouraged high numbers of births owing to the scarcity of labor in the new lands. With the onset of industrialization in the nineteenth century, a demographic transition resulted in fewer births per female. Integenerational reproduction, therefore, mediated through production, has impact on the local ecology.[8]

Second, people (as well as other living things) must reproduce their own energy on a daily basis through food and must conserve that energy through clothing (skins, furs, or other methods of bodily temperature control) and shelter. Gathering or planting food crops, fabricating clothing, and constructing houses are directed toward the reproduction of daily life.

In addition to these biological aspects of reproduction, human communities reproduce themselves socially in two additional ways. People pass on skills and behavioral norms to the next generation of producers, and that allows a culture to reproduce itself over time. They also structure systems of governance and laws that maintain the social order of the tribe, town, or nation. Many such laws and policies deal with the allocation and regulation of natural resources, land, and property rights. They are passed by legislative bodies and administered through government agencies and a system of justice. Law in this interpretation is a means of maintaining and modifying a particular social order. These four aspects of reproduction (two biological and two social) interact with ecology as mediated by a particular mode of production.[9]

---

7. Merchant, *Death of Nature.* See also Evelyn Fox Keilet, *Reflections on Gender and Science* (New Haven, 1985), 33-65. On gender in American perceptions of nature, see Annette Kolodny, *The Lay of the Land: Metaphor as Experience and History in American Life and Letters* (Chapel Hill, 1975); and Annette Kolodny, *The Land before Her: Fantasy and Experience of the American Frontier,* 1630–1860 (Chapel Hill, 1984).

8. Ester Bosrup, *The Conditions of Agricultural Growth: The Economics of Agrarian Change under Population Pressure* (Chicago, 1965); Ester Bosrup, *Women's Role in Economic Development* (New York, 1970); Marvin Harris, *Cultural Materialism: The Struggle for a Science of Culture* (New York, 1979); Carolyn Merchant, ''The Realm of Social Relations: Production, Reproduction, and Gender in Environmental Transformations,'' in *The Earth as Transformed by Human Action,* ed. B. L. Turner II (New York, forthcoming); Robert Wells, *Uncle Sam's Family: Issues and Perspectives in American Demographic History* (Albany, 1985), 28-56.

9. For a more detailed elaboration of reproduction as an organizing category see Merchant, *Ecological Revolutions.*

Such an analysis of production and reproduction in relation to ecology helps to delineate changes in forms of patriarchy in different societies. Although in most societies governance may have been vested in the hands of men (hence patriarchy), the balance of power between the sexes differed. In gatherer-hunter and horticultural communities, extraction and production of food may have been either equally shared by or dominated by women, so that male (or female) power in tribal reproduction (chiefs and shamans) was balanced by female power in production. In subsistence-oriented communities in colonial and frontier America, men and women shared power in production, although men played dominant roles in legal-political reproduction of the social whole. Under industrial capitalism in the nineteenth century, women's loss of power in outdoor farm production was compensated by a gain of power in the reproduction of daily life (domesticity) and in the socialization of children and husbands (the moral mother) in the sphere of reproduction. Thus the shifts of power that Worster argues occurs in different environments are not only those between indigenous and invading cultures but also those between men and women.[10]

A gender perspective on environmental history therefore both offers a more balanced and complete picture of past human interactions with nature and advances its theoretical frameworks. The ways in which female and male contributions to production, reproduction, and cognition are actually played out in relation to ecology depends on the particular stage and the actors involved. Yet within the various acts of what Timothy Weiskel has called the global eco-drama should be included scenes in which men's and women's roles come to center stage and scenes in which nature "herself" is an actress. In this way

gender in environmental history can contribute to a more holistic history of various regions and eras.[11]

DISCUSSION TOPICS

1. How might our environmental concerns differ if Western society were matriarchal rather than patriarchal?
2. How might the inclusion of gender analysis affect current perceptions in Western society about environmental history?

READING 24

Anglo-American Land Use Attitudes

Eugene C. Hargrove

Eugene C. Hargrove (b. 1944), Professor of Philosophy at the University of North Texas, Denton, Texas, has been editor-in-chief of the journal, Environmental Ethics, *since its founding in 1979.*

In his selection, Hargrove traces the philosophical strands underlying contemporary attitudes in the United States toward land and land use which account for the powerful position of landowners. He describes three major sources of influence: practices of German and Saxon freemen, Thomas Jefferson's theory of allodial rights, and John Locke's theory of property.

Freemen among early German tribes set important precedents. For example, primogeniture, in which the oldest child eventually received the family land, often relegated landless offspring to serfdom; the landowners soon became a powerful minority. In addition, the practice of taxation, which began as a customary annual offering to local nobles, became a large burden for poor freemen, while rich landowners remained exempt. The practices of primogeniture and taxation ultimately

---

10. *Ibid.,* Nancy F. Cott, *The Bonds of Womanhood: "Women's Sphere" in New England, 1780–1835* (New Haven, 1977); Barbara Leslie Epstein, *The Politics of Domesticity: Women, Evangelism, and Temperance in Nineteenth Century America* (Middletown, 1981); Ruth Bloch, "American Feminine Ideals in Transition: The Rise of the Moral Mother, 1785–1815," *Feminist Studies,* 4 (June 1978): 101-126; Barbara Welter, "The Cult of True Womanhood, 1820–1860," *American Quarterly,* 18 (Summer 1966): 151-174.

---

11. On environmental history as an ecodrama, see Timothy Weiskel, "Agents of Empire: Steps toward an Ecology of Imperialism," *Environmental Review,* 11 (Winter 1987): 275-288.

resulted in a shift from a society in which there were many landholders to one characterized by feudal conditions in which a few, wealthy landholders held political and economic power.

Saxon freemen developed county courts (moots) which originally were composed of the freemen themselves. Special consideration given by moots to the interests of local landowners still is evident in U.S. courts today.

Thomas Jefferson advocated the notion of allodial rights, in which landowners could own small freehold farmsteads with little or no obligation to governmental authority. Jefferson considered agriculturalists to be among the most vigorous, independent, and virtuous of people; he believed that if they felt tied to the land, they would remain committed to the country. However, Hargrove notes that these independent landowners did not share Jefferson's aesthetic appreciation for nature, nor his respect for sound agricultural practices; instead, they exploited the land for personal gain.

John Locke believed that a farmer's labor determined his or her right to own and use land, and that society should have little role in managing a landowner's property. Locke advocated for transferring the property rights of the crown to each individual landowner. However, the sense of moral responsibility associated with royal ownership was replaced by moral apathy toward the land among individual landowners.

INTRODUCTION

Such protected areas as Yosemite, Yellowstone, and the Grand Canyon are often cited as great successes of the environmental movement in nature preservation and conservation. Yet, not all natural objects and areas worthy of special protection or management are of such national significance and these must be dealt with at state, regional, or local levels. In such cases, environmentalists almost always plead their cause before a county court, a local administrative political body, usually consisting of three judges elected by the rural community, who may or may not have legal backgrounds.

Here the environmentalists are probably in for a great shock. Inevitably, some rural landowner will defend his special property rights to the land in question. He will ask the court rhetorically, ''What right do these outsiders, these so-called environmentalists,

have to come in here and try to tell me what to do with my land?'' and answering his own question, he will continue, ''They don't have any right. I worked the land; it's my property, and no one has the right to tell me what to do with it!'' The environmentalists may be surprised that the farmer does not bother to reply to any of their carefully made points, but the real shock comes at the end when the county court dismisses the environmental issues, ruling in favor of the landowner.

While the environmentalists may suspect corruption (and such dealings are not unlikely), usually both the judges and the landowner are honestly convinced that they have all acted properly. The property rights argument recited by the rural landowner is a very powerful defense, particularly when presented at this level of government. The argument is grounded in a political philosophy almost three centuries old as well as in land use practices which go back at least to Saxon and perhaps even to Celtic times in Europe and England. When the argument is presented to county court judges who share these beliefs and land use traditions, the outcome of the court decision is rarely in doubt. On the other hand, the tradition that natural objects and areas of special beauty or interest ought to be protected from landowners claiming special property rights, and from the practice of landowning in general, is of very recent origin, and without comparable historical and emotional foundations. . . .

My present purpose is to examine traditional land use attitudes. First, I examine the ancient land use practices which gave rise to these attitudes, second, the political activities and views of Thomas Jefferson which secured a place for them in American political and legal thought, and, finally, the political philosophy of John Locke which provided them with a philosophical foundation.

LANDHOLDING AMONG EARLY GERMAN AND SAXON FREEMAN

About two thousand years ago most of Europe was occupied by tribes of peoples known collectively as the Celts. At about that time, these peoples came under considerable pressure from the Romans moving up from the south and from Germanic tribes entering central Europe from the east. Five hundred years later, the Celts had either been subjugated by the German and Roman invaders or pushed back into Ireland and fringe areas of England. The Roman Empire, too, after asserting its presence as far north as England, was in decay. Roman influence would continue in the south, but in northern and central Europe as well as in most of England German influence would prevail.

The Germanic tribes which displaced the Celts and defeated the Romans were composed of four classes: a few nobles or earls, a very large class of freemen, a smaller class of slaves, and a very small class of semi-free men or serfs. Freemen were the most common people in early German society. They recognized no religious or political authority over their own activities, except to a very limited degree. As *free* men, they could, if they desired, settle their accounts with their neighbors and move to another geographical location. Each freeman occupied a large amount of land, his freehold farmstead, on which he grazed animals and, with the help of his slaves, grew crops. When necessary, he joined together with other freemen for defense or, more often, for the conquest of new territories.[1]

Freemen were the key to German expansion. When overcrowding occurred in clan villages and little unoccupied land remained, freemen moved to the border and with other freemen defeated and drove away the neighboring people. Here they established for themselves their own freehold farmsteads. Their descendants then multiplied and occupied the vacant land between the original freehold estates. When land was no longer available, clan villages began to form again and many freemen moved on once more to the new borders to start new freehold farmsteads. In this way, the Germans slowly but surely moved onward across northern and central Europe with freemen leading the way until no more land was available.

Strictly speaking, a freeman did not own his land. The idea of landownership in the modern sense was still many centuries away. In England, for example, landowning did not become a political and legal reality until 1660 when feudal dues were finally abolished once and for all. Freemen, however, lived in prefeudal times. They usually made a yearly offering to the local

noble or earl, but technically this offering was a gift rather than a feudal payment and had nothing to do with their right to their land. As the term *freehold* suggests, a freeman held his land freely without any forced obligations to an overlord or to his neighbors.

In early times, when land was readily available, each freeman occupied as much land as he needed. There was no set amount that a freeman ought to have and no limit on his holdings, except that he could not hold more land than he could use. Thus, in effect, his personal dominion was restricted only by the number of animals that he had available for grazing and the number of slaves he had for agricultural labor. Sometimes, when the land began to lose its fertility, he would abandon his holdings and move to some other unoccupied location nearby. The exact location of each holding was only vaguely determined, and when disputes arose about boundaries, they were settled with the help of the testimony of neighbors or, when that failed, by armed combat between the parties involved.

Much of the unoccupied land was held in common with other freemen in accordance with various local arrangements. Sometimes the use was regulated by establishing the number of cattle that each freeman could place on the land. In other cases, plots were used by different freeman every year on a rotational basis.

When occupied border lands were no longer available for new freemen to settle, the way of life of the freemen began to change. The primary problem was one of inheritance. In the beginning, land had never been divided; rather, it has always been "multiplied" as sons moved to adjacent areas and established new freehold farmsteads. Eventually, however, it became necessary for the sons to divide the land which had been held by their father. A serious problem then developed, for, if division took place too many times, then the holdings became so small that they had little economic value, and the family as a whole slipped into poverty.

The solution was *entail,* i.e., inheritance along selected family lines. The most common form of entail was *primogeniture,* according to which the eldest son inherited everything and the others little or nothing. In this way, the family head remained powerful by keeping his landholdings intact, but most of his brothers were condemned to the semifree and poverty-stricken life of serfdom. As a result of these new inheritance practices, the number of freemen became an increasingly smaller portion of the society as a whole as most of the rest of the population, relatives included, rapidly sank to the level of serfs.

Another problem affecting freemen was taxation. The custom of giving an offering to the local noble was gradually replaced by a tax, and once established, taxes often became large burdens on many of the poorer freemen who in many instances paid taxes while other richer landholders were exempted. In such circumstances, freemen often gave up their status and their lands to persons exempted from the taxes and paid a smaller sum in rent as tenants.

Germans thus made a transition from prefeudal to feudal conditions, and freemen ceased to be an important element in the community as a whole. While freemen never disappeared altogether, most lost the economic freedom that they had formerly had. Although theoretically free to move about as they pleased, they often lacked the economic means of settling their accounts, and so in most cases were little better off than the serfs.

These feudal conditions did not appear in England until long after they were firmly established in Europe. At the time of the conquest of England by William the Conqueror most Englishmen were freemen. Thus, in England, unlike in Germanic Europe, prefeudal conditions did not slip away gradually but were abruptly replaced by a feudal system imposed on much of the native population by the victorious Normans. Under such circumstances, freemen declined in numbers, but struggled as best they could to maintain their freeman status in opposition to Norman rule and as a part of their Saxon heritage. As a result, freemen managed to maintain a presence in England no longer conceivable in Europe. Through them, memories of the heyday of the flamboyant Saxon freemen remained to shade political thought and to shape land use attitudes for centuries after the conquest. Ironically, the conquest drew attention to a class status which might otherwise have quietly passed away.

There were four major political divisions in Saxon England: the kingdom, the shire (called the *county* after the arrival of the Normans), the hundred, and the township, the last two being subdivisions of the shire or county. Throughout English history the exact nature of the government of the kingdom fluctuated, sometimes very radically. Changes occurred in the hundreds and the townships as the courts at these levels were gradually replaced by those of the local nobility, probably with the support of the government of the kingdom. The shire or county and its court or moot, however, persisted unchanged and continued to be one of the most important political units from the earliest Saxon times in England to the present day in both England and the United States.

The county court met to deal with cases not already handled by the hundred moots and with other business of common importance to the community. The meetings were conducted by three men: the alderman, representing the shire; the sheriff, representing the king; and the bishop, representing the church. All freemen in the county had the right to attend the court and participate in the decision process. Most of them, of course, were usually too busy to come except when personal interests were at stake.

There are only small differences between the county courts of Saxon and Norman times and those of modern rural America. The three judges, alderman, sheriff, and bishop, have been replaced by elected judges. Court procedure in most of these courts, however, remain as informal today as it was in pre-Norman England. In many, no record is kept by the court of its decisions and, in such cases, except for word of mouth and intermittent coverage by the news media, little is known of what goes on there. Court judges are primarily concerned with keeping the local landowners contented by resolving local differences and by providing the few community services under the administrative jurisdiction of the court, e.g., maintaining dirt or gravel roads. This casual form of government is replaced only when the county becomes urbanized, thereby, enabling residents to incorporate it and enjoy extensive new administrative and legal powers and, of course, responsibilities.

The special considerations given to the local landowner by the modern rural county court reflects the relationship of Saxon freemen to the court at the time when such courts first came into existence. The court evolved out of the freemen's custom of consulting with his neighbors during local disputes as an alternative to physical combat between the parties involved. Thus, rather than being something imposed on the freemen from above, the court was created by them for their own convenience. Since the freemen gave up little or none of their personal power, the power of the court to enforce its decisions was really nothing more than the collective power of the freemen ultimately comprising the membership of the court. From the earliest times, freemen had had absolute control over all matters pertaining to their own landholdings. When county courts were formed, freemen retained this authority over what they considered to be their own personal affairs. This limitation on the power of the court was maintained for more than a thousand years as part of the traditional conception of what a county court is, and how it is supposed to function. Today, when a landowner demands to know what right the court or anyone else has to tell him what to do with his own land he is referring to the original limitations set on the authority of the county court, and is appealing to the rights which he has informally inherited from his political ancestors, Saxon or German freemen—specifically, the right to do as he pleases without considering any interests except his own.

A modern landowner's argument that he has the right to do as he wishes is normally composed of a set series of claims given in a specific order. First, he points out that he or his father or grandfather worked the land in question. Second, he asserts that his ownership of the land is based on the work or labor put into it. Finally, he proclaims the right of uncontrolled use as a result of his ownership claim. Not all of this argument is derived directly from the freemen's world view. As mentioned above, the modern concept of ownership was unknown to freemen who were engaged in landholding rather than landowning. In other respects, however, there are strong similarities between the views of modern landowners and those of the freemen.

Landholding among German freemen was based on work. A freeman, like the nineteenth-century American homesteader, took possession of a tract of land by clearing it, building a house and barns, and dividing the land into fields for the grazing of animals and for the growing of crops. In this way, his initial work established his claim to continued use.

This emphasis on work as the basis for landholding is especially clear in connection with inheritance. When plenty of vacant land was available, landholdings were never divided among the sons, but, as described above, the sons moved to unoccupied land nearby and started their own freehold farmsteads. Thus, inheritance in those early times was not the acquisition of land itself but rather the transferral of the right to acquire land through work. This distinction is reflected in the early German word for inheritance, *Arbi* in Gothic and *Erbi* in Old High German, both of which have the same root as the modern High German word *Arbeit,* meaning work.[2]

Thus freemen were interested in land use rather than landownership. The right to land was determined by their social status as freemen and not by the fact that they or their fathers had occupied or possessed a particular piece of ground. The specific landholdings, thus, were not of major importance to the early freemen. Conceivably, they might move several times to new landholdings abandoning the old without the size of their landholdings being affected in any way. As mentioned above, it was their ability to use their holdings, the number of grazing animals, and slave workers they owned, not some form of ownership, which determined the size of their landholdings at any particular time in their lives.

Of course, once unoccupied land ceased to be readily available, freemen started paying much more attention to their land as property, encouraging the development of the idea of landownership in the modern sense. When the inheritance of sons became only the right to work a portion of their father's holdings, the transition from landholding to landowning was well on its way.

Until the time when there were no more unoccupied lands to move to, there was really no reason for freemen to be concerned with proper use or management of their land or for them to worry about possible long-term problems for themselves or their neighbors resulting from misuse and abuse of particular pieces of land. When a freeman lost his mobility, however, he did start trying to take somewhat better care of his land, occasionally practicing crop rotation and planting trees to replace those he cut down, but apparently these new necessities had little influence on his general conviction that as a freeman he had the right to use and even abuse his land as he saw fit.

Today's rural landowner finds himself in a situation not unlike that of freemen in the days when inheritance became the division of land rather than the multiplication of it. In the late eighteenth century and during most of the nineteenth, American rural landowners led a way of life much like that of prefeudal German freemen; now modern landowners face the same limitations their freemen ancestors did as feudal conditions began to develop. Although willing to take some steps toward good land management, especially those which provide obvious short-term benefit, when faced with broader issues involving the welfare of their neighbors and the local community and the protection and the preservation of the environment as a whole, they claim ancient rights which have come down to them from German freemen, and take advantage of their special influence with the local county court, a political institution as eager to please them today as it was more than a thousand years ago.

THOMAS JEFFERSON AND THE ALLODIAL RIGHTS OF AMERICAN FARMERS

When British colonists arrived in North America, they brought with them the land laws and land practices that were current in England at that time. These included entail, primogeniture, and most other aspects of the feudal tenure system which had taken hold in England after the Norman Conquest. The American Revolution called into question the right of the king of England to lands in North America which in turn led to attempts to bring about major land reform—specifically, efforts to remove all elements of the feudal system from American law and practice and replace them with the older Saxon freehold tenure system. At the forefront of this movement was a young Virginian lawyer named Thomas Jefferson. . . .

From the first moment that Jefferson began airing his land tenure opinions, however, he made it completely clear that they were based entirely on Saxon, and not on Norman, common law. Thus, he consistently spoke of allodial rights—*allodial* being the adjectival form of the Old English word *allodium* which refers to an estate held in absolute dominion without obligation to a superior—i.e., the early Germany and Saxon freehold farmstead. . . .

Noting the right of a Saxon freeman to settle his accounts and move to another realm at his own pleasure without obligation to the lord of his previous domain, Jefferson argues that this is also the case with the British citizens who moved to North America. According to this analogy, England has no more claim over residents of America than Germany has over residents of England. In accordance with Saxon tradition, the lands of North America belong to the people living there and not to the king of England.[3] . . .

It is not the king, Jefferson declares, but the individual members of a society collectively or their legislature that determine the legal status of land, and, if they fail to act, then, in accordance with the traditions of Saxon freemen, "each individual of the society may appropriate to himself such lands as he finds vacant, and occupancy will give him title."[4] . . . Jefferson, of course, did not succeed in refuting the claim of the king of England to all land in British America, but by arguing in terms of this old dispute, he gives his position a legal basis which would have strong appeal among Englishmen with Saxon backgrounds, assuring some political support of the American cause in England.

In 1776, Jefferson got the opportunity to try to turn his theory into practice. Although Jefferson is most famous for writing the *Declaration of Independence,* most of his time that year was spent working on his draft of the Virginia constitution and on the reform of various Virginia laws including the land reform laws. In his draft constitution, Jefferson included a provision which gave each person of full age the right to fifty acres of land "in full and absolute dominion." In addition, lands previously "holden of the crown in feesimple" and all other lands appropriated in the future were to be "holden in full and absolute dominion, of no superior whatever.''[5] Although these provisions were deleted, and similar bills submitted to the legislature failed to pass, Jefferson, nevertheless, did succeed in getting the legislature to abolish the feudal inheritance laws, entail and primogeniture. . . .

As for the government selling the land, Jefferson was completely opposed. ''I am against selling the land at all,'' he writes to Pendleton, ''By selling the lands to them, you will disgust them, and cause an avulsion of them from the common union. They will settle the lands in spite of every body.'' This prediction proved to be remarkably correct as evidenced by the fact that the next eighty years of American history was cluttered with squatters illegally occupying government land and then demanding compensation for their ''improvements'' through special preemption laws.[6]

In 1784, when he was appointed to head the land committee in the Congress of the Confederacy, Jefferson had a second opportunity to reestablish the Saxon landholding system. Whether Jefferson tried to take advantage of this opportunity is not known because the report of the committee, called the Ordinance of 1784, contains nothing about allodial rights to land. In addition, it even contains recommendations for the selling of western lands as a source of revenue for the government. It should be noted, however, that in one respect at least the document still has a very definite Saxon ring to it. Jefferson managed to include in his report a recommendation that settlers be permitted to organize themselves into new states on an equal footing with the original colonies. This recommendation, which was retained in the Ordinance of 1787, a revised version of the earlier ordinance, not only created the political structure necessary to turn the thirteen colonies into a much larger union of states, but also provided future generations of Americans with an independence and mobility similar to that enjoyed by the early Saxon and German freemen. In his *Summary View* of 1774, as mentioned above, Jefferson had argued that just as the Saxons invading England had had the right to set up an independent government, so British Americans had the right to an independent government in North America. The Ordinances of 1784 and 1787 extended his right to movement and self-determination of American set-

tlers leaving the jurisdiction of established states and moving into the interior of the continent. In large measure, it is thanks to this provision that Americans today are able to move from state to state without any governmental control in the form of visas, passports, immigration quotas, or the like as unhassled by such details as were early German freemen.

The absence of any provisions specifically granting landowners full and absolute dominion over their land, however, does not mean that Jefferson abandoned this conception of landholding or ownership. Privately and in his published writings he continued to champion the right of Americans to small freehold farmsteads. The only major change seems to be that Jefferson stopped trying to justify his position in terms of historical precedents and instead began speaking in moral terms claiming that small independent landholders were the most virtuous citizens any state could ever hope to have. In a letter to John Jay in 1785, Jefferson writes:

> Cultivators of the earth are the most valuable citizens. They are the most vigorous, the most independent, the most virtuous, and they are tied to their country and wedded to it's liberty and interests by the most lasting bands.[7]

In a letter to James Madison in the same year, he adds:

> Whenever there is in any country, uncultivated lands and unemployed poor, it is clear that the laws of property have been so far extended as to violate natural right. The earth is given as a common stock for man to labour and live on. If, for the encouragement of industry we allow it to be appropriated, we must take care that other employment be furnished to those excluded from that appropriation. If we do not the fundamental right to labour the earth returns to the unemployed. It is too soon yet in our country to say that every man who cannot find employment but who can find uncultivated land, shall be at liberty to cultivate it, paying a moderate rent. But it is not too soon to provide by every possible means that as few as possible shall be without a little portion of land. The small landholders are the most precious part of the state.[8]

. . . These remarks are probably . . . the basis for the position of rural landowners today when faced with environmental issues. They are defending the American moral virtues which they have always been told their style of life and independence represents.

Had Jefferson been alive in the late nineteenth century when his views were being cited in opposition to the preservation of Yellowstone or were he alive today to see his Saxon freemen busily sabotaging county planning and zoning, he might have become disillusioned with his faith in the virtues of independent rural landowners. Jefferson, after all, as a result of his purchase of the Natural Bridge, perhaps the first major act of nature preservation in North America, ranks as a very important figure in the history of the nature preservation movement. Unfortunately, however, Jefferson's homesteaders and their modern day descendants did not always retain his aesthetic interest in nature or his respect for sound agricultural management which he interwove with his Saxon land use attitudes to form a balanced land use philosophy.

In part, the callousness and indifference of most rural landowners to environmental matters reflects the insensitivity of ancient Saxon freemen who viewed land as something to be used for personal benefit and who, being semi-nomadic, were unconcerned about whether that use would result in irreparable damage to the particular piece of land that they held at any given point in their lives. In addition, however, it can also be traced back to the political philosophy and theory of property of John Locke, a seventeenth-century British philosopher, who had a major impact on the political views of Jefferson and most other American statesmen during the American Revolution and afterwards. This influence is the subject of the next section.

JOHN LOCKE'S THEORY OF PROPERTY

As noted above, German and Saxon freemen did not have a concept of landownership, but only of landholding. As long as there was plenty of land for everyone's use, they did not concern themselves with exact boundaries. Disputes arose only when two freemen wanted to use the same land at the same time. By the end of the Middle Ages, however, with land in short supply, landholders began enclosing their landholdings to help ensure exclusive use. Enclosure kept the grazing animals of others away and also provided a

sign of the landholder's presence and authority. Although enclosure was only a small step towards the concept of landownership, it, nonetheless, proved useful as a pseudo-property concept in early seventeenth-century New England where Puritans were able to justify their occupation of Indian lands on the grounds that the lack of enclosures demonstrated that the lands were vacant. Landownership became an official legal distinction in England after 1660 with the abolishment of feudal dues. The concept of landownership was introduced into British social and political philosophy thirty years later as part of John Locke's theory of property. This theory was presented in detail in Locke's *Two Treatises of Government,* a major work in political philosophy first published in 1690.[9]

Jefferson had immense respect and admiration for Locke and his philosophical writings. On one occasion, he wrote to a friend that Locke was one of the three greatest men that had ever lived—Bacon and Newton being the other two. Jefferson's justification of the American Revolution in "The Declaration of Independence" was borrowed directly from the *Second Treatise.* Many of Jefferson's statements in the document are almost identical to remarks made by Locke. For example, when Jefferson speaks of "life, liberty, and the pursuit of happiness," he is closely paraphrasing Locke's own views. His version differs from Locke's in only one minor respect: Jefferson substitutes for Locke's "enjoyment of property" the more general phrase "the pursuit of happiness," a slight change made to recognize other enjoyments in addition to those derived from the ownership of property. . . .

In the *Second Treatise* Locke bases property rights on the labor of the individual:

> Though the Earth, and all inferior Creatures be common to all Men, yet, every Man has a *Property* in his own *Person.* This no Body has any Right to but himself. The *Labour* of his Body, and the *Work* of his Hands, we may say, are properly his. Whatsoever then he removes out of the State that Nature hath provided, and left in, he hath mixed his *Labour* with, and joyned to it something that is his own, and thereby makes it his *Property.*[10]

This theory of property served Locke's friends well since it made their property rights completely independent of all outside interest. According to Locke, property rights are established without reference to kings, governments, or even the collective rights of other people. If a man mixes his labour with a natural object, then the product is his.

The relevance of Locke's labor theory to the American homestead land use philosophy becomes especially clear when he turns to the subject of land as property:

> But the *chief matter of Property* being now not the Fruits of the Earth, and the Beasts that subsist on it, but the *Earth it self* as that which takes in and carries with it all the rest; I think it is plain, that *Property* in that too is acquired as the former. *As much land* as a Man Tills, Plants, Improves, Cultivates, and can use the Product of, so much is his *Property.* He by his Labour does, as it were, inclose it from the Common. . . . God, when He gave the World in common to all Mankind, commanded Man also to labour, and the penury of his Condition required it of him. God and his Reason commanded him to subdue the Earth, *i.e.* improve it for the benefit of Life, and therein lay out something upon it that was his own, his labour. He that in Obedience to this Command of God, subdued, tilled, sowed any part of it, thereby annexed to it something that was his *Property,* which another had no Title to, nor could without injury take from him.[11]

In this passage, the right of use and ownership is determined by the farmer's labor. When he mixes his labor with the land, the results are *improvements,* the key term in homesteading days and even today in rural America where the presence of such improvements may qualify landowners for exemption from planning and zoning under a grandfather clause. Since property rights are established on an individual basis independent of a social context, Locke's theory of property also provides the foundation for the landowner's claim that society has little or no role in the management of his land, that nobody has the right to tell him what to do with his property.

Locke reenforces the property owner's independence from societal restraints with an account of the origins of society in which property rights are supposedly more fundamental than society itself. According to Locke, the right to the enjoyment of prop-

erty is a presocietal *natural right.* It is a natural right because it is a right which a person would have in a state of nature. Locke claims that there was once, at some time in the distant past, a true state of nature in which people possessed property as a result of their labor, but, nevertheless, did not yet have societal relations with one another. This state of nature disappeared when these ancient people decided to form a society, thereby giving up some of their previous powers and rights. They did not, however, Locke emphatically insists, relinquish any of their natural rights to their own property, and the original social contract establishing the society did not give society any authority at all over personal property. In fact, the main reason that society was formed, according to Locke's account, was to make it possible for individuals to enjoy their own property rights more safely and securely. Thus, society's primary task was and allegedly still is to protect private property rights, not to infringe on them. A government which attempts to interfere with an individual's natural and uncontrolled right to the enjoyment of his property, moreover, deserves to be overthrown and the citizens of the society are free to do so at their pleasure. In effect, Locke is arguing along lines completely compatible with the early Saxon and Jeffersonian doctrine that a landowner holds his property in full and absolute dominion without any obligation to a superior.

The similarity of Locke's position to this doctrine invites the conclusion that Locke, like Jefferson, was drawing inspiration from Saxon common law and that Locke's social contract was actually the establishment of the shire or county court by Saxon freemen. Curiously, however, Locke makes no mention of the Saxons in these contexts and, even more curiously, no political philosopher ever seems to have considered the possibility that Locke might have been referring to this period of English history. In his chapter on conquest, nevertheless, Locke does demonstrate (1) that he knew what a freeman was, (2) that he was aware of the legal conflicts resulting from the Norman Conquest, and (3) that he sided with the Saxons in that controversy. In the one paragraph where he mentions the Saxons by name, he flippantly remarks that, even if they did lose their rights as freemen at the time of the conquest, as a result of the subsequent six centuries of intermarriage all Englishmen of Locke's day could claim freeman status through some Norman ancestor and it would "be very hard to prove the contrary."[12] Locke may have chosen not to mention the specifics of Saxon history fearing that if he did so, his political philosophy might have been treated as nothing more than just another call for a return to Saxon legal precedents. It is hard to imagine, nonetheless, that Locke's readers in the seventeenth century were not aware of these unstated connections considering the ease with which Jefferson saw them eighty years later in colonial North America. It is also possible, of course, that Locke may have been ignorant of the details of Saxon common law and may have simply relied on the popular land use attitudes of his day without being aware of their Saxon origin. At any rate, however, the ultimate result would be the same—a political philosophy which provides philosophical foundations for the ancient Saxon land use attitudes and traditions. . . .

Not everyone in the first half of the nineteenth century shared Jefferson's enthusiasm for land reform based on Saxon common law modified by Locke's theory of property, and for a time the idea of landholding independent of landowning continued to be influential in American political and legal thought. Early versions of the homestead bill before the beginning of the Civil War, for example, often contained inalienability and reversion clauses. According to these, a homesteader had the right to use the land, but could not subdivide it, sell it, or pass it on to his children after his death. These limitations, however, were not compatible with the wishes of potential homesteaders who wanted to be landowners, not just landholders, and, as a result, they were not included in the Homestead Act of 1862. It is unlikely that homesteading based entirely on Saxon common law ever had much chance of passing Congress because early nineteenth-century settlers squatting illegally on Western lands and demanding the enactment of special preemption laws had always had landownership as their primary objective.[13]

Because it was probably Locke's theory of property as much as Saxon common law which encour-

aged American citizens and immigrants to move westward, both should be given a share of the credit for the rapid settlement of the American West which ultimately established a national claim to all the lands west of the Appalachians as far as the Pacific. This past benefit to the American people, nevertheless, should not be the only standard for evaluating this doctrine's continuing value. We must still ask just how well the position is suited to conditions in twentieth-century America.

MODERN DIFFICULTIES WITH LOCKE'S POSITION

One obvious problem with Locke's theory today is his claim that there is enough land for everyone.[14] This premise is of fundamental importance to Locke's argument because, if a present or future shortage of land can be established, then any appropriation of land past or present under the procedure Locke recommends, enclosure from the common through labor, is an injustice to those who must remain unpropertied. By Locke's own estimates there was twice as much land at the end of the seventeenth century as all the inhabitants of the Earth could use. To support these calculations Locke pointed to the "in-land, vacant places of America"—places which are now occupied.[15] Since Locke's argument depends on a premise which is now false, Locke would have great difficulty advancing and justifying his position today.

Another problem is Locke's general attitude toward uncultivated land. Locke places almost no value on such land before it is improved and after improvement he says the labor is still the chief factor in any value assessment:

> . . . when any one hath computed, he will then see, how much *labour makes the far greatest part of the value* of things we enjoy in this World: And the ground which produces the materials, is scarce to be reckon'd in, as any, or at most, but a very small part of it; So little, that even amongst us, Land that is left wholly to Nature, that hath no improvement of Pasturage, Tillage, or Planting, is called, as indeed it is, *waste* and we shall find the benefit of it amount to little more than nothing.

According to Locke's calculations, 99 to 99.9 percent of the value of land even after it is improved still results from the labor and not the land. Although these absurdly high figures helped strengthen Locke's claim that labor establishes property rights over land, by making it seem that it is primarily the individual's labor mixed with the land rather than the land itself which is owned, such estimates, if presented today, would be considered scientifically false and contrary to common sense.[16]

Locke's land-value attitudes reflect a general desire prevalent in Locke's time as well as today for maximum agricultural productivity. From Locke's point of view, it was inefficient to permit plants and animals to grow naturally on uncultivated land:

> . . . I ask whether in the wild woods and uncultivated waste of America left to Nature, without any improvement, tillage, or husbandry, a thousand acres will yield the needy and wretched inhabitants as many conveniences of life as ten acres of equally fertile land doe in Devonshire where they are well cultivated?[17]

The problem, however, is not just productivity and efficiency, but also a general contempt for the quality of the natural products of the Earth. Locke writes with great conviction that ''*Bread* is more worth than Acorns, *Wine* than Water, and *Cloth* or *Silk* than Leaves, Skins or Moss.''[18] Even though we might be inclined to agree with Locke's pronouncements in certain contexts, the last two hundred years of the American experience have provided us with new attitudes incompatible with those of Locke and his contemporaries, and apparently completely unknown to them, which place high value on trees, water, animals, and even land itself in a wholly natural and unimproved condition. Unlike Locke, we do not always consider wilderness land or uncultivated land synonymous with waste.

At the very core of Locke's land-value attitudes is his belief that ''the Earth, and all that is therein, is given to Men for the Support and Comfort of their being.'' In one sense, this view is very old, derived from the biblical and Aristotelian claims that the Earth exists for the benefit and use of human beings. At the same time, it is very modern because of Locke's twin emphasis on labor and consumption. Both of these activities are of central importance in communistic and capitalistic political systems, and they became so important precisely because the founders and ideologists of each system originally took their ideas about labor and consumption from Locke's philosophy. In accordance with these ideas, the Earth is nothing more than raw materials waiting to be transformed by labor into consumable products. The Greeks and Romans would have objected to this view on the grounds that labor and consumption are too low and demeaning to be regarded as primary human activities.[19] From a twentieth-century standpoint, given the current emphasis on consumption, the neglect of the aesthetic and scientific (ecological) value of nature seems to be a more fundamental and serious objection to this exploitative view.

The worst result of Locke's property theory is the amoral or asocial attitude which has evolved out of it. Locke's arguments have encouraged landowners to behave in an antisocial manner and to claim that they have no moral obligation to the land itself, or even to the other people in the community who may be affected by what they do with their land. This amoral attitude, which has been noted with dismay by Aldo Leopold, Garrett Hardin, and others, can be traced directly to Locke's political philosophy, even though Locke himself may not have intended to create this effect. The reasons why this moral apathy developed are complex.

First, the divine rights of kings had just been abolished. In accordance with this doctrine, the king had had *ultimate* and *absolute* property rights over all the land in his dominion. He could do whatever he wanted with this land—give it away, take it back, use it himself, or even destroy it as he saw fit. Locke's new theory of property stripped the king of this power and authority and transferred these *ultimate* and *absolute* rights to each and every ordinary property owner. This transfer has been a moral disaster in large part because the king's rights involved moral elements which did not carry over to the new rights of the private landowner. As God's agent on Earth, the king was morally obligated to adhere to the highest standards of right and wrong. Furthermore, the king, as the ruler of the land, had a moral and political obligation to consider the general welfare of his entire kingdom whenever he acted. Of course, kings did not always behave as they should have, but, nevertheless, there were standards recognized by these kings and their subjects as to what constituted proper and kingly moral behavior. Private landowners, however, did not inherit these sorts of obligations. Because they were not instruments of church or state, the idea that they should have moral obligations limiting their actions with regard to their own property does not seem to have come up. The standard which landowners adopted to guide their actions was a purely selfish and egotistical one. Because it involved nothing more than the economic interest of the individual, it was devoid of moral obligation or moral responsibility. . . .

Theoretically, Locke's qualification of the right to destroy property is compatible with the American conception of checks and balances and it might have provided a *political* solution to the problem, though not a moral one. Unfortunately, however, it has not been carried over into our political and legal system as successfully as the right to destroy. A man certainly has a right in the United States to sue for damages in court after the fact, when the actions of others have clearly injured him or his property, but the right of the government to take preventive action before the damage is done has not been effectively established. It is this preventive action which private landowners are assailing when they assert their right to use and even destroy their land as they see fit without any outside interference. The success of landowners in this area is amply demonstrated by the great reluctance of most state legislatures to place waste management restrictions on small private *landowners* which have long governed the activities of rural land *developers.*

Government regulation of individual private landowners has been ineffective historically because, from the very beginnings of American government, representation at state and federal levels has nearly always been based on landownership, an approach which has usually assured rural control of the legislature even when most of the citizens in the state lived in urban population centers. Government leaders in-

tent on acting primarily in the interests of landowners could hardly have been expected to play the preventive role which Locke recommends. The unwillingness of legislators to act in this way in the nineteenth century and most of the twentieth, moreover, further contributed to the amoral belief of rural landowners that they can do whatever they want without being concerned about the welfare or rights of others.

When Jefferson attempted to build American society on a Lockeian foundation of small landowners, he did so in large measure because he believed that small landowners would make the most virtuous citizens. He failed to foresee, however, that the independence provided by Locke's presocietal natural rights would discourage rather than encourage social responsibility, and, therefore, would contribute little to the development of moral character in American landowners. Since social responsibility is basic to our conception of morality today, the claim of landowners that their special rights relieve them of any obligation or responsibility to the community can be regarded only as both socially and morally reprehensible. The position of such rural landowners is analogous to that of a tyrannical king. Tyranny is always justified, when it is justified at all, by a claim that the tyrant has the *right* to do as he pleases regardless of the consequences. In practice, however, the impact of rural landowners more closely approaches anarchy than tyranny, but only because landowners, though sharing a common desire to preserve their special rights, do not always have common economic interests. As a result, landowners are usually more willing to promote the theoretical rights of their fellow property owners than their specific land use and development projects, which as members of society, they may find objectionable or even despicable—in spite of their Saxon and Lockeian heritage rather than because of it.

A landowner cannot justify his position morally except with the extravagant claim that his actions are completely independent and beyond any standard of right and wrong—a claim which Locke, Jefferson, and even Saxon freemen would probably have hesitated to make. Actually, there is only one precedent for such a claim. During the Middle Ages, church philosophers concluded that God was independent of all moral standards. They felt compelled to take this position because moral limitations of God's actions would have conflicted with His omnipotence. Therefore, they reasoned that God's actions created moral law—i.e., defined moral law—and that theoretically moral law could be radically changed at any moment. Descartes held this position in the seventeenth century, and in the nineteenth and twentieth centuries some atheistic existential philosophers have argued that because God is dead each man is now forced to create his own values through his individual actions. Although this position could be adopted as a defense of the landowners's extraordinary amoral rights, it would probably be distasteful to most landowners. Without it, this aspect of the rural landowners' position may be indefensible.[20]

Today, of course, whenever Locke's theory of property and the heritage of the ancient Saxon freeman surface in county courts, at planning and zoning meetings, and at state and federal hearings on conservation and land management, they still remain a formidable obstacle to constructive political action. As they are normally presented, however, they are certainly not an all-purpose answer to our environmental problems or even a marginally adequate reply to environmental criticism. When a landowner voices a Lockeian argument he is consciously or unconsciously trying to evade the land management issues at hand and to shift attention instead to the dogmatic recitation of his special rights as a property owner.

As I noted above, some of Locke's fundamental assumptions and attitudes are either demonstrably false or no longer generally held even among landowners. These difficulties need to be ironed out before the landowners can claim that they are really answering their environmental critics. Furthermore it is likely that, even if the position can be and is modernized, the moral issues will still be unresolved.

As it stands, the force of the rural landowners' arguments depends on their historical associations—their Biblical trappings, the echoes of Locke's political philosophy, the Saxon common-law tradition, the feudal doctrine of the divine rights of kings, and the spirit of the nineteenth-century American land laws.

Can they be modernized? That remains to be seen. Until they are, however, landowners, environmentalists, politicians, and ordinary citizens should regard them with some suspicion.

NOTES

1. The account given in this section is based most directly on Denman W. Ross, *The Early History of Land-Holding Among the Germans* (Boston: Soule and Bugbee, 1883), and Walter Phelps Hall, Robert Greenhalgh Albion, and Jennie Barnes Pope, *A History of England and the Empire-Commonwealth,* 4th ed. (Boston: Ginn and Company, 1961).
2. Ross, *Land-Holding,* p. 24.
3. Thomas Jefferson, ''A Summary View of the Rights of British America,'' in *The Portable Thomas Jefferson,* ed. Merrill D. Peterson (New York: Viking Press, 1975), pp. 4-5.
4. Ibid., pp. 17-19.
5. Thomas Jefferson, ''Draft Constitution for Virginia,'' in *Portable Jefferson,* p. 248.
6. Jefferson to Edmund Pendleton, 13 August 1776, in *Papers of Thomas Jefferson,* 1: 492.
7. Jefferson to John Jay, 23 August 1785, in *Portable Jefferson,* p. 384.
8. Jefferson to James Madison, 28 October 1785, in *Portable Jefferson,* p. 397.
9. John Locke, *Two Treatises of Government,* ed. Thomas I. Cook (New York and London: Hafner Press, 1947).
10. Locke, *Second Treatise,* sec. 27.
11. Ibid., sec. 32.
12. Ibid., sec. 177.
13. Paul W. Gates, *History of Public Land Law Development* (Washington D.C.: Public Land Law Commission, 1968), pp. 390-393.
14. Locke, *Second Treatise,* sec. 33.
15. Ibid., sec. 36.
16. Ibid., secs. 42-43.
17. Ibid., sec. 37.
18. Ibid., sec. 42.
19. Ibid., sec. 26; for a full discussion of labor and consumption see Hannah Arendt, *The Human Condition* (Chicago and London: University of Chicago Press, 1958), chap. 3.
20. Jean-Paul Sartre, *Existentialism and Human Emotions* (New York: Philosophical Library, 1957), pp. 13-18.

DISCUSSION TOPICS

1. In what ways is the policy of primogeniture fair or unfair? What policy might be better?
2. How important should historical precedents be in determining the laws governing land use today? What other factors should be considered?
3. John Locke proposed that property rights should be based primarily on the investment of a person's labor. Is that philosophy still valid today? Explain. If not, what is a better approach?

Nature in Industrial Society

Neil Evernden

Lorne Leslie Neil Evernden is on the Faculty of Environmental Studies, Department of Environmental Science, York University, Downsview, Ontario, Canada. He also has written The Natural Alien, *a critique of the philosophies in the environmental movement.*

Evernden analyzes variations in definitions of nature commonly used in industrial society. He notes that nature has been defined according to the different values predominating in society and that the connotations which prevail strongly affect people's ideas about what constitutes proper behavior toward nature.

Evernden explores three definitions of nature. The perception of "nature-as-object," a connotation consistent with humanistic and technocratic assumptions in Western society, results in exploitation of nature. The view of "nature-as-self" implies the extension of a separate selfhood to nature; this view allows thinking about environmental ethics and rights of nature. Evernden believes that Aldo Leopold's land ethic reflects this conception. Finally, the perception of "nature-as-miracle" counters the more traditional assumptions about nature's homogeneous and predictable qualities by emphasizing its uncanny and unpredictable characteristics. In contrast to traditional scientific conceptions of nature, Evernden proposes that the

"nature-as-miracle" definition allows an understanding compatible with human experience. He suggests that this view may be an essential element in the process of changing the human relationship with nature.

Evernden proposes that Rachel Carson's success in challenging conventional notions about controlling nature resulted from her calling attention back to the larger support systems on which human survival depends, and to the human repercussions of environmental abuse. However, by focusing on an enlightened self-interest definition of nature as full of objects important to human well-being (nature-as-object), Evernden contends that Carson abandoned the view of a personal nature that was intrinsically valuable (nature-as-self).

Nature, to all appearances, remains remarkably "popular" in America. It is part of everyone's vocabulary, something we all have knowledge of and opinions about, and something many are moved to defend. Nature is very much a part of "popular culture." But *which* nature?

The question seems nonsensical, of course. There is nature, and there is culture, separate and distinct from each other. But while we acknowledge that we do not all dwell in the same culture or subculture, it is seldom acknowledged that we might not all share the same nature or "subnature." So firmly embedded is the notion of nature as a unitary entity, entirely separate from or even antithetical to, culture, that it is very difficult to entertain the notion of there being more than one understanding of nature. (Arthur Lovejoy once listed 66 uses of the word "nature" in politics, ethics, and metaphysics, and another 20 as used in aesthetics.)[1] In colloquial usage, nature is often simply "the world as given," the force that determines the way things are as well as the clutter of objects that we see interspersed between the "developments" of civilization. In the latter sense, it is nearly synonymous with "environment," or at least with "natural environment," and the "environmental movement" is widely understood as a defense of nature. However, in recent years the very prominence of that movement has been the cause of some reflection on just what this "nature" is that is being defended. As a result, it is becoming increasingly clear that people do not always have the same thing in mind when they speak of nature. This might be most easily illustrated by reviewing one of the success stories of the environmental movement.

[The year] 1987 marks the anniversary of one of the most remarkable incidents in the history of nature preservation in America, and indeed the world. In 1962, a biologist named Rachel Carson made a brave and inspired decision to try a different means of defending nature. The result was a book called *Silent Spring,* which evoked a reaction that has never entirely subsided. To the surprise of many, the resulting ''environmental movement'' has endured remarkably well, and most people still rank environmental issues above all others in importance. Yet it is doubtful whether, twenty-five years ago, they would have been concerned at all. Rachel Carson changed all that when she challenged our collective right to manipulate nature at will. ''Control of nature,'' she said, ''is a phrase conceived in arrogance, born in the Neanderthal age of biology and philosophy, when it was supposed that nature exists for the convenience of man.''[2] But isn't ''control of nature'' what our civilization is principally concerned with? Did Carson genuinely challenge that assumption? Or did she merely wish to?

Although Rachel Carson had spent her life in the defense of nature, she concentrated in *Silent Spring* on one problem only: the widespread and indiscriminate use of pesticides. Her challenge drew the inevitable response from those whose oxen were being gored, and she suffered considerably as a result. Her own integrity was impugned, her publisher was threatened with loss of textbook sales, and the popular media attempted to dismiss her out of hand. A sympathetic but patronizing review in Time Magazine concluded that while many scientists might sympathize with her intentions, they ''fear that her emotional and inaccurate outburst in *Silent Spring* may do harm by alarming the nontechnical public,'' who should be reassured that while some pesticides may be dangerous, many ''are roughly as harmless as DDT,''[3] (which is, of course, now banned in most industrial countries). The Time review now seems dated; Carson's book does not. People reading it for the first

time today are struck by the fact that all that seems to have changed are the names of the poisons. Despite Carson's apparent effectiveness as an advocate, the problem she addresses remains a serious one. Was she actually successful, or did the attempt fail? Or did she, perhaps, accomplish something other than what she intended?

The American debate over the best uses of nature has been unique, and the tradition Rachel Carson represents, following the likes of Henry David Thoreau and John Muir, is a noble one. But because the defense mounted was usually very personal, the audience tended to be made up of those who shared, in some measure, the valued experience of nature that motivated these famous advocates. In other words, they spoke to a constituency of nature-lovers, and however many prestigious names might figure among them, it was still a minority interest. In contrast, everyone had a stake in the economic development of the nation, and everyone was therefore a partner in the quest for control of nature. It was Carson's acceptance of this simple, arithmetic fact—that there were more of ''them'' than of ''us''—that led, however indirectly, to the revolution that was *Silent Spring.* Its success led to widespread concern, and from ''Earth Day'' in 1970 the environmental movement became a force to be reckoned with.

But Carson's book was revolutionary not because it challenged the indiscriminate use of pesticides. Others had sounded the warning long before she did, and it was common knowledge in ''wildlife'' circles that many species were being harmed by this practice. Carson's originality lay in the manner in which she chose to speak and the audience she chose to address. She did not try to appeal to nature-lovers alone: she addressed the entire adult population. She did not speak to the protection of particular organisms that most people had no experience of or concern for, but instead created an entirely new protagonist. Rachel Carson made ''environment'' the endangered entity, rather than a wildlife species.[4] And since humans are similarly dependent on environment, on ''ecosystems,'' she immediately got our collective attention. The endangered species of concern was not the peregrine falcon or the whooping crane: it was us.

This may seem no more than a tactical improvement on her part: by showing each of us "what's in it for me," she made environmental protection a cause with extremely wide support. The introduction of such legislation as the National Environmental Policy Act of 1969 indicates just how widely accepted it has become. But strangely enough, in order to bring about this widespread popularity Carson had effectively to redefine what she meant by "nature." She had to describe a nature that mattered to "the man in the street." *She had to make nature popular.*

Of course, to make something popular is to make it universally understandable and appealing. Accomplishing this usually entails using language that is already in circulation: to be understandable one must say what is already understood. In Carson's case, this meant abandoning the older rhetoric which presumed a kind of valuing of nature that was not widespread, and replacing it with a valuing that was. Rather than rely on the nature-lover's assumption of a personal nature that is intrinsically valuable and must be defended for its own sake, she asserted, albeit only implicitly, that *human beings* are intrinsically valuable and must be defended at all costs—even if that means restraining development so that we can continue to have clean air and water. The nature she defended, then, was the nature that provides a stockpile of essential objects for humans to utilize. Of course, by linking these to the somewhat mysterious concept of an ecosystem, in which all players are assumed to have an essential role, she was also to extract some measure of protection for her beloved wildlife at the same time: people were afraid to exterminate toads for fear the ecosystem might collapse. But despite whatever short-term protection this might have provided, the effect has been the reinforcing of a particular understanding of nature.

NATURE AS OBJECT

Nature—that is, nature-as-object—was now perceived to be vulnerable in a way few had imagined before. It was still perceived to be a collection of objects, but now it was a collection of *important* objects. The general understanding of nature was not challenged in any significant way. For that reason, the consequences of the environmental movement have been less dramatic than one might have predicted of such a broadly supported venture. To understand why this might be so, we have to bear in mind something about the understanding we all have of nature. It might help, as a first step, to imagine what would have happened if Rachel Carson had chosen to speak as a nature-lover, rather than as a resource conservationist.

One of the common means of dismissing a writer like Carson was to accuse her of being "emotional" (as the Time reviewer did), or of being "anthropomorphic": of acting as if animals or nature in general had human characteristics and could feel the harm done to them. In the view of many, even to suggest that there are human characteristics (feelings, intelligence, awareness) in other organisms is to be a victim of the "Bambi syndrome," and to be afflicted with emotional delusions about useful natural resources. Since this kind of criticism enjoys the reputation of being hard-nosed and "objective," it is dangerous for an author to expose herself to it. The consequence was that Carson and others like her were totally vulnerable whenever they allowed their feeling for nature to show through. The notion of a world containing "persons" of other species, or even of nature as a kind of extended self, was simply unacceptable. To encourage nature preservation, she had to speak instead of the nature that most of society understands: a small price to pay for credibility, one might think.

This much is quite understandable. But why is it that a person is so vulnerable to criticism when she implies that nature is in any way sensate, anything more than a collection of objects? The history of the understanding of nature would very nearly amount to a history of human society, since every social group has had a conception of nature which it uses in maintaining its own internal stability. Mary Douglas, the eminent anthropologist, once suggested that every "environment," that is, every understanding of the non-human world around us, is "a mask and support for a certain kind of society." Were we able to describe each of these conceptions, we would have a kind of cultural fingerprint with which to identify any society that has ever existed. Like us, they had a notion of the necessity of nature and of their vulnerability if it is damaged or "polluted." The pollution they encountered was not always of the "contamination drinking water" variety, but of course the dictionary definition of pollution is somewhat wider than our colloquial usage: the destruction of the purity or sanctity of something. Anything that threatens the purity of the world around us, physically or conceptually, is an instance of pollution. And since polluters put the whole of society at risk, they must be made to mend their ways. The understanding of the vulnerability of nature is, therefore, also a means of social control, since it enables the group to argue against a particular action by one of its members. The consequence is that both the physical environment and the social beliefs of the group are maintained intact.

Given our understanding of nature as a collection of physical properties or objects, it is easy for us to understand the dangers of contaminating these. We have more trouble understanding some other kinds of pollution: the eating of "summer food" (caribou) in winter, for instance, which cost an Eskimo girl her life, or the participation of women in "male" ceremonies. Yet these can also threaten the purity of the social conception of nature, because as Mary Douglas argues,

> The deepest emotional investment of all is in the assumption that there is a rule-obeying universe, and that its rules are objective, independent of social validation. Hence the most odious pollutions are those which threaten to attack a system at its intellectual base.[5]

And we too have trouble with this kind of contamination, whether we recognize it or not. In fact, it may have been fear of just such contamination that made it impossible for Rachel Carson to talk about her own understanding of nature, which we might call "nature-as-self."

THE CONCEPTUAL POLLUTION OF NATURE

My suggestion that there was some conflict between Rachel Carson's personal understanding of nature and the one she espoused publicly in *Silent Spring* is, of course, conjecture. But we can say with confidence that she exemplifies the plight of a great many people who have been faced with this dilemma, and she certainly serves as a useful illustration of the way cultural premises dictate the very mode of communication an individual must select if he or she wishes to be taken seriously. It is a very subtle form of censorship which all societies practice, although perhaps not so massively and effectively as is the case in western industrialized countries. Thanks to modern mass communications, all of us are given daily instruction in the acceptable range of belief and expression. If we wish to share our ideas, we must make our message adhere to the required format and presuppositions. Even if this was less dramatically true in Carson's day, it may well have been the circumstance that provoked her to the kind of discourse she finally chose in *Silent Spring* and that that denied her the ability to state the message that she, as a nature-lover of long standing, would have wished to deliver.

I suggested earlier that one of the things that forced her decision was the fact that she would have been thought foolish had she been overtly emotional or anthropomorphic in putting her case. If someone claims to perceive feelings in nature, it is generally assumed to be because that person is "projecting" some of his or her inner feelings into nature. But it is too mild a statement to say that this is regarded as erroneous. At a deeper level, it is also sensed to be a dangerous act of pollution. Just how this could be so might be more apparent if we briefly consider the notion of "projection" before returning to our main issue, the kind of "nature" that exists in popular culture today.

J. H. van den Berg spoke of the phenomenon of projection in his classic book *The Changing Nature of Man*. Van den Berg is a Dutch psychiatrist who initiated a study of "historical psychology" to discover how humans and their understanding of reality have changed over time. One of the beliefs that is widely held today is that of projection, even though no one has ever successfully explained just how this phenomenon might work. It is essentially an explanatory mechanism to account for the fact that some people see something in the world that the rest of us do not believe to be there. Van den Berg illustrates this with a number of examples from his psychiatric practice. When the patient claims to see a world that is different from our own, we assure him that it is ''all in his head,'' that it is ''not real'' but merely ''projected.'' And if the patient denies being aware of any such projecting activity, as he almost surely will, then we explain that he is doing it ''subconsciously.'' We cannot, of course, prove a word of what we say. It is simply a means of explaining a discrepancy in world-view which is discomforting to both the patient and ourselves, and of dismissing the patient's version of reality. We could instead accept what the patient says at face value, and conclude that he is gifted with a different insight, that he can see aspects of the world that the rest of us cannot. Some societies have been quite willing to do so, and even to admire the ability of the ''insane'' to reveal these other faces of nature. But we do not. And, according to van den Berg, we dare not.

> . . . it is quite clear that the patient cannot be permitted a brick—or a street, house, city, train *or nature*—of his own. He must be projecting; *what he sees are his own personal impurities* . . . We smile reassuringly and say, ''You are projecting, what you are seeing is within yourself.'' (emphasis added)[6]

The patient has contaminated the world with the impurities of his inner self—he has *polluted.* That is, he has threatened the sanctity of the world and, in doing so, has threatened us all in some degree. The same is true of the nature-lover for whom nature is what we are calling ''nature-as-self'' rather than the conventional ''nature-as-object'': he or she contaminates reality by finding the qualities of persons in the world of nature. Since our agreement is that only physical objects can be said to populate nature, then the assertion of personal qualities is a breach of the accord, and must be a consequence of illegal ''projection'' on the part of the polluter. But so what? Even if we find this silly, what harm does it do? Why must we ridicule such a person and conjure up the stereotype of the ''little old lady in tennis shoes,'' implying mental incompetence, in order to dismiss the perception out of hand? Van den Berg's answer would be that

we can't collectively *afford* to have society members constituting their own personal understandings of nature. With the rise of humanism and the notion that the individual human is the only authority and the only source of value and meaning, the belief of each individual is potentially critical. If each of us is an authority, then it is crucial that we *agree* on what is. And the basis of our agreement, our lowest common denominator of perception, is nature-as-object, a bare-bones nature with no subjectivity and no personal variables at all: just stuff. According to van den Berg, we need agreement on nature-as-object because that is virtually the only thing we can agree on, and therefore the only piece of ''certainty'' we can cling to for social cohesion.

These specifications for nature have been with us a long time now. Hans Jonas has argued that the rejection of projection, and specifically of anthropomorphism, has been a condition of the modern scientific worldview from its inception: a condition, not a conclusion. It was dismissed by Francis Bacon, without any real attempt to justify the exclusion. Jonas comments that Bacon and his successors succeeded

> in putting a severe ban on any transference of features of internal experience into the interpretation of the external world . . . Anthropomorphism at all events, and even zoomorphism in general, became scientific high treason. It is in this dualistic setting that we meet the ''nature of man'' as a source of defilement for ''philosophy'' (natural science), and the objection to ''final'' explanation is that it is anthropomorphic.[7]

Again, we find the charge that it is a ''defilement''—a pollution—to find any human properties in nature. Is it any wonder, then, that authors like Rachel Carson had to take great pains to make nature-as-object the center of their discourse? To do otherwise would be to risk instant dismissal, except among the small sector of society that shares an understanding of the world as nature-as-self.

NATURE AS SELF

However, the consequences of that decision are difficult to assess. To some, it would appear that

Carson's decision was an inspired one, and that the popularity that environmental issues have enjoyed was a consequence of that choice. However, one has to question whether anything more than popularity was gained by this subterfuge. Has the natural environment enjoyed a significantly greater degree of protection as a result? We cannot "re-run the experiment," so to speak, and so can never know for sure. But the very fact that Carson's book still seems so relevant raises serious doubts. Nature is still at risk, still being polluted, still being encroached upon, still being driven to extinction piece by piece, species by species. It may be, some now feel, that more was lost than was gained in the rise to prominence, because the price paid for public attention was the ability to speak of what matters. We cannot know whether Carson would agree with this assessment, but some of her successors have certainly found this to be the case. So many, in fact, that alternate schools of environmentalism have arisen to attempt to repair the damage.

With the realization that the translation to technocratic respectability has enucleated the subject of concern, there have been a variety of attempts to speak in defense of nature without resorting to the language of nature-as-object. One such attempt which has enjoyed a certain vogue is known as "deep ecology," referring to the attempt to attend to the root assumptions that lead to environmental destruction rather than simply to the technical symptoms of that malaise.[8] Proponents of this approach differ from each other in some respects, but they tend to concur in their notion of nature as "extended self." That is, they resist the idea of an individual being entirely restricted to what R. D. Laing calls a "skin-encapsulated ego" and suggest instead that people have a field of concern which they experience as self. Consequently, the nature they perceive is, in some measure, a portion of themselves. The loss of nature is therefore also a loss of self, rather like an amputation of an appendage done without the patient's permission.

But the nature-as-self can also imply a slightly different understanding. Instead of being "extended self," it may instead imply an extension of self-hood to nature—an understanding of nature as "like-self"

or as a community of selves, of persons, with whom one has relationships similar to those within human society.[9] It therefore makes sense to think of rights and obligations within nature, or even of a morality of nature. The arguments are complex, but obviously they lead in quite a different direction than does the resourcism implicit in the nature-as-object conception. And they quite commonly lead to talk of environmental ethics and rights,[10] although not among all practitioners (some would argue that the idea of ethics and rights presumes discrete, atomistic individuals, the very kind of dualism they are seeking to avoid).[11] For our purposes, however, the significant point is simply that there is an alternative understanding of nature present in contemporary society which is apparently growing in popularity. And while it is certainly far from challenging the hegemony of nature-as-object, its expansion is significant. Obviously the understanding of nature we have will effect the kind of expectations we have, both of nature and of ourselves in relation to nature: what seems proper and appropriate behavior toward an object is not necessarily appropriate toward a "self." The question one asks of nature-as-object is "what's in it *for* me?"; whereas of nature-as-self one might ask "what is it *to* me?" The former implies simple exploitation, whether "well managed" or not, while the latter implies a concern with the relationship of humans and non-humans.

But while these may be the two contending understandings of nature that figure most prominently in popular culture at the moment, they probably do not exhaust the possibilities.

NATURE AS MIRACLE

We believe in facts, just the facts. We do not, generally speaking, believe in miracles. It is highly unlikely, therefore, that many of us would hold a conception of nature as "miracle." Many nature-lovers no doubt have had experiences that one might consider "miraculous," even though they would probably choose a more prudent adjective such as "aesthetic." But the possibility of regarding nature as uncanny and unpredictable needs to be mentioned here, even though it is not possible to do more than hint at its possible significance.

It is commonly understood that a miracle, were such to exist, would be something that runs contrary to the laws of nature. Given that, it would make little sense to speak of nature-as-miracle. However, whether something is ''against nature'' would depend on our definition of nature. Given that we believe we have discovered ''laws'' of nature, then of course anything that seems to break those laws would be, by definition, unnatural—if not absurd. But to treat the possibility of nature-as-miracle seriously, one would have to ask just where these ''laws'' come from and what they actually apply to, which is not a simple task.

One of the reasons that the miracle has largely disappeared from our lives is that we have come to know the world as homogeneous and continuous. That is to say, since it is composed of matter which is similar in composition and behaves in a consistent manner, we are able to predict the result of actions confidently. Of course, it has been understood for centuries that one cannot actually *prove* a causal relationship—it could change on the next trial—but we can nevertheless act as if that were so, since nature seems seldom to surprise us. It is interesting, however, where the initial assumption came from. Why did we decide that nature is sufficiently homogeneous and continuous for us to assume consistent causal relationships?

We find the assumption firmly entrenched by the late seventeenth century, when Gottfried Leibniz could assert that ''nature does not leap''—''Tout va par degrés dans la nature et rien par saut.''[12] And of course such ''natural laws'' made possible all sorts of revised understandings, the most obvious being Charles Lyell's theory of gradual geological change which in turn fed Charles Darwin's belief in continuous biological evolution. But as J. H. van den Berg observed, the real germ of this idea lies in the meditations of René Descartes, for whom it bore intellectual fruit almost immediately. Once he concluded that discontinuity is inconceivable, that nature never

''jumps'' or makes abrupt, unexpected changes, he felt assured that the ''stuff'' of nature is everywhere the same: there are no pockets of resistance, no surprises. Nature is homogeneous.

This expectation permitted Descartes to take a new turn in his reflections on reality, one which continues to affect each of our lives today. If nature is homogeneous, if it is all essentially the same, then all we need to be concerned with is what he called ''extensiveness'': an object occupies space. Furthermore, what has extensiveness can be subdivided and can be understood in terms of mathematical analysis, which was of course one of Descartes's intentions. In fact, the very notion of a law of continuity may have come from his mathematical theorizing in which he realized that ''if the first two or three terms of any progression are known, it is not difficult to find the other terms.''[13] Whatever differences there may be between objects must be the result of differences in motion. His success in arguing this conception laid the groundwork for what we now know as nature, and for the tools of analysis—science—which we regard as the only valid means of knowing nature.

Nothing above should come as any surprise, for we are all heirs of Descartes and we all know nature to be a continuous and predictable phenomenon. The ''laws of nature'' could not permit such rebelliousness. It comes as something of a surprise, therefore, to find a reputable author like van den Berg making such a description and then saying ''Yet it is not true.'' He denies Descartes's assumption, the one we all take for granted.

> The reader who might think that I do not mean this seriously is mistaken. I *am* serious. The way Descartes treats objects is not fair. If science wants to consider objects as they are, in the form they have as objects, then it is not permitted to speak of objects which consist of nothing but extensiveness. There is no such thing—and there was no such thing. But Descartes' ideas have penetrated so deeply into reality that nobody knows where the idea ends and reality (or, if preferred, another idea of reality) begins.[14]

Van den Berg is simply pointing out that what Descartes did was make an assumption about the nature of reality, an assumption that we, henceforth, have taken as indisputable fact. Certainly it has had useful consequences. But it is, nevertheless, an assumption, and one which, like all assumptions, rules out all other possibilities. Van den Berg argues that much of value is lost in this exclusion, including an understanding of nature that is genuinely compatible with our own *experience* of it rather than with an abstract *conception* of it—we know pigeons and sunsets, but only believe in ecosystems. In order to believe in Descartes's nature, we had to expunge all the qualities we thought we knew, all the colors, smells, weights, and textures—"projection" is a crime, remember—and attend only to what the model requires be there. We had to withdraw ourselves and our senses from the understanding of nature altogether.

> Withdrawing from the things means dehumanizing them. Only if we withdraw, can we find the "laws of nature." These exist, however, only in a close unity, one which does not include us. As a rule, this condition of withdrawal is not mentioned, and therefore it seems that the laws of nature are always valid. But they are only valid in an artificial reality, a reality from which we are excluded. Only tautologies can make them seem valid in our world.[15]

So according to van den Berg (among others),[16] the understanding of nature which we take as obvious is in fact a rather complex and abstract one which we acquire in a lengthy cultural exercise in indoctrination. Without schooling, who could possibly conceive of it? Even in the 1920s, it was apparent that our educational system was firmly committed to its dissemination. Alfred North Whitehead commented that the view of nature as "a dull affair, soundless scentless, colourless; merely the hurrying of material, endlessly, meaninglessly" was ubiquitous. Every university "organizes itself in accordance with it." And yet, he concluded, it is quite unbelievable. This conception of the universe is surely framed in terms of high abstractions, and the paradox only arises because we have "mistaken our abstraction for concrete realities."[17] We are persuaded by abstractions—"ecosystems"—in a way we seldom are by realities—

frogs and mourning doves. We have become victims of the "fallacy of misplaced concreteness" which requires that we regard our abstractions about nature as actual objects of nature, while simultaneously dismissing as trivial or as "projections" our actual experiences of nature. But experience cannot be entirely suffocated by belief, and even extensive schooling cannot remove all vestiges of the direct experience of a nature from which we are *not* withdrawn and in which the "laws of nature" do not always apply. Heterogeneity cannot be entirely exercised, and the occasional miracle just might still occur.

The reason this may be significant is that the idiosyncratic experience of the world may actually transcend the cultural heritage that has given us an understanding of nature that entails the "environmental crisis" as its consequence. That is, if it is so that nature-as-object is the inevitable consequence of a series of cultural interpretations, it may be that the whole of our behavior, including that which leads to the abuse of nature that we now characterize as the environmental crisis, is a consequence of our belief in nature-as-object. The only long term possibility of alleviating that crisis would be to transcend the understanding of nature that gives rise to it. The alternative could be something like what we have been calling nature-as-self, since this at least entails a greater sense of life in nature and some measure of personal responsibility and obligation towards it. But it might also be that something like nature-as-miracle, some experience that transcends the normal understanding and holds it temporarily in abeyance so that the personal awareness of the living world is restored, is a prerequisite to any real change in the awareness of individuals and therefore also to a change in the conception of nature in popular culture.

I suggested earlier that an understanding of nature-as-object implies a stance toward the world that could only prompt one to ask "what's in it for me"—the very question Carson exploited by appearing to answer it. An understanding of nature-as-self involves the premise of persons in the world beyond the human community alone, and therefore entails a search for some understanding of our relationship to the others:

the question asked is, ''what is it *to* me.'' But the third nature, nature-as-miracle, does not prompt questions of control or even questions of kinship. The stance towards the world as miraculous, as awesome, or even as beautiful, could only prompt one to ask ''what *is* it?''—a metaphysical question rather than an economic or a political one.

THE SOCIAL CONSTRUCTION OF NATURE

The sense of nature we have will obviously affect our idea of what constitutes proper behavior toward it. The nature that dominates popular culture today is one that is consistent with our humanistic and technocratic assumptions. Nature-as-object is the only understanding of the three that facilitates exploitation and the resourcist rhetoric that legitimizes and facilitates it. The rise of nature-as-self in popular culture is an interesting phenomenon which may or may not entail a substantial change. It seems more in keeping with Aldo Leopold's expectation that we will expand our range of moral responsibility (his famous ''land ethic'')[18] to include the non-human, than with Rachel Carson's public stance as the advocate of human well-being through the defense of ecosystemic integrity. As for nature-as-miracle, as long as it is limited to the experience of relatively few individuals, or even to rather minor experiences interpreted as merely ''aesthetic'' by a larger section of society, it is probably nothing more than a source of pleasure or puzzlement to the individuals involved. But it *may* be more widespread than we realize: perhaps the occasional experiences of wonder which we all enjoy are symptomatic evidence of the continued possibility of the miraculous. And should this possibility ever gain credence in a larger way, it is conceivable that it might challenge our fundamental perception of the way the world is. Nature-as-miracle challenges the ''nothing-but-ness'' of contemporary technocratic explanation. It challenges the assumptions of homogeneity and continuity that permit us to exclude the possibility of surprise and to assume confidently public acceptance of a ''lowest common nature'' that can never be challenged without villainy or ''projection.'' It is, per-

haps, the refugium in which alternative ''natures'' still reside.

There will always be ''nature'' in popular culture: nature is a hypothesis that every society needs. We all like to claim to be doing what is ''natural,'' and like our ancestors we often admonish each other to ''follow nature.'' However there is some hypocrisy in this, because we only want to follow if nature is willing to lead in our chosen direction. If we have a dog named ''nature,'' we can cheerfully claim to be following it by walking a step or two behind. But to be confident the dog will not deny us this pleasure, we keep it on a leash, lest it take a turn not of our choosing. But our desire to have some sort of control over the direction nature leads us, even while proclaiming to be followers only, is not a perversion unique to our society. In fact, it may be the rule of the day where humans are concerned. Marshall Sahlins described this tendency in his remarkably concise study, *The Use and Abuse of Biology,* in which he used the recent debate surrounding ''sociobiology'' to illustrate this tendency at work in contemporary society. But he also described the general and possibly essential propensity of human societies to invent the nature they desire or need, and then to use it to justify the social pattern they have developed. He concludes that

> We seem unable to escape from this perpetual movement, back and forth between the culturalization of nature and the naturalization of culture. It frustrates our understanding at once of society and of the organic world.[19]

The nature that functions in the lives of the majority, that functions as a vital part of popular culture, is inevitably a consequence of this pendular movement between the world of nature and human culture. Nature is never irrelevant. It is used habitually to justify and legitimate the actions we wish to regard as normal, and the behavior we choose to impose on each other. The fact that we are content to construe nature as an object at the moment is symptomatic of our desire to avoid any constraints and to have a free hand to manipulate the world into the forms suited to the exchanges of modern technocracy. The investment we have in the maintenance of this understanding of nature is enormous. And yet, it is not secure. Nature-as-self is also a contemporary reality. It is certainly not the norm, but it is credible enough to generate widespread discussion. And if we ever find that nature-as-miracle has found its way into the columns of Time Magazine, we may begin to wonder whether nature, whatever it may be, is about to slip its leash.

NOTES

1. Cited by Marjorie Hope Nicolson, *Mountain Gloom and Mountain Glory* (New York: W. W. Norton & Co., 1959), pp. 22-23. See also ''Nature as aesthetic norm'' in Arthur O. Lovejoy, *Essays in the History of Ideas* (New York: G. P. Putnam's Sons, 1960), pp. 69-77.

2. Rachel Carson, *Silent Spring* (Boston: Houghton Mifflin Co., 1962), p. 297.

3. ''Pesticides: The Price of Progress,'' *Time* (September 28, 1962), p. 45.

4. For further elaboration of this see Neil Evernden, *The Natural Alien* (Toronto: University of Toronto Press, 1985).

5. Mary Douglas, ''Environments at Risk,'' in Jonathon Benthall, ed., *Ecology: The Shaping Enquiry* (London, Longman, 1972), p. 144.

6. J. H. van den Berg, *The Changing Nature of Man: Introduction to a Historical Psychology* (New York: Delta, 1975), pp. 225-226.

7. Hans Jonas, *The Phenomenon of life* (Chicago: University of Chicago Press, 1966), pp. 35-36.

8. See Bill Devall and George Sessions, *Deep Ecology: Living as if Nature Mattered* (Salt Lake City: Peregrine Smith Books, 1985).

9. See Erazim Kohak, *The Embers and the Stars* (Chicago: University of Chicago Presss, 1984).

10. See, for example, Peter Singer's *Animal Liberation* (New York: Avon Books, 1975).

11. Warwick Fox, *Deep Ecology: A Response to Richard Sylvan's Critique of Deep Ecology* (Hobart, Tasmania: University of Tasmania, Environmental Studies Occasional Paper #20, 1986).

12. Van den Berg, *Changing Nature,* p. 52.

13. Van den Berg, *Changing Nature,* p. 53.

14. Van den Berg, *Changing Nature,* p. 56.

15. Van den Berg, *Changing Nature,* p. 125.

16. Similar arguments have been put by many writers. See for instance John Livingston, *One Cosmic Instant* (Toronto: McClelland, 1973); Morris Berman, *The Re-Enchantment of the World* (Ithaca: Cornell University Press, 1981); Theodore Roszak, *Where the Wasteland Ends* (New York, Doubleday, 1972); Neil Evernden, *The Natural Alien;* David Ehrenfeld, *The Arrogance of Humanism* (New York, Oxford University Press, 1978).

17. Alfred North Whitehead, *Science and the Modern World* (New York: The Free Press, 1925), pp. 54-55.

18. Aldo Leopold, *A Sand County Almanac* (New York, Oxford University Press, 1949), pp. 201-226.

19. Marshall Sahlins, *The Use and Abuse of Biology* (London: Tavistock Publishers, 1977), p. 105.

DISCUSSION TOPICS

1. To what extent do you agree with Evernden that there were conflicts between Rachel Carson's personal understanding of nature and the view she espoused in *Silent Spring?*

2. What views of nature might be equally valid with those proposed by Evernden? What is your view of nature, and how does it compare to Evernden's view?

CASE FOR CLASS DEBATE

It has been proposed that 25 percent of all lands designated as wilderness would be reclassified as ''sacred space.'' These lands would be totally closed to any human visitation, including wilderness hiking, ecological monitoring, fire fighting, law enforcement, or activities related to public health.

Using the debating techniques outlined in Appendix A, debate the merits of this plan. What arguments and strategies were used by each side? Which were persuasive?

FOR FURTHER READING

Bilsky, Lester J. *Historical Ecology: Essays on Environment and Social Change.* Port Washington, N.Y.: Kennikat Press, 1980. A series of essays by eleven scholars on past environmental crises and past human relationships with nature, starting from prehistoric times. Most attention is focused on Europe, but some information is presented about China and other parts of the world.

Conviser, Richard. ''Toward Agricultures of Context.'' *Environmental Ethics* 6: 71-85, 1984. The author explores origins of agricultural organization, particularly the movements toward scientism and capitalism. Forms of agriculture, consistent with holism and localism, are recommended as better alternatives.

Environmental History Review (formerly *Environmental Review*) is a publication of the American Society for Environmental History. Established in 1976, the focus of the journal is on scholarly research on past environmental change. Many pertinent articles are published here.

Evernden, Neil. *The Natural Alien.* Toronto: University of Toronto Press, 1985. An insightful and thought-provoking perspective on the deficiencies inherent in the environmental movement's ideology. Evernden maintains that humans become alienated from the richness of nature and life when viewing the world primarily in terms of its technological value.

Hargrove, Eugene C. ''The Historical Foundations of American Environmental Attitudes.'' *Environmental Ethics* 1: 209-240, 1979. The author claims that American environmental attitudes developed from an interplay of Western science and art over the last three centuries. He views these attitudes as part of broad scientific and aesthetic changes that will probably become a permanent part of Western values.

Hughes, J. Donald. ''Effects of Classical Cities on the Mediterranean Landscape.'' *Ekistics* 42(253): 332-342, 1976. Practices in ancient cities resulted in environmental problems similar to those experienced in modern cities, including air, water, and noise pollution. Land use and urban planning decisions also were difficult during ancient times.

Hughes, J. Donald. ''The Environmental Ethics of the Pythagoreans.'' *Environmental Ethics* 2: 195-213, 1980. Identifies two conflicting perspectives among the Pythagoreans: a sense of reverence for nature and kinship with all life, and a doctrine of separability of soul and body that devalued the body and the external world of which it is a part.

Hughes, J. Donald. ''How the Ancients Viewed Deforestation.'' *Journal of Field Archeology* 10: 437-445. 1983.

Hughes evaluates the causes and effects of deforestation in ancient lands. He describes how the demands of human use superseded traditional values supporting the preservation of forested lands.

Hughes, J. Donald. ''Pan: Environmental Ethics in Classical Polytheism,'' in *Religion and Environmental Crisis,* Eugene C. Hargrove, ed. Athens, Ga.: University of Georgia Press, 1986, pp. 7-24. Provides a perspective on the role the Great Pan played in ancient times as an all-pervasive spiritual power and the unversal god of nature. Notes that the death of Pan occurred when Christianity arose. Probes the role that these ancient ideas may have played in the development of an explicit environmental ethic.

Merchant, Carolyn. *Ecological Revolution: Nature, Gender and Science in New England.* Chapel Hill, N.C.: University of North Carolina Press, 1989. Merchant analyzes the colonial and capital revolutions in New England as an example of ''ecological revolutions'' in the relation between humans and nonhumans in nature. She covers the ecological and social transformations in New England from the seventeenth century to the present. Extensive notes and bibliography.

Nash, Roderick F. *The Rights of Nature: A History of Environmental Ethics.* Madison, Wis.: University of Wisconsin Press, 1989. An interesting tracing of the ideas that led some in our society away from simple anthropocentrism to the belief that nature has rights that must be respected.

Oelschlager, Max. *The Idea of Wilderness: From Prehistory to the Age of Ecology.* New Haven, Conn.: Yale University Press, 1991. A thoughtful and scholarly look at the history of ideas focusing on the notion of wilderness.

Shepherd, Paul. *The Tender Carnivore and the Sacred Game.* New York: Charles Scribner's Sons, 1973. A thoughtful look at the human place in the natural world, and its historical foundations. Addresses fundamental assumptions in the relationship of Western society to nature, including human-nature dualism.

Thomas, Keith. *Man and the Natural World: A History of Modern Sensibility.* New York: Pantheon Books, 1983. The author delineates the assumptions which underlay the perceptions and feelings of men and women toward nature, in early England.

Vest, Jay H. ''Nature Awe: Historical Views of Nature.'' *Western Wildlands* 1: 39-43, 1983. An interesting and insightful look at the relationships ancient Celts had toward nature, and the foundation this culture had for some Western practices and perceptions.

Worster, Donald. *Nature's Economy: The Roots of Ecology.* San Francisco: Sierra Club Books, 1977. The author presents a history of ideas in the field of ecology. Three of the chapters in the final part of the text lead into a general discussion of the ethical implications of ecology.

Worster, Donald. "History as Natural History: An Essay on Theory and Method." *Pacific Historical Review* 53: 1-19, 1984. Analyzes the contributions of an ecological perspective to the study of human history. Reviews several American historians and anthropologists who have adopted an ecological perspective. Suggests that historians can add specificity to the generalizations of ecological analysis.

CHAPTER FIVE

Economic/ Political/ Legal Issues

In this chapter we identify and evaluate economic, political, and legal issues underlying environmental policy, including policies of using publicly owned resources.

Many scholars argue that contemporary economic paradigms and political processes have serious shortcomings for making environmental decisions. Robert Costanza and Herman Daly maintain that the integration of ecological considerations into these paradigms and processes is of the utmost importance.[1]

HOMO ECONOMICUS

The term *Homo economicus* is used to refer to economic man, an abstract concept of the man or woman who is concerned only with his or her own satisfaction (personal utility) and indifferent to where that satisfaction comes from. Many environmental theorists maintain that the assumptions which underlie this abstraction result in deeply flawed environmental policies. For example, Herman Daly and John Cobb, Jr. argue that the concept is empirically false and also

dangerous in encouraging the uninhibited pursuit of personal gain.[2] Steven Edwards, however, maintains in his essay, "In Defense of Environmental Economics," that the model offers testable hypotheses concerning economic behavior.

PERSONAL PREFERENCES AS NORMATIVE

Many economists argue that normative evaluation of an individual's desires by others is unacceptable. Only the Pareto-efficiency criterion is used: by this criterion an action is considered economically efficient if no one is harmed while at least one person benefits. Whether an individual benefits is left to the sole judgment of that individual. The source of value is found in subjective individual wants, not in the needs of other human beings or other species. While this subjective treatment of the individual's wants is often criticized, Edwards suggests that there is an

---

1. Robert Costanza and Herman E. Daly, "Toward an Ecological Economics," *Ecological Modelling,* 38 (1987): 1-7.

2. Herman E. Daly and John B. Cobb, Jr., *For the Common Good: Redirecting the Economy Toward Community, the Environment, and a Sustainable Future* (Boston: Beacon Press, 1989), pp. 85-96.

unacceptable presumptuousness in judging the wants of others, and Anderson and Leal argue that allowing the voluntary exchange of property rights between consenting owners promotes individual liberty.[3]

SUSTAINABLE RESOURCE USE AND PREVENTING IRREVERSIBLE LOSSES

Defining sustainable use of a natural resource is a fundamental issue in environmental economics. In Goodland and Ledec's essay, "Neoclassical Economics and Principles of Sustainable Development," sustainable use is defined as the level of use at which the benefits of a resource are maximized without jeopardizing the potential for similar benefits in the future. The authors point out that many environmental consequences of contemporary development projects are either completely irreversible or reversible only over a very long time. Examples include species extinctions, groundwater contamination, fossil fuel depletion, loss of traditional knowledge of indigenous tribal peoples when they are acculturated, soil erosion, human-induced climatic changes, and removal of coral reefs and certain forest types. Such irreversible losses traditionally are not considered in cost-benefit analyses.

Sustainability also refers to a key concept in steady-state economics, an approach associated with Herman E. Daly's work and that of others beginning in the 1970s. Steady-state economics stresses the limits to resource use based on the carrying capacity of the earth. This view also affirms a view of human beings as capable of stewardship and kinship with both future generations and nonhuman life.[4]

EXTERNALITIES

Externalities are "spillover effects of someone's production or consumption that affect the well-being of other producers and consumers."[5] These effects are not directly reflected in market transactions; externalities are sometimes referred to as the problem of "missing markets." Such externalities can include pollution, soil erosion, and losses or gains in wildlife habitat.

NONMONETIZED VALUES

Comparing economic values with values that cannot be easily given a monetary value often is a controversial issue. Edwards argues that the concept of economic value can encompass any instrumental value. Nonmonetized values (values not easily converted into monetary terms) can be converted to monetary terms by methods which assess the individual's willingness-to-pay (how much a person is willing to pay to obtain or retain a resource) or willingness-to-be-reimbursed (how much a person would require to be reimbursed for the loss or degradation of a resource.) Edwards does note, however, that such assessments assume the applicability of the *Homo economicus* model. Economists sometimes suggest assigning shadow or surrogate prices to goods or services which have no market price, or creating and assigning exchangeable property rights (such as pollution or depletion quotas) which are then priced in markets as they are traded.[6] Christopher Stone's essay, "Should Trees Have Standing?" recommends the use of shadow-pricing in order to allow incorporation of natural objects into the legal system.

In their essay Goodland and Ledec note that some

3. Terry Lee Anderson and Donald R. Leal, *Free Market Environmentalism* (San Francisco: Pacific Research Institute for Public Policy, 1991), pp. 4-8.

4. Herman E. Daly, *Steady-State Economics* (Washington, D.C.: Island Press, 1991), pp. 14-49. Steady-state economists see the economy as a subsystem of the environment; the economy lives by importing low-entropy matter-energy (raw materials) and exporting high-entropy matter-energy (waste). Since the environment is finite, so must the economy be.

5. Eric L. Hyman and Bruce Stiftel, *Combining Facts and Values in Environmental Impact Assessment: Theories and Techniques* (Boulder, Colo.: Westview Press, 1988), p. 64.

6. "As a lark, the Environmental Protection Agency staff estimated the dollar value of a living tree, including its value to the ecosystem and its aesthetic and recreation values, to be $500,000." Michael Edesess, *The Christian Science Monitor,* September 15, 1989.

environmental consequences, while tangible, cannot easily be assigned a monetary value due to difficulties in estimating both their physical and economic impacts. Educated guesswork is all that is available.

Ascribing intrinsic value to natural entities may further complicate economic considerations, because such ascription often greatly enhances value or involves intangible value. Intrinsic values are not readily accounted for in strictly economic terms.

SOCIAL TRAPS: SHARING THE COMMONS

A social trap occurs when individuals base their decisions on what they believe will benefit them personally in the short term, but produce circumstances which work to everyone's detriment, including their own.

One form of social trap which has received wide attention is the "tragedy of the commons," as described by Garrett Hardin in his essay. According to Hardin, if individuals use natural resources held in common in a way which will maximize their own benefit, disaster for all will follow.

The existence of social traps challenges Adam Smith's idea of the "invisible hand," according to which if each pursues his or her own prosperity all will benefit. However, it should be noted that social traps could be used as evidence of the usefulness of the *Homo economicus* model.

LEGAL RIGHTS AS REFORMATIVE AND PROTECTIVE

Legal rights are conventional (based on social institutions) and hence can develop in ways which may reform social awareness. Christopher Stone urges the extension of legal rights to include natural objects in order to reform human perceptions of the importance of the natural world. Such inclusion requires not only shadow-pricing but the use of legal guardianships to represent the interests of natural objects.

Sagoff points out in his essay, "Some Problems with Environmental Economics," the protective role of legal rights in circumstances in which individuals do not wish to sell their property to the highest bidder. Legal rights can limit the wholesale use of cost-benefit analysis in setting environmental policy.

ENVIRONMENTAL POLITICS—SOMETHING NEW?

In their essay, "Environmental Politics and the Administrative State," Robert Paehlke and Douglas Torgerson maintain that environmental politics is a movement which originated about twenty years ago. It is composed of private environmental groups and environmental professionals, united by a sense of urgency. Environmental politics cannot easily be classified as conservative or liberal; its institutional form is still emerging. In his essay Sagoff stresses that environmental decisions should be made in the political process of deliberation and argumentation rather than based on cost-benefit economic analysis and consumer surveys.

The Tragedy of the Commons

Garrett Hardin

Garrett Hardin (b. 1915) is Emeritus Professor of Human Ecology, University of California, Santa Barbara.

Hardin argues that many problems have no technical solution, but rather require changes in moral values. He asserts that in a commons—a publicly owned resource—general public good does not follow from everyone serving their own interest, in contrast to Adam Smith's theories. Hardin uses sheepherders on a common pasture as an example. As a rational being, each sheepherder would find it advantageous to increase the size of his or her own herd, but the result of each engaging in the most rational behavior would be ruin of the commons for all.

Hardin points to overgrazing of public lands in the western United States, overfishing in the oceans, and overuse of national parks as real-life examples of the tragedy of the commons. Hardin presents pollution as a similar problem in reverse: the cost of discharging wastes for any individual is less than the cost of purifying the wastes before their release. Likewise, Hardin argues that the decision to have children should not rest with individual families, as long as it is believed that everyone born has an equal right to the commons.

The solution recommended by Hardin is some mutually agreed-upon public coercion, such as taxation. Even if imperfect, such a system would be preferable to the status quo in which selfish individuals can damage many others.

. . . *The Wealth of Nations* (1776) popularized the "invisible hand," the idea that an individual who "intends only his own gain," is, as it were, "led by an invisible hand to promote . . . the public interest."[1] Adam Smith did not assert that this was invariably true, and perhaps neither did any of his followers. But he contributed to a dominant tendency of thought that has ever since interfered with positive action based on rational analysis, namely, the tendency to assume that decisions reached individually will, in fact, be the best decisions for an entire society. If this assumption is correct it justifies the continuance of our present policy of laissez-faire in reproduction. If it is correct we can assume that men will control their individual fecundity so as to produce the optimum population. If the assumption is not correct, we need to reexamine our individual freedoms to see which ones are defensible.

TRAGEDY OF FREEDOM IN A COMMONS

The rebuttal to the invisible hand in population control is to be found in a scenario first sketched in a little-known pamphlet[2] in 1833 by a mathematical amateur named William Forster Lloyd (1794–1852). We may well call it "the tragedy of the commons," using the word "tragedy" as the philosopher Whitehead used it[3]: "The essence of dramatic tragedy is not unhappiness. It resides in the solemnity of the remorseless working of things." He then goes on to say, "This inevitableness of destiny can only be illustrated in terms of human life by incidents which in fact involve unhappiness. For it is only by them that the futility of escape can be made evident in the drama."

The tragedy of the commons develops in this way. Picture a pasture open to all. It is to be expected that each herdsman will try to keep as many cattle as possible on the commons. Such an arrangement may work reasonably satisfactorily for centuries because tribal wars, poaching, and disease keep the numbers of both man and beast well below the carrying capacity of the land. Finally, however, comes the day of reckoning, that is, the day when the long-desired goal of social stability becomes a reality. At this point, the inherent logic of the commons remorselessly generates tragedy.

As a rational being, each herdsman seeks to maximize his gain. Explicitly or implicitly, more or less consciously, he asks, "What is the utility *to me* of adding one more animal to my herd?" This utility has one negative and one positive component.

(1) The positive component is a function of the increment of one animal. Since the herdsman receives all the proceeds from the sale of the additional animal, the positive utility is nearly $+1$.

(2) The negative component is a function of the additional overgrazing created by one more animal. Since, however, the effects of overgrazing are shared by all the herdsmen, the negative utility for any particular decision-making herdsman is only a fraction of -1.

Adding together the component partial utilities, the rational herdsman concludes that the only sensible course for him to pursue is to add another animal to his herd. And another; and another. . . . But this is the conclusion reached by each and every rational herdsman sharing a commons. Therein is the tragedy. Each man is locked into a system that compels him to increase his herd without limit—in a world that is limited. Ruin is the destination toward which all men rush, each pursuing his own best interest in a society that believes in the freedom of the commons. Freedom in a commons brings ruin to all.

Some would say that this is a platitude. Would that it were! In a sense, it was learned thousands of years ago, but natural selection favors the forces of psychological denial.[4] The individual benefits as an individual from his ability to deny the truth even though society as a whole, of which he is a part, suffers. . . .

In an approximate way, the logic of the commons has been understood for a long time, perhaps since the discovery of agriculture or the invention of private property in real estate. But it is understood mostly only in special cases which are not sufficiently generalized. Even at this late date, cattlemen leasing national land on the western ranges demonstrate no more than an ambivalent understanding, in constantly pressuring federal authorities to increase the head count to the point where overgrazing produces erosion and weed-dominance. Likewise, the oceans of the world continue to suffer from the survival of the philosophy of the commons. Maritime nations still respond automatically to the shibboleth of the "freedom of the seas." Professing to believe in the "inexhaustible resources of the oceans," they bring species after species of fish and whales closer to extinction.[5]

The National Parks present another instance of the working out of the tragedy of the commons. At present, they are open to all, without limit. The parks themselves are limited in extent—there is only one

Yosemite Valley—whereas population seems to grow without limit. The values that visitors seek in the parks are steadily eroded. Plainly, we must soon cease to treat the parks as commons or they will be of no value to anyone.

What shall we do? We have several options. We might sell them off as private property. We might keep them as public property, but allocate the right to enter them. The allocation might be on the basis of wealth, by the use of an auction system. It might be on the basis of merit, as defined by some agreed-upon standards. It might be by lottery. Or it might be on a first-come, first-served basis, administered to long queues. These, I think, are all the reasonable possibilities. They are all objectionable. But we must choose—or acquiesce in the destruction of the commons that we call our National Parks.

POLLUTION

In a reverse way, the tragedy of the commons reappears in problems of pollution. Here it is not a question of taking something out of the commons, but of putting something in—sewage, or chemical, radioactive, and peat wastes into water; noxious and dangerous fumes into the air; and distracting and unpleasant advertising signs into the line of sight. The calculations of utility are much the same as before. The rational man finds that his share of the cost of the wastes he discharges into the commons is less than the cost of purifying his wastes before releasing them. Since this is true for everyone, we are locked into a system of "fouling our own nest," so long as we behave only as independent, rational, free-enterprisers.

The tragedy of the commons as a food basket is averted by private property, or something formally like it. But the air and waters surrounding us cannot readily be fenced, and so the tragedy of the commons as a cesspool must be prevented by different means, by coercive laws or taxing devices that make it cheaper for the polluter to treat his pollutants than to discharge them untreated. We have not progressed as far with the solution of this problem as we have with the first. Indeed, our particular concept of private property, which deters us from exhausting the positive resources of the earth, favors pollution. The owner of a factory on the bank of a stream—whose property extends to the middle of the stream—often has difficulty seeing why it is not his natural right to muddy the waters flowing past his door. The law, always behind the times, requires elaborate stitching and fitting to adapt it to this newly perceived aspect of the commons.

The pollution problem is a consequence of population. It did not much matter how a lonely American frontiersman disposed of his waste. ''Flowing water purifies itself every 10 miles'' my grandfather used to say, and the myth was near enough to the truth when he was a boy, for there were not too many people. But as population became denser, the natural chemical and biological recycling processes became overloaded, calling for a redefinition of property rights. . . .

MUTUAL COERCION MUTUALLY AGREED UPON

The social arrangements that produce responsibility are arrangements that create coercion, of some sort. . . . The only kind of coercion I recommend is mutual coercion, mutually agreed upon by the majority of the people affected.

To say that we mutually agree to coercion is not to say that we are required to enjoy it, or even to pretend we enjoy it. Who enjoys taxes? We all grumble about them. But we accept compulsory taxes because we recognize that voluntary taxes would favor the conscienceless. We institute and (grumblingly) support taxes and other coercive devices to escape the horror of the commons. . . .

RECOGNITION OF NECESSITY

Perhaps the simplest summary of this analysis of man's population problems is this: the commons, if justifiable at all, is justifiable only under conditions of low-population density. As the human population has increased, the commons has had to be abandoned in one aspect after another.

First we abandoned the commons in food gather-

ing, enclosing farm land and restricting pastures and hunting and fishing areas. These restrictions are still not complete throughout the world.

Somewhat later we saw that the commons as a place for waste disposal would also have to be abandoned. Restrictions on the disposal of domestic sewage are widely accepted in the Western world; we are still struggling to close the commons to pollution by automobiles, factories, insecticide sprayers, fertilizing operations, and atomic energy installations. . . . Every new enclosure of the commons involves the infringement of somebody's personal liberty.

. . . But what does ''freedom'' mean? When men mutually agreed to pass laws against robbing, mankind became more free, not less so. Individuals locked into the logic of the commons are free only to bring on universal ruin: once they see the necessity of mutual coercion, they become free to pursue other goals. I believe it was Hegel who said, ''Freedom is the recognition of necessity.''

The most important aspect of necessity that we must now recognize, is the necessity of abandoning the commons in breeding. No technical solution can rescue us from the misery of overpopulation. Freedom to breed will bring ruin to all. At the moment, to avoid hard decisions many of us are tempted to propagandize for conscience and responsible parenthood. The temptation must be resisted, because an appeal to independently acting consciences selects for the disappearance of all conscience in the long run, and an increase in anxiety in the short.

The only way we can preserve and nurture other and more precious freedoms is by relinquishing the freedom to breed, and that very soon. ''Freedom is the recognition of necessity''—and it is the role of education to reveal to all the necessity of abandoning the freedom to breed. Only so, can we put an end to this aspect of the tragedy of the commons.

NOTES

1. A. Smith, *The Wealth of Nations* (New York: Modern Library 1937), p. 423.
2. W.F. Lloyd, *Two Lectures on the Checks to Population* (Oxford: University Press, 1833), reprinted (in part) in

Population, Evolution and Birth Control, ed. G. Hardin. (San Francisco: Freeman, 1964), p. 37.

3. A.N. Whitehead, *Science and the Modern World* (New York: Mentor, 1948), p. 17.

4. G. Hardin, Ed., *Population, Evolution, and Birth Control,* (San Francisco: Freeman, 1964), p. 56.

5. S. McVav, *Scientific American* 216, No. 8 (1966): 13.

DISCUSSION TOPICS

1. Identify a commons in your geographical area. Is this commons falling into the pattern described by Hardin? Explain.

2. What other forms of mutual coercion besides taxation might reduce individual exploitation of a commons?

3. Do you agree with Hardin that the freedom to breed will bring ruin to all? Explain your reasoning.

READING 27

Understanding the Commons

Gary Snyder

Gary Snyder (b. 1930) is author of several volumes of essays and seven collections of poetry, including the Pulitzer Prize winning Turtle Island. *He teaches literature and wilderness thought at the University of California at Davis.*

In the following passage from Practice of the Wild, *he contrasts historical and contemporary examples of the commons. He notes that Hardin really is talking about contemporary common-pool resources, not the historic form of a commons. Shared natural areas in both Asia and Europe that served as historic commons were based on small plots of land operated by traditional, local communities.*

Snyder recommends a return to local control of commons land rather than control by a central government or large corporations aiming at development or extraction. Snyder sees no alternative but to restore the historic commons as an organization in which human and nonhuman join in "the web of the wild world," although he recognizes that the existence of a world marketplace will make such local organization difficult.

I stood with my climbing partner on the summit of Glacier Peak looking all ways round, ridge after ridge and peak after peak, as far as we could see. To the west across Puget Sound were the farther peaks of the Olympic Mountains. He said: "You mean there's a senator for all this?" As in the Great Basin, crossing desert after desert, range after range, it is easy to think there are vast spaces on earth yet unadministered, perhaps forgotten, or unknown (the endless sweep of spruce forest in Alaska and Canada)—but it is all mapped and placed in some domain. In North America there is a lot that is in public domain, which has its problems, but at least they are problems we are all enfranchised to work on. David Foreman, founder of the Earth First! movement, recently stated his radical provenance. Not out of Social Justice, Left Politics, or Feminism did I come—says David—but from the Public Lands Conservation movement—the solid stodgy movement that goes back to the thirties and before. Yet these land and wildlife issues were what politicized John Muir, John Wesley Powell, and Aldo Leopold—the abuses of public land.

American public lands are the twentieth-century incarnation of a much older institution known across Eurasia—in English called the "commons"—which was the ancient mode of both protecting and managing the wilds of the self-governing regions. It worked well enough until the age of market economies, colonialism, and imperialism. Let me give you a kind of model of how the commons worked.

Between the extremes of deep wilderness and the private plots of the farmstead lies a territory which is not suitable for crops. In earlier times it was used jointly by the members of a given tribe or village. This area, embracing both the wild and the semi-wild, is of critical importance. It is necessary for the health of the wilderness because it adds big habitat, overflow territory, and room for wildlife to fly and run. It is essential even to an agricultural village economy because its natural diversity provides the many necessities and amenities that the privately held plots cannot. It enriches the agrarian diet with game and fish. The shared land supplies firewood, poles and stone for building, clay for the kiln, herbs, dye plants, and much else, just as in a foraging economy. It is especially important as seasonal or full-time open range for cattle, horses, goats, pigs, and sheep.

In the abstract the sharing of a natural area might be thought of as a matter of access to "common pool resources" with no limits or controls on individual exploitation. The fact is that such sharing developed over millennia and always within territorial and social contexts. In the peasant societies of both Asia and Europe there were customary forms that gave direction to the joint use of land. They did not grant free access to outsiders, and there were controls over entry and use by member households. The commons has been defined as "the undivided land belonging to the members of a local community as a whole." This definition fails to make the point that the commons is both specific land *and* the traditional community institution that determines the carrying capacity for its various subunits and defines the rights and obligations of those who use it, with penalties for lapses. Because it is traditional and *local,* it is not identical with today's "public domain," which is land held and managed by a central government. Under a national state such management may be destructive (as it is becoming in Canada and the United States) or benign (as it often has been in the past)—but in no case is it locally managed. One of the ideas in the current debate on how to reform our public lands is that of returning them to regional control.

An example of traditional management: what would keep one household from bringing in more and more stock and tempting everyone toward overgrazing? In earlier England and in some contemporary Swiss villages (Netting, 1976), the commoner could only turn out to common range as many head of cattle as he could feed over the winter in his own corrals. This meant that no one was allowed to increase his herd from outside with a cattle drive just for summer grazing. (This was known in Norman legal language

as the rule of *levancy and couchancy:* you could only run the stock that you actually had "standing and sleeping" within winter quarters.)

The commons is the contract a people make with their local natural system. The word has an instructive history: it is formed of *ko,* "together," with (Greek) *moin,* "held in common." But the Indo-European root *mei* means basically to "move, to go, to change." This had an archaic special meaning of "exchange of goods and services within a society as regulated by custom or law." I think it might well refer back to the principle of gift economies: "the gift must always move." The root comes into Latin as *munus,* "service performed for the community" and hence "municipality."

There is a well-documented history of the commons in relation to the village economies of Europe and England. In England from the time of the Norman Conquest the enfeoffed knights and overlords began to gain control over the many local commons. Legislation (the Statute of Merton, 1235) came to their support. From the fifteenth century on the landlord class, working with urban mercantile guilds and government offices, increasingly fenced off village-held land and turned it over to private interests. The enclosure movement was backed by the big wool corporations who found profit from sheep to be much greater than that from farming. The wool business, with its exports to the Continent, was an early agribusiness that had a destructive effect on the soils and dislodged peasants. The arguments for enclosure in England—efficiency, higher production—ignored social and ecological effects and served to cripple the sustainable agriculture of some districts. The enclosure movement was stepped up again in the eighteenth century: between 1709 and 1869 almost five million acres were transferred to private ownership, one acre in every seven. After 1869 there was a sudden reversal of sentiment called the "open space movement" which ultimately halted enclosures and managed to preserve, via a spectacular lawsuit against the lords of fourteen manors, the Epping Forest.

Karl Polanyi (1975) says that the enclosures of the eighteenth century created a population of rural homeless who were forced in their desperation to become the world's first industrial working class. The enclosures were tragic both for the human community and for natural ecosystems. The fact that England now has the least forest and wildlife of all the nations of Europe has much to do with the enclosures. The takeover of commons land on the European plain also began about five hundred years ago, but one-third of Europe is still not privatized. A survival of commons practices in Swedish law allows anyone to enter private farmland to pick berries or mushrooms, to cross on foot, and to camp out of sight of the house. Most of the former commons land is now under the administration of government land agencies.

A common model can still be seen in Japan, where there are farm villages tucked in shoestring valleys, rich growing in the *tanbo* on the bottoms, and the vegetable plots and horticulture located on the slightly higher ground. The forested hills rising high above the valleys are the commons—in Japanese called *iriai,* "joint entry." The boundary between one village and the next is often the very crests of the ridges. On the slopes of Mt. Hiei in Kyoto prefecture, north of the remote Tendai Buddhist training temples of Yokkawa, I came on men and women of Ohara village bundling up slender brush-cuttings for firewood. They were within the village land. In the innermost mountains of Japan there are forests that are beyond the reach of the use of any village. In early feudal times they were still occupied by remnant hunting peoples, perhaps Japanese-Ainu mixed-blood survivors. Later some of these wildlands were appropriated by the government and declared "Imperial Forests." Bears became extinct in England by the thirteenth century, but they are still found throughout the more remote Japanese mountains, even occasionally just north of Kyoto.

In China the management of mountain lands was left largely to the village councils—all the central government wanted was taxes. Taxes were collected in kind, and local specialties were highly prized. The demands of the capital drew down Kingfisher feathers, Musk deer glands, Rhinoceros hides, and other exotic products of the mountains and streams, as well as rice, timber, and silk. The village councils may have resisted overexploitation of their resources, but

when the edge of spreading deforestation reached their zone (the fourteenth century seems to be a turning point for the forests of heartland China), village land management crumbled. Historically, the seizure of the commons—east or west—by either the central government or entrepreneurs from the central economy has resulted in degradation of wild lands and agricultural soils. There is sometimes good reason to kill the Golden Goose: the quick profits can be reinvested elsewhere at a higher return.

In the United States, as fast as the Euro-American invaders forcefully displaced the native inhabitants from their own sorts of traditional commons, the land was opened to the new settlers. In the arid West, however, much land was never even homesteaded, let alone patented. The native people who had known and loved the white deserts and blue mountains were now scattered or enclosed on reservations, and the new inhabitants (miners and a few ranchers) had neither the values nor the knowledge to take care of the land. An enormous area was de facto public domain, and the Forest Service, the Park Service, and the Bureau of Land Management were formed to manage it. (The same sorts of land in Canada and Australia are called "Crown Lands," a reflection of the history of English rulers trying to wrest the commons from the people.)

In the contemporary American West the people who talk about a "sagebrush rebellion" might sound as though they were working for a return of commons land to local control. The truth is the sagebrush rebels have a lot yet to learn about the place—they are still relative newcomers, and their motives are not stewardship but development. Some westerners are beginning to think in long-range terms, and these don't argue for privatization but for better range management and more wilderness preservation.

The environmental history of Europe and Asia seems to indicate that the best management of commons land was that which was locally based. The ancient severe and often irreversible deforestation of the Mediterranean Basin was an extreme case of the misuse of the commons by the forces that had taken its management away from regional villages (Thirgood, 1981). The situation in America in the nineteenth and early twentieth centuries was the reverse. The truly local people, the Native Americans, were decimated and demoralized, and the new population was composed of adventurers and entrepreneurs. Without some federal presence the poachers, cattle grazers, and timber barons would have had a field day. Since about 1960 the situation has turned again: the agencies that were once charged with conservation are increasingly perceived as accomplices of the extractive industries, and local people—who are beginning to be actually local—seek help from environmental organizations and join in defense of the public lands.

Destruction extends worldwide and "encloses" local commons, local peoples. The village and tribal people who live in the tropical forests are literally bulldozed out of their homes by international logging interests in league with national governments. A well-worn fiction used in dispossessing inhabitory people is the declaration that the commonly owned tribal forests are either (1) private property or (2) public domain. When the commons are closed and the villagers must buy energy, lumber, and medicine at the company store, they are pauperized. This is one effect of what Ivan Illich calls "the 500-year war against subsistence."

So what about the so-called tragedy of the commons? This theory, as now popularly understood, seems to state that when there are open access rights to a resource, say pasturage, everyone will seek to maximize his take, and overgrazing will inevitably ensue. What Garrett Hardin and his associates are talking about should be called "the dilemma of common-pool resources." This is the problem of overexploitation of "unowned" resources by individuals or corporations that are caught in the bind of "If I don't do it the other guy will" (Hardin and Baden, 1977). Oceanic fisheries, global water cycles, the air, fertility—all fall into this class. When Hardin et al. try to apply their model to the historic commons it doesn't work, because they fail to note that the commons was a social institution which, historically, was

never without rules and did not allow unlimited access (Cox, 1985).

In Asia and parts of Europe, villages that in some cases date back to neolithic times still oversee the commons with some form of council. Each commons is an entity with limits, and the effects of overuse will be clear to those who depend on it. There are three possible contemporary fates for common pool resources. One is privatization, one is administration by government authority, and the third is that—when possible—they become part of a true commons, of reasonable size, managed by local inhabitory people. The third choice may no longer be possible as stated here. Locally based community or tribal (as in Alaska) landholding corporations or cooperatives seem to be surviving here and there. But operating as it seems they must in the world marketplace, they are wrestling with how to balance tradition and sustainability against financial success. The Sealaska Corporation of the Tlingit people of southeast Alaska has been severely criticized (even from within) for some of the old-growth logging it let happen.

We need to make a world-scale "Natural Contract" with the oceans, the air, the birds in the sky. The challenge is to bring the whole victimized world of "common pool resources" into the Mind of the Commons. As it stands now, any resource on earth that is not nailed down will be seen as fair game to the timber buyers or petroleum geologists from Osaka, Rotterdam, or Boston. The pressures of growing populations and the powers of entrenched (but fragile, confused, and essentially leaderless) economic systems warp the likelihood of any of us seeing clearly. Our perception of how entrenched they are may also be something of a delusion.

Sometimes it seems unlikely that a society as a whole can make wise choices. Yet there is no choice but to call for the "recovery of the commons"—and this in a modern world which doesn't quite realize what it has lost. Take back, like the night, that which is shared by all of us, that which is our larger being. There will be no "tragedy of the commons" greater than this: if we do not recover the commons—regain personal, local, community, and peoples' direct involvement in sharing (in *being*) the web of the wild world—that world will keep slipping away. Eventually our complicated industrial capitalist/socialist mixes will bring down much of the living system that supports us. And, it is clear, the loss of a local commons heralds the end of self-sufficiency and signals the doom of the vernacular culture of the region. This is still happening in the far corners of the world.

The commons is a curious and elegant social institution within which human beings once lived free political lives while weaving through natural systems. The commons is a level of organization of human society that includes the nonhuman. The level above the local commons is the bioregion. Understanding the commons and its role within the larger regional culture is one more step toward integrating ecology with economy.

NOTES

Cox, Susan Jane Buck, ''No Tragedy in the Commons,'' *Environmental Ethics* 7.2 (1985): 49-62.

Hardin, Garrett and John Baden, *Managing the Commons,* San Francisco: W.H. Freeman, 1977.

Netting, R., ''What Alpine Peasants Have in Common: Observations on Communal Tenure in a Swiss Village,'' *Human Ecology* 4.2 (1976): 135-146.

Polanyi, Karl, *The Great Transformation,* New York: Octagon Books, 1975.

''The so-called Statute of Merton, 1236'' *English Historical Documents, III* ed. Harry Rothwell, New York and Oxford: Oxford University Press, 1975, pp. 351-354.

Thirgood, J.V., *Man and the Mediterranean Forest: A History of Resource Depletion,* New York: Academic Press, 1981.

DISCUSSION TOPICS

1. What aspects of the environment could be treated as a historic commons under local control? Explain your reasoning.
2. What solutions do you recommend for management of common-pool resources such as oceanic fisheries, global water cycles, air, and soil?
3. Do you agree with Snyder that some people who live in an area are not ''truly local''? How would you distinguish between those who merely live in an area and those who are truly local?

READING 28

In Defense of Environmental Economics

Steven F. Edwards

Steven F. Edwards (b. 1954) is a resource economist working for the National Marine Fisheries Service in Woods Hole, Massachusetts.

Edwards argues that economic valuations can be used wherever the assumptions of Homo economicus *hold. These assumptions include that individuals are selfishly interested only in their own satisfaction (''personal utility'') and that they are indifferent to where that satisfaction comes from. As* Homo economicus *becomes more satisfied, his or her willingness-to-pay for additional units of whatever is satisfying diminishes. This simple abstraction yields testable hypotheses about willingness-to-pay.*

Anything that is valued instrumentally can in principle be dealt with economically. Economic value does not require markets and prices to be expressed, since personal utility also can be determined by such mechanisms as the taxes a governmental body chooses to impose and membership in conservation organizations. These allocations of economic value require neither consumption nor use.

Instrumental value is determined solely by the utility something yields. The contingent valuation method (surveys in which resources go in a hypothetical market to the highest bidder) is used to assess nonuse values. Edwards notes that economists concentrate on ascertaining peoples' real preferences rather than presumptuously focusing on what someone else thinks they should be.

Edwards points out that altruistic preferences do not

fit within the model of Homo economicus. *The altruist's personal utility is not the primary motivation, and the altruist is not indifferent to the various sources of personal utility.*

. . . In the economic model of egoistic man, definitions of economic value are derived from a preference structure called indifference.[1] That is, economic man is indifferent between amounts and assortments of things that provide equal satisfaction, or utility.[2] Because choices are constrained by personal assets, economic behavior is characterized broadly by the allocation of income (and time in some cases) among things that provide personal utility.

It is crucial to understand the importance of indifference and the relationship between income and personal utility in order to understand definitions of economic value and why economic values are monetized. Clearly if economic man's income increases, so will personal utility, since more money is available to increase the amounts of things that provide personal satisfaction. Similarly, if income decreases, utility will decrease. Looked at another way, we ask, if something changes to reduce the availability, amount, or quality of something that provides instrumental value, what is the maximum that the person is willing to pay to prevent the change? Notice that the change (e.g., price increase for a marketed commodity, reduction in ground water quality, reduction in the population size of the endangered blue whale) would lower utility for economic man, and that maximum willingness-to-pay is the reduction in income that prevents the change. That is, maximum willingness-to-pay is *the change in income that holds personal utility constant.* A similar process could be followed to define a willingness-to-be-compensated in terms of the minimum acceptable change in income that keeps personal utility constant when the conditions are allowed to change. These utility-held-constant or Hicksian values are the theoretical notions of economic value that economists presume to measure with assessments of willingness-to-pay.[3]

Four important points are implicit in this brief characterization of economic man and economic value. The first three concerning indifference, monetization, and the relationships among economic value, markets, and prices are elaborated in this section. The measurement of nonconsumptive and nonuse values with willingness-to-pay surveys is discussed in [the] section [on measurement of nonconsumptive and nonuse values].

Indifference is the cornerstone of rigorous definitions of economic values. Something's economic value—whether it be a marked commodity, an unpriced environmental resource, or sympathy for future generations—is determined entirely by its ability to yield personal utility. Furthermore, the measure of something's instrumental value to economic man decreases as its level increases because the person moves toward satiation. That is, while something's total instrumental value manifest in total willingness-to-pay increases with its level, marginal willingness-to-pay for incremental units decreases. In this context, the cold truth is that there is nothing unique about an apple, a day of fishing, a scenic vista, a blue whale, or a bequest of clean ground water to future genera-

---

1. I assume that everyone agrees that profit is a well-defined notion of value in economics. Therefore, I will not discuss economic values associated with market supply. See Richard E. Just, Darrell Hueth and Andrew Schmitz, *Applied Welfare Economics and Public Policy* (Englewood Cliffs, N.J.: Prentice-Hall, 1982), for a discussion of economic profit, economic rent, and producer's surplus.

2. *Indifference does not imply a lack of interest* in any one thing or assortment of things. Indifference is a *relative* term for things that provide equal levels of personal utility. Also, my inelegant use of the word *thing* to refer generally to everything animate and inanimate is merely a matter of convenience and should not carry negative connotations.

3. This is not the place to teach microeconomics and welfare economics. Those interested in achieving a clear understanding of the relationships among price, marginal willingness-to-pay, total willingness-to-pay, utility, marginal utility, consumer's (Marshallian) surplus, and the four Hicksian surpluses might begin with Just, Hueth, and Schmitz's book, *Applied Welfare Economics.* This is recommended given the confusion that is apparent in critiques of economics.

tions. Economic man trades these off at the margin to identify positions of equal personal satisfaction.

Nor is there anything special about the money metric. Monetization simply reflects economic man's allocation of income over things that yield personal utility. If choices were constrained by time or beads, economic value would be measured in minutes or numbers of beads. Dollars, or more accurately changes in income, are convenient and legitimate proxies for the change in commodities that leaves economic man indifferent between initial and final conditions.

This brings us to a third and crucial point: markets and prices are not necessary conditions for economic value. Rather, markets and prices emerge from collective economic behavior when people can be excluded from the use and benefits of things unless they pay for them.[4] Property rights protect owners' claims to things while prices facilitate an allocation of their claims. Without exclusivity, there is little reason for people other than a philanthropist to supply a commodity or an environmental resource, since without it they would not be compensated. Without exclusivity on the supply side and a sufficient interest or demand on the part of others to pay for something, markets and prices would not emerge.

Contrast things that are exchanged in markets with scenic vistas, clean ground water, national forests, and blue whales. Although the latter usually are not priced in traditional single-commodity markets, economic man still gets personal satisfaction from their existence. In fact, it seems difficult to argue that market-like mechanisms, albeit nontraditional, do not allocate resources to protect environmental quality, wilderness, wildlife, and the likely interests of future generations when we pay taxes (and in many cases vote to raise taxes) for pollution control, ecosystem preservation, endangered species programs, and so on. In addition, conservation organizations are in effect voluntary, market-like systems for providing nonconsumptive recreation, species preservation, and environmental protection. Traditional markets and prices provide only one mechanism whereby these values are revealed. Limiting economics to the analysis of traditional markets is arbitrary. . . .

There also seems to be general agreement [among critics of environmental economics—eds.] with Kelman's view that monetizing environmental values somehow cheapens the resource, making the process inappropriate.[5] As examples of this curious assertion that markets/prices form preferences rather than vice–versa, he cites praise that is bought, the sale of humans, and prostitution. While pitiable or reprehensible to others, the value to those who engage in these actions *voluntarily* is consistent with egoistic motives and preferences. That is, Kelman uses the preferences of others to reject the preferences of self a priori. In addition, Kelman presumes incorrectly that the instrumental value of superficially similar things will be equal—he compares apples with oranges, so to speak. Or, to use his example, it seems unlikely that ''prostitute services'' and ''sex that consummates love'' are identical for most people.[6] Clearly, these acts are quite different and should be expected to yield different levels of instrumental value. In the context of this paper, it would not be surprising for someone to value a commercialized campground and a domestic rabbit differently from a remote national forest and a wild rabbit, since the things themselves are different. Economic assessments of individual, instrumental values are indeed appropriate for economic man.

MEASUREMENT OF NONCONSUMPTIVE AND NONUSE VALUES

. . . Anything that is valued instrumentally and in comparison to the instrumental value derived from other things can in principle be handled by economics,

---

4. See Alan Randall's characterization of environmental resources according to divisibility, exclusivity, and rivalry, *Resource Economics: An Economic Approach to Natural Resource and Environmental Policy* (New York: John Wiley and Sons, 1981).

---

5. Kelman, ''Cost-Benefit Analysis'' and *What Price Incentives.*
6. Kelman, *What Price Incentives,* p. 71.

be it acts of friendship or love[7] or wilderness recreation, aesthetics, levels of species preservation, or bequests of natural resources to future generations. Although this might be disquieting, it is, nevertheless, true for economic man, since something's instrumental value is determined solely by the utility that it yields, and since changes in income standardize changes in market and nonmarket things.

This final point must be elaborated given its relationship to the contingent valuation method. Kevin Boyle and Richard Bishop distinguish among: (1) consumptive use values such as hunting whereby economic man derives personal satisfaction from harvesting natural resources; (2) nonconsumptive use values such as wildlife photography and nature walks whereby personal satisfaction is derived from using, but not consuming, wildlife and wilderness; (3) indirect use values where, for example, wildlife and the outdoors are enjoyed indirectly through television and literature; and (4) nonuse values whereby personal satisfaction is derived from preserving wildlife or the environment, but where use is not involved.[8] The unifying characteristic of these values and their definitions in the economics literature is that their assignment is based solely on personal utility and indifference. Rolston acquiesces somewhat on the recreational value of "wildlands."[9] However, he focuses on market prices involved with travel costs rather than on the individual's motivation to be willing to incur these costs.

The nonuse category is tantamount to the economist's notions of existence values.[10] Stated simply, preservation value is the personal satisfaction that one receives from preserving wildlife. It is defined rigorously in terms of maximum willingness-to-pay which is presumed to keep personal utility constant. Similarly, bequest value is defined as the personal satisfaction (also manifest in willingness-to-pay) from leaving natural resources for the possible use by future generations. Since future amounts of these things and/or one's future preferences may be uncertain, an additional component called option value can be defined loosely as the willingness-to-pay to eliminate supply uncertainty.[11] Each type of nonuse value (and use value) has an option value complement. Finally, and for the sake of completeness, option "price" is one's total willingness-to-pay against/for a change in the natural environment, including the expected value of relevant use and nonuse benefits plus the associated option values.[12]

While it is a relatively easy matter to define these values for economic man, their assessment awaited methodological advances. Economists responded to the need to internalize human impacts on the environment in policy decisions by developing an array of market-related and nonmarket methods which are consistent with utility theory. Of the methods that are now available, the contingent valuation method is required to assess the nonuse values, and it has distinct

7. Kelman seems to agree that "in principle the analysis can be extended to valued feelings as well as valued material goods" (*What Price Incentives,* p. 21).

8. Kevin Boyle and Richard C. Bishop, "The Total Value of Wildlife Resources: Conceptual and Empirical Issues," presented at the Association of Environmental and Resource Economists' Workshop on Recreation and Demand Modeling. Boulder, Colo., 17-18 May 1985.

9. Rolston, "Valuing Wildlands," *Environmental Ethics* 7 (1985): 23-48.

10. Rolston ("Valuing Wildlands") used a somewhat dated value typology from environmental economics. As discussed above, existence value subsumes preservation value and bequest value; it is not separate from bequest value. Furthermore, these concepts are not separable from option value in the sense used by Rolston. In fact, each use and nonuse value concept in economics has an option value component when demand or supply is uncertain. See Alan Randall and John R. Stoll, "Existence Value in a Total Valuation Framework," in R.D. Rowe and L.G. Chestnut, eds., *Managing Air Quality and Scenic Resources at National Parks and Wilderness Areas* (Boulder, Colo.: Westview Press, 1983), for a discussion of a complete value typology.

11. Sagoff might prefer inchoate to uncertain ("At the Shrine"). Either way, these notions of economic value are not undermined when a person's intent is to value the environment relative to the personal benefits that other things provide.

12. Terms like option *price* and *consumers* surplus are regrettable when one tries to overcome semantical as well as substantive barriers between disciplines. While economists are comfortable with unnecessary references to market concepts, critics may find false corroboration when the words price and consumption are used to discuss nonmarket and nonconsumptive valuations. I hope that the reader will look beyond sometimes confusing and careless nomenclature and into the underlying meaning of the concepts.

advantages when the so-called market-related approaches are faced with significant empirical problems.[13] It is being used increasingly to assess the economic value of recreation, scenic beauty, air quality, water quality, species preservation, and bequests to future generations.[14] In essence, people are presented with an expected change in the level of an environmental resource and usually asked for their maximum willingness-to-pay to prevent the change, if it is a reduction, or to promote the change, if it is an improvement. . . .

IMPLICATIONS OF COMMITMENTS TO OTHERS FOR ECONOMIC ANALYSIS

Lest the reader think differently, I have not argued that economic man actually characterizes mankind. Nor have I argued that markets, prices, and people's willingness-to-pay for environmental resources necessarily proves the existence of economic man. This reasoning would be circular and illogical. Instead, my discussion focuses on the proposition that *if* man's preferences are selfish and structured by indifference, then economic value is well-defined and measured appropriately in monetary terms. This simple abstraction of man is powerful in the sense that it yields testable hypotheses about willingness-to-pay.

For much economic inquiry—positive (vis-à-vis normative) economics—it is sufficient to predict behavior from the model of economic man. The realistic detail of the model is irrelevant when one seeks only accurate predictions of behavior. For example, contingent valuation experiments facilitate tests of whether and how much people are willing-to-pay for environmental resources. Difficulty arises, however, when it is necessary to interpret the meaning of willingness-to-pay. Whether willingness-to-pay is a rigorous measure of economic value where personal utility is held constant depends entirely on the validity of the assumptions about motivations and preferences. On this subject, environmental ethicists describe points of view that compete with the model of economic man.

Discussions of moralistic and social preferences found in thoughtful papers by Daly, Kelman, Rolston, and Tribe cause one to consider the implications of alternative motivations and preference structures for economic valuations.[15] Indeed, ethical views that argue for the intrinsic value or rights of other humans, wildlife, and future generations could be personified by a genuine altruist with unselfish commitments to the well-being of others.[16] The question thus arises: does such a stereotype of altruistic man—the antithesis of economic man—have implications for interpreting expressions of willingness-to-pay?

As Amartya Sen, an economist, argues, attitudes and behavior that are motivated by genuine commitments to others have profound implications for economic valuation:

> [C]ommitment does involve, in a very real sense, counterpreferential choice, destroying the crucial assumption that a chosen alternative must be better than (or at least as good as) the others for the person choosing it, and this would certainly require that models be formulated in an essentially different way. . . . Commitment is, of course, closely related to one's morals; . . . it drives a wedge between personal choice and personal welfare, and much of traditional economic theory relies on the identity of the two.[17]

---

13. See A. Myrick Freeman, *The Benefits of Environmental Improvement: Theory and Practice* (Washington, D.C.: Resources for the Future, 1979), for a discussion of the various methods in environmental economics and of their comparative advantages.

14. Rolston (''Valuing Wildlands'') cited many of these studies in footnote 3. For additional studies see issues of *Land Economics* and the *Journal of Environmental Economics and Management.*

15. Daly, ''Alternative Strategies''; Kelman, *What Price Incentives;* Rolston, *Valuing Wildlands;* Sen, ''Rational Fools''; Tribe, ''Ways Not to Think About Plastic Trees.''

16. Most environmental economists agree that some form of altruism motivates existence values. However, Boyle and Bishop (''Total Value''), Randall and Stoll (''Existence Value''), and others actually describe what D. A. Kennett, ''Altruism and Economic Behavior: I. Developments in the Theory of Public and Private Redistribution,'' *American Journal of Economics and Sociology* 39 (1980): 183-198, would call *quasi-altruism,* whereby ostensibly altruistic acts or statements actually are motivated by self-interest.

17. Sen, ''Rational Fools,'' p. 328-389.

Although Sen discusses intragenerational commitments and an individual's social preferences, his rationale extends to moral principles that involve commitments to wildlife and future generations.[18] The "wedge between personal choice and personal welfare" requires a preference structure that differs radically from personal utility and indifference. A suitable candidate is a lexicographic ordering of preferences whereby changes in the population size of blue whales, in bequests of clean ground water to future generations, and so on are viewed as being morally right or wrong by the altruist.[19] Tribe touched on the possibility of lexicographic preferences for environmental protection, but did not delve into its technical implications for economic analysis.[20]

Elsewhere I examine some of the technical implications of altruistic choice which are revealed by a lexicographic preference structure.[21] While the details cannot be illustrated here, the implications of commitments to others are straightforward. Most importantly, indifference is undefined for the altruist, since no two states of the world involving trade-offs between the well-being of others and personal utility can have equal ranking. This is not to say, however, that willingness-to-pay and personal utility are undefined. For example, a person committed to stopping the killing of whales would always sacrifice income to prevent whaling and the accidental bicatch of whales in fisheries, since he always prefers more whales to fewer. The altruist's willingness-to-pay is defined, and in terms of it personal well-being obviously declines since disposable income decreases. However, this relationship is asymmetric, since willingness-to-pay is not based on changes in personal utility, and, therefore, does not match rigorous notions of economic values.

The upshot of this brief inspection of an altruist's preferences is that neither willingness-to-pay nor willingness-to-be-compensated approximates rigorous notions of economic values which hold personal utility constant (i.e., Hicksian values). This is true simply because self-interest is a secondary concern to the altruist. For example, a maximum willingness-to-pay of $x to Greenpeace, Inc. to help reduce the killing of whales worldwide from N to n whales cannot be interpreted as the amount of money that leaves the altruist indifferent between a situation with the loss of N whales and an income of $X (where $X is greater than $x) and a situation with a loss of n whales and an income of $(X − x).

CONCLUSIONS

After erecting a value taxonomy, Rolston asks rhetorically, "Can the preceding array of value levels and types be reduced, wholly or in part, to economic terms as a prerequisite for cost-benefit analysis?"[22] The answer is a qualified yes, although the word *reduced* has unnecessary connotations. Monetization of non-market, environmental values by individuals is relevant and appropriate when a person's preferences are based on self-interest and on indifference between amounts of things that provide equal satisfaction. There is no category mistake in these cases since all use and nonuse concepts for economic man are ho-

18. For similar viewpoints on the rights of wildlife and future generations see: Joel Feinberg, "The Rights of Animals and Future Generations," in W.T. Blackstone, ed., *Philosophy and Environmental Crisis* (Athens: University of Georgia Press, 1974); J. Ferejohn and T. R. Page, "On the Foundations of Intertemporal Choice," *American Journal of Agricultural Economics* 60 (1978): 269-275; Peter Singer, *Animal Liberation: A New Ethics for Our Treatment of Animals* (New York: New York Review, 1975); Taylor, "Are Humans Superior to Animals?"; Tribe, "Ways Not to Think about Plastic Trees; E.B. Weiss, "The Planetary Trust: Conservation and Intergenerational Equity," *Ecology Law Quarterly* 11 (1984): 495-581.

19. Just as words in a dictionary are ordered, lexicographical orderings over states of the world are ranked according to priorities. That is, more of a thing is always preferred to less regardless of what happens to other things that are ranked lower. This is in contrast to indifference whereby different things can be exchanged to identify positions of indifference.

20. Tribe, "Ways Not to Think about Plastic Trees."

21. Steven F. Edwards, "Environmental Ethics and the Assessment of Existence Values: Does the Neoclassical Fit?" *Northeastern Journal of Agricultural and Resource Economics* 15.2 (1986): 145-150.

22. Rolston, "Valuing Wildlands," p. 38.

mologous.[23] Methodologies that are used to assess these values, including the contingent valuation method, are also relevant, being limited only by empirical problems in some applications. Whether cost-benefit analysis can be used to amalgamate these values across individuals is another matter for consideration at the macro level of analysis.[24]

The qualification involves empirical ignorance about underlying motivations and preference structures. I have argued that willingness-to-pay is not a proxy for utility-held-constant notions of economic value when choices are not motivated by self-interest and indifference is undefined. Ethicists challenge economists for presuming, a priori, that people attempt to think and behave like economic man, and that the ''total'' value of the natural environment can be measured in economic terms. However, most critics of environmental economics are also presumptuous when they take strongly normative positions on what preferences *should be* without also attending to what they actually *are*.

From an objective perspective, the disagreement between economists and ethicists on individual ethics is an empirical matter. Adam Smith's inductive reasoning and Richard Dawkins' discussion of the genetic basis for selfish behavior argue for the existence of economic man.[25] However, Stephen Kellert's studies of attitudes toward animals suggest a richer, pluralistic system of preferences within individuals and throughout society.[26] For example, of the ten attitudes that he identifies, the humanistic, moralistic, and utilitarian attitudes were dominant in 35%, 20%, and 20% of his sample, respectively. The issue is complicated further by the possibility of complex preference structures such as ''preferences over preferences'' whereby economic man and altruistic man might exist in one person.[27]

DISCUSSION TOPICS

1. Edwards argues that the abstraction of *Homo economicus* can be useful when people's actions are based on self-interest and indifference. In your view, what kind of circumstances lend themselves to this model? Under what circumstances might this model not hold?

2. How do you believe assigning dollar amounts to environmental values affects our relationship to the environment? Explain your reasoning.

---

23. Sagoff criticizes economists for allegedly making category mistakes when monetizing the values of the natural environment (''At the Shrine''). However, no logical mistake is made when concepts are homologous. That is, market and nonmarket values for economic man are derived from personal utility and indifference, and, therefore, have a common derivative. This is in contrast to things that are similar, or as taxonomists in the biological sciences emphasize, analogous but which lack a common derivative.

24. It is interesting to note, however, that well defined economic values ascertained for individuals could be amalgamated in ways other than cost-benefit analysis. For example, they could be used in an egalitarian framework to undertake policies that make individual welfare more equal. Alternatively, the individual assessments could be used within a libertarian framework to determine if a policy reduces the welfare of any one individual.

---

25. Richard Dawkins, *The Selfish Gene* (New York: Oxford University Press, 1976).

26. Stephen R. Kellert, ''Contemporary Values of Wildlife in American Society,'' in W.W. Shaw and E.H. Zube, eds., *Wildlife Values,* Institutional Series Report No. 1, Center for Assessment of Noncommodity Natural Resource Values, Rocky Mountain Forest and Range Experiment Station, U.S. Forest Service, 1980); Kellert, ''Assessing Wildlife and Environmental Values in Cost-Benefit Analysis,'' *Journal of Environmental Management* 18 (1984): 353-363.

27. R.C. Jeffrey, ''Preferences Among Preferences,'' *Journal of Philosophy* 71 (1974): 377-391; H. Margolis, ''A New Model of Rational Choice,'' *Ethics* 91 (1981): 265-279; Sen, ''Rational Fools.''

Some Problems with Environmental Economics

Mark Sagoff

Mark Sagoff received his Ph.D. in 1970 from the University of Rochester and is a research scholar at the Center for Philosophy and Public Policy, University of Maryland. His most recent book is The Economy of the Earth: Philosophy, Law, and the Environment *(London: Cambridge University Press, 1988). Sagoff responds to Steven Edwards' article by arguing, first, that willingness-to-pay as used in environmental economics does not measure personal satisfaction but only the results of contingent valuation surveys. Second, Sagoff argues that economic analysis is indeed limited to markets, because traditionally the willingness to sell is just as important as the willingness to buy. Some people may prefer not to sell at any price. Third, Sagoff interprets the increasing incidence of very high protest bids on willingness-to-pay surveys as evidence that many people believe that the natural resources in question are not for sale.*

Sagoff believes that environmental law, including property rights and rules, protects the owner from being forced to sell when he or she might not want to. If it were not for property rights, agencies enforcing conflict resolution by means of economy efficiency, based on cost-benefit analysis, could require that the owner sell out to the highest bidder. Sagoff interprets legislation such as the Clean Air Act and the Endangered Species Act as expressions of the public's insistence that they do not wish to market clean air and other natural resources but rather to regulate their use.

Sagoff presents some of the difficulties inherent in creating and interpreting preference surveys. Rather than setting policy merely on the basis of surveys of preferences or on the basis of cost-benefit analysis, he believes that decision makers must become educated about the natural world, and incorporate such virtues as careful deliberation and intellectual honesty. Economic considerations are significant in making environmental policy in the sense that they can provide guidelines for comparing alternative solutions to resource problems, after these solutions have been determined to be environmentally and culturally acceptable. Sagoff concludes by asserting that citizens are thinking and political beings capable of making objective judgments, not simply subjects with preferences.

. . . Edwards writes that cost-benefit analysis is a special case of utilitarianism, but this is not so, since welfare economics and the techniques of cost-benefit analysis it employs have no relation to substantive conceptions of the good, such as pleasure or happiness, of the kind that utilitarianism values. Welfare economists earlier in this century, imbued with a positivistic philosophy of science popular at the time, took pains to divorce their theory from any such substantive conception of utility, like happiness, since it could not be quantified, and insisted instead on defining utility in relation to measureable quantities, such as willingness-to-pay, even if these have no normative significance and no basis, therefore, in utilitarianism. Thus, sophisticated advocates of welfare economics, like Richard Posner, point out that the efficiency criterion is independent of utilitarian ethical theory. "The most important thing to bear in mind about the concept of value [in the economist's sense]," he writes, "is that it is based on what people are willing to pay for something rather than the happiness they would derive from having it."[1]

Let me now turn to Edwards' second point [p. 233], namely, that it is arbitrary to limit economic analysis to traditional markets. While this is true, it leads us to ask whether the kind of economic analysis that is relevant to the "contingent" valuation of resources applies to traditional markets in the first place. I believe, on the contrary, that it is arbitrary to *limit* it

---

1. Richard Posner, *The Economics of Justice* (Cambridge, Mass.: Harvard University Press, 1981), p. 60.

because it is arbitrary to *apply* this sort of analysis to traditional markets.

The big difference between traditional markets, in which property rights are well defined, and "contingent" markets, in which resources go, in principle, to the highest bidder, is this. In traditonal markets people can and do refuse to sell their property even to those who will pay the highest price for it; rather than sell out to a trespasser at the highest price, an individual is likely to try to enjoin the trespass. Thus, if your neighbor starts operating a stamping mill, drowning you in noise, you may proceed against him, and a court will enjoin the nuisance, especially if the zoning ordinances are on your side. The rights in question here are not for sale to the highest bidder; the owner may defend them in court. The rights to exclude and not to transfer are the most common incidents of ownership; they cannot be overridden, even by theorists who believe, for some reason, that all resources should be put up for auction to the highest bidder.

It is a commonplace that traditional markets will not allocate resources to those willing to pay the most for them, because of market "failures" and for other reasons, one of which is that many owners will refuse on principle to "sell out," e.g., to polluters.[2] If resources are to be allocated efficiently, an agency of the government must transfer them to the highest bid-

---

2. Many commentators recognize that cost-benefit analysis is an instrument of centralized government planning and that efficiency can be achieved only in an authoritarian system that substitutes bureaucratic control for free markets. The central authority, to justify its authoritarian allocation, need only say it is correcting a market failure. As Duncan Kennedy writes, it is rare that an analyst "lacks a handy externality to justify a particular . . . measure" (Duncan Kennedy, "Cost-Benefit Analysis of Entitlement Problems: A Critique," *Standard Law Review* 33 (1980): 419.) I am urging an additional reason for the same conclusion, namely, that in traditional markets owners for ethical, cultural, or other reasons can refuse to sell, while in the hypothetical markets envisioned by economic analysis, resources essentially are auctioned off to the highest bidder. The point I am making here has nothing to do with the gap between "bid" and "asked" prices for property rights, which economists recognize. My point is that environmental law deals with resources that people in fact refuse to sell at all—and this includes publicly as well as privately owned resources.

ders whether the original owners (including the public that owns "common" resources) consent to that transfer or not.

The economic analysis that Edwards defends applies to an auction in which every item is determined beforehand to be for sale to the highest bidder. Edwards may believe that "publicly" owned resources are essentially "unowned" and should be auctioned off; hence, economic analysis applies to them at least as well as it does to privately owned resources. An enormous structure of public law, like the Clean Air and Clean Water Acts, however, establishes that the public knows it owns environmental resources and has decided not to market them even to the highest bidder. The public has decided to prohibit or enjoin certain takings, as it were, rather than simply to accept them for a price. Likewise in traditional markets, an owner may refuse to sell to polluters rights to person and property even for a profit. . . .

To see this distinction, imagine you are a farmer and your neighbor, a rancher, sends his sheep to graze on your corn. In a traditional market—one which backs up property rights with property rules—you can get an injunction to compel your neighbor to stop the trespass. This is true because traditional markets recognize the traditional incidents of property, including the right to exclude.

In the sort of "market" welfare economists envision, injunctive relief of this sort is unavailable; you have to bargain with your neighbor to reach an "efficient" allocation of the resource. If bargaining breaks down, a court determines what your corn is "objectively" worth and awards you damages in that amount. What matters is how much each of you is willing to pay; ownership determines at most the direction in which payment is made.

If a victim of some market "externality," such as pollution, refuses to sell the relevant rights and seeks injunctive relief instead, this signifies, to the economic theorist, that the property owner is "uncooperative;" he or she is trying to "gouge" the tortfeasor by holding out for a higher price. The economic theorist, by interpreting the actions of property holders in this way, easily overrides their right not to sell, and has the state impose an "efficient" bargain, e.g., by awarding damages, instead.[3] ...

TWO APPROACHES TO RATIONALITY

In order to evaluate the economic approach to enviromental policy, it is important to distinguish two senses in which social policy decisions might be described as "rational" and as "scientific."[4] In one sense, a decision is "rational" if it uses mathematical criteria and methodologies, laid down in advance, to infer policy recommendations from independent or exogenous preferences in the client society. This approach conforms to a philosophy of science that stresses notions like "value neutrality," "replicable experiments," and "correspondence to an independent reality."

A decision or policy might be described as "rational" or as "scientific" in another sense if it is based on good reasons—reasons that are open and yet stand up to criticism. The words *rational* and *scientific* in this second sense, as Richard Rorty writes, means something more like "sane" and "reasonable" than "methodical." The term *rationality,* on this second approach, "names a set of moral virtues: tolerance, respect for the opinions of others, willingness to listen, reliance on persuasion rather than force."[5]

In accordance with the first approach, economists study data that have to do with prices and with the preferences consumers reveal or express in actual and surrogate markets. Economic analysts can then answer questions like "how safe, clean, etc., is safe or clean enough?" in terms of data about preferences—data that therefore represent independent variables or exogenous states of the world. In doing so, they are able to balance the benefits of environmental protection, measured in this way, against the opportunity costs of economic development.

The second approach, in contrast, uses a juridical or deliberative model to weigh various normative constraints, established by statute, against these opportunity costs. In accordance with this approach, public officials must not only recognize both the legal and ethical force of these constraints, but at the same time take account of technical, economic, and other realities, since no one can pursue a goal without adjusting to the obstacles that stand in the way of achieving it. Because there is no methodology for making this sort of judgment, public officials have only statutory language, judicial interpretation of that language, their general knowledge and experience, and the virtues of inquiry to rely upon. This is the reason why statutes generally require that officials respond to views presented at public hearings that they set policies that are reasonable and feasible, and that they create a record of their deliberations which can be reviewed by the courts.

The problem-solving approach of the Endangered Species Act, which sets up a committee to mitigate conflicts, illustrates this ethical and juridical approach to social regulation. This approach ties the rationality of the policy-making process to virtues, particularly, the virtues of deliberation, for example, intellectual honesty, civility, willingness to see a problem in a larger context, and openness of mind. It does not require decisions to conform to criteria, methodologies, or guidelines laid down in advance. Rather, it depends upon an open process in which decision makers respond on the record to the merits of arguments and proposals.

Economists, in measuring the value of "unpriced" social and environmental benefits, approach situa-

---

3. This is the reason that "libertarianism rejects in principle the use of cost-benefit analysis as a basis to justify pollution." Libertarians recognize that in traditional markets, where property rules are backed by property rights, "processes of production which involve pollution, so long as the harmful imposition upon others occurs without the consent of the victims, . . . may not be carried out." Tibor R. Machan, "Pollution and Political Theory," in *Earthbound,* ed. Tom Regan (New York: Random House, 1984), p. 98. A society that takes property rights and consent seriously, such as ours, will then at least enact environmental laws that seek to minimize and eventually eliminate pollution. A planned or centralized economy, in contrast, may permit and may even require pollution and any other transfer of property rights, without the consent of the initial owners, as long as the transfer is efficient or the benefits exceed the costs.

4. I have explained this distinction in more detail in "Where Ickes Went Right or Reason and Rationality in Environmental Law," *Ecology Law Quarterly* 14 (1987): 265-323.

5. Richard Rorty, "Science as Solidarity," unpublished manuscript, 1984, p. 3.

tions in a way that brings these two conceptions of science and rationality into serious conflict. This conflict becomes apparent when analysts must decide how much information to present to subjects and how much discussion, deliberation, and education to allow as part of a survey experiment. An analysis or assessment can be "scientific" in the sense of "gathering data on exogenous variables" only if it allows no discussion, education, or deliberation to take place. An approach which is "scientific" and "neutral" in this way, however, cannot be "scientific" in the sense of being "reasonable," "civilized," or "intelligent."

THE WYOMING EXPERIMENT

The Wyoming economists[6] attempted to make their analyses "scientific" by basing them on quantitative methodologies and on independently existing data that can be verified through replicable experiments. Accordingly, these economists sought to develop quantified methodologies to identify exogenous preferences as data and to aggregate them in a way that permits the calculation of a social decision. In other words, they tried to make intangible values tangible. Can this be done?

Anyone trying to deal with these intangibles has to answer a lot of questions. How valuable is atmospheric visibility in parks, wilderness areas, and so on? How important is it for us to be able to stand on a mountaintop in Yosemite and contemplate an "integral vista" free of power plants, hotels, highways, or other signs of industrial civilization? What are the expressive or symbolic values of nature untouched by man and how much are these worth to us? How draconian should prohibitions on development be in order to keep the wilderness experience pristine?

Let us stick to the example of visibility in and near national parks. In measuring the value of visibility, we need to know, first, how a loss of atmospheric clarity or quality is caused. A mist or fog hanging on the mountains, for example, can be very beautiful, perhaps more beautiful than a clear view, as the Japanese show us in their paintings. A mist or fog, then, need not impair aesthetic value. Even a volcano which distributes ash over hundreds of miles may be viewed as an aesthetic marvel; people will come from as far just to see it. If soot and precipitates from a power plant impede visibility, however, the resulting loss of air quality, even if indistinguishable from that caused by a volcano, has a completely different meaning. We no longer think of it as natural or compare it with aspects of nature and its beauty; we may perceive it, rather, as an assault on nature and as destructive of its integrity.

The Wyoming economists faced something of a dilemma when they designed their experiment: they had to decide whether or not to explain to the participants how the visibility would be lost in the vistas presented in the photographs. If they let the participants assume that the cause would be natural, e.g., an approaching storm, then they might elicit a preference for *less* visibility, since oncoming storms in deserts can be considered beautiful. If the experimenters identified the cause as the belching smokestacks of Humongous Megawatt, a coal-fired utility, however, the respondents might not reveal aesthetic but political preferences. They might express opinions, for example, about the inadvisability of increasing supply as opposed to decreasing demand for energy through conservation. They might even offer legal arguments based on the PSD provisions of the Clean Air Act.

In fact, this is what happened. The Wyoming team (appropriately, I believe) informed the respondents that the visibility would be obscured by pollution from a power plant. They described the amount of

---

6. [This material appeared earlier in the article—eds.]. In 1975, the Environmental Protection Agency, enforcing the "Prevention of Significant Deterioration" (PSD) requirement of the Clean Air Act, directed states to amend their implementation plans to protect air quality in areas where it exceeds national health and safety minimums. . . .

In a recent article, "An Experiment on the Economic Value of Visibility," three economists from the University of Wyoming have tackled this problem. The authors attempt to interpret and to evaluate PSD requirements in economic terms. "Aesthetics," the authors say, "will play a major role. The PSD requirements amount to formal governmental admission that aesthetics, at least as embodied in atmospheric visibility, is a 'good' that might have a positive value." See R. Rowe, R. D'Arge, and D. Brookshire, "An Experiment on the Economic Value of Visibility," *Journal of Environmental Economics and Management* (1980): 1.

energy (in kilowatt hours) to be produced, the location of the facilities, the levels of emission of various pollutants, and so on. I do not know whether the economists gave the subjects of the experiment information about the PSD requirements of the Clean Air Act; the respondents, however, may have had that information. The economists asked the subjects, first, how much they would pay (the "equivalent" or "ES" measure of consumer surplus) to prevent the deterioration of the visibility caused by the power plant. They then asked for "compensating" or "CS" values, which is to say, the amounts that the respondents would accept to allow the power plant to emit that much pollution.

When the respondents were asked how much they would demand in compensation (the "CS" or "WTA" value) to permit the loss of visibility shown in the photographs, at least half of them used the question as an occasion to express a political opinion. The Wyoming experimenters report:

> The CS values . . . put the liability for maintaining visibility with the power companies and presupposes [*sic*] that the power companies will attempt to buy off consumers rather than cleanse the air. If respondents reject this concept of "being bought off to permit pollution" they might increase their compensation. Strategically, respondents may give large or infinite valuations as an indication that this concept is unacceptable. This is partially supported in that slightly over one-half of the sample required infinite compensation or refused to cooperate with the CS portion of the survey instrument.[7]

The experimenters found even in their own experiment that a majority of a sample of citizens rejected a cost-benefit or "consumer surplus" approach to trade-offs between health, safety, or environmental quality and economic growth, an approach which also seems to be precluded by the Clean Air Act, the Occupational Safety and Health Act, and by other legislation.[8] Attempting to make their approach practicable, if not legal, they ended up in an awkward

position: they asked citizens participating in the experiment to accept the concept of trading dollars for pollution "rights," a concept that many citizens reject,[9] and most of the subjects responded by entering protest bids or by refusing to cooperate with the experiment.

THE PROBLEM OF INFORMATION

In an excellent paper on "Information Disclosure and Endangered Species Evaluation," a group of economists from Hawaii described bidding games and surrogate markets, i.e., the contingent valuation method (CVM), they used to determine citizen willingness to pay to preserve endangered species. The Hawaii group observed that WTP values are deeply influenced by the information subjects receive in the survey or experiment. These authors write:

> . . . willingness to pay (WTP) to preserve a particular animal is significantly influenced by information provided about the animal's physical and behavioral characteristics, and about its endangered status. While this proposition may appear obvious, it bears important implications for the proper type and amount of information disclosed in preservation valuation studies.[10]

In the Hawaii experiment, subjects were asked how much they were willing to contribute to a fund for preserving humpback whales, an endangered species. Then an experimental group saw *The Singing Whale,* a Jean Cousteau film describing the humpback and the threats to its survival. A control group viewed a film unrelated to whales, *The Sixty Minute Spot: The Making of a Television Commercial.* All subjects were then asked to reevaluate or reconsider their bids. After seeing the films, one-third of the experimental group and one-fifth of the control group increased their bids. The authors note that this "lends support

---

7. Rowe et al., "An Experiment," p. 9.

8. *American Textile Manufacturers v. Donovan (Cotton Dust),* 452 U.S. 490 (1981).

9. For discussion, see Steven Kelman, *What Price Incentives: Economists and the Environment* (Boston: Auburn House, 1981).

10. Karl Samples, John Dixon, and Marcia Gowen, "Information Disclosure and Endangered Species Evaluation," *Land Economics* 62 (1986): 306-312; quotation at 306.

to the view that preferences are learned during the interview process, even in the absence of new relevant information.''[11]

The Hawaii economists point out that relevant information can influence preservation bids in many ways. An individual is likely to decrease his bid, for example, if he learns that the population of a particular species is so large that it will survive or so small that it will go extinct no matter how much he and others contribute. A reasonable individual, in other words, is likely to apply some principle of triage to deal with the number and characteristics of endangered species. The economists conclude that ''information disclosure can influence perceived marginal efficiency investment in a preservation fund, and thereby result in changes in an individual's budget allocation strategy.''[12]

The Hawaii experimenters recognized the importance of their results for the contingent valuation of preservation, amenity, and other benefits of environmental protection. They identified a methodological question about the extent to which respondents are given information or otherwise allowed to educate themselves, discuss, or deliberate over the issues. Should valuation be based on the immediate, untutored, *ex ante* preferences of the respondents or should valuation refer to their informed or educated judgment instead?

One alternative, the authors note, ''is to accept the state of the respondents' ignorance about the resource as given, and provide only enough information about the resource to create a realistic market situation.'' This alternative has the advantage of keeping the response exogenous to or independent of the experiment. It has the disadvantage (as we saw in the Wyoming experiment), however, ''that respondents may not readily accept operating in a hypothetical market situation with unknown payoffs and opportunity costs.''[13]

At the other extreme, ''the analyst could provide

vast amounts of information to respondents about the resource being valued, along with complete information about its substitutes and complements.'' The respondents might discuss, in the visibility case, for example, various alternatives to constructing power plants near national parks, e.g., the possibility of energy conservation. They might try to size up or define the problem in terms which allow a different sort of solution. This kind of approach, the Hawaii economists point out, ''could change the preference mappings of respondents and therefore make individual values endogenous to the valuation process.''[14]

How should we choose between these alternatives? Should we accept the first alternative, insisting that the valuation of environmental benefits be ''rational'' in the sense of being methodical, derived from exogenous variables, and determined by criteria laid down in advance? Should we prefer the second alternative, emphasizing the virtues of deliberation rather than the methods of derivation, and hence a conception of ''rationality'' which is less akin to ''methodological'' than to ''civilized,'' ''reasonable,'' and ''sane''?

An analogy may help us answer this question. Let us suppose that a person has been called to perform jury duty. The judge informs each juror that a Mr. Smith has been accused of robbing a liquor store. Then the judge asks each juror separately whether Mr. Smith is guilty. If the judge is methodologically sophisticated, indeed, he or she may ask how much each juror is willing to pay for the preferred verdict. The judge may then report the verdict in terms of the mean, the average, or some statistical tranformation of the weighted average of the jurors' preferences.

If you were a juror, how would you respond to the judge? You might complain that the methodology is flawed—the judge should use the average rather than the mean bid to set the sentence. The judge may point, however, to a large literature which investigates all the ins and outs of the statistical methodologies—perhaps the software—used by the court. He or she may reply, moreover, that the verdict rests entirely on

11. Ibid., p. 310.
12. Ibid., p. 311.
13. Ibid., p. 312.

14. Ibid.

ex ante preferences which remain completely independent or exogenous to the decision-making process.

You might, on the other hand, ask the judge to let the jury hear the case—the evidence for and against—and to deliberate to reach a consensus in good faith. The judge could rule this out on the grounds that the verdict would then be biased by the means of obtaining it. What is more, he could point out that no quantified methodology exists for reaching a verdict through deliberation on the evidence. To be scientific, so the judge might reason, the verdict must be derived from exogenous variables by quantified criteria laid down in advance. Jurors might be permitted to make use of any hearsay evidence that they may have picked up beforehand from the newspapers. No further inquiry, however, may bias or prejudice preference.

If you were faced with this situation, what would you think? You would think that the judge is *crazy*. You would probably refuse to cooperate with this sort of ''valuation.'' You might protest, for example, or just vote to acquit Mr. Smith.

Economists often confront this kind of resistance to their surveys. Their subjects may reject cost-benefit balancing as an inappropriate and illegal framework for making social policy. Two resource economists observe:

> Bidding questions for changes in air quality are not always well received by respondents due to rejection of the hypothetical scenario, rejection of the implied property rights or liability rules presented in a situation, or rejection for moral and ethical reasons. . . . Rejection and protest bids have varied from 20 percent to 50 percent for specific applications of the bidding technique. *In these cases, respondents' true values remains unknown and unaccounted for.*[15]

I contend that just the reverse is true: it is only in this way—by lodging a protest—that respondents can begin to make their values known. These respondents may not perceive themselves as bundles of exogenous preferences, but rather as thinking beings capable of reaching informed judgments in the context of public inquiry and deliberation. They may regard themselves as a jury who might reach a considered judgment after discussion of all relevant views and information, including the relevant statutes. The contingent valuation method (CVM), however, insofar as it tries to make respondents express preferences rather than form judgments, denies their status both as thinking and political beings.[16] This is possibly the major reason that respondents so often enter protest bids or otherwise resist this sort of experiment.

DISCUSSION TOPICS

1. Should environmental decisions be based solely on the public good? What other factors would be important to consider?
2. What should be the proper role of cost-benefit analysis in determining environmental policy?

READING 30

Neoclassical Economics and Principles of Sustainable Development

Robert Goodland and George Ledec

Robert Goodland and George Ledec are employed in the Department of Environmental and Scientific Affairs of the World Bank, Washington, D.C. They argue that environmental concerns can be integrated into

---

15. Rowe and Chestnut, *The Value of Visibility*, pp. 80-81 (citations omitted, italics added). These authors cite three studies that encountered a 50 percent protest or rejection rate.

16. I have argued elsewhere that resource economists commit a ''category mistake'' by asking of objective beliefs and judgments a question that is appropriate only to subjective preferences and wants. See ''Economic Theory and Environmental Law,'' *Michigan Law Review* 79 (1981): 1393-1419, esp. pp. 1410-1418.

neoclassical (market-oriented capitalist) economic theory, and illustrate their ideas using projects of the World Bank. They point out that the traditional criterion of economic efficiency, Pareto optimality, can occur with both ecologically unsustainable patterns of resource use and with unjust income distributions.

Goodland and Ledec maintain that cost-benefit analysis, while possessing many deficiencies, still is necessary for advancing environmental goals. However, environmentalists should insist that all costs are taken into account. Also, safe minimum legal standards are needed, such as toxicity laws.

They point out various flaws in the use of the Gross National Product (GNP) as a complete measure of the wealth or welfare of a country: it does not measure income distribution, social well-being, or the value of nonutilized but available resources. The Gross National Product includes economic activity which is devoted to compensating for environmental damage, and it ignores natural resource depletion as well as production for subsistence, even though self-sufficient production may often be preferable to market-oriented production.

Goodland and Ledec argue that industrialized countries may not provide suitable development models for the Third World, and that the real goal of all development should be the production of adequate living standards for the world's population on a sustainable basis. They also note that environmental damages should be considered in cost-benefit analyses.

Future benefits and costs often are discounted by economists in favor of short-term benefits and costs. Goodman and Ledec note that such discounting can severely underestimate the environmentally stabilizing value of the natural world. Discounting future costs and benefits can discourage investment with long-term benefits and promote those with long-term costs.

Goodland and Ledec propose to define sustainable development as development which optimizes the benefits in the present without jeopardizing the potential for similar benefits in the future. Benefits can include economic efficiency, just distribution of economic resources, and political, religious, moral, and aesthetic values. They note that much current use of natural resources is not sustainable by these criteria.

Goodland and Ledec conclude by affirming the value of safe minimum standards, criteria which projects must meet to be approved, such as environmental and social criteria regardless of cost-benefit analysis. They provide a list of such standards.

PERSPECTIVE

. . . Economics is the study of allocating the resources available to society in a way that maximizes social well-being. If something must be foregone or sacrificed in order to achieve a social goal, the economic choices are involved. Economics attempts to tell us how we can make the trade-offs among tangible, material goods in the most efficient, or 'Pareto-optimal,' manner. A Pareto optimum is defined as a state of the economy in which all economic resources are allocated and used 'efficiently,' such that it is impossible to make anyone economically better off without making someone else economically worse off.

A major advantage of efficient markets is their ability to attain Pareto-optimal resource allocation (which is no small achievement). However, a Pareto-optimal allocation can occur at an ecologically unsustainable pattern of resource use, just as it can occur at an ethically undesirable pattern of income distribution (D. Pearce, 1976b). Pareto optimality is defined independently of both income distribution and the physical scale of resource use. Public policy decision-making which relies exclusively on market criteria (and, by extension, cost-benefit analysis centered on present-value maximizations) can effectively address only short-term allocative efficiency—not many of the other important factors which determine human welfare. These factors include income distribution, intangible environmental goods, and the prospect of a safer future that can be achieved by sustainable natural resource use (Daly, 1977; Hueting, 1980a, 1984). Therefore sustainability, like equitable income distribution, cannot be properly determined with typical efficiency criteria, using techniques such as conventional economic cost-benefit analysis [CBA]. . . .

Despite the many deficiencies of CBA, it can still be useful for advancing environmental goals. Even unreasonably low or highly inaccurate estimates of environmental benefits and costs are better than none, because the alternative is to assume implicitly that these benefits and costs are zero. Rather than abandoning CBA, environmentalists should insist that it take environmental and other social costs explicitly into account. As is discussed in [the section on safe minimum standards], CBA is most useful from an environmental perspective when it is 'constrained' by safe minimum standards.

PROBLEMS OF PHYSICAL MEASUREMENTS

Development projects have many 'tangible' environmental consequences which, while very real, cannot readily be assigned a monetary value. This is due to the difficulties inherent in both physical estimation and monetary valuation of the relevant environmental effects. In terms of physical effects, it may be difficult, as an example, to predict a priori to what extent the building of a rural road through a forested area may affect soil erosion, as well as downstream sedimentation and water quality. Similarly, it may be very difficult to predict to what extent the projected use of agricultural chemicals in an irrigation project may reduce downstream fish catches, particularly in the longer term. In practice, physical estimation of the environmental effects of a proposed project usually amounts to little more than educated guesswork. This uncertainty is due in part to the relative lack of appropriate scientific data in most developing countries, as well as the site-specific nature of many environmental effects.

Difficulties in the physical estimation of relevant environmental effects are further compounded by the fact that relatively gradual changes in resource use can sometimes produce discontinuous and catastrophic effects in multi-species ecosystems. These changes may be counter-intuitive and irreversible. For example, there have already been a number of unexpected ecological collapses in economically important ocean fisheries (WRI and IIED, 1986). There is a gradation of confidence in the physical measurement of environmental impacts, depending on what types of effects are being measured (Kneese and Sweeney, 1985).

Even when the physical environmental effects of a proposed project can be predicted with some accuracy, monetary valuation of these effects can still prove impossible or exceedingly difficult. This is particularly evident in the case of many 'environmental

services.' Environmental services are beneficial functions performed by natural ecosystems, such as maintenance of water flow patterns, protection of soil, biodegradation of pollutants, recycling of wastes, support of fisheries and other economically important living resources, and regulation of climate. Despite their actual economic value and importance to meeting human needs, environmental services are frequently ignored or underestimated in CBA because they are usually public goods, not priced in the market-place. Some environmental services, such as soil fertility on private land in areas where land tenure is secure and efficient land markets exist, can be private goods, and may therefore be reflected in market values and captured in economic analyses. However, situations such as this are the exception, rather than the rule. This is particularly the case in many developing countries, where land markets are highly distorted and land tenure is often insecure.

A variety of different techniques have been used to estimate the shadow prices of environmental services (D. Pearce, 1976a, 1978; Ahmad, 1983). . . . Despite these methodologies, estimation of shadow prices[1] for tangible environmental goods and services remains incomplete and is rarely practiced on a systematic basis in project analysis.

PROBLEMS OF VALUING 'INTANGIBLE' ENVIRONMENTAL BENEFITS

Intangible environmental values derive from the belief that many features of the natural world have a significant intrinsic value, quite apart from any 'practical' or utilitarian (i.e., economic) value which they may have. Clearly, if a need to preserve a known species is perceived and sacrifices have to be made to achieve this need, then economic choices enter. However, the need to preserve 'utilitarian' species is not yet adequately perceived; much less perceived is the need to preserve unknown species for their intrinsic

---

1. 'Shadow prices' are economic values which are imputed to goods or services that have no market price (or for which the market price is considered 'distorted,' such that it does not accurately reflect actual social costs and benefits).

value, or to avoid eliminating natural areas likely to harbor unknown or rare species. A significant and growing number of people believe that human beings should take care to avoid causing the extinction of other living species—even those species not yet known to have any practical value to humanity. Similarly, many people appreciate the mere existence of free-flowing rivers, or other undeveloped natural wonders, even when these people have no plans to visit or directly use them. Efforts to measure environmental values such as these, many of which have an ethical or spiritual basis, as an economic 'willingness to pay' have yet to become satisfactory (Hueting, 1980c; D. Pearce, 1980).

There are a number of reasons why valuing 'intangible' environmental benefits is so difficult. For example, people's preferences as self-interested, market-oriented consumers are often not consistent with their public policy opinions as socially-minded citizens (Lind, 1982; Sagoff, 1983). This does not mean that people are necessarily irrational—just that human valuation is too complex to be reduced to a simple summation of subjective individual wants. People cannot be perfectly knowledgeable, nor can all their wants be satisfied through the market place. Many ethical values are not revealed by market-place activity, nor by Net Present Value (NPV) or other forms of CBA. To the extent that ethics are important contributors to human happiness, policy makers should attempt to accommodate such ethical values, whether or not they can be measured by CBA.

GROSS NATIONAL PRODUCT AND ENVIRONMENTAL ACCOUNTING

Gross National Product (GNP), a national account statistic that measures aggregate national generation of income, was never intended to be a complete measure of wealth or welfare, and few economists would argue that it is. Nonetheless, many institutions use GNP for exactly this purpose. As an example, many World Bank publications rank countries according to their per-capita GNP. The implicit message of such rankings is that rapid growth in per-capita GNP is an important goal of economic development. However, GNP (or the rather similar Gross Domestic Product, GDP) is seriously flawed as a measure of development success, for the following reasons:

1. GNP does not measure income distribution or even the material well-being of the bulk of a country's population. Some countries (such as China and Sri Lanka) have managed to meet the basic needs of the great majority of their populations at very low levels of per-capita GNP. Other countries (such as Brazil or Algeria) have attained much higher GNP levels and rapid growth rates, while comparatively failing to meet the basic needs of many of their citizens.

2. GNP measures only market transactions, not self-sufficient production. For example, households which grow their own food, without using purchased seeds, chemical fertilizers, biocides or other marketed inputs, do not have the value of their production reflected in GNP accounts. Self-sufficient production of food, clothing, and other goods still predominates in many developing countries, and may often be preferable to market-oriented production for a variety of environmental and social reasons.

3. GNP measures the aggregate level of economic activity, but often this activity does not actually reflect social well-being. For example, more rapid obsolescence of consumer products can increase GNP. To use a hypothetical illustration, assume that person A buys five stoves, each lasting only 2 years, and person B buys one stove that lasts 10 years. Both consumers will have gotten the same level of utility, i.e., 10 years' worth of cooking service. However, in all likelihood, person A will have contributed considerably more to the GNP account than person B.

4. Some of the economic activity measured by GNP is devoted to restoring, replacing, or compensating for environmental services lost through modern production systems. For example, sewage treatment plants reduce the water pollution that results from no longer recycling human waste as fertilizer; medical expenses help compensate for health damage due to asbestos or other unsafe products; and

more frequent painting reduces corrosion damage from air pollution and acid rain. GNP therefore uncritically combines all market expenditures, irrespective of whether those expenditures are due to social 'goods' or 'bads.' If everyone who owns a car suddenly has an accident with it, GNP will go up; if everyone who owns a house installs a solar heater, GNP will ultimately go down!

5. GNP measures economic 'flows,' rather than the standing or 'asset' value of natural resource or other economic 'stocks.' This aspect, inherent in GNP accounting, can also short-change environmental concerns. Policy makers (who have been repeatedly told that rapid GNP growth is an important measure of successful development) may seek to 'liquidate' their natural resource base (e.g., forests or minerals) in order to convert a stock asset into a measurable economic flow.

Resource-rich countries, or those with unused renewable resources,[2] can temporarily pursue such a policy of liquidation. But resource-poor countries, or those experiencing heavy population pressure on the natural resource base, may find that the undesirable effects of overexploitation (e.g., resource depletion, pollution) outweigh the benefits (Dasgupta, 1982; Mahar, 1985).

To the extent that privately held resources earn rent (e.g., a landlord's rented field), GNP accounts for resource depletion—but GNP includes such depletion as a benefit! However, national accounts statistics do not generally record depletion of natural resources incurred in generating income, even though this represents a loss to the country's natural resource wealth. Because many environmental services and resources are common property or public goods, their value is not reflected in the market place. Resources that are

not accounted for are apt to be wasted or managed inefficiently. It is therefore important for governments to monitor their use, in order to make better-informed decisions. Modified accounting procedures would assist governments in improving resource management, including the management of consumption rates. To this end, the United Nations Environment Program (UNEP) and the World Bank have been collaborating through 'environmental accounting' workshops held in 1983, 1984 and 1985. The purpose of these workshops has been to develop methods that internalize natural resource stocks and environmental services in national accounts. The main problem is how best to operationalize this concept and incorporate it in policy. Complete correction of national accounts to reflect natural resource depletion is not yet possible due to the lack of appropriate shadow prices.

NORTH-SOUTH LINKAGES

It is frequently argued that the world's developed nations will help the developing nations by promoting their own economic growth, thereby increasing their demand for goods from the developing world (World Bank, 1984a). However, there is less than consensus on this point. Increasing affluence in the North appears more likely to increase the demand for services and high-technology goods, rather than for primary commodities from the South (Drucker, 1985). Furthermore, growth in industrialized countries consumes limited or scarce energy resources and often further encroaches upon the limited natural resource base of developing countries, thereby perhaps undermining their prospects for long-term sustainable development. For example, increased demand in the North for luxury or non-essential uses of finite resources, such as petroleum, is likely to drive up the prices that poor people in the South must pay for them to satisfy their more basic needs. Such increased prices may, for example, compel more poor people to strip available forests for fuelwood to meet their cooking needs. Thus, the alternative hypothesis, that increased resource consumption in the North actually hurts development prospects in the South, merits closer attention.

A related question concerns the wisdom of using

---

2. 'Unused renewable resources' is preferred over the somewhat environmentally deterministic concept of carrying capacity. Carrying capacity is defined as the maximum number of a given species that can be supported indefinitely by a particular habitat, allowing for seasonal and random change, without any degradation of the natural resource base that would diminish the maximum population in the future. Carrying capacity is analogous to the sustainable rate of harvest and is in turn dependent on the size of the resource stock.

the industrialized countries of North America, Europe, and Japan as development models for the Third World. To the extent that present-day natural resource consumption patterns in these countries are unsustainable over the long term, it seems imprudent to attempt to generalize such patterns to the rest of the world. For example, Brown et al. (1984) make the case that universal private ownership of automobiles is not a desirable (or attainable) goal throughout the world, because automobiles are such extravagant consumers of natural resources. Instead, Brown et al. suggest that modern transportation systems be promoted, which can benefit most of the world's population, rather than only an affluent elite. The idea is not for people to forego the benefits of modern technology, nor to remain impoverished. Rather, it is to promote those technologies and development strategies which can provide an adequate, if not extravagant, living standard for essentially the entire population on a sustainable basis.

IRREVERSIBILITY AND PRESERVATION OF FUTURE OPTIONS

Many of the environmental consequences of development projects or policies are either completely irreversible, or reversible only over a very long time scale (by human standards). Examples of more or less irreversible environmental effects include species extinctions, groundwater contamination, fossil fuel depletion, loss of the traditional knowledge of indigenous tribal peoples when they are rapidly acculturated, soil erosion, human-induced climatic changes, and the removal of slowly-reproducing ecosystems such as coral reefs and certain type of forests. Many of the natural resources which are being irreversibly lost could be of major, through largely incalculable, value to future generations. For example, even if no economic or other human use is currently known for the millions of as-yet-unstudied species and the associated evolutionary processes that exist in the world's remaining natural ecosystems, past experience indicates that some of them will prove very valuable indeed (Ehrlich and Ehrlich, 1981; World Bank, 1987). This concern is particularly urgent for the developing countries of the tropics, where species di-

versity is greatest and scientific knowledge is poorest. As noted recently by E. O. Wilson, species extinctions or other irreversible environmental losses are the ones which future generations are least likely to forgive this generation (Wilson, 1984).

Preventing irreversible environmental losses would preserve many of the options available to future generations, so that they might more effectively meet the challenges of an uncertain future. It is prudent for the present generation to pursue courses of action which foreclose relatively fewer options for the future. Some economists have therefore suggested that relative to the benefits of preservation, there is a point in many projects where the sacrifice of short-term gain is desirable in order to preserve reversibility (i.e., prevent the permanent elimination of future options).

CBA techniques usually treat irreversible costs (if they have even been considered and quantified) no differently from more readily reversible ones. . . . The inattention of CBA techniques to the special problems posed by irreversibility is unfortunate but not surprising, since CBA is based on the mechanistic concept of a readily reversible 'market equilibrium' (Norgaard, 1984c).

COMPARATIVE ADVANTAGE IN AGRICULTURE

The economic principle of comparative advantage is analogous to its ecological counterpart—division of labor or ecological specialization. Both can bring enormous advantage to the individuals of a community. However, comparative advantage is commonly invoked in international trade theory to justify the case for specialization among nations. As historically applied, comparative advantage has encouraged many developing nations to depend on a small number of agricultural export commodities, while attending less to domestic food production. The theory holds that it may be advantageous to sell the agricultural commodity (e.g., cocoa, palm oil) for foreign exchange and buy cheap foreign food (e.g., United States wheat). This pattern can help explain why more and more countries are importing grain, that former food exporting nations are now net importers, and that in some countries—particularly in Sub-Saharan Africa—per-capita food production has declined markedly over the past two decades. Relative emphasis on export crops rather than local food production is only one of several factors which can be blamed for the decline in food production growth, soil erosion and other environmental degradation, and inappropriate agricultural pricing policies (Mahar, 1985). Certainly, the ability to import food from climatically dissimilar areas provides a buffer to natural disasters such as droughts. This should be weighed against the local maintenance of some buffer capacity.

The extent to which countries should emphasize export crops versus domestic food production has sparked lively debate among economists and others concerned. . . .

To this widespread questioning of export crop promotion strategies, we now seek to add an environmental perspective. Agricultural commodity projects are usually sited on prime agricultural land in order to maximize the yields needed to support the investment. This can impair indigenous food production, which is often pushed to more marginal land as a result. Indigenous food production on marginal land often threatens watersheds and slopes that are better left intact in forest or other protective cover. Overgrazing is also more difficult to avoid on marginal land. Agricultural commodity projects need modern highways, with all their environmental impacts, including unplanned settlement and inappropriate land use in ecologically fragile areas. Many cash crops are often grown as large-scale monocultures, while food grown for local consumption by small farmers is more readily adapted to polyculture and agro-forestry systems. Monocultures are less desirable from an environmental standpoint because of their vulnerability to pests and diseases, their often heavy reliance on biocides and chemical fertilizers, and their suitability for using heavy machinery (which often compacts or otherwise damages the soil). From an environmental point of view, export crop promotion (unless it is unusually well-managed) appears to be a less desirable or riskier strategy than local food production. This argument is not to suggest that export crop production is never appropriate or desirable. Rather, we merely recommend that environmental concerns be ade-

quately considered when recommendations are formulated for national agricultural policies and strategies, or when the pros and cons of export crop production are debated.

DISCOUNT RATE

The discount rate (r) is a time preference concept. If we choose to believe that the concept of a 'socially optimum' discount rate actually exists, we must acknowledge that such a discount rate can never be precisely known because the preferences and circumstances of future generations remain unknown (Hueting, 1980a; Lind, 1982). However, we know that sound environmental management often imposes minor, short-term costs in order to gain substantial benefits over the long term. Thus, discounting of future benefits (and costs) to net present value can severely undervalue many environmental functions and services. Although many organizations rely on CBA and discounting, some economists have recognized the significance of this flaw (e.g., Mishan, 1967; D. Pearce, 1975, 1978; Daly, 1977; Page, 1977; Hueting, 1980a).

The use of any particular discount rate r in CBA calculations operationalizes a subjective judgment of the relative importance of the present and the future. It is a normative proposition expressed in mathematical terms, rather than a neutral or objective quantitative assessment. We cannot prove that r for environmental functions (with the risk of irreversible losses) has to be equal to r for investment to produce market goods. The high discount rates currently used in project analysis, commonly 10% and more, discourage investments with long-term benefits, while promoting projects with long-term costs. High discount rates also imply excessive discounting of possible future environmental catastrophes (such as groundwater contamination by leaking radioactive wastes).

The most fundamental question involving discounting concerns the extent to which today's society should sacrifice material consumption to improve the well-being of the future. . . . Since the future is inherently highly uncertain, discounting many valuable natural resources at today's opportunity cost of capital (as per Barnett and Morse's ''intergenerational invisible hand'') is not a very prudent or risk-averse option from the point of view of the future.

SOME PRINCIPLES OF SUSTAINABLE DEVELOPMENT

Sustainable Development Defined

Although 'sustainable development' has seldom been precisely defined, it has become a popular slogan among conservationists and even within elements of the mainstream development community. We therefore seek to provide in this paper a tentative definition of this important concept, as follows. Sustainable development is here defined as *a pattern of social and structural economic transformations (i.e., 'development') which optimizes the economic and other societal benefits available in the present, without jeopardizing the likely potential for similar benefits in the future.* A primary goal of sustainable development is to achieve a reasonable (however defined) and equitably distributed level of economic well-being that can be perpetuated continually for many human generations. Sustainability implies a transition away from economic growth based on depletion of non-renewable resource stocks and towards progress (i.e., improvement in the quality of life) based more on renewable resources over the long run.

This definition has major implications for economic development theory and practice, including the following five points:

(1) Human well-being depends upon at least three categories of value: (a) economic efficiency (i.e., Pareto optimality), (b) equitable distribution of economic resources, and (c) 'non-economic' values (e.g., religious and spiritual concerns, human dignity and pride, aesthetics, and civil liberties). It therefore makes sense for development plans to seek to optimize among these values, rather than to maximize any one (e.g., economic efficiency or growth in production), since some trade-offs are inevitable. Van Praag and Spit (1982) use the welfare economic theory to make the case for more equitable income distribution.

(2) Although it is impossible to predict with much precision the likely interests of future generations, it is prudent to assume that their need for natural resources (soil, air, water, forests, fisheries, plant and animal species, energy, and minerals) will not be markedly less than ours. Therefore, sustainable development implies using renewable natural resources in a manner which does not eliminate or degrade them, or otherwise diminish their usefulness for future generations. Sustainable development therefore implies usually harvesting renewable resources on a sustained-yield basis, rather than 'mining' them to near-extinction. Whales, tropical rain forests, and coral reefs are examples of renewables that are often mined rather than harvested sustainably. This policy need not be absolute, if the flow of natural products or environmental services to be lost can be readily replaced in a sustainable manner (e.g., by maintaining genetic stocks). However, exceptions to this rule need to be justified more carefully than has often been the case.

(3) Sustainable development further implies using non-renewable (exhaustible) mineral resources in a manner which does not unnecessarily preclude easy access to them by future generations. For example, it will surely be easier in the future to make use of today's scrap metal if it is recycled, than if it is dumped as waste in a dispersed manner.

(4) Sustainable development also implies depleting non-renewable energy resources at a slow enough rate so as to ensure the high probability of an orderly societal transition to renewable energy sources (including solar, wood and other biomass, wind, hydroelectric and other water-based sources) when non-renewable energy becomes substantially more costly. Sustainability implies using long-term planning (rather than merely short-term market forces) to guide the transition to renewable energy sources. The price of petroleum, arguably the world's most important non-renewable resource, has actually dropped sharply in the last five years in the United States, for example, tending to encourage more rapid depletion by consumers. In cases such as these, the market does not adequately reflect future scarcity.

(5) In the context of agricultural or other biologi-

cally-based projects sustainability implies the permanent maintenance of biological productivity on the site, with the costs of imported inputs such as energy (e.g., diesel, biocides) and nutrients (e.g., fertilizer) not exceeding the commercial value of the site's production. Even when the crop pays for its inputs, production is not sustainable if the biological productivity of the site is impaired (e.g., by soil compaction or decrease in organic matter). In a wider context, the long-term availability of energy, fertilizers, and other exhaustible agricultural inputs must be addressed.

Steady State Economics and Limits to Growth

Conventional economic theory typically assumes that there are no limits to growth in the physical scale of production and consumption, or that these limits are so distant as to be irrelevant. Over the past decade, a great deal of evidence has surfaced which indicates that this is no longer the case. For example, recent data indicate that the productivity of forests, fisheries, croplands, and grasslands—the fundamental renewable resource systems—is on the decline worldwide in many countries (Brown, 1981; WRI and IIED, 1986). The marginal cost of discovering and exploiting new mineral and fossil fuel deposits is increasingly exponentially. Despite such evidence as this, even the theoretical possibility of limits to growth (not just their imminence) is flatly denied by many neoclassical economists. In this context, an interesting contrast appears to emerge between neoclassical microeconomic and macroeconomic theory. In microeconomics, growth in production (or consumption) is possible or is considered desirable only to the point where the marginal benefit (e.g., revenue) equals the marginal cost. In macroeconomic theory, there is usually no concept of the optimum size of an economy over the long term; rather, bigger is always better. This approach neglects the often severe environmental and other social costs associated with high and growing rates of per-capita natural resource consumption. Once these costs are taken into account, the limits to growth become visible.

The 'limits to growth' debate can be clarified by distinguishing between growth in natural resource consumption (or 'throughput') and in economic output per se (as measured by GNP or a related index) (Daly, 1984a). Notwithstanding any conceivable technological advances, growth in natural resource consumption (whether due to an increase in population, per-capita consumption, or both) is ultimately constrained by the physical laws of thermodynamics and by the finite size of the planet. However, growth in economic output may not be similarly constrained, since innovation may continue to find ways to squeeze more 'value added' from a natural resource bundle. Thus, governments concerned with long-term sustainability need not seek to limit growth in economic output, so long as they seek to stabilize aggregate natural resource consumption.

SAFE MINIMUM STANDARDS

'Safe minimum standard' (SMS) analysis (Ciriacy-Wantrup, 1963; Bishop, 1982; Bishop and Anderson, 1985) is one decision methodology which can be used to address those ecological concerns which are given little or no attention in economic CBA. An SMS is any non-economic criterion which a project must meet to be approved. SMS analysis is a time-tested, standard operating procedure that is widespread throughout engineering design, health planning, industrial worker safety, and other sectors. For example, a bridge is commonly designed with a safety factor of three or more to accommodate the unexpected and the unknown.

When used in the appraisal of development projects, SMSs constrain the economic CBA by specifying environmental, social, or other criteria which the project must meet in all cases. If a project is modified to meet SMS criteria, any extra costs of such modification are automatically added to other project costs in the CBA. If a proposed project cannot be modified to meet SMS criteria, it is abandoned in favor of more environmentally or socially prudent investments. CBA which incorporates SMSs is therefore a type of constrained economic optimization.

Up to this time, the World Bank has publicly committed itself to the following SMSs in the projects it supports:

(1) Projects depending on the harvest of renew-

able natural resources (such as forests, fisheries, and grazing lands) shall adhere to sustained-yield principles, to minimize the risk of overexploitation and degradation (through overcutting, overfishing, or overgrazing) (World Bank, 1984b).

(2) Projects shall not clear, inundate, or otherwise convert ecologically important wildland ecosystems, including (but not limited to) officially designated protected areas, without adequate compensatory measures (World Bank, 1984b, 1986).

(3) Projects shall avoid knowingly causing the extinction or endangerment of plant or animal species, unless adequate mitigatory measures are provided (World Bank, 1984b, 1986).

(4) Any project based in one country shall not affect the environment or natural resource base of any neighboring countries without their full consent (World Bank, 1984b). Judgment is necessary in determining the cut-off point, particularly where data are inadequate (such as with acid rain).

(5) Projects shall not contravene any international environmental agreement to which the borrowing country is party (World Bank, 1984b).

(6) Any groups seriously disadvantaged by Bank-supported projects (such as vulnerable ethnic minorities or communities undergoing involuntary resettlement) shall be appropriately compensated to a degree that makes them no worse off (and may make them better off) than without the project. This is to be done even if the compensatory project components do not contribute to the stream of economic benefits (World Bank, 1982, 1984b).

(7) Projects shall not compromise public health and safety to any degree which would be widely regarded as unacceptable by the affected people or by experienced, impartial third parties (World Bank, 1982, 1984b).

REFERENCES CITED

Ahman, Y.J. (Ed.), 1983. Environmental Decision Making. UNEP, Nairobi, 36 pp.

Berry, B.J., 1977. The Social Burdens of Environmental Pollution. Ballinger, Cambridge, Mass., 613 pp.

Bishop, R.C. and Anderson, S.O., 1985. Economics, Institutions, and Natural Resources: Collected Works of S.V. Ciriacy-Wantrup. Westview Press, Boulder, Colo. 225 pp.

Brown, L.R., 1981. Building a Sustainable Society. Norton, New York, 433 pp.

Brown, L.R. et al., 1984. State of the World. Norton, New York, 252 pp.

Ciriacy-Wantrup, S.V. 1963. Resource Conservation: Economics and Policies. University of California, Berkeley, Calif. 395 pp.

Clark, C.W., 1973b. Profit maximization and the extinction of animal species. J. Pol. Econ., 81: 950-961.

Clark, C.W., 1976. Mathematical Bioeconomics: The Optimal Management of Renewable Resources. Wiley, New York, 352 pp.

Daly, H.E., 1977. Steady-State Economics. Freeman, San Francisco, Calif. 185 pp.

Daly, H.E., 1984a. Alternative strategies for integrating economics and ecology. In: A.-M. Jansson (Ed.), Integration of Economy and Ecology—An Outlook for the Eighties. Wallenberg Foundation for International Cooperation in Science, Stockholm, pp. 19-30.

Drucker, P., 1985. Out of the depression cycle. Wall Street J., January 9:26.

Ehrlich, P.R. and Ehrlich, A.H., 1981. Extinction: The Causes and Consequences of the Disappearance of Species. Random House, New York, 305 pp.

Hueting, R., 1980a. New Scarcity and Economic Growth. North-Holland, Amsterdam, 270 pp.

Hueting, R., 1980c. The Use of Environmental Data in the Economic Decision-Making Process. Netherlands Bureau of Statistics, Voorburg, 17 pp.

Hueting, R., 1984. Economic aspects of environmental accounting. UNEP First Environmental Accounting Workshop, 5-8 November, at The World Bank, Washington, D.C., 24 pp.

Kneese, A.V. and Sweeney, J.L. (eds.), 1985 Handbook of Natural Resource and Energy Economics, Vols. I and II. Elsevier, New York, 470 + 294 pp.

Mahar, D. (Ed.) 1985. Rapid Population Growth and Human Carrying Capacity: Two Perspectives. Staff Workshop Paper 960. The World Bank, Washington, D.C., 89 pp.

Mishan, E.J., 1967. The Costs of Economic Growth. Staples Press, London, 190 pp.

Norgaard, R.B., 1984c. Environmental Economics: An Evolutionary Critique and a Plea for Pluralism. Work paper 299. Berkeley, Calif., 34 pp.

Page, T., 1977. Conservation and Economic Efficiency: An Approach to Materials Policy. Resources of the Future/

Johns Hopkins University Press, Baltimore, Md., 266 pp.

Pearce, D.W. (eds.), 1975. The Economics of National Resource Depletion. Macmillan, London, 220 pp.

Pearce, D.W., 1976a. The limits of cost-benefit analysis as a guide to environmental policy. Kyklos, 29, Fasc. 1:97-112.

Pearce, D.W., 1976b. Environmental Economics. Longmans, London, 202 pp.

Pearce, D.W. (Ed.), 1978. The Valuation of Social Cost. Allen and Unwin, London, 197 pp.

Rawls, J., 1972. A Theory of Justice. Clarendon Press, Oxford, 607 pp.

Van Praag, B.M.S. and Spit, J.S., 1982. The Social Filter Process and Income Evaluation. Rep. 82.08, Leyden University Center for Research in Public Economics, Leiden, The Netherlands.

Wilson, E.O., 1984. Biophilia: The Human Bond with Other Species. Harvard University Press, Cambridge, Mass., 157 pp.

World Bank, 1984b. Environmental Policies and Procedures of the World Bank. Office of Environmental and Scientific Affairs, World Bank, Washington, D.C., 8 pp.

World Bank, 1986. The World Bank's Operational Policy on Wildlands: Their Protection and Management in Economic Development. Office of Environmental and Scientific Affairs, World Bank, Washington, D.C., 20 pp.

World Bank, 1987. Wildlands: Their Protection and Management in Economic Development. World Bank, Washington, D.C., 333 pp.

WRI and IIED (World Resources Institute and International Institute for Environment and Development), 1986. World Resources 1986: An Assessment of the Resource Base That Supports the Global Economy. Basic Books, New York, 353 pp.

DISCUSSION TOPICS

1. Does the list of safe minimum standards provided by Goodland and Ledec omit any important standards?

2. Does the comprehensive approach advocated by Goodland and Ledec have any disadvantages?

Should Trees Have Standing?

Christopher D. Stone

Christopher D. Stone teaches law at the University of Southern California in Los Angeles. Publication of Should Trees Have Standing? *in 1972 was an important influence on the development of the field of environmental ethics. He has recently published* Earth and Other Ethics: The Case for Moral Pluralism *(New York: Harper & Row, 1987).*

Stone proposes giving legal rights to natural objects. While such an extension of rights may seem unthinkable, he points out that such extensions have always seemed unthinkable before they occurred, and that there are currently a number of inanimate legal persons, such as railroads and corporations.

Stone summarizes what it means for something to have legal standing and how natural objects currently do not possess legal standing. He proposes an extension of the legal guardianship model for legal incompetents, and explains some of the advantages of such a strategy.

. . . Throughout legal history, each successive extension of rights to some new entity has been, theretofore, a bit unthinkable. We are inclined to suppose the rightlessness of rightless ''things'' to be a decree of Nature, not a legal convention acting in support of some status quo. It is thus that we defer considering the choices involved in all their moral, social, and economic dimensions. . . .The fact is, that each time there is a movement to confer rights onto some new ''entity,'' the proposal is bound to sound odd or frightening or laughable.[1] This is partly because until the rightless thing receives its rights, we cannot see it as anything but a *thing* for the use of ''us''—those who are holding rights at the time.[2] . . .

The reason for this little discourse on the unthinkable, the reader must know by now, if only from the title of the paper. I am quite seriously proposing that we give legal rights to forests, oceans, rivers and other so-called ''natural objects'' in the environment—indeed, to the natural environment as a whole.[3]

As strange as such a notion may sound, it is neither fanciful nor devoid of operational content. In fact, I do not think it would be a misdescription of recent developments in the law to say that we are already on the verge of assigning some such rights, although we have not faced up to what we are doing in those particular terms.[4] We should do so now, and begin to explore the implications such a notion would hold.

TOWARD RIGHTS FOR THE ENVIRONMENT

Now, to say that the natural environment should have rights is not to say anything as silly as that no one should be allowed to cut down a tree. We say human beings have rights, but—at least as of the time of this writing—they can be executed.[5] Corporations have rights, but they cannot plead the fifth amendment[6]; *In re Gault* gave 15-year-olds certain rights in juvenile proceedings, but it did not give them the right to vote. Thus, to say that the environment should have rights is not to say that it should have every right we can imagine, or even the same body of rights as human beings have. Nor is it to say that everything in the environment should have the same rights as every other thing in the environment.

What the granting of rights does involve has two sides to it. The first involves what might be called the legal-operational aspects; the second, the psychic and socio-psychic aspects. I shall deal with these aspects in turn.

THE LEGAL-OPERATIONAL ASPECTS

What it Means to be a Holder of Legal Rights

There is, so far as I know, no generally accepted standard for how one ought to use the term ''legal rights.'' Let me indicate how I shall be using it in this piece.

First and most obviously, if the term is to have any content at all, an entity cannot be said to hold a legal right unless and until *some public authoritative body* is prepared to give *some amount of review* to actions that are colorably inconsistent with that "right." For example, if a student can be expelled from a university and cannot get any public official, even a judge or administrative agent at the lowest level, either (i) to require the university to justify its actions (if only to the extent of filling out an affidavit alleging that the expulsion "was not wholly arbitrary and capricious") or (ii) to compel the university to accord the student some procedural safeguards (a hearing, right to counsel, right to have notice of charges), then the minimum requirements for saying that the student has a legal right to his education do not exist.[7]

But for a thing to be *a holder of legal rights,* something more is needed than that some authoritative body will review the actions and processes of those who threaten it. As I shall use the term, "holder of legal rights," each of three additional criteria must be satisfied. All three, one will observe, go towards making a thing *count* jurally—to have a legally recognized worth and dignity in its own right, and not merely to serve as a means to benefit "us" (whoever the contemporary group of rights-holders may be). They are, first, that the thing can institute legal actions *at its behest*; second, that in determining the granting of legal relief, the court must take *injury to it* into account; and, third, that relief must run to the *benefit of it.* . . .

Toward Having Standing in Its Own Right

It is not inevitable, nor is it wise, that natural objects should have no rights to seek redress in their own behalf. It is no answer to say that streams and forests cannot have standing because streams and forests cannot speak. Corporations cannot speak either; nor can states, estates, infants, incompetents, municipalities or universities. Lawyers speak for them, as they customarily do for the ordinary citizen with legal problems. One ought, I think, to handle the legal problems of natural objects as one does the problems of legal incompetents—human beings who have become vegetable. If a human being shows signs of becoming senile and has affairs that he is de jure incompetent to manage, those concerned with his well being make

such a showing to the court, and someone is designated by the court with the authority to manage the incompetent's affairs. The guardian[8] (or "conservator"[9] or "committee"[10]—the terminology varies) then represents the incompetent in his legal affairs. Courts make similar appointments when a corporation has become "incompetent"—they appoint a trustee in bankruptcy or reorganization to oversee its affairs and speak for it in court when that becomes necessary.

On a parity of reasoning, we should have a system in which, when a friend of a natural object perceives it to be endangered, he can apply to a court for the creation of a guardianship.[11] Perhaps we already have the machinery to do so. California law, for example, defines an incompetent as "any person, whether insane or not, who by reason of old age, disease, weakness of mind, or other cause, is unable, unassisted, properly to manage and take care of himself or his property, and by reason thereof is likely to to be deceived or imposed upon by artful or designing persons."[12] Of course, to urge a court that an endangered river is "a person" under this provision will call for lawyers as bold and imaginative as those who convinced the Supreme Court that a railroad corporation was a "person" under the fourteenth amendment, a constitutional provision theretofore generally thought of as designed to secure the rights of freedmen.[13] (As this article was going to press, Professor Byrn of Fordham petitioned the New York Supreme Court to appoint him legal guardian for an unrelated foetus scheduled for abortion so as to enable him to bring a class action on behalf of all foetuses similarly situated in New York City's 18 municipal hospitals. Judge Holtzman granted the petition of guardianship.[14]) If such an argument based on present statutes should fail, special environmental legislation could be enacted along traditional guardianship lines. Such provisions could provide for guardianship both in the instance of public natural objects and also, perhaps with slightly different standards, in the instance of natural objects on "private" land.[15]

The potential "friends" that such a statutory scheme would require will hardly be lacking. The Sierra Club, Environmental Defense Fund, Friends of the Earth, Natural Resources Defense Counsel, and the Izaak Walton League are just some of the many groups which have manifested unflagging dedication to the environment and which are becoming increasingly capable of marshalling the requisite technical experts and lawyers. If, for example, the Environmental Defense Fund should have reason to believe that some company's strip mining operations might be irreparably destroying the ecological balance of large tracts of land, it could, under this procedure, apply to the court in which the lands were situated to be appointed guardian.[16] As guardian, it might be given rights of inspection (or visitation) to determine and bring to the court's attention a fuller finding on the land's condition. If there were indications that under the substantive law some redress might be available on the land's behalf, then the guardian would be entitled to raise the land's rights in the land's name, *i.e.,* without having to make the roundabout and often unavailing demonstration, discussed below, that the "rights" of the club's members were being invaded. Guardians would also be looked to for a host of other protective tasks, *e.g.,* monitoring effluents (and/or monitoring the monitors), and representing their "wards" at legislative and administrative hearings on such matters as the setting of state water quality standards. Procedures exist, and can be strengthened, to move a court for the removal and substitution of guardians, for conflicts of interest or for other reasons,[17] as well as for the termination of the guardianship.[18]

The guardianship approach, however, is apt to raise two objections, neither of which seems to me to have much force. The first is that a committee or guardian could not judge the needs of the river or forest in its charge; indeed, the very concept of "needs," it might be said, could be used here only in the most metaphorical way. The second objection is that such a system would not be much different from what we now have: is not the Department of Interior already such a guardian for public lands, and do not most states have legislation empowering their attorneys general to seek relief—in a sort of *parens patriae* way—for such injuries as a guardian might concern himself with?

As for the first objection, natural objects *can* communicate their wants (needs) to us, and in ways that are not terribly ambiguous. I am sure I can judge with more certainty and meaningfulness whether and when my lawn wants (needs) water, than the Attorney General can judge whether and when the United States wants (needs) to take an appeal from an adverse judgment by a lower court. The lawn tells me that it wants water by a certain dryness of the blades and soil—immediately obvious to the touch—the appearance of bald spots, yellowing, and a lack of springiness after being walked on; how does "the United States" communicate to the Attorney General? For similar reasons, the guardian-attorney for a smog-endangered stand of pines could venture with more confidence that his client wants the smog stopped, than the directors of a corporation can assert that "the corporation" wants dividends declared. We make decisions on behalf of, and in the purported interests of, others every day; these "others" are often creatures whose wants are far less verifiable, and even far more metaphysical in conception, than the wants of rivers, trees, and land.[19]

As for the second objection, one can indeed find evidence that the Department of Interior was conceived as a sort of guardian of the public lands.[20] But there are two points to keep in mind. First, insofar as the Department already is an adequate guardian it is only with respect to the federal public lands as per Article IV, section 3 of the Constitution.[21] Its guardianship includes neither local public lands nor private lands. Second, to judge from the environmentalist literature and from the cases environmental action groups have been bringing, the Department is itself one of the bogeys of the environmental movement. (One thinks of the uneasy peace between the Indians and the Bureau of Indian Affairs.) Whether the various charges be right or wrong, one cannot help but observe that the Department has been charged with several institutional goals (never an easy burden), and is currently looked to for action by quite a variety of interest groups, only one of which is the environmentalists. In this context, a guardian outside the institution becomes especially valuable. Besides, what a person wants, fully to secure his rights, is the ability to retain independent counsel even when, and perhaps especially when, the government is acting "for him" in a beneficent way. I have no reason to doubt, for example, that the Social Security System is being managed "for me"; but I would not want to abdicate my right to challenge its actions as they affect me, should the need arise.[22] I would not ask more trust of national forests, vis-à-vis the Department of Interior. The same considerations apply in the instance of local agencies, such as regional water pollution boards, whose members' expertise in pollution matters is often all too credible.[23]

. . . The guardian would urge before the court injuries not presently cognizable—the death of eagles and inedible crabs, the suffering of sea lions, the loss from the face of the earth of species of commercially valueless birds, the disappearance of a wilderness area. One might, of course, speak of the damages involved as "damages" to us humans, and indeed, the widespread growth of environmental groups shows that human beings do feel these losses. But they are not, at present, economically measurable losses: how can they have a monetary value for the guardian to prove in court?

The answer for me is simple. Wherever it carves out "property" rights, the legal system is engaged in the process of *creating* monetary worth. One's literary works would have minimal monetary value if anyone could copy them at will. Their economic value to the author is a product of the law of copyright; the person who copies a copyrighted book has to bear a cost to the copyright-holder because the law says he must. Similarly, it is through the law of torts that we have made a "right" of—and guaranteed an economically meaningful value to—privacy. (The value we place on gold—a yellow inanimate dirt—is not simply a function of supply and demand—wilderness areas are scarce and pretty too—but results from the actions of the legal systems of the world, which have institutionalized that value; they have even done a remarkable job of stabilizing the price). I am proposing we do the same with eagles and wilderness areas as we do with copyrighted works, patented inventions, and privacy: *make* the violation of rights in them to be a cost by declaring the "pirating" of them to be the

invasion of a property interest.[24] If we do so, the net social costs the polluter would be confronted with would include not only the extended homocentric costs of his pollution (explained above) but also costs to the environment *per se*.

How, though, would these costs be calculated? When we protect an invention, we can at least speak of a fair market value for it, by reference to which damages can be computed. But the lost environmental "values" of which we are now speaking are by definition over and above those that the market is prepared to bid for: they are priceless.

One possible measure of damages, suggested earlier, would be the cost of making the environment whole, just as, when a man is injured in an automobile accident, we impose upon the responsible party the injured man's medical expenses. Comparable expenses to a polluted river would be the costs of dredging, restocking with fish, and so forth. It is on the basis of such costs as these, I assume, that we get the figure of $1 billion as the cost of saving Lake Erie.[25] As an ideal, I think this is a good guide applicable in many environmental situations. It is by no means free from difficulties, however.

One problem with computing damages on the basis of making the environment whole is that, if understood most literally, it is tantamount to asking for a "freeze" on environmental quality, even at the costs (and there will be costs) of preserving "useless" objects.[26] Such a "freeze" is not inconceivable to me as a general goal, especially considering that, even by the most immediately discernible homocentric interests, in so many areas we ought to be cleaning up and not merely preserving the environmental status quo. In fact, there is presently strong sentiment in the Congress for a total elimination of all river pollutants by 1985,[27] notwithstanding that such a decision would impose quite large direct and indirect costs on us all. Here one is inclined to recall the instructions of Judge Hays, in remanding Consolidated Edison's Storm King application to the Federal Power Commission in *Scenic Hudson:*

The Commission's renewed proceedings must include as a basic concern the preservation of natural beauty and of natural historic shrines, keeping in mind that, in our affluent society, the cost of a project is only one of several factors to be considered.[28]

Nevertheless, whatever the merits of such a goal in principle, there are many cases in which the social price tag of putting it into effect are going to seem too high to accept. Consider, for example, an oceanside nuclear generator that could produce low cost electricity for a million homes at a savings of $1 a year per home, spare us the air pollution that comes of burning fossil fuels, but which through a slight heating effect threatened to kill off a rare species of temperature-sensitive sea urchins; suppose further that technological improvements adequate to reduce the temperature to present environmental quality would expend the entire one million dollars in anticipated fuel savings. Are we prepared to tax ourselves $1,000,000 a year on behalf of the sea urchins? In comparable problems under the present law of damages, we work out practicable compromises by abandoning restoration costs and calling upon fair market value. For example, if an automobile is so severely damaged that the cost of bringing the car to its original state by repair is greater than the fair market value, we would allow the responsible tortfeasor to pay the fair market value only. Or if a human being suffers the loss of an arm (as we might conceive of the ocean having irreparably lost the sea urchins), we can fall back on the capitalization of reduced earning power (and pain and suffering) to measure the damages. But what is the fair market value of sea urchins? How can we capitalize their loss to the ocean, independent of any commercial value they may have to someone else?

One answer is that the problem can sometimes be sidestepped quite satisfactorily. In the sea urchin example, one compromise solution would be to impose on the nuclear generator the costs of making the ocean whole somewhere else, in some other way, *e.g.,* re-establishing a sea urchin colony elsewhere, or making a somehow comparable contribution.[29] In the debate over the laying of the trans-Alaskan pipeline, the builders are apparently prepared to meet conservationists' objections half-way by re-establishing wildlife away from the pipeline, so far as is feasible.[30]

But even if damage calculations have to be made, one ought to recognize that the measurement of damages is rarely a simple report of economic facts about "the market," whether we are valuing the loss of a foot, a foetus, or a work of fine art. Decisions of this sort are always hard, but not impossible. We have increasingly taken (human) pain and suffering into account in reckoning damages, not because we think we can ascertain them as objective "facts" about the universe, but because, even in view of all the room for disagreement, we come up with a better society by making rude estimates of them than by ignoring them.[31] We can make such estimates in regard to environmental losses fully aware that what we are really doing is making implicit normative judgments (as with pain and suffering)—laying down rules as to what the society is going to "value" rather than reporting market evaluations. In making such normative estimates decision-makers would not go wrong if they estimated on the "high side," putting the burden of trimming the figure down on the immediate human interests present. All burdens of proof should reflect common experience; our experience in environmental matters has been a continual discovery that our acts have caused more long-range damage than we were able to appreciate at the outset. . . .

The strongest case can be made from the perspective of human advantage for conferring rights on the environment. Scientists have been warning of the crises the earth and all humans on it face if we do not change our ways—radically—and these crises make the lost "recreational use" of rivers seem absolutely trivial. The earth's very atmosphere is threatened with frightening possibilities: absorption of sunlight, upon which the entire life cycle depends, may be diminished; the oceans may warm (increasing the "greenhouse effect" of the atmosphere), melting the polar ice caps, and destroying our great coastal cities; the portion of the atmosphere that shields us from dangerous radiation may be destroyed. Testifying before Congress, sea explorer Jacques Cousteau predicted that the oceans (to which we dreamily look to feed our booming populations) are headed toward their own death: "The cycle of life is intricately tied up with the cycle of water . . . the water system has to remain alive if we are to remain alive on earth.''[32] We are depleting our energy and our food sources at a rate that takes little account of the needs even of humans now living.

These problems will not be solved easily; they very likely can be solved, if at all, only through a willingness to suspend the rate of increase in the standard of living (by present values) of the earth's ''advanced'' nations, and by stabilizing the total human population. For some of us this will involve forfeiting material comforts; for others it will involve abandoning the hope someday to obtain comforts long envied. For all of us it will involve giving up the right to have as many offspring as we might wish. Such a program is not impossible of realization, however. Many of our so-called ''material comforts'' are not only in excess of, but are probably in opposition to, basic biological needs. Further, the ''costs'' to the advanced nations is not as large as would appear from Gross National Product figures. G.N.P. reflects social gain (of a sort) without discounting for the social *cost* of that gain, *e.g.*, the losses through depletion of resources, pollution, and so forth. As has well been shown, as societies become more and more ''advanced,'' their real marginal gains become less and less for each additional dollar of G.N.P.[33] Thus, to give up ''human progress'' would not be as costly as might appear on first blush.

Nonetheless, such far-reaching social changes are going to involve us in a serious reconsideration of our consciousness towards the environment. . . . What is it within us that gives us this need not just to satisfy basic biological wants, but to extend our wills over things, to object-ify them, to make them ours, to manipulate them, to keep them at a psychic distance? Can it all be explained on ''rational'' bases? Should we not be suspect of such needs within us, cautious as to why we wish to gratify them? When I first read that passage of Hegel, I immediately thought not only of the emotional contrast with Spinoza, but of the passage in Carson McCullers' *A Tree, A Rock, A Cloud,* in which an old derelict has collared a twelve year old boy in a streetcar cafe. The old man asks whether the boy knows ''how love should be begun'':

The old man leaned closer and whispered:
''A tree. A rock. A cloud.''
. . .
''The weather was like this in Portland,'' he said. ''At the time my science was begun. I meditated and I started very cautious. I would pick up something from the street and take it home with me. I bought a goldfish and I concentrated on the goldfish and I loved it. I graduated from one thing to another. Day by day I was getting this technique. . . .
. . .
. . . ''For six years now I have gone around by myself and built up my science. And now I am a master. Son. I can love anything. No longer do I have to think about it even. I see a street full of people and a beautiful light comes in me. I watch a bird in the sky. Or I meet a traveler on the road. Everything, Son. And anybody. All stranger and all loved! Do you realize what a science like mine can mean?''[34]

To be able to get away from the view that Nature is a collection of useful senseless objects is, as McCullers' ''madman'' suggests, deeply involved in the development of our abilities to love—or, if that is putting it too strongly, to be able to reach a heightened awareness of our own, and others' capacities in their mutual interplay. To do so, we have to give up some psychic investment in our sense of separateness and specialness in the universe. And this, in turn, is hard giving indeed, because it involves us in a flight backwards, into earlier stages of civilization and childhood in which we had to trust (and perhaps fear) our environment, for we had not then the power to master it. Yet, in doing so, we—as persons—gradually free ourselves of needs for supportive illusions.

. . . What is needed is a myth that can fit our growing body of knowledge of geophysics, biology and the cosmos. In this vein, I do not think it too remote that we may come to regard the Earth, as some have suggested, as one organism, of which Mankind is a functional part—the mind, perhaps: different from the rest of nature, but different as a man's brain is from his lungs. . . .

To shift from such a lofty fancy as the planetarization of consciousness to the operation of our municipal legal system is to come down to earth hard.

Before the forces that are at work, our highest court is but a frail and feeble—a distinctly human—institution. Yet, the Court may be at its best not in its work of handing down decrees, but at the very task that is called for: of summoning up from the human spirit the kindest and most generous and worthy ideas that abound there, giving them shape and reality and legitimacy.[35] Witness the School Desegregation Cases which, more importantly than to integrate the schools (assuming they did), awakened us to moral needs which, when made visible, could not be denied. And so here, too, in the case of the environment, the Supreme Court may find itself in a position to award "rights" in a way that will contribute to a change in popular consciousness. It would be a modest move, to be sure, but one in furtherance of a large goal: the future of the planet as we know it.

How far we are from such a state of affairs, where the law treats "environmental objects" as holders of legal rights, I cannot say. But there is certainly intriguing language in one of Justice Black's last dissents, regarding the Texas Highway Department's plan to run a six-lane expressway through a San Antonio Park.[36] Complaining of the Court's refusal to stay the plan, Black observed that "after today's decision, the people of San Antonio and the birds and animals that make their home in the park will share their quiet retreat with an ugly, smelly stream of traffic. . . . Trees, shrubs, and flowers will be mown down."[37] Elsewhere he speaks of the "burial of public parks," of segments of a highway which "devour parkland," and of the park's heartland.[38] Was he, at the end of his great career, on the verge of saying— just saying—that "nature has 'rights' on its own account"? Would it be so hard to do?

NOTES

1. Recently, a group of prison inmates in Suffolk County tamed a mouse that they discovered, giving him the name Morris. Discovering Morris, a jailer flushed him down the toilet. The prisoners brought a proceeding against the Warden complaining, *inter alia*, that Morris was subjected to discriminatory discharge and was otherwise unequally treated. The action was unsuc-

cessful, on grounds that the inmates themselves were "guilty of imprisoning Morris without a charge, without a trial, and without bail," and that other mice at the prison were not treated more favorably. "As to the true victim the Court can only offer again the sympathy first proffered to his ancestors by Robert Burns. . . ." The Judge proceeded to quote from Burns' "To a Mouse." Morabito v. Cyrta, 9 CRIM. L. REP. 2472 (N.Y. Sup. Ct. Suffolk Co. Aug. 26, 1971).

The whole matter seems humorous, of course. But what we need to know more of is the function of humor in the unfolding of a culture, and the ways in which it is involved with the social growing pains to which it is testimony. Why do people make jokes about the Women's Liberation Movement? Is it not on account of— rather than in spite of—the underlying validity of the protests, and the uneasy awareness that a recognition of them is inevitable? A. Koestler rightly begins his study of the human mind, ACT OF CREATION (1964), with an analysis of humor, entitled "The Logic of Laughter." And *cf.* Freud, *Jokes and the Unconscious,* 8 Standard Edition of the Complete Psychological Works of Sigmund Freud (J. Strachey transl. 1905). (Query too: what is the relationship between the conferring of proper *names, e.g.,* Morris, and the conferring of social and legal *rights?*)

2. Thus it was that the Founding Fathers could speak of the inalienable rights of all men, and yet maintain a society that was, by modern standards, without the most basic rights for Blacks, Indians, children and women. There was no hypocrisy; emotionally, no one *felt* that these other things were men.

3. In this article I essentially limit myself to a discussion of non-animal but natural objects. I trust that the reader will be able to discern where the analysis is appropriate to advancing our understanding of what would be involved in giving "rights" to other objects not presently endowed with rights—for example, not only animals (some of which already have rights in some senses) but also humanoids, computers, and so forth. *Cf.* the National Register for Historic Places, 16 U.S.C. § 470 (1970), discussed in Ely v. Velde, 321 F. Supp. 1088 (E.D. Va. 1971). . . .

4. The statement in text is not quite true; *cf.* Murphy, *Has Nature Any Right to Life?,* 22 Hast. L.J. 467 (1971). An Irish court, passing upon the validity of a testamentary trust to the benefit of someone's dogs, observed in dictum that " 'lives' means lives of human beings, not

of animals or trees in California.'' Kelly v. Dillon, 1932 Ir. R. 255, 261. (The intended gift over on the death of the last surviving dog was held void for remoteness, the court refusing ''to enter into the question of a dog's expectation of life,'' although prepared to observe that ''in point of fact neighbor's [sic] dogs and cats are unpleasantly long-lived. . . .'' *Id.* at 260-61).

5. Four cases dealing with the Constitutionality of the death penalty under the eighth and fourteenth amendments are pending before the United States Supreme Court. Branch v. Texas, 447 S.W.2d 932 (Tex. 1969), *cert. granted,* 91 S. Ct. 2287 (1970); Aikens v. California, 70 Cal. 2d 369, 74 Cal. Rptr. 882, 450 P.2d 258 (1969), *cert. granted,* 91 S. Ct. 2280 (1970); Furman v. Georgia, 225 Ga. 253, 167 S.E.2d 628 (1969), *cert. granted,* 91 S. Ct. 2282 (1970); Jackson v. Georgia, 225 Ga. 790, 171 S.E.2d 501 (1969), *cert. granted,* 91 S. Ct. 2287 (1970).

6. *See* George Campbell Painting Corp. v. Reid, 392 U.S. 286 (1968); Oklahoma Press Pub. Co. v. Walling, 327 U.S. 186 (1946); Baltimore & O.R.R. v. ICC, 221 U.S. 612 (1911); Wilson v. United States, 221 U.S. 361 (1911); Hale v. Henkel, 201 U.S. 43 (1906).

7. *See* Dixon v. Alabama State Bd. of Educ., 294 F.2d 150 (5th Cir.), *cert. denied,* 368 U.S. 930 (1961).

8. *See, e.g.,* Cal. Prob. Code §§ 1460-62 (West Supp. 1971).

9. Cal. Prob. Code § 1751 (West Supp. 1971) provides for the appointment of a ''conservator.''

10. In New York the Supreme Court and county courts outside New York City have jurisdiction to appoint a committee of the person and/or a committee of the property for a person ''incompetent to manage himself or his affairs.'' N.Y. Mental Hygiene Law § 100 (McKinney 1971).

11. This is a situation in which the ontological problems discussed in note 3 *supra* become acute. One can conceive a situation in which a guardian would be appointed by a county court with respect to a stream, bring a suit against alleged polluters, and lose. Suppose now that a federal court were to appoint a guardian with respect to the larger river system of which the stream were a part, and that the federally appointed guardian subsequently were to bring suit against the same defendants in state court, now on behalf of the river, rather than the stream. (Is it possible to bring a still subsequent suit, if the one above fails, on behalf of the entire hydrologic cycle, by a guardian appointed by an international court?)

While such problems are difficult, they are not impossible to solve. For one thing, pre-trial hearings and rights of intervention can go far toward their amelioration. Further, courts have been dealing with the matter of potentially inconsistent judgments for years, as when one state appears on the verge of handing down a divorce decree inconsistent with the judgment of another state's courts. Kempson v. Kempson, 58 N.J. Eg. 94, 43 A. 97 (Ch. Ct. 1899). Courts could, and of course would, retain some natural objects in the res nullius classification to help stave off the problem. Then, too, where (as is always the case) several ''objects'' are interrelated, several guardians could all be involved, with procedures for removal to the appropriate court— probably that of the guardian of the most encompassing ''ward'' to be acutely threatened. And in some cases subsequent suit by the guardian of more encompassing ward, not guilty of laches, might be appropriate. The problems are at least no more complex than the corresponding problems that the law has dealt with for years in the class action area.

12. Cal. Prob. Code § 1460 (West Supp. 1971). The N.Y. Mental Hygiene Law (McKinney 1971) provides for jurisdiction ''over the custody of a person and his property if he is incompetent to manage himself or his affairs by reason of age, drunkenness, mental illness or other cause. . . .''

13. Santa Clara County v. Southern Pac. R.R., 118 U.S. 394 (1886). Justice Black would have denied corporations the rights of ''persons'' under the fourteenth amendment. *See* Connecticut Gen. Life Ins. Co. v. Johnson, 303 U.S. 77, 87 (1938) (Black, J. dissenting): ''Corporations have neither race nor color.''

14. *In re* Byrn, L. A. Times, Dec. 5, 1971, § 1, at 16 col. 1. A preliminary injunction was subsequently granted, and defendant's cross-motion to vacate the guardianship was denied. Civ. 13113/71 (Sup. Ct. Queens Co., Jan. 4, 1972) (Smith, J.). Appeals are pending. Granting a guardianship in these circumstances would seem to be a more radical advance in the law than granting a guardianship over communal natural objects like lakes. In the former case there is a traditionally recognized guardian for the object—the mother—and her decision has been in favor of aborting the foetus.

15. The laws regarding the various communal resources had to develop along their own lines, not only because so many different persons' ''rights'' to consumption and usage were continually and contemporaneously involved, but also because no one had to bear the costs

of his consumption of public resources in the way in which the owner of resources on private land has to bear the costs of what he does. For example, if the landowner strips his land of trees, and puts nothing in their stead, he confronts the costs of what he has done in the form of reduced value of his land; but the river polluter's actions are costless, so far as he is concerned—except insofar as the legal system can somehow force him to internalize them. The result has been that the private landowner's power over natural objects on his land is far less restrained by law (as opposed to economics) than his power over the public resources that he can get his hands on. If this state of affairs is to be changed, the standard for interceding in the interests of natural objects on traditionally recognized "private" land might well parallel the rules that guide courts in the matter of people's children whose upbringing (or lack thereof) poses social threat. The courts can, for example, make a child "a dependent of the court" where the child's "home is an unfit place for him by reason of neglect, cruelty, or depravity of either of his parents. . . ." Cal. Welf. & Inst. Code § 600(b) (West 1966). *See also id* at § 601: any child "who from any cause is in danger of leading an idle, dissolute, lewd, or immoral life [may be adjudged] a ward of the court."

16. *See* note *supra.* The present way of handling such problems on "private" property is to try to enact legislation of general application under the police power, *see* Pennsylvania Coal Co. v. Mahon, 260 U.S. 393 (1922), rather than to institute civil litigation which, though a piecemeal process, can be tailored to individual situations.

Despite these protections, the problem of overseeing the guardian is particularly acute where, as here, there are no immediately identifiable human beneficiaries whose self-interests will encourage them to keep a close watch on the guardian. To ameliorate this problem, a page might well be borrowed from the law of ordinary charitable trusts, which are commonly placed under the supervision of the Attorney General. *See* Cal. Corp. Code §§ 9505, 10207 (West 1955).

18. *See* Cal. Prob. Code §§ 1472, 1590 (West 1956 and Supp. 1971).

19. Here, too, we are dogged by the ontological problem discussed in note 3 *supra.* It is easier to say that the

smog-endangered stand of pines "wants" the smog stopped (assuming that to be a jurally significant entity) then it is to venture that the mountain, or the planet earth, or the cosmos, is concerned about whether the pines stand or fall. The more encompassing the entity of concern, the less certain we can be in venturing judgments as to the "wants" of any particular substance, quality, or species within the universe. Does the cosmos care if we humans persist or not? "Heaven and earth . . . regard all things as insignificant, as though they were playthings made of straw." Lao-Tzu, Tao Teh King 13 (D. Goddard transl. 1919).

20. *See* Knight v. United States Land Ass'n, 142 U.S. 161, 181 (1891).

21. Clause 2 gives Congress the power "to dispose of and make all needful Rules and Regulations respecting the Territory or other Property belonging to the United States."

22. *See* Flemming v. Nestor, 363 U.S. 603 (1960).

23. *See* the L. A. Times editorial *Water: Public vs. Polluters* criticizing: . . . the ridiculous built-in conflict of interests on Regional Water Quality Control Board. By law, five of the seven seats are given to spokesmen for industrial, governmental, agricultural or utility users. Only one representative of the public at large is authorized, along with a delegate from fish and game interests. Feb. 12, 1969, Part II, at 8, cols. 1-2.

24. Of course, in the instance of copyright and patent protection, the creation of the "property right" can be more directly justified on homocentric grounds.

25. *See* Schrag, *Life on a Dying Lake,* in The Politics of Neglect 167, at 173 (R. Meek & J. Straayer, eds. 1971).

26. One ought to observe, too, that in terms of real effect on marginal welfare, the poor quite possibly will bear the brunt of the compromises. They may lack the wherewithal to get out to the countryside—and probably want an increase in material goods more acutely than those who now have riches.

27. On November 2, 1971, the Senate, by a vote of 86-0, passed and sent to the House the proposed Federal Water Pollution Control Act Amendments of 1971, 117 Cong. Reg. S17464 (daily ed. Nov. 2, 1971). Sections 101(a) and (a)(1) of the bill declare it to be "national policy that, consistent with the provisions of this Act— (1) the discharge of pollutants into the navigable waters be eliminated by 1985." S.2770, 92d Cong., 1st Sess., 117 Cong. Rec. S17464 (daily ed. Nov. 2, 1971).

28. 354 F.2d 608, 624 (2d Cir. 1965).

17. Cal. Prob. Code § 1580 (West Supp. 1971) lists specific causes for which a guardian may, after notice and a hearing, be removed.

29. Again, there is a problem involving what we conceive to be the injured entity. *See* notes 3, 19 *supra.*

30. N.Y. Times, Jan. 14, 1971, § 1, col. 2, and at 74, col. 7.

31. Courts have not been reluctant to award damages for the destruction of heirlooms, literary manuscripts or other property having no ascertainable market value. In Willard v. Valley Gas Guel Co., 171 Cal. 9, 151 Pac. 286 (1915), it was held that the measure of damages for the negligent destruction of a rare old book written by one of plaintiff's ancestors was the amount which would compensate the owner for all detriment including sentimental loss proximately caused by such destruction. The court, at 171 Cal. 15, 151 Pac. 289, quoted approvingly from Southern Express Co. v. Owens, 146 Ala. 412, 426, 41 S. 752, 755 (1906). . . .

32. J. Cousteau, "The Oceans: No Time to Lose," *L. A. Times,* Oct. 24, 1971, § (opinion), at 1, col. 4.

33. *See* J. Harte & R. Socolow, Patient Earth (1971).

34. C. McCullers, The Ballad of the Sad Cafe and Other Stories 150-51 (1958).

35. C. D. Stone, *Existential Humanism and the Law,* in Existential Humanistic Psychology 151 (1971).

36. San Antonio Conservation Soc'y v. Texas Highway Dep't, *cert. denied,* 400 U.S. 968 (1970) (Black, J. dissenting to denial of certiorari).

37. *Id.* at 969.

38. *Id.* at 971.

DISCUSSION TOPICS

1. On what basis does Stone argue for the extension of legal rights to natural objects?

2. What disadvantages do Stone's proposals have?

3. In a critique of Stone's proposed extension to natural objects of the guardianship of legal incompetents model, John Rodman has written: "Is this, then, the new enlightenment—to see nonhuman animals as imbeciles, wilderness as a human vegetable?"[7] How might Stone defend himself against this criticism?

---

7. John Rodman, "The Liberation of Nature?" Inquiry 20 (1977): 83-145.

Environmental Politics and the Administrative State

Robert Paehlke and Douglas Torgerson

Robert Paehlke is Professor of Political Studies and Environmental and Resource Studies at Trent University. Author of Environmentalism and the Future of Progressive Politics, *he is the founding editor of the journal* Alternatives: Perspectives on Society, Technology and Environment. *Douglas Torgerson teaches political theory and organization theory at Trent University, where he is Associate Professor and Director of Administrative Studies. Author of* Industrialization and Assessment: Social Impact Assessment as a Social Phenomenon, *he is the current editor of the journal* Policy Sciences.

Paehlke and Torgerson argue that environmental politics is a distinctive aspect of contemporary politics, different from the usual divisions of left, right, and center. Environmental politics is made up of both environmental organizations and environmental professionals who share the sense of environmental crisis, a crisis which requires fundamental revisions in administrative practice. According to Paehlke and Torgerson, environmental politics stands apart from conventional interest-group politics because environmental groups are concerned with a broad public interest rather than their own economic advantage.

Environmentalism logically implies a new form of administration which is more openly political than the conventional agenda of the administrative state. Environmental administration is fluid, noncompartmentalized, open, and involves a new integration of centralized and decentralized decision-making which is still emerging. Such administration is anti-technocratic and yet requires noncompartmentalized expertise which unifies systems and includes the common sense of local inhabitants.

Paehlke and Torgerson note that environmental politics has become institutionalized during the last twenty years and contains tensions between the methods and goals of groups such as the Audubon Society and Earth First! Nevertheless, environmental administration

includes both citizens and experts and may be able to manage ''Leviathan,''[8] without sacrificing democracy.

In the context of advancing industrialization, the fiction of apolitical administration readily appears plausible. Made in the image of the machine, the administrative apparatus becomes both an achievement and instrument of rationalization—of technological progress in an increasingly mechanized universe: ''mechanical technology is impersonal and dispassionate, and its end is very simply to serve human needs, without fear or favor or respect of persons, prerogatives, or politics.''[1] Bureaucratic organization emerges as a mechanism especially well suited to promoting a natural and necessary course of development. The administrative state, in particular, can thus appear as a form of governance beyond politics.

The advent of environmental politics has not been able completely to dispel this technocratic illusion, but has challenged it. With the established pattern of development drawn into question, the conventional agenda no longer appears simply as natural and necessary, but stands out clearly as a matter of choice—as something subject to revision. As this agenda comes under scrutiny, attention also turns to the process in which it is formulated and in which concrete policy decisions are made. Here the divide between politics and administration collapses: the two intermingle in a way which violates rationalistic expectations and prevailing canons of administrative legitimacy. The technocratic imagery now appears as a veil, obscuring the normal interplay of forces in the administrative sphere of state and economy. What is drawn into question is not only the historical direction created and maintained by the convergence of these forces, but also the institutional form which they collectively constitute.

ENVIRONMENTAL POLITICS

Environmental politics disturbs the composure of the administrative state. Even though Leviathan endeav-

---

8. Paehlke and Torgerson refer to the administrative state as ''Leviathan,'' the name given by Thomas Hobbes in 1651 to his theory of a state governed by a central power of absolute authority.

ors to force environmental problems onto the procrustean bed of conventional administrative thought and practice, the goal proves to be elusive. With the dramatic outburst of environmental concern some two decades ago, officials were generally quick to align their statements with the prevailing sentiment. Just as quickly, however, there emerged among them a sense that environmental problems had either been solved by modest reforms or displaced by more serious and pressing economic difficulties. Environmentalism, many hopefully believed, was going out of style and would not hold public attention for long. It seemed safe for officials to slight environmental concerns, and eventually neo-conservative forces were able to mount a determined assault upon environmentalism and the reforms it had initiated in the administrative state. Nonetheless, environmental politics had been animated by a particular perception of environmental problems—a perception which was strong and pervasive enough to sustain environmental concern in a substantial network of environmental organizations and among a significant proportion of environmental professionals. Once again, it now does not seem safe for public officials to ignore environmental concerns or simply to repeat the clichéd promises of progress.[2]

To say that environmental politics is animated by a particular perception of environmental problems is not to say that this perception is universally shared by all actors in this arena. Indeed, it is a perception which has often been ridiculed by forces committed to the conventional vision of order and progress. Nonetheless, environmental politics has emerged as an identifiable arena of contemporary politics and administration through the impetus of actors sharing a view which challenges the complacent notion that there is nothing new to environmental problems—that these are really just problems like any others and can be handled in the ordinary way.[3]

In a manner necessarily irritating to the administrative mind, environmental problems are deemed both enormously complex and serious—as raising in a dramatic fashion moral issues which once seemed settled and technical questions which few had even imagined. Against the expectations of the administrative mind, this view focuses on problems which may be entirely unmanageable and which, at the very least,

call for a thorough revision of administrative inquiry and practice. In its view of the complexity and seriousness of environmental problems, this perception contains a paradox. The problems seem virtually beyond comprehension yet enough is known to demand urgent action.

Environmental problems are perceived as being multidimensional, interconnected, interactive and dynamic. They point beyond the controlled setting of the laboratory or the production process to an ambiguous world where innumerable variables elude identification, much less measurement. The very scope of the unknown seems to expand dramatically with each little bit learned. Yet the problems appear not only extraordinarily complex, but also extremely threatening to particular concerns and, indeed, to the general interests of humanity.

A sense of crisis demands action and innovative directions in problem-solving. No single fact or model demonstrates an emerging crisis, but a litany of difficulties becomes increasingly impressive. Environmental impacts appear largely cumulative, moreover, and it becomes increasingly hard to deny that the maximum sustainable level of imposition of economy on environment has been reached or exceeded. Human populations and activities are encroaching in some way on the habitats of other species on nearly every square mile of land on the planet. Virtually all the best agricultural land now carries human-imposed eco-systems, maintained in many cases through the use of toxic chemicals. Ground water, river water, lake water, and the oceans are laced with chemicals: polar bears carry toxic chemicals in their livers. Precipitation around the world appears altered in both quantity and quality, and the ozone layer has been disrupted. Tropical rainforests seem headed for rapid elimination. Human beings are silently, surreptitiously being killed by unacceptable—and ''acceptable''—levels of pollution.

The perception alternates, then, between a sense of human limits and a confidence that human action has at least a chance of solving environmental problems. This ambivalence allows for differing approaches, including the reflex response of looking to established authority as some environmentalists have done. What that approach fails to recognize, however, is that established authority is itself seldom bothered by a sense of human limits and instead typically exudes unshakable confidence in prevailing institutions and their capacity to resolve problems. Of course, this capacity cannot, in principle, be disproven. Problems which seem to be insoluble in the context of established institutions could—however dim the possibility—conceivably be resolved through some unanticipated innovation, or through some unforeseen way of defining the problems. What remains striking, nonetheless, is the unshakable character of this confidence, for its foundation is as suspect as the rationalistic imagery which adorns it: "The achievements of modern science and technology, however impressive, do not of themselves provide solid evidence that the problems which they confront and, in fact, create, can actually be overcome."[4] There is, indeed, reason for doubt. The administrative sphere, while singularly successful in promoting the established pattern of development, has not shown itself to be effective in either restraining or qualitatively redirecting industrialization. The administrative sphere, moreover, craves that which is definite, precise, and calculable—tolerating little in the way of ambivalence. Nonetheless, such ambivalent perception may well be in accord with an organizational form oriented toward a balance between the humility of recognizing limits and the confidence needed for effective action.

While environmental politics is animated by a particular view of environmental problems, it is also characterized by the rather distinctive perspective and interests of those advancing environmental concerns. Environmental politics is a dimension of political life which is different from the politics of left, right, and center. While the center has typically endorsed environmental concern—even reducing the environment to a so-called "motherhood" issue—environmentalism has also been portrayed as a mere extension of the socialist movement or of the earlier progressive conservation movement. Despite the frequently unabashed hostility of neo-conservatism to the environmental movement and its goals, there is also an ambiguous relationship between environmentalism and the appeals of neo-conservatism.[5] Environmental politics, moreover, stands apart from conventional interest-group politics and thus bears a distinctive

relationship to the state and the administrative world generally.

The intriguing ambiguity in the relationship between environmentalism and neo-conservatism turns largely on how the two view the administrative state. Both exhibit a notable hostility. For neo-conservatives the goal has been economic recovery and expansion through deregulation, entrepreneurship, and the "magic of the market." Environmentalists, in turn, have often emphasized alternative patterns of development, comprising grass-roots citizen participation and empowerment, responsible individual action, and both public and private decentralized initiatives. For environmentalism, this emphasis in part represents a reaction against the administrative orientation of the earlier conservation movement. Neo-conservatives are reacting against the seemingly unidirectional growth of the "positive state."

In terms of concrete policy thrusts, neo-conservatism has ironically pursued a course ensuring the continued growth and presence of the administrative state in economy and society. This course has included the financing of megaprojects, direct and indirect subsidies to private corporations, bailouts for companies and industries "too big to fail," grants for technological development, and—especially in the American context—mammoth expenditures amounting to a "military Keynesianism."[6] Nor was such a course really avoidable because neo-conservatism has by no means replaced the prevailing consensus which attributes to the administrative state ultimate responsibility for the economic management of advanced industrial society. A further irony is that neo-conservatism in America, Canada, and Britain has had to make a concerted effort to restrain a seemingly visceral hostility to environmentalism in order to project at least an appearance of environmental concern. One of the most dramatic adjustments in current political life, this change suggests that continuing public support for environmental protection may prove to be a significant chink in the neo-conservative armor. . . .

Besides its unique orientation to the prevailing ideological map, environmental politics also departs from the conventional framework of interest-group politics. The focus of environmental groups, that is, is concerned more with a broad public interest than with a narrow, particular interest. This point is implicit in the literature on ''post-materialist'' values; and environmentalism is central to discussions of the ''new social movements'' that challenge conventional politics.[7] Those devoted to environmental politics are not typically seeking economic advantages. Instead, environmentalists see themselves generally as representing a universal human interest (including future generations) or as speaking for other species and especially threatened parts of non-human nature—indeed, more comprehensively, as working in the interests of the planet and its inhabitants as a whole.

The distinctive orientation of environmentalism is significant in the politics of the administrative state. For this realm works smoothly only if those seeking favors are uniformly professional and responsible— if they speak the proper language of precision and instrumentality while standing ready to make the trade-offs necessary for compromise solutions. With their particular perspective and interests, environmentalists often do not measure up to these standards. Yet as they seek concrete results in the policy process, they are bound to interact over time with the administrative state and the corporate world. Then environmentalists do—often in a dramatic and deliberate fashion—become increasingly professional and ''responsible.'' Indeed, participation in environmental impact assessment hearings and other administrative procedures often requires time and expertise. Since environmentalists are hardly less likely than others to need a means of livelihood, they may well become reliant on the continuing success and stability of an environmental organization or network—even if remuneration tends to be meagre. Moreover, with the frankly moral character of its demands, environmentalism can appear overbearing and untrustworthy in a world where one gets along by going along. Environmentalists are pressed to compromise simply in order not to appear uncompromising.

Yet this is not the entire story, for professionalized environmentalists are frequently eclipsed by events and ''out-greened'' by others.[8] This tension runs through existing groups, and is increased with the

entry of new groups and individuals into environmental politics. A significant impetus in this regard arises with the so-called NIMBY syndrome, or— in distinctly different terms—with opposition to LULUs: locally unwanted land uses. Here local residents may generally oppose development which would degrade the recreational amenities of the area. Or landowners could object to particular projects which would decrease the sale value of their property. Clearly, these motives are common to interest-group politics, and there is an arsenal of compensatory devices available in conventional politics and administration. Yet, typically in such situations, there are two elements which resist ready compromise and a smooth resolution to disputes. One is the attachment that people may feel to a place with which they identify. The other is the fact that some who object to a landfill, a toxic waste dispository, or an oil refinery do so not only with their particular interests in view, but also with concern for a broader, interrelated context of environmental problems. Indeed, when such opposition resists conventional compromises, more than an immediate difficulty is created for the administrative state. For these situations also direct the attention of a broader citizenry to environmental concerns; face-to-face with particular consequences of industrialization, some are led to perceive broader questions and perhaps to inject a vigorous and uncompromising attitude into environmental politics.

ENVIRONMENTAL ADMINISTRATION

In its collision with the administrative state, as we have seen, environmental politics is influenced by an historically unique perception which takes environmental problems not to be ordinary problems, easily remedied or administered in the conventional manner. Environmental politics thereby clearly departs from the earlier politics of conservation and its tendency to align itself with the administrative apparatus of an emerging industrialism. Indeed, at times environmental politics seems moved by an impulse to have done with administration altogether.[9] Yet this impulse would appear to be based in a recognition of the inadequacies of conventional administration in grappling with environmental problems. What the impulse obscures is that administration cannot simply be abolished: the historical possibility is for a form of administration more adequate to the environmental problems which are emerging as we move into the aftermath of industrialization. The at least implicit logic of environmentalism, of environmental politics, is to realize this new kind of administration.

Environmental administration possesses no completed form or systematic program, but is an emerging orientation of inquiry and practice distinctly at odds with the conventional agenda. . . .

In order to grasp the idea of environmental administration more fully, we can briefly and provisionally characterize it with an interrelated and incomplete list of adjectives: (1) non-compartmentalized, (2) open, (3) decentralized, (4) anti-technocratic, and (5) flexible. Here we will focus, in turn, on each characteristic.

(1) *Non-compartmentalized.* Environmental administration resists the typical bureaucratic tendency toward compartmentalization. Because it recognizes a pervasive complex of problems, environmental administration has indefinite boundaries and has, indeed, challenged early efforts to confine environmental concerns to a single, often marginal, sub-division of government. The institutionalization of environmental impact assessment, for example, has—despite its limitations—prompted a broad range of government departments and agencies to think environmentally. . . .

(2) *Open.* While the hallmark of conventional administration is secrecy in a cloistered decision-making process, the hallmark of environmental administration is openness. . . . Public administrators, and even private decision-makers, are more and more likely to find themselves at a public hearing or in a courtroom, rather than closeted in the offices of a confidential world. . . .

(3) *Decentralized.* The slogan ''think globally, act locally'' reflects a significant ambivalence in environmental administration. . . . Global problems in some cases require common, cooperative global solutions, with little room for wide variations in approach: diverse initiatives here need coordination to be effective. Prompt efforts to stem the depletion of ozone in

the upper atmosphere, to take an obvious example, could well be pointless if China should embark upon a program of providing CFC-based refrigerators to its vast population. Some central administration is necessary, moreover, to prevent havens for pollution in areas where authorities are inclined to trade environmental quality for economic opportunities: the air of much of a continent can be fouled from within a single, neglectful political jurisdiction. . . .

If environmental administration must deal with global problems, so too must it deal with the local and the particular, with peculiar geographical and cultural contexts. Here necessary knowledge and initiative cannot be the preserve of a centralized administrative structure, staffed by remote and anonymous personnel. Knowledge and initiative, indeed, arise from intimate involvement in the context.[10] . . . Obviously, environmental administration anticipates some kind of new balance, integration, or alignment of centralization and decentralization.

(4) *Anti-technocratic.* . . . Environmental administration necessarily draws heavily on the findings and opinions of experts. Sciences such as ecology, epidemiology, and toxicology, indeed, provide important foundations for environmentalism as a perspective which informs environmental administration in its challenge to technocracy. But expertise, almost by definition, is specialized and thus insufficient by itself for handling environmental problems. With its features of non-compartmentalization and openness, environmental administration clearly draws attention to the importance of the generalist capable of viewing problems in a broader configuration, of perceiving and judging collectivities, interactions, and relationships across systems. The importance of the generalist suggests, moreover that the boundary between relevant expertise and common sense is often fluid and indistinct.[11] The door is thus open to citizen participation in a process which could educate *both* citizens and experts.

The insufficiency of specialized expertise means that the administrative process needs to remain open to a range of influences and experiences which are typically excluded in conventional practice. This point reinforces the importance of the knowledge and initiative to be gained through a relatively decentralized pattern of interaction involving both citizens and experts.

. . . No doubt there is often a rationale to exclude such influences. For example, there is often concern about the supposedly unwarranted delays occasioned by the NIMBY syndrome. Yet this concern is based upon the assumption that administrative officials have both the competence and commitment to handle environmental problems effectively without external influences. To take a case in point, the failure of the administrative sphere—both public and private—to prevent or effectively respond to the massive Valdez oil spill was followed by a rapid mobilization of local communities attempting, with inadequate and makeshift equipment, to contain the damage.[12] This spontaneous, decentralized response suggests that the initial planning of the damage control system might well have relied upon local knowledge and initiative; and this would have required the active involvement of local communities. Of course, this approach would have elicited concern and many questions from these communities, and the conventional administrative view would take this to be a sufficient reason for the approach to be rejected. It is indeed possible that intense opposition would have been encountered, but it is also possible that this very opposition would have promoted the design of a more effective damage control system—or, indeed, the choice and design of a transportation system which would have made damage on such a scale impossible in the first place. This observation is no doubt relevant to many major projects and LULUs. What often seems to be the danger of unwarranted delay might also be viewed as a necessary trial for projects which would render less likely at least some major mistakes. More broadly considered, indeed, such an orientation to the administrative process would alter its present commitment and enhance the prospect of a pattern of development consistent with environmental concerns. . . .

(5) *Flexible.* Conventional problem-solving focuses on a form of analysis which proceeds from a fairly fixed conceptual framework, seeking impatiently to reduce ambiguity and diversity in the subject-matter to something manageable and familiar.

What is lost is a sensitivity to those changes and differences which resist ready recognition, much less classification. Following from its non-compartmentalized, open, decentralized, and anti-technocratic characteristics, environmental administration remains flexible in its orientation to problems. Indeed, environmental administration is also flexible in another—perhaps perplexing—sense: it resists precisely the type of characterization we are trying to give it, for it is an emergent phenomenon. Environmental administration is taking shape, and remains to be shaped further. But no one is in a position to offer a comprehensive description or prescription. The very vocabulary now available is inadequate, distorting environmental administration even while describing, prescribing, and emerging along with it. For it would be ridiculous to say, taking the opposites of the terms employed here, that environmental administration possesses no features which could be considered somehow compartmentalized, closed, centralized, technocratic, or fixed. Such a notion of environmental administration would itself be absurdly rigid, yet such a distortion is certainly possible given the prevailing political and administrative context. Obviously, to speak of environmental administration is a task more complex than coming down on one side or another of a polar opposition. Yet the words to grasp and convey the right balance, integration, or realignment are not yet part of the available vocabulary. To create such a vocabulary is part of an intellectual—indeed political—task which would change the prevailing agenda of inquiry and practice.

ENVIRONMENTAL ADMINISTRATION AND THE ADMINISTRATIVE STATE

. . . Environmentalism betrays differences and tensions as some groups tend toward professionalism, compromise, and workable solutions while other groups accentuate an oppositional posture accompanied by direct action and sensational stunts. Both these elements are necessary, though perhaps not sufficient, in the emergence of environmental administration.

Impatience with Leviathan should not obscure

what is both obvious and paradoxical: moving beyond Leviathan would also mean initially helping to manage it. This is not to deny that the process could be long, even interminable—that opposition could significantly be absorbed through accommodation. Yet institutionalization has a memory that is more than momentary. Once established and set in motion, an administrative process gains a dynamism of its own and may see something through, especially if there are pressures which will not allow it to forget what it might prefer to forget. Institutional changes which tend to make the administrative process more open and participatory introduce an element of unpredictability which can be denied only through the illusion which the administrative mind fosters of its unbounded capacity to control events. Innovation of this kind, moreover, raises the prospect not only of citizens interacting with experts, but also of citizens *as* experts and experts *as* citizens. The strengthening of this already-present tendency would be a key event in the emergence of environmental administration: Leviathan might then become manageable.

NOTES

1. Thorstein Veblen, *The Engineers and the Price System* (New York: Viking Press, 1933 [1921]), pp. 135-136. This book inspired the Technocracy movement of the 1930's; the term *technocracy* has since, of course, come to have a broader application.

2. In the midst of an outburst of environmental concern, the Nixon Administration quickly embraced a series of environmental measures in 1970, in particular with the President signing the *National Environmental Policy Act* of 1969 with much fanfare on the first day of the new decade. Yet the high priority of the environment did not last long. In mid-1971, the President clearly suggested the need for a shift: "We are not going to allow the environment issue to be used sometimes falsely and sometimes in a demagogic way basically to destroy the [industrial] system." By 1973, risk of an environmental crisis had apparently passed: "When we came to office in 1969," Nixon said, "we tackled this problem with all the power at our command. Now there is encouraging evidence that the United States has moved away from the environmental crisis that could have been toward a new era of restoration and renewal.

Today . . . we are well on the way to winning the war against environmental degradation—well on the way to making our peace with nature. . . ." Fuel shortages now placed an urgent new priority high on the agenda—that of securing expanded energy supplies. A key measure in this regard was the construction of the Trans-Alaska pipeline. See Richard N.L. Andrews, *Environmental Policy and Administrative Change* (Lexington, MA: Lexington Books, 1976), ch. 3, esp. pp. 24-25 for quotations. Recently, the final communiqué of the 1989 economic summit in Paris "devoted more space to the environment than to any other subject. . . . Being politicians, the leaders did not suddenly decide to go green because they liked the color. Powerful public sentiment in their respective countries drove them toward the fine words of their communiqué. . . . Environmental groups . . . are right to remain skeptical. . . ." Jeffrey Simpson, "The Greening of the G7," *The Globe and Mail* (July 19, 1989), p. A6. *Cf.* Anthony Downs, "Up and Down with Ecology: The 'Issue-Attention Cycle'," *The Public Interest* 38 (1972), pp. 38-50.

3. The distinctive character of the environmental perspective is emphasized in Robert Paehlke, *Environmentalism and the Future of Progressive Politics* (New Haven: Yale University Press, 1989).

4. Douglas Torgerson, *Industrialization and Assessment: Social Impact Assessment as a Social Phenomenon* (Toronto: York University, 1980), p. 72. Also see ch. 2 generally and pp. 186-189.

5. On the relationship of environmentalism to the major political ideologies, see Paehlke, *Environmentalism and the Future of Progressive Politics,* ch. 7.

6. See Robert Paehlke, "Environmentalism: 'Motherhood,' Revolution, or Just Plain Politics?" *Alternatives* 13:1 (1985), pp. 29-33; Robert M. Campbell, "From Keynesianism to Monetarism," *Queen's Quarterly* 88 (1981), pp. 635-650.

7. See, *e.g.,* Vaughan Lyon, "The Reluctant Party: Ideology versus Organization in Canada's Green Movement," *Alternatives* 13:1 (1985), pp. 3-8.

8. See Michael W. McCann, "Public Interest Liberalism and the Modern Regulatory State," *Polity* 21:1 (1988), pp. 373-400; Ronald Inglehart, "Post-Materialism in an Environment of Insecurity," *American Political Science Review* 75 (1981), pp. 880-900; Claus Offe, "New Social Movements: Challenging the Boundaries of Institutional Politics," *Social Research* 52:4 (1985), pp. 817-868. Also see Robyn Eckersley, "Green Poli-

tics: A Practice in Search of a Theory?'' *Alternatives* 15:4 (1988), pp. 52-61.

9. Tension within and among environmental groups became apparent as Pollution Probe in Toronto joined with Loblaws, a major supermarket chain, in developing and promoting ''green'' products. This involvement with the private sector of the administrative sphere followed from and reinforced a deliberate effort to develop a more professionalized environmental organization. The outcome was conflict within Pollution Probe, the resignation of the executive director, and criticism—at least of Loblaws—by Greenpeace Canada. In response to the controversy, various environmentalists affirmed the need for a diversity of groups. See Craig McInnes, ''Environment Groups Face a Crisis of Identity,'' *The Globe and Mail* (July 15, 1989), p. D2.

10. For a convenient summary of some relevant literature, see Brian Martin, ''Self-Managing Environmentalism,'' *Alternatives* 13:1 (1985), pp. 34-39.

11. See Douglas Torgerson, ''Between Knowledge and Politics: Three Faces of Policy Analysis,'' *Policy Sciences* 19 (1986), p. 51. No doubt resistance to this prospect is to be expected. Consider in this regard the comment of a citizen dealing with officials in a case involving the problem of radioactive waste: ''They got nervous when someone started using the same technological jargon. They were always presuming that no one was going to do that, and . . . that they would just intimidate everyone, and that everyone would just shut up.'' Quoted in Donald Alexander, ''Eldorado: Local Citizen Activism and the Nuclear Establishment, 1933-1988,'' M.A. Thesis, Trent University, Peterborough, Ontario, 1989, p. 76.

12. In an NBC News report on April 14, 1989 from Valdez, Don Molina described Homer, Alaska as a ''town under siege,'' bracing for the oil spill to reach it and with 4,400 people fashioning improvised oil collecting booms. ''There are finally some signs of order among the chaos of the clean-up,'' he added, ''the beginning of coordination for all the equipment in place or on the way three weeks after the spill.''

DISCUSSION TOPICS

1. Does the urgency of environmental problems require a centralized administration rather than the somewhat decentralized environmental administration described by Paehlke and Torgerson?

2. Paehlke and Torgerson argue that the underlying political agenda of the administrative state is to foster continued technological progress and economic growth, regardless of cumulative environmental damage. Does the administration of your state government fit this description?

3. Have human beings reached the maximum sustainable level of economic development? Why or why not?

4. Must environmentalists be liberals? Explain your reasoning.

CHAPTER EXERCISES

Divide the students into five groups:

1. Owners of a hypothetical mining corporation
2. Local property owners in the area being considered for mining
3. Environmental economists using a cost-benefit approach based on contingent valuation surveys
4. Representatives of an environmental organization
5. Members of a government agency regulating mining

Have the corporation present a brief proposal, giving the type of mine and expected benefits to the community. The proposed mine adjoins a national forest with endangered species of wildlife. Have the economists design a brief survey and then survey the property owners, on whether a mine should be established. The results of the survey and the views of the environmental organization are then presented to the government agency at a hearing attended by the parties involved. The agency renders its decision with an explanation of its basis.

This exercise can be adapted to deal with local controversies.

FOR FURTHER READING

Anderson, Terry Lee and Donald R. Leal. *Free Market Environmentalism*. San Francisco: Pacific Research Institute for Public Policy, 1991. A readable, forceful defense of the use of well-specified property rights to natural resources, including suggestions for air pollution problems.

Bandyopadhyay, Jayanta and Vandana Shiva. "Chipko: Rekindling India's Forest Culture." *The Ecologist* 17: 26-34, 1987. A historical account of the development of the important Chipko movement to save India's forests.

Buttel, Frederick H., Martin Kenney, and Jack Kloppenburg, Jr. "From Green Revolution to Biorevolution: Some Observations on the Changing Technological Bases of Economic Transformation in the Third World." *Economic Development and Cultural Change* 34: 31-55, 1985. A thorough discussion (pp. 31-55) of the comparative impacts on the Third World of the Green Revolution and the Biorevolution (manipulation of living organisms in order to produce a desired product). A main concern is ignoring the needs of the rural poor in the less-developed countries by the private system of research.

Callicott, J. Baird. "The Wilderness Idea Revisited: The Sustainable Development Alternative." *The Environmental Professional* 13: 235-247, 1991. An important article in which Callicott argues for an integration of human economic activities with biological conservation. He maintains that the popular idea of wilderness perpetuates the man-nature split, is ethnocentric, and ignores the dynamism of natural processes. He provides several examples of mutually enhancing human/nature symbioses. Extensive references.

Cleveland, Cutler J. "Biophysical Economics: Historical Perspective and Current Research Trends." *Ecological Modelling* 38: 47-73, 1987. Cleveland traces biophysical economists from the eighteenth century physiocrats to contemporary economists such as Nicholas Georgescu-Roegen and Herman Daly and others, and argues that economics must no longer ignore the role of natural resources.

Costanza, Robert. "Social Traps and Environmental Policy." *BioScience* 37: 407-412, 1987. Argues that the long-term social cost of activities with environmental impacts should be charged to the responsible parties in the short run.

Edwards, Steven F. "Ethical Preferences and the Assessment of Existence Values: Does the Neoclassical Model Fit?" *Northeastern Journal of Agricultural and Resource Economics* 15: 145-150, 1986. Recommends that contingent valuation surveys collect data on underlying motives as well as monetary valuation in order to distinguish between egoists and altruists.

Environmental Values. A journal published in England which began publication in 1992. Contains interdisciplinary articles.

Georgescu-Roegen, Nicholas. *The Entrophy Law and the Economic Process.* Cambridge, Mass.: Harvard University Press, 1971. A highly influential book arguing that economics must take seriously the fact that human activity is limited by the stock of low entropy on the globe. Any use of natural resources for nonvital needs diminishes future life.

Hardin, Garrett and John Baden, eds. *Managing the Commons.* San Francisco: W.H. Freeman, 1977. An anthology concerned with cultural changes needed to ensure human survival.

Hays, Samuel P. *Beauty, Health, and Permanence: Environmental Politics in the United States, 1955–1985.* Cambridge: Cambridge University Press, 1987. A clearly written and wide-ranging account of American environmental politics, intended for a general audience.

Hubbard, Harold M. "The Real Cost of Energy." *Scientific American* 264: 36-42, 1991. Argues for various strategies of incorporating all the costs of energy into the market.

Hueting, Roefie. "An Economic Scenario that Gives Top Priority to Saving the Environment." *Ecological Modelling* 38: 123-140, 1987. An argument that environmental conservation can increase jobs and improve living conditions, based on a 1980–1984 experiment in The Netherlands.

Mitchell, Robert Cameron and Richard T. Carson. "Property Rights, Protest, and the Siting of Hazardous Waste Facilities." *AEA Papers and Proceedings* 76: 285-290, 1986. Presents an argument for recognizing community property rights by allocating hazardous waste facilities by means of a referendum tied with a compensation package.

Norgaard, Richard B. "Economics as Mechanics and the Demise of Biological Diversity." *Ecological Modelling* 38: 107-121, 1987. Argues that biological diversity has declined with economic diversity. Economic decisions by human beings should be understood as part of the ecological system.

Ostrom, Elinor. *Governing the Commons: The Evolution of Institutions for Collective Action.* Cambridge: Cambridge University Press, 1990. Ostrom has studied collective action by individuals using common-pool resources (CPR) for over 30 years. The book provides descriptions of both successful and unsuccessful CPR arrangements. Includes a framework for comprehensive further study and extensive notes and references.

Pearce, David. "Foundations of an Ecological Economics." *Economic Modelling* 38: 9-18, 1987. Argues that a sustainable society is one in which Rawls-style distributional justice is applied intergenerationally.

Rice, Richard E. "Old-Growth Logging Myths: The Ecological Impact of the US Forest Service's Management Policies." *The Ecologist* 20: 141-146, 1990. Argues that old-growth timber harvesting in national forests does not benefit other forest resources. Subsidized logging should be phased out and current harvest methods altered.

Rodman, John. "The Liberation of Nature?" *Inquiry* 20: 83-145, 1977. An important article arguing against the extension of human moral systems as proposed by Singer and Stone and in favor of a new myth involving the defense of diversity and richness of potential on biological, social, and psychological levels.

Rolston, Holmes, III. "The Wilderness Idea Reaffirmed." *The Environmental Professional* 13: 1-9, 1991. Rolston argues that Callicott's account of human beings as entirely natural is incorrect. Rolston maintains that wilderness has intrinsic value and should be protected from human utilization.

Rolston, Holmes, III and James Coufal. "A Forest Ethic and Multivalue Forest Management." *Journal of Forestry* 89.4: 35-40, 1991. Provides ten categories of values: life support; economic, scientific, recreational, and aesthetic use; wildlife; biotic diversity; natural history; spiritual and intrinsic.

Rosenbaum, Walter A. *Environmental Politics and Policy.* Washington, D.C.: Congressional Quarterly Press, 1991. Clear presentation of how public policy is formed, together with a discussion of risk assessment for air and water, toxics, energy, and public lands use.

Sagoff, Mark. *The Economy of the Earth: Philosophy, Law, and the Environment.* Cambridge: Cambridge University Press, 1988. A collection of important essays arguing against market failure as the basis of social regulation and in favor of the thesis that social regulation expresses what we believe as a nation.

Schramm, Gunter and Jeremy J. Warford, eds. *Environment, Management and Economic Devleopment.* Baltimore: Johns Hopkins University Press, 1989. A readable anthology concerning environmental management in developing countries, arguing that economic development and environmental protection are not always mutually exclusive.

Underwood, Daniel A. and Paul G. King. "On the Ideological Foundations of Environmental Policy." *Ecological Economics* 1: 315-334, 1989. Contrasts steady-state and neoclassical economic schools of thought and argues that steady-state economic theory is in accord with scientific knowledge.

CHAPTER SIX

Anthropocentrism

In this chapter we first define anthropocentrism and identify two major types (strong anthropocentrism and weak anthropocentrism), and then focus on some ethical issues within the context of an anthropocentric world view.

CONCEPTUAL FRAMEWORK

Anthropocentrism is the philosophical perspective asserting that ethical principles apply to humans only, and that human needs and interests are of highest, and even exclusive, value and importance. Thus, concern for nonhuman entities is limited to those entities having value to humans. Anthropocentrism can be traced back at least to the time of Mesopotamia,[1] and is probably one of the older ethical positions in Western civilization.

In contemporary Western society, anthropocentrism often serves as a "default ethic," a position assumed without careful consideration of alternative world views. However, anthropocentrism also is a position held by many thoughtful and reflective people as the most morally correct perspective to advocate. It is this latter position that we describe and analyze in this chapter.

Roots of anthropocentrism in Western society can be found both in religious and secular philosophies. Since the persuasiveness of a religious-based ethic depends on sharing a common faith and world view, those who are not adherents are less likely to find its tenets compelling. Therefore, many contemporary scholars have appealed to the more universal, secular themes first developed among ancient Greek philosophers. Our focus in this chapter is primarily on secular anthropocentric philosophies, but also includes the anthropocentrism found in the work of St. Thomas Aquinas, who strongly influenced both secular and religious perspectives in Western society. Other religious-based moral perspectives are included in Chapters 10 and 11.

Bryan G. Norton, in his essay, "Contemporary Expressions of Anthropocentrism: Environmental Ethics and Weak Anthropocentrism," argues that there are two types of anthropocentrism prevalent in Western society. The first, *strong anthropocentrism*, is characterized by the notion that nonhuman species and natural objects have value only to the extent that they satisfy a "felt preference." A "felt preference"

---

1. J. Donald Hughes, *Ecology in Ancient Civilization.* (Albuquerque, N.M.: University of New Mexico Press, 1975).

is any fulfillable human desire—whether or not it is based on thought and reflection. The readings from St. Thomas Aquinas, René Descartes, Immanuel Kant, W. J. McGee, and R. D. Guthrie in this chapter generally illustrate this perspective.

The second type, *weak anthropocentrism,* is distinguished by the affirmation that nonhumans and natural objects can satisfy ''considered preferences'' as well as ''felt preferences.'' A ''considered preference'' is a human desire or need which is based on careful deliberation, and is compatible with a rationally adopted worldview, incorporating sound metaphysics, scientific theories, aesthetic values, and moral ideals. Thus, weak anthropocentrists value nonhuman entities for more than their use in meeting unreflective human needs: they value them for enriching the human experience. In this chapter, F. Fraser Darling, W. H. Murdy, and Stephen Jay Gould present positions more closely allied with weak anthropocentrism. Keep in mind, however, that strong and weak anthropocentrism are not always sharply distinguished. Anthropocentric positions can fall in a range between strong and weak anthropocentrism.

LIMITING MORAL CONCERN TO HUMAN BEINGS

Clarifying the moral responsibility of humans to the rest of nature is one of the most difficult and controversial tasks in formulating an environmental ethic in our society. Anthropocentrists restrict the object of our moral concern largely or exclusively to human beings, who are viewed as superior to other creatures and to nature. Anthropocentrists commonly justify their position by citing unique characteristics which emphasize the importance of the human species. For example, the human capacity to reason plays a central role in the arguments of Aquinas, Descartes, and Kant. Descartes and Kant also stress the development and use of language in maintaining the extension of moral concern only to humans. Another justification for anthropocentrism is couched in negative terms: that is, all of the arguments for extending moral concern beyond humans are illogical or infeasible. Guth-

rie holds this perspective. Some anthropocentrists, such as Fraser Darling and Murdy, base their positions on the observed power and biological superiority of humans in the natural world. Murdy also argues for the evolutionary necessity of taking this philosophic position.

In contrast, those who oppose anthropocentrism believe that a moral system restricted to humans is arbitrary, unjust, and illogical.[2] For example, in many well-established ethical systems, moral worth is extended not only to nonhuman animals, but to spiritual beings and sacred places as well. Some scholars point to the many similarities between humans and other animals, especially mammals, in arguing that any ethic which includes all humans and excludes all nonhumans is unjust since there are no morally relevant characteristics (for example, rationality, consciousness, language) which all humans possess, and no nonhumans possess. If all humans qualify for moral concern, then any objective criteria would require that some nonhuman entities also qualify. Because of the controversy surrounding the issue of who ought to be accorded moral concern, most readings in this chapter offer a thoughtful defense of anthropocentrism.

The authors represented in this chapter hold varying perspectives on the moral limits which should be sanctioned in human treatment of nonhumans and the environment. Descartes suggests that nonhumans are little more than intricate machines lacking a soul and does not place any clear limits on how humans ought to treat them. Aquinas, Kant, and Guthrie refer to indirect duties toward humans, and propose the consideration of human sensibilities when making decisions about the treatment of nonhumans. However, Guthrie also insists that as long as people are not forced to experience or witness possibly offensive acts they must allow others to exploit organisms for their own education and enjoyment. In Guthrie's view, how humans treat nonhumans is merely a matter of taste.

---

2. Bernard E. Rollin, in *Animal Rights and Human Morality* (Buffalo, N.Y.: Prometheus Books, 1981), pp. 3-22.

ENLIGHTENED SELF-INTEREST

A central question which merits careful consideration is, ''Will anthropocentrism eventually lead the human species to self-destruction, and perhaps to the destruction of many other species as well?'' As an essentially self-serving ethic, anthropocentrism may lack the necessary safeguards to protect the planet from the effects of the human species' steadily increasing numbers and demands on world resources. The response of anthropocentrists to this question is built largely on the notion of ''enlightened self-interest.'' From this perspective, many anthropocentrists acknowledge the human potential for environmental destruction and recognize that long-term human existence and well-being depend on the health and stability of the planet's ecological support system. They advocate that humans must take responsibility for maintaining this support system in a healthy, useful condition.

This point of view is found most commonly among weak anthropocentrists. For example, Fraser Darling in his essay, ''Man's Responsibility for the Environment,'' proposes that humans accept their superiority as a species and view themselves as biological aristocrats, assuming a *noblesse oblige* responsibility toward the natural world. Human survival is a key foundation of this responsibility. In ''Anthropocentrism: A Modern View,'' Murdy also acknowledges human superiority, and maintains that human survival and well-being depend on the health and stability of the whole ecological support system. Murdy stresses the great destructive potential exhibited by humans, and points out that dependence on the ecological support system must lead humans to be careful not to destroy this fragile planet. In Murdy's view, humans should ascribe value to nonhumans and the rest of the natural world in accordance with how these entities benefit humanity. Gould discounts the notion of the earth as a fragile planet needing protection, but argues that an enlightened self-interest makes it prudent for humans to treat nature more gently than they have in the past.

DISTRIBUTING BENEFITS FROM THE NATURAL WORLD

All of the authors in this chapter identify human needs as the primary consideration in making environmental decisions. However, McGee in his essay, ''The Conservation Mentality of Natural Resources,'' seeks to ensure that all citizens of the United States share the benefits from the country's natural resources—not only the entrepreneurs developing these resources. McGee also stresses that natural resources must be managed so that they are available to future generations. Guthrie, Fraser Darling, and Murdy likewise recommend long-term human benefit as the basis for making environmental decisions. None of the authors addresses global responsibilities for sharing resources with other countries or social groups who lack them.

Differences Between Rational and Other Creatures

St. Thomas Aquinas

One of the most influential early thinkers is St. Thomas Aquinas (1225–1274), a medieval philosopher and theologian who was declared a saint in 1323. Among other accomplishments, he was a major contributor to Scholasticism, in which he posited the compatibility of faith and reason.

St. Thomas Aquinas holds that rationality is what determines the excellence of a thing; the greater the intellect, the more excellent a being, with God viewed as pure intellect and hence perfect Being. St. Thomas believes only humans possess intellects on earth, and he considers that the remainder of God's earthly creation is under human dominion.

In part, St. Thomas Aquinas bases his reasoning on the concept of the Great Chain of Being. Advocates for this idea propose an ordering of all life forms on a continuous scale according to how closely each approaches the perfect self-sufficiency and plentitude of Being found in God; they range from the most meager kinds of existents, which barely escape nonexistence, up to the ens perfectissimum, *or God. Elements of this concept are derived from Plato and Aristotle and later were elaborated by the Neoplatonist, Plotinus.*

Following in the tradition of the Great Chain of Being, St. Thomas Aquinas infers that less perfect beings should properly be subordinated to more perfect ones. Thus, in his views, humans and other animals can treat plants as they please, and humans can use lower animals as they desire (but not vice versa). Likewise, humans are subordinate to angels and God.

St. Thomas Aquinas believes that Biblical passages mandating human concern toward animals and nature fundamentally are grounded in human concerns and duties toward other humans. Thus, only humans deserve moral concern. St. Thomas does believe cruelty to nonhumans is wrong, but only because it might encourage cruelty toward other humans. Logically extended, however, St. Thomas' perspective could be used to condone torturing *"lower"* animals if this behavior diffuses sadism toward humans.

In the first place then, the very condition of the rational creature, in that it has dominion over its actions, requires that the care of providence should be bestowed on it for its own sake: whereas the condition of other things that have not dominion over their actions shows that they are cared for, not for their own sake, but as being directed to other things. Because that which acts only when moved by another, is like an instrument; whereas that which acts by itself, is like a principal agent. Now an instrument is required, not for its own sake, but that the principal agent may use it. Hence whatever is done for the care of the instruments must be referred to the principal agent as its end: whereas any such action directed to the principal agent as such, either by the agent itself or by another, is for the sake of the same principal agent. Accordingly intellectual creatures are ruled by God, as though He cared for them for their own sake, while other creatures are ruled as being directed to rational creatures.

Again. That which has dominion over its own act, is free in its action, because *he is free who is cause of himself:* whereas that which by some kind of necessity is moved by another to act, is subject to slavery. Therefore every other creature is naturally under slavery; the intellectual nature alone is free. Now, in every government provision is made for the free for their own sake; but for slaves that they may be useful to the free. Accordingly divine providence makes provision for the intellectual creature for its own sake, but for other creatures for the sake of the intellectual creature.

Moreover. Whenever certain things are directed to a certain end, if any of them are unable of themselves to attain to the end, they must needs be directed to those that attain to the end, which are directed to the end for their own sake. Thus the end of the army is victory, which the soldiers obtain by their own action in fighting, and they alone in the army are required for their own sake; whereas all others, to whom other duties are assigned, such as the care of horses, the preparing of arms, are requisite for the sake of the soldiers of the army. Now, it is clear from what has been said, that God is the last end of the universe, whom the intellectual nature alone obtains in Himself, namely by knowing and loving Him, as was proved above. Therefore the intellectual nature alone is requisite for its own sake in the universe, and all others for its sake.

Further. In every whole, the principal parts are requisite on their own account for the completion of the whole, while others are required for the preservation or betterment of the former. Now, of all the parts of the universe, intellectual creatures hold the highest place, because they approach nearest to the divine likeness. Therefore divine providence provides for the intellectual nature for its own sake, and for all others for its sake.

Besides. It is clear that all the parts are directed to the perfection of the whole: since the whole is not on account of the parts, but the parts on account of the whole. Now, intellectual natures are more akin to the whole than other natures: because, in a sense, the intellectual substance is all things, inasmuch as by its intellect it is able to comprehend all things; whereas every other substance has only a particular participation of being. Consequently God cares for other things for the sake of intellectual substances.

Besides. Whatever happens to a thing in the course of nature happens to it naturally. Now, we see that in the course of nature the intellectual substance uses all others for its own sake; either for the perfection of the intellect, which sees the truth in them as in a mirror; or for the execution of its power and development of its knowledge, in the same way as a craftsman develops the conception of his art in corporeal matter; or again to sustain the body that is united to an intellectual soul, as is the case in man. It is clear, therefore, that God cares for all things for the sake of intellectual substances.

Moreover. If a man seek something for its own sake, he seeks it always, because *what is per se, is always:* whereas if he seek a thing on account of something else, he does not of necessity seek it always but only in reference to that for the sake of which he seeks it. Now, as we proved above, things derive their

being from the divine will. Therefore whatever is always is willed by God for its own sake; and what is not always is willed by God, not for its own sake, but for another's. Now, intellectual substances approach nearest to being always, since they are incorruptible. They are, moreover, unchangeable, except in their choice. Therefore intellectual substances are governed for their own sake, as it were; and others for the sake of intellectual substances.

The fact that all the parts of the universe are directed to the perfection of the whole is not in contradiction with the foregoing conclusion: since all the parts are directed to the perfection of the whole, in so far as one part serves another. Thus in the human body it is clear that the lungs belong to the body's perfection, in that they serve the heart: wherefore there is no contradiction in the lungs being for the sake of the heart, and for the sake of the whole animal. In like manner that other natures are on account of the intellectual is not contrary to their being for the perfection of the universe: for without the things required for the perfection of the intellectual substance, the universe would not be complete.

Nor again does the fact that individuals are for the sake of the species militate against what has been said. Because through being directed to their species, they are directed also to the intellectual nature. For a corruptible thing is directed to man, not on account of only one individual man, but on account of the whole human species. Yet a corruptible thing could not serve the whole human species, except as regards its own entire species. Hence the order whereby corruptible things are directed to man, requires that individuals be directed to the species.

When we assert that intellectual substances are directed by divine providence for their own sake, we do not mean that they are not also referred by God and for the perfection of the universe. Accordingly they are said to be provided for on their own account, and others on account of them, because the goods bestowed on them by divine providence are not given them for another's profit: whereas those bestowed on others are in the divine plan intended for the use of intellectual substances. Hence it is said (Deut. iv. 19): *Lest thou see the sun and the moon and the other stars, and being deceived by error, thou adore and serve them, which the Lord thy God created for the service of all the nations that are under heaven:* and (Ps. viii. 8): *Thou hast subjected all things under his feet, all sheep and oxen: moreover, the beasts also of the field:* and (Wis. xii. 18): *Thou, being master of power, judgest with tranquillity, and with great favour disposest of us.*

Hereby is refuted the error of those who said it is sinful for a man to kill dumb animals: for by divine providence they are intended for man's use in the natural order. Hence it is no wrong for man to make use of them, either by killing or in any other way whatever. For this reason the Lord said to Noe (Gen. ix. 3): *As the green herbs I have deliverd all flesh to you.*

And if any passages of Holy Writ seem to forbid us to be cruel to dumb animals, for instance to kill a bird with its young: this is either to remove man's thoughts from being cruel to other men, and lest through being cruel to animals one become cruel to human beings: or because injury to an animal leads to the temporal hurt of man, either of the doer of the deed, or of another: or on account of some signification: thus the Apostle expounds the prohibition against *muzzling the ox that treadeth the corn.*

DISCUSSION TOPICS

1. St. Thomas Aquinas argues that beings with greater rationality (intellect) are to rule over those beings with lesser intellect which, in turn, are to rule over those with no intellect. Do you agree that rationality (intellect) is the best criterion to use in establishing the importance of beings? Explain your reasoning.

2. What are the advantages and disadvantages of using rationality as the criterion for determining the moral worth of a species?

Animals Are Machines

René Descartes

*René Descartes (1596–1650), often called "the father of
modern philosophy," shaped the view that humans are
distinctly different from other animals and the rest of the
natural world. In Descartes' view, language and reason
are the features that set humans apart from all other
species. Using the principle of parsimony, in which one
always must begin with the simplest explanation of
observed phenomena, Descartes argues that the observed
behaviors of all nonhuman creatures can be explained
without ascribing minds and consciousness to them. He
concludes that nonhuman animals can be viewed as no
more than machines with parts assembled in intricate
ways. Based on Descartes' rationale, humans have little
responsibility to other animals or the natural world,
unless the treatment of them affects other humans.*

I

I had explained all these matters in some detail in the
Treatise which I formerly intended to publish. And
afterwards I had shown there, what must be the fabric
of the nerves and muscles of the human body in order
that the animal spirits therein contained should have
the power to move the members, just as the heads of
animals, a little while after decapitation, are still observed to move and bite the earth, notwithstanding
that they are no longer animate; what changes are
necessary in the brain to cause wakefulness, sleep and
dreams; how light, sounds, smells, tastes, heat and all
other qualities pertaining to external objects are able
to imprint on it various ideas by the intervention of
the senses; how hunger, thirst and other internal affections can also convey their impressions upon it;
what should be regarded as the "common sense" by
which these ideas are received, and what is meant by
the memory which retains them, by the fancy which
can change them in diverse ways and out of them
constitute new ideas, and which, by the same means,

distributing the animal spirits through the muscles,
can cause the members of such a body to move in as
many diverse ways, and in a manner as suitable to the
objects which present themselves to its senses and to
its internal passions, as can happen in our own case
apart from the direction of our free will. And this will
not seem strange to those, who, knowing how many
different *automata* or moving machines can be made
by the industry of man, without employing in so doing
more than a very few parts in comparison with the
great multitude of bones, muscles, nerves, arteries,
veins, or other parts that are found in the body of each
animal. From this aspect the body is regarded as a
machine which, having been made by the hands of
God, is incomparably better arranged, and possesses
in itself movements which are much more admirable,
than any of those which can be invented by man. Here
I specially stopped to show that if there had been such
machines, possessing the organs and outward form of
a monkey or some other animal without reason, we
should not have had any means of ascertaining that
they were not of the same nature as those animals. On
the other hand, if there were machines which bore a
resemblance to our body and imitated our actions as
far as it was morally possible to do so, we should
always have two very certain tests by which to recognise that, for all that, they were not real men. The first
is, that they could never use speech or other signs as
we do when placing our thoughts on record for the
benefit of others. For we can easily understand a machine's being constituted so that it can utter words,
and even emit some responses to action on it of a
corporeal kind, which brings about a change in its
organs; for instance, if it is touched in a particular part
it may ask what we wish to say to it; if in another part
it may exclaim that it is being hurt, and so on. But it
never happens that it arranges its speech in various
ways, in order to reply appropriately to everything
that may be said in its presence, as even the lowest
type of man can do. And the second difference is, that
although machines can perform certain things as well
as or perhaps better than any of us can do, they infallibly fall short in others, by the which means we may
discover that they did not act from knowledge, but
only from the disposition of their organs. For while

reason is a universal instrument which can serve for all contingencies, these organs have need of some special adaptation for every particular action. From this it follows that it is morally impossible that there should be sufficient diversity in any machine to allow it to act in all the events of life in the same way as our reason causes us to act.

By these two methods we may also recognise the difference that exists between men and brutes. For it is a very remarkable fact that there are none so depraved and stupid, without even excepting idiots, that they cannot arrange different words together, forming of them a statement by which they make known their thoughts; while, on the other hand, there is no other animal, however perfect and fortunately circumstanced it may be, which can do the same. It is not the want of organs that brings this to pass, for it is evident that magpies and parrots are able to utter words just like ourselves, and yet they cannot speak as we do, that is, so as to give evidence that they think of what they say. On the other hand, men who, being born deaf and dumb, are in the same degree, or even more than the brutes, destitute of the organs which serve the others for talking, are in the habit of themselves inventing certain signs by which they make themselves understood by those who, being usually in their company, have leisure to learn their language. And this does not merely show that the brutes have less reason than men, but that they have none at all, since it is clear that very little is required in order to be able to talk. And when we notice the inequality that exists between animals of the same species, as well as between men, and observe that some are more capable of receiving instruction than others, it is not credible that a monkey or a parrot, selected as the most perfect of its species, should not in these matters equal the stupidest child to be found, or at least a child whose mind is clouded, unless in the case of the brute the soul were of an entirely different nature from ours. And we ought not to confound speech with natural movements which betray passions and may be imitated by machines as well as be manifested by animals; nor must we think, as did some of the ancients, that brutes talk, although we do not understand their

language. For if this were true, since they have many organs which are allied to our own, they could communicate their thoughts to us just as easily as to those of their own race. It is also a very remarkable fact that although there are many animals which exhibit more dexterity than we do in some of their actions, we at the same time observe that they do not manifest any dexterity at all in many others. Hence the fact that they do better than we do, does not prove that they are endowed with mind, for in this case they would have more reason than any of us, and would surpass us in all other things. It rather shows that they have no reason at all, and that it is nature which acts in them according to the disposition of their organs, just as a clock, which is only composed of wheels and weights is able to tell the hours and measure the time more correctly than we can do with all our wisdom.

I had described after this the rational soul and shown that it could not be in any way derived from the power of matter, like the other things of which I had spoken, but that it must be expressly created. I showed, too, that it is not sufficient that it should be lodged in the human body like a pilot in his ship, unless perhaps for the moving of its members, but that it is necessary that it should also be joined and united more closely to the body in order to have sensations and appetites similar to our own, and thus to form a true man. In conclusion, I have here enlarged a little on the subject of the soul, because it is one of the greatest importance. For next to the error of those who deny God, which I think I have already sufficiently refuted, there is none which is more effectual in leading feeble spirits from the straight path of virtue, than to imagine that the soul of the brute is of the same nature as our own, and that in consequence, after this life we have nothing to fear or to hope for, any more than the flies and ants. As a matter of fact, when one comes to know how greatly they differ, we understand much better the reasons which go to prove that our soul is in its nature entirely independent of body, and in consequence that it is not liable to die with it. And then, inasmuch as we observe no other causes capable of destroying it, we are naturally inclined to judge that it is immortal.

II

I cannot share the opinion of Montaigne and others who attribute understanding or thought to animals. I am not worried that people say that men have an absolute empire over all the other animals; because I agree that some of them are stronger than us, and believe that there may also be some who have an instinctive cunning capable of deceiving the shrewdest human beings. But I observe that they only imitate or surpass us in those of our actions which are not guided by our thoughts. It often happens that we walk or eat without thinking at all about what we are doing; and similarly, without using our reason, we reject things which are harmful for us, and parry the blows aimed at us. Indeed, even if we expressly willed not to put our hands in front of our head when we fall, we could not prevent ourselves. I think also that if we had no thought we would eat, as the animals do, without having to learn to; and it is said that those who walk in their sleep sometimes swim across streams in which they would drown if they were awake. As for the movements of our passions, even though in us they are accompanied with thought because we have the faculty of thinking, it is none the less very clear that they do not depend on thought, because they often occur in spite of us. Consequently they can also occur in animals, even more violently than they do in humans beings, without our being able to conclude from that that they have thoughts.

In fact, none of our external actions can show anyone who examines them that our body is not just a self-moving machine but contains a soul with thoughts, with the exception of words, or other signs that are relevant to particular topics without expressing any passion. I say words or other signs, because deaf-mutes use signs as we use spoken words; and I say that these signs must be relevant, to exclude the speech of parrots, without excluding the speech of madmen, which is relevant to particular topics even though it does not follow reason. I add also that these words or signs must not express any passion, to rule out not only cries of joy or sadness and the like, but also whatever can be taught by training to animals. If you teach a magpie to say good-day to its mistress,

when it sees her approach, this can only be by making the utterance of this word the expression of one of its passions. For instance it will be an expression of the hope of eating, if it has always been given a titbit when it says it. Similarly, all the things which dogs, horses, and monkeys are taught to perform are only expressions of their fear, their hope, or their joy; and consequently they can be performed without any thought. Now it seems to me very striking that the use of words, so defined, is something peculiar to human beings. Montaigne and Charron may have said that there is more difference between one human being and another than between a human being and an animal; but there has never been known an animal so perfect as to use a sign to make other animals understand something which expressed no passion; and there is no human being so imperfect as not to do so, since even deaf-mutes invent special signs to express their thoughts. This seems to me a very strong argument to prove that the reason why animals do not speak as we do is not that they lack the organs but that they have no thoughts. It cannot be said that they speak to each other and that we cannot understand them; because since dogs and some other animals express their passions to us, they would express their thoughts also if they had any.

I know that animals do many things better than we do, but this does not surprise me. It can even be used to prove they act naturally and mechanically, like a clock which tells the time better than our judgement does. Doubtless when the swallows come in spring, they operate like clocks. The actions of honeybees are of the same nature, and the discipline of cranes in flight, and of apes in fighting, if it is true that they keep discipline. Their instinct to bury their dead is no stranger than that of dogs and cats who scratch the earth for the purpose of burying their excrement; they hardly ever actually bury it, which shows that they act only by instinct and without thinking. The most that one can say is that though the animals do not perform any action which shows us that they think, still, since the organs of their body are not very different from ours, it may be conjectured that there is attached to those organs some thoughts such as we experience in ourselves, but of a very much less perfect kind. To which I have nothing to reply except that if they thought as we do, they would have an immortal soul like us. This is unlikely, because there is no reason to believe it of some animals without believing it of all, and many of them such as oysters and sponges are too imperfect for this to be credible. But I am afraid of boring you with this discussion, and my only desire is to show you that I am, etc.

III

But there is no prejudice to which we are all more accustomed from our earliest years than the belief that dumb animals think. Our only reason for this belief is the fact that we see that many of the organs of animals are not very different from ours in shape and movement. Since we believe that there is a single principle within us which causes these motions—namely the soul, which both moves the body and thinks—we do not doubt that some such soul is to be found in animals also. I came to realize, however, that there are two different principles causing our motions: one is purely mechanical and corporeal and depends solely on the force of the spirits and the construction of our organs, and can be called the corporeal soul; the other is the incorporeal mind, the soul which I have defined as a thinking substance. Thereupon I investigated more carefully whether the motions of animals originated from both these principles or from one only. I soon saw clearly that they could all originate from the corporeal and mechanical principle, and I thenceforward regarded it as certain and established that we cannot at all prove the presence of a thinking soul in animals. I am not disturbed by the astuteness and cunning of dogs and foxes, or all the things which animals do for the sake of food, sex, and fear; I claim that I can easily explain the origin of all of them from the constitution of their organs.

But though I regard it as established that we cannot prove there is any thought in animals, I do not think it is thereby proved that there is not, since the human mind does not reach into their hearts. But when I investigate what is most probable in this matter, I see no argument for animals having thoughts except the fact that since they have eyes, ears, tongues, and other sense-organs like ours, it seems likely that they have sensation like us; and since thought is included in our mode of sensation, similar thought seems to be attributable to them. This argument, which is very obvious, has taken possession of the minds of all men from their earliest age. But there are other arguments, stronger and more numerous, but not so obvious to everyone, which strongly urge the opposite. One is that it is more probable that worms and flies and caterpillars move mechanically than that they all have immortal souls.

It is certain that in the bodies of animals, as in ours, there are bones, nerves, muscles, animal spirits, and other organs so disposed that they can by themselves, without any thought, give rise to all animals the motions we observe. This is very clear in convulsive movements when the machine of the body moves despite the soul, and sometimes more violently and in a more varied manner than when it is moved by the will.

Second, it seems reasonable, since art copies nature, and men can make various automata which move without thought, that nature should produce its own automata, much more splendid than artificial ones. These natural automata are the animals. This is especially likely since we have no reason to believe that thought always accompanies the disposition of organs which we find in animals. It is much more wonderful that a mind should be found in every human body than that one should be lacking in every animal.

But in my opinion the main reason which suggests that the beasts lack thought is the following. Within a single species some of them are more perfect than others, as men are too. This can be seen in horses and dogs, some of whom learn what they are taught much better than others. Yet, although all animals easily communicate to us, by voice or bodily movement, their natural impulses of anger, fear, hunger and so on, it has never yet been observed that any brute animal reached the stage of using real speech, that is to say, of indicating by word or sign something pertaining to pure thought and not to natural impulse. Such speech is the only certain sign of thought hidden in a body. All men use it, however stupid and insane they may be, and though they may lack tongue and organs of voice; but no animals do. Consequently it can be taken as a real specific difference between men and dumb animals.

For brevity's sake I here omit the other reasons for denying thought to animals. Please note that I am speaking of thought, and not of life or sensation. I do not deny life to animals, since I regard it as consisting simply in the heat of the heart; and I do not deny sensation, in so far as it depends on a bodily organ. Thus my opinion is not so much cruel to animals as indulgent to men—at least to those who are not given to the superstitions of Pythagoras—since it absolves them from the suspicion of crime when they eat or kill animals.

Perhaps I have written at too great length for the sharpness of your intelligence; but I wished to show you that very few people have yet sent me objections which were as agreeable as yours. Your kindness and candour has made you a friend of that most respectful admirer of all who seek true wisdom, etc.

DISCUSSION TOPICS

1. What major differences does Descartes use to distinguish humans from other animals?
2. What arguments do you believe would be most persuasive in countering Descartes' position that nonhuman animals can be described as complicated machinery?

READING 35

Duties to Animals

Immanuel Kant

Immanuel Kant (1724–1804), a German philosopher during the Age of Enlightenment is considered to be one of the great philosophical thinkers of all time. Kant asserts that only rational beings merit moral concern. He believes that for a rational being, rationality has intrinsic value, and thus is a goal worth seeking in itself. Since rationality is the same for all rational beings, all rational beings work for a common goal, which is to achieve a rational world. Kant argues that rational beings cannot achieve a rational world if they compete with or hinder each other for personal gain such as wealth or power. Thus, morally correct behavior for rational beings entails helping other rational beings, because this contributes to their common goal of achieving a rational world. Kant asserts that only rational beings contribute directly to achieving the intrinsic good of a rational world. He maintains that since nonrational beings do not contribute directly, their treatment by rational beings does not affect the effort to achieve a rational world. Consequently, it is proper for nonrational beings to be used as means to an end (that is, a rational world).

Kant defines rationality as the ability to universalize details into broader, general concepts. He recognizes that many animals can communicate by signs, but believes that animals do not use symbols. Since the symbolic structure of language is necessary to express general concepts, beings without language cannot express general concepts, and hence are not rational. Since nonhuman animals and natural entities are not rational, they do not merit moral concern. Kant concludes that human beings have little or no responsibility toward animals or the natural world.

Baumgarten speaks of duties towards beings which are beneath us and beings which are above us. But so far as animals are concerned, we have no direct duties. Animals are not self-conscious and are there merely as a means to an end. That end is man. We can ask, ''Why do animals exist?'' But to ask, ''Why does man exist?'' is a meaningless question. Our duties towards animals are merely indirect duties towards humanity. Animal nature has analogies to human nature, and by doing our duties to animals in respect of manifestations of human nature, we indirectly do our duty towards humanity. Thus, if a dog has served his master long and faithfully, his service, on the analogy of human service, deserves reward, and when the dog has grown too old to serve, his master ought to keep him until he dies. Such action helps to support us in our duties towards human beings, where they are bounden duties. If then any acts of animals are analogous to human acts and spring from the same principles, we have duties towards the animals because thus we cultivate the corresponding duties towards human beings. If a man shoots his dog because the animal is no longer capable of service, he does not fail in his duty to the dog, for the dog cannot judge, but his act is inhuman and damages in himself that humanity which it is his duty to show towards mankind. If he is not to stifle his human feelings, he must practise kindness towards animals, for he who is cruel to animals becomes hard also in his dealing with men. We can judge the heart of a man by his treatment of animals. Hogarth depicts this in his engravings. He shows how cruelty grows and develops. He shows the child's cruelty to animals, pinch the tail of a dog or a cat; he then depicts the grown man in his cart running over a child; and lastly, the culmination of cruelty in murder. He thus brings home to us in a terrible fashion the rewards of cruelty, and this should be an impressive lesson to children. The more we come in contact with animals and observe their behaviour, the more we love them, for we see how great is their care for their young. It is then difficult for us to be cruel in thought even to a wolf. Leibnitz used a tiny worm for purposes of observation, and then carefully replaced it with its leaf on the tree so that it should not come to harm through any act of his. He would have been sorry—a natural feeling for a humane man—to destroy such a creature for no reason. Tender feelings towards dumb animals develop humane feelings towards mankind. In England butchers and doctors do not sit on a jury because they are accustomed to the sight of death and hardened. Vivisectionists, who use living animals for their experiments, certainly act cruelly, although their aim is praiseworthy, and they can justify their cruelty, since animals must be regarded as man's instruments; but any such cruelty for sport cannot be justified. A master who turns out his ass or his dog because the animal can no longer earn its keep manifests a small mind. The Greeks' ideas in this respect were highminded, as can be seen from the fable of the ass and the bell of ingratitude. Our duties towards animals, then, are indirect duties towards mankind.

DISCUSSION TOPICS

1. Do you believe that humans are the only rational beings? Explain your reasoning.
2. What are the benefits of viewing rationality as an end in itself? What are the possible losses?

Environmental Ethics and Weak Anthropocentrism

Bryan G. Norton

Bryan G. Norton (b. 1944) is Professor of Philosophy at the University of South Florida. He has been an active contributor to the growing field of environmental ethics. His books include The Preservation of Species, The Spice of Life, *and* Why Preserve Natural Diversity?

Norton proposes and defines two forms of anthropocentrism: weak and strong. He argues that weak anthropocentrism provides an adequate basis from which to criticize destructive environmental practices, to acknowledge human affinity to nature, and to account for the distinctive nonindividualistic nature of environmental ethics. He believes that since weak anthropocentrism is an adequate ethic, and does not depend on the controversial assumption of ascribing intrinsic value to nature, weak anthropocentrism should be favored over other, nonanthropocentric forms of environmental ethics.

ANTHROPOCENTRISM AND NONANTHROPOCENTRISM

. . . I suggest that the distinction between anthropocentrism and nonanthropocentrism has been given more importance in discussions of the foundations of environmental ethics than it warrants because a crucial ambiguity in the term *anthropocentrism* has gone unnoticed.[1] Writers on both sides of the controversy apply this term to positions which treat humans as the only loci of intrinsic value.[2] Anthropocentrists are therefore taken to believe that every instance of value originates in a contribution to human values and that all elements of nature can, at most, have value instrumental to the satisfaction of human interests.[3] Note that anthropocentrism is defined by reference to the position taken on *loci* of value. Some nonanthropocentrists say that human beings are the *source* of all values, but that they can designate nonhuman objects as loci of fundamental value.[4]

It has also become common to explain and test views on this point by reference to "last man examples" which are formulated as follows.[5] Assume that a human being, *S*, is the last living member of *Homo sapiens* and that *S* faces imminent death. Would *S* do wrong to wantonly destroy some object *X*? A positive answer to this question with regard to any nonhuman *X* is taken to entail nonanthropocentrism. If the variable *X* refers to some natural object, a species, an ecosystem, a geological formation, etc., then it is thought that positions on such questions determine whether a person is an anthropocentrist or not, because the action in question cannot conceivably harm any human individual. If it is wrong to destroy *X*, the wrongness must derive from harm to *X* or to some other natural object. But one can harm something only if it is a good in its own right in the sense of being a locus of fundamental value.

Or so the story goes. I am unconvinced because not nearly enough has been said about what counts as a human interest. In order to explore this difficult area, I introduce two useful definitions. A *felt preference* is any desire or need of a human individual that can at least temporarily be sated by some specifiable experience of that individual. A *considered preference* is any desire or need that a human individual would express after careful deliberation, including a judgment that the desire or need is consistent with a rationally adopted world view—a world view which includes fully supported scientific theories and a metaphysical framework interpreting those theories, as well as a set of rationally supported aesthetic and moral ideals.

When interests are assumed to be constructed merely from felt preferences, they are thereby insulated from any criticism or objection. Economic approaches to decision making often adopt this approach because it eschews "value judgments"—decision makers need only ask people what they want, perhaps correct these preferences for intensity, compute the preferences satisfied by the various possible courses of action, and let the resulting ordinal ranking imply a decision.

A considered preference, on the other hand, is an idealization in the sense that it can only be adopted after a person has rationally accepted an entire world view and, further, has succeeded in altering his felt preferences so that they are consonant with that world view. Since this is a process no one has ever completed, references to considered preferences are hypothetical—they refer to preferences the individual would have if certain contrary-to-fact conditions were fulfilled. Nonetheless, references to considered pref-

---

1. My thoughts on this subject have been deeply affected by discussions of the work of Donald Regan and J. Baird Callicott. See, Donald Regan, "Duties of Preservation," and J. Baird Callicott, "On the Intrinsic Value of Nonhuman Species," in *The Preservation of Species,* edited by Bryan G. Norton. Princeton, Princeton University Press, 1986. 305 pages.

2. I borrow this phrase from Donald Scherer, "Anthropocentrism, Atomism, and Environmental Ethics," *Environmental Ethics* 4 (1982): 115-123.

3. I take anthropocentrism to be interchangeable with homocentrism. See R. and V. Routley, "Against the Inevitability of Human Chauvinism," in *Ethics and Problems of the 21st Century,* edited by K.E. Goodpaster and K.M. Sayre (Notre Dame, Ind.: University of Notre Dame Press, 1979), pp. 56-57. Routley and Routley show that "human chauvinism" (anthropocentrism, homocentrism) are equivalent to the thesis of man's "dominion," which they describe as "the view that the earth and all its nonhuman contents exist or are available for man's benefit and to serve his interests."

4. See J. Baird Callicott, "On the Intrinsic Value of Nonhuman Species," in Norton, *The Preservation of Species,* and Pluhar, "The Justification of an Environmental Ethic."

5. See, for example, Richard Routley, "Is There a Need for a New, an Environmental, Ethic?" p. 207; Routley and Routley, "Human Chauvinism and Environmental Ethics," in *Environmental Philosophy,* edited by D.S. Mannison, M.A. McRobbie and R. Routley (Canberra: Australian National University, Department of Philosophy, 1980), p. 121; and Donald Regan, "Duties of Preservation," in Norton, *The Preservation of Species.*

erences remain useful because it is possible to distinguish felt preferences from considered preferences when there are convincing arguments that felt preferences are not consistent with some element of a world view that appears worthy of rational support.

It is now possible to define two forms of anthropocentrism. A value theory is *strongly anthropocentric* if all value countenanced by it is explained by reference to satisfactions of felt preferences of human individuals. A value theory is *weakly anthropocentric* if all value countenanced by it is explained by reference to satisfaction of some felt preference of a human individual or by reference to its bearing upon the ideals which exist as elements in a world view essential to determinations of considered preferences.

Strong anthropocentrism, as here defined, takes unquestioned felt preferences of human individuals as determining value. Consequently, if humans have a strongly consumptive value system, then their ''interests'' (which are taken merely to be their felt preferences) dictate that nature will be used in an exploitative manner. Since there is no check upon the felt preferences of individuals in the value system of strong anthropocentrism, there exists no means to criticize the behavior of individuals who use nature merely as a storehouse of raw materials to be extracted and used for products serving human preferences.

Weak anthropocentrism, on the other hand, recognizes that felt preferences can be either rational or not (in the sense that they can be judged not consonant with a rational world view). Hence, weak anthropocentrism provides a basis for criticism of value systems which are purely exploitative of nature. In this way, weak anthropocentrism makes available two ethical resources of crucial importance to environmentalists. First, to the extent that environmental ethicists can make a case for a world view that emphasizes the close relationship between the human species and other living species, they can also make a case for ideals of human behavior extolling harmony with nature. These ideals are then available as a basis for criticizing preferences that merely exploit nature.

Second, weak anthropocentrism as here defined also places value on human experiences that provide the basis for value formation. Because weak anthropocentrism places value not only on felt preferences, but also on the process of value formation embodied in the criticism and replacement of felt preferences with more rational ones, it makes possible appeals to the value of experiences of natural objects and undisturbed places in human value formation. To the extent that environmentalists can show that values are formed and informed by contact with nature, nature takes on value as a teacher of human values. Nature need no longer be seen as a mere satisfier of fixed and often consumptive values—it also becomes an important source of inspiration in value formation.[6]

. . . Within the limits set by weak anthropocentrism as here defined, there exists a framework for developing powerful reasons for protecting nature. Further, these reasons do not resemble the extractive and exploitative reasons normally associated with strong anthropocentrism.

And they do not differ from strongly anthropocentric reasons in merely theoretical ways. Weakly anthropocentric reasoning can affect behavior as can be seen by applying it to last man situations. Suppose that human beings choose, for rational or religious reasons, to live according to an ideal of maximum harmony with nature. Suppose also that this ideal is taken seriously and that anyone who impairs that harmony (by destroying another species, by polluting air and war, etc.) would be judged harshly. But such an ideal need not attribute intrinsic value to natural objects, nor need the prohibitions implied by it be justified with nonanthropocentric reasoning attributing intrinsic value to nonhuman natural objects. Rather, they can be justified as being implied by the ideal of harmony with nature. This ideal, in turn, can be justified either on religious grounds referring to human spiritual development or as being a fitting part of a rationally defensible world view. . . .

---

6. For fuller discussions of this point, see Mark Sagoff, ''On Preserving the Natural Environment,'' *Yale Law Journal* 84 (1974): 205-67; Holmes Rolston, III, ''Can and Ought We to Follow Nature?'' *Environmental Ethics* 1 (1979): 7-1; and Bryan G. Norton, *The Spice of Life* (in preparation).

DISCUSSION TOPICS

1. Do you agree with Norton's position that the differences between anthropocentrism and nonanthropocentrism have been given more importance than they warrant? Justify your answer.
2. Norton argues that weak anthropocentrism is a preferable environmental ethic to other, nonanthropocentric forms because it requires fewer assumptions (that is, one does not need to ascribe intrinsic value to nonhuman entities). Do you agree with Norton? Explain your position.

READING 37

The Conservation Mentality of Natural Resources

W. J. McGee

W. J. McGee (1853–1912), who helped spearhead the early conservation movement in the United States with Gifford Pinchot, James Garfield, and Theodore Roosevelt, firmly believes that the benefits from the U.S.'s natural resources belong to every citizen. His contributions to the early conservation movement in this country helped ensure that the benefits went to the public good rather than merely to private enterprise. However, McGee does not appear to view natural resources as having value beyond fulfilling human needs and contributing to human prosperity. Thus he is best described as a strong anthropocentrist. In exploring the moral arguments behind the conservation movement, McGee alludes to the importance of considering future generations in justifying the protection of natural resources.

. . . [America's Founding Fathers] saw Land as the sole natural resource of the country, so the succeeding generations remained indifferent to the values residing in the minerals below and the forest above. . . .

Herein lay what now seems the most serious error in the world's greatest Republic. Monarchs are accustomed to retaining royal or imperial rights in the forests and minerals, and these eventually inure to the benefit of their people; ecclesiastic institutions allied with monarchial rule have commonly held rein over rarer resources until they were reclaimed by the growing generations of men; but through a lamentable lack of foresight our Republic hasted to give away, under the guise of land to live on, values far greater than the land itself—and this policy continued for generations. . . .

The policy of free giving grew into thoughtless habit, and this into a craze which spread apace. . . . States and cities followed the national lead, and all manner of franchises—rights of way, water rights, and the rest—were given for long terms or in perpetuity to all comers, generally without money and without price. In all the world's history no other such saturnalia of squandering the sources of permanent prosperity was ever witnessed! In the material aspect, our individual liberty became collective license, and our legislative and administrative prodigality grew into national profligacy; the balance between impulse and responsibility was lost, the future of the People and Nation was forgotten, and the very name of posterity was made a by-word by men in high places; and worst of all the very profligacies came to be venerated as law and even crystallized foolishly in decisions or more questionably in enactments—and for long there were none to stand in the way of the growing avalanche of extravagance. The waste was always wildest in the West, for as settlement followed the sun new resources were discovered or came into being through natural growth. . . .

. . . [T]he free gift of these resources . . . opened the way to monopoly, and the resources passed under monopolistic control with a rapidity never before seen in all the world's history; and it is hardly too much to say that the Nation has become one of the Captains of Industry first, and one of the People and their chosen representatives only second. With the free gift, under the title of land, of resources far exceeding the land in value, the aspiration of the Fathers for a land of free families failed; for the mineral-bearing and wood-bearing lands were devoted to mining and milling and manufacturing instead of homes, and the People became in large measure industrial dependents rather than free citizens. . . .

Done in a few lines, the history of the country and its resources . . . [has been one of] wealth beyond the visions of avarice and power above the dreams of tyranny . . . [coming] to the few—at vast cost to the just patrimony of the multitude—while much of the substance of the Nation has been wasted and many of the People have passed under the domination of the beneficiaries of Privilege. Ample resources indeed remain—enough to insure the perpetuity of the People—but the question also remains whether these shall be held and used by the People, whose travail gave them value and whose rights therein are inalienable and indefeasible under the Declaration of Independence and the Constitution, or whether they shall go chiefly into the hands of the self-chosen and self-anointed few, largely to forge new shackles for the wrists and ankles of the many! This problem of history is not one of passion or for reckless action. The simple facts are that the inequities arose chiefly in the confusion of other resources with Land, and that the inequalities in opportunity due to this confusion have arisen so insidiously as to escape notice. Yet the question remains: How may American freemen proceed decently and in order to reclaim their own?

. . . [Gifford] Pinchot and [James R.] Garfield especially, and [Theodore] Roosevelt in his turn, sought to counteract the tendency toward wholesale alienation of the public lands for the benefit of the corporation and the oppression or suppression of the settler; and in the end their efforts resulted in what is now known as the Conservation Movement. . . .

On its face the Conservation Movement is material—ultra-material. . . . Yet in truth there has never been in all human history a popular movement more firmly grounded in ethics, in the eternal equities, in the divinity of human rights! Whether we rise into the spritual empyrean or cling more closely to the essence of humanity, we find our loftiest ideals made real in the Cult of Conservation. . . .

. . . What *right* has any citizen of a free country,

whatever his foresight and shrewdness, to seize on sources of life for his own behoof that are the common heritage of all; what *right* has legislature or court to help in the seizure; and striking still more deeply, what *right* has any generation to wholly consume, much less to waste, those sources of life without which the children or the children's children must starve or freeze? These are among the questions arising among intelligent minds in every part of this country, and giving form to a national feeling which is gradually rising to a new plane of equity. The questions will not down. Nay, like Banquo's ghost they tarry, and haunt, and search! How shall they find answer? The ethical doctrine of Conservation answers: by a nobler patriotism, under which citizen-electors will cleave more strongly to their birthright of independence and strive more vigorously for purity of the ballot, for rightness in laws, for cleanness in courts, and for forthrightness in administration; by a higher honesty of purpose between man and man; by a warmer charity, under which the good of all will more fairly merge with the good of each; by a stronger family sense, tending toward a realization of the rights of the unborn; by deeper probity, maturing in the realizing sense that each holder of the sources of life is but a trustee for his nominal possessions, and is responsible to all men and for all time for making the best use of them in the common interest; and by a livelier humanity, in which each will feel that he lives not for himself alone but as a part of a common life for a common world and for the common good. . . .

Whatever its material manifestations, every revolution is first and foremost a revolution in thought and in spirit. . . . [The last of humanity's great revolutions] was inspired in the New World by the new realization that all men are equally entitled to life, liberty, and the pursuit of happiness. . . . Still the hope of the Fathers for a freehold citizenry joined in equitable and indissoluble Union is not fully attained. The American Revolution was fought for Liberty; the American Constitution was framed for Equality; yet that third of the trinity of human impulses without which Union is not made perfect—Fraternity—has not been established: full brotherhood among men and generations has not yet come. The duty of the

Fathers was done well according to their lights; but some new light has come out of the West where their sons have striven against Nature's forces no less fiercely than the Fathers against foreign dominion. So it would seem to remain for Conservation to perfect the concept and the movement started among the Colonists one hundred and forty years ago—to round out the American Revolution by framing a clearer Bill of Rights. Whatever others there may be, surely these are inherent and indefeasible:

1. The equal Rights of all men to opportunity.
2. The equal Rights of the People in and to resources rendered valuable by their own natural growth and orderly development.
3. The equal Rights of present and future generations in and to the resources of the country.
4. The equal Rights (and full responsibilities) of all citizens to provide for the perpetuity of families and States and the Union of States.

The keynote of all these is Fraternity. They look to the greatest good for the greatest number and for the longest time; they are essential to perfect union among men and States; and until they are secured to us we may hardly feel assured that government of the People, by the People, and for the People shall not perish from the earth.

DISCUSSION TOPICS

1. In light of how environmental history has developed since McGee wrote his four points for "framing a clearer Bill of Rights," rewrite any of the points you believe could be improved. Explain your rationale.
2. In what ways could McGee's vision of the conservation movement infringe on the rights of private property owners? How could these conflicts be resolved?

The Ethical Relationship Between Humans and Other Organisms

R. D. Guthrie

A recent defense of strong anthropocentrism is offered by R. Dale Guthrie (b. 1936), a University of Alaska zoologist specializing in evolutionary mechanics and vertebrate paleontology. Guthrie views ethics as strictly an intrahuman phenomenon, and advocates the notion that human rules of conduct are for human benefit only. Humans are under no moral obligation to extend their own internal codes of behavior to other species; in fact, it can be a serious error to do so. Guthrie argues that it is both illogical and impractical to extend moral concern beyond the human community.

The nature of our responsibilities toward other organisms is certainly no new issue, but the controversy has been re-ignited recently by legislative action to regulate the care and maintenance of laboratory stock. Although this specific issue involves a decision of immediate concern to scientists, it also raises the even more basic question as to the general role that other organisms should occupy in our ethical system. It seems prudent that we should first examine the problem in its broadest context before further legislative action and the firm lines of political alignment are drawn.

An analysis of one aspect of our ethical system necessarily involves some dealings with the system as a whole. Unfortunately, the area of ethical theory can sometimes be an ideological quagmire from which few return enlightened. Much of the difficulty arises from our being drawn, by tradition, into thinking that our moral scaffolding is suspended from some outside agency. Rather, I would subscribe to the concept that moral principles, and the standards by which they are judged, are human constructs and thus can be evaluated on an empirical basis, even though the criteria are complex and the judgments sometimes

difficult. Inherent in this position is the idea that our judgments are dependent upon generalizations from past experiences and may have to be altered as new situations are encountered. The only aprioristic element is the underlying assumption that man's rules of conduct are to be to his benefit. For the limited purposes of this essay, I will thus assume that the most desirable rules governing human behavior are those which, now and in the future, promote the welfare of the human population as an aggregate of individuals and contribute to the smooth functioning of its social machinery, while at the same time allowing for the greatest freedom of individual expression and fulfilment. Such a conceptual distillation necessarily includes academic deficiencies with which philosophers of ethical theory will quibble; but, by and large, this has become the gauge by which we evaluate political systems, economic policies, codes of sexual behavior, technological innovations, planned parenthood, and so forth. This assumption of the most desirable code of conduct forms the basis of the idea that I wish to present.

My thesis is that the inclusion of other organisms as primary participants in our ethical system is both logically unsound and operationally unfeasible. It is illogical because we cannot consider other organisms as moral bodies and amoral bodies simultaneously. By *moral bodies* I mean those entities ultimately to be considered in evaluating the action. As an example of this categorization, let us say that, as part of an experiment, a mineralogist wishes to dissolve a unique crystal. On what basis does he decide that the destruction will be worthwhile? The judgment has to be made on the effect of his action on living and future humans—the immediate benefits derived from the crystal's destruction weighed against the assets of its continued existence. The rare crystal is an amoral body, since our concern is with the ultimate effect on humans (the moral bodies which made this a moral question) and not with the welfare of the rock per se.

The relationships among non-human organisms are also not generally defined as moral or immoral. Most would agree that a wild wolf killing a wild deer is, in and of itself, not subject to moral analysis. We as humans may wish to keep the wolf from killing a game species, or the weeds from stunting the turnips, but we do not contend that the wolves and weeds are immoral for so doing. We wish to curtail the wolf and weed population, not ultimately for the sake of the deer and turnips, but for our own ends. In my categorization, then, rare crystals, wolves, deer, weeds, and turnips are all amoral bodies. Likewise, an act of another organism toward humans, say a mosquito bite, could also be classified as amoral. The mosquito is an amoral body, and we do not hold it morally responsible for having bitten us. Thus, at two bonds of a triangular relationship, we recognize the amoral nature of the non-human's act toward another non-human organism and, second, a non-human organism's act toward a human as being amoral. It is difficult not to conclude that the final bond—a human's act toward other organisms—is, in and of itself, an amoral one. It becomes a moral act only when humans are affected, because our moral codes are rules of human behavior, as I assumed in the beginning, and, as such, exclude other organisms as primary participants.

The fallacy of giving other organisms the status of moral bodies and amoral bodies simultaneously leads us into what we might refer to as "Schweitzer's dilemma." In his *reverence for life* philosophy, Schweitzer considered each organism as an individual whose suffering and death were to be avoided if at all possible.[1] If one supports this philosophy—that it is the organism's discomfort, the welfare of the organism itself, that is our concern—he is confronted with the perplexing situation of having to regard pain that occurs "in the wild" as bad. Since it is an individual organism's discomfort that is emphasized and not the effect upon the human causing it, the pain will be just as real no matter what the origin. One is, as Schweitzer was,[2] forced to regard predators as evil. However, predators avoid the pains of starvation and eventual death by causing pain and death to other organisms. This relationship is an inherent part of the community structure where energy is transferred from one trophic level to the next, ergo, the dilemma. Failure to have reverence for the predator's life is itself a contradiction of the basic tenet of Schweitzer's philosophy, yet to have reverence for the predator's life is to revere

those processes which result in pain and death. Furthermore, if it is the organism's pain, in and of itself, that we wish to prevent, we incur responsibilities beyond our own species' actions. The Schweitzerian philosophy implies that the billions of non-human animals (and plants?) which are being mutilated and killed in nature are the unattended wards of humankind.

Within our own species, if a fellow member becomes mentally or physically incapacitated to function within the moral code, we make corresponding adjustments by withholding some of those freedoms which are given to others (we confine him to a mental institution or hospital ward or require glasses while driving). To extend a similar sliding scale of conduct toward, or expected conduct from, other organisms is operationally unfeasible. First of all, we would have to formulate some sort of discriminatory system which would define the nature and extent of preferential moral treatment. Which organisms would we include in our moral system, and to what degree?

Some who apply our moral code to other organisms do so only to higher organisms. However, the concept of a "higher" organism is a rather nebulous affair. Which is "higher," a bee, apple tree, elephant, sailfish, or winter wheat? The ideas of "progressive," "advanced," or "higher" may be applied, with meaning, to a phylogenetic sequence—the older being more primitive—or with reference to one particular character—horses exhibiting a more advanced state of digit reduction than man. However, as a generalized concept, "higher" is interlaced with teleological overtones that are rejected by virtually all evolutionists.

The concept of phylogenetic proximity has also been suggested as a discriminatory basis for evaluating the behavior of other organisms. As well as having anthropocentric underwear, this idea also involves other problems; for example, sewer rats are probably just as close phylogenetically to humans as are cocker spaniels. Relying on something like the potential for learned behavior seems just as arbitrary and shallow. All organisms which rely more on the equally successful "instinctive" behavior would be whimsically bypassed.

Not only do we face absurd decisions as to what organisms we are to apply the code among the different taxa, but the question can also be posed as to how individual variation within each species is to be regarded. There is even the problem of the fluctuation of our code through time. Does the evaluation of what constitutes ''indecent exposure'' also change for other organisms? These and many other questions arise. If, however, we are to consider our morality as an entirely human phenomenon, and apply it only to humans, many problems are eliminated, and the system is workable. We need not cringe in sin every time we bite into a pork chop, trim the hedge, or order the pooch to get the paper. The human ramifications of any deed are ponderous enough.

My contention that human acts committed toward other organisms can only be evaluated by their human effects should be interpreted in its broadest sense. One could even argue that a highly pathogenic species of bacteria should not be driven to extinction. It may be wise to maintain the species as a protected laboratory culture in the event that future development may be able to utilize the species as a valuable source of information or a unique research tool. Although hunting, fishing, butterfly collecting, and wildflower picking provide immediate recreation, these species must also be managed with regard to their recreational use by future generations of humans. The health of our livestock, both those in the private laboratory and those raised for commercial purposes, must necessarily have high priority because our health as consumers and the information that we as scientists derive from them depend upon their physical condition. In the management of livestock and game species, our concern is mainly with population parameters and not with specific individuals. This is not the case with pets. Since one of the chief functions of a pet is to provide companionship, the owner must be concerned about his pet as an individual—an organism from which he receives pleasure by exchanging affection—and should be able to expect that other people will treat his pet with this in mind. I do not wish to imply in the presentation of this philosophy of our relationships with other organisms that the owner should look upon his Rover without emotion or affection, for to do so would destroy the relationship from which the owner is receiving satisfaction. However, he should not deceive himself by thinking that he is giving the dog attention solely for the dog's sake. The motivation for domesticating and continuing to raise pets is not the improvement of these animals' welfare.

In general practice, we do not bring laboratory and domestic animals under the same moral consideration that we do other humans. We regulate their diet, decide on breeding time and specific mate, compel them to do tasks against their volition, eat them, and put them to death when they become senile. Only in rare instances have human slaves received similar treatment.

The basic distinction in the human interpretation of the two phenomena, slavery of other humans and slavery of other organisms, is rather revealing. We do not hesitate in our discrimination against those organisms who are not our own species. The categorization is discrete and operationally meaningful in its broadest application. Those times in the past when human slavery has been condoned, and those sentiments among us today that are sympathetic with human enslavement, can be tied to the idea that the subjugated are ''other''—something else radically different from me and mine. A fairer criticism of the mistake of the *apartheid* attitude is not so much a breach of the moral code as it is bad taxonomy. The growing world pressure against racial discrimination is perhaps due to the increasing recognition that we are all one species with very little, if any, interpopulational variation in potential ability to accumulate information, to formulate ideas, and to experience the varied forms of social interaction.

Although it is but a small minority of humans that wish to extend such moral codes as ''freedom from servitude'' to other organisms, many rebel in revulsion when they witness other organisms experiencing pain. This, I believe, is because we have stronger emotions relating to the prevention of human pain than we do for preventing such things as freedom infringements, and have been more thorough in our anthropomorphic transference of these to other organisms. Yet, in the attempt to incorporate the pain experienced by other organisms directly into our moral judgments, we are courting the same logical and practical difficulties which we encounter in any consideration of them as moral bodies.

A current example will bring the question into better focus. Suppose society is faced with the decision whether to permit students the freedom to experiment with live laboratory animals, bred and maintained for that purpose, or to withhold this freedom by law on the basis that the animal's pain and ensuing death caused by the inexperienced hands of the student is not worth the information and experience that the student derives. It is difficult to imagine any basis of equivalency by which we could evaluate education in terms of some translatable value of rat pain. I contend that there is no common denominator. Even the problems that we face within our own moral system, in attempting to weigh the immediate discomforts of the varied forms of child discipline, and the dangers of testing a new drug, against their long-term advantages, border on being insurmountable. However, we still have a common foundation for our judgments—human welfare.

A recurrent thread in most discussions on the relationship of our ethics to other animals is the concept that none should be hurt or caused to die unnecessarily. Certainly all would agree with this in theory. However, we have no common basis to judge *necessity* in this context. One group contends that all vivisection is unnecessary; another feels that most is necessary. How does one judge if it is necessary to kill or cause other organisms pain for the aesthetic enjoyments of fishing, recovering from a mild parasitic infection, training a retriever dog, or having a mosquito-free back yard? What unresolvable quandaries we are led into! The act that is unnecessary to one is quite necessary to another, and we eventually return to the *effect upon humans* as the final basis of evaluation.

Also, if one wishes to assume the position that killing and causing other organisms pain is "justified when necessary for sustenance," but nevertheless immoral, then we must surely classify meat-eating societies, like the Eskimos, as more evil than some vegetarian agriculturists. Our own meat-eating habits would also have to be abandoned, for who among us would take the hypocritical position that we eat prime

T-bone only for the necessary protein? We, by heritage and necessity, are organisms with heterotrophic habits and tastes and, therefore, are tethered to continued existence by the inexorable expenditure of the lives of other organisms. Our heterotrophic nature precludes any philosophy which would judge killing of other organisms as a sinful act against those organisms.

Throughout the evolution of social thought, man has not always visualized himself as separate from other organisms, just as he drew no distinct line between animate and inanimate objects. But the growing trend in the modern world to anthropomorphize the acts of other organisms arises from a rather different source. Early man had an intimate contact with other organisms, and his incorporation of these other species into his philosophy and religion no doubt was a result of this dependency upon and fear of other species. In the process of our self-domestication we have removed ourselves farther and farther from our contact with other species, and it is because of this lack of first hand understanding and familiarity that we attribute human feelings and motivations to other organisms. Although science has enabled us to place ourselves in the proper phylogenetic scheme, it has also removed humanity as a whole from the first hand contact with, and appreciation of, some basic ecological processes. We have seldom seen the organisms that we eat, when they were alive. It is not uncommon to meet people who are upset at the thought of eating the same lobster that they chose from the live-box earlier in the evening. Although perhaps small by comparison, the price that we pay for the benefits of modern society is the loss in breadth of experience gained from seeing ourselves "in the system," as direct participants in the life and death of other organisms somewhat similar to ourselves. Moreover, we can expect further increases in this price as society's relationship with other organisms becomes even more indirect. Perhaps the current boom and rising influence of animal suffrage groups exemplifies this trend.

One can identify the changes in attitude within this century as we grade from a rural to an urban society. On the farm there was a sharper line between humans and other organisms. The pigs were butchered and the peas canned. As urbanites, our contact with other organisms is usually with pets or even the more humanized cartoon characters. Children reared in our urban society may misread ''roast duck'' on the menu as roast Donald, and bears are those furry people who wear ranger hats in ads that tell you to use care with matches. Our increasingly limited experience with other organisms has caused us to extend further our moral code outside its sphere of applicability. What a black day for the nation if Alfred the alligator ended up in the last frame of Tuesday's Special chomping a half-skinned, intestines-dangling, Pogo—but, of course, that is part of the real relationship between alligators and opossums.

We have generated a phobia of seeing viscera of other organisms and of seeing them killed. The idea that insides are repugnant, and our distaste for non-human death, probably originated as extensions of the fear of human death or witnessing human viscera. Relating emotionally to other organisms is no doubt a natural by-product of the breakdown of our sharp value delineation between humans and non-humans, resulting from our increasing lack of contact with other organisms. However, this transference of our fears and concerns about humans to other species may detract from the welfare of our own species. If we are to sterilize our view of life by editing the realities of nature to suit our anthropomorphic attitudes, we can anticipate attendant limitations in our potential for understanding ourselves and the real world about us. To become involved in the births and deaths of other organisms in the laboratory or in the field, if it can be done without any recognizable loss to human welfare, may help us understand or at least feel more deeply the natural processes of life and death, of which we are a part. Also, witnessing the inner complexities of individual function surely contributes to our appreciation of the phenomenon of life. Denying ourselves these perspectives by letting our emotions completely humanize other organisms may be no trivial loss.

If we are to accept the idea that our moral system was designed by man for regulating the behavior of his own species and that it is improper to apply it to other organisms, we can then attempt to deal with a related issue—the nature of our moral obligation to other humans as it relates to our conduct toward other organisms. How must we behave if our treatment of a non-human organism offends others who empathize more than we do? In its extreme form, one pressure group attempts to legislate its tastes or emotional sensitivities on the minority group. Consider bullfighting and live pigeon shoots, both of which are illegal in the United States. Those who wish to outlaw these events have two alternative arguments, assuming that they themselves are not forced to experience or witness the event: they can take the position that it is detrimental either to the bull's welfare or to the welfare of those who are attending. In the case of the first position, one courts some of the problems that I have been reviewing. The basis of the second position has yet to be demonstrated. We are told by some who attend these events that they can be enjoyable and rewarding experiences, and in those countries where they occur now, we can but conclude that they are enjoyed by many people. Those who disagree take the position that an emphasis on the ''humane'' treatment of other organisms will further nurture those qualities in our relationship with other humans. In some situations this is probably true, but, unfortunately, blurring this difference also invites the other part of the association; and disposing of an intestinal parasite would be a poor analogy to our disposition toward a fellow human drawing unemployment compensation. I would rather take the other view, that it is the distinction between human welfare and the welfare of other things that will provide deeper meaning to the preciousness of the human individual. Debasing the value of human relationships by a loose analogy with our relationship to other organisms has affected, and no doubt could further affect, the esteem of human worth.

I refer again to the criteria for evaluating moral actions, stated in the beginning, that the rules governing human behavior should be constructed to regard the welfare of humans not only as a group but also as individuals. This necessitates maintaining the greatest possible latitude of individual behavior without markedly encroaching on the welfare of the unit as a whole. We must then make sure that to allow one segment to perform an act does not, in consequence, detract materially from the freedom of another segment, and, if so, some mutual compromise will have to be made. Performing a physiology experiment with the exposed viscera of a live horse in the middle of a public park does not show moral regard for the individuals who, by witnessing it, would experience considerable discomfort. Even though the physiologist may feel that the squeamishness of the lady passerby is unjustified, he nevertheless has the responsibility to consider her emotional sensitivities. Likewise, the same lady must allow other segments of society to use other organisms in their education and enjoyment, so long as she is not personally forced to experience or witness those acts. This is, of course, the same principle that we use in other matters of individual taste (e.g., nudity, intoxication, and loud parties).

The classroom is a slightly different situation. The teacher has been given the responsibility to aid people in their education in the best way he knows. The teacher's judgment to require the student to work on living organisms (or to read *Catcher in the Rye,* for that matter) may be intended to give the student a more intimate contact with other perspectives that cannot be communicated by just reading a lab manual or a literary review. Thus a teacher has a less restricted license to expose his students to other ways of feeling and thinking than does one stranger to another. But certainly there are still limitations. Interestingly enough, almost all of the opposition to vivisection in schools has been directed, not toward the question of the students' rights and discomforts, but of the animals'.

The error of extending moral judgment outside the system is widespread among scientists. Biologists are particularly susceptible. Most biologists were attracted to their discipline because they were fascinated with animals in their youth, and in the modern world this fascination is generally on an individual basis with pets, cartoon characters, circus performers, and zoo inhabitants. We as biologists are hesitant to accord other organisms the same moral status as inorganic objects because of the striking kinship we share morphologically, physiologically, and behaviorally (those areas with which biologists are most familiar). And, of course, the philosophical tendency to include other organisms directly in human codes of behavior stems, indirectly, from these phylogenetic bonds. However, our ethical constructs apply to an entirely different level of organization, a level with which biologists typically do not deal professionally. Value judgments of human conduct are in the same realm as concepts such as citizenship and taxation where we do categorize other animate objects in the same set with inorganic ones, and would consider as ludicrous the application of an idea such as proportional representation—"one individual, one vote"—to include gophers.

Although many other species have, like the human species, evolved their own codes of social behavior, they have only done so directly or indirectly to increase the welfare of the members of their own species. Not unexpectedly, these codes are not the same ones that we have constructed for ourselves.

The key theme of this essay is that the human species, or for that matter any species, is under no moral obligation to extend its own internal code of behavior to other species and that it can be a serious error to do so; however, it would be an equal or greater error to take the short sighted view that a species' welfare is merely an intraspecific matter. Any species is a segment of the entire community, and its integrity and continued existence cannot be evaluated aside from the larger community unit. The quality of our future as humans will depend on the quality of our management of the community of organisms of which we are an integral part. To impede this management by misunderstanding the nature of *either* our ecological or moral relationships can only be to the human detriment.

NOTES

1. T. Kiernan, *A Treasury of Albert Schweitzer.* (New York: Citadel, 1965), p. 349.
2. P. Shepard, 24th N. Amer. Wildlife Conf., Trans., pp. 504-512, 1959.

DISCUSSION TOPICS

1. Why does Guthrie believe it is wrong to "humanize" nonhuman organisms, that is, to ascribe human qualities to their behavior? Do you agree with Guthrie's position? Explain.

2. Do you agree with the position that as long as ''squeamish'' people do not have to witness or experience offensive acts, they ought to be tolerant when others exploit animals for their own education and enjoyment?

Man's Responsibility for the Environment

F. Fraser Darling

Frank Fraser Darling (1903–1979), a geneticist and biologist who was knighted in 1970, was an early advocate of weak anthropocentrism. Fraser Darling notes the great superiority humans have over the rest of the natural world and advocates the position that humans are ''biological aristocrats'' exercising dominion over the planet by virtue of their superiority as a species. Using the analogy of an aristocratic ideal, however, Fraser Darling advocates that as true aristocrats humans must be servants of their wards and assume a noblesse oblige responsibility to the natural world. But he never loses sight of the fact that human survival is a key component underlying this responsibility. An interesting feature of Fraser Darling's perspective is that both privilege and responsibility are tied to the notion of human superiority.

Man is biologically an aristocrat. He has dominion over the creatures, the plant cover and the very landscape of his planet. Man, indeed, is privileged. Ecologically, he occupies the summits of food chains and pyramids. Man is the lord of the living manor and privilege is implicit in superiority.

I do not think aristocracy is a humanly conceived notion but an observable phenomenon. Beneath man are lesser lords on the summits of their own little pyramids, be they tiger or eagle, robin or mole, dragonfly or spider. The aristocratic ideal, however, is a conception of the human mind, very old, very beautiful, and a potential ecological factor of great significance in the world. Few races of men have quite failed to conceive this ideal though too little of it may have been practised either by groups, classes or individuals.

Briefly put, the ideal is expressed by saying that the aristocrat is the servant of his people. It involves the notion of restraint, what the Greek meant in the word *''aidos.''* Superiority is accepted, not assumed in conceit, nor disclaimed in mock modesty; when superiority is known to its holder it is accepted humbly as a burden proudly carried.

I have no intention of giving myself to the wolves by discussing the virtue of the aristocratic ideal in its practice between man and man even if such a discussion would not be wholly irrelevant in relation to clean air and water as human rights, but I do take it as the basis of an ethic of responsible behaviour between man and his total environment. This includes all other living things, the landscape, air and water, and the various products of art in man's history, art being considered as an emanation of nature.

Civilization is itself a flower of evolution, one which man could not have achieved had he not learned to tap the immense stores of mineral and organic matter which the earlier planet had produced, and to modify the habitats in which he found himself. Immediately he ceased being an indigenous animal, recycling his products and wastes within his own habitat, he began to impoverish his world. Naturally, he could not see this straightaway, especially as he was still struggling to survive as a species. Nevertheless, there is evident in primitive cultures a rudimentary sense of reciprocation to the environment or an identification as being part of the wholeness of it. When an Athabascan Indian asks the forgiveness of the bear he is about to hunt and kill because of his need, he is philosophically conscious and understanding of his own ecological situation which demands what the bear has to offer to his continued survival. His prayer is a beautiful example of restraint, no new-fangled hyper-sophisticated preciousness.

The earth has been rich enough to bear the strain of emergent civilization on its organic resources, and the gain is the beauty of the human mind, the glory of the human spirit. Yet all the time there has been a painfully conscious sorrow that the beauty and glory have been distilled from a mash of baser behaviour, emotions and physical evidence. Awe for nature and its expressions has, I believe, always been present, but the responses to that awe would make an interesting study of man facing and coping with his whole environment. Comparative religion is part of such a study and I think we should find that polytheism was an expression of man's sense of belonging to a whole of multiple checks and balances. An earth mother was functional and comforting even if terrible on occasion.

When certain wild crops could not be harvested and certain animals not be hunted until certain propitious dates, man was reaching to some scarcely articulate notion of conservation, to a facet of identity with other living things. The Dinka of the Bahr-el-Ghazal honours the giraffe calf born among his cattle by anointing it with cattle fat, and you will see even today how tame giraffes are in that part of the world. I have sat among a dozen Dinka men and women sprawled under one of their raised huts of boughs and thatch, and watched a tiny poisonous snake in the floor above us, weaving its way as confidently as a gecko. The little snake, an insect eater, was accepted; it was not outside the Dinka's world. The West Highlander still has in the back of his mind a half memory of Finoula's kindred; he will not kill a swan and is disturbed if some infidel does such a thing. This is more than mere taboo. The polytheistic attitude makes for a slow rate of change.

Monotheism was a powerful thrust forward for the human being, concentrating spiritual force, especially when man identified the image of God with his own—though he puts it the opposite way, that God created him in His own image. Now comes a process of dissociation with other living things and in the example of the Jews it extends to the notion of being God's chosen people. Here is enormous strength—at a cost usually unimagined and perhaps unseen until our own era. Western man, having adopted the Judaic-Christian religion, has not only banished all living things other than his own species from the partnership of God and himself, but has developed the convenient conviction that God created the rest of living things

for the *use* and delectation of man. Orthodox religion may be tottering, but not this mental attitude; so-called rationality even strengthens it. My own plea for a preservation of a natural oakwood drew from a righteous and aggrieved timber merchant the expostulation ''But it's ripe!''

Once life other than human has been relegated to the status of useful material, or material awaiting the discovery of usefulness to the human being, the return to an ethical system of thought relating to it is very difficult. I am not greatly moved when I hear supporters of the national park and nature reserve movement argue that living things have educational value, that the beauties of nature give pleasure to humanity, that they are of scientific value or of potential usefulness, and that we cannot afford to lose them. The essential attitude is not far in advance of that of the timber merchant.

Life exists in its own right and this we must acknowledge.

During my lifetime, philosophy, religion and science have come a long way nearer together. The philosophy of wholeness is grasped and accepted, and science now is less sure of any absolute distinction between living and non-living. ''I was born a mineral and arose a plant. . . .'' The truth of Zoroastrianism comes back to us, that we are all of one stuff, difference is only in degree, and God can be conceived as being in all and of all, the sublime and divine immanence.

If this is the point to which we have come, it is time for us to exercise the ideal of our aristocratic nature, to be the servant of the planet to which we were born and to which we are still bound. Neither life nor matter is to be squandered, but as yet the mercantile outlook remains paramount. If the cancerous growth of human population needs the destruction of more wilderness, then the human population must be indulged and more wilderness will be destroyed. I say cancerous growth because it is uncontrolled and out of control, resulting in the *barrios* of South American cities, the seething port cities of Asia where the food comes in—growth without form.

Pollution of the environment is a concomitant of over-population, but it is of two kinds, passive in that which no one can avoid, and positive in failing to act when the preventive process is known, either in sewage disposal or the control of industrial wastes. Here the aristocratic ideal is directly applicable between man and man. I think the National Coal Board has set an excellent example in its treatment of landscapes after open-cast coal extraction, and only the other day this body gave a subsidence area in Kent as a National Nature Reserve.

I spoke of man being a biological aristocrat living at the summits of ecological pyramids. The Scythians of the Kuban and the Ukraine, the Plains Indians of the prairies and peoples of deltas and marshes were comparatively few in number, living on high protein diets. As far as we can see, such ecological summit cultures are self-conserving of animal natural resources, but the descent from the aristocratic position in the change-over in land use to cereal production of wheat, maize and rice for sustenance and export has put such people or their invading successors in the position of shortening the food chain, going to plant food direct and finding wild animals either superfluous or a nuisance. The agriculturist feels an animosity to wild animals and they come more and more to be of some lower creation to be harried and slaughtered. The relinquishment of his ecologically aristocratic position has now landed man into the ultimate condition of rabbit and vole, without the merciful phenomenon of resorption of foetuses in times of excessive numbers. Yes, the potato will feed more mouths per acre than any other crop we have, but look at Van Gogh's ''Potato Eaters,'' a striking social document, and read Salaman's *History and Social Influence of the Potato.* After that you can scarcely exclude dietary policy from ethics.

An ethical attitude toward animal life and towards landscape, pure air and clean water, has grown as our condition has deteriorated. The aristocratic ideal is there among the few but the real thrust forward towards conservation and care has come from realization of our growing plight and is not so much ethical as hygienic, concerned with survival. Even so, I think we are losing out. But such a complete pessimist as I sound to be must be a man of overweening conceit; in reality, we cannot take on the mantle of infallibility. Whatever we feel, we must act up to our convictions

of the conservation notion, possibly putting back the catastrophe far enough that all men will have changed in heart. There are evidences in detail already in that the outlook for wild life in Africa is brighter than it was ten years ago, and this year at the International Union for Conservation of Nature research workers of five nations in whose hands the fate of polar bears is held, came together under a neutral chairman to discuss their work for the benefit of the bear. Even so, the inability of the powers to settle positively for conservation of the whale stocks of the world is a reproach to us. I think most of us do think of our behaviour towards the whales in the last forty years in direct ethical terms. The ethic of conservation is perhaps quite primitive, in that we recognize that we are not vegetarians and are not prepared to be so for some high-falutin' principle, but the stocks of animals must be treated with reverence near to veneration, not only because we need them and use them, but because they are worthy of respect in their own right as fellow members of the world community of living things. Such a view does not land us into any fantastic unreal world of Jainism. Aldo Leopold put it shortly over twenty years ago, ''That land is a community is the basic concept of ecology, but that land is to be loved and respected is an extension of ethics.'' Land in Leopold's sense included the farmers' land and the whole terrain in which communities of living things lived; another short couple of sentences of his were, ''We abuse land because we regard it as a commodity belonging to us. When we see land as a community to which we belong, we may begin to use it with love and respect.''

Ecology as a science makes possible understanding as well as insight into what might be called the physiology of community. To use the ecosystem approach to study and assessment of land use and its problems is to make us readier to accept the ethical principles of conservation. An understanding of the intricacies of niche structure in biological communities causes us to hesitate in taking short cuts in practical thinking. We do not rush in with a spray gun at some apparent pest before we know what it does in its total community. Even the word pest is a doubtful one in the ecologist's vocabulary, for so often the pest is a consequence of earlier misdirected human activity. To instigate a chain reaction in ecological relations within a community on grounds of expedience is not only foolish but in my opinion unethical. We have done this in the past through ignorance, as in malaria control of the *Anopheles* mosquito, to find that we have brought other vectors out of the trees which are less easy to control. We did it with red mite control in British orchards. We could do it with tsetse control in Africa. The professed aim is always to solve an immediate problem or to provide urgently needed food for a not urgently needed human population. Sometimes it has been for the plain profit motive.

Ecologists facing social problems of biological equilibrium may be so far in the van in ethical thinking that they may be considered unrealistic. I think we need much discussion between agriculturists and the fringe industries with ecologists on the whole subject of ethical standards. Few of us can be happy with the degradation of living creatures now being suffered in the name of increased food production. Veal production by intensive methods, the de-beaking of hens and suchlike practices are the antithesis of the aristocratic ideal. It is doubtful whether such so-called farmers have really managed to lie to themselves (that purely human ability) that they are contributing to a worthy cause of food production for the masses. They are moved by the profit motive.

Orthodox religions of the Judaic-Christian phylum have failed us badly, historically in the Scriptures, philosophically in having split the community of life by the figment of soul as a human prerogative in association with God, and currently in their tardiness to face the consequences of uncontrolled human increase. Yet within the churches there are fine men with their eyes open and we should get in touch with them on the ideas of conservation. I tried this years ago with a Hebridean minister of hard-shell Presbyterian convictions and was told he did not concern himself with secular affairs; again, after drinking coffee with an Anglican bishop after a harvest festival service, I mooted the cogency of the conservation ethic at such a service and received the comment, ''Candidly, I had never considered harvest thanksgiving in those terms.'' But it is time we tried again.

Finally, we should not lose sight of the fact that it is largely from Western man, deriving from the Judaic-Christian ethos, that the new ethic of responsibility for the environment is growing, but in so small a segment of power. Within it there is compassion as well as logic.

Ecologists are discoverers, not preachers, but how can they keep quiet in our present world? Nevertheless, let them not be mere expostulators, as so-called conservationists are apt to be. The ethic of conservation has grown up in a period of declining religious conviction, but I think this would be an inadmissible correlation. It has grown with our increasing straits, but not fast enough. As I implied at the outset, the social disciplines of subsistence cultures were often self-conserving of the habitat: a world which has so largely emerged from subsistence culture has tended to shed parts of these disciplines without understanding them and the habitat often breaks down along with the culture itself, and more so when technology is so powerful as to give false confidence. One might say this is digressing from ethics into social studies of an ecological character. All well and good, but there is a point in these processes at which ethical questions of behaviour and culture present themselves and worry us if we put them aside. At this moment we can evade them no longer. I, along with most of us, am seeking, seeking in the spirit of science, but with the feeling that science and religion cannot be far apart in such truth as may be vouchsafed to us.

As the dominant mammal on the face of the earth, as the clever one, the only one as far as we know capable of reflection and of accumulating knowledge, our duty is plain, to serve the lesser creation, to keep our world clean and pass on to posterity a record of which we shall not feel shame.

DISCUSSION TOPICS

1. Why does Fraser Darling advocate polytheism over monotheism as a belief system? Do you agree with this position? Explain your reasoning.
2. It has been suggested that a doctrine of aristocracy can lead to a paternalistic attitude toward one's charges. Do you agree? What advantages or disadvantages are inherent in such an attitude toward nature?

Anthropocentrism: A Modern View

W. H. Murdy

Another representative of weak anthropocentrism, William H. Murdy (b. 1928), a botanist at Emory University specializing in genetics and reproductive biology, builds on the notion that concern for our own species has a strong evolutionary precedent. Murdy asserts that all species exist as ends for themselves; in biological terms, they seek to maximize their own reproductive success. Thus it is natural for humans to value other humans more highly than the rest of nature; in fact, it would be logical for members of any species to view themselves as most valuable. Murdy acknowledges, however, that human survival and well-being depend on the health and stability of our whole ecological support system. From an enlightened self-interest perspective, he advocates that humans ascribe value to all elements of the natural world.

The capacity of man to affect the environment beyond himself is an evolutionary emergent, continuous with the much more limited ability of other organisms to affect the environment beyond themselves. It enables man to modify environments to suit his needs, which is a root cause of both his biological success and ecological problems. It also enables man to enhance values beyond himself, and this is a major feature of the new anthropocentrism expressed in this article.

PRE-DARWINIAN ANTHROPOCENTRISM

Socrates, in a dialogue with Euthydemus,[1] is reported to have said:

Tell me, Euthydemus, has it ever occurred to you to reflect on the care the gods have taken to furnish man with what he needs? . . . Now, seeing that we need food, think how they make the earth to yield it, and provide to that end appropriate seasons which furnish in abundance the diverse things that minister not only to our wants but to our enjoyment.

The idea that nature was created to benefit man was a popular belief throughout Western history and was still very much alive in the 19th century. Cuvier, "father" of comparative anatomy and paleontology, "could think of no better reason for the existence of fishes . . . than that they provided food for man,"[2] and Lyell, a leading geologist of the 19th century, in his early years, believed that domestic animals had been expressly designed for man's use. He writes[3]:

The power bestowed on the horse, the dog, the ox, the sheep, the cat, and many species of domestic fowls, of supporting almost every climate, was given expressly to enable them to follow man throughout all parts of the globe in order that we might obtain their services, and they our protection.

DARWINIAN ANTHROPOCENTRISM

Charles Darwin, in *The Origin of Species,* provided sufficient evidence to finally inter the idea that nature exists to serve man. According to William Paley, 18th-century exponent of natural theology, the rattlesnake's rattle was expressly designed to give warning to its prey. Darwin[4] asserts that "natural selection cannot possibly produce any modification in a species exclusively for the good of another species" and makes the following declaration:

If it could be proved that any part of the structure of any one species had been formed for the exclusive good of another species it would annihilate my theory, for such could not have been produced through natural selection. (p. 196)

Species exist as ends in themselves. They do not exist for the exclusive benefit of any other species. The purpose of a species, in biological terms, is to survive to reproduce. Potter[5] writes: "all successful living organisms behave purposefully in terms of their own or their species survival." (p. 16) Species that failed to do so became extinct.

A MODERN VIEW OF ANTHROPOCENTRISM

To be anthropocentric is to affirm that mankind is to be valued more highly than other things in nature—

by man. By the same logic, spiders are to be valued more highly than other things in nature—by spiders. It is proper for men to be anthropocentric and for spiders to be arachnocentric. This goes for all other living species. The following statement by Simpson[6] expresses the modern version of anthropocentrism:

> Man is the highest animal. The fact that he alone is capable of making such judgment is in itself part of the evidence that this decision is correct. And even if he were the lowest animal, the anthropocentric point of view would still be manifestly the only proper one to adopt for consideration of his place in the scheme of things and when seeking a guide on which to base his actions and his evaluations of them.

Anthropocentrism is a pejorative in many of the articles which deal with the so-called ''ecological crisis.'' Lynn White,[7] in his widely quoted article, ''The historical roots of our ecological crisis,'' upbraids Christianity for being the most anthropocentric religion the world has seen:

> Christianity, in absolute contrast to ancient paganism and Asia's religions (except perhaps Zoroastrianism), not only established a dualism of man and nature but also insisted that it is God's will that man exploit nature for his proper ends.

White is right to remind us of how tragically myopic has been our exploitation of nature. However, he is wrong to infer that it is somehow wrong for man to exploit nature for ''his proper ends.'' We must exploit nature to live. The problem lies in our difficulty to distinguish between ''proper ends,'' which are progressive and promote human values, and ''improper ends,'' which are retrogressive and destructive of human values.

Another attitude toward nature that eschews anthropocentrism is the ''Franciscan'' belief in the fundamental equality of all life. In this view, man is merely one of several million different species comprising a ''democracy of all God's creatures.''[7] Jordan[8] states: ''The time will come when civilized man will feel that the rights of all living creatures on earth are as sacred as his own.'' Julian Huxley[9] expresses a similar opinion: ''In ethical terms, the

golden rule applies to man's relations with nature as well as to relations between human beings.''

If we affirm that all species have ''equal rights,'' or, that the rights of man are not of greater value than the rights of other species, how should it affect our behavior toward nature? The golden rule, ''As ye would that men should do to you, do ye to them likewise,'' is a moral axiom which requires reciprocity among ethicizing beings. How does such a principle apply to nonethicizing forms of life which cannot reciprocate? The callous, wanton destruction of life is surely not a proper end for man, but what about our destruction of pathogenic bacteria, in order that we might remain healthy, or our destruction of plant and animal life, in order that we might be nourished? To affirm that men, dogs, and cats have more rights than plants, insects, and bacteria is a belief that species do not have equal rights. If, however, we believe in the equality of all species, none should be genetically manipulated or killed for the exclusive benefit of another.

To ascribe value to things of nature as they benefit man is to regard them as instruments to man's survival or well-being. This is an anthropocentric point of view. As knowledge of our dependent relationships with nature grows, we place instrumental value on an ever greater variety of things. Phytoplankton of the oceans becomes valuable when we recognize the key role of these organisms in providing the earth's free oxygen. Continued growth of knowledge may lead to an awareness that no event in nature is without some effect on the whole of which we are a part and therefore we should value all items in nature. Basic to the kind of anthropocentrism expounded in this article is the recognition that an individual's well-being depends on the well-being of both its social group and ecological support system.

Birch contends that to evaluate things of nature in terms of instrumental value, regardless of how enlightened our evaluation might be, will not provide us with a ''valid ethic of nature.'' He writes[10]: ''Conservation will rest on very uncertain foundations unless it comes to be based on a view that living creatures besides man have intrinsic worth. Unless they have, there seems no sound reason for conservation other than to suit the purposes of man, and these change from time to time and place to place.'' To have a ''valid ethic of nature,'' according to Birch, we must affirm ''the intrinsic value of every item in creation.''

An anthropocentric attitude toward nature does not require that man be the source of all value, nor does it exclude a belief that things of nature have intrinsic value. According to Laszlo[11]: ''There is nothing in all the realms of natural systems which would be value-free when looked at from the vantage point of the systems themselves'' (p. 105). Whitehead[12] writes: ''The element of value, of being valuable, of having value, of being an end in itself, of being something which is for its own sake, must not be omitted in any account of an event as the most concrete actual something'' (p. 93).

I may affirm that every species has intrinsic value, but I will behave as though I value my own survival and that of my species more highly than the survival of other animals or plants. I may assert that a lettuce plant has intrinsic value, yet I will eat it before it has reproduced itself because I value my own nutritional well-being above the survival of the lettuce plant. Birch[10] writes: ''Man left only with his self-interest, however enlightened, will not provide sufficient motivation for ecological survival.'' Even this statement can be interpreted in terms of instructional value, that is, man should acknowledge the intrinsic value of things; otherwise he will not have sufficient motivation for ecological survival, which I assume includes human survival individually and as a species.

MAN'S PLACE IN NATURE

Whitehead[12] writes:

> That which endures is limited, obstructive, intolerant, infecting its environment with its own aspects. But it is not self-sufficient. The aspects of all things enter into its very nature. It is only itself as drawing together into its own limitation the larger whole in which it finds itself. Conversely it is only itself by lending its aspects to this same environment in which it finds itself. (p. 94)

Ecologists have a saying: ''You cannot do just one thing.'' Many of our actions, motivated by a desire to improve the quality of human life, have, to our detriment, caused unexpected consequences because we failed to recognize the essential interrelatedness of all things. ''Man's first realization that he was not identical with nature'' was a crucial step in evolution, writes Bohm,[13] ''because it made possible a kind of autonomy in his thinking, which allowed him to go beyond the immediately given limits of nature, first in his imagination, and ultimately in his practical work.'' Realization that our freedom of choice is ''bounded by the limits of compatibility with the dynamic structure of the whole'' (p. 75)[11] and must ''remain within the limits of natural systems values'' (p. 107)[11] is yet another crucial step in evolution. ''Not until man accepts his dependency on nature and puts himself in place as part of it,'' writes Iltis,[14] ''not until then does man put man first. This is the greatest paradox of human ecology.''

A human being is both a hierarchical system (composed of subsystems such as organs, cells, and enzyme systems) and a component of supra-individual, hierarchical systems (populations, species, ecosystems, cultural systems). Man is therefore a set within a hierarchical system of sets. ''In hierarchies a given set must be described not only for itself but in terms both of what is within it, and what it is within.''[15] Because science up to now has been strongly reductionist, we know more about the systems that make up our bodies and our cells than we do about those that transcend our individual lives—the evolutionary, ecologic, and social 'wholes'' of which we are ''parts.''

In an evolutionary sense, the life that animates us has existed in an unbroken line of descent, in numerous forms adapted to myriad environments, since life first appeared on earth some 3 billion years ago. Beside life, our ancestry extends back through billions of years of molecular change to the nuclei of former stars. Here the elements necessary for life were built up from hydrogen, the simplest and most abundant element in the universe. Beyond primordial hydrogen, our ancestral roots became lost in a profound mystery—the beginning of things, the origin of the universe of matter, energy, space, and time.

In an ecologic sense, our existence depends upon

the proper functioning of the earth's present ecosystem. In the course of cosmic evolution the forces of matter and energy produced a planet fit to support life. In the course of biologic evolution, the activities of living things produced an environment fit to support human life. The day-to-day maintenance of our "life-support system" depends on the functional interaction of countless, interdependent biotic and physio-chemical factors. The movement of ocean currents and the activity of soil microbes are as essential to our existence as the oxygen we breathe.

In a social sense, we are as much a product of our culture as of our genes. "We are not ourselves only," writes Wells,[16] "We are also part of human experience and thought." We possess no greater innate intelligence, artistic skill, or emotional feeling than did our prehistoric predecessors, who painted vivid images on cave walls over 30,000 years ago. We are different from Cro-Magnon man because we are heirs to a greater store of knowledge collected by the human species over thousands of years of cultural evolution. In large measure, our personalities are determined by a collective consciousness which we can contribute to and which is itself evolving.

CULTURE, KNOWLEDGE, AND POWER

Once the evolutionary process produced a species with culture, it was inevitable that knowledge of nature would accrue to such a species at an accelerating pace. Culture represents a unique way of acquiring, storing, and transmitting knowledge about the world. Knowledge acquired by one generation may be transmitted to succeeding generations by the agency of social learning. While each newborn person must acquire cultural knowledge anew, the amount of cultural knowledge available to the social group tends to grow in a cumulative fashion. "Cultures may die," writes Hawkins,[17] "as cells may; but death is not built into them, as it is into multicellular animals. And through cultures learning becomes cumulative, evolutionary."

A species that can learn from the experiences of its predecessors can, potentially, build new knowledge upon an ever-expanding base. Cumulative

knowledge provides man, the cultural species, with ever-increasing power to exploit nature and, as a result, he is a great biological success. The human species successfully occupies a greater variety of habitats, over a greater geographic range, with greater numbers, than any other species. Man is recognized as the latest dominant type in a succession of dominant types which emerged during the process of evolution, and represents the first time a species, and not a group of species, has achieved world dominance.

In acquiring his present position of dominance, the human species has radically reshaped the face of nature. "Whole landscapes are now occupied by man-dominated (and in part man-created) faunas and floras."[18] For the first time in earth's evolution, one species can genetically manipulate other species to their detriment, but to its own advantage. Darwin (p. 46) remarks:

> One of the most remarkable features in our domesticated races is that we see in them adaptation, not indeed to the animal's or plant's own good, but to man's use or fancy.[4]

Maize (*Zea mays*) is a species which was molded into an artifact by our prehistoric ancestors. It is unable to survive in nature without man's intervention. Maize was the agricultural base of the great pre-Columbian civilizations of the New World. European colonists encountered it almost everywhere in America, but they found it only in cultivation. The "ear" or pistillate inflorescence of maize was modified by prehistoric man into a botanical monstrosity. There is "no natural way by which the grains can be detached from the cob, escape from the husks, and be dispersed." When the entire ear falls to the ground, "the germinating grains produce a compact cluster of seedlings, none of which has much chance to survive."[19]

Man's ability to exploit nature has been limited by the amount of energy available to the species. For most of human history, energy for man's activities came exclusively from the consumption of plants and animals. "The earliest culture systems developed techniques of hunting, fishing, trapping, collecting, gathering, etc. as means of exploiting the plant and animal resources of nature" (p. 371).[20] The first quantum jump in the energy resources for culture building took place with the domestication of plants and animals. White asserts that a few thousand years after this event, "the great civilizations of antiquity . . . came quickly into being." The second quantum jump in the amount of energy available to man was the tapping of fossil fuel deposits of coal, oil, and natural gas. "The consequences of the fuel revolution," writes White (p. 373), "were in general much like those of the agricultural revolution: an increase in population, larger political units, bigger cities, an accumulation of wealth, a rapid development of the arts and sciences, in short, a rapid and extensive advance of culture as a whole."[20]

Creation of the Cathedral of Chartres or the Declaration of Independence required the existence of civilizations based on artificial ecosystems. Natural ecosystems have intrinsic value, but the realization of value in human evolution, a proper end for man, has depended upon their replacement by artificial systems, which produce more energy.

INEVITABLE CRISIS IN CULTURAL EVOLUTION

Aristotle[21] began his *Metaphysica* with the sentence: "All men by nature desire to know." Throughout history, in spite of prophetic warnings that "knowledge increaseth sorrow," the fund of knowledge available to the human species has continued to expand. Major milestones in this process of knowledge accumulation include the invention of writing and the emergence of modern science.

Scientific knowledge has given us power to do miraculous things as well as monstrous things. We can eliminate diseases, transplant organs, explore the moon, while at the same time we can poison the earth's life-support system or engage in chemical, biological, and nuclear warfare. Nineteenth-century scientists saw the growth and application of scientific knowledge "leading infallibly upward to an empyrean noon hour for mankind," writes Monod,[22] "whereas what we see opening before us today is an abyss of darkness."

We live at a time in human history when the knowledge crisis has become acute. Our current knowledge enables us to "move mountains," but we are still ignorant about whether to do so would be in our best interest. Our collective knowledge of nature has outgrown our collective wisdom, which Potter (p. 1) defines as the "knowledge of how to use knowledge for man's survival and for improvement in the quality of life."[5]

In our frustration we sometimes blame science and technology or a particular ideology for our problems, or we wish that evolution had taken a different direction. If, however, modern society were wiped out and we were to begin again with our paleolithic ancestors, cultural evolution would inevitably lead to a similar knowledge crisis even though its course and time of development would be different. The knowledge crisis is one that every cultural species on every inhabitable planet in the universe must surmount at a point in its evolution, or become extinct. George Wald once remarked in a lecture that it took the planet earth 4.5 billion years to discover that it was 4.5 billion years old and he added: "Having got to that point . . . have we got much longer?"

MAN'S THREAT TO HIS OWN SURVIVAL

Whitehead[12] writes:

> The key to the mechanism of evolution is the necessity for the evolution of a favorable environment, conjointly with the evolution of any specific type of enduring organisms of great permanence. Any physical object which by its influence deteriorates its environment, commits suicide. (p. 109)

Darwin[4] states in *The Origin of Species* (p. 78): "Never forget that every single organic being may be said to be striving to the utmost to increase its numbers," and Bertrand Russell[23] writes: "Every living thing is a sort of imperialist, seeking to transform as much as possible of its environment into itself and its seed." Man's unprecedented power to exploit nature has been used in part to improve the quality of human life, but also in part to transform as much as possible of the environment into ever more human beings. The latter process in our time threatens to undermine the former. George Wald[24] supposes that "man is the first living species, animal or plant, on this planet that has ever been threatened by its own reproductive success.''

The maximization of reproductive potential is, from the biological point of view, in the best interest of most species. This was true for man throughout most of his history. In a world with small human populations at the mercy of environmental vicissitudes, with vast areas of unoccupied space and great stores of untapped resources, the biblical injunction, ''Be fruitful and multiply and subdue the earth,'' had adaptive value and was in the species' best interest, but in the modern world such an injunction is an anachronism.

Negative feedback from the environment has done more to convince us of the essential interrelatedness of things than the prophetic preachments of philosophers ever could do. Unlimited growth of human numbers and human activities within the earth's limited ecosystem is a root cause of our ecological problems. The planet earth, except for a continuous input of solar energy, is essentially a closed system. Its supply of space, air, water, and other natural resources is definitely limited. Widespread pollution, scarcity of resources, and overcrowding are telltale signs that man is becoming maladapted to his niche.

Sinnott[25] writes: ''Organisms often fail to act in such a way as to favor their survival.'' The production of ever more human biomass at the expense of ever greater environmental degradation is anti-anthropocentric in that it is maladaptive for the species. Sinnott continues: ''Natural selection . . . preserves individuals which tend to react in a favorable way, which have 'purposes' that are conducive to successful life and survival, which 'want' the right things.'' The same could be said for populations, species, and cultures.

In order to survive as individuals and as a species we must choose to do the things which will preserve our ''life-support system.'' However, to be anthropocentric is not to seek merely for biological survival. Man is not only an evolving biological entity, but an evolving cultural one as well. Eisenberg[26] asks: ''Is mere perpetuation of the species, without concern for the quality of life, a sufficient criterion for man, even if it has been so for nature?'' Our greatest danger is

not that the human species will become extinct, which is unlikely to occur in the foreseeable future, but that the cultural values that make us human will become extinct.

The ''ecological crisis'' is basically a crisis in human evolution. Modern man stands at a crossroads. Continued geometric growth in human numbers, consumption of resources, and pollution of environments will propel mankind down a road of diminished options. A short way down this road, a point will be reached where the only alternative to extinction will be the regimented ant-heap. This is a process of evolutionary retrogression in which higher, emergent values are destroyed in behalf of the fundamental value of biological survival.

It is anthropocentric to value the factors that make us uniquely human, to seek to preserve and enhance such factors and to counter antihuman forces which threaten to diminish or destroy them. Nature outside of man will not act to preserve human values: it is our responsibility alone.

PARTICIPATION IN OUR OWN EVOLUTION

If all of man's actions were determined, he could not hope to constructively affect the course of human evolution by conscious intent, even if he were to conclude that its direction is inimical to personal freedom and human values. He could only hope to ''fathom the direction of the process'' in order to ''make it less painful by accepting it rather than fighting it'' (p. 355).[20] In this view, since man cannot direct change toward human purposes, his only recourse is to endlessly adjust human purposes to accommodate purposeless change.

The dismal portrayal of man as a passive entity in an evolutionary drama totally dominated by the environment is only one side of the evolutionary process. Evolution is more than the molding of entities by their surroundings. It also involves the ability of entities to interact with, adapt to, and change environments in creative, intelligent, and novel ways.

Man, because of his power of projection, has greater potential for affecting his own evolution than any other species. He is the only species, as far as is known, with the capacity to project purposes (goal-ideas), which arise in his mind from hopes, fantasies, and dreams about the future, and then proceed to work toward their realization. Birch[27] writes: "Possibilities are unseen realities. So far as our human lives are concerned they are potent causes that guide and transform our lives." Thus, the image of the future that man adopts is not merely an illusion, but an element in the chain of causality.

Birth, death, and reproduction are common to all life, but man, because he is capable of reflection and of planning his own actions, does not blindly respond to nature like other organisms: he assimilates and transforms nature and invests it with a meaning and intelligible moral value (p. 40).[28] "We cannot recapture the animal security of instinct," writes Teilhard de Chardin (p. 44).[28] "Because, in becoming men, we have acquired the power of looking to the future and assessing the value of things. We cannot do nothing, since our very refusal to decide is a decision in itself."

FAITH IN THE POTENTIALITIES OF MANKIND

Man is not the measure of all things. He is not the center of the universe, nor the source of all value, nor the culmination of terrestrial evolution. Nevertheless, he is "the present crest of the evolutionary wave" (p. 237),[28] the entity in which the evolutionary trends of greater organizational complexity and greater consciousness have their most advanced development. It is in human evolution that the higher values of truth, justice, love, and beauty have their greatest expression. Further progress toward the realization of higher states of these values, if it is to occur at all, must develop in and through man. He is the key not only to his own survival, but to the survival and furtherance of values of cosmic significance.

In order to influence evolution in wise and responsible ways, we must strive for an ever fuller understanding of our relationship to greater wholes—society, nature, and ultimately to the primary source of order and value in the world. Personal identification with greater wholes is essential to the discovery of

our own wholeness. An entity is only itself, according to Whitehead, "as drawing together into its own limitation the larger whole in which it finds itself. Conversely it is only itself by lending its aspects to this same environment in which it finds itself" (p. 94).[12]

Effective participation in our own evolution requires not only that we establish a harmonious relationship to larger wholes, but, in addition, that we affirm the human phenomenon to be a vitally significant process in its own right and our individual selves to be holistic centers "of spontaneity and self-creation contributing distinctively to the world."[29]

Teilhard de Chardin (p. 296) saw, as a possibility, "mankind falling suddenly out of love with its own destiny. This disenchantment would be conceivable, and indeed inevitable," he writes, "if as a result of growing reflection we came to believe that our end could only be collective death in an hermetically sealed world."[28] Boulding[30] concurs: "An ideology which states that the world is essentially meaningless but that we ought to strive, suffer and fight for it is unlikely to be powerful because of the essential contradictions among its components. If an interpretation of history says the world is meaningless, then our value system is likely to be pure hedonism—'Eat, drink, and be merry, for tomorrow we die'—or else one of apathy or stoic resignation."

Unbridled self-indulgence on the part of one generation without regard to future ones is the modus operandi of biological evolution and may be regarded as rational behavior. Heilbroner[31] asks: "On what private, 'rational' considerations, after all, should we make sacrifices now to ease the lot of generations whom we will never live to see?" If man, with his extraordinary power to multiply, consume, and pollute, seeks only to maximize short-term gain, global disaster will result in the very near future. The only possible answer to the above question, according to Heilbroner, "lies in our capacity to form a collective bond of identity with future generations." To do so is to affirm that the human enterprise has value which transcends our individual lives.

An anthropocentric faith in mankind affirms that we are not isolated monads acting out absurd roles within a meaningless context, but that we are essential elements of a meaningful whole and that our individual acts are vitally significant to the self-actualization of the process of human evolution itself and to the enhancement of value in the world.

SUMMARY

Anthropocentrism is proposed as a valid and necessary point of view for mankind to adopt for consideration of his place in nature. Our current ecological problems do not stem from an anthropocentric attitude per se, but from one too narrowly conceived. Anthropocentrism is consistent with a philosophy that affirms the essential interrelatedness of things and that values all items in nature since no event is without some effect on wholes of which we are parts. The ecological crisis is viewed as an inevitable crisis in human evolution. Through cultures knowledge becomes cumulative. A crisis occurs when our knowledge of nature, which determines our power to exploit nature, exceeds our knowledge of how to use knowledge for our own survival and for improvement in the quality of our lives. An anthropocentric belief in the value, meaningfulness, and creative potential of the human phenomenon is considered a necessary motivating factor to participatory evolution which, in turn, may be requisite to the future survival of the human species and its cultural values.

NOTES

1. Xenophon *Memorabilia and Oeconomicus* (Harvard University Press, Cambridge, Mass., 1959), p. 299.
2. G.G. Simpson, *This View of Life* (Harcourt, Brace & World, New York, 1964), p. 101.
3. C. Lyell, *Principles of Geology* (Kay, Jun, and Brother, Philadelphia, 1837), vol. 1, p. 512.
4. C. Darwin, *The Origin of Species* (Doubleday, Garden City, N.Y., 1872 ed).
5. V.R. Potter, *Bioethics* (Prentice-Hall, Englewood Cliffs, N.J., 1971).
6. G.G. Simpson, *The Meaning of Evolution* (Yale University Press, New Haven, Conn., 1949), p. 286.
7. L. White, Jr., *Science* 155, 1205 (1967).
8. D.S. Jordan, quoted in H.M. Smith, *Biologist* 52, 56 (1970).
9. J. Huxley, *The Human Crisis* (Univ. of Washington Press, Seattle, 1963), p. 24.
10. C. Birch, *Zygon* 8, 255 (1973).
11. E. Laszlo, *The Systems View of the World* (Braziller, New York, 1972).
12. A.N. Whitehead, *Science and the Modern World* (Macmillan, New York, 1925).
13. D. Bohm, *The Van Leer Jerusalem Foundation Series* (Humanities Press, New York, 1973), p. 18.
14. H.H. Iltis, *BioScience* 20, 820 (1970).
15. C. Grobstein, in *Hierarchy Theory,* H.H. Pattee, Ed. (Braziller, New York, 1973), p. 31.
16. H.G. Wells, in *Living Philosophies* (Simon & Schuster, New York, 1931), p. 83.
17. D. Hawkins, *The Language of Nature* (Freeman, San Francisco, 1964), p. 276.
18. E. Anderson, *Smithson. Inst. Annu. Rep.* (1956), p. 461.
19. P. Weatherwax, *Indian Corn in Old America* (Macmillan, New York, 1954), p. 179.
20. L. White, *The Science of Culture* (Farrar & Straus, New York, 1949), pp. 371-373.
21. Aristotle, *The Works of Aristotle,* vol. 8. *Metaphysica,* W.D. Ross, Transl. (Clarendon, Oxford, ed. 2, 1928), p. 980a.
22. J. Monod, *Chance and Necessity* (Knopf, New York, 1971), p. 170.
23. B. Russell, *Philosophy* (Norton, New York, 1927), p. 27.
24. G. Wald, *Zygon* 5, 168 (1970).
25. E.W. Sinnott, *Cell and Psyche* (Harper & Row, New York, 1961), pp. 82-83.
26. L. Eisenberg, *Science* 176, 126 (1972).
27. C. Birch, *J. Am. Acad. Rel.* 40, 158 (1972).
28. P. Teilhard de Chardin, *The Future of Man* (Harper & Row, New York, 1964).
29. I.G. Barbour, *Issues in Science and Religion* (Prentice-Hall, Englewood Cliffs, N.J., 1966), p. 131.
30. K.E. Boulding, *The Meaning of the Twentieth Century* (Harper & Row, New York, 1965), p. 163.
31. R.L. Heilbroner, *An Inquiry into the Human Prospect* (Norton, New York, 1974), p. 115.

DISCUSSION TOPICS

1. Summarize the reasoning Murdy uses to support his position that the only reasonable environmental ethic is an enlightened self-interest in which we

affirm human value, work for its good, and plan for its future and long-term survival.

2. Murdy claims that all species behave purposefully in terms of their own or their species survival, and that those which have failed to do so have become extinct. Do you agree with this idea? Explain your reasoning.

3. Some might argue that Murdy's position is more concerned with the practical issue of human survival than questions of moral right and wrong. Do you agree? How would you separate these issues? Explain your reasoning.

4. Do you agree with Murdy that survival of such higher values as truth, justice, beauty, love, etc., justify doing what is necessary to ensure human survival? Explain your reasoning.

READING 41

The Golden Rule—A Proper Scale for Our Environmental Crisis

Stephen Jay Gould

Stephen Jay Gould (b. 1941) is an evolutionary biologist who teaches biology, geology, and the history of science at Harvard University. A McArthur Prize fellow, he and Niles Eldredge proposed the idea of punctuated equilibrium, a modification of the theory of evolution which holds that most new species arise relatively quickly (over geological time), rather than through the slow, gradual accumulation of modifications.

Gould addresses two linked arguments: (1) that humans live in a fragile world at serious risk to disruption from human impacts, and (2) that we must learn to become stewards of the planet to prevent further destruction. He argues that human impact is greatly overrated, particularly on a geological time scale, and that humans have much less importance as a species than we would like to think. However, Gould acknowledges that over the short term, humans could be quite self-destructive. Rather than stewardship, Gould advocates an environmental ethic based on enlightened self-interest, and patterned after the Golden Rule; he believes that humans ought to treat nature as they would want to be treated by nature.

Patience enjoys a long pedigree of favor. Chaucer pronounced it "an heigh vertu, certeyn" ("The Franklin's Tale"), while the New Testament had already made a motto of the Old Testament's most famous embodiment: "Ye have heard of the patience of Job" (James 5:11). Yet some cases seem so extended in diligence and time that another factor beyond sheer endurance must lie behind the wait. When Alberich, having lost the Ring of the Nibelungen fully three operas ago, shows up in act 2 of *Götterdämmerung* to advise his son Hagen on strategies for recovery, we can hardly suppress a flicker of admiration for this otherwise unlovable character. (I happen to adore Wagner, but I do recognize that a wait through nearly all the *Ring* cycle would be, to certain unenlightened folks, the very definition of eternity in Hades.)

Patience of this magnitude usually involves a deep understanding of a fundamental principle, central to my own profession of geology but all too rarely grasped in daily life—the effects of scale. Phenomena unfold on their own appropriate scales of space and time and may be invisible in our myopic world of dimensions assessed by comparison with human height and times metered by human life spans. So much of accumulating importance at earthly scales— the results of geological erosion, evolutionary changes in lineages—is invisible by the measuring rod of a human life. So much that matters to particles in the microscopic world of molecules—the history of a dust grain subject to Brownian motion, the fate of shrunken people in *Fantastic Voyage* or *Inner Space*—either averages out to stability at our scale or simply stands below our limits of perception.

It takes a particular kind of genius or deep understanding to transcend this most pervasive of all conceptual biases and to capture a phenomenon by grasping a proper scale beyond the measuring rods of our own world. Alberich and Wotan know that pursuit of the Ring is dynastic or generational, not personal. William of Baskerville (in Umberto Eco's *Name of the Rose*) solves his medieval mystery because he alone understands that, in the perspective of centuries, the convulsive events of his own day (the dispute between papacies of Rome and Avignon) will be forgotten, while the only surviving copy of a book by Aristotle may influence millennia. Architects of medieval cathedrals had to frame satisfaction on scales beyond their own existence, for they could not live to witness the completion of their designs.

May I indulge in a personal anecdote on the subject of scale? As a child, I loved to memorize facts but rebelled at those I deemed unimportant (baseball stats were in, popes of Rome and kings of England out). In sixth grade, I had to memorize the sequence of land acquisitions that built America. I could see the rationale for learning about the Louisiana Purchase and the Mexican Cession—since they added big chunks to our totality. But I remember balking, and publicly challenging the long-suffering Ms. Stack, at the Gadsden Purchase of 1853. Why did I have to know about a sliver of southern Arizona and New Mexico?

Now I am finally hoist by my own petard (blown up by my own noxious charge, according to the etymologies). After a lifetime of complete nonimpact by the Gadsden Purchase, I have become unwittingly embroiled in a controversy about a tiny bit of territory within this smallest of American growing points. A little bit of a little bit; so much for effects of scale and the penalties of blithe ignorance.

The case is a classic representative of a genre (environmentalists versus developers) made familiar in recent struggles to save endangered populations—the snail darter of a few years back, the northern spotted owl versus timber interests (decided, properly in my view, for the birds on the day that I write this essay, June 2, 1990). The University of Arizona, with the backing of an international consortium of astronomers, wishes to build a complex of telescopes atop Mount Graham in southeastern Arizona (part of the Gadsden Purchase). But the old-growth spruce-fir habitat on the mountaintop forms the heart of the range for *Tamiasciurus hudonicus grahamensis,* the Mount Graham red squirrel—a distinct subspecies

that lives nowhere else and that forms the southernmost population of the entire species. The population has already been reduced to some 100 survivors, and destruction of several acres of spruce-fir growth (to build the telescopes) within the 700 or so remaining acres of best habitat might well administer a *coup de grâce* to this fragile population.

I cannot state an expert opinion on details of this controversy (I have already confessed my ignorance about everything involving the Gadsden Purchase and its legacy). Many questions need to be answered. Is the population already too small to survive in any case? If not, could the population, with proper management, coexist with the telescopes in the remaining habitat? (Environmentalists fear change of microclimate as much or more than loss of acreage. Reduction of forest canopy will increase wind and sun, producing a drop in humidity. The squirrels survive winter by storing unopened cones in food caches beside trees. If humidity falls, cones may dry out and open, causing loss of seeds and destruction of food.)

I do not think that, practically or morally, we can defend a policy of saving every distinct local population of organisms. I can cite a good rationale for the preservation of species—for each species is a unique and separate natural object that, once lost, can never be reconstituted. But subspecies are distinct local populations of species with broader geographical ranges. Subspecies are dynamic, interbreedable, and constantly changing; what then are we saving by declaring them all inviolate? Thus, I confess that I do not agree with all arguments advanced by defenders of the Mount Graham red squirrel. One leaflet, for example, argues: ''The population has been recently shown to have a fixed, homozygous allele which is unique in Western North America.'' Sorry folks. I will stoutly defend species, but we cannot ask for the preservation of every distinctive gene, unless we find a way to abolish death itself (for many organisms carry unique mutations).

No, I think that for local populations of species with broader ranges, the brief for preservation must be made on a case by case basis, not a general principle of preservation (lest the environmental movement ultimately lose popular support for trying to freeze a dynamic evolutionary world *in statu quo*). On this proper basis of individual merit, I am entirely persuaded that the Mount Graham red squirrel should be protected and the astronomical observatory built elsewhere—and for two reasons.

First, the red squirrel itself: the Mount Graham red is an unusually interesting local population within an important species. It is isolated from all other populations and forms the southernmost extreme of the species' range. Such peripheral populations, living in marginal habitats, are of special interest to students of evolution.

Second, the habitat: environmentalists continually face the political reality that support and funding can be won for soft, cuddly, and "attractive" animals, but not for slimy, grubby, and ugly creatures (of potentially greater evolutionary interest and practical significance) or for habitats. This situation has led to the practical concept of "umbrella" or "indicator" species—surrogates for a larger ecological entity worthy of preservation. Thus, the giant panda (really quite a boring and ornery creature despite its good looks) raises money to save the remaining bamboo forests of China (and a plethora of other endangered creatures with no political clout); the northern spotted owl has just rescued some magnificent stands of old-growth giant cedars, Douglas fir, and redwoods (and I say hosanna); and the Mount Graham red squirrel may save a rare and precious habitat of extraordinary evolutionary interest.

The Pinaleno Mountains, reaching 10,720 feet at Mount Graham, are an isolated fault-block range separated from others by alluvial and desert valleys that dip to less than 3,000 feet in elevation. The high peaks of the Pinalenos contain an important and unusual fauna for two reasons. First, they harbor a junction of two biogeographic provinces: the Nearctic, or northern, by way of the Colorado Plateau, and the Neotropical, or southern, via the Mexican Plateau. The Mount Graham red squirrel (a northern species) can live this far south because high elevations reproduce the climate and habitat found near sea level in the more congenial north. Second, and more important to evolutionists, the old-growth spruce-fir habitats on the high peaks of the Pinalenos are isolated "sky is-

lands"—10,000-year-old remnants of a habitat more widely spread over the region of the Gadsden Purchase during the height of the last Ice Age. In evolutionary terms, these isolated pieces of habitat are true islands—patches of more northern microclimate surrounded by southern desert. They are functionally equivalent to bits of land in the ocean. Consider the role that islands (like the Galápagos) have played both in developing the concepts of evolutionary theory and in acting as cradles of origin (through isolation) or vestiges of preservation for biological novelties.

Thus, whether or not the telescopes will drive the Mount Graham red squirrel to extinction (an unsettled question well outside my area of expertise), the sky islands of the Pinalenos are precious habitats that should not be compromised. Let the Mount Graham red squirrel, so worthy of preservation in its own right, also serve as an indicator species for the unique and fragile habitat that it occupies.

But why should I, a confirmed eastern urbanite who has already disclaimed all concern for the Gadsden Purchase, choose to involve myself in the case of the Mount Graham red squirrel? The answer, unsurprisingly, is that I have been enlisted—involuntarily, unawares, and on the wrong side to boot. I am simply fighting mad, and fighting back.

The June 7, 1990, *Wall Street Journal* ran a prodevelopment, antisquirrel opinion piece by Michael D. Copeland (identified as "executive director of the Political Economy Research Center in Bozeman, Montana") under the patently absurd title: "No Red Squirrels? Mother Nature May Be Better Off." (I can at least grasp, while still rejecting, the claim that nature would be no worse off if the squirrel died, but I am utterly befuddled at how anyone could argue that the squirrels inflict a positive harm upon the mother of us all!) In any case, Copeland misunderstood my writings in formulating a supposedly scientific argument for his position.

Now, scarcely a day goes by when I do not read a misrepresentation of my views (usually by creationists, racists, or football fans, in order of frequency). My response to nearly all misquotation is the effective retort of preference: utter silence. (Honorable intellectual disagreement should always be addressed;

misquotation should be ignored, when possible and politically practical.) I make an exception in this case because Copeland cited me in the service of a classic false argument—indeed, the standard, almost canonical misuse of my profession of paleontology in debates about extinction. Paleontologists have been enlisted again and again, in opposition to our actual opinions and in support of attitudes that most of us regard as anathema, to uphold arguments by developers about the irrelevance (or even, in this case, the benevolence) of modern anthropogenic extinction. This standard error is a classic example of failure to understand the importance of scale—thus I return to the premise and structure of my introductory paragraphs (did you really think that I waffled on so long about scale only so that I could talk about the Gadsden Purchase?).

Paleontologists do discuss the inevitability of extinction for all species—in the long run and on the broad scale of geological time. We are fond of saying that 99 percent or more of all species that ever lived are now extinct. (My colleague Dave Raup often opens talks on extinction with a zinging one-liner: "To a first approximation, all species are extinct.") We do therefore identify extinction as the normal fate of species. We also talk a lot—more of late since new data have made the field so exciting—about the mass extinctions that punctuate the history of life from time to time. We do discuss the issue of eventual "recovery" from these extinctions, in the sense that life does rebuild or surpass its former diversity after several million years. Finally, we do allow that mass extinctions break up stable faunas and, in this sense, permit or even foster evolutionary innovations well down the road (including the dominance of mammals and the eventual origin of humans, following the death of dinosaurs).

From this set of statements about extinction in the fullness of geological time (on scales of millions of years), some apologists for development have argued that extinction at any scale (even of local populations within years or decades) poses no biological worry but, on the contrary, must be viewed as a comfortable part of an inevitable natural order. Or so Copeland states:

Suppose we lost a species. How devastating would that be? "Mass extinctions have been recorded since the dawn of paleontology," writes Harvard paleontologist Stephen Gould . . . the most severe of these occurred approximately 250 million years ago . . . with an estimated 96 percent extinction of species, says Mr. Gould. . . . There is general agreement among scientists that today's species represent a small proportion of all those that have ever existed—probably less than 1 percent. This means that more than 99 percent of all species ever living have become extinct.

From these facts, largely irrelevant to red squirrels on Mount Graham, Copeland makes inferences about the benevolence of extinction in general (although the argument applies only to geological scales):

Yet, in spite of these extinctions, both Mr. Gould and University of Chicago paleontologist Jack Sepkoski say that the actual number of living species has probably increased over time. [True, but not as a result of mass extinctions, despite Copeland's next sentence.] The "niches" created by extinctions provide an opportunity for a vigorous development of new species. . . . Thus, evolutionary history appears to have been characterized by millions of species extinctions and subsequent increases in species numbers. Indeed, by attempting to preserve species living on the brink of extinction, we may be wasting time, effort and money on animals that will disappear over time, regardless of our efforts.

But all will "disappear over time, regardless of our efforts"—millions of years from now for most species if we don't interfere. The mean life span of marine invertebrate species lies between 5 and 10 million years; terrestrial vertebrate species turn over more rapidly, but still average in the millions. By contrast, *Homo sapiens* may be only 250,000 years old or so and may enjoy a considerable future if we don't self-destruct. Similarly, recovery from mass extinction takes its natural measure in millions of years—as much as 10 million or more for fully rekindled diversity after major catastrophic events.

These are the natural time scales of evolution and geology on our planet. But what can such vastness possibly mean for our legitimately parochial interest in ourselves, our ethnic groups, our nations, our cultural traditions, our bloodlines? Of what conceivable significance to us is the prospect of recovery from mass extinction 10 million years down the road if our entire species, not to mention our personal family lineage, has so little prospect of surviving that long?

Capacity for recovery at geological scales has no bearing whatever upon the meaning of extinction today. We are not protecting Mount Graham red squirrels because we fear for global stability in a distant future not likely to include us. We are trying to preserve populations and environments because the comfort and decency of our present lives, and those of fellow species that share our planet, depend upon such stability. Mass extinctions may not threaten distant futures, but they are decidedly unpleasant for species in the throes of their power (particularly if triggered by such truly catastrophic events as extraterrestrial impact). At the appropriate scale of our lives, we are just a species in the midst of such a moment. And to say that we should let the squirrels go (at our immediate scale) because all species eventually die (at geological scales) makes about as much sense as arguing that we shouldn't treat an easily curable childhood infection because all humans are ultimately and inevitably mortal. I love geological time—a wondrous and expansive notion that sets the foundation of my chosen profession, but such immensity is not the proper scale of my personal life.

The same issue of scale underlies the main contributions that my profession of paleontology might make to our larger search for an environmental ethic. This decade, a prelude to the millennium, is widely and correctly viewed as a turning point that will lead either to environmental perdition or stabilization. We have fouled local nests before and driven regional faunas to extinction, but we have never been able to unleash planetary effects before our current concern with ozone holes and putative global warming. In this context, we are searching for proper themes and language to express our environmental worries.

I don't know that paleontology has a great deal to offer, but I would advance one geological insight to combat a well-meaning, but seriously flawed (and all too common), position and to focus attention on the right issue at the proper scale. Two linked arguments are often promoted as a basis for an environmental ethic:

1. That we live on a fragile planet now subject to permanent derailment and disruption by human intervention;

2. That humans must learn to act as stewards for this threatened world.

Such views, however well intentioned, are rooted in the old sin of pride and exaggerated self-importance. We are one among millions of species, stewards of nothing. By what argument could we, arising just a geological microsecond ago, become responsible for the affairs of a world 4.5 billion years old, teeming with life that has been evolving and diversifying for at least three-quarters of that immense span? Nature does not exist for us, had no idea we were coming, and doesn't give a damn about us. Omar Khayyám was right in all but his crimped view of the earth as battered when he made his brilliant comparison of our world to an eastern hotel:

> Think, in this battered Caravanserai
> Whose Portals are alternate
> Night and Day,
> How Sultan after Sultan with his Pomp
> Abode his destined Hour, and
> went his way.

This assertion of ultimate impotence could be countered if we, despite our late arrival, now held power over the planet's future (argument number one above). But we don't, despite popular misperception of our might. We are virtually powerless over the earth at our planet's own geological time scale. All the megatonnage in our nuclear arsenals yield but one ten-thousandth the power of the asteroid that might have triggered the Cretaceous mass extinction. Yet the earth survived that larger shock and, in wiping out dinosaurs, paved the road for the evolution of large mammals, including humans. We fear global warming, yet even the most radical model yields an earth far cooler than many happy and prosperous times of a prehuman past. We can surely destroy ourselves, and take many other species with us, but we can barely dent bacterial diversity and will surely not remove many million species of insects and mites. On geological scales, our planet will take good care of itself and let time clear the impact of any human malfeasance. The earth need never seek a henchman to wreak Henry's vengeance upon Thomas à Becket: "Who will free me from this turbulent priest?" Our planet simply waits.

People who do not appreciate the fundamental principle of appropriate scales often misread such an argument as a claim that we may therefore cease to worry about environmental deterioration—just as Copeland argued falsely that we need not fret about extinction. But I raise the same counterargument. We cannot threaten at geological scales, but such vastness is entirely inappropriate. We have a legitimately parochial interest in our own lives, the happiness and prosperity of our children, the suffering of our fellows. The planet will recover from nuclear holocaust, but we will be killed and maimed by the billions, and our cultures will perish. The earth will prosper if polar icecaps melt under a global greenhouse, but most of our major cities, built at sea level as ports and harbors, will founder, and changing agricultural patterns will uproot our populations.

We must squarely face an unpleasant historical fact. The conservation movement was born, in large part, as an elitest attempt by wealthy social leaders to preserve wilderness as a domain for patrician leisure and contemplation (against the image, so to speak, of poor immigrants traipsing in hordes through the woods with their Sunday picnic baskets). We have never entirely shaken this legacy of environmentalism as something opposed to immediate human needs, particularly of the impoverished and unfortunate. But the Third World expands and contains most of the pristine habitat that we yearn to preserve. Environmental movements cannot prevail until they convince people that clean air and water, solar power, recycling, and reforestation are best solutions (as they are) for human needs at human scales—and not for impossibly distant planetary futures.

I have a decidedly unradical suggestion to make about an appropriate environmental ethic—one rooted, with this entire essay, in the issue of appropriate human scale versus the majesty, but irrelevance, of geological time. I have never been much attracted to the Kantian categorical imperative in searching for an ethic—to moral laws that are absolute and unconditional and do not involve any ulterior motive or end. The world is too complex and sloppy for such uncompromising attitudes (and God help us if we embrace the wrong principle, and then fight wars, kill, and maim in our absolute certainty). I prefer the messier "hypothetical imperatives" that invoke desire, negotiation, and reciprocity. Of these "lesser," but altogether wiser and deeper, principles, one has stood out for its independent derivation, with different words but to the same effect, in culture after culture. I imagine that our various societies grope toward this principle because structural stability, and basic decency necessary for any tolerable life, demand such a maxim. Christians call this principle the "golden rule"; Plato, Hillel, and Confucius knew the same maxim by other names. I cannot think of a better principle based on enlightened self-interest. If we all treated others as we wish to be treated ourselves, then decency and stability would have to prevail.

I suggest that we execute such a pact with our planet. She holds all the cards and has immense power over us—so such a compact, which we desperately need but she does not at her own time scale, would be a blessing for us, and an indulgence for her. We had better sign the papers while she is still willing to make a deal. If we treat her nicely, she will keep us going for a while. If we scratch her, she will bleed, kick us out, bandage up, and go about her business at her planetary scale. Poor Richard told us that "necessity never made a good bargain," but the earth is kinder than human agents in the "art of the deal." She will uphold her end; we must now go and do likewise.

DISCUSSION TOPICS

1. How does Gould make the argument that we should not let a species (for example, the Mount Graham red squirrel) become extinct, in light of of the fact that over 99% of all species have become

extinct, and all eventually are expected to do so.

2. Do you believe Gould is correct in his view that humans have much less importance over a long-term (geological) time scale than we would like to think? What reasons would you give to support or reject this position?

3. Will a ''Golden Rule'' relationship with our planet work if only one side (humans) can consciously agree to the terms? Explain your reasoning.

CHAPTER EXERCISES

With which of the authors in this chapter do you find yourself in closest agreement, and at greatest odds? What are the decisive points made by each respective author that most influenced your decision?

CASE FOR CLASS DEBATE

The proposal to purchase a 40,000-hectare parcel of private timber lands and form a national park is estimated to cost about 1300 local jobs over the next eight years in a community of 55,000 people.

Using the debate guidelines presented in Appendix A, have a class debate over the wisdom of this proposal on the basis of anthropocentric considerations only. Thus, economics, aesthetic considerations, and impacts on current people and future generations would be acceptable, whereas arguments based on extending moral consideration to animals or the natural environment itself would be excluded. Which human concerns and values were appealed to by each side? Which were most persuasive?

FOR FURTHER READING

Donagan, A. *The Theory of Morality.* Chicago: University of Chicago Press, 1977. A clear statement of traditional morality as grounded in reason, of the Kantian variety. Chapter 7, pp. 229-243 is especially relevant.

Ehrenfeld, David. *The Arrogance of Humanism.* New York: Oxford University Press, 1978. Ehrenfeld provides an excellent commentary on problems associated with a dominionistic attitude toward nature, particularly with the belief that technology can be used to solve all of humans ills.

Ferré, Frederick. *Philosophy of Technology.* Englewood Cliffs, N.J: Prentice-Hall, 1988. With so much of the human capacity to dominate the rest of the natural world based on technology, this book by Ferré provides an insightful look at the relationship of technology to intelligence, modern existence, ethics, religion and metaphysics, and life in general.

Frey, R. G. ''Rights, Interests, Desires and Beliefs(?).'' *American Philosophical Quarterly* 16:233-239, 1979. While concerned predominantly with the relationship of humans to nonhuman animals, many of the arguments presented by Frey are easily applicable to wildlife in particular and the natural environment in general.

Hardin, G. *Exploring New Ethics for Survival.* New York: Viking Press, 1972. Initially written to clarify the logic of his article, ''Tragedy of the Commons,'' this book provides a strong statement on the necessity for humans to plan and take charge of their destiny. An articulate presentation of one anthropocentric vision.

Hughes, J. Donald. *Ecology in Ancient Civilization.* Albuquerque, N.M.: University of New Mexico Press, 1975. Hughes presents an environmental history from the ancient world through Jewish, Greek, Roman, and Christian cultures, to gain insights on attitudes found in modern Western societies.

Hughes, J. Donald. ''Ecology in Ancient Greece.'' *Inquiry* 18: 115-125, 1975. Hughes provides insight into two major strands of Greek thinking, as espoused by Aristotle and Theophrastus, and their relation to anthropocentric environmental ethics in Western society.

Kozlovsky, Daniel G. *An Ecological and Evolutionary Ethic,* Englewood Cliffs, N.J.: Prentice-Hall, 1974. Written by a biologist-philosopher who developed lines of thought similar to some deep ecologists. Assesses current anthropocentric perspectives.

McCloskey, A.J. *Ecological Ethics and Politics.* Totowa, N.J.: Rowman and Littlefield, 1983. An argument for an enlightened self-interest. Author adopts a liberal ''ecologically informed'' position in rejecting the ''preservationist authoritarian'' approach. He welcomes increased technological management of nature.

Nash, Roderick F. *American Environmentalism: Readings in Conservation History,* 3rd ed. New York: McGraw-Hill, An excellent selection of readings from leaders in the American environmentalist movement, 1832 to 1988. Several provide insights on the role of anthropocentrism on our environmental impacts. Examples include that of Wilbur Jacobs (pp. 25-30), who summarizes the devastating impact of pioneers on North

American lands, and Gifford Pinchot's (pp. 73-79) elucidation of his philosophy that conservation means the greatest good of our natural resources to the greatest number for the longest time.

Norton, Bryan G. *Why Preserve Natural Diversity?* Princeton, N.J.: Princeton University Press, 1987. Provides a clarification and taxonomy of anthropocentrism in the introductory chapter (pp. 3-22).

Partridge, Ernest. ''On the Rights of Future Generations,'' in *Upstream/Downstream,* Donald Scherer, ed. Philadelphia: Temple University Press, 1990. Thoughtfully evaluates five arguments (pp. 40-66) used to discount extending moral concern to future human generations, and finds all of them lacking.

Rollin, Bernard E. *Animal Rights and Human Morality.* Buffalo, N.Y.: Prometheus Books, 1981. A clear, articulate account of anthropocentrism (pp. 3-64) developed as part of his larger theme of justifying moral concern for nonhuman animals.

Shrader-Frechette, K.S. *Environmental Ethics.* Pacific Grove, Calif.: The Boxwood Press, 1981. A collection of readings on many aspects of environmental ethics; pages 1 to 56 cover the pros and cons of several forms of secular anthropocentrism.

Spiro, J.G., and N. Carter. Where were you when I laid the foundations of the Earth? IUCN Bulletin 16(10-12): 127-128, 1985. A short paper pointing out evidence for the conservation concept of ''wise use'' in the Torah.

Squiers, E.R. (ed). The environmental crisis: The ethical dilemma. AuSable Trails Institute of Environmental Studies, Mancelona, Michigan, 1982. A collection of papers presenting environmental ethics from a Christian perspective.

White, L.R., Jr. The historical roots of our ecological crisis. Science 155: 1203-1207, 1967. The classic paper on how Christianity, as an anthropocentric religion, has played a leading role in bringing about the environmental crisis.

CHAPTER SEVEN

Individualism

In this chapter we discuss several perspectives which affirm the moral standing of nonhuman as well as human individuals. We identify what these approaches have in common and the differences between those views which include only individual animals and those which include individual plants as well.

THE REJECTION OF HOLISM

All of the authors in this section affirm that only individuals can be meaningfully said to have moral value in and of themselves. Neither species (populations of individuals) nor ecosystems embody moral value. For example, Regan points out in his essay, "The Case for Animal Rights," that individuals are the paradigmatic holders of rights, since it is individuals who are conscious, who feel and make decisions, who care about what happens to them, who are centers of life. He maintains that it is unclear what could be meant by attributing rights to *collections* of individuals.

Singer's position, addressed in his essay, "Equal-

ity for Animals?," is equally individualistic, although he talks in terms of interests rather than of rights. Singer follows the utilitarian lead of Jeremy Bentham in locating moral good and bad in the happiness or unhappiness of sentient individuals (those individuals capable of feeling pleasure and pain). Utilitarianism is an aggregative ethic. Thus, to arrive at the best moral choice, a moral agent must consider the probable consequences issuing from his or her actions for all of the sentient individuals affected by the action. The moral agent then sums these positive and negative consequences to decide whether to engage in the proposed action. Bentham tells us that in this summation each one counts for one, and no one counts for more than one.

Paul Taylor in an excerpt from *Respect for Nature* tries to account for the relationships between individuals in an ecosystem while still retaining the moral locus within the individual. He proposes that while the good of an individual is the full development of its biological powers, the good of a population of individuals is arrived at by assessing the optimal *average* good of individuals in that population. Thus even though ''good'' primarily applies to the welfare of individuals, we can speak of the ''statistical good'' of a species or a population.[1]

TAKING EQUALITY SERIOUSLY

Peter Singer and Tom Regan both have developed theories building on the principle of equality. Singer argues that equality means the equal consideration of the interests of individuals rather than equal treatment of individuals. He maintains that any individual with interests or with sentience must be morally considered. The species membership of the individual is irrelevant to this consideration.

Tom Regan bases his argument for animal rights on the notion of the equality of inherent value. Inherent value is used by Regan to mean what we termed ''intrinsic value'' in Chapter 2. This value is possessed by all individuals who are ''subjects of a life.'' Subjects of a life have some sense of the past and anticipation of the future, as well as a sufficiently unified consciousness to make it meaningful to talk of their life being better or worse for *them*.[2] Regan distinguishes between moral agents and moral patients. Moral agents can be held morally accountable for the acts they perform or fail to perform, whereas moral patients cannot. Moral patients are unable to formulate or to act upon moral principles, although they are conscious, sentient, and have a psychophysical identity over time.[3] Regan maintains that moral patients have inherent value equal to that of moral agents and have an equal right to respectful treatment.

James Rachels in his essay, ''Morality Without the Idea that Humans are Special,'' develops Singer's arguments against speciesism by arguing that speciesism violates the principle of ''relevant difference.'' This principle holds that differences in the treatment of individuals must be based on morally relevant differences between those individuals. Simply citing species membership is not sufficient to justify different treatments of individuals.

The ''reverence for life'' philosophy espoused by Albert Schweitzer in his essay,'' The Ethics of Reverence for Life,'' affirms the equality of value of everything that lives, and rejects as human arrogance the attempt to assign more value to one life than another. Similarly, Paul Taylor's ''respect for nature'' view includes the strong affirmation of the equal inherent value of all organisms as teleological centers of life. Taylor distinguishes between the inherent worth of organisms and their merit, as judged by the standards of some external criterion, such as that of usefulness to human beings. However, Goodpaster states that it is consistent to both acknowledge the moral considerability of all life forms and to acknowledge degrees of moral significance.[4]

DO ALL INDIVIDUALS COUNT MORALLY?

''Zootic individualism'' is the name we have given to the position that animals and only animals are conscious subjects of a life and therefore deserve moral consideration. Singer, Regan, and Rachels are representative of this view. Regan restricts his account to adult mammals, because such animals clearly exhibit the conscious individuality which is the basis of his concept of inherent value. Singer casts his net a bit wider and includes all organisms which possess a

---

1. Paul Taylor, *Respect for Nature: A Theory of Environmental Ethics* (Princeton, N.J.: Princeton University Press, 1986), pp. 69-71.

2. Rachels has recently used the term ''biographical life'' to refer to those individuals who are subjects of a life. See James Rachels, *Created from Animals: The Moral Implications of Darwinism* (Oxford: Oxford University Press, 1990), p. 199.

3. Sapontzis argues that animals can be virtuous (do good actions) even though they do not fulfill the other criteria for moral agents. See S.F. Sapontzis, ''Are Animals Moral Beings?'' *American Philosophical Quarterly* 17, No. 1 (January 1980): 45-52.

4. For a brief critique of Regan from the standpoint of a theory attributing intrinsic but differing value to all individuals, see Susan Armstrong-Buck, ''Whitehead's Metaphysical System as a Foundation for Environmental Ethics,'' *Environmental Ethics* 8 (Fall 1986): 241-259, especially 254-256.

central nervous system. There is considerable empirical evidence for animal consciousness.[5]

"Biotic individualism" refers to the position that all living organisms have interests or a good of their own and hence moral value. Schweitzer, Taylor, and Goodpaster argue that being alive is sufficient for an individual to deserve respectful treatment. Schweitzer's well-known concept of reverence for life is updated and refined by Taylor in his "respect for nature" doctrine. Goodpaster in his essay, "On Being Morally Considerable," maintains that there is no good reason to restrict moral considerability to sentient individuals, because plants have discernible interests as well.[6]

---

5. Much recent investigation is discussed in *The Unheeded Cry: Animal Consciousness, Animal Pain and Science,* by Bernard E. Rollin (Oxford: Oxford University Press, 1990). Donald Griffin challenges contemporary behaviorism in *Animal Thinking* (Cambridge, Mass.: Harvard University Press, 1984).

6. Goodpaster's argument has been refined by Gary E. Varner in "Biological Functions and Biological Interests," *The Southern Journal of Philosophy* 28, No. 2 (1990): 251-270. Tom Birch has recently argued that the entire project of determining criteria for moral considerability should be abandoned in favor of extending moral consideration to all entities without regard to their meeting a standard which human beings have created. See Tom Birch, "Universal Considerability: All the Way Down with Considerability," *Environmental Ethics* (in press).

The Case for Animal Rights

Tom Regan

Tom Regan (b. 1938) teaches philosophy at North Carolina State University in Raleigh. He has been a prolific author and editor and is a leader in the animal rights movement. Regan's concept of "subject-of-a-life" encompasses those individuals who have beliefs and desires, an emotional life, and a psychophysical identity over time (their experience is psychologically continuous and associated with the same body). He states that this definition applies most clearly to normal adult mammals.[7] Subjects-of-a-life can be either moral agents or moral patients.[8] Moral patients are those individuals who are not morally accountable (for example, human infants, the mentally deranged, and most other mammals). Regan postulates that both moral agents and moral patients have inherent value, and that they have it equally. Inherent value refers to the value of an individual as a subject-of-a-life. This value is independent of the instrumental value of the individual for others and also is independent of the value of that individual's experiences, such as how much pleasure that individual has or how "cultivated" its tastes are.

According to Regan, those who have inherent value are entitled to respectful treatment. Thus, Regan rules out hunting and trapping as well as most forms of wildlife management as the promotion of maximum sustainable yield of game. Members of an endangered species are no more valuable than members of other species. Since all animals deserve respectful treatment, it is mainly human practices which need management. For Regan, holistic views such as Aldo Leopold's land ethic are "environmental fascism" because the individual has no value in itself. Regan believes that if human beings show proper respect for the rights of the individuals who make up the biotic community, the biotic community itself will be preserved.

---

7. Tom Regan, *The Case for Animal Rights* (Berkeley: University of California Press, 1983), p. 239.

8. Tom Regan, *The Case for Animal Rights,* pp. 151-156.

. . . To be the subject-of-a-life, in the sense in which this expression will be used, involves more than merely being alive and more than merely being conscious. . . . [I]ndividuals are subjects-of-a-life if they have beliefs and desires; perception, memory, and a sense of the future, including their own future; an emotional life together with feelings of pleasure and pain; preference- and welfare-interests; the ability to initiate action in pursuit of their desires and goals; a psychophysical identity over time; and an individual welfare in the sense that their experiental life fares well or ill for them, logically independently of their utility for others and logically independently of their being the object of anyone else's interests. Those who satisfy the subject-of-a-life criterion themselves have a distinctive kind of value—inherent value—and are not to be viewed or treated as mere receptacles. . . .

The subject-of-a-life criterion identifies a similarity that holds between moral agents and patients. Is this similarity a relevant similarity, one that makes viewing them as inherently valuable intelligible and nonarbitrary? The grounds for replying affirmatively are as follows: (1) A relevant similarity among all those who are postulated to have equal inherent value must mark a characteristic shared by all those moral agents and patients who are here viewed as having such value. The subject-of-a-life criterion satisfies this requirement. *All* moral agents and *all* those moral patients with whom we are concerned *are* subjects of a life that is better or worse for them, in the sense explained, logically independently of the utility they have for others and logically independently of their being the object of the interests of others. (2) Since inherent value is conceived to be a categorical value, admitting of no degrees, any supposed relevant similarity must itself be categorical. The subject-of-a-life criterion satisfies this requirement. This criterion does not assert or imply that those who meet it have the status of subject of a life to a greater or lesser degree, depending on the degree to which they have or lack some favored ability or virtue (e.g., the ability for higher mathematics or those virtues associated with artistic excellence). One either *is* a subject-of-a-life, in the sense explained, or one *is not*. All those who are, are so equally. The subject-of-a-life criterion thus demarcates a categorical status shared by all moral agents and those moral patients with whom we are concerned. (3) A relevant similarity between moral agents and patients must go some way toward illuminating why we have direct duties to both and why we have less reason to believe that we have direct duties to individuals who are neither moral agents nor patients, even including those who, like moral agents and those patients we have in mind, are alive. This requirement also is satisfied by the subject-of-a-life criterion. Not all living things are subjects of a life, in the sense explained; thus not all living things are to be viewed as having the same moral status, given this criterion, and the differences concerning our confidence about having direct duties to some (those who are subjects) and our not having direct duties to others (those who are not subjects) can be at least partially illuminated because the former meet, while the latter fail to meet, the subject-of-a-life criterion. For these reasons, the subject-of-a-life criterion can be defended as citing a relevant similarity between moral agents and patients, one that makes the attribution of equal inherent value to them both intelligible and nonarbitrary. . . .

If individuals have equal inherent value, then any principle that declares what treatment is due them as a matter of justice must take their equal value into account. The following principle (*the respect principle*) does this: *We are to treat those individuals who have inherent value in ways that respect their inherent value.* . . . The principle does not apply only to how we are to treat some individuals having inherent value (e.g., those with artistic or intellectual virtues). It enjoins us to treat *all* those individuals having inherent value in ways that respect their value, and thus it requires respectful treatment of all who satisfy the subject-of-a-life criterion. Whether they are moral agents or patients, we must treat them in ways that respect their equal inherent value. . . .

It is not an act of kindness to treat animals respectfully. It is an act of justice. It is not ''the sentimental interests'' of moral agents that grounds our duties of justice to children, the retarded, the senile, or other moral patients, including animals. It is respect for

their inherent value. The myth of the privileged moral status of moral agents has no clothes.

WHY HUNTING AND TRAPPING ARE WRONG

Since animals can pose innocent threats and because we are sometimes justified in overriding their rights when they do, one cannot assume that all hunting or trapping must be wrong. If rabid foxes have bitten some children and are known to be in the neighboring woods, and if the circumstances of their lives assume future attacks if nothing is done, then the rights view sanctions nullifying the threat posed by these animals. When we turn from cases where we protect ourselves against the innocent threats wild animals pose, to the activities of hunting and trapping, whether for commercial profit or ''sport,'' the rights view takes a dim view indeed. Standard justifications of the ''sport'' of hunting—that those who engage in it get exercise, take pleasure in communion with nature, enjoy the camaraderie of their friends, or take satisfaction in a shot well aimed—are lame, given the rights view. All these pleasures are obtainable by engaging in activities that do not result in killing any animal (walking through the woods with friends and a camera substitutes nicely), and the aggregate of the pleasures hunters derive from hunting could only override the rights of these animals if we viewed them as mere receptacles, which, on the rights view, they are not.

The appeal to tradition—an appeal one finds, for example, in support of fox hunting in Great Britain—has no more force in the case of hunting than it does in the case of any other customary abuse of animals—or humans. All that appeals to tradition signal in this case, and all they signify in related contexts, is that it is traditional to view animals as mere receptacles or as renewable resources. These appeals to tradition, in other words, are themselves symptomatic of an impoverished view of the value animals have in their own right and thus can play no legitimate role in defending a practice that harms them. Such appeals are as deficient in Great Britain, when made in behalf of the ''sport'' of fox hunting, as they are when made in Japan or Russia in defense of commercial whaling,[1] or in Canada in defense of the annual slaughter of seals. To allow these practices to continue, if certain quotas are not exceeded, is wrong, given the rights view, for reasons that will become clearer as we proceed.

Of course, those who hunt and trap sometimes rest their case on other considerations. It is not *their* pleasure that justifies what they do; rather, it is the humane service they perform for *the animals* that does. The situation, we are enjoined to believe, is this: If a certain number of animals are not hunted or trapped, there will be too many animals belonging to a given species for a given habitat to support. That being so, some of these animals will die of starvation because of their inability to compete successfully with the other animals in the habitat. To cull or harvest a certain number of these animals thus has the humane purpose and achieves the humane goal of sparing these animals the ordeal of death by starvation. How can the rights view, or any other view that is sensitive to the welfare of animals, find fault with that?

The rights view finds fault with this defense of hunting and trapping on several counts. First, the defense assumes that the death endured by hunted and trapped animals is always better (i.e., always involves less suffering) than the death these animals would endure as a result of starvation. This is far from credible. Not all hunters are expert shots, and not all trappers tend their traps responsibly or use traps that exhibit their ''humane'' concern for animals, the infamous leg-hold trap being perhaps the most notorious example to the contrary. Is it obvious that animals who experience a slow, agonizing death as a result of a hunter's poor shot or a poorly tended trap have a ''better death'' than those who die from starvation? One looks for an argument here and finds none. Unless or until one does, the defense of hunting and trapping on the grounds that they kill ''more humanely'' is specious.

Second, appeals to ''humane concern'' are dramatically at odds with the philosophy of current hunting and trapping practices, as well as with wildlife management generally. This philosophy, or the creed

of maximum sustainable yield, applies to hunting and trapping in the following way. Those who hunt and trap are legally permitted, within specified seasons, to ''harvest'' or ''crop'' a certain number of wildlife of various species, the quota for that season, both collectively and for each individual hunter, to be fixed by determining whether, together with the best estimates of natural mortality, those who hunt and trap will be able to ''harvest'' the same number next season, and the next, and so on. In this way the maximum sustainable yield is established. If this philosophy is applied successfully, hunters and trappers will be legally licensed to do the same thing in future seasons as others were licensed to do in the past—namely, kill up to a certain number (a certain quota) of animals. If, that is, restraint is exercised in each season, the *total* number of animals that can be harvested over time will be larger, or, to put the point in its simplest, starkest terms, if fewer animals are killed now, future generations of hunters will be able to kill a larger (aggregate) number of animals in the future, which will be better. This implication of the creed of maximum sustainable yield unmasks the rhetoric about ''humane service'' to animals. It must be a perverse distortion of the ideal of humane service to accept or engage in practices the explicit goal of which is to insure that there will be a larger, rather than a smaller, number of animals to kill! With ''humane friends'' like that, wild animals certainly do not need any enemies.

Essentially the same point can be made regarding the aggregate amount of suffering animals will endure if the creed of maximum sustainable yield is successful. If successful, the total number of animals who will die an agonizing death as a result of the poor shooting of hunters, plus those who die in similar agony as a result of poorly tended ''humane'' traps, plus those who die by natural causes will be larger than if other options were adopted. It is a moral smokescreen, therefore, to defend sport hunting and trapping by appeal to their humane service. The actions allowed by the philosophy of maximum sustainable yield speak louder than the lofty words uttered in its defense. The success of this philosophy would guarantee that more, not fewer, animals will be killed, and that more, not fewer, animals will die horrible deaths, either at the hands of humans or in the course of nature.

But it is not only the inconsistency between what it proclaims and what it implies that marks the undoing of the creed of maximum sustainable yield. That approach to decision making regarding wildlife management policies profoundly fails to recognize or respect the rights of wild animals. No approach to wildlife can be morally acceptable if it assumes that policy decisions should be made on the basis of aggregating harms and benefits. In particular, these decisions should not be made by appeal to the minimize harm principle. That principle sets before us what seems to be a laudatory goal—namely, to minimize the total amount of harm in general and suffering in particular. But that principle lacks the moral wherewithal to place any limits on how this laudatory goal is to be achieved; it lacks the means to assess the means used to achieve this end. If the rights of individuals are violated, that simply does not compute morally, given the minimize harm principle, if violating these rights is instrumental in achieving the goal of minimizing total harm. The rights view categorically denies the propriety of this approach to decision making. Policies that lessen the total amount of harm at the cost of violating the rights of individuals, whether these individuals are moral agents or patients, and, if the latter, human or animal, are wrong. Even if it were true, which it is not, that the philosophy of maximum sustainable yield would lead to a reduction in the total amount of death and suffering for undomesticated animals, it still would not follow that we should accept that philosophy. As it systematically ignores the rights of wild animals, so does it systematically violate them.

The rights view categorically condemns sport hunting and trapping. Though those who participate in it need not be cruel or evil people, what they do is wrong. And what they do is wrong because they are parties to a practice that treats animals as if they were a naturally recurring renewable resource, the value of which is to be measured by, and managed by reference to, human recreational, gustatory, aesthetic, social,

and other interests. Animals do renew themselves. Normally, they do not require human assistance to reproduce, any more than do trees, for example; but wild animals are not natural resources *here for us.* They have value apart from human interests, and their values is not reducible to their utility relative to our interests. To make a sport of hunting or trapping them is to do what is wrong because it is to fail to treat them with the respect they are due as a matter of strict justice.

Shorn of their appeal to their ''humane concern'' for wildlife, defenders of hunting and trapping are likely to protest that what they do is no different in kind from what other animals do in the state of nature. Animals routinely kill members of other (though only infrequently members of their own) species, and the death they suffer at the hands of other animals is gruesome enough to make even the most hardened heart wince. When it comes to interspecies relations, nature *is* red in tooth and claw. If the rights view professes to condemn sport hunting and trapping, it might be claimed, then it should do the same when it comes to the fatal interaction between animals themselves.

The rights view rejects this argument. Animals are not moral agents and so can have none of the same duties moral agents have, including the duty to respect the rights of other animals. The wolves who eat the caribou do no moral wrong, though the harm they cause is real enough. So it is that, according to the rights view, the overarching goal of wildlife management should not be to insure maximum sustainable yield; it should be to protect wild animals from those who would violate their rights—namely, sport hunters and trappers, commercial developers who destroy or despoil their natural habitat in the name of economic interest, and the like. *It is, in short, human wrongs that need managing, not the ''crop'' of animals.* Put affirmatively, the goal of wildlife management should be to defend wild animals in the possession of their rights, providing them with the opportunity to live their own life, by their own lights, as best they can, spared that human predation that goes by the name of ''sport.'' We owe this to wild animals, not out of kindness, nor because we are against cruelty, but out of respect for their rights. If, in reply, we are told that respecting the rights of animals in the wild in the way the rights view requires does not guarantee that we will minimize the total amount of suffering wild animals will suffer over time, our reply should be that this cannot be the overarching goal of wildlife management, once we take the rights of animals seriously. The total amount of suffering animals cause one another in the wild is not the concern of morally enlightened wildlife management. Being neither the accountants nor managers of felicity in nature, wildlife managers should be principally concerned with *letting animals be,* keeping human predators out of their affairs, allowing these ''other nations''[2] to carve out their own destiny.

When we move from sport to the commercial exploitation of wildlife, the moral scene is the same, only worse because the number of animals involved is greater. The rights view condemns the business of killing wild animals. Even if it is true that those whose present quality of life is tied to commerce in wild animals would be made worse-off if their business failed, that is no reason why we should continue to allow it. Like anyone else who enters the world of business, those whose business it is to kill wild animals must understand that they waive their right not to be made worse-off if their business fails. We have no duty to buy their products, and they have no right to require that we keep either their business or their present quality of life afloat. To appeal to the risk of diminished welfare in the case of their dependents is as lame in the present case as it was in the case of animal agriculture, as a defense in support of those whose business it is to kill wild animals. Moreover, while those in this business, like the rest of us, have the right to do what they can to avoid being made worse-off, they, like the rest of us, exceed this right when what they do violates the rights of others. And the commercial exploitation of wildlife does this— with a vengeance. Animals in the wild are treated as renewable resources, as if they had value only relative to the economic interests of those who feed off their dead carcasses. The rights view categorically condemns the commercial harvesting of wild animals, not because those embarked on this business are, or

must be, cruel or evil people, but because what they do is wrong. Justice will be done when, and only when, we refuse to allow these commercial ventures to continue.

One can imagine someone accepting the letter but not the spirit of the foregoing. For there are, after all, many nonhumans who are killed, either for sport or commerce, who are not animals in the limited sense in which this word has been used throughout this [discussion]—who are not, that is, normal mammalian animals, aged one year or more. A voice might be heard in support of duck hunting, for example, or in defense of the commercial exploitation of baby seals. Because similar protests might be raised in different contexts (for example, one might claim that what one does to nonmammals in science or to poultry in agriculture should not be covered by the same principles that apply to what is done to mammals), a review of this defense . . . will be deferred . . . [See p. 358 of *The Case for Animal Rights*—eds.]

Here it will suffice to raise a simple question. Let us assume that newly born *wild mammalian animals* (e.g., baby seals) do not yet meet the subject-of-a-life criterion; still, they clearly have the potential to do so. Why, then, should the moral standards that apply to how they may be treated differ in any way from those that apply to how human infants should be? The rights view denies that there is a nonarbitrary difference one could cite to justify treating the two differently. Unless one would be willing to approve of harming human infants in pursuit of sport or profit, one cannot approve of the similar treatment of infant mammalian animals.

No even partial assessment of hunting and trapping could be adequate if it failed to mention the matter of predator control. Sheep farmers in the southwestern United States, for example, are troubled by predatory animals, most notably coyotes, who attack grazing sheep, sometimes killing more than they need to subsist. The economic loss suffered by these farmers occasions their public outcry, and they have taken steps, with the assistance of federal funds and personnel, to control these predators.

Those who accept the rights view must work to bring an end to such predator control programs. The official justification of these programs assumes that the predators cause losses to persons engaged in a justified enterprise—namely, the animal industry. Since the rights view denies that this industry's treatment of animals is morally justified, the harm done to predatory animals in the name of minimizing the financial losses of those engaged in this industry is morally to be condemned. In the struggle between those involved in the animal industry and those predatory animals who inhabit the lands used in the name of this industry, it is the industry, not the predators, that ought to go. And if in response those in this industry appeal to their legal rights to the land and their legal ownership of the animals in their business, those who accept the rights view should reply, first, that the appeal to legal rights by itself never settles any moral question and, second, that the present legal status of farm animals, as owned property, is itself one of the traditions the rights view seeks to change.

HOW TO WORRY ABOUT ENDANGERED SPECIES

The rights view is a view about the moral rights of individuals. Species are not individuals, and the rights view does not recognize the moral rights of species to anything, including survival. What it recognizes is the prima facie right of individuals not to be harmed, and thus the prima facie right of individuals not to be killed. That an individual animal is among the last remaining members of a species confers no further right on that animal, and its right not to be harmed must be weighed equitably with the rights of any others who have this right. If, in a prevention situation, we had to choose between saving the last two members of an endangered species or saving another individual who belonged to a species that was plentiful but whose death would be a greater prima facie harm to that individual than the harm that death would be to the two, then the rights view requires that we save that individual. Moreover, numbers make no difference in such a case. If the choice were between saving the last thousand or million members of the species to which the two belong, that would make no

moral difference. The aggregate of their lesser harms does not harm any individual in a way that is prima facie comparable to the harm that would be done to this solitary individual. Nor would aggregating the losses of other interested parties (e.g., human aesthetic or scientific interests) make any difference. The sum of these losses harms no individual in a way that is prima facie comparable to the harm that would be done to the single individual if we chose to override his right.

The rights view is not opposed to efforts to save endangered species. It only insists that we be clear about the reasons for doing so. On the rights view, the reason we ought to save the members of endangered species of animals is not because the species is endangered but because the individual animals have valid claims and thus rights against those who would destroy their natural habitat, for example, or who would make a living off their dead carcasses through poaching and traffic in exotic animals, practices that unjustifiably override the rights of these animals. But though the rights view must look with favor on any attempt to protect the rights of any animal, and so supports efforts to protect the members of endangered species, these very efforts, aimed specifically at protecting the members of species that are endangered, can foster a mentality that is antagonistic to the implications of the rights view. If people are encouraged to believe that the harm done to animals matters morally *only when* these animals belong to endangered species, then these same people will be encouraged to regard the harm done to *other* animals as morally acceptable. In this way people may be encouraged to believe that, for example, the trapping of plentiful animals raises no serious moral question, whereas the trapping of rare animals does. This is not what the rights view implies. The mere size of the relative population of the species to which a given animal belongs makes no moral difference to the grounds for attributing rights to that individual animal or to the basis for determining when that animal's rights may be justifiably overridden or protected.

Though said before, it bears repeating: *the rights view is not indifferent to efforts to save endangered species. It supports these efforts.* It supports them, however, not because these animals are few in number; primarily it supports them because they are equal in value to all who have inherent value, ourselves included, sharing with us the fundamental right to be treated with respect. Since they are not mere receptacles or renewable resources placed here for our use, the harm done to them as individuals cannot be justified merely by aggregating the disparate benefits derived by commercial developers, poachers, and other interested third parties. That is what makes the commercial exploitation of endangered species wrong, not that the species are endangered. On the rights view, the same principles apply to the moral assessment of rare or endangered animals as apply to those that are plentiful, and the same principles apply whether the animals in question are wild or domesticated.

The rights view does not deny, nor is it antagonistic to recognizing, the importance of human aesthetic, scientific, sacramental, and other interests in rare and endangered species or in wild animals generally. What it denies is that (1) the value of these animals is reducible to, or is interchangeable with, the aggregate satisfaction of these human interests, and that (2) the determination of how these animals should be treated, including whether they should be saved in preference to more plentiful animals, is to be fixed by the yardstick of such human interests, either taken individually or aggregatively. Both points cut both ways, concerning, as they do, both how animals may and how they may not be treated. In particular, any and all harm done to rare or endangered animals, done in the name of aggregated human interests, is wrong, according to the rights view, because it violates the individual animal's right to respectful treatment. With regard to wild animals, the general policy recommended by the rights view is: *let them be!* Since this will require increased human intervention in *human* practices that threaten rare or endangered species (e.g., halting the destruction of natural habitat and closer surveillance of poaching, with much stiffer fines and longer prison sentences), the rights view sanctions this intervention, assuming that those hu-

mans involved are treated with the respect they are due. Too little is not enough.

Rights and Environmental Ethics: An Aside

The difficulties and implications of developing a rights-based environmental ethic should be abundantly clear by now and deserve brief comment before moving on. The difficulties include reconciling the *individualistic* nature of moral rights with the more *holistic* view of nature emphasized by many of the leading environmental thinkers. Aldo Leopold is illustrative of this latter tendency. "A thing is right," he states, "when it tends to preserve the integrity, stability, and beauty of the biotic community. It is wrong when it tends otherwise."[3] The implications of this view include the clear prospect that the individual may be sacrificed for the greater biotic good, in the name of "the integrity, stability, and beauty of the biotic community." It is difficult to see how the notion of the rights of the individual could find a home within a view that, emotive connotations to one side, might be fairly dubbed "environmental fascism." To use Leopold's telling phrase, man is "*only* a member of the biotic team,"[4] and as such has the same moral standing as any other "member" of "the team." If, to take an extreme, fanciful but, it is hoped, not unfair example, the situation we faced was either to kill a rare wildflower or a (plentiful) human being, and if the wildflower, as a "team member," would contribute more to "the integrity, stability, and beauty of the biotic community" than the human, then presumably we would not be doing wrong if we killed the human and saved the wildflower. The rights view cannot abide this position, not because the rights view categorically denies that inanimate objects can have rights (more on this momentarily) but because it denies the propriety of deciding what should be done to individuals who have rights by appeal to aggregative considerations, including, therefore, computations about what will or will not maximally "contribute to the integrity, stability, and beauty of the biotic community." Individual rights are not to be outweighed by such considerations (which is not to say that they are never to be outweighed). Environmental fascism and the rights view are like oil and water: they don't mix.

The rights view does not deny the possibility that collections or systems of natural objects might have inherent value—that is, might have a kind of value that is not the same as, is not reducible to, and is incommensurate with any one individual's pleasures, preference-satisfactions, and the like, or with the sum of such goods for any number of individuals. The beauty of an undisturbed, ecologically balanced forest, for example, might be conceived to have value of this kind. The point is certainly arguable. What is far from certain is how moral rights could be meaningfully attributed to the *collection* of trees or the ecosystem. Since neither is an individual, it is unclear how the notion of moral rights can be meaningfully applied. Perhaps this difficulty can be surmounted. It is fair to say, however, that no one writing in this important area of ethics has yet done so.[5]

Because paradigmatic right-holders are individuals, and because the dominant thrust of contemporary environmental efforts (e.g., wilderness preservation) is to focus on the whole rather than on the part (i.e., the individual), there is an understandable reluctance on the part of environmentalists to ''take rights seriously,'' or at least a reluctance to take them as seriously as the rights view contends we should. But this may be a case of environmentalists not seeing the forest for the trees—or, more accurately, of not seeing the trees for the forest. The implications of the successful development of a rights-based environmental ethic, one that made the case that individual inanimate natural objects (e.g., *this* redwood) have inherent value and a basic moral right to treatment respectful of that value, should be welcomed by environmentalists. If individual trees have inherent value, they have a kind of value that is not the same as, is not reducible to, and is incommensurate with the intrinsic values of the pleasures, preference-satisfactions, and the like, of others, and since the rights of the individual never are to be overridden merely on the grounds of aggregating such values for all those affected by the outcome, a rights-based environmental ethic would bar the door to those who would uproot wilderness in the name of ''human progress,'' whether this progress be aggregated economic, educational, recreational, or other human interests. On the rights view, assuming this could be successfully extended to inanimate natural objects, our general policy regarding wilderness would be precisely what the preservationists want—namely, let it be! Before those who favor such preservation dismiss the rights view in favor of the holistic view more commonly voiced in environmental circles, they might think twice about the implications of the two. There is the danger that the baby will be thrown out with the bath water. A rights-based environmental ethic remains a live option, one that, though far from being established, merits continued exploration. It ought not to be dismissed out of hand by environmentalists as being in principle antagonistic to the goals for which they work. It isn't. Were we to show proper respect for the rights of the individuals who make up the biotic community, would not the *community* be preserved? And is not that what the more holistic, systems-minded environmentalists want? . . .

NOTES

1. A fuller argument critical of commercial whaling is contained in my ''Why Whaling is Wrong,'' in Tom Regan, *All That Dwell Therein* (Berkeley: University of California Press, 1982).
2. The suggestion that we view wild animals as ''other nations, caught with ourselves in the net of life and time, fellow prisoners of the splendour and travail of the earth,'' comes from Henry Beston, *The Outermost House: A Year of Life on the Great Beach of Cape Cod* (New York: Viking Press, 1971), p. 25.
3. Aldo Leopold, *A Sand County Almanac* (New York: Oxford University Press, 1949), p. 217.
4. Ibid., p. 209, emphasis added.
5. For further remarks on these matters, see my ''What Sorts of Beings Can Have Rights?'' and ''The Nature and Possibility of an Environmental Ethic,'' both in Tom Regan, *All That Dwell Therein.*

DISCUSSION TOPICS

1. Do you find Regan's postulation of inherent value in individuals who are subjects-of-a-life to be convincing? Why or why not?

2. Do you agree with Regan that ecocentrism is environmental fascism? How do you think Leopold would respond to Regan's charge? (See Chapter Eight.)
3. Is Regan correct that protection of individual animals will protect the biotic community? Give an example supporting your position.
4. Explain and evaluate Regan's theory by applying it to endangered species of plants, plants harmful to animals, and plants beneficial to animals.

CLASS EXERCISE

You are a member of your state's fish and game commission. If you applied Regan's theories, what would be the outcome concerning:

1. Sport hunting of a deer population which is too large for its habitat?
2. Control of coyote predation on domestic sheep? Do you agree with Regan's position?

READING 43

Equality for Animals?

Peter Singer

Peter Singer (b. 1946) is an Australian philosopher who is Professor of Philosophy and Director of the Center for Human Bioethics at Monash University. His book Animal Liberation *(1975) was important in bringing the question of animal suffering to the attention of the general public. In the following reading from* Practical Ethics *(1979) Singer argues that racism and sexism are immoral because they violate the principle of equality of interests. Likewise, Singer argues, ''speciesism'' is immoral. It is immoral to discriminate against an individual simply because he or she is not a member of one's own species, rather than to consider the interests of that individual as equal to those of all other individuals.*

Singer proposes that any sentient individual has interests which must be given moral consideration. Singer argues that there is no good reason to deny that animals suffer: animals provide external signs of suffering which are similar to those of a human being; animals have central nervous systems with developed centers of emotion; and the capacity to feel pain is of survival benefit to animals. Also, language is not essential to suffering; human infants do not talk but we still accept that they experience pain. There is no morally defensible reason to consider animal suffering of less moral significance than human suffering, unless in a particular situation the mental powers of normal adult humans would either diminish or add to the suffering.

Singer distinguishes between causing suffering and killing on the grounds that the life of a self-aware being is more valuable than the life of a being without self-awareness. After considering several objections to his view, Singer concludes by arguing that ethical obligations are not limited to those who can reciprocate.

RACISM AND SPECIESISM

In the previous chapter I gave reasons for believing that the fundamental principle of equality, on which the equality of all human beings rests, is the principle of equal consideration of interests. Only a basic moral principle of this kind can allow us to defend a form of equality which embraces all human beings, with all the differences that exist between them. I shall now contend that while this principle does provide an adequate basis for human equality, it provides a basis which cannot be limited to humans. In other words I shall suggest that, having accepted the principle of equality as a sound moral basis for relations with others of our own species, we are also committed to accepting it as a sound moral basis for relations with those outside our own species—the nonhuman animals.

This suggestion may at first seem bizarre. We are used to regarding the oppression of blacks and women as among the most important moral and political issues facing the world today. These are serious matters, worthy of the time and energy of any concerned persons. But animals? Surely the welfare of animals is in a different category altogether, a matter for old ladies in tennis shoes to worry about. How can anyone waste their time on equality for animals when so many humans are denied real equality?

This attitude reflects a popular prejudice against taking the interests of animals seriously—a prejudice no better founded than the prejudice of white slave-owners against taking the interests of blacks seriously. It is easy for us to criticize the prejudices of our grandfathers, from which our fathers freed themselves. It is more difficult to distance ourselves from our own beliefs, so that we can dispassionately search for prejudices among them. What is needed now is a willingness to follow the arguments where they lead, without a prior assumption that the issue is not worth attending to.

The argument for extending the principle of equality beyond our own species is simple, so simple that it amounts to no more than a clear understanding of the nature of the principle of equal consideration of interests. We have seen that this principle implies that our concern for others ought not to depend on what they are like, or what abilities they possess (although precisely what this concern requires us to do may vary according to the characteristics of those affected by what we do). It is on this basis that we are able to say that the fact that some people are not members of our race does not entitle us to exploit them, and similarly the fact that some people are less intelligent than others does not mean that their interests may be disregarded. But the principle also implies that the fact that beings are not members of our species does not entitle us to exploit them, and similarly the fact that other animals are less intelligent than we are does not mean that their interests may be disregarded.

. . . [M]any philosophers have advocated equal consideration of interests, in some form or other, as a basic moral principle. Few recognized that the principle has applications beyond our own species. One of the few who did was Jeremy Bentham, the founding father of modern utilitarianism. In a forward-looking passage, written at a time when black slaves in the British dominions were still being treated much as we now treat nonhuman animals, Bentham wrote:

> The day *may* come when the rest of the animal creation may acquire those rights which never could have been withholden from them but by the hand of tyranny. The

French have already discovered that the blackness of the skin is no reason why a human being should be abandoned without redress to the caprice of a tormentor. It may one day come to be recognised that the number of the legs, the villosity of the skin, or the termination of the *os sacrum,* are reasons equally insufficient for abandoning a sensitive being to the same fate. What else is it that should trace the insuperable line? Is it the faculty of reason, or perhaps the faculty of discourse? But a full-grown horse or dog is beyond comparison a more rational, as well as a more conversable animal, than an infant of a day, or a week, or even a month, old. But suppose they were otherwise, what would it avail? The question is not, Can they reason? nor Can they *talk*? but, *Can they suffer?*[1]

In this passage Bentham points to the capacity for suffering as the vital characteristic that entitles a being to equal consideration. The capacity for suffering—or more strictly, for suffering and/or enjoyment or happiness—is not just another characteristic like the capacity for language, or for higher mathematics. Bentham is not saying that those who try to mark 'the insuperable line' that determines whether the interests of a being should be considered happen to have selected the wrong characteristic. The capacity for suffering and enjoying things is a prerequisite for having interests at all, a condition that must be satisifed before we can speak of interests in any meaningful way. It would be nonsense to say that it was not in the interests of a stone to be kicked along the road by a schoolboy. A stone does not have interests because it cannot suffer. Nothing that we can do to it could possibly make any difference to its welfare. A mouse, on the other hand, does have an interest in not being tormented, because it will suffer if it is.

If a being suffers, there can be no moral justification for refusing to take that suffering into consideration. No matter what the nature of the being, the principle of equality requires that its suffering be counted equally with the like suffering—in so far as rough comparisons can be made—of any other being. If a being is not capable of suffering, or of experiencing enjoyment or happiness, there is nothing to be taken into account. This is why the limit of sentience (using the term as a convenient, if not strictly accurate, shorthand for the capacity to suffer or experience enjoyment or happiness) is the only defensible boundary of concern for the interests of others. To mark this boundary by some characteristic like intelligence or rationality would be to mark it in an arbitrary way. Why not choose some other characteristic, like skin colour?

Racists violate the principle of equality by giving greater weight to the interests of members of their own race when there is a clash between their interests and the interests of those of another race. White racists do not accept that pain is as bad when it is felt by blacks as when it is felt by whites. Similarly those I would call 'speciesists' give greater weight to the interests of members of their own species when there is a clash between their interests and the interests of those of other species. Human speciesists do not accept that pain is as bad when it is felt by pigs or mice as when it is felt by humans.

That, then, is really the whole of the argument for extending the principle of equality to nonhuman animals; but there may be some doubts about what this equality amounts to in practice. In particular, the last sentence of the previous paragraph may prompt some people to reply: 'Surely pain felt by a mouse just is not as bad as pain felt by a human. Humans have much greater awareness of what is happening to them, and this makes their suffering worse. You can't equate the suffering of, say, a person dying slowly from cancer, and a laboratory mouse undergoing the same fate.'

I fully accept that in the case described the human cancer victim normally suffers more than the nonhuman cancer victim. This in no way undermines the extension of equal consideration of interests to nonhumans. It means, rather, that we must take care when we compare the interests of different species. In some situations a member of one species will suffer more than a member of another species. In this case we should still apply the principle of equal consideration of interests but the result of so doing is, of course, to give priority to relieving the greater suffering. A simpler case may help to make this clear.

If I give a horse a hard slap across its rump with my open hand, the horse may start, but it presumably feels little pain. Its skin is thick enough to protect it against a mere slap. If I slap a baby in the same way,

however, the baby will cry and presumably does feel pain, for its skin is more sensitive. So it is worse to slap a baby than a horse, if both slaps are administered with equal force. But there must be some kind of blow—I don't know exactly what it would be, but perhaps a blow with a heavy stick—that would cause the horse as much pain as we cause a baby by slapping it with our hand. That is what I mean by 'the same amount of pain' and if we consider it wrong to inflict that much pain on a baby for no good reason then we must, unless we are speciesists, consider it equally wrong to inflict the same amount of pain on a horse for no good reason.

There are other differences between humans and animals that cause other complications. Normal adult human beings have mental capacities which will, in certain circumstances, lead them to suffer more than animals would in the same circumstances. If, for instance, we decided to perform extremely painful or lethal scientific experiments on normal adult humans, kidnapped at random from public parks for this purpose, adults who entered parks would become fearful that they would be kidnapped. The resultant terror would be a form of suffering additional to the pain of the experiment. The same experiments performed on nonhuman animals would cause less suffering since the animals would not have the anticipatory dread of being kidnapped and experimented upon. This does not mean, of course, that it would be *right* to perform the experiment on animals, but only that there is a reason, which is not speciesist, for preferring to use animals rather than normal adult humans, if the experiment is to be done at all. It should be noted, however, that this same argument gives us a reason for preferring to use human infants—orphans perhaps—or retarded humans for experiments, rather than adults, since infants and retarded humans would also have no idea of what was going to happen to them. So far as this argument is concerned nonhuman animals and infants and retarded humans are in the same category; and if we use this argument to justify experiments on nonhuman animals we have to ask ourselves whether we are also prepared to allow experiments on human infants and retarded adults. If we make a distinction between animals and these humans, how can we do it, other than on the basis of a morally indefensible preference for members of our own species?

There are many areas in which the superior mental powers of normal adult humans make a difference: anticipation, more detailed memory, greater knowledge of what is happening, and so on. These differences explain why a human dying from cancer is likely to suffer more than a mouse. It is the mental anguish which makes the human's position so much harder to bear. Yet these differences do not all point to greater suffering on the part of the normal human being. Sometimes animals may suffer *more* because of their more limited understanding. If, for instance, we are taking prisoners in wartime we can explain to them that while they must submit to capture, search, and confinement they will not otherwise be harmed and will be set free at the conclusion of hostilities. If we capture a wild animal, however, we cannot explain that we are threatening its life. A wild animal cannot distinguish an attempt to overpower and confine from an attempt to kill; the one causes as much terror as the other.

It may be objected that comparisons of the sufferings of different species are impossible to make, and that for this reason when the interests of animals and humans clash the principle of equality gives no guidance. It is probably true that comparisons of suffering between members of different species cannot be made precisely. Nor, for that matter, can comparisons of suffering between different human beings be made precisely. Precision is not essential. As we shall see shortly, even if we were to prevent the infliction of suffering on animals only when the interests of humans will not be affected to anything like the extent that animals are affected, we would be forced to make radical changes in our treatment of animals that would involve our diet, the farming methods we use, experimental procedures in many fields of science, our approach to wildlife and to hunting, trapping and the wearing of furs, and areas of entertainment like circuses, rodeos, and zoos. As a result, a vast amount of suffering would be avoided.

So far I have said a lot about the infliction of suffering on animals, but nothing about killing them. This omission has been deliberate. The application of the principle of equality to the infliction of suffering is, in theory at least, fairly straightforward. Pain and suffering are bad and should be prevented or minimized, irrespective of the race, sex, or species of the being that suffers. How bad a pain is depends on how intense it is and how long it lasts, but pains of the same intensity and duration are equally bad, whether felt by humans or animals. When we come to consider the value of life, we cannot say quite so confidently that a life is a life, and equally valuable, whether it is a human life or an animal life. It would not be speciesist to hold that the life of a self-aware being, capable of abstract thought, of planning for the future, of complex acts of communication, and so on, is more valuable than the life of a being without these capacities. (I am not saying whether this view is justifiable or not; only that it cannot simply be rejected as speciesist, because it is not on the basis of species itself that one life is held to be more valuable than another.) The value of life is a notoriously difficult ethical question, and we can only arrive at a reasoned conclusion about the comparative value of human and animal life after we have discussed the value of life in general. . . . Meanwhile there are important conclusions to be derived from the extension beyond our own species of the principle of equal consideration of interests, irrespective of our conclusions about the value of life. . . .

SOME OBJECTIONS

This [writing] is not the first occasion on which I have put forward the position for which I have argued. . . . On previous occasions I have encountered a variety of questions and objections, some straightforward and predictable, some more subtle and unexpected. In this final section . . . I shall attempt to answer the most important of these objections. I shall begin with the more straightforward ones.

How Do We Know That Animals Can Feel Pain?

We can never directly experience the pain of another being, whether that being is human or not. When I see my daughter fall and scrape her knee, I know that she feels pain because of the way she behaves—she cries, she tells me her knee hurts, she rubs the sore spot, and so on. I know that I myself behave in a somewhat similar—if more inhibited—way when I feel pain, and so I accept that my daughter feels something like what I feel when I scrape my knee.

The basis of my belief that animals can feel pain is similar to the basis of my belief that my daughter can feel pain. Animals in pain behave in much the same way as humans do, and their behaviour is sufficient justification for the belief that they feel pain. It is true that, with the exception of those apes who have been taught to communicate by sign language, they cannot actually say that they are feeling pain—but then when my daughter was a little younger she could not talk either. She found other ways to make her inner states apparent, however, so demonstrating that we can be sure that a being is feeling pain even if the being cannot use language.

To back up our inference from animal behaviour, we can point to the fact that the nervous systems of all vertebrates, and especially of birds and mammals, are fundamentally similar. Those parts of the human nervous system that are concerned with feeling pain are relatively old, in evolutionary terms. Unlike the cerebral cortex, which developed only after our ancestors diverged from other mammals, the basic nervous system evolved in more distant ancestors common to ourselves and the other 'higher' animals. This anatomical parallel makes it likely that the capacity of animals to feel is similar to our own.

It is significant that none of the grounds we have for believing that animals feel pain hold for plants. We cannot observe behaviour suggesting pain—sensational claims to the contrary have not been substantiated—and plants do not have a centrally organized nervous system like ours.

Animals Eat Each Other, So Why Shouldn't We Eat Them?

This might be called the Benjamin Franklin Objection. Franklin recounts in his *Autobiography* that he was for a time a vegetarian but his abstinence from animal flesh came to an end when he was watching some friends prepare to fry a fish they had just caught. When the fish was cut open, it was found to have a smaller fish in its stomach. 'Well,' Franklin said to himself, 'if you eat one another, I don't see why we may not eat you' and he proceeded to do so.[2]

Franklin was at least honest. In telling this story, he confesses that he convinced himself of the validity of the objection only after the fish was already in the frying pan and smelling 'admirably well'; and he remarks that one of the advantages of being a 'reasonable creature' is that one can find a reason for whatever one wants to do. The replies that can be made to this objection are so obvious that Franklin's acceptance of it does testify more to his love of fried fish than his powers of reason. For a start, most animals that kill for food would not be able to survive if they did not, whereas we have no need to eat animal flesh. Next, it is odd that humans, who normally think of the behavior of animals as 'beastly' should, when it suits them, use an argument that implies we ought to look to animals for moral guidance. The decisive point, however, is that nonhuman animals are not capable of considering the alternatives open to them or of reflecting on the ethics of their diet. Hence it is impossible to hold the animals responsible for what they do, or to judge that because of their killing they 'deserve' to be treated in a similar way. Those who read these lines, on the other hand, must consider the justifiability of their dietary habits. You cannot evade responsibility by imitating beings who are incapable of making a choice.

Sometimes people point to the fact that animals eat each other in order to make a slightly different point. This fact suggests, they think, not that animals deserve to be eaten, but rather that there is a natural law according to which the stronger prey upon the weaker, a kind of Darwinian 'survival of the fittest' in which by eating animals we are merely playing our part.

This interpretation of the objection makes two basic mistakes, one a mistake of fact and the other an error of reasoning. The factual mistake lies in the assumption that our own consumption of animals is part of the natural evolutionary process. This might be true of a few primitive cultures which still hunt for food, but it has nothing to do with the mass production of domestic animals in factory farms.

Suppose that we did hunt for our food, though, and this was part of some natural evolutionary process. There would still be an error of reasoning in the assumption that because this process is natural it is right. It is, no doubt, 'natural' for women to produce an infant every year or two from puberty to menopause, but this does not mean that it is wrong to interfere with this process. We need to know the natural laws which affect us in order to estimate the consequences of what we do; but we do not have to assume that the natural way of doing something is incapable of improvement. . . .

Ethics and Reciprocity

In the earliest surviving major work of moral philosophy in the Western tradition, Plato's *Republic*, there is to be found the following view of ethics:

> They say that to do injustice is, by nature, good; to suffer injustice, evil; but that there is more evil in the latter than good in the former. And so when men have both done and suffered injustice and have had experience of both, any who are not able to avoid the one and obtain the other, think that they had better agree among themselves to have neither; hence they begin to establish laws and mutual covenants; and that which is ordained by law is termed by them lawful and just. This, it is claimed, is the origin and nature of justice—it is a mean or compromise, between the best of all, which is to do injustice and not be punished, and the worst of all, which is to suffer injustice without the power of retaliation. (*Republic* II 359)

This was not Plato's own view; he put it into the mouth of Glaucon in order to allow Socrates, the hero of his dialogue, to refute it. It is a view which has never gained general acceptance, but has not died away either. Echoes of it can be found in the ethical theories of contemporary philosophers like John Rawls, Gilbert Harman and John Mackie; and it has been used, by these philosophers and others, to justify the exclusion of animals from the sphere of ethics, or at least from its core. For if the basis of ethics is that I refrain from doing nasty things to others as long as

they don't do nasty things to me, I have no reason against doing nasty things to those who are incapable of appreciating my restraint and controlling their conduct towards me accordingly. Animals, by and large, are in this category. When I am surfing far out from shore and a shark attacks, my concern for animals will not help; I am as likely to be eaten as the next surfer, though he may spend every Sunday afternoon taking potshots at sharks from a boat. Since animals cannot reciprocate, they are, on this view, outside the limits of the ethical contract.

In assessing this conception of ethics we should distinguish between *explanations* of the origin of ethical judgments, and *justifications* of these judgments. The explanation of the origin of ethics in terms of a tacit contract between people for their mutual benefit is quite plausible (though not more plausible than a number of alternative accounts). But we could accept this account, as a historical explanation, without thereby committing ourselves to any views about the rightness or wrongness of the ethical system that has resulted. No matter how self-interested the origins of ethics may be, it is possible that once we have started thinking ethically we are led beyond these mundane premises. For we are capable of reasoning, and reason is not subordinate to self-interest. When we are reasoning about ethics we are using concepts that, as we saw in the first chapter of this book, take us beyond our own personal interest, or even the interest of some sectional group. According to the contract view of ethics, this universalizing process should stop at the boundaries of our community; but once the process has begun we may come to see that it would not be consistent with our other convictions to halt at that point. Just as the first mathematicians, who may have started counting in order to keep track of the number of people in their tribe, had no idea that they were taking the first steps along a path that would lead to the infinitesimal calculus, so the origin of ethics tells us nothing about where it will end.

When we turn to the question of justification we can see that contractual accounts of ethics have many problems. Clearly, such accounts exclude from the ethical sphere a lot more than nonhuman animals. Since permanent mental defectives are equally incapable of reciprocating, they must also be excluded. The same goes for infants and very young children; but the problems of the contractual view are not limited to these 'marginal cases.' The ultimate reason for entering into the ethical contract is, on this view, self-interest. Unless some additional universal element is brought in, one group of people has no reason to deal ethically with another if it is not in their interest to do so. If we take this seriously we shall have to revise our ethical judgments very drastically. For instance, the white slave traders who landed on a lonely part of the African coast and captured blacks to sell in America had no self-interested reason for treating blacks any better than they did. The blacks had no way of retaliating. If they had only been contractualists, the slave traders could have rebutted the abolitionists by explaining to them that ethics stops at the boundaries of the community, and since blacks are not part of their community they have no duties to them.

Nor is it only past practices that would be affected by taking the contractual model seriously. Though people often speak of the world today as a single community, there is no doubt that the power of people in, say, Chad, to reciprocate either good or evil that is done to them by, say, citizens of the United States is very limited. Hence it does not seem that the contract view provides for any obligations on the part of wealthy nations to poorer nations.

Most striking of all is the impact of the contract model on our attitude to future generations. 'Why should I do anything for posterity? What has posterity ever done for me?' would be the view we ought to take if only those who can reciprocate are within the bounds of ethics. There is no way in which those who will be alive in the year 2100 can do anything to make our lives better or worse. Hence if obligations only exist where there can be reciprocity, we need have no worries about problems like the disposal of nuclear waste. True, some nuclear wastes will still be deadly for a quarter of a million years; but as long as we put it in containers that will keep it away from us for 100 years, we have done all that ethics demands of us.

These examples should suffice to show that, whatever its origin, the ethics we have now does go beyond a tacit understanding between beings capable of rec-

iprocity, and the prospect of returning to such a basis is not appealing. Since no account of the origin of morality compels us to base our morality on reciprocity, and since no other arguments in favour of this conclusion have been offered, we should reject this view of ethics.

NOTES

1. Bentham, Jeremy, *An Introduction to the Principles of Morals and Legislation, Works,* XIX (New York: Russell and Russell, 1962), sec. 1, footnote to paragraph 4.
2. Benjamin Franklin, *Autobiography* (New Haven and London: Yale University Press, 1964), pp. 87-88.

DISCUSSION TOPICS

1. Do you find Singer's arguments against speciesism convincing? Why or why not?
2. Do you accept Singer's distinction between causing suffering and killing? Does Singer's argument allow the ''putting to sleep'' of homeless dogs?
3. Singer argues that the pain suffered by a rat generally is morally equivalent to that suffered by a human being in a similar situation. Do you agree? Why or why not?

READING 44

Morality Without the Idea that Humans are Special

James Rachels

James Rachels teaches philosophy at the University of Alabama at Birmingham. In this excerpt from Created From Animals: The Moral Implications of Darwinism *he elaborates the attack on speciesism begun by Singer by discussing four of its forms: radical, mild, unqualified, and qualified. ''Unqualified speciesism'' is the view that mere species alone are morally important. ''Qualified speciesism'' is the more sophisticated view that species-*

membership is correlated with morally significant differences. Qualified speciesism can focus on rationality and autonomy, linguistic ability, membership in the moral community, or sensitivity to harm. Rachels rejects all forms of speciesism on the basis of the principle of equality: that comparable interests of individuals should be given comparable moral weight. Only differences relevant to the situation justify different treatment. The excerpt concludes with Rachels' argument that this view of ''moral individualism'' requires that individuals who are subjects of a biographical life (that is, who have a psychologically continuous experience of past-present-future) be valued, and that the more complex an individual's life, the more wrong it is to kill that individual.

SPECIESISM

Recent writers on animal welfare have introduced the term 'speciesism' to refer to systematic discrimination against non-humans. (The term was coined by Richard Ryder, a British psychologist who quit experimenting on animals after he became convinced this was immoral, although Peter Singer's book *Animal Liberation* was responsible for popularizing the term.) Speciesism is said to be analogous to racism: it is the idea that the interests of the members of a particular species count for more than the interests of the members of other species, just as racism is the notion that the interests of the members of a particular race count for more. As Singer puts it:

> The racist violates the principle of equality by giving greater weight to the interests of members of his own race when there is a clash between their interests and the interests of those of another race. The sexist violates the principle of equality by favoring the interests of his own sex. Similarly the speciesist allows the interests of his own species to override the greater interests of members of other species. The pattern is identical in each case.

The traditional doctrine of human dignity is speciesist to the core, for it implies that the interests of humans have priority over those of all other creatures. But let me try to be a little more precise about this. Human speciesism can take two forms, one much more plausible than the other:

Radical speciesism: Even the relatively trivial interests of humans take priority over the vital interests of non-humans. Thus, if we have to choose between causing mild discomfort to a human, and causing excruciating pain to a non-human, we should prefer to cause pain to the non-human and spare the human.

Thus is the version of speciesism that Singer describes: one allows the interests of one's own species to override the *greater* interests of members of other species. We can, however, define a milder and more plausible version:

Mild speciesism: When the choice is between a relatively trivial human interest and a more substantial interest of a non-human, we may choose for the non-human. Thus it may be better to cause a little discomfort for a human than to cause agony for an animal. However, if the interests are comparable—say, if the choice is between causing the *same* amount of pain for a human or for a non-human—we should give preference to the human's welfare.

Many defenders of traditional morality have embraced the radical form of speciesism. Aquinas and Kant . . . both held that the interests of non-humans count for nothing, and therefore may be outweighed by any human interest whatever. Indeed, on their view there is no point in doing any 'weighing' at all: the human always wins, no matter what. Descartes even denied that non-humans have any interests that *could* be weighed. Contemporary readers might find their views too extreme, and yet still find mild speciesism to be an attractive doctrine.

The principle of equality, on the other hand, involves the rejection of even mild speciesism: it implies that humans and non-humans are, in a sense, moral equals—that is, it implies that the interests of non-humans should receive the *same* consideration as the comparable interests of humans. I suspect that, viewed in this light, the principle of equality will seem implausible to many readers. The doctrine of human dignity, at least when it is interpreted as involving only mild speciesism, might appear to be a much more plausible view. Therefore, if I am to defend the principle of equality, I need to explain why even mild speciesism should be rejected.

Unqualified Speciesism

In addition to distinguishing between radical and mild speciesism, we may distinguish between qualified and unqualified versions of the doctrine. The former distinction has to do with the extent of the view; the latter has to do with its logical basis.

Unqualified speciesism is the view that mere species alone is morally important. On this view, the bare fact that an individual is a member of a certain species, unsupplemented by any other consideration, is enough to make a difference in how that individual should be treated.

This is not a very plausible way of understanding the relation between species and morality, and generally it is not accepted even by those who defend traditional morality. To see why it is not plausible, consider the old science-fiction story 'The Teacher from Mars' by Eando Binder. The main character in that story is a Martian who has come to earth to teach in a school for boys. Because he is 'different'—seven feet tall, thin, with tentacles and leathery skin—he is taunted and abused by the students until he is almost driven out. Then, however, an act of heroism makes the boys realize they have been wrong, and the story ends happily with the ring-leader of the bullies vowing to mend his ways.

Written in 1941, the story is a not-so-thinly-disguised morality tale about racism. But the explicit point concerns species, not race. The teacher from Mars is portrayed as being, psychologically, exactly like a human: he is equally as intelligent, and equally as sensitive, with just the same cares and interests as anyone else. The only difference is that he has a different kind of body. And surely *that* does not justify treating him with less respect. Having appreciated this point, the reader is obviously expected to draw a similar conclusion about race: the fact that there are physical differences between whites and blacks—skin colour, for example—should make no moral difference either. . . .

Qualified Speciesism

But there is a more sophisticated view of the relation between morality and species, and it is this view that defenders of traditional morality have most often adopted. On this view, species alone is not regarded as morally significant. However, species-membership is correlated with *other* differences that *are* significant. The interests of humans are said to be more important, not simply because they are human, but because humans have morally relevant characteristics that other animals lack. This view might take several forms.

(1) *The idea that humans are in a special moral category because they are rational, autonomous agents.* Humans, it might be said, are in a special moral category because they are rational, autonomous agents. Humans can guide their own conduct according to their own conceptions of what ought to be done. (Since Kant, this has been the most popular way of describing the difference between humans and other animals, at least among philosophers.) It is this fact, rather than the 'mere' fact that they are human, that qualifies them for special consideration. This is why their interests are more important, morally speaking, than the interests of other species, although, it might be admitted, if the members of any other species were rational, autonomous agents, they would also go into the special moral category and would qualify for the favoured treatment. However, defenders of traditional morality insist that as a matter of fact no other species has this characteristic. So humans alone are entitled to full moral consideration.

Darwin, as we have seen, resisted the idea that humans have characteristics that are not shared by other animals. Instead he emphasized the continuities between species: if man is more rational than the apes, it is only a matter of degree, not of kind. But it may be of some interest to see what would follow *if* this were true. So let us set aside the Darwinian objection, and grant for the purpose of argument that humans are the only fully rational, autonomous agents. What would follow from this assumption?

Does the fact that someone is a rational autonomous agent make a difference in how he should be treated? Certainly it may. For such a being, the self-direction of his own life is a great good, valued not only for its instrumental worth but for its own sake. Thus paternalistic interference may be seen as an evil. To take a simple example: a woman might have a certain conception of how she wants to live her life. This conception might involve taking risks that we think are foolish. We might therefore try to change her mind; we might call attention to the risks and argue that they are not worth it. But suppose she will not heed our warnings: Are we then justified in forcibly preventing her from living her life as she chooses? It may be argued that we are not justified, for she is, after all, a rational, autonomous agent. It is different for someone who is *not* a fully rational being—a small child, for example. Then we feel justified in interfering with his conduct, to prevent him from harming himself. The fact that the child is not (yet, anyway) a fully rational agent justifies us in treating him differently from how we would treat someone who is a fully rational agent.

Of course, the same thing could be said to justify treating a human differently from a non-human. If we forcibly intervened to protect an animal fron danger, but did not do the same for a human, we might justify this by pointing to the fact that the human is a rational autonomous agent, who knew what she was doing and who had the right to make her own choice, while this was not true of the animal.

Now notice two points about this reasoning. First, the fact that one individual is a rational autonomous agent, while another is not, sometimes justifies treating a human differently from a non-human, but it also justifies treating some humans differently from other humans. This consideration does not simply separate humans from animals; it separates humans from other humans as well. Thus, even if we grant (as a good Darwinian would not) that humans are the only rational, autonomous agents, we still have not identified a characteristic that separates all humans from all non-humans.

Secondly, and more important, once we understand *why* being a rational agent makes a difference in how one may be treated, in those cases in which it does make a difference, it becomes clear that posses-

sion of this quality is not always relevant. As we have already observed, whether a difference is relevant depends on the kind of treatment that is in question. When the issue is paternalistic interference, it is relevant to note whether the individual whose behavior might be coerced is a rational agent. Suppose, however, that what is in question is not paternalistic interference, but putting chemicals in rabbits' eyes to test the safety of a new shampoo. To say that rabbits may be treated in this way, but humans may not, because humans are rational agents, is comparable to saying that one law-school applicant may be accepted, and another rejected, because one has a broken arm while the other has an infection.

Therefore, the observation that humans are rational autonomous agents cannot justify the whole range of differences between our treatment of humans and our treatment of non-humans. It can justify some differences in treatment, but not others.

There is still another problem for this form of qualified speciesism. Some unfortunate humans—perhaps because they have suffered brain damage—are not rational agents. What are we to say about them? The natural conclusion, according to the doctrine we are considering, would be that their status is that of mere animals. And perhaps we should go on to conclude that they may be used as non-human animals are used—perhaps as laboratory subjects, or as food?

Of course, traditional moralists do not accept any such conclusion. The interests of humans are regarded as important no matter what their 'handicaps' might be. The traditional view is, apparently, that moral status is determined by what is normal for the species. Therefore, because rationality is the norm, even non-rational humans are to be treated with the respect due to the members of a rational species. Carl Cohen, a philosopher at the University of Michigan, apparently endorses this view in his defence of using animals, but not humans, in medical experiments. Cohen writes:

> Persons who are unable, because of some disability, to perform the full moral functions natural to human beings are certainly not for that reason ejected from the moral community. *The issue is one of kind.* Humans are of such a kind that they may be the subject of experiments

only with their voluntary consent. The choices they make freely must be respected. Animals are of such a kind that it is impossible for them to give or withhold voluntary consent or to make a moral choice. What humans retain when disabled, animals never had.[1]

Let us pass over the obvious point that animals do seem to be able to withhold consent from participation in experiments—their frantic efforts to escape from the research setting, particularly when they are being caused acute discomfort, suggests that very strongly. But it is the more general theoretical point that we want to consider.

This idea—that how individuals should be treated is determined by what is normal for their species—has a certain appeal, because it does seem to express our moral intuitions about mentally deficient humans. 'We should not treat a person worse merely because he has been so unfortunate,' we might say about someone who has suffered brain damage. But the idea will not bear close inspection. A simple thought-experiment will expose the problem. Suppose (what is probably impossible) that an unusually gifted chimpanzee learned to read and speak English. And suppose he eventually was able to converse about science, literature, and morals. Finally he expresses a desire to attend university classes. Now there might be various arguments about whether to permit this, but suppose someone argued as follows: 'Only humans should be allowed to attend these classes. Humans can read, talk, and understand science. Chimps cannot.' But this chimp *can* do those things. 'Yes, but *normal* chimps cannot, and that is what matters.' Following Cohen, it might be added that 'The issue is one of kind,' and not one of particular abilities accidental to particular individuals.

Is this a good argument? Regardless of what other arguments might be persuasive, this one is not. It assumes that we should determine how an individual is to be treated, not on the basis of *its* qualities, but on the basis of *other* individuals' qualities. The argument is that this chimp may be barred from doing something that requires reading, despite the fact that he can read, because other chimps cannot read. That seems not only unfair, but irrational.

(2) *The idea that humans are in a special moral category because they can talk.* Traditionally, when Western thinkers characterized the differences between humans and other animals, the human capacity for language was among the first things mentioned. Descartes, as we have seen, thought that man's linguistic capacity was the clearest indication that he has a soul; and when Huxley was challenged by his working men to explain why kinship with the apes did not destroy 'the nobility of manhood,' he replied that 'man alone possesses the marvelous endowment of intelligible and rational speech.'

Is the fact that humans are masters of a syntactically complicated language, vastly superior to any communication-system possessed by non-humans, relevant to decisions about how they may be treated? In the preceding paragraphs I have already made some observations that bear on this. Clearly, it is sometimes relevant. It is relevant, for example, to the question of who will be admitted to universities. A knowledge of English is required to be a student in many universities, and humans, but not chimpanzees, meet this requirement. But not all humans qualify in this regard, and so it is reasonable to refuse admission to those humans. This means that it is the individual's particular linguistic capacity that is relevant to the admissions decision, and not the general capacities of 'mankind.' Moreover, there are many forms of treatment to which the question of linguistic ability is not relevant—torture, for example. (The reason why it is wrong to torture has nothing to do with the victim's ability to speak.) Therefore, the most that can be said about this 'marvelous endowment' is that *most* humans have it, and that it is relevant to *some* decisions about how they should be treated. This being so, it cannot be the justification of a principled policy of always giving priority to human interests.

It might be objected that this underrates the importance of language, because the implications of language are so diffuse. It isn't *simply* that knowing English enables one to read books, to ask and answer questions, to qualify for admission to universities, and so on. In addition to such discrete achievements, we have to consider the way that having a language enriches and extends all of one's other psychological capacities as well. A being with a language can have moral and religious beliefs that would otherwise be impossible; such a being's hopes, desires, and disappointments will be more complex; its activities will be more varied; its relationships with others will be characterized by greater emotional depth; and on and on. In short, its whole life will be richer and more complex. The lives of creatures who lack such a language will be correspondingly simpler. In light of this, it will be argued, isn't it reasonable to think that human language makes human life morally special?

There is obviously something to this. I think it is true that possession of a human language enriches almost all of one's psychological capacities; that this has consequences that ramify throughout one's life; and that this is a fact that our moral outlook should accommodate. But it is not obvious exactly how this fact should figure into our moral view. What, exactly, is its significance? It does not seem right to say that, because of this, human interests should always have priority over the interests of non-humans, for there may still be cases in which even the enriched capacities of humans are irrelevant to a particular type of treatment. I want to make a different suggestion about its significance.

Suppose the type of treatment in question is killing: say, we have to choose between causing the death of a human, and causing the death of a non-human animal. On what grounds may this choice be made? Although killing is a specific type of treatment, its implications are especially broad: one's death puts an end to all one's activities, projects, plans, hopes, and relationships. In short, it puts an end to one's whole life. Therefore, in making this decision it seems plausible to invoke a broadly inclusive criterion: we may say that the *kind of life* that will be destroyed is relevant to deciding which life is to be preferred. And in assessing the kind of life involved, we may refer, not just to particular facts about the creatures, but to summary judgements about what all the particular facts add up to. Humans, partly because of their linguistic capacities, have lives that are richer and more complex than the lives of other animals. For this reason, one may reasonably conclude that killing a human is worse than killing a non-human.

If this account is correct, it would also explain why it is worse to kill some non-humans than others. Suppose one had to choose between killing a rhesus monkey and swatting a fly. If we compare the two, we find that the life of the monkey is far richer and more complex than that of the fly, because the monkey's psychological capacities are so much greater. The communicative abilities of the monkey, we may note, also make an important difference here. Because the monkey is able to communicate with others of its own kind—even though its communicative skills are inferior to those of humans—its relations with its peers are more complex than they would otherwise be. (This is a clear illustration of Darwin's thesis that the differences between humans and non-humans are matters of degree, not kind.) In light of all this, we may conclude that it is better to swat the fly. This result is intuitively correct, and it lends additional plausibility to the general idea that, where killing is concerned, it is the richness and complexity of the life that is relevant to judgements about the wrongfulness of its destruction.

This is compatible with moral individualism only if we add a certain qualification, namely, that it is the richness and complexity of the *individual* life that is morally significant. Some humans, unfortunately, are not capable of having the kind of rich life that we are discussing. An infant with severe brain damage, even if it survives for many years, may never learn to speak, and its mental powers may never rise above a primitive level. In fact, its psychological capacities may be markedly inferior to those of a typical rhesus monkey. In that case, moral individualism would see no reason to prefer its life over the monkey's. This will strike many people as implausible. Certainly, the traditional doctrine of human dignity would yield a different result. Nevertheless, I think that moral individualism is correct on this point, and I will have more to say about this below. . . .

Where does this leave the relation between species and morality? The picture that emerges is more complex, but also more true to the facts, than traditional morality. The fact is that human beings are not simply 'different' from other animals. In reality, there is a complex pattern of similarities and differences. The matching moral idea is that in so far as a human and a member of another species are similar, they should be treated similarly, while to the extent that they are different they should be treated differently. This will allow the human to assert a right to better treatment whenever there is some difference between him and the other animal that justifies treating him better. But it will not permit him to claim greater rights simply because he is human, or because humans in general have some quality that he lacks, or because he has some characteristic that is irrelevant to the particular type of treatment in question. . . .

RETHINKING THE MORAL STATUS OF NON-HUMAN ANIMALS

One of the fundamental ideas expressed by moral individualism is that moral rules are species-neutral: the same rules that govern our treatment of humans should also govern our treatment of non-humans. . . .

[O]ur theory should shed some light on the question of the value of non-human life. Once we have become clear about the reasons why killing humans is wrong, we are in a position to ask whether the same reasons, or similar ones, also apply in the case of non-humans.

Humans, we observed, are the subjects of lives—not just biological lives, but biographical lives. It is our lives in the biographical sense that we value, and the point of the rule against killing is to protect the interests that we have in virtue of the fact that we are the subjects of such lives. Do non-human animals also have biographical lives? Clearly, many do not. Having a life requires some fairly sophisticated mental capacities. Bugs and shrimp do not have those capacities. They are too simple. But consider a more complex animal such as the rhesus monkey. The rhesus is a favourite research animal for experimental psychologists because, being so close to us from an evolutionary point of view, they share many of our psychological characteristics. They are intelligent and live in organized social groups; they communicate with one another; they care about each other and, as we have seen, they behave altruistically towards one

another. Monkey mothers and infants are bonded much as humans are. Moreover, they are not all alike: the lives and personalities of individual animals are surprisingly diverse. Their lives are not as intellectually and emotionally complex as those of humans, but clearly they do have lives.

Other examples could be given easily enough; twentieth-century investigators have confirmed Darwin's observation that the mental capacities of all the 'higher mammals' are similar to the capacities of humans. The situation seems to be that, when we consider the mammals closest to ourselves in the old phylogenetic scale, we find that they do have lives. Then the further down the scale we go, the less confidence we have that there is anything like a biographical life, until we reach the bugs and shrimp, where the notion of a biographical life has only the most doubtful application.

The moral view suggested by this is that animals, human and non-human, come under the protection of the rule against killing just to the extent that they are the subjects of biographical lives. But more needs to be said. There is no reason the wrongness of killing has to be an all-or-nothing matter; one killing could be more objectionable than another. Thus, killing an animal that has a rich biographical life might be more objectionable than killing one that has a simpler life. This corresponds fairly well to our pre-reflective intuitions. We think that killing a human is worse than killing a monkey, but we also think that killing a monkey is a more morally serious matter than squashing a bug. From an evolutionary perspective, this is fair enough. The lives of humans and non-humans need not be accorded exactly the same value, for the extra psychological capacities of humans provides reason why their lives may be valued more. At the same time, this does not mean that the lives of all other animals may be held cheap: on the contrary, consistency requires that to the extent that they have lives similar to our own, killing them must be regarded with a similar seriousness. The more complex their lives are, the greater the objection to destroying them.

This accords with some of our pre-reflective feelings, but it goes against others. The triumph of Darwinism during the past century has modified some of our intuitions about humans and other animals, but the transformation has by no means been complete. Our feelings are still largely shaped by pre-Darwinian notions. Thus many of us think nothing of killing even 'higher mammals' for food, to use their skins as ornamental clothing, or simply as sport. Moral individualism would require that these practices be reconsidered. Moreover, we feel instinctively that the life of *every* human being has what Kant called 'an intrinsic worth' or 'dignity' and so we tend to value every human life more than any non-human life, regardless of its particular characteristics. That is why the biological life of a Tay-Sachs infant, who will never develop into the subject of a biographical life, may be treated with greater respect than the life of an intelligent, sensitive animal such as a chimpanzee. Moral individualism would also imply that this judgement is mistaken. . . .

NOTE

1. Cohen, Carl, ''The Case for the Use of Animals in Biomedical Research,'' *The New England Journal of Medicine* 315: 865-870, 1986 (emphasis added).

DISCUSSION TOPICS

1. How would you classify your own views on the relationship between species membership and moral considerability?
2. Do you agree with Rachels' interpretation of the principle of equality? Why or why not?
3. Apply Rachels' view to whether some gazelles suspected of carrying a disease should be killed in order to scientifically study the condition of their internal organs in order to determine if they *are* carrying a disease transmissible to humans. What if the disease is transmissible to other wild animals? to livestock?

CLASS EXERCISE

1. Design a questionnaire to survey the views on speciesism of students in another class and their reasons for it. Classify the responses according to Rachels' four forms.

READING 45

The Ethics of Reverence for Life

Albert Schweitzer

Albert Schweitzer (1875–1965), a Swiss physician, musician, theologian, and philosopher, received the Nobel Prize in 1952. He established a world-famous medical hospital serving the people of equatorial Africa on the forested banks of the Ogowe River.

Schweitzer's ethics of reverence for life begins with the fundamental experience of reverence for one's own will to live amid other lives which will to live. The basic ethical principle is that maintaining and encouraging life is good, whereas destroying or obstructing life is bad. Reverence for life applies to all life, including that of insects and plants.

Schweitzer acknowledges that in the biological world one thing lives by destroying another, but he maintains that in human beings life manifests the yearning to unify itself. Each time we help another being, we are united with the divine will ''in which all life is one.'' His response to the inevitability of injuring other life is to bear the individual responsibility for causing such injury and to be careful to cause no more injury than is absolutely necessary.

. . . True philosophy must start from the most immediate and comprehensive fact of consciousness, which says: ''I am life which wills to live, in the midst of life which wills to live.'' This is not an ingenious dogmatic formula. Day by day, hour by hour, I live and move in it. At every moment of reflection it stands fresh before me. There bursts forth from it again and again as from roots that can never dry up, a living world- and life-view which can deal with all the facts of Being. A mysticism of ethical union with Being grows out of it.

As in my own will-to-live there is longing for wider life and for the mysterious exaltation of the will-to-live which we call pleasure, with dread of annihilation and of the mysterious depreciation of the will-to-live which we call pain; so is it also in the will-to-live all around me, whether it can express itself before me, or remains dumb.

Ethics consist, therefore, in my experiencing the compulsion to show to all will-to-live the same reverence as I do to my own. There we have given us that basic principle of the moral which is a necessity of thought. It is good to maintain and to encourage life; it is bad to destroy life or to obstruct it.

As a matter of fact, everything which in the ordinary ethical valuation of the relations of men to each other ranks as good can be brought under the description of material and spiritual maintenance or promotion of human life, and of effort to bring it to its highest value. Conversely, everything which ranks as bad in human relations is in the last analysis material or spiritual destruction or obstruction of human life, and negligence in the endeavour to bring it to its highest value. Separate individual categories of good and evil which lie far apart and have apparently no connection at all with one another fit together like the pieces of a jig-saw puzzle, as soon as they are comprehended and deepened in this the most universal definition of good and evil.

The basic principle of the moral which is a necessity of thought means, however, not only an ordering and deepening, but also a widening of the current views of good and evil. A man is truly ethical only when he obeys the compulsion to help all life which he is able to assist, and shrinks from injuring anything that lives. He does not ask how far this or that life deserves one's sympathy as being valuable, nor, beyond that, whether and to what degree it is capable of feeling. Life as such is sacred to him. He tears no leaf from a tree, plucks no flower, and takes care to crush no insect. If in summer he is working by lamplight, he prefers to keep the window shut and breathe a stuffy atmosphere rather than see one insect after another fall with singed wings upon his table.

If he walks on the road after a shower and sees an earthworm which has strayed on to it, he bethinks himself that it must get dried up in the sun, if it does not return soon enough to ground into which it can burrow, so he lifts it from the deadly stone surface, and puts it on the grass. If he comes across an insect which has fallen into a puddle, he stops a moment in order to hold out a leaf or a stalk on which it can save itself.

He is not afraid of being laughed at as sentimental. It is the fate of every truth to be a subject for laughter until it is generally recognized. Once it was considered folly to assume that men of colour were really men and ought to be treated as such, but the folly has become an accepted truth. To-day it is thought to be going too far to declare that constant regard for everything that lives, down to the lowest manifestations of life, is a demand made by rational ethics. The time is coming, however, when people will be astonished that mankind needed so long a time to learn to regard thoughtless injury to life as incompatible with ethics.

Ethics are responsibility without limit towards all that lives.

As a general proposition the definition of ethics as a relationship within a disposition to reverence for life, does not make a very moving impression. But it is the only complete one. Compassion is too narrow to rank as the total essence of the ethical. It denotes, of course, only interest in the suffering will-to-live. But ethics include also feeling as one's own all the circumstances and all the aspirations of the will-to-live, its pleasure, too, and its longing to live itself out to the full, as well as its urge to self-perfecting.

Love means more, since it includes fellowship in suffering, in joy, and in effort, but it shows the ethical only in a simile, although in a simile that is natural and profound. It makes the solidarity produced by ethics analogous to that which nature calls forth on the physical side, for more or less temporary purposes between two beings which complete each other sexually, or between them and their offspring.

Thought must strive to bring to expression the nature of the ethical in itself. To effect this it arrives at defining ethics as devotion to life inspired by reverence for life. Even if the phrase reverence for life sounds so general as to seem somewhat lifeless, what is meant by it is nevertheless something which never lets go of the man into whose thought it has made its way. Sympathy, and love, and every kind of valuable enthusiasm are given within it. With restless living force reverence for life works upon the mind into which it has entered, and throws it into the unrest of a feeling of responsibility which at no place and at no time ceases to affect it. Just as the screw which churns its way through the water drives the ship along, so does reverence for life drive the man.

Arising, as it does, from an inner compulsion, the ethic of reverence for life is not dependent on the extent to which it can be thought out to a satisfying conception of life. It need give no answer to the question of what significance the ethical man's work for the maintenance, promotion, and enhancement of life can be in the total happenings of the course of nature. It does not let itself be misled by the calculation that the maintaining and completing of life which it practises is hardly worth consideration beside the tremendous, unceasing destruction of life which goes on every moment through natural forces. Having the will to action, it can leave on one side all problems regarding the success of its work. The fact in itself that in the ethically developed man there has made its appearance in the world a will-to-live which is filled with reverence for life and devotion to life is full of importance for the world.

In my will-to-live the universal will-to-live experiences itself otherwise than in its other manifestations. In them it shows itself in a process of individualizing which, so far as I can see from the outside, is bent merely on living itself out to the full, and in no way on union with any other will-to-live. The world is a ghastly drama of will-to-live divided against itself. One existence makes its way at the cost of another; one destroys the other. One will-to-live merely exerts its will against the other, and has no knowledge of it. But in me the will-to-live has come to know about other wills-to-live. There is in it a yearning to arrive at unity with itself, to become universal.

Why does the will-to-live experience itself in this

way in me alone? Is it because I have acquired the capacity of reflecting on the totality of Being? What is the goal of this evolution which has begun in me?

To these questions there is no answer. It remains a painful enigma for me that I must live with reverence for life in a world which is dominated by creative will which is also destructive will, and destructive will which is also creative.

I can do nothing but hold to the fact that the will-to-live in me manifests itself as will-to-live which desires to become one with other will-to-live. That is for me the light that shines in the darkness. The ignorance in which the world is wrapped has no existence for me; I have been saved from the world. I am thrown, indeed, by reverence for life into an unrest such as the world does not know, but I obtain from it a blessedness which the world cannot give. If in the tenderheartedness produced by being different from the world another person and I help each other in understanding and pardoning, when otherwise will would torment will, the division of the will-to-live is at an end. If I save an insect from a puddle, life has devoted itself to life, and the division of life against itself is ended. Whenever my life devotes itself in any way to life, my finite will-to-live experiences union with the infinite will in which all life is one, and I enjoy a feeling of refreshment which prevents me from pining away in the desert of life.

I therefore recognize it as the destiny of my existence to be obedient to this higher revelation of the will-to-live in me. I choose for my activity the removal of this division of the will-to-live against itself, so far as the influence of my existence can reach. Knowing now the one thing needful, I leave on one side the enigma of the universe and of my existence in it.

The surmisings and the longings of all deep religiousness are contained in the ethics of reverence for life. This religiousness, however, does not build up for itself a complete philosophy, but resigns itself to the necessity of leaving its cathedral unfinished. It finishes the chancel only, but in this chancel piety celebrates a living and never-ceasing divine service. . . .

But what is the position of the ethics of reverence for life in the conflicts which arise between inward compulsion to self-sacrifice, and the necessary upholding of the ego?

I too am subject to division of my will-to-life against itself. In a thousand ways my existence stands in conflict with that of others. The necessity to destroy and to injure life is imposed upon me. If I walk along an unfrequented path, my foot brings destruction and pain upon the tiny creatures which populate it. In order to preserve my own existence, I must defend myself against the existence which injures it. I become a persecutor of the little mouse which inhabits my house, a murderer of the insect which want to have its nest there, a mass-murderer of the bacteria which may endanger my life. I get my food by destroying plants and animals. My happiness is built upon injury done to my fellow-men.

How can ethics be maintained in face of the horrible necessity to which I am subjected through the division of my will-to-live against itself?

Ordinary ethics seek compromises. They try to dictate how much of my existence and of my happiness I must sacrifice, and how much I may preserve at the cost of the existence and happiness of other lives. With these decisions they produce experimental, relative ethics. They offer as ethical what is in reality not ethical but a mixture of non-ethical necessity and ethics. They thereby bring about a huge confusion, and allow the starting of an ever-increasing obscuration of the conception of the ethical.

The ethics of reverence for life know nothing of a relative ethic. They make only the maintenance and promotion of life rank as good. All destruction of and injury to life, under whatever circumstances they take place, they condemn as evil. They do not keep in store adjustments between ethics and necessity all ready for use. Again and again and in ways that are always original they are trying to come to terms in man with reality. They do not abolish for him all ethical conflicts, but compel him to decide for himself in each case how far he can remain ethical and how far he must submit himself to the necessity for destruction of and injury to life, and therewith incur guilt. It is

not by receiving instruction about agreement between ethical and necessary, that a man makes progress in ethics, but only by coming to hear more and more plainly the voice of the ethical, by becoming ruled more and more by the longing to preserve and promote life, and by becoming more and more obstinate in resistance to the necessity for destroying or injuring life.

In ethical conflicts man can arrive only at subjective decisions. No one can decide for him at what point, on each occasion, lies the extreme limit of possibility for his persistence in the preservation and furtherance of life. He alone has to judge this issue, by letting himself be guided by a feeling of the highest possible responsibility towards other life.

We must never let ourselves become blunted. We are living in truth, when we experience these conflicts more profoundly. The good conscience is an invention of the devil.

What does reverence for life say about the relations between man and the animal world?

Whenever I injure life of any sort, I must be quite clear whether it is necessary. Beyond the unavoidable, I must never go, not even with what seems insignificant. The farmer, who has mown down a thousand flowers in his meadow as fodder for his cows, must be careful on his way home not to strike off in wanton pastime the head of a single flower by the roadside, for he thereby commits a wrong against life without being under the pressure of necessity.

Those who experiment with operations or the use of drugs upon animals, or inoculate them with diseases, so as to be able to bring help to mankind with the results gained, must never quiet any misgivings they feel with the general reflection that their cruel proceedings aim at a valuable result. They must first have considered in each individual case whether there is a real necessity to force upon any animal this sacrifice for the sake of mankind. And they must take the most anxious care to mitigate as much as possible the pain inflicted. How much wrong is committed in scientific institutions through neglect of anaesthetics, which to save time or trouble are not administered!

How much, too, through animals being subjected to torture merely to demonstrate to students generally known phenomena! By the very fact that animals have been subjected to experiments, and have by their pain won such valuable results for suffering humanity, a new and special relation of solidarity has been established between them and us. From that springs for each one of us a compulsion to do to every animal all the good we possibly can. By helping an insect when it is in difficulties, I am only attempting to cancel part of man's ever new debt to the animal world. Whenever an animal is in any way forced into the service of man, every one of us must be concerned with the sufferings which for that reason it has to undergo. None of us must allow to take place any suffering for which he himself is not responsible, if he can hinder it in any way. He must not soothe his conscience with the reflection that he would be mixing himself up in something which does not concern him. No one must shut his eyes and regard as non-existent the sufferings of which he spares himself the sight. Let no one regard as light the burden of his responsibility. While so much ill-treatment of animals goes on, while the moans of thirsty animals in railway trucks sound unheard, while so much brutality prevails in our slaughter-houses, while animals have to suffer in our kitchens painful death from unskilled hands, while animals have to endure intolerable treatment from heartless men, or are left to the cruel play of children, we all share the guilt.

We are afraid of making ourselves conspicuous, if we let it be noticed how we feel for the sufferings which man brings upon the animals. At the same time we think that others have become more "rational" then we are, and regard what we are excited about as usual and a matter of course. Yet suddenly they will let slip a word which shows us that they too have not yet learnt to acquiesce. And now, though they were strangers, they are quite near us. The mask in which we deceived each other falls off. We know now, from one another, that we feel alike about being unable to escape from the gruesome proceedings that are taking place unceasingly around us. What a making of a new acquaintance!

The ethics of reverence for life guard us from let-ting each other believe through our silence that we no longer experience what, as thinking men, we must experience. They prompt us to keep each other sensitive to what distresses us, and to talk and to act together, just as the responsibility we feel moves us, and without any feeling of shyness. They make us join in keeping on the look-out for opportunities of bringing some sort of help to animals, to make up for the great misery which men inflict on them, and thus to step for a moment out of the incomprehensible horror of existence. . . .

DISCUSSION TOPICS

1. Having read Schweitzer, how do you think he might respond to Guthrie's description (Chapter Six) of the predator-prey relationship as "Schweitzer's dilemma"?
2. What are some strong points of Schweitzer's view?
3. Do you think Schweitzer's view is too idealistic to be helpful in developing an environmental ethic? Why or why not?

READING 46

On Being Morally Considerable

Kenneth Goodpaster

Kenneth Goodpaster (b. 1944) teaches in the Department of Management at Harvard Business School, Cambridge, Massachusetts. Goodpaster observes that moral philosophy of the last few centuries has assumed a position of "ethical egoism": moral considerability must be based on what satisfies self-interested human moral agents. Goodpaster argues, however, that the only plausible criterion for what counts morally is being alive.[9]

Goodpaster maintains that such issues as whether something has rights, the relative degree of moral significance of something with respect to other things, and whether a moral agent could live according to a particular moral view, are narrower issues than whether or not something deserves moral consideration at all. Goodpaster agrees with Singer, Feinberg[10] and others that a being does not have to be rational in order to be morally considerable, but does not agree with those who limit moral considerability to sentience. Goodpaster points out that trees have needs and interests in remaining alive.

A thing is right when it tends to preserve the integrity, stability, and beauty of the biotic community. It is wrong when it tends otherwise.

Aldo Leopold

What follows is a preliminary inquiry into a question which needs more elaborate treatment than an essay can provide. The question can be and has been addressed in different rhetorical formats, but perhaps G. J. Warnock's formulation of it[1] is the best to start with:

> Let us consider the question to whom principles of morality apply from, so to speak, the other end—from the standpoint not of the agent, but of the "patient." What, we may ask here, is the condition of moral *relevance?* What is the condition of having a claim to be *considered,* by rational agents to whom moral principles apply? (p. 148)

In the terminology of R. M. Hare (or even Kant), the same question might be put thus: In universalizing our putative moral maxims, what is the scope of the variable over which universalization is to range? A more legalistic idiom, employed recently by Chris-

topher D. Stone,[2] might ask: What are the requirements for "having standing" in the moral sphere? However the question gets formulated, the thrust is in the direction of necessary and sufficient conditions on X in

$$\text{For all } A, X \text{ deserves moral consideration} \atop \text{from } A. \qquad (1)$$

where A ranges over rational moral agents and moral 'consideration' is construed broadly to include the most basic forms of practical respect (and so is not restricted to "possession of rights" by X).

I

. . . Modern moral philosophy has taken ethical egoism as its principle foil for developing what can fairly be called a *humanistic* perspective on value and obligation. That is, both Kantian and Humean approaches to ethics tend to view the philosophical challenge as that of providing an epistemological and motivational generalization of an agent's natural self-interested concern. Because of this preoccupation with moral "take-off," however, too little critical thought has been devoted to the flight and its destination. One result might be a certain feeling of impotence in the minds of many moral philosophers when faced with the sorts of issues mentioned earlier, issues that question the breadth of the moral enterprise more than its departure point. To be sure, questions of conservation, preservation of the environment, and technology assessment *can* be approached simply as application questions, e.g., "How shall we evaluate the alternatives available to us instrumentally in relation to humanistic satisfactions?" But there is something distressingly uncritical in this way of framing such issues—distressingly uncritical in the way that deciding foreign policy solely in terms of "the national interest" is uncritical. Or at least, so I think.

It seems to me that we should not only wonder

---

9. Goodpaster does suggest that ecosystems as wholes might have interests, but does not develop the point.

10. Joel Feinberg, "The Rights of Animals and Unborn Generations," in William T. Blackstone, ed., *Philosophy and Environmental Crisis* (Athens: University of Georgia, 1974).

1. *The Object of Morality* (New York: Methuen, 1971); parenthetical page references to Warnock will be to this book.

2. *Should Trees Have Standing?* (Los Altos, Calif.: William Kaufmann, 1974); parenthetical page references to Stone will be to this book.

about, but actually follow "the road not taken into the wood." Neither rationality nor the capacity to experience pleasure and pain seem to me necessary (even though they may be sufficient) conditions on moral considerability. And only our hedonistic and concentric forms of ethical reflection keep us from acknowledging this fact. Nothing short of the condition of *being alive* seems to me to be a plausible and nonarbitrary criterion. What is more, this criterion, if taken seriously, could admit of application to entities and systems of entities heretofore unimagined as claimants on our moral attention (such as the biosystem itself). Some may be inclined to take such implications as a *reductio* of the move "beyond humanism." I am beginning to be persuaded, however, that such implications may provide both a meaningful ethical vision and the hope of a more adequate action guide for the long-term future. Paradigms are crucial components in knowledge—but they can conceal as much as they reveal. Our paradigms of moral considerability are individual persons and their joys and sorrows. I want to venture the belief that the universe of moral consideration is more complex than these paradigms allow.

II

My strategy, now that my cards are on the table, will be to spell out a few rules of the game (in this section) and then to examine the "hands" of several respected philosophers whose arguments seem to count against casting the moral net as widely as I am inclined to. . . . [Finally,] I will discuss several objections and touch on further questions needing attention.

The first . . . distinction that must be kept clear in addressing our question has already been alluded to. It is that between moral *rights* and moral *considerability*. My inclination is to construe the notion of rights as more specific than that of considerability, largely to avoid what seem to be unnecessary complications over the requirements for something's being an appropriate "bearer of rights." The concept of rights is used in wider and narrower senses, of course. Some authors (indeed, one whom we shall consider later in this paper) use it as roughly synonymous with Warnock's notion of "moral relevance." Others believe that being a bearer of rights involves the satisfaction of much more demanding requirements. The sentiments of John Passmore[3] are probably typical of this narrower view:

> The idea of "rights" is simply not applicable to what is non-human . . . It is one thing to say that it is wrong to treat animals cruelly, quite another to say that animals have rights (pp. 116/7).

I doubt whether it is so clear that the class of rights-bearers is or ought to be restricted to human beings, but I propose to suspend this question entirely by framing the discussion in terms of the notion of moral considerability (following Warnock), except in contexts where there is reason to think the widest sense of 'rights' is at work. Whether beings who deserve moral consideration in themselves, not simply by reason of their utility to human beings, also possess moral *rights* in some narrow sense is a question which will, therefore, remain open here—and it is a question the answer to which need not be determined in advance.

A second distinction is that between what might be called a *criterion of moral considerability* and a *criterion of moral significance.* The former represents the central quarry here, while the latter, which might easily get confused with the former, aims at governing *comparative* judgments of moral "weight" in cases of conflict. Whether a tree, say, deserves any moral consideration is a question that must be kept separate from the question of whether trees deserve more or less consideration than dogs, or dogs than human persons. We should not expect that the criterion for having "moral standing" at all will be the same as the criterion for adjudicating competing claims to priority among beings that merit that standing. . . .

III

Let us begin with Warnock's own answer to the question, now that the question has been clarified some-

---

3. *Man's Responsibility for Nature* (New York: Scribner's, 1974).

what. In setting out his answer, Warnock argues (in my view, persuasively) against two more restrictive candidates. The first, what might be called the *Kantian principle,* amounts to little more than a reflection of the requirements of moral *agency* onto those of moral considerability:

For *X* to deserve moral consideration from *A,*　(4)
　　X must be a rational human person.

Observing that such a criterion of considerability eliminates children and mentally handicapped adults, among others, Warnock dismisses it as intolerably narrow.

The second candidate, actually a more generous variant of the first, sets the limits of moral considerability by disjoining ''potentiality'':

For all *A, X* deserves moral consideration from　(5)
A if and only if *X* is a rational human person or
　　is a potential rational human person.

Warnock's reply to this suggestion is also persuasive. Infants and imbeciles are no doubt potentially rational, but this does not appear to be the reason why we should not maltreat them. And we would not say that an imbecile reasonably judged to be incurable would thereby reasonably be taken to have no moral claims (p. 151). In short, it seems arbitrary to draw the boundary of moral *considerability* around rational human beings (actual or potential), however plausible it might be to draw the boundary of moral *responsibility* there.[4]

Warnock then settles upon his own solution. The basis of moral claims, he says, may be put as follows:

> . . . just as liability to be judged as a moral agent follows from one's general capability of alleviating, by moral action, the ills of the predicament, and is for that reason confined to rational beings, so the condition of being a

proper ''beneficiary'' of moral action is the capability of *suffering* the ills of the predicament—and for that reason is not confined to rational beings, nor even to potential members of that class (p. 151).

The criterion of moral considerability then, is located in the *capacity to suffer:*

For all *A, X* deserves moral consideration from　(6)
A if and only if *X* is capable of suffering pain
　　(or experiencing enjoyment).

And the defense involves appeal to what Warnock considers to be (analytically) the *object* of the moral enterprise: amelioration of the predicament.'' . . .

W. K. Frankena, in a recent paper,[5] joins forces:

> Like Warnock, I believe that there are right and wrong ways to treat infants, animals, imbeciles, and idiots even if or even though (as the case may be) they are not persons or human beings—just because they are capable of pleasure and suffering, and not just because their lives happen to have some value to or for those who clearly are persons or human beings.

And Peter Singer[6] writes:

> If a being is not capable of suffering, or of experiencing enjoyment or happiness, there is nothing to be taken into account. This is why the limit of sentience (using the term as a convenient, if not strictly accurate, shorthand for the capacity to suffer or experience enjoyment or happiness) is the only defensible boundary of concern for the interests of others (p. 154).

I say that the mood is aggravated because, although I acknowledge and even applaud the conviction expressed by these philosophers that the capacity to suffer (or perhaps better, *sentience*) is sufficient for moral considerability, I fail to understand their reasons for thinking such a criterion necessary. To be sure, there are hints at reasons in each case. Warnock

---

4. Actually, it seems to me that we ought not to draw the boundary of moral responsibility just here. See my ''Morality and Organizations,'' in *Proceedings of the Second National Conference on Business Ethics* (Waltham, Mass.: Bentley College, 1978).

5. ''Ethics and the Environment,'' in Kenneth Goodpaster and K.M. Sayre, eds., *Ethics and Problems of the 21st Century* (Notre Dame, Ind.: University Press, 1978).

6. ''All Animals Are Equal,'' in Tom Regan and Peter Singer, *Animal Rights and Human Obligations* (Englewood Cliffs, N.J.: Prentice-Hall, 1976). See p. 316.

implies that nonsentient beings could not be proper "beneficiaries" of moral action. Singer seems to think that beyond sentience "there is nothing to take into account." And Frankena suggests that nonsentient beings simply do not provide us with moral reasons for respecting them unless it be potentiality for sentience.[7] Yet it is so clear that there *is* something to take into account, something that is not merely "potential sentience" and which surely does qualify beings as beneficiaries and capable of harm—namely, *life*—that the hints provided seem to me to fall short of good reasons.

Biologically, it appears that sentience is an adaptive characteristic of living organisms that provides them with a better capacity to anticipate, and so avoid, threats to life. This at least suggests, though of course it does not prove, that the capacities to suffer and to enjoy are ancillary to something more important rather than tickets to considerability in their own right. In the words of one perceptive scientific observer:

> If we view pleasure as rooted in our sensory physiology, it is not difficult to see that our neurophysiological equipment must have evolved via variation and selective retention in such a way as to record a positive signal to adaptationally satisfactory conditions and a negative signal to adaptationally unsatisfactory conditions . . . The pleasure signal is only an evolutionarily derived indicator, not the goal itself. It is the applause which signals a job well done, but not the actual completion of the job.[8]

Nor is it absurd to imagine that evolution might have resulted (indeed might still result?) in beings whose capacities to maintain, protect, and advance their lives did not depend upon mechanisms of pain and pleasure at all.

So far, then, we can see that the search for a criterion of moral considerability takes one quickly and plausibly beyond humanism. But there is a tendency, exhibited in the remarks of Warnock, Frankena, and Singer, to draw up the wagons around the notion of sentience. I have suggested that there is reason to go further and not very much in the way of argument not to. But perhaps there is a stronger and more explicit case that can be made for sentience. I think there is, in a way, and I propose to discuss it in detail in the section that follows.

IV

Joel Feinberg offers what may be the clearest and most explicit case for a restrictive criterion on moral considerability (restrictive with respect to life). . . .

The central thesis defended by Feinberg is that a being cannot intelligibly be said to possess moral rights (read: deserve moral consideration) unless that being satisfies the "interest principle," and that only the subclass of humans and higher animals among living beings satisfies this principle:

> . . . the sorts of being who can have rights are precisely those who have (or can have) interests. I have come to this tentative conclusion for two reasons: (1) because a right holder must be capable of being represented and it is impossible to represent a being that has no interests, and (2) because a right holder must be capable of being a beneficiary in his own person, and a being without interests is a being that is incapable of being harmed or benefited, having no good or "sake" of its own (p. 51).

Implicit in this passage are the following two arguments, interpreted in terms of moral considerability:

Only beings who can be represented can deserve moral consideration. (A1)

Only beings who have (or can have) interests can be represented.

Therefore, only beings who have (or can have) interests can deserve moral consideration.

---

7. "I can see no reason, from the moral point of view, why we should respect something that is alive but has no conscious sentiency and so can experience no pleasure or pain, joy or suffering, unless perhaps it is potentially a consciously sentient being, as in the case of a fetus. Why, if leaves and trees have no capacity to feel pleasure or to suffer, should I tear no leaf from a tree? Why should I respect its location any more than that of a stone in my driveway, if no benefit or harm comes to any person or sentient being by my moving it?" ("Ethics and the Environment.")

8. Mark W. Lipsey, "Value Science and Developing Society," paper delivered to the Society for Religion in Higher Education, Institute on Society, Technology and Values (July 15-Aug. 4, 1973), p. 11.

Only beings capable of being beneficiaries   (A2)
can deserve moral consideration.

Only beings who have (or can have) interests
are capable of being beneficiaries.

Therefore, only beings who have (or can
have) interests can deserve moral consideration.

I suspect that these two arguments are at work between the lines in Warnock, Frankena, and Singer,
though of course one can never be sure. In any case,
I propose to consider them as the best defense of the
sentience criterion in recent literature.

I am prepared to grant, with some reservations, the
first premises in each of these obviously valid arguments. The second premises, though, are *both* importantly equivocal. To claim that only beings who have
(or can have) interests can be represented might mean
that ''mere things'' cannot be represented because
they have nothing to represent, no ''interests'' as opposed to ''usefulness'' to defend or protect. Similarly,
to claim that only beings who have (or can have)
interests are capable of being beneficiaries might
mean that ''mere things'' are incapable of being benefited or harmed—they have no ''well-being'' to be
sought or acknowledged by rational moral agents. So
construed, Feinberg seems to be right; but he also
seems to be committed to allowing any *living* thing
the status of moral considerability. For as he himself
admits, even plants

> . . . are not ''mere things''; they are vital objects with
> inherited biological propensities determining their nat-
> ural growth. Moreover we do say that certain conditions
> are ''good'' or ''bad'' for plants, thereby suggesting that
> plants, unlike rocks, are capable of having a ''good'' (p.
> 51).

But Feinberg pretty clearly wants to draw the nets
tighter than this—and he does so by interpreting the
notion of ''interests'' in the two second premises
more narrowly. The contrast term he favors is not
'mere things' but 'mindless creatures.' And he makes
this move by insisting that ''interests'' logically presuppose *desires* or *wants* or *aims,* the equipment for
which is not possessed by plants (nor, we might add,
by many animals or even some humans?)

But why should we accept this shift in strength of
the criterion? In doing so, we clearly abandon one
sense in which living organisms like plants do have
interests that can be represented. There is no absurdity
in imagining the representation of the needs of a tree
for sun and water in the face of a proposal to cut it
down or pave its immediate radius for a parking lot.
We might of course, on reflection, decide to go ahead
and cut it down or do the paving, but there is hardly
an intelligibility problem about representing the tree's
interest in our deciding not to. In the face of their
obvious tendencies to maintain and heal themselves,
it is very difficult to reject the idea of interests on the
part of trees (and plants generally) in remaining alive.[9]

Nor will it do to suggest, as Feinberg does, that the
needs (interests) of living things like trees are not
really their own but implicitly *ours:* ''Plants may need
things in order to discharge their functions, but their
functions are assigned by human interests, not their
own'' (p. 54). As if it were human interests that assigned to trees the tasks of growth or maintenance!
The interests at stake are clearly those of the living
things themselves, not simply those of the owners or
users or other human persons involved. Indeed, there
is a suggestion in this passage that, to be capable of
being represented, an organism must *matter* to human
beings somehow—a suggestion whose implications
for human rights (disenfranchisement) let alone the
rights of animals (inconsistently for Feinberg, I
think)—are grim.

The truth seems to be that the ''interests'' that
nonsentient beings share with sentient beings (over
and against ''mere things'') are far more plausible as
criteria of *considerability* than the ''interests'' that
sentient beings share (over and against ''mindless
creatures''). This is not to say that interests construed
in the latter way are morally irrelevant—for they may
play a role as criteria of moral *significance*—but it is
to say that psychological or hedonic capacities seem
unnecessarily sophisticated when it comes to locating
the minimal conditions for something's deserving to

---

9. See Albert Szent-Gyorgyi, *The Living State* (New York:
Academic Press, 1972), esp. ch. VI, ''Vegetable Defense Systems.''

be valued for its own sake. Surprisingly, Feinberg's own reflections on ''mere things'' appear to support this very point:

> . . . mere things have no conative life: no conscious wishes, desires, and hopes; or urges and impulses; or unconscious drives, aims, and goals; or latent tendencies, direction of growth, and natural fulfillments. Interests must be compounded somehow out of conations; hence mere things have no interests (p. 49).

Together with the acknowledgment, quoted earlier, that plants, for example, are not ''mere things,'' such observations seem to undermine the interest principle in its more restrictive form. I conclude, with appropriate caution, that the interest principle either grows to fit what we might call a ''life principle'' or requires an arbitrary stipulation of psychological capacities (for desires, wants, etc.) which are neither warranted by (A1) and (A2) nor independently plausible. . . .

Let us now turn to several objections that might be thought to render a ''life principle'' of moral considerability untenable quite independently of the adequacy or inadequacy of the sentience or interest principle.

(O1) A principle of moral respect or consideration for life in all its forms is mere Schweitzerian romanticism, even if it does not involve, as it probably does, the projection of mental or psychological categories beyond their responsible boundaries into the realms of plants, insects, and microbes.

(R1) This objection misses the central thrust of my discussion, which is *not* that the sentience criterion is necessary, but applicable to all life forms—rather the point is that the possession of sentience is not necessary for moral considerability. Schweitzer himself may have held the former view—and so have been ''romantic''—but this is beside the point.

(O2) To suggest seriously that moral considerability is coextensive with life is to suggest that conscious, feeling beings have no more central role in the moral life than vegetables, which is downright absurd—if not perverse.

(R2) This objection misses the central thrust of my discussion as well, for a different reason. It is consistent with acknowledging the moral considerability of

all life forms to go on to point out differences of moral significance among these life forms. And as far as perversion is concerned, history will perhaps be a better judge of our civilization's treatment of animals and the living environment on that score.

(O3) Consideration of life can serve as a criterion only to the degree that life itself can be given a precise definition; and it can't.

(R3) I fail to see why a criterion of moral considerability must be strictly decidable in order to be tenable. Surely rationality, potential rationality, sentience, and the capacity for or possession of interests fare no better here. Moreover, there do seem to be empirically respectable accounts of the nature of living beings available which are not intolerably vague or open-textured:

> The typifying mark of a living system . . . appears to be its persistent state of low entropy, sustained by metabolic processes for accumulating energy, and maintained in equilibrium with its environment by homeostatic feedback processes.[10]

Granting the need for certain further qualifications, a definition such as this strikes me as not only plausible in its own right, but ethically illuminating, since it suggests that the core of moral concern lies in respect for self-sustaining organization and integration in the face of pressures toward high entropy.

(O4) If life, as understood in the previous response, is really taken as the key to moral considerability, then it is possible that larger systems besides our ordinarily understood ''linear'' extrapolations from human beings (e.g., animals, plants, etc.) might satisfy the conditions, such as the biosystem as a whole. This surely would be a *reductio* of the life principle.

(R4) At best, it would be a *reductio* of the life principle in this form or without qualification. But it seems to me that such (perhaps surprising) implications, if true, should be taken seriously. There is some evidence that the biosystem as a whole exhibits behavior approximating to the definition sketched

---

10. K.M. Sayre, *Cybernetics and the Philosophy of Mind* (New York: Humanities, 1976), p. 91.

above,[11] and I see no reason to deny it moral considerability on that account. Why should the universe of moral considerability map neatly onto our medium-sized framework of organisms?

(O5) There are severe epistemological problems about imputing interests, benefits, harms, etc. to non-sentient beings. What is it for a tree to have needs?

(R5) I am not convinced that the epistemological problems are more severe in this context than they would be in numerous others which the objector would probably not find problematic. Christopher Stone has put this point nicely:

> I am sure I can judge with more certainty and meaningfulness whether and when my lawn wants (needs) water than the Attorney General can judge whether and when the United States wants (needs) to take an appeal from an adverse judgment by a lower court. The lawn tells me that it wants water by a certain dryness of the blades and soil—immediately obvious to the touch—the appearance of bald spots, yellowing, and a lack of springiness after being walked on; how does "the United States" communicate to the Attorney General? (p. 24).

We make decisions in the interests of others or on behalf of others every day—"others" whose wants are far less verifiable than those of most living creatures.

(O6) Whatever the force of the previous objections, the clearest and most decisive refutation of the principle of respect for life is that one cannot *live* according to it, nor is there any indication in nature that we were intended to. We must eat, experiment to gain knowledge, protect ourselves from predation (macroscopic and microscopic), and in general deal with the overwhelming complexities of the moral life while remaining psychologically intact. To take seriously the criterion of considerability being defended, all these things must be seen as somehow morally wrong.

(R6) This objection, if it is not met by implication in (R2), can be met, I think, by recalling the distinction made earlier between regulative and operative moral consideration. It seems to me that there clearly are limits to the operational character of respect for living things. We must eat, and usually this involves killing (though not always). We must have knowledge, and sometimes this involves experimentation with living things and killing (though not always). We must protect ourselves from predation and disease, and sometimes this involves killing (through not always). The regulative character of the moral consideration due to all living things asks, as far as I can see, for sensitivity and awareness, not for suicide (psychic or otherwise). But it is not vacuous, in that it does provide a *ceteris paribus* encouragement in the direction of nutritional, scientific, and medical practices of a genuinely life-respecting sort. . . .

DISCUSSION TOPICS

1. Define the notion of "interests." Do you agree with Goodpaster that plants have interests? How would you evaluate those interests compared with those of an animal?
2. Regan's moral theory rejects the moral considerability of plants. What argument might Regan give against Goodpaster's view? How might Goodpaster respond?

READING 47

Respect for Nature

Paul Taylor

Paul Taylor teaches philosophy at Brooklyn College, City University of New York. In Respect for Nature *he develops the view that human beings are members of the earth's living community but are not inherently superior to other living things. Each organism is a "teleological center of life"—a unique individual pursuing its own good in its own way.*

---

11. See J. Lovelock and S. Epton, "The Quest for Gaia," *The New Scientist*, LXV, 935 (Feb. 6, 1975): 304-309.

Taylor offers four duties toward nature, the fundamental duty being ''nonmaleficence,'' to do no harm. The other three rules are those requiring restitution of harm done, refraining from interfering in the natural world, and faithfulness to the trust placed in human beings by wild animals. (Taylor maintains that human beings should conduct themselves consistently with an animal's needs and expectations, the latter based on past interactions with human beings.) Taylor does not argue that animals and plants have moral rights in the same sense that human persons do,[11] but rather that the attitude of respect for nature requires moral agents to live in accord with the four duties toward nature.

In order to resolve conflicting claims between human beings and wild living creatures, Taylor provides five principles: self-defense, proportionality, minimum harm, distributive justice, and restitutive justice. In order to apply these principles, he distinguishes between basic and nonbasic interests. Overall, when wild animals and plants are not harmful to human beings, the basic interests of wild animals and plants override the nonbasic interests of human beings. If the basic interests of both humans and nonhumans are involved, conflicts are to be decided according distributive justice—that is, species-impartial fairness.

THE BIOCENTRIC OUTLOOK AND THE ATTITUDE OF RESPECT FOR NATURE

. . . The beliefs that form the core of the biocentric outlook are four in number:

(a) The belief that humans are members of the Earth's Community of Life in the same sense and on the same terms in which other living things are members of that Community.

(b) The belief that the human species, along with all other species, are integral elements in a system of interdependence such that the survival of each living thing, as well as its chances of faring well or poorly, is determined not only by the physical

conditions of its environment but also by its relations to other living things.

(c) The belief that all organisms are teleological centers of life in the sense that each is a unique individual pursuing its own good in its own way.

(d) The belief that humans are not inherently superior to other living things. . . .

INDIVIDUAL ORGANISMS AS TELEOLOGICAL CENTERS OF LIFE

So far the biocentric outlook has been presented as a belief-system that sets a framework for viewing ourselves in relation to other species and for understanding how we and they alike fit into the whole natural environment of our planet. The third component of that outlook, in contrast with the first two, focuses our attention on the lives of individual organisms. The biocentric outlook includes a certain way of conceiving of each entity that has a life of its own. To accept the outlook is to sharpen and deepen our awareness of what it means to be a particular living thing.

Our knowledge of individual organisms has expanded rapidly with advances in the biological and physical sciences in the past century. Organic chemistry and microbiology have brought us close to every cell and every molecule that make up the physical structure of the bodies of organisms. We have greatly increased our understanding of how living things function as physical and chemical systems. We are acquiring ever more accurate and complete explanations of why organisms behave as they do. As we thus come to know more about their life cycles, their interactions with other organisms and with the environment, we become increasingly aware of how each of them is carrying out its life functions according to the laws of its species-specific nature. But besides this, our increasing knowledge and understanding also enable us to grasp the uniqueness of each organism as an individual. Scientists who have made careful and detailed studies of particular plants and animals have often come to know their subjects as identifiable individuals. Close observation over extended periods, whether in the laboratory or in the field, has led them

---

11. Paul Taylor, *Respect for Nature* (Princeton, N.J.: Princeton University Press, 1986), pp. 245ff.

to an appreciation of the unique "personalities" of their subjects. Sometimes a scientist develops a special interest in a particular animal or plant, all the while remaining strictly objective in the gathering and recording of data.[1]

Nonscientists may likewise experience this development of interest when, as amateur naturalists, they make accurate observations over a sustained period of close acquaintance with a plant or animal. As one becomes more and more familiar with the organism being observed, one acquires a sharpened awareness of the particular way it is living its life. One may become fascinated by it and even get to be involved with its good and bad fortunes. The organism comes to mean something to one as a unique, irreplaceable individual. Finally one achieves a genuine understanding of its point of view. One can then imaginatively place oneself in the organism's situation and look at the world from its standpoint.

This progressive development from objective, detached knowledge to the recognition of individuality, and from the recognition of individuality to a full awareness of an organism's standpoint, is a process of heightening our consciousness of what it means to be an individual living thing.

. . . To say it is a teleological center of life is to say that its internal functioning as well as its external activities are all goal-oriented, having the constant tendency to maintain the organism's existence through time and to enable it successfully to perform those biological operations whereby it reproduces its kind and continually adapts to changing environmental events and conditions. It is the coherence and unity of these functions of an organism, all directed toward the realization of its good, that make it one teleological center of activity. Physically and chemically it is in the molecules of its cells that this activity occurs,

but the organism as a whole is the unit that responds to its environment and so accomplishes (or tends to accomplish) the end of sustaining its life.[2]

Understanding individual organisms as teleological centers of life does not mean that we are falsely anthropomorphizing. It does not involve "reading into" them human characteristics. We need not, for example, consider them to have consciousness. That a particular tree is a teleological center of life does not entail that it is intentionally aiming at preserving its existence, that it is exerting efforts to avoid death, or that it even cares whether it lives or dies. As we saw [earlier], organisms like trees and one-celled protozoa do not have a conscious life. They are not aware of a world around them. They have no thoughts or feelings and hence no interest in anything that happens to them. Yet they have a good of their own around which their behavior is organized. All organisms, whether conscious or not, are teleological centers of life in the sense that each is a unified, coherently ordered system of goal-oriented activities that has a constant tendency to protect and maintain the organism's existence.

Under this conception of individual living things, each is seen to have a single, unique point of view. This point of view is determined by the organism's particular way of responding to its environment, interacting with other individual organisms, and undergoing the regular, lawlike transformations of the various stages of its species-specific life cycle. As it sustains its existence through time, it exemplifies all the functions and activities of its species in its own peculiar manner. When observed in detail, its way of existing is seen to be different from that of any other

---

1. It is nowadays standard practice for biologists conducting research in the field to study organisms not only by observing natural differences by which to identify particular individuals but also by tagging or marking individuals for purposes of ready recognition.

2. Three books have explored in depth the use of teleological concepts and explanations in biology. Although they are in sharp disagreement about the correct analysis to be made of such concepts and explanations, there is general acknowledgment that those concepts and explanations are integral to the biological sciences. See Michael Ruse, *The Philosophy of Biology* (London: J. M. Dent, 1973); Andrew Woodfield, *Teleology* (New York: Cambridge University Press, 1976); and Larry Wright, *Teleological Explanation* (Los Angeles: University of California Press, 1976).

organism, including those of its species. To be aware of it not only as *a* center of life, but as *the* particular center of life that it is, is to be aware of its uniqueness and individuality. The organism is the individual it is precisely in virtue of its having its own idiosyncratic manner of carrying on its existence in the (not necessarily conscious) pursuit of its good.

This mode of understanding a particular individual is not possible with regard to inanimate objects. Although no two stones are exactly alike in their physical characteristics, stones do not have points of view. In pure fantasy, of course, we can play at performing the imaginative act of taking a stone's standpoint and looking at the world from its perspective. But we are then moving away from reality, not getting closer to it. The true reality of a stone's existence includes no point of view. This is not due to the fact that it lacks consciousness. As we have noted, plants and simple animal organisms also lack consciousness, but have points of view nonetheless. What makes our awareness of an individual stone fundamentally different from our awareness of a plant or animal is that the stone is not a teleological center of life, while the plant or animal is. The stone has no good of its own. We cannot benefit it by furthering its well-being or harm it by acting contrary to its well-being, since the concept of well-being simply does not apply to it.

This point holds even for those complex mechanisms (such as self-monitoring space satellites, chess-playing computers, and assembly-line "robots") that have been constructed by humans to function in a quasi-autonomous, self-regulating manner in the process of accomplishing certain purposes. Though such machines are understandable as teleological systems, they remain in actual fact inanimate objects. The ends they are programmed to accomplish are not purposes of their own, independent of the human purposes for which they were made. This is not to deny that in certain contexts it is perfectly proper to speak of what is good or bad for them. These would be conditions that add to or detract from their effectiveness as instruments for bringing about the (human) ends they were made to serve. But it is precisely this fact that separates them from living things.

The goal-oriented operations of machines are not inherent to them as the goal-oriented behavior of organisms is inherent to *them*. To put it another way, the goals of a machine are derivative, whereas the goals of a living thing are original. The ends and purposes of machines are built into them by their human creators. It is the original purposes of humans that determine the structures and hence the teleological functions of those machines. Although they manifest goal-directed activities, the machines do not, as independent entities, have a good of their own. Their "good" is "furthered" only insofar as they are treated in such a way as to be an effective means to human ends.

A living plant or animal, on the other hand, has a good of its own in the same sense that a human being has a good of its own. It is, independently of anything else in the universe, itself a center of goal-oriented activity. What is good or bad for it can be understood by reference to its own survival, health, and well-being. As a living thing it seeks its own ends in a way that is not true of any teleologically structured mechanism. It is in terms of *its* goals that we can give teleological explanations of why it does what it does. We cannot do the same for machines, since any such explanation must ultimately refer to the goals their human producers had in mind when they made the machines.

I should add as a parenthetical note that this difference between mechanism and organism may no longer be maintainable with regard to those complex electronic devices now being developed under the name of artificial intelligence. Perhaps some day computer scientists and engineers will construct beings whose internal processes and electrical responses to their surroundings closely parallel the functions of the human brain and nervous system. Concerning such beings we may begin to speak of their having a good of their own independently of the purposes of their creators. At that point the distinction drawn above between living things and inanimate machines may break down. It is best, I think, to have an open mind about this. But for our present purposes we need not go into this matter. In working out a life-centered theory of environmental ethics that is applicable to the relations between humans and the natural world, we can use for practical purposes the distinction as it is made above. If mechanisms (organisms?) of artificial intelligence were ever to be produced, another system of ethics might have to be applied to the treatment of such entities by moral agents. . . .

THE DENIAL OF HUMAN SUPERIORITY

. . . [C]onsider one of the most frequently repeated assertions concerning the superiority of humans over nonhumans. This is the claim that we humans are *morally* superior beings because we possess, while animals and plants lack, the capacities that give us the status of moral agents. Such capacities as free will, accountability, deliberation, and practical reason, it is said, endow us with the special nobility and dignity that belong only to morally responsible beings. Because human existence has this moral dimension it exemplifies a higher grade of being than is to be found in the amoral, irresponsible existence of animals and plants. In traditional terms, it is freedom of the will and the moral responsibility that goes with it that together raise human life above the level of the beasts.

There is a serious confusion of thought in this line of reasoning if the conclusion drawn is understood as asserting that humans are morally superior to nonhumans. One cannot validly argue that humans are morally superior beings on the ground that they possess, while others lack, the capacities of a moral agent. The reason is that, as far as moral standards are concerned, only beings that have the capacities of a moral agent can meaningfully be said to be *either* morally good *or* morally bad. Only moral agents can be judged to be morally better or worse than others, and the others in question must be moral agents themselves. Judgments of moral superiority are based on the comparative merits or deficiencies of the entities being judged, and these merits and deficiencies are all moral ones, that is, ones determined by moral standards. One entity is correctly judged morally superior to another if it is the case that, when valid moral standards are applied to both entities, the first fulfills them to a

greater degree than the second. Both entities, therefore, must fall within the range of application of moral standards. This would not be the case, however, if humans were being judged superior to animals and plants, since the latter are not moral agents. Just as animals and plants can be neither good nor bad scientists, engineers, critics, or Supreme Court justices, so they can be neither good nor bad moral agents. More precisely, it is meaningless to speak of them as morally good or bad. Hence it is meaningless to say either that they are morally inferior to humans or that humans are morally superior to them. I conclude that it is not false but simply confused to assert that humans are the moral superiors of animals and plants. . . .

THE BASIC RULES OF CONDUCT

. . . I shall now set out and examine four rules of duty in the domain of environmental ethics. This is not supposed to provide an exhaustive account of every valid duty of the ethics of respect for nature. It is doubtful whether a complete specification of duties is possible in this realm. But however that may be, the duties to be listed here are intended to cover only the more important ones that typically arise in everyday life. I suggest later on, in connection with the discussion of priority principles, that in all situations not explicitly or clearly covered by these rules we should rely on the attitude of respect for nature and the biocentric outlook that together underlie the system as a whole and give it point. Right actions are always actions that express the attitude of respect, whether they are covered by the four rules or not. . . .

The four rules will be named (a) the Rule of Nonmaleficence, (b) the Rule of Noninterference, (c) the Rule of Fidelity, and (d) the Rule of Restitutive Justice.

(a) *The Rule of Nonmaleficence.* This is the duty not to do harm to any entity in the natural environment that has a good of its own. It includes the duty not to kill an organism and not to destroy a species-population or biotic community, as well as the duty to refrain from any action that would be seriously detrimental to the good of an organism, species-population, or life community. Perhaps the most fundamental wrong in the ethics of respect for nature is to harm something that does not harm us. . . .

(b) *The Rule of Noninterference.* Under this rule fall two sorts of negative duties, one requiring us to refrain from placing restrictions on the freedom of individual organisms, the other requiring a general ''hands off'' policy with regard to whole ecosystems and biotic communities, as well as to individual organisms. . . .

(c) *The Rule of Fidelity.* This rule applies only to human conduct in relation to individual animals that are in a wild state and are capable of being deceived or betrayed by moral agents. The duties imposed by the Rule of Fidelity, though of restricted range, are so frequently violated by so many people that this rule needs separate study as one of the basic principles of the ethics of respect for nature.

Under this rule fall the duties not to break a trust that a wild animal places in us (as shown by its behavior), not to deceive or mislead any animal capable of being deceived or misled, to uphold an animal's expectations, which it has formed on the basis of one's past actions with it, and to be true to one's intentions as made known to an animal when it has come to rely on one. Although we cannot make mutual agreements with wild animals, we can act in such a manner as to call forth their trust in us. The basic moral requirement imposed by the Rule of Fidelity is that we remain faithful to that trust.

The clearest and commonest examples of transgressions of the rule occur in hunting, trapping, and fishing. Indeed, the breaking of a trust is a key to good (that is, successful) hunting, trapping, and fishing. Deception with intent to harm is of the essence. . . .

(d) *The Rule of Restitutive Justice.* In its most general terms this rule imposes the duty to restore the balance of justice between a moral agent and a moral subject when the subject has been wronged by the agent. Common to all instances in which a duty of restitutive justice arises, an agent has broken a valid moral rule and by doing so has upset the balance of justice between himself or herself and a moral subject. To hold oneself accountable for having done such an act is to acknowledge a special duty one has taken upon oneself by that wrongdoing. This special duty is the duty of restitutive justice. It requires that one make amends to the moral subject by some form of compensation or reparation.

. . . It will be helpful to summarize our findings by taking an overall look at the priority relations holding among the four rules of duty. The general picture we then get shows the Rule of Nonmaleficence to be at the top. Our most fundamental duty toward nature (putting aside possible conflicts with the duties of human ethics) is to do no harm to wild living things as far as this lies within our power. Our respect for nature primarily expresses itself in our adhering to this supreme rule.

With regard to the other three rules, we have found that it is usually possible to avoid violations of each of them by carefully choosing how we make restitution and when we set up the conditions that lead to the development of an animal's trust in us. But where conflicts cannot be avoided, the priority principles that generally hold are: (a) Fidelity and restitutive justice override noninterference when a great good is brought about and no creature is permanently harmed by the permitted interference. (b) Restitutive justice outweighs fidelity when a great good is brought about and no serious harm is done to a creature whose trust in us is broken.

It must be added that the two negative rules, to refrain from doing harm and to refrain from interfering in the natural world, are in ordinary circumstances almost always possible to comply with. We can usually find methods of making restitution that do not cause harm to or impose constraints upon living things. The same is true of developing in them the bonds of trust. The major modes of restitution are setting aside wilderness areas, protecting endangered and threatened species, restoring the quality of an environment that has been degraded, and aiding plants and animals to return to a healthy state when they have been weakened or injured by human causes. All of these measures can normally be taken without the necessity of breaking faith with or imposing restrictions upon the creatures of the wild. . . .

FIVE PRIORITY PRINCIPLES FOR THE FAIR RESOLUTION OF CONFLICTING CLAIMS

I shall now consider . . . five . . . principles, to be designated as follows:

a. The principle of self-defense.
b. The principle of proportionality.
c. The principle of minimum wrong.
d. The principle of distributive justice.
e. The principle of restitutive justice.

Although I believe these five principles cover all the major ways of adjudicating fairly among competing claims arising from clashes between the duties of human ethics and those of environmental ethics, I must emphasize at the outset that they do not yield a neat solution to every possible conflict situation. . . .

The Principle of Self-Defense

The principle of self-defense states that it is permissible for moral agents to protect themselves against dangerous or harmful organisms by destroying them. This holds, however, only when moral agents, using reasonable care, cannot avoid being exposed to such organisms and cannot prevent them from doing serious damage to the environmental conditions that make it possible for moral agents to exist and function as moral agents. Furthermore, the principle does not allow the use of just any means of self-protection, but only those means that will do the least possible harm to the organisms consistent with the purpose of preserving the existence and functioning of moral agents. There must be no available alternative that is known to be equally effective but to cause less harm to the ''attacking'' organisms.

The principle of self-defense permits actions that are absolutely required for maintaining the very existence of moral agents and for enabling them to ex-

ercise the capacities of moral agency. It does not permit actions that involve the destruction of organisms when those actions simply promote the interests or values which moral agents may have as persons. Self-defense is defense against *harmful* and *dangerous* organisms, and a harmful or dangerous organism in this context is understood to be one whose activities threaten the life or basic health of those entities which need normally functioning bodies to exist as moral agents.

. . . The principle of self-defense is formulated in such a way as to be species-blind. The statement of the principle refers only to moral agents and organisms (of whatever species) that are not moral agents. No mention is made of humans and nonhumans. Of course, in discussing various aspects and implications of the principle, one ordinarily refers to humans defending themselves against nonhumans as typical of situations in which the principle applies to the practical circumstances of life. Strictly speaking, however, no reference to any species need be made. The fact that (most) humans are moral agents and (most) nonhumans are not is a contingent truth which the principle does not take to be morally relevant. Moral agents are permitted to defend themselves against harmful or dangerous organisms that are not moral agents. This is all the principle of self-defense allows. If there happen to be nonhuman moral agents whose existence as moral agents is endangered by the actions of humans who are not moral agents (such as the insane and the severely retarded), then the principle states that it is permissible for the nonhumans in question to kill those humans who endanger them, if this is required for the preservation of the nonhumans' status as moral agents and there is no alternative way to protect themselves. . . .

The Principle of Proportionality

Before considering in detail each of the four remaining priority principles, it is well to look at the way they are interrelated. First, all four principles apply to situations where the nonhuman organisms involved are *harmless*. If left alone their activities would not endanger or threaten human life and health. Thus all four principles apply to cases of conflict between humans and nonhumans that are not covered by the principle of self-defense.

Next we must make a distinction between basic and nonbasic interests.[3] Using this distinction, the arrangement of the four principles can be set out as follows. The principles of proportionality and minimum wrong apply to cases in which there is a conflict between the *basic* interests of animals or plants and the *nonbasic* interests of humans. The principle of distributive justice, on the other hand, covers conflicts where the interests of all parties involved are *basic*. Finally, the principle of restitutive justice applies only where, in the past, either the principle of minimum wrong or that of distributive justice has been used. Each of those principles creates situations where some form of compensation or reparation must be made to nonhuman organisms, and thus the idea of restitution becomes applicable. . . .

---

3. In one of the few systematic studies of priority principles holding between humans and nonhumans, Donald VanDeVeer argues that the distinction between basic and ''peripheral'' (nonbasic) interests, which applies to all species that can be said to have interests, is a morally relevant difference; see VanDeVeer, ''Interspecific Justice,'' *Inquiry* 22/1-2 (Summer 1979): 55-79. VanDeVeer would not, however, be likely to accept any of the priority principles I set out since he considers the psychological capacity to live a satisfying life a ground for counting the interests of beings possessing that capacity to be of greater weight than the equally basic interests of beings lacking it. His main reason for opposing pure egalitarianism among species seems to be that such a view is counterintuitive, being incompatible with ''our deepest and strongest pre-theoretical convictions about specific cases'' (p. 58; see also pp. 66 and 76).

VanDeVeer's position has recently been defended, with certain qualifications, by Robin Attfield in *The Ethics of Environmental Concern* (New York: Columbia University Press, 1983), chapter 9. Attfield holds that ''. . . varying degrees of *intrinsic* value attach to lives in which different capacities are realized'' (Attfield's italics, p. 176). This is a view similar to that of Louis G. Lombardi, which I critically examined in Chapter Three [of *Respect for Nature*.] Attfield's arguments, unlike Lombardi's, are marred by a failure to distinguish the concept of intrinsic value from that of inherent worth. The utilitarianism Attfield espouses is not seen to be logically incompatible with the principle that each organism has inherent worth as an individual, a principle he also appears to hold. The incompatibility of these two ideas has been clearly explained by Tom Regan in *The Case for Animal Rights,* chapters 7 and 8.

It is possible for us to make judgments of the comparative importance of interests of nonhuman animals and plants because, once we become factually enlightened about what protects or promotes their good, we can *take their standpoint* and judge what is, from their point of view, an important or unimportant event in their lives as far as their overall well-being is concerned. Thus we are able to make a reasonable estimate of how seriously they would be harmed or deprived of something good if a certain condition were absent from their lives.

What counts as a serious harm or deprivation will, of course, depend on the kind of organism concerned. If each organism has a good of its own, so that it makes sense to speak of its faring well or poorly to the extent that it is able or unable to live a life fitted for its species-specific nature, then we may consider a serious harm or deprivation as being whatever severely impairs its ability to live such a life or makes it totally unable to do so.

In the case of humans a serious harm or deprivation will be whatever takes away or greatly reduces their powers of rationality and autonomy, including conditions of mental or physical incapacity that make it impossible for them to live a meaningful life. Since properly functioning organs and the soundness and health of other components of one's body are essential to human well-being, whatever injures these parts of one's body is a harm. The seriousness of the harm depends on the extent and permanence of damage done to those parts and on their contribution to the ability of the organism as a whole to function in a healthy way. With regard to the psychological aspects of a human being, a serious harm will include anything that causes insanity, severe emotional disorder, or mental retardation of a kind that prevents the development or exercise of the basic powers of rationality and autonomy.

I might note that with reference to humans, basic interests are what rational and factually enlightened people would value as an essential part of their very existence as *persons*. They are what people need if they are going to be able to pursue those goals and purposes that make life meaningful and worthwhile. Thus for human persons their basic interests are those

interests which, when morally legitimate, they have a *right* to have fulfilled. . . . We do not have a right to whatever will make us happy or contribute to the realization of our value system; we do have a right to the necessary conditions for the maintenance and development of our personhood. These conditions include subsistence and security ("the right to life"), autonomy, and liberty. A violation of people's moral rights is the worst thing that can happen to them, since it deprives them of what is essential to their being able to live a meaningful and worthwhile life. And since the fundamental, necessary conditions for such a life are the same for everyone, our human rights have to do with universal values or primary goods. They are the entitlement we all have as persons to what makes us persons and preserves our existence as persons.

In contrast with these universal values or primary goods that constitute our basic interests, our nonbasic interests are the particular ends we consider worth seeking and the means we consider best for achieving them that make up our individual value systems. The nonbasic interests of humans thus vary from person to person, while their basic interests are common to all.

This discussion of basic and nonbasic interests has been presented to introduce the second and third priority principles on our list, proportionality and minimum wrong. Both principles employ the distinction between basic and nonbasic interests, so it was necessary to clarify this distinction before examining them.

The principles apply to two different kinds of conflicts among competing claims. In both cases we are dealing with situations in which the *basic* interests of animals and plants conflict with the *nonbasic* interests of humans. But each principle applies to a different type of nonbasic human interests. In order to differentiate between these types we must consider various ways in which the nonbasic interests of humans are related to the attitude of respect for nature.

First, there are nonbasic human interests which are *intrinsically incompatible with* the attitude of respect for nature. The pursuit of these interests would be given up by anyone who had respect for nature since

the kind of actions and intentions involved in satisfying them directly embody or express an exploitative attitude toward nature. Such an attitude is incompatible with that of respect because it means that one considers wild creatures to have merely instrumental value for human ends. To satisfy nonbasic interests of this first kind is to deny the inherent worth of animals and plants in natural ecosystems. Examples of such interests and of actions performed to satisfy them are the following (all actually occur in the contemporary world):

> Slaughtering elephants so the ivory of their tusks can be used to carve items for the tourist trade.
>
> Killing rhinoceros so that their horns can be used as dagger handles.
>
> Picking rare wildflowers, such as orchids and cactuses, for one's private collection.
>
> Capturing tropical birds, for sale as caged pets.
>
> Trapping and killing reptiles, such as snakes, crocodiles, alligators, and turtles, for their skins and shells to be used in making expensive shoes, handbags, and other "fashion" products.
>
> Hunting and killing rare wild mammals, such as leopards and jaguars, for the luxury fur trade.
>
> All hunting and fishing which is done as an enjoyable pastime (whether or not the animals killed are eaten), when such activities are not necessary to meet the basic interests of humans. This includes all sport hunting and recreational fishing.

The ends and purposes of these practices and the human interests that motivate them are inherently incompatible with the attitude of respect for nature in the following sense. If we consider the various practices along with their central purposes as representing a certain human attitude toward nature, this attitude can only be described as exploitative. Those who participate in such activities with the aim of accomplishing the various purposes that motivate and direct them, as well as those who enjoy or consume the products while knowing the methods by which they were obtained, cannot be said to have genuine respect for nature. For all such practices treat wild creatures as mere instruments to human ends, thus denying their inherent worth. Wild animals and plants are being valued only as a source of human pleasure or as things that can be manipulated and used to bring about human pleasure.

It is important to realize that the human interests that underlie these practices are nonbasic. Even when hunters and fishermen eat what they have killed, this is incidental to the central purpose and governing aim of their sport. (I am not at this point considering the very different case of subsistence hunting and fishing, where such activities are not done as enjoyable pastimes but out of necessity.) That eating what they kill is a matter of pleasure and hence serves only a nonbasic interest is shown by the fact that they would continue to hunt or fish even if, for some reason of health or convenience, they did not eat the mammal, bird, or fish they killed. They are not hunting or fishing in order to have enough food to live.

With reference to this and to all the other examples given, it should be noted that none of the actions violate human rights. Indeed, if we stay within the boundaries of human ethics alone, people have a moral right to do such things, since they have a freedom-right to pursue without interference their legitimate interests and, within those boundaries, an interest is "legitimate" if its pursuit does not involve doing any wrong *to another human being*.

It is only when the principles of environmental ethics are applied to such actions that the exercise of freedom-rights in these cases must be weighed against the demands of the ethics of respect for nature. We then find that the practices in question are wrong, *all things considered*. For if they were judged permissible, the basic interests of animals and plants would be assigned a lower value or importance than the nonbasic interests of humans, which no one who had the attitude of respect for nature (as well as the attitude of respect for persons) would find acceptable. After all, a human being can still live a good life even if he or she does not own caged wild birds, wear apparel made from furs and reptile skins, collect rare wildflowers, engage in hunting and fishing as recreational pastimes, buy ivory carvings, or use horn dagger handles. But every one of these practices treats wild animals and plants as if their very existence is something

having no value at all, other than as means to the satisfaction of human preferences.

Let us now consider another type of nonbasic human interest that can come into conflict with the basic interests of wild animals and plants. These are human interests which, in contrast with those just considered, are not *in themselves* incompatible with respect for nature. Nevertheless, the pursuit of these interests has *consequences* that are undesirable from the perspective of respect for nature and should therefore be avoided if possible. Sometimes the nonbasic human interests concerned will not be valued highly enough to outweigh the bad consequences of fulfilling them. In that case a person who has respect for nature would willingly forego the pursuit of those interests. Other times the interests will be so highly valued that even those who genuinely respect nature will not be willing to forego the pursuit of the interests. In the latter case, although having and pursuing the interests do not embody or express the attitude of respect for nature, neither do they embody or express a purely exploitative attitude toward nature. Wild animals and plants are not being used or consumed as mere means to human ends, though the consequences of actions in which the interests are pursued are such that wild creatures suffer harm. Examples of nonbasic interests of this type are:

> Building an art museum or library where natural habitat must be destroyed.
>
> Constructing an airport, railroad, harbor, or highway involving the serious disturbance of a natural ecosystem.
>
> Replacing a native forest with a timber plantation.
>
> Damming a free-flowing river for a hydroelectric power project.
>
> Landscaping a natural woodland in making a public park.

Whether people who have true respect for nature would give up the activities involved in these situations depends on the value they place on the various interests being furthered. This in turn would depend on people's total systems of value and on what alternatives were available—in particular, whether substitutes less damaging to the environment could be found and whether some or all of the interests could be satisfied in other ways.

Let us recapitulate this classification of nonbasic human interests, since it is crucial to the examination of the priority principles I will consider below. First there are interests that directly express an exploitative attitude toward nature; actions taken to satisfy such interests are intrinsically incompatible with respect for nature. Second, there are interests that do not exemplify in themselves an exploitative attitude toward nature, but in many practical circumstances the means taken to satisfy those interests bring about effects on the natural world which, in the eyes of those who have respect for nature, are to be avoided whenever possible. Among this second class of interests are those which are not important enough to (not so highly valued by) a person to make the gains of their pursuit outweigh the undesirable consequences for wildlife. Others are such that their value does outweigh the undesirable consequences, even when such weight is assigned by one who has full respect for nature.

This classification bears on the two priority principles we are now about to consider: the principle of proportionality and that of minimum wrong. Each of the two kinds of nonbasic human interests mentioned above determines the range of application of one of these principles. The principle of proportionality applies to situations of conflict between the basic interests of wild animals and plants and those nonbasic human interests that are intrinsically incompatible with respect for nature. The principle of minimum wrong, on the other hand, applies to conflicts between the basic interests of wild animals and plants and those nonbasic human interests that are so highly valued that even a person who has respect for nature would not be willing to abstain from pursuing them, knowing that the pursuit of such interests will bring about conditions detrimental to the natural world.

Figure 7-1 schematically represents the relations among the five priority principles and their ranges of application.

Putting aside consideration of the principle of minimum wrong until later, I shall now discuss that of proportionality. The central idea of the principle of proportionality is that, in a conflict between human values and the good of (harmless) wild animals and plants, greater weight is to be given to basic than to nonbasic interests, no matter what species, human or other, the competing claims arise from. Within its proper range of application the principle prohibits us from allowing nonbasic interests to override basic ones, even if the nonbasic interests are those of humans and the basic are those of animals and plants. . . .

The Principle of Minimum Wrong

. . . The principle states that, when rational, informed, and autonomous persons *who have adopted the attitude of respect for nature* are nevertheless unwilling to forego the two sorts of values mentioned above, even though they are aware that the consequences of pursuing those values will involve harm to wild animals and plants, it is permissible for them to pursue those values only so long as doing so involves fewer wrongs (violations of duties) than any alternative way of pursuing those values. . . .

How does the principle of minimum wrong determine a fair resolution of competing claims in situations of that kind? The following considerations are the relevant ones to be taken into account. First we must ask ourselves whether the human values being furthered are really worth the extreme cost being imposed on wild creatures. In this connection we should reflect on our own value system and on the way of life of our community to see whether a modification in values or a shift in perspective could not be made, consistent with the most fundamental aspects of that system or way of life, which would obviate at least some of the direct killing of nonhumans. Secondly, we should examine carefully all alternative possibilities open to us with regard to the manner of pursuing our values and way of life. The principle of minimum wrong demands that we choose the alternative that either eliminates direct killing entirely or that involves the least numbers killed. Finally, our respect for nature makes us respond with abhorrence to whatever killing is done, and gives rise to the recognition of our duty to make reparation or some form of compen-

Wild Animals and Plants	Harmful to Humans	Harmless to Humans (Or: their harmfulness can reasonably be avoided)		
		Basic Interests		*Basic Interests*
. . . in conflict with . . .		. . . in conflict with . . .		. . . in conflict with . . .
		Nonbasic interests		*Basic interests*
		Intrinsically incompatible with respect for nature.	Intrinsically compatible with respect for nature, but extrinsically detrimental to wildlife and natural ecosystems.	
Humans				
Priority Principles	(1) *Self-defense*	(2) *Proportionality*	(3) *Minimum wrong*	(4) *Distributive justice*
			. . . when (3) or (4) have been applied . . . (5) *Restitutive justice*	

FIGURE 7-1

sation for the harm we have done to living things in the natural world. . . .

We might say that the system of *intrinsically valued ends* shared by a whole society as the focus of its ways of life, along with those human creations and productions that are judged as *supremely inherently valuable* by rational and enlightened members of the society, determine the set of human interests that are to be weighed against the interests of animals and plants in the situations of conflict to which the principle of minimum wrong is applicable.

The Principle of Distributive Justice

This fourth priority principle applies to competing claims between humans and nonhumans under two conditions. First, the nonhuman organisms are not harming us, so the principle of self-defense does not apply. Secondly, the interests that give rise to the competing claims are on the same level of comparative importance, all being *basic* interests, so the principles of proportionality and of minimum wrong do not apply. The range of application of the fourth principle covers cases that do not fall under the first three.

This principle is called the principle of distributive justice because it provides the criteria for a just distribution of interest-fulfillment among all parties to a conflict when the interests are all basic and hence of equal importance to those involved. Being of equal importance, they are counted as having the same moral weight. This equality of weight must be preserved in the conflict-resolving decision if it is to be fair to all. The principle of distributive justice requires that when the interests of the parties are all basic ones and there exists a natural source of good that can be used for the benefit of any of the parties, each party must be allotted an equal share. A fair share in those circumstances is an equal share.

When we try to put this principle of distributive justice into practice, however, we find that even the fairest methods of distribution cannot guarantee perfect equality of treatment to each individual organism. Consequently we are under the moral requirement to supplement all decisions grounded on distributive justice with a further duty imposed by the fifth priority principle, that of restitutive justice. . . .

In working out the various methods by which the principle of distributive justice can be put into practice, we must keep in mind the fact that the wild animals and plants we are concerned with are not themselves harmful to us. Consequently we are not under any necessity to kill them in self-defense. Since they are not "attacking" us, we can try to avoid or eliminate situations where we are forced to choose between their survival and ours. Thus the principle of distributive justice requires us to devise ways of transforming situations of confrontation into situations of mutual accommodation whenever it is possible to do so. In this way we can share the beneficial resources of the Earth equally with other members of the Community of Life. Our aim is to make it possible for wild animals and plants to carry on their natural existence side by side with human cultures.

Sometimes, however, the clash between basic human interests and the equally basic interests of nonhumans cannot be avoided. Perhaps the most obvious case arises from the necessity of humans to consume nonhumans as food. Although it may be possible for most people to eat plants rather than animals, I shall point out in a moment that this is not true of all people. And why should eating plants be ethically more desirable than eating animals?

Let us first look at situations where, due to severe environmental conditions, humans must use wild animals as a source of food. In other words, they are situations where subsistence hunting and fishing are necessary for human survival. Consider, for example, the hunting of whales and seals in the Arctic, or the

killing and eating of wild goats and sheep by those living at high altitudes in mountainous regions. In these cases it is impossible to raise enough domesticated animals to supply food for a culture's populace, and geographical conditions preclude dependence on plant life as a source of nutrition. The principle of distributive justice applies to circumstances of that kind. In such circumstances the principle entails that it is morally *permissible* for humans to kill wild animals for food. This follows from the equality of worth holding between humans and animals. For if humans refrained from eating animals in those circumstances they would in effect be sacrificing their lives for the sake of animals, and no requirement to do that is imposed by respect for nature. Animals are not of *greater* worth, so there is no obligation to further their interests at the cost of the basic interests of humans.

However, since it is always a prima facie duty of environmental ethics not to destroy whole ecosystems (the duties of nonmaleficence and noninterference), it follows that wherever possible the choice of animal food source and the methods used in hunting should be guided by the principle of minimum wrong. The impact on natural ecosystems of the practice of killing wild animals for food must not involve a greater number of wrongs than any available alternative.

The same considerations apply to the practice of culling wild animals for food (as is done with the Wildebeest and the Water Buffalo in Africa) where environmental conditions make it impossible to use domesticated animals or to grow edible plants for human survival. Here the morally right decision is determined, first by the permissibility of consuming wild animals under the principle of distributive justice, and second, by the obligation to choose the species of animal to be taken and the manner of taking them that entail least harm to all the wild living things in the area. Thus severe damage to nature ecosystems and whole biotic communities must be avoided wherever possible.

I turn now to the issue of meat-eating versus vegetarianism, at least as far as the principles of environmental ethics apply to it. There are two main points to be considered. The first is that, when we raise and slaughter animals for food, the wrong we do to them does not consist simply in our causing them pain.

Even if it became possible for us to devise methods of killing them, as well as ways of treating them while alive, that involved little or no pain, we would still violate a prima facie duty in consuming them. They would still be treated as mere means to our ends and so would be wronged. Now, we see above that it is permissible to kill animals when this is necessary for our survival. But will not the very same be true of our killing plants, in the light of the fact that plants, just like animals, are our equals in inherent worth? Although no pain or conscious suffering to living things is involved here, we are nevertheless using plants wholly for our own purposes. They are therefore being wronged when we kill them to eat them. Yet it is permissible to do this, since we have no duty to sacrifice ourselves to them. Whether we are dealing with animals or with plants, then, the principle of distributive justice applies (and along with it, as we shall see later, the principle of restitutive justice).

Still, the factor of animal suffering does raise important considerations in practice even if no greater wrong is committed in eating animals than in eating plants. Granted that susceptibility to pain does not give animals a higher inherent worth; nevertheless any form of conscious suffering is an intrinsically bad occurrence in the life of a sentient creature. From the standpoint of the animals involved, a life without such experiences is better than a life that includes them. Such a being's good is not fully realized when it is caused to suffer in ways that are not contributory to its overall well-being. We know that this is so in our own case, and must therefore infer that it is so in their case.

Now, insofar as respect is due to sentient animals, moral consideration and concern for their well-being will accordingly include attempts to minimize intrinsic evils in their lives. So when there is a choice between killing plants or killing sentient animals, it will be less wrong to kill plants if animals are made to suffer when they are taken for food.

I consider now the main point regarding the relevance of the principles of environmental ethics to the issue of vegetarianism versus meat eating. It will become clear that, in the light of this second point, anyone who has respect for nature will be on the side of vegetarianism, even though plants and animals are regarded as having the same inherent worth. The point that is crucial here is the amount of arable land needed for raising grain and other plants as food for those animals that are in turn to be eaten by humans when compared with the amount of land needed for raising grain and other plants for direct human consumption. . . . We can drastically reduce the amount of cultivated land needed for human food production by changing from a meat-eating culture to a vegetarian culture. The land thus saved could be set aside as sanctuaries for wildlife. . . .

The Principle of Restitutive Justice

. . . As a priority principle in our present context, the principle of restitutive justice is applicable whenever the principles of minimum wrong and distributive justice have been followed. In both cases harm is done to animals and plants that are harmless, so some form of reparation or compensation is called for if our actions are to be fully consistent with the attitude of respect for nature. (In applying the minimum wrong and distributive justice principles, no harm is done to harmless *humans,* so there occurs an inequality of treatment between humans and nonhumans in these situations.) In its role as a priority principle for determining a fair way to resolve conflicts between humans and nonhumans, the principle of restitutive justice must therefore supplement those of minimum wrong and distributive justice.

What kinds of reparation or compensation are suitable? Two factors can guide us in this area. The first is the idea that the greater the harm done, the greater the compensation required. Any practice of promoting or protecting the good of animals and plants which is to serve to restore the balance of justice between humans and nonhumans must bring about an amount of good that is comparable (as far as can be reasonably estimated) to the amount of evil to be compensated for.

The second factor is to focus our concern on the soundness and health of whole ecosystems and their biotic communities, rather than on the good of particular individuals. As a practical measure this is the most effective means for furthering the good of the greatest number of organisms. Moreover, by setting aside certain natural habitats and by maintaining certain types of physical environments in their natural condition, compensation to wild creatures can be ''paid'' in an appropriate way.... To set aside habitat areas and protect environmental conditions in those areas so that wild communities of animals and plants can realize their good is the most appropriate way to restore the balance of justice with them, for it gives full expression to our respect for nature even when we have done harm to living things in order to benefit ourselves. We can, as it were, return the favor they do us by doing something for their sake. Thus we need not bear a burden of eternal guilt because we have used them—and will continue to use them—for our own ends. There is a way to make amends.

DISCUSSION TOPICS

1. Give examples of your own of a plant and an animal having a good of its own. Do you agree with Taylor that a stone does not have a good of its own?

2. Taylor includes plants in his system of respect for nature, whereas Regan does not consider plants to have moral rights. Which author do you agree with? Why?

3. Apply Taylor's four duties to nature to the attempt to save the California condor with a captive breeding program. Is this program morally right?

4. Using Taylor's system of five priority principles, how would you decide:
   (a) Whether to construct an airport, if you were a member of a board of supervisors in a rural area.
   (b) Whether to build a shelter for the homeless on land currently used as a wildlife refuge by your city, if you were mayor.

CLASS EXERCISES

The students have each recently purchased a 100-acre forest. Assuming they were limited to the views presented in this chapter, which theory would they use to guide their decisions in dealing with this forest?

Would they choose a different theory if they were deciding how to raise a herd of dairy cows on a farm?

FOR FURTHER READING

Armstrong-Buck, Susan. ''Nonhuman Experience: A Whiteheadian Analysis.'' *Process Studies* 18, No. 1: 1-18, 1989. An analysis of recent findings concerning nonhuman experience, in particular primate experience. Includes a proposed typology of self-consciousness.

Between the Species, an ethics journal published quarterly by the Schweitzer Center of the San Francisco Bay Institute/Congress of Cultures (P.O. Box 254, Berkeley, Calif. 94701). A good source of philosophical and literary essays and poetry concerning the human-animal relationship.

Botzler, R.G. and S.B. Armstrong-Buck. ''Ethical Considerations in Research on Wildlife Diseases.'' *Journal of Wildlife Diseases* 21: 341-354, 1985. Suggests guidelines for use of animals in wildlife research.

Cheney, Dorothy L. and Robert M. Seyforth. *How Monkeys See the World: Inside the Mind of Another Species.* Chicago: University of Chicago Press, 1990. A thorough and detailed study of wild vervets and captive primates, co-authored by an anthropologist and a psychologist. The book examines the communicative and cognitive abilities of primates living under natural conditions, emphasizing their social interactions. Extensive bibliography.

Clark, Stephen R.L. *The Nature of the Beast: Are Animals Moral?* Oxford: Oxford University Press, 1984. An Aristotelian discussion which attempts to see animals for their own sake and for what we can learn about ourselves.

Dombrowski, Daniel A. *Hartshorne and the Metaphysics of Animal Rights.* Albany N.Y.: State University of New York Press, 1988. A perceptive study of Hartshorne's theory of God and his thoughts on animals, including the aesthetics of birdsong.

Dombrowski, Daniel A. *The Philosophy of Vegetarianism* Amherst: University of Massachusetts Press, 1984. A well-written study emphasizing ancient Greek philosophy. Contains an extensive annotated bibliography.

Godlovitch, Stanley, and Roslind Godlovitch, eds. *Animals, Men, and Morals: An Equity into the Maltreatment of Non-Humans.* New York: Taplinger, 1972. The book, by philosophers and sociologists, which arguably began the contemporary animal rights movement.

Gould, James L. ''Do Honeybees Know What They are Doing?'' *Natural History* 88.6: 66-75, 1979. Discusses intriguing evidence of learning in bees.

Griffin, D.R. *Animal Thinking,* Cambridge, Mass.: Harvard University Press, 1984. A persuasive argument that animal consciousness is the simplest explanation of much animal behavior.

Griffin, D.R., ed. *Animal Mind–Human Mind.* New York: Springer-Verlag, 1982. A collection of valuable papers interpreting the animal mind.

Howard, Walter E. *Animal Rights vs. Nature.* Davis, Calif.: W.E. Howard, 1990. A highly polemical argument against animal rights by a zoologist.

Lorenz, Konrad. *Man Meets Dog.* Middlesex, England: Penguin, 1953. A classic by a distinguished ethologist, describing the complexity of the human-dog relationship and the depth of canine personalities he has known.

Mitchell, Robert W. and Nicholas S. Thompson, eds. *Deception: Perspectives on Human and Nonhuman Deceit.* Albany, N.Y.: State University of New York Press, 1986. A fine collection of essays dealing with many aspects of deception.

Partridge, Ernest. "Three Wrong Leads in a Search for an Environmental Ethic: Tom Regan on Animal Rights, Inherent Values, and Deep Ecology," *Ethics and Animals* 3: 61-74, 1983. A clear exposition of the basic individualistic-holistic problem.

Patterson, Francine and Eugene Linden. *The Education of Koko.* New York: Holt, Rinehart and Winston, 1981. An intriguing introduction to Koko, the first gorilla to learn human language.

Radner, Daisie and Michael Radner. *Animal Consciousness.* Buffalo, N.Y.: Prometheus Books, 1989. A valuable analysis of the Cartesian concept of consciousness as involving reflective and nonreflective consciousness. The Radners argue that granting animals moral status requires recognizing species-specific interests.

Regan, Tom, ed. *Animal Sacrifices: Religious Perspectives on the Use of Animals in Science.* Philadelphia: Temple University Press, 1986. Contains articles on animal experimentation from Western and non-Western religious views.

Regan, Tom and Peter Singer, eds. *Animal Rights and Human Obligations.* Englewood Cliffs, N.J.: Prentice Hall, 1989. A useful collection of contemporary and historical essays within the Western tradition. Includes some essays on wildlife.

Rollin, Bernard E. *Animal Rights and Human Morality.* Buffalo, N.Y.: Prometheus Books, 1981. A lucid and critical assessment of the Western view of animals, utilizing the concept of *telos.* Contains thoughtful chapters on experimentation on animals in laboratories and schools, and our obligations to pet animals.

Rollin, Bernard E. *The Unheeded Cry: Animal Consciousness, Animal Pain and Science.* Oxford: Oxford University Press, 1990. A thoroughly researched study by the first philosopher to teach courses in veterinary ethics. Rollin discusses the attitude toward animal consciousness, beginning with George Romanes in the nineteenth century and including both American and European views. Extensive bibliography from 1879 to the present.

Rose, John M. "Nothing of the Origin and Destiny of Cats: The Remainder of the Logos." *Between the Species* 6, No. 2: 53-62, 1990. A helpful analysis of Aristotle's and Heidegger's understanding of animal logos, which concludes that both thinkers are caught up in the understanding of animals as equipment.

Sapontzis, S.F. "Are Animals Moral Beings?" *American Philosophic Qurterly* 17, No. 1: 45-52, 1980. Sapontzis argues that animals act morally in the sense that they can do good though they may not be aware of the moral value of the action. Animals who do good must be respected and given rights to life and dignity.

Singer, Peter. *Animal Liberation.* New York: Avon, 1975. A strong utilitarian argument for considering the interests of animals equally with those of any other sentient being. May be the only philosophical book to contain recipes.

Singer, Peter. *Practical Ethics.* Cambridge: Cambridge University Press, 1979. A well-written book which further develops his 1975 *Animal Liberation.* Addresses hunger, abortion and euthanasia.

Singer, Peter, ed. *In Defense of Animals.* New York: Harper & Row, 1986. A readable collection of essays by both theorists and practitioners in the animal rights movement, including discussions of factory farming, experimentation, zoos, and endangered species.

Varner, Gary E. "Biological Functions and Biological Interests." *Southern Journal of Philosophy* 23, No. 2: 251-270, 1990. Varner refines Goodpaster's view by making a useful distinction between biological and preference interests.

CHAPTER EIGHT

Ecocentrism

In this chapter we define ecocentrism and distinguish its two major forms. We then address several ethical issues that emerge from an ecocentric world view.

Ecocentrism is based on the philosophical premise that the natural world has inherent or intrinsic value. There are two types of ecocentrism: the land ethic and deep ecology. Proponents of the land ethic advocate that humans have an ethical responsibility toward the natural world. Although the roots of the land ethic can be traced to many different cultures, its expression in Western philosophical thought is relatively recent, and was first clearly articulated by Aldo Leopold in the late 1940s.

In contrast to anthropocentrists and extensionists, proponents of the land ethic advocate a true environmental ethic, valuing nature in and of itself, rather than only in relation to its significance for the survival and well-being of humans or other select species. The land ethic implies human responsibility for natural communities. In the first essay of this chapter, "The Land Ethic," Aldo Leopold asserts that "A thing is right when it tends to preserve the integrity, stability, and beauty of the biotic community. It is wrong when it tends otherwise." In Leopold's view, adherence to the land ethic results in a change of human self-per-ception; humans cease to see themselves as conquerors or as members of a superior species on the planet, but rather see themselves as plain members and participating citizens of the land community.

Deep ecology is a more recent ecocentric philosophy. Deep ecology involves an intensive questioning of the values and lifestyles that originally led to serious environmental problems. The term *deep ecology* was coined in 1974 by Arne Naess, a Norwegian philosopher, to contrast with the notion of shallow ecology, which includes all superficial, short-term reform approaches to solving such environmental problems as pollution and resource depletion.

Deep ecologists' ideas do not constitute an ethical theory defendable by rational argument in the usual Western sense.[1] Rather, deep ecologists call for a transformation of the fundamental principles guiding a long-term relationship with the environment. These principles may include living a life that is simple in means but rich in ends; honoring the right of all life forms to live and flourish; empathizing with other life

---

1. George Sessions, "The Deep Ecological Movement: A Review," *Environmental Review* 11 (1987): 105-125.

forms; maximizing the diversity of human and non-human life; and maximizing long-range universal self-realization. Deep ecologists share a commitment to a new vision of the world. They advocate an ecological wisdom, or ecosophy, rather than an environmental ethic per se. However, it can be seen that many of the human choices based on deep ecology values are similar to the choices based on land ethic values.

JUSTIFICATIONS USED FOR AN ECOCENTRIC PERSPECTIVE

All of the authors in this chapter state or imply that the natural world has inherent or intrinsic value. While some of the authors do not defend their views, most provide at least some rationale for their perspectives.

Leopold explicitly articulates only a limited justification for the land ethic. For example, he describes some of the serious environmental problems for which humans were responsible, paticularly in the southwestern United States, as reason for a land ethic. However, in his essay, "Ecological Sensibility," John Rodman maintains that the whole of Leopold's book, *The Sand County Almanac,* provides implicit justification for the land ethic, inducing readers to take a sympathetic view of the natural world and to perceive natural communities and their respective members as subjects rather than mere objects.

In "The Conceptual Foundations of the Land Ethic" J. Baird Callicott argues that human ethics originally evolved out of moral feelings or social sentiments. He notes that this perspective was first developed by Adam Smith and David Hume, that it later served as a basis for Darwin's views on the evolution of ethics, and that Leopold built the land ethic on this philosophical foundation. Callicott further proposes that a justification of the land ethic can be grounded on three scientific cornerstones: evolution, ecology, and Copernican astronomy.

Using the Aristotelian notion of *telos,* Rodman argues that moral consideration ought to be extended to anything that is autonomous and has the capacity for self-direction or self-regulation. In a radical proposal, Rodman extends the notion of *telos* to characterize not only individual living entities, but natural systems as well. However, application of the notion of *telos* to ecosystems has provoked controversy.[2,3]

James D. Heffernan proposes in his essay, "The Land Ethic: A Critical Appraisal" that all living things, including ecosystems, have interests that can be benefited or harmed. Heffernan thus justifies an ecocentric perspective by arguing that all things which can be benefited or harmed, including natural systems, deserve moral concern.

Naess in his essay, "The Deep Ecological Movement: Some Philosophical Aspects," traces the principles of deep ecology to fundamental insights found in Christianity, Buddhism, Taoism, Baha'i, and other philosophies. Dave Foreman in "Putting the Earth First" bases his ecocentric perspective on the conviction that the natural world has intrinsic value, but offers no further justification.

DOES A LAND ETHIC ASCRIBE RIGHTS OR RESPECT TO THE BIOTIC COMMUNITY?

Many traditional ethical systems incorporate the notion that certain rights are ascribed to those members falling under moral concern. Rodman ascribes rights to ecosystems and proposes certain duties humans have toward ecosystems based on these rights. In contrast, Callicott believes that the notion of respect is a more appropriate perspective than rights with regard to the natural world. Leopold implies the notion of respect when he points out that moral consideration for the land does not prevent the alteration, use, or management of biotic communities, but does affirm their right to a continued existence, and at least in some places their continued existence in a natural state.

---

2. H. Cahen, "Against the Moral Considerability of Ecosystems," *Environmental Ethics* 10 (1988): 195-216.

3. S.N. Salthe and B.M. Salthe, "Ecosystem Moral Considerability: A Reply to Cahen," *Environmental Ethics* 11 (1989): 355-361.

THE RELATIONSHIP OF HUMANS TO NATURE

One concern related to the land ethic is how to resolve the conflicting needs that exist between humans and nature. For example, Heffernan points out that feeding starving people through intense agriculture may lead to the disruption of healthy ecosystems, but ceasing these agricultural efforts may lead to immoral consequences.

The concern that ecocentrism may be a totalitarian rather than a humanistic philosophy is addressed by Don E. Marietta, Jr. in his essay, ''Environmental Holism and Individuals.'' He points out that there are several versions of holism (ecocentrism), each having several forms ranging from modest to extreme. In Marietta's view, only the extreme forms of ecocentrism that subordinate the interests and rights of individuals to the good of the natural world might justify the claim of critics that ecocentrism is a totalitarian position.

Most land ethic philosophers view the land ethic as an additional rule to a primary duty to humans. Heffernan interprets the land ethic to provide an additional moral principle: that human survival interests ought to outweigh survival interests of nonhumans, but that the survival interests of nonhumans ought to outweigh the nonsurvival interests of humans.

Likewise, Callicott argues that land ethic values do not replace or preempt previous moral responsibilities toward humans; rather, they enhance them. Callicott draws on parallel concepts among Native American groups, such as the value for maintaining an attitude of respect toward individual creatures while still using them or allowing them their natural fates.

In contrast, some deep ecologists deemphasize the importance of the human species. Foreman, for example, stresses that humans are only one of many species, and argues that, in fact, there simply are too many people in the world. Foreman asserts that human lives have no greater value than do other lives, and that the long-term health of the biosphere should take precedence over human welfare.

A more moderate perspective is advocated by Naess, who believes that humans have overriding obligations to their own species. Like Heffernan, however, he believes that vital needs of nonhumans ought to take precedence over nonvital needs of humans. Naess argues that excessive pressures on planetary life stem primarily from the human population explosion, particularly among industrialized nations, and that population reduction might be the highest priority in these societies.

RANKING CONFLICTING VALUES WITHIN THE NATURAL WORLD

Another concern related to the land ethic is how to resolve conflicts between the needs of various ecosystems, as well as among the different components within them. Rodman provides a cluster of values that can apply to both individual natural entities and to natural systems; these values include diversity, complexity, integrity, harmony, stability, and scarcity. Rodman proposes that these values be used as criteria for comparing alternative courses of permissible actions to optimize good effects.

THE ROLE OF WILDERNESS IN THE NATURAL ENVIRONMENT

Naess recognizes that humans always have altered their environment and probably always will, but argues that the nature and extent of these alterations is the key concern. In his view, human destruction of nature has been excessive, and there should be a continued effort to preserve and extend areas of wilderness. Naess argues that large wilderness areas are required for continued evolutionary speciation of biotic organisms.

Foreman believes that preservation of wilderness is of greatest importance. He considers wilderness to be the real and permanent part of the world, and human constructions such as cities or the global business community to be artificial and transitory parts. Virtually all of human history has been played out in wilderness; wilderness also is the arena for evolution and the home of many other species with whom humans share the planet.

THE RELATIONSHIP OF ENLIGHTENED SELF-INTEREST TO THE LAND ETHIC

There are similarities between the positions advocated by proponents of the land ethic and proponents of an enlightened self-interest form of anthropocentrism. Both, for example, advocate concern for the long-term health and well-being of the biosphere, although based upon different underlying assumptions or values. Callicott questions whether Leopold genuinely accords true moral standing to nonhuman entities and nature as a whole, or whether the land ethic is based on enlightened self-interest. Callicott argues that the land ethic has elements of both perspectives, but believes that Leopold clearly goes beyond advocating only enlightened self-interest, and truly extends moral consideration to nature.

Naess (p. 16) recognizes the effectiveness of homocentric arguments to protect the natural world, but gives several reasons why he believes it is not wise to argue solely from this point of view.

The Land Ethic

Aldo Leopold

Aldo Leopold (1887–1948), one of the earliest and most influential voices among Western scholars elucidating an ecocentric perspective, was a forester, wildlife manager, and creative thinker. Leopold graduated from the Yale School of Forestry, and worked several years for the U.S. Forest Service. Later Leopold was instrumental in establishing wildlife management as a profession. At the University of Wisconsin, Madison, he served as the country's first professor of wildlife management.

Leopold was greatly concerned by the detrimental impact of humans on the land and particularly by the rapid deterioration of the environment in the southwestern United States. Before Leopold's time, American conservationists had justified most of their concerns about the environment by pointing to its importance for human survival and well-being. Leopold believed that a basic lack of human regard for the land itself lay at the heart of most natural resource and agricultural problems. He argued strongly that the biotic world and natural environment themselves have intrinsic value. Rather than dominating and exploiting the natural world, Leopold believed that humans should see themselves as "plain members and citizens" of the biotic community.

Leopold's essay, "The Land Ethic," one of the final selections in his book, A Sand County Almanac, is considered by many to be a modern classic. In it, Leopold first clarified the notion of human moral responsibility to the natural environment. The heart of this ethic is summarized in a few, often quoted words: "A thing is right when it tends to preserve the integrity, stability, and beauty of the biotic community. It is wrong when it tends otherwise." The land ethic essay appears to be a single coherent statement that easily might have been written over a short period of time, but actually was written in four phases over a 14-year period.[4]

---

4. Curt Meine, "Building The Land Ethic," in J. Baird Callicott, *Companion to a Sand County Almanac* (Wisconsin: Universityof Wisconsin Press, 1987), p. 173.

When god-like Odysseus returned from the wars in Troy, he hanged all on one rope a dozen slave-girls of his household whom he suspected of misbehavior during his absence.

This hanging involved no question of propriety. The girls were property. The disposal of property was then, as now, a matter of expediency, not of right and wrong.

Concepts of right and wrong were not lacking from Odysseus' Greece: witness the fidelity of his wife through the long years before at last his black-prowed galleys clove the wine-dark seas for home. The ethical structure of that day covered wives, but had not yet been extended to human chattels. During the three thousand years which have since elapsed, ethical criteria have been extended to many fields of conduct, with corresponding shrinkages in those judged by expediency only.

THE ETHICAL SEQUENCE

This extension of ethics, so far studied only by philosophers, is actually a process in ecological evolution. Its sequences may be described in ecological as well as well as in philosophical terms. An ethic, ecologically, is a limitation on freedom of action in the struggle for existence. An ethic, philosophically, is a differentiation of social from anti-social conduct. These are two definitions of one thing. The thing has its origin in the tendency of interdependent individuals or groups to evolve modes of co-operation. The ecologist calls these symbioses. Politics and economics are advanced symbioses in which the original free-for-all competition has been replaced, in part, by co-operative mechanisms with an ethical content.

The complexity of co-operative mechanisms has increased with population density, and with the efficiency of tools. It was simpler, for example, to define the anti-social uses of sticks and stones in the days of the mastodons than of bullets and billboards in the age of motors.

The first ethics dealt with the relation between individuals; the Mosaic Decalogue is an example. Later accretions dealt with the relation between the individual and society. The Golden Rule tries to integrate the individual to society; democracy to integrate social organization to the individual.

There is as yet no ethic dealing with man's relation to land and to the animals and plants which grow upon it. Land, like Odysseus' slave-girls, is still property. The land-relation is still strictly economic, entailing privileges but not obligations.

The extension of ethics to this third element in human environment is, if I read the evidence correctly, an evolutionary possibility and an ecological necessity. It is the third step in a sequence. The first two have already been taken. Individual thinkers since the days of Ezekiel and Isaiah have asserted that the despoliation of land is not only inexpedient but wrong. Society, however, has not yet affirmed their belief. I regard the present conservation movement as the embryo of such an affirmation.

An ethic may be regarded as a mode of guidance for meeting ecological situations so new or intricate, or involving such deferred reactions, that the path of social expediency is not discernible to the average individual. Animal instincts are modes of guidance for the individual in meeting such situations. Ethics are possibly a kind of community instinct in-the-making.

THE COMMUNITY CONCEPT

All ethics so far evolved rest upon a single premise: that the individual is a member of a community of interdependent parts. His instincts prompt him to compete for his place in that community, but his ethics prompt him also to co-operate (perhaps in order that there may be a place to compete for).

The land ethic simply enlarges the boundaries of the community to include soils, waters, plants, and animals, or collectively: the land.

This sounds simple: do we not already sing our love for and obligation to the land of the free and the home of the brave? Yes, but just what and whom do we love? Certainly not the soil, which we are sending helter-skelter downriver. Certainly not the waters, which we assume have no function except to turn turbines, float barges, and carry off sewage. Certainly not the plants, of which we exterminate whole com-

munities without batting an eye. Certainly not the animals, of which we have already extirpated many of the largest and most beautiful species. A land ethic of course cannot prevent the alteration, management, and use of these 'resources,' but it does affirm their right to continued existence, and, at least in spots, their continued existence in a natural state.

In short, a land ethic changes the role of *Homo sapiens* from conqueror of the land-community to plain member and citizen of it. It implies respect for his fellow-members, and also respect for the community as such.

In human history, we have learned (I hope) that the conqueror role is eventually self-defeating. Why? Because it is implicit in such a role that the conqueror knows, *ex cathedra,* just what makes the community clock tick, and just what and who is valuable, and what and who is worthless, in community life. It always turns out that he knows neither, and this is why his conquests eventually defeat themselves.

In the biotic community, a parallel situation exists. Abraham knew exactly what the land was for: it was to drip milk and honey into Abraham's mouth. At the present moment, the assurance with which we regard this assumption is inverse to the degree of our education.

The ordinary citizen today assumes that science knows what makes the community clock tick; the scientist is equally sure that he does not. He knows that the biotic mechanism is so complex that its workings may never be fully understood.

That man is, in fact, only a member of a biotic team is shown by an ecological interpretation of history. Many historical events, hitherto explained solely in terms of human enterprise, were actually biotic interactions between people and land. The characteristics of the land determined the facts quite as potently as the characteristics of the men who lived on it.

Consider, for example, the settlement of the Mississippi valley. In the years following the Revolution, three groups were contending for its control: the native Indian, the French and English traders, and the American settlers. Historians wonder what would have happened if the English at Detroit had thrown a little more weight into the Indian side of those tipsy scales which decided the outcome of the colonial migration into the cane-lands of Kentucky. It is time now to ponder the fact that the cane-lands, when subjected to the particular mixture of forces represented by the cow, plow, fire, and axe of the pioneer, became bluegrass. What if the plant succession inherent in this dark and bloody ground had, under the impact of these forces, given us some worthless sedge, shrub, or weed? Would Boone and Kenton have held out? Would there have been any overflow into Ohio, Indiana, Illinois, and Missouri? Any Louisiana Purchase? Any transcontinental union of new states? Any Civil War?

Kentucky was one sentence in the drama of history. We are commonly told what the human actors in this drama tried to do, but we are seldom told that their success, or the lack of it, hung in large degree on the reaction of particular soils to the impact of the particular forces exerted by their occupancy. In the case of Kentucky, we do not even know where the bluegrass came from—whether it is a native species, or a stowaway from Europe.

Contrast the cane-lands with what hindsight tells us about the Southwest, where the pioneers were equally brave, resourceful, and persevering. The impact of occupancy here brought no bluegrass, or other plant fitted to withstand the bumps and buffetings of hard use. This region, when grazed by livestock, reverted through a series of more and more worthless grasses, shrubs, and weeds to a condition of unstable equilibrium. Each recession of plant types bred erosion; each increment to erosion bred a further recession of plants. The result today is a progressive and mutual deterioration, not only of plants and soils, but of the animal community subsisting thereon. The early settlers did not expect this: on the ciénegas of New Mexico some even cut ditches to hasten it. So subtle has been its progress that few residents of the region are aware of it. It is quite invisible to the tourist who finds this wrecked landscape colorful and charming (as indeed it is, but it bears scant resemblance to what it was in 1848).

This same landscape was 'developed' once before, but with quite different results. The Pueblo Indians settled the Southwest in pre-Columbian times, but

they happened *not* to be equipped with range livestock. Their civilization expired, but not because their land expired.

In India, regions devoid of any sod-forming grass have been settled, apparently without wrecking the land, by the simple expedient of carrying the grass to the cow, rather than vice versa. (Was this the result of some deep wisdom, or was it just good luck? I do not know.)

In short, the plant succession steered the course of history; the pioneer simply demonstrated, for good or ill, what successions inhered in the land. Is history taught in this spirit? It will be, once the concept of land as a community really penetrates our intellectual life.

THE ECOLOGICAL CONSCIENCE

Conservation is a state of harmony between man and land. Despite nearly a century of propaganda, conservation still proceeds at a snail's pace; progress still consists largely of letterhead pieties and convention oratory. On the back forty we still slip two steps backward for each forward stride.

The usual answer to this dilemma is 'more conservation education.' No one will debate this, but is it certain that only the *volume* of education needs stepping up? Is something lacking in the *content* as well?

It is difficult to give a fair summary of its content in brief form, but, as I understand it, the content is substantially this: obey the law, vote right, join some organizations, and practice what conservation is profitable on your own land; the government will do the rest.

Is not this formula too easy to accomplish anything worth-while? It defines no right or wrong, assigns no obligation, calls for no sacrifice, implies no change in the current philosophy of values. In respect of land-use, it urges only enlightened self-interest. Just how far will such education take us? An example will perhaps yield a partial answer.

By 1930 it had become clear to all except the ecologically blind that southwestern Wisconsin's topsoil was slipping seaward. In 1933 the farmers were told that if they would adopt certain remedial practices for five years, the public would donate CCC labor to install them, plus the necessary machinery and materials. The offer was widely accepted, but the practices were widely forgotten when the five-year contract period was up. The farmers continued only those practices that yielded an immediate and visible economic gain for themselves.

This led to the idea that maybe farmers would learn more quickly if they themselves wrote the rules. Accordingly the Wisconsin Legislature in 1937 passed the Soil Conservation District Law. This said to farmers, in effect: *We, the public, will furnish you free technical service and loan you specialized machinery, if you will write your own rules for land-use. Each county may write its own rules, and these will have the force of law.* Nearly all the counties promptly organized to accept the preferred help, but after a decade of operation, *no county has yet written a single rule.* There has been visible progress in such practices as strip-cropping, pasture renovation, and soil liming, but none in fencing woodlots against grazing, and none in excluding plow and cow from steep slopes. The farmers, in short, have selected those remedial practices which were profitable anyhow, and ignored those which were profitable to the community, but not clearly profitable to themselves.

When one asks why no rules have been written, one is told that the community is not yet ready to support them; education must precede rules. But the education actually in progress makes no mention of obligations to land over and above those dictated by self-interest. The net result is that we have more education but less soil, fewer healthy woods, and as many floods as in 1937.

The puzzling aspect of such situations is that the existence of obligations over and above self-interest is taken for granted in such rural community enterprises as the betterment of roads, schools, churches, and baseball teams. Their existence is not taken for granted, nor as yet seriously discussed, in bettering the behavior of the water that falls on the land, or in the preserving of the beauty or diversity of the farm landscape. Land-use ethics are still governed wholly by economic self-interest, just as social ethics were a century ago.

To sum up: we asked the farmer to do what he conveniently could to save his soil, and he has done just that, and only that. The farmer who clears the woods off a 75 per cent slope, turns his cows into the clearing, and dumps its rainfall, rocks, and soil into the community creek, is still (if otherwise decent) a respected member of society. If he puts lime on his fields and plants his crops on contour, he is still entitled to all the privileges and emoluments of his Soil Conservation District. The District is a beautiful piece of social machinery, but it is coughing along on two cylinders because we have been too timid, and too anxious for quick success, to tell the farmer the true magnitude of his obligations. Obligations have no meaning without conscience, and the problem we face is the extension of the social conscience from people to land.

No important change in ethics was ever accomplished without an internal change in our intellectual emphasis, loyalties, affections, and convictions. The proof that conservation has not yet touched these foundations of conduct lies in the fact that philosophy and religion have not yet heard of it. In our attempt to make conservation easy, we have made it trivial.

SUBSTITUTES FOR A LAND ETHIC

When the logic of history hungers for bread and we hand out a stone, we are at pains to explain how much the stone resembles bread. I now describe some of the stones which serve in lieu of a land ethic.

One basic weakness in a conservation system based wholly on economic motives is that most members of the land community have no economic value. Wildflowers and songbirds are examples. Of the 22,000 higher plants and animals native to Wisconsin, it is doubtful whether more than 5 per cent can be sold, fed, eaten, or otherwise put to economic use. Yet these creatures are members of the biotic community, and if (as I believe) its stability depends on its integrity, they are entitled to continuance.

When one of these non-economic categories is threatened, and if we happen to love it, we invent subterfuges to give it economic importance. At the beginning of the century songbirds were supposed to be disappearing. Ornithologists jumped to the rescue with some distinctly shaky evidence to the effect that insects would eat us up if birds failed to control them. The evidence had to be economic in order to be valid.

It is painful to read these circumlocutions today. We have no land ethic yet, but we have at least drawn nearer the point of admitting that birds should continue as a matter of biotic right, regardless of the presence or absence of economic advantage to us.

A parallel situation exists in respect of predatory mammals, raptorial birds, and fish-eating birds. Time was when biologists somewhat overworked the evidence that these creatures preserve the health of game by killing weaklings, or that they control rodents for the farmer, or that they prey only on 'worthless' species. Here again, the evidence had to be economic in order to be valid. It is only in recent years that we hear the more honest argument that predators are members of the community, and that no special interest has the right to exterminate them for the sake of a benefit, real or fancied, to itself. Unfortunately this enlightened view is still in the talk stage. In the field the extermination of predators goes merrily on: witness the impending erasure of the timber wolf by fiat of Congress, the Conservation Bureaus, and many state legislatures.

Some species of trees have been 'read out of the party' by economics-minded foresters because they grow too slowly, or have too low a sale value to pay as timber crops: white cedar, tamarack, cypress, beech, and hemlock are examples. In Europe, where forestry is ecologically more advanced, the non-commercial tree species are recognized as members of the native forest community, to be preserved as such, within reason. Moreover some (like beech) have been found to have a valuable function in building up soil fertility. The interdependence of the forest and its constituent tree species, ground flora, and fauna is taken for granted.

Lack of economic value is sometimes a character not only of species or groups, but of entire biotic communities: marshes, bogs, dunes, and 'deserts' are examples. Our formula in such cases is to relegate their conservation to government as refuges, monuments, or parks. The difficulty is that these communities are usually interspersed with more valuable private lands; the government cannot possibly own or control such scattered parcels. The net effect is that we have relegated some of them to ultimate extinction over large areas. If the private owner were ecologically minded, he would be proud to be the custodian of a reasonable proportion of such areas, which add diversity and beauty to his farm and to his community.

In some instances, the assumed lack of profit in these 'waste' areas has proved to be wrong, but only after most of them had been done away with. The present scramble to reflood muskrat marshes is a case in point.

There is a clear tendency in American conservation to relegate to government all necessary jobs that private landowners fail to perform. Government ownership, operation, subsidy, or regulation is now widely prevalent in forestry, range management, soil and watershed management, park and wilderness conservation, fisheries management, and migratory bird management, with more to come. Most of this growth in governmental conservation is proper and logical, some of it is inevitable. That I imply no disapproval of it is implicit in the fact that I have spent most of my life working for it. Nevertheless the question arises: What is the ultimate magnitude of the enterprise? Will the tax base carry its eventual ramifications? At what point will governmental conservation, like the mastodon, become handicapped by its own dimensions? The answer, if there is any, seems to be in a land ethic, or some other force which assigns more obligation to the private landowner.

Industrial landowners and users, especially lumbermen and stockmen, are inclined to wail long and loudly about the extension of government ownership and regulation to land, but (with notable exceptions) they show little disposition to develop the only visible alternative: the voluntary practice of conservation on their own lands.

When the private landowner is asked to perform some unprofitable act for the good of the community, he today assents only with outstretched palm. If the act costs him cash this is fair and proper, but when it costs only forethought, open-mindedness, or time, the issue is at least debatable. The overwhelming growth of land-use subsidies in recent years must be ascribed, in large part, to the government's own agencies for conservation education: the land bureaus, the agricultural colleges, and the extension services. As far as I can detect, no ethical obligation toward land is taught in these institutions.

To sum up: a system of conservation based solely on economic self-interest is hopelessly lopsided. It tends to ignore, and thus eventually to eliminate, many elements in the land community that lack commercial value, but that are (as far as we know) essential to its healthy functioning. It assumes, falsely, I think, that the economic parts of the biotic clock will function without the uneconomic parts. It tends to relegate to government many functions eventually too large, too complex, or too widely dispersed to be performed by government.

An ethical obligation on the part of the private owner is the only visible remedy for these situations.

THE LAND PYRAMID

An ethic to supplement and guide the economic relation to land presupposes the existence of some mental image of land as a biotic mechanism. We can be ethical only in relation to something we can see, feel, understand, love, or otherwise have faith in.

The image commonly employed in conservation education is 'the balance of nature.' For reasons too lengthy to detail here, this figure of speech fails to describe accurately what little we know about the land mechanism. A much truer image is the one employed in ecology: the biotic pyramid. I shall first sketch the pyramid as a symbol of land, and later develop some of its implications in terms of land-use.

Plants absorb energy from the sun. This energy flows through a circuit called the biota, which may be represented by a pyramid consisting of layers. The bottom layer is the soil. A plant layer rests on the soil, an insect layer on the plants, a bird and rodent layer on the insects, and so on up through various animal groups to the apex layer, which consists of the large carnivores.

The species of a layer are alike not in where they came from, or in what they look like, but rather in what they eat. Each successive layer depends on those below it for food and often for other services, and each in turn furnishes food and services to those above. Proceeding upward, each successive layer decreases in numerical abundance. Thus, for every carnivore there are hundreds of his prey, thousands of their prey, millions of insects, uncountable plants. The pyramidal form of the system reflects this numerical progression from apex to base. Man shares an intermediate layer with the bears, raccoons, and squirrels which eat both meat and vegetables.

The lines of dependency for food and other services are called food chains. Thus soil-oak-deer-Indian is a chain that has now been largely converted to soil-corn-cow-farmer. Each species, including ourselves, is a link in many chains. The deer eats a hundred plants other than oak, and the cow a hundred plants other than corn. Both, then, are links in a hundred chains. The pyramid is a tangle of chains so complex as to seem disorderly, yet the stability of the system proves it to be a highly organized structure. Its functioning depends on the co-operation and competition of its diverse parts.

In the beginning, the pyramid of life was low and squat; the food chains short and simple. Evolution has added layer after layer, link after link. Man is one of thousands of accretions to the height and complexity of the pyramid. Science has given us many doubts, but it has given us at least one certainty: the trend of evolution is to elaborate and diversify the biota.

Land, then, is not merely soil; it is a fountain of energy flowing through a circuit of soils, plants, and animals. Food chains are the living channels which conduct energy upward; death and decay return it to the soil. The circuit is not closed; some energy is dissipated in decay, some is added by absorption from the air, some is stored in soils, peats, and long-lived forests; but it is a sustained circuit, like a slowly augmented revolving fund of life. There is always a net loss by downhill wash, but this is normally small and offset by the decay of rocks. It is deposited in the ocean and, in the course of geological time, raised to form new lands and new pyramids.

The velocity and character of the upward flow of energy depend on the complex structure of the plant and animal community, much as the upward flow of sap in a tree depends on its complex cellular organization. Without this complexity, normal circulation would presumably not occur. Structure means the characteristic numbers, as well as the characteristic kinds and functions, of the component species. This interdependence between the complex structure of the land and its smooth functioning as an energy unit is one of its basic attributes.

When a change occurs in one part of the circuit, many other parts must adjust themselves to it. Change does not necessarily obstruct or divert the flow of energy; evolution is a long series of self-induced changes, the net result of which has been to elaborate the flow mechanism and to lengthen the circuit. Evolutionary changes, however, are usually slow and local. Man's invention of tools has enabled him to make changes of unprecedented violence, rapidity, and scope.

One change is in the composition of floras and faunas. The larger predators are lopped off the apex of the pyramid; food chains, for the first time in history, become shorter rather than longer. Domesticated species from other lands are substituted for wild ones, and wild ones are moved to new habitats. In this world-wide pooling of faunas and floras, some species get out of bounds as pests and diseases, others are extinguished. Such effects are seldom intended or foreseen; they represent unpredicted and often untraceable readjustments in the structure. Agricultural science is largely a race between the emergence of new pests and the emergence of new techniques for their control.

Another change touches the flow of energy through plants and animals and its return to the soil. Fertility is the ability of soil to receive, store, and release energy. Agriculture, by overdrafts on the soil, or by too radical a substitution of domestic for native species in the superstructure, may derange the channels of flow or deplete storage. Soils depleted of their storage, or of the organic matter which anchors it, wash away faster than they form. This is erosion.

Waters, like soil, are part of the energy circuit. Industry, by polluting waters or obstructing them with dams, may exclude the plants and animals necessary to keep energy in circulation.

Transportation brings about another basic change: the plants or animals grown in one region are now consumed and returned to the soil in another. Transportation taps the energy stored in rocks, and in the air, and uses it elsewhere; thus we fertilize the garden with nitrogen gleaned by the guano birds from the fishes of seas on the other side of the Equator. Thus the formerly localized and self-contained circuits are pooled on a world-wide scale.

The process of altering the pyramid for human occupation releases stored energy, and this often gives rise, during the pioneering period, to a deceptive exuberance of plant and animal life, both wild and tame. These releases of biotic capital tend to becloud or postpone the penalties of violence.

This thumbnail sketch of land as an energy circuit conveys three basic ideas:

(1) That land is not merely soil.

(2) That the native plants and animals kept the energy circuit open; others may or may not.

(3) That man-made changes are of a different order than evolutionary changes, and have effects more comprehensive than is intended or foreseen.

These ideas, collectively, raise two basic issues: Can the land adjust itself to the new order? Can the desired alterations be accomplished with less violence?

Biotas seem to differ in their capacity to sustain violent conversion. Western Europe, for example, carries a far different pyramid than Caesar found there. Some large animals are lost; swampy forests have become meadows or plowland; many new plants and animals are introduced, some of which escape as pests; the remaining natives are greatly changed in distribution and abundance. Yet the soil is still there and, with the help of imported nutrients, still fertile; the waters flow normally; the new structure seems to function and to persist. There is no visible stoppage or derangement of the circuit.

Western Europe, then, has a resistant biota. Its inner processes are tough, elastic, resistant to strain. No matter how violent the alterations, the pyramid, so far, has developed some new *modus vivendi* which preserves its habitability for man, and for most of the other natives.

Japan seems to present another instance of radical conversion without disorganization.

Most other civilized regions, and some as yet barely touched by civilization, display various stages of disorganization, varying from initial symptoms to advanced wastage. In Asia Minor and North Africa diagnosis is confused by climatic changes, which may have been either the cause or the effect of advanced wastage. In the United States the degree of disorganization varies locally; it is worst in the Southwest, the Ozarks, and parts of the South, and least in New England and the Northwest. Better land-uses may still arrest it in the less advanced regions. In parts of Mexico, South America, South Africa, and Australia a violent and accelerating wastage is in progress, but I cannot assess the prospects.

This almost world-wide display of disorganization in the land seems to be similar to disease in an animal, except that it never culminates in complete disorganization or death. The land recovers, but at some reduced level of complexity, and with a reduced carrying capacity for people, plants, and animals. Many biotas currently regarded as 'lands of opportunity' are in fact already subsisting on exploitative agriculture, i.e., they have already exceeded their sustained carrying capacity. Most of South America is overpopulated in this sense.

In arid regions we attempt to offset the process of wastage by reclamation, but it is only too evident that the prospective longevity of reclamation projects is often short. In our own West, the best of them may not last a century.

The combined evidence of history and ecology seems to support one general deduction: the less violent the man-made changes, the greater the probability of successful readjustment in the pyramid. Violence, in turn, varies with human population density; a dense population requires a more violent conversion. In this respect, North America has a better chance for permanence than Europe, if she can contrive to limit her density.

This deduction runs counter to our current philosophy, which assumes that because a small increase in density enriched human life, that an indefinite increase will enrich it indefinitely. Ecology knows of no density relationship that holds for indefinitely wide limits. All gains from density are subject to a law of diminishing returns.

Whatever may be the equation for men and land, it is improbable that we as yet know all its terms. Recent discoveries in mineral and vitamin nutrition reveal unsuspected dependencies in the up-circuit: incredibly minute quantities of certain substances determine the value of soils to plants, of plants to animals. What of the down-circuit? What of the vanishing species, the preservation of which we now regard as an esthetic luxury? They helped build the soil; in what unsuspected ways may they be essential to its maintenance? Professor Weaver proposes that we use prairie flowers to reflocculate the wasting soils of the dust bowl; who knows for what purpose cranes and condors, otters and grizzlies may some day be used?

LAND HEALTH AND THE A-B CLEAVAGE

A land ethic, then, reflects the existence of an ecological conscience, and this in turn reflects a conviction of individual responsibility for the health of the land. Health is the capacity of the land for self-renewal. Conservation is our effort to understand and preserve this capacity.

Conservationists are notorious for their dissensions. Superficially these seem to add up to mere confusion, but a more careful scrutiny reveals a single plane of cleavage common to many specialized fields. In each field one group (A) regards the land as soil, and its function as commodity-production; another group (B) regards the land as a biota, and its function as something broader. How much broader is admittedly in a state of doubt and confusion.

In my own field, forestry, group A is quite content to grow trees like cabbages, with cellulose as the basic forest commodity. It feels no inhibition against violence; its ideology is agronomic. Group B, on the other hand, sees forestry as fundamentally different from agronomy because it employs natural species, and manages a natural environment rather than creating an artificial one. Group B prefers natural reproduction on principle. It worries on biotic as well as economic grounds about the loss of species like chestnut, and the threatened loss of the white pines. It worries about a whole series of secondary forest functions: wildlife, recreation, watersheds, wilderness areas. To my mind, Group B feels the stirrings of an ecological conscience.

In the wildlife field, a parallel cleavage exists. For Group A the basic commodities are sport and meat; the yardsticks of production are ciphers of take in pheasants and trout. Artificial propagation is acceptable as a permanent as well as a temporary recourse— if its unit costs permit. Group B, on the other hand, worries about a whole series of biotic side-issues. What is the cost in predators of producing a game crop? Should we have further recourse to exotics? How can management restore the shrinking species, like prairie grouse, already hopeless as shootable game? How can management restore the threatened rarities, like trumpeter swan and whooping crane? Can management principles be extended to wildflowers? Here again it is clear to me that we have the same A-B cleavage as in forestry.

In the larger field of agriculture I am less competent to speak, but there seem to be somewhat parallel cleavages. Scientific agriculture was actively developing before ecology was born, hence a slower penetration of ecological concepts might be expected. Moreover the farmer, by the very nature of his techniques, must modify the biota more radically than the forester or the wildlife manager. Nevertheless, there are many discontents in agriculture which seem to add up to a new vision of 'biotic farming.'

Perhaps the most important of these is the new evidence that poundage or tonnage is no measure of the food-value of farm crops; the products of fertile soil may be qualitatively as well as quantitatively superior. We can bolster poundage from depleted soils by pouring on imported fertility, but we are not necessarily bolstering food-value. The possible ultimate ramifications of this idea are so immense that I must leave their exposition to abler pens.

The discontent that labels itself 'organic farming,' while bearing some of the earmarks of a cult, is nevertheless biotic in its direction, particularly in its insistence on the importance of soil flora and fauna.

The ecological fundamentals of agriculture are just as poorly known to the public as in other fields of land-use. For example, few educated people realize that the marvelous advances in technique made during recent decades are improvements in the pump, rather than the well. Acre for acre, they have barely sufficed to offset the sinking level of fertility.

In all of these cleavages, we see repeated the same basic paradoxes: man the conqueror *versus* man the biotic citizen; science the sharpener of his sword *versus* science the searchlight on his universe; land the slave and servant *versus* land the collective organism. Robinson's injunction to Tristram may well be applied, at this juncture, to *Homo sapiens* as a species in geological time:

Whether you will or not
You are a King, Tristram, for you are one
Of the time-tested few that leave the world,
When they are gone, not the same place it was.
Mark what you leave.

THE OUTLOOK

It is inconceivable to me that an ethical relation to land can exist without love, respect, and admiration for land, and a high regard for its value. By value, I of course mean something far broader than mere economic value; I mean value in the philosophical sense.

Perhaps the most serious obstacle impeding the evolution of a land ethic is the fact that our educational and economic system is headed away from, rather than toward, an intense consciousness of land. Your true modern is separated from the land by many middlemen, and by innumerable physical gadgets. He has no vital relation to it; to him it is the space between cities on which crops grow. Turn him loose for a day on the land, and if the spot does not happen to be a golf links or a 'scenic' area, he is bored stiff. If crops could be raised by hydroponics instead of farming, it would suit him very well. Synthetic substitutes for wood, leather, wool, and other natural land products suit him better than the originals. In short, land is something he has 'outgrown.'

Almost equally serious as an obstacle to a land ethic is the attitude of the farmer for whom the land is still an adversary, or a taskmaster that keeps him in slavery. Theoretically, the mechanization of farming ought to cut the farmer's chains, but whether it really does is debatable.

One of the requisites for an ecological comprehension of land is an understanding of ecology, and this is by no means co-extensive with 'education'; in fact, much higher education seems deliberately to avoid ecological concepts. An understanding of ecology does not necessarily originate in courses bearing ecological labels; it is quite as likely to be labeled geography, botany, agronomy, history, or economics. This is as it should be, but whatever the label, ecological training is scarce.

The case for a land ethic would appear hopeless but for the minority which is in obvious revolt against these 'modern' trends.

The 'key-log' which must be moved to release the evolutionary process for an ethic is simply this: quit thinking about decent land-use as solely an economic problem. Examine each question in terms of what is ethically and esthetically right, as well as what is economically expedient. A thing is right when it tends to preserve the integrity, stability, and beauty of the biotic community. It is wrong when it tends otherwise.

It of course goes without saying that economic feasibility limits the tether of what can or cannot be done for land. It always has and it always will. The fallacy the economic determinists have tied around our collective neck, and which we now need to cast off, is the belief that economics determines *all* land-use. This is simply not true. An innumerable host of actions and attitudes, comprising perhaps the bulk of all land relations, is determined by the land-users' tastes and predilections, rather than by his purse. The bulk of all land relations hinges on investments of time, forethought, skill, and faith rather than on investments of cash. As a land-user thinketh, so is he.

I have purposely presented the land ethic as a product of social evolution because nothing so important as an ethic is ever 'written.' Only the most superficial student of history supposes that Moses 'wrote' the Decalogue; it evolved in the minds of a thinking community, and Moses wrote a tentative summary of it for a 'seminar.' I say tentative because evolution never stops.

The evolution of a land ethic is an intellectual as well as emotional process. Conservation is paved with good intentions which prove to be futile, or even dangerous, because they are devoid of critical understanding either of the land, or of economic land-use. I think it is a truism that as the ethical frontier advances from the individual to the community, its intellectual content increases.

The mechanism of operation is the same for any ethic: social approbation for right actions: social disapproval for wrong actions.

By and large, our present problem is one of attitudes and implements. We are remodeling the Alhambra with a steam-shovel, and we are proud of our yardage. We shall hardly relinquish the shovel, which after all has many good points, but we are in need of gentler and more objective criteria for its successful use.

DISCUSSION TIPS

1. Is there a specifically *new* environmental ethic presented by Leopold? Explain why you do or do not believe so.
2. Give two weaknesses you perceive in Leopold's land ethic.

READING 49

Ecological Sensibility

John Rodman

John Rodman, Professor of Political Studies and Environmental Studies at Pitzer College and Claremont Graduate School, Claremont, California, presents ideas that build on and extend beyond those presented in Leopold's essay. Rodman's philosophy has three components. First, he argues that natural objects deserve moral concern based on their intrinsic value. Second, he extends moral concern beyond the level of the individual and stresses the reality and importance of systems and relationships in nature. Finally, he introduces the notion that the qualities of ecosystems lead humans to have certain correlative responsibilities toward them.

Rodman proposes that natural beings, including

communities and ecosystems, each have a telos *or end of their own—that is, they are autonomous and have the capacity for internal self-direction and self-regulation. Rodman asserts that we ought to treat each thing with a* telos *with respect for its own particular ends or purposes. While Aristotle saw segments of nature as having a* telos, *this notion traditionally has been applied only to persons, as done by Kant. Rodman's proposal is to extend the concept of* telos *to the community or ecosystem, thus applying it to a totally new level of biological organization.*

Rodman also offers a description of value-giving characteristics which he believes should be applied to both individuals and communities when making decisions about alternative courses of action that involve conflicting values. Finally, based on what he considers to be the rights of natural objects, Rodman advocates a series of human duties, including noninterference with natural processes, repair of severe environmental damage, and a respectful style of cohabitation with nature.

. . . The last form that I shall discuss is still emergent, so that description is not easily separated from prescription. The term "sensibility" is chosen to suggest a complex pattern of perceptions, attitudes, and judgments which, if fully developed, would constitute a disposition to appropriate conduct that would make talk of rights and duties unnecessary under normal conditions. At this stage of development, however, we can analytically distinguish three major components of an Ecological Sensibility: a theory of value that recognizes intrinsic value in nature without (hopefully) engaging in mere extensionism (in the sense discussed in section 3); a metaphysics that takes account of the reality and importance of relationships and systems as well as of individuals; and an ethics that includes such duties as noninterference with natural processes, resistance to human acts and policies that violate the noninterference principle, limited intervention to repair environmental damage in extreme circumstances, and a style of coinhabitation that involves the knowledgeable, respectful, and restrained use of nature. Since there is not space to discuss all these components here, and since I have sketched

some of them elsewhere,[1] I shall focus here on two basic dimensions of the theory of value, drawing primarily upon the writings of Leopold,[2] the Routleys,[3] and Rodman.

The first dimension is simple but sweeping in its implications. It is based upon the obligation principle that one ought not to treat with disrespect or use as a mere means anything that has a *telos* or end of its own—anything that is autonomous in the basic sense of having a capacity for internal self-direction and self-regulation. This principle is widely accepted but has been mistakenly thought (e.g., by Kant and others) to apply only to persons. Unless one engages in a high redefinition of terms, however, it more properly applies to (at least) all living natural entities and natural systems. (I leave aside in this essay the difficult and important issue of physical systems.) The vision of a world composed of many things and many kinds of things, all having their own *telē*, goes back (except for the recognition of ecosystems) to Aristotle's metaphysics and philosophy of nature and does therefore not involve us in the kinds of problems that arise from extending the categories of modern Liberal ethics to a natural world made up of the dead "objects" of modern thought. (To mention Aristotle is not, of course, to embrace all of his opinions, especially the very anthropocentric *obiter dicta*—e.g., that plants exist for the sake of animals, animals for humans, etc.—that can be found in his *Ethics* and *Politics*.) This notion of natural entities and natural systems as having intrinsic value in the specific and basic form, of having *telē* of their own, having their own characteristic patterns of behavior, their own stages of development, their own business (so to speak), is the

---

1. "Ecological Resistance: John Stuart Mill and the Case of the Kentish Orchid," paper presented at the annual meeting of the American Political Science Association, 1977.

2. Aldo Leopold, *A Sand County Almanac* (New York: Oxford University Press, 1949).

3. Richard and Val Routley, "Human Chauvinism and Environmental Ethics," in *Environmental Philosophy,* eds. Don Mannison, Michael McRobbie, and Richard Routley (Department of Philosophy, Research School of Social Sciences, The Australian National University, 1980); Val and Richard Routley, "Social Theories, Self Management, and Environmental Problems," in ibid.

basic ground in which is rooted the attitude of respect, the obligation of noninterference, etc. In it is rooted also the indictment of the Resource Conservation standpoint as being, at bottom, an ideology of human chauvinism and human imperialism.

It may be objected that our paradigmatic notion of a being having a *telos* is an individual human being or a person, so that viewing nature in terms of *telē* involves merely another extension of an all-too-human quality to (part of) nature, retaining the conventional atomistic metaphysics and reinstating the conventional moral pecking order. I do not think that this is the case. It seems to me an observable fact that thistles, oak trees, and wombats, as well as rainforests and chaparral communities, have their own characteristic structures and potentialities to unfold, and that it is as easy to see this in them as it is in humans, if we will but look.

For those unaccustomed to looking, Aldo Leopold's *Sand County Almanac* provides, in effect, a guidebook. Before the reader is introduced to the "land ethic" chapter (which is too often read out of the context of the book as a whole), (s)he is invited to accompany Leopold as he follows the tracks of the skunk in the January snow, wondering where the skunk is heading and why; speculating on the different meanings of a winter thaw for the mouse whose snow burrow has collapsed and for the owl who has just made dinner of the mouse; trying to understand the honking of the geese as they circle the pond; and wondering what the world must look like to a muskrat eye-deep in the swamp. By the time one reaches Leopold's discussion of the land ethic, one has grown accustomed to thinking of different animals—and (arguably), by extension, different natural entities in general—as subjects rather than objects, as beings that have their own purposes, their own perspectives on the world, and their own goods that are differentially affected by events. While we can never get inside a muskrat's head and know exactly what the world looks like from that angle, we can be pretty certain that the view is different from ours. What melts away as we become intrigued with this plurality of perspectives is the assumption that any one of them

(for example, ours) is privileged. So we are receptive when the "land ethic" chapter suggests that other natural beings deserve respect and should be treated as if they had a "right" in the most basic sense of being entitled to continue existing in a natural state. To want from Leopold a full-scale theory of the rights of nature, however, would be to miss the point, since the idea of rights has only a limited application. Moreover, Leopold does not present logical arguments for the land ethic in general, because such arguments could not persuade anyone who still looked at nature as if it were comprised of objects or mere resources, and such arguments are unnecessary for those who have come to perceive nature as composed of subjects. When perception is sufficiently changed, respectful types of conduct seem "natural," and one does not have to belabor them in the language of rights and duties. Here, finally, we reach the point of "paradigm change."[4] What brings it about is not exhortation, threat, or logic, but a rebirth of the sense of wonder that in ancient times gave rise to philosophers but is now more often found among field naturalists.

In further response to the objection that viewing nature in terms of *telē* is simply another version of anthropocentric Moral Extensionism, consider that a forest may be in some ways more nearly paradigmatic than an individual human for illustrating what it means to have a *telos*. A tropical rainforest may take 500 years to develop to maturity and may then maintain a dynamic, steady-state indefinitely (for millions of years, judging from fossils) if not seriously interfered with. It exhibits a power of self-regulation that may have been shared to some extent by millennia of hunter-gatherer societies but is not an outstanding characteristic of modern humans, taken either as individuals or as societies. While there may therefore be some differences in the degree to which certain aspects of what it means to have a *telos* are present in one organism or one system compared with another, the basic principle is that all items having a *telos* are

---

4. Obviously, I believe that those who see Leopold's land ethic as a mere extension of conventional ethics are radically mistaken.

entitled to respectful treatment. Comparisons are more fruitfully made in terms of the second dimension of the theory of value.

The second dimension incorporates a cluster of value-giving characteristics that apply both to natural entities and (even more) to natural systems: diversity, complexity, integrity, harmony, stability, scarcity, etc. While the *telos* principle serves primarily to provide a common basic reason for respectful treatment of natural entities and natural systems (ruling out certain types of exploitative acts on deontological grounds), and to provide a criterion for drawing morally relevant distinctions between natural trees and plastic trees, natural forests and timber plantations, etc., this cluster of value-giving qualities provides criteria for evaluating alternatives courses of permissible action in terms of optimizing the production of good effects, the better action being the one that optimizes the qualities taken as an interdependent, mutually constraining cluster. Aldo Leopold seems to have had something like this model in mind when he stated the land ethic in these terms:

> A thing is right when it tends to preserve the integrity, stability, and beauty of the biotic community. It is wrong when it tends otherwise.

(We may wish to modify Leopold's statement, omitting reference to beauty and adding additional criteria, especially diversity [which stands as a principle in its own right, not merely as a means to stability]; moreover, an action can be right or wrong in reference to individuals as well as communities—but Leopold was redressing an imbalance, calling our attention to the supra-individual level, and can be forgiven for overstating his case.) More controversially, the cluster of ecological values can also be used to appraise the relative value of different ecosystems when priorities must be set (given limits on time, energy, and political influence) by environmentalists working to protect nature against the bulldozer and the chain saw. The criteria of diversity, complexity, etc., will sometimes suggest different priorities than would result from following the esthetic of the sublime or a criterion such as sentience, while a fully pantheistic philosophy

of preservation provides no criteria at all for discriminating cases.

What can be said in justification of this cluster of ecological values? It is possible for human beings to hold such values. Those who do not, and those who are not sure whether they do or not, may wish to imagine alternative worlds, asking whether they prefer the diverse world to the monocultural world, and so forth. But it would be naive to assume that such thought experiments are conducted without any significant context. For example, I am aware that my preference for diverse, complex, and stable systems occurs in a time that I perceive as marked by an unprecedentedly high rate of species extinction and ecosystem simplification. In this situation, diversity has scarcity value in addition to its intrinsic value, in addition to its instrumental value as conducive to stability. This illustrates a general characteristic of the cluster of ecological values: the balance is not static but fluctuates in response to changes in the environment, so that different principles are more or less prominent at different times.

Since the cluster of value-giving principles applies generally throughout the world to living natural entities and systems, it applies to human beings and human societies as well as to the realm of nonhuman nature. To the extent that diversity on an individual human level is threatened by the pressures of conformity in mass society, and diversity of social ways of life is threatened by the pressures of global resource exploitation and an ideology of world-wide "development" in whose name indigenous peoples are being exterminated along with native forests, it would be short-sighted to think of "ecological issues" as unrelated to "social issues." From an ecological point of view, one of the most striking socio-political phenomena of the twentieth century—the rise of totalitarian dictatorships that forcibly try to eliminate the natural condition of human diversity in the name of some monocultural ideal (e.g., an Aryan Europe or a classless society)—is not so much a freakish aberration from modern history as it is an intensification of the general spirit of the age. Ecological Sensibility, then is "holistic" in a sense beyond that usually thought of: it grasps the underlying principles that manifest themselves in what are ordinarily perceived as separate ''social'' and ''environmental'' issues.[5] More than any alternative environmental ethic, it attains a degree of comprehension that frees environmentalists from the charge of ignoring ''people problems'' in their preoccupation with saving nature. Insofar as Ecological Sensibility transcends ''ecology'' in the strict sense, its very name is metaphorical, drawing on a part to suggest the whole. Starting with issues concerning human treatment of the natural environment, we arrive at principles that shed light on the total human condition.

DISCUSSION TOPICS

1. How does Rodman's ecocentric ethic differ from the one proposed by Leopold?
2. Can the notion of *telos* appropriately be ascribed to biotic communities? Why or why not?

5. See also Rodman, ''Paradigm Change in Political Science,'' *American Behavioral Scientist* 24, No. 1 (September-October 1980): 67-69.

Callicott identifies the influences of past ecologists such as Clements, Forbes, Elton, and Tansley on Leopold's ideas. He also contrasts Judeo-Christian tenets with Darwinian perspectives on how ethical concern arose. Callicott points out that an important foundation of the land ethic is Leopold's perception that all ethics are based on the idea that each individual belongs to an interdependent community, and that Leopold extended the notion of community beyond humans to encompass the natural environment. Callicott justifies the land ethic on three scientific perspectives: evolutionary theory, the science of ecology, and insights from the Copernican revolution in astronomy.

Callicott argues that Leopold's land ethic provides a basis for extending moral consideration both to the individual members and to the whole of a biotic community, but maintains that Leopold's land ethic is primarily holistic. The land ethic places more emphasis on maintaining the complex structure of the land and its proper functioning as an energy unit than on the individual members and material components of the ecosystem.

READING 50

The Conceptual Foundations of the Land Ethic

J. Baird Callicott

J. Baird Callicott (b. 1941), Professor of Philosophy and Natural Resources at the University of Wisconsin at Stevens Point, has taught environmental ethics courses since the early 1970s and has been a prolific writer in the field. In his article, Callicott outlines the major elements of Leopold's land ethic, and details how they fit into a new moral theory. He then evaluates some of the controversial features of this moral philosophy.

As Wallace Stegner observes, *A Sand County Almanac* is considered ''almost a holy book in conservation circles,'' and Aldo Leopold a prophet, ''an American Isaiah.'' And as Curt Meine points out, ''The Land Ethic'' is the climactic essay of *Sand County,* ''the upshot of 'The Upshot.' ''[1] One might, therefore, fairly say that the recommendation and justification of moral obligations on the part of people to nature is what the prophetic *A Sand County Almanac* is all about.

But, with few exceptions, ''The Land Ethic'' has not been favorably received by contemporary academic philosophers. Most have ignored it. Of those who have not, most have been either nonplussed or hostile. Distinguished Australian philosopher John Passmore dismissed it out of hand, in the first book-length academic discussion of the new philosophical subdiscipline called ''environmental ethics.''[2] In a more recent and more deliberate discussion, the equally distinguished Australian philosopher H. J. McCloskey patronized Aldo Leopold and saddled ''The Land Ethic'' with various far-fetched ''interpretations.'' He concludes that ''there is a real problem in attributing a coherent meaning to Leopold's statements, one that exhibits his land ethic as representing a major advance in ethics rather than a retrogression to a morality of a kind held by various primitive peoples.''[3] Echoing McCloskey, English philosopher Robin Attfield went out of his way to impugn the philosophical respectability of ''The Land Ethic.'' And Canadian philosopher L. W. Sumner has called it ''dangerous nonsense.''[4] Among those philosophers more favorably disposed, ''The Land Ethic'' has usually been simply quoted, as if it were little more than a noble, but naive, moral plea, altogether lacking a supporting theoretical framework—i.e., foundational principles and premises which lead, by compelling argument, to ethical precepts.

The professional neglect, confusion, and (in some cases) contempt for ''The Land Ethic'' may, in my judgment, be attributed to three things: (1) Leopold's extremely condensed prose style in which an entire conceptual complex may be conveyed in a few sentences, or even in a phrase or two; (2) his departure from the assumptions and paradigms of contemporary philosophical ethics; and (3) the unsettling practical implications to which a land ethic appears to lead. ''The Land Ethic,'' in short, is, from a philosophical point of view, abbreviated, unfamiliar, and radical.

Here I first examine and elaborate the compactly expressed abstract elements of the land ethic and expose the ''logic'' which binds them into a proper, but revolutionary, moral theory. I then discuss the controversial features of the land ethic and defend them against actual and potential criticism. I hope to show that the land ethic cannot be ignored as merely the groundless emotive exhortations of a moonstruck conservationist or dismissed as entailing wildly untoward practical consequences. It poses, rather, a serious intellectual challenge to business-as-usual moral philosophy.

''The Land Ethic'' opens with a charming and poetic evocation of Homer's Greece, the point of which is to suggest that today land is just as routinely and remorselessly enslaved as human beings then were. A panoramic glance backward to our most distant cultural origins, Leopold suggests, reveals a slow but steady moral development over three millennia. More of our relationships and activities (''fields of conduct'') have fallen under the aegis of moral principles (''ethical criteria'') as civilization has grown and matured. If moral growth and development continue, as not only a synoptic review of history, but recent past experience suggest that it will, future generations will censure today's casual and universal environmental bondage as today we censure the casual and universal human bondage of three thousand years ago. . . .

The history of moral practice, however, is not identical with the history of moral consciousness. Morality is not descriptive; it is prescriptive or normative. In light of this distinction, it is clear that today, despite rising rates of violent crime in the United States and institutional abuses of human rights in Iran, Chile, Ethiopia, Guatemala, South Africa, and many other places, and despite persistent organized social injustice and oppression in still others, moral consciousness is expanding more rapidly now than ever before. Civil rights, human rights, women's liberation, children's liberation, animal liberation, etc., all indicate, as expressions of newly emergent moral ideals, that ethical consciousness (as distinct from practice) has if anything recently accelerated—thus confirming Leopold's historical observation.

Leopold next points out that ''this extension of ethics, so far studied only by philosophers''—and therefore, the implication is clear, not very satisfactorily studied—''is actually a process in ecological evolution'' (p. 202). What Leopold is saying here, simply, is that we may understand the history of ethics, fancifully alluded to by means of the Odysseus vignette, in biological as well as philosophical terms. From a biological point of view, an ethic is ''a limitation on freedom of action in the struggle for existence'' (p. 202). . . .

. . . How . . . did ethics originate and, once in existence, grow in scope and complexity?

The oldest answer in living human memory is theological. God (or the gods) imposes morality on people. And God (or the gods) sanctions it. . . . Western philosophy, on the other hand, is almost unanimous in the opinion that the origin of ethics in human experience has somehow to do with human reason. . . . Darwin . . . turned to a minority tradition of modern philosophy for a moral psychology consistent with and useful to a general evolutionary account of ethical phenomena. A century earlier, Scottish philosophers David Hume and Adam Smith had argued that ethics rest upon feelings or ''sentiments''—which, to be sure, may be both amplified and informed by reason.[5] And since in the animal kingdom feelings or sentiments are arguably far more common or widespread than reason, they would be a far more likely starting point for an evolutionary account of the origin and growth of ethics.

Darwin's account, to which Leopold unmistakably (if elliptically) alludes in ''The Land Ethic,'' begins with the parental and filial affections common, perhaps, to all mammals.[6] Bonds of affection and sympathy between parents and offspring permitted the formation of small, closely kin social groups, Darwin argued. Should the parental and filial affections bonding family members chance to extend to less closely related individuals, that would permit an enlargement of the family group. And should the newly extended community more successfully defend itself and/or more efficiently provision itself, the inclusive fitness of its members severally would be increased, Darwin reasoned. Thus, the more diffuse familial affections, which Darwin (echoing Hume and Smith) calls the ''social sentiments,'' would be spread throughout a population.[7]

Morality, properly speaking—i.e., morality as oppsoed to mere altruistic instinct—requires, in Darwin's terms, ''intellectual powers'' sufficient to recall the past and imagine the future, ''the power of language'' sufficient to express ''common opinion,'' and ''habituation'' to patterns of behavior deemed, by common opinion, to be socially acceptable and beneficial.[8] Even so, ethics proper, in Darwin's account, remains firmly rooted in moral feelings or social sentiments which were—no less than physical faculties, he expressly avers—naturally selected, by the advantages for survival and especially for successful reproduction, afforded by society.[9]

The protosociobiological perspective on ethical phenomena, to which Leopold as a natural historian was heir, leads him to a generalization which is remarkably explicit in his condensed and often merely resonant rendering of Darwin's more deliberate and extended paradigm: Since ''the thing [ethics] has its origin in the tendency of interdependent individuals or groups to evolve modes of co-operation, . . . all ethics so far evolved rest upon a single premise: that the individual is a member of a community of interdependent parts'' (pp. 202-203).

Hence, we may expect to find that the scope and specific content of ethics will reflect both the perceived boundaries and actual structure or organization of a cooperative community or society. *Ethics and society or community are correlative.* This single, simple principle constitutes a powerful tool for the analysis of moral natural history, for the anticipation of future moral development (including, ultimately, the land ethic), and for systematically deriving the specific precepts, the prescriptions and proscriptions, of an emergent and culturally unprecedented ethic like a land or environmental ethic.

Anthropological studies of ethics reveal that in fact the boundaries of the moral community are generally coextensive with the perceived boundaries of society.[10] And the peculiar (and, from the urbane point of view, sometimes inverted) representation of virtue and vice in tribal society—the virtue, for example, of sharing to the point of personal destitution and the vice of privacy and private property—reflects and fosters the life way of tribal peoples.[11] Darwin, in his leisurely, anecdotal discussion, paints a vivid picture of the intensity, peculiarity, and sharp circumscription of ''savage'' mores: ''A savage will risk his life to save that of a member of the same community, but will be wholly indifferent about a stranger.''[12] As Darwin portrays them, tribes-people are at once paragons of virtue ''within the limits of the same tribe'' and enthusiastic thieves, manslaughterers, and torturers without.[13]

For purposes of more effective defense against common enemies, or because of increased population density, or in response to innovations in subsistence methods and technologies, or for some mix of these or other forces, human societies have grown in extent or scope and changed in form or structure. Nations—like the Iroquois nation or the Sioux nation—came into being upon the merger of previously separate and mutually hostile tribes. Animals and plants were domesticated and erstwhile hunter-gatherers became herders and farmers. Permanent habitations were established. Trade, craft, and (later) industry flourished. With each change in society came corresponding and correlative changes in ethics. The moral community expanded to become coextensive with the newly drawn boundaries of societies and the representation of virtue and vice, right and wrong, good and evil, changed to accommodate, foster, and preserve the economic and institutional organization of emergent social orders. . . .

Most educated people today pay lip service at least to the ethical precept that all members of the human species, regardless of race, creed, or national origin, are endowed with certain fundamental rights which it is wrong not to respect. According to the evolutionary scenario set out by Darwin, the contemporary moral ideal of human rights is a response to a perception—however vague and indefinite—that mankind worldwide is united into one society, one community—however indeterminate or yet institutionally unorganized. As Darwin presciently wrote:

> As man advances in civilization, and small tribes are united into larger communities, the simplest reason would tell each individual that he ought to extend his social instincts and sympathies to all the members of the same nation, though personally unknown to him. This point being once reached, there is only an artificial barrier to prevent his sympathies extending to the men of all nations and races. If, indeed, such men are separated from him by great differences of appearance or habits, experience unfortunately shows us how long it is, before we look at them as our fellow-creatures.[14]

According to Leopold, the next step in this sequence beyond the still incomplete ethic of universal humanity, a step that is clearly discernible on the horizon, is the land ethic. The "community concept" has, so far, propelled the development of ethics from the savage clan to the family of man. "The land ethic simply enlarges the boundary of the community to include soils, waters, plants, and animals, or collectively: the land" (p. 204).

As the foreword to *Sand County* makes plain, the overarching thematic principle of the book is the inculcation of the idea—through narrative description, discursive exposition, abstractive generalization, and occasional preachment—"that land is a community" (p. viii). The community concept is "the basic concept of ecology" (p. viii). Once land is popularly perceived as a biotic community—as it is professionally perceived in ecology—a correlative land ethic will emerge in the collective cultural consciousness.

Although anticipated as far back as the mid-eighteenth century—in the notion of an "economy of nature"—the concept of the biotic community was more fully and deliberately developed as a working model or paradigm for ecology by Charles Elton in the 1920s.[15] The natural world is organized as an intricate corporate society in which plants and animals occupy "niches," or as Elton alternatively called them, "roles" or "professions," in the economy of nature.[16] As in a feudal community, little or no socioeconomic mobility (upward or otherwise) exists in the biotic community. One is born to one's trade.

Human society, Leopold argues, is founded, in large part, upon mutual security and economic interdependency and preserved only by limitations on freedom of action in the struggle for existence—that is, by ethical constraints. Since the biotic community exhibits, as modern ecology reveals, an analogous structure, it too can be preserved, given the newly amplified impact of "mechanized man," only by analogous limitations on freedom of action—that is, by a land ethic (p. viii). A land ethic, furthermore, is not only "an ecological necessity," but an "evolutionary possibility" because a moral response to the natural environment—Darwin's social sympathies, sentiments, and instincts translated and codified into a body of principles and precepts—would be automatically triggered in human beings by ecology's social representation of nature (p. 203).

Therefore, the key to the emergence of a land ethic is, simply, universal ecological literacy.

The land ethic rests upon three scientific corner-stones: (1) evolutionary and (2) ecological biology set in a background of (3) Copernican astronomy. Evolutionary theory provides the conceptual link between ethics and social organization and development. It provides a sense of ''kinship with fellow-creatures'' as well, ''fellow-voyagers'' with us in the ''odyssey of evolution'' (p. 109). It establishes a diachronic link between people and non-human nature.

Ecological theory provides a synchronic link—the community concept—a sense of social integration of human and nonhuman nature. Human beings, plants, animals, soils, and waters are ''all interlocked in one humming community of cooperations and competitions, one biota.''[17] The simplest reason, to paraphrase Darwin, should, therefore, tell each individual that he or she ought to extend his or her social instincts and sympathies to all the members of the biotic community though different from him or her in appearance or habits.

And although Leopold never directly mentions it in *A Sand County Almanac,* the Copernican perspective, the perception of the Earth as ''a small planet'' in an immense and utterly hostile universe beyond, contributes, perhaps subconsciously, but nevertheless very powerfully, to our sense of kinship, community, and interdependence with fellow denizens of the Earth household. It scales the Earth down to something like a cozy island paradise in a desert ocean.

Here in outline, then, are the conceptual and logical foundations of the land ethic: Its conceptual elements are a Copernican cosmology, a Darwinian protosociobiological natural history of ethics, Darwinian ties of kinship among all forms of life on Earth, and an Eltonian model of the structure of biocenoses all overlaid on a Humean-Smithian moral psychology. Its logic is that natural selection has endowed human beings with an affective moral response to perceived bonds of kinship and community membership and identity; that today the natural environment, the land, is represented as a community, the biotic community; and that, therefore, an environmental or land ethic is both possible—the biopsychological and cognitive conditions are in place—and necessary, since human beings collectively have acquired the power to destroy the integrity, diversity, and stability of the environing

and supporting economy of nature. In the remainder of this essay I discuss special features and problems of the land ethic germane to moral philosophy.

The most salient feature of Leopold's land ethic is its provision of what Kenneth Goodpaster has carefully called ''moral considerability'' for the biotic community per se, not just for fellow members of the biotic community[18]:

> In short, a land ethic changes the role of *Homo sapiens* from conqueror of the land-community to plain member and citizen of it. It implies respect for his fellow-members, *and also respect for the community as such.* (p. 204, emphasis added)

The land ethic, thus, has a holistic as well as an individualistic cast.

Indeed, as ''The Land Ethic'' develops, the focus of moral concern shifts gradually away from plants, animals, soils, and waters severally to the biotic community collectively. Toward the middle, in the subsection called Substitutes for a Land Ethic, Leopold invokes the ''biotic rights'' of *species*—as the context indicates—of wildflowers, songbirds, and predators. In The Outlook, the climactic section of ''The Land Ethic,'' nonhuman natural entities, first appearing as fellow members, then considered in profile as species, are not so much as mentioned in what might be called the ''summary moral maxim'' of the land ethic: ''A thing is right when it tends to preserve the integrity, stability, and beauty of the biotic community. It is wrong when it tends otherwise'' (pp. 224-225).

By this measure of right and wrong, not only would it be wrong for a farmer, in the interest of higher profits, to clear the woods off a 75 percent slope, turn his cows into the clearing, and dump its rainfall, rocks, and soil into the community creek, it would also be wrong for the federal fish and wildlife agency, in the interest of individual animal welfare, to permit populations of deer, rabbits, feral burros, or whatever to increase unchecked and thus to threaten the integrity, stability, and beauty of the biotic communities of which they are members. The land ethic not only provides moral considerability for the biotic community per se, but ethical consideration of its individual members is preempted by concern for the preservation of the integrity, stability, and beauty of the biotic community. The land ethic, thus, not only has a holistic aspect; it is holistic with a vengeance.

The holism of the land ethic, more than any other feature, sets it apart from the predominant paradigm of modern moral philosophy. It is, therefore, the feature of the land ethic which requires the most patient theoretical analysis and the most sensitive practical interpretation.

. . . Goodpaster convincingly argues that mainstream modern moral theory is based, when all the learned dust has settled, on this simple paradigm of ethical justification and logic exemplified by the Benthamic and Kantian prototypes.[19] If the criterion of moral values and consideration is pitched low enough—as it is in Bentham's criterion of sentiency—a wide variety of animals are admitted to moral entitlement.[20] If the criterion of moral value and consideration is pushed lower still—as it is in Albert Schweitzer's reverence-for-life ethic—all minimally conative things (plants as well as animals) would be extended moral considerability.[21] The contemporary animal liberation/rights, and reverence-for-life/life-principle ethics are, at bottom, simply direct applications of the modern classical paradigm of moral argument. But this standard modern model of ethical theory provides no possibility whatever for the moral consideration of wholes—of threatened *populations* of animals and plants, or of endemic, rare, or endangered *species,* or of biotic *communities,* or most expansively, of the *biosphere* in its totality—since wholes per se have no psychological experience of any kind.[22] Because mainstream modern moral theory has been ''psychocentric,'' it has been radically and intractably individualistic or ''atomistic'' in its fundamental theoretical orientation.

Hume, Smith, and Darwin diverged from the prevailing theoretical model by recognizing that altruism is as fundamental and autochthonous in human nature as is egoism. According to their analysis, moral value is not identified with a natural quality objectively present in morally considerable beings—as reason and/or sentiency is objectively present in people and/or animals—it is, as it were, projected by valuing subjects.[23] . . .

Theoretically then, the biotic community owns what Leopold, in the lead paragraph of The Outlook,

calls ''value in the philosophical sense''—i.e., direct moral considerability—because it is a newly discovered proper object of a specially evolved ''public affection'' or ''moral sense'' which all psychologically normal human beings have inherited from a long line of ancestral social primates (p. 223).[24]

In the land ethic, as in all earlier stages of social-ethical evolution, there exists a tension between the good of the community as a whole and the ''rights'' of its individual members considered severally. . . .

In any case, the conceptual foundations of the land ethic provide a well-formed, self-consistent theoretical basis for including both fellow members of the biotic community and the biotic community itself (considered as a corporate entity) within the purview of morals. The preemptive emphasis, however, on the welfare of the community as a whole, in Leopold's articulation of the land ethic, while certainly *consistent* with its Humean-Darwinian theoretical foundations, is not *determined* by them alone. The overriding holism of the land ethic results, rather, more from the way our moral sensibilities are informed by ecology.

Ecological thought, historically, has tended to be holistic in outlook.[25] Ecology is the study of the *relationships* of organisms to one another and to the elemental environment. These relationships bind the *relata*—plants, animals, soils, and waters—into a seamless fabric. The ontological primacy of objects and the ontological subordination of relationships, characteristic of classical Western science, is, in fact, reversed in ecology.[26] Ecological relationships determine the nature of organisms rather than the other way around. A species is what it is because it has adapted to a niche in the ecosystem. The whole, the system itself, thus, literally and quite straightforwardly shapes and forms its component parts.

Antedating Charles Elton's community model of ecology was F. E. Clements' and S. A. Forbes' organism model.[27] Plants and animals, soils and waters, according to this paradigm, are integrated into one superorganism. Species are, as it were, its organs; specimens its cells. Although Elton's community paradigm (later modified, as we shall see, by Arthur Tansley's ecosystem idea) is the principal and morally fertile ecological concept of ''The Land Ethic,'' the more radically holistic superorganism paradigm of Clements and Forbes resonates in ''The Land Ethic'' as an audible overtone. . . .

In an early essay, ''Some Fundamentals of Conservation in the Southwest,'' Leopold speculatively flirted with the intensely holistic superorganism model of the environment as a paradigm pregnant with moral implications.[28] . . .

Had Leopold retained this overall theoretical approach in ''The Land Ethic,'' the land ethic would doubtless have enjoyed more critical attention from philosophers. The moral foundations of a land or, as he might then have called it, ''earth'' ethic, would rest upon the hypothesis that the Earth is alive and ensouled—processing inherent psychological characteristics, logically parallel to reason and sentiency. This notion of a conative whole Earth could plausibly have served as a general criterion of intrinsic worth and moral considerability, in the familiar format of mainstream moral thought. . . .

. . . Leopold may have abandoned the ''earth ethic'' because ecology had abandoned the organism analogy, in favor of the community analogy, as a working theoretical paradigm. And the community model was more suitably given moral implications by the social/sentimental ethical natural history of Hume and Darwin. . . .

The Land Pyramid is the pivotal section of ''The Land Ethic''—the section which effects a complete transition from concern for ''fellow-members'' to the ''community as such.'' It is also its longest and most technical section. A description of the ''ecosystem'' (Tansley's deliberately nonmetaphorical term) begins with the sun. Solar energy ''flows through a circuit called the biota'' (p. 215). It enters the biota through the leaves of green plants and courses through plant-eating animals, and then on to omnivores and carnivores. At last the tiny fraction of solar energy converted to biomass by green plants remaining in the corpse of a predator, animal feces, plant detritus, or other dead organic material is garnered by decomposers—worms, fungi, and bacteria. They recycle the participating elements and degrade into entropic equilibrium any remaining energy. According to this paradigm

land, then, is not merely soil; it is a fountain of energy flowing through a circuit of soils, plants, and animals. Food chains are the living channels which conduct energy upward; death and decay return it to the soil. The circuit is not closed; . . . but it is a sustained circuit, like a slowly augmented revolving fund of life. (p. 216)

In this exceedingly abstract (albeit poetically expressed) model of nature, process precedes substance and energy is more fundamental than matter. Individual plants and animals become less autonomous beings than ephemeral structures in a patterned flux of energy.

. . . The maintenance of ''the complex structure of the land and its smooth functioning as an energy unit'' emerges in The Land Pyramid as the *summum bonum* of the land ethic (p. 216).

From this good Leopold derives several practical principles slightly less general, and therefore more substantive, than the summary moral maxim of the land ethic distilled in The Outlook. ''The trend of evolution [not its ''goal,'' since evolution is ateleological] is to elaborate and diversify the biota'' (p. 216). Hence, among our cardinal duties is the duty to preserve what species we can, especially those at the apex of the pyramid—the top carnivores. ''In the beginning, the pyramid of life was low and squat; the food chains short and simple. Evolution has added layer after layer, link after link'' (pp. 215-216). Human activities today, especially those, like systematic deforestation in the tropics, resulting in abrupt massive extinctions of species, are in effect ''devolutionary''; they flatten the biotic pyramid; they choke off some of the channels and gorge others (those which terminate in our own species).[29]

The land ethic does not enshrine the ecological status quo and devalue the dynamic dimension of nature. Leopold explains that ''evolution is a long series of self-induced changes, the net result of which has been to elaborate the flow mechanism and to lengthen the circuit. Evolutionary changes, however, are usually slow and local. Man's invention of tools has enabled him to make changes of unprecedented violence, rapidity, and scope'' (pp. 216-217). ''Natural'' species extinction, i.e., species extinction in the normal course of evolution, occurs when a species is replaced by competitive exclusion or evolves into another form.[30] Normally speciation outpaces extinction. Mankind inherited a richer, more diverse world than had ever existed before in the 3.5 billion-year odyssey of life on Earth.[31] What is wrong with anthropogenic species extirpation and extinction is the *rate* at which it is occurring and the *result:* biological impoverishment instead of enrichment.

Leopold goes on here to condemn, in terms of its impact on the ecosystem, "the world-wide pooling of faunas and floras," i.e., the indiscriminate introduction of exotic and domestic species and the dislocation of native and endemic species; mining the soil for its stored biotic energy, leading ultimately to diminished fertility and to erosion; and polluting and damming water courses (p. 217).

According to the land ethic, therefore: Thou shalt not extirpate or render species extinct; thou shalt exercise great caution in introducing exotic and domestic species into local ecosystems, in extracting energy from the soil and releasing it into the biota, and in damming or polluting water courses; and thou shalt be especially solicitous of predatory birds and mammals. Here in brief are the express moral precepts of the land ethic. They are all explicitly informed—not to say derived—from the energy circuit model of the environment.

The living channels—"food chains"—through which energy courses are composed of individual plants and animals. A central, stark fact lies at the heart of ecological processes: Energy, the currency of the economy nature, passes from one organism to another, not from hand to hand, like coined money, but, so to speak, from stomach to stomach. Eating *and being eaten,* living *and dying* are what make the biotic community hum.

The precepts of the land ethic, like those of all previous accretions, reflect and reinforce the structure of the community to which it is correlative. Trophic asymmetries constitute the kernel of the biotic community. It seems unjust, unfair. But that is how the economy of nature is organized (and has been for thousands of millions of years). The land ethic, thus, affirms as good, and strives to preserve, the very inequities in nature whose social counterparts in human communities are condemned as bad and would be eradicated by familiar social ethics, especially by the more recent Christian and secular egalitarian exemplars. A "right to life" for individual members is not consistent with the structure of the biotic community and hence is not mandated by the land ethic. This disparity between the land ethic and its more familiar social precedents contributes to the apparent devaluation of individual *members* of the biotic community and augments and reinforces the tendency of the land ethic, driven by the systemic vision of ecology, toward a more holistic or community-per-se orientation.

Of the few moral philosophers who have given the land ethic a moment's serious thought, most have regarded it with horror because of its emphasis on the good of the community and its deemphasis on the welfare of individual members of the community. Not only are other sentient creatures members of the biotic community and subordinate to its integrity, beauty, and stability; so are *we.* . . .

Of course Leopold never intended the land ethic to have either inhumane or antihumanitarian implications or consequences. But whether he intended them or not, a logically consistent deduction from the theoretical premises of the land ethic might force such untoward conclusions. And given their magnitude and monstrosity, these derivations would constitute a *reductio ad absurdum* of the whole land ethic enterprise and entrench and reinforce our current human chauvinism and moral alienation from nature. If this is what membership in the biotic community entails, then all but the most radical misanthropes would surely want to opt out.

The land ethic, happily, implies neither inhumane nor inhuman consequences. That some philosophers think it must follows more from their own theoretical presuppositions than from the theoretical elements of the land ethic itself. Conventional modern ethical theory rests moral entitlement, as I earlier pointed out, on a criterion or qualification. If a candidate meets the criterion—rationality or sentiency are the most commonly posited—he, she, or it is entitled to equal moral standing with others who possess the same qualification in equal degree. Hence, reasoning in this philosophically orthodox way, and forcing Leopold's theory to conform: if human beings are, with other animals, plants, soils, and waters, equally members of the biotic community, and if community membership is the criterion of equal moral consideration, then not only do animals, plants, soils, and waters have equal (highly attenuated) ''rights,'' but human beings are equally subject to the same subordination of individual welfare and rights in respect to the good of the community as a whole.

But the land ethic, as I have been at pains to point out, is heir to a line of moral analysis different from that institutionalized in contemporary moral philosophy. From the biosocial evolutionary analysis of ethics upon which Leopold builds the land ethic, it (the land ethic) neither replaces nor overrides previous accretions. Prior moral sensibilities and obligations attendant upon and correlative to prior strata of social involvement remain operative and preemptive.

Being citizens of the United States, or the United Kingdom, or the Soviet Union, or Venezuela, or some other nation-state, and therefore having national obligations and patriotic duties, does not mean that we are not also members of smaller communities or social groups—cities or townships, neighborhoods, and families—or that we are relieved of the peculiar moral responsibilities attendant upon and correlative to these memberships as well. Similarly, our recognition of the biotic community and our immersion in it does not imply that we do not also remain members of the human community—the ''family of man'' or ''global village''—or that we are relieved of the attendant and correlative moral responsibilities of that membership, among them to respect universal human rights and uphold the principles of individual human worth and dignity. The biosocial development of morality does not grow in extent like an expanding balloon, leaving no trace of its previous boundaries, so much as like the circumference of a tree.[32] Each emergent, and larger, social unit is layered over the more primitive, and intimate, ones.

Moreover, as a general rule, the duties correlative to the inner social circles to which we belong eclipse

those correlative to the rings farther from the heartwood when conflicts arise. Consider our moral revulsion when zealous ideological nationalists encourage children to turn their parents in to the authorities if their parents should dissent from the political or economic doctrines of the ruling party. A zealous environmentalist who advocated visiting war, famine, or pestilence on human populations (those existing somewhere else, of course) in the name of the integrity, beauty, and stability of the biotic community would be similarly perverse. Family obligations in general come before nationalistic duties and humanitarian obligations in general come before environmental duties. The land ethic, therefore, is not draconian or fascist. It does not cancel human morality. The land ethic may, however, as with any new accretion, demand choices which affect, in turn, the demands of the more interior social-ethical circles. Taxes and the military draft may conflict with family-level obligations. While the land ethic, certainly, does not cancel human morality, neither does it leave it unaffected.

Nor is the land ethic inhumane. Nonhuman fellow members of the biotic community have no ''human rights,'' because they are not, by definition, members of the human community. As fellow members of the biotic community, however, they deserve respect.

How exactly to express or manifest respect, while at the same time abandoning our fellow members of the biotic community to their several fates or even actively consuming them for our own needs (and wants), or deliberately making them casualties of wildlife management for ecological integrity, is a difficult and delicate question.

Fortunately, American Indian and other traditional patterns of human-nature interaction provide rich and detailed models. Algonkian woodland peoples, for instance, represented animals, plants, birds, waters, and minerals as other-than-human persons engaged in reciprocal, mutually beneficial socioeconomc intercourse with human beings.[33] Tokens of payment, together with expressions of apology, were routinely offered to the beings whom it was necessary for these Indians to exploit. Care not to waste the usable parts, and care in the disposal of unusable animal and plant remains, were also an aspect of the respectful, albeit necessarily consumptive, Algonkian relationship with fellow members of the land community. As I have more fully argued elsewhere, the Algonkian portrayal of human-nature relationships is, indeed, although certainly different in specifics, identical in abstract form to that recommended by Leopold in the land ethic.[34] . . .

. . . Is the land ethic prudential or deontological? Is the land ethic, in other words, a matter of enlightened (collective, human) self-interest, or does it genuinely admit nonhuman natural entities and nature as a whole to true moral standing?

The conceptual foundations of the land ethic, as I have here set them out, and much of Leopold's hortatory rhetoric, would certainly indicate that the land ethic is deontological (or duty oriented) rather than prudential. In the section significantly titled The Ecological Conscience, Leopold complains that the then-current conservation philosophy is inadequate because "it defines no right or wrong, assigns no obligation, calls for no sacrifice, implies no change in the current philosophy of values. In respect of land-use, it urges *only* enlightened self-interest" (pp. 207–208, emphasis added). Clearly, Leopold himself thinks that the land ethic goes beyond prudence. In this section he disparages mere "self-interest" two more times, and concludes that "obligations have no meaning without conscience, and the problem we face is the extension of the social conscience from people to land" (p. 209).

In the next section, Substitutes for a Land Ethic, he mentions rights twice—the "biotic right" of birds to continuance and the absence of a right on the part of human special interest to exterminate predators.

Finally, the first sentences of The Outlook read: "It is inconceivable to me that an ethical relation to land can exist without love, respect, and admiration for land, and a high regard for its value. By value, I of course mean something far broader than mere economic value; I mean value in the philosophical sense" (p. 223). By "value in the philosophical sense," Leopold can only mean what philosophers more technically call "intrinsic value" or "inherent worth."[35] Something that has intrinsic value or inherent worth

is valuable in and of itself, not because of what it can do for us. "Obligation," "sacrifice," "conscience," "respect," the ascription of rights, and intrinsic value—all of these are consistently opposed to self-interest and seem to indicate decisively that the land ethic is of the deontological type.

. . . Leopold does frequently lapse into the language of (collective, long-range, human) self-interest. Early on, for example, he remarks, "in human history, we have learned (I hope) that the conqueror role is eventually *self*-defeating" (p. 204, emphasis added). And later, of the 95 percent of Wisconsin's species which cannot be "sold, fed, eaten, or otherwise put to economic use," Leopold reminds us that "these creatures are members of the biotic community, and if (as I believe) its stability depends on its integrity, they are entitled to continuance" (p. 210). The implication is clear: the economic 5 percent cannot survive if a significant portion of the uneconomic 95 percent are extirpated; nor may *we,* it goes without saying, survive without these "resources."

Leopold, in fact, seems to be consciously aware of this moral paradox. Consistent with the biosocial foundations of his theory, he expresses it in sociobiological terms:

> An ethic may be regarded as a mode of guidance for meeting ecological situations so new or intricate, or involving such deferred reactions, that the path of social expediency is not discernible to the average individual. Animal instincts are modes of guidance for the individual in meeting such situations. Ethics are possibly a kind of community instinct in-the-making. (p. 203)

From an objective, descriptive sociobiological point of view, ethics evolve because they contribute to the inclusive fitness of their carriers (or, more reductively still, to the multiplication of their carriers' genes); they are expedient. However, the path to self-interest (or to the self-interest of the selfish gene) is not discernible to the participating individuals (nor, certainly, to their genes). Hence, ethics are grounded in instinctive feeling—love, sympathy, respect—not in self-conscious calculating intelligence. Somewhat like the paradox of hedonism—the notion that one cannot achieve happiness if one directly pursues happiness per se and not other things—one can only secure self-interest by putting the interests of others on a par with one's own (in this case long-range collective human self-interest and the interest of other forms of life and of the biotic community per se).

So, is the land ethic deontological or prudential, after all? It is both—self-consistently both—depending upon point of view. From the inside, from the lived, felt point of view of the community member with evolved moral sensibilities, it is deontological. It involves an affective-cognitive posture of genuine love, respect, admiration, obligaton, self-sacrifice, conscience, duty, and the ascription of intrinsic value and biotic rights. From the outside, from the objective and analytic scientific point of view, it is prudential. "There is no other way for land to survive the impact of mechanized man," nor, therefore, for mechanized man to survive his own impact upon the land (p. viii).

NOTES

1. Wallace Stegner, "The Legacy of Aldo Leopold," in J. Baird Callicott, ed., *Companion to A Sand County Almanac* (Madison: The University of Wisconsin Press, 1987). Curt Meine, "Building 'The Land Ethic,' " in J. Baird Callicott, ed., *Companion to A Sand County Almanac* (Madison: The University of Wisconsin Press, 1987). The oft-repeated characterization of Leopold as a prophet appears traceable to Roberts Mann, "Aldo Leopold: Priest and Prophet," *American Forests* 60, no. 8 (August 1954): 23, 42-43; it was picked up, apparently, by Ernest Swift, "Aldo Leopold: Wisconsin's Conservationist Prophet," *Wisconsin Tales and Trails* 2, no. 2 (September 1961): 2-5; Roderick Nash institutionalized it in his chapter, "Aldo Leopold: Prophet," in *Wilderness and the American Mind* (New Haven: Yale University Press, 1967; revised edition, 1982).

2. John Passmore, *Man's Responsibility for* [significantly not *"to"*] *Nature: Ecological Problems and Western Traditions* (New York: Charles Scribner's Sons, 1974).

3. H.J. McCloskey, *Ecological Ethics and Politics* (Totowa, N.J.: Rowman and Littlefield, 1983), 56.

4. Robin Attfield, in "Value in the Wilderness," *Metaphilosophy* 15 (1984), writes, "Leopold the philosopher is something of a disaster, and I dread the thought of the student whose concept of philosophy is modeled principally on these extracts. (Can value 'in the philosophical sense' be contrasted with instrumental value? If concepts of right and wrong did not apply to slaves in Homeric Greece, how could Odysseus suspect the slavegirls of 'misbehavior'? If all ethics rest on interdependence how are obligations to infants and small children possible? And how can 'obligations have no meaning without conscience,' granted that the notion of conscience is conceptually dependent on that of obligation?)" (294). L.W. Sumner, "Review of Robin Attfield, *The Ethics of Environmental Concern*," *Environmental Ethics* 8 (1986): 77.

5. See Adam Smith, *Theory of the Moral Sentiments* (London and Edinburgh: A Millar, A. Kinkaid, and J. Bell, 1759) and David Hume, *An Enquiry Concerning the Principles of Morals* (Oxford: The Clarendon Press, 1777; first published in 1751). Darwin cites both works in the key fourth chapter of *Descent* (pp. 106 and 109, respectively).

6. Darwin, *Descent*, 98ff.

7. Ibid., 105f.

8. Ibid., 113ff.

9. Ibid., 105.

10. See, for example, Elman R. Service, *Primitive Social Organization: An Evolutionary Perspective* (New York: Random House, 1962).

11. See Marshall Sahlins, *Stone Age Economics* (Chicago: Aldine Atherton, 1972).

12. Darwin, *Descent*, III.

13. Ibid., 117ff. The quoted phrase occurs on p. 118.

14. Ibid., 124.

15. See Donald Worster, *Nature's Economy: The Roots of Ecology* (San Francisco: Sierra Club Books, 1977).

16. Charles Elton, *Animal Ecology* (New York: Macmillan, 1927).

17. Aldo Leopold, *Round River* (New York: Oxford University Press, 1953), 148.

18. Kenneth Goodpaster, "On Being Morally Considerable," *Journal of Philosophy* 22 (1978): 308-325. Goodpaster wisely avoids the term *rights,* defined so strictly albeit so variously by philosophers, and used so loosely by nonphilosophers.

19. Goodpaster, "Egoism to Environmentalism." Actually Goodpaster regards Hume and Kant as the co-fountainheads of this sort of moral philosophy. But Hume does not reason in this way. For Hume, the other-oriented sentiments are as primitive as self-love.

20. See Peter Singer, *Animal Liberation: A New Ethics for Our Treatment of Animals* (New York: Avon Books,

1975) for animal liberation; and see Tom Regan, *All That Dwell Therein: Animal Rights and Environmental Ethics* (Berkeley: University of California Press, 1982) for animal rights.

21. See Albert Schweitzer, *Philosophy of Civilization: Civilization and Ethics,* trans. John Naish (London: A. & C. Black, 1923). For a fuller discussion see J. Baird Callicott, "On the Intrinsic Value of Non-human Species," in *The Preservation of Species,* ed. Bryan Norton (Princeton: Princeton University Press, 1986), 138-172.

22. Peter Singer and Tom Regan are both proud of this circumstance and consider it a virtue. See Peter Singer, "Not for Humans Only: The Place of Nonhumans in Environmental Issues" in *Ethics and Problems of the 21st Century,* 191-206; and Tom Regan, "Ethical Vegetarianism and Commercial Animal Farming" in *Contemporary Moral Problems,* ed. James E. White (St. Paul, Minn.: West Publishing Co. 1985), 279-294.

23. See J. Baird Callicott, "Hume's Is/Ought Dichotomy and the Relation of Ecology to Leopold's Land Ethic," *Environmental Ethics* 4 (1982): 163-174, and "Non-anthropocentric Value Theory and Environmental Ethics," *American Philosophical Quarterly* 21 (1984): 299-309, for an elaboration.

24. I have elsewhere argued that "value in the philosophical sense" means "intrinsic" or "inherent" value. See J. Baird Callicott, "The Philosophical Value of Wildlife," in *Valuing Wildlife: Economic and Social Values of Wildlife,* ed. Daniel J. Decker and Gary Goff (Boulder, Colo.: Westview Press, 1986), 214-221.

25. See Worster, *Nature's Economy.*

26. See J. Baird Callicott, "The Metaphysical Implications of Ecology," *Environmental Ethics* 8 (1986): 300-315, for an elaboration of this point.

27. Robert P. McIntosh, *The Background of Ecology: Concept and Theory* (Cambridge: Cambridge: Cambridge University Press, 1985).

28. Aldo Leopold, "Some Fundamentals of Conservation in the Southwest," *Environmental Ethics* 1 (1979): 139-140, emphasis added.

29. I borrow the term "devolution" from Austin Meredith, "Devolution," *Journal of Theoretical Biology* 96 (1982): 49-65.

30. Holmes Rolston, III, "Duties to Endangered Species," *Bioscience* 35 (1985): 718-726. See also Geerat Vermeij, "The Biology of Human-Caused Extinction," in Norton, *Preservation of Species,* 28-49.

31. See D.M. Raup and J.J. Sepkoski, Jr., "Mass Extinctions in the Marine Fossil Record," *Science* 215 (1982): 1501-1503.

32. I owe the tree-ring analogy to Richard and Val Routley (now Sylvan and Plumwood, respectively), "Human Chauvinism and Environmental Ethics," in *Environmental Philosophy,* ed. D. Mannison, M. McRobbie, and R. Routley (Canberra: Department of Philosophy, Research School of the Social Sciences, Australian National University, 1980), 96-189. A good illustration of the balloon analogy may be found in Peter Singer, *The Expanding Circle: Ethics and Sociobiology* (New York: Farrar, Straus and Giroux, 1983).

33. For an elaboration see Thomas W. Overholt and J. Baird Callicott, *Clothed-in-Fur and Other Tales: An Introduction to an Ojibwa World View* (Washington, D.C.: University Press of America, 1982).

34. J. Baird Callicott, "Traditional American Indian and Western European Attitudes Toward Nature: An Overview," *Environmental Ethics* 4 (1982): 163-174.

35. See Worster, *Nature's Economy.*

DISCUSSION TOPICS

1. Callicott presents the notion that Leopold's land ethic is founded on evolutionary theory, ecology, and Copernican astronomy. How convincing is the logic he uses to justify the land ethic? Explain your position.

2. Callicott suggest that if Leopold had maintained the model of nature as a superorganism rather than accepting Elton's model of nature as community, the land ethic may have received more critical attention from philosophers. Which model of nature (superorganism or community) do you believe to be more defensible? Explain your reasoning.

The Land Ethic: A Critical Appraisal

James D. Heffernan

James D. Heffernan (b. 1940) is a professor of philosophy at the University of the Pacific, Stockton, California. His interests include the philosophy of mind and artificial intelligence, philosophy of science, and environmental ethics.

Heffernan focuses on Aldo Leopold's maxim: "A thing is right when it tends to preserve the integrity, stability, and beauty of the biotic community. It is wrong when it tends otherwise." To Heffernan, stability is the characteristic with the greatest ecological significance, and he interprets Leopold to mean that one should preserve the characteristic structure of an ecosystem and its capacity to withstand change or stress.

Heffernan evaluates how the integrity, stability, and beauty of the biotic community are goods such that preserving them is right. He argues that living things, including ecosystems, have interests which can be benefited or harmed, and thus have intrinsic value. It is right to preserve the integrity, stability, and beauty of entities with intrinsic value.

Heffernan addresses the issue of whether Leopold's land ethic should be interpreted as a single new moral value, a summum bonum, *or whether it is an additional rule of conduct in which ecosystemic good is to be weighed along with human good in deciding the rightness or wrongness of certain actions. He concludes that to view Leopold's ethic as a* summum bonum *would lead to immoral consequences. Instead, Heffernan proposes that Leopold's maxim be viewed as offering a* prima facie *rule of conduct: "Provided that in doing so I commit no greater wrong, a thing is right when it tends to preserve the integrity, stability, and beauty of an ecosystem." He further proposes as a general principle that human survival should take precedence over survival of nonhumans, but that the survival interests of the biotic community ought to take precedence over the nonsurvival interests of humans.*

I

No maxim is more often cited in discussions of environmental ethics than Aldo Leopold's: "A thing is right when it tends to preserve the integrity, stability, and beauty of the biotic community. It is wrong when it tends otherwise."[1] Yet relatively little has been done by way of sustained critical appraisal of this principle.[2] In this essay I contribute to the task of appraisal by answering three questions: (1) what is referred to by the phrase "the integrity, stability, and beauty of the biotic community"? (2) What "things" tend to preserve or threaten the integrity, stability, and beauty of the biotic community? (3) Are the integrity, stability, and beauty of the biotic community goods such that preserving them is right and failing to do so wrong?

II

In his essay "The Land Ethic" Leopold asserts: "All ethics so far evolved rest upon a single premise: that the individual is a member of a community of interdependent parts."[3] What is distinctive about the land ethic, he continues, is that it "enlarges the boundaries of the community to include soils, waters, plants, and animals, or collectively: the land."[4] Since Leopold includes the nonliving environment in his notion of the *biotic community,* he can be understood to be

---

1. Aldo Leopold, *A Sand County Almanac and Sketches Here and There* (New York: Oxford University Press, 1968), pp. 224-255.

2. The reader will find some perfunctory criticism of Leopold's maxim in John Passmore's *Man's Responsibility for Nature: Ecological Problems and Western Traditions* (New York: Charles Scribner's Sons, 1974), p. 116. A response to Passmore's criticism as well as further analysis of Leopold's maxim can be found in J. Baird Callicott's article "Elements of an Environmental Ethic: Moral Considerability and the Biotic Community" (*Environmental Ethics* 1 (1979): 71-81). Callicott's "Animal Liberation: A Triangular Affair," in *Environmental Ethics* 2 (1980): 311-338, adds some further analysis. Finally, Holmes Rolston's "Is There an Ecological Ethic?" in *Ethics* 85 (1975): 93-109, is an important contribution as well. I am indebted to Rolston for reminding me of several of these earlier discussions.

3. Leopold, *Sand County Almanac,* p. 203.

4. Ibid., p. 204.

referring to what contemporary ecologists call an *ecosystem.* For example, G. Tyler Miller, Jr. in his *Living in the Environment* defines an ecosystem as a "community of living things interacting with one another and with their physical environment (solar energy, air, water, soil, heat, wind, and various essential chemicals)."[5] Some examples of ecosystems are forests, ponds, lakes, rivers, grasslands, deserts, even the entire planet Earth. This last example, the totality of terrestrial ecosystems, is often called the *biosphere.*[6]

Of the triad of characteristics—integrity, stability, and beauty—only stability seems to have found a secure place in ecological literature. In his *Fundamentals of Ecology,* Eugene Odum defines *stability* as the "tendency for biological systems to resist change and to remain in a state of equilibrium."[7] Miller defines it as the "ability to withstand or to recover from externally imposed changes or stresses."[8] Moreover, Miller maintains that stability implies "persistence of structure over time."[9] In similar fashion Leopold speaks of "land health" as the "capacity of the land for self-renewal."[10] Leopold also suggests a connection between structure and stability:

> Structure means the characteristic numbers, as well as the characteristic kinds and functions, of the component species. This interdependence between the complex structure of the land and its smooth functioning as an energy unit is one of its basic attributes.[11]

The characteristic structure of an ecosystem seems to be what Leopold means by its integrity, for he suggests that the "stability (of an ecosystem) depends on its integrity." He seems also to think of the complex structure of an ecosystem as its beauty; for he refers to "the incredible intricacies of the plant and animal community" as "the intrinsic beauty of the organism called America"[12]

Hence, when Leopold talks of preserving the "integrity, stability, and beauty of the biotic community" he is referring to preserving the characteristic structure of an ecosystem and its capacity to withstand change or stress. Moreover, maintaining the characteristic structure of the ecosystem, its objective beauty, is the key to preserving its stability.

III

The claim that the stability of an ecosystem is a function of its structural complexity is related to a hypothesis frequently discussed in ecological literature, viz., the "diversity-stability" hypothesis. The initial plausibility of this hypothesis is explained in the following fashion by Miller:

> Intuitively it seems that species diversity (the number of different species and their relative abundance) and food-web complexity should help stabilize ecosystems. With so many different species and ecological niches, risk is widely spread; the system should have more ways to respond to environmental stress, and it should be more efficient in capturing and using matter and energy. The diversity of negative feedback controls should tend to keep the ecosystem functioning smoothly. A complex food-web should also promote stability. If one species is eliminated many predators can shift to another food source. In other words, it seems intuitively obvious that it is better not to have all of one's eggs in the same basket.[13]

However, if the diversity-stability hypothesis is taken to mean that the more diverse an ecosystem is the more stable it is, there has been some disconfirming evidence. One of the most diverse ecosystems yet investigated is the tropical rainforest; yet it also appears to be the most fragile, in that clearing a sufficiently large area for agriculture or too frequently clearing a small area leads to complete breakdown.

5. G. Tyler Miller, Jr., *Living in the Environment,* 2d ed. (Belmont, Calif.: Wadsworth, 1979), p. 43.

6. Ibid.

7. Eugene P. Odum, *Fundamentals of Ecology,* 3rd ed. (Philadelphia: W.B. Saunders, 1971), p. 140.

8. Miller, *Living in the Environment,* p. 82.

9. Ibid.

10. Leopold, *Sand County Almanac,* p. 221.

11. Ibid., p. 216.

12. Ibid., p. 174.

13. G. Tyler Miller, Jr., *Living in the Environment,* p. 87.

David Ehrenfeld in *The Arrogance of Humanism* reports that mathematical modeling of the diversity-stability hypothesis has shown that "the most diverse systems ought to be the most delicate; they were the ones at greatest risk of collapse following human-induced change."[14] Moreover, according to Ehrenfeld, there is direct evidence from conservation work that "the diverse, 'mature' communities were almost always the first to fall apart under heavy human-imposed stress and were always the most difficult to protect."[15] This kind of evidence leads ecologists like Miller to treat the diversity-stability hypothesis with caution. Miller says: "The idea that diversity leads to ecosystem stability may be valid in some types of ecosystems, especially if stress is not enough to wipe out the dominant species. But we should be wary of applying this idea to all situations."[16] John Passmore expresses similar reservations in his *Man's Responsibility for Nature*:

> There are, then, two principles which seem to be untenable: the first, that it is always better to increase the diversity of an ecosystem; the second, that it is never better to do so. All that can be properly said is that in modifying the degree of diversity there are always inherent dangers, biological dangers, and there is also the real risk of destroying the 'character' of a landscape, the complex set of relationships which constitute its attractiveness.[17]

It might be objected, however, that Leopold's ethical directive implies no commitment to the diversity-stability hypothesis unless *diversity* is understood to mean "characteristic diversity." It seems plausible to claim that the stability of an ecosystem is a function of its characteristic diversity. The characteristic diversity of an ecosystem cannot be raised (e.g., by introducing exotic species) or lowered (e.g., by removing indigenous species) without disturbing its integrity; and that in turn may, in Leopold's judgment, threaten its stability.

It also needs to be pointed out that stability is a relational property. Ecosystems are stable relative to the characteristic climactic, geological, and biological fluctuations in which they have evolved. No ecosystem is stable relative to all possible fluctuations. For example, no terrestrial ecosystem could withstand the stress induced by the burning out of the sun. Along the same lines, ecosystems that are stable relative to characteristic fluctuations or stresses in which they have evolved may not be stable relative to human-induced stress no matter how diverse they are, simply because shifts in the characteristic diversity induced by high technology or large population influxes are not the kinds of stress to which even the most diverse ecosystems have evolved a resistance.

Thus, we have a reply to the second question raised above: what "things" tend to preserve or threaten the integrity, stability, and beauty of the biotic community? They are the things that preserve or threaten the characteristic structure and characteristic diversity of ecosystems, or things that involve uncharacteristic stresses. Examples of such things are rife: depletion of the ozone layer in the atmosphere, eutrophication of lakes and other bodies of water, elimination of important species by pesticides or herbicides, introduction of certain exotic species, and desertification.

Leopold's principle proscribes such "things" and any activities that lead to such changes. Proscribed actions would probably include the use of fluorocarbons in aerosal sprays, the dumping of industrial wastes in fresh water, the use of broad-spectrum pesticides and herbicides in agriculture, and the over-grazing of pasture lands. Presumably to refrain from activities that threaten ecosystem stability is the best way to preserve it.

IV

Now that we have examined the principal concepts of Leopold's maxim we can deal with the last question: are the integrity, stability, and beauty of the biotic community goods such that preserving them is right and failing to do so wrong?

---

14. David W. Ehrenfeld, *The Arrogance of Humanism* (New York: Oxford University Press, 1978), p. 195.

15. Ibid.

16. G. Tyler Miller, Jr., *Living in the Environment*, p. 88.

17. John Passmore, *Man's Responsibility for Nature* (New York: Scribner's, 1974), p. 120.

In general a thing may be either good in itself, i.e., intrinsically good, or good because it leads to something good in itself, i.e., instrumentally good. There is relatively little difficulty in showing that the integrity, stability, and beauty of the biosphere are instrumentally good for human beings and other forms of life. Ecology has acquainted us with the various ways in which the continuance of life on this planet depends on the integrity and stability of the biosphere. For example, J. E. Lovelock has argued that if the proportion of oxygen in the atmosphere were to be increased to twenty-five percent by destruction of the biological controls on oxygen, the planet would be plagued by virtually uncontrollable lightning-initiated fires that would destroy almost everything flammable in a relatively short time.[18] The integrity and stability of the biosphere, then, are instrumentally good in that they constitute the conditions within which life can continue.

With regard to lesser ecosystems the task of establishing that their integrity and stability is instrumentally good for human life is not so easy. The modification of ecosystems in agriculture certainly is a case in which the destruction or at least radical reduction in the integrity and stability of a wild ecosystem leads to good for human life. The flooding of a wild river canyon for a reservoir is an instance in which the integrity and stability of riparian and other habitat are destroyed for the human goods of flood control, hydroelectric power, irrigation water, and boating. Sometimes the preservation of individual ecosystems may be good for human beings either economically (habitat for valuable species) or scientifically (natural laboratory) or aesthetically (especially beautiful places) or recreationally (places for hiking). But one would be hard pressed to show that the preservation of ecosystems always leads to something good for humans. Often, the opposite is the case, that the destruction of the integrity and stability of an ecosystem leads to good for humans. For example, the city of Los Angeles derives the benefit of water from the

destruction of Mono Lake and numerous people derive recreational benefits from the destruction of desert habitats by trail bikes and other off-road vehicles.

Recognizing this last difficulty a number of philosophers have been led to attempt to establish that the integrity, stability, and beauty of an ecosystem are intrinsic goods. This is perhaps what Leopold meant by "value in the philosophical sense":

> It is inconceivable to me that an ethical relation to land can exist without love, respect, and admiration for land, and a high regard for its value. By value, I of course mean something far broader than mere economic value; I mean value in the philosophical sense.[19]

Some philosophers have thought that to say that the integrity, stability, and beauty of an ecosystem are intrinsic goods is incomprehensible. For such philosophers the concept of intrinsic goods (or bads) is intimately bound up with concept of benefits (or harms). For example, William Frankena in a critique of reverence-for-life ethics says the following:

> The difficulty about it, to my mind, is that I can see no reason, from the moral point of view, why we should respect something that is alive but has no conscious sentiency and so can experience no pleasure or pain, joy or suffering, unless perhaps it is potentially a consciously sentient being, as in the case of a fetus. Why, if leaves and trees have no capacity to feel pleasure or to suffer, should I tear no leaf from a tree? Why should I respect its location any more than that of a stone in my driveway, if no benefit or harm comes to any person or sentient being by my moving it?[20]

Frankena seems here to be committed to a principle something like the following: it is only possible to benefit or harm a consciously sentient being or one that is potentially so.

Peter Singer takes a similar position in his *Animal Liberation*:

18. J.E. Lovelock, *Gaia: A New Look at Life on Earth* (New York: Oxford University Press, 1979), pp. 70-71.

19. Leopold, *Sand County Almanac*, p. 223.
20. W.K. Frankena, "Ethics and the Environment," in K.E. Goodpaster and K.M. Sayre, eds., *Ethics and the Problems of the 21st Century* (Notre Dame: University of Notre dame Press, 1979), p. 11.

The capacity for suffering and enjoyment is a *prerequisite for having interests at all,* a condition that must be satisfied before we can speak of interests in a meaningful way. It would be nonsense to say that it was not in the interests of a stone to be kicked along the road by a schoolboy. A stone does not have interests because it cannot suffer. Nothing that we can do to it could possibly make any difference to its welfare. A mouse, on the other hand, does have an interest in not being kicked along the road, because it will suffer if it is.[21]

Thus far then we seem to be left with the dilemma: either a creature is consciously sentient (at least potentially) or it is incapable of being benefited or harmed. Since ecosystems are not consciously sentient, they are incapable of being benefited or harmed.

Recently Kenneth Goodpaster has argued contra Frankena and Singer that it is possible to benefit or harm anything that is alive:

There is no absurdity in imagining the representation of the needs of a tree for sun and water in the face of a proposal to cut it down or pave its immediate radius for a parking lot. . . . In the face of their obvious tendencies to maintain and heal themselves, it is very difficult to reject the idea of interests on the part of trees (and plants generally) in remaining alive.[22]

Similar remarks can be made about ecosystems and the biosphere as a whole. . . .

At this point, then, it seems appropriate to claim, contra Frankena and Singer, that living things and even ecosystems, are things that have interests and, hence, may be benefited or harmed by having their interests nurtured or thwarted, even though these things are not sentient creatures. Notice that in arguing that it is not possible to harm a nonsentient being Frankena talks about plucking a leaf from a tree or not respecting its location. But these examples are both things not (at least, not necessarily) harmful to trees. Plucking a leaf and transplanting may both be done without harming a tree, whereas girdling or uprooting may not.

If those things that can be benefited or harmed are those things that have intrinsic value, then ecosystems and their inhabitants have intrinsic value. If this is true, then preserving the integrity, stability, and beauty of an ecosystem is right. Not to do so is wrong. But this last claim raises a further problem.

The problem is this: is Leopold proposing a new standard of right and wrong that will replace or supplement the old? For example, he may be suggesting: "Hitherto we have used benefit or harm to human beings as the intrinsic good to be done or evil to be avoided, but I now propose to replace benefit and harm to human beings by benefit and harm to ecosystems as the intrinsic good to be done or evil to be avoided." Or he may be suggesting: "Hitherto we have used benefit or harm to human beings as the sole intrinsic good to be done or evil to be avoided, but I now propose to supplement benefit and harm to human beings with benefit and harm to ecosystems as another intrinsic good to be done or evil to be avoided."

If the former interpretation were the correct one it would have morally unacceptable consequences, for it would imply that the standard against which our actions are measured would be benefit and harm to ecosystems. On this interpretation, then, feeding starving peoples on the African Sahel would be wrong precisely insofar as their continued existence leads to deterioration of the ecosystems they inhabit through their practices of wood gathering and dung burning. Agriculture, except of the most primitive kind, would be wrong precisely insofar as cultivation threatens the integrity and stability of wild ecosystems. Indeed, almost the only right actions on this interpretation of Leopold's principle would be the cessation of most human projects and the setting up of wilderness preserves. . . .

The second interpretation of Leopold's maxim avoids the morally unacceptable implications of the first interpretation suggested above, but it does so at a price. On the second interpretation there are numerous goods to be considered alongside human good, i.e., the good of ecosystems and the good of their

21. Peter Singer, *Animal Liberation: A New Ethics for Our Treatment of Animals* (New York: Avon Books, 1977), p. 8 (author's emphasis).

22. Kenneth E. Goodpaster, "On Being Morally Considerable," *The Journal of Philosophy* 75 (1978): 319.

nonhuman components, and these goods can conflict with one another. Perhaps then Leopold should be interpreted as proposing a new rule of conduct, but a rule having exceptions, because on occasion it can conflict with other rules, e.g., "A thing is right when it tends to preserve the life of an innocent human being. It is wrong when it tends otherwise." A classical example of conflict between rules is the conflict between the rule regarding promise keeping and that of preserving human life: a person to whom I have promised a gun has decided to use the gun to hold up a store. Should I give the person the gun and thus keep my promise or withhold the gun and thus protect human lives?

Some philosophers have tried to deal with exceptions to rules by claiming that they are *prima facie* rules of conduct, not *actual* rules of conduct.[23] They are rules to be followed unhesitatingly, just in case no other rules apply to the situation. This condition is represented by saying that rules of conduct have an implicit *ceteris paribus* clause ("other things being equal"). So, for example, provided that in doing so I commit no wrong, it is right to keep a promise. And, providing that I am not avoiding a supervening moral wrong, it is wrong not to keep a promise.

Some philosophers have attempted to provide ranking systems, e.g., claiming that preventing a death is more important than keeping a promise. However, others have been persuaded by the complexity of actual situations to forego the attempt to rank these rules and claim that such rules indicate wrong-making (or right-making) features that may be outweighed in various circumstances by other such features. Thus, if an act involves breaking a promise, that is a moral stroke against it; but that may be outweighed by other strokes for or against it, i.e., that it involves saving a life. On this interpretation Leopold may be viewed as offering a *prima facie* rule of conduct: "Provided that in doing so I commit no greater wrong, a thing is right when it tends to preserve the integrity, stability, and beauty of an ecosystem."

_____
23. Cf. W.K. Frankena, *Ethics,* 2d ed. (Englewood Cliffs: Prentice-Hall, 1973), pp. 24-28.

Now this interpretation of Leopold's maxim rids it of the absurd consequence of condoning the refusal to feed a people that is destroying its ecosystem, but it does so, perhaps at the price of rendering it innocuous or unhelpful in moral decision making. Because moral rules, on this interpretation, do not prescribe or proscribe an act on all occasions or because a set of moral rules does not come with a precise ranking, they are considered useless. This, however, is like arguing that geometrical relationships are useless in construction because no physical structure precisely embodies them. Such rules can guide moral thinking without determining it. For example, guided by the rule that there is *prima facie* wrong involved in interfering with the integrity, stability, and beauty of an ecosystem, I disapprove of the use of ORVs in desert landscapes because, although recreation is important, it can be gotten in other ways. I do not disapprove of agriculture (at least not in a blanket way) since it is not clear that humans can be fed without it. However, even in agriculture I am on the lookout for ways of raising food that are less destructive of ecosystems than current energy-intensive methods. I do suppose this means that one might permit or acquiesce in the destruction of ecosystems to save human lives.

But this does not mean that saving human lives always outweighs preserving the integrity and stability of ecosystems. I think most people would find it absurd to turn the Appalachian or the John Muir trails into asphalt highways on the grounds that it contributes to the preservation of human life by making rescue operations easier. To say that the integrity and stability of ecosystems and human lives are intrinsic values does not imply that everything must be sacrificed to preserve them.

To say that something is intrinsically valuable is to say that, *ceteris paribus,* to preserve it is right, to destroy it wrong. But in life, as in ecology, *ceteris non paribus.* In certain circumstances it may not be wrong to destroy an ecosystem and in certain circumstances it may not be wrong not to satisfy a human interest. The human interest in ORV recreation perhaps should be sacrificed to the integrity, stability, and beauty of the Mojave desert, whereas the stability of the tall grass prairie may have to yield to the reduced stability of the cornfield. The human interest in the convenience of fluorocarbon aerosols should yield to the interests of the biosphere, whereas I find it difficult to recognize as an ethic one that condones not giving aid to a country simply on the grounds that it is destroying its own ecosystems.

Perhaps we can venture a general principle at this point: the survival interests of human beings ought to outweigh those of the rest of the biotic community and the survival interests of the rest of the biotic community ought to outweigh the nonsurvival interests of human beings. This helps decide some cases. For example, the human interest in attractive shoes should not outweigh the survival interests of alligators, for clearly an interest in *attractive* shoes is not a survival interest, but the interest in some kind of food for native Africans may for a time outweigh the preservation of rainforest ecosystems, for the interest in food is a survival interest in human beings. Of course, widespread destruction of rainforests could lead to an upset in the integrity of the biosphere and this lends some urgency to finding ways of feeding people or reducing their numbers that do not involve destruction of the rainforests.

I am not sanguine about the possibility of providing a rule so precisely formulated that all cases of conflict can be easily resolved, but even an imprecise rule provides guidance, without determination, in many cases, i.e., those cases in which it is clear that the human interest at stake is or is not a survival interest and/or the ecosystemic interest is or is not a survival interest.

V

In this essay I have provided a critical analysis of Aldo Leopold's land ethic as summarized in the maxim: "A thing is right when it tends to preserve the integrity, stability, and beauty of the biotic community. It is wrong when it tends otherwise." Current ecological literature suggests a rephrasing of this maxim as follows: "A thing is right when it tends to preserve the characteristic diversity and stability of an ecosystem (or the biosphere). It is wrong when it tends otherwise." Those things that threaten the stability of an ecosystem tend not to be minor changes in the structure, i.e., in the "characteristic numbers, as well as the characteristic kinds and function, of the component species," but rather major ones. Ecological science cannot supply us with a simple way of characterizing stability-threatening activities, not, for instance, through the "diversity-stability hypothesis." Nonetheless, in practice numerous examples of such activities are easy to find.

Against those philosophers who contend that the stability of an ecosystem is not an intrinsic value, since it is not possible to harm or benefit anything not at least potentially sentient, I have argued, following Goodpaster, that it is possible to harm or benefit anything that exhibits "self-sustaining organization and integration in the face of pressures toward high entropy." Lastly I have argued that it is more appropriate to interpret Leopold as offering an additional prima facie rule of conduct rather than a single new standard of right and wrong. The latter way of interpreting the maxim has, in my estimation, immoral consequences, whereas the former way allows recognition of the intrinsic value of the stability of ecosystems without the consequence that it is never permissible to sacrifice the stability of ecosystems. While this interpretation does not make our duties toward ecosystems precisely calculable, that seems only reasonable. "Weighing the alternatives" has always seemed to me a metaphor for hard thinking rather than something we can do precisely.

DISCUSSION TOPICS

1. Heffernan advocates that stability is the only ecological term Leopold uses in his land ethic maxim, and that the notion of integrity is closely tied to the characteristic diversity of an ecosystem. Heffernan also deemphasizes beauty as a distinctive characteristic and suggests rephrasing Leopold's maxim to read, "A thing is right when it tends to preserve the characteristic diversity and stability of an ecosystem (or the biosphere). It is wrong when it tends otherwise." Explain why you agree or disagree with this proposal.

2. In what ways can ecosystems be characterized as having interests? Explain.

3. Do you agree with Heffernan's rule that the survival interests of human beings ought to outweigh those of the rest of the biotic community and the survival interests of the biotic community ought to outweigh the nonsurvival interests of human beings? Explain your reasons. How might Heffernan's rule be applied to environmental decisions?

<hr>

READING 52

Environmental Holism and Individuals

Don E. Marietta, Jr.

Don E. Marietta, Jr. (b. 1926), is professor and department chair of the Philosophy Department at Florida Atlantic University, Boca Raton, Florida. His research interests and writing include phenomenology and environmental ethics.

Marietta addresses the concern that environmental holism (ecocentrism) may be totalitarian because it subordinates the interests and rights of individuals to the good of the biosphere. He points out that there are not only several versions of holism, but several possible forms of each version. One version, scientific holism, holds that all living things are interrelated and share a common dependence on the nonliving parts of the world. Scientific holism can be stated as no more than a series of empirical findings about the natural world, but also can be stated in more extreme forms in which an ecological perspective becomes the dominant idea guiding the search for new knowledge.

Axiological holism is the perspective that the value of a natural entity is based on the importance of that entity's role in a natural system. In a modest form of axiological holism, the contribution of an entity to the ecosystem as a whole would be merely one basis for determining its value. In a more extreme form, its contribution would be the only basis for its value.

Deontic holism holds that our moral duties toward organisms and their moral standing are founded on their membership in the biospheric community. Forms of deontic holism may range from the perspective that duties

to whole ecosystems are one of many aspects of moral duty, to the notion that duties to ecosystems are the only source of duties. Despite the differences in these ideas, Marietta believes that axiological and deontic holism often are not clearly distinguished by environmental philosophers.

In Marietta's view, only the more extreme forms of axiological and deontic holism might justify the fears of critics that holism is a totalitarian philosophy. He argues that the extreme forms of holism are not logically necessary conclusions of holding a holistic perspective, and further, these extreme forms easily can lead to immoral consequences. Marietta also finds these extreme forms to be very reductionistic, and so abstract that they become meaningless. In his view, claims of environmental integrity and claims of justice and liberty as well as realization of human potentials must be given due consideration in developing a sound environmental philosophy.

I. CHARGES AGAINST HOLISTIC ENVIRONMENTALISM

Some very serious charges have been raised against the environmental philosophy on which a number of environmental ethicists have based their ethics. This philosophy, which has been known by such terms as *deep ecology, biocentrism,* and *holism,* is seen as a development of Aldo Leopold's land ethic, with emphasis placed on the concept of human beings as equals of other species in the biosphere. The biosphere is viewed as the source of value and/or obligation, and the well-being of the biosphere is the primary ethical good; human interests must be seen in the broad holistic perspective of the good of the whole biosphere.[1]

Since this holistic approach seems to subordinate the good of the individual to the good of the whole, it has been called ''totalitarian'' by Marti Kheel, and Tom Regan has charged that ''what holism gives us

<hr>

1. Aldo Leopold wrote, ''A thing is right when it tends to preserve the integrity, stability, and beauty of the biotic community. It is wrong when it tends otherwise.'' See Aldo Leopold, *A Sand Country Almanac* (London, Oxford, and New York: Oxford University Press, 1949), pp. 224–225.

is a fascist understanding of the environment."[2] Eric Katz holds that the holistic approach is unacceptable because of "the substitution problem," i.e., that one individual can be substituted for another in transactions of moral import, thus weakening respect for the intrinsic value of individuals.[3] William Aiken holds that the implications of holism are "astounding, staggering," for there would be a total loss of individual rights.[4] Eric Katz and Mark Sagoff hold that holistic environmentalism is not compatible with animal rights.[5] Feminists also have grounds for reservations about holistic environmentalism, that it could work against the goals of women's liberation, especially in respect to freedom in reproduction.[6]

These charges against, and reservations about, holism are serious. If they are well-founded, a holistic approach to the environment is a rejection of humanistic ethics, with its concern for individual worth and individual rights. This would mean that holistic environmental ethics is a radical repudiation of centuries of moral philosophy.

Are these fears about the effects of holistic environmentalism reasonable? Is holism likely to result in an overthrowing of humanistic ethics and individual rights? Some of the writings of holistic philosophers do sound extreme and uncompromising. George Sessions and Bill Devall say that human interests should be considered "only as a part of the larger whole." Paul W. Taylor argues that human beings have no moral claim to superiority over other animals. J. Baird Callicott holds that the degree to which environmentalism is biocentric may be measured in the degree to which it is misanthropic.[7]

In spite of these strong expressions of principle, however, these same philosophers do not advocate the draconian measures that seem to be indicated. Arne Naess, who coined the term *deep ecology,* advocated biospherical equality only "in principle," holding that the qualifying clause was necessary "because any realistic praxis necessitates some killing, exploitation, and suppression." Devall and Sessions recognize that nonhuman nature can be used for "vital needs," and they recognize that a needed decrease in human population may take a thousand years to achieve. Paul W. Taylor grants that the killing of wild animals or plants can be justified by adequate moral reasons; he does not hold that humans must further the good of wild creatures at whatever cost to humans.[8]

In a careful reply to the charges against biocentric ethics that we are considering, J. Baird Callicott says that the new holistic environmental perspective toward the global biotic community does not override the humanitarian ethical concerns of the human community. He considers "morally skewed" the suggestion that most of the human population should be destroyed in the interest of the biotic community. He says that biocentric environmental ethics requires that we assume some obligation to the Earth and make *some* sacrifice for its sake. Callicott recognizes that we have nested rings of involvement in society and in nature, with obligations to family and friends, professional obligations, and obligations to the commu-

2. Marti Kheel, "The Liberation of Nature: A Circular Affair," *Environmental Ethics* 7 (1985): 135–149; Tom Regan, *The Case for Animal Rights* (Berkeley: University of California Press, 1983), p. 372.

3. Eric Katz, "Organicism, Community, and the 'Substitution Problem,'" *Environmental Ethics* 7 (1985): 241-256.

4. William Aiken, "Ethical Issues in Agriculture," in Tom Regan, ed., *Earthbound* (New York: Random House, 1984), p. 269.

5. Eric Katz, "Is There a Place for Animals in the Moral Consideration of Nature?" *Ethics and Animals* 4 (1983): 75; Mark Sagoff, "Animal Liberation and Environmental Ethics: Bad Marriage, Quick Divorce," *Report from the Center for Philosophy and Public Policy* 4 (1984): 6.

6. I am indebted to Sara Ann Ketchum for my awareness of this concern about holism.

7. Bill Devall and George Sessions, "The Development of Natural Resources and the Integrity of Nature," *Environmental Ethics* 6 (1984): 305; Paul W. Taylor, "The Ethics of Respect for Nature," *Environmental Ethics* 3 (1980): 211-218, J. Baird Callicott, "Animal Liberation: A Triangular Affair," *Environmental Ethics* 2 (1979): 326.

8. Arne Naess, "The Shallow and Deep, Long-Range Ecology Movement. A Summary," *Inquiry* 16 (1973): 95; Bill Devall and George Sessions, "The Development of Natural Resources and the Integrity of Nature," pp. 303, 318; Paul. W. Taylor, "In Defense of Biocentricism," p. 242.

nity and to the country nestled within, not overridden by obligations to humanity and the natural environment. Duties growing out of our various levels of involvement must be weighed and seen in relation to each other when we decide what we must do.[9]

II. THE SERIOUSNESS OF THE CHARGES

Does the moderate talk of advocates of holism answer the charges made by humanistic critics? Will the critics be reassured? Will their fears be put to rest? They probably will not, and certainly should not. The dire picture of the effects of holism is not simply a response to what the holists have said. It is also based on possibilities that the holists did not mention and that they may not have foreseen. It is based on what the critics think might be the logical outcome of the holistic approach. While it is a welcome thing that the present generation of holists does not reject the practices of humanistic ethics, the next generation might not be so bound to the ethics of an earlier day. They might be more consistent and take holism to its logical conclusions.

In order to answer the charges made against holism, it is not enough to show that holists are not advocating the abandonment of concerns for justice, liberty, peace, kindness, and personal growth. It must be shown that a wholesale replacement of humanistic values and duties is not the logical outcome of holism. It must be shown that holists have no logical basis for letting obligation to the biosphere override all the traditional moral concerns.

Can this assurance be given? I am going to attempt to do so, but first it is necessary to point out that holism is not a simple doctrine. It appears in several aspects and in different degrees. I am not going to deal with the debate over the advantages of an organismic, community, or cellular model of biological interdependence. I do not mean to imply that this debate is not important. It is an important matter which has been treated in the literature, and there will surely be a continuing discussion of the meaning and implications of these models. Each of these models of interdependence seems, however, to raise the same fears about the overthrow of humanistic ethics out of concern for a more inclusive entity, no matter how the latter is modeled. I, therefore, focus on other distinctions between aspects of holism that have received less attention.

One way holism appears is as a scientific notion. Scientific holism is the claim that all living things are interrelated. They are interdependent and they share a common dependence on the nonliving parts of the world. This point of view can be stated in scientific terms; it is the basic theme of the instructional program at two nature centers with which I have been associated. It can be expressed in terms of evolution, trophic webs, and ecosystems. It can also be expressed in terms of kinship, family, common citizenship, and nature's economy. This interdependence of all living things can even be the theme of poets such as Gary Snyder and Francis Thompson.

Scientific holism can be stated in modest fashion, claiming no more than scientific research has demonstrated in the study of actual plant and animal species and of observable relationships between them, and between them and the inorganic aspects of their habitats. It can, however, be stated as a conceptual model, a presupposition that guides the search for knowledge and around which knowledge is organized. It can be used in environmental education as an overall world picture to make biological knowledge vivid and memorable. It can be stated in what must be an exaggerated manner, as in Francis Thompson's poetic reference to troubling a star.[10] The biologist who says, "every living thing is dependent upon every other living thing," probably would admit that

9. J. Baird Callicott, "The Search for An Environmental Ethic," in Tom Regan, ed., *Matters of Life and Death,* 2d ed. (New York: Random House, 1980), p. 411. See also his essay, "The Conceptual Foundations of the Land Ethic," in J. Baird Callicott, ed., *Companion to A Sand County Almanac* (Madison: University of Wisconsin Press, 1987).

10. "thou canst not stir a flower | Without troubling of a star."

the statement goes beyond what can be demonstrated; one philosopher admits to having overstated the idea of dependency.[11]

Another version of holism is axiological. This is the ascription of value on the basis of the role that an organism or something useful to an organism plays in the system of nature. This version of holism can be seen in the writing of several holists. It is presented clearly in Baird Callicott's paper on animal liberation.[12]

As with scientific holism, axiological holism can come in several degrees. According to a restrained version, the contribution to the ecosystem as a whole is merely one source of value. That it is the most important source of value is a stronger claim. The most extreme claim is that it is the only valid source of value. Statements of the axiological approach to holism are usually not explicit enough to place them on this scale, and most defenders of a biocentric ethic seem to fall short of the extreme view when their works are read as a whole, although isolated statements do sound like advocacy of the extreme approach.

Another version of holism is deontic holism, which holds that moral duty and moral standing derive from membership in the biospheric community. A modest version of this claim treats duty to the whole system of nature as one aspect of moral duty. A stronger claim presents such duties as primary ones that override lesser duties. The most extreme claim is that it is the only source of duty. It seems that Devall, Taylor, Sessions, Callicott, and other holistic philosophers do not accept the extreme claim, in spite of isolated statements that could be interpreted this way.

Deontic holism and axiological holism are frequently, perhaps usually, seen together. The connection between them has not, to my knowledge, been fully worked out by anyone, but their use in virtually the same breath indicates that they are thought by the holist to be related in some significant way.

I do not claim that each of the possible positions I have indicated has been staked out by someone. Whether they actually have been advocated does not matter for my purposes: they may be treated now as logically possible points of view which might have supporters in the future. Major points on each continuum have been occupied by capable advocates, and seeing the possible positions helps to clarify the issues involved.

I am interested in uncovering which positions should be supported. I do not claim to be competent to deal technically with the various positions on the scientific holism continuum. Since the axiological and deontic types of holism are what I wish to discuss, and since they do not seem to be logically derived from specific versions of scientific holism, technical and scientific aspects of holism can be left in more capable hands. When the several versions of holism are defined, it seems clear that what the critics fear is extreme axiological and deontic holism, according to which the biosphere is the *only* significant source of value and duty or is, at least, the final consideration in cases of disagreement. In light of the critics' fears, the question to ask is whether the extreme expressions of axiological and deontic holism should be adopted.

I argue that these extreme versions of holism are not required by consistency and that they are not the logical conclusion to which holism is leading. I also hold that they are not only unacceptable to our present state of moral sensibility, but that they are unjustifiable assumptions. They are extremely reductionistic, and they tend to be so abstract that they become meaningless by losing touch with our knowledge and experience.

III. THE LOGICAL OUTCOME OF HOLISM

Consistency does not require a new generation of holists to reject the humanistic ethics of individual rights and interests and duties which human beings have toward other human beings. There are several ways to see that this is so. I do not intend to belabor

---

11. Paul W. Taylor, "In Defense of Biocentrism," *Environmental Ethics* 4 (1983): 239. Taylor admits that some of the claims he makes about interdependency in "Ethics of Respect for Nature" are exaggerated.

12. Callicott, "Animal Liberation," p. 324.

the point that value judgments and ethical norms are not derived from factual information. The connection between knowledge and moral judgment is a complicated matter; moralists see the relationship between knowledge and obligation in various ways. However the philosophers of a new generation interpret the relationship between factual knowledge and ethical norms, it is quite unlikely that the lack of a deductive link between biological knowledge and ethical standards, by itself, will prevent the acceptance of an extreme form of holism. Whether extreme holism is accepted will depend on other reasons. Will it commend itself to a new generation of moralists? Will they see the extreme approach as the fitting ethical stance to take in light of their knowledge of ecology and their understanding of the nature of ethics?

At first it may seem the appropriate moral position. In his article on animal rights, for example, Callicott correlates a biocentric environmental perspective with misanthropy.[13] Other articles have cited literary works written from a holistic perspective that express a disregard for or even an antipathy toward human concerns. Are these just overstatements brought on by the emotional nature of arguments about nature? Or do they show the appropriate attitude to take in the face of what we know?

I argue that the extreme position is not justified because it is too reductionistic and too abstract. When extreme atomistic and extreme holistic positions are seen as polar opposites, this polarization makes them too abstract. Holism is taken beyond its basis in biological science, and it treats both persons and the system of nature as abstractions, without attention to the actual individuals of which the system is composed. The system of nature is no longer the interworking of organisms and inorganic features of which we have actual knowledge. Interdependence becomes an abstract notion. It is thought of in vague images and terms: symbolic thinking ignores the things which are out there in the world. The whole is not simply greater than its parts; it becomes a vague concept in which the parts become hazily perceived or lost. The individual whose interests are to be sacrificed to the good of the whole becomes a sort of cipher. This is seen in the substitution problem as depicted by Eric Katz.[14]

This abstraction is extremely reductionistic. The individual person is viewed only in terms of functions related to the whole: the significance and value of the individual is reduced to the significance that individual has as a part in the whole. The only important ethical aspect of the individual is the ethical importance of membership in the whole. This sort of reductionism has the same faults as other reductionistic approaches. It ignores far too much that is morally relevant.

It is a mistake to define a human person solely in terms of the concepts employed in biological science. It is the same sort of mistake that was made by those who defined human persons reductionistically in terms of rationality, religious destiny, social organization, or any other single aspect. In addition to biological functions, such as reproduction and nutrition, the human person has cognitive, psychological, aesthetic, and moral capacities that must be considered in defining the person. If, as many of us believe, these functions and capacities have a biological basis, to view the person in the narrow terms of the science of biology is an ironic reduction. Instead of a perspective that looks at the broad significance of biology in understanding the human person, it takes only a small part of humanness, the effect of the species on the natural environment, as all that matters. The rich life of the person is reduced to an abstraction that can be disposed of in terms of numbers on a graph.

An ethical system needs to take into consideration everything that can be morally relevant. None of the facets of humanness can be left out of consideration. Even one who is not a utilitarian must recognize the moral relevance of the human capacity to feel pain.

---

13. Ibid., p. 326.

14. Eric Katz, ''Organism, Community, and the 'Substitution Problem','' pp. 241-256.

That humans can feel a great many different types of pain, perhaps types experienced by no other organism, is ethically significant. That humans are rational and self-conscious does not justify the crudely anthropocentric attitudes of which we have been guilty, but these aspects of human life are important morally.

Traditional ethical systems were developed in response to basic needs of human persons and human society. Now we must realize the ethical importance of our impact upon the natural system. To do that, however, we do not need to see ourselves solely as organisms acting upon our environment or to reduce our ethical concern to environmental concerns. We have no alternative to confronting the many complex decisions in which our traditional ethical concerns will conflict with our environmental concerns. We will need to approach these difficult decisions without making our task look easier by being reductionistic and refusing to give due consideration to one part of the difficulty. The claims of environmental integrity and the claims of justice, liberty, and the realization of human potentiality must be given due consideration. It would be a mistake to try to subsume all of ethics under extreme holistic environmental ethics. Our situation is similar to the one W. D. Ross describes when he discusses choosing between *prima facie* duties in his classic work *The Right and the Good.* There is no way to avoid a careful weighing of obligations. It is a risky business without specific rules to guide it. As Ross puts it, when we make a correct moral judgment, we have been lucky. To be sure, we have developed a few principles to guide us in making judgments in hard cases.[15] We will need to use these and others that might be developed in the future to make the best judgments we can in the morally complex situations we now face and will face.

Predicting what future generations of philosophers will think is a risky business. We do not know what

situations they will face or what draconian measures may be needed for the survival of life on this planet. We do not know what political philosophies or ideologies will hold sway when philosophers make ethical judgments generations from now. We do not know what will be possible in light of prevailing political, social, and economic conditions. It is possible that future generations of philosophers will adopt ethical principles that would seem to us now to be needlessly stern or even misanthropic. If, for example, timely measures are not taken to control human population, there may be a time when extremely severe measures may need to be taken to save humanity. In the face of such a crisis many humanistic values may be sacrificed. This could happen even without the adoption of a holistic moral perspective; atomistic anthropocentrists could act to preserve the human race. My point is that such draconian measures would be a response to the environmental crisis: they would not follow by an inexorable logic from holism.

Person/Planet, the title of a book by Theodore Roszak, gives us, I believe, the clue we are looking for. On the one hand, our perspective must be person-planetary if we are to develop our ethics by the standards we have been working out through many generations. We would fail to take into account the findings of science if we did not recognize the importance of our role as inhabiters of this planet and as its potential destroyers. On the other hand, we would be crudely reductionistic and turn ourselves and our world into empty abstractions if we did not take into account what we are as persons. In thinking holistically we need not cast aside that product of centuries of thought and effort, humanistic ethics. Indeed we must not; any adequate approach to ethical thinking forbids it.

---

15. We tend, for example, to respect individual rights and to keep commitments unless there is an urgent social need or a clear and present danger to society. We tend to put urgent needs of persons (such as saving lives) above less urgent needs. Similar priorities are based on familiar utilitarian and deontological principles.

DISCUSSION TOPICS

1. Within the holistic framework described by Marietta, how would you classify each of the authors you have read in this chapter? Explain your reasoning.

2. If you identify yourself as an ecocentrist, how

would you classify yourself within Marietta's framework? Explain your position.

•**3.** Are there other holistic philosophies which you believe do not fit readily in Marietta's scheme? Explain your position.

READING 53

The Deep Ecological Movement: Some Philosophical Aspects

Arne Naess

Arne Naess (b. 1912) is head of the Philosophy Department at the University of Oslo, Norway. Naess first coined the term deep ecology *in 1974, and has written extensively on the topic since that time.*

Deep ecology is a movement designed to encourage people to question more deeply the fundamental presuppositions underlying the dominant economic approach of Western society in terms of value priorities, philosophy, and religion. Naess points out that deep ecology is not a proper academic philosophy, nor an institutionalized set of ideas as found in a religion or ideology. It is better characterized as a movement among people who share certain fundamental attitudes and beliefs, support a similar lifestyle, and agree on a variety of political issues. Naess presents eight points which help define a deep ecology perspective. He contrasts deep ecology with the shallow ecology position by their differing perspectives on pollution, use of natural resources, the human population explosion, cultural diversity and appropriate technology, land/sea use, and education and science. Naess identifies some of the underlying values or assumptions from which deep ecology can be derived in Christianity, Buddhism, Taoism, and Baha'i, as well as other philosophies. He then elaborates a well-defined personal philosophy ("Ecosophy T") which is founded on one ultimate norm: maximizing long-range, universal self-realization.

1. DEEP ECOLOGY ON THE DEFENSIVE

Increasing pressures for continued growth and development have placed the vast majority of environmental professionals on the defensive. . . .

If professional ecologists persist in voicing their value priorities, their jobs are often in danger, or they tend to lose influence and status among those who are in charge of overall policies.[1] Privately, they admit the necessity for deep and far-ranging changes, but they no longer speak out in public. As a result, people deeply concerned about ecology and the environment feel abandoned and even betrayed by the "experts" who work within the "establishment."

In ecological debates, many participants know a lot about particular conservation policies in particular places, and many others have strong views concerning fundamental philosophical questions of environmental ethics, but only a few have both qualities. When these people are silent, the loss is formidable. . . .

2. A CALL TO SPEAK OUT

What I am arguing for is this: even those who completely subsume ecological policies under the narrow ends of human health and well-being cannot attain their modest aims, at least not fully, without being joined by the supporters of deep ecology. They need what these people have to contribute, and this will work in their favor more often than it will work against them. Those in charge of environmental policies, even if they are resource-oriented (and growth tolerating?) decision makers, will increasingly welcome, if only for tactical and not fundamental reasons, what deep ecology supporters have to say. Even though the more radical ethic may seem nonsensical or untenable to them, they know that its advocates are, in practice, doing conservation work that sooner or later must be done. They concur with the practice even though they operate from diverging theories. The time is ripe for professional ecologists to break their silence and express their deepest concerns more freely. A bolder advocacy of deep ecological concerns by those working within the shallow, resource-oriented environmental sphere is the best strategy for regaining some of the strength of this movement among the general public, thereby contributing, however modestly, to a turning of the tide.

. . . Conservation strategies are more eagerly implemented by people who love what they are conserving, and who are convinced that what they love is intrinsically loveable. Such lovers will not want to hide their attitudes and values, rather they will increasingly give voice to them in public. They possess a genuine ethics of conservation, not merely a tactically useful instrument for human survival.

In short, environmental education campaigns can fortunately combine human-centered arguments with a practical environmental ethic based on either a deeper and more fundamental philosophic or religious perspective, and on a set of norms resting on intrinsic values. But the inherent strength of this overall position will be lost if those who work professionally on environmental problems do not freely give testimony to fundamental norms. . . .

3. WHAT IS DEEP ECOLOGY?

The phrase "deep ecology movement" has been used up to this point without trying to define it. In what follows, a set of principles or key terms and phrases (or a platform), agreed upon by George Sessions and myself, are tentatively proposed as basic to deep ecology.[2] More accurately, the sentences have a double function. They are meant to express important points which the great majority of supporters accept, implicitly or explicitly, at a high level of generality. Furthermore, they express a proposal to the effect that those who solidly reject one or more of these points should not be viewed as supporters of deep ecology. This might result because they are supporters of a shallow (or reform) environmental movement or rather they may simply dislike one or more of the 8 points for semantical or other reasons. But they may well accept a different set of points which, to me, has roughly the same meaning, in which case I shall call them supporters of the deep ecology movement, but add that they *think* they disagree (maybe Henryk Skolimowski is an example of the latter). The 8 points are:

1. The well-being and flourishing of human and non-human Life on Earth have value in themselves (synonyms: intrinsic value, inherent worth). These values are independent of the usefulness of the non-human world for human purposes.
2. Richness and diversity of life forms contribute to the realization of these values and are also values in themselves.
3. Humans have no right to reduce this richness and diversity except to satisfy vital needs.
4. The flourishing of human life and cultures is compatible with a substantially smaller human population. The flourishing of non-human life *requires* a smaller human population.
5. Present human interference with the non-human world is excessive, and the situation is rapidly worsening.
6. Policies must therefore be changed. These policies affect basic economic, technological, and ideological structures. The resulting state of affairs will be deeply different from the present.
7. The ideological change will be mainly that of appreciating life quality (dwelling in situations of inherent value) rather than adhering to an increasingly higher standard of living. There will be a profound awareness of the difference between bigness and greatness.
8. Those who subscribe to the foregoing points have an obligation directly or indirectly to try to implement the necessary changes.

Comments on the Basic Principles

RE (1): This formulation refers to the biosphere, or more professionally, to the ecosphere as a whole (this is also referred to as "ecocentrism"). This includes individuals, species, populations, habitat, as well as human and non-human cultures. Given our current knowledge of all-pervasive intimate relationships, this implies a fundamental concern and respect.

The term "life" is used here in a more comprehensive non-technical way also to refer to what biologists classify as "non-living": rivers (watersheds), landscapes, ecosystems. For supporters of deep ecology, slogans such as "let the river live" illustrate this broader usage so common in many cultures.

Inherent value, as used in (1), is common in deep ecology literature, e.g., (''The presence of inherent value in a natural object is independent of any awareness, interest, or appreciation of it by any conscious being'').[3]

RE (2): The so-called simple, lower, or primitive species of plants and animals contribute essentially to the richness and diversity of life. They have value in themselves and are not merely steps toward the so-called higher or rational life forms. The 2nd principle presupposes that life itself, as a process over evolutionary time, implies an increase of diversity and richness. . . .

RE (3): The term ''vital need'' is deliberately left vague to allow for considerable latitude in judgment. Differences in climate and related factors, together with differences in the structures of societies as they now exist, need to be taken into consideration.

RE (4): People in the materially richest countries cannot be expected to reduce their excessive interference with the non-human world overnight. The stabilization and reduction of the human population will take time. Hundreds of years! Interim strategies need to be developed. But in no way does this excuse the present complacency. The extreme seriousness of our current situation must first be realized. And the longer we wait to make the necessary changes, the more drastic will be the measures needed. Until deep changes are made, substantial decreases in richness and diversity are liable to occur: the rate of extinction of species will be 10 or 100 or more times greater than in any other short period of earth history.

RE (5): This formulation is mild. For a realistic assessment, see the annual reports of the World Watch Institute in Washington, D.C.

The slogan of ''non-interference'' does not imply that humans should not modify some ecosystems, as do other species. Humans have modified the earth over their entire history and will probably continue to do so. At issue is the *nature and extent* of such interference. The per capita destruction of wild (ancient) forests and other wild ecosystems has been excessive in rich countries; it is essential that the poor do not imitate the rich in this regard.

The fight to preserve and extend areas of wilderness and near-wilderness (''free Nature'') should continue. The rationale for such preservation should focus mainly on the ecological functions of these areas (one such function: large wilderness areas are required in the biosphere for the continued evolutionary speciation of plants and animals). Most of the present designated wilderness areas and game reserves are not large enough to allow for such speciation.

RE (6): Economic growth as it is conceived of and implemented today by the industrial states is incompatible with points (1)–(5). There is only a faint resemblance between ideal sustainable forms of economic growth and the present policies of industrial societies.

Present ideology tends to value things because they are scarce and because they have a commodity value. There is prestige in vast consumption and waste (to mention only several relevant factors).

Whereas ''self-determination,'' ''local community,'' and ''think globally, act locally,'' will remain key terms in the ecology of human societies, nevertheless the implementation of deep changes requires increasingly global action: action across borders.

Governments in Third World countries are mostly uninterested in deep ecological issues. When institutions in the industrial societies try to promote ecological measures through Third World governments, practically nothing is accomplished (e.g., with problems of desertification). Given this situation, support for global action through non-governmental international organizations becomes increasingly important. Many of these organizations are able to act globally ''from grassroots to grassroots'' thus avoiding negative governmental interference.

Cultural diversity today requires advanced technology, that is, techniques that advance the basic goals of each culture. So-called soft, intermediate, and alternative technologies are steps in this direction.

RE (7): Some economists criticize the term ''quality of life'' because it is supposedly vague. But, on closer inspection, what they consider to be vague is actually the non-quantifiable nature of the term. One cannot quantify adequately what is important for the quality of life as discussed here, and there is no need to do so.

RE (8): There is ample room for different opinions about priorities: what should be done first; what next? What is the most urgent? What is clearly necessary to be done, as opposed to what is highly desirable but not absolutely pressing? The frontier of the environmental crisis is long and varied, and there is a place for everyone.

The above formulations of the 8 points may be useful to many supporters of the deep ecology movement. But some will certainly feel that they are imperfect, even misleading. If they need to formulate in a few words what is basic to deep ecology, then they will propose an alternative set of sentences. I shall of course be glad to refer to them as alternatives. There ought to be a measure of diversity in what is considered basic and common.

Why should we call the movement ''the deep ecological movement''?[4] There are at least six other designations which cover most of the same issues: ''Ecological Resistance,'' used by John Rodman in important discussions; ''The New Natural Philosophy'' coined by Joseph Meeker; ''Eco-philosophy,'' used by Sigmund Kvaloy and others to emphasize (1) a highly critical assessment of the industrial growth societies from a general ecological point of view, and (2) the ecology of the human species; ''Green Philosophy and Politics,'' (while the term ''green'' is often used in Europe, in the United States ''green'' has a misleading association with the rather ''blue'' Green agricultural revolution; ''Sustainable Earth Ethics,'' as used by G. Tyler Miller; and ''Ecosophy'' (eco-wisdom), which is my own favorite term. Others could be mentioned as well.

And so, why use the adjective ''deep''? This question will be easier to answer after the contrast is made between shallow and deep ecological concerns. ''Deep ecology'' is not a philosophy in any proper academic sense, nor is it institutionalized as a religion or an ideology. Rather, what happens is that various persons come together in campaigns and direct actions. They form a circle of friends supporting the same kind of lifestyle which others may think to be ''simple,'' but which they themselves see as rich and many-sided. They agree on a vast array of political issues, although they may otherwise support different political parties. As in all social movements, slogans and rhetoric are indispensible for ingroup coherence. They react together against the same threats in a predominately nonviolent way. Perhaps the most influential participants are artists and writers who do not articulate their insights in terms of professional philosophy, expressing themselves rather in art or poetry. For these reasons, I use the term ''movement'' rather than ''philosophy.'' But it is essential that fundamental attitudes and beliefs are involved as part of the motivation for action.

4. DEEP VERSUS SHALLOW ECOLOGY

A number of key terms and slogans from the environmental debate will clarify the contrast between the shallow and the deep ecology movements.[5]

Pollution

Shallow approach: Technology seeks to purify the air and water and to spread pollution more evenly. Laws limit permissible pollution. Polluting industries are preferably exported to developing countries.

Deep approach: Pollution is evaluated from a biospheric point of view, not focusing exclusively on its effects on human health, but rather on life as a whole, including the life conditions of every species and system. . . .

The priority is to fight the deep causes of pollution, not merely the superficial, short-range effects. The Third and Fourth world countries cannot afford to pay the total costs of the war against pollution in their regions; consequently they require the assistance of the First and Second world countries. Exporting pollution is not only a crime against humanity, it is a crime against life in general.

Resources

Shallow approach: The emphasis is upon resources for humans, especially for the present generation in affluent societies. On this view, the resources of the earth belong to those who have the technology to exploit them. There is confidence that resources will not be depleted because, as they get rarer, a high market price will conserve them, and substitutes will be found through technological progress. Further, plants, animals, and natural objects are valuable only as resources for humans. If no human use is known, or seems likely ever to be found, it does not matter if they are destroyed..

Deep approach: The concern here is with resources and habitats for all life forms for their own sake. No natural object is conceived of solely as a resource. This leads, then, to a critical evaluation of human modes of production and consumption. . . . From a deep perspective, there is an emphasis upon an ecosystem approach rather than the consideration merely of isolated life forms or local situations. There is a long-range maximal perspective of time and place.

Population

Shallow approach: The threat of (human) ''overpopulation'' is seen mainly as a problem for developing countries. One condones or even applauds population increases in one's own country for shortsighted economic, military, or other reasons; an increase in the number of humans is considered as valuable in itself or as economically profitable. The issue of an ''optimum population'' for humans is discussed without reference to the question of an 'optimum population'' for other life forms. . . . A long-term substantial reduction of the global human population is not seen to be a desirable goal. In addition, the right is claimed to defend one's borders against ''illegal aliens,'' regardless of what the population pressures are elsewhere.

Deep approach: It is recognized that excessive pressures on planetary life stem from the human population explosion. The pressure stemming from the industrial societies is a major factor, and population reduction must have the highest priority in those societies.

Cultural Diversity and Appropriate Technology

Shallow approach: Industrialization of the Western industrial type is held to be the goal of developing countries. The universal adoption of Western tech-

nology is held to be compatible with cultural diversity, together with the conservation of the positive elements (from a Western perspective) of present nonindustrial societies. There is a low estimate of deep cultural differences in non-industrial societies which deviate significantly from contemporary Western standards.

Deep approach: Protection of non-industrial cultures from invasion by industrial societies. The goals of the former should not be seen as promoting lifestyles similar to those in the rich countries. Deep cultural diversity is an analogue on the human level to the biological richness and diversity of life forms. A high priority should be given to cultural anthropology in general education programs in industrial societies.

There should be limits on the impact of Western technology upon present existing non-industrial countries and the Fourth World should be defended against foreign domination. Political and economic policies should favor subcultures within industrial societies. Local, soft technologies should allow for a basic cultural assessment of any technical innovations, together with freely expressed criticism of so-called advanced technology when this has the potential to be culturally destructive.

Land and Sea Ethics

Shallow approach: Landscapes, ecosystems, rivers, and other whole entities of nature are conceptually cut into fragments, thus disregarding larger units and comprehensive gestalts. These fragments are regarded as the properties and resources of individuals, organizations or states. Conservation is argued in terms of ''multiple use'' and ''cost/benefit analysis.'' The social costs and long-term global ecological costs of resource extraction and use are usually not considered. Wildlife management is conceived of as conserving nature for ''future generations of humans.'' Soil erosion or the deterioration of ground water quality, for example, is noted as a human loss, but a strong belief in future technological progress makes deep changes seem unnecessary.

Deep approach: The earth does not belong to humans. For example, the Norwegian landscapes, rivers, flora and fauna, and the neighboring sea are not the property of Norwegians. Similarly, the oil under the North Sea or anywhere else does not belong to any state or to humanity. And the "free nature" surrounding a local community does not belong to the local community.

Humans only inhabit the lands, using resources to satisfy vital needs. And if their non-vital needs come in conflict with the vital needs of nonhumans, then humans should defer to the latter. The ecological destruction now going on will not be cured by a technological fix. Current arrogant notions in industrial (and other) societies must be resisted.

Education and the Scientific Enterprise

Shallow approach: The degradation of the environment and resource depletion requires the training of more and more "experts" who can provide advice concerning how to continue combining economic growth with maintaining a healthy environment. We are likely to need an increasingly more dominating and manipulative technology to "manage the planet" when global economic growth makes further environmental degradation inevitable. The scientific enterprise must continue giving priority to the "hard sciences" (physics and chemistry). High educational standards with intense competition in the relevant "tough" areas of learning will be required.

Deep approach: If sane ecological policies are adopted, then education should concentrate on an increased sensitivity to non-consumptive goods, and on such consumables where there is enough for all. Education should therefore counteract the excessive emphasis upon things with a price tag. There should be a shift in concentration from the "hard" to the "soft" sciences which stress the importance of the local and global cultures. The educational objective of the World Conservation Strategy ("building support for conservation") should be given a high priority, but within the deeper framework of respect for the biosphere.

In the future, there will be no shallow environmental movement if deep policies are increasingly adopted by governments, and thus no need for a special deep ecological social movement.

5. BUT WHY A "DEEP" ECOLOGY?

The decisive difference between a shallow and a deep ecology, in practice, concerns the willingness to question, and an appreciation of the importance of questioning, every economic and political policy in public. This questioning is both "deep" and public. It asks "why" insistently and consistently, taking nothing for granted!

Deep ecology can readily admit to the practical effectiveness of homocentric arguments:

> It is essential for conservation to be seen as central to human interests and aspirations. At the same time, people—from heads of state to the members of rural communities—will most readily be brought to demand conservation if they themselves recognize the contribution of conservation to the achievement of their needs as perceived by them, and the solution of their problems, as perceived by them.[6]

There are several dangers in arguing solely from the point of view of narrow human interests. Some policies based upon successful homocentric arguments turn out to violate or unduly compromise the objectives of deeper argumentation. Further, homocentric arguments tend to weaken the motivation to fight for necessary social change, together with the willingness to serve a great cause. In addition, the complicated arguments in human-centered conservation documents such as the World Conservation Strategy go beyond the time and ability of many people to assimilate and understand. They also tend to provoke interminable technical disagreements among experts. Special interest groups with narrow short-term exploitive objectives, which run counter to saner ecological policies, often exploit these disagreements and thereby stall the debate and steps toward effective action.

Writers with the deep ecology movement try to articulate the fundamental presuppositions underlying the dominant economic approach in terms of value priorities, philosophy, and religion. In the shallow movement, questioning and argumentation come to a halt long before this. The deep ecology movement is therefore "the ecology movement which questions deeper." A realization of the deep changes which are required, as outlined in the deep ecology 8 point platform (discussed in section 3 above) makes us realize the necessity of ''questioning everything.'' . . .

6. DEEP ECOLOGY ILLUSTRATED AS A DERIVATIONAL SYSTEM

Underlying the 8 tenants or principles presented in section 3, there are even more basic positions and norms which reside in philosophical systems and in various world religions. Schematically (Figure 8-1) we may represent the total views logically implied in the deep ecology movement by streams of derivations from the most fundamental norms and descriptive assumptions (level 1) to the particular decisions in actual life situations (level 4). . . .

As we dig deeper into the premises of our thinking, we eventually stop. Those premises we stop at are our ultimates. When we philosophize, we all stop at different places. But we all use premises which, for us, are ultimate. They belong to level 1 in the diagram. Some will use a sentence like ''Every life form has intrinsic value'' as an ultimate premise, and therefore place it at level 1. Others try, as I do, to conceive of

it as a conclusion based on a set of premises. For these people, this sentence does not belong to level 1. There will be different ecosophies corresponding to such differences.

Obviously, point 6 of the 8 point deep ecology tenants (see section 3) cannot belong to level 1 of the diagram. The statement ''there must be new policies affecting basic economic structures'' needs to be justified. If no logical justification is forthcoming, why not just assert instead that ecologically destructive ''business as usual'' economic policies should continue? In the diagram I have had ecosophies as ultimate premises in mind at level 1. None of the 8 points of the deep ecology principles belong at the ultimate level; they are derived as conclusions from premises at level 1.

Different supporters of the deep ecology movement may have different ultimates (level 1), but will nevertheless agree about level 2 (the 8 points). Level 4 will comprise concrete decisions in concrete situations which appear as conclusions from deliberations involving premises at levels 1 to 3. An important point: supporters of the deep ecology movement act from deep premises. They are motivated, in part, from a philosophical or religious position.

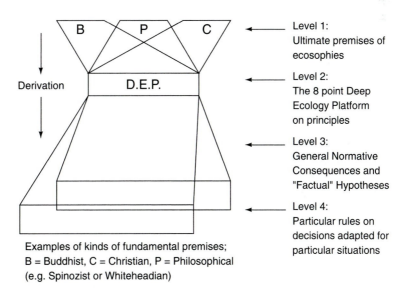

Examples of kinds of fundamental premises;
B = Buddhist, C = Christian, P = Philosophical
(e.g. Spinozist or Whiteheadian)

Level 1:
Ultimate premises of ecosophies

Level 2:
The 8 point Deep Ecology Platform on principles

Level 3:
General Normative Consequences and "Factual" Hypotheses

Level 4:
Particular rules on decisions adapted for particular situations

FIGURE 8-1.
The apron diagram.

7. MULTIPLE ROOTS OF THE DEEP ECOLOGY PRINCIPLES

The deep ecology movement seriously questions the presuppositions of shallow argumentation. Even what counts as a rational decision is challenged, because what is "rational" is always defined in relation to specific aims and goals. If a decision is rational in relation to the lower level aims and goals of our pyramid, but not in relation to the highest level, then this decision should not be judged to be rational. This is an important point! If an environmentally oriented policy decision is not linked to intrinsic values or ultimates, then its rationality has yet to be determined. The deep ecology movement connects rationality with a set of philosophical or religious foundations. But one cannot expect the ultimate premises to constitute rational conclusions. There are no "deeper" premises available.

Deep ecological questioning thus reveals the fundamental normative orientations of differing positions. Shallow argumentation stops before reaching fundamentals, or it jumps from the ultimate to the particular; that is, from level 1 to level 4.

But it is not only normative claims that are at issue. Most (perhaps all) norms presuppose ideas about how the world functions. Typically the vast majority of assertions needed in normative systems are descriptive (or factual). This holds at all the levels. . . .

Those engaged in the deep ecology movement have so far revealed their philosophical or religious homes to be mainly in Christianity, Buddhism, Taoism, Baha'i, or in various philosophies. The top level of the derivational pyramid can, in such cases, be made up of normative and descriptive principles which belong to these religions and philosophies.

Since the late 70's, numerous Christians in Europe and America, including some theologians, have actively taken part in the deep ecology movement. Their interpretations of the Bible, and their theological positions in general, have been reformed from what was, until recently, a crude dominating anthropocentric emphasis.

There is an intimate relationship between some forms of Buddhism and the deep ecology movement. The history of Buddhist thought and practice, especially the principles of non-violence, non-injury, and reverence for life, sometimes makes it easier for Buddhists to understand and appreciate deep ecology than it is for Christians, despite a (sometimes overlooked) blessedness which Jesus recommended in peace-making. I mention Taoism chiefly because there is some basis for calling John Muir a Taoist, for instance, and Baha'i because of Lawrence Arturo.

Ecosophies are not religions in the classical sense. They are better characterized as *general* philosophies, in the sense of total views, inspired in part by the science of ecology. At level 1, a traditional religion may enter the derivational pyramid through a set of normative and descriptive assumptions which would be characteristic of contemporary interpretations (hermeneutical efforts) of that religion.

Supporters of the deep ecology movement act in contemporary conflicts on the basis of their fundamental beliefs and attitudes. This gives them a particular strength and a joyful expectation or hope for a greener future. But, naturally, few of them are actively engaged in a systematic verbal articulation of where they stand.

8. ECOSOPHY T AS AN EXAMPLE OF A DEEP ECOLOGICAL DERIVATIONAL SYSTEM

I call the ecosophy I feel at home with "Ecosophy T" (Figure 8-2). . . . Ecosophy T has only one ultimate norm: "Self-realization!" I do not use this expression in any narrow, individualistic sense. I want to give it an expanded meaning based on the distinction between a large comprehensive Self and a narrow egoistic self as conceived of in certain Eastern traditions of *atman*.[7] This large comprehensive Self (with a capital "S") embraces all the life forms on the planet (and elsewhere?) together with their individual selves (*jivas*). If I were to express this ultimate norm in five words, I would say: "Maximize (long-range, universal) Self-realization!" Another more colloquial way to express this ultimate norm would be to say "Live and let live!" (referring to all of the life forms and natural processes on the planet). If I had to give up the term fearing its inevitable misunderstanding, I would use the term "universal symbiosis." "Maxi-

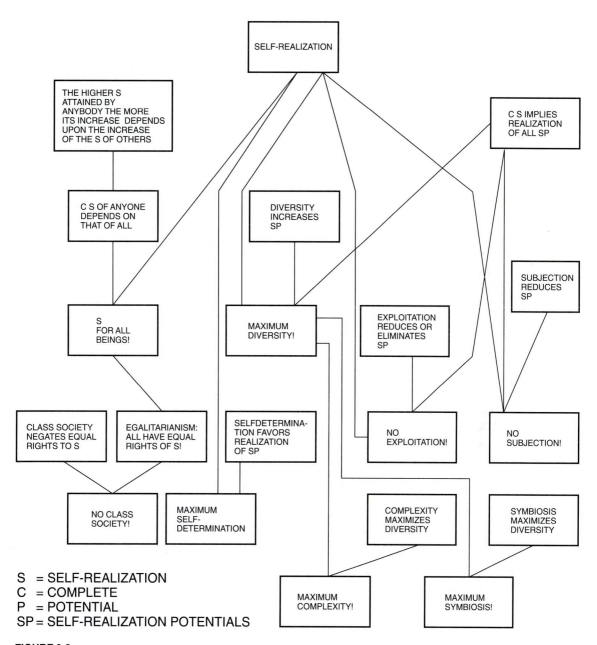

FIGURE 8-2.
Ecosophy T diagram.

mize Self-realization!'' could, of course, be misinterpreted in the direction of colossal ego trips. But ''Maximize symbiosis!'' could be misinterpreted in the opposite direction of eliminating individuality in favor of collectivity.

Viewed systematically, not individually, maximum Self-realization implies maximizing the manifestations of all life. So next I derive the second term, ''Maximize (long range, universal) diversity!'' A corollary is that the higher the levels of Self-realization attained by any person, the more any further increase depends upon the Self-realization of others. Increased self-identity involves increased identification with others. ''Altruism'' is a natural consequence of this identification.

This leads to an hypothesis concerning an inescapable increase of identification with other beings when one's own Self-realization increases. As a result, we increasingly see ourselves in other beings, and others see themselves in us. In this way, the Self is extended and deepened as a natural process of the realization of its potentialities in others.

By universalizing the above, we can derive the norm, ''Self-realization for every being!'' From the norm, ''Maximize diversity!'' and a hypothesis that maximum diversity implies a maximum of symbiosis, we can derive the norm ''Maximize symbiosis!'' Further, we work for life conditions such that there is a minimum of coercion in the lives of others. And so on![8] The 8 points of the deep ecology platform are derived in a fairly simple way.

A philosophy as a world view inevitably has implications for practical situations. Like other ecosophies, Ecosophy T therefore moves on, without apologies, to the concrete questions of lifestyles. These will obviously show great variation because of differences in hypotheses about the world in which each of us lives, and in the ''factual'' statements about the concrete situations in which we make decisions.

I shall limit myself to a discussion of a couple of areas in which my ''style'' of thinking and behaving seem somewhat strange to friends and others who know a little about my philosophy.

First, I have a somewhat extreme appreciation of diversity; a positive appreciation of the existence of styles and behavior which I personally detest or find nonsensical (but which are not clearly incompatible with symbiosis); an enthusiasm for the ''mere'' diversity of species, or varieties within a genus of plants or animals; I support, as the head of a philosophy department, doctrinal theses completely at odds with my own inclinations, with the requirement only that the authors are able to understand fairly adequately some basic features of the kind of philosophy I myself feel at home with; an appreciation of combinations of *seemingly* incompatible interests and behaviors, which makes for an increase of subcultures within industrial states and which might to some extent help future cultural diversity. So much for ''diversity!''

Second, I have a somewhat extreme appreciation of what Kant calls ''beautiful actions'' (good actions based on inclination), in contrast with actions which are performed out of a sense of duty or obligation. The choice of the formulation ''Self-realization!'' is in part motivated by the belief that maturity in humans can be measured along a scale from selfishness to an increased realization of Self, that is, by broadening and deepening the Self, rather than being measured by degrees of dutiful altruism. I see joyful sharing and caring as a natural process of growth in humans.

Third, I believe that multifaceted high-level Self-realization is more easily reached through a lifestyle which is ''simple in means but rich in ends'' rather than through the material standard of living of the average citizens of industrial states.

The simple formulations of the deep ecology platform and Ecosophy T are not meant primarily to be used among philosophers, but also in dialogues with the ''experts.'' When I wrote to the ''experts'' and environmental professionals personally, asking whether they accept the 8 points of the platform, many answered positively in relation to most or all of the points. And this includes top people in the ministries of oil and energy! Nearly all were willing to let their written answers be widely published. It is an open question, however, as to what extent they will try to influence their colleagues who use only shallow argumentation. But the main conclusion to be drawn is moderately encouraging: there are views of the human/nature relationship, widely accepted among established experts responsible for environmental decisions, which require pervasive, substantial changes of present policies in favor of our ''living'' planet, and these views are held not only on the basis of shortsighted human interests.

NOTES

1. These problems are discussed further in Naess' keynote address to the second international Conference on Conservation Biology held at The University of Michigan in May 1985; published as ''Intrinsic Value: Will the Defenders of Nature Please Rise?'', *Conservation Biology* (1986): 504-515.
2. The Deep Ecology principles (or platform) were agreed upon during a camping trip in Death Valley, California (April, 1984) and first published in George Sessions (ed.), *Ecophilosophy VI* newsletter (May, 1984). They have subsequently appeared in a number of publications.
3. Tom Regan, ''The Nature and Possibility of an Environmental Ethic,'' *Environmental Ethics* 3 (1981): 19-34, citation on p. 30.
4. I proposed the name, ''Deep, Long-Range Ecology Movement'' in a lecture at the Third World Future Research conference in Bucharest in September, 1972. A summary of that lecture (''The Shallow and the Deep, Long-Range Ecology Movement'') was published in *Inquiry* 16 (1973): 95-100. Within the deep ecology movement it is fairly common to use the term ''deep ecologist,'' whereas ''shallow ecologist,'' I am glad to say, is rather uncommon. Both terms may be considered arrogant and slightly misleading. I prefer to use the awkward, but more egalitarian expression 'supporter of the deep (or shallow) ecology movement,' avoiding personification. Also, it is common to call deep ecology consistently anti-anthropocentric. This has led to misconceptions: see my ''A Defense of the Deep Ecology Movement,'' *Environmental Ethics* 5 (1983).
5. The ''shallow/deep'' dichotomy is rough. Richard Sylvan has proposed a much more subtle classification; see his ''A Critique of Deep Ecology,'' *Discussion Papers in Environmental Philosophy,* RSSS, Australian National University, No. 12 (1985).
6. *World Conservation Strategy,* section 13 (concluding paragraph).
7. The term *atman* is not taken in its absolutistic senses (not as a permanent indestructible ''soul''). This makes it consistent with those Buddhist denials (the *avatman doctrine*) that the *atman* is to be taken in absolutist senses. Within the Christian tradition some theologians distinguish ''ego'' and ''true self'' in ways similar to these distinctions in Eastern religions. See the ecophilosophical interpretation of the gospel of Luke in Stephen Verney's *Onto the New Age* (Glasgow: Collins, 1976), pp. 33-41.
8. Many authors take some steps toward derivational structures, offering mild systematizations. The chapter ''Environmental Ethics and Hope'' (in G. Tyler Miller, *Living in the Environment,* 3rd ed. [Belmont, Calif.: Wadsworth, 1983]) is a valuable start, but the derivational relations are unclear. The logic and semantics of simple models of normative systems are briefly discussed in my ''Notes on the Methodology of Normative Systems,'' *Methodology and Science* 10 (1977): 64-79. For a defense of the thesis that as soon as people assert anything at all, they assume a total view, implicitly involving an ontology, methodology, epistemology, and ethics, see my ''Reflections about Total Views,'' *Philosophy and Phenomenological Research* 25 (1964-65): 16-29. The best and wittiest warning against taking systematizations too seriously is to be found in Soren Kierkegaard, *Concluding Unscientific Postscript.*

   For criticism and defense of my fundamental norm (''Self-realization''), together with my answer, see *In Sceptical Wonder: Essays in Honor of Arne Naess* (Oslo: University Press, 1982). My main exposition of Ecosophy T was originally offered in the Norwegian work, *Okologi, samfunn og livsstil* (Oslo: University Press, 5th ed., 1976). Even there, the exposition is sketchy. [Editor's note: Naess' Norwegian book has been revised and reissued as Arne Naess, *Ecology, Community and Lifestyle,* trans. and ed. David Rothenberg (Cambridge: Cambridge University Press, 1989)].

DISCUSSION TOPICS

1. How do you define human vital needs? To what degree do these needs vary among persons? Elaborate.
2. In what way is Naess' vision of deep ecology similar to, and different from, Leopold's land ethic? Explain.

Putting the Earth First

Dave Foreman

Dave Foreman is founder of the Earth First! movement. He has been actively engaged as an advocate for environmental protection, and has written a number of articles on the topic.

Foreman outlines the assumptions or values which underlie the Earth First! movement. To Foreman, preservation of wilderness is the fundamental issue. He stresses the need to act quickly and decisively on behalf of the biosphere, and he views intuitive, instinctive awareness to be just as valid as rationality as a basis for action.

Foreman consistently stresses the need to deemphasize the importance of human beings, and to recognize that humans have no more value than do other creatures. He maintains that there are far too many people on earth to preserve the earth and its natural diversity. Foreman calls for the acceptance of a deep ecology lifestyle which is more harmonious with preserving natural diversity on the planet.

In July 1987, seven years after the campfire gathering that spawned Earth First!, I rose among the Ponderosa Pines and scattered shafts of sunlight on the North Rim of the Grand Canyon and mounted a stage festooned with Earth First! banners and American flags. Before me sat several hundred people: hippies in tie-dyed shirts and Birkenstocks, rednecks for wilderness in cowboy boots and hats, middle-class hikers in waffle stompers, graybeards and children. The diversity was impressive. The energy was overpowering. Never in my wildest dreams had I imagined the Earth First! movement would attract so many. Never had I hoped that we would have begun to pack such a punch. We were attracting national attention; we were changing the parameters of the debate about ecological issues; we had become a legend in conservation lore.

Yet, after seven years, I was concerned we were losing some of our clarity of purpose, and blurring our focus. In launching Earth First!, I had said, ''Let our actions set the finer points of our philosophy.'' But now I was concerned that the *what* of our actions might be overwhelming the *why*. For some of those newly attracted to Earth First!, action seemed to be its own justification. I felt a need to return to wilderness fundamentalism, to articulate what I thought were the principles that defined the Earth First! movement, that gave it a specific identity. The response to the principles I offered that day was so overwhelmingly positive that I elaborated on them in the *Earth First! Journal* later that fall. Here they are.

A placing of Earth first in all decisions, even ahead of human welfare if necessary. Our movement is called ''Earth First!'' not ''People First!'' Sometimes what appears to be in the short-term interest of human beings as a whole, a select group of human beings, or individual human beings is detrimental to the short-term or long-term health of the biosphere (and to the actual long-term welfare of human beings). Earth First! does not argue that native diversity should be preserved if it can be done without negatively impacting the material ''standard of living'' of a group of human beings. We simply state that native diversity should be preserved, that natural diversity a-building for three and a half billion years should be left unfettered. Human beings must adjust to the planet; it is supreme arrogance to expect the planet and all it contains to adjust to the demands of humans. In everything human society does, the primary consideration should be for the long-term health and biological diversity of Earth. After that, we can consider the welfare of humans. We should be kind, compassionate, and caring with other people, but Earth comes first.

A refusal to use human beings as the measure by which to value others. An individual human life has no more intrinsic value than does an individual Grizzly Bear life. Human suffering resulting from drought and famine in Ethiopia is tragic, yes, but the destruction there of other creatures and habitat is even more tragic. This leads quickly into the next point.

An enthusiastic embracing of the philosophy of Deep Ecology or biocentrism. This philosophy states simply and essentially that all living creatures and communities possess intrinsic value, inherent worth. Natural things live for their own sake, which is another way of saying they have value. Other beings (both animal and plant) and even so-called "inanimate" objects such as rivers and mountains are not placed here for the convenience of human beings. Our biocentric worldview denies the modern concept of "resources." The dominant philosophy of our time (which contains Judeo-Christianity, Islam, capitalism, Marxism, scientism, and secular humanism) is anthropocentrism. It places human beings at the center of the universe, separates them from nature, and endows them with unique values. EF!ers are in direct opposition to that philosophy. Ours is an ecological perspective that views Earth as a community and recognizes such apparent enemies as "disease" (e.g., malaria) and "pests" (e.g., mosquitoes) not as manifestations of evil to be overcome but rather as vital and necessary components of a complex and vibrant biosphere.

A realization that wilderness is the real world. The preservation of wilderness is the fundamental issue. Wilderness does not merely mean backpacking parks or scenery. It is the natural world, the arena for evolution, the caldron from which humans emerged, the home of the others with whom we share this planet. Wilderness is the real world; our cities, our computers, our airplanes, our global business civilization all are but artificial and transient phenomena. It is important to remember that only a tiny portion of the history of the human species has occurred outside of wilderness. The preservation of wildness and native diversity is *the* most important issue. Issues directly affecting only humans pale in comparison. Of course, ecology teaches us that all things are connected, and in this regard all other matters become subsets of wilderness preservation—the prevention of nuclear war, for example—but the most important campaigns being waged today are those directly on behalf of wilderness.

A recognition that there are far too many human beings on Earth. There are too many of us everywhere—in the United States, in Nigeria; in cities, in rural areas; with digging hoes, with tractors. Although there is obviously an unconscionable maldistribution of wealth and the basic necessities of life among humans, this fact should not be used—as some leftists are wont to do—to argue that overpopulation is not the problem. It *is* a large part of the problem; there are far too many of us *already*—and our numbers continue to grow astronomically. Even if inequitable distribution could be solved, six billion human beings converting the natural world to material goods and human food would devastate natural diversity.

This basic recognition of the overpopulation does not mean that we should ignore the economic and social causes of overpopulation, and shouldn't criticize the accumulation of wealth in fewer and fewer hands, the maldistribution of "resources," and the venality of multinational corporations and Third World juntas alike, but simply that we must understand that Great Blue Whales, Jaguars, Black Rhinoceroses, and rain forests are not compatible with an exploding human population.[1]

A deep questioning of, and even an antipathy to, "progress" and "technology." In looking at human history, we can see that we have lost more in our "rise" to civilization than we have gained. We can see that life in a hunter-gatherer society was on the whole healthier, happier, and more secure than our lives today as peasants, industrial workers, or business executives. For every material "achievement" of progress, there are a dozen losses of things of profound and ineffable value. We can accept the pejoratives of "Luddite" and "Neanderthal" with pride.

---

1. Two excellent books on the population issue that are also sensitive to social and economic issues are William R. Catton, Jr.'s *Overshoot: The Ecological Basis of Revolutionary Change* (Urbana, Ill., and Chicago: University of Illinois Press, 1982), and *The Population Explosion*, by Paul and Anne Ehrlich (New York: Simon and Schuster, 1990). No one concerned with the preservation of biological diversity should be without these.

(This does not mean that we must immediately eschew all the facets of technological civilization. We are *of* it, and use it; this does not mean that we can't critique it.)

A refusal to accept rationality as the only way of thinking. There is room for great diversity within Earth First! on matters spiritual, and nowhere is tolerance for diversity more necessary. But we can all recognize that linear, rational, logical left brain thinking represents only part of our brain and consciousness. Rationality is a fine and useful tool, but it is just that—a tool, one way of analyzing matters. Equally valid, perhaps more so, is intuitive, instinctive awareness. We can become more cognizant of ultimate truths by sitting quietly in the wild than by studying in a library. Reading books, engaging in logical discourse, and compiling facts and figures are necessary in the modern context, but they are not the only ways to comprehend the world and our lives. Often our gut instincts enable us to act more effectively in a crisis than does careful rational analysis. An example would be a patient bleeding to death in a hospital emergency room—you can't wait for all the tests to be completed. Your gut says, ''Act!'' So it is with Earth First!'s actions in Earth's current emergency.

A lack of desire to gain credibility or ''legitimacy'' with the gang of thugs running human civilization. It is basic human nature to want to be accepted by the social milieu in which you find yourself. It hurts to be dismissed by the arbiters of opinion as ''nuts,'' ''terrorists,'' ''wackos,'' or ''extremists.'' But we are not crazy; we happen to be sane humans in an insane human society in a sane natural world. We do not have ''credibility'' with Senator Mark Hatfield or Maxxam chairman Charles Hurwitz—but they do not have credibility with us! (We do have their attention, however.) They are madmen destroying the pure and beautiful. Why should we ''reason'' with them? We do not share the same worldview or values. There is, however, a dangerous pitfall here that some alternative groups fall into. That is that we gain little by being consciously offensive, by trying to alienate

others. We can be strong and unyielding without being obnoxious.

The American system is very effective at co-opting and moderating dissidents by giving them attention and then encouraging them to be ''reasonable'' so their ideas will be taken seriously. Putting a critic on the evening news, on the front page of the newspaper, in a national magazine—all of these are methods the establishment uses to entice one to share their worldview and to enter the negotiating room to compromise. The actions of Earth First!—both the bold and the comic—have gained attention. If they are to have results, we must resist the siren's offer of credibility, legitimacy, and a share in the decision-making. We are thwarting the system, not reforming it. While we are therefore not concerned with political credibility, it must be remembered that the arguments and actions of Earth First! are based on the understanding of ecology. It is vitally important that we have biological credibility.

An effort to go beyond the tired, worn-out dogmas of left, right, and middle-of-the-road. These doctrines, whether blaming capitalism, communism, or the devil for all the problems in the world, merely represent internecine squabbles between different factions of humanism. Yes, multinational corporations commit great evil (the Soviet Union is essentially a state-run multinational corporation); there is a great injustice in the world; the rich are getting richer and the poor poorer—but all problems cannot be simplistically laid at the feet of evil capitalists in the United States, Europe, and Japan. Earth First! is not left or right; we are not even in front. Earth First! should not be in the political struggle between humanists sects at all. We're in a wholly different game.

An unwillingness to set any ethnic, class, or political group of humans on a pedestal and make them immune from questioning. It's easy, of course, to recognize that white males from North America and Europe (as well as Japanese males) hold a disproportionate share of responsibility for the mess we're in; that upper- and middle-class consumers from the First

World take an excessive portion of the world's "resources" and therefore cause greater per capita destruction than do other peoples. But it does not follow that everyone else is blameless.

The Earth First! movement has great affinity with aboriginal groups throughout the world. They are clearly in the most direct and respectful relationship with the natural world. Earth First! should back such tribes in the common struggle whenever possible without compromising our ideals. For example, we are supportive of the Dine (Navajo) of Big Mountain against relocation, but this does not mean we overlook the severe overgrazing by domestic sheep on the Navajo Reservation. We may be supportive of subsistence life-styles by natives in Alaska, but we should not be silent about clearcutting old-growth forest in southeast Alaska by native corporations, or about the Eskimo Doyon Corporation's push for oil exploration and development in the Arctic National Wildlife Refuge. It is racist either to condemn or to pardon someone based on their ethnic background.

Similarly, we are inconsistent when we castigate Charles Hurwitz for destroying the last wildnerness redwood forest, yet feel sympathy for the loggers working for him. Industrial workers, by and large, share the blame for the destruction of the natural world. They may be yoked by the big-money boys, but they are generally willing servants who share the worldview of their bosses that Earth is a smorgasbord of resources for the taking. Sometimes, in fact, it is the sturdy yeoman from the bumpkin proletariat who holds the most violent and destructive attitudes toward the natural world (and toward those who would defend it).[2] Workers are victims of an unjust economic system, but that does not absolve them of what they do. This is not to deny that some woods workers oppose the destruction of ancient forests, that some may even be Earth First!ers, but merely that it is inappropriate to overlook abuse of the natural world simply because of the rung the perpetrators occupy on the economic ladder.

Some argue that workers are merely struggling to feed their families and are not delighting in destroying the natural world. They say that unless you deal with the needs of loggers to make a living, you can't save the forest. They also claim that loggers are manipulated by their bosses to express anti-wilderness viewpoints. I find this argument to be patronizing to loggers and other workers. When I read comments from timber fellers expressing hatred toward pristine forests and toward conservationists, it is obvious that they willingly buy into the worldview of the lumber barons. San Francisco's *Image Magazine* reports on a letter to the editor written by one logger: "Working people trying to feed their families have little time to be out in the woods acting like children and making things hard for other working people. . . . Anyone out there have a recipe for spotted owl? Food stamps won't go far, I'm afraid. And since they're always being shoved down my throat, I thought I'd like mine fried."[3] Bumper stickers proclaiming "Kill an owl. Save a logger." are rife in the Northwest. I at least respect the logger who glories in felling a giant tree and who hunts Spotted Owls enough to grant him the mental ability to have his own opinions instead of pretending he is a stupid oaf, manipulated by his bosses and unable to think for himself.

Of course the big timber companies do manipulate their workers with scare tactics about mill closings and wilderness lockups, but many loggers (or cat-skinners, oilfield workers, miners, and the like) simply hate the wild and delight in "civilizing" it. Even educating workers about ecological principles will not necessarily change the attitudes of many; there are basic differences of opinion and values. Conservationists should try to find common ground with loggers and other workers whenever possible, but the sooner we get rid of Marxist views about the noble proletariat, the better.

---

2. A case in point involves the Spotted Owl, a Threatened species dependent on ancient forests. These little owls are easily attracted by playing tapes of their call. Loggers in the Northwest are going into old-growth forests with tape recorders and shotguns to exterminate Spotted Owls. They feel that if they do so, they will eliminate a major reason to stop the logging of these pristine forests.

---

3. Jane Kay, "Tree Wars," *San Francisco Examiner Image Magazine* (December 17, 1989).

A willingness to let our actions set the finer points of our philosophy and a recognition that we must act. It is possible to debate endlessly the finer points of dogma, to feel that every nuance of something must be explored before one can act. Too often, political movements become mere debating societies where the participants engage in philosophical masturbation and never get down to the vital business at hand. Others argue that you have no right to argue for environmental preservation until you are living a pure, non-impacting life-style. We will never figure it all out, we will never be able to plan any campaign in complete detail, none of us will ever entirely transcend a polluting life-style—but we can act. We can act with courage, with determination, with love for things wild and free. We can't be perfect, but we can *act*. We are warriors. Earth First! is a warrior society. We have a job to do.

An acknowledgment that we must change our personal life-styles to make them more harmonious with natural diversity. We must eschew surplusage. Although to varying degrees we are all captives of our economic system and cannot break entirely free, we must practice what we preach to the best of our ability. Arne Naess, the Norwegian philosopher and originator of the term "Deep Ecology," points out that we are not able to achieve a true "Deep Ecology" life-style, but it is the responsibility of each of us to move in that direction. Most of us still need to make a living that involves some level of participation in "the system." Even for activists, there are trade-offs—flying in a jetliner to help hang a banner on the World Bank in Washington, D.C., in order to bring international attention to the plight of tropical rain forests; using a computer to write a book printed on tree pulp that will catalyze people to take action; driving a pickup truck down a forest road to gain access to a proposed timber sale for preventive maintenance. We need to be aware of these trade-offs, and to do our utmost to limit our impact.

A commitment to maintaining a sense of humor, and a joy in living. Most radicals are a dour, holier-

than-thou, humorless lot. Earth First!ers strive to be different. We aren't rebelling against the system because we're losing in it. We're fighting for beauty, for life, for joy. We kick up our heels in delight in the wilderness, we smile at a flower and a hummingbird. We laugh. We laugh at our opponents—and, more important, we laugh at ourselves.

An awareness that we are animals. Human beings are primates, mammals, vertebrates. EF!ers recognize their animalness; we reject the New Age eco-la-la that says we must transcend our base animal nature and take charge of our evolution in order to become higher, moral beings. We believe we must return to being animal, to glorying in our sweat, hormones, tears, and blood. We struggle against the modern compulsion to become dull, passionless androids. We do not live sanitary, logical lives; we smell, taste, see, hear, and feel Earth; we live with gusto. We *are* Animal.

An acceptance of monkeywrenching as a legitimate tool for the preservation of natural diversity. Not all Earth First!ers monkeywrench, perhaps not even the majority, but we generally accept the idea and practice of monkeywrenching. Look at an EF! T-shirt. The monkeywrench on it is a symbol of resistance, an heir of the *sabot*—the wooden shoe dropped in the gears to stop the machine, from whence comes the word *sabotage*. The mystique and lore of "night work" pervades our tribe, and with it a general acceptance that strategic monkeywrenching is a legitimate tool for defense of the wild.

And finally: Earth First! is a warrior society. In addition to our absolute commitment to and love for this living planet, we are characterized by our willingness to defend Earth's abundance and diversity of life, even if that defense requires sacrifices of comfort, freedom, safety, or, ultimately, our lives. A warrior recognizes that her life is not the most important thing in her life. A warrior recognizes that there is a greater reality outside her life that must be defended. For us in Earth First!, that reality is Earth, the evolutionary process, the millions of other species with which we share this bright sphere in the void of space.

Not everyone can afford to make the commitment of being a warrior. There are many other roles that can—and must—be played in defense of Earth. One may not constantly be able to carry the burden of being a warrior; it may be only a brief period in one's life. There are risks and pitfalls in being a warrior. There may not be applause, there may not be honors and awards from human society. But there is no finer applause for the warrior of the Earth than the call of the loon at dusk or the sigh of wind in the pines.

Later that evening as I looked out over the darkening Grand Canyon, I knew that whatever hardships the future might bring, there was nothing better and more important for me to do than to take an intransigent stand in defense of life, to not compromise, to continue to be a warrior for the Earth. To be a warrior for the Earth regardless of the consequences.

DISCUSSION TOPICS

1. Do you agree with Foreman that concern for the long-term health and biological diversity of the earth should take precedence over human welfare? Justify your position.
2. Do you agree with Foreman that intuitive, instinctive awareness is just as valid as rationality, and perhaps more so, as a basis for action? Explain your view.

CLASS DISCUSSION

Small Groups

1. How does the land ethic differ from the predominant ethics of Western society?
2. How do the ecocentric ethics presented in this chapter differ from the perceptions held by Native American groups with which you are familiar?
3. What sort of ecocentric ethic, if any, might be applicable in food-poor countries such as Bangladesh, or countries in sub-Saharan Africa?
4. To what degree do each of the following scholars

share perspectives with deep ecology: Leopold, Rodman, Callicott, Heffernan, Marietta?
5. What morally relevant features may be missing from Leopold's land ethic or the deep ecology perspective presented by Naess? Explain.
6. All things considered, how might you improve Leopold's statement of the land ethic or Naess' vision of deep ecology?

CASE FOR CLASS DEBATE

A plan has been proposed to reintroduce peregrine falcons to a 308,000-hectare national forest in which they formerly lived. However, the horned lark, a common prey species for the peregrine, has been at a low population in that forest for several years. It is estimated that while the peregrine would readily survive on alternate prey species, there is about a 10% risk that peregrines could drive the lark population to extinction.

Using the techniques outlined in Appendix A, debate the merits of this plan, on the basis of ecocentric arguments only. Thus, anthropocentric arguments such as economics or impacts on current or future humans would be excluded, as would arguments based on concern for individual animals. Arguments based on intrinsic or inherent values in nature would be acceptable. Which arguments were used by each side? Which were most effective?

FOR FURTHER READING

Armstrong-Buck, Susan. "What Process Philosophy Can Contribute to the Land Ethic and Deep Ecology." *Trumpeter* 8: 29-34, 1991. A summary of Callicott's and Rolston's positions on value, as well as a brief discussion of self in deep ecology. Some weaknesses in these positions are discussed, and a brief introduction to process metaphysics as a possible remedy is presented.

Attfield, Robin. "Methods of Ecological Ethics." *Metaphilosophy* 14: 195-208, 1983. A criticism of the positions advocated by John Rodman and J. Baird Callicott that one should ascribe value to nature.

Callicott, J. Baird. "Non-Anthropocentric Value Theory and Environmental Ethics." *American Philosophical Quarterly* 21: 299-309, 1984. A thoughtful and critical review of various non-anthropocentric value theories for environmental ethics. Among these are animal liberation, ethical conativism, theistic axiology, holistic rationalism, and Leopold's land ethic. Callicott argues for Leopold's land ethic.

Devall, Bill. *Simple in Means, Rich in Ends: Practicing Deep Ecology.* Utah: Salt Lake City, Peregrine Smith Books, 1988. The author discusses practicing deep ecology at all levels, whether through inner clarification and insight, developing intellectual arguments to respect and protect nature, or by political action.

Devall William, and George Sessions. *Deep Ecology: Living as if Nature Mattered.* Salt Lake City, Utah: Gibbs M. Smith, 1985. A book designed to help raise ecological consciousness. Calls for a rejection of most current values of Western society in favor of biospheric egalitarianism. Favors low-energy, low technology, and small decentralized communities.

Ferré, Frederick. "Obstacles on the Path to Organismic Ethics." *Environmental Ethics* 11: 231-241, 1989. Advocates an organismic viewpoint over the more traditional mechanistic consciousness. Addresses some of the criticisms of organicism, and proposes a form of personalistic organicism as the foundation for an environmental ethic.

Fox, Warwick. "Deep Ecology: A New Philosophy of our Time." *The Ecologist* 14: 194-204, 1984. Fox summarizes the distinguishing features of this philosophy and addresses some of the criticisms directed to the movement. Includes a reply by Arne Naess and additional comments by Fox.

Golley, Frank B. "Deep Ecology from the Perspective of Environmental Science." *Environmental Ethics* 9: 45-55, 1987. Concludes that two norms of deep ecology, self-realization and biocentric equality, can be compatibly interpreted through the perspective of scientific ecology.

Livingston, John A. "Moral Concern and the Ecosphere." *Alternatives* 12: 3-9, 1985. A review of several philosophies which address the human–nature relationship.

Martin, Michael. "Ecosabotage and Civil Disobedience." *Environmental Ethics* 12: 291-310, 1990. Argues that ecosabotage is not a form of civil disobedience, but that both of these phenomena are special cases of a more general notion of conscientious wrong-doing. Evaluates two possible justifications of ecosabotage and concludes that utilitarian arguments could justify some forms of ecosabotage.

Moline, Jon N. "Aldo Leopold and the Moral Community" *Environmental Ethics* 8: 47-58, 1986. Moline provides an interpretation of Leopold that avoids the problems of extreme holism and extreme individualism.

Naess, Arne. *Ecology, Community and Lifestyle: Outline of an Ecosophy.* Edited and translated by David Rothenberg. Cambridge: Cambridge University Press, 1989. The translator, David Rothenberg, in conjunction with Naess, developed an English text to present Naess' own system of reasoning that led to his personal philosophy, Ecosophy T. Naess is less interested in building one standard philosophy than in teaching the readers to develop their own systems in their own ways.

Naess, Arne. "A Defence of the Deep Ecology Movement." *Environmental Ethics* 6: 265-270, 1984. Responds to Watson's criticisms that a deep ecology perspective requires that humans be set apart from nature. Rather, deep ecologists insist that life on earth has intrinsic value and that human behavior must change drastically.

Nash, Roderick F. *American Environmentalism: Readings in Conservation History*, 3rd ed. New York: McGraw-Hill, 1990. An annotated collection of many of the most pertinent writings in the development of environmental philosophy, including a number by biocentric thinkers.

Nash, Roderick F. *The Rights of Nature: A History of Environmental Ethics.* Madison, Wisc.: The University of Wisconsin Press, 1989. Provides an in-depth history of the idea that ethical standing should include the natural world.

Rolston, Holmes, III. *Environmental Ethics: Duties to and Values in the Natural World.* Philadelphia: Temple University Press, 1987. Rolston presents a philosophy of nature encompassing a theory of objective natural value, a view of how humans ought to fit into the natural world, and recommendations for environmental decision making.

Rolston, Holmes, III. *Philosophy Gone Wild: Essays in Environmental Ethics.* Buffalo, N.Y.: Prometheus Books, 1986. A collection of 15 essays in which a leading thinker in the field of environmental ethics addresses the problem of defining and justifying the values found in nature, and defining an ecocentric ethic.

Rolston, Holmes, III. "In Defense of Ecosystems." *Garden (New York Botanical Garden)* 12: 2-5; 32, 1988. A nontechnical introduction to ecosystems and the basis for valuing them, and to ecocentric ethics.

Scarce, R. *Eco-Warriors.* Chicago: Noble Press, 1990. An overview of radical environmentalism, including some of the philosophical foundations, major players, and some of the practices.

Sessions, George. "The Deep Ecological Movement: A Review." *Environmental Review* 11: 105-125, 1987. A history of the deep ecology movement by the major bibliographer of the deep ecology movement.

Sylvan, Richard. "A Critique of Deep Ecology." *Radical Philosophy* 40: 2-12; 41, 1985. Provides an insightful evaluation of the deep ecology movement. A major criticism offered by Sylvan is that deep ecologists are too vague and inconsistent, in part due to their deemphasis on rational argument.

Watson, Richard A. "A Critique of Anti-Anthropocentric Biocentrism." *Environmental Ethics* 5: 245-256, 1983. Watson argues that deep ecology logically separates humans from nature, and that a true biocentrism would not restrict humans any more than other animals; this latter position would be environmentally destructive. Rather, the author advocates that human interest in survival (anthropocentrism) is the best foundation of a sound environmental ethic.

Zimmerman, Michael E. "Feminism, Deep Ecology and Environmental Ethics." *Environmental Ethics* 9: 21-44, 1987. The ecofeminist criticism that patriarchalism has played a crucial role in shaping the attitudes of Western society toward nature is evaluated in relation to both reform environmentalism and deep ecology.

CHAPTER NINE

The Challenge of Ecofeminism

In this chapter we define "ecofeminism," delineate its challenge to other forms of environmental ethics, and identify several central issues within ecofeminism.

"Ecofeminism" was coined in 1974 by the French ecofeminist Francoise d'Eaubonne[1] in order to emphasize the potential of women to create an ecological revolution. Since then there have been many ecofeminist political events, conferences, and publications.[2] Although they adopt various approaches, ecofeminists agree that the dominance of nature is linked in inescapable ways with the dominance of women, and that any analysis which comes to terms with the subordination of one must come to terms with the subordination of the other.

Ecofeminism can be considered a subsidiary branch of feminism, or as the form which feminism as a whole should take. One fundamental purpose of feminist theory is to analyze the concept of gender in its many forms.[3] Feminism is a dynamic, broad-based philosophic perspective with a number of distinct theoretical approaches.[4]

As Karen Warren points out in her analysis of the "logic of domination" in her essay, "The Power and Promise of Ecological Feminism," the subordination of one group by another generally requires a conceptual dichotomy in which the first group is seen not only as different but as inferior to the other. In rejecting such value-laden, dualistic patterns of thinking, ecofeminism is, as Stephanie Lahar states in her essay, "Ecofeminist Theory and Grassroots Politics," trans-

---

1. Francoise d'Eaubonne, *Le Feminisme ou La Mort* (Paris: Pierre Horay, 1974).

2. For an ecofeminist bibliography and resource list, contact Ecofeminist Resources, Women's Studies Program, University of Maine, 94 Bedford Street, Portland, Maine, 94102.

3. Jane Flax, "Postmodern and Gender Relations in Feminist Theory," *Signs* 12 (1987): 621-643.

4. Feminism can be differentiated into such categories as Marxist, socialist, radical, liberal, postmodern, and spiritual feminism. For essays illustrating the first four types, see Alison M. Jaggar and Paula S. Rothenberg, eds., *Feminist Frameworks: Alternative Theoretical Accounts of the Relations Between Woman and Men* (New York: McGraw-Hill, 1984). For a treatment of postmodern feminism as well as "psychoanalytic feminism" and "existentialist feminism," see Rosemarie Tong, *Feminist Thought: A Comprehensive Introduction* (Boulder, Colo.: Westview Press, 1989). *Hypatia* 3, No. 3 (1989) is a special issue on French Feminist Philosophy, edited by Nancy Fraser and Sandra Bartky.

formational rather than merely reformist. Ecofeminists believe that social and political institutions must be radically restructured to eliminate such pernicious dualisms as the superior male vs. the inferior female, or superior human beings versus the rest of nature. Ecofeminism is nonhierarchical, egalitarian, and nonviolent.

WHY MUST ENVIRONMENTAL ETHICS BE FEMINIST?

''Patriarchy,'' the systematic, institutional dominance of women by men, has characterized virtually all historical societies. Patriarchy characterizes Western science and Western ethics, including, to some extent, environmental ethics.[5] Feminists point out that modern science is still often practiced from a ''masculine,'' reductivist, and domineering attitude toward nature as a resource for human beings.[6] Western ethics has often insisted on the supreme value of human ''reason,'' as exclusive of sensation, feeling, intuition, and relatedness.

Patriarchy has not yet been significantly affected in Western society by the feminist movement, as indicated by the information collected during the United Nations Decade for Women (1975–1985).[7] Given the persistence of patriarchy, any theory of environmental ethics which ignores the linking of women and nature is, as Warren states, historically inaccurate, as well as conceptually and morally inadequate.

---

5. Ariel Kay Salleh, ''Deeper than Deep Ecology: the Eco-Feminist Connection,'' *Environmental Ethics* 6 (1984): 339-345.

6. Evelyn Fox Keller, *Reflections on Gender and Science* (New Haven, Conn.: Yale University Press, 1985), Chaps. 4, 5, 6 and 9.

7. Despite the increasing participation of women in society, the status of women is still universally regarded as secondary to that of men. Women experience high illiteracy rates, low educational and economic levels, and devaluation of their productive and reproductive roles. The major media in every country continue to stereotype women. For a discussion, see Arvonne S. Fraser, *The U.N. Decade for Women: Documents and Dialogue* (Boulder, Colo.: Westview Press, 1987), pp. 159-176.

ARE WOMEN CLOSER TO NATURE THAN MEN?

One of the major differences among ecofeminist thinkers is found in their view of the relationship of women to nature. Theorists such as Warren and Lahar reject biologically based gender roles. They argue that the claim that women are closer to nature than men ignores the role of cultural conditioning over the centuries, in which women have been ''lumped together'' with nature, children, and indigenous peoples as more ''primitive'' and simpler than men. Warren and Lahar maintain that once this cultural conditioning is changed, no special relationship between women and nature will remain.

Thinkers such as Charlene Spretnak, however, maintain that women's physical experiences of menstruation, pregnancy, birthgiving, and lactation do provide women with a biologically based, special closeness to natural processes, a closeness which is to be recognized and honored, as she espouses in her essay, ''States of Grace.''[8]

IS THE EARTH OUR MOTHER?

Disagreements similar to those mentioned above also surround the ''sex-typing'' of the planet.[9] Lahar and others are concerned that personifying the earth as female nurturer will tend to solidify oppressive gender stereotypes; these thinkers also argue that if the earth is identified as the mother of human beings, the powerful human projections involved in ''mother'' will tend to obscure the independence and indeed strangeness of nonhuman life. These theorists recommend that the same sentiments of respect and love for our earth home can and should be expressed in gender-neutral symbolism.

However, in her essay, ''Women in Nature,'' Van-

---

8. Starhawk develops an earth-based religion which builds on these womanly experiences in *The Spiral Dance: Rebirth of the Ancient Religion of the Goddess* (San Francisco: Harper & Row, 1979).

9. Patrick Murphy, ''Sex-Typing the Planet,'' *Environmental Ethics* 10 (1988): 155-168.

dana Shiva maintains that it is appropriate to view the earth as the mother of humans. She develops the Indian concept of "Prakriti" as a nondualistic insight into the Mother of Nature. Julia Scofield Russell in her essay, "The Evolution of an Ecofeminist," also uses the powerful symbol of earth mother in the meditation which begins her article.

THE CONNECTIONS BETWEEN THEORY AND PRACTICE

Ecofeminism is a call to thoughtful integration of what has been separated: nature and culture, mind and body, male and female, reason and feeling, theory and practice. Ecofeminists affirm the intimate relationship of theory and practice. In their articles, Lahar and Spretnak stress the importance of practice and commend the creation of equitable and ecologically sound lifestyles and communities. Russell explains the deep connections between personal lifestyle and the creation of a "nurturer society."

THE CAUSES OF PATRIARCHY

One of the important debates among ecofeminist theorists concerns the origins of patriarchy, and the resulting domination of women and nature. One view, associated with the archaeological research of Marija Gimbutas,[10] is that such domination first manifested itself around 4500 B.C.E.[11] with the invasion of Old Europe (geographically from the Atlantic Ocean to the Dniper River, 7000 to 3500 B.C.E.) by cattle-herding Indo-European tribes, which she refers to as the "Kurgan" culture.[12] These tribes, with domesti-

cated horses and lethal weapons, emerged in the Volga river basin of South Russia. By the middle of the fifth millennium, even cultures west of the Black Sea had become patriarchal.

According to Gimbutas, the earlier Old European cultures were Goddess-centered "gylanies,"[13] in which women were heads of clans or queen-priestesses. These peaceful, earth-centered, nonpatriarchal, and nonmatriarchal social systems were destroyed by the invasions of the Kurgan people, which changed them from gylanic to androcratic and from matrilineal to patrilineal.[14]

Some ecofeminists, however, reject such a theory as a "Neolithic mystique" which is politically naive and irrelevant to the current situation.[15] Theorists such as Carolyn Merchant concentrate on the analysis of more recent historical periods in the belief that the concepts of nature and women are historical and social constructions.[16] Still others, such as the historian Gilda Lerner, locate the origins of patriarchy in the division of labor necessitated by child-bearing and lactation.[17] Lahar argues for the development of a number of models of the dynamics of oppression, so that the route to transformative change, both personal and political, will be made more evident.

THE IMPORTANCE OF THE INDIVIDUAL

Ecofeminist theorists stress the importance of individuals and their relationships, as well as the appre-

---

10. Marija Gimbutas has authored a number of books, including *Gods and Goddesses of Old Europe* (Berkeley: Univ. of California, 1974) and most recently, *The Civilization of the Goddess* (New York: Harper Collins, 1991).

11. "B.C.E." (Before the Common Era) and "C.E." (the Common Era) are increasingly used by both Christian and non-Christian scholars (although not by Gimbutas herself), to avoid dating world history according to an exclusively Christian framework.

12. *Kurgan* means "barrow" in Russian. These peoples buried their dead in round barrows that covered the mortuary houses of important males. Consult Marija Gimbutas, *The Language of the Goddess* (New York: Harper Collins, 1989), p. xx.

13. Gimbutas adopts Riana Eisler's term *gylany* for the social structure in which both sexes were equal. See Riana Eisler, *The Chalice and the Blade: Our History Our Future* (San Francisco: Harper & Row, 1987), pp. 105-106.

14. "Matrilineal" and "patrilineal" refer to how the inheritance of power and property are inherited: according to the female and male line, respectively.

15. Janet Biehl, *Rethinking Ecofeminist Politics* (Boston: South End Press, 1991), pp. 29-56.

16. Carolyn Merchant, *The Death of Nature: Women, Ecology, and the Scientific Revolution* (San Francisco: Harper & Row, 1980), especially Chap. 1.

17. Lerner states that the feminist critique of patriarchy, together with changes in women's reproductive lives, health and education, are helping to build a truly human world, free of dominance and hierarchy. See her book, *The Creation of Patriarchy* (New York: Oxford University Press, 1986).

ciation of genuine differences between peoples, organisms, and individual human beings. Marti Kheel has pointed out that some writers have defended hunting as an opportunity for their own "merging" with nature, and thereby overlooked the significance of the loss of life of individual animals.[18] In this respect the insights of ecofeminism parallel those of zootic individualism, in which the standpoint of the individual animal is honored.[19]

In her essay Karen Warren calls attention to the importance for ecofeminism of the relationships between particular people, as well as the affirmation of differences both between individual people and between groups of humans and nonhumans. This emphasis on individuals has been developed by Val Plumwood, who has explained that the ecofeminist emphasis on relationships does not mean that people are merged or indistinguishable. Rather, ecofeminism rejects the dualistic false dichotomy between egoism and altruism, between the self as atomistic or merged. Instead, self is understood as "embedded in a network of essential relationships with distinct others.[20]

---

18. Marti Kheel, "Ecofeminism and Deep Ecology: Reflections on Identity and Difference," in Irene Diamond and Gloria Feman Orenstein, *Reweaving the World: The Emergence of Ecofeminism* (San Francisco: Sierra Club Books, 1990), pp. 128-137.

19. Carol J. Adams provides an incisive critique of ecofeminism as failing to give enough attention to the domination of animals. See Carol J. Adams, "Ecofeminism and the Eating of Animals," *Hypatia* 6 (1991): 125–145.

20. Val Plumwood, "Nature, Self, and Gender: Feminism, Environmental Philosophy, and the Critique of Rationalism," *Hypatia* 6 (1991): 3-27. Plumwood provides a profound critique of rationalism. For a brief critique of deep ecology's inclusive self, see Susan Armstrong-Buck, "What Process Philosophy Can Contribute to the Land Ethic and Deep Ecology," *The Trumpeter* 8 (1991): 29-35.

The Power and Promise of Ecological Feminism

Karen J. Warren

Karen J. Warren (b. 1947) teaches philosophy at Macalester College in St. Paul, Minnesota. She has made important contributions to the development of ecofeminist theory, and conducts workshops in philosophy and critical thinking for students in grades K through 12.

Warren argues that ecological feminism points out the connections between the domination of women and the domination of nature. Ecofeminist philosophers claim that the most important of such connections include basic beliefs, attitudes, and values. Oppressive conceptual frameworks are those which justify one party dominating another. Oppressive conceptual frameworks are ''patriarchal'' when they justify the domination of women by men.

Warren points out three features of oppressive conceptual frameworks: ''value-hierarchical'' thinking, ''value dualisms,'' and a ''logic of domination.'' According to Warren, the problem in Western society is not value-dualism or value-hierarchical thinking in itself, but the historical use of these conceptual frameworks in the logic of domination, which has justified both the domination of nature and women by men.

Warren points out that while there are disagreements among ecofeminists on the relationship between women and nature, all ecofeminists agree that the logic of domination historically has justified the twin dominations of women and nature. Furthermore, because ''naturism'' (the view that nature is inferior to the human realm) is linked by the logic of domination to sexism, feminism is also committed to ending naturism.

According to Warren, narrative (storytelling) is an important resource to both feminism and environmental ethics. Narrative stresses relationships, expresses the diverse attitudes one can take toward the world, shows that ethics emerges out of particular situations, and

provides a fitting conclusion.[21] Warren points to Marilyn Frye's concept of the ''loving eye''[22] as appreciating the complexity and difference of the other, as opposed to the ''arrogant'' attitude of conquest which characterizes patriarchal culture.

Ecofeminism is anti-naturist, contextualist, pluralistic, uses narrative, is inclusive, nonobjective, values care, love, friendship and trust, and takes relationships seriously. Warren concludes that feminism must embrace ecofeminism and that environmental ethics must embrace feminism for historical and conceptual as well as feminist reasons.

. . . I argue that the promise and power of ecological feminism is that *it provides a distinctive framework both for reconceiving feminism and for developing an environmental ethic which takes seriously connections between the domination of women and the domination of nature.* I do so by discussing the nature of a feminist ethic and the ways in which ecofeminism provides a feminist and environmental ethic. I conclude that any feminist theory *and* any environmental ethic which fails to take seriously the twin and interconnected dominations of women and nature is at best incomplete and at worst simply inadequate.

FEMINISM, ECOLOGICAL FEMINISM, AND CONCEPTUAL FRAMEWORKS

Whatever else it is, feminism is at least the movement to end sexist oppression. It involves the elimination of any and all factors that contribute to the continued and systematic domination or subordination of women. While feminists disagree about the nature of and solutions to the subordination of women, all fem-

---

21. Barry Lopez maintains that good stories can renew the individual's sense of purpose in life. The landscape within and without the story is perceived by means of the relationships of its components. This relationship is conveyed in a story which ''rings true.'' See Barry Lopez, ''Landscape and Narrative,'' in *Crossing Open Ground* (New York: Charles Scribner's Sons, 1988), pp. 61-71.

22. Marilyn Frye, ''In and Out of Harm's Way: Arrogance and Love,'' in *The Politics of Reality* (Trumansburg, N.Y.: Crossing Press, 1983), pp. 66-72.

inists agree that sexist oppression exists, is wrong, and must be abolished.

A "feminist issue" is any issue that contributes in some way to understanding the oppression of women. Equal rights, comparable pay for comparable work, and food production are feminist issues wherever and whenever an understanding of them contributes to an understanding of the continued exploitation or subjugation of women. Carrying water and searching for firewood are feminist issues wherever and whenever women's primary responsibility for these tasks contributes to their lack of full participation in decision making, income producing, or high status positions engaged in by men. What counts as a feminist issue, then, depends largely on context, particularly the historical and material conditions of women's lives.

Environmental degradation and exploitation are feminist issues because an understanding of them contributes to an understanding of the oppression of women. In India, for example, both deforestation and reforestation through the introduction of a monoculture species tree (e.g., eucalyptus) intended for commercial production are feminist issues because the loss of indigenous forests and multiple species of trees has drastically affected rural Indian women's ability to maintain a subsistence household. Indigenous forests provide a variety of trees for food, fuel, fodder, household utensils, dyes, medicines, and income-generating uses, while monoculture-species forests do not.[1] Although I do not argue for this claim here, a look at the global impact of environmental degradation on women's lives suggests important respects in which environmental degradation is a feminist issue.

Feminist philosophers claim that some of the most important feminist issues are *conceptual* ones: these issues concern how one conceptualizes such mainstay philosophical notions as reason and rationality, ethics, and what it is to be human. Ecofeminists extend this feminist philosophical concern to nature. They argue that, ultimately, some of the most important connections between the domination of women and the domination of nature are conceptual. To see this, consider the nature of conceptual frameworks.

A *conceptual framework* is a set of *basic* beliefs, values, attitudes, and assumptions which shape and reflect how one views oneself and one's world. It is a socially constructed lens through which we perceive ourselves and others. It is affected by such factors as gender, race, class, age, affectional orientation, nationality, and religious background.

Some conceptual frameworks are oppressive. An *oppressive conceptual framework* is one that explains, justifies, and maintains relationships of domination and subordination. When an oppressive conceptual framework is *patriarchal,* it explains, justifies, and maintains the subordination of women by men.

I have argued elsewhere that there are three significant features of oppressive conceptual frameworks: (1) value-hierarchical thinking, i.e., "up-down" thinking which places higher value, status, or prestige on what is "up" rather than on what is "down"; (2) value dualisms, i.e., disjunctive pairs in which the disjuncts are seen as oppositional (rather than as complementary) and exclusive (rather than as inclusive), and which place higher value (status, prestige) on one disjunct rather than the other (e.g., dualisms which give higher value or status to that which has historically been identified as "mind," "reason," and "male" than to that which has historically been identified as "body," "emotion," and "female"); and (3) logic of domination, i.e., a structure of argumentation which leads to a justification of subordination.[2]

The third feature of oppressive conceptual frameworks is the most significant. A logic of domination is not *just* a logical structure. It also involves a substantive value system, since an ethical premise is

---

1. I discuss this in my paper, "Toward An Ecofeminist Ethic."

2. The account offered here is a revision of the account given earlier in my paper "Feminism and Ecology: Making Connections." I have changed the account to be about "oppressive" rather than strictly "patriarchal" conceptual frameworks in order to leave open the possibility that there may be some patriarchal conceptual frameworks (e.g., in non-Western cultures) which are *not* properly characterized as based on value dualisms.

needed to permit or sanction the "just" subordination of that which is subordinate. This justification typically is given on grounds of some alleged characteristic (e.g., rationality) which the dominant (e.g., men) have and the subordinate (e.g., women) lack.

Contrary to what many feminists and ecofeminists have said or suggested, there may be nothing *inherently* problematic about "hierarchical thinking" or even "value-hierarchical thinking" in contexts other than contexts of oppression. Hierarchical thinking is important in daily living for classifying data, comparing information, and organizing material. Taxonomies (e.g., plant taxonomies) and biological nomenclature seem to require *some* form of "hierarchical thinking." Even "value-hierarchical thinking" may be quite acceptable in certain contexts. (The same may be said of "value dualisms" in non-oppressive contexts.) For example, suppose it is true that what is unique about humans is our conscious capacity to radically reshape our social environments (or "societies"), as Murray Bookchin suggests.[3] Then one could truthfully say that humans are better equipped to radically reshape their environments than are rocks or plants—a "value-hierarchical" way of speaking.

The problem is not simply *that* value-hierarchical thinking and value dualisms are used, but *the way* in which each has been used *in oppressive conceptual frameworks* to establish inferiority and to justify subordination.[4] It is the logic of domination, *coupled with* value-hierarchical thinking and value dualisms, which "justifies" subordination. What is explanatorily basic, then, about the nature of oppressive conceptual frameworks is the logic of domination.

For ecofeminism, that a logic of domination is explanatorily basic is important for at least three rea-

sons. First, without a logic of domination, a description of similarities and differences would be just that—a description of similarities and differences. Consider the claim, "Humans are different from plants and rocks in that humans can (and plants and rocks cannot) consciously and radically reshape the communities in which they live; humans are similar to plants and rocks in that they are both members of an ecological community." Even if humans are "better" than plants and rocks with respect to the conscious ability of humans to radically transform communities, one does not *thereby* get any *morally* relevant distinction between humans and nonhumans, or an argument for the domination of plants and rocks by humans. To get *those* conclusions one needs to add at least two powerful assumptions, viz., (A2) and (A4) in argument A below:

(A1)   Humans do, and plants and rocks do not, have the capacity to consciously and radically change the community in which they live.

(A2)   Whatever has the capacity to consciously and radically change the community in which it lives is morally superior to whatever lacks this capacity.

(A3)   Thus, humans are morally superior to plants and rocks.

(A4)   For any X and Y, if X is morally superior to Y, then X is morally justified in subordinating Y.

(A5)   Thus, humans are morally justified in subordinating plants and rocks.

Without the two assumptions that *humans are morally superior* to (at least some) nonhumans, (A2), and that *superiority justifies subordination,* (A4), all one has is some difference between humans and some nonhumans. This is true *even if* that difference is given in terms of superiority. Thus, it is the logic of domination, (A4), which is the bottom line in ecofeminist discussions of oppression.

Second, ecofeminists argue that, at least in Western societies, the oppressive conceptual framework which sanctions the twin dominations of women and

3. Murray Bookchin, "Social Ecology versus 'Deep Ecology'," in *Green Perspectives: Newsletter of the Green Program Project,* No. 4-5 (Summer 1987): 9.

4. It may be that in contemporary Western society, which is so thoroughly structured by categories of gender, race, class, age, and affectional orientation, that there simply is no meaningful notion of "value-hierarchical thinking" which does not function in an oppressive context. For purposes of this paper, I leave that question open.

nature is a patriarchal one characterized by all three features of an oppressive conceptual framework. Many ecofeminists claim that, historically, within at least the dominant Western culture, a patriarchal conceptual framework has sanctioned the following argument B:

(B1)   Women are identified with nature and the realm of the physical; men are identified with the ''human'' and the realm of the mental.

(B2)   Whatever is identified with nature and the realm of the physical is inferior to (''below'') whatever is identified with the ''human'' and the realm of the mental; or, conversely, the latter is superior to (''above'') the former.

(B3)   Thus, women are inferior to (''below'') men; or, conversely, men are superior to (''above'') women.

(B4)   For any X and Y, if X is superior to Y, then X is justified in subordinating Y.

(B5)   Thus, men are justified in subordinating women.

If sound, argument B establishes *patriarchy,* i.e., the conclusion given at (B5) that the systematic domination of women by men is justified. But according to ecofeminists, (B5) is justified by just those three features of an oppressive conceptual framework identified earlier: value-hierarchical thinking, the assumption at (B2); value dualisms, the assumed dualism of the mental and the physical at (B1) and the assumed inferiority of the physical vis-à-vis the mental at (B2); and a logic of domination, the assumption at (B4), the same as the previous premise (A4). Hence, according to ecofeminists, insofar as an oppressive patriarchal conceptual framework has functioned historically (within at least dominant Western culture) to sanction the twin dominations of women and nature (argument B), both argument B and the patriarchal conceptual framework, from whence it comes, ought to be rejected.

Of course, the preceding does not identify which premises of B are false. What is the status of premises

(B1) and (B2)? Most, if not all, feminists claim that (B1), and many ecofeminists claim that (B2), have been assumed or asserted within the dominant Western philosophical and intellectual tradition.[5] As such, these feminists assert, as a matter of historical fact, that the dominant Western philosophical tradition has assumed the truth of (B1) and (B2). Ecofeminists, however, either deny (B2) or do not affirm (B2). Furthermore, because some ecofeminists are anxious to deny any ahistorical identification of women with nature, some ecofeminists deny (B1) when (B1) is used to support anything other than a strictly historical claim about what has been asserted or assumed to be true within patriarchal culture—e.g., when (B1) is used to assert that women properly are identified with the realm of nature and the physical.[6] Thus, from an ecofeminist perspective, (B1) and (B2) are properly viewed as problematic though historically sanctioned claims: they are problematic precisely because of the way they have functioned historically in a patriarchal conceptual framework and culture to sanction the dominations of women and nature.

---

5. Many feminists who argue for the historical point that claims (B1) and (B2) have been asserted or assumed to be true within the dominant Western philosophical tradition do so by discussion of that tradition's conceptions of reason, rationality, and science. For a sampling of the sorts of claims made within that context, see ''Reason, Rationality, and Gender,'' ed. Nancy Tuana and Karen J. Warren, a special issue of the American Philosophical Association's *Newsletter on Feminism and Philosophy* 88, No. 2 (March 1989): 17-71. Ecofeminists who claim that (B2) has been assumed to be true within the dominant Western philosophical tradition include: Gray, *Green Paradise Lost;* Griffin, *Woman and Nature: The Roaring Inside Her;* Merchant, *The Death of Nature;* Ruether, *New Woman/New Earth.* For a discussion of some of these ecofeminist historical accounts, see Plumwood, ''Ecofeminism.'' While I agree that the historical connections between the domination of women and the domination of nature is a crucial one, I do not argue for that claim here.

6. Ecofeminists who deny (B1) when (B1) is offered as anything other than a true, descriptive, historical claim about patriarchal culture often do so on grounds that an objectionable sort of biological determinism, or at least harmful female sex-gender stereotypes, underlie (B1). For a discussion of this ''split'' among those ecofeminists (''nature feminists'') who assert and those ecofeminists (''social feminists'') who deny (B1) as anything other than a true historical claim about how women are described in patriarchal culture, see Griscom, ''On Healing the Nature/History Split.''

What *all* ecofeminists agree about, then, is the way in which *the logic of domination* has functioned historically within patriarchy to sustain and justify the twin dominations of women and nature.[7] Since *all* feminists (and not just ecofeminists) oppose patriarchy, the conclusion given at (B5), all feminists (including ecofeminists) must oppose at least the logic of domination, premise (B4), on which argument B rests—whatever the truth-value status of (B1) and (B2) *outside of* a patriarchal context.

That *all* feminists must oppose the logic of domination shows the breadth and depth of the ecofeminist critique of B: it is a critique not only of the three assumptions on which this argument for the domination of women and nature rests, viz., the assumptions at (B1), (B2), and (B4); it is also a critique of patriarchal conceptual frameworks generally, i.e., of those oppressive conceptual frameworks which put men ''up'' and women ''down,'' allege some way in which women are morally inferior to men, and use that alleged difference to justify the subordination of women by men. Therefore, ecofeminism is necessary to *any* feminist critique of patriarchy, and, hence, necessary to feminism (a point I discuss again later).

Third, ecofeminism clarifies why the logic of domination, and any conceptual framework which gives rise to it, must be abolished in order both to make possible a meaningful notion of difference which does not breed domination and to prevent feminism from becoming a ''support'' movement based primarily on shared experiences. In contemporary society, there is no one ''woman's voice,'' no *woman* (or *human*) *simpliciter*: every woman (or human) is a woman (or human) of some race, class, age, affectional orientation, marital status, regional or national background, and so forth. Because there are no ''monolithic experiences'' that all women share, feminism must be a ''solidarity movement'' based on shared beliefs and interests rather than a ''unity in sameness'' movement based on shared experiences and shared victimization.[8] In the words of Maria Lugones, ''Unity—not

to be confused with solidarity—is understood as conceptually tied to domination.''[9]

Ecofeminists insist that the sort of logic of domination used to justify the domination of humans by gender, racial or ethnic, or class status is also used to justify the domination of nature. Because eliminating a logic of domination is part of a feminist critique—whether a critique of patriarchy, white supremacist culture, or imperialism—ecofeminists insist that *naturism* is properly viewed as an integral part of any feminist solidarity movement to end sexist oppression and the logic of domination which conceptually grounds it. . . .

CLIMBING FROM ECOFEMINISM TO ENVIRONMENTAL ETHICS

Many feminists and some environmental ethicists have begun to explore the use of first-person narrative as a way of raising philosophically germane issues in ethics often lost or underplayed in mainstream philosophical ethics. Why is this so? What is it about narrative which makes it a significant resource for theory and practice in feminism and environmental ethics? Even if appeal to first-person narrative is a helpful literary device for describing ineffable experience or a legitimate social science methodology for documenting personal and social history, how is first-person narrative a valuable vehicle of argumentation for ethical decision making and theory building? One fruitful way to begin answering these questions is to ask them of a particular first-person narrative.

Consider the following first-person narrative about rock climbing:

> For my very first rock climbing experience, I chose a somewhat private spot, away from other climbers and on-lookers. After studying ''the chimney,'' I focused all my energy on making it to the top. I climbed with intense determination, using whatever strength and skills I had to accomplish this challenging feat. By midway I was exhausted and anxious. I couldn't see what to do next—where to put my hands or feet. Growing increasingly

---

7. I make no attempt here to defend the historically sanctioned truth of these premises.

8. See, e.g., Bell Hooks, *Feminist Theory: From Margin to Center* (Boston: South End Press, 1984), pp. 51-52.

9. Maria Lugones, ''Playfulness, 'World-Travelling,' and Loving Perception,'' *Hypatia* 2, No. 2 (Summer 1987): 3.

more weary as I clung somewhat desparately to the rock, I made a move. It didn't work. I fell. There I was, dangling midair above the rocky ground below, frightened but terribly relieved that the belay rope had held me. I knew I was safe. I took a look up at the climb that remained. I was determined to make it to the top. With renewed confidence and concentration, I finished the climb to the top.

On my second day of climbing, I rappelled down about 200 feet from the top of the Palisades at Lake Superior to just a few feet above the water level. I could see no one—not my belayer, not the other climbers, no one. I unhooked slowly from the rappel rope and took a deep cleansing breath. I looked all around me—really looked—and listened. I heard a cacophony of voices—birds, trickles of water on the rock before me, waves lapping against the rocks below. I closed my eyes and began to feel the rock with my hands—the cracks and crannies, the raised lichen and mosses, the almost imperceptible nubs that might provide a resting place for my fingers and toes when I began to climb. At that moment I was bathed in serenity. I began to talk to the rock in an almost inaudible, child-like way, as if the rock were my friend. I felt an overwhelming sense of gratitude for what it offered me—a chance to know myself and the rock differently, to appreciate unforeseen miracles like the tiny flowers growing in the even tinier cracks in the rock's surface, and to come to know sense of *being in relationship* with the natural environment. It felt as if the rock and I were silent conversational partners in a longstanding friendship. I realized then that I had come to care about this cliff which was so different from me, so unmovable and invincible, independent and seemingly indifferent to my presence. I wanted to be with the rock as I climbed. Gone was the determination to conquer the rock, to forcefully impose my will on it; I wanted simply to work respectfully with the rock as I climbed. And as I climbed, that is what I felt. I felt myself *caring* for this rock and feeling thankful that climbing provided the opportunity for me to know it and myself in this way.

There are at least four reasons why use of such a first-person narrative is important to feminism and environmental ethics. First, such a narrative gives voice to a felt sensitivity often lacking in traditional analytical ethical discourse, viz., a sensitivity to conceiving of oneself as fundamentally "in relationship with" others, including the nonhuman environment.

It is a modality which *takes relationships themselves seriously.* It thereby stands in contrast to a strictly reductionist modality that takes relationships seriously only or primarily because of the nature of the *relators* or parties to those relationships (e.g., relators conceived as moral agents, right holders, interest carriers, or sentient beings). In the rock-climbing narrative above, it is the climber's relationship with the rock she climbs which takes on special significance—which is itself a locus of value—in addition to whatever moral status or moral considerability she or the rock or any other parties to the relationship may also have.[10]

Second, such a first-person narrative gives expression to a variety of ethical attitudes and behaviors often overlooked or underplayed in mainstream Western ethics, e.g., the difference in attitudes and behaviors toward a rock when one is "making it to the top" and when one thinks of oneself as "friends with" or "caring about" the rock one climbs.[11] These different attitudes and behaviors suggest an ethically germane contrast between two different types of relationship humans or climbers may have toward a rock: an imposed conqueror-type relationship, and an emergent caring-type relationship. This contrast grows out of, and is faithful to, felt, lived experience.

---

10. Suppose, as I think is the case, that a necessary condition for the existence of a moral relationship is that at least one party to the relationship is a moral being (leaving open for our purposes what counts as a "moral being"). If this is so, then the Mona Lisa cannot properly be said to have or stand in a moral relationship with the wall on which she hangs, and a wolf cannot have or properly be said to have or stand in a moral relationship with a moose. Such a necessary-condition account leaves open the question whether *both* parties to the relationship must be moral beings. My point here is simply that however one resolves *that* question, recognition of the relationships themselves as a locus of value is a recognition of a source of value that is different from and not reducible to the values of the "moral beings" in those relationships.

11. It is interesting to note that the image of being friends with the Earth is one which cytogeneticist Barbara McClintock uses when she describes the importance of having "a feeling for the organism," "listening to the material [in this case the corn plant]," in one's work as a scientist. See Evelyn Fox Keller, "Women, Science, and Popular Mythology," in *Machina Ex Dea: Feminist Perspectives on Technology,* ed. Joan Rothschild (New York: Pergamon Press, 1983), and Evelyn Fox Keller, *A Feeling For the Organism: The Life and Work of Barbara McClintock* (San Francisco: W.H. Freeman, 1983).

The difference between conquering and caring attitudes and behaviors in relation to the natural environment provides a third reason why the use of first-person narrative is important to feminism and environmental ethics: it provides a way of conceiving of ethics and ethical meaning as *emerging out of* particular situations moral agents find themselves in, rather than as being *imposed on* those situations (e.g., as a derivation or instantiation of some predetermined abstract principle or rule). This emergent feature of narrative centralizes the importance of *voice*. When a multiplicity of cross-cultural *voices* are centralized, narrative is able to give expression to a range of attitudes, values, beliefs, and behaviors which may be overlooked or silenced by imposed ethical meaning and theory. As a reflection of and on felt, lived experiences, the use of narrative in ethics provides a stance from which ethical discourse can be held accountable to the historical, material, and social realities in which moral subjects find themselves.

Lastly, and for our purposes perhaps most importantly, the use of narrative has argumentative significance. Jim Cheney calls attention to this feature of narrative when he claims, "To contextualize ethical deliberation is, in some sense, to provide a narrative or story, from which the solution to the ethical dilemma emerges as the fitting conclusion."[12] Narrative has argumentative force by suggesting *what counts* as an appropriate conclusion to an ethical situation. One ethical conclusion suggested by the climbing narrative is that what counts as a proper ethical attitude toward mountains and rocks is an attitude of respect and care (whatever that turns out to be or involve), not one of domination and conquest.

In an essay entitled "In and Out of Harm's Way: Arrogance and Love," feminist philosopher Marilyn Frye distinguishes between "arrogant" and "loving" perception as one way of getting at this difference in the ethical attitudes of care and conquest.[13]

Frye writes:

> The loving eye is a contrary of the arrogant eye.
>
> The loving eye knows the independence of the other. It is the eye of a seer who knows that nature is indifferent. It is the eye of one who knows that to know the seen, one must consult something other than one's own will and interests and fears and imagination. One must look at the thing. One must look and listen and check and question.
>
> The loving eye is one that pays a certain sort of attention. This attention can require a discipline but *not* a self-denial. The discipline is one of self-knowledge, knowledge of the scope and boundary of the self. . . . In particular, it is a matter of being able to tell one's own interests from those of others and of knowing where one's self leaves off and another begins. . . .
>
> The loving eye does not make the object of perception into something edible, does not try to assimilate it, does not reduce it to the size of the seer's desire, fear and imagination, and hence does not have to simplify. It knows the complexity of the other as something which will forever present new things to be known. The science of the loving eye would favor The Complexity Theory of Truth [in contrast to The Simplicity Theory of Truth] and presuppose The Endless Interestingness of the Universe.[14]

According to Frye, the loving eye is not an invasive, coercive eye which annexes others to itself, but one which "knows the complexity of the other as something which will forever present new things to be known."

When one climbs a rock as a conqueror, one climbs with an arrogant eye. When one climbs with a loving eye, one constantly "must look and listen and check and question." One recognizes the rock as something very different, something perhaps totally indifferent to one's own presence, and finds in that difference joyous occasion for celebration. One knows "the boundary of the self," where the self—the "I," the climber—leaves off and the rock begins. There is no fusion of two into one, but a complement of two entities *acknowledged* as separate, different, independent, yet *in relationship;* they are in relationship if

---

12. Cheney, "Eco-Feminism and Deep Ecology," p. 144.

13. Marilyn Frye, "In and Out of Harm's Way: Arrogance and Love," in *The Politics of Reality* (Trumansburg, N.Y.: The Crossing Press, 1983), pp. 66–72.

---

14. Ibid., pp. 75–76.

only because the loving eye is perceiving it, responding to it, noticing it, attending to it.

An ecofeminist perspective about both women and nature involves this shift in attitude from "arrogant perception" to "loving perception" of the nonhuman world. Arrogant perception of nonhumans by humans presupposes and maintains *sameness* in such a way that it expands the moral community to those beings who are thought to resemble (be like, similar to, or the same as) humans in some morally significant way. Any environmental movement or ethic based on arrogant perception builds a moral hierarchy of beings and assumes some common denominator of moral considerability in virtue of which like beings deserve similar treatment or moral consideration and unlike beings do not. Such environmental ethics are or generate a "unity in sameness." In contrast, "loving perception" presupposes and maintains *difference*— a distinction between the self and order, between human and at least some nonhumans—in such a way that perception of the other as other *is* an expression of love for one who/which is recognized at the outset as independent, dissimilar, different. As Maria Lugones says, in loving perception, "Love is seen not as fusion and erasure of difference but as incompatible with them."[15] "Unity in sameness" alone is an *erasure of difference*.

"Loving perception" of the nonhuman natural world is an attempt to understand what it means *for humans* to care about the nonhuman world, a world *acknowledged* as being independent, different, perhaps even indifferent to humans. Humans *are* different from rocks in important ways, even if they are also both members of some ecological community. A moral community based on loving perception of oneself *in relationship with* a rock, or with the natural environment as a whole, is one which acknowledges and respects difference, whatever "sameness" also exists.[16] The limits of loving perception are determined only by the limits of one's (e.g., a person's, a community's) ability to respond lovingly (or with appropriate care, trust, or friendship)—whether it is to other humans or to the nonhuman world and elements of it.[17]

If what I have said so far is correct, then there are very different ways to climb a mountain and *how* one climbs it and *how* one narrates the experience of climbing it matter ethically. If one climbs with "arrogant perception," with an attitude of "conquer and control," one keeps intact the very sorts of thinking that characterize a logic of domination and an oppressive conceptual framework. Since the oppressive conceptual framework which sanctions the domination of nature is a patriarchal one, one also thereby keeps intact, even if unwittingly, a patriarchal conceptual framework. Because the dismantling of patriarchal conceptual frameworks is a feminist issue, *how* one climbs a mountain and *how* one narrates— or tells the story—about the experience of climbing also are *feminist issues*. In this way, ecofeminism makes visible why, at a conceptual level, environmental ethics is a feminist issue. I turn now to a consideration of ecofeminism as a distinctively feminist and environmental ethic. . . .

All the props are now in place for seeing how ecofeminism provides the framework for a distinctively feminist and environmental ethic. It is a feminism that critiques male bias wherever it occurs in ethics (including environmental ethics) and aims at providing an ethic (including an environmental ethic) which is not male biased—and it does so in a way that satisfies the preliminary boundary conditions [the "quilt"] of a feminist ethic.

First, ecofeminism is quintessentially anti-naturist. Its anti-naturism consists in the rejection of any way of thinking about or acting toward nonhuman nature that reflects a logic, values, or attitude of domination. Its anti-naturist, anti-sexist, anti-racist, anti-classist (and so forth, for all other "isms" of social domination) stance forms the outer boundary of the quilt: nothing gets on the quilt which is naturist, sexist, racist, classist, and so forth.

---

15. Maria Lugones, "Playfulness," p. 3.
16. Cheney makes a similar point in "Eco-Feminism and Deep Ecology," p. 140.

---

17. Ibid., p. 138.

Second, ecofeminism is a contextualist ethic. It involves a shift *from* a conception of ethics as primarily a matter of rights, rules, or principles predetermined and applied in specific cases to entities viewed as competitors in the contest of moral standing, *to* a conception of ethics as growing out of what Jim Cheney calls ''defining relationships,'' i.e., relationships conceived in some sense as defining who one is.[18] As a contextualist ethic, it is not that rights, or rules, or principles are *not* relevant or important. Clearly they are in certain contexts and for certain purposes.[19] It is just that what *makes* them relevant or important is that those to whom they apply are entities *in relationship with* others.

Ecofeminism also involves an ethical shift *from* granting moral consideration to nonhumans *exclusively* on the grounds of some similarity they share with humans (e.g., rationality, interests, moral agency, sentiency, right-holder status) *to* ''a highly contextual account to see clearly what a human being is and what the nonhuman world might be, morally speaking, *for* human beings.''[20] For an ecofeminist, *how* a moral agent is in relationship to another becomes of central significance, not simply *that* a moral agent is a moral agent or is bound by rights, duties, virtue, or utility to act in a certain way.

Third, ecofeminism is structurally pluralistic in that it presupposes and maintains difference—difference among humans as well as between humans and at least some elements of nonhuman nature. Thus, while ecofeminism denies the ''nature/culture'' split,

it affirms that humans are both members of an ecological community (in some respects) and different from it (in other respects). Ecofeminism's attention to relationships and community is not, therefore, an erasure of difference but a respectful acknowledgement of it.

Fourth, ecofeminism reconceives theory as theory in process. It focuses on patterns of meaning which emerge, for instance, from the storytelling and first-person narratives of women (and others) who deplore the twin dominations of women and nature. The use of narrative is one way to ensure that the content of the ethic—the pattern of the quilt—may/will change over time, as the historical and material realities of women's lives change and as more is learned about women-nature connections and the destruction of the nonhuman world.[21]

Fifth, ecofeminism is inclusivist. It emerges from the voices of women who experience the harmful domination of nature and the way that domination is tied to their domination as women. It emerges from listening to the voices of indigenous peoples such as Native Americans who have been dislocated from their land and have witnessed the attendant undermining of such values as appropriate reciprocity, sharing, and kinship that characterize traditional Indian culture. It emerges from listening to voices of those who, like Nathan Hare, critique traditional approaches to environmental ethics as white and bourgeois, and as failing to address issues of ''black ecology'' and the ''ecology'' of the inner city and urban spaces.[22] It also emerges out of the voices of Chipko women who see the destruction of ''earth, soil, and

---

18. Henry West has pointed out that the expression ''defining relations'' is ambiguous. According to West, ''the 'defining' as Cheney uses it is an adjective, not a principle—it is not that ethics defines relationships; it is that ethics grows out of conceiving of the relationships that one is in as defining what the individual is.''

19. For example, in relationships involving contracts or promises, those relationships might be correctly described as that of moral agent to rights holders. In relationships involving mere property, those relationships might be correctly described as that of moral agent to objects having only instrumental value, ''relationships of instrumentality.'' In comments on an earlier draft of this paper, West suggested that possessive individualism, for instance, might be recast in such a way that an individual is defined by his or her property relationships.

20. Cheney, ''Eco-Feminism and Deep Ecology,'' p. 144.

21. One might object that such permission for change opens the door for environmental exploitation. This is not the case. An ecofeminist ethic is anti-naturist. Hence, the unjust domination and exploitation of nature is a ''boundary condition'' of the ethic; no such actions are sanctioned or justified on ecofeminist grounds. What it *does* leave open is some leeway about what counts as domination and exploitation. This, I think, is a strength of the ethic, not a weakness, since it acknowledges that *that* issue cannot be resolved in any practical way in the abstract, independent of a historical and social context.

22. Nathan Hare, ''Black Ecology,'' in *Environmental Ethics*, ed. K.S. Shrader-Frechette (Pacific Grove, Calif.: Boxwood Press, 1981), pp. 229-236.

water'' as intimately connected with their own inability to survive economically.[23] With its emphasis on inclusivity and difference, ecofeminism provides a framework for recognizing that what counts as ecology and what counts as appropriate conduct toward both human and nonhuman environments is largely a matter of context.

Sixth, as a feminism, ecofeminism makes no attempt to provide an ''objective'' point of view. It is a social ecology. It recognizes the twin dominations of women and nature as social problems rooted both in very concrete, historical, socioeconomic circumstances and in oppressive patriarchal conceptual frameworks which maintain and sanction these circumstances.

Seventh, ecofeminism makes a central place for values of care, love, friendship, trust, and appropriate reciprocity—values that presuppose that our relationships to others are central to our understanding of who we are.[24] It thereby gives voice to the sensitivity that in climbing a mountain, one is doing something in relationship with an ''other,'' an ''other'' whom one can come to care about and treat respectfully.

Lastly, an ecofeminist ethic involves a reconception of what it means to be human, and in what human ethical behavior consists. Ecofeminism denies abstract individualism. Humans are who we are in large part by virtue of the historical and social contexts and the relationships we are in, including our relationships with nonhuman nature. Relationships are not something extrinsic to who we are, not an ''add on'' feature of human nature; they play an essential role in shaping what it is to be human. Relationships of humans to the nonhuman environment are, in part, constitutive of what it is to be a human.

By making visible the interconnections among the dominations of women and nature, ecofeminism shows that both are feminist issues and that explicit acknowledgement of both is vital to any responsible environmental ethic. Feminism *must* embrace ecological feminism if it is to end the domination of women because the domination of women is tied conceptually and historically to the domination of nature.

A responsible environmental ethic also *must* embrace feminism. Otherwise, even the seemingly most revolutionary, liberational, and holistic ecological ethic will fail to take seriously the interconnected dominations of nature and women that are so much a part of the historical legacy and conceptual framework that sanctions the exploitation of nonhuman nature. Failure to make visible these interconnected, twin dominations results in an inaccurate account of how it is that nature has been and continues to be dominated and exploited and produces an environmental ethic that lacks the depth necessary to be truly *inclusive* of the realities of persons who at least in dominant Western culture have been intimately tied with that exploitation, viz., women. Whatever else can be said in favor of such holistic ethics, a failure to make visible ecofeminist insights into the common denominators of the twin oppressions of women and nature is to perpetuate, rather than overcome, the source of that oppression.

This last point deserves further attention. It may be objected that as long as the end result is ''the same''—the development of an environmental ethic which does not emerge out of or reinforce an oppressive conceptual framework—it does not matter whether that ethic (or the ethic endorsed in getting there) is feminist or not. Hence, it simply is *not* the case that any adequate environmental ethic must be feminist. My argument, in contrast, has been that it *does* matter, and for three important reasons. First, there is the scholarly issue of accurately representing historical reality, and that, ecofeminists claim, requires acknowledging the historical feminization of nature and naturalization of women as part of the exploitation of nature. Second, I have shown that the conceptual connections between the domination of women and the domination of nature are located in an oppressive and, at least in Western societies, patriarchal conceptual framework characterized by a logic of domination. Thus, I have shown that failure to notice the nature of this connection leaves at best an incomplete, inaccurate, and partial account of what

---

23. For an ecofeminist discussion of the Chipko movement, see my ''Toward an Ecofeminist Ethic,'' and Shiva's *Staying Alive*.
24. See Cheney, ''Eco-Feminism and Deep Ecology,'' p. 122.

is required of a conceptually adequate environmental ethic. An ethic which *does not* acknowledge this is simply *not* the same as one that does, whatever else the similarities between them. Third, the claim that, in contemporary culture, one can have an adequate environmental ethic which is *not* feminist assumes that, in contemporary culture, the label *feminist* does not add anything crucial to the nature or description of environmental ethics. I have shown that at least in contemporary culture this is false, for the word *feminist* currently helps to clarify just *how* the domination of nature is conceptually linked to patriarchy and, hence, how the liberation of nature, is conceptually linked to the termination of patriarchy. Thus, because it has critical bite in contemporary culture, it serves as an important reminder that in contemporary sex-gendered, raced, classed, and naturist culture, an un-labeled position functions as a privileged and "un-marked" position. That is, without the addition of the word *feminist,* one presents environmental ethics as if it has no bias, including male-gender bias, which is just what ecofeminists deny: failure to notice the con-nections between the twin oppressions of women and nature *is* male-gender bias.

One of the goals of feminism is the eradication of all oppressive sex-gender (and related race, class, age, affectional preference) categories and the creation of a world in which *difference does not breed domina-tion*—say, the world of 4001. If in 4001 an "adequate environmental ethic" is a "feminist environmental ethic," the word *feminist* may then be redundant and unnecessary. However, this is *not* 4001, and in terms of the current historical and conceptual reality the dominations of nature and of women are intimately connected. Failure to notice or make visible that con-nection in 1990 perpetuates the mistaken (and privi-leged) view that "environmental ethics" is *not* a fem-inist issue, and that *feminist* adds nothing to environmental ethics.[25] . . .

---

25. I offer the same sort of reply to critics of ecofeminism such as Warwick Fox who suggest that for the sort of ecofeminism I defend, the word *feminist* does not add anything significant to environmental ethics and, consequently, that an ecofeminist like

DISCUSSION TOPICS

1. State in your own words an argument which illus-trates what Warren refers to as the "logic of dom-ination."
2. Do you agree with Warren that "naturism" is linked to sexism? Give an example supporting your position. Is naturism the same thing as an-thropocentrism?
3. Warren states that only in the far future (4001) might the recognition of differences not breed domination. Describe your vision of such a world. What might be some steps on the way to such a society?
4. Do you agree with Warren that no ethical thinking can escape gender-bias? Why or why not?

READING 56

Ecofeminist Theory and Grassroots Politics

Stephanie Lahar

Stephanie Lahar teaches in the environmental studies and women's studies programs at the University of Vermont. She chairs the Burlington, Vermont, Conservation Board.

Lahar points out that ecofeminism seeks to integrate personal, social, and environmental issues that are often

---

myself might as well call herself a deep ecologist. He asks: "Why doesn't she just call it [i.e., Warren's vision of a transformative feminism] deep ecology? Why specifically attach the label *feminist* to it . . . ?" (Warwick Fox, "The Deep Ecology-Ecofeminism Debate and Its Parallels," *Environmental Ethics* 11, No. 1 [1989]: 14, n. 22). Whatever the important similarities between deep ecol-ogy and ecofeminism (or, specifically, my version of ecofemi-nism)—and, indeed, there are many—it is precisely my point here that the word *feminist* does add something significant to the con-ception of environmental ethics, and that any environmental ethic (including deep ecology) that fails to make explicit the different kinds of interconnections among the domination of nature and the domination of women will be, from a feminist (and ecofeminist) perspective such as mine, inadequate.

separated, providing directions for a potential transformation of social institutions. Ecofeminist theorists have drawn from many positions, for example Ynestra King's use of feminist political theory and Starhawk's earth-centered spirituality.

The woman/nature association is a fundamental concern for ecofeminism, and various theories have been proposed to account for that association and the widespread oppression of women and nature in patriarchy. Lahar maintains that rather than seeking the seed of domination of woman and nature in the remote past, ecofeminists should continue to examine current cultural, scientific, and economic sources of oppression.

Lahar argues that ecofeminists should continue their emphasis on political activism if they are to function in a creative and reconstructive way. She urges the development of a moral theory which does not sacrifice individual needs to a social or planetary whole such as Gaia. Lahar warns against confusing symbolic and concrete realities, as found in the imaging of the Earth as Mother and in seeing women as biologically determined to be closer to nature than men.

. . . GRASSROOTS ACTIVISM

In the New England town of Brattleboro, Vermont, a handful of women and men from an ecofeminist affinity group gathered on Mother's Day in 1987. On a dewy hillside surrounded by woods and marsh, they looked over a prototypical scene: a developer from another state had cleared much of the land in an area that had rapidly been losing open space and valuable wetlands. Eighty-six condominiums were to be built, second and third homes far beyond the means of most area residents. A long strip had been bulldozed near the condos right through the marsh. A member of the group describes their action:

> Eight of us went out early in the morning, with plants and gardening tools, and began to plant the strip. A great colorful, wonderful garden emerged—it didn't feel as though we were working on it, it just happened. The people who lived neighboring the development started to come out, and they brought flowers to plant and seeds. We claimed the strip as a community garden.[1]

In the afternoon the developer arrived, and the group blocked his way until he agreed to talk with

them about their concerns. Several hours later, the protesters gave him "permission" to plow under the community garden. A week later the neighbors, who had not previously organized, went to a selectmen's meeting to object to the developer's plan to close the road for a week to blast to lay pipes—and they won. The victory was small but important. The Mother's Day Garden, like many ecofeminist actions, accomplished several goals. It was a direct protest as well as an invitation to the developer to consider community and environmental impacts. It also empowered people who were not initially involved to take responsibility for the community and area in which they lived.

The largest identifiably ecofeminist actions that have taken place in the history of the movement were the Women's Pentagon Actions in November of 1980 and November of 1981, which were organized by participants in the "Women and Life on Earth: Ecofeminism in the 1980s" conference in Amherst, Massachusetts. In these nonviolent direct actions, women surrounded the Pentagon, issuing a Unity Statement that called for social, economic, and reproductive rights as well as an end to the arms race and the exploitation of resources, people, and the environment. In the 1980s ecofeminism became a presence and, in some cases, an organizing principle in decentralized movements on the American and international left. Initiatives that ecofeminism has both drawn from and contributed to include the peace movement, the direct action movement, and Green party politics.[2] Ecofeminism shares overlapping goals with these other loosely organized movements including equitable and peaceful social relations, and sustainable and nonexploitative economic systems and life-styles. It also shares a spirit of resistance to institutionalized power structures and is committed to nonviolence and open processes of communication. As has been the case in other activist movements, ecofeminists have attempted to implement these ideals among each other and outwardly. They have encountered through debates and differences a struggle to find ground between two poles: on the one hand a prematurely unified theory and political praxis that obscures and suppresses differences, and on the other an indiscriminate pluralism that results in vague thinking, passivity, and political inertia.

THEORETICAL ORIGINS

Ecofeminism draws theoretical concepts from ecology, especially a principle of life's interdependence, and from feminism, especially a social analysis of the domination of women that is also linked with racism and classism. Disparate strands from these sources and others including feminist spirituality and issue-oriented activism do not make for an easy, definitive synthesis, and various theorists have weighted their analyses differently.

Well-known theorists such as Ynestra King and Starhawk trace different lineages for ecofeminist theory, often echoing their own intellectual and political journeys. King acknowledges a debt to Murray Bookchin's philosophy of social ecology as well as to a long study of social and political theory and to feminist social analyses. She advocates a "critical analysis of and opposition to the uniformity of technological, industrial culture—capitalist and socialist—[that] is crucial to feminism, ecology and the struggle of indigenous peoples" (1989, p. 177). This is a rational and politically anarchist position. According to Noel Sturgeon, King "has prominently figured in the promulgation of ecofeminism as a position on the American left which is deeply rooted in the politics and practice of the direct action movement" (1989, p. 15). King differentiates her conception of ecofeminism from other liberatory political movements, however, which according to her "see themselves as outgrowths of the past—even possibly as a vindication or revenge for the past, rather than as preceding or anticipating the future." She frames ecofeminism as "the practice of hope," explaining that "to have hope . . . is to believe that [the] future can be created by intentional human beings who now take responsibility [for it]."[3]

Starhawk, on the other hand, finds a base for ecofeminism in a very different background of feminist spirituality, claiming that "Ecofeminism is a movement with an implicit and sometimes explicit spiritual base." She outlines feminist, or earth-centered spirituality as a source for a value system for ecofeminism. For example, "the second base concept of earth-centered spirituality is that of interconnection . . . [this] translates into compassion, our ability to feel and identify with others—human beings, natural cycles and processes, animals and plants" (1989, p. 178). Starhawk draws a political agenda from principles she has developed through a practice of an earth-based religion.

King and Starhawk exemplify different backgrounds in thought and experience among ecofeminists, especially as they urge, in King's case, a conceptual/rational transformation and, in Starhawk's, a spiritual/psychological one as the motivational core of social change. As a result of these different paths to a similar, often identical activist politics, there is some friction and some complementarity in tracing ecofeminism's heritage as well as its fundamental principles.

A point of departure for ecofeminist theory in its earliest formulations was analyzing a transcultural symbolic association and devaluation of women and nature. Ecofeminists were, and are, interested not only in confronting the fallacies of biologically determined gender roles but in delving into the deeper psychological and cultural/mythic base of a value-laden polarization between "primitive" nature and "civilized" society. The so-called domestic sphere of women's work and activities across many times and cultures includes caring for children, the elderly, and the sick and working close to the land. This has traditionally been regarded as less "civilized" and therefore lesser in value, than the public sphere of men's work and activities. Sherry Ortner analyzed this deep attitudinal split in an article written from a structuralist perspective and often cited by ecofeminist theorists, "Is Female to Male as Nature Is to Culture?" (1974).

The dark side of the woman/nature association is especially vivid in the intersections of women's oppression and the exploitation of nature in many developing countries today. For example, all over the world Western "green revolution" agricultural methods have been imported into developing countries either through a misplaced altruism or, increasingly, under pressure as a short-term intensive method of cash-crop production to pay off Third World debts. Green-revolution methods include growing crops in monocultures using genetically engineered seed, chemical pesticides, deep plowing, and intensive irrigation, which permanently destroys indigenous soils. These have replaced traditional methods that have long sustained soil fertility, including mixed and rotational cropping that renews soil nutrients and repels pests, using appropriate plowing depths and irrigation methods for the local soils, and integrating practices of animal husbandry, forestry, and agriculture. Vandana Shiva has shown how in India, as in many parts of the world, women's impoverishment has increased and their status decreased relative to men as the environment has been degraded, exacerbating prior gender inequities. A direct correlation has been noted between regions that have adopted the most green-revolution technology and increased violence and discrimination against women. As one example, Shiva notes:

> The Kallars, a landless community in Tamil Nadu, have, over the last 10 to 15 years, started routinely dispensing with their girl children. The logic of dispensability is linked to the green revolution which, through commercialisation, introduces a differential wage labour, on the one hand (with men getting Rs. 13 a day and women getting Rs. 6) and, on the other, creates a demand for dowry which has driven the poverty-stricken community to female infanticide. (1988, p. 119).

Through explicit and measurable links between environmental degradation and violence against women, Shiva shows that "in the perspective of women engaged in survival struggles which are, simultaneously, struggles for the protection of nature, women and nature are intimately related, and their domination and liberation similarly linked" (1988, p. 47).

One of the primary debates in ecofeminist theory concerns the causes of domination and the exploitation of women, nature, and others, as well as where and when these should be located. Riane Eisler and Charlene Spretnak, for example, each argue that prototypical patterns of domination can be traced to the invasion of Indo-European societies by nomadic tribes from Eurasia about 4500 B.C. According to this analysis European society in the Neolithic period was free of modern forms of oppression, and, significantly, was also "matrifocal, matrilineal, peaceful [and] agrarian" until "barbarian invaders from the barren fringes of the globe [left] in their wake destruction . . . what characterizes these invaders is that they [brought] with them male dominance along with their angry gods of thunder and war" (Eisler 1990, p. 29).

Aside from the questionable interpretations of the archaeological evidence on which this argument is based, some ecofeminist and feminist theorists have regarded a theory of domination describing origins in a collectively misogynist, anti-natural male consciousness that suddenly "arrives" as politically naive and irrelevant to a modern analysis and deconstruction of the dynamics of oppression (Biehl 1989; Prentice 1988). Such a claim based in ancient history does not address the processes by which a "dominator" consciousness and social practices originally developed. Instead, alternative models have connected the exploitation of women and nature to cultural, scientific, and economic factors that are more historically accessible, on the premise that examining the convergence of these factors can lead to an understanding of how to deconstruct them. Carolyn Merchant (1980, 1989) and Vandana Shiva (1988) both do this by tracing the transformations of cultural practices and symbols from the Enlightenment to the present day. Shiva claims that "the reductionist world-view, the industrial revolution, and the capitalist economy were the philosophical, technological, and economic components of the same process" (1988, p. 23). She calls the practices by which this complex expands "maldevelopment."

One manifestation of the combination of developments and maldevelopments Shiva refers to is the commodification of both "natural resources" and people. When landscapes and ecosystems are regarded as commodities, then members of an ecosystem, including human beings, are treated as "isolated and extractable units" (Cronon 1983, p. 21). One face of the problem lies in the values and reinforcing structures of most social and economic systems, but it is also internalized in individuals. Even with a high degree of personal awareness and maturity, we are conditioned by collective perceptual filters to experience in predetermined ways the subjectivity/objectivity of other persons, beings, and things. This means that social projects must be both deeply personal and political to render transformative changes. Ecofeminism's context for social analysis is nature, since it contains and includes all humans and human creations as well as nonhuman existence.

Ecofeminism must continue to dissemble the multiple layers and strands of ideologies and practices that power a dysfunctional society and make it dangerous to individuals and to the totality of life. I believe that the search for some singular and original seed of domination in the distant past does not really help us with this. We should proceed, instead, to further develop models of the interlocking dynamics of oppression, so that when we are working for liberation in one area we are able to see links and contribute to opening up other areas as well.

PARAMETERS AND CAUTIONS FOR A PROGRESSIVE THEORY

Ecofeminist theory aspires to an integrated and intersubjective view of human life and society in/as part of nature. Ultimately, this is an encompassing natural philosophy that we should think of not as a blueprint to be developed by one or two utopian thinkers but as a cultural revolution. In the face of various claims about key concepts and themes for ecofeminism, can and should we try to establish a set of general principles? What purposes would this serve?

My assertion is that we need to define guiding parameters for our theory that can continually be refined but that provide recognizable directives and contexts for the development of ecofeminist analyses and social projects. These are important for many reasons, but among them is the historical demonstration that some philosophies lend themselves to contemplation and inaction—for example, the largely mental politic of postmodernist deconstruction in its academic and literary forms, or the inward mysticism of metaphysicians such as Heidegger, touted by ecological theorists such as Arne Naess who advise us to

think like a mountain.[4] Other philosophies lend themselves to action, the expression of will, and political participation; for example, the political analyses of Emma Goldman, foremother of direct action as protest. Ecofeminist theory has in the past developed in close dialogue with political praxis. In ecofeminist dialogue in the past several years, however, particularly in debates about environmental ethics and the relation of ecofeminism to feminist spirituality, reference to political praxis has decreased relative to earlier discussions.[5]

Ecofeminism is highly critical of most current social and political institutions and thereby serves a deconstructive or dissembling function that supports political resistance. To fulfill this deconstructive potential, its criticisms must continue to be acted upon by the expression of resistance through direct action on life-threatening issues (militarism, violence against women, the nuclear industry, pollution and toxics, environmental destruction). Ecofeminism also aspires to a creative and reconstructive function in society, as King's ''practice of hope.'' To fulfill a reconstructive potential, a social philosophy must extend a social critique and utopian vision into imperatives for action. This means that life-preserving values and policies must be promoted and carried out beyond circles of personal affinity and academic philosophy and brought into public arenas. Reconstructive projects that ecofeminist theory and activism has contributed to include, for example, community forums on social or environmental issues and those at intersections such as biotechnology; state legislation supporting the civil rights and safety of groups that historically have had little political power; the reallocation of private and public resources and funds to socially responsible uses; alternative housing and land-use arrangements; and local alternative economic systems.[6] Unlike the largely mental politics of postmodern, poststructuralist social critiques in the academy as well as some systems of environmental ethics, ecofeminism's popular and political base in grassroots organizing and direct action has fanned the will to personal and collective action from its inception.

Maintaining a balance of critical and creative directions is crucial to the continued political potency of ecofeminism. Can we afford not to have an action-oriented philosophy at a crisis point in social and natural history, when we are literally threatened on a global scale by annihilation by nuclear war or ecological destruction? Ecofeminism's promise is that it provides not only an orientation and worldview but also a basis for responsible action. In order for the movement to fulfill this promise, I believe that it is necessary to establish broad parameters that diverse ideas and actions can be referred to, and to maintain critical and vitalizing links between theory and praxis.

I offer the following four points of focus to help create and maintain a firm ground for social and ecological responsibility and political participation. These are that we (1) treat ecofeminism as a moral theory, (2) engage in the project of working out an integrated philosophy of humanity and nonhuman nature, (3) view this theory as a living process inseparable from the individuals and groups who think and practice it, and (4) maintain an active political and participatory emphasis that is both deconstructive (reactive to current injustices) and reconstructive (proactive in creating new forms of thinking and doing).

The first parameter I have outlined is that ecofeminism be treated as a moral theory—a prescriptive psychological and social model that includes an idea of future potential and how best to unfold it, not just an analysis of how things were in the past or are currently. Philosopher Amélie Rorty defines such a theory and what it should do.:

> Besides characterizing the varieties of well-lived lives, and formulating general principles and ideals for regulating conduct, a moral theory should tell us something about how to get from where we are to where we might better be. While it needn't prescribe a decision procedure for determining every detail of every choice and action, it should, in a general way, be action-guiding: constructing a robust ethical theory requires an astute understanding of *psychology and of history* (1988, p. 15; italics added).

Furthermore, a moral theory must emerge out of a felt sense of need and personal connection with the issues at hand, not just out of an abstract process of reasoning. Ethical systems based only in abstracted values fail to draw real commitments and can too easily be used as tools of manipulation and deception—for example, to rationalize military aggression on the basis of furthering democracy. Ecofeminism must be adequately grounded and contextualized to be a "robust" and action-guiding ethical theory. It should, therefore, have a foundational characterization of reality (an ontology) and escape some of the traps of classical philosophy that have helped to support conceptual splitting and dualisms. In particular, ecofeminism needs to avoid assumptions of either classical materialism or classical idealism, with connotations of inanimate substance set in opposition to a purely subjective, psychic, or spiritual quality. This means that we must develop concepts and personal sensibilities of self and world that move beyond conceptual dichotomies. Our paradigms and experiences of self and world must be monistic but differentiated to reflect their real basis in earthly life, accounting for both the integrity of individuals and collective realities and functions.

Basically, we are looking to develop a better alternative to a classically Western atomistic, materialist worldview—without simply flipping to its polar opposite, a holistic, idealist one with a mirror-image set of problems. Ultimately, an atomistic view that reduces life to its smallest increments endangers our lives through a fascination with the manipulation of genes and nuclear power, ignoring the interlocking relations, functions, and activities of natural and social communities. And yet holism as a principle that gives superior explanatory power and/or value to a collective entity or community can also endanger our lives by undermining the integrity of individuals and their specific needs and interests. Women and other oppressed categories of people should be especially wary of paradigms that could be construed as advocating the sacrifice of individual needs to a "greater whole"—whether that be the family, society, or "Gaia," a planetary entity. The latter has made its appearance as an ideal in some ecofeminist writing after James Lovelock took the ancient Greek earth goddess's name to describe his scientific theory of the earth as a self-regulating organism, and this was taken up by various poets, philosophers, and ethicists as a paradigm for nature. I believe, along with Marti Kheel, who writes from the context of animal liberation, that ecofeminist theory must be especially careful in outlining its guiding principles to ''address the importance of individual beings *as well as* the larger whole'' (1990, p. 19).

The key to incorporating the integrity of individual and collective realities is an expanded concept of nature that we, as gendered human beings, can then find a place in. We must understand ''natural'' and ''social'' histories (as well as our personal lives) as processes of differentiation and incorporation that are expressions of nature rather than emerging *out* of nature. This way we neither annihilate ourselves in nature (reducing ourselves to a small and therefore expendable part) nor sever ourselves from the nonhuman environment and from those aspects of ourselves unmediated by social processes.

At the core of the expanded concept of nature that I advocate is the rejection of a subject/object split at its root—the opposition of human consciousness and a mechanical nature—and the adoption, instead, of an ontology of nature as *fundamentally material and subjective.* This acknowledges different types of subjectivity in natural phenomena that include (but are not limited to) human life and mental processes. In these terms human consciousness is a specialized form of subjectivity but in no way exclusive or original. Imbuing nature with both materiality and subjectivity provides a substantial basis for commonality as well as differences between human beings and nonhuman life, without the mystification of a discontinuous conceptual leap from nature to human existence.

In a realm of human possibilities that exists continuously with, and as an aspect of, nature, we can proceed to explore gender, race, and other categories of human difference as particulars rather than as oppositional qualities. They are specific elaborations of the human species, complex constructs of biological givens and subjective mediations. In actuality, biological sex or genetic heritage is only a small part of what we experience as gender or race. As Donna Haraway reminds us, ''race and gender are the world-changing products of specific, but very large and durable histories'' (1989, p. 8). An expanded concept of nature affects our thinking and experience of human diversity in terms such as gender and race in two important ways: first, it prevents our collapsing them into purely biological/materialist explanations, thereby dismissing our own subjective creation and participation in those differences; second it renders nonsensical the total detachment that characterizes extreme processes of objectification by providing us with an irrefutable basis for mutual identification with others, in a shared natural heritage and physical/subjective existence.

The purpose of working out an integrated philosophy of humanity and nature is not only to challenge dualisms to reflect more clearly our lived experience in theory but also to describe relations among women, men, society, and nonhuman nature in a way that is conducive to a high quality of life and antithetical to oppression and exploitation. There are a few potential pitfalls we need to be cognizant of as we develop a synthesis that relates an expanded sensibility of nature and specific social agendas. In outlining parameters for ecofeminism that are aimed at transforming personal sensibilities as well deconstructing conceptual splits, it is important to acknowledge and integrate rational, emotional, visceral, imaginative, and intuitive modes of experience and expression. It is also critical, however, to distinguish ontological and phenomenological descriptions and emphasize a necessary discrimination between symbolic and literal existence.

In popular ecofeminist literature one commonly comes across feminized earth and nature images, but there is a troubling absence of critical discussion about them. To relate to the earth as a mother—an entreaty from bumper stickers as well as scholarly essays—is an analogy that is imaginatively inspiring. But ''Mother Earth'' and the pronouns ''she'' and ''her'' in philosophical/theoretical discourse (as in ''her forests, rivers, and different creatures have intrinsic value'' [Diamond and Orenstein 1990, p. xi] tend to reify precisely the unexamined woman/nature associations ecofeminism has challenged since its beginnings. Additionally, the psychological effect of understanding the earth as a fundamentally feminine parent is to reduce our sense of the vast and varied subjectivities of the planet and all its life to our projections of human consciousness and to blur the diversified forms of the natural world with our associations to human bodies, or even the particular human body of our own mother. When Paula Gunn Allen calls to ''the planet, our mother, Grandmother Earth,'' and to us to attend to ''her'' as she ''is giving birth'' (1990, pp. 52-54), the anthropomorphization diminishes more than expands our awareness, evoking good and bad psychological associations with parenting that we have received and given rather than a sense of wonder that comes from stretching our consciousness to relate to something much bigger than human existence.

Another potential pitfall, which is related to the confusion of symbolic and concrete realities, is for ecofeminists to promote unintentionally an essentialist view of gender differences. This confirms a fear of many outside of ecofeminism that it is a new version of biological determinism that privileges women's relationship to nonhuman nature. This happens, for example, in Brian Swimme's essay, which appears in the most recently published anthology of ecofeminist writing:

> My proposal is that we learn to interpret the data provided by the fragmented scientific mind with the holistic poetic vision alive in ecofeminism. What is this holistic vision? . . . I would simply point to the perspective, awareness and consciousness found most clearly *in primal peoples and women generally* (1990, p. 17; italics added).

Marti Kheel and others have noted that conceptual and ethical frameworks marked by care, compassion, and person-to-person accountability can help model the type of thinking and decisionmaking that can help reconstruct human relations to nature, and perhaps this is what Swimme means to suggest (Kheel 1985). Feminist theorists have made phenomenological studies of predominately female traits that include an ethical/moral orientation—an ''ethic of care''—and alternative epistemologies, or ''women's ways of knowing'' (Gilligan 1982; Belenky et al. 1986). These are useful as historically specific descriptions.

There is a danger, however, for ecofeminism to reify unwittingly an ''ethic of care'' or ''women's ways of knowing'' as universal and biologically determined qualities (and thereby imply that women are limited to these) by dropping them into ecofeminist theory without the historical and cultural contexts in which they developed.

For ecofeminism to fulfull its promise as an emancipatory theory, we must be especially careful in accounting for traits that for complex historical reasons have become gender associated in our culture, even though these may at present describe collective norms. This means that we must be cognizant of what we omit from our theories as well as what we include. Our admission of a specific physical, cultural, and temporal position can give our ideas life and credibility while empowering others to articulate their own unique contribution. This helps us understand a body of ideas such as ecofeminism as embodied ideas—not an abstractable theory but a process inseparable from the persons who think, struggle with, carry, and live it in specific times and places.

CONCLUSION

Ecofeminism is a growing theoretical and political movement. In its short history it has been characterized by considerable diversity among its participants as well as in some of its premises and assumptions. In general, ecofeminism brings strands of several philosophical orientations together in an incisive synthesis, including ecological principles of diversity and interdependence in human and nonhuman communities, and a particular feminist analysis of power relations and interlocking dominations. It also develops a utopian vision of human society integrated with the natural world. I have argued that ecofeminism can best be developed in the future by defining several parameters or points of focus that would serve as references for diverse ideas and claims. These would lend coherence to ecofeminist analyses while helping to avoid some pitfalls of theoretical contradiction and to maintain accountability between theory and political practice. One of the points of focus I suggest is the crucial philosophical project of continuing to develop an expanded concept of nature that can serve as a ground and context for social analyses and can also serve to connect us with our own embodiment and natural heritage. This needs to be worked out very carefully, with special attention to deconstructing cultural dualisms that have supported the association and concurrent devaluation of women, nonhuman nature, and other significant categories of people and things.

Ecofeminism's political goals include the deconstruction of oppressive social, economic, and political systems and the reconstruction of more viable social and political forms. No version of ecofeminist theory dictates exactly what people should do in the face of situations they encounter in personal and public life, nor is it a single political platform. The relation of ecofeminist theory to political activism is ideally informative and generative and not one of either prescribing or ''owning'' particular actions. Ecofeminist theory advocates a combined politics of resistance and creative projects, but the specific enactment of these is a result of dialogue between the individuals involved and the actual situation or issue. Ecofeminism contributes an overall framework and conceptual links to the political understanding of the interplay between social and environmental issues, and routes to political empowerment through understanding the effects of one's actions extended through multiple human and nonhuman communities.

Ecofeminism faces a challenge in maintaining, and to a certain degree, recovering a politically potent activist emphasis. Ecofeminism's critical frameworks and utopian visions are exciting and energizing—in one sense, it is a focus term for philosophies that integrate human society and nature and aim for an entirely new intellectual/perceptual/sensate experience of self and world. It is in no way ahistorical, however, as it is developed and lived by people with different backgrounds and assumptions about the nature of gender roles, social arrangements, and human/environmental relations. Ecofeminism does make big promises. Their fulfillment depends on theorists and activists who can embody the broad and integrated sensibilities of self and world that ecofeminism helps develop and advocate and who can find the power and the energy to act on those sensibilities to make real social and political changes.

NOTES

I would like to thank Ariel Salleh, Karin Aguilar-San Juan, and other members of the South End Press collective, Karen Warren, and anonymous reviewers for their comments on earlier versions of this essay.

1. From a conversation with Sue Swain who was one of the organizers and participants in the Mother's Day Garden.
2. For specific treatments of ecofeminism's relation to the peace movement see King (1986), to the direct action movement see Sturgeon (1989), and to Green Party politics see Tokar (1987, pp. 39, 85, 137) and Spretnak (1988).
3. From a plenary discussion at the ''Culture, Nature and Theory: Ecofeminist Perspectives'' conference at USC-Los Angeles, March 1987.
4. See Naess (1985), who is credited with introducing the term deep ecology. Murray Bookchin (1988) has critiqued deep ecology's strange reverence for Martin Heidegger, whose mystical philosophy and ideological connection to Hitler's Nazi party give rise to profound questions about the suitability of his ideas as a basis for social revision and reconstruction.
5. In the three anthologies of ecofeminist essays that have been published (Caldecott and Leland 1983; Plant 1989; Diamond and Orenstein 1990) there is a progressive trend away from activist issues, which almost completely constitute the first anthology (in essays like ''Black Ghetto Ecology'' and ''Greening the Desert: Women of Kenya Reclaim Land''), toward a greater proportion of philosophical discussions of ecofeminism's relation to environmental ethics and feminist spirituality in the last (in essays like ''The Origins of God in the Blood of the Lamb'' and ''Deep Ecology and Ecofeminism: The Emerging Dialogue''). To what degree this trend is beneficial in rounding out and developing a more sophisticated theoretical base for ecofeminism and to what degree it may indicate a diminishment of political involvement and power or an unexamined change in who is defining ecofeminism are extremely important questions for ecofeminists to take up.
6. An example of one project that functions in several of the ways I have listed is Julia Russell's Eco-Home in Los Angeles, a demonstration home and community network that implements and distributes information on solar technology, water-conserving organic gardens, recycling, and composting; in addition it sponsors a community bartering system and revolving loan fund. In my home state of Vermont ecofeminists have organized forums on reproductive technologies and environ-

mental conservation through the Burlington Women's Council, and ecofeminists were among those who lobbied against state legislation legalizing surrogate mother contracts and for a bill that recognizes and prosecutes ''hate crimes'' against minority groups, gays and lesbians.

REFERENCES

Allen, Paula Gunn. 1990. The woman I love is a planet, the planet I love is a tree. In *Reweaving the world*. See Diamond and Orenstein 1990.

Belenky, Mary, Blythe Clinchy, Nancy Goldberger, and Jill Tarule. 1986. *Women's ways of knowing*. New York: Basic Books.

Biehl, Janet. 1989. Goddess mythology in ecological politics. *New Politics* 2: 84-105.

Bookchin, Murray. 1988. Social Ecology Versus Deep Ecology. *Socialist Review* 3: 9-29.

Caldecott, Leonie and Stephanie Leland, eds. 1983. *Reclaim the earth: Women speak out for life on earth*. London: The Women's Press.

Cameron, Anne. 1989. First Mother and the rainbow children. In *Healing the wounds*. See Plant 1989.

Cronon, William. 1983. *Changes in the land: Indians, colonists, and the ecology of New England*. New York: Hill and Wang.

Diamond, Irene and Gloria Feman Orenstein eds. 1990. *Reweaving the world: The emergence of ecofeminism*. San Francisco: Sierra Club Books.

Eisler, Riane. 1987. *The chalice and the blade*. San Francisco: Harper and Row.

Gilligan, Carol. 1982. *In a different voice*. Cambridge: Harvard University Press.

Haraway, Donna. 1989. *Primate visions: Gender, race and nature in the world of modern science*. New York: Routledge.

Kheel, Marti. 1985. The liberation of nature: A circular affair. *Environmental Ethics* 7: 135-49.

Kheel, Marti. 1990. Animal liberation and environmental ethics: Can ecofeminism bridge the gap? Paper presented at the 1990 National Women's Studies Association conference.

King, Ynestra. 1986. In the interest of peace: Feminism, women and politics. Unpublished paper.

King, Ynestra. 1989. Healing the wounds: Feminism, ecology, and nature/culture dualism. In *Gender/body/knowledge: Feminist reconstructions of being and knowing*.

Alison Jaggar and Susan Bordo, eds. New Brunswick and London: Rutgers University Press.

Merchant, Carolyn. 1980. *The death of nature: Women, ecology and the scientific revolution*. San Francisco: Harper and Row.

Merchant, Carolyn. 1989. *Ecological revolutions*. Chapel Hill and London: University of North Carolina Press.

Naess, Arne. 1985. Identification as a source of deep ecological attitudes. In *Deep ecology*. Michael Tobias, ed. San Diego: Avant Books.

Ortner, Sherry. 1974. Is female to male as nature is to culture? In *Woman, culture and society*. Michelle Rosaldo and Louise Lamphere, eds. Stanford, CA: Stanford University Press.

Plant, Judith. 1989. *Healing the wounds: The promise of ecofeminism*. Philadelphia: New Society Publishers.

Prentice, Susan. 1988. Taking sides: what's wrong with eco-feminism? *Women and Environments* (Spring): 9-10.

Rorty, Amélie. 1988. *Mind in action*. Boston: Beacon Press.

Shiva, Vandana. 1988. *Staying alive: women, ecology and development*. London: Zed.

Spretnak, Charlene. 1988. Ecofeminism: our roots and flowering. *Woman of Power* 9: 6-10.

Starhawk. 1989. Feminist, earth-based spirituality and ecofeminism. In *Healing the wounds*. See Plant 1989.

Sturgeon, Noel. 1989. What does the politics of poststructuralist feminism look like? Ecofeminism, positional feminism and radical feminism revisited. Paper presented at the 1989 National Women's Studies Association Conference.

Swimme, Brian. 1990. How to heal a lobotomy. In *Reweaving the world*. See Diamond and Orenstein 1990.

Tokar, Brian. 1987. *The green alternative*. San Pedro, CA: R. and E. Miles.

DISCUSSION TOPICS

1. Lahar states that ecofeminism makes big promises. Do you think these promises are too broad and idealistic to be effective in changing society?

2. Do you agree with Lahar that human beings should not relate to the earth as their mother? Are there any positive aspects of such a relationship which she does not mention?

3. Lahar calls for an integrated view of nature and human nature. What are some points such a view should include?

The Evolution of an Ecofeminist

Julia Scofield Russell

Julia Scofield Russell has studied under two Zen masters for over 18 years. In 1980 she founded Eco-Home, a demonstration home in Los Angeles, California, for urban ecological living. In the following essay she invokes a powerful experience of the earth as a living being and explains how this overarching sense can and should be integrated into the individual's daily life. She maintains that ''as we transform ourselves, we transform our world.''

Breathe. Feel the air enter your lungs. Breathe. Feel millions of oxygen atoms permeating your lung membranes, entering your bloodstream, being delivered to every cell in your body, fueling the fire of life within you. Mother is feeding you. She feels you and sustains your life with every breath.

Let your consciousness move now down to your feet. Keep going down through the floor, to the ground. Penetrate the ground with your consciousness as though you were growing roots into the Earth. Deeper and deeper. Sense her massiveness. Her ever-abidingness.

Feel her hold you to her. Gravity is her embrace. Feel her love. Allow her love to flow into you, up through the soles of your feet, through your legs and torso to your heart, your shoulders, your head. Bathe in her love. Breathe.

Let her love permeate every cell. Let your heart fill with her love. Let it swell with love, from her, for her.

She nurtures you in every way.

The air you breathe is her.

The food you eat is her.

Let your love and gratitude grow. Let it flow out to her, to Father Sun, and to all your brothers and sisters of the plant and animal kingdom.

We are all mother's children, beloved by her, nurtured and protected from the harsh reality of outer space.

I think, perhaps, the single most important fact to be known by every person on the planet is that the Earth is a living being. This is ancient wisdom. Lost and now refound. James Lovelock learned it by compar-

ing the Earth's atmosphere to that of other planets in his book, *Gaia: A New View of Life on Earth* (New York: Oxford University Press, 1979). But it can be learned in many ways.

I learned it from a compost pile, in an initiation whose beginnings were humble indeed. I constructed three bottomless boxes, 18 inches square and about 6 inches high, according to instructions I came across in *Woman's Day*. I placed the boxes on top of one another, covered them with a piece of plywood and began disposing of my table scraps in there. Occasionally, I would add a handful of dirt.

After about 6 weeks the pile almost filled the boxes. It was time to turn it. I took the box off the top and placed it on the ground next to the others. Then I dug in with my hand spade to transfer the top layers into the box I had just removed. I was assailed by a revolting stench of vomit! I was horrified. As I proceeded down further the odor began to change, but not for the better! It smelled intensely like human feces!

What was going on? *Women's Day* had said nothing about this! I switched the second box to the new site. Ugh! Now it began to smell like dog or cat feces. Not much better than human, but I kept on and soon began to perceive a barnyard scent. Having spent some years as a girl in dairy country, this smell of horse and cow manure I recognized at least as something more earthy, less a putrefying waste. The farmers had used manure to fertilize their fields.

Now I was down to the bottom box. I lifted it and placed it on top of the other two. My next spadeful revealed something amazing! I didn't quite know what at first. It was dark, dark brown and somewhat chunky. I gingerly leaned forward for a whiff. It smelled—clean! I took a piece of it in my hand. It was crumbly. I smelled it again. It smelled like the ground after a spring rain! No doubt about it. It was soil! Fresh, rich, clean soil.

As I crouched there with this fragrant new soil in my hand, my mind boggled and the knowledge came through loud and clear: The Earth turns everything given to it into itself, just as my body does and all living bodies do. The Earth is a living being!

I know now that the ghastly odors I encountered

as I turned the pile were due to the lack of air circulation. Lack of oxygen causes anaerobic digestion, which is characterized by foul odor. An aerated pile does not smell bad.

However, it was that progression of smells from vomit through feces to soil that enabled me to recognize that it was a process of digestion that was taking place, and it was this recognition that was the great learning for me. Needless to say, this learning has changed and continues to change my life, as I think it must anyone's life, who learns it. Sometimes it is very painful, as when I see the abuses being heaped upon the Earth's body: toxic wastes, ozone depletion, species extinction, desertification, smog, acid rain, famine, forest death, poverty, cancer, genocide, dead rivers and lakes, nuclear contamination.

Many of our cities are, by now, actually uninhabitable, though we continue to live in them, wondering why we are miserable, sick, furious, frightened. But moving out of the cities is no escape. Toxic waste will find you wherever you are. It will bubble up in your backyard, seep into your drinking water, or waft on a summer breeze into your bedroom and nursery.

"Progress" is mindlessly polluting our air, sea, soil, minds, souls, and bodies. The mad absurdity of the entire socioeconomic/cultural structure is evident. Ecofeminists have realized that we must question the entire civilization that mankind has contrived—all of its values, its goals, its achievements. It is not merely antifeminine, it is antihuman, antilife.

We have discovered that we cannot ignore the larger sickness to rail against isolated symptoms for we then betray ourselves and the world. To succeed merely in the limited objectives of social equality is to succeed in locking ourselves more tightly into a system that is fatal to us all.

It is true that our civilization has been robbed of the healthy balance of masculine and feminine influence necessary for survival. We women must manifest our half of the whole. But not a tacked-on half. Our course is to permeate the whole, changing it all.

As victim consciousness fades, we are discovering that which we uniquely have to give as women, female human beings, aware children of our Mother Earth, loving kin to all our relatives in this biosphere.

It's becoming clear to us that women's liberation cannot be separate from the liberation of all—men, women, children, old, middle aged, Black, White, Yellow, Red, and mixed, rich and poor, animals, plants, and Mother Earth herself—from the tyranny of the conqueror society that now dominates the world. Whether it calls itself capitalistic, communistic, socialist, democratic, republican, multinational, or whatever is incidental to the primary characteristic they all share—the drive to conquest, the exploitation of women, nature, and each other.

How do we move from a conqueror society to a nurturer society? First, we should recognize that the process is already well under way. We're facilitating meetings instead of running them, we're mediating disagreements instead of litigating them. We can and have introduced a new style of management into business that acknowledges the whole individual. We're spearheading social responsibility in investment and economics as though people and the Earth mattered. The Green movement is growing, worldwide. Citizen diplomacy is creating person-to-person peace. The patriarchal psychology of Freud is being superseded by a more nurturing and wholistic view of the human personality. The illusion of pure objectivity is disappearing with the emerging reality of quantum physics. Health care is becoming care of the whole person rather than symptom suppression.

We can and do write books, hold conferences, join groups, go to meetings, vote, sponsor legislation, lobby our representatives, participate in campaigns, and run for office ourselves. Perhaps we demonstrate and commit civil disobedience. All this is important and effective and needs to be done.

Yet there is still another level of empowerment, commitment, and opportunity that is often overlooked when we discuss social change and that is the essential role our individual life-styles, our everyday choices and behavior, play in maintaining the status quo or effecting change. I call it the politics of life-style and I think it is a distinctly feminine politics in that it is both inner and universal, personal and all-inclusive. It is based on the understanding that lasting societal transformation begins with and rests on transformation of the individual.

It may be hard at first to see how our life-styles are political. So I should begin by explaining what I mean by politics. I define the word in a broader sense than is usual. Economist Hazel Henderson defines the politics to which I'm referring in *The Politics of the Solar Age*. She says:

> I am talking about all the newer "politics by other means," the more fundamental politics of: redefining issues and reshaping questions; restating old "problems"; re-visioning alternative futures, alternative life-styles; reweaving the split between work and leisure, the "public" and "private" sectors, money and wealth, "success" and well-being, psychic riches and deeper human satisfaction. I am talking about the new "issue politics," which is supplanting geographical politics, not in its narrow, vengeful form but in the broader issues: the politics of planetary awareness and ecological understanding, and the new demands growing out of it: global laws concerning equitable resource use, new conflict-resolution mechanisms, universal human rights, freedom of information and media access, a new international economic order, and a global framework of accountability for multinational corporate enterprises and the impacts of science and technologies.[1]

What is the justification for such a wholistic definition of politics?

It is generally thought that we may choose to become politically involved and take part in the political process at special times, in special places, but that it is something that normally takes place elsewhere and involves other people, the famous "they" and "them." It is politicians, we think, who choose to live and work in the so-called political arena full time. There are the parties and the platforms, the elections and the coups, all of them seen as sometimes affecting us but separate from us, from our daily lives.

But are they? Is the body separate from the head? Are the fingers separate from the hand? In a certain way, yes. But in a more important way, no. They are all parts of one body. All the parts are affected by the actions and general health of all the other parts, and all those parts and their interrelationships make up the whole body. A finger with nerves that don't send or receive messages is severely handicapped, as is a hand with missing or paralyzed fingers. And the body as a whole is handicapped by any damaged or unhealthy limb or organ.

We're all part of a body politic, presently in the form of a nation, and that body politic derives its character, its health, its effectiveness, its very existence from us. We are its lifeblood, its nerves, its brain. *It will not function without our continual cooperation.* For instance, its present economic structure depends on our agreement to use Federal Reserve banknotes as the measure of exchange between us and to consume certain things at a certain rate and hundreds and thousands of other actions and nonactions that support the status quo.

At the same time, a body, a nation, exists in a larger context in which it functions as a part. The nation exists in the context of all nations that make up the whole political body of humanity. And all of humanity exists in a biosphere that is the body of the whole Earth. We exist as part of a seamless whole in which everything is connected to everything else. Seen in this context, I think, it is evident that the movies we choose to see, the food we eat, what we throw away and where, our relationships, our means of livelihood—everything—has effects that emanate out from our personal lives into our society and ultimately the whole living planet.

If we go to meetings and stage demonstrations protesting industrial pollution or unfair employment practices and then get in our car and stop off on our way home to buy the products manufactured by those same companies, we may be doing more to perpetuate the problems than alleviate them. When we consume goods and services without regard for their environmental and social costs, we are supporting technologies and policies that are laying waste to our world. If we resort, or accede, to domination and exploitation in our personal and business lives, we are practicing modes of behavior that are bringing us to the brink of disaster on an international scale. Do we protest government spending on nuclear weaponry, yet continue to fund it through our taxes?

Not that we should stop protesting, but we also need to start changing *ourselves.* Healing the planet begins with us, in our daily lives.

There has been something in me that has always

striven for integration and suffered from the fragmentation and compartmentalizing that is the normal life-style of today. But it wasn't until my thirties that I began to encounter writings by others who found today's demands and deprivations onerous and stressful. Rachel Carson[2] documented the havoc our way of life was wreaking on our natural environment, and before I knew it almost everything I picked up was confirming my long, albeit secretly held, objections to the typical middle-class U.S. life-style—its goals, its values, its products and by-products, its technologies, and on and on down the list.

As my ecological consciousness grew, I perceived that our species was behaving as a cancer on the Earth. Through unlimited and undifferentiated growth, we are infecting and spreading our toxic wastes throughout the world. But I also saw that I had the choice to live as a healthy cell, joining with other healthy cells, to function as part of the Earth's immune system. This was the genesis of Eco-Home, a demonstration home in Los Angeles for ecological living in the city. Our focus is on reducing the toxicity our habit of clumping together has on our environment by bringing an ecologically sensitive consciousness to our everyday lives.

At Eco-Home we reduce and recycle our wastes, we conserve energy and water, and we support decentralized, nonpolluting, renewable resource energy production. We have climate-appropriate and organic food gardens, and we're developing a demonstration home to model all these systems and more. We support local organic food growers through an organic farmers' market. We support the development of a local exchange trading system and help each other find or create right livelihood. We make socially responsible investments and, in cooperation with the Co-op Resources and Services Project (CRSP), we have our own revolving loan fund that will provide capital for ecologically sound businesses. Also in cooperation with CRSP, we're sponsoring the creation of an ecologically integrated community here in Los Angeles. In general, then, we work to promulgate a view of reality that recognizes the interrelatedness of all phenomena.

We take our role as consumers seriously and fulfill it thoughtfully. We understand that when we purchase a product we are supporting the entire system that produced it. We are also responsible for its effect on us and our world while we own it and even after we no longer want or need it. What is its effect then? Does it trash up our landscape? Does it pollute the water or the air or the soil? Or is it recyclable, reusable. Does it conform to the law of the circle—the fact that the Earth's natural life-support systems are circular. There is no "out." Everything is in the system, and everything we put into the system comes back to us, for good or for ill. If the product can be reused or recycled, it is life supporting. If it can't be, it follows the law of entropy, increases chaos, and is antilife. We try to support life in everything we do and to withhold our support from products and processes that degrade life in any way.

We withdraw support from companies and/or practices that are socially and ecologically damaging. We support those that are ecologically sound and ethical. If there aren't any, we start our own with our friends. When confronted with blockage or even sabotage in personal or business life, we recognize it as an opportunity to practice win/win conflict resolution instead of resorting to legal, physical, or even psychological revenge. We bring our lives into harmony with the natural cycles and systems that sustain life.

As we transform ourselves, we transform our world. Not later. Now. Simultaneously. How can this be so? The practice of the politics of life-style springs from an understanding of how things actually happen rather than the linear, cause-and-effect model. As we align ourselves with the regenerative powers of the Earth and the evolutionary thrust of our species, we tap abilities beyond the ordinary. We move into the Tao.

How do you initiate this process in your life? You can start just about anywhere. You can start with recycling, with your means of transportation, with your diet and food-buying practices, with composting, with your relationships, with meditation, tax resistance, right livelihood, housing, gardening, conservation—it's up to you. What seems easiest, most obvious, or most urgent to you? Start there.

Most important: start becoming aware of yourself

as an integral part of the body of humanity, and the body of humanity as a child of Mother Earth, still cradled in her womb with all our brothers and sisters of the plant and animal kingdoms. Doing the meditation that opens this essay every day will help to build your conscious bonding with her. A new sense of security will subtly alter your consciousness. As your awareness grows, so will your actions be informed by greater sensitivity to the impact you're having on all around you. Mothering Earth in your everyday life will become a personal imperative.

And so we move, from a conqueror society to a nurturer society.

NOTES

1. Hazel Henderson, *The Politics of the Solar Age: Alternatives to Economics* (Garden City, NY: Anchor/Doubleday, 1981), p. xiii.
2. Rachel Carson, *Silent Spring* (Boston: Houghton Mifflin, 1962).

DISCUSSION TOPICS

1. Russell maintains that the earth is our living Mother and that we should in turn mother the earth. Based on this essay, do you think this view nourishes or hinders Russell's political activism? What response do you think Lahar would have to Russell's approach?
2. Russell states that lifestyles are political. What reasons does she give for this view? Do you agree?

READING 58

Women in Nature

Vandana Shiva

Vandana Shiva is the director of the Research Foundation for Science and Ecology in Dehra Dun, India. After receiving a doctorate in theoretical physics, she worked for the Indian Institute for Management in Bangalore. She is active in the Chipko *movement, in which village women have acted nonviolently to protect the forests from destruction.*

Shiva points out that the world views of ancient civilizations such as India have much to contribute to the creation of ecologically sustainable societies. In the following excerpts from her book, Women in Nature, *she discusses the Indian concept of ''Prakriti,'' a name for the primordial energy which is worshipped in India as the Mother of Nature from which all life arises. Indian cosmology is nondualistic: human beings and nature complement and sustain each other.*

Shiva calls attention to real productivity, in which women cooperate with nature. The productive women of whom Shiva speaks are not the ''ecologically alienated, consumerist elite women'' of both the Third World and the West, but the women who quietly work to sustain human and natural life in harmony with local ecosystems and needs. Such sustenance work has been devalued and ignored in favor of what she terms ''maldevelopment,'' the domination of women, the Third World, and nature by the ''colonising male'' who imposes a political economy of commodity and cash flows. Western-imposed development or economic growth is really maldevelopment because of its destructiveness to both rural peoples and the natural world which sustains them. Gross National Product measures only some costs, ignoring indirect costs such as ecological devastation. Such maldevelopment benefits only the elites in both the wealthy nations and the Third World and only for the short term. Resources needed for renewal are diverted to the market economy, generating deprivation and misery for the poorer members of society. Development can lead to less water, less fertile soil, and less satisfaction of basic and vital needs.

Shiva argues that it is a mistake to conceive of Third World women as simply victims of environmental degradation. In fact, these rural women are in a privileged position to lead their societies to ecological recovery: their minds are still free from the distortions of maldevelopment, and they possess knowledge both from bearing the costs of maldevelopment and from using holistic, locally appropriate ecological practices. Only the producers of life can be its protectors.

According to Shiva, masculinity and femininity are socially constructed ideas: they reflect the patriarchal view of the masculine as creative and violent and the feminine as passive and nonviolent. Shiva presents a ''trans-gender'' concept of liberation, which affirms that the feminine principle as creative nonviolence is present in nature, women, and men. Liberation begins with the colonized, but it must also embrace the colonizer.

NATURE AS THE FEMININE PRINCIPLE

Women in India are an intimate part of nature, both in imagination and in practise. At one level nature is symbolised as the embodiment of the feminine principle, and at another, she is nurtured by the feminine to produce life and provide sustenance.

From the point of view of Indian cosmology, in both the exoteric and esoteric traditions, the world is produced and renewed by the dialectical play of creation and destruction, cohesion and disintegration. The tension between the opposites from which motion and movement arises is depicted as the first appearance of dynamic energy (Shakti). All existence arises from this primordial energy which is the substance of everything, pervading everything. The manifestation of this power, this energy, is called nature (Prakriti).[1] Nature, both animate and inanimate, is thus an expression of Shakti, the feminine and creative principle of the cosmos; in conjunction with the masculine principle (Purusha), Prakriti creates the world.

Nature as Prakriti is inherently active, a powerful, productive force in the dialectic of the creation, renewal and sustenance of *all* life. In *Kulacudamim Nigama*, Prakriti says:

There is none but Myself
Who is the Mother to create.[2]

Without Shakti, Shiva, the symbol for the force of creation and destruction, is as powerless as a corpse. 'The quiescent aspect of Shiva is, by definition, inert . . . Activity is the nature of Nature (Prakriti).'[3]

Prakriti is worshipped as Aditi, the primordial vastness, the inexhaustible, the source of abundance. She is worshipped as Adi Shakti, the primordial power. All the forms of nature and life in nature are the forms, the children, of the Mother of Nature who is nature itself born of the creative play of her thought.[4] Hence Prakriti is also called Lalitha,[5] the Player, because *lila* or play, as free spontaneous activity, is her nature. The will-to-become many (Bahu-Syam-Prajayera) is her creative impulse and through this impulse, she creates the diversity of living forms in nature. The common yet multiple life of mountains, trees, rivers, animals is an expression of the diversity that Prakriti gives rise to. The creative force and the created world are not separate and distinct, nor is the created world uniform, static and fragmented. It is diverse, dynamic and inter-related.

The nature of Nature as Prakriti is activity *and* diversity. Nature symbols from every realm of nature are in a sense signed with the image of Nature. Prakriti lives in stone or tree, pool, fruit or animal, and is identified with them. According to the *Kalika Purana*:

> Rivers and mountains have a dual nature. A river is but a form of water, yet it has a distinct body. Mountains appear a motionless mass, yet their true form is not such. We cannot know, when looking at a lifeless shell, that it contains a living being. Similarly, within the apparently inanimate rivers and mountains there dwells a hidden consciousness. Rivers and mountains take the forms they wish.[6]

The living, nurturing relationship between man and nature here differs dramatically from the notion of

---

1. 'Prakriti' is a popular category, and one through which ordinary women in rural India relate to nature. It is also a highly evolved philosophical category in Indian cosmology. Even those philosophical streams of Indian thought which were patriarchal and did not give the supreme place to divinity as a woman, a mother, were permeated by the prehistoric cults and the living 'little' traditions of nature as the primordial mother goddess.

2. For an elaboration of the concept of the feminine principle in Indian thought see Alain Danielon, *The Gods of India,* New York: Inner Traditions International Ltd., 1985; Sir John Woodroffe, *The Serpent Power,* Madras: Ganesh and Co., 1931; and Sir John Woodroffe, *Shakti and Shakta,* London: Luzaz and Co., 1929.

---

3. Woodroffe, *op. cit.,* (1931), p 27.

4. W.C. Beane, *Myth, Cult and Symbols in Sakta Hinduism: A Study of the Indian Mother Goddess,* Leiden: E.J. Brill, 1977.

5. *Lalitha Sahasranama,* (Reprint), Delhi: Giani Publishing House, 1986.

6. *Kalika Purana,* 22.10-13, Bombay: Venkateshwara Press, 1927.

man as separate from and dominating over nature. A good illustration of this difference is the daily worship of the sacred tulsi within Indian culture and outside it. Tulsi (*Ocimum sanctum*) is a little herb planted in every home, and worshipped daily. It has been used in Ayurveda for more than 3000 years, and is now also being legitimised as a source of diverse healing powers by western medicine. However, all this is incidental to its worship. The tulsi is sacred not merely as a plant with beneficial properties but as Brindavan, the symbol of the cosmos. In their daily watering and worship women renew the relationship of the home with the cosmos and with the world process. Nature as a creative expression of the feminine principle is both in ontological continuity with humans as well as above them. Ontologically, there is no divide between man and nature, or between man and woman, because life in all its forms arises from the feminine principle.

Contemporary western views of nature are fraught with the dichotomy or duality between man and woman, and person and nature. In Indian cosmology, by contrast, person and nature (Purusha-Prakriti) are a duality in unity. They are inseparable complements of one another in nature, in woman, in man. Every form of creation bears the sign of this dialectical unity, of diversity within a unifying principle, and this dialectical harmony between the male and female principles and between nature and man, becomes the basis of ecological thought and action in India. Since, ontologically, there is no dualism between man and nature and because nature as Prakriti sustains life, nature has been treated as integral and inviolable. Prakriti, far from being an esoteric abstraction, is an everyday concept which organises daily life. There is no separation here between the popular and elite imagery or between the sacred and secular traditions. As an embodiment and manifestation of the feminine principle it is characterised by (a) creativity, activity, productivity; (b) diversity in form and aspect; (c) connectedness and inter-relationship of all beings, including man; (d) continuity between the human and natural; and (e) sanctity of life in nature.

Conceptually, this differs radically from the Cartesian concept of nature as 'environment' or a 'resource.' In it, the environment is seen as separate from man: it is his surrounding, not his substance. The dualism between man and nature has allowed the subjugation of the latter by man and given rise to a new world-view in which nature is (a) inert and passive; (b) uniform and mechanistic; (c) separable and fragmented within itself; (d) separate from man; and (e) inferior, to be dominated and exploited by man.

The rupture within nature and between man and nature, and its associated transformation from a life-force that sustains to an exploitable resource characterises the Cartesian view which has displaced more ecological world-views and created a development paradigm which cripples nature and woman simultaneously.

The ontological shift for an ecologically sustainable future has much to gain from the world-views of ancient civilisations and diverse cultures which survived sustainably over centuries. These were based on an ontology of the feminine as the living principle, and on an ontological continuity between society and nature—the humanisation of nature and the naturalisation of society. Not merely did this result in an ethical context which excluded possibilities of exploitation and domination, it allowed the creation of an earth family.

The dichotomised ontology of man dominating woman and nature generates maldevelopment because it makes the colonising male the agent and model of 'development.' Women, the Third World and nature become underdeveloped, first by definition, and then, through the process of colonisation, in reality.

The ontology of dichotomisation generates an ontology of domination, over nature and people. Epistemologically, it leads to reductionism and fragmentation, thus violating women as subjects and nature as an object of knowledge. This violation becomes a source of epistemic and real violence—I would like to interpret ecological crises at both levels—as a disruption of ecological perceptions of nature.

Ecological ways of knowing nature are necessarily participatory. Nature herself is the experiment and women, as sylviculturalists, agriculturists and water resource managers, the traditional natural scientists. Their knowledge is ecological and plural, reflecting both the diversity of natural ecosystems and the diversity in cultures that nature-based living gives rise to. Throughout the world, the colonisation of diverse peoples was, at its root, a forced subjugation of ecological concepts of nature and of the Earth as the repository of all forms, latencies and powers of creation, the ground and cause of the world. The symbolism of Terra Mater, the earth in the form of the Great Mother, creative and protective, has been a shared but diverse symbol across space and time, and ecology movements in the West today are inspired in large part by the recovery of the concept of Gaia, the earth goddess.[7]

The shift from Prakriti to 'natural resources,' from Mater to 'matter' was considered (and in many quarters is still considered) a progressive shift from superstition to rationality. Yet, viewed from the perspective of nature, or women embedded in nature, in the production and preservation of sustenance, the shift is regressive and violent. It entails the disruption of nature's processes and cycles, and her interconnectedness. For women, whose productivity in the sustaining of life is based on nature's productivity, the death of Prakriti is simultaneously a beginning of their marginalisation, devaluation, displacement and ultimate dispensability. The ecological crisis is, at its root, the death of the feminine principle, symbolically as well as in contexts such as rural India, not merely in form and symbol, but also in the everyday processes of survival and sustenance.

NATURE AND WOMEN AS PRODUCERS OF LIFE

With the violation of nature is linked the violation and marginalisation of women, especially in the Third World. Women produce and reproduce life not merely biologically, but also through their social role in providing sustenance. All ecological societies of forest-dwellers and peasants, whose life is organised on the principle of sustainability and the reproduction of life

in all its richness, also embody the feminine principle. Historically, however, when such societies have been colonised and broken up the men have usually started to participate in life-destroying activities or have had to migrate; the women meanwhile, usually continue to be linked to life and nature through their role as providers of sustenance, food and water. The privileged access of women to the sustaining principle thus has a historical and cultural, and not merely biological, basis. The principle of creating and conserving life is lost to the ecologically alienated, consumerist elite women of the Third World and the over-consuming west, just as much as it is conserved in the lifestyle of the male and female forest-dwellers and peasants in small pockets of the Third World.

Maria Mies has called women's work in producing sustenance the *production of life* and views it as a truly productive relationship to nature, because 'women not only collected and consumed what grew in nature but they *made things grow*.'[8] This organic process of growth in which women and nature work in partnership with each other has created a special relationship of women with nature, which, following Mies, can be summarised as follows:

a. Their interaction with nature, with their own nature as well as the external environment, was a reciprocal process. They conceived of their own bodies as being productive in the same way as they conceived of external nature being so.

b. Although they appropriate nature, their appropriation does not constitute a relationship of dominance or a property relation. Women are not owners of their own bodies or of the earth, but they co-operate with their bodies and with the earth in order 'to let grow and to make grow.'

c. As producers of new life they also became the first subsistence producers and the inventors of the first productive economy, implying from the beginning social production and the creation of social relations, i.e., of society and history.

7. Erich Neumann, *The Great Mother,* New York: Pantheon Books, 1955.

8. Maria Mies, *Patriarchy and Accumulation on a World Scale,* London: Zed Books, 1986, pp. 16-17, 55.

Productivity, viewed from the perspective of survival, differs sharply from the dominant view of the productivity of labour as defined for processes of capital accumulation. 'Productive' man, producing commodities, using some of nature's wealth and women's work as raw material and dispensing with the rest as waste, becomes the only legitimate category of work, wealth and production. Nature and women working to produce and reproduce life are declared 'unproductive.'

With Adam Smith, the wealth created by nature and women's work was turned invisible. Labour, and especially male labour, became the fund which originally supplies it with all the necessities and conveniences of life. As this assumption spread to all human communities, it introduced dualities within society, and between nature and man. No more was nature a source of wealth and sustenance; no more was women's work in sustenance 'productive' work; no more were peasant and tribal societies creative and productive. They were all marginal to the framework of the industrial society, except as resources and inputs. The transforming, productive power was associated only with male western labour, and economic development became a design of remodelling the world on that assumption. The devaluation and derecognition of nature's work and productivity has led to the ecological crises; the devaluation and de-recognition of women's work has created sexism and inequality between men and women. The devaluation of subsistence, or rather sustenance economies, based on harmony between nature's work, women's work and man's work has created the various forms of ethnic and cultural crises that plague our world today.

The crisis of survival and the threat to sustenance arises from ecological disruption that is rooted in the arrogance of the west and those that ape it. This arrogance is grounded in a blindness towards the quiet work and the invisible wealth created by nature and women and those who produce sustenance. Such work and wealth are 'invisible' because they are decentred, local and in harmony with local ecosystems and needs. The more effectively the cycles of life, as essential ecological processes, are maintained, the more invisible they become. Disruption is violent and

visible; balance and harmony are experienced, not seen. The premium on visibility placed by patriarchal maldevelopment forces the destruction of invisible energies and the work of women and nature, and the creation of spectacular, centralised work and wealth. Such centralisation and the uniformity associated with it works further against the diversity and plurality of life. Work and wealth in accordance with the feminine principle are significant precisely because they are rooted in stability and sustainability. Decentred diversity is the source of nature's work and women's productivity; it is the work of 'insignificant' plants in creating significant changes which shift the ecological equilibrium in life's favour. It is the energy of all living things, in all their diversity, and together, the diversity of lives wields tremendous energy. Women's work is similarly invisible in providing sustenance and creating wealth for basic needs. Their work in the forest, the field and the river creates sustenance in quiet but essential ways. Every woman in every house in every village of rural India works invisibly to provide the stuff of life to nature and people. It is this invisible work that is linked to nature and needs, which conserves nature through maintaining ecological cycles, and conserves human life through satisfying the basic needs of food, nutrition and water. It is this essential work that is destroyed and dispensed with by maldevelopment: the maintenance of ecological cycles has no place in a political economy of commodity and cash flows.

The existence of the feminine principle is linked with diversity and sharing. Its destruction through homogenisation and privatisation leads to the destruction of diversity and of the commons. The sustenance economy is based on a creative and organic nature, on local knowledge, on locally recycled inputs that maintain the integrity of nature, on local consumption for local needs, and on the marketing of surplus beyond the imperatives of equity and ecology. The commodity and cash economy destroys natural cycles and reduces nature to raw materials and commodities. It creates the need for purchase and sale to centralised inputs and commodity markets. When production is specialised and for export, surplus becomes a myth. There is only indebtedness, of peoples and nations.

The debt trap is part of global commodity production and sale which destroys nature and nurturing economies in the name of development.

Sustenance, in the final analysis, is built on the continued capacity of nature to renew its forests, fields and rivers. These resource systems are intrinsically linked in life-producing and life-conserving cultures, and it is in managing the integrity of ecological cycles in forestry and agriculture that women's productivity has been most developed and evolved. Women transfer fertility from the forests to the field and to animals. They transfer animal waste as fertilizer for crops and crop by-products to animals as fodder. They work with the forest to bring water to their fields and families. This partnership between women's and nature's work ensures the sustainability of sustenance, and it is this critical partnership that is torn asunder when the project of 'development' becomes a patriarchal project, threatening both nature and women. The forest is separated from the river, the field is separated from the forest, the animals are separated from the crops. Each is then separately developed, and the delicate balance which ensures sustainability and equity is destroyed. The visibility of dramatic breaks and ruptures is posited as 'progress.' Marginalised women are either dispensed with or colonised. Needs go unfulfilled, nature is crippled. The drama of violence and fragmentation cannot be sustained and the recovery of the feminine principle thus becomes essential for liberating not only women and nature, but also the patriarchal reductionist categories which give rise to maldevelopment.

The revolutionary and liberational potential of the recovery of the feminine principle consists in its challenging the concepts, categories and processes which have created the threat to life, and in providing oppositional categories that create and enlarge the spaces for maintaining and enriching all life in nature and society. The radical shift induced by a focus on the feminine principle is the recognition of maldevelopment as a culture of destruction. The feminine principle becomes a category of challenge which locates nature and women as the source of life and wealth, and as such, active subjects, maintaining and creating life-processes.

There are two implications that arise from the recognition of nature and women as producers of life. First, that what goes by the name of development is a maldevelopment process, a source of violence to women and nature throughout the world. This violence does not arise from the misapplication of an otherwise benign and gender-neutral mode, but is rooted in the patriarchal assumptions of homogeneity, domination and centralisation that underlie dominant models of thought and development strategies. Second, that the crises that the maldevelopment model has given rise to cannot be solved within the paradigm of the crisis mind. Their solution lies in the categories of thought, perception and action that are life-giving and life-maintaining. In contemporary times, Third World women, whose minds have not yet been dispossessed or colonised, are in a privileged position to make visible the invisible oppositional categories that they are the custodians of. It is not only as victims, but also as leaders in creating new intellectual ecological paradigms, that women are central to arresting and overcoming ecological crises. Just as ecological recovery begins from centres of natural diversity which are gene pools, Third World women, and those tribals and peasants who have been left out of the processes of maldevelopment, are today acting as the intellectual gene pools of ecological categories of thought and action. Marginalisation has thus become a source for healing the diseased mainstream of patriarchal development. Those facing the biggest threat offer the best promise for survival because they have two kinds of knowledge that are not accessible to dominant and privileged groups. First, they have the knowledge of what it means to be the victims of progress, to be the ones who bear the costs and burdens. Second, they have the holistic and ecological knowledge of what the production of life is about. They retain the ability to see nature's life as a *precondition* for human survival and the integrity of interconnectedness in nature as a precondition for life. Women of the Third World have been dispossessed of their base for sustenance, but not of their minds, and in their uncolonised minds are conserved the oppositional categories that make the sustenance of life possible for all. The producers of life alone can be its real protectors. Women embedded in nature, producing life with nature, are therefore taking the initiative in the recovery of nature.

To say that women and nature are intimately associated is not to say anything revolutionary. After all, it was precisely just such an assumption that allowed the domination of both women and nature. The new insight provided by rural women in the Third World is that women and nature are associated *not in passivity but in creativity and in the maintenance of life.*

This analysis differs from most conventional analyses of environmentalists and feminists. Most work on women and environment in the Third World has focussed on women as special victims of environmental degradation. Yet the women who participate in and lead ecology movements in countries like India are not speaking merely as victims. Their voices are the voices of liberation and transformation which provide new categories of thought and new exploratory directions. In this sense, this study is a post-victimology study. It is an articulation of the categories of challenge that women in ecology movements are creating in the Third World. The women and environment issue can be approached either from these categories of challenge that have been thrown up by women in the struggle for life, or it can be approached through an extension of conventional categories of patriarchy and reductionism. In the perspective of women engaged in survival struggles which are, simultaneously, struggles for the protection of nature, women and nature are intimately related, and their domination and liberation similarly linked. The women's and ecology movements are therefore one, and are primarily counter-trends to a patriarchal maldevelopment. Our experience shows that ecology and feminism can combine in the recovery of the feminine principle, and through this recovery, can intellectually and politically restructure and transform maldevelopment.

Maldevelopment is seen here as a process by which human society marginalises the play of the feminine principle in nature and in society. Ecological breakdown and social inequality are intrinsically related to the dominant development paradigm which puts man

against and above nature and women. The underlying assumptions of dialectical unity and cyclical recovery shared by the common concern for the liberation of nature and of women, contrast deeply with the dominant western patriarchal assumptions of duality in existence and linearity in process. Within the western paradigm, the environmental movement is separate from the women's movement. As long as this paradigm with its assumptions of linear progress prevails, 'environmentalism' and 'feminism' independently ask only for concessions *within* maldevelopment, because in the absence of oppositional categories, that is the only 'development' that is conceivable. Environmentalism then becomes a new patriarchal project of technological fixes and political oppression. It generates a new subjugation of ecological movements and fails to make any progress towards sustainability and equity. While including a few women as tokens in 'women and environment,' it excludes the feminine visions of survival that women have conserved. Fragmented feminism, in a similar way, finds itself trapped in a gender-based ideology of liberation—taking off from either the 'catching-up-with-men' syndrome (on the grounds that the masculine is superior and developed), or receding into a narrow biologism which accepts the feminine as gendered, and excludes the possibility of the recovery of the feminine principle in nature and women, *as well as* men.

GENDER-IDEOLOGY VS. THE RECOVERY OF THE FEMININE PRINCIPLE

We see the categories of 'masculine' and 'feminine' as socially and culturally constructed. A gender-based ideology projects these categories as biologically determined. The western concept of masculinity that has dominated development and gender relations has excluded all that has been defined by culture as feminine and has legitimised control over all that counts as such. The category of masculinity as a socially constructed product of gender ideology is associated with the creation of the concept of woman as the 'other.' In this asymmetrical relationship, femininity is ideologically constructed as everything that is not masculine and must be subjected to domination. . . .

Gender ideology has created the dualism and disjunction between male and female. Simultaneously it has created a conjunction of activity and creativity with violence and the masculine, and a conjunction of passivity with non-violence and the feminine. Gender-based responses to this dualism have retained these conjunctions and disjunctions, and within these dichotomised categories, have prescribed either the masculinisation or feminisation of the world.

There is, however, a third concept and process of liberation that is trans-gender. It is based on the recognition that masculine and feminine as gendered concepts based on exclusiveness are ideologically defined categories, as is the association of violence and activity with the former, and non-violence and passivity with the latter. Rajni Kothari has observed, The feminist input serves not just women but also men. There is no limiting relationship between feminist values and being a woman.[9] In this non-gender based philosophy the feminine principle is not exclusively embodied in women, but is the principle of activity and creativity in nature, women and men. One cannot really distinguish the masculine from the feminine, person from nature, Purusha from Prakriti. Though distinct, they remain inseparable in dialectical unity, as two aspects of one being. The recovery of the feminine principle is thus associated with the non-patriarchal, non-gendered category of creative non-violence, or 'creative power in peaceful form,' as Tagore stated in his prayer to the tree.

It is this conceptual framework within which this book, and the experiences and struggles discussed in it are located. This perspective can recover humanity not in its distorted form of the victim and oppressor, but by creating a new wholeness in both that transcends gender because gender identity is, in any case, an ideological, social and political construct.

The recovery of the feminine principle is a response to multiple dominations and deprivations not just of women, but also of nature and non-western cultures. It stands for ecological recovery and nature's liberation, for women's liberation and for the liberation of men who, in dominating nature and women, have sacrificed their own human-ness. Ashis Nandy says, one must choose the slave's standpoint not only because the slave is oppressed but also because he represents a higher-order cognition which perforce includes the master as a human, whereas the master's cognition has to exclude the slave except as a 'thing.'[10] Liberation must therefore begin from the colonised and end with the coloniser. As Gandhi was to so clearly formulate through his own life, freedom is indivisible, not only in the popular sense that the oppressed of the world are one, but also in the unpopular sense that the oppressor, too, is caught in the culture of oppression.

The recovery of the feminine principle is based on inclusiveness. It is a recovery in nature, woman and man of creative forms of being and perceiving. In nature it implies seeing nature as a live organism. In woman it implies seeing women as productive and active. Finally, in men the recovery of the feminine principle implies a relocation of action and activity to create life-enhancing, not life-reducing and life-threatening societies.

The death of the feminine principle in women and nature takes place through the association of the category of passivity with the feminine. The death of the feminine principle in men takes place by a shift in the concept of activity from creation to destruction, and the concept of power from empowerment to domination. Self-generated, non-violent, creative activity as the feminine principle dies simultaneously in women, men and nature when violence and aggression become the masculine model of activity, and women and nature are turned into passive objects of violence. The problem with a gender-based response to a gender-based ideology is that it treats ideologically constructed gender categorisation as given by nature. It treats passive non-violence as biological givens in women, and violence as a biological given in men, when both non-violence and violence are

---

9. Rajni Kothari, 'Lokayan's Efforts to Overcome the New Rift,' IFDA Dossier, Vol. 52, March-April 1986, p. 9.

10. Ashis Nandy, *The Intimate Enemy,* Delhi: Oxford University Press, 1986, p. *xv.*

socially constructed and need have no gender association. Gandhi, the modern world's leading practitioner and preacher of non-violence was, after all, a man. The historical creation of a gender divide by a gender ideology cannot be the basis of gender liberation. And a gender-based ideology remains totally inadequate in either responding to the ecological crisis created by patriarchal and violent modes of relating to nature, or in understanding how Third World women are leading ecological struggles based on values of conservation which are immediately generalised as the concern for entire communities and regions, and even humanity as a whole.

DISCUSSION TOPICS

1. According to Shiva, rural Third World women have been dispossessed of their natural resources but not of their minds. Do you agree that such women can provide needed ecological leadership? Explain your position.
2. What types of Western-style development are maldevelopment, and which are not?
3. Shiva argues for the recovery of the feminine principle in nature, women and men, but she argues that masculinity and femininity are socially constructed categories. Is her position consistent?

READING 59

States of Grace

Charlene Spretnak

Charlene Spretnak has authored several books, including Lost Goddesses of Early Greece[23] *and* Green Politics: The Global Promise, *with Fritjof Capra. In the following essay she notes the lack of cultural support from a*

dualistic, anthropocentric culture for the experience of "ecocommunion," of our sacred oneness with the natural world. The experience of grace is the experience of ourselves as particular expressions of the cosmic body. Spretnak argues for the recognition of the reality of our larger self, as found in the bioregion of which we as individuals are a part. She provides suggestions to develop awareness of these ecocommunities, including a description of a spring equinox ritual.

Spretnak speaks for those ecofeminists who experience nature in the form of the Goddess, one of Whose names is "Gaia."[24] For Spretnak, the Goddess is a metaphor for the divinity of the sacred whole of the Earthbody. Spretnak summarizes some of the archaeological evidence describing the Goddess-centered culture in Old Europe; she notes the importance of this historical Goddess religion for many women. For Spretnak, such importance lies partly in the centrality of the "elemental power of the female body" to Neolithic cultures. Goddess spirituality does not mire women in their bodies, outside of culture, but respects their bodies as part of the Earthbody. The divine is immanent, present within nature. As human beings share in this body, they are empowered and able to embrace the regenerative cycles of natural life.

. . . To hone our awareness of the ecocommunity, most of us need to begin with basics, such as learning to recognize a dozen native plants, a dozen birds, and other local animals. Professional naturalists in city and regional parks can be of assistance, but it is also worth the effort to seek out the amateur naturalists in one's community. In both my former and present homes, I have enjoyed many half-day bird walks with white-haired ladies who were extremely knowledgeable and encouraging to novices. (All the naturalists I have known were good-natured and wore their knowledge lightly, perhaps because long periods of immersion in the larger reality have imbued them with an existential security that requires no grandstanding. In any case, getting out into nature seems to be good for the disposition, and even beginners find it nearly

---

23. Charlene Spretnak, *Lost Goddesses of Early Greece: A Collection of Pre-Hellenic Myths* (Boston: Beacon Press, 1981).

24. *Gaia* is the Greek Earth goddess whose name is often used to suggest that life on Earth functions as one organism. Anthony Weston, "Forms of Gaian Ethics," *Environmental Ethics* 9, No. 3 (1987): 217-230.

impossible to return home from birding in a negative mood.) Having a sense of one's bioregion may some-day be considered as essential as knowing the local streets and highways. Newcomers might ask their neighbors, "On what day of the week is the local farmers' market held around here? What time of year is the all-species parade?[1] Oh, and who are the local naturalists—we don't want to remain know-nothings for long!"

As we begin to develop a sense of the ecocommunity in which we live, we grow to cherish it. Without much forethought we find ourselves creating personal rituals of communion—making visitations to a particular spot, suspending thought for a long moment at the beginning of the day to let the backyard bird song fill our mind/body, or feeling drawn to observe the daily progress of a budding tree. As our sensitivity increases, certain narrowly focused rituals within the human community seem to cry out for greater fullness. While saying grace before a meal, why not express gratitude not only for our food but for the presence of the animals, plants, landforms, and water? Participating in worship services, why not suggest various ways that the presence of the bioregion can be included? Celebrations of baptism, confirmation, Bar Mitzvah, Bat Mitzvah, and weddings could all include the ritual planting of a tree. Certainly the annual slaughter of millions of firs to celebrate the birth of Christ could be replaced with purchasing live firs, or, better still, native trees, which could later be planted or donated to a regional park.

Beyond that, each of our religious rituals, those that mark the stages in an individual's spiritual life as well as those that are communal celebrations in the liturgical cycle, could be enriched by greater recognition of the cosmic web of life.[2] In this era of ecological awakening, the living presence of the ceremonies of native peoples—inspiring acts of regeneration of their sense of interrelatedness with the sacred whole—is a great gift. Perhaps the growing appreciation of their embodied wisdom will lead to an interfaith deepening of the spirituality of Earthlings.

While some people work to "cosmologize" organized religion, others have taken to grow-your-own

ceremonies of cosmological celebration, especially at the solstices and equinoxes. The two days with the longest and shortest gift of light from our sun, plus the two days with light and darkness of equal length, plus the midpoint days between those four were celebrated in pre-Christian Europe as natural markers in the majestic cycles of Earth's body. Two of the midpoint holy days are preserved in modern times as May Day and All Saints Day (or All Hallows Day, preceded immediately by Hallows Eve, or "Halloween").[3] Today the solstices and equinoxes have become occasions for groups of friends and family to gather in celebration of the Earth community and to focus awareness on the particular turning of the seasons. With friends, I have given thanks at autumn equinox for the bountiful harvests of the soil and in our lives, turned inward on the long night of winter solstice to look directly at the dark, known regeneration at spring equinox as Earth's exuberance burst forth, and felt the fullness of fruition at summer solstice when Earth's day is long and sensuous.

Of all those images, the most beautiful that remains with me is the spring equinox ritual we evolved over time.[4] A group of some forty people in spring colors walk from our cars in procession to a gentle rise in a spacious park, carrying armfuls of flowers and greens, food and drink, and burning incense. Musicians among us play instruments as the children toss a trail of petals. We form a circle and place the flowers and greens at our feet, forming a huge garland for the Earth, one foot wide and half as high. In the center on colorful cloths we set baskets of food and objects of regeneration—feathers shed by eagles and other birds, a bowl of water, a small statue of a pregnant female, and several sprays of pink and white blossoms. We breathe together and plant our feet squarely on the warming earth, drawing up its procreative powers into our being. Working mindfully, we take some flowers and ivy from the Earth garland and make individual garlands with trailing ribbons for ourselves, then weave together the stems and greens in the grand garland. Standing, we call upon the presence of the East and the cleansing winds that clear our minds. We call upon the presence of the South and the fires of warmth and energy that enliven us. We call upon the presence of the West and the water that soothes and renews us. We call upon the presence of the North and the earth that grounds and feeds us. We sing, perhaps the Indian song ''The Earth Is Our Mother.'' We seat ourselves around the garland and offer into the circle one-word poems about spring in our bioregion. Someone reads a favorite poem. A storyteller, accompanied by soft drumming and birdsong flute, tells an ancient tale of the meaning of spring. We sing a lilting song with her. A second storyteller tells another story of spring. We sing a rhythmic chant with him. The two bards put on masks they have made and dance and leap around the circle, sprung with vernal energies. In counterpoint, the men sing his song, the women hers. We rise and sway like saplings as we sing. We move as the spirit moves us, dancing, turning. When we come to rest, we sit, emptied of song, on the ground and let the flute song fill our bodies. We pass around a bowl of berries, each person taking one and offering into the circle thoughts of thanksgiving for particular gifts of spring. Brimming with love for the embodied wisdom of Gaia, we bid farewell to the presence of the four directions and break the circle. Then come feasting and visiting. Thus do we welcome spring.

THE ECOLOGICAL IMPERATIVE

. . . Our species is but one expression of the cosmos. We have always played an interactive role with the rest of the Earth community. There is no possibility that we could refrain from intervention; even walking down a street, we probably crush countless tiny creatures. Our bodies require food, warmth, clothing, and shelter—all of which we take from earth-stuff. The *problem* is the denial of humility and care that marks the modern and ultra-modern revolutions against the integrity of Gaia, a dynamic unfolding that was well established long before our emergence. Our species' ethics should include the fulfilling of our vital needs with minimal damage to our cosmic relations. If that were our guideline, we would surely have to admit that our knowledge of the intricacies of Gaian life is so far from complete that we should make far-reaching changes in the ecosystems only with great caution.

Since the dominant culture continues to rush in the opposite direction—cleaning up a few production processes, for example, while still maintaining ravenous growth economies that devour habitats with dazzling efficiency—Gaian spirituality calls for ''action prayers,'' activist engagement with those human systems that are furthering the gratuitous destruction of the Earth community. Much ''green'' activism in the industrialized nations as well as the Third and Fourth Worlds has been sustained by spiritual commitment.

Commitment, to be effective, must also be informed. Understanding basic principles of ecology—interdependence, diversity, resilience, adaptability, and limits—is necessary in opposing unwise human intervention.[5] People with untempered faith in the supposedly value-free, objective life of technology often insist that environmental dynamics are so complicated that the public should back off and let commissions of scientific experts make all decisions, which would then be enacted by government. If memory serves, that course of action gave us scores of dangerous nuclear power plants; numerous disastrous assaults on the ecological integrity of watersheds by the U.S. Army Corps of Engineers; approval of hundreds of toxic compounds for agricultural, industrial, and medical uses; and a flood of federal research funding for the development of genetically engineered animals, pesticides, and crops without adequate testing of *dynamic* interaction, such as will occur in a real ecosystem once a new microorganism leaves the lab. The burden of proof (of safety) should be on the people pushing for novel, substantial change in the ecosystems, not on the citizens calling for caution.

Not only is it difficult for concerned citizens working through existing channels in modern technocracies to defend sustainability against destructive projects that will boost the GNP (a tally that includes costs of attempted environmental cleanup as if it were merely part of value-free production and services), but the voices of millions of other residents are not heard at all. In a parliament of all species, humans' expansionist schemes for industrial mastery of the biosphere would no doubt be hooted off the floor as too unbearably callous, greedy, and murderous to merit a formal vote. Because the existing governmental channels in societies with growth economies are not designed to welcome sustainable earth ethics in more than superficial ways, grassroots movements have had to mount direct, usually nonviolent, challenges to ecocide. Such campaigns demand much time and energy and often yield frustration. Yet, for increasing numbers of people worldwide, that work is experienced not merely as attempts to save enough of the biosphere for human survival, but as moral acts that embody our felt connection with the sacred whole. John Seed, a defender of the rain forests in Australia, has described the Gaian spiritual transformation he underwent in the course of his activism: " 'I am protecting the rainforest' develops to 'I am part of the rainforest protecting myself. I am that part of the rainforest recently emerged into thinking.' " Through continuing engagement, he has found, one's Gaian memory improves.[6] . . .

CULTURAL FEMINISM AND THE HISTORY OF GODDESS SPIRITUALITY

Since the midseventies a movement of spiritual renewal that honors nature, the female, and the body has flourished in our society: the reclaiming of Goddess spirituality. The genesis of this recovery was part of the movement by many women from radical to cultural feminism, although there is still much overlap. In the initial burst of the current wave of feminism, the source of women's oppression was located in "male chauvinism" and "white males." Some feminists still cite the latter term as the cause of social ills. Many of us, however, came to focus attention on the dynamics of *acculturation* that maintained attitudes devaluing women. We located the problem in socialization rather than in oppressive types of supposedly inherent masculine behavior. Hence there is a good deal of common ground between cultural feminism and certain aspects of deconstructive-postmodern feminism.[7]

In my own life, I can recall the exact moment of the shift to a cultural analysis. I was traveling to a meditation retreat in 1974 in New Mexico from southern Illinois in a Volkswagen "Beetle" with two friends from our local women's center. Someone had recommended *The First Sex* by Elizabeth Gould Davis, which I had purchased and was reading in the backseat. Over the engine noise I would call out,

"Amazing! Listen to this!" and read passage after passage. Davis revealed countless examples of how woman's cultural and legal status declined as Christianity gradually transformed the Celtic societies in France, England, Ireland, the Rhineland, and elsewhere. She also noted that Christian conversion succeeded in Celtic Europe only when the people agreed to accept "Mary" as a new name for the Goddess. As I read on with sustained astonishment, the fixed entity that had been taught to me as "history" disassembled along Interstate 40, and I saw for the first time that *patriarchy is a cultural construct*—although I did not conclude, as deconstructionists do, that there is *nothing but* cultural construction in human experience. (Even though I could see that Davis made a number of unwarranted leaps in her conclusions, I hope her memory will be honored as a catalyst for the more careful studies that followed.)

Cultural feminism has focused on prepatriarchal culture (such as Neolithic Old Europe), nonpatriarchal culture (such as the Hopi), dynamics of oppression in patriarchal culture, and creative possibilities for postpatriarchal culture. From this branch of feminism the terms "patriarchal culture," "patriarchal religion," and so forth have spread to the others. That the informing expressions of the prepatriarchal Neolithic era stood out in our readings, fixing the attention of women who had been raised in patriarchal religion, is not surprising. Feminist critiques of the Jewish and Christian traditions were already in the air,[8] but they did not offer the spark of possibility that we found in poring over statues, symbols, and mythic narratives from the age of the Goddess. We discovered powerful female bodies of all sizes honored and revered; statues that were half bird and half female, linking humanity with the rest of nature; ritual figurines of female bodies incised with representations of life-giving water; symbols of the sacred pelvic triangle of the female; and sacred myths of the transformative powers of the Earth and the female celebrated in ecstatic dance and holy rite. Imagine our surprise.

During that period of awakening I became engrossed with reconstructing the pre-Olympian myths of early Greece, the sacred stories and symbolism of the pre-Hellenic goddesses, whose artifacts, shrines, and other historic documentation long predate the arrival of the Indo-European thunderbolt god, Zeus, and his patriarchal soap opera on Mount Olympus.[9] The shift from the pre–Indo-European religion (centered on goddesses, who were enmeshed with people's daily experiencing of the energy forces in life and who were powerful sources of compassion and protection, as well as inspiration for divine wisdom and just law) to the Indo-Europeanized Greek religion (centered on a chieftain sky-god who was "up there" and remote, judgmental, warlike, and often involved in local strife) was well established. Yet I and other "spirituality feminists" were curious to know more about the societal transformation in which the disempowerment of the Goddess was embedded.

Over the years numerous studies have appeared documenting widespread occurrences of Goddess spirituality in Old Europe, the Middle East, Asia, Africa, and the Americas. It would be most interesting if an international task force of cultural historians were constituted to assemble and synthesize all the evidence regarding the myriad incidents of societal shift from Goddess to God, from matrifocal to patriarchal culture. (Most feminist cultural historians interested in the long era of the Goddess in various societies avoid the term "matriarchal," since the archaeological findings usually indicate a roughly gender-egalitarian society or are inconclusive regarding sex-role dominance—although many excavated sites clearly do reflect the centrality of women's social roles. Because "matriarchy" connotes the inverse of a power-over, male-dominant society, cultural feminists and several archaeologists prefer to use *matrifocal, matristic, matricentric, gynecentric,* and so forth, since the cultural artifacts demonstrate a focus on the transformative powers of the female regardless of whatever the exact form of government may have been.) Eventually, many matrifocal, matrilineal cultures were pressured to shift to patriarchal arrangements when they were confronted with dominant forces of Christianity, Islam, or Eurocentric colonialism.[10] Male-dominant cultures certainly existed before those powerful forces of social, economic, and religious conversion spread out over the world, but they did account for a sizable boost in the incidence of patriarchal societies. . . .

EARTHBODY AND PERSONAL BODY AS SACRED

The contemporary renaissance of Goddess spirituality draws on a growing body of knowledge about historical Goddess religion but is shaped and energized by the living practice, which is both personal and communal, ancient and spontaneous. The initial response to learning of the historical presence of Goddess religion, at least for myself, was wonder, followed by gratitude that the entire phenomenon, which had nearly been paved over by patriarchal culture, might now be known. That wonder was followed by puzzlement at what Goddess religion might mean to the spiritual lives of women in contemporary circumstances. Poring over the hundreds of photographs of Goddess figurines, bas-reliefs, and frescoes, one could not fail to grasp the centrality of the elemental power of the female body, jarring as that was to any reader raised under patriarchy.[11] Absorbing even a little of that orientation made it easy to see why our Neolithic, and probably even our Paleolithic, ancestors perceived the bountiful manifestations of the Earth as emanating from a fertile body—an immense female whose tides moved in rhythm with the moon, whose rivers sustained life, whose soil/flesh yielded food, whose caves offered ritual womb-rooms for ceremonies of sacred community within her body, whose vast subterranean womb received all humans in burial. It is not difficult to understand why they held Her sacred.

To even attempt to surmise the Neolithic thought processes that informed the artistic expressions of female forms and the ritual practices that must have surrounded them, however, was more difficult, even though Gimbutas's work has helped to sort the multiplicity of forms and focus on the recurring symbols of water, birth, regeneration, and so forth.[12] Stare as one might at, say, a small sculpted circle of ritual female dancers, one could not know, more than five thousand years later, what the actual and entire practice has been. Hence the contemporary expressions of Goddess spirituality, including its flowering in the arts,[13] are not simply attempts to replicate the extremely ancient religion that long preceded "the lost weekend" of patriarchal culture. Rather, they are creative spiritual practice, which is embedded in a profound historical tradition and, more fundamentally, in the female dimension of being.

Some forms of contemporary Goddess spirituality are entirely "free-form," creating practices by drawing directly on inspiration from the artifacts, myths, and other remnants of Goddess religion in early Greece, the biblical lands, Africa, Asia, and the pre-Columbian Americas. Other forms involved participation in mediating traditions, that is, systems of worship such as Goddess-centered "native European" witchcraft or the African-based folk religions of the Caribbean and Brazil. Some ancient traditions of Goddess spirituality, such as that of the Goddess Akonedi in Ghana, have spread to Europe and the Americas in recent decades through immigration. While there is great diversity within contemporary Goddess spirituality, the common threads among the forms that grew out of feminist renewal are the desire to honor the Earthbody and one's personal body via an ongoing birthing process of cosmological unfolding—the intention to articulate as deeply and fully as possible one's ontological potential as an embodied Earthbeing, a weaver of the cosmic web. . . .

The contemporary practice of Goddess spirituality includes creative participation in myth, symbol, and ritual. Because this spiritual orientation honors the elemental power of the female and its embeddedness in nature, it was perceived as regressive, embarrassing, or even horrifying to liberal and material/socialist feminists, who apparently accepted the patriarchal dualism of nature-versus-culture and had internalized the patriarchal rationalization that the reason women had traditionally been blocked from participation in culture was their bodily "plight" of being mired in the reproductive processes of nature. Investing their consciousness within such an orientation, it is quite understandable that "modern" feminists recoil (I use the present tense here because it still occurs today) when "spiritual feminists" celebrate our bodies and our elemental connectedness with nature. If one subscribes to the patriarchal view of culture as human endeavor pursued in opposition to nature, drawing attention to such connections automatically places women outside the realm of culture as "biological

agents" *instead of* "cultural agents." The renewal of Goddess spirituality, however, rejected the patriarchal dualism from the outset. Like countless prepatriarchal and nonpatriarchal societies, we women who had drifted out of patriarchal religion[14] view culture not as a struggle in opposition to nature but as a potentially harmonious extension of nature, a human construction inclusive of creative tensions and reflective of our embeddedness in the Earthbody and the teachings of nature: diversity, subjectivity, adaptability, interrelatedness. Within such an orientation—let's call it ecological sanity—the bodily affinity of females and males with nature is respected and culturally honored, rather than denied and scorned.

The central understanding in contemporary Goddess spirituality is that the divine—creativity in the universe, or ultimate mystery—is laced throughout the cosmic manifestations in and around us. The divine is immanent, not concentrated in some distant seat of power, a transcendent sky-god. Instead of accepting the notion in patriarchal religion that one must spiritually transcend the body and nature, it is possible to apprehend divine transcendence as the sacred whole, or the infinite complexity of the universe. The Goddess, as a metaphor for divine immanence and the transcendent sacred whole, expresses ongoing regeneration with the cycles of her Earthbody and contains the mystery of diversity within unity: the extraordinary range of differentiation in forms of life on Earth issued from her dynamic form and are kin. A second aspect of contemporary Goddess spirituality is the empowerment experienced by people as they come to grasp their heritage and presence in terms of the cosmological self, the dimension of human existence that participates in the larger reality. Such empowerment is far different from a dominating "power-over," the binding force of social constructions in a patriarchal culture. Rather, it is a strengthening of one's capabilities of subjectivity and cosmic unfolding within a web of caring and solidarity that extends backward and forward in time, drawing one from the fragmentation and lonely atomization of modernity to the deepest levels of connectedness. A third aspect of Goddess spirituality is the perceptual shift from the death-based sense of existence that underlies patriarchal culture to a regeneration-based awareness, an embrace of life as a cycle of creative rebirths, a dynamic participation in the processes of infinity.

. . . Goddess spirituality celebrates the power of the erotic as the sparking of cosmic potential, rather than wrestling with the erotic as a process that potentially yields a new generation and hence the signal of one's approaching end. The erotic and the sensuous, expressed through the aesthetic, draw forth not only physical generation but unpredictably creative waves of spiritual, intellectual, and emotional renewal. . . .

NOTES

1. All-species parades are community celebrations of the animal citizens in the bioregion. Generally they feature children in costumes of local animals. Further information is available from the All-Species Project, 804 Apodaca Hill, Santa Fe, NM 85701.

2. For example, a tree-planting ceremony at home or on public land needing more vegetation could be part of rites of baptism, First Communion, marriage, and funerals. The liturgical language used in all of those ceremonies could be enriched by including awareness and appreciation of the creation.

   An example of moving in the other direction, that is, bringing rituals of blessing and thanksgiving to events of the natural world, is offered by Gertrude Mueller Nelson in "Blessing for First Fruits and Herbs," using Psalm 65 and derived from "the old ones found in the Roman Ritual" in her inspiring book *To Dance with God: Family Ritual and Community Celebration* (Mahwah, NJ: Paulist Press, 1986), 211.

3. People who observe all eight of the old "Earth holy days" usually consider themselves part of the neo-Pagan movement. "Pagan" means "country person."

4. The spring garland for the Earth in that ritual was the idea of the late Leslie Mahler, a creative and inspiring ritualist whose presence is deeply missed. Some of the other elements, including the songs, traveled from other ritual groups. A cassette tape of several widely used Earth-ritual songs, *Reclaiming Chants,* is available from the Reclaiming Collective, P.O. Box 14404, San Francisco, CA 94114.

5. A good textbook on ecology is *Living in the Environment* by G. Tyler Miller, Jr. (Belmont, CA: Wadsworth Publishing, 1982).

6. John Seed, "Beyond Anthropocentrism," in John Seed, Joanna Macy, Pat Fleming, and Arne Naess, *Thinking Like a Mountain: Towards a Council of All Beings* (Philadelphia and Santa Cruz: New Society Publishers, 1988), 36.

7. . . . Two . . . expressions of cultural feminism are my "Naming the Cultural Forces that Push Us toward War" in *Exposing Nuclear Phallacies,* ed. Diana E.H. Russell (New York: Pergamon Press, 1989) and my introduction to *The Politics of Women's Spirituality* (Garden City, NY: Doubleday, 1982), which proposes, among other things, that cultural power hoarded by males is a compensatory response to a fearful perception of the elemental power of the female, and that Jungian notions of the "eternal feminine" and the passive receptivity it entails are cultural constructions of patriarchy rather than universal truths about females.

8. See Mary Daly, *The Church and the Second Sex* (New York: Harper & Row, 1968) and Elizabeth Cady Stanton and the Revising Committee, *The Woman's Bible* (1985), republished as *The Original Feminist Attack on the Bible* (New York: Arno Press, 1974). Also available by then was Mary Daly's *Beyond God the Father: Toward a Philosophy of Women's Liberation* (Boston: Beacon Press, 1973), which she refers to in the introduction as a sequel to *The Church and the Second Sex* and which advocated women's charting a postpatriarchal path.

   It is important to note that Canaan was one of the last, not first, areas in the eastern Mediterranean region and southeastern Europe to "go patriarchal." The Yahwehists who migrated into Canaan definitely were not the sole cause of the destruction of all Goddess religion.

9. See Charlene Spretnak, *Lost Goddesses of Early Greece: A Collection of Pre-Hellenic Myths* (Boston: Beacon Press, 1981).

10. See, for example, Peggy Reeves Sanday, "The Decline of the Women's World: The Effect of Colonialism," chapter seven, in *Female Power and Male Dominance: On the Origins of Sexual Inequality* (Cambridge: Cambridge University Press, 1981).

11. For a thoughtful exploration of this experience, see Adrienne Rich, "Prepatriarchal Female/Goddess Images," in *The Politics of Women's Spirituality* (Garden City, NY: Doubleday, 1982), excerpted from her *Of Woman Born: Motherhood as Experience and Institution* (New York: W.W. Norton, 1976).

12. See Gimbutas, *Language of the Goddess.*

   Skeptics sometimes accuse feminist cultural historians of "prettifying" the pre-Indo-European goddesses by ignoring the bloodthirsty, devouring ones, which they are certain must have existed. Actually, those forms seem to arise with the advent of patriarchal culture. The prepatriarchal goddesses represented the entire cycle of being—birth, maturation, death, regeneration—but apparently not as demonic forces. Even Kali, the devouring Hindu goddess, is believed by many scholars to be a revised version of an indigenous Earth goddess who long predated the Aryan invasion; see the discussion by David R. Kinsley in chapter three of *The Sword and the Flute: Kali and Krsna* (Berkeley: University of California Press, 1975).

13. See Elinor W. Gadon, *The Once and Future Goddess* (San Francisco: Harper & Row, 1989) and Gloria Feman Orenstein, *The Reflowering of the Goddess* (New York: Pergamon Press, 1990).

   Also see Mary Beth Edelson, *Seven Cycles: Public Rituals; Seven Sites: Painting on Walls;* and *Shape Shifters: Seven Mediums* (all available from the artist: 110 Mercer St., New York, NY 10012).

   Also see Janine Canan, ed., *She Rises Like the Sun; Invocations of the Goddess by Contemporary American Women Poets* (Freedom, CA: The Crossing Press, 1989).

14. Although the focus of this chapter is the renewal of Goddess spirituality by women who left institutional patriarchal religion, I do not mean to imply that only those women who left were feminist. A strong feminist movement exists today within both Judaism and Christianity. . . .

DISCUSSION TOPICS

1. Have you had experiences of oneness with nature? Have these experiences seemed remote from your daily life? Why do you believe that such experiences should (or should not) be cultivated?

2. Spretnak affirms that women have a special connection with the Earthbody. Do you agree with her? Why or why not?

3. Do you believe it is important to establish whether Earth Goddess-worshipping cultures have existed? What relevance, if any, would these be to environmental ethics? Explain.

CLASS EXERCISES

1. Have students write down their associations with the terms "masculine," "feminine," and "na-

ture." Which terms overlap the most? The least? Have the students share these results in small groups, with one student then summarizing the results to report to the class.

CLASS DEBATE

Organize a debate with Resolved: Women are closer to nonhuman animals and the earth than are men. (See the description of classroom debates in Appendix A.)

FOR FURTHER READING

Biehl, Janet. *Rethinking Ecofeminist Politics.* Boston: South End Press, 1991. A critique of ecofeminism by a social ecologist. Biehl argues that ecofeminism is a regressive force, particularly in its embrace of goddess worship, emphasis on metaphors and myths, and its glorification of the early Neolithic. Ecofeminism situates women outside of Western culture as essentially "natural."

Collard, Andree, with Joyce Contrucci. *Rape of the Wild: Man's Violence against Animals and the Earth.* Bloomington, Ind.: Indiana University Press, 1989. A powerful and eloquent statement of the patriarchal connection between the violation of nature, animals, and women. Includes animal experimentation, hunting, and space exploration.

Dexter, Miriam Robbins. *Whence the Goddesses: A Source Book.* New York: Pergamon Press, 1990. A clearly written, scholarly study of ancient female- and male-centered theologies, the assimilation of eight groups of Neolithic European and Near Eastern goddesses, and a discussion of the functions of the female in male-centered society. Extensive notes in original languages.

Diamond, Irene and Gloria Feman Orenstein. *Reweaving the World: The Emergence of Ecofeminism.* San Francisco: Sierra Club Books, 1990. A valuable collection of essays expressive of the many facets of ecofeminism.

Griffin, Susan. *Woman and Nature: The Roaring Inside Her.* New York: Harper & Row, 1980. A pioneering, lyrical, and immensely powerful account which juxtaposes patriarchal judgments about the nature of matter and the nature of women.

Hallen, Patsy. "Making Peace with the Environment: Why Ecology Needs Feminism." *The Trumpeter* 4:3-14, 1987. A wide-ranging, clearly written argument for the feminist reconstruction of society, including natural science.

Hypatia: A Journal of Feminist Philosophy, 6:1-218, 1991. Special Issue on Ecological Feminism, ed. Karen J. Warren. The first collection of explicitly philosophical essays on ecological feminism.

Keller, Evelyn Fox. *A Feeling for the Organism: The Life and Work of Barbara McClintock.* San Francisco: W.H. Freeman and Co., 1983. A perceptive study of a scientist, often cited by ecofeminists, whose exceptional work in plant genetics and cytology has incorporated respect and love for plants.

Matthews, Freya. *The Ecological Self.* Savage, Md.: Barnes and Noble, 1991. Matthews presents a metaphysical vision of the ''geometrodynamical universe'' as a self.

Merchant, Carolyn. *The Death of Nature: Women, Ecology and Scientific Revolution.* San Francisco: Harper & Row, 1989. A masterly study of how during 1500 to 1700 the organic conception of the cosmos with a ''living female earth at its center'' gave way to a mechanistic model, with a dead and passive nature. Merchant argues that concepts of nature and women are historical and social constructions. Contains extensive notes.

Orenstein, Gloria Feman. *The Reflowering of the Goddess.* New York: Pergamon Press, 1990. An integration of art, literature, history, and spirituality. Extensive bibliography.

Plant, Judith, ed. *Healing the Wounds: The Promise of Ecofeminism.* Philadelphia: New Society Publishers, 1989. A collection of accessible essays and some poetry from a spectrum of ecofeminists.

Ruether, Rosemary. *New Woman/New Earth: Sexist Ideologies and Human Liberation.* New York: Seabury Press, 1975. A historical critique of patriarchy and a sketch of an egalitarian society by a prominent Christian theologian.

CHAPTER TEN

Judeo-Christian Perspectives

Judaism and Christianity have strongly influenced philosophical perspectives in contemporary Western society, even among those who are not religious adherents. It is difficult, if not impossible, to evaluate Western values and behaviors without assessing the historical contributions of these pervasive and powerful traditions. In this chapter we begin by identifying the key problems associated with using Judeo-Christian sources in formulating an environmental ethic. We then summarize the Biblical view of God's relationship to nature, and identify central ideas that might underly a biblically based environmental ethic. Although we recognize that Judaism and Christianity are distinct religious traditions, there is sufficient continuity between the Hebrew and Christian scriptures to permit an integrated discussion about their perspectives toward the natural world.

PROBLEMS IN USING JUDAISM AND CHRISTIANITY AS SOURCES FOR AN ENVIRONMENTAL ETHIC

There are at least three problems in using Judeo-Christian sources as a foundation for developing an environmental ethic. One general problem confronting any ethic based on a religion is that its appeal may be limited to the community of believers. Another problem is that Judaism and Christianity are considered by some to be the sources of many of the most negative attitudes toward nature held in Western society. A less commonly noted problem is that the Bible does not explicitly address environmental issues, per se, and thus environmental ethics based on Biblical sources are necessarily derived from scholars' interpretations of what they consider to be relevant passages.

As mentioned, basing a universal environmental ethic on a particular religious perspective can limit its appeal. In addition, within the Judeo-Christian framework there are many sects and systems of belief. Representatives of the various denominations often disagree with one another, making it difficult to identify a core of common doctrines and beliefs on which to build an environmental ethic. Despite these problems, any major religion providing the foundation for a cogent and workable environmental ethic could serve as a powerful unifying force in determining the environmental choices and actions for a large number of people.

Of greater concern is the charge that the tenets of Christianity and Judaism held by adherents may be among the principal causes of the environmental crisis. Lynn White, Jr.[1] presents an articulate summary of this charge. White's thesis is that Christianity bears a major responsibility for the current environmental crisis in Western society. He believes the solutions lie either in altering the Christian religion significantly, or in abandoning it altogether. White's first preference is to use St. Francis of Assisi as a model for Christian living. Alternatively, he suggests replacing Christianity with Zen Buddhism or another more ecologically sensitive non-Western religion. While numerous writers have echoed White's perception, many others have opposed it; representatives of both perspectives are included in a selection of references at the end of this chapter. However, as summarized earlier in Chapter 4, Historical Context, the consensus of authors is that the influence of Greek philosophy on Western attitudes toward the environment probably is as great as, or greater than, that exercised by Judaisim and Christianity.

Other writers, such as Christopher Stone,[2] have argued that the environmental destruction in Western society may not have been caused by any specific ideology. Stone suggests a simpler scenario. There has been an increasing number of humans, with increasing wants, and there has been an increasing technology to satisfy those wants at cost to the environment. Stone's scenario suggests a dominance of strong anthropocentrism, as defined in Chapter 6.

Hargrove[3] suggests that White's thesis is inadvertently framed to ensure that no useful outcome would result. While many acknowledge that Christianity makes an important contribution to current Western attitudes toward nature, almost no one is willing to accept either of the alternative solutions White presents. Thus, with the guilt of Christianity at least partly justified, but the solutions to the problem unacceptable, the argument has little likelihood of yielding a satisfactory resolution. Hargrove argues it is time to move beyond this debate and seek new directions. He proposes evaluating how major religions, including Christianity, can best respond to the environmental crisis. Whatever eventual responsibility is assigned to Christianity for the environmental attitudes currently held in Western society, we believe Hargrove is correct in moving beyond the White debate. His proposal to determine if Christianity and other major religions are able to provide a strong and workable foundation for an environmental ethic is a good place to start.

In addressing the potential of Judaism and Christianity to provide such a foundation, some might question whether they have enough of substance to say about environmental ethics in contemporary Western society. Biblical writers are most concerned about understanding the proper relationship between God and humanity, and, secondarily, in understanding the proper relationships among human beings. Insights about human responsibility toward the land, wildlife, and ecosystems seem, at best, distant considerations. Indeed, the ecological concepts which underlie contemporary environmental perspectives were not a part of the Biblical writers' world view. However, the authors in this chapter all believe that a careful interpretation of Biblical literature, and a thoughtful evaluation of Judeo-Christian insights can provide a firm foundation for an environmental ethic.

THE RELATION OF GOD TO NATURE IN JUDEO-CHRISTIAN THEOLOGY

There is a rich variety of perspectives about God's relationship to nature represented in the Judeo-Christian tradition. A few preliminary definitions may help clarify some of these perspectives. The terms *deism* and *theism* signify alternative views of God's role in the universe. Proponents of deism believe that after creation God exerted no further control over the universe, including in the lives of human beings. In contrast, proponents of theism believe that God continues to care about and exert some control over the universe, the natural world, and humans. Also, theists believe that God is known through revelation, both through

1. Lynn R. White, Jr., ''The Historical Roots of our Ecological Crisis,'' *Science* 155 (1967): 1203-1207.

2. Christopher D. Stone, ''Should Trees Have Standing?—Toward Legal Rights for Natural Objects,'' *Southern California Law Review* 45 (1972): 450-501.

3. Eugene C. Hargrove, *Religion and Environmental Crisis* (Athens, Ga.: The University of Georgia Press, 1986), pp. ix-xix.

divine interaction with humans in history, and through increasing knowledge and insight about the natural world (creation). All of the authors in this chapter advocate some form of theism.

Transcendent monotheism is the traditional Judeo-Christian perspective. Proponents of this view affirm that God existed prior to the universe, created it, and rules over it. God is separate from and superior to the creation (nature). Susan Bratton in "Christian Ecotheology and the Old Testament" and Wendell Berry in "The Gift of Good Land" develop environmental ethics founded primarily on a transcendent monotheistic perspective. Both writers draw almost exclusively on Old Testament writings.

A view generally rejected in Judaism and Christianity, and which offers a striking contrast to transcendent monotheism, is pantheism. Pantheism is the doctrine that God is everything, and that everything collectively comprises God. In pantheism, the universe and God are considered to be the same. Harold Wood[4] has proposed pantheism as a basis for an environmental ethic.

In contrast to pantheism, an alternative to transcendent monotheism which generally is acceptable to Judaism and Christianity is panentheism, the perspective that God includes the world, but the world is not the whole of God's being. Thus, God is not identical with nature, but is both immanent in and transcendent to nature. Michael Zimmerman in his essay, "Quantum Theory, Intrinsic Value, and Panentheism," presents an environmental ethic from a panentheistic perspective. Evolutionary panentheism is founded on the notion that God is present in and continues to evolve along with the creation.

An idea closely related to evolutionary panenthe-

ism is process theology, which is founded on Alfred North Whitehead's ideas[5] that the universe is not composed of inert matter, but instead is a continuous series of events and interactions—a process. Jay McDaniel, a theologian, in his essay, "Christian Spirituality as Openness to Fellow Creatures," has incorporated the tenets of process theology into an environmental theology.

St. Francis of Assisi does not easily fit into any of these categories. In his writing, as exemplified in the poem, "The Canticle of Brother Sun," St. Francis deemphasizes hierarchies and dualism, and maintains that everything has a direct relationship to God. Thus, he probably is best described as expressing a panentheistic perspective.

IDEAS UNDERLYING A JUDEO-CHRISTIAN ENVIRONMENTAL ETHIC

There are at least three ideas articulated by the authors of this chapter that can serve as a foundation for a Judeo-Christian-based environmental ethic. One notion is that the world is God's creation. Second, God is pleased with the results of this creative handiwork. Finally, God values all of the creation—the individual members of creation as well as the underlying processes and relations among them.

These three ideas support the view that each part of nature is something precious to God. It follows readily that to honor God, one must honor the creation which God loves. Each author shares a vision of how this can and should occur.

---

4. Harold W. Wood, "Modern Pantheism as an Approach to Environmental Ethics," *Environmental Ethics* 7 (1985): 151-163.

5. Alfred North Whitehead (1861–1947) is one of the greatest philosophers of the twentieth century. His best known work is *Science and the Modern World* (New York: The Macmillan Company, 1925). Whitehead's major work was *Process and Reality: An Essay in Cosmology* (New York: Social Science Book Store, 1929).

The Canticle of Brother Sun

St. Francis of Assisi

St. Francis of Assisi (1182?–1226) was born Giovanni di Bernardone in Assisi, Umbria, Italy. He exemplified humility, absolute poverty, unconditional love and devotion to others, and great religious fervor. He founded the Franciscan order of friars in the Roman Catholic Church.

In his famous poem, "The Canticle of Brother Sun," St. Francis is believed to express some of his deepest feelings and insights. The poem provides a clear contrast to a more traditional anthropocentric Christian perspective by stressing a nonhierarchical spiritual egalitarianism with nature. St. Francis does not believe that the elements of nature belong to the category of "things"; rather, he emphasizes his personal relationship with them, much like the I-Thou relationship articulated by Martin Buber. In "The Canticle of Brother Sun" St. Francis joyously celebrates the close spiritual relationship of all of nature to God.

1. Most High, all-powerful, good Lord,
   Yours are the praises, the glory, the honor, and all blessing.[1]
2. To You alone, Most High, do they belong,
   and no man is worthy to mention Your name.
3. Praised be You, my Lord, with all your creatures,
   especially Sir Brother Sun,
   Who is the day and through whom You give us light.
4. And he is beautiful and radiant with great splendor;
   and bears a likeness of You, Most High One.
5. Praised be You, my Lord, through Sister Moon and the stars,[2]
   in heaven You formed them clear and precious and beautiful.
6. Praised be You, my Lord, through Brother Wind,
   and through the air, cloudy and serene, and every kind of weather
   through which You give sustenance to Your creatures.
7. Praised be You, my Lord, through Sister Water,
   which is very useful and humble and precious and chaste.
8. Praised be You, my Lord, through Brother Fire,
   through whom You light the night
   and he is beautiful and playful and robust and strong.
9. Praised be You, my Lord, through our Sister Mother Earth,
   who sustains and governs us,
   and who produces varied fruits with colored flowers and herbs.
10. Praised be You, my Lord, through those who give pardon for Your love[3]
    and bear infirmity and tribulation.
11. Blessed are those who endure in peace
    for by You, Most High, they shall be crowned.
12. Praised be You, my Lord, through our Sister Bodily Death,[4]
    from whom no living man can escape.
13. Woe to those who die in mortal sin.
    Blessed are those whom death will find in Your most holy will,
    for the second death shall do them no harm.[5]
14. Praise and bless my Lord and give Him thanks
    and serve Him with great humility.

NOTES

1. Cf. Rev. 4:9, 11.
2. It is important to penetrate the meaning of the word *per,* which Saint Francis uses throughout the remainder of his first section. It suggests a corruption of the Latin *per,* or the French *pour,* and the developing Italian *par.* Thus it may be translated "for," suggesting an attitude of thanksgiving; "by," expressing a sense of instrumentality; or "through," indicating instrumentality as well as a deeper sense of mysticism in perceiving God's presence in all creation. All translations are acceptable. [We] accept the final translation, since it is more consistent with the witness of Saint Bonaventure's theology of exemplarism, e.g., *Itinerarium mentis in Deum, Legenda major,* IX, 1.
3. The second section of the Canticle begins with this stanza. Since the human person is not part of the chorus of the previous section, he now enters into the hymn through an identification with the God-man, Jesus

Christ, i.e., by suffering weakness and tribulation, pardoning out of love, and enduring in peace.

4. The third section begins with this stanza.

5. Cf. Rev. 2:11; 20:6. Saint Fulgentius of Ruspe comments on these verses in his treatise on forgiveness: ''Here on earth they are changed by the first resurrection, in which they are enlightened and converted, thus passing from death to life, sinfulness to holiness, unbelief to faith, and evil actions to holy life. For this reason the second death has no power over them. . . . As the first resurrection consists of the conversion of the heart, so the second death consists of unending torment'' (cf. Saint Fulgentius of Ruspe, *On Forgiveness,* Liber 2, 11, 2–12, 1. 3–4, *Corpus Christianoum* 91A, 693–695).

DISCUSSION TOPICS

1. What are some of the key features of St. Francis's environmental philosophy that can be derived from his canticle?

2. In what ways is your own environmental ethic similar to and different from the convictions expressed by St. Francis?

READING 61

Christian Ecotheology and the Old Testament

Susan Power Bratton

Susan Power Bratton (b. 1948) is a professional research biologist with the U.S. National Park Service Cooperative Unit at the University of Georgia, Athens, Georgia. She conducted her work at the Institute of Ecology, at The University of Georgia.

Bratton seeks to define the proper relationship between humans and the environment through an analysis of Old Testament themes, including the stories of God's creation. She maintains that many significant themes have been misunderstood or overlooked, in part because of the theocentric nature of the Old Testament and the wide dispersion of relevant passages within these texts. Bratton believes that God's role as Creator should be seen within

the context of other major Old Testament themes such as the covenant relationship and salvation. Bratton analyzes the role of the Creator God and the role of humans in developing a Christian ecotheology, and she argues that while Old Testament writers clearly separate God from nature, they do give intrinsic value to nature. Bratton also asserts that humans hold dominion and have special responsibilities toward God's creation, requiring them to be faithful, self-disciplined, diligent, giving, and forgiving stewards.

INTRODUCTION

The role of Judeo-Christian theology in developing environmental ethics has often been portrayed as negative or inadequate to modern problems. Historians, such as Lynn White, Jr. and Roderick Nash, have blamed either the Church or Biblical writings for encouraging abuse of nature.[1] Even modern theologians from the Christian tradition, such as John B. Cobb, Jr., find the traditional Judeo-Christian view inadequate and have suggested we must seek new theological or philosophical alternatives.[2] The question is a complex one, however, because the Western Church has, through the centuries, neglected the study of creation.[3] Interest in creation theology has been minor compared to other doctrinal issues such soteriology and Christology, and many Christian scholars have a better understanding of the Greek texts than of the older Hebrew writings. The attitude of the Church may, therefore, not have been based on a thorough analysis of Scripture. Further, the recognition of a global environmental crisis is a recent phenomenon; our current scientific understanding of the processes of environmental change was not available at the time the scriptures were written.

One possible way to develop a sound Christian

---

1. Lynn White, Jr., ''The Historical Roots of Our Ecological Crisis,'' *Science* 155 (1967): 1203-1207; Roderick Nash, *Wilderness and the American Mind* (New Haven: Yale University Press, 1970).

2. John B. Cobb, Jr., *Is It Too Late? A Theology of Ecology* (Beverly Hills, Calif.: Bruce, 1972).

3. James B. Packer, ''The Gospel: Its Content and Communication,'' in John Scott and Robert Coote, eds., *Down to Earth: Studies in Christianity and Culture* (Grand Rapids: William B. Eerdmans, 1980), pp. 97–114.

ecotheology, and to determine a proper Christian approach to environmental ethics, is first to analyze scriptural texts concerning God-creation and man-creation relationships. We can then draw an accurate picture of what the Biblical writers originally meant when discussing creation. My purpose in this paper is to look at the works of modern Old Testament scholars, particularly Walther Eichrodt, Gerhard von Rad, and Claus Westermann, who have made substantial contributions to our current understanding of Hebrew theology, including theology of creation. I begin with an overview of important components of Old Testament thinking on both creation and God as creator, and discuss these ideas in relation to the development of a viable Christian ecotheology.

It should be pointed out at the beginning that modern Old Testament critics are not in agreement regarding the best methodology for analysis; nor do they all handle the question of the historical content of the texts in the same way. Some critics treat the Old Testament as if it has one central theme; others see it as presenting several themes. Some authors, such as Gerhard von Rad and Brevard Childs, attempt to include the entire canon in their work, or at least hold that all the books must be considered, while others, such as Claus Westermann, do not see all the books as equally important or interpretable in terms of central themes. (Westermann omits the wisdom literature from consideration in developing Old Testament theology.) Writers also differ greatly in how they relate the Old Testament to the New Testament: some disregard the New Testament entirely; others attempt to integrate the two sets of works, even though they are the products of different historical and cultural environments and were composed in different languages.[4] Although these disagreements among scholars are important to the detailed study of the Old Testament, they are generally beyond the scope of this paper. I attempt to avoid these conflicts by using the principles for Old Testament theology outlined by Hasel.[5] These are (in edited form):

(1) Biblical theology is to be treated as a historical-

theological discipline,[6] and (2) the method must be historical and theological from the starting point.[7] These are quite different from many attempts at constructing ecotheologies or at evaluating the potential success of a Judeo-Christian ecotheology, in that most such efforts are either historical or theological, but not both.

(3) The only appropriate source for Old Testament theology is the Old Testament, not related literatures and traditions.[8] This principle is important to ecotheologies where authors have seen passages such as the Genesis accounts only as versions of myths derived from other sources. Hasel would reject this treatment as inadequate.

(4) An analysis need not follow the order of books in the canon, but should be based, as best can be determined, on the dates of the writings.[9]

(5) "An OT [Old Testament] theology not only seeks to know the theology of the various books, or groups of writings; it also attempts to draw together and present the major themes of the OT. . . . OT theology must allow its themes, motifs, and concepts to be formed for it by the OT itself."[10] We must, therefore, be careful not to do what many environmental writers have done and see the Old Testament largely from the point of view of our own current philosophical interests and cultural environment. If we are to evaluate Old Testament thought, we must do this with a recognition both of the writers original intentions and the Hebrew world view. Old Testament theology must be based on what the Old Testament itself actually says about something. Further, we must discriminate between those concepts, events, or practices merely recorded or described in the texts and those which are affirmed or condoned. Since any discussion of creation theology must attempt to be eclectic, care must be taken not to replace the priorities of the ancient Hebrews with our own.

(6) "As the OT is interrogated for its theology, it answers first of all by yielding various theologies,

---

4. Gerhard Hasel, *Old Testament Theology: Basic Issues in the Current Debate* (Grand Rapids: William B. Eerdmans, 1972).
5. Ibid., pp. 169-183.

6. Ibid., p. 169.
7. Ibid., p. 171.
8. Ibid., p. 177.
9. Ibid., p. 179.
10. Ibid., p. 180.

namely those of the individual books and groups of writings, and then by yielding the theologies of various longitudinal themes. But the name of our discipline as theology of the OT is not only concerned to present and explicate the variety of different theologies. The concept foreshadowed by the name of the discipline has one theology in views, namely the theology of the OT.''[11] For our purposes, this implies that in analyzing creation theology of the Old Testament, one has to look both at individual books and at the overall presentation of all the books. In light of Hasel's remarks, creation theology might be better termed the ''creation theme'' and seen as one of many theological strands, intimately connected to the other themes that combine to make Old Testament theology. In pursing the creation theme one cannot depend solely on the first few chapters of Genesis, nor can one ignore the wisdom literature. Many writers who have tackled the question of the adequacy of Judeo-Christian environmental ethics, have relied on one or two passages of Scripture and may thus have misunderstood the total thrust of the scriptural texts.[12]

(7) ''The name 'theology of the Old Testament' implies the larger context of the Bible of which the New Testament is the other part. An integral OT theology must demonstrate its basic relationship to the NT or to NT theology.''[13] This is, of course, critical in determining how the Old Testament should relate to Christian ecotheology.

Within this theological framework then, I attempt to develop an overview of the creation theology of the Old Testament, and try to avoid both excessive cultural distortion of the Old Testament's meaning and incomplete analysis of the Hebrew position.

THE CREATOR GOD

Although many environmental commentators begin the discussion of Judeo-Christian ecotheology with the question of man's dominion, most Old Testament commentators begin the discussion of creation theology with an investigation of God as creator. The modern reader tends to look for passages explaining man's relationship to nature, but this is of itself a poor way to start analyzing Old Testament texts, which are very theocentric. Westermann, for example, states: ''A theology of the Old Testament has the task of summarizing and viewing together what the Old Testament as a whole, in all its sections, says about God.''[14]

In order to answer our first question—how does the Old Testament present God as acting in the original creation?—we can begin by comparing the Hebrew presentation to those of neighboring cultures. The Old Testament has some striking parallels to Babylonian creation accounts[15] and was, of course, developed in an environment where there was considerable threat of syncretism with Caanite and Egyptian cultures. Despite some borrowing of imagery, the Hebrew picture of God as creator was quite distinct. In the Babylonian accounts, the god Marduk fights chaos and in the process creates life and order. In the Genesis accounts chaos is mentioned, but is conceptually different. The ''Enuma Elish'' epic of the Babylonians describes a watery chaos that is not only living matter, but is part of the first two principles, Apsu and Tiamat, ''in whom all elements of the future universe were comingled.''[16] Thus, in the Babylonian epic the universe is preexisting. In Genesis, God creates all matter and imparts life to His creatures via His divine breath.[17] The gods of the Babylonians arise out of the primeval chaos and are, therefore, merely deified nat-

11. Ibid., p. 181.

12. Discussions of some of the cultural results of this sort of limited interpretation may be found in Clarence Glacken, *Traces on the Rhodian Shore* (Berkeley: University of California Press, 1967) and in Keith Thomas, *Man and the Natural World: A History of Modern Sensibility* (New York: Pantheon Books, 1983).

13. Gerhard Hasel, *Old Testament Theology*, p. 183.

14. Claus Westermann, *Elements of Old Testament Theology* (Atlanta: John Knox Press, 1982), p. 9. Hereafter cited as Westermann, OTT.

15. Bernhard W. Anderson, *Creation Versus Chaos: The Reinterpretation of Mythical Symbolism in the Bible* (New York: Association Press, 1967).

16. Alexander Heidel, *The Babylonian Genesis* (Chicago: University of Chicago Press, 1951), p. 97.

17. Biblical scholars disagree on the question of whether the first chapter of Genesis really describes creation from nothing. Genesis 1:1 could also imply there was something present before creation, even if it were ''chaos.'' Gerald Wilson has pointed out to me this is a semantic question, and alternate readings are possible.

ural forces. In the Hebrew accounts, even when Yahweh confronts chaos, "creation does not draw the deity into the flux of the world process . . . ,"[18] much less generate God or the godly. The Old Testament presents the universe as a creation of God, which He transcends. This is in marked contrast to both Babylonian and Caanite religions, where heavenly bodies, trees, and other natural objects were credited with supernatural power and thereby deified.

From the very beginning Yahweh is seen as acting spiritually and personally to create order. In the Genesis account and in the prophets, Yahweh creates through His word. These accounts provide us "with an idea of the absolute effortlessness of the divine creative action . . ." and also make clear that "if the world is the product of the creative word, it is therefore . . . sharply separated in nature from God himself—it is neither an emanation nor a mythically understood manifestation of the divine nature and power."[19] This has a number of implications for the relationship between God and creation. As Langdon Gilkey observes, no part of creation shares "divinity in any of its aspects, as if the being or substance of God had separated itself into many pieces to become the being of each creature."[20] Furthermore, the difference between God and His creation "is the result of God's creative act, not of a 'fall' or turning away from God . . ." and God's transcendence is itself a source of the "alienation" of creation from God.[21]

The spirit, or in Hebrew "Ruah" (breath of God), is instrumental in the original creative act, and is held throughout the Old Testament to be the very principle of life. Both man and animals come to life through this breath of God. If God withdraws His spirit, then "every creature must sink down in death."[22] It should be noted that this spirit is also seen as "the instrument

of God in salvation history,"[23] "the consumating power of the new age,"[24] and "the power behind the life of the people of God."[25] Neither the spirit nor the creation event are independent of other major Old Testament themes. As Claus Westermann points out:

> . . . only he who is active in everything could be savior. Since God is One, the savior must also be the creator. It follows that in the Old Testament the history established by God's saving deed was expanded to include the beginning of everything that happens. The savior of Israel is the creator; the creator is the savior of Israel. What began in creation issues into Israel's history.[26]

Environmental commentators who restrict their reading to Genesis often miss the complex interweaving of the Old Testament concept of creation with other themes. Von Rad even proposes "that Israel was interested in creation not because of nature and its problems, but because of history."[27] The "history only" point of view is extreme, but a careful reading of the entire Old Testament shows creation as relating to history, salvation, the people of Israel, wisdom, and eschatological events. The references are scattered throughout the Old Testament, but are most numerous in Psalms, the Prophets, and the wisdom literature.

In the middle section of the Book of Isaiah[28] (chaps. 40-55), for example, the author combines two major Hebrew traditions, that of God the creator and of Yahweh of the Exodus as God active in history.[29] As von Rad suggests:

> A special feature in Deutero-Isaiah's thought about creation is, of course, that he does not regard creation as a work by itself, something additional to Yahweh's his-

---

18. Walther Eichrodt, *Theology of the Old Testament,* vol. 2 (Philadelphia: Westminster Press, 1967), p. 98.

19. Gerhard von Rad, *Old Testament Theology,* vol. 1 (New York: Harper & Row, 1962), p. 142 (hereafter cited as von Rad, OTT). This tradition is not without parallels in other cultures. The Egyptian god, Ptah, also creates by his word.

20. Langdon Gilkey, *Maker of Heaven and Earth* (New York: Doubleday and Co., 1959), p. 86.

21. Ibid., p. 87.

22. Eichrodt, *Theology,* p. 48.

23. Ibid., p. 50.

24. Ibid., p. 57.

25. Ibid., p. 60.

26. Westermann, OTT, p. 86.

27. Gerhard von Rad, *God at Work in Israel* (Nashville: Abingdon, 1980), p. 99.

28. There is some scholarly disagreement over the number of authors of the Book of Isaiah. Conservatives hold to one author. Some critics propose three or more. The term Deutero-Isaiah is used both for chapters 40-55 and the supposed author of this section.

29. Carroll Stuhlmueller, *The Prophets and the Word of God* (Notre Dame: Fides Publishers, 1964), p. 200.

torical acts. . . . [F]or him creation is the first of Yahweh's miraculous historical acts and a remarkable witness to his will to save. The conclusive evidence for this 'soteriological' conception of creation is the fact that Deutero-Isaiah can at one time speak of Yahweh, the creator of the world and at another of Yahweh, the creator of Israel.[29]

In Isaiah 40-55, the original act of creation and the creation of the people of Israel through the Exodus become types for a ''new saving event'' and thus are integrated into eschatology. Yahweh can, through the power of His word and His spirit, create a new kingdom of Israel. Deutero-Isaiah makes frequent use of the word *bara,* which is also used in the first chapters of Genesis to imply a creative act, such as the creation of Adam, which only God can perform. *Bara* is used not only to refer to the first creation, but also in establishing God's loving kindness toward Israel. Since both the original creation and the new saving event are accomplished by the Word and the Spirit of God, these deeds of creation are ''personal, responsible'' acts of God.[30]

Having established that God the creator is transcendent and that his creative acts include not only the creation of the universe via His word, but also the creation and salvation of his people, we now can ask, what are the characteristics, according to the Old Testament, of creation itself? Returning to the Genesis account we find that after the earth is separated from the seas ''God saw that it was good . . . ,''[31] and that at the very end of the creation effort, ''God saw everything that he had made, and behold, it was very good.''[32] The English translation misses the full meaning of the Hebraic adjective *tob,* which can mean good and beautiful:

In the concluding sentence the listener can thus also hear the echo: ''Behold, it was very beautiful.'' The beauty of creation has its foundation in the will of the creator;

beauty belongs to God's works. Whoever speaks about the work of the creator also speaks about the beautiful.[33]

The creation accounts include a judgment by God and it is a highly favorable one.

A second characteristic of creation is that it is blessed by God. When God said, ''Be fruitful and multiply . . .,'' he gave a blessing that continues outside of the events of salvation history.[34] Although many environmental critiques mention this statement, only in regard to humankind or actually treat the statement as if it were curse, the original intent was both universal and beneficial.

A third characteristic of creation is that it praises or glorifies God. In Psalm 148:3-10, for example, all creation is called on to praise God:

Praise him, sun and moon,
    praise him, all you shining stars!
Praise him you highest heavens,
    and you waters above the heavens!. . . .
Praise the Lord from the earth,
    you sea monsters and all deeps,
fire, hail, snow and frost,
    stormy wind fulfilling his command!

Mountains and all hills.
    fruit trees and all cedars!
Beasts and all cattle,
    creeping things and flying birds!

The same type of imagery is found in other books such as Job and Isaiah. Isaiah 55:12 reads:

For you shall go out in joy,
    and be led forth in peace;
the mountains and the hills before you
    shall break forth into singing,
and all the trees of the field shall
    clap their hands.

Creation may also act as a party in a covenant lawsuit concerning the sins of the people of Israel, as in Micah 6:1-2:

---

30. Gerhard von Rad, *The Message of the Prophets* (New York: Harper & Row, 1962), p. 208.

31. Gen. 1:10; all translations are from *The New Oxford Annotated Bible* (New York: Oxford University Press, 1973).

32. Gen. 1:31.

---

33. Westermann, OTT, p. 93.

34. Gen. 1:22; Westermann, OTT, pp. 102–04.

Hear what the Lord says:
Arise, plead your case before the mountains
and let the hills hear your voice.
Hear, you mountains, the controversy of the Lord,
and you enduring foundations of the earth;
for the Lord has a controversy with his people;
and he will contend with Israel.

All this implies that God has a continuing concern for creation and that creation is continually able to respond to God. Further, in Deutero-Isaiah, creation is described as participating in the new saving event.

It should be noted that the Old Testament usually deals with creation in its entirety and there is no divine hierarchy within the whole. All is good and beautiful, while none is in any way God. For the ancient Hebrew, evil is not a necessary element in creation, and the evil now operating on and through creation will ultimately be defeated by the ''new saving event'' which will also be a new creative act.

ADAM IN CREATION

Having looked at the role of God, we now need to analyze how humankind relates to God in the midst of creation, and thereby relates to creation. The first problem concerns the statement in Genesis 1:26: ''Then God said: 'Let us make man in our image, after our likeness. . . .' '' This has been interpreted by some authors as simply setting man above creation, but it might be better interpreted as setting man in an especially close relationship to God. Von Rad states in his commentary on the passage that ''God participates more intimately and intensively in this than in the earlier works of creation.''[35] Westermann goes further and suggests that ''this is not primarily a statement about human life, but about the creation of human life by God. The creature God is now planning is to stand in relationship to him; humans are to correspond to God so that something can happen between them and God, so that God can speak to them and they can answer.''[36]

In the same verse, immediately after God declares that Adam is to be made in the divine image, we find the controversial passage: ''. . . and let them have dominion over the fish of the sea, and over the birds of the air, and over cattle, and over all the earth and over every creeping thing that creeps upon the earth.'' Many environmental commentators have taken this as a presentation of earth to human beings as a gift to them, when in reality it is a more complex matter of setting man to work under the continuing authority of God. Even the creation in the image of God is not a gift or a declaration of simple superiority but a necessity required before Adam can rule. As Von Rad suggests:

> This commission to rule is not considered as belonging to the definition of God's image; but is its consequence, i.e., that for which man is capable because of it. . . . Just as powerful earthly kings, to indicate their claim to dominion, erect an image of themselves in the provinces of their empire where they do not personally appear, so man is placed upon earth in God's sovereign emblem. He is really only God's representative, summoned to maintain and enforce God's claim to dominion over the earth.[37]

Eichrodt basically concurs when he writes:

> The connection between Man's creation in the image of God and his dominant position within the world of creatures is . . . indeed associated with the declaration of God's intention to create Man, being mentioned as a consequence of the especially close relationship of this creature to his Creator; but in the detailed exposition of the divine plan it is then quite clearly distinguished from this relationship as a separate item which has to be promised by a special creative act of blessing. Subjugation of the earth and dominion over its creatures bestows on the human race a common universal task, and in the execution of this task Man's special nature is to become visibly effective in that he is hereby made the responsible representative of the divine cosmic Lord.[38]

The command to take dominion was necessary for man to assume his special responsibility. That is, the command was both enabling and differentiating.

---

35. Gerhard von Rad, *Genesis* (Philadelphia: Westminster Press, 1972), p. 57.

36. Westermann, OTT, p. 97.

37. Gerhard von Rad, *Genesis,* pp. 57-58.

38. Eichrodt, *Theology,* p. 127.

Man's dominion was not a simple transfer of civil power, but was actually a spiritual transfer of authority centered in a special creative act.

After giving man dominion, God repeats the blessing given to the creatures and applies it to humankind: "And God blessed them, and God said multiply, and fill the earth and subdue it; and have dominion over the fish of the sea and over the birds of the air and over every living thing that moves upon the earth."[39] Again, environmental commentators have tended to emphasize the dominion aspect and have neglected the fact that God gives mankind exactly the same blessing as the rest of creation and that He requires that man assume the responsibility of representing God's interests. As Westermann states:

> These verses sum up what it means to be a human being; man is what he is precisely as a creature of God; his creature-state determines his capability and the meaning of his existence. What man is capable of is bestowed on him by the blessing. The blessing seen as controlling the power of fertility is a gift which man shares with the animals. It is something that binds man and beasts together.[40]

Thus, we have in this short text, man set in the image of God and therefore in special relationship to Him. Man is set above creation, but because he is given the same blessing as creation, he is therefore insured of creatureliness.

In Genesis 2, which scholars hold to be a second separate creation account combined with Genesis 1, "The Lord God took the man and put him in the garden of Eden to till it and keep it."[41] This passage does not give a portrait of man called to be despot, but presents man as called to serve. The verb *abad* translated as "to till" has the connotation not only of work, but of service, and can be translated as "to serve" or "to be a slave to." The word *shamar* "to keep" might also be translated "to watch" or "to preserve."[42] It is important that God's power placed

man in Eden to serve and preserve the earth. God then allowed man to eat the fruits of the garden. Nowhere is it implied man has a right to do this, or that the earth is man's servant to be done with as he pleases.

Some authors have pointed out that the command "to take dominion" uses the Hebrew words *rada* and *kabas,* which are very strong and imply treading down or trampling.[43] All relevant texts need to be interpreted in a compatible fashion, however, and in this context some form of ravishing the earth is clearly not intended in Genesis 2:15. James Barr has suggested that nothing more is to be read into the Hebrew words of the dominion passage than "the basic needs of settlement and agriculture," including tilling the ground, and this interpretation is satisfactorily within the limits imposed by the passage on the keeping of Eden.[44]

Following Adam's placement in Eden comes the temptation and spread of sin in Genesis 3. Man, having been given a special relationship to God and a position of power over creation, breaks his relationship with God, who then reacts to the "increasingly grave violation of his order."[45] Adam's power is limited, and these limitations affect his ability to understand and know God. Adam also ceases to comprehend godly matters, such as executing dominion and receiving the blessings of Genesis 2.[46]

In the course of rebuking Adam and Eve for the transgression in Eden, God pronounces His punishment via a curse, which includes a curse of the ground. This curse puts a stumbling block in front of Adam who is still under the commission to work given in Genesis 2:15. Henceforth, "man's work is always in some way tied up with toil and effort; every area of work throws up its thorns and thistles which can not be avoided. . . ."[47] In basic recognition that what man needs must come from creation, the passage declares that the barriers to man successfully completing his

---

39. Gen. 1:28.

40. Claus Westermann, *Creation* (Philadelphia: Fortress Press, 1974), p. 49.

41. Gen. 2:15.

42. Loren Wilkinson, ed., *Earth Keeping: Christian Stewardship of Natural Resources* (Grand Rapids: Eerdmans, 1980), p. 209.

43. von Rad, *Genesis,* p. 59.

44. James Barr, "Man and Nature: The Ecological Controversy and the Old Testament," in David and Ellen Spring, eds., *Ecology and Religion in History* (New York: Harper & Row, 1974), pp. 63-64.

45. von Rad, *Genesis,* p. 155.

46. Claus Westermann, *Creation,* pp. 89-112.

47. Ibid., p. 102.

tasks are found in his broken relationship with creation itself. Although theologians disagree as to whether all creation fell with Adam, nature is, at the very least, an innocent victim, under a curse because of man's sin and does not now fully produce its full fruits because of it.[48] From this it can be inferred that proper dominion is not an easy matter for man, who is struggling, because of the effects of sin, to relate not only to God, but also to other humans and all of nature. The breaking of the relationship with God and the expulsion from the garden also imply that dominion, as God intended it, can only be carried out with careful attention to the will of God and a tremendous effort. If dominion originally required God as both a lord and cooperator, God becomes even more necessary after the curse, because only God can lift it.

It should be recognized that much of the remainder of the Old Testament deals directly with the character of God, man's relationship to God, and other issues relevant to God's expectations of man. The establishment of covenant relationships, such as those made with Abraham or with Moses, present man with an opportunity to reestablish open communication with Yahweh. In the process of describing the expected man-God relationships the Prophets, for example, used a theology that included God as creator. Creation had "opened up the dimension of history and saving history" for Israel and therefore is repeatedly mentioned in her sacred texts.[49]

One last series of passages deserve analysis in regard to man's relationship to nature, and these are the references to creation and wisdom in the wisdom literature. This literature is relatively late and is the beginning of an attempt to seek out the mysteries of nature. It presents wisdom as preexisting before the rest of creation and as immanent in the world. God gave an order to his works at the very beginning and this order is separate from the activities of men. Unlike the modern who considers wisdom and knowledge to be solely the product of human endeavor, the scholars who wrote the wisdom literature considered wisdom something created by God which existed in creation, whether man was there or not. This literature also held that the way to wisdom was through fear (not literally fear, perhaps respect or awe is a better term) of Yahweh. If someone cares to pursue it, therefore, wisdom, the key not only to order in the universe, but also the key to correct behavior or proper action before God, is available.[50] A characteristic of the wisdom literature is "the determined effort to relate the phenomenon of the world, of 'nature' with its secrets of creation, to the saving revelation addressed to man."[51] These concerns are rarely discussed in the environmental literature; yet, they represent an extensive block of "how to" texts which have parallels in other religions, including those of the Far East.

GOD'S CONTINUING INTERACTION WITH CREATION

Rather than stop with the Genesis accounts, we can now pose the question: does God continue to interact in creation and if so, how? Since there are relatively few direct references to creation in the New Testament and the references in the Old Testament are scattered, it is easy to concentrate on the Genesis passages and to begin to take a deist view, that is, to see God as creator only at the beginning of time. In the Old Testament God continues as creator throughout.

As mentioned previously, God acts in creation by both blessing and saving. Blessing is different from saving in that the continuing blessing of God "is a quiet, continuous, flowing, and unnoticed working . . . which can not be captured in moments or dates. . . . Evening and morning songs speak about the activity of a blessing God."[52] In addition, God also

---

48. Paul Santmire, *Brother Earth: Nature God and Ecology in Time of Crisis* (New York: Thomas Nelson, 1970), pp. 163-68.

49. von Rad, OTT, p. 450.

50. Gerhard von Rad, *Wisdom in Israel* (Nashville: Abingdon, 1972), pp. 144-76.

51. von Rad, OTT, p. 449.

52. Westermann, OTT, p. 103.

saves individuals and communities and will ultimately redeem creation as a whole. "The entire Old Testament thus speaks of God's continuous action in addition to the acts which occur once in his saving and judging deeds."[53]

Heschel makes the point that "the fundamental thought in the Bible is not creation, but God's care for his creation."[54] On one hand, we have what modern theologians call providence: the very ordering of nature is "a revelation of God's goodness, particularly his mercy and long suffering,"[55] and on the other hand, we have God working to bring about salvation. This includes miracles (or in Old Testament terms, God's mighty deeds) which may be regarded as creative acts. The Exodus, for example, was marked by a series of miraculous events, each of which may be viewed independently as a move of God the creator exercising his prerogatives with His handiwork. One may also see the entire Exodus, however, as a single new creative act of Yahweh.[56]

THE OLD TESTAMENT AND CHRISTIAN ECOTHEOLOGY

In the preceding discussion of the Old Testament, I showed that creation theology was more to the ancient Hebrew than a theology of original creative acts, it was a theology of God's continuing interaction with both humankind and nature. The concept of an ecotheology, based on relationships between God and humankind, God and nature, and humankind and nature, therefore, has a foundation in the ancient writings and is by scriptural precedent a legitimate Christian concern.

In developing a sound Christian ecotheology, we have to accept the fact that the majority of scriptural texts directly mentioning creation are in the Old Testament, and that any dependable theology of creation

must be founded on extensive Hebrew scholarship.[57] We also have to accept the fact that some common criticisms of Judeo-Christian thinking—that it desacredizes nature and that it sets humankind in a special position—are basically correct interpretations of Old Testament theology. Concluding that these theological attributes of Judeo-Christian thinking produce an inadequate view of nature is an oversimplification, however.

Although the Old Testament clearly and purposefully removes any trace of divinity from nature, its discussions of creation are so spiritualized that they are difficult for the modern secular reader to comprehend fully. The very fact that nature praises God gives nature continuing intrinsic value. The Old Testament stresses the spiritual and aesthetic, neither of which can be given the definite material values our modern minds would prefer. We may actually be more comfortable with the sacred groves of the Baal worshipers, because they give individual natural features a special value and avoid the problem of having to grasp the entirety of creation as the work of God remaining under his care. The holism of the Old Testament in regard to nature presents an ironic stumbling block to categorized, materialistic modern thinking.

A second area of weakness in modern Christian interpretation concerns the ideas of "man in the image of God" and of "dominion." Many people remove these from their proper spiritual context and simply assume that the earth was placed here for the benefit of humankind. This is not, however, what the texts say. What the Genesis passages and much of the rest of the Old Testament speak for is a servitude of man to God, and as a result, to God's interests. The Old Testament records many failures in this regard, and man's inability to see his responsibilities begins when Cain asks: "Am I my brother's keeper?"[58]

---

53. Ibid.

54. Abraham Heschel, *The Prophets,* vol. 2 (New York: Harper & Row, 1962), p. 264.

55. William Dyrness, *Themes in Old Testament Theology* (Downers Grove: InterVarsity Press, 1979), p. 76.

56. Ibid., p. 77.

57. David Ehrenfeld justly criticized a draft of this paper for its lack of references to Jewish exegetes such as Rashni. Jewish interpretation of the Old Testament could not, of course, be based on Hasel's principles since Hasel accepts the New Testament as canonical. A thorough overview of Jewish scholarship on creation is a very needed addition to the environmental literature and would add further depth to our understanding of the Old Testament.

58. Gen. 4:9; Wilkinson, *Earthkeeping,* p. 212.

The themes of servitude and of covenant relationships requiring responsibility to God are woven into the entire Old Testament. In the poetic crown of the Prophets, the second half of Isaiah, we find the "suffering servant" of Yahweh, and "might see in this description of one 'despised and rejected by men' the increasingly familiar pattern . . . dominion is servitude."[59] The Old Testament also makes clear that to serve God adequately one must be faithful, diligent, self-disciplined, giving, forgiving, etc. Dominion is not an easy task and can only be executed by continuing hard labor and overcoming major obstacles. The effort must be under God's direction and must be accomplished for God, not for personal gain.

In the United States, concepts of God and nature have had a variety of cultural associations. Barbara Novak claims that in the nineteenth century, for example, "Ideas of God's nature and of God in nature became hopelessly entangled, and only the most scrupulous theologians even tried to separate them."[60] Further, Americans have often seen the natural bounty of the continent as a special blessing, and have often extended their patriotism into a perceived divine appointment as the New Jerusalem.[61] The intent of the ancient Hebrews not withstanding, the romantic tendency to equate nature with God, on one hand, and the conservative tendency to promote civil religion as part of the national destiny, on the other, are likely to perpetuate the confusion and misinterpretation surrounding the "dominion passage."

Since the theme of creation in the Old Testament is not independent of other themes, current Christian attitudes about creation cannot be independent of other related issues such as salvation. The attitude that "the Lord will fix it all in the end" is eschatologically correct but ignores God's continuing care and blessing via his servants. Christ's parables of the householder who returns to check on the tenants working his estate and of the king who returns to see what his servants have done with the money they have been given are good models, since God has given us both a responsibility and a blessing.

If God created the cosmos as *tob,* humankind should help to maintain it as such and preserve its aesthetic values. Unfortunately, modern English translations miss the impact of the Hebrew word, and the modern reader may secularize the passage: "And God saw that it was good for something . . ." or "And God saw that it was full of material value." In "taking dominion" the Old Testament shows a concern both for the maintenance of the aesthetic values of creation and, in the Pentateuch and the writings of the prophets, for the just distribution of the resources available.

The Old Testament provides numerous texts on how one can serve God and the entire wisdom literature is dedicated to the topic of righteous action. The idea that the ancient writings are too weak and their view of the environment too primitive to be of much help today comes from superficial analysis or actual ignorance of the texts. The Old Testament attitude toward creation is so strongly spiritualized that it is hard for us to understand it. Moreover, the standards set on service to God are so high that most people, as the Old Testament so candidly illustrates in the case of the nation Israel, have no inclination to even try to meet them. Passages written centuries ago can be both difficult to understand and difficult to set in a meaningful modern context. It is important, however, that we avoid hasty judgments on one of the central roots of the Western spiritual heritage and that our approach to the Old Testament be both thoughtful and scholarly. Those interested in developing a Christian ecotheology should not be too cursory in their treatment of the Old Testament texts nor too glib in their assumptions concerning the will of God for creation. In-depth studies of specific writings and literatures, i.e., the psalms or the wisdom literature, and a search for more strands in the creation theme, will produce a better formed and sounder ecotheology and may also help to compensate for any past Christian theological neglect of God's role as creator.

---

59. Ibid., p. 214.

60. Barbara Novak, *Nature and Culture: American Landscape Painting, 1825–1875* (New York: Oxford University Press, 1980), p. 3.

61. See, for example, Robert Linder and Richard Pierard, *Twilight of the Saints: Biblical Christianity and Civil Religion in America* (Downers Grove, Ill.: InterVarsity Press, 1978).

DISCUSSION TOPICS

1. Do you believe that the Old Testament, in and of itself, is an adequate source for formulating a coherent environmental ethic? Give examples to support your position.

2. How does Bratton interpret the Biblical theme of human dominion in relation to human activity in the world? Is this an accurate assessment? Explain your reasoning.

READING 62

The Gift of Good Land

Wendell Berry

Wendell Berry (b. 1934), a contemporary Christian scholar who bases his environmental ethic on the Bible, is a novelist, professor, and farmer. Berry believes that the theme of stewardship in the Bible defines the proper relationship between humans and nature. He maintains that the oft-cited Genesis passages counseling humans to subdue the earth have been misinterpreted. Berry asserts that the story of God's giving the Promised Land to the Israelites is a more revealing passage for understanding human responsibility toward creation.

My purpose here is double. I want, first, to attempt a Biblical argument for ecological and agricultural responsibility. Second, I want to examine some of the practical implications of such an argument. I am prompted to the first of these tasks partly because of its importance in our unresolved conflict about how we should use the world. That those who affirm the divinity of the Creator should come to the rescue of His creation is a logical consistency of great potential force.

The second task is obviously related to the first, but the origin of my motive here is somewhat more personal. I wish to deal directly at last with my own long-held belief that Christianity, as usually presented by its organizations, is not *earthly* enough—that a valid spiritual life in this world must have a practice and a practicality—it must have a material result. (I am well aware that in this belief I am not alone.) What I shall be working toward, then, is some sort of practical understanding of what Arthur O. Lovejoy called the "this-worldly" aspect of Biblical thought. I want to see if there is not at least implicit in the Judeo-Christian heritage a doctrine such as that the Buddhists call "right livelihood" or "right occupation."

Some of the reluctance to make a forthright Biblical argument against the industrial rape of the natural world seems to come from the suspicion that this rape originates with the Bible, that Christianity cannot cure what, in effect, it has caused. The best known spokesman for this view is Professor Lynn White, Jr., whose essay, "The Historical Roots of Our Ecologic Crisis," has been widely published.

Professor White asserts that it is a "Christian axiom that nature has no reason for existence save to serve man." He seems to base his whole argument on one Biblical passage, Genesis 1:28, in which Adam and Eve are instructed to "subdue" the earth. "Man," says Professor White, "named all the animals, thus establishing his dominance over them." There is no doubt that Adam's superiority over the rest of Creation was represented, if not established, by this act of naming; he *was* given dominance. But that this dominance was meant to be tyrannical, or that "subdue" meant to destroy, is by no means a necessary inference. Indeed, it might be argued that the correct understanding of this "dominance" is given in Genesis 2:15, which says that Adam and Eve were put into the Garden "to dress it and to keep it."

But these early verses of Genesis can give us only limited help. The instruction in Genesis 1:28 was, after all, given to Adam and Eve in the time of their innocence, and it seems virtually certain that the word "subdue" would have had a different intent and sense for them then than it could have for them, or for us, after the Fall.

It is tempting to dispute at length various statements in Professor White's essay, but he himself has made that unnecessary by giving us two sentences that very neatly define both his problem and my task. He writes, first, that "God planned all of this [the Creation] explicitly for man's benefit and rule: no item in the physical creation had any purpose save to serve man's purposes." And then, only a few sentences later, he says: "Christianity . . . insisted that it is God's will that man exploit nature for his *proper* ends." [Author's emphasis.]

It is certainly possible that an extremely critical difference exists between "man's purposes" and "man's *proper* ends." And one's belief or disbelief in that difference, and one's seriousness about the issue of propriety, will tell a great deal about one's understanding of the Judeo-Christian tradition.

I do not mean to imply that I see no involvement between that tradition and the abuse of nature. I know very well that Christians have often been not only indifferent to such abuse, but often have condoned and perpetrated it. That is not the issue. The issue is whether or not the Bible explicitly or implicitly defines a *proper* human use of Creation or the natural world. Proper use, as opposed to improper use, or abuse, is a matter of great complexity, and to find it adequately treated it is necessary to turn to a more complex story than that of Adam and Eve.

The story of the giving of the Promised Land to the Israelites is more serviceable to this issue than the story of the giving of the Garden of Eden, because the Promised Land is a divine gift to a *fallen* people. For that reason the giving is more problematical, and the receiving is more conditional and more difficult. In the Bible's long working-out of the understanding of this gift, it seems to me, we find the beginning—and, by implication, the completion too—of the definition of an ecological discipline.

But first I have to acknowledge that, to me, the effort to make sense of this story involves a considerable difficulty. The tribes of Israel, though they see the Promised Land as a gift to them from God, are also obliged to take it by force from its established inhabitants. And so a lot of the "divine sanction" by which they act sounds like the sort of rationalization that invariably accompanies nationalistic aggression and theft. It is impossible to ignore the similarities to the westward movement of our own frontier. The

Israelites followed their own doctrine of "manifest destiny," which for them, as for us, disallowed the human standing of their opponents. In Canaan, as in America, the conquerors acted upon the broadest possible definition of idolatry and the narrowest possible definition of justice. They conquered with the same ferocity and with the same genocidal intent.

But for all these similarities, there is a significant difference. Whereas the greed and violence of the American frontier produced an ethic of greed and violence that justified American industrialization, the ferocity of the conquest of Canaan was accompanied from the beginning by the working out of an ethical system antithetical to it—and antithetical, for that matter, to the American conquest that I have compared to it. The difficulty, then, but also the wonder of the story of the Promised Land is that, there, the primordial and still continuing dark story of human rapaciousness begins to be accompanied by a vein of light, one that, however improbably and uncertainly, still accompanies us. This light originates largely, it seems to me, in the idea of the land as a gift—not a free or a deserved gift, but a gift given only upon certain rigorous conditions.

It is a gift because the people who are to possess it did not create it. It is accompanied by careful warnings and demonstrations of the folly of saying that "My power and the might of mine hand hath gotten me this wealth" (Deuteronomy 8:17). Thus deeply implicated in the very definition of this gift is a specific warning against *hubris,* the great ecological sin, just as it is the great sin of politics. People are not gods. They must not act like gods or assume a godly authority. If they do, terrible retributions are in store. In this warning we have the root of the issue of propriety, of *proper* human purposes and ends. We must not use the world as though we had created it ourselves.

The Promised Land, moreover, is not a permanent gift. It is "given," but only for a time, and only for so long as it is properly used. It is stated unequivocally, and repeated again and again, that "the heaven and the heaven of heavens is the Lord's thy God, the earth also, with all that therein is" (Deuteronomy 10:14). What is given is not ownership, but a sort of tenancy, the right of habitation and use: "The land shall not be sold forever: for the land is mine; for ye are strangers and sojourners with me'' (Leviticus 25:23).

In token of His landlordship, God required a sabbath for the land, which was to be left fallow every seventh year; and a sabbath of sabbaths every fiftieth year, a ''year of jubilee,'' during which not only would the fields lie fallow, but the land would be returned to its original owners, as if to free it of the taint of trade and the conceit of human ownership. But beyond their agricultural and social intent, these sabbaths ritualize an observance of the limits of ''my power and the might of mine hand''—the limits of human control. Looking at their fallowed fields, the people are to be reminded that the land is theirs only by gift; it exists in its own right, and does not begin or end with any human purpose.

The Promised Land, moreover, is ''a land which the Lord thy God careth for: the eyes of the Lord thy God are always upon it . . .'' (Deuteronomy 11:12). And this care promises a repossession by the true landlord, and a fulfillment not in the power of its human inhabitants: ''. . . as truly as I live, all the earth shall be filled with the glory of the Lord'' (Numbers 14:21)—a promise recalled by St. Paul in Romans 8:21: ''. . . the Creature [the Creation] itself shall be delivered from the bondage of corruption into the glorious liberty of the children of God.''

Finally, and most difficult, the good land is not given as a reward. It is made clear that the people chosen for this gift do not deserve it, for they are ''a stiffnecked people'' and have been wicked and faithless. To such a people such a gift can be given only as a moral predicament: Having failed to deserve it beforehand, they must prove worthy of it afterwards; they must use it well, or they will not continue long in it.

How are they to prove worthy?

First, they must be faithful, grateful and humble; they must remember that the land is a gift: ''When thou hast eaten and art full, then thou shalt bless the Lord thy God for the good land which he hath given thee'' (Deuteronomy 8:10).

Second, they must be neighborly. They must be just, kind to one another, generous to strangers, honest in trading. These are social virtues, yet, as they in-variably do, they have ecological and agricultural implications. For the land is described as an ''inheritance''; the community is understood to exist not just in space, but also in time. One lives in the neighborhood, not just of those who now live ''next door,'' but of the dead who have bequeathed the land to the living, and of the unborn to whom the living will in turn bequeath it. The demanding fact here is that we can have no direct behavioral relation to those who are not yet alive. The only neighborly thing we can do for them is to preserve their inheritance: We must take care, among other things, of the land, which is never a possession, but an inheritance to the living, borrowed from the unborn.

And so the third thing the possessors of the land must do to be worthy of it is to practice good husbandry. The story of the Promised Land has a good deal to say on this subject, and yet its account is rather fragmentary. We must depend heavily on implication. Let us consider just a couple of verses (Deuteronomy 22:6-7):

> If a bird's nest chance to be before thee in the way in any tree, or on the ground, whether they be young ones, or eggs, and the dam sitting upon the young, or upon the eggs, thou shalt not take the dam with the young.
>
> But thou shalt in any wise let the dam go, and take the young to thee; that it may be well with thee, and that thou mayest prolong thy days.

This, obviously, is a perfect paradigm of ecological and agricultural discipline, in which the idea of inheritance is necessarily paramount. The inflexible rule is that the source must be preserved. You may take the young, but you must save the breeding stock. You may eat the harvest, but you must save seed, and you must preserve the fertility of the fields.

What we are talking about, of course, is an extremely elaborate understanding of charity. It is so elaborate because of the perception, implicit here—explicit in the New Testament—that charity by its very nature cannot be selective—that it is, so to speak, out of human control. It cannot be selective because between any two humans, or any two creatures, all Creation exists as a bond. Charity cannot be just human, any more than it can be just Jewish or just Samaritan. Once begun, wherever it begins, it cannot stop until it includes all Creation, for all creatures are parts of a whole upon which each is dependent, and it is a contradiction in terms to love your neighbor and despise the great inheritance on which all life depends. Charity even for one person does not make sense except in terms of an effort to love all Creation in response to the Creator's love for it.

And how is this charity answerable to "man's purposes"? It is not, any more than is the Creation itself. Professor White's contention that the Bible proposes such a thing is, so far as I can see, simply wrong. It is not allowable to love the Creation according to the purposes one has for it, any more than it is allowable to love one's neighbor in order to borrow tools. The wild ass and the wild ox are said in the Book of Job (39:5-12) to be "free," precisely in the sense that they are not subject or serviceable to human purposes. The same point—though it is not the main point of that passage—is made in the Sermon on the Mount in reference to "the fowls of the air" and "the lilies of the field." Faced with this problem in Book VIII of *Paradise Lost,* Milton scrupulously observes this same reticence. Adam asks about "celestial Motions," and Raphael refuses to explain, making the mystery a test of intellectual propriety and humility:

. . . for the Heav'n's wide Circuit, let it speak
the Maker's high magnificence, who built
So spacious, and his Line stretcht out so far;
That Man may know he dwells not in his own;
An Edifice too large for him to fill,
Lodg'd in a small partition, and the rest
Ordain'd for uses to his Lord best known.

(Lines 100-106)

The Creator's love for the Creation is mysterious precisely because it does not conform to human purposes. The wild ass and the wild lilies are loved by God for their own sake; and yet they are part of a pattern that we must love because of our dependence on it. This is a pattern that humans can understand well enough to respect and preserve, though they cannot "control" it or even hope to understand it completely. The mysterious and the practical, the Heavenly and the earthly, are thus joined. Charity is a theological virtue and is prompted, no doubt, by a

theological emotion, but it is also a practical virtue because it must be practiced. The requirements of this complex charity cannot be fulfilled by smiling in abstract beneficence on our neighbors and on the scenery. It must come to acts, which must come from skills. Real charity calls for the study of agriculture, soil husbandry, engineering, architecture, mining, manufacturing, transportation, the making of monuments and pictures, songs and stories. It calls not just for skills but for the study and criticism of skills, because in all of them a choice must be made: They can be used either charitably or uncharitably.

How can you love your neighbor if you don't know how to build or mend a fence, how to keep your filth out of his water supply and your poison out of his air; or if you do not produce anything and so have nothing to offer, or do not take care of yourself and so become a burden? How can you be a neighbor without *applying* principle—without bringing virtue to practical issues? And how will you practice virtue without skills?

The ability to be good surely is not the ability to do nothing. It is not negative or passive. It is the ability to do something well—to do good work for good reasons. In order to be good you have to know how—and this knowing is vast, complex, humble and humbling; it is of the mind and of the hands, of neither alone.

The divine mandate to use the world justly and charitably, then, defines every person's moral predicament as that of a steward. But this is hopeless and meaningless unless it produces an appropriate discipline: stewardship. And stewardship is hopeless and meaningless unless it involves long-term courage, perseverance, devotion and skill. This skill is not to be confused with any accomplishment or grace of spirit or of intellect. It has to do with everyday proprieties in the practical use and care of created things—with "right livelihood."

If "the earth is the Lord's" and we are His stewards, then obviously some livelihoods are "right" and some are not. Is there, for instance, any such thing as a Christian stripmine? A Christian atomic bomb? A Christian nuclear power plant or radioactive waste dump? What might be the design of a Christian transportation or sewer system? Does not Christianity imply limitations on the scale of technology, architecture, and land holding? Is it Christian to profit or otherwise benefit from violence? Is there not, in Christian ethics, an implied requirement of practical separation from a destructive or a wasteful economy? Do not Christian values require the enactment of a distinction between an organization and a community?

It is clear, I hope, that it is impossible to understand, much less to answer, such questions except in reference to issues of practical skill, because they all have to do with distinctions between kinds of action. These questions, moreover, are intransigently personal, for they ask, ultimately, how each livelihood and each life will be taken from the world, and what each will cost of the livelihoods and lives of others. Organizations and even communities cannot hope to answer such questions until persons have begun to ask them.

But here we must acknowledge, I think, one inadequacy of Judeo-Christian tradition. This tradition, at least in its most prominent and best-known examples, doesn't provide us with a precise enough understanding of the commonplace issues of livelihood. There are two reasons for this.

One is the "otherworldly philosophy" that, according to Lovejoy, "has, in one form or another, been the dominant official philosophy of the larger part of civilized mankind through most of its history. . . . The greater number of the subtler speculative minds and of the great religious teachers have . . . been engaged in weaning man's thought or his affections, or both, from . . . Nature. . . ." (*The Great Chain of Being,* p. 26). The connection here seems to me to be plain enough to need no elaboration.

The second reason, which does require some elaboration, is that the Judeo-Christian tradition as embodied in its art and literature, including the Bible, is so strongly heroic. The poets and storytellers in this tradition have tended to be interested in the extraordinary actions of "great men"—actions unique in grandeur, such as may occur only once in the history of the world. These extraordinary actions do indeed bear a universal significance, but they cannot very well serve as examples of ordinary behavior. Ordinary behavior belongs to a different dramatic mode, a different understanding of action, even a different un-

derstanding of virtue. The drama of heroism raises, above all, the issue of physical and/or moral courage: Does the hero have, in extreme circumstances, the courage to obey—to perform the task, the sacrifice, the resistance, the pilgrimage that he is called on to perform? The drama of ordinary or daily behavior also raises the issue of courage, but it raises at the same time the issue of skill; and, because ordinary behavior lasts so much longer than heroic action, it raises in a more complex and difficult way the issue of perseverance. It may, in some ways, be easier to be Samson than to be a good husband or wife day after day for 50 years.

Heroic works are meant to be (among other things) instructive and inspiring to ordinary people in ordinary life, and they are, grandly and deeply so. But there are two issues they are precluded by their nature from raising: the issue of lifelong devotion and perseverance in unheroic tasks, and the issue of good workmanship or "right livelihood."

It can be argued, I believe, that until fairly recently there was simply no need for attention to such matters, for there existed yeoman or peasant or artisan classes, whose birthright was the fundamental skills of earthkeeping. These were the people who did the work of feeding and clothing and housing, and who were responsible for the necessary skills, disciplines and restraints. As long as these classes and their traditions were strong, there was at least the hope that the world would be well used. But probably the most revolutionary accomplishment of the industrial revolution was to destroy the traditional livelihoods and so break down the cultural lineage of those classes.

The industrial revolution has held in contempt not only the "obsolete skills" of those classes, but the concern for quality, for responsible workmanship and good work that supported those skills. For the principle of good work it substituted a secularized version of the heroic tradition: the ambition to be a "pioneer" of science or technology, to make a "breakthrough" that will "save the world" from some "crisis," which by now is usually the result of some previous "breakthrough."

The best example we have of this kind of hero, I am afraid, is the fallen Satan of *Paradise Lost*—Milton undoubtedly having observed in his own time the prototypes of industrial heroism. This is a hero who instigates and influences the actions of others, but does not act himself. His heroism is of the mind only—escaped, as far as possible, not only from divine rule, from its place in the order of Creation or the Chain of Being, but also from the influence of material creation:

A mind not to be chang'd by Place or Time.
The mind is its own place, and in itself
Can make a Heav'n of Hell, a Hell of Heav'n.
(Book I, lines 253-255)

This would-be heroism is guilty of two evils that are prerequisite to its very identity: *hubris* and abstraction. The industrial hero supposes that "mine own *mind* hath saved me"—and moreover that it may save the world. Implicit in this is the assumption that one's mind is one's own and that it may choose its own place in the order of things; one usurps divine authority, and thus, in classic style, becomes the author of results that one can neither foresee nor control.

And because this mind is understood only as a cause, its primary works are necessarily abstract. We may need to remind ourselves at this point that materialism in the sense of the love of material things is not in itself an evil. As C. S. Lewis pointed out, God too loves material things; He invented them. The Devil's work is abstraction—not the love of material things, but the love of their quantities—which, of course, is why "David's heart smote him after that he had numbered the people" (II Samuel 24:10). It is not the lover of material things but the abstractionist who defends long-term damage for short-term gain, or who calculates the "acceptability" of industrial damage to ecological or human health, or who counts dead bodies on the battlefield. The true lover of material things does not think in this way, but is answerable instead to the paradox in the parable of the lost sheep: that each is more precious than all.

But perhaps we cannot understand this secular heroic mind until we understand its opposite: the mind obedient and in place. And for that we can look again at Raphael's warning in Book VIII of *Paradise Lost:*

. . . apt the Mind or Fancy is to rove
Uncheckt, and of her roving is no end;

Till warn'd, or by experience taught, she learn
That not to know at large of things remote
From use, obscure and subtle, but to know
That which before us lies in daily life,
Is the prime Wisdom; what is more, is fume,
Or emptiness, or fond impertinence,
And renders us in things that most concern
Unpractic'd, unprepar'd, and still to seek.
Therefore from this high pitch let us descend
A lower flight, and speak of things at hand
Useful . . .
(Lines 188-200)

In its immediate sense this is a warning against thought that is theoretical or speculative (and therefore abstract), but in its broader sense it is a warning against disobedience—the eating of the forbidden fruit, and act of *hubris,* which Satan proposes as a compellingly reasonable theory and which Eve undertakes as a speculation.

An excellent example of the conduct of industrial heroism is to be found in the present rush of experts to "solve the problem of world hunger," known in industrial heroic jargon as "the world food problematique." As is characteristic of industrial heroism, the professed intention is entirely salutary: nobody should starve. The trouble is that "world hunger" is not a problem that can be solved by a "world solution." Except in a very limited sense, it is not an industrial problem, and industrial attempts to solve it—such as the "Green Revolution" and "Food for Peace"—have often had grotesque and destructive results. "The problem of world hunger" cannot be solved until it is understood and dealt with by local people as a multitude of local problems of ecology, agriculture, and culture.

The most necessary thing in agriculture for instance, is not to invent new technologies or methods, not to achieve "breakthroughs," but to determine what technologies and methods are appropriate to specific people, places and needs, and to apply them correctly. Application is the crux (and is critical here because the heroic approach ignores it) because no two farms or farmers are alike; no two fields are alike. Just the changing shape or topography of the land makes for differences of the most formidable kind. Abstractions never cross these gaps without either doing damage or ceasing to be abstractions. And prefabricated industrial methods and technologies *are* abstractions. The bigger and more expensive, the more heroic they are, the harder they are to apply considerately and conservingly.

Application is the most important work, but also the most modest, complex, difficult and long—and so it goes against the grain of industrial heroism. It destroys forever the notions that the world can be thought of (by humans) as a whole and that humans can ''save'' it as a whole—notions we can well do without, for they prevent us from understanding our problems and from growing up.

To use knowledge and tools in a particular place with good long-term results is not heroic. It is not a grand action visible from a long distance or for a long time. It is a small action, but more complex and difficult, more skillful and responsible, more whole and enduring than most grand actions. It comes of a willingness to devote oneself to work that perhaps only the eye of Heaven will see in its full intricacy and excellence. Perhaps the real work, like real prayer and real charity, must be done in secret.

The great study of stewardship, then, is ''to know / That which before us lies in daily life'' and to be practised and prepared ''in things that most concern.'' The angel is talking about good work, which is to talk about skill. With the loss of skill we lose stewardship; in losing stewardship we lose fellowship; we become outcasts from the great neighborhood of Creation. It is possible—as our experience in *this* good land shows—to exile ourselves from Creation and to ally ourselves with the principle of destruction—which is, ultimately, the principle of nonentity. It is to be willing, in general, for beings to not-be. And once we have allied ourselves with that principle, we are foolish to think that we can control the results. The ''regulation'' of abominations is a modern governmental exercise that never succeeds. If we are willing to pollute the air—to harm the elegant creature known as the atmosphere—by that token we are willing to harm all creatures that breathe, ourselves and our children among them. There is no begging off or ''trading off.'' You cannot affirm the power plant and condemn the smokestack, or affirm the smoke and condemn the cough.

That is not to suggest that we can live harmlessly, or strictly at our own expense; we depend upon other creatures and survive by their deaths. To live we must daily break the body and shed the blood of Creation. When we do this lovingly, knowingly, skillfully, reverently, it is a sacrament. When we do it greedily, clumsily, ignorantly, destructively, it is a desecration. By such desecration we condemn ourselves to spiritual and moral loneliness, and others to want.

DISCUSSION TOPICS

1. How does Berry counter the claim by Lynn White, Jr. that Christianity caused the environmental crisis? What is your opinion?
2. Do you believe that Berry's conception of Christian stewardship is a workable environmental ethic? Support your position.

READING 63

Quantum Theory, Intrinsic Value, and Panentheism

Michael E. Zimmerman

Michael E. Zimmerman (b. 1946) is professor and department chair of Philosophy, Newcomb College, Tulane University, New Orleans, Louisiana. He also is author of Eclipse of the Self: The Development of Heidegger's Concept of Authenticity.

Zimmerman believes that to espouse a valid environmental ethic, one must reject the dominant dualism in Western society, and affirm a conception of nature which recognizes and values the relatedness of all things. Zimmerman recognizes that it often is difficult for people in an anthropocentric society to acknowledge intrinsic value in the natural world. He proposes that this problem can be resolved by adopting a nondualistic philosophy such as panentheism. From a panentheistic perspective, the universe began when God emptied a portion of the divine being into the lowest level—matter and energy. Evolution of the natural world is the slow return of this creation to the original level of divine reality. Christian panentheists view all creatures as valuable, both in and of themselves and as manifestations of the divine. Obeying the will of God is to accept and respect all being that emanates from God's creative act. A nondualistic perspective leads to compassion and love for all being.

THE CONTRIBUTION OF NONDUALISM TO ENVIRONMENTAL ETHICS

. . . The deep ecologists Arne Naess and Warwick Fox have argued that only a process of wider identification with all beings, an identification which acknowledges the internal relatedness of all beings, can provide the basis for a satisfactory environmental ethics. In a commentary on Callicott's quantum theory essay, Fox says that

> the problem of justifying intrinsic value could be said to shift from the environmental axiological question ''What is it about the nature or being of *x* that makes it intrinsically valuable?'' to the normative ''autological'' question ''Why ought one relate to *x* as to one's self (or in an 'I-Thou' rather than an 'I-It' manner)?'' . . . Thus the term ''intrinsic value'' can still do useful philosophical work in deep ecological theorizing if it is understood as making a claim about the nature of the relationship that one has or ought to have with *x* (and, hence, about the *state of being to which one ought to aspire*), rather than as making a claim about the nature or being of *x*.[1]

The paradigm of internal relationships is, in Fox's point of view, important in overcoming previous delusions about the separateness of the self from nature. Yet Fox acknowledges that cognitive insight into internal relatedness is not in itself sufficient to bring about a new relationship between oneself and the rest of the world. This new relationship requires a new ''state of being,'' one that is nondualistic. But how to bring about this new state of being?

---

1. Fox, ''Deep Ecology and Intrinsic Value.'' Emphasis added. By *autological* Fox means ''having to do with self.''

Callicott argues that knowledge about the interrelatedness of all life may lead a rational humanity to a deeper appreciation of the need to live on Earth appropriately. Knowledge about the paradoxes of quantum theory, moreover, may have the effect of showing the limits to dualistic thinking and of promoting cosmological speculation that is consistent with a metaphysics of internal relations. As I've already mentioned, these trends in the sciences may be helping to prepare the way for the emergence of a more inclusive, nondualistic level of awareness.

Nondualistic awareness involves direct apprehension of the fact that there are no boundaries, that all dualisms are artificial (though often helpful). Even the division between ego states (thoughts, memories, fantasies, etc.) and so-called external objects is revealed as artificial. All things, including ego states and external objects, are seen as manifestations emerging from what is apprehended as a fertile ''no-thing-ness.'' The ''I'' itself appears as a temporary phenomenon, an energy pattern maintaining itself according to certain intentions and habits. The true ''self'' is not the ego, but instead the ''no-thing-ness'' from which all things emerge.

Within Eastern and Western nondualistic traditions there is disagreement about the meaning of the ''non-thing-like'' source for all beings, a source that is itself not ''located'' anywhere, but provides the context for space, time, matter, energy, perception, and ego consciousness. Some nondualistic Eastern traditions, such as Buddhism, refer to this nothingness *(sunyata)* in metaphysical terms as the nonpersonal awareness that perceives/engenders all things. In some nondualistic Western traditions, including Western mysticism, the primordial ''no-thing-like'' source is conceived in more personalized terms, as the Godhead beyond God. Mystical Christianity claims that the ordinary concept of God (a divine entity in heaven) is a misleading product of dualistic consciousness. The God beyond God cannot be said to ''be'' at all, but instead must be conceived as ''no-thing-ness,'' as beyond but somehow inclusive of all creatures. The apparent proximity of the Buddhist and mystical Christian view has not gone unnoticed. Recent decades have witnessed an extraordinary dialogue between Buddhists and Christians, who have discovered such a remarkable convergence of themes from their nondualistic traditions.[2]

Nondualistic experience leads to compassion and love for all beings. Nondualistic awareness no longer identifies itself with a particular entity (the rational ego) and so no longer is forced to adopt a defensive posture toward entities that are other than ego. Freed from false identification with a dualistic state (ego consciousness), awareness can now discern and have compassion for the suffering undergone by people who remain at dualistic levels of awareness. Nondualistic awareness does not cling or hinder, but instead lets all things come forth as they are. The Christian mystical tradition maintains that such awareness is divine, and to the extent that humans share such awareness, they participate in the divine. This is the esoteric meaning of Jesus' claim that ''I and the Father are One.''[3] Nondualistic awareness would not only lead humanity to treat all beings, human and nonhuman, with a profound respect, but would also free humanity from many of the cravings, aversions, and delusions that are responsible for wars and for production methods that threaten to destroy the biosphere.

As I mentioned earlier, while the experiential dimension of nondualism is reported to be the same by various traditions, those traditions have different interpretations of the ''meaning'' of such nondualistic experience. Certain versions of mystical Christianity, for example, hold that nondualistic experience reveals the truth of the doctrine of *panentheism.* Panentheism, seeking to reconcile divine transcendence with divine immanence, maintains that God is present in but not identical with creation. Divine awareness gives rise to creatures and in some measure participates in the

life of those creatures, but is not wholly identical with them. Evolutionary panentheists, whose doctrines resemble those of Hegel, claim that God is present in and continues to develop through the evolving existence of creatures, thereby overcoming the otherworldliness of traditional Christianity.

In one essay, Callicott maintains that traditional Christianity has promoted the human exploitation of nature, but nevertheless recognizes that

> Historically the first and theoretically the most obvious possibility [for a nonanthropocentric axiology] is theistic axiology. If God is posited as the arbiter of value, anthropocentrism is immediately and directly overcome. If God, moreover, is conceived as in the Judeo-Christian tradition to be the creator of the natural world, and to have declared his creation to be *good,* then the creation as a whole, including, as its centerpiece, the biosphere, and the components of the creation, species prominently among them, have, by immediate inference, intrinsic value. . . .
>
> This theistic axiology has one main drawback as a nonanthropocentric value theory for environmental ethics. It is primitive, essentially mythic, ambiguous, and inconsistent with modern science, and more especially with modern ecological, evolutionary biology. It is therefore metaphysically discordant with the world view in which environmental problems are perceived as fundamentally important and morally charged in the first place.[4]

Callicott is right in suggesting that theocentrism provides the basis for a nonanthropocentric axiology: everything is good if it is a manifestation of and in relationship with the divine. Callicott agrees with theocentrism that modern humanity is arrogant, but—at least in the essay from which the quotation is taken—he does not accept the theocentric diagnosis of or solution to such arrogance. He identifies theocentrism as such with a particular interpretation of Judeo-Christian theocentrism. He then dismisses that tradition as ''primitive, essentially mythic, ambiguous, and inconsistent with modern science. . . .''

It is important to note that nondualistic panenthe-

2. See, for example, Hans Waldenfels, *Absolute Nothingness: Foundations for Buddhist-Christian Dialogue,* trans. J.W. Heisig (New York: Paulist Press, 1980); J.K. Kadowaki, S.J., *Zen and the Bible: A Priest's Experience,* trans. Joan Rieck (London: Routledge & Kegan Paul), 1980; Dom Aelred Graham, *Zen Catholicism* (New York: Harcourt Brace & World, 1963); Thomas Merton, *Mystics and Zen Masters* (New York: Dell Publishing Co., 1967).

3. On this topic, see Wilber, *Up from Eden;* Fritjof Schuon, *The Transcendent Unity of Religions* (Wheaton, Ill.: Quest Books, 1984); Alan Watts, *The Supreme Identity* (New York: Vintage Books, 1972).

4. J. Baird Callicott, ''Non-Anthropocentric Value Theory and Environmental Ethics,'' *American Philosophical Quarterly* 21 (1984): 302.

ists would agree with much of Callicott's assessment of traditional Christianity. The Christian panentheist would say that Christ was indeed the Son of God, the first human being to make his way back to the highest level of consciousness. Yet Christ's nondualistic awareness could not be shared by later "Christians," who were still struggling to move beyond the stage of collective consciousness to dualistic ego consciousness and were deeply influenced theologically by neo-Platonic disdain for matter and preference for soul. Because of their soul-matter dualism, early Christians tended to dissociate themselves from creation and to seek an other-worldly home. This dissociation, when combined with the doctrine that humanity had been given "dominion" over creation, helped to justify modern exploitation of the natural world.[5] Such exploitation was spurred on by Reformation doctrines regarding the necessity of "developing" one's talents and the Earth through industry. Indeed, the quest to create a technological-industrial "paradise" on Earth can be regarded as a secular version of the Judeo-Christian promise of a New Jerusalem.[6]

Fortunately, the Judeo-Christian tradition can be interpreted panentheistically, in such a way that the tradition calls for humans to do God's will "on Earth as it is in Heaven." For panentheism, obeying the "will of God" on Earth means accepting and respecting all beings as the fruit of God's creative activity. Such obedience stems automatically from nondualistic awareness, which discerns that divine awareness is not radically separate, but merely concealed from dualistic human awareness.

As a theory, panentheism cannot in and of itself bring about nondualistic experience any more than quantum theory can. Nevertheless, the growing interest on the part of Christian theologians in panentheistic doctrines may be yet another sign of the emergence of nondualistic awareness. Some panentheists describe the evolution of creation in the following way.[7] For "reasons" beyond rational comprehension, the timeless presence of the divine is disturbed by a "disturbance" or "ripple" in which a separate level comes forth from the divine. This separate level falls

5. It is important to note that feminist authors interpret this soul-body dualism, along with other features of ego consciousness, as symptoms of the primary dichotomy in Western civilization: male vs. female. Patriarchalism is allegedly responsible for the domination of nature. To a large extent, the nondualistic mode of awareness described in the present essay is consistent with the nonsexist mode of awareness called for by eco-feminists. On this topic, see my essay "Feminism, Environmental Ethics, and Deep Ecology," *Environmental Ethics* 9 (1987): 21-44. See also Marti Kheel, "The Liberation of Nature: A Circular Affair," *Environmental Ethics* 7 (1985): 135-149; Rosemary Radford Reuther, *New Woman New Earth* (New York: Seabury, 1975); Ynestra King, "Toward an Ecological Feminism and a Feminist Ecology," in *Machina Ex Dea: Feminist Perspectives on Technology,* ed. Joan Rothschild (New York: Pergamon Press, 1983); Ariel Kay Salleh, "Deeper than Deep Ecology: The Eco-Feminist Connection," *Environmental Ethics* 6 (1984): 339-345; Naomi Flax, "Political Philosophy and the Patriarchal Unconscious," *Discovering Reality: Feminist Perspectives on Epistemology, Metaphysics, Methodology, and Philosophy of Science,* ed. Sandra Harding and Merrill Hintikka (Boston: D. Reidel Publishing Company, 1983); Marilyn French, *Beyond Power: On Women, Men, and Morals* (New York: Summit Books, 1985); Carol Gilligan, *In a Different Voice* (Cambridge: Harvard University Press, 1982).

6. The pioneering essay criticizing the Judeo-Christian tradition is Lynn White, Jr.'s, "The Historical Roots of Our Ecologic Crisis," *Science* 155 (1967): 1203-1207. See also David Crownfield,

"The Curse of Abel," *North American Review* 258 (1973): 58-63, and John Passmore, *Man's Responsibility for Nature* (New York: Charles Scribner's Sons, 1974). Passmore argues that the Jewish tradition was more respectful of creation, while the Christian tendency to dominate nature can be traced back to the influence of Greek stoicism on Christian theology. For the most famous feminist critique of patriarchal Christianity, see Mary Daly, *Beyond God the Father* (Boston: Beacon Press, 1973). Since the appearance of White's article in 1967, an enormous literature has arisen to defend the Judaeo-Christian tradition against the charge that it justifies the domination of nature. See, for example, Thomas S. Derr, "Religious Responsibility for Ecological Crisis: An Argument Run Amok," *Worldview* 18 (1975): 39-45; Gordon Kaufman, "A Problem for Theology: The Concept of Nature," *Harvard Theological Review* 65 (1972): 337-366; Daniel O'Connor and Francis Oakley, eds., *Creation: The Impact of an Idea* (New York: Scribner, 1969); Alfred Stefferud, ed., *Christians and the Good Earth* (New York: Friendship Press, 1972); Zachary Hayes, *What Are They Saying about Creation?* (Ramsey, N.J.: Paulist Press, 1980); Loren Wilkinson, *Earthkeeping: Christian Stewardship of Natural Resources* (Grand Rapids, Mich.: Eerdman, 1980); Wesley Granberg-Michaelson, *A Worldly Spirituality: The Call to Redeem the Earth* (New York: Harper & Row, 1985); and David and Eileen Spring, eds., *Ecology and Religion in History* (New York: Harper & Row, 1974).

7. See Wilbur, *Up from Eden;* and Watts, *The Supreme Identity.* Other panentheists, such as Charles Hartshorne, offer a rather different account of creation and evolution. See also the important book by Charles Birch and John Cobb, Jr., *The Liberation of Life* (Cambridge: Cambridge University Press, 1981).

into still lower levels until it manifests itself as the level of matter-energy. This manifestation may correspond with what Genesis calls creation, and with what nondualistic thinkers call "involution." In creation, as Arthur Peacocke has argued, God surrenders or empties Himself/Herself to the lowest level of reality, that of matter-energy.[8] Then, over billions of years of cosmic evolution, matter-energy moves toward ever greater complexity; later stages of development include the earlier stages. Life emerges, and then self-conscious life. The emergence of self-conscious life is a crucial stage in the divine process of reconstituting the levels of reality that were temporarily forgotten when God emptied Himself/Herself into the level of matter-energy and "forgot" Himself/Herself.

Ego consciousness is a constricted form of the self-awareness that is emerging through the history of creation. Even at the level of ego consciousness, humanity has some sense of the divine presence. But ego conscious humanity is stricken with the death anxiety that comes with sensing itself to be separate from and threatened by everything else. Inflated by self-importance and driven by anxiety, the ego engages in the God project: the attempt to turn the finite, mortal ego into the infinite, eternal Divine. Denying its own mortality, the ego projects mortality onto nature: by controlling and even by destroying nature, the ego thinks that it will somehow conquer its own mortality. In addition, the ego projects its mortality and evil onto enemies: by destroying the enemy, the ego believes it destroys its own mortality and evil. This is an important key for understanding the nuclear arms race.[9]

To avoid self destruction, it would appear that humanity must evolve into a more inclusive, nondualistic level of awareness which dissolves the dualisms of ego vs. nature, and of ego vs. ego. Nondual awareness includes, but transcends the level of ego con-

sciousness. Just as someone existing at a collective level of consciousness cannot conceive of what it means to be an autonomous individual, a self-directed ego consciousness, so too someone existing at the stage of ego consciousness cannot appreciate what the next level of consciousness might be. According to panentheists, nondualistic experience discloses that the ego's isolation is illusory and that the ego is not a substantial entity at all, but instead merely a temporary, constricted mode of divine experience.

An important question for panentheists is the degree of independent "reality" that creatures have with respect to their divine source.[10] Many Christian panentheists maintain that although creatures are manifestations of the divine, they also make their own contribution to the creative unfolding of God through creation. Other types of panentheists emphasize that even the relative independence of creatures is an illusion; all creation is a phenomenal form through which the will of God is at work. This view is more typical of certain Vedantic versions of panentheisms.

Such considerations are not a problem for those nondualists who are not panentheists, for example, the Buddhists. Buddhism does not ascribe divinity to the openness/emptiness *(sunyata)* in which all things emerge and dwell. Callicott seems to be more comfortable with Eastern forms of nondualism, as can be seen in his recently published essay on Asian religions and environmental ethics.[11] In this essay, Callicott seems to agree with the view for which I have been arguing: namely, that a transformation of rational awareness is necessary to achieve the nondualism consistent with a doctrine of internal relations.

Warning against a naive conflation of the multifarious Asian traditions into a lump called "Eastern thought," Callicott makes important distinctions

---

8. A.R. Peacocke, *Creation and the World of Science* (New York: Oxford University Press, 1979).

9. See Michael E. Zimmerman, "Humanism, Ontology, and the Nuclear Arms Race," *Research in Philosophy and Technology* 6 (1983): 157-172; Zimmerman, "Anthropocentric Humanism and the Arms Race," *Nuclear War: Philosophical Perspectives,* ed. Michael Fox and Leo Groarke (New York: Peter Lang Publishers, 1985).

10. For this point, and for others as well, I am indebted to an anonymous reviewer of this essay. It would take another essay to develop sufficiently the many important suggestions that he made with regard to the present essay.

11. J. Baird Callicott, "Conceptual Resources for Environmental Ethics in Asian Traditions of Thought: A Propaeduetic," *Philosophy East and West* 37 (1987): 115-130. See also Callicott, "The Metaphysical Implications of Ecology," *Environmental Ethics* 8 (1986): 301-316. Because of constraints of time and space, I have not been able fully to incorporate into the present essay the important ideas found in these recent works by Callicott.

among Vedanta, Confucianism, Taoism, Buddhism, and Zen Buddhism. While he regards Vedanta as too given to monism, and Buddhism as too life denying, Callicott suggests that Confucianism, Taoism, and Zen Buddhism are capable of providing the foundation for a profound environmental ethics. Zen Buddhism, for example, which was influenced by Taoism, offers a nondualistic, aesthetic appreciation of all phenomena, an appreciation that promotes right treatment of all beings. Callicott notes that "The inherent aesthetic quality of the momentary/eternal state of *satori* in Zen distinguishes it from the apparent negativity of *nirvana* in traditional Indian Buddhism."[12] *Satori* is not achieved by cognitive insight into "internal relations," but involves direct, noncognitive, nondualistic experience. There is no longer a cognitive subject contemplating the "fact" of internal relations; instead, there is the *direct manifestation* of this internal relatedness.

Similarly, we can conceive of the relationship between Creator and creation nondualistically. Traditionally, God has been conceived as an entity "out there," while creation is another entity "over here." This dualistic conception was motivated by the proper insight that God cannot be identified with any creature, not even with creation. Pantheism makes such an identification. Panentheism, however, claims that the Creator is both transcendent of and immanent in creation. This state of affairs is paradoxical for cognitive rationality, but not for nondualistic awareness. Panentheistic seers proclaim that while the "Godhead" transcends all creation, creation, nevertheless, is a completely sufficient manifestation of God within the limitations of matter and energy. An "enlightened" human being, then, experiences the divine in the here and now. No longer identifying with the separate "I," and hence no longer driven to protect the "I" from its inevitable death, the enlightened person becomes, in effect, the divine openness in which all creatures can manifest themselves and "be" what they are. Such a person is godlike insofar as he or she bears witness to, marvels at, and participates in the ongoing event of creation. Here we may think of St. Francis of Assisi.

Callicott seems to be moving toward a nondualistic position, one that is consistent with many of the principles of panentheism. His preference for religious traditions—such as Taoism and Zen Buddhism—which both appreciate nature and do not appeal to a transcendent creator, and his antipathy toward the transcendent deity of traditional theocentrism, can be reconciled in a properly constituted panentheistic view. Western people, however, are unlikely to be converted to Zen or Taoism. If an evolution of Western awareness is to occur, it may well need to take place in terms of the Judeo-Christian tradition. A Christian panentheism offers a different interpretation of the meaning of Jesus Christ than do more traditional anthropocentric views. For example, the doctrine of Christ's Incarnation can be interpreted as meaning that the divine is present in creation, not removed from it, and that God is present in *all* creation, not just in human beings. Christ was resurrected only after he had surrendered to his incarnate, mortal status. Hence, redemption does not mean that the eternal soul flies off to an otherworldly heaven; instead, redemption means experiencing eternity here and now in incarnate form.

For the panentheist, the history of the universe is purposive, but its details are not planned in advance. Hence, panentheists are comfortable with recent cosmological speculation which holds that the universe is open-ended, creative, and characterized by novelty. Evidently, God trusts that the interaction of matter-energy will eventually give rise to self-conscious forms of life that will evolve toward divine awareness. Although it was not necessary that *human* life emerge, an increasing number of scientists as well as theologians are saying that it appears to have been inevitable that in a universe like our own *some* form of self-consciousness would emerge.[13]

Recently, cosmologists have been discussing the "anthropic principle," the "strong" version of which maintains that our universe inevitably produces beings capable of observing and in some sense capable of helping to complete that universe.[14] Human

---

12. Callicott, "Conceptual Resources."

13. See Peacocke, *Creation and the World of Science.*
14. Barrow and Tipler, *The Cosmological Anthropic Principle.*

interaction with the rest of creation/nature would then not only give rise to new forms of value, but would also *recognize* the value of creation/nature as it was before human life emerged. Panentheism affirms that creation/nature has intrinsic value, although as noted above panentheists differ with respect to the degree of relative independence to assign to creatures.

While I have not provided an exhaustive account of nondualism, I have shown that a certain kind of nondualistic panentheism is consistent with the wider sense of identification that Callicott holds as the necessary basis for environmental ethics. The search for a solution to the problem of the intrinsic value of nonhuman beings leads to a nondualistic solution. One interpretation of nondualism is panentheism, one form of which holds that all creatures are valuable both in and of themselves *and* insofar as they are manifestations of the divine, and another form of which holds that all creatures are intrinsically valuable only because they are manifestations of the divine. Panentheists tend to agree that humankind has evolved as a result of self-organizing processes of the physical universe, the history of which is the history of God remembering Himself or Herself. Our present, dualistic-anthropocentric level of awareness is an inevitable stage of the evolution toward a more inclusive level of awareness.

Quantum theory and ecology are in many respects consistent at the rational-dualistic level with the experiential insight into internal relationships at the level attained by the awakened person. That increasing numbers of people, even in our anthropocentric age, are recognizing the intrinsic value of nature, suggests that humanity is continuing to evolve toward a more inclusive level of awareness.

CONCLUDING REMARKS

In closing, I want to entertain two objections to what I have been saying: first, that my talk of nondualism, panentheism, and human transformation is utopian and provides no guidance for life in the present; second, that talk of a new, nondomineering humanity-nature relationship is usually accompanied by talk about the need for humanity to become passive with regard to nature.

The first objection correctly perceives the need for moral guidance in the here and now for the great number of people who still operate primarily at the level of ego awareness. At this level of awareness, prudential appeals are most effective for protecting the biosphere from human abuse. Reform environmentalism, which seeks to preserve the environment for human use, will be with us for a long time. There is no contradiction in seeking to reform current ways of using nature while simultaneously seeking a shift toward a more inclusive level of awareness, in light of which nature would manifest itself as something other than an object for domination. Moreover, there is no contradiction between promoting human ''rights'' while at the same time preparing the way for a new level of awareness in which *all* beings are accorded moral respect; indeed, winning universal human rights is a necessary step in consolidating ego awareness. Before such consolidation has taken place, humanity will not be capable of moving to a more inclusive stage of awareness, one that will engender respect for nonhuman reality.

The level of attainment of those who promote a shift to higher consciousness can be discerned, in part, by their attitude toward the ego, dualism, and rationality. If the promoters condemn and call for the destruction of ego consciousness, if they dissociate themselves from rationality, then they themselves remain caught in dualistic thinking. A higher consciousness does not dissociate itself from prior stages, but instead *includes* those stages within itself.

According to the second objection, talk of enlightenment is tied to human passivity and such passivity is incompatible with the obvious need for the human organism to be active in using nature. Moreover, a passive person cannot fulfill or realize him/herself. Hence, so the argument goes, the search for nondualistic awareness and for a more profound humanity-nature relationship ends up stifling human existence.[15]

---

15. See Richard Watson, ''A Critique of Anti-Anthropocentric Biocentrism,'' *Environmental Ethics* 5 (1983): 245-256, and ''Eco-Ethics: Challenging the Underlying Dogmas of Environmentalism,'' *Whole Earth Review,* No. 45 (March 1985): 5-13.

I reply to this objection by arguing that nondualistic awareness neither leads to passivity nor stifles human existence. Indeed, a level of awareness that is more inclusive than ego consciousness promotes a more profound activity and makes possible a more fulfilled human existence than is possible at the level of ego consciousness. Arne Naess, a deep ecologist and student of nondualistic pathways, maintains that a way of life rooted in domination corrupts the master as well as the slave.[16] An awakened humanity would presumably seek to develop the technical means necessary to provide for human welfare and self-development in ways that would not treat the rest of nature/creation merely as raw material. Learning to "let beings be" is not at all incompatible with an active human life that utilizes trees, animals, water, and minerals for life-sustaining, creative, and self-fulfilling purposes.[17] As contrasted with ego consciousness which has no sense of limits, however, enlightened awareness respects the limits proper to him/herself as well as those proper to the rest of creation. Existing fully within one's limits is the sign of wisdom.

In essence, religion promotes more inclusive levels of awareness which overcome the separateness, isolation, and fragmentation caused by dualisms. All too often historical forms of theocentrism have been governed by dualistic thinking (heaven vs. Earth, man vs. nature, man vs. woman, God vs. creation, etc.). In contrast, nondualistic traditions (including panentheism) point beyond the limits of such dualism. Essentially, religion is a linking up *(re-ligio)*, a "re-membering" of what has been disassociated. A glance at any newspaper will reveal the consequences of such disassociation. Whether or not the "remembering" necessary for a sense of limits will occur in time to avert ecological disaster remains to be seen.

If the theocentric traditions are right, however, a disaster that would be catastrophic for our civilization would not be a permanent obstacle to the process whereby the divine "re-members" itself through world history. It may well be that what we have been taught to regard as the pinnacle of the history of consciousness, rational, scientific, technological civilization is in fact a temporary stage that will be *aufgehoben* as a more inclusive stage comes on the scene. Yet it is also possible that a less painful process is already underway, one that will help to move us away from the paradigm of power to the paradigm of mutuality, from the drive toward an already receding goal of total control to the appreciation of loving creativity present in the here and now. It is this process that Callicott seeks to further in his admirable quest for a nondualistic basis for humanity's relation with nature.

DISCUSSION TOPICS

1. How does Zimmerman's interpretation of the creation of the universe differ from your perception of this creation? In what ways might different interpretations affect one's environmental ethic?
2. With which entities in the world do you personally feel the strongest sense of kinship and oneness? From which entities in the world do you feel a sense of separation? What characteristics constitute the consistent differences between those entities?

16. Arne Naess, "A Defense of the Deep Ecology Movement," *Environmental Ethics* 6 (1984): 265-270.

17. The philosopher Martin Heidegger made a significant contribution to the humanity-nature relation with his notion of "letting beings be." On this topic, see Michael E. Zimmerman, "Towards a Heideggerean *Ethos* for Radical Environmentalism," *Environmental Ethics* 5 (1983): 99-131, and "Ontology, Science, and the Humanity-Nature Relationship," *The Modern Schoolman* 64 (1986): 19-43. See also Neil Evernden, *The Natural Alien* (Toronto: The University of Toronto Press, 1985).

READING 64

Christian Spirituality as Openness to Fellow Creatures

Jay McDaniel

Jay McDaniel is an associate professor of religion and the director of the Marshall T. Steel Center for the Study of Religion and Philosophy, Hendrix College, Conway, Arkansas. In addition to his work on the relationship of process theology to environmental ethics, McDaniel also is interested in the dialogues among adherents of Christianity, Buddhism, and liberation theology.

Building on the notion of "feeling for the organism" articulated by Barbara McClintock, Nobel laureate for her work in the genetics of corn, McDaniel addresses four questions. What is the "feeling for the organism?" Why is this feeling important to Christian spirituality? What are its implications for an understanding of nonhuman life within the context of process theology? And finally, how might this feeling be understood in relation to God? McDaniel's answers provide the foundation for an environmental ethic grounded in process theology.

INTRODUCTION

Barbara McClintock is a Nobel laureate who pioneered discoveries in gene transposition through years of work with corn plants. In a recently published biography Evelyn Fox Keller describes McClintock's approach to these plants and in so doing reveals aspects of McClintock's understanding of nature. As she studies her corn plants, we are told, McClintock brings with her not simply the observational and analytical skills characteristic of all good scientists, but also a certain intuitive sensitivity: an inward openness to fellow creatures. McClintock tells Keller that in good biological research, a person must have the patience to "hear what the material has to say to you," the openness to "let it come to you." Above all, she says, one must have a "feeling for the organism."[1]

The purpose of this essay is to interpret this feeling and show its relevance to Christian spirituality. Four questions are addressed. What is the feeling? Why is it important to Christian spirituality? How, within a specific theological context, might its implications for an understanding of nonhuman life be understood? And how might its relation to God be understood? The essay is divided into four sections corresponding to these questions.

A FEELING FOR THE ORGANISM

What is McClintock's "feeling for the organism"? Judging from her comments and Keller's commentary, it is an appreciative and intuitive apprehension of an organism in three of its aspects. In the first place, it is a feeling for the organism as a *unique individual.* "No two plants are alike," McClintock tells Keller, "they're all different, and as a consequence, you have to know that difference." McClintock continues: "I start with the seedling, and I don't want to leave it. I don't feel I really know the story if I don't watch the plant all the way along. So I know every plant in the field, I know them intimately, and I find it a great pleasure to know them"[2]

In the second place, it is a feeling for the organism as a *mysterious other.* Keller quotes Einstein as saying that science often proceeds from "a deep longing to understand even a faint reflexion of the reason revealed in the world," but then she tells us that on this point McClintock may differ. "McClintock's feeling for the organism is not simply a longing to behold the 'reason revealed in this world'." Rather it is "a longing to embrace the world in its very being, through reason and beyond." And how does the organism supercede reason? "For McClintock, reason—at least in the conventional sense of the word—is not by itself adequate to describe the vast complexity—even mystery—of living forms. Organisms have a life and order of their own that scientists can only partially fathom."[3] This life of its own is the organism's otherness, and the intuitable and yet ungraspable elusiveness of this life is the organism's mystery.

In the third place, McClintock's feeling for the organism is a sensitivity to the creature as a *fellow subject.*[4] Keller writes that "over the years a special kind of sympathetic understanding grew in McClintock, heightening her powers of discernment, until finally, the objects of her study have become subjects in their own right." These objects "claim from her a special kind of attention that most of us expe-

---

1. Evelyn Fox Keller, *A Feeling for the Organism: The Life and Work of Barbara McClintock* (San Francisco: W.H. Freeman and Company, 1983), p. 200.

---

2. Ibid., p. 198.
3. Ibid., p. 199.
4. In this essay I use the word *fellow* reluctantly, hoping that it can be understood in a manner free from gender bias.

rience only in relation to other persons.''[5] In fact, as Keller explains, the natural objects are not simply objects for McClintock; they are organisms.

> Organism is for her a code word—not simply a plant or animal (''Every component of the organism is as much of an organism as every other part'')—but the name of a living form, of object-as-subject. With an uncharacteristic lapse into hyperbole, McClintock says: ''Every time I walk on grass I feel sorry because I know the grass is screaming at me.''[6]

Judging from Keller's assumption that McClintock's comment concerning walking on grass is hyperbole, we can surmise that the quality of a corn plant's life for itself—that is, its life as a subject—would be markedly different from that of a human's life for himself or herself. Compared to human subjectivity, corn plant subjectivity would undoubtedly seem mysterious in its otherness. Yet McClintock's orientation suggests that humans can feel a sense of kinship amid this mystery, because, after all, humans and other forms of life are fellow subjects with common evolutionary roots. Corn plants are distant, perhaps *very* distant, cousins: strange and yet lovable kin.

THE NEED FOR A NEW SPIRITUALITY

Let us assume that McClintock's sensitivities are accurate, and that organisms are in fact strange kin to which we can be sympathetically attuned. The question is: can a feeling for the organism of the sort exemplified by McClintock be understood religiously, that is, as a distinctive mode of spirituality in which humans are directly attuned to God? Stated another way, can a love of flora and fauna as they exist in and for themselves, rather than as they exist for industrial or economic purposes, be understood as feeling with God?

This question is important because it has so often been neglected or answered negatively in Christianity, the world's most populous religion. In particular it has been neglected by Western Christians. The roots

of this neglect go as far back as the ancient Hebrew renunciation of fertility cults and the early Christian adoption of a spirit-matter dichotomy as learned from the Greeks. Beginning with these roots Western Christians traditionally have been encouraged to find God indirectly through charitable relations with other people and through self-examination, and directly through prayer and meditation, but rarely, with a few important exceptions, through attunement to plants and animals. To Western Christian ears the discovery of God through attunement to fellow creatures has smacked of pantheism: an idolatrous identification of God with nature.

Given this heritage it is no accident that many environmentalists have seen Christianity as a dangerously unecological, and indeed anti-ecological, tradition. An ecological religious tradition is one that recognizes the intrinsic value of nonhuman forms of life, such that they are approached as ends in themselves and not simply as means to other ends. By contrast, the Christian tradition has often stressed only the instrumental value of nonhuman forms of life, either their instrumentality for human purposes or for divine ends. In emphasizing the sovereignty of humans or a supernatural God, Christians have either ignored or denied nature's value *in itself*. The inadequacy of this orientation has been brought to light in Lynn White's much publicized article ''The Historical Roots of Our Ecological Crisis.''[7] Despite various attempts at rebuttal, there remains truth to White's claim that Christian habits of thought are partly responsible for environmental problems in the West and in regions that have become Westernized.[8] As White puts it, ''Christianity bears a huge burden of guilt.''[9]

---

5. Ibid., p. 200.
6. Ibid.

7. Lynn White, Jr., ''The Historical Roots of our Ecological Crisis,'' *Science* 155 (1967): 1203-1207.

8. It may be that biblical habits of thought, particularly those found in the Hebrew Bible, are more ecological than post-biblical ways of thinking developed by Christian theology. For a demonstration of certain ''ecological'' dimensions of biblical thinking, see Susan Power Bratton, ''Christian Ecotheology and the Old Testament,'' *Environmental Ethics* 6 (1984): 195-209.

9. Ibid., p. 1207.

Given the truth in White's claim, and given the increasing influence of Christianity among the peoples of the world, particularly in Africa and Latin America, one thing is clear. Any long-term solution to environmental problems will depend, at least in part, on a change within Christianity itself. What is needed is a shift in the very nature of Christian spirituality: a shift from an unecological to an ecological spiritual orientation.

The shift can be accomplished in the West in at least three ways. It can be effected (1) by a rediscovery of subdominant emphases within the Western heritage itself, such as those of Francis of Assisi and the Rhineland mystics.[10] This is the transition White recommends. It can be generated (2) by an appropriation of insights from Eastern Orthodoxy, a rich and often neglected tradition which has generally emphasized a sacramental understanding of the natural world. Or the shift can be accomplished (3) by learning from emerging Christian traditions that seek explicit disengagement from Western habits of thought. Here I am speaking of the new forms of Christian self-understanding that are emerging in subdominant perspectives in North America, such as Black, Feminist, and Native American Christian theologies, and in "liberation" perspectives from Asia, Africa, and Latin America. In the latter context, Christian spirituality can be transformed by an inclusion of ecological insights from women's experience, from Primal (e.g., Native American and African) perspectives, and from Eastern (e.g., Buddhist and Taoist) points of view.[11] In any or all of these three ways, the transition within Western Christianity must be from a spirituality that sees nature *apart* from God, as is typical of

a great deal of Western Christian past, to a spirituality that sees nature *in* God, as can be typical of a global and yet culturally diverse Christian future.

Besides the three types of transformation just noted, however, there is a fourth type, and one that is perhaps closer to home for some Christians in the West. Christian spirituality can be transformed by learning from the sensitive naturalist. By "naturalist" I mean someone such as Henry Thoreau, Walt Whitman, John Muir, Aldo Leopold, or Annie Dillard: someone who spends a good deal of time in nature itself, who seeks to learn as much about nature as he or she can from direct observation, and who does so out of a deep respect for its beauties and mysteries. I mean someone, to take a particular example, like Barbara McClintock.

PROCESS THEOLOGY AS ECOLOGICAL THEOLOGY

It is fortunate that today there is a theological resource available for appropriating McClintock's insights. It is process theology: a religious perspective that is being developed predominantly, though not exclusively, in Christian circles, and that is deeply influenced by the philosophies of Alfred North Whitehead and Charles Hartshorne. Following Whitehead and Hartshorne, yet also drawing from certain biblical points of view, process thinkers such as John B. Cobb, Jr., L. Charles Birch, Marjorie Suchocki, and David Ray Griffin agree with McClintock that each living organism is a unique individual, a mysterious other, and a fellow subject.[12] In these respects and others their theology has many parallels to Primal and Eastern perspectives, and thus represents a bridge by which Christians can learn, not only from Mc-

---

10. See Matthew Fox, "Creation-Centered Spirituality from Hildegard of Bingen to Julian of Norwich: 300 Years of An Ecological Spirituality in the West," in *Cry of the Environment: Rebuilding the Christian Creation Tradition,* ed. Philip N. Joranson and Ken Butigan (Sante Fe: Bear and Company, 1984), pp. 84-106.

11. For an example of how Christianity might become more environmentally sensitive through an inclusion of insights from women's experience, see Rosemary Radford Ruether, *Sexism and God-Talk: Toward a Feminist Theology* (Boston: Beacon Press, 1983), pp. 72-92.

12. For a good introduction to process theology, see John B. Cobb, Jr. and David Ray Griffin, *Process Theology: An Introductory Exposition* (Philadelphia: Westminster Press, 1976). Of particular interest to those concerned with a theology of nature is chapter 4. The best statement to date of the process theology of ecology, particularly with reference to its implications for environmental ethics, is John B. Cobb, Jr. and L. Charles Birch, *The Liberation of Life: From Cell to Community* (Cambridge: Cambridge University Press, 1981).

Clintock, but also from other ecologically oriented religious traditions. Amid such learning, so process thinkers suggest, Christianity can itself be transformed. Indeed, a new Christianity can emerge.[13]

Those who first encounter the process perspective rightly ask at the outset how such a process of learning, and hence of change within Christianity, can be justified? At least as process theologians understand Christianity, a change is justified because Christianity is itself an ongoing process capable of growth and change rather than a settled and static fact that is doomed to repeat every aspect of its past. Christianity is a continuing historical movement within which, in each new age, new generations with new ideas rightly participate. Through their participation, the religion can itself take new forms. A new generation's faithfulness to Christ does not lie in absolutizing the Christian past, even though some aspects of that past may be quite resourceful and are appropriately appreciated and repeated. Rather, faithfulness lies in being open to a God whose call perpetually comes from the future rather than the past, beckoning for openness to truth, goodness, and beauty, whatever their sources. Such openness is itself responsive to what process thinkers such as Cobb call the living Christ, the divine Logos revealed in, but not exhausted by, Jesus.[14] It is because Christianity is a process, initiated but not completed by Jesus, that it can become more ecological despite its ambiguous past.[15]

As must all who espouse an ecological religious orientation, process thinkers affirm that in its individuality a living organism is of intrinsic value. In these affirmations they recommend a new Christianity that is responsive, in a constructive rather than defensive way, to the critique of Lynn White. In order to evaluate whether or not they succeed in their intentions, and in order to see how they might learn from McClintock, we do well to clarify further their notion of intrinsic value. In a process context to feel another organism as a unique individual, a mysterious other, and a fellow subject is to be aware of it as having—that is, as inwardly embodying and outwardly expressing—such value.

The process affirmation of an organism's intrinsic value does not exclude a concomitant recognition of the organism's instrumentality. Nor does it deny that an organism has its identity in relation to, rather than independence from, other creatures and the surrounding environment. Consider, for example, how a process thinker might understand a single animal, for example, a deer.

From a process perspective an individual deer embodies and expresses intrinsic value. Yet, it also has instrumental value for other creatures in its natural environment. Instrumentally understood, for example, the deer may be an object of prey for wolves, and it may also be an object of instrumental value for humans who hunt it for food. It is part of an ecosystem in which it plays an instrumental role. Furthermore, as attention to systemic realities makes clear, the deer's existence, both as an object for others and as a subject for itself, is relational. Without its surroundings, it would not be what it is, and, indeed, it would not be at all.

It is amid rather than apart from this relationality that the deer has intrinsic value. It has this value because, even with its instrumentality, it is an experiencing subject with reality for itself and hence value to itself. It has—or, better, *is*—a living psyche concerned with its own survival and well-being. Of course, this psyche is not an isolated ego of the sort Descartes envisioned. The deer's psyche, like a human psyche, is an ongoing process of taking into account data from its own point of view, and of subjectively synthesizing these data into immediately prehended gestalts. The data may be physical stimulants such as internal pains and pleasures, or extrabodily influences such as trees, leaves, and other animals. In any case, the objects are appropriated by the

---

13. For an example of how process thinkers believe Christianity might be transformed through its encounter with Buddhism, see John B. Cobb, Jr., *Beyond Dialogue: Toward a Mutual Transformation of Christianity and Buddhism* (Philadelphia: Fortress Press, 1982).

14. John B. Cobb, Jr., *Christ in a Pluralistic Age* (Philadelphia: Westminster Press, 1975), pp. 82-94.

15. The most extensive survey of this ambiguous past has been made by Paul Santmire in *The Travail of Nature: The Ambiguous Ecological Promise of Christian Theology* (Philadelphia: Fortress Press, 1985).

deer through its conscious and unconscious feelings of them. These feelings—or "prehensions," as Whitehead speaks of them—are the very way in which the deer, as a subject for itself, is inextricably related to its body and to the surrounding world. These relations are not adventitious to the deer's reality as a subject; rather they are constitutive of that reality. It is in the deer's relational subjectivity, and in its attendant richness of experience, that the deer has value in and for itself, and hence intrinsic value.

In accordance with the tradition of Leibniz in the West, various religious traditions in the East, the Primal traditions the world over, process theologians suggest that all creatures are instances of relational subjectivity, and hence that all creatures have intrinsic value. A "creature" can be understood as any entity that is created through its relationships with, and responses to, other entities, including God. A creature may be an energy event within the depths of an atom, an individual molecule, a living cell, or a psychophysical organism such as a deer or human. In process theology there is no sharp line between creatures that are sentient and those that are insentient, although sentience or subjectivity need not be "conscious" or "reflective" in ways with which humans and other animals may be familiar. There was never a time in cosmic evolution when all creatures were utterly devoid of sentience and when, out of sheer inert matter, sentience appeared. Rather evolution has been, and continues to be, an unfolding process, proceeding sometimes gradually and sometimes by leaps and spurts, of different types of creatures with different types of physical organization, and with different degrees and ways of being sentient.

How does this view of nature compare with that of McClintock? For purposes of comparison it is important to note that for process thinkers there are two different ways in which a creature can exemplify such subjectivity. A creature can be (1) a system of relational subjects with a psyche, that is, with a presiding or dominant subject that consciously or unconsciously receives input from all the other members and either consciously or unconsciously initiates responses. Or it can be (2) a system of relational subjects without a presiding or dominant subject that thus re-

ceives influences and initiates responses. Stated another way, a creature can be a *monarchical* system whose complex unity, oftentimes called its body, houses a dominant subject, oftentimes called its psyche or soul; or it can be a *democratic* system whose body, though a complex totality of interrelated subjects, has no dominant member.

It is important to note that a psyche or soul as thus understood is not a supernatural entity. It is not something of an ontological type entirely different from that of cells and molecules, implanted in an organism by God. Rather it is a series of experiences, a series of relational subjects, each of which inherit from their predecessors with particular intimacy, and each of which, upon occurrence, receive data from the body and surrounding environment, therein initiating responses. The soul, like a cell or molecule, is natural rather than supernatural.

A hypothetical example may help. The deer alluded to above was conceived as a monarchy. It was understood as a psychophysical organism, as an organism with a psyche. In discussing its intrinsic value, the focus was on its psyche, its reality for itself. The deer was understood as a living subject. The cells in the deer's body, too, can be conceived as monarchies, that is, as living subjects. Amid their complexity they seem to exhibit a capacity for unified response which suggests that they have reality for themselves as well as reality for others. They, too, have intrinsic value as psyches, though the richness of their experience, in terms of their capacity for intensity, is probably less than that of the deer's psyche. In any case, the deer, at this level of analysis, is a psychic monarchy of cellular monarchies.[16]

---

16. Even the organelles within these cells might even be monarchies. The molecules of which these organelles are composed might best be conceived as democracies, as might the atoms composing these molecules. Molecules and atoms seem to lack subjective centers, even though the energy events composing them exhibit small degrees of subjective responsiveness. As a psychophysical organism, then, the deer can be conceived as a monarchy of cellular monarchies, each of which are themselves monarchies of organellic monarchies, which are themselves monarchies of democratically organized subcellular parts.

But what of plants? Process theologians generally suggest that individual plants, considered as unified organisms, are democracies rather than monarchies. While the cells in a given plant are monarchies, an individual plant seems to be a complex system of such monarchies, with no overriding subject.[17] A plant is a democracy of cellular monarchies.

If we agree with the judgment of most process theologians that plants are democracies rather than monarchies, we might easily infer that individual plants, in contrast to individual animals, cannot be correctly perceived as subjects. Plants are, after all, not unified subjects in their own right. They are only aggregates of subjects. It would seem that, by virtue of their status as aggregates, they cannot be appropriately felt as fellow subjects.

If we take McClintock's perspective normatively, as I do in this essay, we realize that such a conclusion is false. McClintock does indeed perceive individual plants as subjects, and as "unique" subjects at that. "No two plants are alike," she tells us, "they're all different. . . . So I have to know every plant in the field. I know them intimately."

To date process theologians have not taken up the challenge of McClintock's perspective, primarily because they have not devoted much attention to the various ways in which plants can be directly experienced. Their focus has been on a theoretical interpretation of plants and animals such as that proffered above, but not on a phenomenological description of how, in the immediacy of experience, plants and animals might be directly and appreciatively perceived. If they are to carry through the development of an ecological Christianity, process thinkers still have much to learn from phenomenological studies of how humans can perceive plants and animals.

It may be that, following further empirical investigation by phenomenologists and scientists, process theologians will conclude that at a theoretical level plants, too, are monarchies. This would open the door in an unambiguous way for an appropriation of McClintock's sensitivities. But perhaps they need not alter their theoretical perspective in order to learn from McClintock. Keeping their current distinction between plants as democracies and some animals as monarchies, they can affirm that there are at least two ways in which macroscopic flora and fauna might be truthfully and appreciatively perceived: as *unifying subjects,* as in the case of animals with psyches, or as *aggregate subjects,* as in the case of most plants.

To perceive an organism as a *unifying subject* is to perceive it as having a perspective, or point of view, of its own. That perspective may be strangely different from one's own; and indeed it may be quite mysterious. But it is a perspective nonetheless, and it cannot be reduced to a totality of parts that compose the organism's body, not even the totality of neurons composing the brain. It is the organism's psyche or soul: a whole that is greater than the sum of the parts. This whole is more than the sum of its parts, not in the sense that it is independent of those parts, but rather in the sense that it is a subjective synthesis of those parts into a perspective of its own. A unifying subject is a living synthesis of many data, bodily and extra-bodily, into a single whole, enjoyed by the subject itself.

To perceive an organism as an *aggregate subject* is to perceive it as a subjective unity, but not as a unifying subject. One recognizes that the organism's unity is actually the sum of the various perspectives composing the organism's body. Considered as a whole, the organism is not greater than its parts; rather the organism is its parts. As it appears to the human senses, this organismic whole can be perceived as a singular, outward manifestation of various types of inward subjective energy; and in the singularity of this manifestation the organism is thus perceived as a subjective unity. Yet, as in the case of a corn plant, this inward subjective energy belongs to the cells and the subcellular organisms that compose them. As McClintock put it in describing her plants: "Every component of the organism is as much of an organism as every other part." Her statement implies that the cells are the organisms, the living subjects, with which the larger organism, the plant as aggregate subject, is identical. McClintock's intuitions reveal that one can well have a feeling for this aggregate subject. This

---

17. Cobb and Griffin, *Process Theology,* p. 78.

would be an intuition of the plant's various cellular modes of subjective being as they exist, and display themselves, in a single presentation of interrelated unity. One can have, as McClintock affirms, "a feeling for the organism."

Through this distinction between aggregate subjects, which are democratic systems, and unifying subjects, which are monarchical systems, process theology can affirm along with McClintock that all living organisms—plants and animals—are fellow subjects to which a person can be sympathetically attuned. It is important to reiterate that a feeling for the organism—either as unifying subject of as aggregate subject—involves a respect, not only for the organism's unique individuality, but for its *otherness*. This reiteration is important as a response to an objection that can easily and understandably be directed at panexperiential perspectives of the sort process thinkers endorse.

It can be argued that what process thinkers and McClintock might take as a recognition of subjectivity in nonhuman forms of life is actually an illegitimate projection of human traits onto nonhuman organisms: perhaps an unjustified way of "raising organisms up" to a human level in order to argue for their worth.[18] The objectors would argue that the process perspective fails to appreciate the genuine "otherness" of nonhuman ways of being, and that the perspective therefore expresses and encourages a form of human arrogance.

Process thinkers and McClintock will appreciate the motives behind the objection. They, too, are interested in undercutting human arrogance, and they, too, want to affirm the idea that nonhuman forms of life exemplify modes of being that are radically and beautifully *different* from those with which humans are familiar. Yet they argue that the reluctance to admit subjectivity in nonhuman forms of life can itself express and encourage a form of arrogance. It can suggest that human experience, even in its subconscious and prereflective depths, is a supreme exception to, rather than expression of, that which is found throughout nature, and hence that there is a sharp dichotomy between human and nonhuman forms of existence. It is in order to avoid such dualism and its attendant arrogance that process thinkers affirm a continuity between human and nonhuman experience. Yet they recognize that amid this continuity there are different degrees and kinds of subjectivity. Some types of organisms may have greater degrees of subjectivity than others, and all organisms have unique types of subjectivity: types that can indeed seem strange and "other," and yet mysteriously beautiful, to humans.

Particularly exemplary of this strangeness will be the kind of subjectivity expressed in inorganic materials. For Whiteheadians even rocks are aggregate expressions of subjective energy that is constitutive of the energy events within the depths of atoms. In its quality and degree this subjective energy is undoubtedly quite different from anything known by living beings. Compared to plant and animal sentience its degree of intensity may seem quite negligible and its value quite trivial. But the intensity and value are not nonexistent. The living vibrancy of rocks can be felt in mountains and boulders experienced in certain types of outdoor experiences; it can be sensed in a different way in Zen rock gardens and in certain forms of sculpture; it has been expressed in many of the paintings of artists such as Ruskin and Cezanne; and it is perhaps implied by the most advanced frontiers of contemporary science.[19] As William Barrett has

---

18. In understanding the import of, and motivations behind, this objection, I have been aided by conversations with Holmes Rolston, III. Rolston has also pointed out the possible limitations of doctrines of intrinsic value. See his article "Are Values in Nature Subjective or Objective?" *Environmental Ethics* 4 (1982): 146. He writes: "But the 'for what it is itself' facet of intrinsic becomes problematic in a holistic web. It is too internal and elementary; it forgets relatedness and externality." The process affirmation of intrinsic value avoids Rolston's critique. It does not succumb to that forgetfulness of relatedness to which Rolston rightly objects.

---

19. See Jay McDaniel, "Physical Matter as Creative and Sentient," *Environmental Ethics* 5 (1983): 291-317, for a discussion of how quantum mechanics can imply a panpsychist view of physical matter, and for a discussion of the kind of spiritual attunement that might be involved with inorganic matter.

written: "Whoever thinks matter is mere inert stuff has not looked long at rocks."[20]

In the last analysis, then, a "feeling for the organism" need not be limited to fellow plants and animals. It can extend to *all* fellow creatures. All existents are, in one way or another, organisms. A feeling for their organismic quality can unfold within the human psyche in many different ways, some of which may seem to the experiencer more "aesthetic" than "religious" given ordinary connotations of the terms. All such feelings will involve a realization that an existent's outer form is an expression of its inward energy, and that this energy has a quality of conscious or unconscious for-itself-ness. This for-itself-ness can be felt either as the presence of a subject in its own right, as when with sympathetic attunement we apprehend a deer, or as the presence of something that exudes living energy because it is expressive of things that are subjects in their own right, as when we apprehend plants and inorganic realities. Our apprehension of this for-itself-ness will always be dim and vague. As conscious or unconscious, it will be interfused with other sorts of feelings that obstruct its purity. A "feeling for the organism" is almost never a clear and distinct perception of the sort Descartes cherished. But it is nonetheless important, because it reveals to us our fellow creatures and our solidarity with them. Additionally it is important because, for Christians and others who are thus inclined, it is a distinctive way of dwelling with God.

FEELING FOR THE ORGANISM AS COMMUNION WITH GOD

Spirituality in a theistic context can be one or some combination of several types of experiences. It can be an openness to God as God transcends the world, as is the case in certain forms of private prayer and apophatic mysticism. It can be an openness to God as immanent within the world, as is the case in certain forms of this-worldly mysticism in which one sees God in other people and fellow creatures. Or it can be an openness to the world as it is known and loved by God, as is the case with a "feeling for the organism." In what follows I focus on the latter.

Openness to the world as known and loved by God is a contemporary and ecologically minded version of what Paul conceived as putting on the mind of God.[21] It is feeling the presence of the world as God feels it. In a process context this feeling need not be understood simply as a mirroring by humans of God's way of feeling, as if God were "up there" and humans and the rest of nature "down here." Rather it can be understood as an actual internalization of divine feeling within the human psyche: a lived participation in the divine consciousness.[22] To put on the mind of God is to allow God to feel the world through oneself, and thus to allow God's consciousness to become one's own, subject of course to human limitations.

Considered in its own right, at least as process thinkers imagine it, God's consciousness has at least three qualities. First, it feels each creature on its own terms: that is, as that creature uniquely synthesizes the many data of its world into a single whole. This is God's feeling of each individual in its relational particularity and its intrinsic value. Second, God's consciousness feels the totality of creatures as a single, ongoing system: a kingdom of God in which all things are directly or indirectly related to all other things, in which new events continually occur, and in which new creatures continually emerge. This is God's feeling of the world as an unfinished and yet momentarily complete whole. Third, the divine consciousness feels both the individual creature, and the

---

20. William Barrett, *The Illusion of Technique* (New York: Anchor Books, 1979), pp. 368–369.

21. Romans 12:2: "Do not be conformed to this world but be transformed by the renewal of your mind, that you may prove what is the will of God, what is good and acceptable and perfect." See also Eph. 4:24; Col. 3:10 and 3:14. For an interesting discussion of this type of spirituality in a different context, see John B. Cobb, Jr., "Traditional Religions in Japan and Christianity," *School of Theology at Claremont Bulletin,* vol. 26, no. 5.

22. In technical process terminology, this can be understood as a repetition of divine "subjective forms," particularly those subjective forms which qualify God's "consequent nature." The repetition can itself be understood as a certain way of experiencing God's consequent nature in the mode of causal efficacy.

world as a whole, in light of their interconnected possibilities for the future. This is God's feeling of the world in light of what can become the case, or ought to become the case, if maximum richness of experience is to be realized.

A Christian spirituality will put on the mind of God in each of these three ways. First, to whatever degree is possible given human limitations, individuals who embody this spirituality will be sensitive to individual creatures as they exist in and for themselves. Each will have a mind and heart for the concrete and the particular, human and nonhuman, in its inwardness and in its varying degrees and kinds of intrinsic value. Second, they will be aware of themselves as existing within a vast network of existing creatures, all of which form a single, cosmic ecosystem, or a "great economy," as Wendell Berry speaks of it. They will not grasp the whole as a totality in relation to which they are spectators; rather they will feel it as an ultimate and mysterious context within which, in reverence and humility, they live and die. Third, they will be open to, and hopeful concerning, growth for as many individuals as they can, and for the whole. They will feel themselves as part of a cosmic adventure greater than themselves, though an adventure whose destiny partially depends on their actions in the present.

In the latter context, Christians' spirituality will naturally unfold as an ethic. Their concern for well-being of individuals and for the whole will lead them toward an active advocacy of those ideals which best enhance the well-being of life in its ongoing adventure: namely, peace, social justice, and ecological sustainability. What these ideals mean in terms of public policy has been spelled out in some amount of detail by Charles Birch and John Cobb. Considered as a whole, they are aspects of what these thinkers call an "ethic of life."[23]

McClintock's "feeling for the organism" embodies the first of the three dimensions of a holistic spir-

ituality noted above. It is putting on the mind of God, and therein being sensitive to individual creatures as they exist in and for themselves. Considered in itself, it is not sufficient for an adequate environmental ethic or even a satisfying spirituality. It cannot and should not be separated from the other dimensions, which is to say that it should be accompanied by a sense for the cosmos and the Earth's biosphere as systems within which humans and other animals reside, and by a concern for the well-being and future of these systems and the various micro-systems of which they consist. But a feeling for systems in which individuals participate is insufficient without a concomitant feeling for individuals themselves. If one is to participate in the ongoing adventure of the kingdom with gentleness, one must learn to see, not just the systems, but the individual participants, in God.

To see the creature *in* God is to see it as the very content of God's feeling and indeed God's life. Such seeing presupposes, of course, that there is a God and that this God feels: a presupposition which is essential to most biblical perspectives, and which process theologians share. What must be noted, however, is the special character of God's experience, at least as process thinkers understand it. In a Whiteheadian context God's experience is best understood, not on the analogy of external sense perception, in which the objects experienced are thought to be external to the subject experiencing, but rather on the analogy of memory, in which the objects remembered (past events) are felt as immanent within the subject remembering, or even better on the analogy of immediate bodily experience, in which the objects felt (for example, a pain in one's stomach) are felt as immanent with the subject experiencing the pain. From a process perspective God feels the world as within, rather than external to, God's own life.

Indeed, process thinkers believe that there is nothing in the universe outside the divine life, although, as within the divine life, creatures have autonomous creativity and sentience. The universe as a whole is a monarchy rather than a democracy. It has a dominant soul, or a subjective center, which at any given moment feels all things, much in the manner that a mind feels things in its body. This universal soul—a whole

---

23. For an elaboration of this "ethic of life" as it transcends anthropocentrism, and as it involves specific proposals of justice and sustainability, see Birch and Cobb, *The Liberation of Life*, pp. 141-175.

that is greater than, and yet includes, its parts—is God, understood as the ongoing Psyche of the universe. The totality of creatures in the universe constitutes God's own body.

The divine Psyche feels things as they are, in their inward as well as outward properties, and loves them. A Christian spirituality that sees nature in God will attempt to feel nonhuman organisms as God feels them, that is, with openness to what they are in and for themselves, and with love. It will recognize that nonhuman organisms are parts of the divine body, and it will recognize that humans, too, are parts of that body. Such recognition will not preclude an awareness of the instrumental value various parts can have for one another. It will not preclude a *use* of the land, of animals in certain ways, and of plants in others. Indeed, it will not preclude a use of other people. But such use will not be wanton, and it will be complemented whenever circumstances allow by a willingness to let things be, to allow them to flourish in their own right. It will be in Wendell Berry's terms, ''kindly use.''[24] Its underlying spirit, like God's own, will be a reverence for life.

It is primarily through the development of such a spirituality and its attendant ethic, not through historical defense, that Christians can adequately respond to Lynn White's critique of their tradition. Christians need not defend all that they have been in the past. Such defensiveness usually indicates idolatry. It is absolutizing the past and therein failing to respond to the divine Logos, whom they name the living Christ. This Christ, enfleshed but not exhausted by Jesus, is none other than the divine Psyche itself, immanent as a cosmic Lure. In different ways and forms, Christ is present within all creatures, human and nonhuman. Within humans, Christ comes as an inwardly felt and continuously present invitation to love life more fully and deeply. When Christians learn to walk lightly on the earth, having cultivated that feeling for the organism of which McClintock speaks, they will have extended their horizons of care. A feeling, which in certain ways they have often already cultivated in relation to fellow humans, will then be enjoyed in relation to fellow creatures. Amid such enjoyment they will be responding even more fully to the call of Christ.

DISCUSSION TOPICS

1. McDaniel describes three qualities of God's consciousness from the perspective of a process theologian. Which quality do you find least compelling or valid? Why? What additional qualities might be descriptive of God's consciousness?
2. Using McDaniel's metaphors, do you believe the universe is more like a monarchy or a democracy? Explain your rationale.

CASE FOR CLASS DEBATE

Many scholars have addressed the question of whether the Judeo-Christian religious tradition, or some alternative such as Greek philosophy, has contributed more to destructive environmental values found in Western society.

Using the guidelines presented in Appendix A, debate the two sides of this issue. Which arguments were appealed to by each side? Which were most effective?

FOR FURTHER READING

Anglemyer, M., E.R. Seagraves, and C.C. LeMaistre. *A Search for Environmental Ethics: An Initial Bibliography.* Smithsonian Institution Press, Washington, D.C.: 1980. An excellent annotated bibliography (119 pp.) of books and papers up to the late 1970s that deal with the moral and religious aspects of human relationships to the environment. This collection is particularly strong in its summary of Judeo-Christian literature.

Attfield, Robin. ''Western Traditions and Environmental Ethics,'' in *Environmental Philosophy,* Robert Elliot and Arran Gare, eds. University Park, Pa.: 1983. Attfield disputes a number of the criticisms leveled against the Judeo-Christian tradition as a source of the environmental crisis in the West, and argues that the best hope for an environmental ethic lies in the Western cultural tradition, rather than in a new philosophy.

---

24. Wendell Berry, *The Unsettling of America: Culture and Agriculture* (New York: Avon Books, 1977), p. 31.

Barbour, Ian G. *Western Man and Environmental Ethics: Attitudes Toward Nature and Technology.* Reading, Mass.: Addison-Wesley Publishing Company, 1972. Sixteen scholars examine the basic assumptions about nature, humans, and society. They address the social priorities, value judgments, and ethical issues involved in policy decisions about the environment. A number of the scholars focus on the role of the Judeo-Christian tradition as a contributor to the environmental crisis. Others evaluate the potential role of the Judeo-Christian tradition as a source for an environmental philosophy.

Berman, Morris. *The Reenchantment of the World.* Ithaca, N.Y.: Cornell University Press 1981. An analysis of the meaning of nature in religion.

Black, John. *The Dominion of Man: The Search for Ecological Responsibility.* Edinburgh: University Press, 1970. Chapter 2 (''The Western World-View''), Chapter 3 (''Dominion Over Nature''), and Chapter 4 (''The Concept of Stewardship'') address the relationship of the Judeo-Christian tradition to contemporary Western views about nature.

Bratton, Susan Power. ''The Original Desert Solitaire: Early Christian Monasticism and Wilderness.'' *Environmental Ethics* 10: 31-53, 1988. Argues that St. Francis was not unusual in his posture of humility and respect toward the natural world, but rather part of a long monastic tradition.

Buber, Martin. *I and Thou.* New York: Charles Scribner's Sons, 1970. A very difficult, but perceptive discussion on building intimate relationships between the self and the rest of the world, including God.

Callicott, J. Baird. ''Genesis and John Muir.'' *Revision* 12: 31-47, 1990. Presents John Muir's view that God cares for the creation as a whole and all its parts equally. In contrast, anthropocentrism may be original sin.

Callicott, J. Baird. ''The Search for an Environmental Ethic,'' in *Matters of Life and Death,* T. Regan, ed. Prospect Heights, Ill.: Waveland Press, 1990. Offers a thoughtful and critical look at the environmental ethics derived from the Judeo-Christian tradition.

Cobb, John B., Jr. and L. Charles Birch. *The Liberation of Life: From Cell to Community.* Cambridge: Cambridge University Press, 1981. An excellent statement on process theology in relation to ecology. Good insights on the implications of process theology for environmental ethics.

Cobb, John B., Jr. and David Ray Griffin. *Process Theology: An Introductory Exposition.* Philadelphia: Westminster Press, 1976. A good introduction to process theology, with insights on a theology of nature presented in Chapter 4.

Elsdon, Ron. *Bent World: A Christian Response to the Environmental Crisis.* Downers Grove, Ill.: InterVarsity Press, 1981. The views of a conservative Christian who accepts the Bible as the supreme authority. A valuable guide for conservative Protestants and others desiring insights into a conservative Christian perspective.

Fox, Matthew. *The Coming of the Cosmic Christ.* San Francisco: Harper & Row, 1988. An excellent introduction to creation spirituality, a contemporary Christian vision for dealing with the environmental crisis and other significant problems.

Fritsch, A.J. *Environmental Ethics: Choices for Concerned Citizens.* Garden City, N.Y.: Doubleday/Anchor, 1980. An exploration of the values that underlie environmental degradation and the sets of principles that humans must apply to improve the situation. Written from a Roman Catholic perspective.

Hargrove, Eugene C. *Religion and Environmental Crisis.* Athens, Ga.: University of Georgia Press, 1985. A valuable collection of papers summarizing various religious perspectives on human responsibility to the environment. A variety of perspectives are presented for the Judeo-Christian tradition, among others.

Helfand, Jonathan. ''The Earth is the Lord's: Judaism and Environmental Ethics,'' in *Religion and Environmental Crisis,* Eugene C. Hargrove, ed. Athens, Ga.: University of Georgia Press, 1985. Summarizes the evidence to show that Jews are encouraged to love and be responsible to the land and nature. Judaism requires humans to exercise restraint and respect others—a perspective that is key to conservation ethics.

Hiers, Richard H. ''Ecology, Biblical Theology and Methodology: Biblical Perspectives on the Environment,'' *Zygon* 19: 43-59, 1984. The author responds to the Lynn White debate by asserting that there is no single Biblical viewpoint on ecology nor were the Biblical writers addressing twentieth century problems. But Biblical texts point out that God cares for all beings, and that humans have a responsibility toward, as well as dominion over, other creatures.

Joranson, Philip N. and Ken Butigan. *Cry of the Environment: Rebuilding the Christian Creation Tradition.* Santa Fe, N.M.: Bear & Company, 1984. An excellent selection of papers on the Judeo-Christian creation tradition as it relates to human perspectives on the environmental crisis.

Kay, Jeanne. ''Concepts of Nature in the Hebrew Bible.''

Environmental Ethics 10: 309-327, 1988. Evaluates the degree of environmental despotism and stewardship found in the Bible. Assets that the Hebrew Bible's principal environmental theme is of nature's assistance in divine retribution. There is also a moral and multisided view of nature presented in the Bible.

Linzey, Andrew. *Christianity and the Rights of Animals.* New York: The Crossroad Publishing Company, 1987. A challenge to the traditional Christian perspective that animals do not fall within the purview of moral concern; develops the case for living in greater peace and empathy with nonhuman animals.

McDaniel, Jay B. *Earth, Sky, Gods and Mortals.* Mystic, Conn.: Twenty-third Publications, 1990. A thoughtful look at living the life of a mature, reflective, ecological Christian.

McHarg, Ian. "Values, Process and Form," in *The Fitness of Man's Environment,* Smithsonian Annual II. Washington, D.C.: Smithsonian Institute Press, 1968. An indictment of anthropocentric values that have led to despoliation of the natural world, and the problems associated with modern cities. In particular, the role of the Judeo-Christian tradition is cited as a major contributor to these ills.

Nash, Roderick F. "The Greening of Religion," in *The Rights of Nature: A History of Environmental Ethics.* Madison, Wis.: The University of Wisconsin Press, 1989. Provides an excellent short introduction (pp. 87-120) to the development of environmental consciousness in contemporary religions, especially Christianity.

Passmore, John. *Man's Responsibility for Nature: Ecological Problems and Western Traditions.* New York: Scribners, 1974. In Part I of this book, the author addresses the historical foundations of Western attitudes toward nature. He argues that Bacon and Descartes distorted the Genesis passage to mean humans could modify nature as they please. Argues that Western traditions are very complex and diversified.

Rolston, Holmes, III. "Wildlife and Wildlands: A Christian Perspective." *Church and Society* 80: 16-40, 1990. Addresses values, aesthetic features, and ethics about the natural world from a Christian perspective.

Santmire, H. Paul. *The Travail of Nature: The Ambiguous Ecological Promise of Christian Theology.* Philadelphia: Fortress Press, 1985. A study tracing the role of nature in Christian thought. Compares a spiritual motif to an ecological motif as competing interpretive frameworks.

Schaeffer, F. *Pollution and the Death of Man: The Christian View of Ecology.* New York: Hodder and Stoughton, 1970. A discussion of environmental ethics from a predominantly Protestant perspective. Schaeffer develops the notion that nature deserves respect because it is God's creation.

Schwarzschild, Steven S. "The Unnatural Jew." *Environmental Ethics* 6: 347-362. Presents a scholarly discussion of the separateness of nature and ethics in Jewish history and culture. Argues that from a traditional Jewish standpoint, nature remains subject to human ends.

Seed, John. *Thinking Like a Mountain: Towards a Council of All Beings.* Philadelphia: New Society Publishers, 1988. Brief selections including a "Council of All Beings" ritual and sample workshop agendas.

Simmons, Deborah A. *Environmental Ethics: A Selected Bibliography for the Environmental Professional.* Council of Planning Librarians Bibliography 213. Chicago, Ill.: Council of Planning Librarians, This fourteen-page bibliography of environmental ethics materials includes a section on religion.

Spiro, J.G. and N. Carter. "Where Were You When I Laid the Foundations of the Earth?" *IUCN Bulletin* 16(10-12): 127-128, 1985. A short paper pointing out evidence for the conservation concept of "wise use" in the Torah.

Spring, David and Eileen Spring, eds. *Ecology and Religion in History.* New York: Harper & Row, 1974. A series of essays by seven scholars addressing the relationships of the Judeo-Christian tradition to the current environmental crises.

Squiers, E.R., ed. *The Environmental Crisis: The Ethical Dilemma.* Mancelona, Mich.: AuSable Trails Institute of Environmental Studies, 1982. A collection of papers presenting environmental ethics from a Christian perspective.

White, Lynn, Jr. "Continuing the conversation," in *Western Man and Environmental Ethics,* Ian G. Barbour, ed. Reading, Mass.: Addison-Wesley Publishing Company, 1973. The author replies to critics of his earlier article, "The Historical Roots of Our Ecological Crisis." He affirms that human beliefs and priorities shape political patterns, and he cites further evidence of the distinctive moral approval of technological innovation in medieval Christianity. He concludes that an ecological ethic must be based on more than enlightened self-interest; it must include a recognition of obligations to all creatures.

White, Lynn R., Jr. "The Historical Roots of Our Ecological Crisis." *Science* 155: 1203-1207, 1967. The classic paper on how Christianity, as an anthropocentric religion, has played a leading role in bringing about the environmental crisis.

Wood, Harold W., Jr. ''Modern Pantheism as an Approach to Environmental Ethics.'' *Environmental Ethics* 7: 151-163, 1985. Argues that pantheism promotes a theological basis for achieving oneness with God through knowledge, devotion, and works, and that pantheism can establish an enlightened theory for environmental ethics.

CHAPTER ELEVEN

Multicultural Perspectives

In this chapter, we delineate the value of considering multicultural perspectives in developing principles in environmental ethics. We then analyze non-Western religions and philosophies as possible sources of ecological wisdom, and discuss the merits of integrating Eastern conceptions into Western environmental ethics. We conclude the chapter by evaluating these non-Western perspectives for common elements.

VALUE OF CONSIDERING MULTICULTURAL PERSPECTIVES IN DEVELOPING PRINCIPLES IN ENVIRONMENTAL ETHICS

In the process of developing principles of environmental ethics, it is of great value to consider multicultural perspectives. One contribution of considering multicultural perspectives is that different cultural groups have world views which could aid contemporary Western society in better reframing the issues of the environmental crisis, and in seeking more satisfying solutions to ecological problems. The insights of diverse cultural groups have been tested and refined over eons of human history, and yet have resulted in strikingly different perspectives. To reject or discount the perspectives of other cultural groups reflects a parochial and elitist outlook, and severely limits the wealth of insights available to Western society for effectively dealing with environmental problems.

In addition, Hargrove[1] argues that the East needs to develop a more judicious environmental ethic as much as the West does. He believes that comparative studies of Eastern attitudes toward the environment and Western environmental philosophies can contribute to developing wiser contemporary Eastern environmental philosophies. In his essay, ''Radical American Environmentalism and Wilderness Preservation: A Third World Critique,'' Ramachandra Guha evaluates the applicability of one Western philosophy, deep ecology, to Third World cultures and environments.

A less commonly expressed contribution which multicultural studies provide is an improved understanding in Western society of the varying perspectives among all who share the planet and who must make decisions regarding the natural world. It is increasingly recognized that environmental decisions made in any one society have the potential of affecting other societies as well. Knowledge and respect for

---

1. Eugene C. Hargrove, ''Forward,'' in *Nature in Asian Traditions of Thought,* ed. J. Baird Callicott and Roger T. Ames (Albany: State University of New York Press, 1989), pp. xiii-xxi.

other members of the global community are essential if humans are to develop effective strategies for solving common environmental problems.

ARE NON-WESTERN RELIGIONS AND PHILOSOPHIES POSSIBLE SOURCES OF ECOLOGICAL WISDOM?

Guha challenges two views commonly expressed by Western scholars about Eastern religions and philosophies: that Eastern conceptions are biocentric in outlook, and that the "primal" peoples of the East subordinated themselves to the integrity of their biotic universe. Guha believes that these two Western perceptions are little more than projections of Western prejudices about the East. Guha points out that there is too much variation between the diverse cultural traditions represented to easily generalize about their perspectives. While some mystics certainly did reflect on the human relationship to nature, Guha points out that these mystics lived in a society of cultivators actively using nature. Guha acknowledges that there often has been a skilled manipulation of nature in the East, but he points out that Eastern knowledge about the natural world was not infallible, as reflected by the well-documented ecological disasters found in Eastern societies.

Tuan[2] has argued that Buddhism and Taoism may have precepts which promote respectful attitudes toward nature, in theory, but that did not prevent the Chinese from engaging in a long history of environmental changes and destruction. Yet, Hargrove[3] points out that environmental values are the ideals for how people *ought* to live, rather than a description of how they necessarily always do behave. In any society, there is a broad range of responses as to how thoroughly its members accept and follow prescribed societal values. Hargrove also points out that the gradual environmental degradation in the East may have resulted from empirical ignorance; he notes that empirical ignorance also may explain some of the problems in the West. Thus, the environmental problems observed in non-Western societies may very well be due to causes other than a lack of wisdom about the proper human relationship to the natural environment.

In their essay, "Ties That Bind: Native American Beliefs as a Foundation for Environmental Consciousness," Annie Booth and Harvey Jacobs argue that Native Americans provide a contemporary model of how humans can learn to live in harmony with the natural world. Booth and Jacobs note that some elements of Native American philosophies already have been integrated into contemporary Western views such as deep ecology and ecofeminism. Several other authors in this section, notably Po-keung Ip, Mawil Izzi Deen (Samarrai), and Lily de Silva, suggest that Taoism, Islam, and Buddhism, respectively, offer good foundations for an environmental ethic.

SHOULD EASTERN CONCEPTIONS BE INTEGRATED INTO WESTERN ENVIRONMENTAL ETHICS?

Hargrove[4] summarizes the substantial body of thought among Western scholars which maintains that it would be very difficult, if not impossible, to have an extensive integration of Eastern conceptions into Western environmental ethics. The major arguments against such integration are the fear that Eastern conceptions gradually might destroy Western society by undermining its basic values, the belief that Eastern values are too incompatible to be assimilated into Western civilization, and the judgment that Eastern ideas have been too ineffective in preventing ecological disasters in the East to be of much value in the West. Hargrove points out some of the contradictions among these positions and challenges the validity of each; he also argues that the West has successfully integrated many Eastern cultural values without damaging effects.

Hargrove proposes that the major contribution of Eastern thought to contemporary Western society

---

2. Yi-Fu Tuan, "Discrepancies Between Environmental Attitude and Behaviour Examples from Europe and China," *Canadian Geographer* 13 (1968): 176-191.

3. See note 1.

---

4. See note 1.

probably will be to provide a limited number of isolated ideas that will be selectively integrated and gradually assimilated until they cease to seem exotic; but he does not believe that Eastern thought will lead to changes in the main strands and course of Western philosophy.

However, Booth and Jacobs, and Gerald James Larson in his essay, " 'Conceptual Resources' in South Asia for 'Environmental Ethics,' " challenge the notion that one can selectively lift ideas out of their cultural and historical contexts and successfully integrate them into another culture. Yet, Booth and Jacobs acknowledge that some Native American ideas already have become integrated in ecofeminism and deep ecology.

The authors of these readings also raise a different but related issue. They challenge the propriety of one cultural group selecting and adopting some of the values of another cultural group. Booth and Jacobs note that there often is a fine line between respectful learning and intellectual plundering. Larson notes a parallel between the exploitation of Asian natural resources by Europeans in earlier years, and the contemporary trend for Westerners to "mine" the cultural wealth of Eastern religions and philosophy. However, as Hargrove notes, cultural exchanges have not been one-sided only; ideas and values have flowed in both directions between East and West.

ARE THERE COMMON ELEMENTS AMONG NON-WESTERN PERSPECTIVES?

There are difficulties in attempting to identify common elements among non-Western perspectives. There is, of course, no one ideology that can be said to represent "the Native American perspective," "the Buddhist perspective," or any other perspective. Making generalizations about diverse perspectives does not allow proper acknowledgment of the richness and distinctiveness of values found within each tradition. Common elements among some strands of each philosophy might not be generalizable to all.

Also, non-Western perspectives are very different from one other. For example, Buddhism focuses primarily on human suffering, and probably cannot be considered a theistic religion, whereas Hinduism, Taoism, and Native American belief systems include numerous gods and spirits. In contrast, Islam is a monotheistic religion. Thus, the probability of identifying common elements among such diverse perspectives is limited.

Finally, each of these perspectives is dynamic, and is steadily changing over time. Some of these changes take place gradually, following the inevitable growth and evolution of a philosophy as its scholars study and probe its limits in a changing society. Some changes can occur in violent and rapid succession, as when Native American groups were invaded by Europeans.

Despite these limitations, one element which does seem to be common among several non-Western perspectives discussed in this chapter is the deemphasis on dualism, and the human sense of connectedness with the natural world, particularly when contrasted with Western views. Booth and Jacobs insist that most scholars have a very limited appreciation for the deep sense of connection Native Americans feel with the land of which they are a part. Po-Keung Ip in his essay, "Taoism and the Foundations of Environmental Ethics," believes that humans are fully linked to the Tao as well as to everything else in the world. In her essay, "The Buddhist Attitude Towards Nature," de Silva acknowledges that in Buddhism humans are expected to rise above nature, but she emphasizes that humans and nature are bound in a reciprocal causal relationship; there is a close tie between human morality and events and the conditions in the natural environment. As can be seen in the essay by Mawil Izzi Deem, "Islamic Environmental Ethics, Law, and Society," and in an article by Zaidi,[5] Islam promulgates a dualism similar to that often reflected in the Judeo-Christian world view.

---

5. Iqtidar H. Zaidi, "On the Ethics of Man's Interaction with the Environment: An Islamic Approach," *Environmental Ethics* 3 (1981): 35-47.

Ties That Bind: Native American Beliefs as a Foundation for Environmental Consciousness

Annie L. Booth and Harvey M. Jacobs

Annie L. Booth (b. 1960) and Harvey M. Jacobs both have been associated with the Institute for Environmental Studies at the University of Wisconsin in Madison, Wisconsin. Booth's interests include ecological feminism, deep ecology, Native American world views, bioregionalism, environmental policy, and human-land relationships. Jacobs also is a member of the Department of Urban and Regional Planning at the University of Wisconsin, Madison. His teaching and research interests include policy techniques and issues for land use and environmental management.

Although they recognize the significant diversity among Native American cultures, Booth and Jacobs believe that a number of common strands occur among these groups and that, despite some exceptions, the attitudes of Native Americans toward their lands is one which tends to preserve the biological integrity within natural communities. Booth and Jacobs identify and describe Native American conceptions about the natural world that are relevant to environmental ethics. For example, the animate and inanimate world is not viewed as empty in Native American cultures; everything has a being, a life, and a self-consciousness. In many of the cultures, the earth itself is perceived as a living, conscious being which must be treated with respect and care. Most Native American societies have a strong sense of identity with a particular place such as a river, mountain, or other natural geographical feature. Another common cultural theme among diverse groups is a sense of kinship with other living beings; many Native American legends speak of other species as beings who shed fur masks, look human, and once shared a common language with humans. In fact, this common spiritedness allows humans to enter into social relationships with these beings, and these relationships often involve a sense of mutual obligation, reciprocity, balance, and respect.

The authors suggest that Native American perspectives can provide elements for a contemporary ecological model of living in harmony with the natural world, and that some elements already have been incorporated into deep ecology and ecofeminism. While one cannot "borrow" a culture, the authors suggest that ideas in Native American cultures can lead to the discovery of new directions for contemporary Western society.

In a conversation with us, Booth stressed that the following article is only a summary of some very complex ideas and encouraged all interested scholars to read the original sources for the full richness of these Native American perspectives.

. . . Both deep ecologists and ecofeminists call for the development of a new human consciousness, one of humility, which recognizes the importance of all life, including the life of the organism Earth.[1] As radical activists and philosophers begin to articulate and implement their ideas for a truly ecological world, they find themselves drawn, again and again, to the beliefs and traditions of North America's Native Americans.[2] Native Americans are often portrayed as model ecological citizens, holding values and beliefs that industrialized humans have long since sacrificed in the pursuit of progress and comfort. This interest in Native American relationships with the natural world has an old history. As Cornell points out, influential members of the early American conservation movement were deeply impressed by Native Americans and their knowledge of and relations with the natural world.[3] Such interest is shared even by less radical elements in the environmental movement.[4]

Native American statements about the integrity and inherent importance of the natural world . . . stir many Western people, but there seems to be surprisingly little understanding of Native Americans' actual

---

1. James E. Lovelock, *Gaia: A New Look at Life on Earth* (New York: Oxford University Press, 1979).

2. For one set of prominent examples see Devall, "The Deep Ecology Movement," and Green Party, *Politics For Life,* p. 13.

3. George L. Cornell, "The Influence of Native Americans on Modern Conservationists," *Environmental Review* 9 (1985): 105-117.

4. See for instance Stewart L. Udall, "Indians: First Americans, First Ecologists," in *Readings in American History–73/74* (Connecticut: Dushkin Publishing Group, 1973).

relationships with their environment. Even so, this does not keep elements of the environmental movement, mainstream and radical, recent and historical, from using Native Americans for their own ends. In this chapter we attempt to redress this situation by offering a synthetic, detailed discussion of Native American beliefs and relationships with the natural world as presented by Native Americans and by anthropologists and historians. As such, we take a broad approach to the nature of Native American culture, addressing it as a singular phenomenon. Although we are aware of the significant differences among Native American cultures, there is enough similarity in environmental views to warrant this type of cross-cutting approach. More detailed descriptions of the works used here are available in a related annotated bibliography.[5] It is our hope that this chapter will help the environmental movement develop an empathic and analytic understanding of traditions that they now use so loosely.

BELOVED MOTHER TO CONQUERED ENEMY

Although they varied significantly between different cultures, Native American relationships with the natural world tended to preserve biological integrity within natural communities, and did so over a significant period of historical time. These cultures engaged in relationships of mutual respect, reciprocity, and caring with an Earth and fellow beings as alive and self-conscious as human beings. Such relationships were reflected and perpetuated by cultural elements including religious belief and ceremonial ritual.[6]

We do not claim that natural communities remained unchanged by human activities, for they did change, considerably so, and in some instances, negatively so. However, the great majority of natural communities remained ecologically functional while supporting both Native American cultures and a great diversity of different plant and animal species.

In contrast, invading Europeans brought with them cultures that practiced relationships of subjugation and domination, even hatred, of European lands. They made little attempt to live *with* their natural communities, but rather altered them wholesale. The impoverishment of the ecological communities of sixteenth and seventeenth-century Europe was so great that, in contrast, early settlers of the New World found what they described as either a marvelous paradise or a horrendous wilderness, but certainly something completely outside their experience.[7]

Native American cultures had adapted their needs to the capacities of natural communities; the new inhabitants, freshly out of Europe, adapted natural communities to meet their needs. The differences between these two approaches have had profound impacts on the diversity and functioning of natural communities in North America.

NO SUCH THING AS EMPTINESS

In the songs and legends of different Native American cultures it is apparent that the land and her creatures are perceived as truly beautiful things. There is a sense of great wonder and of something which sparks a deep sensation of joyful celebration. Above all else, Native Americans were, and are, life-affirming; they respected and took pleasure in the life to be found around them, in all its diversity, inconsistency, or inconvenience. Everything had a place and a being, life and self-consciousness, and everything was treated accordingly. Hughes points out that only the newly arrived Europeans considered the land to be a "wilderness," barren and desolate.[8] To Native Americans, it was a bountiful community of living beings, of whom the humans were only one part. It was a place of great sacredness, in which the workings of the Great Spirit, or Great Mystery, could always be felt.

---

5. Annie L. Booth and Harvey M. Jacobs, *Environmental Consciousness: Native American Worldviews and Sustainable Natural Resource Management: An Annotated Bibliography,* CPL Bibliography no. 214 (Chicago: Council of Planning Librarians, 1988).

6. J. Donald Hughes, *American Indian Ecology* (El Paso: Texas University Press, 1983).

---

7. See William Cronan, *Changes in the Land: Indians, Colonists and the Ecology of New England* (New York: Hill and Wang, 1983); and Hughes, *American Indian Ecology.*

8. Hughes, *American Indian Ecology.*

Hultkrantz argues that it is only because nature reflected the presence of the Great Mystery that it was considered to be sacred.[9] His interpretation suggests that the Indians' appreciation of nature, whether for its beauty or for its productivity, was influenced by the presence of other values. Hultkrantz felt that the Native American's relationship with nature reflected a dynamic tension, which was inherent in a relationship which both loves and exploits the natural world. This tension was reflected, in part, in the Native American's view of nature, which often included some quite terrifying aspects such as cannibalistic and malevolent spirits. Nature is both nurturing and attractive as well as destructive and dangerous.

In distinct contrast to Hultkrantz's interpretations, however, Native American writers focus on the wonders of the land. Standing Bear, a Lakota Sioux, wrote that Native Americans felt a special joy and wonder for all the elements and changes of season which characterized the land.[10] They felt that they held the spirit of the land within themselves, and so they met and experienced the elements and seasons rather than retreating from them. For Standing Bear and the Lakota, the Earth was so full of life and beings that they never actually felt alone. . . .

[A] very central belief which seems consistent across many Native American cultures [is] that the Earth is a living, conscious being that must be treated with respect and loving care. The Earth may be referred to as Mother, or Grandmother, and these are quite literal terms, for the Earth is the source, the mother of all living beings, including human beings. Black Elk, a Lakota, asked, ''Is not the sky a father and the earth a mother and are not all living things with feet and wings or roots their children?''[11] The Earth, and those who reside upon her, take their sacredness from that part of the Great Spirit which resides in all living beings. They are not the source of

sacredness, but are no less sacred for that circumstance. . . .

Interestingly, the idea of the Earth as a living, conscious being, Gaia, has recently been the subject of discussion and debate within the mainstream Western scientific community.[12] A very old and sacred idea appears to be in the process of being rediscovered.

WE ARE THE LAND

The belief in a conscious, living nature is not simply an intellectual concept for Native American cultures. For most, perception of the landscape is important in determining perception of self. Vine Deloria, Jr. argues that Native Americans hold a perception of reality which is bound up in spatial references, references which refer to a physical place.[13] In Deloria's view, a spatial reference is important in establishing positive relationships with the natural world. Because of its basis in a particular land or place, a spatial orientation requires an intimate and respectful relationship with that land. . . .

Not only do Native Americans see themselves as part of the land, they consider the land to be part of them. This goes beyond the romanticized love of nature that modern-day environmentalists are said to indulge in, for the Native American faced the best and worst of the land, and still found it to be sacred, a gift from the Great Mystery of great meaning and value: it offered them their very being. . . . In a very organic sense, the roots of the Native American peoples were always, and still are, in the natural communities in which they have lived.[14]

This theme is echoed by Luther Standing Bear when he describes the elders of the Lakota Sioux as growing so fond of the Earth that they preferred to sit or lie directly upon it.[15] In this way, they felt that they approached more closely the great mysteries in life

9. Ake Hultkrantz, *Belief and Worship in Native North America* (Syracuse: Syracuse University Press, 1981).

10. Luther Standing Bear, *Land of the Spotted Eagle* (Lincoln: University of Nebraska Press, 1933).

11. John G. Neihardt, *Black Elk Speaks: Being the Life Story of a Holy Man of the Oglala Sioux* (New York: Pocket Books, 1975), p. 6.

12. Lovelock, *Gaia: A New Look at Life on Earth.*

13. Vine Deloria, Jr., *God Is Red* (New York: Grosset & Dunlap, 1973).

14. Paula Gunn Allen, *The Sacred Hoop: Recovering the Feminine in American Indian Traditions* (Boston: Beacon Press, 1986).

15. Standing Bear, *Land of the Spotted Eagle*, p. 192.

and saw more clearly their kinship with all life. Indeed, Standing Bear comments that the reason for the white culture's alienation from their adopted land is that they are not truly of it; they have no roots to anchor them for their stay has been too short.[16] . . .

This interconnection between person and land is not merely a thing of historical significance. Present-day Native Americans continue to acknowledge their ties to their land. Utes in the Southwest faced with the question of mining on their lands are deeply troubled, for the land is more than mere resource;[17] . . . [it is a part of who and what they are as a people and as a culture.]

RELATIVES IN FUR MASKS

Recognizing that they were part of the land meant that many Native American cultures did not intellectually or emotionally isolate themselves from the land and her other inhabitants, as did European-derived cultures. The idea which appears over and over is "kinship" with other living beings.[18] . . .

Brown comments that while humans serve as the intermediary between earth and sky, this does not lessen the importance of other beings, as they are the links between humans and the Great Mystery.[19] To realize the self, kinship with all beings must be realized. To gain knowledge, humans must humble themselves before all creation, down to and including the lowliest ant, and realize their own nothingness. Knowledge may come through vision quests, and this knowledge is transmitted and offered by animals. Nature is a mirror which reflects all things, including that which it is important to learn about, understand and value throughout life.

Standing Bear explains that all beings share in the life force which flows from Wakan Tanka, the Great Mystery, including "the flowers of the plains, the blowing winds, rocks, trees, birds, animals," as well as man. "Thus all things were kindred and brought together by the same Great Mystery."[20] The other animals had rights, the right to live and multiply, the right to freedom, and the right to man's indebtedness. The Lakota Sioux, says Standing Bear, respected those rights.

Most Native American legends speak of other species as beings who could shed their fur mask and look human, as beings who once shared a common language with humans, and who continued to understanding humans after the humans had lost their ability to understand them. Callicott quotes the Sioux holy man Black Elk, who describes the world as sharing in spiritedness.[21] Because everything shares in this spiritedness, it is possible for humans to enter into social and kin relations with other beings.

Martin, discussing subarctic bands, also notes that Native Americans felt and acknowledged a spiritual kinship with the animals they dealt with.[22] A sympathy built up between the human person who hunted and the animal persons who were hunted, a sympathy which pervaded human life. Animals lived in a world that was spiritual, although they assumed a fleshy body in the physical world. Their connection with the spiritual world made them mediators in all things to do with the spiritual world, such as when humans attempted to enter that world.

According to Nelson, the Alaskan Koyukon sense that the world they live in is a world full of aware, sensate, personified, feeling beings, who can be offended and who at all times must be treated with the

---

16. Ibid., p. 248.

17. Stephanie Romeo, "Concepts of Nature and Power: Environmental Ethics of the Northern Ute," *Environmental Review* 9 (1985): 160-161.

18. Paula Gunn Allen, "The Sacred Hoop: A Contemporary Indian Perspective on American Literature," in Geary Hobson (ed.), *The Remembered Earth,* (Albuquerque: Red Earth Press, 1979), p. 225.

19. Joseph Epes Brown, *The Spiritual Legacy of the American Indian* (New York: Crossroad Publishing Co., 1985).

20. Standing Bear, *Land of the Spotted Eagle,* p. 193.

21. J. Baird Callicott, "Traditional American Indian and Traditional Western European Attitudes towards Nature: An Overview," in Robert Elliot and Arran Gare, eds. *Environmental Philosophy: A Collection of Readings* (University Park: Pennsylvania State University Press, 1983), pp. 231-259.

22. Calvin Martin, "Subarctic Indians and Wildlife," in C. Vecsey and R.W. Venables, eds., *American Indian Environments: Ecological Issues in Native American History* (Syracuse: Syracuse University Press, 1980), pp. 38-45.

proper respect.[23] The animals with which the Koyu-kons interact are among these powerful, watchful beings. Legend states that they once were human, becoming animals when they died. Animals and humans are distinct beings, their souls being quite different, but the animals are powerful beings in their own right. They are not offended at being killed for use, but killing must be done humanely, and there should be no suggestion of waste. Nor can the body be mistreated: it must be shown respect according to any number of taboos. Consequently a complex collection of rules, respectful activities, and taboos surround everyday life and assist humans in remaining within the moral code that binds all life. . . .

The practical consequences of such relationships with animals are profound. There is considerable archaeological evidence to suggest that the great prairies and the northeastern forests discovered by the Europeans were a product of modification. Hughes argues that the difference between these historical modifications and those made by the present-day inhabitants is demonstrated by the fact that the first Europeans found a forested and abundant country easily supporting the inhabitants, a country so different from fifteenth-century Europe that it was taken to be an unspoiled paradise.[24] Although animals were taken, sometimes in large numbers, rarely were species endangered or exterminated, for trying to exterminate a species would have meant trying to eliminate not only an essential of life, but a kindred being.

Hughes believes that the ''ecological consciousness'' of the Native American was in part due to their sense of kinship with the rest of the world, and in part made up of an extensive working knowledge and understanding of the world with which they lived. Much of this knowledge was codified and passed on through the medium of myths and legends handed down between generations. Such intimate knowledge permitted careful and judicious hunting, based on the knowledge of what animals resided in the area, how many there were, and how many were required to ensure a healthy population. Hunting territories were shared by families or bands, but misuse, such as excessive killing, might be grounds for war.

RECIPROCITY AND BALANCE IN ALL THINGS

Interactions with these important beings, these fur-covered kin, required careful consideration. Reciprocity and balance were required from both sides in the relationships between humankind and other living beings. Balance was vital: the world exists as an intricate balance of parts, and it was important that humans recognized this balance and strove to maintain and stay within this balance. All hunting and gathering had to be done in such a way as to preserve the balance. Human populations had to fit within the balance. For everything that was taken, something had to be offered in return, and the permanent loss of something, such as in the destruction of a species, irreparably tore at the balance of the world. Thus, offerings were not so much sacrifices, as whites were inclined to interpret them, but rather a fair exchange for what had been taken, to maintain the balance. In this way, the idea of reciprocity emerges. From the Native American perspective, as Hughes puts it, ''mankind depends on the other beings for life, and they depend on mankind to maintain the proper balance.''[25] According to the Koyukons, for example, humans interact with natural things on the basis of a moral code, which, if properly attended to, contributes to a proper spiritual balance between humans and nonhumans.[26]

Momaday, a Kiowa writer and teacher, describes the necessary relationship as an act of reciprocal ap-

23. Richard K. Nelson, Make Prayers to the Raven (Chicago: University of Chicago Press, 1983); Richard K. Nelson, ''A Conservation Ethic and Environment: The Koyukon of Alaska,'' in Nancy M. Williams and Eugene S. Hunn, eds., *Resource Managers: North American and Australian Hunter Gatherers,* AAAS Selected Symposium no. 67 (Boulder: Westview Press, 1982), pp. 211-228.

24. J. Donald Hughes, ''Forest Indians: The Holy Occupation,'' *Environmental Review* 2 (1977): 2-13.

25. Hughes, *American Indian Ecology,* p. 17.

26. Nelson, ''A Conservation Ethic and Environment: The Koyukon of Alaska.''

probation, ''approbations in which man invests himself in the landscape, and at the same time incorporates the landscape into his own most fundamental experience.''[27] The respect and approval is two-way: humans both give and receive value and self-worth from the natural world. According to Momaday, this act of approbation is an act of the imagination, and it is a moral act. All of us are what we imagine ourselves to be, and the Native Americans imagine themselves specifically in terms of relationships with the physical world, among other things. Native Americans have been determining themselves in their imagination for many generations, and in the process, the landscape has become part of a particular reality. In a sense, for the Native American, the process is more intuitive and evolutionary than is the white Western rational linear process. The Native American has a personal investment in vision and imagination as a reality, or as part of a reality, whereas many whites believe such things have very little to do with what we call reality.

Toelken examines the idea of reciprocity between the Navaho people and what he describes as ''the sacred *process* going on in the world.''[28] Religion embodies a reciprocal relationship between the people and this process, and everything becomes a part of this circular, sacred give and take. Part of the idea of reciprocity is the necessity and importance of interaction. Participation in reciprocity is vital; a failure to interact, or a breakdown in interaction, leads to disease and calamity. Thus, everything that is used in everyday life is used for its part in that interaction; it becomes a symbol of sacred interaction and relationship between the people, the plants, the animals, and the land. Rituals such as those used for healing are not designed to ward off illness or directly cure the ill person. Rather, they are designed to remind the ill person of a frame of mind which is in proper relationship with the rest of the world, a frame of mind which is essential to the maintenance of good health.

LIFE AND RELIGION

. . . As Toelken points out, Native Americans rarely distinguish between their religious life and their secular life.[29] Instead there is nothing in life that is *not* religious, whether it is hunting or gathering, or greeting the sun as it rises each morning. . . .

Everything from hunting to healing is a recognition and affirmation of the sacredness of life. In the weaving of a basket is the creation of the whole world. In a proper life there is never a sense of disconnectedness from the Earth. . . .

Both action and contemplation are interrelated for many Native Americans, and every action may be an opportunity for meditation and reflection, an opportunity to search for new truths and meanings. . . .

The ability to recognize and learn from such living symbols is not something unique to Native Americans. Everyone has or can acquire such openness if he or she is receptive and willing to try to understand with the heart. . . .

DEVELOPING AN ENVIRONMENTAL CONSCIOUSNESS

. . . For more than a century concerned Western environmentalists have held up Native Americans as one contemporary model of a way humans can learn to live in harmony with the natural world. Our detailed investigation of this assertion, cutting across Native American cultures, suggests that the basic premise of those holding this position is correct. However, it is likely that for many who hold this position, their conception of the Native American world view is limited in its appreciation of the depth and breath of Native Americans integration with the land of which they are a part. For example, the extent to which Native Americans understand the Earth and all life upon it as fully alive and needing and deserving of a reciprocal, respectful relationship, and the thoroughly religious character of Native American relationships with the natural world, demonstrate how far a construction of a Western environmental consciousness has to go to

27. N. Scott Momaday, ''Native American Attitudes towards the Environment,'' in Walter H. Capps, ed., *Seeing with a Native Eye* (New York: Harper & Row, 1976), p. 80.

28. Barre Toelken, ''Seeing with a Native Eye: How many Sheep Will It Hold?'' in Walter H. Capps, ed., *Seeing with a Native Eye* (New York: Harper & Row, 1976), p. 14.

29. Toelken, ''Seeing with a Native Eye.''

truly learn from and draw upon that which Native Americans have to teach.

Yet this is exactly the type of understanding which is reflected in the contemporary scholarship of environmental philosophy, particularly with regard to deep ecology and ecological feminism. Concerns and articulations of reciprocal respect for all life forms, a recognition of the Earth itself as a living being, and the recognition of the critical place of some form of spirituality in environmental consciousness permeate both strands of ecophilosophy. But these two approaches to a Western environmental consciousness have come to be characterized as oppositional, rather than integrative.[30] One lesson to be drawn from Native American beliefs is the unity of integrating these two approaches to ecophilosophy so they can work together in the construction of a Western environmental consciousness in which the Earth and all its beings, including humans, have a niche, and humans in particular have an awareness of the importance of all other life forms.

As we turn to Native American cultures for their wisdom, however, it is important to keep in mind that their cultures and relationship with the natural world will not provide any instantaneous solutions to the problems Western culture is presently facing. Cultures, or selected bits of one or two, cannot and should not be arbitrarily grafted onto one another.

Native American traditions, as in all cultures, are embedded in a particular context. The impact and meaning of a tradition stems from lifelong conditioning, preparation, and participation. It is built into the language, into the way day-to-day life is lived and experienced over time, and within a specific physical/social context. Attempts to borrow culture, whether it be wholesale or piecemeal, are doomed to failure.

If we ignore this fact, we risk harm not only to ourselves, but to Native Americans as well. There is a delicate line between respectful learning and intellectual plundering. Richard White questions our cas-

ual and constant habit of using the Native American as a symbol without reference or regard to real Native Americans or their attitudes and feelings.[31] In doing so, White argues, we are just as guilty of using and exploiting these cultures as we are when we steal their lands or their lives and spirits.

But there are less imperialistic approaches to Native American cultures. They can be studied as a contrast to our own destructive relationships with the natural world, and as a reminder that positive relationships can and do exist. An open hearted and respectful investigation of Native American cultures, particularly when members of these cultures voluntarily share with us their understandings and perceptions, can help us discover new directions in which to travel to realize our own potentials. . . .

Luther Standing Bear believed that it took generations of dying and being reborn within a land for that land to become a part of an individual and of a culture.[32] Deloria suggests that it is possible for peoples and lands to adapt and to relate to one another very powerfully, leading to a spiritual union which benefits both; a particular land determines and encourages the nature of a religion that will spring up upon it, and within a religion lies an entire way of life.[33] This is, in fact, exactly the premise of bioregionalists, who add a third strand to the deep ecology-ecofeminism discourse by stressing the need to become intimately aware of particular places, not just place in general.[34] The next step, then, in learning from Native Americans may be to move beyond general study to an examination of individual tribes and cultural groups to understand how the more universal themes ad-

---

30. See for example Janet Biehl, ''Ecofeminism and Deep Ecology: Unresolvable Conflict?'' *Our Generation* 19 (1988): 19-31, and Warwick Fox, ''The Deep Ecology-Ecofeminism Debate and Its Parallels,'' *Environmental Ethics* 11 (1989): 5-25.

31. Richard White, ''Introduction'' [to special issue on the American Indian and the environment], *Environmental Review* 9 (1985): 101-103.

32. Standing Bear, *Land of The Spotted Eagle*, p. 248.

33. Deloria, *God Is Red*, p. 294.

34. See for example, Peter Berg, ed., *Reinhabiting a Separate Country* (San Francisco: Planet Drum Foundation, 1978); Kirkpatrick Sale, *Dwellers in the Land: The Bioregional Vision* (San Francisco: Sierra Club Books, 1985); James J. Parsons, ''On 'Bioregionalism' and 'Watershed Consciousness,' '' *The Professional Geographer* 37 (1985): 1-6; Peter Berg, Beryl Magilavy, and Seth Zuckerman, *A Green City Program for San Francisco Bay Area Cities and Towns* (San Francisco: Planet Drum Books, 1989).

dressed in this chapter were and are articulated in particular places.

All told, we may well be on the path to a sustainable Western environmental consciousness. At least in the case of Native Americans we appear to have encountered and long recognized enduring environmental wisdom, even if we have been unable to integrate it into the mainstream of Western culture. At present, the active discourse among deep ecologists, ecofeminists, and bioregionalists suggests serious work on the shaping of an environmental consciousness in a form appropriate to Western culture. We can and should look for assistance in this effort from Native Americans; they appear willing, even anxious, to aid, as long as in so doing we recognize the boundary between learning and exploiting.

DISCUSSION TOPICS

1. With which Eastern philosophy do you believe Native American perspectives summarized by Booth and Jacobs have the most in common? The greatest difference? Give examples to support your opinion.

2. What differing consequences would you expect between an environmental ethic integrating a strong identification with a ''place,'' as is characteristic of many Native American cultures, and an ethic integrating an identification as ''world citizen,'' often occurring in Western society?

3. Which parts of Native American perceptions do you believe can most easily be integrated into your own environmental ethic? Which perceptions would you find difficult to integrate?

Islamic Environmental Ethics, Law, and Society

Mawil Y. Izzi Deen (Samarrai)

Mawil Y. Izzi Deen (Samarrai) is an assistant professor at King Abdul Aziz University, Jeddah, Saudi Arabia. The author also is consultant to the Saudi Arabian Center for Science and Technology, and co-author of Islamic Principles for the Conservation of the Natural Environment.

Deen believes that the foundation for environmental protection in the Islamic faith is based on the religious principle that all aspects of the natural world were created by God, with different functions that were determined and balanced by God. Islamic values are considered unalterably accurate, and Muslims are obliged to obey what God has ordered.

The role of humans is to enjoy, use, and benefit from the environment. This can involve subjugation, use, construction, and development. It also includes meditation, contemplation, and enjoyment of the earth's beauty. Since the earth also is a source of beauty and a place to worship God, humans must intervene to protect it. A theory of sustainable utilization can be derived from the Islamic assertion that life is maintained with a due balance in everything. Proper behavior goes beyond mere enlightened self-interest since the existence of the world testifies to the greatness of God.

Islamic practices in the realm of environmental ethics include the protection of certain zones (ḥimā) for the welfare of the people; establishment of certain inviolable zones (ḥarīm) often associated with wells, springs, or waterways; and the development of environmental projects in several countries, especially Saudi Arabia.

Islamic environmental ethics, like all other forms of ethics in Islam, is based on clear-cut legal foundations which Muslims hold to be formulated by God. Thus, in Islam, an acceptance of what is legal and what is ethical has not involved the same processes as in cultures which base their laws on humanistic philosophies.

Muslim scholars have found it difficult to accept the term 'Islamic Law,' since 'law' implies a rigidity and dryness alien to Islam. They prefer the Arabic word *Sharī'ah* (Shariah) which literally means the 'source of water,' The Shariah is the source of life in that it contains both legal rules and ethical principles. This is indicated by the division of the Shariah relevant to human action into the categories of: obligatory actions (*wājib*),—those which a Muslim is required to perform; devotional and ethical virtues (*mandūb*),—those actions a Muslim is encouraged to perform, the non-observance of which, however, incurs no liability; permissible actions (*mubāh*),—those in which a Muslim is given complete freedom of choice; abominable actions (*makrūh*),—those which are morally but not legally wrong; and prohibited actions (*ḥaram*),—all those practices forbidden by Islam.

A complete separation into the two elements, law and ethics, is thus unnecessary in Islam. For a Muslim is obliged to obey whatever God has ordered, his philosophical questions having been answered before he became a follower of the faith.

THE FOUNDATION OF ENVIRONMENTAL PROTECTION

In Islam, the conservation of the environment is based on the principle that all the individual components of the environment were created by God, and that all living things were created with different functions, functions carefully measured and meticulously balanced by the Almighty Creator. Although the various components of the natural environment serve humanity as one of their functions, this does not imply that human use is the sole reason for their creation. The comments of the medieval Muslim scholar, Ibn Taymīyah, on those verses of the Holy Qur'ān which state God created the various parts of the environment to serve humanity, are relevant here:

> In considering all these verses it must be remembered that Allah in His wisdom created these creatures for reasons other than serving man, for in these verses He only explains the benefits of these creatures [to man].[1]

The legal and ethical reasons for protecting the environment can be summarized as follows[2]: First, the environment is God's creation and to protect it is to preserve its values as a sign of the Creator. To assume that the environment's benefits to human beings are the sole reason for its protection may lead to environmental misuse of destruction.

Second, the component parts of nature are entities in continuous praise of their Creator. Humans may not be able to understand the form or nature of this praise, but the fact that the Qur'ān describes it is an additional reason for environmental preservation:

> The seven heavens and the earth and all that is therein praise Him, and there is not such a thing but hymneth his praise; but ye understand not their praise. Lo! He is ever Clement, Forgiving (Sūrah 17: 44).[3]

Third, all the laws of nature are laws made by the Creator and based on the concept of the absolute continuity of existence. Although God may sometimes wish otherwise, what happens, happens according to the natural law of God (sunnah), and human beings must accept this as the will of the Creator. Attempts to break the law of God must be prevented. As the Qur'ān states:

> Hast thou not seen that unto Allah payeth adoration whosoever is in the heavens and whosoever is in the earth, and the sun, and the moon, and the stars, and the hills, and the trees, and the beasts, and many of mankind (Sūrah 22: 18).

Fourth, the Qur'ān's acknowledgment that humankind is not the only community to live in this world—''There is not an animal in the earth, nor a flying creature flying on two wings, but they are peoples like unto you' (Sūrah 6: 38)—means that while humans may currently have the upper hand over other 'peoples,' these other creatures are beings and, like us, are worthy of respect and protection. The Prophet Muhammad (peace be upon him) considered all living creatures worthy of protection (hurmah) and kind treatment. He was once asked whether there will be a reward from God for charity shown to animals. His reply was very explicit: 'For [charity shown to] each creature which has a wet heart there is a reward.'[4] Ibn Hajar comments further upon this tradition, explaining that wetness is an indication of life (and so charity extends to all creatures), although human beings are more worthy of the charity if a choice must be made.[5]

Fifth, Islamic environmental ethics is based on the concept that all human relationships are established on justice (‘adl) and equity (iḥsān): ‘Lo! Allah enjoineth justice and kindness' (Sūrah 16: 90). The prophetic tradition limits benefits derived at the cost of animal suffering. The Prophet Muhammad instructed: ‘Verily Allah has prescribed equity (iḥsān) in all things. Thus if you kill, kill well, and if you slaughter, slaughter well. Let each of you sharpen his blade and let him spare suffering to the animal he slaughters.'

Sixth, the balance of the universe created by God must also be preserved. For ‘Everything with Him is measured' (Sūrah 13: 8). Also, ‘There is not a thing but with Us are the stores thereof. And We send it not down save in appointed measure' (Sūrah 15: 21).

Seventh, the environment is not in the service of the present generation alone. Rather, it is the gift of God to all ages, past, present, and future. This can be understood from the general meaning of Sūrah 2:29: ‘He it is Who created for you all that is in the earth' The word ‘you' as used here refers to all persons with no limit as to time or place.

Finally, no other creature is able to perform the task of protecting the environment. God entrusted humans with the duty of viceregency, a duty so onerous and burdensome that no other creature would accept it: ‘Lo! We offered the trust unto the heavens and the earth and the hills, but they shrank from bearing it and were afraid of it. And man assumed it' (Sūrah 33:72).

THE COMPREHENSIVE NATURE OF ISLAMIC ETHICS

Islamic ethics is founded on two principles—human nature, and religious and legal grounds. The first principle, natural instinct (fitrah), was imprinted in the human soul by God at the time of creation (Sūrah 91: 7–8). Having natural instinct, the ordinary individual can, at least to some extent, distinguish not only between good and bad, but also between these and that which is neutral, neither good nor bad.[6] However, an ethical conscience is not a sufficient personal guide. Due to the complexities of life an ethical conscience alone cannot define the correct attitude to every problem. Moreover, a person does not live in a vacuum, but is affected by outside influences which may corrupt the ability to choose between good and evil. Outside influences include customs, personal interests, and prevailing concepts concerning one's surroundings.[7]

The religious and legal grounds upon which Islamic ethics is founded were presented by the messengers of God. These messengers were possessed of a special nature, and since they were inspired by God, they were able to avoid the outside influences which may affect other individuals.

Legal instructions in Islam are not negative in the sense of forcing the conscience to obey. On the contrary, legal instructions have been revealed in such a way that the conscience approves and acknowledges them to be correct. Thus the law itself becomes a part of human conscience, thereby guaranteeing its application and its success.

An imported, alien law cannot work because, while it may be possible to make it legally binding, it cannot be made morally binding upon Muslims. Muslims willingly pay the poor-tax (*zakāh*) because they know that if they fail to do so they will be legally and ethically responsible. Managing to avoid the legal consequences of failure to pay what is due will not help them to avoid the ethical consequences, and they are aware of this. Although a Muslim poacher may be able to shoot elephants and avoid park game wardens, if a framework based on Islamic principles for the protection of the environment has been published, he knows that he will not be able to avoid the everwatchful divine Warden. The Muslim knows that Islamic values are all based on what God loves and wants: 'And when he turns away [from thee] his effort in the land is to make mischief therein and to destroy the crops and the cattle; and Allah loveth not mischief' (Sūrah 2: 205).

When the Prophet Solomon and his army were about to destroy a nest of ants, one ant warned the rest of the colony of the coming destruction. When Solomon heard this he begged God for the wisdom to do the good thing which God wanted him to do. Solomon was obviously facing an environmental problem and needed an ethical decision; he begged God for guidance:

> Till, when they reached the Valley of the Ants, an ant exclaimed: O, ants! Enter your dwellings lest Solomon and his armies crush you, unperceiving.
>
> And [Solomon] smiled, laughing at her speech, and said: My Lord, arouse me to be thankful for Thy favor wherewith Thou hast favored me and my parents, and to do good that shall be pleasing unto Thee, and include me among [the number of] Thy righteous slaves (Sūrah 27: 18–19).

Ethics in Islam is not based on a variety of separate scattered virtues, with each virtue, such as honesty or truth, standing isolated from others. Rather virtue in Islam is a part of a total, comprehensive way of life which serves to guide and control all human activity.[8] Truthfulness is an ethical value, as are protecting life, conserving the environment, and sustaining its development within the confines of what God has ordered. When 'Āïsha, the wife of the Prophet Muḥammad, was asked about his ethics she replied: 'His ethics are the whole Qur'ān.' The Qur'ān does not contain separate scattered ethical values. Rather it contains the instructions for a complete way of life. There are political, social and economic principles side by side with instructions for the construction and preservation of the earth.

Islamic ethical values are based not on human reasoning, as Aristotle claimed values to be, nor on what society imposes on the individual, as Durkheim thought, nor on the interests of a certain class, as Marxists maintain. In each of these claims values are affected by circumstances. In Islam, ethical values are held to be based on an accurate scale which is unalterable as to time and place.[9] Islam's values are those without which neither persons nor the natural environment can be sustained.

THE HUMAN–ENVIRONMENT RELATIONSHIP

As we have seen, within the Islamic faith, an individual's relationship with the environment is governed by certain moral precepts. These originate with God's creation of humans and the role they were given upon the Earth. Our universe, with all its diverse component elements was created by God and the human being in an essential part of His Measured and Balanced Creation. The role of humans, however, is not only to enjoy, use and benefit from their surroundings. They are expected to preserve, protect and promote their fellow creatures. The Prophet Muḥammad (peace be upon him) said: 'All creatures are God's dependents and the best among them is the one who is most useful to God's dependents.'[10] The Prophet of Islam looked upon himself as responsible for the trees and the animals and all natural elements. He also said: 'The only reasons that God does not cause his punishment to pour over you are the elderly, the suckling babes, and the animals which graze upon your land'[11] Muḥammad prayed for rain when he was reminded that water was short, the trees suffering from drought, and animals dying. He begged God's mercy to fall upon his creatures.[12]

The relationship between human beings and their environment includes many features in addition to subjugation and utilization. Construction and development are primary but our relationship to nature also includes meditation, contemplation and enjoyment of its beauties. The most perfect Muslim was the Prophet Muḥammad who was reported by Ibn 'Abbās to have enjoyed gazing at greenery and running water.[13]

When reading verses about the Earth in the Holy Qur'ān, we find strong indications that the Earth was originally a place of peace and rest for humans:

> Is not He [best] Who made the earth a fixed abode, and placed rivers in the folds thereof, and placed firm hills therein, and hath set a barrier between the two seas? Is there any God beside Allah? Nay, but most of them know not! (Sūrah 27: 61)

The Earth is important to the concept of interrelation. Human beings are made from two components of the Earth—dust and water.

> And Allah hath caused you to grow as a growth from the earth, And afterward He maketh you return thereto, and He will bring you forth again, a [new] forthbringing. And Allah hath made the earth a wide expanse for you That ye may thread the valleyways thereof (Sūrah 71: 17–20).

The word 'earth (arḍ) is mentioned twice in this short quotation and in the Qur'ān the word occurs a total of 485 times, a simple measure of its importance.

The Earth is described as being subservient to humans: 'He it is Who hath made the earth subservient unto you, so walk in the paths thereof and eat of His providence' (Sūrah 67: 15). The Earth is also described as a receptacle: 'Have we not made the earth a receptacle both for the living and the dead' (Sūrah 77: 25–26).[14] Even more importantly, the Earth is considered by Islam to be a source of purity and a place for the worship of God. The Prophet Muḥammad said: 'The earth is made for me [and Muslims] as a prayer place (masjid) and as a purifier.' This means that the Earth is to be used to cleanse oneself before prayer if water is unobtainable.[15] Ibn 'Umar reported that the Prophet of Islam said: 'God is beautiful and loved everything beautiful. He is generous and loves generosity and is clean and loves cleanliness.'[16]

Thus it is not surprising that the Islamic position with regard to the environment is that humans must intervene in order to protect the Earth. They may not stand back while it is destroyed. 'He brought you forth from the earth and hath made you husband it' (Sūrah 11: 61). For, finally, the Earth is a source of blessedness. And the Prophet Muḥammad said: 'Some trees are as blessed as the Muslim himself, especially palm.'[17]

THE SUSTAINABLE CARE OF NATURE

Islam permits the utilization of the natural environment but this utilization should not involve unnecessary destruction. Squandering is rejected by God: 'O Children of Adam! Look to your adornment at every place of worship, and eat and drink, but be not prodigal. Lo! He loveth not the prodigals' (Sūrah 7: 31). In this Qur'ānic passage, eating and drinking refer to the utilization of the sources of life. Such utilization is not without controls. The component elements of life have to be protected so that their utilization may continue in a sustainable way. Yet even this preservation must be undertaken in an altruistic fashion, and not merely for its benefit to human beings. The

Prophet Muḥammad said: 'Act in your life as though you are living forever and act for the Hereafter as if you are dying tomorrow.'[18]

These actions must not be restricted to those which will derive direct benefits. Even if doomsday were expected imminently, humans would be expected to continue their good behaviour, for Muḥammad said, 'When doomsday comes if someone has a palm shoot in his hand he should plant it.[19] This *hadīth* encapsulates the principles of Islamic environmental ethics. Even when all hope is lost, planting should continue for planting is good in itself. The planting of the palm shoot continues the process of development and will sustain life even if one does not anticipate any benefit from it. In this, the Muslim is like the soldier who fights to the last bullet.

A theory of the sustainable utilization of the ecosystem may be deduced from Islam's assertion that life is maintained with due balance in everything: 'Allah knoweth that which every female beareth and that which the wombs absorb and that which they grow. And everything with Him is measured' (Sūrah 13: 8). Also: 'He unto Whom belongeth the sovereignty of the heavens and the earth, He hath chosen no son nor hath He any partner in the sovereignty. He hath created everything and hath meted out for it a measure' (Sūrah 25: 2).

Humans are not the owners, but the maintainers of the due balance and measure which God provided for them and for the animals that live with them.

> And after that He spread the earth,
> And produced therefrom water thereof and the pasture thereof,
> And He made fast the hills,
> A provision for you and for your cattle (Sūrah 79: 30–33).

The Qur'ān goes on to say:

> But when the great disaster cometh,
> The day when man will call to mind his [whole] endeavor (Sūrah 79:34–35).

Humans will have a different home (*ma' wā*) or place of abode, different from the Earth and what it contains. The word *ma' wā* is the same word used in modern Arabic for 'environment.' One cannot help but wonder if these verses are an elaboration on the concept of sustainable development, a task that humans will undertake until their home is changed.

Sayyid Quṭb, commenting on these verses, observes that the Qur'ān, in referring to the origin of ultimate truth, used many correspondences (*muwāfaqāt*)—such as building the heavens, darkening the night, bringing forth human beings, spreading the earth, producing water and plants, and making the mountains fast. All these were provided for human beings and their animals as providence, and are direct signs which constitute proof as to the reality of God's measurement and calculation. Finally, Sayyid Quṭb observes that every part of God's creation was carefully made to fit into the general system, a system that testifies to the Creator's existence and the existence of a day of reward and punishment.

At this point, one must ask whether it is not a person's duty to preserve the proof of the Creator's existence while developing it. Wouldn't the wholesale destruction of the environment be the destruction of much which testifies to the greatness of God?

The concept of the sustained care of all aspects of the environment also fits into Islam's concept of charity, for charity is not only for the present generation but also for those in the future. A story is told of 'Umar ibn al-Khaṭṭab, the famous companion of the Prophet. He once saw that an old man, Khuzaymah ibn Thābit, had neglected his land. 'Umar asked what was preventing him from cultivating it. Khuzaymah explained that he was old and could be expected to die soon. Whereupon, Umar insisted that he should plant it.' Khuzaymah's son, who narrated the story, added that his father and 'Umar planted the uncultivated land together.'[20]

This incident demonstrates how strongly Islam encourages the sustained cultivation of the land. Land should not be used and then abandoned just because the cultivator expects no personal benefit.

In Islam, law and ethics constitute the two interconnected elements of a unified world view. When considering the environment and its protection, this Islamic attitude may constitute a useful foundation for the formulation of a strategy throughout, at least, the Muslim world. Muslims who inhabit so much of the developing world may vary in local habits and customs but they are remarkably united in faith and in their attitude to life.

Islam is a religion of submission to God, master of all worlds. The Earth and all its inhabitants were created and are dominated by God. All Muslims begin their prayers five times a day with the same words from the Holy Qur'ān: 'Praise be to Allah, Lord of the Worlds' (Sūrah 1:1). These opening words of the Qur'ān have become not only the most repeated but also the most loved and respected words for Muslims everywhere. Ibn Kathīr, like many other Qur'ānic commentators, considers that the word 'worlds' (*ālamīn*) means the different kinds of creatures that inhabit the sky, the land, and the sea. Muslims submit themselves to the Creator who made them and who made all other worlds. The same author mentions that Muslims also submit themselves to the signs of the existence of the Creator and His unity. This secondary meaning exists because 'worlds' comes from the same root as signs; thus the worlds are signs of the Creator.[21]

A Muslim, therefore, has a very special relationship with those worlds which in modern times have come to be known as the environment. Indeed, that these worlds exist and that they were made by the same Creator means that they are united and interdependent, each a part of the perfect system of creation. No conflict should exist between them; they should exist in harmony as different parts of the whole. Their coexistence could be likened to an architectural masterpiece in which every detail has been added to complete and complement the structure. Thus the details of creation serve to testify to the wisdom and perfection of the Creator.

THE PRACTICE OF ISLAMIC ENVIRONMENTAL ETHICS

Islam has always had a great influence on the formation of individual Muslim communities and the policy making of Muslim states. Environmental policy has been influenced by Islam and this influence has remained the same throughout the history of the Islamic faith.

The concept of *ḥimā* (protection of certain zones) has existed since the time of the Prophet Muḥammad. *Ḥimā* involved the ruler or government's protection of specific unused areas. No one may build on them or develop them in any way. The Mālikī school of Islamic law described the requirements of *ḥimā* to be the following.[22] First, the need of the Muslim public for the maintenance of land in an unused state. Protection is not granted to satisfy an influential individual unless there is a public need. Second, the protected area should be limited in order to avoid inconvenience to the public. Third, the protected area should not be built on or cultivated. And fourth, the aim of protection (Zuhaylī 5:574) is the welfare of the people, for example, the protected area may be used for some restricted grazing by the animals of the poor.

The concept of *ḥimā* can still be seen in many Muslim countries, such as Saudi Arabia, where it is practised by the government to protect wildlife. In a less formal way it is still practised by some bedouin tribes as a custom or tradition inherited from their ancestors.

The *ḥarīm* is another ancient institution which can be traced back to the time of the Prophet Muḥammad. It is an inviolable zone which may not be used or developed, save with the specific permission of the state. The *ḥarīm* is usually found in association with wells, natural springs, underground water channels, rivers and trees planted on barren land or *mawāt*.[23] There is careful administration of the *ḥarīm* zones based on the practice of the Prophet Muḥammad and the precedent of his companions as recorded in the sources of Islamic law.

At present the role of Islam in environmental protection can be seen in the formation of different Islamic organizations and the emphasis given to Islam as a motive for the protection of the environment.

Saudi Arabia has keenly sought to implement a number of projects aimed at the protection of various aspects of the environment, for example, the late King Khalid's patronage of efforts to save the Arabian oryx from extinction.

The Meteorology and Environmental Protection Administration (MEPA) of Saudi Arabia actively promotes the principles of Islamic environmental protection. In 1983 MEPA and the International Union for the Conservation of Nature and Natural Resources commissioned a basic paper on the Islamic principles for the conservation of natural environment.[24]

The Islamic faith has great impact on environmental issues throughout the Arab and Muslim world. The first Arab Ministerial Conference took as its theme 'The Environmental Aspects of Development' and one of the topics considered was the Islamic faith and its values.[25] The Amir of Kuwait emphasized the fundamental importance of Islam when he addressed the General Assembly of the United Nations in 1988. He explained that Islam was the basis for justice, mercy, and cooperation between all humankind; and he called for an increase in scientific and technological assistance from the North to help conserve natural and human resources, combat pollution and support sustainable development projects.

Finally, it is imperative to acknowledge that the new morality required to conserve the environment which the World Conservation Strategy (Section 13.1) emphasizes, needs to be based on a more solid foundation. It is not only necessary to involve the public in conservation policy but also to improve its morals and alter its attitudes. In Muslim countries such changes should be brought about by identifying environmental policies with Islamic teachings. To do this, the public education system will have to supplement the scientific approach to environmental education with serious attention to Islamic belief and environmental awareness.

NOTES

1. Aḥmad Ibn Taymīyah, *Majamūʿ Fatawā* (Rabat: Saudi Educational Attaché, n.d.), 11:96-97.
2. Mawil Y. Izzi Deen (Samarrai), ''Environmental Protection and Islam,'' *Journal of the Faculty of Arts and Humanities, King Abdulaziz University* 5 (1985).
3. All references to the Holy Qur'ān are from *The Meaning of the Glorious Koran,* trans. Mohammed M. Pickthall, (New York: Mentor, n.d.).
4. Ibn Hajar al-ʿAsqalānī, *Fatḥ al-Bārī bi-Sharḥ Ṣaḥīḥ al-Bukhārī,* edited by M.F. ʿAbd al-Bāqī, M. al-Khāṭib, and A. B. Bāz 1959; 1970 (Beirut: Dār al-Maʿrifah, 195; 197), 5: 40.
5. Ibid., 5: 42.
6. Muḥammad ʿAbd Allah Draz, *La Morale du Koran,*

trans. into Arabic by A. Shahin and S.M. Badāwī (Kuwait: Dār al-Risālah, 1973), 28.
7. Ibid.
8. Sayyid Quṭb, *Muqāwamāt al-Tasawwur al-Islāmī* (Cairo: Dār al-Shurūq, 1985), 289.
9. Ibid., 290.
10. Ismāʿil Ibn Muḥammad al-ʿAjlūnī, *Kashf al-Khafāʾ wa Muzīl al-Ilbās,* edited by A. al-Qallash (Syria Damascus: Muʾassasat al-Risālah, 1983), 1:458.
11. Ibid., 1:213.
12. Ibn Ḥajar, *Fatḥ al Bārī,* 2: 512.
13. ʿAjlūnī, *Kash al-Khafāʾ,* 1: 387.
14. N.J. Dawood, trans. *The Koran* (New York: Penguin, 1974): 54.
15. Muḥammad Ibn Ismāʿīl al-Bukhāri, *Ṣaḥīḥ al-Bukhāri* (Istanbul: Dār al-Ṭibaʿah al-Amīrah, 1897), 1: 86.
16. Ajlūnī, *Kashf al-Khafāʾ,* 1: 260.
17. Bukhāri, *Ṣaḥīḥ al-Bukhāri,* 1: 22, 6: 211.
18. Aḥmad Ibn al-Ḥusayn al-Bayhāqī, *Sunan al-Bayhaqī al-Kubrā* (Hyderabad, India: n.d.), 3: 19.
19. Ibid., 3: 184.
20. Soūti, *al-Jāmi ʿal-Kabīr,* manuscript (Egyptian General Committee for Publication, n.d.).
21. M.A. al-Sabuni, *Mukhtaṣar Tafsīr Ibn Kathīr* (Beirut: Dār al-Qurʾān al-Karīm, 1981), 1: 21.
22. Wahbah Muṣtafa Zuḥayli, *al-Fiqh al-Islāmī wa ʿAdilatuhu* (Damascus: Muʾassasat al-Risālah 1985).
23. Ibid., 5: 574.
24. A.H. Bakader, A.T. al-Sabbagh, M.A. al-Gelinid, and M.Y. Izzi Deen (Samarrai), *Islamic Principles for the Conservation of the Natural Environment* (Gland, Switzerland: International Union for the Conservation of Nature and MEPA, 1983).
25. *Habitat and the Environment* (Tunis: Economic Affairs Department of the Directorate of the Arab League, 1986).

DISCUSSION TOPICS

1. What similarities and differences are there between the Islamic view and the views presented by St. Thomas Aquinas (Chapter 6) and Bratton (Chapter 10)?
2. What particular insights from Islam might be applicable in developing a more judicious environmental ethic in Western society? Justify your position.

The Buddhist Attitude Towards Nature

Lily de Silva

Lily de Silva is professor of Buddhist Studies at the University of Peradeniya, Sri Lanka. Her professional background is particularly strong in the Theravada form of Buddhism predominating in Southeast Asia.

De Silva notes that Buddhism is concerned primarily with seeking an end to human suffering, and does not directly address issues in environmental ethics. However, she believes that a characteristic Buddhist attitude toward nature can be inferred from Buddhist writings. In the Buddhist world view, the natural world passes through alternating states of evolution and dissolution. Yet, adherents also believe that natural processes are affected by human moral behavior, as recorded in a number of Buddhist writings and legends.

Buddhists advocate a gentle, nonaggressive attitude toward nature. A simple existence with few, easily satisfied wants is considered to be an exemplary life. Humans are admonished to use nature in order to rise above it, and to realize their innate human spiritual potential.

A follower of Buddhism cultivates an attitude of compassion and sympathy for living things. Mettā refers to feelings of boundless loving-kindness toward all creatures. Buddhist reverence exhibits itself in a gentle, nonviolent attitude toward plants—especially long-standing gigantic trees.

De Silva maintains that humans are alienated both from themselves and from nature, and that human greed has led to violent and aggressive attitudes toward nature. In Buddhist thought, the mind is supreme and a clean environment results from a proper moral and spiritual lifestyle. De Silva believes that Buddhism provides a model for such a lifestyle.

. . . Buddhism strictly limits itself to the delineation of a way of life designed to eradicate human suffering. The Buddha refused to answer questions which did not directly or indirectly bear on the central problem of human suffering and its ending. Furthermore, environmental pollution is a problem of the modern age, unheard of and unsuspected during the time of the Buddha. Therefore it is difficult to find any specific discourse which deals with the topic we are interested in here. Nevertheless, as Buddhism is a full-fledged philosophy of life reflecting all aspects of experience, it is possible to find enough material in the Pali Canon to delineate the Buddhist attitude towards nature.

The word ''nature'' means everything in the world which is not organised and constructed by man. The Pali equivalents which come closest to ''nature'' are *loka* and *yathābhūta*. The former is usually translated as ''world'' while the latter literally means ''things as they really are.'' The words *dhammatā* and *niyāma* are used in the Pali Canon to mean ''natural law or way.''

NATURE AS DYNAMIC

According to Buddhism changeability is one of the perennial principles of nature. Everything changes in nature and nothing remains static. This concept is expressed by the Pali term *anicca*. Everything formed is in a constant process of change (*sabbe sankhārā aniccā*).[1] The world is therefore defined as that which disintegrates (*lujjatī ti loko*); the world is so called because it is dynamic and kinetic, it is constantly in a process of undergoing change.[2] In nature there are no static and stable ''things''; there are only ever-changing, ever-moving processes. . . .

MORALITY AND NATURE

The world passes through alternating cycles of evolution and dissolution, each of which endures for a long period of time. Though change is inherent in nature, Buddhism believes that natural processes are affected by the morals of man. . . . Buddhism believes that though change is a factor inherent in nature, man's moral deterioration accelerates the process of change and brings about changes which are adverse to human well being and happiness. . . .

[S]everal suttas from the Pali Canon show that early Buddhism believes there to be a close relationship between human morality and the natural environment. This idea has been systematised in the theory of the five natural laws (*pañca niyāmadhammā*) in the later commentaries.[3] According to this theory, in the cosmos there are five natural laws or forces at work, namely *utuniyāma* (lit. "season-law"), *bīja-niyāma* (lit. "seed-law"), *cittaniyāma, kammani-yāma* and *dhammaniyāma*. They can be translated as physical laws, biological laws, psychological laws, moral laws and causal laws, respectively. While the first four laws operate within their respective spheres, the last-mentioned law of causality operates *within* each of them as well as *among* them.

This means that the physical environment of any given area conditions the growth and development of its biological component, i.e., flora and fauna. These in turn influence the thought pattern of the people interacting with them. Modes of thinking determine moral standards. The opposite process of interaction is also possible. The morals of man influence not only the psychological make-up of the people but the biological and physical environment of the area as well. Thus the five laws demonstrate that man and nature are bound together in a reciprocal causal relationship with changes in one necessarily bringing about changes in the other.

The commentary on the *Cakkavattisīhanāda Sutta* goes on to explain the pattern of mutual interaction further.[4] When mankind is demoralised through greed, famine is the natural outcome; when moral degeneration is due to ignorance, epidemic is the inevitable result; when hatred is the demoralising force, widespread violence is the ultimate outcome. If and when mankind realizes that large-scale devastation has taken place as a result of his moral degeneration, a change of heart takes place among the few surviving human beings. With gradual moral regeneration conditions improve through a long period of cause and effect and mankind again starts to enjoy gradually increasing prosperity and longer life. The world, including nature and mankind, stands or falls with the type of moral force at work. If immorality grips society, man and nature deteriorate; if morality reigns, the quality of human life and nature improves. Thus greed, hatred and delusion produce pollution within and without. Generosity, compassion and wisdom produce purity within and without. This is one reason the Buddha has pronounced that the world is led by the mind, *cittena niyata loko.*[5] Thus man and nature,

according to the ideas expressed in early Buddhism, are interdependent.

HUMAN USE OF NATURAL RESOURCES

For survival mankind has to depend on nature for his food, clothing, shelter, medicine and other requisites. For optimum benefits man has to understand nature so that he can utilise natural resources and live harmoniously with nature. By understanding the working of nature—for example, the seasonal rainfall pattern, methods of conserving water by irrigation, the soil types, the physical conditions required for growth of various food crops, etc.—man can learn to get better returns from his agricultural pursuits. But this learning has to be accompanied by moral restraint if he is to enjoy the benefits of natural resources for a long time. Man must learn to satisfy his needs and not feed his greeds. The resources of the world are not unlimited whereas man's greed knows neither limit nor satiation. Modern man in his unbridled voracious greed for pleasure and acquisition of wealth has exploited nature to the point of near impoverishment. . . .

Buddhism tirelessly advocates the virtues of non-greed, non-hatred and non-delusion in all human pursuits. Greed breeds sorrow and unhealthy consequences. Contentment (*santuṭṭhi*) is a much praised virtue in Buddhism.[6] The man leading a simple life with few wants easily satisfied is upheld and appreciated as an exemplary character.[7] Miserliness[8] and wastefulness[9] are equally deplored in Buddhism as two degenerate extremes. Wealth has only instrumental value; it is to be utilised for the satisfaction of man's needs. Hoarding is a senseless anti-social habit comparable to the attitude of the dog in the manger. The vast hoarding of wealth in some countries and the methodical destruction of large quantities of agricultural produce to keep the market prices from falling, while half the world is dying of hunger and starvation, is really a sad paradox of the present affluent age.

Buddhism commends frugality as a virtue in its own right. Once Ānanda explained to King Udena the thrifty economic use of robes by the monks in the following order. When new robes are received the old robes are used as coverlets, the old coverlets as mattress covers, the old mattress covers as rugs, the old rugs as dusters, and the old tattered dusters are kneaded with clay and used to repair cracked floors and walls.[10] Thus nothing usable is wasted. Those who waste are derided as "wood-apple eaters."[11] A man shakes the branch of a wood-apple tree and all the fruits, ripe as well as unripe, fall. The man would collect only what he wants and walk away leaving the rest to rot. Such a wasteful attitude is certainly deplored in Buddhism as not only anti-social but criminal. The excessive exploitation of nature as is done today would certainly be condemned by Buddhism in the strongest possible terms.

Buddhism advocates a gentle non-aggressive attitude towards nature. According to the *Sigālovāda Sutta* a householder should accumulate wealth as a bee collects pollen from a flower.[12] The bee harms neither the fragrance nor the beauty of the flower, but gathers pollen to turn it into sweet honey. Similarly, man is expected to make legitimate use of nature so that he can rise above nature and realise his innate spiritual potential.

ATTITUDE TOWARDS ANIMAL AND PLANT LIFE

The well-known Five Precepts (*pañca sīla*) form the minimum code of ethics that every lay Buddhist is expected to adhere to. Its first precept involves abstention from injury to life. It is explained as the casting aside of all forms of weapons, being conscientious about depriving a living being of life. In its positive sense it means the cultivation of compassion and sympathy for all living beings.[13] The Buddhist layman is expected to abstain from trading in meat too.[14]

The Buddhist monk has to abide by an even stricter code of ethics than the layman. He has to abstain from practices which would involve even unintentional injury to living creatures. For instance, the Buddha promulgated the rule against going on a journey during the rainy season because of possible injury to worms and insects that come to the surface in wet weather.[15] The same concern for non-violence prevents a monk from digging the ground.[16] Once a monk who was a

potter prior to ordination built for himself a clay hut and set it on fire to give it a fine finish. The Buddha strongly objected to this as so many living creatures would have been burnt in the process. The hut was broken down on the Buddha's instructions to prevent it from creating a bad precedent for later generations.[17] The scrupulous non-violent attitude towards even the smallest living creatures prevents the monks from drinking unstrained water.[18] It is no doubt a sound hygienic habit, but what is noteworthy is the reason which prompts the practice, namely, sympathy for living creatures.

Buddhism also prescribes the practice of *mettā*, "loving-kindness" towards all creatures of all quarters without restriction. The *Karanīyamettā Sutta* enjoins the cultivation of loving-kindness towards all creatures, timid and steady, long and short, big and small, minute and great, visible and invisible, near and far, born and awaiting birth.[19] All quarters are to be suffused with this loving attitude. Just as one's own life is precious to oneself, so is the life of the other precious to himself. Therefore a reverential attitude must be cultivated towards all forms of life. . . .

The understanding of kamma and rebirth, too, prepares the Buddhist to adopt a sympathetic attitude towards animals. According to this belief it is possible for human beings to be reborn in subhuman states among animals. The *Kukkuravatika Sutta* can be cited as a canonical reference which substantiates this view.[20] The Jātakas provide ample testimony to this view from commentarial literature. It is possible that our own close relatives have been reborn as animals. Therefore it is only right that we should treat animals with kindness and sympathy. The Buddhist notion of merit also engenders a gentle non-violent attitude towards living creatures. It is said that if one throws dish-washing water into a pool where there are insects and living creatures, intending that they feed on the tiny particles of food thus washed away, one accumulates merit even by such trivial generosity.[21] According to the *Macchuddāna Jātaka* the Bodhisatta threw his leftover food into a river in order to feed the fish, and by the power of that merit he was saved from an impending disaster.[22] Thus kindness to animals, be they big or small, is a source of merit—merit needed for human beings to improve their lot in the cycle of rebirths and to approach the final goal of Nibbāna.

Buddhism expresses a gentle non-violent attitude towards the vegetable kingdom as well. It is said that one should not even break the branch of a tree that has given one shelter.[23] Plants are so helpful to us in providing us with all necessities of life that we are expected not to adopt a callous attitude towards them. The more strict monastic rules prevent monks from injuring plant life.[24]

Prior to the rise of Buddhism people regarded natural phenomena such as mountains, forests, groves and trees with a sense of awe and reverence.[25] They considered them as the abode of powerful non-human beings who could assist human beings at times of need. Though Buddhism gave man a far superior Triple Refuge (*tisaraṇa*) in the Buddha, Dhamma and Sangha, these places continued to enjoy public patronage at a popular level, as the acceptance of terrestrial non-human beings such as *devatās*[26] and *yakkhas*[27] did not violate the belief system of Buddhism. Therefore among the Buddhists there is a reverential attitude towards specially long-standing gigantic trees. They are called *vanaspati* in Pali, meaning ''lords of the forests.''[28] As huge trees such as the ironwood, the sāla and the fig are also recognised as the Bodhi trees of former Buddhas, the deferential attitude towards trees is further strengthened.[29] It is well known that the *ficus religiosa* is held as an object of great veneration in the Buddhist world today as the tree under which the Buddha attained Enlightenment.

The construction of parks and pleasure groves for public use is considered a great meritorious deed.[30] Sakka the lord of gods is said to have reached this status as a result of social services such as the construction of parks, pleasure groves, ponds, wells and roads.[31]

The open air, natural habitats and forest trees have a special fascination for the Eastern mind as symbols of spiritual freedom. The home life is regarded as a fetter (*sambādha*) that keeps man in bondage and misery. Renunciation is like the open air (*abbhokāsa*), nature unhampered by man's activity.[32] . . . The Buddha's constant advice to his disciples also was to re-

sort to natural habitats such as forest groves and glades. There, undisturbed by human activity, they could zealously engage themselves in meditation.[33]

ATTITUDE TOWARDS POLLUTION

. . . Cleanliness was highly commended by the Buddhists both in the person and in the environment. They were much concerned about keeping water clean, be it in the river, pond or well. These sources of water were for public use and each individual had to use them with proper public-spirited caution so that others after him could use them with the same degree of cleanliness. Rules regarding the cleanliness of green grass were prompted by ethical and aesthetic considerations. Moreover, grass is food for most animals and it is man's duty to refrain from polluting it by his activities.

Noise is today recognised as a serious personal and environmental pollutant troubling everyone to some extent. . . .

The Buddha and his disciples revelled in the silent solitary natural habitats unencumbered by human activity. Even in the choice of monasteries the presence of undisturbed silence was an important quality they looked for.[34] Silence invigorates those who are pure at heart and raises their efficiency for meditation. But silence overawes those who are impure with ignoble impulses of greed, hatred and delusion. . . .

The psychological training of the monks is so advanced that they are expected to cultivate a taste not only for external silence, but for inner silence of speech, desire and thought as well. The sub-vocal speech, the inner chatter that goes on constantly within us in our waking life, is expected to be silenced through meditation.[35] The sage who succeeds in quelling this inner speech completely is described as a *muni,* a silent one.[36] His inner silence is maintained even when he speaks! . . .

NATURE AS BEAUTIFUL

The Buddha and his disciples regarded natural beauty as a source of great joy and aesthetic satisfaction. The saints who purged themselves of sensuous worldly pleasures responded to natural beauty with a detached sense of appreciation. The average poet looks at nature and derives inspiration mostly by the sentiments it evokes in his own heart; he becomes emotionally involved with nature. For instance, he may compare the sun's rays passing over the mountain tops to the blush on a sensitive face, he may see a tear in a dew drop, the lips of his beloved in a rose petal, etc. But the appreciation of the saint is quite different. He appreciates nature's beauty for its own sake and derives joy unsullied by sensuous associations and self-projected ideas. . . .

CONCLUSION

. . . In the present ecocrisis man has to look for radical solutions. "Pollution cannot be dealt with in the long term on a remedial or cosmetic basis or by tackling symptoms: all measures should deal with basic causes. These are determined largely by our values, priorities and choices."[37] Man must reappraise his value system. The materialism that has guided his lifestyle has landed him in very severe problems. Buddhism teaches that mind is the forerunner of all things, mind is supreme. If one acts with an impure mind, i.e., a mind sullied with greed, hatred and delusion, suffering is the inevitable result. If one acts with a pure mind, i.e., with the opposite qualities of contentment, compassion and wisdom, happiness will follow like a shadow.[38] Man has to understand that pollution in the environment has been caused because there has been psychological pollution within himself. If he wants a clean environment he has to adopt a lifestyle that springs from a moral and spiritual dimension.

Buddhism offers man a simple moderate lifestyle eschewing both extremes of self-deprivation and self-indulgence. Satisfaction of basic human necessities, reduction of wants to the minimum, frugality and contentment are its important characteristics. Each man has to order his life on moral principles, exercise self-control in the enjoyment of the senses, discharge his duties in his various social roles, and conduct himself with wisdom and self-awareness in all activities. It is only when each man adopts a simple moderate lifestyle that mankind as a whole will stop polluting the environment. This seems to be the only way

of overcoming the present ecocrisis and the problem of alienation. With such a lifestyle, man will adopt a non-exploitative, non-aggressive, gentle attitude towards nature. He can then live in harmony with nature, utilising its resources for the satisfaction of his basic needs. The Buddhist admonition is to utilise nature in the same way as a bee collects pollen from the flower, neither polluting its beauty nor depleting its fragrance. Just as the bee manufacturers honey out of pollen, so man should be able to find happiness and fulfilment in life without harming the natural world in which he lives.

NOTES

All Pali texts referred to are editions of the Pali Text Society, London. Abbreviations used are as follows:

A.   Anguttara Nikāya
D.   Dīgha Nikāya
Dh.   Dhammapada
Dh. A. Dhammapada Aṭṭhakathā
J.   Jātaka
M.   Majjhima Nikāya
S.   Saṁyutta Nikāya
Sn.   Sutta-nipāta
Thag.   Theragāthā
Vin.   Vinaya Pitaka

1. A. IV, 100.
2. S. IV, 52.
3. Atthasālini, 854.
4. D. A. III, 854.
5. S. I, 39.
6. Dh. v. 204.
7. A. IV, 2, 220, 229.
8. Dh. A. I, 20 ff.
9. Dh. A. III, 129 ff.
10. Vin. II, 291.
11. A. IV, 283.
12. D. III, 188.
13. D. I, 4.
14. A. III, 208.
15. Vin. I, 137.
16. Vin, IV, 125.
17. Vin. III, 42.
18. Vin. IV, 125.
19. Sn. vv. 143-152.
20. M. I, 387 f.
21. A. I, 161.
22. J. II, 423.

23. Petavatthu II, 9, 3.
24. Vin. IV, 34.
25. Dh. v. 188.
26. S. I, 1-45.
27. S. I, 206-215.
28. S. IV, 302; Dh. A. I, 3.
29. D. II, 4.
30. S. I, 33.
31. J. I, 199 f.
32. D. I, 63.
33. M. I 118; S. IV, 373.
34. A. V, 15.
35. S. IV, 217, 293.
36. Sn. vv. 207-221; A. I, 273.
37. Robert Arvill, *Man and Environment* (Penguin Books, 1978), p. 170.
38. Dh. vv. 1, 2.

DISCUSSION TOPICS

1. What similarities and differences are there between the Buddhist conception of how nature works and your own conception of how nature works? How do you think these differences could be resolved?

2. In what ways is the Buddhist concern for finding an end to human suffering related to the development of an environmental ethic?

3. What Buddhists beliefs could contribute to developing a more workable environmental ethic in Western society?

READING 68

Taoism and the Foundations of Environmental Ethics

Po-Keung Ip

Po-Keung Ip earned undergraduate and graduate degrees from the Chinese University of Hong Kong, and has conducted graduate work at the University of Western Ontario, London, Ontario, Canada. His research interests include the philosophy of science and environmental ethics.

Ip proposes that an environmental ethic ought to provide answers to the following three questions: What is the nature of nature? What is the human relationship to nature? How should humans relate themselves to nature? In elucidating the Taoist perspective, Ip believes that both science and ethics provide vital resources for addressing environmental problems. Ip believes that the Tao symbolizes the ultimate reality of nature which is, in essence, wholly depersonalized. Humans are linked to the Tao, and through the Tao to everything else.

According to the Tao, there is a moral imperative to be virtuous toward nature. Everything is viewed as ontologically equal. An anthropocentric outlook conflicts with the egalitarian valuing of all being, and is antithetical to the Tao.

Ip challenges the traditional interpretation of the Taoist concept of ''wu-wei'' as ''inaction.'' Rather, he suggests that wu-wei *means acting in accordance with nature, that is, in harmony with the Tao. In Ip's view, Taoism helps break the false barriers separating humans from the rest of nature, and affirms inherent valuing of nonhumans that goes beyond their use merely for meeting human needs.*

I. INTRODUCTION

I take it that the major task of environmental ethics is the construction of a system of normative guidelines governing man's attitudes, behavior, and action toward his natural environment. The central question to be asked is: how *ought* man, either as an individual or as a group, to behave, to act, toward nature? By *nature* I mean the nonhuman environment man finds himself in. Surely, a question of this sort presupposes the appropriateness of the application of moral, ethical concepts to nature, viz., stones, fish, bears, trees, water, and so on. Questions about the legitimacy and meaningfulness of such an application automatically arise. However, in the present paper I presume such legitimacy without arguing for it.[1]

---

1. Tom Regan recently has given a detailed discussion on this issue in ''The Nature and Possibility of an Environmental Ethic,'' *Environmental Ethics* 3 (1981): 19-34.

Any viable environmental ethics, it seems to me, should provide adequate answers to three questions: (1) what is the nature of nature? (2) What is man's relationship to nature? (3) How should man relate himself to nature? In this paper I show that Taoism gives reasonably good answers to these questions and I argue that Taoism, in this sense, is capable of providing a metaphysical foundation for environmental ethics.

II. SCIENCE AND ETHICS

Contemporary environmental crises, such as pollution of various sorts, overusage of natural resources, and extinction of rare species, force us to reconsider exactly what the relationships between man and nature are. At the same time they compel us to reflect once again on what sort of attitudes we ought to have toward nature. The kinds of questions raised here are both scientific and ethical. On the one hand, they are scientific because only recently has man come to realize how ignorant he is of the natural surrounding he is in. It is certainly an irony to twentieth-century man that even though modern science has made tremendous strides in probing both the very large and the very small, it has little to say about the middle, i.e., our surrounding ecosphere. The still immature state of the environmental sciences, nonetheless, sadly bears this out. On the other hand, the questions envisaged here are clearly ethical both in the descriptive and the normative senses. First, we need to understand how man actually conceives his relationship with nature. This is clearly an empirical problem that invites both sociological as well as historical studies. However, we also need to go beyond these empirical questions and ask ourselves whether such attitudes are morally justified. This inevitably involves us in the problems of moral criteria.

I regard both the scientific and ethical approaches to our environmental problems to be vitally important. Both should work closely with the other. Both need the help of the other. Without either, our understanding of environmental problems must remain very limited and incomplete. But what sort of relationship should science and ethics have? I do not try to enter into this thorny problem here.[2] It is important to note, however, that by urging a close working relationship between science and ethics, I am not attempting to *derive* ethics from science. I take the position, without arguing for it, that ethics can never be derived from science, if *derived* is understood in the logical sense of deduction. That this is so is due to the fact that one can never derive *ought* from *is*—a too familiar problem in moral philosophy. The sense in which I say that ethics should work closely with science is this: suppose we have a system of ethics, *E*, which is capable of generating a set of normative guidelines, *G*. Suppose that *G* in conjoining with the knowledge of the situation in which the agent is about to take action yields morally acceptable attitudes and actions. This set of attitudes and actions is not only morally acceptable, but is also according to the knowledge available at the time, workable or realizable. In other words, the relationship between science and ethics is an oblique one. Scientific knowledge only supports ethics indirectly in the way that it provides evidence that the set of actions and attitudes "derivable" from the ethical system in question is workable, realizable.

Let me give a brief example. Suppose we have an ethic which exhorts people to act selflessly regardless of causes and occasions. Scientific results may suggest, however, that self-interest is a primary motivation of human behavior and action. In this case, we have an ethic which runs counter to the evidences of human nature arrived at by scientific research. We say that such an ethic is not supported by science and hence is not involved in the kind of working relationship that we hope for between the two. On the other hand, if we have an ethic which is not only compatible with science, but also receives support from it (in the sense explained), then we say that we have reason to believe that it is plausible.

Two concepts will be useful in my discussion. I take an ethic to be *minimally coherent* if and only if (1) it is coherent and (2) it is compatible with science. An ethic is *maximally coherent* if and only if (1) it is coherent and (2) it receives support from science. The

---

2. See Don Marietta, Jr.'s "The Interrelationships between ecological Science and Environmental Ethics," *Environmental Ethics* 1 (1979): 195-207.

minimally coherent ethic is a weak version of environmental ethics. The maximally coherent ethic, which requires more scientific data, and hence more research, presumably is harder to construct. Due to inadequate ecological information concerning the man-nature relation, nevertheless, I think the kind of ethic that is workable at present is the minimally coherent one. If such understanding is correct, the first step toward an adequate theory for environmental ethics depends on the possibility of establishing such minimally coherent ethics. In the light of such understanding, I show that Taoism, as chiefly represented by the teachings of Lao Tzu and Chuang Tzu, can provide us with such an ethic.

III. THE TAOIST CONCEPTION OF NATURE

Recall the three questions posed at the beginning of the paper, viz., what is the nature of nature, of the man-nature relationship, of the right attitudes to nature? The first two questions are clearly metaphysical in nature and the last one ethical. Let us see how Taoism responds to these questions.

To understand the Taoist conception of nature, one must start with the notion of *Tao.* Using a mystical and poetical language, Lao Tzu in *Tao Té Ching* gives a rich but at times amorphous representation of how nature works. This is done by means of the notion of *Tao.* At the very beginning of *Tao Té Ching,* it is said:

> The Tao (Way) that can be told is not the eternal Tao,
> The name that can be named is not the eternal name,
> The nameless is the origin of Heaven and Earth. . . .
> (chap. 1)[3]

In other places, we are also told that "Tao is eternal and has no name" (chap. 32) and that

> There was something undifferentiated and yet complete, which existed before Heaven and Earth.
> Soundless and formless, It depends on nothing and does not change,
> It operates everywhere and is free from danger,

> It may be considered the mother of the Universe,
> I do not know its name; I call it Tao. (chap. 25)

From similiar utterances in *Tao Té Ching,* we gather that Tao has the following attributes: it is nameless, intangible, empty, simple, all-pervasive, eternal, life-sustaining, nourishing.[4] Indeed, for Lao Tzu, *Tao* stands for the ultimate reality of nature. Unlike *Tien* (Heaven) and *Ti* (God),[5] *Tao* is not anything like a creator god. Rather it is a totally depersonalized concept of nature.

The namelessness of *Tao* is due to its infinite nature, since Lao Tzu believes that only finite things can be attached a name. To give a name to a thing is to individuate it and to give it a definite identity. However, *Tao* by virtue of its infinite nature certainly rejects all names. In other words, *Tao* cannot be exhaustively individuated in the domain of empirical beings, though the latter owe their existence to *Tao.* Hence, *Tao* is not characterizable in any finite manner. Therefore, although we can, in a sense, say we "know" *Tao* by knowing this or that finite being, yet the knowledge thus arrived at is very incomplete. In this way, the nature of *Tao* is at best indeterminable insofar as human knowledge is concerned.

There is also a dynamic side of *Tao.* We are told that "reversion is the action of *Tao*" (chap. 40). *Tao* is also depicted as a process of change and transformation. In fact, everything in the universe is the result of self- and mutual-transformations which are governed by the dialectical interactions of *Tao*'s two cosmic principles—*Ying* and *Yang*[6]—which explain the rhythmic processes which constitute the natural world.

---

3. All quotations from *Tao Té Ching* are from Chan Wing-Tsit, *A Source Book in Chinese Philosophy* (Princeton: Princeton University Press, 1963), pp. 139-173. They are identified in the text by chapter number.

4. See *Tao Té Ching,* chaps. 1, 74, 21, 35, 4, 6, 32.

5. The origins of the notions of *Ti* (God) and *Tien* (Heaven) were closely tied with ancestor worship in ancient China. *Ti* apparently represented a personal god and was supposed to be the perennial source of life. However, it was subsequently replaced by a less personalistic notion of *Tien.* The latter was a highly naturalistic notion which had no strong religious connotation, but was mainly used to stand for the physical sky. See Chang Chung-ying, "Chinese Philosophy: A Characterization," in A. Naess and A. Hannay, eds., *Introduction to Chinese Philosophy* (Oslo: Universitetsforlaget, 1972), pp. 141-165.

6. See Derk Bodde, "Harmony and Conflict in Chinese Philosophy," in A.F. Wright, ed., *Studies in Chinese Thought* (Chicago: University of Chicago Press, 1953), p. 121.

Since *Tao* nourishes, sustains, and transforms beings, a natural relationship is built between them. This relationship is best understood if we understand the meaning of the *Té* of *Tao*. *Té* signifies the potency, the power, of *Tao* that nourishes, sustains, and transforms beings. As a result, the nourishment, development and fulfilment of beings are the consequence of *Té*. Because of the nature of *Té*, it is both a potency as well as a virtue, and by virtue of the possession of *Té*, *Tao* is itself virtuous as well. Since *Té* is internalized in all beings in the universe, there is no problem of relating beings in the world. Indeed, things are related to each other not only metaphysically but also morally. The *Té* of *Tao* provides the essential connections. Man, being a member of beings, is without exception internally linked to *Tao* as well as to everything else. Moreover, being endowed with *Té*, man is also endowed with the capacity of doing virtuous things toward his cosmic counterparts. Thus, a crucial metaphysical linkage between man and nature is established. In the Taoist world view, there is no unbridgeable chasm between man and nature, because everything is inherently connected to everything else. The *Tao* is not separated from the natural world of which it is the source. In Taoism, therefore, chaos is impossible.

The moral imperative to be virtuous toward nature is made possible by another feature of *Tao,* impartiality. According to Lao Tzu, *Tao* "being all embracing, is impartial" (chap. 16). *Tao* is impartial in the sense that everything is to be treated on an equal footing. To use a more apt term, everything is which is seen as being "ontologically equal."[7] Man receives no special attention or status from *Tao*. Homocentrism is simply an alien thing in the Taoist axiological ordering of beings. As a matter of fact, the Taoist holds that there is a kind of egalitarian axiology of beings. The notion of ontological and axiological equality of beings receives further elaborations in the hands of Chuang Tzu. For Chuang Tzu, beings are onotologically equal because they are formed as a result of a process of self- and mutual-transforma-

tions. The alleged individuality and uniqueness of beings can be determinable only in such process. Everything is related to everything else through these processes of self- and mutual-transformations.[8]

IV. THE DOCTRINE OF WU WEI

Acknowledging the fact that man-nature is an inherently connected whole, and that man and other beings, animated or otherwise, are ontologically as well as axiologically equal, the question of how man should behave or act toward his natural surroundings is readily answerable, for the Taoist would take the doctrine of *Wu Wei* as the proper answer to this question.

Although the doctrine of *Wu Wei* is relatively well-known, care must be taken as to how one construes the meaning of *wu wei*. I am taking a position which is at variance with the classical rendition. A majority of writers, to my knowledge, translate the meaning of *wu wei* as inaction,[9] but I think there is a better way of translating it which is more coherent with the system of thought presented in *Tao Té Ching* and other representative Taoist texts. Perhaps the translation of *wu wei* as nonaction is the result of relying too heavily on the literal understanding of the meanings of the words *wu* and *wei*. Literally, *wu* means "not"; *wei,* on the hand, means "action" or "endeavor." However, the meaning of *wu wei* need not literally be translated as "inaction." The reasons are as follows. Although we are told that "*Tao* invariably takes no action [*wu wei*],[10] and yet there is nothing left undone" (chap. 37), given that Tao nourishes, sustains, and fulfills, *Tao* is invariably action-in-itself. To say *Tao wu wei* here is tantamount to saying that *Tao* acts in accordance with its own nature. Since *Tao* is action-in-itself, it certainly requires no additional action to act. To say *Tao* takes no action can best be understood as *Tao* taking no *exogenous* action to act, since such action would be redundant.

7. For more on the notion of ontological equality, see Chang, "Chinese Philosophy," p. 149.

8. For more on the self- and mutual-transformation of beings, see *Chuang Tzu,* chapter two, in Chan, *Source Book.*

9. See Fung Yu-lan, *A History of Chinese Philosophy,* vol. 1, trans. D. Bodde (Princeton: Princeton University Press, 1952), p. 187; Chan, *Source Book.*

10. I systematically replaced *wu wei* in all places in Chan's original translations.

This construal of *wu wei* indeed has other textual support as well. For example, in characterizing the sage, Lao Tzu says, that he

Deal[s] with things before they appear.
Put[s] things in order before disorder arises. . . .
A tower of nine storeys begins with a heap of earth.
The journey of a thousand *li* [1/3 mile] starts from where one stands,
He who takes an action fails.
He who grasps things loses them.
For this reason the sage takes no action and therefore does not fail. . . . (chap. 64)

To make sense of the above paragraph, *wu wei* should not be interpreted as nonaction. To do otherwise would make one very difficult to make sense of the phrases, ''Deal[s] with things before they appear. Put[s] things in order before disorder arises.'' Surely, not only are they not nonaction, they are indeed well-planned and deliberative actions. Moreover, when Lao Tzu says, ''A tower of nine storeys begins with a heap of earth. The journey of a thousand *li* starts from where one stands,'' he seems to be saying that things simply work in accordance with the laws of nature. Anyone who tries to do things in violation of the laws of nature is doomed to failure. Therefore, the statements, ''He who takes an action fails'' and ''the sage takes no action and therefore does not fail'' are consistently [to] be interpreted as ''he who takes action in violation of the laws of nature fails'' and ''the sage acts in accordance with the laws of nature and therefore does not fail.'' The sage, being the ideal Taoist man, surely understands the *Tao* well and is thus capable of not acting against nature.[11]

The moral to be drawn from the doctrine of *Wu Wei* is clear and straightforward, given our interpretation of the meaning of *wu wei*. That is, insofar as ecological action is concerned, the Taoist's recommendation is so simple that it almost amounts to a truism: act in accordance with nature. However, one should be reminded of the fact that such a proposal is

well supported both by the metaphysical and axiological conceptions of the man-nature relation. It is exactly this kind of metaphysical grounding that an environmental ethic needs.

V. CONCLUSION—THE TAOIST REVERSION

Western man inherited from the Enlightenment legacy a conception of nature which is patently anti-environmentalistic. The world is depicted, chiefly through the work of Descartes, as a big machine consisting only of extended matter. It has no life of its own and no value of its own. Its value can only be defined in terms of human needs and purposes. It does not have intrinsic value of any sort, but has only instrumental value defined in terms of human desires. Man, being the processor of mind, can willfully subject this allegedly lifeless world to his desires and purposes. The extreme consequence of such homocentrism is the ruthless and unlimited exploitation of the environment.

Such an attitude assumes a clear dichtomy between subjectivity and objectivity. On the subjective side, we find man with his feels, desires, sentiments, passions, reasons, purposes, sensations etc., all of these regarded as needing to be satisfied, fulfilled or worthy of preserving and cultivating. On the objective side, we find the nonhuman world totally devoid of any sentience, functioning blindly according to mechanical laws. Such a machine-like world certainly cannot have any value and worth of its own except as a means to the satisfaction and fulfillment of human needs and wants. Such human needs and wants could range from the most notable to the most mean, from the purely aesthetic to the cognitively epistemic and to the practically technological. The physical world is there for us to comprehend (Greek philosophers), to experiment with (Francis Bacon), to transform into a humanized or human nature (Karl Marx), and to exploit for material goods (Adam Smith and Milton Friedman).

Nevertheless, the man-nature relationship envisaged here is at best an external and instrumental one. The world is simply something out there, ready to be subjected to human control and use. It is simply an ''otherness.'' As the Enlightenment teaches us: there

---

11. For other textual evidence to support my interpretation, see *Haai Nan Tzu,* quoted in J. Needham, *Science and Civilization in China,* vol. 2 (Cambridge: Cambridge University Press, 1956), p. 51 and *Chuang Tzu* in Chan, *Source Book.*

is no internal link between us and it. We do not feel that it is part of us, nor do we feel that we are part of it. We are, cast into a seemingly unsurpassable gap between subject and object, between man and nature.

To transcend this human predicament, we need a philosophy which can break this metaphysical barrier that separates man from his world, one which can reconnect the essential link which has been mistakenly severed for so long between human and nonhuman counterparts. We need a philosophy which can attribute values to nonhuman objects independently of human needs. That is, nonhuman beings should be regarded as having intrinsic values of their own rather than having only extrinsic or instrumental values. Moreover, we also need a philosophy which can tell us that we are part of a universe whose parts mutually nourish, support, and fulfill each other.

It seems to me that one philosophy which satisfies the above mentioned features is the Taoist philosophy we have been discussing. Most important of all, one cannot find in it the metaphysical schism that divides subject and object, for the supposed gap between man and nature simply has no place in the Taoist conception of the man-nature relationship. Subject and object, through self- and mutual-transformations, are metaphysically fused and unified. Moreover, the thesis of ontological equality of beings, and hence the axiological equality of beings, completely annihilates the kind of homocentrism at the center of the Enlightenment world view. In addition, it also opens up the possibility of ascribing values to nonhuman objects regardless of the latter's usefulness to human beings. Thus, a theory of intrinsic value for nature is indeed forthcoming within the Taoist framework. These features are vitally important to the construction of environmental ethics of any sort, and are, I believe, capable of providing the necessary metaphysical underpinnings upon which an environmental ethics has to rest.

Taoism, moreover, is compatible with science and is thus capable of providing a minimally coherent ethics. First, it is not anti-scientific, for despite all its mystical overtones, Taoism is in fact a version of naturalism. The doctrine of *Wu Wei* implicitly entails

a notion of observation which is germane to science.[12] Second, ecology as a science teaches us the interdependence of all life forms and nonliving things. It takes man as only one part of the interdependent whole. Every member of this intricately integrated complex is, in a very real sense, ecologically equal because each member depends on all others for survival, sustenance, and fulfillment. Analogously, the Taoist concept of ontological equality undoubtedly expresses the same idea, although in a more metaphysical way.

Note also that the Taoist metaphysics, the notion of axiological equality comes together with the notion of ontological equality. This is due to the fact that in Taoist metaphysics fact and value are fused together, just as subject and object are. Such metaphysical unification of value and fact is crucial in giving us a foundation upon which we can bring science and ethics together. It also makes it possible and meaningful to say that science and ethics coheres in this metaphysical sense. Although it seems presumptuous to assert that the Taoist ideas anticipates cognate concepts in modern ecology, nevertheless, one certainly cannot deny that the insights of the Taoist are explicitly acknowledged and endorsed by the latter.

DISCUSSION TOPICS

1. What particular insights from Taoism do you believe might be relevant in developing a workable environmental ethic in Western society? How does the evidence that Chinese citizens continued to damage the environment despite the precepts of Taoism affect your assessment of the value of Taoism in developing an environmental ethic?

2. Do you agree with Ip about the relationship between science and ethics? Explain your position.

3. What similarities and differences are there between environmental perspectives in Taoism and in Buddhism? In Taoism and Islam?

---

12. Needham incidentally holds such a view, see Colin A. Ronan, *The Shorter Science and Civilization in China,* vol. 1 (Cambridge: Cambridge University Press, 1978), p. 98.

"Conceptual Resources" in South Asia for "Environmental Ethics"

Gerald James Larson

Gerald James Larson (b. 1938) is Professor and Department Chair of Religious Studies at the University of California, Santa Barbara, California. His research interests include South Asian religion and philosophy, Sanskrit, and Hindi.

Larson describes three traditional types of ethical perspectives found in South Asian thought, and evaluates how effectively they might be used as foundations for an environmental ethic. Larson also challenges the approach many Westerners take of exploiting ideas related to environmental ethics from Eastern religions and philosophies, likening them to the ways in which earlier Europeans exploited natural resources from Asia. He argues that Eastern ideas cannot sensibly be lifted out of their larger philosophical and social contexts and successfully applied to Western problems. Larson believes that there is no definitive philosophical solution to the environmental crisis, and holds that Western philosophy itself is a cause of the problem.

Larson contends that there are three fallacies which must be avoided in order to clarify this problem: misplaced symmetry, disembedded ideas, and sovereignty of the subject. Finally, he suggests that comparative philosophers could contribute to solving the environmental crisis in three ways: by providing improved metaphors for identifying the environmental crisis, by encouraging more cross-cultural and interdisciplinary research, and by helping to facilitate the inevitable changes in the economic and political spheres which would follow adoption of a new ecological world view.

It is a reasonably simple exercise for a South Asianist to address the subject of this book by setting forth a purely descriptive and/or analytic discussion of traditional South Asian metaethical positions that could be construed as "conceptual resources" for doing "environmental ethics." Such an exercise involves, in my judgment, identifying at least three basic positions.

First, it is possible to identify what a metaethicist might characterize as a perspective of "nonnaturalistic, intuitionist, noncognitivism," or in the indigenous idiom of traditional South Asia, the perspective of Mīmāṁsā, either of the Bhāṭṭa type or of the Prābhākara type. From such a perspective, what is good is not a natural property of the world. The good cannot be defined but is realized directly in intuition, and it cannot be dealt with in terms of the notions of true and false. What is good, rather, has to do with the direct, injunctive prescriptions set forth in the *Veda* about what we should do at certain crucial points in our lives. The Vedas do not tell us anything about the world, but they enjoin us to act in a certain way (or, in other words, the act-deontology of the Bhāṭṭas) or to follow certain rules (the rule-deontology of the Prābhākaras).

Second, it is possible to identify what a metaethicist might characterize as a perspective of "naturalistic, nonintuitionist cognitivism," or in the indigenous idiom, the so-called "realist" perspectives in traditional Indian philosophy, namely, the Nyāya-Vaiśeṣika, the Jaina, and the early Buddhist positions. From such a perspective, what is good is a natural property of the world. The good can be defined and talked about in terms of the world in which we live, and it can be discussed in terms of what is true and false. Moreover, there are predictable consequences which provide the basic motivation for behaving in a moral way. The cultural trappings for such a position involve psychological hedonism (the *sukha-duḥkha* continuum), *karman* and *saṁsāra,* and *dharma* as a theory of obligation. It is a commonsense point of view given the presuppositions of the South Asian culture frame, and it is the most obvious moral position or moral theory to assume in such a context. As a normative position, it could be tagged as a kind of teleological cognitivism (or what Potter has called "path-philosophy").

Third, it is possible to identify what a metaethicist might characterize as a perspective of "nonnaturalistic, intuitionist a-moralism" (or what I like to call the "wild card" in the Indian deck), or, in the indigenous idiom of traditional South Asia, the perspective of Sāṃkhya, Yoga, Vedānta, and certain varieties of Mahāyāna Buddhist reflection (Mādhyamika and Yogācāra). From such a perspective, there is nothing that is truly or intrinsically good. To be sure, many things appear to be good either in terms of minimizing frustration (*duḥkha*), or in terms of maximizing more favorable rebirths, or in terms of sheer contemplation, or in terms of intellectual reflection. Serious discrimination reveals, however, that all determinate formulations or awarenesses of what is good prove to be temporary, limited, and most important, inextricably allied with dialectical modalities (*sukha-duḥkha-moha*) that undercut the perception, inference, or intuition that *anything* is intrinsically good. There may be some contributory or instrumental (or, in other words, extrinsic) "value" in the world in that it can point one in a certain direction or prepare one for ultimate insight, but, finally, the ultimate experience itself is *not* a moral experience—it is "beyond good and evil," or, putting the matter directly, it is the denial that moral and ethical theorizing has any value at all! As a normative position, one might tag such a perspective with (the admittedly barbaric) expression "gnoseological intuitionism" or the claim that the ultimate experience is a non-moral or a-moral intuition that arises through an extraordinary modality of knowing.

Among these three traditional perspectives in South Asian theorizing, the first perspective, namely, the act-deontology or rule-deontology of Mīmāṃsā, is an unlikely candidate for environmental ethics, since its injunctions are based on a corpus of texts, the Vedas, the authority of which is barely relevant even in orthodox communities in modern India, quite apart from nonorthodox South Asian environments or environments altogether outside of South Asia. This leaves us, then, with the second perspective, or, in other words, the "teleological cognitivism" of the Indian realist traditions (Nyāya, Vaiśeṣika, Jaina, and early Buddhist thought), and the third perspective, or what I have called the "gnoseological intuitionism" of Sāṃkhya, Yoga, Vedānta, and Mahāyāna Buddhist thought. In terms of environmental ethical discussions, I am inclined to agree that the South Asian

realist traditions (Nyāya, Vaiśeṣika, Jaina, and early Buddhist thought) could be employed fruitfully as a way of undergirding a "pragmatic" approach to environmental ethics, as David Kalupahana has forcefully argued in his paper "Man and Nature: Towards a Middle Path of Survival."[1] I am also inclined to agree that the South Asian "gnoseological intuitionist" views of Sāṃkhya, Yoga, Vedānta, and Mahāyāna Buddhist thought could be employed fruitfully as a way of establishing a somewhat new approach to "natural reverence," as Eliot Deutsch has argued in his paper, "A Metaphysical Grounding for Natural Reverence: East-West."[2] Moreover, J. Baird Callicott's critique of Deutsch has a South Asian answer, in my view. Callicott argues that the South Asian notion of Oneness is "substantive and essential . . . and the experience of it homogeneous and oceanic," whereas "in both contemporary ecology and quantum theory at their respective levels of phenomena the oneness of nature is systemic and (internally) relational."[3] Such a basic difference may be said to be valid in terms of Vedānta and Mahāyāna Buddhist accounts of "gnoseological intuitionism," but, as is well known to South Asianists, such a difference would not hold in Sāṃkhya and Yoga accounts. The notion of *prakṛti* as *triguṇa* (*sattva, rajas, tamas*) is clearly "systemic and (internally) relational" in Callicott's sense, and environmental ethicists could possibly find powerful conceptual resources for developing "organic" and/or "holistic" perspectives on nature within the traditions of Sāṃkhya and Yoga in South Asian thought.

In any case, as mentioned at the outset, from a purely descriptive and/or analytic point of view, it is a reasonably simple exercise to proceed in the manner I have briefly been outlining by finding "conceptual resources" in Asian traditions for doing "environmental ethics." To be sure, we could debate whether I have been sufficiently precise in formulating the various South Asian options, and more than that, whether it is possible to identify additional perspectives as well—for example, one could, I suppose, suggest "conceptual resources" from South Asian theistic, Tantric, or Śākta traditions, and so forth.

Overall, however, I am increasingly troubled and/

or frustrated *(duḥkha)* by such purely descriptive approaches to comparative philosophizing as the ones I have been outlining and which are implicit in our work as a whole, and my frustration is both methodological and theoretical. My methodological frustration can easily be pinpointed. We appear to be using, albeit unconsciously, a particular metaphor that, in my view, is methodologically loaded and seriously misleading. If one substitutes the word ''natural'' for ''conceptual'' in the expression ''conceptual resources,'' it becomes immediately apparent that we are using an economic metaphor in our undertaking. Since the eighteenth century, European nation-states have been utilizing Asia to supply a variety of resources: spices, tea, cotton, minerals, oil, natural gas, cheap labor, and hosts of other commodities. Now it seems that we are setting out again, only this time we are on the lookout for ''conceptual resources.'' We appear to be using, in other words, an economic metaphor of raw materials. The needed ''ideas'' for environmental ethics are presumably in short ''supply'' in our own environment, but we recognize that there is an increasing ''demand'' for some new intellectual commodities.

What is methodologically loaded and seriously misleading about such an economic metaphor of raw materials is the corollary component of such a metaphor, namely, that we are not really interested in the raw materials in their natural state. We want, rather, to appropriate the raw materials so that we can use them for making what *we* want. We all know full well that the ''ideas'' and/or ''concepts'' that we need are not available directly in Asian contexts. They are deeply embedded in culture frames, kinship systems, traditional institutional frameworks, and so forth, from which they must be detached or ''dug out'' as it were and then imported into our own frameworks. Moreover, if they are to be utilized profitably, these ''resources'' will have to be processed, manufactured, mass-produced, and, finally, distributed. Of course, we recognize that the market for the eventual product is worldwide or global, and in that sense we can congratulate ourselves that what we are doing will subsequently benefit not only Asia but all people everywhere. This, of course, is exactly the rationale that the British used in India during the Raj. Raw materials were purchased in South Asia at a remarkably cheap price; factories in England then processed and manufactured the raw materials into useful consumer items which were subsequently sold in markets in India and elsewhere for a significant profit (and taxed as well). The rationale for the whole process was that the British were actively developing the Indian economy!

The methodological point for our work is that when we proceed by using an economic metaphor in this fashion, we are committing ourselves to a comparative enterprise of external appropriation. Ideas and concepts come to be construed as ''things'' or ''entities'' that can be disembedded from their appropriate frameworks and then processed and made to fit into our own frameworks. Such a method for comparative philosophy is, in my view, one-dimensional, overly selective, forced, anachronistic, sociologically unsophisticated, and, perhaps worst of all, unpersuasive. Surely we can develop more sophisticated methodological approaches in our comparative philosophizing.

As already indicated, however, my frustration *(duḥkha)* is not only methodological but also substantive and/or theoretical. My substantive or theoretical concern can be expressed by referring to some comments made by J. Baird Callicott in his article, ''Non-Anthropocentric Value Theory and Environmental Ethics.'' Callicott suggests that environmental ethics may be thought of in two quite different ways, either (a) a sort of subdivision of applied ethics (on analogy, say, with business ethics), that is to say as ''an *application* of well-established conventional philosophical categories to emergent practical environmental problems''; or (b) a creative enterprise that ''may be understood to be an *exploration* of alternative moral and even metaphysical principles, forced upon philosophy by the magnitude and recalcitrance of these [environmental] problems.'' Moreover, says Callicott, if understood in the latter, more ambitious sense, the task of the environmental ethicist ''is that of a theoretician or philosophical architect (as in Descartes' self-image).''[4] My substantive concern has to do with Callicott's way of putting the problem, namely, the environmental ethicist as a "theoretician or philosophical architect (as in Descartes' self-image)." To me as a comparativist, this way of putting the matter does not go far enough in identifying what is really at issue. It simply is a paraphrase of the basic problem, or, putting the matter somewhat differently, this very idiom is itself a part of the problem. The notion of the philosopher as a "theoretician or philosophical architect (as in Descartes' self-image)" is itself part of the conceptual framework that emerged in the seventeenth century for the first time and which included the rise of quantitative science, technology, manipulative reasoning, and the political economies of the emerging nation-state. It is a conceptual framework or mind-set that divides, classifies, quantifies, and distinguishes discreet "universes of meaning" (to use Thomas Luckmann's idiom).[5] Modern philosophy itself, in other words, as a distinct, separate discipline that analyzes, explores, and applies concepts, is symptomatic of a world view that causes "environmental pollution, the aesthetic degradation of nature, human overpopulation, resource depletion, ecological destruction and . . . abrupt massive species extinction," according to Callicott.[6] My point here is not an ethical or moral one. I am not regretting what has happened since the seventeenth century, nor am I seeking to assign some sort of blame. My point, rather, is a theoretical one, and I am inclined to express it in the following Zen-like way: We have not understood the environmental crisis until we realize that there is *no* philosophical answer to it. If we seriously think that we can find "conceptual resources" in Asia and then work them into our own philosophizing, *and* that such an effort would have a serious impact on the environmental crisis, then we really have not understood the environmental crisis at all! Put differently, our effort is itself a part of the problem. We are spinning our wheels, and nothing at all will or can change. It is a bit like the Vedānta of Śaṅkara: cleverly tinkering with concepts that deny everything on one level while allowing everything to remain just as it is on another level.

My substantive and/or theoretical frustration, in other words, is that philosophy (including comparative philosophy) as conventionally construed in the modern world since Descartes cannot adequately deal with the environmental crisis. Rather it is part of the crisis and cannot itself be used as a way of dealing with the crisis. This entails, furthermore, that all of the other "divisions" of modern academia, namely, economics, sociology, political science, physics, mathematics, chemistry, the biological sciences, and so forth, cannot as separate "language games" or "universes of meaning" deal adequately with the crisis either. It is this very predilection in European intellectual history since Descartes (and its progeny) to divide and separate intellectual tasks, and, more than that, to isolate and professionalize cognitive pursuits from other dimensions of human functioning (for example, trade, commerce, kinship relations, sexuality, and so forth) that is itself reflective of our current environmental crisis. One way of putting the point is to suggest that what we thought was a Weberian process of "rationalization" (increased efficiency, goal-oriented behavior, and so forth) has turned out to be a Freudian defense-mechanism notion of "rationalization" and that, therefore, what we had anticipated to be a modern, sophisticated, efficient, and civilized world has, in fact, turned out to be yet another highly neurotic world system even more dangerous than earlier ones, since its capacity for self-destruction is global and species-wide. Nor do I think, let me hasten to add, that we can retreat into premodern religious visions or apologetically contrived modernist versions of those same visions. Such visions may provide solace or salvation or "release" from issues such as the environmental crisis, as indeed they always have, but they tend largely to be either question-begging alternatives to dealing with the environmental crisis or else, like philosophy and other isolated cognitive domains, themselves symptomatic of the crisis.

What is needed instead, in my view, is a radical reorientation of the manner in which we might construe the problem, and I would like to call attention to some fundamental considerations that should be kept in mind as we seek to determine a starting point for bringing about such a reorientation. I shall mention three such fundamental considerations which, if taken together, might provide a kind of prolegomenon to a serious discussion of the environmental crisis from the perspective of comparative studies. The considerations are hardly new, nor are they particularly controversial, but they are frequently lost sight of in contemporary discussion.

First, I should like to call attention to what Charles Hartshorne has characterized as "the fallacy of misplaced symmetry," a problem that Hartshorne finds in much of Asian thought (Śaṁkara, Nāgārjuna, and so forth) as well as in European thought (Bradley, Bergson, and so forth). In a recent paper, Hartshorne refers to the fallacy as follows:

> I find a common fallacy in these widely separated thinkers. A relation between two terms is really two relations, the one of A to B, and the one of B to A. Neither Bradley nor Nāgārjuna take this duality into account. . . . Past events are realities, not unrealities. This doctrine is missing both from Bradley's and from Nāgārjuna's account. Hence they clearly begged the question. . . . They overlooked time's arrow, the asymmetry of temporal relations. They committed the fallacy of misplaced symmetry. Another way to put the matter is, both thinkers refuted only a static view of multiplicity. They spatialized time. . . . Relations of dependence in space are indeed symmetrical, but not those in time.
>
> Do effects depend on causes? Of course. Do we depend on our ancestors? Of course. Do causes depend on effects? Of course not. Do we depend on our descendants? Whatever our descendants turn out to be, we are what we are. But it is absurd to say, whatever our ancestors were, we are what we are. Without them we would not have been, period. But our existing now is absolute fact that no occurrence or non-occurrence in the future can nullify. . . . It is the indispensable foundation of any tenable rationality. All our living implies a real past, immune to alteration, and a merely potential future, whose exact characters are in the process of being created, step by step, beginning now.[7]

Whether one would follow Hartshorne's asymmetry-of-relations argument all the way to his process metaphysics is, of course, debatable; but in this context I wish to press what I take to be a nondebatable claim regarding the environmental crisis, namely, that it is something totally new and that there is an asymmetrical relation between it and all earlier natural crises. The survival of life on earth as we now know it is seriously in jeopardy. To use a Sāṃkhya idiom from South Asia, we have reached the "curds" stage of an earlier "milk" stage in the unfolding of our natural habitat as a species, and we cannot wish away the "curds" stage by arguing for a symmetrical relationship between milk and curds. The curds can only become milk again at the time of the great dissolution (mahā-pralaya), but, of course, when that happens, there can no longer be anything alive to enjoy the milk!

Second, I should like to call attention to what might be called the fallacy of disembedded ideas. Philosophy (and comparative philosophy) operates on the level of conceptual analysis, but we have learned from the history of Asian thought (East Asian and South Asian) as well as from much of modern European thought (Marx, Weber, Freud, Wittgenstein, and so forth) that conceptual frameworks are always embedded in larger culture frames insofar as they are vital components for a "form of life." We have learned from Kuhn and Feyerabend that even our most treasured abstractions, that is to say, the conceptual apparatus of our modern science, exists or "has life" only in such environments ("paradigms," frames," and so forth). In our comparative work we have discovered over three thousand languages on our planet and hundreds of "culture frames" and "paradigms." In our scientific work we have discovered that there is a statistical probability that perhaps as many as one million planets in our own galaxy alone are capable of supporting "intelligent life." Yet in view of all of this, we still ask ourselves if archaic notions such as the "Tao," brahman-ātman, Allah, God, dharma, or whatever, all of which notions are derived from premodern, qualitative-science "frames" or "paradigms," can be disembedded, dusted off, and somehow utilized in dealing with the environmental crisis. It is my inclination to think that we would do better, rather, as comparativists, to inquire into the manner in which ideas and/or concepts function in their respective "frames" and "paradigms" as a way of getting a handle on how our modern "concept clusters" might be generating and are being generated by the contemporary "frames" and "paradigms" in which we live.

Third, I should like to call attention to what might be called the fallacy of "the sovereignty of the subject.'' I take the expression from Foucault's *The Archaeology of Knowledge,* in which he inquires into the reasons for the difficulty of developing what he calls a ''general theory of discontinuity.''

> There is a reason for this. If the history of thought could remain the locus of uninterrupted continuities . . . it would provide a privileged shelter for the sovereignty of consciousness. Continuous history is the indispensable correlative of the founding function of the subject: the guarantee that everything that has eluded him may be restored to him; the certainty that time will disperse nothing without restoring it in a reconstituted unity. . . .
>
> In various forms, this theme has played a constant role since the nineteenth century: to preserve, against all decenterings, the sovereignty of the subject, and the twin figures of anthropology and humanism.[8]

I am neither a post-structuralist nor a deconstructionist, but I think that Foucault's point is well taken in any properly framed discussion of the environmental crisis. I mentioned earlier that, using statistical probability, it has been determined that ''intelligent life'' may be present on as many as one million planets within our own galaxy. Using similar procedures in mathematical astronomy, it has been estimated that there may be as many as ten million planets within our galaxy that are able to support ''life'' in some sense. Our own planet is about 4.6 billion years old, and there is mounting evidence that some forms of life have been present almost from the beginning. Hominid forms have existed from about five hundred thousand years ago, but ''civilized'' life (in the sense of animal husbandry, agriculture, polished tools, pottery, some form of social life, and so forth) has only existed since about 6000 B.C.E. (or, in other words, from what is usually called the ''Neolithic'' period in such areas as the ancient Near East, Mohenjo-Daro, and so forth). Cognitive and affective capacities sufficient to support ''civilized'' life, in other words, are quite recent from within the perspective of the ''history'' of life forms on our own planet, and the self-reflective images we have of ourselves as so-called ''modern'' hominids are a bit over two hundred years old. Remarkable strides have been made recently in such areas as brain physiology, biochemistry, mathematical astronomy, and so on, but similar strides

have been lacking for the most part in theoretical formulations of the role and function of self-awareness in the hominid life-form. We still operate with ''philosophies'' and ''psychologies'' of self-awareness but have very little grasp of the evolutionary significance of such constructions. Putting the matter another way, we have very little understanding of the human need for or the evolutionary significance of the self-awareness of the human life-form. We have very little sense of the ''meaning of meaning,'' and we appear to be stuck with interpretations of self-awareness that may have long outlived their usefulness. I suspect that future progress in dealing with the environmental crisis will have to address critically the problem of ''the sovereignty of the subject'' and to avoid the fallacy of assuming that what we think we are is in any sense an adequate, accurate, consistent, or clear measure of what we are.

The fly is still alive and well in the bottle. What I mean by alluding to Wittgenstein in this context is that we have not yet succeeded in framing our problem in a way that allows us to escape from a mind-set that is itself a part of the problem. Comparative reflection is, I think, helpful in enabling us to see this—in enabling us, as it were, to uncork the bottle.

Far be it from me to predict what will happen if the fly gets out of the bottle, but if we take seriously the sorts of considerations I have briefly been describing, namely, ''the fallacy of misplaced symmetry,'' ''the fallacy of disembedded ideas,'' and ''the fallacy of the sovereignty of the subject,'' we as comparativists may well have much to contribute by way of addressing problems related to our present ''environmental crisis.'' Let me conclude by programmatically mentioning at least a few of these contributions.

First, comparativists could be helpful in generating better metaphors for construing the problem. As comparativists, we know full well that an economic metaphor of ''conceptual resources'' with all of its negative connotations of exploitation and external appropriation, is not at all an apt way of thinking about conceptual frameworks. Conceptual systems or schemes are inextricably a part of a comprehensive way of life, and indeed are frequently symptomatic for helping to uncover the latent or hidden forces and/

or processes that are operative in a given culture or society. In this regard, it seems to me, a biological science metaphor along the lines of comparative anatomy comes close to highlighting the problem of the environmental crisis. An arm is not a fin, and a lung is not a gill, but there are nevertheless interesting affinities between these pairs in concrete life forms over time. In a similar fashion, one conceptual framework is not identical to another, nor can simple substitutions be made between them, but nevertheless there can be illuminating comparisons about the manner in which conceptual frameworks or networks operate in larger, concrete social realities. Such a metaphor of comparative anatomy would focus attention on thinking or conceptualization, not necessarily as a *cause* or a *prescription* for a society's or a culture's problems, but, rather, as a *symptom* or a *diagnosis* regarding society's or a culture's self-understanding. Why is it, for example, that we tend to think of the environmental crisis as a "philosophical" or "ethical" problem when it is obviously so much more than that? What do our conceptual frameworks regarding "ethics" tell us about our Western historical experience, our "anatomy," as it were, as a culture or as a set of genetically related cultures? Classical Chinese thought is symptomatic of quite a different "anatomy," as is classical Indian thought, Eskimo thought, Islamic thought, and so forth. I am speaking here, of course, only in terms of metaphor, and I am not arguing for a naturalistic reductionism. I am simply suggesting that as a comparativist I find a biological science metaphor much more to the point of what is at issue in any interesting discussion of the environmental crisis. There are undoubtedly a number of other metaphors which could be helpful, and as comparativists we are nicely positioned because of our training to discuss them.

Second, comparativists could be helpful in encouraging more broadly based cross-cultural and interdisciplinary research in an area such as the environmental crisis. The comparativist in the course of training early along learns that one cannot simply do linguistics, philosophy, religion, anthropology, and so forth, nor can one isolate one's research in only one cultural context. As suggested earlier, in almost every instance, our Western scholarly specializations are little more than heuristic and historical divisions derived from the vicissitudes and power struggles of our own developing social reality. There again, "philosophy" (or any other division in the modern academy) is a symptom of rather than a prescription for the environmental crisis. To look to "philosophy" for solutions to the environmental crisis is to acquiesce in the marginalization of the cognitive life that has been occurring in European and American culture since the seventeenth century. The time has come, perhaps, to criticize such compartmentalization as itself a major symptom of our current environmental crisis and to launch cross-cultural and interdisciplinary inquiries that bring together humanists, scientists, politicians, and the rest—inquiries that do not permit specialists to hide behind their narrowly conceived expertise.

Third, and finally, uncorking the bottle and allowing the fly to escape will surely have some intriguing political implications. If it is the case that conceptual schemes or networks make up part of the "anatomy" of every culture or society, and if it is the case that the "philosopher" must relinquish his privileged (and marginalized) isolation in order to begin to get a handle on the scope of the environmental issue, then this surely means that the conventional centers of power and wealth of our modern way of life will be seriously threatened and, as Marx has taught us, will hardly roll over and play dead. The committees for determining comfortable government grants, private fellowships, and legislative funding for higher education, all of which dispense their largess on the premises of marginalization and the maintenance of the status quo, will undoubtedly not be happy, and yet these structures of modernity are deeply implicated in the environmental crisis and cry out for criticism in any serious treatment of the issues. But by what authority would one issue the criticism or carry out a given program for political action? In the name of Reason? Civility? Justice? Fairness? As comparativists, we know that such notions are construed differently from culture to culture and that one important factor in shaping the differences is the set of power relations that operate in a particular social reality.

Hence, to begin rethinking a problem such as the environmental crisis in our modern world is at one and same time to begin reshaping the power relations in that world—in other words, the intellectual work is in an important sense a political act. To some extent, of course, this is a sort of Marxian point with the important difference, however, that unlike the Marxist, the comparativist has no platform of certainty, no ''vanguard'' status by means of which to pursue a political program. The comparativist is simply one more participant in an ongoing effort to attain some sort of reflexive grasp of what is happening to the human species in our own time.

To put all of this somewhat differently, the truly important task for the comparativist in the environmental debate is not to offer up non-Western, alternative ''world views'' for possible adoption, but, rather, precisely the opposite, namely, through comparative analysis to come to a more critical understanding of what it means to be human at a time when all of the old certainties of our Western and non-Western traditions have largely collapsed.

NOTES

1. David J. Kalupahana, ''Man and Nature: Toward a Middle Path of Survival,'' in J. Baird Callicott and Roger T. Ames, eds., *Nature in Asian Traditions of Thought* (Albany: State University of New York Press, 1989), p. 247.
2. Eliot Deutsch, ''A Metaphysical Grounding for Natural Reverence: East-West'' in J. Baird Callicott and Roger T. Ames, eds., *Nature in Asian Traditions of Thought* (Albany: State University of New York Press, 1989), p. 259.
3. J. Baird Callicott, ''Conceptual Resources or Environmental Ethics in Asian Traditions of Thought: A Propaedeutic,'' *Philosophy East and West* 37 (1987): 124.
4. J. Baird Callicott, ''Non-anthropocentric Value Theory and Environmental Ethics,'' *American Philosophical Quarterly* 21 (1984): 299.
5. See Peter Berger and Thomas Luckmann, *The Social Construction of Reality: A Treatise in the Sociology of Knowledge* (Garden City, N.Y.: Anchor/Doubleday, 1967).
6. Callicott, ''Conceptual Resources,'' p. 116.
7. Charles Hartshorne, ''Saṅkara, Nāgārjuna, and Fa Tsang,'' in Gerald James Larson and Eliot Deutsch, eds., *Interpreting Across Boundaries: New Essays in Comparative Philosophy* (Princeton: Princeton University Press, 1988), 104-105.
8. Michel Foucault, *The Archaeology of Knowledge,* trans. A.M. Sheridan Smith (New York: Pantheon Books, 1972), p. 12.

DISCUSSION TOPICS

1. In relation to Larson's argument against lifting Eastern ideas out of their philosophical and cultural contexts, do you believe it is ever appropriate to integrate nonwestern ideas into Western environmental ethics? Explain your position.
2. What other fallacies in addition to those raised by Larson ought to be considered in reformulating the environmental crisis?
3. In order to implement a workable environmental ethic in Western society, what changes in political and economic structures might be necessary?

READING 70

Radical American Environmentalism and Wilderness Preservation: A Third World Critique

Ramachandra Guha

Ramachandra Guha is a scholar at the Centre for Ecological Sciences, Indian Institute for Science, Bangalore, India. His research interests include environmentalism in India.

This essay by Guha is among the very few evaluations by Eastern scholars of the applicability of ideas from the Western environmental movement to non-Western societies. Guha analyzes environmental problems and concerns in the Third World using the perspectives from the deep ecology movement. He then examines four basic tenets of deep ecology: the call for a shift from an anthropocentric to a biocentric perspective; the strong focus on the value of wilderness preservation; the widespread reference to Eastern spiritual tradition as a forerunner of deep ecology perspectives; and the conviction that the deep ecology movement is at the forefront of the environmental movement.

Guha identifies a number of serious disadvantages in applying a deep ecology perspective to Third World problems. He views the emphasis on preserving biotic diversity to the detriment of human needs as unacceptable, and maintains that the anthropocentrism/biocentrism dichotomy is irrelevant because it ignores two fundamental causes underlying environmental crises on the planet: overconsumption and growing militarism. Guha believes that the emphasis on wilderness preservation by the deep ecology movement is harmful to the Third World in three ways: it tends to benefit the rich and deprive the poor; it leads to neglect of more pressing environmental problems; and it encourages imperialistic yearnings of Western conservationists. Guha argues that Western scholars often idealize and misinterpret Eastern viewpoints by underestimating the impacts which Eastern societies have on their environments, and by failing to distinguish the wide variety of perspectives represented among Eastern religions and philosophies. Finally, Guha categorizes the deep ecology movement as a radical trend primarily within the wilderness preservation movement of America, and asserts that radical environmental movements in other parts of the world have developed different goal orientations than in the American movement.

Even God dare not appear to the poor man except in the form of bread.

Mahatma Gandhi

I. INTRODUCTION

The respected radical journalist Kirkpatrick Sale recently celebrated ''the passion of a new and growing movement that has become disenchanted with the environmental establishment and has in recent years mounted a serious and sweeping attack on it—style,

substance, systems, sensibilities and all.''[1] The vision of those whom Sale calls the ''New Ecologists''— and what I refer to in this article as deep ecology—is a compelling one. Decrying the narrowly economic goals of mainstream environmentalism, this new movement aims at nothing less than a philosophical and cultural revolution in human attitudes toward nature. In contrast to the conventional lobbying efforts of environmental professionals based in Washington, it proposes a militant defence of ''Mother Earth,'' an unflinching opposition to human attacks on undisturbed wilderness. With their goals ranging from the spiritual to the political, the adherents of deep ecology span a wide spectrum of the American environmental movement. As Sale correctly notes, this emerging strand has in a matter of a few years made its presence felt in a number of fields: from academic philosophy (as in the journal *Environmental Ethics*) to popular environmentalism (for example, the group Earth First!).

In this article I develop a critique of deep ecology from the perspective of a sympathetic outsider. I critique deep ecology not as a general (or even a foot soldier) in the continuing struggle between the ghosts of Gifford Pinchot and John Muir over control of the U.S. environmental movement, but as an outsider to these battles. I speak admittedly as a partisan, but of the environmental movement in India, a country with an ecological diversity comparable to the U.S., but with a radically dissimilar cultural and social history.

My treatment of deep ecology is primarily historical and sociological, rather than philosophical, in nature. Specifically, I examine the cultural rootedness of a philosophy that likes to present itself in universalistic terms. I make two main arguments: first, that deep ecology is uniquely American, and despite superficial similarities in rhetorical style, the social and political goals of radical environmentalism in other cultural contexts (e.g., West Germany and India) are

---

1. Kirkpatrick Sale, ''The Forest for the Trees: Can Today's Environmentalists Tell the Difference,'' *Mother Jones* 11, No. 8 (November 1986): 26.

quite different; second, that the social consequences of putting deep ecology into practice on a worldwide basis (what its practitioners are aiming for) are very grave indeed.

II. THE TENETS OF DEEP ECOLOGY

While I am aware that the term *deep ecology* was coined by the Norwegian philosopher Arne Naess, this article refers specifically to the American variant.[2] Adherents of the deep ecological perspective in this country, while arguing intensely among themselves over its political and philosophical implications, share some fundamental premises about human–nature interactions. As I see it, the defining characteristics of deep ecology are fourfold:

First, deep ecology argues, that the environmental movement must shift from an "anthropocentric" to a "biocentric" perspective. In many respects, an acceptance of the primacy of this distinction constitutes the litmus test of deep ecology. A considerable effort is expended by deep ecologists in showing that the dominant motif in Western philosophy has been anthropocentric—i.e., the belief that man and his works are the center of the universe—and conversely, in identifying those lonely thinkers (Leopold, Thoreau, Muir, Aldous Huxley, Santayana, etc.) who, in assigning man a more humble place in the natural order, anticipated deep ecological thinking. In the political realm, meanwhile, establishment environmentalism (shallow ecology) is chided for casting its arguments in human-centered terms. Preserving nature, the deep ecologists say, has an intrinsic worth quite apart from any benefits preservation may convey to future human generations. The anthropocentric-biocentric distinction is accepted as axiomatic by deep ecologists, it structures their discourse, and much of the present discussion remains mired within it.

The second characteristic of deep ecology is its focus on the preservation of unspoilt wilderness—and the restoration of degraded areas to a more pristine condition—to the relative (and sometimes absolute) neglect of other issues on the environmental agenda. I later identify the cultural roots and portentous consequences of this obsession with wilderness. For the moment, let me indicate three distinct sources from which it springs. Historically, it represents a playing out of the preservationist (read *radical*) and utilitarian (read *reformist*) dichotomy that has plagued American environmentalism since the turn of the century. Morally, it is an imperative that follows from the biocentric perspective; other species of plants and animals, and nature itself, have an intrinsic right to exist. And finally, the preservation of wilderness also turns on a scientific argument—viz., the value of biological diversity in stabilizing ecological regimes and in retaining a gene pool for future generations. Truly radical policy proposals have been put forward by deep ecologists on the basis of these arguments. The influential poet Gary Snyder, for example, would like to see a 90 percent reduction in human populations to allow a restoration of pristine environments, while others have argued forcefully that a large portion of the globe must be immediately cordoned off from human beings.[3]

Third, there is a widespread invocation of Eastern spiritual traditions as forerunners of deep ecology. Deep ecology, it is suggested, was practiced both by major religious traditions and at a more popular level by "primal" peoples in non-Western settings. This complements the search for an authentic lineage in Western thought. At one level, the task is to recover those dissenting voices within the Judeo-Christian

---

2. One of the major criticisms I make in this essay concerns deep ecology's lack of concern with inequalities *within* human society. In the article in which he coined the term *deep ecology,* Naess himself expresses concerns about inequalities between and within nations. However, his concern with social cleavages and their impact on resource utilization patterns and ecological destruction is not very visible in the later writings of deep ecologists. See Arne Naess, "The Shallow and the Deep, Long-Range Ecology Movement: A Summary," *Inquiry* 16 (1973): 96 (I am grateful to Tom Birch for this reference).

3. Gary Snyder, quoted in Sale, "The Forest for the Trees," p. 32. See also Dave Foreman, "A Modest Proposal for a Wilderness System," *Whole Earth Review,* No. 53 (Winter 1986-87): 42-45.

tradition; at another, to suggest that religious traditions in other cultures are, in contrast, dominantly if not exclusively ''biocentric'' in their orientation. This coupling of (ancient) Eastern and (modern) ecological wisdom seemingly helps consolidate the claim that deep ecology is a philosophy of universal significance.

Fourth, deep ecologists, whatever their internal differences, share the belief that they are the ''leading edge'' of the environmental movement. As the polarity of the shallow/deep and anthropocentric/biocentric distinctions makes clear, they see themselves as the spiritual, philosophical, and political vanguard of American and world environmentalism.

III. TOWARD A CRITIQUE

Although I analyze each of these tenets independently, it is important to recognize, as deep ecologists are fond of remarking in reference to nature, the interconnectedness and unity of these individual themes.

(1) Insofar as it has begun to act as a check on man's arrogance and ecological hubris, the transition from an anthropocentric (human-centered) to a biocentric (humans as only one element in the ecosystem) view in both religious and scientific traditions is only to be welcomed.[4] What is unacceptable are the radical conclusions drawn by deep ecology, in particular, that intervention in nature should be guided primarily by the need to preserve biotic integrity rather than by the needs of humans. The latter for deep ecologists is anthropocentric, the former biocentric. This dichotomy is, however, of very little use in understanding the dynamics of environmental degradation. The two fundamental ecological problems facing the globe are (i) overconsumption by the industrialized world and by urban elites in the Third World and (ii) growing militarization, both in a short-term sense (i.e., ongoing regional wars) and in a long-term sense (i.e., the arms

race and the prospect of nuclear annihilation). Neither of these problems has any tangible connection to the anthropocentric-biocentric distinction. Indeed, the agents of these processes would barely comprehend this philosophical dichotomy. The proximate causes of the ecologically wasteful characteristics of industrial society and of militarization are far more mundane: at an aggregate level, the dialectic of economic and political structures, and at a micro-level, the life style choices of individuals. These causes cannot be reduced, whatever the level of analysis, to a deeper anthropocentric attitude toward nature; on the contrary, by constituting a grave threat to human survival, the ecological degradation they cause does not even serve the best interests of human beings! If my identification of the major dangers to the integrity of the natural world is correct, invoking the bogy of anthropocentrism is at best irrelevant and at worst a dangerous obfuscation.

(2) If the above dichotomy is irrelevant, the emphasis on wilderness is positively harmful when applied to the Third World. If in the U.S. the preservationist/utilitarian division is seen as mirroring the conflict between ''people'' and ''interests,'' in countries such as India the situation is very nearly the reverse. Because India is a long settled and densely populated country in which agrarian populations have a finely balanced relationship with nature, the setting aside of wilderness areas has resulted in a direct transfer of resources from the poor to the rich. Thus, Project Tiger, a network of parks hailed by the international conservation community as an outstanding success, sharply posits the interests of the tiger against those of poor peasants living in and around the reserve. The designation of tiger reserves was made possible only by the physical displacement of existing villages and their inhabitants; their management requires the continuing exclusion of peasants and livestock. The initial impetus for setting up parks for the tiger and other large mammals such as the rhinoceros and elephant came from two social groups, first, a class of ex-hunters turned conservationists belonging mostly to the declining Indian feudal elite and second, representatives of international agencies, such as the

---

4. See, for example, Donald Worster, *Nature's Economy: The Roots of Ecology* (San Francisco: Sierra Club Books, 1977).

World Wildlife Fund (WWF) and the International Union for the Conservation of Nature and Natural Resources (IUCN), seeking to transplant the American system of national parks onto Indian soil. In no case have the needs of the local population been taken into account, and as in many parts of Africa, the designated wildlands are managed primarily for the benefit of rich tourists. Until very recently, wildlands preservation has been identified with environmentalism by the state and the conservation elite; in consequence, environmental problems that impinge far more directly on the lives of the poor—e.g., fuel, fodder, water shortages, soil erosion, and air and water pollution—have not been adequately addressed.[5]

Deep ecology provides, perhaps unwittingly, a justification for the continuation of such narrow and inequitable conservation practices under a newly acquired radical guise. Increasingly, the international conservation elite is using the philosophical, moral, and scientific arguments used by deep ecologists in advancing their wilderness crusade. A striking but by no means atypical example is the recent plea by a prominent American biologist for the takeover of large portions of the globe by the author and his scientific colleagues. Writing in a prestigous scientific forum, the *Annual Review of Ecology and Systematics,* Daniel Janzen argues that only biologists have the competence to decide how the tropical landscape should be used. As "the representatives of the natural world," biologists are "in charge of the future of tropical ecology," and only they have the expertise and mandate to "determine whether the tropical agroscape is to be populated only by humans, their mutualists, commensals, and parasites, or whether it will also contain some islands of the greater nature— the nature that spawned humans, yet has been vanquished by them." Janzen exhorts his colleagues to advance their territorial claims on the tropical world more forcefully, warning that the very existence of these areas is at stake: "if biologists want a tropics in which to biologize, they are going to have to buy it with care, energy, effort, strategy, tactics, time, and cash."[6]

This frankly imperialist manifesto highlights the multiple dangers of the preoccupation with wilderness preservation that is characteristic of deep ecology. As I have suggested, it seriously compounds the neglect by the American movement of far more pressing environmental problems within the Third World. But perhaps more importantly, and in a more insidious fashion, it also provides an impetus to the imperialist yearning of Western biologists and their financial sponsors, organizations such as the WWF and IUCN. The wholesale transfer of a movement culturally rooted in American conservation history can only result in the social uprooting of human populations in other parts of the globe.

(3) I come now to the persistent invocation of Eastern philosophies as antecedent in point of time but convergent in their structure with deep ecology. Complex and internally differentiated religious traditions—Hinduism, Buddhism, and Taoism—are lumped together as holding a view of nature believed to be quintessentially biocentric. Individual philosophers such as the Taoist Lao Tzu are identified as being forerunners of deep ecology. Even an intensely political, pragmatic, and Christian influenced thinker such as Gandhi has been accorded a wholly undeserved place in the deep ecological pantheon. Thus the Zen teacher Robert Aitken Roshi makes the strange claim that Gandhi's thought was not human-centered and that he practiced an embryonic form of deep ecology which is "traditionally Eastern and is

---

5. See Centre for Science and Environment, *India: The State of the Environment 1982: A Citizens Report* (New Delhi: Centre for Science and Environment, 1982); R. Sukumar, "Elephant-Man Conflict in Karnataka," in Cecil Saldanha, ed., *The State of Karnataka's Environment* (Bangalore: Centre for Taxonomic Studies, 1985). For Africa, see the brilliant analysis by Helge Kjekshus, *Ecology Control and Economic Development in East African History* (Berkeley: University of California Press, 1977).

6. Daniel Janzen, "The Future of Tropical Ecology," *Annual Review of Ecology and Systematics* 17 (1986): 305-306; emphasis added.

found with differing emphasis in Hinduism, Taoism and in Theravada and Mahayana Buddhism.''[7] Moving away from the realm of high philosophy and scriptural religion, deep ecologists make the further claim that at the level of material and spiritual practice ''primal'' peoples subordinated themselves to the integrity of the biotic universe they inhabited.

I have indicated that this appropriation of Eastern traditions is in part dictated by the need to construct an authentic lineage and in part a desire to present deep ecology as a universalistic philosophy. Indeed, in his substantial and quixotic biography of John Muir, Michael Cohen goes so far as to suggest that Muir was the ''Taoist of the [American] West.''[8] This reading of Eastern traditions is selective and does not bother to differentiate between alternate (and changing) religious and cultural traditions; as it stands, it does considerable violence to the historical record. Throughout most recorded history the characteristic form of human activity in the ''East'' has been a finely tuned but nonetheless conscious and dynamic manipulation of nature. Although mystics such as Lao Tzu did reflect on the spiritual essence of human relations with nature, it must be recognized that such ascetics and their reflections were supported by a society of cultivators whose relationship with nature was a far more *active* one. Many agricultural communities do have a sophisticated knowledge of the natural environment that may equal (and sometimes surpass) codified ''scientific'' knowledge; yet, the elaboration of such traditional ecological knowledge (in both material and spiritual contexts) can hardly be said to rest on a mystical affinity with nature of a deep ecological kind. Nor is such knowledge infallible; as the archae-ological record powerfully suggests, modern Western man has no monopoly on ecological disasters.

In a brilliant article, the Chicago historian Ronald Inden points out that this romantic and essentially positive view of the East is a mirror image of the scientific and essentially pejorative view normally upheld by Western scholars of the Orient. In either case, the East constitutes the Other, a body wholly separate and alien from the West; it is defined by a uniquely spiritual and nonrational ''essence,'' even if this essence is valorized quite differently by the two schools. Eastern man exhibits a spiritual dependence with respect to nature—on the one hand, this is symptomatic of his prescientific and backward self, on the other, of his ecological wisdom and deep ecological consciousness. Both views are monolithic, simplistic, and have the characteristic effect—intended in one case, perhaps unintended in the other—of denying agency and reason to the East and making it the privileged orbit of Western thinkers.

The two apparently opposed perspectives have then a common underlying structure of discourse in which the East merely serves as a vehicle for Western projections. Varying images of the East are raw material for political and cultural battles being played out in the West; they tell us far more about the Western commentator and his desires than about the ''East.'' Inden's remarks apply not merely to Western scholarship on India, but to Orientalist constructions of China and Japan as well:

> Although these two views appear to be strongly opposed, they often combine together. Both have a similar interest in sustaining the Otherness of India. The holders of the dominant view, best exemplified in the past in imperial administrative discourse (and today probably by that of 'development economics'), would place a traditional, superstition-ridden India in a position of perpetual tutelage to a modern, rational West. The adherents of the romantic view, best exemplified academically in the discourses of Christian liberalism and analytic psychology, concede the realm of the public and impersonal to the positivist. Taking their succour not from governments and big business, but from a plethora of religious foundations and self-help institutes, and from allies in

---

7. Robert Aitken Roshi, ''Gandhi, Dogen, and Deep Ecology,'' reprinted as appendix C in Bill Devall and George Sessions, *Deep Ecology: Living as if Nature Mattered* (Salt Lake City: Peregrine Smith Books, 1985). For Gandhi's own views on social reconstruction, see the excellent three volume collection edited by Raghavan Iyer, *The Moral and Political Writings of Mahatma Gandhi* (Oxford: Clarendon Press, 1986-87).

8. Michael Cohen, *The Pathless Way* (Madison: University of Wisconsin Press, 1984), p. 120.

the 'consciousness industry,' not to mention the important industry of tourism, the romantics insist that India embodies a private realm of the imagination and the religious which modern, western man lacks but needs. They, therefore, like the positivists, but for just the opposite reason, have a vested interest in seeing that the Orientalist view of India as 'spiritual,' 'mysterious,' and 'exotic' is perpetuated.[9]

(4) How radical, finally, are the deep ecologists? Notwithstanding their self-image and strident rhetoric (in which the label "shallow ecology" has an opprobrium similar to that reserved for "social democratic" by Marxist-Leninists), even within the American context their radicalism is limited and it manifests itself quite differently elsewhere.

To my mind, deep ecology is best viewed as a radical trend within the wilderness preservation movement. Although advancing philosophical rather than aesthetic arguments and encouraging political militancy rather than negotiation, its practical emphasis—viz., preservation of unspoilt nature—is virtually identical. For the mainstream movement, the function of wilderness is to provide a temporary antidote to modern civilization. As a special institution within an industrialized society, the national park "provides an opportunity for respite, contrast, contemplation, and affirmation of values for those who live most of their lives in the workaday world."[10] Indeed, the rapid increase in visitations to the national parks in postwar America is a direct consequence of economic expansion. The emergence of a popular interest in wilderness sites, the historian Samuel Hays points out, was "not a throwback to the primitive, but an integral part of the modern standard of living as people sought to add new 'amenity' and 'aesthetic' goals and desires to their earlier preoccupation with necessities and conveniences."[11]

Here, the enjoyment of nature is an integral part of the consumer society. The private automobile (and the life style it has spawned) is in many respects the ultimate ecological villain, and an untouched wilderness the prototype of ecological harmony; yet, for most Americans it is perfectly consistent to drive a thousand miles to spend a holiday in a national park. They possess a vast, beautiful, and sparsely populated continent and are also able to draw upon the natural resources of large portions of the globe by virtue of their economic and political dominance. In consequence, America can simultaneously enjoy the material benefits of an expanding economy and the aesthetic benefits of unspoilt nature. The two poles of "wilderness" and "civilization" mutually coexist in an internally coherent whole, and philosophers of both poles are assigned a prominent place in this culture. Paradoxically as it may seem, it is no accident that Star Wars technology and deep ecology both find their fullest expression in that leading sector of Western civilization, California.

Deep ecology runs parallel to the consumer society without seriously questioning its ecological and socio-political basis. In its celebration of American wilderness, it also displays an uncomfortable convergence with the prevailing climate of nationalism in the American wilderness movement. For spokesmen such as the historian Roderick Nash, the national park system is America's distinctive cultural contribution to the world, reflective not merely of its economic but

9. Ronald Inden, "Orientalist Constructions of India," *Modern Asian Studies* 20 (1986): 442. Inden draws inspiration from Edward Said's forceful polemic, *Orientalism* (New York: Basic Books, 1980). It must be noted, however, that there is a salient difference between Western perceptions of Middle Eastern and Far Eastern cultures respectively. Due perhaps to the long history of Christian conflict with Islam, Middle Eastern cultures (as Said documents) are consistently presented in pejorative terms. The juxtaposition of hostile and worshiping attitudes that Inden talks of applies only to Western attitudes toward Buddhist and Hindu societies.

10. Joseph Sax, *Mountains Without Handrails: Reflections on the National Parks* (Ann Arbor: University of Michigan Press, 1980), p. 42. Cf. also Peter Schmitt, *Back to Nature: The Arcadian Myth in Urban America* (New York: Oxford University Press, 1969), and Alfred Runte, *National Parks: The American Experience* (Lincoln: University of Nebraska Press, 1979).

11. Samuel Hays, "From Conservation to Environment: Environmental Politics in the United States since World War Two," *Environmental Review* 6 (1982): 21. See also the same author's book entitled *Beauty, Health and Permanence: Environmental Politics in the United States, 1955-85* (New York: Cambridge University Press, 1987).

of its philosophical and ecological maturity as well. In what Walter Lippman called the American century, the ''American invention of national parks'' must be exported worldwide. Betraying an economic determinism that would make even a Marxist shudder, Nash believes that environmental preservation is a ''full stomach'' phenomenon that is confined to the rich, urban, and sophisticated. Nonetheless, he hopes that ''the less developed nations may eventually evolve economically and intellectually to the point where nature preservation is more than a business.''[12]

The error which Nash makes (and which deep ecology in some respects encourages) is to equate environmental protection with the protection of wilderness. This is a distinctively American notion, borne out of a unique social and environmental history. The archetypal concerns of radical environmentalists in other cultural contexts are in fact quite different. The German Greens, for example, have elaborated a devastating critique of industrial society which turns on the acceptance of environmental limits to growth. Pointing to the intimate links between industrialization, militarization, and conquest, the Greens argue that economic growth in the West has historically rested on the economic and ecological exploitation of the Third World. Rudolf Bahro is characteristically blunt:

> The working class here [in the West] is the richest lower class in the world. And if I look at the problem from the point of view of the whole of humanity, not just from that of Europe, then I must say that the metropolitan working class is the worst exploiting class in history. . . . What made poverty bearable in eighteenth or nineteenth-century Europe was the prospect of escaping it through exploitation of the periphery. But this is no longer a possibility, and continued industrialism in the Third World will mean poverty for whole generations and hunger for millions.[13]

Here the roots of global ecological problems lie in the disproportionate share of resources consumed by the industrialized countries as a whole *and* the urban elite within the Third World. Since it is impossible to reproduce an industrial monoculture worldwide, the ecological movement in the West must begin by cleaning up its own act. The Greens advocate the creation of a ''no growth'' economy, to be achieved by scaling down current (and clearly unsustainable) consumption levels.[14] This radical shift in consumption and production patterns requires the creation of alternate economic and political structures—smaller in scale and more amenable to social participation—but it rests equally on a shift in cultural values. The expansionist character of modern Western man will have to give way to an ethic of renunciation and self-limitation, in which spiritual and communal values play an increasing role in sustaining social life. This revolution in cultural values, however, has as its point of departure an understanding of environmental processes quite different from deep ecology.

Many elements of the Green program find a strong resonance in countries such as India, where a history of Western colonialism and industrial development has benefited only a tiny elite while exacting tremendous social and environmental costs. The ecological battles presently being fought in India have as their epicenter the conflict over nature between the subsistence and largely rural sector and the vastly more powerful commercial-industrial sector. Perhaps the most celebrated of these battles concerns the Chipko (Hug the Tree) movement, a peasant movement against deforestation in the Himalayan foothills. Chipko is only one of several movements that have sharply questioned the nonsustainable demand being placed on the land and vegetative base by urban centers and industry. These include opposition to large dams by displaced peasants, the conflict between

---

12. Roderick Nash, *Wilderness and the American Mind,* 3rd ed. (New Haven: Yale University Press, 1982).

13. Rudolf Bahro, *From Red to Green* (London: Verso Books, 1984).

14. From time to time, American scholars have themselves criticized these imbalances in consumption patterns. In the 1950s, William Vogt made the charge that the United States, with one-sixteenth of the world's population, was utilizing one-third of the globe's resources. (Vogt, cited in E.F. Murphy, *Nature, Bureaucracy and the Rule of Property* [Amsterdam: North Holland, 1977, p. 29]). More recently, Zero Population Growth has estimated that each American consumes thirty-nine times as many resources as an Indian. See *Christian Science Monitor,* 2 March 1987.

small artisan fishing and large-scale trawler fishing for export, the countrywide movements against commercial forest operations, and opposition to industrial pollution among downstream agricultural and fishing communities.[15]

Two features distinguish these environmental movements from their Western counterparts. First, for the sections of society most critically affected by environmental degradation—poor and landless peasants, women, and tribals—it is a question of sheer survival, not of enhancing the quality of life. Second, and as a consequence, the environmental solutions they articulate deeply involve questions of equity as well as economic and political redistribution. Highlighting these differences, a leading Indian environmentalist stresses that "environmental protection per se is of least concern to most of these groups. Their main concern is about the use of the environment and who should benefit from it."[16] They seek to wrest control of nature away from the state and the industrial sector and place it in the hands of rural communities who live within that environment but are increasingly denied access to it. These communities have far more basic needs, their demands on the environment are far less intense, and they can draw upon a reservoir of cooperative social institutions and local ecological knowledge in managing the "commons"—forests, grasslands, and the waters—on a sustainable basis. If colonial and capitalist expansion has both accentuated social inequalities and signaled a precipitous fall in ecological wisdom, an alternate ecology must rest on an alternate society and polity as well.

This brief overview of German and Indian environmentalism has some major implications for deep ecology. Both German and Indian environmental traditions allow for a greater integration of ecological concerns with livelihood and work. They also place a greater emphasis on equity and social justice (both within individual countries and on a global scale) on the grounds that in the absence of social regeneration environmental regeneration has very little chance of succeeding. Finally, and perhaps most significantly, they have escaped the preoccupation with wilderness preservation so characteristic of American cultural and environmental history.[17]

IV. A HOMILY

In 1958, the economist J. K. Galbraith referred to overconsumption as the unasked question of the American conservation movement. There is a marked selectivity, he wrote, "in the conservationist's approach to materials consumption. If we are concerned about our great appetite for materials, it is plausible to seek to increase the supply, to decrease waste, to make better use of the stocks available, and to develop substitutes. But what of the appetite itself? Surely this is the ultimate source of the problem. If it continues its geometric course, will it not one day have to be restrained? Yet in the literature of the resource problem this is the forbidden question. Over it hangs a nearly total silence."[18]

The consumer economy and society have expanded tremendously in the three decades since Galbraith penned these words: yet his criticisms are nearly as valid today. I have said "nearly," for there are some hopeful signs. Within the environmental movement several dispersed groups are working to

---

15. For an excellent review, see Anil Agarwal and Sunita Narain, eds., *India: The State of the Environment 1984-85: A Citizens Report* (New Delhi: Centre for Science and Environment, 1985). Cf. also Ramachandra Guha, *The Unquiet Woods: Ecological Change and Peasant Resistance in the Indian Himalaya* (Berkeley: University of California Press, forthcoming).

16. Anil Agarwal, "Human–Nature Interactions in a Third World Country," *The Environmentalist* 6, No. 3 (1986): 167.

17. One strand in radical American environmentalism, the bioregional movement, by emphasizing a greater involvement with the bioregion people inhabit, does indirectly challenge consumerism. However, as yet bioregionalism has hardly raised the questions of equity and social justice (international, intranational, and intergenerational) which I argue must be a central plank of radical environmentalism. Moreover, its stress on (individual) *experience* as the key to involvement with nature is also somewhat at odds with the integration of nature with livelihood and work that I talk of in this paper. Cf. Kirkpatrick Sale, *Dwellers in the Land: The Bioregional Vision* (San Francisco: Sierra Club Books, 1985).

18. John Kenneth Galbraith, "How Much Should a Country Consume?" in Henry Jarrett, ed., *Perspectives on Conservation* (Baltimore: Johns Hopkins Press, 1958), pp. 91-92.

develop ecologically benign technologies and to encourage less wasteful life styles. Moreover, outside the self-defined boundaries of American environmentalism, opposition to the permanent war economy is being carried on by a peace movement that has a distinguished history and impeccable moral and political credentials.

It is precisely these (to my mind, most hopeful) components of the American social scene that are missing from deep ecology. In their widely noticed book, Bill Devall and George Sessions make no mention of militarization or the movements for peace, while activists whose practical focus is on developing ecologically responsible life styles (e.g., Wendell Berry) are derided as "falling short of deep ecological awareness."[19] A truly radical ecology in the American context ought to work toward a synthesis of the appropriate technology, alternate life style, and peace movements.[20] By making the (largely spurious) anthropocentric-biocentric distinction central to the debate, deep ecologists may have appropriated the moral high ground, but they are at the same time doing a serious disservice to American and global environmentalism.[21]

---

19. Devall and Sessions, *Deep Ecology,* p. 122. For Wendell Berry's own assessment of deep ecology, see his "Amplications: Preserving Wilderness," *Wilderness* 50 (Spring 1987): 39-40, 50-54.

20. See the interesting recent contribution by one of the most influential spokesmen of appropriate technology—Barry Commoner, "A Reporter at Large: The Environment," *New Yorker,* 15 June 1987. While Commoner makes a forceful plea for the convergence of the environmental movement (viewed by him primarily as the opposition to air and water pollution and to the institutions that generate such pollution) and the peace movement, he significantly does not mention consumption patterns, implying that "limits to growth" do not exist.

21. In this sense, my critique of deep ecology, although that of an outsider, may facilitate the reassertion of those elements in the American environmental tradition for which there is a profound sympathy in other parts of the globe. A global perspective may also lead to a critical reassessment of figures such as Aldo Leopold and John Muir, the two patron saints of deep ecology. As Donald Worster has pointed out, the message of Muir (and, I would argue, of Leopold as well) makes sense only in an American context: he has very little to say to other cultures. See Worster's review of Stephen Fox's *John Muir and His Legacy,* in *Environmental Ethics* 5 (1983): 277-281.

DISCUSSION TOPICS

1. Based on the readings, what perspectives do Guha and Larson hold in common? How do their views differ?
2. Do you agree with Guha's assessment that the social consequences of taking a deep ecology approach to solving Third World problems would be very grave? Justify your position.
3. How might a deep ecologist respond to Guha's major points?

CLASS EXERCISES

1. Based on the authors you have read in this chapter, and your own experiences and outside reading, rank the perspectives covered in this chapter from the one showing the greatest ecological wisdom and insight, to the one seeming to encompass the least. Justify your ranking.
2. Among the multicultural perspectives presented in this chapter, which do you believe could be most successfully applied in contemporary Western society? Explain your position.

CASE FOR CLASS DEBATE

Is it possible or proper for Western society to appropriate cultural insights from Eastern or Native American philosophies for its own use?

Using the guidelines presented in Appendix A, debate the two sides of this issue. Which arguments were appealed to by each side? Which were most persuasive?

FOR FURTHER READING

Abram, David. "The Ecology of Magic," *Orion* 10.3: 28-43, 1991. An essay on animism and the ecological role of the shaman in traditional cultures, arguing that animistic beliefs ensure a participatory, non-anthropocentric relationship to animals and plants, and the land itself.

Badiner, Allan H., ed. *Dharma Gaia: A Harvest of Essays in Buddhism and Ecology.* Berkeley: Parallax Press, 1990. Contemporary essays by philosophers, Buddhist scholars and practitioners.

Brown, Joseph Epes, ed. *The Sacred Pipe.* New York: Penguin Books, 1973. A sense of the connectedness between Sioux Indians and the earth clearly emerges in this fascinating account of the seven rites of the Oglala Sioux, as reported by this unique individual, Black Elk.

Callicott, J. Baird, "Conceptual Resources for Environmental Ethics in Asian Traditions of Thought: A Propaedeutic." *Philosophy East and West* 37: 115-130, 1987. Provides a brief evaluation of the potential contributions that can be made to ecological ethics by a variety of Asian traditions.

Callicott, J. Baird. "Traditional American Indian and Western European Attitudes Toward Nature: An Overview." *Environmental Ethics* 4: 293-318, 1982. Argues the American Indians supported an environmental ethic whereas Western Europeans encouraged alienation from, and exploitation of, the environment.

Callicott, J. Baird, and Roger T. Ames, eds. *Nature in Asian Traditions of Thought: Essays in Environmental Philosophy* Albany: State University of New York Press, 1989. An excellent collection of eighteen papers by philosophers addressing world views as seen from the perspective of the science of ecology, Chinese philosophy, Japanese philosophy, Buddhism, and (East) Indian philosophy.

Chawla, Saroj. "Linguistic and Philosophical Roots of Our Environmental Crisis." *Environmental Ethics* 13: 253-262, 1991. Makes a linguistic comparison of Amerindian languages with the English language, and concludes that the English language is not conducive to a holistic and careful attitude toward the environment.

Cheng, Chung-ying. "On the Environmental Ethics of the *Tao* and the *Ch'i.*" *Environmental Ethics* 8: 351-370, 1986. The author proposes five axioms which he believes will provide a foundation for an environmental ethic: the axiom of total interpenetration, the axiom of self-transformation, the axiom of creative spontaneity, the axiom of a will not to will, and the axiom of nonattaching attachment.

Dwivedi, O.P., and B.N. Tiwari. *Environmental Crisis and Hindu Religion.* New Delhi, India: Gitanjali Publishing House, 1987. Presentation and evaluation of the nondualistic, cosmic theory of God's creation, with chapters on Hindu attitudes toward animals, plants, and pollution. Includes primary sources in both English and Sanskrit.

Engel, J. Ronald, and Joan Gibb Engel, eds. *Ethics of Environment and Development: Global Challenge, International Response.* Tucson: The University of Arizona Press, 1990. A collection of twenty-one papers focusing on the ethical principles at stake in the concept of "sustainable development." Presents perspectives from Western Europe and North America, Eastern Europe and the Soviet Union, South and Central America, Africa and the Middle East, and Asia, as well as the experiences of women.

Gardiner, Robert W. "Between Two Worlds: Humans in Nature and Culture." *Environmental Ethics* 12: 339-352, 1990. The author identifies some of the tensions and paradoxes entailed by the view that humans live simultaneously in two worlds: the world of nature and the world of culture.

Goodman, Russell. "Taoism and Ecology." *Environmental Ethics* 2: 73-80, 1980. The author asserts that Taoists of ancient China were keen observers of nature and important early Chinese scientists. On the basis of several principles, he argues that they would have favored such contemporary options as passive solar energy and organic farming.

Guha, Ramachandra. "Ideological Trends in Indian Environmentalism." *Economic and Political Weekly* (3 December 1988): 2578-2581, 1988. Three strands of the environmental movement are identified in India: "crusading Gandhian, appropriate technology, and ecological Marxists." An argument is made supporting this ideological plurality.

Hargrove, Eugene C., ed. *Religion and Environmental Crisis.* Athens, Ga.: The University of Georgia Press, 1985. An excellent selection of eleven papers, with topics including classical polytheism, Native American perspectives, Taoism, Islam, Judaism, and Christianity.

Hughes, J. Donald. *American Indian Ecology.* El Paso, Tex.: Texas Western Press, 1983. Hughes describes the basis of the American Indian relationship to nature, with a focus on the very complex mentality which gives rise to the Indian ecological outlook. He provides insights into the way Indians conceive of the natural world and its life forms.

Johns, David M. "Relevance of Deep Ecology to the Third World: Some Preliminary Comments." *Environmental Ethics* 12: 233-252, 1990. Challenges the criticisms

Guha offers of deep ecology. Argues that deep ecology's distinction between anthropocentrism and biocentrism is useful in dealing with the two critical problems Guha mentions: overconsumption and militarism.

Manazoor, S. Parvez. "Environment and Values: The Islamic Perspective," in *The Touch of Midas: Science, Values and Environment in Islam and the West,* Aiauddin Sardar, ed. Manchester, England: Manchester University Press, 1984. Author argues (pp. 151-169) that the Islamic viewpoint has been neglected, and that Islamic traditions and values provide an effective and comprehensive answer to the environmental crisis.

Nasr, Seyyed Hossein. *The Encounter of Man and Nature: The Spiritual Crisis of Modern Man.* London: George Allen and Unwin Ltd., 1968. A comparative overview of the relation of humans to the natural world in major religions.

Peerenboom, R.P. "Beyond Naturalism: A Reconstruction of Daoist Environmental Ethics." *Environmental Ethics* 13: 3-22, 1991. Offers an alternative interpretation of Taoism, and concludes that it is not much better than Western philosophies in dealing with the environmental crisis.

Reed, Gerard. "A Native American Environmental Ethic: A Homily on Black Elk," in *Religion and Environmental Crisis.* Eugene C. Hargrove, ed., Athens, Ga.: The University of Georgia Press, 1986. Argues (pp. 25-37) that traditional Native American thinkers such as Black Elk maintained an ethic of reverence for nature as a reflection of God. Religious values were tied to ecological attitudes and practices, enabling the Native Americans to live in a healthy balance with the land for millenia.

Rolston, Holmes, III. "Can the East Help the West to Value Nature?" *Philosophy East and West* 37: 172-190, 1987. Concludes that Eastern philosophies probably are not very applicable as bases for valuing nature or for solving environmental problems in Western society.

Rolston, Holmes, III. "Respect for Life: Can Zen Buddhism Help in Forming an Environmental Ethic," in *Zen Buddhism Today, Annual Report of the Kyoto Zen Symposium No. 7.* Kyoto, Japan: The Kyoto Seminary for Religious Philosophy, 1989. Rolston finds (pp. 11-30) that Zen Buddhism has potential applications to environmental ethics, but questions whether it can support objective thinking which values animals, plants, species, or ecosystems.

Schwarz, O. Douglas. "Indian Rights and Environmental Ethics: Changing Perspectives, and a Modest Proposal." *Environmental Ethics* 9: 291-302, 1987. Author argues that the environmental movement has been insensitive to the concerns of American Indians. Rather than advocating taking away rights that Indians have been entitled to for decades, environmentalists should negotiate on these matters.

Shaner, David Edward and R. Shannon Duval. "Conservation Ethics and the Japanese Intellectual Tradition." *Environmental Ethics* 11: 197-214, 1989. Argues that the Japanese philosophical and religious tradition represents a commitment to ecocentrism.

Smith, Huston. "Tao Now: An Ecological Testament," in *Earth Might Be Fair: Reflections on Ethics, Religion, and Ecology,* Ian G. Barbour, ed. Englewood Cliffs, N.J.: Prentice-Hall, 1972. Provides an overview of the Taoist relationship to nature.

Standing Bear, Luther. *Land of the Spotted Eagle.* Lincoln, Nebr.: University of Nebraska Press, 1933. Standing Bear describes traditional Sioux life and culture. Most of the book is ethnographic, with chapters on child rearing, social and political organization, the family, religion, and adulthood. Provides excellent insights on the strengths of traditional Sioux culture and, more generally, on the importance of native cultures and values, and the status of Indian people in American society.

Tuan, Yi-Fu. "Discrepancies Between Environmental Attitude and Behaviour: Examples from Europe and China." *Canadian Geographer* 12: 176-191, 1968. Describes differences between European and Chinese conceptions of nature, contrasting the human dominion over nature among Europeans with the focus on harmony with nature among Taoists and Buddhists. However, notes the great transformations in the environment which occurred in China over the centuries, despite the attitudes toward nature embedded in these philosophies.

Vittachi, Anuradha. *Earth Conference One: Sharing A Vision for Our Planet.* Boston, Mass.: Science Library, 1989. An excellent account of the 1988 Global Forum of Spiritual and Parliamentary Leaders on Human Survival, held in Oxford, England. Two outcomes were the recommendation to model a planetary consciousness which honors tribal memberships, and the distinctions made between outer forms of religion and universal spiritual values.

FOR THE CHILDREN

The rising hills, the slopes,
of statistics
lie before us.
the steep climb
of everything, going up,
up, as we all
go down.

In the next century
or the one beyond that,
they say,
are valleys, pastures,
we can meet there in peace
if we make it.

To climb these coming crests
one word to you, to
you and your children:

stay together
learn the flowers
go light

Class Exercises

Two approaches commonly have been used to increase student participation of students in class discussions: small group discussions and debates.

SMALL GROUP DISCUSSIONS

The students divide themselves into groups of three (or five) each. A question is posed or a problem is presented on which they are asked to present their considered opinions. Some of the Discussion Topics presented after each chapter's readings could be used. After approximately 10 minutes of discussion, a spokesperson from each group presents that group's assessment, with at least one cogent reason to support the group's position. Each group normally has 2 to 4 minutes to summarize its position. The instructor keeps a summary of various answers and opinions on the board, and summarizes them with the class at the end of the exercise. With each new exercise, students are encouraged to participate with students with whom they have not previously worked.

DEBATES

A controversial issue is presented to the class, and all students are allowed to choose the side they wish to represent. Small inequities in numbers on each side can be evened by asking for volunteers to change sides. The issue is then debated by standardized debating procedures, as presented by Infante.[1] We recommend the following schedule:

Introduction
   Advocates for proposal (10 minutes)
   Opponents to proposal (10 minutes)

Rebuttal
   Opponents to proposal (10 minutes)
   Advocates for proposal (10 minutes)

Summary
   Opponents to proposal (7 minutes)
   Advocates for proposal (7 minutes)

A 5-minute break is normally allowed between introduction and rebuttal, and rebuttal and summary. If necessary to accommodate a 50-minute class period, the summary and judges' decisions can be completed during a second class period.

---

1. Dominic A. Infante, *Arguing Constructively* (Prospect Heights, Ill.: Waveland Press, 1988).

Based on our experiences, we recommend the following:

1. To be most effective, each team in the debate should have no more than seven students; a larger class would benefit by having additional debates rather than larger teams.
2. Before the first debate, one class period should be devoted to presenting debating principles and strategies to the students.[2]
3. One class period is set aside for the respective teams to prepare their positions. This gives everyone an opportunity to work together at a time that all have available.
4. The debate should be judged by an independent panel of five students from the class who are not part of either team. The student judges develop their own scoring procedure which they share with the competing teams before the debate. Although the criteria used to judge have varied, some of the criteria judges used in our classes include the currency and adequacy of the evidence, the scientific reliability of the sources of evidence, the relevance of the arguments used, the appearance (voice and posture) of the advocates during their presentation, consistency and logic of ideas used, degree to which emotional appeal is used or avoided, clarity with which underlying assumptions are established, degree to which opposing arguments are directly addressed, and overall persuasiveness.

One variation of this exercise is that after choosing positions, the students are required to switch sides and advocate the opposing view. Despite their initial resistance, students almost uniformly have agreed at the end of the exercise that they learned as much or more than if they had simply argued the position they originally chose.

2. See note 1.

Acknowledgments

CHAPTER ONE

McDonald, L. 1982. The Role of Statistics and the Scientific Method in the Art of Problem Solving.* Symposium: Issues and Technology in the Management of Impacted Western Wildlife. By permission of the author and Thorne Ecological Institute, 5398 Manhattan Circle, Boulder, Co. 80303.

Stevenson, L. 1989. Is Scientific Research Value-Neutral? *Inquiry* 32:213-222. By permission of the author and Scandinavian University Press, *Inquiry*, P.O. Box 2959, Toyen, N-608 Oslo, Norway.

Brown, D. A. 1987. Ethics, science, and environmental regulation. *Environmental Ethics* 9:331-349. Copyright Donald A. Brown. By permission of the author.

Rolston, H., III. 1990. Biology and Philosophy in Yellowstone. *Biology and Philosophy* 5:241-258. By permission of the author and Kluwer Academic Publishers.

Worster, D. 1990. The Ecology of Order and Chaos. *Environmental Review* 14(1-2):1-18. Copyright (c) 1990, The American Society for Environmental History. By permission of Donald Worster and *Environmental History Review*.

---

* Unabridged reading.

CHAPTER TWO:

Rolston, H., III. 1983. Values gone wild. *Inquiry* 26:181-207, and Rolston, H., III. 1989. Reprinted in *Philosophy Gone Wild*; pp.118-143. Buffalo, NY: Prometheus Books. By permission of the author and Scandinavian University Press, Inquiry, P. O. Box 2959, Toyen, N-0608 Oslo, Norway.

Regan, T. 1983. *The Case for Animal Rights*; pp. 126-135. Copyright (c) 1983 The Regents of the University of California. By permission of the University of California Press.

Callicott, J. B. 1986. On the intrinsic value of nonhuman species. *The Preservation of Species: The Value of Biological Diversity*; pp.138-172. B. G. Norton, editor. Copyright (c) 1986 by Princeton University Press. By permission of J. Baird Callicott, Bryan G. Norton, and Princeton University Press.

Stone, C. D. 1988. Moral pluralism and the course of environmental ethics. *Environmental Ethics* 10:139-154. By permission of Christopher D. Stone.

Cheney, J. 1989. Postmodern environmental ethics: ethics as bioregional narrative. *Environmental Ethics* 11:117-134. (Revised.) By permission of Jim Cheney.

Weston, A. 1992. Before Environmental Ethics. *Environmental Ethics* 14. By permission of Anthony Weston.

CHAPTER THREE:

Thoreau, H. D. 1980. Walking. *The Natural History Essays.* By permission of Gibbs Smith, Publisher.

Muir, J. 1913. A Near View of the High Sierras. *The Mountains of California* 4:48-73. Public Domain—no acknowledgment needed.

Terrie, P. G. 1987. John Muir on Mount Ritter: A New Wilderness Aesthetic. *The Pacific Historian* 31:135-144. Copyright 1987 Holt-Atherton Department, University of the Pacific Libraries. By permission of Philip G. Terrie and University of the Pacific.

Dillard, A. C. 1974. Seeing. *Pilgrim at Tinker Creek.* Copyright (c) 1974 by Annie Dillard. By permission of Blanche C. Gregory Literary Agency Inc. and HarperCollins Publishers, Inc.

Fowles, J. 1979. On Seeing Nature Whole. *Harpers* 259 (Nov):49-68. Copyright (c) 1979 by *Harper's Magazine.* All rights reserved. Essay is excerpted from *The Tree* (Boston: Little, Brown and Co.). By special permission of *Harpers Magazine* and Little, Brown & Co.

Carlson, A. 1979. Appreciation and the Natural Environment. *Journal of Aesthetics and Art* 37:267-275. Reprinted by permission of Allen Carlson and *Journal of Aesthetics and Art.*

Callicott, J. B. 1987. *The Land Aesthetic* (Revised). Companion to a *Sand County Almanac*; pp.157-171. By permission of J. Baird Callicott and the University of Wisconsin Press.

Hargrove, E. C. 1989. An Ontological Argument for Environmental Ethics. *Foundations of Environmental Ethics*; pp.191-201. Copyright 1989. By permission of Eugene C. Hargrove and Prentice-Hall, Inc., Englewood Cliffs, N. J.

CHAPTER FOUR:

Hughes, J. D. 1975. The ancient roots of our ecological crisis.* *Ecology in Ancient Civilizations*; pp.147-156. The University of New Mexico Press. Copyright J. Donald Hughes. By permission of J. Donald Hughes, member, advisory board, *Environmental History Review.*

Hughes, J. D. and J. Swan. 1986. How much of the earth is sacred space? *Environmental Review* 10 (4): 247-259. Copyright (c) 1986, The American Society for Environmental History. By permission of *Environmental Review.*

Worster, D. 1990. Transformations of the earth: Toward an agroecological perspective in history. *The Journal of American History* 76: 1087-1113. By permission of Donald Worster and *The Journal of American History.*

Merchant, C. 1990. Gender and environmental history.* *The Journal of American History* 76 (March):1117-1121. Copyright 1990, Organization of American Historians. By permission of Carolyn Merchant and *The Journal of American History.*

Hargrove, E. C. 1980. Anglo-American land use attitudes. Environmental Ethics 2:121-148. By permission of Eugene C. Hargrove.

Evernden, N. 1989. Nature in industrial society. *Cultural politics in contemporary America*; pp.151-164. I. Angus, and S. Jhally, editors. By permission of Neil Evernden.

CHAPTER FIVE:

Hardin, G. 1968. Tragedy of the Commons. *Science* 162:1243-1248. 13 Dec 1968. Copyright 1968, American Association for the Advancement of Science. By permission of Garrett Hardin and Science.

Snyder, G. 1990. *Understanding the Commons. The Practice of the Wild*; pp.29-37. Copyright (c) 1990 by Gary Snyder. North Point Press, publisher. By permission of Farrar, Straus & Giroux, Inc.

Edwards, S. E. 1987. In defense of environment of economics. *Environmental Ethics* 9:73-85. Reprinted by permission of Steven E. Edwards.

Sagoff, M. 1988. Some Problems with Environmental Economics. *Environmental Ethics* 10:55-74. By permission of Mark Sagoff.

Goodland, R., and G. Ledec. 1987. Neoclassical economics and principles of sustainable development. *Ecological Modelling* 38:19-47. By permission of the authors and Elsevier Science Publishers B.V.

Stone, C. D. 1972. Should Trees Have Standing?. *Toward Legal Rights for Natural Objects*; Southern California Law Review 45.2:450-501. By permission of Christopher D. Stone.

Paehlke, R. and D. Torgerson. 1990. Environmental Politics and the Administrative State. *Managing Leviathan: Environmental Politics and the Administrative State*; pp.285-301. R. Paehlke, and D. Torgerson, editors. By permission of the authors and Broadview Press.

CHAPTER SIX:

Saint Thomas Aquinas. 1928. Differences between rational and other creatures.* *Summa Contra Gentiles.* English

Dominican Fathers (Benziger Brothers, 1928), translators. Third Book, Part II, Chapter CXII. By permission of Benziger Publishing.

Descartes, R. Discourse on Method in *Philosophical Works of Descartes* 1:115-118. Haldane, E.S. and Ross, G.R.T., translators. Selections II and III from *Descartes: Philosophical Letters*. Kenny, A., translator and editor. By permission of Cambridge University Press.

Kant, I. 1963. Duties to animals and spirits.* *Lectures on Ethics*; pp.239-241. Infield, L., translator. By permission of Methuen & Company, London.

Norton, B. G. 1984. Anthropocentrism and Nonanthropocentrism. *Environmental Ethics* 6:131-148. By permission of Bryan G. Norton.

McGee, W. J. 1990. The Conservation Mentality. *American Environmentalism*. Originally published 1910—public domain, no acknowledgment needed.

Guthrie, R. D. 1967. The ethical relationship between humans and other organisms.* *Perspectives in Biology and Medicine* 11:52-62. By permission of R. Dale Guthrie and University of Chicago Press.

Fraser Darling, F. 1969. Man's responsibility for the environment.* *Biology and Ethics*; pp.117-122. Ebling, F.J., editor. Reprinted by permission of Biology Symposium Number 18, Academic Press.

Murdy, W. H. 1975. Anthropocentrism: a modern version. *Science* 187:1168-1172. Copyright 1975, American Association for the Advancement of Science. By permission of W. H. Murdy and Science.

Gould, S. J. 1990. The Golden Rule - a proper scale for our environmental crisis. *Natural History* (Sept):24-30. Copyright the American Museum of Natural History, 1990. By permission of *Natural History*.

CHAPTER SEVEN:

Regan, T. 1983. *The Case for Animal Rights*; pp. 243-4, 248, 280, 353-363. Berkeley: University of California Press. Copyright (c) 1983 The Regents of the University of California. By permission of the University of California Press.

Singer, P. 1979. Equality for Animals? *Practical Ethics*. By permission of Peter Singer and Cambridge University Press.

Rachels, J. 1990. *Created from Animals: The Moral Implications of Darwinism*. pp. 181-90; 194; 208-209. Copyright (c) 1990 by James Rachels. By permission of James Rachels and Oxford University Press.

Schweitzer, A. 1964. The ethics of reverence for life. *The Philosophy of Civilization*; pp.240-264. Buffalo: Prometheus Books. Copyright (c) 1987 Rhena Schweitzer Miller. By permission of Rhena Schweitzer Miller.

Goodpaster, K. 1978. On being morally considerable. *Journal of Philosophy* 75:308-325. By permission of Kenneth Goodpaster and Journal of Philosophy.

Taylor, P. W. 1986. *Respect for Nature: A Theory of Environmental Ethics*; Chapters 3, 4, and 6. Copyright (c) 1986 Princeton University Press. By permission of Princeton University Press.

CHAPTER EIGHT:

Leopold, A. 1949. The land ethic. *A Sand County Almanac: And Sketches Here and There*; pp.201-226. Copyright 1949, 1977 by Oxford University Press, Inc. By permission of Oxford University Press.

Rodman, J. 1983. Four forms of ecological consciousness reconsidered: Ecological sensibility. *Ethics and the Environment*; pp.88-92. D. Scherer, and T. Attig, editors. N. J.: Prentice Hall, Inc. By permission of John Rodman.

Callicott, J. B. 1987. The conceptual foundations of the land ethic. *Companion to a Sand County Almanac*; pp. 186-217. By permission of J. Baird Callicott and University of Wisconsin Press.

Heffernan, J. D. 1982. The land ethic: a critical appraisal. *Environmental Ethics* 4:235-247. By permission of James D. Heffernan.

Marietta, D. E., Jr. 1988. Environmental holism and individuals. *Environmental Ethics* 10(3):251-258. Copyright Don E. Marietta, Jr. By permission of Don E. Marietta, Jr.

Naess, A. 1987. The deep ecological movement: Some philosophical aspects. *Philosophical Inquiry*. By permission of Arne Naess.

Foreman, D. 1991. Putting the earth first. *Confessions of an eco-warrior*; pp.25-36. Copyright (c) 1991 by David Foreman. By permission of Harmony Books, a division of Crown Publishers, Inc., courtesy of the Schaffner Agency Inc.

CHAPTER NINE:

Warren, K. 1990. The Power and Promise of Ecological Feminism. *Environmental Ethics* 12:125-146. By permission of Karen Warren.

Lahar, S. 1991. Ecofeminist Theory and Grassroots Politics. Hypatia 6:28-45. By permission of Stephanie Lahar.

Russell, J. S. 1990. *The Evolution of an Ecofeminist.* Reweaving the World: The Emergence of Ecofeminism;

pp.223-230. I. Diamond, and G.F. Orenstein, editors. By permission of Sierra Club Books.

Shiva, V. 1989. Women in Nature. *Staying Alive: Women, Ecology, and Development in India*; pp.38-54. By permission of Zed Books Limited, London.

Spretnak, C. 1991. *States of Grace: The Recovery of Meaning in the Postmodern Age*; pp.106-111, 127-138. Copyright (c) 1991 by Charlene Spretnak. By permission of HarperCollins Publishers, Inc.

CHAPTER TEN:

Saint Francis of Assisi. 1982. *The Canticle of Brother Sun. Francis and Clare: The Complete Works of Francis and Clare.* Armstrong, R. J. OFM, Cap., and Brady, I. OFM, translators. (c) 1982 by The Missionary Society of St. Paul the Apostle in the State of New York. By kind permission of SPCK, London, and Paulist Press.

Bratton, S. P. 1986. Christian ecotheology and the Old Testament.* *Environmental Ethics* 6:195-209. By permission of Susan Power Bratton.

Berry, W. 1981. The gift of good land. The Gift of Good Land.* North Point Press. Also appeared in *Sierra Magazine* 64:20-26. Copyright (c) 1981 by Wendell Berry. By permission of Farrar, Straus & Giroux, Inc. and *Sierra Magazine*.

Zimmerman, M. E. 1988. Quantum theory, intrinsic value, and pantheism. Environmental Ethics 10: 21-30. By permission of Michael E. Zimmerman.

McDaniel, J. 1986. A feeling for the organism: Christian spirituality as openness to fellow creatures.* *Environmental Ethics* 8:33-46. By permission of Jay McDaniel.

CHAPTER ELEVEN:

Booth, A. L.; Jacobs, H. M. 1990. Ties that bind: Native American beliefs as a foundation for environmental consciousness. *Environmental Ethics* 12:27-43.

Deen (Samarai), M.Y.I. 1990. *Islamic Environmental Ethics, Law and Society. Ethics of Environment and Development.* Engel, J. R. and J. G. Engel, editors. By permission of Belhaven Press, London. All rights reserved.

de Silva, L. 1987. *The Buddhist Attitude toward Nature. Buddhist Perspectives on the Ecocrisis*; pp.9-29. Sandell, K., editor. By permission of Lily de Silva and Buddhist Publication Society, Kandy, Sri Lanka.

Ip, P. K. 1986. Taoism and the foundations of environmental ethics.* *Religion and environmental crisis*; pp.94-106. Hargrove, E.C., editor. By permission of University of Georgia Press.

Larson, G. J. 1989. Conceptual Resources in South Asia for Environmental Ethics.* *Nature in Asian Traditions of Thought*; pp.267-277. Callicott, J.B. and R.T. Ames, editors. By permission of the State University of New York Press, Albany.

Guha, R. 1989. Radical American environmentalism and wilderness preservation: A Third World critique.* *Environmental Ethics* 11:71-83. By permission of Ramachandra Guha.

EPILOGUE:

Snyder, G. 1974. *For the Children.* Turtle Island*; p.86. Copyright (c) 1974 by Gary Snyder. By permission of New Directions Publishing Corporation.